Macmillan Encyclopedia of

Architects

Editorial board

Macmillan Encyclopedia of

Architects

ADOLF K. PLACZEK, *editor in chief*

Volume 3

THE FREE PRESS
a division of Macmillan Publishing Co., Inc.
New York
COLLIER MACMILLAN PUBLISHERS
LONDON

THE FREE PRESS
A Division of Macmillan Publishing Co., Inc.
866 Third Avenue, New York, N. Y. 10022

Collier Macmillan Canada, Inc.

Library of Congress Catalog Card Number: 82-17256

Printed in the United States of America

printing number

2 3 4 5 6 7 8 9 10

Library of Congress Cataloging in Publication Data
Main entry under title:

Macmillan encyclopedia of architects.

Includes bibliographies and indexes.
1. Architects—Biography. I. Placzek, Adolf K.
II. Title: Encyclopedia of architects.
NA40.M25 1982 720′.92′2 [B] 82-17256
ISBN 0-02-925000-5 (set)

LHÔTE, FRANÇOIS

Paris-trained, François Lhôte (c.1750–1808) is best known for his work in Bordeaux (from 1768). In major urban projects (Hôtel de Ville with FRANÇOIS BONFIN, the city architect; Theater; Place Royale) he was soon replaced by VICTOR LOUIS. Lhôte built several town houses and in 1790 became director of the Bordeaux Academy.

MYRA DICKMAN ORTH

WORKS

1780s, Hôtel de l'Administration des Hospices; 1780s, Hôtel Basquiant; 1780s, Hôtel Journu; 1780s, Hôtel Piganeau; Bordeaux, France.

BIBLIOGRAPHY

BRAHAM, ALLAN 1980 *The Architecture of the French Enlightenment.* London: Thames & Hudson.

HAUTECOEUR, LOUIS 1952 *Seconde moitié du XVIIIe siècle: Le style Louis XVI, 1750–1792.* Volume 4 in *Histoire de l'architecture classique en France.* Paris: Picard.

PARISET, F. G. 1974–1975 "Architectes parisiens à Bordeaux à la fin du 18e siècle." *Bulletin Archéologique* 10–11:115–125.

PARISET, F. G. 1980 *Victor Louis, 1731–1800: Dessins et Gravures.* Bordeaux. Exhibition catalogue.

L

CONTINUED

LIANG SSU-CH'ENG

Liang Ssu-ch'eng (1901–1972) (pronounced Leong Sss-chung) was China's pre-eminent architectural historian. Before his time, Chinese architecture was undervalued by the educated upper class as a craft taught by apprenticeship to illiterate craftsmen. His leadership in discovering, recording, and analyzing key structures of all eras systematized this neglected subject.

Liang was born in Tokyo where his father, Liang Ch'i-ch'ao, famous scholar and political reformer, was in exile for his political views. After a thorough education in Chinese traditional culture and language, Liang had an eight-year saturation in English language and Western learning at Tsing Hua's middle school and college in Peking. His fiancée, Lin Whei-yin, was determined to be an architect herself, and they both received architectural training at the University of Pennsylvania's School of Fine Arts, graduating with honors in 1927.

PAUL PHILIPPE CRET's curriculum, modeled on that of the Ecole des Beaux-Arts in Paris, introduced the Liangs to European architectural history with assignments such as "design a triumphal arch according to its period," or "finish an existing unfinished cathedral," or "restore an ancient ruin."

The young couple were married in March 1928 and returned to China, where Liang established the department of architecture at Northeastern University in Mukden and also a firm with his wife and two fellow Cret students. In June 1931, shortly before the Japanese military closed the university, the Liangs moved to Peking. He had accepted an appointment as research director of the Society (later Institute) for Research in Chinese Architecture, a post he later shared with Japan-trained LIU TUN-CHEN.

Liang had to learn the technical terminology of the two extant architectural construction manuals, one by LI CHIEH, an official of the Sung Dynasty, published in 1103, and one from the Ch'ing Dynasty, published in 1730. To begin he turned to the old palace carpenters who could point out the structural parts by name and interpret for him directly the technical terms and building methods. This first-hand research resulted in Liang's first book, *Ch'ing-shih ying-tsao tse-li* (Rules for Ch'ing Period Architecture), published in Peking in 1933. The Sung manual he studied all his life.

Between 1932 and 1937, Liang and his wife led field trips for several months each year to find surviving buildings of earlier times, as did his colleague Liu. They published their discoveries (in Chinese) in the Society's quarterly *Bulletin.* On Liang's very first field trip in April 1932 to a Buddhist temple, Tu-le ssu, in Chi Hsien, 60 miles east of Peking, he discovered a well-preserved timber-framed structure erected in 984 A.D. which housed a colossal clay statue 52 feet in height. In 1937, he found an even earlier wooden structure, Fo-kuang ssu, in the Wu-t'ai mountains of Shansi. This impressive T'ang Buddhist temple, Liang's most famous discovery, is with one minor exception China's oldest, erected in 857 A.D. Other important finds in fifteen provinces are too numerous to mention but Liang particularly prized a towering wooden pagoda at Ying Hsien, Shansi, built in 1056 and an amazing open-spandrel stone bridge near Chao Hsien, Hopei, built in the Sui Dynasty (581–618 A.D.). Its principal arch is over 115 feet in length.

Liang's field work involved searching local histories for references, going to promising sites, photographing and measuring old structures in detail, copying historical data usually recorded on related stelae, and promptly publishing the results in the *Bulletin.*

During the war years 1937–1945, the Liangs and the Institute staff were refugees in west China. Though architectural surveys of Yunnan and Szechwan were made, Liang's principal accomplishments of these miserable years were to formulate his analysis of Chinese wood-frame construction in "The Grammar of Chinese Architecture" (*Bulletin* VII-2, 1945, in Chinese) and to prepare manuscripts of two books, one in Chinese, one in English, summarizing his first-hand study of dated architecture from Shang to Ch'ing. Plans and elevations based on field data as well as photographs illustrate these works. Neither book was published in Liang's lifetime but the Chinese manuscript was photo-printed for restricted student use in the 1950s and is being prepared for publication in 1983 in Peking. The English manuscript, *A Pictorial History of Chinese Architecture,* is a briefer version of the former and will be published about the same time by the M.I.T. Press, Cambridge, Massachusetts.

In 1947, Liang made his second and last visit to the United States as visiting professor at Yale. He received an honorary degree from Princeton and was appointed a design consultant to the Planning Office of the United Nations building in New York.

Under the People's Republic after 1949, Liang was given important architectural assignments, but he disputed the official slogan "utility, economy, and if conditions allow, beauty." He tried to establish a new architecture in the Chinese tradition but his buildings were expensive. He was harshly criticized for this and for his protests at the destruction of Peking landmarks. As a professor of architecture at Tsing Hua University, he had a wide influence throughout his life.

WILMA FAIRBANK

BIBLIOGRAPHY

With the exception of the three brief articles by Liang Ssu-ch'eng listed below, all of his writings were in Chinese.

Chung-kuo ying-tsao hsueh-she hui-k'an. 1930–1945 This quarterly published in Chinese the essays and field reports of Liang and his colleagues.

ECKE, GUSTAV 1936–1937 "The Institute for Research in Chinese Architecture: A Short Summary of the Field Work Carried on from Spring 1932 to Spring 1937." *Monumenta Serica* 2, no. 2:448–474.

LIANG SSU-CH'ENG 1938 "Open Spandrel Bridges of Ancient China." *Pencil Points* 10, Jan.:25–32; Mar.:155–160.

LIANG SSU-CH'ENG 1948 "Chinese Architecture and Art." *Encyclopedia Americana.* Danbury, Conn.: Grolier. Liang's article appeared in subsequent editions.

LIANG SSU-CH'ENG 1952 "China's Architectural Heritage and the Tasks of Today." *People's China* no. 21:30–36.

LIBERA, ADALBERTO

In the panorama of Italian architects before and after World War II, Adalberto Libera (1903–1963) is at once original and emblematic. He is decisively original for his moral energy and his spirit and enthusiasm which characterize every design, built or unbuilt; and he is emblematic of many other architects in the profound transformation his designs underwent when he passed from the Fascist to the subsequent democratic period. The quality of his architecture did not change when it is seen simply as a relationship between lines and volumes, but certainly there was a considerable reduction of tension in the work. It was almost as if he lost motivation, and the design research ended up spending itself in a compound equilibrium of plastic rhythms, or rather in the correct application of a sort of accepted, virtually absolute canon which was rarely susceptible to doubts and emotional tension. In this way, the expressive form Libera manifested in his work of the 1930s was transformed, after 1950, into a composition exercise in the constant attempt to join the mechanism of the new industrialized building production to the new social system introduced by the new immigrant masses. Although unknown in their essence, these masses became the obligatory users of an architectural "Rationalism" culturally guaranteed more by a certain aversion to it during the Fascist period than by experienced observations of reality.

For this reason, the works of Libera's later period, such as the Tuscolano Quarter (1953–1954) in Rome, the administrative buildings of the Ministry of the Treasury (1958), the Olympic Village (1959–1960), the residential zone of Kobala, India (1961–1962), the Palazzo della Regione Trentina (1954), and so forth, bespeak a high professionalism, attentive and rigorous but by now generic and almost uniform in the panorama of contemporary Italian architecture.

Libera was born at Villa Lagarina, near Trent, where he attended the Austrian schools until his family fled to Parma during World War I. In Parma, he continued his education and studied architecture at the State Art Institute, receiving his degree in architecture from the Scuola Superiore in 1928. He began his work in 1926, while still a student, when he joined the *Gruppo 7,* where he distinguished himself with his active participation in drawing up the "Manifesto of Italian Rationalism" published in the *Rassegna Italiana* from December 1926 to May 1927. In 1927, he took part in the Stuttgart exhibit organized by Ludwig Mies van der Rohe. The next year, when he had just graduated, he felt the need to give greater prominence and public exposure to the activities of the Rationalist group. Thus he promoted the foundation of the Movimento Italiano Architettura Razionale (MIAR); almost contemporaneously (1928), together with Gaetano Minucci, he organized the first Exposition of Rational Architecture in Rome.

In 1931, with Pier Maria Bardi, he organized a second exhibit, which provided the first major occasion for strong polemical battles between the supporters of a "modern" culture and the most reactionary academic circles, battles which were destined to last throughout the Fascist period and in which both sides claimed victories and defeats. With the dissolution of MIAR, Libera pursued his professional activities, elaborating in practice the theories voiced in the provocative cultural exhibits he promoted. He collaborated from time to time with the best Italian architects of the era. For the Exhibition of the Fascist Revolution to celebrate the tenth anniversary of the March on Rome, Libera collaborated with Mario De Renzi on the façade and with Gino Valenti on the sanctuary room inside. The work was a great success and had considerable architectural influence. The burnished copper lictoral fasces, twenty-five meters high, came to symbolize the exhibit itself, and was then used for subsequent celebrations.

A second major design event for Libera was his participation in the national competition for the Palazzo del Littorio (1935–1936) and the permanent Exhibition of the Fascist Revolution, in via dell'Impero, Rome. The promoters conceived of this event as the time to define a new Fascist style, but Libera distinguished himself in the urban placement of his project and in the original architectural solution of having the work stretched along an arch which contained and exalted the regime's symbol in a didactic expressionism. Naturally, given the cultural and political uncertainties of Fascism—and above all, given its desire not to be compromised by demanding solutions, only a beautiful catalog of all of the projects submitted was printed, putting off for another time the choice of a "lictoral style."

Following this experience, Libera turned resolutely to truly professional work, in which he applied syntheses of the various urban and architectural solutions which he had singled out during his study of the language of architecture. Although he did enter several national competitions (his plan for Aprilia in the reclaimed Pontine Marshes is especially noteworthy), he neither won the competitions nor built any major public projects.

In 1938, Libera designed and built Curzio Malaparte's villa on Capri, with a highly original architectural solution, the apex of his greatest creativity; certainly, this work is a great attempt to integrate nature and design. Indeed, this building has a particularly organic spirit, in an architectural sense; one might venture to hypothesize a certain assonance in the rhythms of the rock on the stairway to the terrace, and the architectural game of water and overhangs in FRANK LLOYD WRIGHT's Kaufmann House.

The last important work of this period was his design for the creatively and compositionally audacious arch for E'42. Here again, the expressive motif is compressed with intense symbolic value; the boundary between architecture and sculpture is unclear, and it offers a particular conception of the relationship between man and urban space.

Following a long period of isolation in the Trentino region during the demise of Fascism, Libera returned to a new political climate in Rome in 1947. He assumed the directorship of the architectural section of INA-Casa, developing the design for the Tuscolano as well as a long string of urban projects. In 1953, following a national competition, he began teaching at the University of Florence. In 1962, he transferred to the University of Rome, where he died the following year.

RICCARDO MARIANI
Translated from Italian by
Diane Ghirardo

WORKS

*1927, Exposition, Stuttgart, Germany. *1929, First Exhibit of Rationalist Architecture (with Gaetano Minucci); 1929–1930, Tor di Quinto Cooperative (with Mario Ridolfi); Rome. *1931, Exhibit of Italian Architecture, Berlin. 1931–1932, Nicoletti House; *1932–1933, Exhibition of Fascist Revolution (façade with Mario De Renzi; sanctuary with Gino Valente); 1933–1934, Ostiense Post Office (with De Renzi); Rome. 1935, Houses for Tirrena Society, Ostia, Italy. *1935–1936, Palazzo Littorio; *1937–1938, Palazzo dei Ricevimenti e Congressi, E'42; Rome. *1938, Villa Malaparte, Capri, Italy. *1953–1954, Tuscolano Housing Quarter, Rome. *1954, Palazzo della Regione Trentino, Trent, Italy. 1958, Ministry of the Treasury Administrative Buildings; *1959–1960, Olympic Village (with others); Rome. 1961–1962, Residential Zone, Kobala, India.

BIBLIOGRAPHY

ARGAN, GIULIO CARLO 1976 *Adalberto Libero.* Rome: Editalia.

BATEY, ANDREW 1980 "Villa Malaparte." *Archetype* 1, no. 4:23–29.

DE' SETA, CESARE (1972)1978 *La cultura architettonica in Italia tra le due guerre.* 2d ed. Bari, Italy: Laterza.

MONTESI, PIO 1959 "Politica e Architettura." Pages 8–11 in *La Casa* 6. Rome: De Luca.

Libergier. Tombstone of Hugues Libergier, Reims Cathedral. France. 1263 or later

LIBERGIER, HUGUES

Hugues Libergier (?–1263) was architect of the Benedictine Abbey Church of Saint-Nicaise at Reims, France, between 1231 and his death in 1263, when he was succeeded by Robert de Coucy. Libergier was responsible for the nave and the west façade and towers of Saint-Nicaise. Traditional and conservative in his nave design, he created one of the most complex and exquisite west façade ensembles anywhere, probably between around 1245 and 1256, when the great bells were hung in the towers. Libergier's principal innovations were a tracery screen across the portal zone which united the buttresses and the openings between them (a scheme adopted from contemporary choir screens) and a huge twin-lancet-and-oculus combination replacing the simpler west rose design.

Libergier is best known today not for his work at Saint-Nicaise (destroyed between 1791 and 1819) but for his tombstone now in Reims Cathedral, where he is shown in fancy costume holding a model of Saint-Nicaise and flanked by the tools of his profession. The tombstone inscription reads: CY GIST MAISTRE HVES LIBERGIERS QVI COMENSA CESTE EGLISE AN [=EN] LAN DE LINCARNATION M.CC. ET XX.I.X [sic., = XXX.I] LE MARDI DE PAQVES ET TRESPASSA LAN DE LINCARNATION M.CC.LXIII LE SEMEDI APRES PAQVES POVR D[I]EV P[R]IEZ PO[V]R LVI.

CARL F. BARNES, JR.

BIBLIOGRAPHY

BIDEAULT, MARYSE, and LAUTIER, CLAUDINE 1977 "Saint-Nicaise de Reims: Chronologie et nouvelles

remarques sur l'architecture." *Bulletin Monumental* 135:295–333.
BRANNER, ROBERT 1965 *Saint Louis and the Court Style in Gothic Architecture.* London: Zwemmer.
GIVELET, FRANÇOIS 1897 *L'église et l'abbaye de Saint-Nicaise de Reims: Notice historique et archéologique.* Reims, France.

LIBON OF ELIS

Libon of Elis (flourished c.470–450 B.C.) was the architect of the Doric temple of Zeus at Olympia; begun probably in 468 B.C., it was one of the largest Doric temples built in Greece. Architecturally normative, even uninspiring, the building was distinguished by the elaborate sculptural programs of its metopes and pediments. It became famous as well for housing the colossal chryselephantine statue of Zeus, by Pheidias. The temple was overthrown by an earthquake in late antiquity, and disappeared from sight until the modern period.

B. M. BOYLE

WORK

*468–457 B.C., Temple of Zeus, Olympia, Greece.

BIBLIOGRAPHY

ASHMOLE, BERNARD 1972 *Architect and Sculptor in Classical Greece.* New York University Press.
DINSMOOR, WILLIAM B. 1973 *The Architecture of Ancient Greece.* Reprint. New York: Biblo Tannen.
LAWRENCE, ARNOLD W. 1975 *Greek Architecture.* Harmondsworth, England: Penguin.

LI CHIEH

Li Chieh (c.1065–1110) lived in China and was editor of *Ying-tsao fa-shih* (Building Standards). This work was compiled during a period when the Chinese government changed its economic system radically. Until the middle of the eleventh century, most taxes and expenditures had been paid in kind, and public work was carried out as labor duty. After this time, most was paid in cash and craftsmen on public work were entitled to receive wages. The new policies were introduced mainly to fill the need for closer control of government expenses. The staff of the ministry of work was enlarged for the same reason, and Li Chieh was employed in 1092. In 1097, the government issued an order for the compilation of the *Ying-tsao fa-shih* to facilitate the accounts for public buildings, and Li Chieh was given charge of the work. In 1100, he finished the manuscript. The *Ying-tsao fa-shih* gives methods for exact calculation of the amount of labor and materials necessary for all sorts of building constructions down to the smallest details.

Li Chieh rose in the ranks of his office, becoming its director in 1105. During his time as official, he supervised the erection of a number of public and imperial buildings in the Chinese capital of that time, the present Kaifeng. All the buildings were destroyed in 1125 when the capital was burned down.

ELSE GLAHN

WORKS

*1098–1100, Wu-wang ti (palace for the five younger brothers of the emperor); *1102, National University; *1103, Building, Imperial Palace; *1103, Department of Ministries; *1104, Sacrificial Building (constructed for the emperor); *1105, Dynastic Ancestral Temple; *1105, Ming-t'ang (temple of imperial sacrifices to heaven); *1106, Buddhist Temple (in commemoration of the emperor's mother); Kaifeng, China.

BIBLIOGRAPHY

CHOU CH'ENG 1731 *Sung tung-ching k'ao.*
GLAHN, ELSE 1976 "Li Chieh." Volume 2, pages 523–529 in Herbert Franke (editor), *Sung Biographies.* Wiesbaden, Germany: Steiner.
LI CHIEH (1103)1925 *Ying-tsao fa-shih.* Reprint. Peking: Ch'i-Ch'ien Chu. In this publication the tomb inscription for Li Chieh by Ch'eng Chü in *Shui-shan hsiao-chi* is reprinted as a colophon.

LICHT, HUGO

Born in the Prussian province of Posen, Hugo Licht (1841–1923) received his architectural training at the Bauakademie in Berlin and at the Polytechnikum in Vienna under HEINRICH VON FERSTEL. After further training in Berlin ateliers, including that of RICHARD LUCAE, and trips abroad to Rome, Paris, and London, Licht entered private practice in Berlin, where he remained from 1871 to 1879. From 1879 to 1906, he was director of the municipal building administration in Leipzig, and he remained in Leipzig until his death.

Between 1883 and 1913, Licht built more than a dozen major buildings in central Leipzig, transforming the face of the city. In these municipal buildings, Licht attempted to find a monumental expression for the buildings of government under the new empire. His solutions to this problem ranged from modest brick buildings, similar to Ferstel's Museum of Applied Art in Vienna, for the Hospital for Incurables (1887–1889) and the Police Headquarters (1889–1890), to rich and lavish interpretations of the baroque and the rococo, as in the remodeled Art Museum (1883–1886) and the Grassi Museum (1892–1895). In the late

1880s, Licht began to develop, in addition, a massive masonry style, distantly neo-Romanesque and also perhaps inspired by H. H. RICHARDSON's Trinity Church, Boston, which Licht admired. This aspect of Licht's work began to be evident in the Market Hall (1889–1891) and came to fruition in the new City Hall (1898–1905). Yet, the City Hall was also a building sui generis; a huge limestone structure, it combined motifs from the past, including gables and a great medievalizing tower, in an entirely new way. Licht was widely admired in Germany for the range of his design ability, his skill in architectural detailing, and for the combination of dignity and practicality evident in the interiors of his municipal buildings.

It was, however, as an architectural publicist and editor that Licht had his greatest influence. Very early in his career, Licht developed close ties to the Ernst Wasmuth publishing house in Berlin; out of this relationship came a long series of extensive compilations of drawings and photographs of German architecture, which helped to make German architects aware of each other and to make their accomplishments available to the outside world. These compilations also stressed new building types—office buildings, stores, and factories—and contributed to the view that such buildings could legitimately be seen as "high architecture." In 1901, Licht persuaded Wasmuth to begin publishing *Die Architektur des XX. Jahrhunderts: Zeitschrift für moderne Baukunst* (1901–1914), an extraordinarily lavish journal consisting principally of photographs, with accompanying commentary in three languages. Under Licht's direction, *Die Architektur des XX. Jahrhunderts* launched the careers of many young architects in Germany and did more than any previous journal had done to overcome provincialism in German architecture. At the same time, it contributed to a new international emphasis in German architectural publications. Licht initiated another periodical in 1906, *Profanbau* (Leipzig, 1906–1922), but *Die Architektur des XX. Jahrhunderts* was his major and lasting contribution to German architecture and to the practices of architectural publishing.

BARBARA MILLER LANE

WORKS

1881–1884, Chapel-Mortuary, New Johannis Cemetery; 1883–1884, Eighth District School; 1883–1886, Art Museum (reconstruction and extensions); 1884, Slaughterhouses; 1885–1887, Conservatory of Music; 1886–1887, Rectory, Nikolaikirche; 1887–1889, Hospital for Incurables; 1889–1890, Municipal Trade School; 1889–1890, Police Headquarters; 1889–1891, Market Hall; 1892–1895, Grassi Museum; 1894–1897, Johanniskirche (remodeling); 1895–1897, Barracks, Möckern; Leipzig. 1896, Kaiser Wilhelm Monument, Breslau, Poland. 1898–1905, New City Hall; 1908–1912, City Hall (extension); Leipzig. 1910, City Hall, Döbeln, Germany. 1912–1913, Leipzig Fire Insurance Company Offices.

BIBLIOGRAPHY

"Dem Andenken an Hugo Licht." 1923 *Zentralblatt der Bauverwaltung* 43:325–328.

Leipzig und seine Bauten. 1892 Leipzig: Gebhardt.

LICHT, HUGO (editor) 1877 *Die Architectur Berlins.* Berlin: Wasmuth.

LICHT, HUGO (editor) 1879–1882 *Die Architektur Deutschlands.* 2 vols. Berlin: Wasmuth.

LICHT, HUGO (editor) 1882 *Die Architektur der Gegenwart.* 2 vols. Berlin: Wasmuth.

LICHT, HUGO (editor) 1886–1900 *Die Architektur der Gegenwart.* 5 vols. Berlin: Wasmuth.

LICHT, HUGO (1894)1900 *Architektonische Details von ausgeführten Bauwerken.* 2d ed. Berlin: Wasmuth.

LICHT, HUGO 1901–1906 *Charakteristische Details zu ausgeführten Bauwerken.* 6 vols. Berlin: Wasmuth.

LICHT, HUGO (editor) 1901–1914 *Die Architektur des XX. Jahrhunderts.*

LICHT, HUGO (editor) 1906–1922 *Profanbau.*

LIENAU, DETLEF

Detlef Lienau (1818–1887) was a professionally trained European architect who made considerable contributions to American architecture in the decades preceding and following the Civil War. His clients, many of whom were prominent figures of the period, greatly respected his abilities, as did leading architects such as RICHARD UPJOHN, LEOPOLD EIDLITZ, and RICHARD MORRIS HUNT, with whom he joined in founding the American Institute of Architects in 1857.

Born in Schleswig-Holstein, he attended elementary and technical schools in Stettin and Berlin. He received a thorough training in carpentry and North German building techniques in Berlin and Hamburg, followed by advanced study at the Königliche Baugewerksschule in Munich the following year. By 1842, he was in Paris, where he spent almost five years in the atelier of HENRI LABROUSTE, then hard at work on the Bibliothèque Sainte-Geneviève. It was to Labrouste that Lienau owed his rationalist approach to planning and construction as well as his classical orientation in design.

After a brief visit to London, Lienau sailed for America, arriving in New York on December 26, 1848. By 1850, he had developed an extensive practice that included almost every kind of building: cottages, mansions, townhouses, rowhouses, an early apartment house and a tenement dwelling, banks, stores, office buildings, lofts, warehouses and factories, as well as schools, libraries, a church, and a museum.

Lienau's first important commission was Grace Church, Jersey City, which opened its doors on May 11, 1853 for the architect's marriage to Catherine van Giesen Booraem. Built to serve a small, still partially rural community, the brownstone structure evidences Lienau's adaptation to current American stylistic practices: the proportions and chief architectural features are those of the early Gothic English parish church in combination with Romanesque elements.

The architect's first city residence, commissioned in 1850 and completed in 1852, was built on Fifth Avenue and Tenth Street for Hart M. Shiff, a wealthy German-born merchant. The Shiff house brought to New York its first example of the French Second Empire style. With low mansard roof, prominent dormers, and a sophisticated handling of brick and brownstone, the house was glowingly described as a French château in contemporary publications. The new style caught on immediately in a city that was rapidly becoming French in its food, dress, manners, and taste. The French mansard style, which was to expand over the entire country in the next two decades, was quickly taken up by other architects such as CALVERT VAUX, JAMES RENWICK, and, upon his return from France in 1855, Richard Morris Hunt.

In 1852, Lienau also built a villa overlooking the Hudson River, near Dobbs Ferry, New York, for Francis Cottenet, a well-to-do French importer. Called Nuits, it was constructed of Caen stone imported from France, and is a classical variation of the popular Italian villa style. Its symmetry is in contrast to the picturesque asymmetrical designs current at the time. At *Beach Cliffe,* in Newport, Rhode Island, built the same year for DeLancey Kane, Lienau's monumental handling of the façade brought to Newport one of its earliest examples of French influence.

Lienau completed his first commission for William Schermerhorn in 1859. It was a large townhouse on Twenty-third Street, west of Fifth Avenue, eminently suited to the lavish entertainments for which the old Knickerbocker family was famous. Faced with brick and brownstone, the façade was simple, straightforward, and restrained in design. More important, however, was the adjoining double mansion (1867–1869) for William's bachelor brother, Edmund H. Schermerhorn. Here, the full impact of French influence, affecting plan as well as elevation, hit New York. The house was quite literally a transplanted Parisian *hôtel particulier.* A carriage drive ran through the building in the French manner, depositing guests at the foot of the grand staircase, then exiting on Twenty-fourth Street.

By far the most ambitious of Lienau's urban residential work was the blockfront of eight attached townhouses, designed in 1868 for Rebecca Colford Jones. Built of light-colored Ohio stone in 1869–1870 and located on the east side of Fifth Avenue, between Fifty-fifth and Fifty-sixth Streets, it achieved standards of monumentality and luxury unequaled in New York until the 1880s. Recognized as a landmark in urban architecture, it not only helped to jolt the city's architecture out of its brownstone rut, but also established an important precedent in planning and design.

Elm Park, in South Norwalk, Connecticut, designed by Lienau for LeGrand Lockwood, a Wall Street broker and railroad magnate, is one of the most grandiose houses of the period, a true precursor of the mansions of the Golden Age. Built around an octagonal court, it was conceived on a princely scale. The superb interiors were finished with imported marbles and rare woods, and the furnishings were designed in part by Lienau's old friend and former partner, Léon Marcotte, one of the most successful designers of furniture and interiors of the day.

In the field of multiple dwellings, after the Civil War, Lienau endeavored to meet the needs of all classes. Grosvenor House, built for Francis Cottenet in 1871–1872 was one of the city's first and finest apartment hotels, well-equipped with modern conveniences, including an elevator. The Schermerhorn Apartments, consisted of four houses designed to appear as one, with shops at street level and flats above, in the French manner. The apartments were well-lit and ventilated by rear courtyards between the buildings and were equipped with conveniences which no French apartment house of that period had. The difference between Lienau's preliminary plan for a tenement house on Elm Street in New York and the house as built in 1879 reflects his concern for the poor.

In the late 1860s and 1870s, Lienau's practice expanded to include a number of institutional and public buildings. In style, these buildings reflect his basic conservatism and that of the institutions he served. Odenheimer Hall (1868) at Saint Mary's Burlington, New Jersey, and Suydam Hall (1871–1873) and the Sage Library (1873–1875) at the General Theological Seminary, New Brunswick, New Jersey, are a great contrast to the Victorian Gothic designs then popular for collegiate architecture. Lienau's concern that a library be as fireproof as possible is reflected in his choice of materials and structural techniques for Hodgson Hall (1873–1876), now the headquarters of the Georgia Historical Society, and the Public Library, both in Savannah, Georgia.

Lienau. Rebecca Jones Blockfront, Fifth Avenue. New York. 1868–1870

Finally, in the commercial and industrial sphere, Lienau's work kept pace with the changes in the economic fabric of the nation during and after the Civil War. In the well-designed much admired warehouse for the French and Belgian Plate Glass Company (1863–1864) in New York, Lienau's rationalist French training and his love of the North German brickwork tradition are clearly apparent.

At the same time, the buildings which Lienau erected for the Matthiessen and Weichers Sugar Refining Company in Jersey City, New Jersey (1862–1870), illustrate the effects of technological changes in production methods upon architectural planning and design. Lienau's building of 1862 served the sugar refining industry as a model for years. It was the first refinery to house the newly invented centrifugal machines, which revolutionized the process of sugar refining. The layout was determined strictly by the sequence of operations, and formal symmetry was sacrificed to a completely functional design. In contrast, Lienau's commercial buildings in New York of the 1870s and 1880s are decidedly retardataire in style.

Lienau's work of the 1870s and 1880s is evidence of a strong undercurrent of conservative, academic traditions running against the mainstream which served as a bridge between the classical traditions of the second quarter of the nineteenth century and their re-emergence in the 1880s in the movement led by McKim, Mead, and White. To the men trained in his office, notably Paul J. Pelz and Henry J. Hardenbergh, Lienau passed on his classical orientation, his respect for rational planning, and his insistence upon sound principles of construction. Lienau's career, begun at Tenth Street and Fifth Avenue in 1850 and ending on the Upper West Side in 1887, reflects the decades of Manhattan's most rapid growth.

Ellen Kramer

WORKS

*1850–1852, Hart M. Shiff House, New York. 1850–1853, Grace Church, Jersey City, N.J. *1852, Beach Cliffe (DeLancey Kane Villa), Newport, R.I. 1852, Nuits (Francis Cottenet Villa), Dobbs Ferry, N.Y. *c.1853–1859, William C. Schermerhorn House, 49 West 23rd Street, New York. *1859, Mechanics' and Traders' Bank, Jersey City, N.J. 1859–1860, Langdon Estate Loft Buildings, 577–581 Broadway, New York. *1862–1870, F. O. Matthiessen and Weichers Sugar Refinery, Jersey City, N.J. 1863–1864, French and Belgian Plate Glass Company, Howard and Crosby Streets, New York. *c.1864, First National Bank of Jersey City, N.J. c.1864–1868, Elm Park (LeGrand Lockwood Mansion), South Norwalk, Conn. *c.1865, New York Life and Trust Company Building; *1867–1869, Edmund H. Schermerhorn House, 45–47 West 23rd Street; New York. 1868, Odenheimer Hall, Saint Mary's Hall, Burlington, N.J. *1868–1870, Rebecca Jones Blockfront, Fifth Avenue; *1870–1871, Schermerhorn Apartments, Third Avenue; New York. *1871, Boeraem Row, Jersey City, N.J. *1871–1872, Grosvenor House, New York. 1871–1873, Suydam Hall, General Theological Seminary, New Brunswick, N.J. 1872, Schloss Düneck, Ueterson, Germany. 1872–1873, Cruickston Park, Blair, Ontario. 1873–1874, DeLancey Kane Loft Building, 676 Broadway, New York. 1873–1874, Sage Library, General Theological Seminary, New Brunswick, N.J. 1873–1876, Hodgson Hall, Savannah, Ga. *1879, Tenement House, 162 Elm Street; *1881–1882, Daniel Parish Estate Office Building, 67 Wall Street; *1880–1882, Panorama Building, Seventh Avenue; New York. 1885–1886, Telfair Academy of Arts and Sciences (alterations), Savannah, Ga. 1886–1887, Houses, 48–54 West 82nd Street, New York.

BIBLIOGRAPHY

Brault, Emile 1893 Volume 3, pages 429–434 in *Les Architectes par leurs oeuvres.* Paris: Laurens.

Hartmann, Sadakichi 1906 "A Conversation with Henry Janeway Hardenbergh." *Architectural Record* 19:376–380.

Kramer, Ellen W. 1955 "Detlef Lienau, an Architect of the Brown Decades." *Journal of the Society of Architectural Historians* 14, Mar.:18–25.

Kramer, Ellen W. 1958 "The Domestic Architecture of Detlef Lienau, a Conservative Victorian." Unpublished Ph.D. dissertation, New York University.

Schaack, Margaret Donald 1967 "The Lockwood-Mathews Mansion." *Interior Design* 38, Mar.: 155–163.

Schuyler, Montgomery 1897 "Works of Henry J. Hardenbergh." *Architectural Record* 6, Jan.–Mar.:335–336.

LIGHTOLER, TIMOTHY

Timothy Lightoler (?–c.1779) was a carver, architect, and author. Most of his designs and engravings are signed "T. Lightoler," but at Burton Constable one design is inscribed "Thos. Lightoler."

The style of his exteriors is Palladian (see ANDREA PALLADIO); his interiors are rococo, with an admixture of Gothick or Chinoiserie. His drawings show landscape settings from within and without and also tables, mirrors, girandoles, and curtains.

IVAN HALL

WORKS

c.1757–1768, Burton Constable (remodeling), North Humberside, England. c.1760, Saint Mary's (altarpiece), Warwickshire, England. c.1762–1764, Platt Hall, Manchester, England. *1763, Bidston Hill Signal House, Cheshire, England. 1763–1765, Stoneleigh Abbey (remodeling), Warwickshire, England. *1763–1769, Saint Paul's Church, Liverpool, England. 1763–1769, Warwick Castle (remodeling), England. *1765–1769, Beverly Minster (organ case), North Humberside, England. *1766, Teddesley Hall (chimneypieces), Staffordshire, England. 1766–1767, Octagon Chapel, Bath, England. 1775–1783, Saint John's Church, Liverpool, England.

BIBLIOGRAPHY

LIGHTOLER, TIMOTHY (1762)1968 *The Gentleman and Farmer's Architect.* Reprint. Farnborough, England: Gregg.

HALFPENNY, WILLIAM; MORRIS, ROBERT; and LIGHTOLER, TIMOTHY 1757 *The Modern Builder's Assistant.* London: Sayer.

LIGORIO, PIRRO

In the mid-sixteenth century, Pirro Ligorio (1513/1514–1583) revived in Rome, Italy, the archeologically oriented architectural style of RAPHAEL and BALDASSARE PERUZZI. The result was a very erudite and refined architecture. Born in Naples of a noble family, he emigrated to Rome about 1534, where his first recorded activity was as a painter in the manner of Polidoro da Caravaggio and Peruzzi. During this period Ligorio began to explore the antiquities of Rome and to compose the first of his two great manuscript encyclopedias on classical antiquity. Later he asserted that he learned perspective and drawing in order to record the antiquities. Probably, at this time, Ligorio met the north Italian architect ANDREA PALLADIO—who was on a trip to Rome—and permitted him to study some of the archeological material Ligorio was assembling. On December 16, 1548, Ligorio was nominated to be a member of the artistic confraternity of the Virtuosi al Pantheon.

In 1549, the Cardinal of Ferrara appointed Ligorio his personal archeologist. With the appointment of the cardinal in the following year as governor of the hilltown of Tivoli, Ligorio began preliminary work on the transformation of the old Franciscan monastery there into the Villa d'Este (1550–1572) with its adjacent gardens. At the same time Ligorio explored the nearby ancient Roman villa of Hadrian which was to influence Ligorio's design of the Villa d'Este gardens, and acquired classical antiquities for the cardinal, some of which were to decorate the gardens. Ligorio's small treatise on the antiquities of Rome appeared in 1553. It is the only publication during his lifetime of his wealth of classical knowledge, which is otherwise preserved in manuscripts.

After the election in 1555 of the Neapolitan Pope Paul IV, the Cardinal of Ferrara was immediately exiled. Although this interrupted Ligorio's work at Tivoli, in April 1557 he was named architect of the Vatican Palace (1557–1565) by his fellow countryman, Pope Paul IV. In addition to revisions within the palace, including the design of the chapel of the new apartment of Paul IV off the Belvedere corridor and an ill-fated project to improve the lighting of the Hall of Constantine, Ligorio began in May 1558 a small summer retreat for the pope in the woods beyond the Belvedere Court, whose construction was interrupted in November.

With the death of Paul IV, the election late in 1559 of Pope Pius IV was even more encouraging to Ligorio's architectural career, as the new pope was determined to pursue vigorously the numerous incomplete papal architectural projects, some of which had languished since their inception under Pope Julius II at the beginning of the century. In May 1560 construction began anew at the casino begun for Pope Paul IV and by 1562, Ligorio completed the structure and most of the decoration of the building, which would henceforth be known as the Casino of Pius IV (1558–1565). A charming small complex of casino, dining loggia, and gateways set around an oval court, it was modeled on a type of ancient Roman garden house (*diaeta*). Richly decorated with stucco, mosaic, and fresco, and enlivened with small fountains, it was described by the nineteenth century historian, Jacob Burckhardt, as "the most beautiful afternoon retreat that modern architecture has created."

By November 1560 work was underway to complete the huge Belvedere Court in the Vatican begun by DONATO BRAMANTE for Julius II, which Ligorio revised by adding curvilinear auditorium seats at the southern end of the lower terrace of the court and by converting the exedra at the northern end into a huge niche as the focus of the vista from the Vatican Palace. At this time, Ligorio undertook other minor, often decorative work, in the palace itself—in the library, the Sala Ducale, the Loggia della Cosmographia, and the Borgia apart-

Ligorio.
Casino of Pius IV.
Rome.
1558–1565

Ligorio.
Lancellotti Palace.
Rome.
c.1560

ment. Pius IV, whose interest in seasonal places of retreat from the Vatican is seen in his immediate completion of the Casino in the Vatican grounds, ordered Ligorio to reerect the elevated corridor, destroyed by Paul IV, which served as a passage from the Palazzo Venezia to the tower erected by Pope Paul III in the Franciscan monastery of Santa Maria d'Aracoeli on the Capitoline Hill, and to redecorate the Tower, with the addition of a new loggia. All of this work was destroyed for the erection in the nineteenth century of the monument to Vittorio Emmanuele. In 1560 Ligorio may have also renovated the exterior elevations and court of the Lancellotti Palace at the southern end of the Piazza Navona. The attribution dates only from the seventeenth century, but the architectural style influenced by the work of Baldassare Peruzzi resembles other work by Ligorio. On December 2, 1560, Ligorio received recognition for his contributions to the culture of Rome by being made an honorary citizen of the city.

As the papal work of Ligorio continued, other architectural projects were undertaken. The problem of the ownership of the Villa Giulia being settled by Pius IV, Ligorio was ordered in 1561 to convert the public fountain on the Via Flaminia at the entrance to the Villa Giulia into a small palace, the so-called Palazzetto of Pius IV, which was given to the papal nephews, Carlo Cardinal Borromeo and Federigo Borromeo, and completed in 1564. In May 1563 Ligorio began in the Vatican a new building north of the Belvedere Court to house papal conclaves, but with the plan of June 1565 to reorganize the papal archives the structure was completed as an archives building. In this century the Archivio was transformed and incorporated into the Vatican Pinacoteca.

Pius IV was also interested in restoring the churches of Rome. In 1561 the bronze doors and lead covering of the dome of the ancient Pantheon, or the church of Santa Maria della Rotonda, were restored under Ligorio's direction, and in April 1564 he was paid for a design to refurbish the façade of the north transept of the Saint John Lateran Basilica, work which is still visible above and behind the double loggia added later by DOMENICO FONTANA. With the death of MICHELANGELO in February 1564, Ligorio was appointed in August architect of the great church of St. Peter's and was soon joined by GIACOMO BAROZZI DA VIGNOLA as assistant architect. Political conflicts among the artistic cliques of Rome delayed Ligorio's appointment, since he was considered hostile to Michelangelo. As an archeologist Ligorio was devoted to the ideas enunciated by the ancient Roman VITRUVIUS in his treatise on architecture and was unhappy with the deviations from Vitruvius that he saw in the work of Michelangelo and his followers. Little work at St. Peter's was accomplished during Ligorio's brief activity, which was limited to completing the northwest side of the entablature of the drum of the dome and to the cutting of capitals for some of the interior chapels. Also in 1564 Ligorio began to rebuild the court of the University of Rome, called the Sapienza, but in October 1565 the work was suspended. It may be at this time that he also refurbished and expanded the old stronghold of the Cenci family in the

Arenula region of Rome, including an adjacent small palace facing the Piazza Cenci, similar in style to the earlier Lancellotti Palace.

Late in July 1565 on the accusation of the sculptor, Guglielmo della Porta, Ligorio was imprisoned on suspicion of defrauding the papacy in some of his architectural work and in the purchase of antiquities. Apparently cleared of the charge, he was released a month later, but his position at the papal court was increasingly threatened by the opposition of the followers and friends of Michelangelo.

The death of Pope Pius IV in December 1565 brought Ligorio's papal career to an end, although he and Sallustio Peruzzi continued in charge of the decorations for the coronation of Pope Pius V in January 1566. With the earlier release from exile of the Cardinal of Ferrara, work had recommenced slowly in 1560 on the Villa d'Este at Tivoli, and Ligorio, no longer involved with papal commissions, could devote more attention to Tivoli, where in 1567 and 1568, he designed fountains and supervised the completion of the gardens. The lavish gardens at Tivoli with their unprecedented wealth of waterworks and intricate iconographical program expressed in antique and modern sculpture, all conceived and designed by Ligorio, represent the climax of Renaissance landscape design and are still one of the great tourist attractions of Italy.

Growing dissatisfied with the Roman cultural ambiance, on December 1, 1568, Ligorio was appointed antiquarian of Alfonso II, duke of Ferrara, and moved to Ferrara early in 1569, where he was also appointed *lector* at the university. Most of his activity in Ferrara was archeological, organizing the ducal collection of antiquities for which in 1571 he made architectural designs to house the collection in the Este Castle. He was also in charge of devising and designing the six temporary triumphal arches erected in 1574 for the visit of King Henry III of France. On December 4, 1580, Ligorio was made an honorary citizen of Ferrara and, dying in October 1583, was buried on October 30 in the former church of Sant'Anna.

David R. Coffin

WORKS

1550–1572, Villa d'Este, Tivoli, Italy. 1557–1565, Vatican Palace; 1558–1565, Casino of Pius IV; 1560–1565, Belvedere Court; *1560–1565, Tower of Paul III (revisions and corridor); c.1560, Lancellotti Palace; 1561, Pantheon (restoration); 1561–1564, Palazzetto of Pius IV; 1564, Saint John Lateran Basilica (north transept); 1564–1565, St. Peter's in the Vatican; 1564–1565, Sapienza; c.1564, Cenci Palace; Rome. *1571, Este Castle (interiors); *1574, arches for entry of Henry III; Ferrara, Italy.

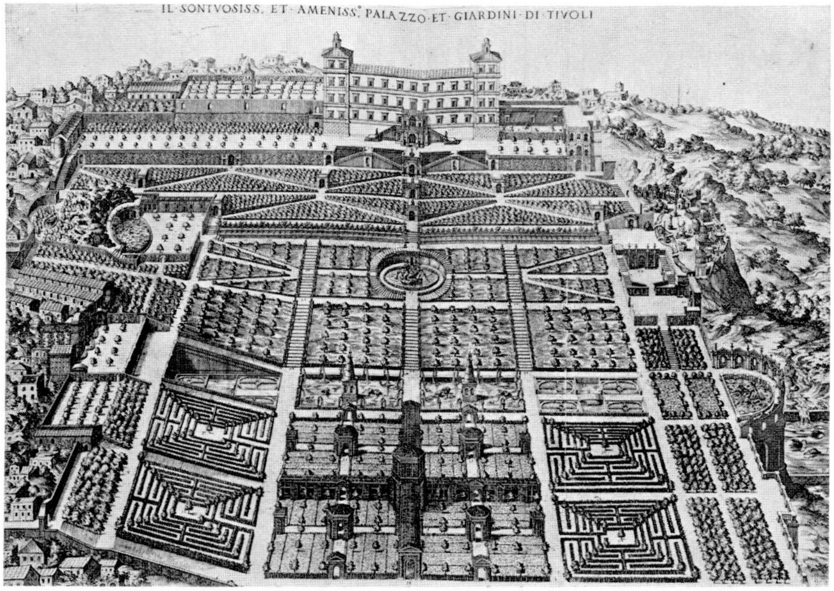

Ligorio.
Tivoli Palace and Gardens (engraving by Dupérac). Italy.

BIBLIOGRAPHY

Ackerman, James S. 1954 *The Cortile del Belvedere.* Biblioteca Apostolica Vaticana.

Ancel, René 1908 "Le Vatican sous Paul IV: Contribution à l'histoire de palais pontifical." *Revue Bénédictine* 24:48–71.

Coffin, David R. 1960 *The Villa d'Este at Tivoli.* N.J.: Princeton University Press.

Coffin, David R. 1964 "Pirro Ligorio on the Nobility of the Arts." *Journal of the Warburg and Courtauld Institutes* 27:191–210.

Coffin, David R. 1979 *The Villa in the Life of Renaissance Rome.* Princeton University Press.

Lamb, Carl 1966 *Die Villa d'Este in Tivoli.* Munich: Prestel.

Smith, Graham 1977 *The Casino of Pius IV.* Princeton University Press.

Venturi, Adolfo 1939 Volume 11, no. 2, pages 977–988 in *Storia dell'arte italiana.* Milan: Hoepli.

LINDEGREN, YRJÖ

Yrjö Lindegren (1900–1952) was the purest of the 1930s Functionalists in Finland. The heroic principles of Functionalism are realized in his major work, the Olympic Stadium in Helsinki (1934–1940). Lindegren designed it with Toivo Jäntti for the 1940 Olympic Games, which were, however, postponed because of the war. The stadium is the finest example of Functionalism in Helsinki; with its 245-foot high slender tower, clean lines, and plain white exterior, it has become a national symbol. The postwar era saw a trend toward more picturesque architecture, which is visible in Lindegren's Serpent House in Helsinki (1951). The building contains 190 apartments turned toward the sun and joined together to form a long continuous curve. The solution was unusual at its time; the vocabulary and the details are, however, basically Functionalist. The separate cubic building in the complex contains the kindergarten, sauna, and swimming pool. After the war, Lindegren, together with VILJO REVELL, assisted ALVAR AALTO in doing a master plan for the city of Rovaniemi in Lapland, which had been destroyed by the Germans. Lindegren also worked with Erik Kråkström on the plan for Helsinki. After Lindegren's premature death, the task was given to Alvar Aalto, on whose plans the present design is based.

PIRKKO-LIISA LOUHENJOKI

WORKS

1934–1940, Olympic Stadium, Helsinki. 1948, Kanavasaari Sports Center, Varkaus, Finland. 1951, Serpent House (apartment complex), Helsinki.

BIBLIOGRAPHY

RICHARDS, J. M. 1978 *800 Years of Finnish Architecture.* London: David & Charles.

SALOKORPI, ASKO 1970 *Modern Architecture in Finland.* London: Weidenfeld & Nicolson; New York: Praeger.

TEMPEL, EGON 1968 *New Finnish Architecture.* Translated by James C. Palmes. London: Architectural Press; New York: Praeger.

WICKBERG, NILS ERIK (1959)1962 *Finnish Architecture.* Helsinki: Otava.

LINDGREN, ARMAS

Armas Lindgren (1874–1929) is known mainly for his association with HERMAN GESELLIUS and ELIEL SAARINEN. The three formed a partnership even before they graduated from the Polytechnic Institute, quickly becoming the most successful office in Finland at that time. Combining elements from Finnish medieval castles and churches, wooden vernacular architecture, and mythology with international Art Nouveau, they were influential in creating the National Romantic style. In 1902, Lindgren became the artistic director for the Central School of Applied Arts; he left the partnership in 1905. For several years, he practiced with Wivi Lönn, one of the first women architects in Finland. The Vanemuinen and Estonia Theaters (1906 and 1912) which they designed in Estonia did not incorporate National Romantic features; they are stylistically closer to late *Jugendstil.* Lindgren combined this with the Renaissance palace style in the New Student House (1910) and in the Suomi and Kaleva Insurance Companies' buildings (1911 and 1913) in Helsinki. With Bertel Liljeqvist, he designed several churches in the 1920s reminiscent of medieval models. Lindgren's interest in Finnish medieval history gave him a fine historical sense, which aided him as the artistic leader of the restoration of Turku Cathedral. Not only was Lindgren a master of ornament and handsome interiors, he was also the designer of unusually high-quality workers' housing and a respected professor at the Helsinki University of Technology.

PIRKKO-LIISA LOUHENJOKI

WORKS

ARMAS LINDGREN, HERMAN GESELLIUS, AND ELIEL SAARINEN

*1899–1900, Finnish Pavilion, World's Fair, Paris. 1900–1901, Pohjola Insurance Company, Helsinki. *1901–1902, Suur-Merijoki Manor House, Viipuri, Finland. 1902–1903, Architect's Studio and House (Huitträsk), Kirkkonummi, Finland. 1902–1905, National Museum; *1903–1904, Northern Joint Stock Bank; Helsinki.

ARMAS LINDGREN AND WIVI LÖNN

1906, Vanemuinen Theater, Tartu, Estonia. 1912, Estonia Theater, Tallinn.

ARMAS LINDGREN

1910, New Student House; 1911, Suomi Insurance Company; 1913, Kaleva Insurance Company; 1913, Kulosaari Casino; Helsinki. 1913, Sakala Student Union House, Tartu, Estonia. 1914, Haikko Manor House, Porvii, Finland. 1917, Rowhouses, Kulosaari, Helsinki. 1923–1928, Turku Cathedral (restoration). 1928, Workers' Housing for Kone ja Silta Oy, Helsinki.

ARMAS LINDGREN AND BERTEL LILJEQVIST

1926, Säynätsalo Church, Finland. 1926, Valkeala Church, Finland.

BIBLIOGRAPHY

CHRIST-JANER, ALBERT (1948)1980 *Eliel Saarinen.* With a foreword by Alvar Aalto. 2d ed., rev. University of Chicago Press.

EATON, LEONARD K. 1972 *American Architecture Comes of Age.* Cambridge, Mass.: M.I.T. Press.

RICHARDS, J. M. 1978 *800 Years of Finnish Architecture.* Newton Abbot, England: David & Charles.

SALOKORPI, ASKO 1970 *Modern Architecture in Finland.* London: Weidenfeld & Nicolson.

SMITH, J. BOULTON 1975 *The Golden Age of Finnish Art.* Helsinki: Ministry of Foreign Affairs.

TUOMI, RITVA 1979 "Kansallisen tyylin etsimisestä:—On the Search for a National Style." Pages 56–96 in *Abacus* (Yearbook of the Museum of Finnish Architecture). Helsinki: The museum.

LINDQVIST, SELIM A.

Selim A. Lindqvist (1867–1939) was a pioneer of Finnish constructivism, an innovator of steel and concrete structures. He received a traditional Beaux-Arts education at the Polytechnic Institute in Helsinki at the height of the neo-Renaissance. At the age of twenty-one, he designed the Merkurius Office Building in Helsinki (1888–1890) with Elia Heikel, a progressive construction designer. The building has a cast-iron structure, vast areas of display windows, but still neo-Renaissance façades. Lindqvist and Heikel developed the constructivist concept further in the Lundqvist office building in Helsinki (1898), first of its kind in Finland, by exposing the structure in the style of the Chicago school. The Hamstern Office Building in Helsinki (1907) was constructed of concrete with only a few ornaments. These buildings were designed when the National Romantic style dominated Finnish architecture; Lindqvist, however, never adopted it. He was always more interested in international trends, especially from Vienna. Lindqvist moved, via a late *Jugendstil* reminiscent of JOSEF HOFFMANN, toward an abstract, classically clear vocabulary. His works, especially the Suvilahti Power Station in Helsinki (1908, 1913), marked the beginning of modernism. It is a progressive and functional building revealing its concrete structure, which, with traces of *Jugendstil* motifs, also functions aesthetically. The power station remains a remarkable example of early constructivism even on the international level, which has contributed to the modern appreciation of Lindqvist.

PIRKKO-LIISA LOUHENJOKI

WORKS

SELIM A. LINDQVIST AND ELIA HEIKEL

1888–1890, Merkurius Office Building; 1898, Lundqvist Office Building; Helsinki.

SELIM A. LINDQVIST

1905, Villa Johanna; 1907, Hamstern Office Building; 1908, Suvilahti Power Station; 1910, Villa Ensi; 1911, Villa Rivera; Helsinki. 1911, Water Tower; 1912, Town Hall; Mikkeli, Finland. 1913, Suvilahti Power Station (enlarged), Helsinki.

BIBLIOGRAPHY

RICHARDS, J. M. 1978 *800 Years of Finnish Architecture.* Newton Abbot, England: David & Charles.

SALOKORPI, ASKO 1970 *Modern Architecture in Finland.* London: Weidenfeld & Nicolson.

SMITH, J. BOULTON 1975 *The Golden Age of Finnish Art.* Helsinki: Ministry of Foreign Affairs.

LINGERI, PIETRO

An early exponent of the Modern movement in Italy, Pietro Lingeri (1894–1968) was born in Tremezzo, on Lake Como, the son of a carpenter. Discovered by the director of the Brera Art Academy to have a special talent for drawing, Lingeri attended the Academy on a scholarship and then went to the Milan Politecnico. There, he came into contact with a number of young architects, some of whom would become the famed *Gruppo 7,* a group that included GIUSEPPE TERRAGNI, with whom Lingeri collaborated on many projects and buildings. Lingeri's own Amila Boat Club was the first completed work of Italian Rationalist architecture, and his buildings before World War II include the artists' houses on Lake Como which are internationally known. Always in the shadow of Terragni, his more vocal and intellectual partner, Lingeri established himself as a talented architect in his own right in the postwar period.

THOMAS L. SCHUMACHER

WORKS

1926–1927, Amila Boat Club, Tremozzo, Como, Italy. 1930, Milione Gallery; 1933–1935, Ghiringelli Apartment House; 1933–1935, Lavezzari Apartment House; 1933–1935, Rustici Apartment House; 1933–1935, Toninello Apartment House; Milan. 1934, Casa Aschieri Apartment House; 1935–1939, Artists' Houses, Isola Comacina; 1938–1942, Campo-Ospedaletto sul Lario; Como, Italy. 1939–1943, Fascist Union of Industrial Workers Headquarters (with A. Cattaneo, Magnoni, Origoni, and Giuseppe Terragni; now the I.N.A.M. Headquarters); 1958, Residential Quarter (INA Casa Subsidized), Vialba, Milan.

BIBLIOGRAPHY

Architectural Design 1981 51, nos. 1–2:1–80.

KOULERMOS, PANOS 1963*a* "Terragni, Lingeri, and Italian Rationalism." *Architectural Design* 33, no.3 108–109.

KOULERMOS, PANOS 1963*b* "The Work of Terragni and Lingeri." *Architectural Design* 33, no. 3:110–136.

SARTORIS, ALBERTO (1948)1954–1957 *Encyclopédie de L'Architecture Nouvelle.* Milan: Hoepli.

SCHUMACHER, THOMAS L. 1980 *Il Danteum di Terragni.* Milan: Officina Edizioni.

LINHART, EVŽEN

Evžen Linhart (1898–1949) lived and worked in Prague, Czechoslovakia. He was a founding member of The Four Purists and of the architecture section of the Devětsil avant-garde association. His own family house, built in 1926–1928, was the very first domestic structure in Prague conceived in the so-called International style, displaying LE CORBUSIER's aesthetical doctrine. He remained true to these principles in other works which he designed and realized, as for instance his Grammar School, Prague (1935), and particularly, soon after

World War II, the Collective House in Litvínov (1946–1958), designed together with Václav Hilský.

VLADIMÍR ŠLAPETA

WORKS

1925, Block of Flats, Žižkov; 1926–1928, Linhart House and Atelier, Dejvice; 1935, Grammar School, Dejvice; Prague. 1946–1958, Collective Dwelling House (with Václav Hilský), Litvínov, Czechoslovakia. 1947, Triennale Exhibition (Czechoslovak Exhibition), Milan.

BIBLIOGRAPHY

BENESŎVÁ, MARIE 1978 "Dvacátá léta v díle E. Linharta." *Architektura ČSR* 37, no. 4:178–180.

STARÝ, OLDŘICH 1950 "Za Evženem Linhartem." *Architektura ČSR* 9, nos. 1–2:48–50.

LINK, THEODORE C.

Theodore Carl Link (1850–1923) was born in Wimpfen, Germany. He emigrated to the United States in 1870. Initially, he worked in New York, Philadelphia, and Texas, and in 1873 established himself in St. Louis, Missouri. His most important work was the St. Louis Union Station. Ninety-nine of his projects are catalogued.

MARY PATRICIA HOLMES

WORKS

1889–1890, Monticello Seminary, Godfrey, Ill. 1891–1894, St. Louis Union Station; 1899, Second Presbyterian Church; St. Louis, Mo. 1900–1903. Mississippi State Capitol, Jackson. 1923, Louisiana State University Campus, Baton Rouge.

BIBLIOGRAPHY

HOLMES, MARY PATRICIA 1970 "A History and Evaluation of the St. Louis Union Station, Constructed 1891–1894." Unpublished M. A. thesis, Washington University, St. Louis, Mo.

HOLMES, MARY PATRICIA 1971 "St. Louis Union Station." *Bulletin of the Missouri Historical Society* 27:248–258.

LIPPI, ANNIBALE

Despite the fact that he built some rather imposing structures in Rome during the third quarter of the sixteenth century, we know remarkably little about the life of Annibale Lippi (?–1580?). The son of Nanni di Baccio Bigio di Bartolommeo Lippi, he was probably born in Florence and trained in the workshop of Francesco Salviati. He may have aided his father, with whom he is sometimes confused, in the construction of the Palazzo Sacchetti, Rome, built for Cardinal Ricci of Montepulciano around 1550. The lower story is probably copied from Antonio da Sangallo the Younger's Palazzo Farnese (see SANGALLO FAMILY). The first work that we can securely attribute to his design is the Church of the Madonna of Loreto, Spoleto (1568–1572), which is strongly reminiscent of the rather severe classicism of GIACOMO BAROZZI DA VIGNOLA and Antonio da Sangallo the Younger.

Although Lippi was a competent architect, he was overshadowed most of his life by others. Not only is his chronology confused—we know neither when he was born nor when he died—but it is difficult to disentangle his contribution from that of others. A case in point is the Villa Medici, Rome, which has traditionally been given to Lippi for its rather loosely ordered paneling and fascinating archeological ornament. The building has also been attributed to Lippi's father. The form of the garden façade of the Villa Medici is especially interesting—it reduces to a kind of random series of openings the traditional High Renaissance Roman palace type of the Palazzo Branconio dell'Aquila or the Palazzo Spada. The Villa Medici was, like the Palazzo Sacchetti, built for Cardinal Ricci. In the early nineteenth century, it was taken over to become the headquarters of the French Academy.

From 1577, Lippi was employed with GIACOMO DELLA PORTA and Martino Longhi (see LONGHI FAMILY) on the construction of the Palazzo dei Conservatori, Rome, the great palace designed by MICHELANGELO on the Capitoline Hill.

NICHOLAS ADAMS

WORKS

1550, Palazzo Sacchetti (possibly under NANNI DI BACCIO BIGIO); 1566–1572, Villa Medici (with or under Bigio); Rome. 1568–1572, Madonna di Loreto, Spoleto, Italy. 1577–1580, Palazzo dei Conservatori (designed by Michelangelo), Rome.

BIBLIOGRAPHY

PORTOGHESI, PAOLO 1972 *Rome of the Renaissance.* London: Phaidon.

LISBOA, ANTONIO FRANCISCO

See ALEIJADINHO.

LISSITZKY, ELEAZAR M.

Eleazar Markovich Lissitzky (1890–1941), who was born near Smolensk, Russia, achieved an international reputation for himself over a wide range of artistic production not only as a painter and graphic designer but also as an exhibition architect.

In 1909, Lissitzky was sent to the Technische Hochschule in Darmstadt, Germany, from which he graduated within a year. After traveling extensively in France and Italy in 1911 and 1912, he returned to Russia in 1914 and obtained his architect's diploma from Riga Technical University in 1916. He exhibited for the first time in 1912, at the Petersburg Artistic Union, although after his graduation from Riga he first earned his living as an architectural assistant in Moscow. In 1916, he was invited to exhibit at the Knave of Diamonds show in which KASIMIR MALEVICH first exhibited his Suprematist drawings. Between 1917 and 1919, Lissitzky worked as an illustrator of Yiddish books, and this undertaking brought him into contact with Marc Chagall, who invited him to teach at the Vitebsk School of Art. This invitation was decisive for Lissitzky who shifted his artistic allegiance to Suprematism, which led to the invention of a generically synthetic art work, which he called a *Proun* and which he regarded as an "interchange station between painting and architecture."

Throughout his subsequent career, Lissitzky sought to adapt the syntax of Suprematism to the demands of applied art, above all, to the fields of typography and exhibition design. His pioneering works in these areas were his 1920 Suprematist *Story of Two Squares* and his *Prounenraum* built for the Greater Berlin Art Exhibition of 1923, where he combined, for the first time, Constructivist detailing and furniture with Suprematist wall reliefs and other Suprematist features. Thereafter, this peculiar synthesis constituted the basis of a whole series of exhibitions throughout the 1920s beginning with his first Exhibition Room built for the International Art Exhibition staged in Dresden, Germany, in 1926. This was followed by his highly kinetic Soviet section, designed for the Cologne Pressa exhibition of 1928. The last major exhibition to be carried out in his *Proun*-style was the Soviet Pavilion which he designed for the International Hygiene Exhibition staged in Dresden in 1930.

With the rise of Social Realism as the official cultural policy of the Soviet Union, Lissitzky's work became much more restrained and national rather than international in tone. His finest works of this period were the brilliant "cinematographic" layouts which he produced from 1932 onward for the magazine *U.S.S.R im Bau* (U.S.S.R. in Construction). These replicated in magazine format the Dziga-Vertov montage techniques which Lissitzky had already developed in the Pressa exhibit four years earlier.

KENNETH FRAMPTON

WORKS

*1923, Proun Room, Greater Berlin Art Exhibition, Berlin. *1926, Exhibition Room (First), International Art Exhibition, Dresden, Germany. *1927, Polygraphic Union Exhibition, Moscow. *1928, Soviet Pavilion, Pressa Exhibition, Cologne. *1928, Exhibition Room (Second), Niedersächsische Landesgalerie, Hannover, Germany. *1929, Soviet Section, International Werkbund Exhibition of Film and Photography, Stuttgart, Germany. *1930, Soviet Pavilion, International Hygiene Exhibition, Dresden, Germany. *1930, Soviet Section, International Fur Trade Exhibition, Leipzig. *1940, Restaurant, Soviet Exhibit at U.S.S.R. Album Isostat, New York.

BIBLIOGRAPHY

ABRAMSKY, C. 1966 "El Lizzitzky as Jewish Illustrator and Typographer." *Studio International* 172, no. 882:182–185.

FRAMPTON, KENNETH 1968 "The Work and Influence of El Lissitzky." *Architects Year Book* 12:253–268.

LISSITZKY, ELEAZAR (1930) 1970 *Russia: An Architecture for World Revolution.* Translated by Eric Dluhasch. Cambridge, Mass.: M.I.T. Press.

LISSITZKY-KÜPPERS, S. 1968 *El Lissitzky/Life, Letters and Text.* New York Graphics Society.

RICHTER, H. 1958 *El Lissitzky: Sieg über die Sonne. Zur Kunst des Kunstruktivismus.* Cologne, Germany: Czwiklitzer.

LITTLE, ARTHUR

Arthur Little (1852–1925) grew up in Boston, attended the Massachusetts Institute of Technology (1871–1876), and apprenticed with PEABODY AND STEARNS. In 1878, he opened his own office in Boston where he later formed a partnership with Herbert Browne (1890). He is best known for his book, *Early New England Interiors* (1877), which consisted of commentary and pen-and-ink drawings of colonial homes in Salem and Marblehead, Massachusetts; Portsmouth, New Hampshire; and Kittery, Maine. His first house, Cliffs, in Manchester, Massachusetts (1879), was influential in the Colonial Revival. Little's work was mainly domestic, typically picturesque in style, frequently shingled, with classical details.

GWEN W. STEEGE

WORKS

1879, Cliffs, Manchester, Mass. 1880–1881, Shingleside; 1882, Grasshead; Swampscott, Mass. 1882–1884, Barn, river, and fort houses, Manchester-by-the-Sea, Mass. 1885, Emerton House (addition), Salem, Mass. 1888,

J. H. Sleeper House, Marblehead Neck, Mass. 1889, Mrs. Ole Bull's House (Joseph Thorpe House), Cambridge, Mass. 1890, House, 2 Raleigh Street, Boston, Mass. *1890, Wirt Dexter House, Chicago. 1902–1905, Larz Anderson House, Washington.

BIBLIOGRAPHY

BACON, EDWIN M., and HERNDON, RICHARD 1892 *Boston of To-day.* Boston: Post Publishing.

BUNTING, BAINBRIDGE 1967 *Houses of Boston's Back Bay.* Cambridge, Mass.: Belknap.

"Colonial Houses and Their Uses to Art." 1978 *American Architect* 3, no. 107:12–13.

LITTLE, ARTHUR 1878 *Early New England Interiors: Sketches in Salem, Marblehead, Portsmouth and Kittery.* Boston: Williams.

RIPLEY, HUBERT GEORGE 1925 "Obituary." *Journal of the American Institute of Architects* 13:191.

SCULLY, VINCENT J., JR. 1955 *The Shingle Style.* New Haven: Yale University Press.

STURGES, WALTER KNIGHT 1973 "Arthur Little and the Colonial Revival." *Journal of the Society of Architectural Historians* 32, no. 2:147–163.

LIVINGSTON, GOODHUE

See TROWBRIDGE and LIVINGSTON.

LLEWELYN-DAVIES, RICHARD

Richard Llewelyn-Davies (1912–1981) was born in London and was educated at Trinity College, Cambridge, the Ecole des Beaux-Arts, Paris, and the Architectural Association School, London. Qualifying as an architect in 1939, he worked as an engineering draftsman with Sir Alexander Gibbs & Partners (1939–1942) and in the engineers department of the London, Midland, and Scottish Railway (1942–1948). This interest in technical research and development proved valuable after his appointment as director of the Investigation into Functions and Design of Hospitals (1948–1960) set up by the Nuffield Foundation. His team work profoundly influenced hospital design, establishing Llewelyn-Davies as an early authority on the subject.

Appointed professor of architecture at University College, London, in 1960, he reorganized the Bartlett School of Architecture, creating in 1967 the Centre for Environmental Studies which embraced related disciplines of town planning and building science, an innovative and influential precedent. In 1969, he became professor of urban planning at University College until his retirement in 1975 whereupon he was elected professor emeritus. Concurrent with his establishment as an influential figure in architectural education, he founded a thriving practice in partnership with JOHN WEEKS (1960–1966) and later as a senior partner (1966–1981) of the successor firm Llewelyn-Davies, Weeks, Forestier-Walker, and Bor. Remaining pre-eminent in the fields of hospital and health care planning and facilities, the firm has constantly expanded its activities internationally in terms of planning, research, studies, and analyses and a wide range of consultancy services. Offices have been opened in North and South America and in the Middle East.

HILARY J. GRAINGER

WORKS

LLEWELYN-DAVIES AND WEEKS

1952, Nuffield House, Musgrave Park Hospital, Belfast, Ireland. 1954, Diagnostic Centre, Corby, Northamptonshire, England. 1955, House, Mayford, Surrey, England. 1957, Mignot Memorial Hospital, Alderney, Channel Islands, England. 1957, Rushbrooke Village Housing, Bury Saint Edmunds, Suffolk, England. 1958, The Times Office Building (with Ellis Clarke and Galleraugh); 1960, Meeting Halls and Laboratories, Zoological Society; 1960, Nuffield Institute of Comparative Medicine; London. 1960, Students Residence and Dining Room (with Colin Laird Associates), Imperial College of Tropical Agriculture, Trinidad, West Indies. 1961, Northwick Park Hospital and Clinical Research Centre, Harrow, Middlesex, England. 1961, Stock Exchange redevelopment; with Fitzroy Robinson); 1961, Sun Alliance Insurance Building (with Robinson); 1963, Tate Gallery (extension); London. 1963, Town Centre Development (phase 1 and Sports Centre; with Ian Fraser Associates), Basingstoke, Hampshire, England.

LLEWELLYN-DAVIES, WEEKS, FORESTIER-WALKER, AND BOR

1966, Barmston Village Housing Project, Washington New Town; 1966, Washington Master Plan; Durham, England. 1967, Milton Keynes Master Plan (with others), Buckinghamshire, England. 1968, Experimental Pathology Research Building, Saint Mary's Hospital, Paddington, London. 1968, Stantonbury Housing Scheme, Milton Keynes, Buckinghamshire, England. 1970, Medical Centre (with the South Australia Department of Public Works), Adelaide, South Australia. 1970, Youth Treatment Centre (with Felix Tanghe and Delarue), Leuven, Belgium. 1971, Salmaniya Medical Centre, Bahrain. 1971, Sciences Laboratories, National Hospital for Nervous Diseases, London. 1971, York District Hospital, England. 1972, General Hospital, Doha, Qatar. 1972, Metal Box Company Headquarters Building, Reading, England. 1972, Singapore General Hospital (with INDECO), Outram Road. 1973, Normanby College Education Centre, King's College Hospital, London. 1974, Health Sciences Centre (with Kingston Reynolds Thom and Allardice), University of Khon Kaen, Thailand. 1975, Cancer Research Foundations, Sutton, Surrey, England. 1975, Rayne Institute Research Laboratories, University College Hospital; 1976, Voluntary Research Trust Research Laboratory Building, King's College Hospital; London. c.1977, School of Business Studies, Gulf Technical College, Bahrain.

BIBLIOGRAPHY

AMERY, COLIN 1979 "Tate Gallery Extension, London." *Architectural Review* 166, no. 990:117–119.

BRITISH HOSPITALS EXPORT COUNCIL (1966)1973 *British Hospitals: Home & Overseas.* 9th ed. London: Trafalgar.

DAVIES, TREVOR 1977 "York District Hospital: Building Study." *Architect's Journal* 165, no. 22:1021–1036.

LLEWELYN-DAVIES, RICHARD 1966*a* "Similarities and Differences in Hospital Design: International Trends." *American Journal of Public Health* 56:1675–1683.

LLEWELYN-DAVIES, RICHARD 1966*b* "Town Design." *Town Planning Review* 37, no. 3:157–172.

LLEWELYN-DAVIES, RICHARD 1967 "Research for Town Planning." *Journal of the Town Planning Institute* 53:221–227.

LLEWELYN-DAVIES, RICHARD 1969 "Educating the Professionals of the Built Environment." *Architectural Record* 147, no. 2:145–150.

LLEWELYN-DAVIES, RICHARD 1976 "The Architect as a Planner." *Journal of the Royal Institute of British Architects* 84, no. 7:282.

ROBERTSON, JAQUELIN T. 1977 "Shahestan Pahlavi: A New Centre for Teheran." *Journal of the Royal Institute of British Architects* 84, no. 4:136–147.

ROPER, HUGH 1969 "The Plan is a Beginning: Some Further Thoughts on Milton Keynes." *Journal of the Town Planning Institute* 56:129–133.

SPRING, MARTIN 1979 "Sixties Panacea: Northwick Park Hospital & Clinical Research Centre." *Building* 236, no. 7081:54–55.

WATSON, F., and LOE, DAVID L. 1970 "Northwick Park: Where Only Growth and Change Are Constant." *Architectural Record* 148, no. 12:101–104.

WATSON, F., and LOE, DAVID L. 1977 "Milton Keynes, the largest new town in Britain." *International Asbestos-Cement Review* 22, no. 2:43–52.

WATSON, F., and LOE, DAVID L. 1979 "Art Box." *Architect's Journal* 169, no. 15:726–727.

LOCKWOOD, HENRY FRANCIS

Henry Francis Lockwood (1811–1878), head of the firm of Lockwood and Mawson, was born at Doncaster and articled to P. F. ROBINSON of London. He set up his own practice in Hull in 1834. In 1849, he moved to Bradford and entered into a partnership with Richard Mawson and William Mawson which lasted until 1874 when he moved to London. He is best remembered for the buildings designed by the firm in Bradford and for the layout of the mill and model town at Saltaire (1851–1876) for Sir Titus Salt. CUTHBERT BRODERICK trained with him.

ROGER DIXON

WORKS

1841–1843, Great Thornton Street Chapel (with Thomas Allom), Hull, England. 1851–1852, Saint George's Hall, Bradford, England. 1851–1876, Mills and Model Town, Saltaire, Yorkshire, England. 1864–1867, Wool Exchange; *1869–1872, Kirkgate Markets; 1869–1873, Bradford Town Hall; 1871, 1873, Warehouses, 62 and 65 Vicar Lane; Bradford, England. 1873–1874, City Temple, Holborn Viaduct; 1874, Saint Stephen's Church, Cambridge Park; London.

BIBLIOGRAPHY

DIXON, ROGER, and MUTHESIUS, STEFAN 1978 *Victorian Architecture.* London: Thames; New York: Oxford University Press.

HITCHCOCK, H. R. (1954)1972 *Early Victorian Architecture in Britain.* Reprint. 2 vols. New York: Da Capo.

PEVSNER, NIKOLAUS 1951 *Middlesex.* Harmondsworth, England: Penguin.

PEVSNER, NIKOLAUS (1959)1974 *Yorkshire: The West Riding.* Revised by Enid Radcliffe. 2d ed. Harmondsworth, England: Penguin.

PHYSICK, JOHN, and DARBY, MICHAEL 1973 *Marble Halls: Drawings and Models For Victorian Secular Buildings.* London: Victoria and Albert Museum.

"Obituary." 1878 *The Builder* 36:788.

LODOLI, CARLO

Fra Carlo Lodoli (1690–1761) has been acknowledged as the most advanced theorist of architecture in the Enlightenment, anticipating twentieth-century ideals. His concepts have been discussed more often than understood, for good reason. Architecture was not his primary concern and Lodoli knew that his theory and occasional forays into architectural design were out of key with the taste and teaching of his day, hence he was in no hurry to order his thoughts for publication. His theory for years was known by word of mouth and only later by two divergent printed texts. The earlier of these, by Count FRANCESCO ALGAROTTI, was published in Pisa (1753) and proved to be a disappointment to the friar; it was in fact a facile caricature of Lodoli's ideas. Long after Lodoli's death, his close friend Andrea Memmo, a fellow Venetian and a Procurator of Saint Mark's, wrote a conscientious, perceptive report, only half of which was printed in 1786. Much later, the efforts of Memmo's daughter, Lucia Mocenigo, resulted in a complete edition (1833–1834) of Memmo's text on Lodoli.

Lodoli.
Cloisters of San Francesco della Vigna (façade).
Venice, Italy.
n.d.

Included were two hitherto unpublished draft outlines of Lodoli's architectural theory, and it seems probable that these were quoted from autograph notes; nothing further by Lodoli himself is known. Lodoli's remaining architectural efforts are similarly slight: a few fragments of stone trim in the monastery of San Francesco della Vigna in Venice, where he lived, and an engraving; none are beautiful, but all are interesting. Why then is Lodoli considered important? The best answer lies in two precepts taken from the draft outlines just mentioned. They remain among the most penetrating statements of principle for a rationalist architecture.

> Proper function and form are the only final, scientific aims of civil architecture. . . . It is desirable to merge them so that they become an indivisible entity.
>
> When a fully suitable material is openly put to use in accord with its characteristics and the purpose of the building, this will always give rise to a structure strong, well proportioned, and convenient.

Originally christened Cristofaro Ignazio Antonio, Fra Carlo was the fourth and youngest son of Count Bernardo Lodoli and his first wife, Anna Maria Alberghetti. The Count was a legal and fiscal expert attached to the Arsenal of Venice and his wife came from a famous clan of metallurgists there. Thus, the boy was familiar with that aura of practical ingenuity and organized planning that had kept the Arsenal pre-eminent over four centuries. He felt at ease with scientific calculation and craft traditions. At home, he felt overpowered by a stepmother and a total of seven sisters; the world of the Friars who guided his education seemed enviable, but it was understood that he had to prepare to help the family as his father grew older.

Nevertheless, at sixteen he slipped onto a boat of the Franciscans which took him to Dalmatia, then a Venetian possession, where he became a novice. His training included mathematics, philosophy, and languages old and modern. When his basic religious instruction was completed by 1708, he took vows as an Observant Friar Minor and the name in religion of Carlo. Four more years of training in Rome made him proficient in theology and in French. He became fascinated by the art and architecture around him, and began to study it with the idea of lecturing on art history. He was sent to Forlì and then to Verona (1715), teaching novices and lecturing in public. He probably visited Florence, whose art he knew well. It was in Verona that he began to attract favorable attention and it was there that he started long-lasting associations with the Marchese Francesco Scipione Maffei and Father Angelo Calogerà, two prominent supporters of the Enlightenment. His reputation reached Venice; in 1720, he transferred to the Monastery of the Vigna where he had been schooled as a boy. He was attentive to the needs of his relatives and became known as a learned, quick-witted, sociable personality of decidedly original opinions. In 1728, he joined Calogerà and others to support the work of Giambattista Vico, the then controversial Neapolitan historian and sociologist, today considered a founder of modern thought; the effort ended unfortunately in a lawsuit.

In 1730, Fra Carlo was struck by a parasitosis that incapacitated him for four years and left him burdened with disagreeable odor and unsightly sores over body and face. He adopted a strict vegetarian diet to no great avail. Lodoli was given new duties; first, to compile a record of all Franciscan writings, a vast task not finished. It did require the reorganization and enlargement of the library at the Vigna, and the friar became interested in local building practices. He drew up tables in Venetian dialect for the workmen, showing the calculated strength and limitaton of materials commonly used. In 1736, Lodoli was appointed by the Riformatori dello Studio, the Regents of the University of Padua, to supervise book publication in the Venetian State; he had to approve all texts before printing and controlled the importation of books printed elsewhere. He aimed to foster ethics, morals, and knowledge and to revive the printing trades of Venice, in decline from their Renaissance vigor. Lodoli became a hero to publishers and printers alike, so effective were his efforts on their behalf.

In 1739, Lodoli was placed in charge of Franciscan pilgrims visiting the Holy Land. They gathered at, and returned to, the Monastery of the Vigna, but they also had to be housed, fed, transported, and guided in Venice, asea, and in the Near East. In his first three-year appointment, Lodoli became familiar with the operation and was made aware of the inadequate quarters at the Vigna. Reappointed, he undertook remodeling of the pilgrims' area, working with minimal funds. His rational, unorthodox provisions owed something to

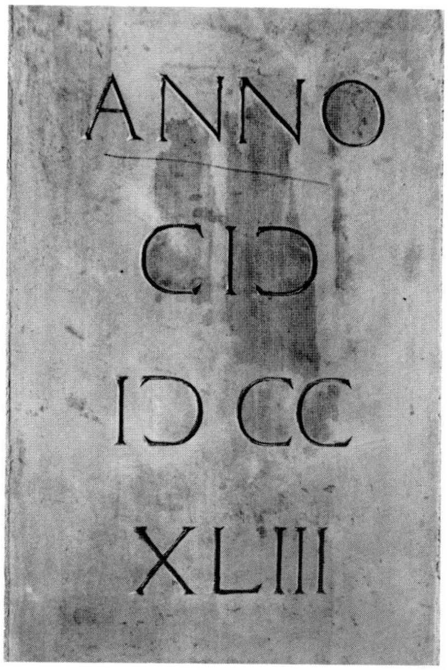

Lodoli.
Cloisters of San Francesco della Vigna (dated inscription).
Venice, Italy.

Lodoli.
Door trim design used as frontispiece to the second part of L'architettura di Jacapo Barozzi da Vignola.

Lodoli.
Cloisters of San Francesco della Vigna (bas-relief, former lintel to door).
Venice, Italy.

the inventive attitudes of the Arsenal. Little remains of this work but the few features in stone previously mentioned. Lodoli was responsible for a decorative bas-relief over the entrance to the pilgrims' rooms. It is a lunette carved to represent a rough fragment of stone fixed to the wall by ordinary screws. The half-figure of a patron saint is shown in stark profile, his halo chipped. Behind the saint lie symbols of the honors he had spurned, while ahead of him lie his religious duties. He holds a monstrance as a lantern to guide him, and the Bible supports him. The symbolism is not esoteric but understandable to unlettered people. Dignity, grace, and artistic rhetoric are abandoned in favor of direct reality and naive craftsmanship. Window trim is equally straightforward and independent. Sills are devised to avoid breaking under the pressure of brick walls settling on wood pile foundations (the usual Venetian construction), and dripstones were similarly set to accept the stresses of time and weather. The engraved Lodolian doorway demonstrates this thinking even more fully since specially constructed jambs are depicted, perhaps inspired by peasant structures seen near Forli. This preoccupation with practical needs rather than canonical moldings and brackets is fully described in Memmo's text. In the monastery, bits of lettering and paving show that Lodoli accepted recondite associations in design as long as no practical consideration was neglected. These fragments refer to rationalist attitudes in antiquity parallel to those Lodoli was stressing in his theory.

Significant as these details are, tucked away from general view, Lodoli's full attitude toward architecture was made clear in another way. Before his duties with the pilgrims began, Lodoli had been approached by Scipione Maffei to undertake an important and delicate task. The Soranzos, one of Venice's distinguished noble families, wanted to complete the education of their young heir so that he would become aware of the great new ideas changing the course of European history. These ideas were not yet current in Venice, and no teachers were concerned with them in a comprehensive manner. The Soranzos turned to Maffei for suggestions; he proposed Lodoli as the ideal instructor. It was discussed that other young nobles might share in the training, and several great families agreed. Lodoli accepted, subject to certain conditions: he was not to be paid but would be free to hire special instructors as need arose; the classes were to be carefully restricted and would be centered in his quarters at the monastery. The main purpose of the enterprise was to prepare young minds to assume hereditary duties, guiding the State with balanced and well-informed attitudes. The chief texts of the Enlightenment in several languages were studied and advantage was taken of the rich resources of Venetian archives; through parents it was possible to study official documents, even confidential ones, bearing on contemporary issues. In this context, architecture appeared as an instrument of statecraft and personal presentation, the most permanent and costly of cultural expressions. Lodoli's theory was meant as a guide to rational and practical judgments controlling architecture, and inevitably it was more than a little critical of contemporary standards.

Many older nobles considered Lodoli's views subversive of the great Venetian traditions. Finally, in 1748, the nobles began to exert pressures and spread innuendos that became more than the physically weakened friar could withstand. He gave up his official duties and reduced his teaching to recuperate his forces. He emerged with the title of Ex-Provincial, allowing him to relax the more severe obligations of an observant friar. A final decade was spent by Lodoli in busy but unregimented re-

Lodoli.
Cloisters of San Francesco della Vigna (drip stone).
Venice, Italy.

Lodoli.
Cloisters of San Francesco della Vigna (window trim).
Venice, Italy.

tirement until his years and ailments made death imminent. On his death, all his papers were quickly confiscated and destroyed partly through carelessness. His friends found almost nothing when they wanted to write about his innovative concepts.

In the late eighteenth and nineteenth centuries, when rationalist theories of architecture proliferated, it was inevitable that Algarotti's fallacious but clever version of Lodoli's ideas should be absorbed into the general flow; after all, Memmo's incomplete and partly inept text seemed unconvincing and he could not cite chapter and verse. Nevertheless, Memmo's criticism of Algarotti's Lodoli is worth considering, it can be summed up in three generalities: Algarotti portrayed a consistent, clear system, but Lodoli's own approach was ad hoc, adaptive, and developmental; Algarotti assumed that all fine arts, including architecture, shared the same pure, ideal goals, but Lodoli developed his architectural concepts from roots in the facts of construction, utility, and physical properties of materials; Algarotti thought that Lodoli was unilaterally utilitarian and that neither ornament nor references to historical values were acceptable to him, contrary to Lodoli's practice and statements. When Memmo's full text finally appeared in the mid 1830s it reached receptive minds, particularly those of two Americans in Italy, Horatio Greenough who lived there and his friend Ralph Waldo Emerson who was visiting. It is not clear that either man knew Memmo's work or Lodoli's reputation but parallels of thought indicate influence however indirect. It has even been claimed that JOHN RUSKIN, who was given the Memmo volumes by Lucia Mocenigo in the 1850s, was influenced by them, but the results are hardly noticeable. Later in the nineteenth century, Lodoli slipped from view, as his key ideas had become common property. In the middle decades of the twentieth century, when art history flourished, Lodoli was rediscovered, first in Algarotti's dogmatic version, but eventually Memmo's more sympathetic record was recognized as representative of Lodoli's seminal insights.

EDGAR KAUFMANN, JR.

BIBLIOGRAPHY

COMOLLI, ANGELO (1792)1964–1965 "Elementi dell'Architettura Lodoliana." Volume 4, pages 50–84 in *Bibliografia Storico-Critica dell'architettura civile ed arti subalterne.* Reprint. Milan: Labor.

KAUFMANN, EDGAR, JR. 1964 "Memmo's Lodoli." *Art Bulletin* 46, no. 2:159–175. Extensive account with approximate translation of Lodoli's(?) outlines of theory.

KAUFMANN, EDGAR, JR. 1982 "Lodoli Architetto." This article, which will be included in a *Festschrift* to be published in honor of H. R. Hitchcock in New York by the Architectural History Foundation Press, includes the best illustrations of Lodoli's designs.

KAUFMANN, EMIL 1955 *Architecture in the Age of Reason.* Cambridge, Mass.: Harvard University Press. Includes the most influential references to Francesco Algarotti's writings on Lodoli.

MEMMO, ANDREA (1833–1834)1973 *Elementi d'architettura Lodoliana, ossia l'arte del fabbricare con solidità scientifica e con eleganza non capricciosa.* Reprint. Milan: Mazzotta. Includes other texts by Lodoli. A few documents subsequently discovered add nothing of substance to these texts.

TORCELLAN, GIANFRANCO 1963 *Una figura della Venezia settecentesca: Andrea Memmo.* Rome and Venice, Italy: Istituto per la collaborazione culturale, Fondazione Cini. The best review of Memmo and Lodoli. For an English language version of similar information, see Edgar Kaufmann, jr., 1964.

VICENTINI, ULDERICO 1955 *Necrologio dei frati minori della provincia veneta.* Venice, Italy: San Nicolo di Lido.

LOGHEM, J. B. VAN

Johannes Bernardus Van Loghem (1881–1940), probably more than any other architect of his generation, embodied the radical changes that took place in the Dutch architectural culture between the end of the nineteenth century and the outbreak of World War II.

Van Loghem grew up in Haarlem in a prosperous bourgeois family. His youth and student days fell in a period marked by an expansive, cyclical economic development and a sharp political and social class struggle. He obtained his diploma as a constructional engineer in 1909 at the Technical University in Delft. His most important teachers were Jacob Klinkhamer, the architect of the neo-Renaissance town hall of Rotterdam, and Henri Evers, who taught utilitarian building science. They trained several engineers who would be of great importance to Dutch architecture, for instance, M. J. GRANPRÉ-MOLIÈRE, and B. Bijvoet and JOHANNES DUIKER. Immediately after his education, Van Loghem started his own office in Haarlem. At first, he designed residences and housing projects for housing associations. The power plant at IJmuiden (1911–1913) shows the great influence of H. P. BERLAGE, whom he came to know at a young age during the construction of the Exchange at Amsterdam.

At least as important, however, were his activities as editor of *Bouwkundig Weekblad* (1915–1918), as a member of the general committee of the Association of Dutch Architects (1917–1919), and as a teacher of engineering. His way of thinking was solidified in 1915, when on the occasion of an architectural exhibition he sharply criticized the leading architects of the time. He reproached MICHEL DE KLERK for making "art without spirit" and K. P. C. DE BAZEL for searching for beauty in the manner of antiquity. He considered Berlage differently. In the latter's design of a Pantheon of Mankind, Van Loghem discovered an informing tragedy, seeing that the idealist has surpassed the artist.

After World War I and under the influence of the successful October Revolution in Russia, many committed intellectuals and artists were radicalized. Van Loghem became a member of the League of Revolutionary Socialistic Intellectuals (1919–1921). Since in his opinion an architect was nothing more than a working man, he proceeded to collectivize his office, without however giving up the aesthetic leadership of the master builder. His work in the field of workers' housing culminated in the design of 120 houses in Betondorp (Concrete Village), Watergraafsmeer (1922–1923), a garden city layed out by the city of Amsterdam. It was also an experiment of the municipal Housing Service to reduce building costs. When as the consequence of an economical recession in the Netherlands the construction of houses stagnated, Van Loghem accepted an invitation to the Soviet Union as a building expert to find out—as he himself stated—whether in a country in which the mechanism of profit making was abolished, tendencies other than those under capitalism were operative. For two years (1926–1927), he stayed in the autonomous mining colony Kemerovo in central Siberia, the most important center of the Kutsnetz basin. He designed a townplan, which, however, never was executed. He did build a series of separate buildings, such as a school, a cooperative building, and a bathhouse.

After his return from the Soviet Union, Van Loghem opened a one-man office in Rotterdam and began writing architectural criticism in the daily newspaper. He also published a book titled *Bouwen, bauen, bâtir building* (1932) in which he set down the principles and directives of modern architecture in the Netherlands, and became a regular contributor to the magazine *de 8 en Opbouw,* also founded in 1932 as the mouthpiece of the association of modern architects of the same name.

As for his designs of the 1930s, the unexecuted competition entries are as interesting as the buildings. His entry in the competition for the Soviet Palace (1931) is an improvement of LE CORBUSIER's design for the League of Nations Palace, on grounds of acoustical, thermal, and building requirements. His entry in a competition for low-cost workers' housing issued by the city of Amsterdam (1934) showed on the available site of 300-by-240 meters twenty-two free-standing high-rise buildings of sixteen stories with four apartments on each floor: an obvious departure from the then generally employed housing types, which,

Van Loghem. Tuinwyk 'Zuid'. Haarlem, Netherlands. 1920–1922

according to Van Loghem, were poor and without any value for the future. Of his executed designs, the nursing home *Blauwvoet* at Driebergen (1930) and several residences are good examples of the white architecture of the *Nieuwe Zakelijkheid* (new functionality). Van Loghem's Swimming Pool in Haarlem (1933–1934) is rightly considered a highlight of modern architecture in the Netherlands.

CEES L. BOEKRAAD

WORKS

1911–1913, Power Plant, IJmuiden, Netherlands. 1922–1923, Betondorp (Concrete Village), Watergraafsmeer, Netherlands. 1926–1927, Townplan, Houses, School, Watertower, and Bathhouse, Kemerovo, Russia. *1930, Rest Home (*de Blauwvoet*), Driebergen, Netherlands. 1933–1934, Swimming Pool, Haarlem, Netherlands.

BIBLIOGRAPHY

OTTENHOF, F. (editor) 1936 *Goedkoope Arbeiderswoningen.* Rotterdam, Netherlands: Brusse.

VAN DE BEEK, JOHAN, and SMIENK, GERRIT 1971 "Ir. J. B. van Loghem b.i., architect." *Plan* (Netherlands) 12, Dec.:2–64.

VAN LOGHEM, J. B. 1915 "Tentoonstelling van Architectura et Amicitia in het stedelijk museum te Amsterdam." *De Nieuwe Amsterdammer* 11, Dec.

VAN LOGHEM, J. B. (1932) 1981 *Bouwen, bauen, bâtir, building.* Reprint. Netherlands: Socialistiese-Uitgeversmaatschappij Nijmegen.

VAN LOGHEM, J. B. 1937 Volume 5, pages 401–403 in Günther Wasmuth (editor), *Lexikon der Baukunst.* Berlin: Wasmuth.

LONDON, GEORGE

George London (?–1714) and his partner HENRY WISE were the major figures in promoting French formal garden design in England around 1700. After training in England and visits to France, London's adaptation of the French style became popular throughout the country. In 1681 he founded the famous Brompton Park Nurseries in London which supplied the wide variety of species required for his gardens. By 1687, Wise was his partner in the nursery business and design practice. Although appointed deputy superintendant of the Royal Gardens in 1688, London left the city work to Wise after 1702. For nearly thirty years he traveled the countryside on horseback supervising the layout and maintenance of his great formal designs.

RICHARD O. SWAIN

WORKS

The dates listed below for each garden are the founding dates.
c.1685, Longleat Gardens (with Henry Wise), Wiltshire, England. 1688, Chatsworth Gardens (with Wise), Derbyshire, England. 1699, Castel Howard (Wray Wood) Gardens, Yorkshire, England. 1704, Marshal Tallard's Garden (with Wise), Nottingham, England. 1706, Wanstead Gardens, Essex, England. 1713, Canons Gardens (unfinished), Middlesex, England.

BIBLIOGRAPHY

GREEN, DAVID 1956 *Gardener to Queen Anne: Henry Wise (1653–1738) and the Formal Garden.* London: Oxford University Press.

HUNT, JOHN DIXON, and WILLIS, PETER (editors) (1975) 1976 *The Genius of the Place: The English Landscape Garden, 1620–1820.* New York: Harper.

LONDON, GEORGE, and WISE, HENRY (editors) 1699 *The Compleat Gard'ner . . . by Monsieur De la Quintinye.* London: M. Gillyflower. Abridgment of John Evelyn's translation, published in 1693.

LONDON, GEORGE, and WISE, HENRY (translators and editors) (1796) 1980 *The Retir'd Gard'ner.* Reprint. New York: Garland. A translation and adaptation "to our English Culture" of French works by François Gentil and Sieur Liger d'Auxerre.

SWITZER, STEPHEN (1718) 1980 *Ichnographia Rustica: Or, the Nobleman, Gentleman and Gardener's Recreation.* Reprint. New York: Garland.

WILLIS, PETER 1977 *Charles Bridgeman and the English Landscape Garden.* London: Zwemmer.

LONG, ROBERT CARY

Robert Cary Long (1810–1849), who was born in Baltimore, Maryland, in 1826 went to New York to train there with an architect who is said to have been MARTIN E. THOMPSON, at the time in partnership with ITHIEL TOWN.

In 1835–1836, Long opened an office for the practice of architecture in Baltimore. His practice and reputation developed rapidly; in 1848, he left Baltimore for New York, where he soon found a place for himself among architects and intellectuals interested in the arts. In June 1849, while supervising a church he had designed in Morristown, New Jersey, he was overcome by cholera and died.

Long's talent and sophisticated tastes should be seen as a result of his contact with Town, ALEXANDER JACKSON DAVIS, and Thompson. Immediately on returning to Baltimore in 1835, he began to produce designs in the classical, Egyptian, and Gothic styles. A drawing (1836) for the Record Office is Egyptian; others (1837) illustrate a classical solution and bear a note that indicates WILLIAM STRICKLAND was reviewing the project. By 1838, he was architect for the newly organized Greenmount Cemetery for which he proposed an Egyptian gateway (1838), but a Gothic building, also by Long, was substituted and built in 1840. At the same time an Egyptian mausoleum he had designed was constructed. His position as Baltimore's leading architect was so firm that in 1840 he was chosen to design the proposed, but never constructed, State Armory and Town Hall, a complex building that would have housed the Hanover Market in a ground story beneath a new Town Hall and Armory, an ingenious urban composition of courtyard, market, and ceremonial center. The style was described by Long as "purely Grecian." Like Davis, Long made a specialty of the design of houses and ornate cottages. Gothic attracted him, but not all his churches are Gothic. He continued to develop a discrete classical manner in the Perine Mansion near Baltimore (1839); the State Institution for the Deaf, Dumb and Blind in Staunton, Virginia (1839–1844); the townhouse for Jerome Bonaparte in Baltimore (1842); and the Baker Mansion in Altoona, Pennsylvania (1844).

Long is now best known for his churches. Not all of them were Gothic, however, and his commissions in the ecclesiastical were varied. Eight of the ten he designed for Baltimore and Maryland survive, while his public, secular works, among them the Athenaeum (1846) and the Roman Amphitheater (1848) have been destroyed. Long was a favorite with religious clients. He became architect for Saint Mary's Cathedral in Natchez, Mississippi (1841–1845), where the bishop was a Sulpician. He added the lodge and iron fence and wall to the west front of the Cathedral in Baltimore by BENJAMIN HENRY LATROBE and repaired and added a spire to Saint Mary's Chapel. Two Roman Catholic churches, Gothic and classical respectively, Saint Alphonsus (begun 1842) and Saint Peter (1843–1844) the Apostle, with its convent and presbytery; the Tudor Franklin Street Presbyterian Church (1844–1846); and the sternly classical Lloyd Street Synagogue (mid-1840s) are his major surviving buildings in Baltimore. The Protestant Episcopal bishop, Whittingham, praised Long's five churches for that denomination; of them only the one in Westminster (1845) survives virtually unchanged.

Long sought to express his ideas through writing and lecturing as well as design. In 1841, he published an article in the *Journal of the Franklin Institute* and he lectured on several occasions to the Mercantile Library Association. On his arrival in New York in 1848, he began to write regularly for *The Literary World,* where he published poetry, reviews, and a series of articles entitled *Architectonics,* of which those on street architecture, polychromy, and shop fronts contain fresh ideas and evidence that Long had been abroad.

At the time of his death, Long was at work on the plans for the Astor Library, a prestigious commission, and he was writing a general book on architecture.

Long.
Saint Peter the Apostle.
Baltimore.
1843–1844

PHOEBE B. STANTON

WORKS

1839, Perine Mansion, near Baltimore. 1839–1844, State Institution for the Deaf, Dumb and Blind, Staunton, Va. 1840–1841, Gothic Gateway, Greenmount Cemetery; 1841–1845, Saint Mary's; Natchez, Mississippi. 1842, Jerome Bonaparte Town House; begun 1842, Saint Alphonsus, Park Avenue at Saratoga; 1843–1844, Saint Peter the Apostle (church, convent, and presbytery), Poppleton Street; Baltimore. 1844, Baker Mansion, Altoona, Pa. 1844–1846, Franklin Street Presbyterian Church, Baltimore. 1845, Church of the Ascension, Westminster, Md. 1846, Athenaeum; 1848, Roman Amphitheater; Baltimore.

BIBLIOGRAPHY

Drawings by Robert Cary Long, Jr., are in the Maryland Historical Society, the Walters Art Gallery, both in Baltimore, the Baltimore City Archives, and the Joseph Downs Manuscript Collection, Henry Francis du Pont Winterthur Museum, Delaware.

DICKSON, HAROLD E. 1958 "The Baker Mansion, Altoona, Pennsylvania." *Journal of the Society of Architectural Historians* 17:25–29.

GHEQUIERE, T. BUCKLER 1876 "The Messrs. Long, Architects." *American Architect and Building News* 1:207.

HOWLAND, R. H., and SPENCER, E. 1953 *The Architecture of Baltimore.* Baltimore: Johns Hopkins University Press.

HUNTER, WILBUR H. 1957 "Robert Cary Long, Jr., and the Battle of the Styles." *Journal of the Society of Architectural Historians* 16:28–30.

LONG, ROBERT CARY, JR. 1842 "On the Development of the Semi-Arch with the Future Advancement of Architectural Art." *Civil Engineer and Architect's Journal* 5:370–372.

LONG, ROBERT CARY, JR. 1843 "On the Alleged Degeneracy of Modern Architecture." *Journal of the Franklin Institute* Series 3 2:346–349.

LONG, ROBERT CARY, JR. 1843 "Gothic Architecture—New Church." *United States Catholic Magazine* 2, no. 5:297–304.

LONG, ROBERT CARY, JR. . 1848–1849 *Literary World.* Long wrote twelve articles for the journal during these years.

Long, Robert Cary, Jr. 1849 *The Ancient Architecture of America.* New York: Bartlett & Welford.

Stanton, Phoebe B. 1968 *The Gothic Revival and American Church Architecture.* Baltimore: Johns Hopkins University Press.

LONGHENA, BALDASSARE

The greatest native-born Venetian architect and one of the principal geniuses of the Italian baroque, Baldassare Longhena (1596/1599–1682) was the son of a stonemason from the Lake of Lugano in the Swiss Alps, Melchisedech Longhena, who worked in Venice for Antonio da Ponte in the 1590s and is further documented at the Churches of San Giuliano (1603) and San Giorgio dei Greci (1604), where he executed the high altar. The family home and workshop were in the Venetian parish of San Severo, where Baldassare is reputed to have been born and where he died; but no secure evidence of his place or date of birth has yet been found, for a search of the San Severo baptismal records has been inconclusive (see Lewis, 1973, for a possibly relevant notice of 12 January 1599). Longhena declared in the last weeks of 1681 (by the Venetian calendar, that is, the first weeks of 1682 modern style) that he had already reached "the decrepit age of eighty-five years": this would argue—if the round figure were strictly accurate—for his birth in 1596. We may suspect, therefore, that Giuseppe Fiocco's selection of 1598 represents a symbolic choice based on Giovanni Lorenzo Bernini's birth in that year; the date has become traditional for Longhena as well and has the advantage of emphasizing the contemporaneity of these two giants of the seventeenth century.

Longhena's training is almost as thinly documented as his birth. His first biographer, Tommaso Temanza, was told by Cavaliere Nicolò Duodo that Baldassare had studied with Vincenzo Scamozzi, whose Venetian residence had been in the same parish of San Severo. Since the aged cavaliere was a nephew of the Procurator Alvise Duodo (one of Longhena's long-time employers) and also a great-grand-nephew of Scamozzi's patron Pietro Duodo, his report may well reflect an accurate family tradition. Further confirmation of such a master–pupil relationship is provided by the patronage of the Contarini family: the same clients who commissioned Scamozzi's late Palazzo Contarini degli Scrigni on the Grand Canal (1609–1616) seem to have ordered young Baldassare's first independent work (probably of about 1616–1620), the Villa Contarini at Mira, whose windmill-like plan of radiating arms was directly lifted from Scamozzi's favorite source, the treatise pages of Sebastiano Serlio.

Since the Villa Contarini survives only in images on contemporary prints, we are left with the singular phenomenon of a very youthful artist, evidently trained in the banalities of late Mannerism, whose earliest buildings decisively document the birth of a new and strikingly coherent style. Directly across the Grand Canal from Scamozzi's Palazzo Contarini—on which Longhena as an apprentice would almost certainly have worked—is his own Palazzo Giustinian-Lolin (1620–1623): whereas the façade of the former is dry, academic, and ambiguously unresolved, Longhena's handling of the latter is vital, inventive, and powerfully focused. It still employs flat-headed apertures flanking the central arcuated ones, and each story terminates at the edges with another sixteenth-century device of isolated single pilasters, only remotely related to a tighter quartet at the center; these last unify the three bays of the main halls in superimposed triumphal arch motifs, set off by projecting balconies. The individual elements may recall Scamozzi by their thinness, but in the successive and analogous Palazzo Widmann (1621–1641/1646) their bolder forms culminate in the first appearance of a Longhena trademark, four huge scrolled brackets that here support a dynamically extruded central balcony. The Palazzo Lezze (1622–1644) first abandons the outer pilasters to concentrate its architectural ornament exclusively on the tetrastyle frontispieces. This initial group of palaces is followed, after the interval of a quarter century, by five others that lead by quick transitions to Longhena's domestic masterworks.

The superficially similar Palazzo Zane façade (1665–1666/1670) retains four central Ionic pilasters only on its first *piano nobile,* with a central aperture restricted to a uniform width with its flanking fellows. The former Corinthian order on the second *piano nobile* is removed entirely, so that five equal bays march in an unbroken rhythm across the upper center; the rusticated basement, which also lacks the Tuscan pilasters of its predecessors, is embellished with twin doors. The exactly contemporaneous landward block (c.1660–1665) of the lost Palazzo Morosini eschewed any order at all and left the regular, open spacing of plain window frames on flat walls to be set off only by a pair of magnificent twin portals at the center of the ground floor. An intermediate solution of the most exalted mastery is Longhena's Palazzo Belloni-Battagia at San Stae (1648–1660?): one great pilastered and pedimented portal rises through a basement zone developed as two equal mezzanines, and five similar tabernacles (with fluted pilasters and broken pediments) enframe al-

Longhena.
Palazzo Belloni-Battagia, Grand Canal.
Venice, Italy.
1648–1660?

Longhena.
Palazzo Pesaro on the Grand Canal.
Venice, Italy.
1649/1652–1682 (completed 1682?–1710 by Gaspari)

ternating window bays in the single *piano nobile.* Instead of an ornamented frontispiece flanked by plain windows, then, Longhena here achieved a brilliant pattern alternating between regularity and variety, as ten almost equally spaced Corinthian shafts are deftly gathered in pairs and larger groups by projecting balconies and segmental pediments. The only remaining wall panels (fronting fireplaces in the lateral rooms) are camouflaged under two lavishly carved coats of arms in the penultimate bays; the result is a captivating but carefully focused sculptural elaboration, three-dimensionally enhanced by continuations of the façade system around the corners onto the first bays of the flanks.

Longhena's domestic designs culminate in two of the most transcendent achievements in the whole history of European palace building, both erected on unlimited budgets, but nonetheless completed only long after his death. The vast bulk of Palazzo Pesaro (begun 1649/1652), completed in the early eighteenth century by Longhena's faithful disciple Antonio Gaspari (the architect of the immense lateral façade on the south), is at the same time one of the most rigorously composed, yet fabulously elaborated, of all Italian palaces. Its double-mezzanine basement sets both window stacks and twin central portals between ponderous wall segments of astonishingly deep-cut diamond rustication: the ornamented sculptural surface steps back to a "true" wall plane at the corners (where the main façade system again wraps boldly around the three-dimensional block), revealing the convoluted mural structure to be many meters thick. This massive density Longhena (and Gaspari) brilliantly lightened on the *piani nobili* by shifting the fireplaces into the interior, to open the upper Canal façade as a "window wall" of almost unbroken glazing, punctuated by rhythmically spaced single and doubled columns, standing far out beyond the "true" plane. This last is further developed by deep window embrasures, lined by paired colonnettes whose receding files move back at right angles to the façade. Larger-than-life sculptures lavishly embellish the whole, and the total impression is of an extraordinarily rich structural web, from whose deep three-dimensional grid there emerges a perfect balance of solid and void, mass and movement, statement and foil.

Longhena's transformation of the Venetian palace tradition achieves its paradigm in Palazzo Rezzonico, begun in 1666 for Filippo Bon, but acquired by Giambattista and Aurelio Rezzonico in 1745, and carefully finished in 1759, at the end of a full century of work, by Giorgio Massari. On Palazzo Pesaro's façade, the wall segments corresponding to internal room divisions still made a vestigial appearance; but at Palazzo Rezzonico, the

Longhena.
Courtyard, Palazzo Pesaro on the Grand Canal.
Venice, Italy.
1649/1652–1682 (completed 1682?–1710 by Gaspari)

Longhena.
Santa Maria della Salute.
Venice, Italy.
1630–1682 (not completed until 1687)

apertures are expanded to fill the entire space between engaged single columns, and the original plane is thus totally dissolved in an apparently regular alternation of glass and pier. The basement is borrowed from MICHELE SANMICHELI's Porta Palio in Verona (1548–1559), the structural system recreates that of JACOPO SANSOVINO's Venetian Library (1536–1560), and the composition of the whole, though grandly simplified and emboldened, returns to the same architect's Palazzo Corner of 1545–1566. Longhena's creative re-use of these sixteenth-century models places his own achievement in a true historical context: as he gradually matured his vision of a continuing and ever grander Venetian classicism, he discarded the planar ambiguities of Scamozzi in favor of the robust and confident massing of these High Renaissance protagonists, whose real successor he was.

As architect to the high official body of the Procuratia de Supra, Longhena's major civic commission was his lengthy completion of Scamozzi's Procuratie Nuove (1640–1663), by which he completed the enclosure of the Piazza San Marco: his western loggia is the perfect vestibule to that great space. Longhena's many monastic commissions (with one exception) are beautiful but not all at the same level of importance. For Palazzo Rezzonico and for the Dominican (1664–1666) and Somascan priories (1670–1682), he created three exceptionally impressive stair halls, but these cannot compete in significance with his great stair for the Benedictine monastery of San Giorgio (1643–1645), whose revolutionary double-branch design places Longhena at the forefront of a long European development. His conventual churches are equally paradigmatic for the future: the Scalzi (1654–1673) is brilliantly evolved from the still tentative prototype of Scamozzi's San Lazzaro dei Mendicanti (1601), and the Ospedaletto façade (1670–1674)—like the Pesaro Monument in the Frari (1665–1669)—adumbrates a decorative extravagance which was to become a dominant motif of the late baroque.

Longhena's crowning masterwork is the central architectural icon of his native city, his sublimely conceived Church of Santa Maria della Salute (1630–1687). This great votive temple to the Queen of Heaven raises its enormous dome over an octagonal rotunda at the pivotal hub of the city, on the point between the Giudecca and Grand Canals, diagonally opposite the Piazzetta and Ducal Palace, and on the converging axes of ANDREA PALLADIO's San Giorgio, Zitelle, and Redentore. Wittkower (1975) and Howard (1981) have established its fundamental importance to the European culture of the seventeenth century: its telescoping internal vistas created a new mode of architectural expression, a "scenographic" concept involving successively revealed focuses of iconographic, as well as aesthetic, intensity. Together with the greatest Roman achievements of Bernini—with which it is perhaps uniquely comparable—the Salute soars beyond mere characterization as the quintessence of high baroque classicism. It establishes one of the most profoundly effective indices of architectural drama and persuasion, triumphantly uniting in one supreme image the philosophical, social, and religious convictions of an extraordinary chapter in the human experience.

DOUGLAS LEWIS

WORKS

*1616–1620, Villa Contarini, River Brenta, Mira, Italy. 1619, San Giorgio dei Greci (Severo Monument); 1620–1623, Palazzo Giustinian-Lolin, Grand Canal; 1621–1641/1646, Palazzo Widmann, San Canciano; 1622–1644, Palazzo Lezze, Misericordia; Venice, Italy. 1624, 1627–1674, Santa Maria, Chioggia, Italy. 1629–1633, Santo Stefano (D'Alviano Monument); (A)1629–1646, Spirito Santo (Paruta Monument); 1630–1682, Santa Maria della Salute (not completed until 1687); (A)1633?–?, Levantine Synagogue; (A)1633?–?, Spanish Synagogue; *1634, House at Santi Filippo e Giacomo; 1635–1638, San Giorgio Maggiore (Michiel Monument, Civran Monument); 1636–1640, Santa Giustina (façade); 1636–1682, San Antonio (rebuilt); 1640–1663, Procuratie Nuove (completion of Vincenzo Scamozzi's design), Piazza San Marco; 1641–1682, Benedictine Monastery of San Giorgio Maggiore (Library [1641–1653], bookcases [1671], great stair [1643–1645], loggia between courtyards [1640s], Noviciate [1657], Infirmary [1677], Foresteria [1680]); *1644/1645–1649, Palazzo Morosini dal Giardin (river wing and *c.1660–1665, calle façade); 1648–1660?, Palazzo Belloni-Battagia, Grand Canal; Venice, Italy. 1648/1649, 1670, Villa Pesaro (completed 1680s?–1710s by Antonio Gaspari), Este, Italy. 1649, Giardino Valmarana (loggia), Vicenza, Italy. 1649–1654, San Pietro di Castello (high altar); 1649–1673, Carmelite Monastery of the Scalzi (*Conventual structures [1649–1659], Santa Maria di Nazareth degli Scalzi [1654–1673], with façade by Giuseppe Sardi and altars by Giuseppe Pozzo); 1649/1652–1682, Palazzo Pesaro on the Grand Canal (completed 1682?–1710 by Gaspari); 1653–1658, Scuola del Santissimo Nome di Dio, Santi Giovanni e Paolo; 1654–1664, Vendramin Chapel, San Pietro di Castello; Venice, Italy. 1655, Church of the Beata Vergine del Soccorso (Santa Maria Rotonda; campanile not completed until 1769–1793), Rovigo, Italy. *1656–1664, Prisons (executed by Antonio Pizzocaro), Vicenza, Italy. 1656/1660?, 1666–1682, Palazzo Bon (later Palazzo Rezzonico; continued 1682?–1712 by Gaspari; completed c.1750–1758 by Giorgio Massari); 1658–1660, Houses for Greek Community, Calle della Madonna, Venice, Italy. 1658/1659–1675, Santa Maria Assunta, Lorto, Italy. 1659/1660–1669, Santa Maria Gloriosa dei Frari (Pesaro Monument); 1661–1672, San Nicolò di Tolentino (high altar); 1664–1674, Dominican Monastery of Santi Giovanni e Paolo (great stair [1664–1666], dormitory ornamentation [1666–1674], library [1669–1674], bookcases [completed 1682 by Giacomo Piazzetta]); 1665–1666/1670, Palazzo Zane at San Stin (façade); 1667–?, San Giorgio Maggiore (Venier Monument); 1667–1678, Ospedaletto of Santi Giovanni e Paolo (kitchen, bakery, washrooms [1667–1670], infirmary, courtyard, wells [1670–1672], Santa Maria dei Derelitti or del Riposo; façade [1670–1674], altars and choir [1671–1678]); *1668–1670, Scuola dei Carmini (project; executed with changes by Girolamo Viviani and Sante Barbiere); *1669, San Marco (Catafalque for François de Beaufort); 1670–1682, Somascan Monastery of Santa Maria della Salute (completed 1682–c.1705 by Domenico Mazzoni and others); 1671–1678, San Basso, Piazzo dei Leoncini; Venice, Italy. 1672–1673, Basilica of Sant' Antonio (Cornaro Monument), Padua, Italy. 1674–1677, Santa Maria delle Vergini (*high altar, executed by Andrea Cominelli), Venice, Italy. *1670s, Villa Lezze, Rovarè (San Biagio di Callalta), Italy. 1670s–1682, Seminary at San Antonio di Castello (Ospedale di Gesù Cristo); 1675–1677, Warehouses, Dogana da Mar or Sea Customhouse; Venice, Italy. (A)1676–1677, Church of the Immaculate Conception (project, constructed 1677–1698 by Giorgio Catenaci and Andrea Catenaci; completed 1718–1780 by Pompeo Ferrari and others), Gostyn, Poland. 1676–1678, Scuola di San Nicolo and Collegio Flangini (both executed 1678–1688 by Alessandro Tremignon); 1678–1679, Ospedale di San Lazzaro dei Mendicanti (decorative arch and wellhead), Venice, Italy. 1678–1682, Villa Rezzonico (not completed until after 1687), Bassano, Italy. 1680?, Houses at San Fantin; 1681–1682, Dominican Convent at Ospizio delle Muneghette, Venice, Italy.

BIBLIOGRAPHY

BASSI, ELENA 1962 "Baldassare Longhena." Pages 83–183 in *Architettura del Sei e Settecento a Venezia.* Naples: Edizioni Scientifiche Italiane.

CRISTINELLI, GIUSEPPE (1972)1978 *Baldassare Longhena.* 2d ed. Padua, Italy: Marsilio.

HOWARD, DEBORAH 1981 *The Architectural History of Venice.* New York: Holmes & Meier; London: Batsford.

LEWIS, DOUGLAS 1973 "Review of Giuseppe Cristinelli, *Baldassare Longhena.*" *Arte Veneta* 27:328–330.

LEWIS, DOUGLAS (1967)1979 *The Late Baroque Churches of Venice.* New York and London: Garland. See pages 306–310 for an annotated Longhena bibliography from the 1967 edition; see also page 10 of the preface to 1979 edition for an update.

MURARO, MICHELANGELO 1973 "Il tempio votivo di Santa Maria della Salute in un poema del Seicento." *Ateneo Veneto* New Series 11:87–119.

TEMANZA, TOMMASO (1738)1963 *Zibaldon de' Memorie Storiche.* Edited by Nicola Ivanoff. Venice and Rome: Istituto per la Collaborazione Culturale.

WITTKOWER, RUDOLF (1963)1975 "Santa Maria della Salute." Pages 125–152 and 286–289 in *Studies in the Italian Baroque.* London: Thames & Hudson; New York: Braziller.

LONGHI FAMILY

Martino Longhi the Elder

Our knowledge of the early years of Martino Longhi (c.1540–1591) is scant. Although he is known to have been born in Viggiù (Lombardy), neither the date of his birth nor his early training has been recorded. The earliest notices of him are in Austria (Schloss Hohenems [1566]) and Piedmont (Santa Croce, Bosco Marengo [1568]), and he appears in Rome for the first time in 1569. In 1573, Longhi began work on the Villa Mondragone in Frascati and at about the same time became papal architect to Gregory XIII, who employed him in the expansion of the Quirinal and Vatican palaces. Although OTTAVIANO MASCARINO replaced him as papal architect in 1577, Longhi remained active throughout the late 1570s with commissions for San Francesco in Frascati (1575), the rebuilding of the portico of Santa Maria Maggiore (1575), a palace for the Altemps (1575–1576) family, and the construction of a new campanile for the Palazzo del Senatore (1578) on the Capitoline. Longhi's fortunes declined somewhat in the early 1580s, but during the pontificate of

Martino Longhi the Elder. San Girolamo degli Schiavoni. Rome. 1588–1589

Sixtus V (1585–1590), his services were again in demand. In the six years before his death, he was involved with a number of Rome's most important architectural enterprises, including the Palazzo Borghese (1586) and the Chiesa Nuova (1586). Of these several late commissions, only the façade of San Girolamo degli Schiavoni (1588–1589), however, came to be fully realized.

Throughout his career, Martino the Elder seldom challenged the prevailing architectural tradition of GIACOMO BAROZZI DA VIGNOLA. His work, like that of his contemporaries DOMENICO FONTANA, Mascarino, and Francesco da Volterra, is characterized by a bland conformity that hardly anticipates the vitality and inventiveness of the coming baroque. Martino's façade of San Girolamo degli Schiavoni typifies in both its flatness and its reliance upon earlier Roman models the timidity and conservatism of its age. Only in the courtyard of the Palazzo Borghese—if it is indeed attributable to him—did Longhi introduce a new vocabulary and a new syntax into the grammar of Roman late mannerism.

Onorio Longhi

Onorio Longhi (c.1569–1619) began his career at about the time of his father Martino's death but it proceeded slowly and was marked by discontinuity. Onorio's bizarre and contentious personality, so colorfully described by his biographers, can hardly have helped his fortunes. He and the painter Caravaggio were forced to flee Rome in 1606 for their part in a homicide, and for the next five years Onorio pursued his career in Lombardy without much success. In 1611, a papal pardon permitted his return to Rome where he was his most productive in the eight remaining years of his life.

His most ambitious undertaking was the vast longitudinal church of Santi Ambrogio e Carlo al Corso (1612–1619), whose interior combines features from both Saint Peter's and the Duomo in Milan. For the façade he intended fully detached columns which, while progressive by Roman standards, were also of north Italian derivation. Few of Onorio's works are securely dated, and his development as an architect is not easily characterized. The diversity of his stylistic repertory may well result from shifting alliances to Roman and Lombard traditions. His church of Santa Maria Liberatrice (1617) or the Palazzo Verospi (1611), for example, remained faithful to the flat, austere conventions of the late Roman cinquecento, whereas other commissions, such as the Vigna Altemps (before 1613) or several of his altar and chapel designs, reveal a fuller appreciation of the sculptural values of his north Italian heritage.

Martino Longhi the Younger

Like his father Onorio and his grandfather who was his namesake, Martino the Younger (1602–1660) was primarily active in Rome, the city of his birth. Onorio, naturally, was his teacher, and Martino no doubt acquired his unruly personality from him along with a knowledge of architecture. Despite this temperamental handicap and a competing interest in writing poetry, the youngest member of the Longhi clan became the most daringly original of the three architects and the one whose creative personality is most clearly defined.

Martino began his career at Santi Ambrogio e Carlo al Corso, directing the works after his father's death in 1619. His first independent commission came a decade later at San Antonio dei Portoghesi (1630) where he designed a conventional, longitudinal interior and a façade whose equally traditional elevation is enlivened by actively shifting planes and a rich assortment of sculptural accents. Martino's most innovative designs were in fact for church façades. In the late 1630s, he proposed a radical new treatment for the still unexecuted front of Santi Ambrogio e Carlo al Corso. Although destined, like his father's 1612 project, to remain on paper, this plan called for two boldly projecting towers and a plethora of free-standing and engaged columns. A few years later, in 1644, he designed an equally innovative façade for the small church of San Giovanni Calabita. This project likewise remained unexecuted; it provided for a concave front that would have been the first of its kind in Rome.

Martino's masterpiece is unquestionably the

façade of Santi Vincenzo ed Anastasio (1646–1650). Here, the architect employed his favorite devices of detached columns, sharply projecting planes, and free-moving sculpture to create a powerful and in some ways prototypical statement of high baroque principles. No fewer than three features make their first appearance on a Roman church façade: fully detached columns, scenographic corner treatments, and compound crowning pediments. The expressive possibilities of these devices were not lost on contemporary architects like PIETRO BERRETTINI DA CORTONA and Carlo Rainaldi.

In his clever reshaping of the nave of San Adriano al Foro Romano (1653), Martino demonstrated his sensitivity to the movement of interior space, an element rarely found in his other ecclesiastical commissions. His two major secular works, the stairway complexes of the Palazzo Caetani in Rome (c.1640) and of the Palazzo Ginnetti in Velletri (c.1642), are more imaginative spatially and, though quite different from one another, also reveal their author's fondness for Mannerist *capricci* in both structure and ornamental detail. Furthermore, in the Palazzo Ginnetti especially, it is clear that Martino never entirely repudiated his father's taste for Lombard sculptural relief. Like FRANCESCO BORROMINI and other progressive architects of his generation, he assimilated all such reminiscences into compositional schemes that were fully baroque.

JOHN VARRIANO

Martino Longhi the Younger. Santi Vincenzo ed Anastasio. Rome. 1646–1650

WORKS

MARTINO LONGHI THE ELDER

1573, Villa Mondragone; 1575, San Francesco; 1575, Santa Maria Maggiore (rebuilding); Frascati, Italy. 1575–1576, Palazzo Altemps; 1578, Palazzo del Senatore (companile); 1585, Palazzo Alessandrino-Bonelli; *1585, Santa Maria Maddalena della Convertite; 1586, Palazzo Borghese; 1586, Santa Maria in Vallicella (Chiesa Nuova); 1587–1590, Cappella Altemps, Santa Maria in Trastevere; 1588, Santa Maria della Consolazione; 1588–1589, San Girolamo degli Schiavoni; 1590, Cappella Olgiati, San Prassede; Rome.

ONORIO LONGHI

c.1600, Cappella Santori, San Giovanni in Laterano; 1603–1604, Cappella di San Filippo Neri, Santa Maria in Vallicella; 1606, Santa Maria Imperatrice; 1611, Palazzo Verospi; 1612–1619, Santi Ambrogio e Carlo al Corso (completed by Martino Longhi the Younger and others); before 1613, Vigna Altemps; *1617, Santa Maria Liberatrice; Rome. n.d., San Antonio Abate, Rieti, Italy.

MARTINO LONGHI THE YOUNGER

After 1619, Santi Ambrogio e Carlo al Corso (with others); 1630, San Antonio dei Portoghesi; c.1639, San Carlo ai Catinari (high altar); *c.1640, Palazzo Cætani (staircase and loggia); Rome. *1642, Palazzo Ginnetti (staircase and loggia), Velletri, Italy. 1643, Santa Maria dell'Umilta (high altar); 1646–1650, Santi Vincenzo ed Anastasio; 1653, San Adriano al Foro Romano (interior restoration); Rome.

BIBLIOGRAPHY

MARTINO LONGHI THE ELDER

BAGLIONE, GIOVANNI (1642)1935 Pages 68–69 and 156–157 in *Le vite de' pittori, scultori, et architetti.* Reprint. Rome: Calzone.

CAFFARELLI, GIOVANNI PIETRO 1851 "Martino Longhi and seine Familie." *Deutsches Kunstblatt* 2:30–31.

CARAVATTI, FRANCESCO 1915 *Viggiu nella storia e nell'arte.* Varese, Italy.

FRIEDEL, HELMUT 1978 "Die Cappella Altemps in S. Maria in Trastevere." *Römisches Jahrbuch für Kunstgeschichte* 17:89–123.

HIBBARD, HOWARD 1962 "Biography of Martino Longhi il Vecchio." Appendix 1, pages 83–93 in *The Architecture of the Palazzo Borghese.* American Academy in Rome.

KOKSA, GIORGIO 1971 *S. Girolamo degli Schiavoni.* Rome: Marietti.

RAUH, R. 1972 "Interessante Archivalien und Bestande des Palastarchivs in Hohenems." *Montfort* 24:300–337.

ONORIO LONGHI

BAGLIONE, GIOVANNI (1642)1935 Page 156 in *Le vite de' pittori, scultori, et architetti.* Reprint. Rome: Calzone.

BARONI, COSTANTINO 1940 Volume 1, part 1, pages 278–279 in *Documenti per la storia dell'architettura a*

Milano nel Rinascimento e nel Barocco. Florence: Sansoni.

BERTOLOTTI, ANTONIO 1881 Volume 2, pages 17–28 in *Artisti lombardi a Roma nei secoli XV, XVI, e XVII.* Milan: Hoepli.

GRASSI, LILIANA 1966 Page 207 in *Province del Barocco e del Rococo.* Milan: Ceschina.

PIETRANGELI, CARLO 1971 "Una'bella faciatella de' travertino' in Campidoglio." *Capitolium* 44, nos. 5–6:20–24.

PUGLIESE, ANTONIO, and RIGANO, SALVATORE 1972 "Martino Longhi il Giovane." Pages 7–192 in M. Fagiolo dell'Arco (editor), *Architettura barocca a Roma.* Rome: Bulzoni.

MARTINO LONGHI THE YOUNGER

BERTOLOTTI, ANTONIO 1881 Volume 2, pages 22–28 in *Artisti lombardi a Roma nei secoli XV, XVI, e XVII.* Milan: Hoepli.

PASCOLI, LIONE (1736)1965 *Vite de' pittori, scultori ed architetti moderni.* Reprint. Amsterdam: Israel.

PASSERI, GIOVANNI BATTISTA 1934 Pages 225–233 in Jacob Hess (editor), *Vite de' pittori, scultori ed architetti che hanno lavorate in Roma.* Vienna: Schrill.

PUGLIESE, ANTONIO, and RIGANO, SALVATORE 1972 "Martino Longhi il Giovane." Pages 7–192 in M. Fagiolo dell'Arco (editor), *Architettura barocca a Roma.* Rome: Bulzoni.

VARRIANO, JOHN 1971 "The Architecture of Martino Longhi the Younger (1602–1660)." *Journal of the Society of Architectural Historians* 30:101–118.

LONGUELUNE, ZACHARIAS

Among the most important French artists working in Dresden in the early eighteenth century, Zacharias Longuelune (1669–1748) first studied painting and then, under ANTOINE LEPAUTRE, architecture in Paris. He worked as building supervisor on the Arsenal Building, Berlin, around 1698 under JEAN DE BODT, who had apparently brought him there from Paris.

Longuelune was sent to Rome to further his education in 1710 by Friedrich I of Prussia and stayed there until 1713 or 1715 when he was called to the Saxon court at Dresden by Frederick Augustus I. In 1715, he visited Berlin and also Warsaw, where he was paid for a drawing from the royal treasury. He remained a part of the Saxon court architectural office throughout his long career, rising to the rank of superior state architect in 1731. As part of a team, Longuelune worked together with several architects and his contributions to their projects are therefore blurred. Few of his many architectural drawings—he was an excellent draftsman—found today in the Saxon State Archives, Dresden, were ever carried out. His considerable influence on Dresden baroque architecture of the 1730s through the 1750s was exerted from his teaching post at the Cadet School of the Engineering Corps. Longuelune's dry and classicizing designs, which particularly affected middle class taste in building, were in contrast to the exuberant baroque style of MATTHÄUS DANIEL PÖPPELMANN who dominated the Dresden scene until his death in 1736. The influential JOHANN CHRISTOPH KNÖFFEL who succeeded Pöppelmann intrigued against Longuelune, limiting his activities.

Longuelune's drawings for palaces in Pillnitz and Gross-Sedlitz both show, in variants, a square plan with a central domed core. His favored treatment of façades, as on the Arsenal Building (1728–1739), Dresden, used shallow risalts, light horizontal drafting, and lisens. In a few drawings, especially for fountains and gardens, an element of fantasy is seen in the architect's otherwise reserved oeuvre.

BEVERLY HEISNER

WORKS

(A)1723–1726, Palace of Gross-Sedlitz (garden), Germany. 1726–1727, Palace of Gross-Sedlitz, Germany. 1726–1730, Übigau Palace (expansion), Germany. 1728–1730, Arsenal (reduced version executed); 1730, Palace (garden wing and interiors; partially executed); Dresden-Neustadt, Germany.

BIBLIOGRAPHY

FRANZ, HEINRICH GERHARD 1953 *Zacharias Longuelune und die Baukunst des 18. Jahrhunderts in Dresden.* Berlin: Deutscher Verein für Kunstwissenschaft.

MERTENS, KLAUS 1962 *Der Park von Gross-Sedlitz.* Germany: Technical University of Dresden.

LOOS, ADOLF

Adolf Loos (1870–1933) has come to be regarded almost universally as one of a small number whose influence did most to create the Modern movement. Ironically, Loos's buildings—which ranged from rather conventional country cottages to austerely planar private houses and large public projects—were little known outside his native Austria during the movement's formative years, and his impact was largely the result of a single written work, in which he vigorously attacked the inappropriate use of ornament.

Loos was born in Bruenn, Moravia (now Brno, Czechoslovakia), the son of a stonemason. At an early age, he worked in his father's shop, an exposure to the craft of building that may have influenced his choice of career, as well as his later fondness for the expressive use of natural materials. Loos attended grammar school in Melk, in Lower Austria, where he already showed signs of a hearing deficiency that would leave him deaf at the end of his life. From there, he went on to the Royal and Imperial State College at Reichenberg in Bohemia and in 1899 was drafted for a year's service in the Austrian army. From 1890 to 1893, Loos studied architecture at the Technical College in Dresden.

In 1893, Loos left Austria for a three-year stay in the United States. While there, he traveled to New York, Philadelphia, St. Louis, and Chicago, where he visited the World's Columbian Exposition. What apparently impressed him most about his trip was not the grandiose academic architecture whose widespread popularity in America the Exposition confirmed, but the innovative and efficient design of American industrial buildings, clothing, and household furnishings. Interested as he was in American examples, he also admired English domestic design, as well as the work of such more immediate sources as JOHANN BERNARD FISCHER VON ERLACH and KARL FRIEDRICH SCHINKEL.

At the time Loos began to make his name known in Vienna, he had executed no complete buildings. His reputation was based on a few interior designs and on a body of polemical articles. Loos had many friends among the artistic and intellectual elite of the city, including Oskar Kokoschka, Ludwig Wittgenstein, and Arnold Schoenberg, but, aloof and independent, he never became a member of any distinct group or movement. In his writing, Loos came increasingly to focus on what he regarded as the excesses of decoration in both traditional Viennese design and in the more recent products of the Vienna Secession and the Wiener Werkstätte. Loos expressed his irritation most strongly in "Ornament and Crime," a short essay published in 1908 that flew in the face of contemporary practice. In it, Loos declared that, "As ornament is no longer organically linked with our culture, it is also no longer an expression of our culture." Lack of ornament, he argued, "is a sign of spiritual strength. Modern man uses the ornaments of earlier and foreign cultures as he thinks fit. He concentrates his own powers of invention on other things."

The essay caused a furor and was widely circulated abroad. (Le Corbusier later referred to it as "an Homeric cleansing" of architecture.) It rapidly became a key document in the modernist literature. However, the international image the essay produced of Loos as inflexibly opposed to all embellishment in architecture did the author a disservice. In his own work, Loos frequently used richly patterned wood and stone, exploiting their naturally decorative effects, and occasionally he even fell back on the classical orders. In 1924, he attempted to clarify the intent of his 1908 essay with another, in which he insisted: "I never meant, as the purists have carried on ad absurdum, that ornament should be systematically and consistently abolished. Only when its time has passed should one not revive it, just as a man will not go back to tattooing his face."

The reason for Loos's frustration with his reputation as a design ascetic is clear from his most important buildings, which tend to be remarkably humane environments. At first glance, the contrast between his austere façades and often sumptuous interiors appointed in colorful marble might suggest a theoretical inconsistency on Loos's part; in fact, the apparent conflict is in keeping with the architect's claim that "we call beautiful that which is most useful." The interiors of Loos's private houses are consummately useful in their accommodation of comfort and visual delight; his exteriors, whose fundamental purpose Loos saw as protection from the weather, offer little more than that. What appear from the outside to be strictly rational proto-modernist surfaces and massing are not so much aesthetic statements as a sort of negative architecture stripped of everything that does not respond to the *Raumplan*, as Loos called his interpenetrating distribution of interior spaces. "Only a very small part of architecture belongs to art: the gravestone and the memorial," he wrote in 1910. "Everything else, everything which serves a purpose, is excluded from art. . . . The artist has only himself to please. The architect has to please everyone."

Loos's most notable early work was the austere interior of the Museum Cafe in Vienna, done in 1899. A more refined work, which reveals in microcosm the architect's great sensitivity to spatial manipulation, is the tiny Kärntner Bar of 1907, also in Vienna. The use of wood paneling and mirrors creates the illusion of an intimate oasis within a much larger space. The architect's store for the firm of Goldman and Salatsch on Vienna's Michaelerplatz (1910), his first major urban building, drew critical fire for the spare surfaces of its upper stories, but the presence of Doric columns at ground level reveals the architect to be less doctrinaire about ornament than his modernist colleagues would claim.

Throughout his career, Loos's most characteristic work remained private houses. Because of their unembellished white façades, these buildings have routinely been associated with the work of Le Corbusier, J. J. P. Oud, and others, but in most cases, Loos was merely cladding living space in the simplest possible manner. Indeed, the composition of the much published Steiner House (1910) and Scheu House (1912), both in Vienna, was determined as much by local zoning ordinances as by any formal theory in the Corbusian mode.

The architect's subsequent work included many more houses (the best of which are the Tzara House in Paris of 1926–1927, the Moller House in Vienna of 1928, and the Mueller House in Prague of 1931), as well as a number of large-scale civic projects. But his best-known project was an entry for the Chicago Tribune Tower competition of 1922. Although Loos's design—a skyscraper in the form of a Doric column—has been widely criticized as either foolish or ironic, it was neither. The design was, in fact, a thoroughly consistent expression of Loos's beliefs. He was simply joining modern (in this case, skyscraper) technology with one of the most durable classical symbols in a building that was altogether useful—and therefore, in Loos's eyes, beautiful—providing a historically resonant monument for a country with few architectural traditions.

In the same year as the Chicago Tribune competition, Loos was appointed chief architect of the Vienna Department of Housing. Disillusioned with the work there, he moved to France, where he was received enthusiastically by the avant-garde. He remained in France until 1927, exhibiting at the Salon d'Automne and becoming the first foreigner to be elected a juror.

Loos returned to Vienna in 1928, and, in 1930, was awarded a life pension by Thomas Masaryk, the president of Czechoslovakia, in which his birthplace then lay. A year later, Loos had an attack of a nervous ailment that had plagued him for years. By late 1932, he was no longer able to work, and he died on August 23, 1933, in many ways a rather traditional architect whose contribution to a revolution in design was, to a large degree, the work of his reading public.

CARTER WISEMAN

WORKS

1899, Museum Cafe; 1907, Kaerntner Bar; 1910, Steiner House; 1910–1911, Store for Goldman & Salatsch Michaelerplatz; 1912, Scheu House; Vienna. 1926–1927, Tristan Tzara House, Paris. 1928, Moller House, Vienna. 1930, Mueller House, Prague.

BIBLIOGRAPHY

BANHAM, REYNER (1960)1970 *Theory and Design in the First Machine Age.* 2d ed. New York: Praeger.

BENEVELO, LEONARDO (1960)1980 *History of Modern Architecture.* 3d ed., rev. Cambridge, Mass.: M.I.T. Press. Originally published in Italian.

GLÜCK, FRANZ 1931 *Adolf Loos.* Paris: Crès.

HITCHCOCK, H. R. (1958)1977 *Architecture: Nineteenth and Twentieth Centuries.* Baltimore: Penguin.

KULKA, HEINRICH (editor) 1931 *Adolf Loos: Das Werk des Architekten.* Vienna: Shroll.

LOOS, ADOLF 1962 Volume 1 in *Sämtliche Schriften.* Edited by Franz Glück. Vienna: Herold.

MÜNZ, LUDWIG, and KÜNSTLER, GUSTAV (1964)1966 *Adolf Loos: Pioneer of Modern Architecture.* Translated from the German by Harold Meek. New York: Praeger.

PEVSNER, NIKOLAUS (1936)1974 *Pioneers of Modern Design.* Baltimore: Penguin. Originally published with the title *Pioneers of the Modern Movement.*

LORD, AUSTIN W.

Born in Rolling Stone, Minnesota, Austin Willard Lord (1860–1922) received his earliest training in various architects' offices in Minneapolis. He attended the Massachusetts Institute of Technology in the mid-1880s, and in 1888 he traveled to Paris, where he entered the atelier of Daumet Girault. Returning to New York City in 1890, he worked for MCKIM, MEAD, AND WHITE, until 1894 when he formed the firm of Lord, [J. Monroe] Hewlett, and [Washington] Hull. Their best known commission was a New York City residence (1897–1907) for Senator William A. Clark. After Hull died in 1909 the firm was renamed Lord, Hewlett, and [Hugh] Tallant. Lord was the first director of the American Academy in Rome (1894–1896), and he later served as director of the School of Architecture at Columbia University (1912–1915).

DENNIS MCFADDEN

WORK

1897–1907, William A. Clark House (with J. Monroe Hewlett and Washington Hull), New York.

BIBLIOGRAPHY

"Austin W. Lord Dies." 1922 *The New York Times* January 20:15.

"Notes." 1922 *American Architect and Building News* 71:168.

LORD, JAMES B.

James Brown Lord (1859–1902) was born in New York City. After graduating from Princeton University, he trained as an architect in the office of WILLIAM A. POTTER. Subsequently, he developed a successful New York practice. His work included several of the King Model Houses (1891), the first branch of the New York Public Library commissioned under the Carnegie bequest (1901), and the Appellate Division Courthouse (1900), all in New York.

DENNIS MCFADDEN

WORKS

1891, King Model Houses; 1900, Appellate Division

Courthouse; 1901, East 76th Street Branch of the New York Public Library; New York.

BIBLIOGRAPHY

"Death of James B. Lord." 1902 *New York Times* June 2, p. 9.

HUSSEY, CHRISTOPHER 1931 *The Work of Sir Robert Lorimer.* London: Country Life.

SAVAGE, PETER 1980*a* *Lorimer and the Edinburgh Craft Designers.* Edinburgh: Harris.

SAVAGE, PETER 1980*b* "The Temper of the Scots Pleasance." *Landscape* 24, no. 3:20–26.

LORIMER, ROBERT S.

Robert Stoddart Lorimer (1864–1929), who was born and trained in Edinburgh, Scotland, developed the vernacular architecture of Scotland; HERMANN MUTHESIUS at the turn of the century saw him as attaining a national perfection of style for Scotland such as R. NORMAN SHAW had achieved thirty years earlier for England.

Lorimer, who worked through a selected group of craftsmen, began practice in Edinburgh in 1893, and rapidly gained notice for his roughcast plastered white cottages. He contributed furniture to the Arts and Crafts exhibitions in London and was elected to the Art Workers Guild in 1896.

He next attracted attention through his country house work, and by 1905, he was pre-eminent in Scotland for restorations, remodelings, garden layouts (some with GERTRUDE JEKYLL), and new mansions. He built a number of churches; the small but highly impressive Thistle Chapel (1909) in Edinburgh made him Scotland's leading Gothic architect. He was knighted in 1911.

During and after World War I, he was much engaged in memorials. He undertook the design of thirty-three British overseas war cemeteries, and the Scottish National War Memorial on Castle Rock in Edinburgh, which opened in 1927, has become a famous shrine.

PETER SAVAGE

WORKS

1892, Earlshall, Fife, Scotland. 1901, Brackenburgh, Cumbria, England 1901, Wayside, Saint Andrews, Scotland. 1902, Marly Knowe, North Berwick, Scotland. 1902, Rowallan, Ayrshire, Scotland. 1902–1908, Barton Hartshorn, Buckingham, England. 1903, Colinton Cottage, Edinburgh. 1906, Ardkinglas, Argyll, Scotland. 1906, Saint Peter's Church, Edinburgh. 1907, Lympne Castle, Kent, England. 1907, Hill of Tarvit, Fife, Scotland. 1907, Rhu-Na-Haven, Aberdeenshire, Scotland. 1908, Formakin, Renfrew, Scotland. 1909. Thistle Chapel, Edinburgh. 1911, Dunderave Castle, Argyll, Scotland. 1916, Balmanno Castle, Perthshire, Scotland. 1919–1927, National War Memorial, Edinburgh.

BIBLIOGRAPHY

DEAS, F. WILLIAM 1931 "The Work of Sir Robert Lorimer." *Journal of the Royal Institute of British Architects* 38, no. 8:239–249; no. 9:292–295.

LOUIS, VICTOR

Victor Louis (1731–1800), born Louis-Nicolas Louis in Paris, studied with Louis Adam Loriot from 1748, trying nine times for the Prix de Rome. Once in Rome (1756–1759), he displeased the director of the Academy, Charles Joseph Natoire. This, in addition to other dubious qualities, excluded him from academic membership which he continued to seek.

The first clear statement of his characteristic neoclassical style emerged early in the unrealized commission for Stanislaw Poniatowski, king of Poland, in Warsaw, where Louis traveled briefly in 1765.

The first important surviving building is the Intendance (Governor's Residence) in Besançon, France (1770–1776). From these early years also date two remodeling projects for Gothic churches: Chartres (1766) and Noyon (1776), where he tried to wed the much admired soaring spaces of the Gothic and the strictness of neoclassical architectural forms.

Louis, by now calling himself Victor, left for Bordeaux in 1773. His patron, the duke of Richelieu, Governor of the Guyenne, for whom he had already worked in Paris, was instrumental in Louis's appointment as architect of the Grand Théâtre, replacing FRANÇOIS LHÔTE. The theater, which became a model for later works, presents a peristyle of twelve free-standing Corinthian columns running the entire length of the façade. Inside, the high rectangular vestibule (the prototype for CHARLES GARNIER'S Paris Opéra) with its symmetrical staircase, leads to a circular auditorium

Louis. Grand Théâtre. Bordeaux, France. 1773–1780

articulated by ten giant Composite columns. There is a small oval concert hall above the vestibule. After financial and administrative tangles, the theater opened in 1780. With the help of his resident studio, Louis built a number of important townhouses to complement the urban fabric, then in full expansion.

With a fête for the duke and duchess of Chartres in Bordeaux (1776), Louis obtained his next major commission, again ousting the incumbent architect, HENRI PIÈTRE. Louis enclosed the gardens of the Palais Royal in Paris (1781–1784) with long wings, monotonously articulated with colossal pilasters over a loggia, providing a popular public promenade. Louis built two more theaters in the Palais Royal, the larger being the present Comédie Française (1786–1790).

The most impressive project for Bordeaux, the Place Ludovise, designed to replace the fortress Château Trompette, was never realized. Only part of his visionary project for the Palladian (see ANDREA PALLADIO) Château of Bouilh was finished when the Revolution intervened.

Louis had little luck in Paris in the 1790s. Planning on emigrating to the United States in 1799, he sent a large trunk of drawings to a friend in Bordeaux. Louis never retrieved the papers, which form the most important part of his documentation, finally exhibited in 1980. Two architects with considerable experience in his Bordeaux studio, LOUIS COMBES and Jean Baptiste Dufart, carried his style into the next century.

MYRA DICKMAN ORTH

WORKS

*1761, Chapel (decoration), Abbey of Notre Dame de Bon Secours; *1765, Chapel of Ames-du-Purgatoire (decoration); Paris. 1766, Cathedral of Chartres (remodeling), France. *1770, Vauxhall of Senor Torré, Boulevard Saint Martin, Paris. 1770–1776, Intendance (Governor's Residence), Besançon, France. *1773, Hôtel of Duke of Richelieu (entrance and courtyard), rue Louis le Grand, Paris. 1773–1780, Grand Théâtre, Bordeaux, France. *1774, Château de Virasel, near Marmande, France. 1774–1780, Hôtel Boyer-Fonfrède; 1774–1780, Hôtel Saige; 1774–1780, Lamolère House; 1774–1780, Legrix House; 1774–1780, Rolly House; 1775, Hôtel Nairac; Bordeaux, France. 1776–1779, Cathedral of Noyon (remodeling), France. 1781–1784, Buildings to enclose the gardens of the Palais Royal; 1782–1783, Théâtre des Petits Comédiens; Paris. 1786–1790, Gobineau House, Bordeaux, France. 1786–1790, Théâtre du Palais Royal (now the Comédie Française); *1791–1793, Théâtre National; 1797, Hôtel Titon (redecoration); Paris.

BIBLIOGRAPHY

BLANCHET, LOUIS, and LAPLACE, ROSELYNE 1978 "L'Architecture de la Comédie Française." *Les Monuments Historiques de la France* 4:35–48.

BRAHAM, ALLAN 1980 *The Architecture of the French Enlightenment.* London: Thames & Hudson.

CHAMPIER, VICTOR, and SANDOZ, G. ROGER 1900 *Le Palais Royal d'après les documents inédits (1629–1900).* 2 vols. Paris: Société de Propagation des livres d'art.

GALLET, MICHEL 1964 *Les Demeures parisiennes: L'Epoque Louis XVI*^e. Paris: Le Temps.

HAUTECOEUR, LOUIS 1952 *Second moitié du XVIII*^e *siècle: Le style Louis XVI, 1750–1792.* Volume 4 in *Histoire de l'architecture classique en France.* Paris: Picard.

KALNEIN, WEND GRAF, and LEVEY, MICHAEL 1972 *Art and Architecture of the Eighteenth Century in France.* Harmondsworth, England: Penguin.

LOUIS, VICTOR 1782 *La Salle de Spectacle de Bordeaux.* Paris: Cailleau.

MARIONNEAU, CHARLES 1881 *Victor Louis.* Bordeaux, France: Gounouilhou. Cites letters and documents.

OTTOMEYER, HANS 1971 "Autobiographies d'architectes parisiens: 1759–1811." *Bulletin de la Société de l'Histoire de Paris et l'Ile de France* 1971:141–206.

PARISET, FRANÇOIS GEORGES 1980 *Victor Louis, 1731–1800: Dessins et Gravures.* France: Revue Historique de Bordeaux. Exhibition catalogue with a full bibliography.

PRUDENT, HENRI, and GAUDET, PAUL 1903 *Les Salles des Spectacles construites par Victor Louis.* Paris: Moderne Librairie de la Construction.

LOWELL, GUY

Boston-born Guy Lowell (1870–1927) studied architecture at the Massachusetts Institute of Technology and the Ecole des Beaux-Arts in Paris. Opening a Boston office in 1900, Lowell received many commissions for large country estates and for landscape designs, serving also as advisory architect for the Boston Metropolitan Parks Commission. He was known for important institutional commissions including the Boston Museum of Fine Arts (1907–1915).

MARJORIE PEARSON

WORKS

1902, Fenway Entrances, Boston. 1902, Lecture Hall, Harvard University, Cambridge, Mass. 1903, Carrie Memorial Tower, Brown University, Providence, R.I. 1903, Emerson Memorial Hall, Harvard University, Cambridge, Mass. 1903–1923, Phillips Academy (twenty-five buildings), Andover, Mass. 1904, John E. Alexandre House, Lenox, Mass. 1904, George O. Knapp House, Lake George, N.Y. 1905, Bayard Thayer House, Lancaster, Mass. 1906–1911, Cumberland County Courthouse (with George Burnham), Portland, Maine. 1907–1915, Museum of Fine Arts, Boston. 1910, James M. Codmar House, Wareham, Mass. 1910–1911, Memorial Hospital, Pawtucket, R.I. 1911, Piping Rock

Club, Locust Valley, N.Y. 1912–1927, New York County Courthouse. *1914, C. K. G. Billings Estate, Locust Valley, N.Y.

BIBLIOGRAPHY

"The Boston Museum of Fine Arts." 1909–1910 *Architects and Builders Magazine* 11:315–322.

LOWELL, GUY 1902 *American Gardens.* Boston: Bates & Guild.

LOWELL, GUY 1916 *Smaller Italian Villas and Farmhouses.* New York: Architectural Publishing.

LOWELL, GUY 1920 *More Small Italian Villas and Farmhouses.* New York: Architectural Publishing.

"Lowell, Guy." (1931)1967 Volume 21, pages 47–49 in *National Cyclopedia of American Biography.* Reprint. Ann Arbor: University Microfilms.

"Museum of Fine Arts, Boston." 1916 *American Architect* 109:214, plates.

"The New York County Court House." 1913 *American Architect* 103:214, plates.

"The New York County Court House." 1919 *American Architect* 116:681–686.

"Obituary." 1927 *American Architect* 131:230.

RUSSELL, BENJAMIN F. W. 1906 "The Works of Guy Lowell." *Architectural Review* (Boston) 13, Feb.:13–40.

LUBETKIN, BERTHOLD

Berthold Lubetkin (1901–), born in Tiflis, Georgia, Russia, was probably the most influential of several European architects who emigrated to Britain in the early 1930s and who were largely responsible for bringing the International style of modern architecture to Britain. Designer, theorist, philosopher, and socialist, he has had an enormous influence on a younger generation of architects despite the small number of his major works.

He began his studies in Moscow and Petrograd (1920–1922), after which he left for study first in Berlin and Warsaw, then in Paris (1925–1927) at the Ecole Spéciale d'Architecture, the Ecole des Beaux-Arts (Atelier AUGUSTE PERRET), the Ecole Supérieure de Béton Armé, and the Institut d'Urbanisme at the Sorbonne. His first success was a winning design in the competition for the Polytechnic of the Urals, Sverdlovsk (1925), during the short period of experiment in the early years of Soviet Russia.

From 1927 to 1930, Lubetkin was in practice in Paris with JEAN GINSBERG. Their 1927 apartment building at 25, avenue de Versailles attracted criticism at the time for the uncompromising horizontality of its façade.

In 1931, Lubetkin moved to England, and in 1932, he became the senior partner in the cooperative partnership TECTON, formed with a group of young graduates of the Architectural Association School, London. Lubetkin was also a founder-member in 1933 of the Modern Architectural Research Group (MARS), formed of young designers, writers, and scientists to exchange and develop technical ideas, to promote the new architectural movement in Britain, and to represent Britain at the meetings of the Congrès Internationaux de l'Architecture Moderne.

In 1932–1933, Tecton built the ingenious Gorilla House for the London Zoo. Several private houses and a small terrace of speculative houses were built in the mid-1930s, but the partnership's first major commission was for the Highpoint Apartment Block (1933–1935) on Highgate Hill, London, which was unique in British architecture at the time and extremely influential for the way in which Tecton had fundamentally rethought every problem down to the smallest details.

Further zoo work followed in 1934 with the sculptural Penguin Pool at the London Zoo and buildings at the new zoo park at Whipsnade, Bedfordshire, and for the zoo in Dudley, Worcestershire (1936–1937). At this time, a second block, different in structure and conception, was added to the Highpoint apartment development (Highpoint II, 1936–1938), which marked a notable change in direction away from pure functionalism in British avant-garde architecture.

The Finsbury Health Centre, Pine Street (1935–1938), for the progressive London Borough of Finsbury, was the first commission in a series of public authority work which thereafter preoccupied Tecton. Here, the Lubetkin concept of the plan both solving functional requirements and generating the form of the building was accomplished with particular success.

After the interruption of World War II, Tecton again regrouped but it dissolved in 1948. A new partnership with Lubetkin, Francis Skinner, and Douglas Bailey was subsequently formed, and Lubetkin was appointed architect-planner for the projected new town of Peterlee, Durham. Tragically, his imaginative scheme foundered through bureaucratic mismanagement, and Lubetkin resigned in 1950, virtually retiring from architectural practice.

BETTY ELZEA

WORKS

1927–1931, Apartments (with Jean Ginsberg), 25 avenue de Versailles, Paris. 1932–1933, Gorilla House (with Tecton), London Zoo. 1933–1935, Highpoint I Apartments (with Tecton), Highgate, London. 1934, Penguin Pool (with Tecton), London Zoo. 1934–1935, Whipsnade Zoo Buildings (with Tecton), Bedfordshire, England. 1935–1938, Finsbury Health Center (with Tecton), Pine Street, London. 1936–1937, Dudley Zoo Buildings (with Tecton), Worcestershire, England.

1936–1938, Highpoint II Apartments (with Tecton), Highgate; 1937–1951, Priory Green Estate (with Tecton; completed by Lubetkin, Bailey and Francis Skinner), Finsbury; 1938–1946, Spa Green Estate (with Tecton; completed by Lubetkin, Bailey and Skinner), Finsbury; 1947–1955, Hallfield Estate (with Tecton; completed by Lasdun and Drake), Paddington; London.

BIBLIOGRAPHY

Coe, Peter, and Reading, Malcolm 1981 *Lubetkin and Tecton: Architecture and Social Commitment.* London: Arts Council of Great Britain.

Furneaux, Jordan, Robert 1955 "Lubetkin." *Architectural Review* 118:36–44.

Jackson, Anthony 1965 "The Politics of Architecture: English Architecture, 1929–1951," *Journal of the Society of Architectural Historians* 24:97–107.

Lubetkin, Berthold 1932 "The Builders." *Architectural Review* 71:201–214.

Lubetkin, Berthold 1937 "Modern Architecture in England." *American Architect* 150:29–42.

Lubetkin, Berthold 1956 "Soviet Architecture: Notes on Developments from 1917 to 1932." *Architectural Association Journal* 71:260–264.

Lubetkin, Berthold 1956 "Soviet Architecture: Notes on Developments from 1932 to 1955." *Architectural Association Journal* 72:85–87.

Nelson, George 1936 "Architects of Europe Today, 12: Tecton." *Pencil Points* 17:527–540.

LUCAE, RICHARD

Born in Berlin, Richard Lucae (1829–1877) was known for rejecting the imitation of Karl Friedrich Schinkel's architecture and criticizing those who emulated his style. Trained at the Berliner Bauakademie (1850–1859), he became an instructor there in 1869 and a director in 1872. He was precise and theoretical in his specialty: architecture designed for the common people.

Architects after 1830 had to respond to the upcoming need for a new building type: housing for the working class. Industrialization had caused the separation of work and living areas, and thus apartment blocks were developed. An example of this type of building was Villa Joachim in Berlin, designed in 1871. Because the design was related totally to the function of living, Lucae rejected symmetrical plans and monumental and representative appearances.

At the same time, the cultural focus shifted from the Church to the public. The public became a more important client, and the architect's response was evident in the construction of numerous neo-Renaissance buildings. According to Lucae, in a comment made in 1878, "the state's duty should be to understand public building not functionally but as monuments of the political system of that time." This statement became the driving force of the German Renaissance movement. These monumental and representative ideas can be easily detected in many buildings of this period. The Opera House of Frankfurt (1873–1880), considered Lucae's masterpiece, was an example of a monumental Renaissance-style building. One of Lucae's best known private buildings was Palais Borsig in Berlin (1873). Lucae's design for the Charlottenburger Polytechnikum (1878–1894) in Berlin was a typical example of exaggerated symbolism in architecture. Symbols that were previously reserved for representative purposes of the Church were now applied to institutional buildings.

Thomas Alexander Bock

WORKS

1871, Villa Joachim; 1873, Palais Borsig; Berlin. 1873–1877, Opera House (not completed until 1880), Frankfurt.

BIBLIOGRAPHY

Gurlitt, Cornelius 1899 *Deutsche Kunst des 19. Jahrhundert.* Berlin: Bondi.

Rosenberg, A. 1884–1889 *Geschichte der modernen Kunst.* 3 vols. Leipzig: Grunow.

LUCANO, GIOVANNI BATTISTA DA

Giovanni Battista da Lucano (also Lugano) (?–1538/1539), a Swiss-born architect, worked in the Marche region of Italy. Outside of Visso, Italy he built the Sanctuary of Macereto from 1528–1538. With his countryman Costantino da Lugano he constructed several palaces and the Cathedral at Matélica, Italy, in the late-fifteenth century.

Howard Shubert

LUCE, CLARENCE SUMNER

Clarence Sumner Luce (1852–1924), an architect specializing in residential buildings, was born in Newport, Rhode Island. Luce practiced in Boston, moving to New York in 1885 when he won a prize for but not the commission of the Boston Public Library. Luce designed hotels and apartment houses in upper Manhattan, but he is primarily remembered for his fine Queen Anne style houses of the late 1870s and early 1880s.

Mosette Glaser Broderick

WORKS

1878–1879, Holyoke Opera House; 1878–1879, Whiting Building; Holyoke, Mass. 1882–1883, Lyman Josephs House, Middletown, R.I. 1882–1884, Walter H. Wesson House, 302 Maple Street, Springfield, Mass. 1886–1887, Conover House, Middletown, R.I. 1891, King Model Houses, Saint Nicholas Historic District; 1891, Hotel Renaissance, Fifth Avenue at 43rd Street; 1901, Hotel Somerset, 150 West 47th Street; New York. 1910, Coindre Hall, Huntingdon, N.Y.

BIBLIOGRAPHY

FRANCIS, DENNIS STEADMAN 1979 *Architects in Practice: New York City 1840–1900.* New York: Committee for the Preservation of Architectural Records.

LENG, CHARLES WILLIAM, and DAVIS, WILLIAM T. 1929–1933 Volume 5 in *Staten Island and Its People.* New York: Lewis Historical Publishing Company.

SCULLY, VINCENT J. (1955)1971 *The Shingle Style and the Stick Style.* Rev. ed. New Haven: Yale University Press.

SHELDON, GEORGE WILLIAM (1886–1887)1979 *Artistic Country Seats.* Reprint. New York: Da Capo.

LUCKHARDT, HANS, and LUCKHARDT, WASSILI

The brothers Hans Luckhardt (1890–1954) and Wassili Luckhardt (1889–1972) worked mainly in Berlin. They are remembered primarily as members of the avant-garde in the circle of BRUNO TAUT in the period 1918–1933. Both were born in Berlin. Wassili studied in Berlin-Charlottenburg and Dresden, and Hans studied in Karlsruhe. Hans died in 1954 before any major postwar works could be realized, but Wassili Luckhardt continued to practice in Berlin through the 1960s as one of the respected founders of modernism.

When they were in their twenties, before World War I, the Luckhardts were influenced by the revolutionary ideas of Expressionism in painting and sculpture. In the immediate postwar period, when there were no opportunities for young architects to build, these Expressionistic influences were coupled with social idealism to produce utopian-fantastic architecture on paper; these ideas were exchanged with other members of the *Gläserne Kette,* a group of like spirits around Bruno Taut who were influenced especially by the writings of PAUL SCHEERBART. Dynamically expressive faceted shapes reflecting the forms of natural crystals—designed as theaters, religious structures, or even as a Monument to Labor—were the result during this heady, revolutionary period.

When the great inflation of 1922 was over and it again became possible to hope for actual commissions, the form vocabulary was changed through the influence of the *Neue Sachlichkeit* (new objectivity) into a type of prismatic cubism, with an emphasis on unadorned planes, right angles, and flat roofs. The Luckhardt brothers—associated with Alfons Anker from 1924—were fascinated with applications of new materials, especially steel and glass, and with new concepts of housing, including openness, clarity, stark simplicity, and light. While their original group of rowhouses on Schorlemerallee in Berlin (1925) was achieved in conventional masonry construction, their houses on the same street from the later 1920s and their villas in Rupenhorn, Berlin (1928), were revolutionary in the application of steel-frame construction and large expanses of glass to residential architecture.

Luckhardt Brothers. Single Family House (with Anker). Schorlemerallee, Berlin. 1925–1928

Forced into inactivity during the Nazi era, the Luckhardts' first building of the postwar era was the Berlin Pavilion at the 1951 Constructa exhibition in Hannover. In a pristine Miesian (see LUDWIG MIES VAN DER ROHE) vein of rectilinear steel frame and a curtain wall largely of glass, this pavilion was characteristic of their favorite motif of lightness achieved through a skeletal frame and the thinnest of curtain walls.

Their contributions to major design competitions all expressed the principles of what had become known as the International style. Among Wassili's realized buildings in the period after the death of Hans in 1954 were the Bavarian Welfare Office in Munich (1957), the architect's own house in Berlin (1957), and the Institutes for Veterinary Medicine (1963–1968) and Plant Physiology (1962–1970) of the Free University in Berlin. His last major commission was the Haus der Bürgerschaft (City Council Building) in Bremen (1962–1969).

RON WIEDENHOEFT

WORKS

HANS AND WASSILI LUCKHARDT

1925–1928, Single-Family Houses (with Alfons Anker), Schorlemerallee; 1928, Villas (with Alfons Anker), Rupenhorn; 1929, Telschow-Haus Commercial Building (with Anker), Potsdamer Platz; Berlin. *1951, Berlin

Pavilion, Constructa exhibition, Hannover, Germany. 1954–1956, Apartment Buildings and Shops, Kottbusser Tor, Berlin.

WASSILI LUCKHARDT

1957, Apartment Building, Interbau exhibition (with Hubert Hoffmann), Hansaviertel, Berlin. 1957, Bavarian Welfare Office, Munich. 1957, Architect's House, Fabeckstrasse, Berlin. 1962–1969, Haus der Bürgerschaft, Bremen, Germany. 1962–1970, Institute for Plant Physiology; 1963–1968, Institute for Veterinary Medicine; Free University, Berlin.

BIBLIOGRAPHY

KLIEMANN, HELGA 1973 *Wassili Luckhardt.* Tübingen, Germany: Wasmuth.

KULTERMANN, UDO 1958 *Wassili und Hans Luckhardt.* Tübingen, Germany: Wasmuth.

LUCKHARDT, HANS 1930 *Zur neuen Wohnform.* Berlin: Bauwelt.

LUCKHARDT, WASSILI, and KOEHLER, WALTER 1956 *Lichtarchitektur.* Berlin: Bauwelt.

LUGAR, ROBERT

The son of a Colchester carpenter, Robert Lugar (1773?–1855) in 1799 began to practice in London and to exhibit at the Royal Academy. He was county surveyor of Essex from 1812 to 1816. Primarily a domestic architect, Lugar executed Italianate designs early in his career, but primarily employed castellated, Gothic, Tudor, and Elizabethan styles later on. He was among the first to apply effectively the ideas of Sir UVEDALE PRICE and HUMPHRY REPTON on picturesque landscaping to the design of dwellings. His *Plans and Views* (1811) was the first important publication of executed designs in nonclassical styles. ARCHIBALD SIMPSON was his pupil.

JOHN ARCHER

WORKS

1806, Gold-Hill, near Shoreham, England. 1808, J. Stirling House, Cordale, near Dumbarton, Scotland. *1808, Tillicheun Castle, Scotland. 1809, Balloch Castle (additions), Scotland. 1809, The Ryes Lodge, Little Henry, Essex, England. By 1811, Brandon Cottage, near Wolston, England. By 1811, Denham Mount, near Uxbridge, England. By 1811, Cottages at The Rookery, Woodford, England. By 1811, Rose Hill Cottage, Wargrave, England. *By 1811, Weddington Hall, near Coventry, England. *By 1816, Oxney Park (enlargements), near Dover, England. 1820–1822, Yaxham Parsonage, England. *1821, Warley Hall, near Birmingham, England. 1821–1824, Swinton Park (additions), England. 1823, Glenlee (enlargements), New Galloway, Scotland. 1825, Cyfarthfa Castle, Wales. c.1825, Hensol, near Castle Douglas, Scotland. By 1828, Betteshanger House, near Sandwich, England. By 1828, New Laithes Hall, Horsforth, England. By 1828, Puckaster Cottage, near Niton, England. 1828–1839, Maeslwch Castle, Wales.

BIBLIOGRAPHY

BLUTMAN, SANDRA 1968 "Books of Designs for Country Houses, 1780–1815." *Architectural History* 11:25–33.

DOBAI, JOHANNES 1977 Volume 3 in *Die Kunstliteratur des Klassizismus und der Romantik in England.* Bern: Benteli.

HITCHCOCK, H. R. (1954)1972 *Early Victorian Architecture in Britain.* 2 vols. Reprint. New York: Da Capo.

LUGAR, ROBERT (1805)1823 *Architectural Sketches for Cottages, Rural Dwellings, and Villas, in the Grecian, Gothic, and Fancy Styles, with Plans.* New ed. London: J. Taylor.

LUGAR, ROBERT (1807)1838 *The Country Gentleman's Architect.* New ed. London: M. Taylor.

LUGAR, ROBERT (1811)1836 *Plans and Views of Ornamental Domestic Buildings.* 2d ed. London: M. Taylor. Originally published with the title *Plans and Views of Buildings.*

LUGAR, ROBERT (1828)1855 *Villa Architecture.* 2d ed. London: M. Taylor.

LYALL, SUTHERLAND 1974 "Minor Domestic Architecture in England and Pattern Books 1790–1840." Unpublished Ph.D. dissertation, University of London.

McMORDIE, MICHAEL 1975 "Picturesque Pattern Books and Pre-Victorian Designers." *Architectural History* 18:43–59.

PILCHER, DONALD 1947 *The Regency Style, 1800–1830.* London: Batsford.

"Robert Lugar." 1848–1892 In *The Dictionary of Architecture.* 8 vols. London: The Architectural Publication Society.

TEYSSOT, GEORGES 1974 "Cottages et pittoresque: Les origines du logement ouvrier en Angleterre, 1781–1818." *Architecture, mouvement, continuité* 34, July:26–37.

LUMSDEN, ANTHONY

Anthony Lumsden (1928–) emigrated to the United States from Australia in 1954; he became principal in charge of design at the firm of Daniel, Mann, Johnson, and Mendenhall in Los Angeles after working with EERO SAARINEN and Associates and ROCHE AND DINKELOO. (1954–1964). Designing office towers and low-rise civic and collegiate buildings, until mid-1968 in collaboration with CESAR PELLI, Lumsden has developed an aesthetic of folded membrane enclosures, separated from any internal structure. Lumsden's most original projects, unbuilt but highly publicized, have wrapped mirrored glass and metal skins over apparently extruding, rolling forms to create a high-tech urban vernacular on a monumental scale.

THOMAS G. BEDDALL

WORKS

1966, Beverly Hills Jewelry Store (with Cesar Pelli); 1969, Century City Medical Plaza (with Pelli); Los Angeles. 1969–1973, Federal Aviation Administration Agency (with Pelli), Lawndale, Calif. 1970–1972, One Park Plaza; 1971–1972, Century Bank; Los Angeles. 1974–1976, Jacksonville Community College (with Reynolds, Smith, and Hills), Fla. 1976, Northlake Community College (with Envirodynamics, Inc.), Irving, Tex. 1978, Los Angeles Valley College, Van Nuys, Calif.

BIBLIOGRAPHY

"Anthony Lumsden, DMJM." 1975 *Architecture and Urbanism* 5, no. 3:61–160.

"Architecture-Promotion et Architecte-Promoteur." 1977 *L'Architecture d'aujourd'hui* 193, Oct.:1–66.

MCCOY, ESTHER 1975 "Post Mies: Architetture di Anthony J. Lumsden." *Domus* 552, Nov.:1–12.

MURPHY, JAMES A. 1972 "A Summation of Parts." *Progressive Architecture* 53, no. 6:72–83.

PAPADEMETRIOU, PETER 1976 "Images from a Silver Screen." *Progressive Architecture* 57, no. 10:70–77.

ROSS, MICHAEL FRANKLIN 1975 "The Development of an Esthetic System at DMJM." *Architectural Record* 157, no. 5:111–120.

SCHMERTZ, MILDRED F. 1979 "Designing the Campus as One Big Building." *Architectural Record* 166, no. 7:87–102.

LUNDY, VICTOR

Victor Alfred Lundy (1923–) was born in New York. He received degrees in architecture from Harvard University (1947, 1948) where he studied under WALTER GROPIUS. Lundy's career began in the office of MARCEL BREUER. Since 1953, he has been in private practice in New York. It is the engineer's aesthetic of structural innovation combined with a lyrical formulism that informs Lundy's architecture. His artistic renderings are testament to his skill in the representational arts. Lundy has always championed the use of wood, believing it to be humanizing and appropriate to American architecture. In his Saint Paul's Lutheran Church (1960) in Sarasota, Florida, the wooden roof is an inverted wooden prow, skylit along its rib. The granite cladding and powerfully cantilevered front section of his U.S. Tax Court (1976) in Washington, demonstrate the influence of Marcel Breuer.

SOPHIE GOBRAN

WORKS

1960, Saint Paul's, Sarasota, Fla. 1961, First Unitarian Church, Westport, Conn. 1976, United States Tax Court, Washington.

BIBLIOGRAPHY

ABERCROMBIE, STANLEY 1976 "Monumental Suspense—United States Tax Court, Washington, D.C." *Progressive Architecture* 57, July:52–59.

LUNDY, VICTOR A. 1959 "Art Alone, Untiring, Stays to Us." *Journal of the American Institute of Architect's* 31, May:15–20.

"New Ideas of Victor Lundy." 1962 *Architectural Record* 131, Feb.:105–120.

LUNTZ, VIKTOR

Viktor Luntz (1840–1903) was a pupil of Friedrich von Schmidt, a Gothic Revivalist and restorer of Viennese Gothic churches, and as such was one of the last representatives of strict historicism in Vienna. However, his main work, the Kaiser-Jubiläumskirche (Emperor's Jubilee Church; 1898–1903) on the Danube in Vienna, is a voluminous building in the Rhenish-Romanesque style. He had won the competition over OTTO WAGNER.

SOKRATIS DIMITRIOU
Translated from German by
Beverley R. Placzek

WORK

1898–1903, Kaiser-Jubiläumskirche (not completed until 1913 by A. Kirstein), Vienna.

BIBLIOGRAPHY

HEVESI, LAJOS 1906 *Acht Jahre Sezession.* Vienna: Konegen.

WAGNER-RIEGER, RENATE 1970 *Wiens Architektur im 19. Jahrhundert.* Vienna: Österreichischer Bundesverlag.

LURAGO, ROCCO

Rocco Lurago (1501–1590) was born in the village of Pelsopra near Como, Italy, and died in Genoa. Member of a family of Lombard sculptors and architects, Lurago migrated south to Genoa in Liguria where he spent his career. Here, in the years following the city's recapture from the French in 1528, Lurago participated in the republic's cultural resurgence under the aegis of Andrea Doria.

Genoa was taken by the French in 1499. The twenty-nine years of foreign occupation which followed isolated the city from the rest of Italy. Thus, when Doria liberated the city and restored the republic, Genoa was essentially a medieval town unfamiliar with the Renaissance. This situation

Lurago.
Palazzo del Municipio.
Genoa, Italy.
1564–1566

accepted the terms of the landscape and worked with its limitations rather than against them: the Palazzo del Municipio is conceived as a series of enclosed terraces built into the hillside and linked by monumental staircases. At the back wall of the first courtyard, a staircase rises and splits, leading the way to the *piano nobile* and a second courtyard built further back into the hillside. The axial sequence of courtyard and staircase recalls DONATO BRAMANTE's Belvedere project at the Vatican in Rome. Lurago's program is an application of landscape design to the problem of urban building.

The Palazzo del Municipio also reflects the Roman ambient in its decoration. The architect's use of the colossal order and an oversized crowning cornice on the building's exterior clearly derives from Michelangelo's designs for the Campidoglio (1538) and the Palazzo Farnese (1546) in Rome.

Lurago's work was imitated throughout Genoa. Bartolomeo Bianco copied the scheme of the Municipio for his own design of the University (1634–1636).

Aside from the Palazzo del Municipio no other documented works of Lurago exist; however, it is generally agreed that the Dominican church and convent commissioned by Pope Paul V at nearby Bosco Alessandrino is also from his hand.

changed rapidly as Doria imported artists from Rome to revive the city's diminished cultural life. Perino del Vaga arrived in 1528 and the sculptor Giovanni Angelo Montorsoli in 1529.

In 1548, GALEAZZO ALESSI was appointed the city's chief architect. Although Genoese, Alessi had spent several years in Rome where he was influenced by the great mannerist experiments of MICHELANGELO and Antonio da Sangallo the Younger (see SANGALLO FAMILY). When he returned to Genoa, Alessi brought with him the style of these architects. In architecture as well as painting and sculpture, mid-century Genoa was thus an outpost of the Roman *maniera.*

It is in this milieu that Lurago first began to work. Although nothing concrete is known about his education or architectural training, it is presumed that Lurago arrived in Genoa well after 1528.

Lurago shows his debt to Alessi and the Romans in many aspects of his only securely identified monument, the Palazzo del Municipio which he erected for Nicolò Grimaldi on Genoa's famed Strada Nuova between 1564 and 1566.

The Palazzo del Municipio is best known for the ingenious solution it offers to the problem of building a palace into a hillside. In the standard Renaissance palace, three stories rise in an enclosed block around a central, rectangular courtyard. In Genoa, where the city's ground level rises and falls dramatically, this formula was often unacceptable. A simple architectural block could not be erected against steep hillsides without a great deal of engineering difficulty. Lurago found an effective solution to this problem by designing a palace which

SARAH E. BASSETT

WORKS

1564–1566, Palazzo del Municipio, Genoa, Italy. 1566–1572, Dominican Church and Monastery, Bosco Alessandrino, Italy. 1581, San Pietro dei Banchi, Genoa, Italy.

BIBLIOGRAPHY

BRINCKMANN, A. E. 1915–1919 *Baukunst des 17. und 18. Jahrhunderts in den Romanischen Ländern.* Berlin: Akademische Verlagsgesellschaft Athenaion.

GROSSO, ORLANDO 1927 *Genova.* Bergamo, Italy: Istituto italiano d'arti grafiche.

HEYDENREICH, LUDWIG H., and LOTS, WOLFGANG 1974 *Architecture in Italy: 1400–1600.* Baltimore: Penguin.

LABÒ, MARIO 1921 "Studi di Architettura Genovese: Palazzo Rosso." *L'Arte* 24:139–151.

SUIDA, WILLIAM EMIL 1906 *Genua.* Leipzig: Seemann.

LURÇAT, ANDRE

Brother of the French artist Jean Lurçat, André Lurçat (1894–1970) studied architecture at the Ecole des Beaux-Arts, Paris. Disenchanted with the forms and design methods promulgated by the Ecole, Lurçat was receptive to arguments in favor of modern architecture put forward after World War I. Early in his career, he rejected the principle of applied ornament and assimilated the functionalist doctrines of LE CORBUSIER, ADOLF LOOS, and others. In the mid-1920s, he produced a number of villas and studio houses which secured his reputation as a designer of considerable talent. In these early designs, Lurçat displayed a preoccupation with the decorative effects obtained through repetition and juxtaposition of simple shapes and volumes, especially on the exterior, which distinguishes his design procedure from that of Le Corbusier during the same period. Nevertheless, his houses are typically less exuberant than those constructed in Paris during the 1920s by ROBERT MALLET-STEVENS.

By no means an architect exploiting a modernist formal vocabulary in response to the dictates of current fashion, Lurçat was strongly committed to modern architecture as an agent of radical social change to be effected through a profound transformation of the built environment. He was a founding member of the Congrès Internationaux d'Architecture Moderne in 1928, and numerous books, articles, and addresses promoted the cause of modern architecture in France.

Lurçat's commitment to this cause was bound up with a left-wing ideological alignment dating back to his membership in the society of *Etudiants Révolutionnaires* during World War I. The first explicit architectural embodiment of Lurçat's political position was his Karl Marx School Complex (1930–1933) in Villejuif, near Paris. Lurçat won the competition for this project with a design elaborated in close collaboration with specialists in education and hygiene. The school as an institution was intended to be a model for pedagogical organization in a classless society recognizing no distinction between material and intellectual labor.

The social and architectural requirements of the working class were of increasing concern to Lurçat from the late 1920s onward. As did many advanced architects during the 1930s, Lurçat devoted attention to the problems of planning the minimum dwelling unit and of organizing residential districts. For community development he favored an arrangement, originated by Le Corbusier in the early 1920s, of low blocks and towers in a parklike setting.

From 1934 to 1936, Lurçat traveled in the Soviet Union, where he participated in the crucial debates of the time regarding the proper character of proletarian architecture. While standing firm in his rejection of academism and archeological revivalism, Lurçat eventually accepted the tendency to monumentality in building recommended by the Stalinist cultural program. None of his several Soviet projects was ever carried out, but his scheme for the Soviet Academy of Sciences figured among the unpremiated finalists in the 1934 competition.

During World War II, Lurçat compiled *Formes, Composition et Lois d'Harmonie* (1953–1957), a treatise on architectural composition which discerns, through formal analyses of great structures of the past, principles of design appropriate for contemporary use. The book constitutes an effort to justify on the level of abstract architectural theory the monumentality and symmetry which Lurçat had come to associate with Marxist building as a result of his experiences in the Soviet Union.

In his later designs, particularly his post-World War II housing schemes, Lurçat attempted to reconcile a will to monumentality (formerly absent in his work) with his functionalist design philosophy, emphasizing the importance of efficiency in spatial distributions and economy in the use of inexpensive materials and prefabricated elements. Critics have frequently dismissed Lurçat's later works as lacking in vitality, but each of these buildings was a straightforward response to specific programmatic requirements and therefore stands as an instance of architectural production more finely attuned to its social purpose than to arbitrary canons of beauty.

ALFRED WILLIS

WORKS

1924, Rousset Villa, Eaubonne, France. 1924–1925, Jean Lurçat Studio-House; 1924–1925, Quillé House, Cité Seurat; 1925, Bertrand House, Cité Seurat; 1925, Georg and Gromaire House; 1925–1926, Huggler House, Cité Seurat; Paris. 1925–1926, Michel House, Versailles, France. 1926–1927, Guggenbuhl House, Paris. 1927, Apartment Block, Bagneux, France. 1927, Barbazanges Gallery, Paris. 1927, Froriep de Salis House, Boulogne-sur-Seine, France. 1930–1931, Hôtel Nord-Sud, Calvi, Corsica, France. 1930–1933, Karl Marx School Complex, Villejuif, France. 1932, Hefferlin Villa, Ville d'Avray, France. 1932, Werkbund Houses, Vienna. 1946–1950, Cité Paul Langevin Housing, Saint-Denis, France. 1946–1950, Maubeuge (reconstruction), France. 1946–1960, Unité de Quartier Fabien Housing, Saint-Denis, France. 1947–1950, Vacation Center, Mériel, France. 1949–1958, Cité Paul Eluard Housing, Saint-Denis, France. 1951, Leduc House, Sceaux, France. 1952–1953, School Complex, Blanc-Mesnil, France. 1952–1953, School in the Quartier Fabien; 1953, Henri Barbuse Day Care Center; Saint-Denis, France. 1953, Michault House, Sceaux, France. 1956–1957, School; 1964–1967, Town Hall; Blanc-Mesnil, France.

BIBLIOGRAPHY

Architecture, Mouvement, Continuité 1976 40:entire issue.

BENEVOLO, LEONARDO (1960)1971 *The Modern Movement.* Volume 2 in *History of Modern Architecture.* Cambridge, Mass.: M.I.T. Press.

CASSETTI, BRUNO (1971)1972 "André Lurçat in

URSS: Il recupero dell'architettura come istituzione." Pages 195–216 in Alberto Rosa et al. (editors), *Socialismo, città, architettura URSS 1917–1937: Il contribuo degli architetti europei.* 2d ed. Rome: officina Edizioni.

GIEDION, SIGFRIED (1926)1938 *Bauen in Frankreich: Bauen in Eisen, Bauen in Eisenbeton.* 2d ed. Leipzig and Berlin: Klinkhardt & Biermann.

HITCHCOCK, H. R. (1929)1970 *Modern Architecture: Romanticism and Reintegration.* Reprint. New York: Hacker.

LURÇAT, ANDRÉ 1929*a* *Architecture.* Paris: Au Sans Pareil.

LURÇAT, ANDRÉ 1929*b* *Projets et Réalisations.* Paris: Vincent, Fréal.

LURÇAT, ANDRÉ 1929*c* *Terrasses et jardins.* Paris: Moreau.

LURÇAT, ANDRÉ 1953–1957 *Formes, Composition et Lois d'Harmonie; éléments d'une science de l'esthétique architecturale.* 5 vols. Paris: Vincent, Fréal.

LURÇAT, ANDRÉ 1961 *Oeuvres récentes I.* Paris: Vincent, Fréal.

"Il Municipio di Blanc-Mesnil de André Lurçat: L'ultima opere di una vittima del 'realismo sovietico.'" 1970 *L'architettura: Cronache e Storia* 16:376–382.

PICCINATO, GIORGIO 1965 *L'architettura contemporanea in Francia.* Rocca San Casciano, Italy: Capelli.

RAGON, MICHEL 1959 *Le livre de l'architecture moderne.* Paris: Laffont.

RAPHAEL, MAX 1976 *Für eine demokratische Architektur.* Frankfurt: Fischer.

SARTORIS, ALBERTO (1932)1941 *Gli elementi dell'architettura funzionale.* 3d ed. Milan: Hoepli.

SARTORIS, ALBERTO (1949)1957 *Encyclopédie de l'architecture nouvelle: Ordre et climat méditerranéens.* 2d ed., rev. Milan: Hoepli.

TAFURI, MANFREDO, and DAL CO, FRANCESCO (1976)1979 *Modern Architecture.* Translated by Robert E. Wolf. New York: Abrams.

TAUT, BRUNO 1929 *Modern Architecture.* London: The Studio.

LUSSON, ADRIEN LOUIS

Born in La Flèche, France, Adrien Louis Lusson (1788–1864) entered the Ecole d'Architecture in Paris in 1806, where he studied under CHARLES PERCIER AND PIERRE FRANÇOIS LEONARD FONTAINE. He was in Italy from 1816 to 1819, and on his return worked for the city of Paris until he retired in 1830. He traveled widely thereafter and published much. An early proponent of iron construction, he is famed as the initial designer of the iron-framed Church of Saint Eugène in Paris. Many of his drawings are in the library at Le Mans.

R. D. MIDDLETON

WORKS

*1822–1826, La Rotonde, Place des Halles, Le Mans, Sarthe, France. 1827, Douane (then Halle de déchargement; later transformed into the Eglise Protestante Evangelique in 1843 by FRANZ CHRISTIAN GAU), rue Chauchat; 1861–1864, Saint François Xavier (later redesigned and reduced in size by Toussaint François Joseph Uchard); Paris. n.d., Château de M. de Chabrol-Volvic, Puy de Dome, France. n.d., Châteaux de Neuville, de Vernay, and de Voisin, France. n.d., Hospital, Néris, Allier, France.

BIBLIOGRAPHY

BAUCHAL, CHARLES 1887 *Nouveau dictionnaire biographique et critique des architectes français.* Paris: Librairie Générale de l'Architecture.

BEUTHER, CHRISTIAN 1965 "Saint-Eugène und die Bibliothèque Nationale: Zwei Esienkonstruktionen und ihr Ideengehalt." In Joseph Hoster and Peter Bloch (editors), *Miscellanea pro arte: Hermann Schnitzler zur Vollendung des 60. Lebensjahres am 13. Januar 1965.* Düsseldorf, Germany: Schwann.

LUSSON, ADRIEN LOUIS (1816)1843 *Plan, coupe, élévation et détail du nouveau marché St. Germain: J. B. Blondel, architecte; A. L. Lusson, inspecteur.* 2d ed., rev. Paris: Bance.

LUSSON, ADRIEN LOUIS 1820 *Description pittoresque de la Sicile.* Paris: The author.

LUSSON, ADRIEN LOUIS 1835 *Projects de trente fontaines pour l'embellissement de la ville de Paris.* Paris: Carilian-Goeury.

LUSSON, ADRIEN LOUIS 1837 *Project d'un archevêché pour la ville de Paris.* Paris: The author.

LUSSON, ADRIEN LOUIS 1838 *Project d'un Collège pour trois cents élèves . . . d'après le programme de M. L'Abbé Nicolle.* Paris: Duverger.

LUSSON, ADRIEN LOUIS 1839 *Spécimen d'architecture gothique . . . .* Paris: Bance.

LUSSON, ADRIEN LOUIS 1842 *Grand Ligne de Chemin de fer de Paris à l'océan, par Orléans, Tours et Nantes . . . .* Paris: Duverger.

LUSSON, ADRIEN LOUIS 1843 *Souvenirs d'un voyage à Munich.* Paris: Breton.

LUSSON, ADRIEN LOUIS 1846 *Project d'un théâtre d'Opéra définitif pour la ville de Paris.* Paris: Gratiot.

LUSSON, ADRIEN LOUIS 1855 *Plans, Coupes, élévations et détails de l'église rue de Montyon, à Paris . . . sous l'invocation de Saint Eugène.* Paris: The author.

LUSSON, ADRIEN LOUIS n.d. *Monuments antiques et modernes de la Sicile, et choix de Palais, maisons et autres édifices de Naples.* Paris: Carilian-Goeury.

LUTYENS, EDWIN

Sir Edwin Landseer Lutyens (1869–1944), the greatest English architect of his generation, dominated the profession during the first four decades of the twentieth century. He was able to sustain his peculiar eminence in many buildings in a wide range of styles and functions during a complex, uncertain, and unstable period of English architecture, he was, above all, a domestic architect. His work brilliantly fused the Romantic and the classical strains in English architecture.

Lutyens was born in London in 1869, the tenth child of Charles Lutyens, a soldier turned painter whose family was ultimately of Dutch origin. Because of ill-health, Lutyens was spared a conventional English education and spent much of his childhood at Thursley, in Surrey, a county near London that was being opened up by the railways. By watching builders and craftsmen at work Lutyens laid the foundations for the superb craftsmanship of his buildings. His study of the outlines and roof planes of old farmhouses and barns may well have encouraged the remarkable sense of architectural form and mass he displayed throughout his long career.

Lutyens's only formal architectural education was at the Kensington School of Art, London, where he did not finish the course, and in the office of Ernest George and Harold PETO (1887–1889), where he first met HERBERT BAKER. In 1889 Lutyens received the commission for Crooksbury, Surrey. At the age of twenty, he set up practice on his own in London. As in all his early work, this first house shows the influence of Ernest George and the two other principal architects of the English domestic revival of the 1870s and 1880s, R. NORMAN SHAW and PHILIP S. WEBB, for whom, in particular, Lutyens had great admiration.

However, none of Lutyens's early Arts and Crafts work is especially remarkable until he came under the influence of GERTRUDE JEKYLL. A remarkable independent woman, who had been influenced by JOHN RUSKIN, Jekyll was interested in country traditions and buildings. Lutyens first masterpiece Munstead Wood, (1896–1897), was built for Jekyll, and demonstrates a sophisticated handling of roof planes, chimneys and gables. The sympathetic and subtle use of traditional materials and building crafts combined with the close relationship between house and garden reflect the strong contribution of Jekyll.

During the following two decades, Jekyll collaborated with Lutyens on the gardens of most of his houses. These gardens are conspicuous for their Romantic combination of the formal and the picturesque as well as for the architectural integration of house and garden. Steps, walls, and terraces developed along dominant axes extended from the interior plan. Some commissions were for gardens only, as at Hestercombe (1906). Jekyll also introduced Lutyens to most of his important early clients as well as to his wife, Lady Emily Lytton. This marriage imposed severe financial demands on Lutyens and encouraged a sometimes overactive search for work, yet the houses designed during the next decade are his most inventive and assured.

Lutyens.
Orchards, Munstead.
Surrey, England.
1897–1899

At the end of the 1890s, Lutyens designed several houses for middle class clients, who wanted a place near London for weekend entertaining. Among his most remarkable and famous houses, Lutyens's love of tradition was enhanced by inventiveness and a compelling mannerism in detail. Houses like Fulbrook (1897–1899) and Orchards (1897–1899) in Surrey are chiefly interesting for the confident development of traditional forms and textures, but further away from London, as at Overstrand in Norfolk (1899–1901), Roseneath, Dumbartonshire (1898), in Scotland and, above all, with Les Bois des Moutiers at Varengeville-sur-mer in France (1898), Lutyens displayed a wilful eccentricity analagous with the work of his contemporary CHARLES RENNIE MACKINTOSH and other architects touched by *l'art nouveau*.

Tigbourne Court, Surrey (1899–1901), with its concave wings, reveals Lutyens's slowly growing interest in geometry combined with an exquisite exploitation of local building traditions. Perhaps the most characteristic example of Lutyens's Romantic and vernacular work is Deanery Garden, Sonning (1899–1902), built for Edward Hudson, who founded *Country Life* in 1897, the perfect vehicle for both English rural nostalgia and for the promotion of Lutyens's architecture. Designed in mellow special brick, with a double height hall of timber and chalk, the use of linking axes in the plan of Deanery Garden may be compared with the contemporary work of FRANK LLOYD WRIGHT.

In the early twentieth century, Lutyens houses were classic statements of Edwardian Romanticism that displayed his love of ambiguity and felicitous appropriateness of detail. At Grey Walls, Gullane, Scotland (1900–1901), where house and gardens were planned generously on forty-five degree geometrical axes, the visitor encounters three ambiguities of direction from the entrance gates to the drawing room. But geometry and the originality of a concave entrance front to the house do not overwhelm the architect's feeling for materials and detail. As a planner of houses, Lutyens was a master at combining domestic comfort with unusual juxtapositions and controlled movement through enclosed spaces that were often arranged around a solid core with a dominating chimney piece at the center of the house. In his chimney pieces, Lutyens was brilliant at invention; in his staircases, he created expansiveness of movement and unexpected vistas. In fact, Lutyens's circulation spaces are often more generously planned than individual rooms.

Lutyens's houses began to show an increasing eclecticism in style. At Little Thakeham (1902), a mellow Tudor exterior contains a grand, double-height classical hall with staircase attached. In Marshcourt (1901–1904), built of an unusual material—chalk—classical details are integrated into a more traditional, vernacular style. Lutyens was evidently responding to the growing interest in classical architecture in the years around 1900. Tired of producing his confident essays in roofs, gables, chimneys, and leaded-light windows, he was anxious to tackle a more demanding architectural discipline. At Homewood, Knebworth (1901), he built a house for his mother-in-law, the Dowager Countess of Lytton. Ionic pilasters appear below an enclosing sweep of roof, while on the entrance front of three weatherboarded gables, the arched entrance porch has an open tympanum above its keystoned lintel. This Mannerist treatment of classical forms, leaving architectural elements hanging free in space, appeared earlier at Overstrand Hall (1899–1901) and later at Marshcourt (1901–1904); it became characteristic of Lutyens's work until the very end of his career.

Neoclassical forms, redolent of the architecture of Claude Nicolas Ledoux, manifested themselves at Papillon Hall (1903–1904), whose eccentric butterfly plan was determined by the incorporation of an earlier house of octagonal form. However, the house that marks Lutyens's wholehearted adoption of the classical system was Heathcote, Ilkley, Yorkshire (1906). In this opulent palazzo, Lutyens adopted the Doric order of Michele Sanmicheli, including pilasters that disappear into the rustication between base and capital. Earlier, in 1903, Lutyens had written in a celebrated letter to Herbert Baker in South Africa: "In architecture Andrea Palladio is the game. It is so big—few appreciate it now and it requires considerable training to value and realize it. The way Christopher Wren handled it was marvellous. Shaw has the gift . . . It is a game that never deceives, dodges never disguises. It means hard thought all through—if it is laboured it fails . . . it is a big game, a high game . . ."

Heathcote shows Lutyens enthusiastically playing the "High Game." Although several writers regard the house as marking the architect's move from a progressive, "Free Style" vernacular to a stiff, reactionary classicism, the house was by no means typical of his domestic practice. At Folly Farm Sulhampstead, Berkshire (1906), the first part of the house was built in brick in a reticent, classical style reminiscent of the period of William and Mary. When Lutyens extended the house in 1912, he added one of his most extreme and extravagant Romantic designs, with vast sweeps of tiled roof around a tiny pool and tall brick chimneys. More typical of Lutyens's later domestic work is a William and Mary, or neo-Georgian, brick style, in which he was following the lead given by Shaw and Ernest Newton some years before. Nashdom (1905–1908), of whitewashed brick, has a perversely understated center and shuttered windows; The Salutation (1911)—perhaps Lutyens's most perfect essay in the style—has exquisitely and unusually proportioned façades placed around a tightly planned interior.

During these same years, however, Lutyens also designed several houses in his "castle" style, often in response to particularly dramatic sites. Elements of this highly Romantic style appear at Overstrand Hall where there are tall mullioned and transomed windows and polygonal bays rising the full height up to a continuous coped parapet. Although in Surrey, Red House at Godalming (1899) exploits a steeply sloping site with these elements, creating a strong castlelike impression from below, it is a small house with rooms arranged in a spiral around a central staircase well. However, Lutyens's principal works in this manner were more farflung. Again for Edward Hudson, Lutyens restored and enlarged Lindisfarne Castle on Holy Island, Northumberland (1903–1904). Here Lutyens respected the old silhouette of the castle and rock while creating interiors that revel in the sophisticated simplicity of bare stone and plaster, heavy Norman columns and arches, timber ceilings, and a succession of different levels. At Lambay Castle in Ireland (1905–1912), Lutyens repaired and enlarged an old house and created an intricate pattern of buildings and gardens within a huge circular rampart wall.

The most extravagant of these castles was Castle Drogo, designed for a successful grocer who wanted a thirteenth-century style castle. An entirely new building on a dramatic bluff in Devon, begun in 1910 and never finished, one-third of the original plan stands today. With its subtly modeled planes of granite wall and carefully placed patterns of mullioned and transomed windows, Drogo would not be mistaken for a real castle, although its interiors and staircases are planned on a heroic scale. Ironically, Lutyens would have preferred to design a straightforward house for this client. By this date, his mind preferred grand conceptions in a classical manner, but an important part of his success as an architect was his willingness to build in whatever style his clients wanted, without losing his own distinctive manner.

The range and quality of Lutyens's work is well shown at Ashby St. Ledgers in Northamptonshire, where he worked intermittently from 1904 until he designed the tomb of his client, Ivor Guest, in 1938. He altered and extended the Elizabethan house, added a dining room in his streamlined castle style, made other additions out of re-erected old timber buildings, laid out the gardens, designed a clever rustic bridge of brick and timber, built stables and lodges, and designed a particularly fine group of six cottages of local stone all under a continuous thatched roof.

In response to the new mood in Britain following the accession of Edward VII to the throne in 1901, Lutyens became eager to expand his practice from the purely domestic and to secure a "big job" in which he could exploit the classical discipline. However he was unsuccessful in securing any commission for the large "Edwardian Baroque" public buildings going up in London at the time. His design for County Hall (1908), strongly influenced by Wren's Greenwich Hospital, was unsuccessful in competition and he had to content himself with smaller jobs. These, nevertheless, show Lutyens strong sense of urban context as well as his immense admiration for the architecture of Wren. The offices for the magazine *Country Life* (1904) are a subtle variation on the brick and stone theme of Hampton Court; the unfinished headquarters for the Theosophical Society (1911–1913) have an immensely grand and simple elevation on the theme of an Italian palazzo. His biggest London commission, however, was not truly urban. This was Hampstead Garden Suburb (1908–1910), where Lutyens created a more formal center for the informal town plan by PARKER and UNWIN. This is dominated by two churches, of similar general style and configuration, in which Lutyens responded to the location by synthesizing town and country in both style and construction. Huge sweeps of roof are combined with Wrenian detail, in two colors of brick, while internally there are both round arches and saucer domes and rustic timber construction.

Lutyens greatest opportunities came in distant parts of the British Empire. In 1910 he was invited to South Africa to design the Art Gallery in Johannesburg (1910–1941). Never finished, this building has a portico derived from St. Paul's Covent Garden by INIGO JONES and giant blank aedicule niches between Doric columns which may have been inspired by old Newgate Prison by GEORGE DANCE THE YOUNGER. Also in Johannesburg is the Rand Regiments Memorial (1911), the first of Lutyens's many memorials on the arch theme.

Lutyens.
Castle Drogo (never completed)
Drewsteignton, Devon, England.
1910–1932

While in South Africa, Lutyens could have seen the monumental classic memorials by his old friend Herbert Baker. Baker's Union Buildings in Pretoria strongly influenced the British Government's choice of architect and style for the new capital of India, which was transferred from Calcuta to Delhi in 1911. In 1912, Lutyens was appointed architect to the Delhi Planning Commission, and was joined by Baker later that year. New Delhi was Lutyens's greatest opportunity. Notwithstanding his quarrel with Baker over the gradient of part of the city's central vista leading up to Lutyens's Viceroy's House, the two architects created the finest example of monumental Beaux-Arts town planning realized in this century. However, with its low density and careful planting of trees, New Delhi is also rooted in the development of the English garden city. It succeeds in combining the formal with the naturalistic. The plan of New Delhi, which was influenced by that for Washington, D.C. and was based on the sixty degree triangle, centered upon the principal building: the Government, or Viceroy's, House (1912–1931).

Viceroy's House, now Rashtrapati Bhavan, is in many respects Lutyens's greatest achievement. A building of prodigious size and an immensely complex plan containing both state and domestic rooms, it demonstrates Lutyens's profound, instinctive understanding of the geometrical essence of classical architecture and his ability to transform it into something new and appropriate to India. Although Lutyens emmployed his version of the Roman Doric—the "Delhi Order"—which rises to the same height from different levels, the character of Viceroy's House is not given by the academic disposition of the classical grammar but by the dynamic monumentality of its mass, with battered walls stepping back at a series of cornices and

Lutyens.
Viceroy's House Complex (now Rashtrapati Bhavan).
New Delhi.
1912–1931

string courses which run inexorably around and through the building. Having resisted the demand to design New Delhi in an Indian rather than a Western style, Lutyens nevertheless grafted Oriental elements onto his architecture: the Moghul roof-top pavilions, or *chattris*, the Moghul projecting cornice, the *chujja*, of thin slices of stone which casts a deep band of shadow; and around the extraordinary monumental dome of Viceroy's House Lutyens wrapped the stone railing motif from the Buddhist *stupa* at Sanchi, India.

A synthesis of East and West, as well as a synthesis of the formal and the naturalistic, also appears in the Moghul Garden to the west of Viceroy's House. Lutyens was inspired by the water gardens of Persia and the Kashmir and created an intricate Romantic pattern of stone, water, trees, flowers, and grass, enhanced by stone walls and pergolas of curious abstracted forms.

Several of the buildings Lutyens proposed for New Delhi were not executed. Apart from the Viceroy's staff quarters and a few official bungalows, the only other buildings designed by Lutyens were the All India Arch and the King George V Memorial at the far end of the central vista, the Record Office and the town houses for the Nizam of Hyderabad and the Gaekwar of Baroda, in which Lutyens employed a more streamlined version of his Delhi Classic style on plans angled at sixty degrees. Sir Herbert Baker designed the Secretariat buildings flanking the approach to Viceroy's House and the circular Council House. Most of the other buildings in New Delhi were designed by younger architects who were strongly influenced by Lutyens, notably ROBERT TOR RUSSELL, A. G. SHOOSMITH, H. A. N. MEDD, and WALTER GEORGE.

By the time New Delhi was inaugurated in 1931, the architectural climate in Britain had changed and the status of classicism, if not Lutyens's own eminence as a practitioner in it, had been weakened. The cause was the human and psychological catastrophe of the Great War of 1914–1918, which undermined the settled world that had made Lutyens's earlier career possible. Paradoxically and ironically, however, Lutyens' war memorials were among his most brilliant and powerful designs. To Lutyens fell the opportunity of designing the principal English national memorial, the Cenotaph in Whitehall in London (1919–1920). A stone sarcophagus standing on a tall, narrow pylon, all of whose planes are curved and converge in accordance with geometrical principles derived from the entasis of the Parthenon, the mass itself steps back alternately on each plane as the structure rises. This personal, abstracted classicism, described as Lutyens's "Elemental Mode" by Christopher Hussey, came increasingly to characterize the architect's work. Anxious to avoid overt religious or national symbolism and increasingly obsessed by the subtleties of geometry, Lutyens was concerned with the emotional power of pure monumental form, comprehensible only in the classical tradition.

In 1917 Lutyens was made one of the Principal Architects to the Imperial War Graves Commission—the others were REGINALD BLOMFIELD, Herbert Baker and C. R. HOLDEN. For the British war cemeteries he designed the Great War Stone, a monolith modeled, again, with a curved entasis. With a team of assistant architects, Lutyens designed many war cemeteries in France and his ideas on the relationship of planting and gardening to the stone walls and buildings strongly influenced the general policy of the I.W.G.C. Many of the small cemeteries show Lutyens's sensitivity to landscape and planting, while amongst the larger cemeteries the most notable is that at Etaples (1923–1924), with pairs of cenotaphs on arched bases and flanked by stone flags.

Lutyens also designed several memorials to the Missing, built in conjunction with the war cemeteries. The most notable of these is the Memorial to the Missing of the Somme at Thiepval (1927-1932), which became the finest executed statement of Lutyens's geometrical abstracted classicism and of the development of his interest in the Roman triumphal arch form. The mass of the memorial is penetrated by a proportioned heirarchy of arch tunnels along two axes, creating sixteen piers on which are carved seventy-three thousand names. As the structure rises it recedes in a series of complex set-backs. One of Lutyens's last designs was the Australian National Memorial at Villers-Bretonneux (1936–1938), in which the more severe and geometrical forms are tempered by classical aedicules standing free in openings—similar to Lutyens's first experiments with classical elements more than three decades earlier.

In the 1920s Lutyens was much less occupied with domestic work. The few houses he designed, such as Gledstone Hall (1922–1926), develop the classical themes of his prewar work. The British Embassy in Washington, D.C. (1927–1928), combined both offices and domestic accommodation in his Neo-Georgian manner, although the rather vertical proportions seem American in character. For most of the decade, however, Lutyens was occupied with New Delhi, war memorials, and, for the first time, commercial designs. In his classical façades for steel-framed office buildings designed by other architects, such as Brittanic House, London (1920–1924), Lutyens relieved the monotonous bulk of such structures by set-backs, varied window treatments, and imaginative classical detail. Much of this work was carried out for the Midland Bank, whose headquarters in the City of London (1924–1939) employed disappearing pilasters and rustication of precise and minute diminution of width and setback as the building rises. The Midland Bank in Piccadilly, London (1921–1925) is in the manner of Wren.

In the 1920s and 1930s, Lutyens undertook other commissions, designing university buildings in sophisticated versions of traditional styles for Magdalene College, Cambridge (1928–1932), and at Campion Hall, Oxford (1935–1942). The essential whimsicality of much of Lutyens's work was given perfect expression in the Dolls' House presented to Queen Mary (1920–1924), which is now on display in Windsor Castle. Lutyens's only venture into designing working-class housing and in using a more modern style was undertaken in 1929 when he designed checkerboard façades for blocks of flats in Page Street, Westminster; these cannot be counted amongst his more successful works.

From 1929 Lutyens was chiefly preoccupied with designing a new Roman Catholic cathedral for the city of Liverpool. This was to be a vast building of brick and granite with a dome larger than those of St. Peter's in Rome and Saint Paul's in London. The design developed the cruciform, centralized plans proposed for St. Peter's and was based on the heirarchy of arch forms employed for the Thiepval Memorial. Externally, the sublime battered walls were to be penetrated by vast arched openings, reflecting the interior spaces, while around the dome were to be grouped spires and belfries, making a tribute to Wren's skyline for the City of London. The power and complexity of this design can now only be appreciated from the wooden model exhibited in 1934 and now stored at the Walker Art Gallery, Liverpool. Only part of the crypt was built before work on the project ceased. For Lutyens, however, the design represented his ultimate statement in the architectural tradition which he thought justified both by geometry and by humanist ideals.

During World War II, Lutyens was preoccupied with the Royal Academy Planning Committee's plan for rebuilding London. Dominated by traffic management and sterile symmetries in the Beaux-Arts manner, it seems sadly lacking in the subtlety and sympathy for tradition characteristic of his earlier work.

When he died, Lutyens's contemporaries were in no doubt of his greatness. The Memorial Volumes of 1950 paid him a tribute not granted to any architect since Wren. For many of his generation who adhered to the classical tradition, Lutyens was the greatest English architect since Wren—if not the greatest English architect—but it was as a classicist that they admired him. Similarly, the recent revival of interest in Lutyens in the United States has tended to interpret his work in terms of Beaux-Arts classicism. However, Lutyens was not an orthodox classicist either by training or inclination. He developed and expanded the "High Game" with a geometrical abstraction unparalleled among the work of his contemporaries, yet in his treatment of mass and in his attention to detail he remained in debt to the Gothic Revival and to the English Arts and Crafts movement.

Charles F. A. Voysey and Frank Lloyd Wright had nothing but admiration for Lutyens's early Romantic vernacular houses, which form an important part of the architectural achievement of the Arts and Crafts movement. Voysey, however, greatly regretted Lutyens's adoption of classicism which, he felt, lead the younger generation of English architects away from the possibility of developing a modern craft-based architecture. Certainly Lutyens must bear much of the responsibility for the direction taken by English architecture in the first third of the twentieth century. Although always sympathetic to the aspirations of young architects, he regarded the International style with suspicion because of its crudity, industrial aesthetic and rejection of craftsmanship and tradition. However, in one respect Lutyens's work itself betrayed the ideals of the Arts and Crafts movement. He never allowed the craftsman any creative independence and only tolerated sculpture or mural decoration that was under his complete control.

Both his son, Robert Lutyens, and his biographer, Christopher Hussey, attempted to identify a body of architectural principles and theory which governed Lutyens's later work, but Lutyens himself was impatient with theory and found his son's book incomprehensible. Verbally inarticulate, Lutyens communicated architectural ideas on paper; "Don't talk, draw it," he would say to his assistants. Yet, paradoxically, Lutyens was a man of verbal wit, delighting in puns and jokes, and Lutyens's personality explains both his social success and the character of his work. His delight in ambiguity and his wit are seen in the deliberate dualities of his plans and in such details as the disappearing pilaster. There was often a degree of arch whimsicality in his work which found its happiest expression in his designs for furniture and light fittings, yet behind his jovial public façade he was an artist of absolute seriousness. Although not a distinguished draftsman in the formal, architectural sense, Lutyens was extraordinarily expressive in his worm's-eye-view sketches of buildings and was a caricaturist of genius.

Lutyens's reputation suffered a degree of eclipse after his death, but has revived dramatically in recent years. Despite the peculiarly English character of the man and his work, he was the subject of an exhibition at the Museum of Modern Art in New York in 1978. In 1981 a major exhibition about Lutyens was held in London. Above all, perhaps, it is the ambiguities, the paradoxes, and the jokes in Lutyens's buildings that appeal to the present generation of postmodern architects, who are anxious to be free of the strict canons of both the International style and Beaux-Arts classicism.

Edwin Lutyens was knighted in 1918 and awarded the Order of Merit in 1942. He was awarded the Gold Medal of the Royal Institute of British Architects in 1921, and the Medal of the American Institute of Architects in 1924. He was master of the Art-Workers' Guild in 1933 and president of the Royal Academy from 1938 until his death in 1944. Lutyens's funeral was in Westminster Abbey and his ashes are interred in the crypt of Saint Paul's Cathedral.

GAVIN STAMP

WORKS

Compiled with Margaret Richardson.

1888, The Corner (additions), Thursley; 1889–1914, Crooksbury (gardener's cottage, house, stables); 1890, Lodges, Park Hatch, Hascombe; 1890, Sheephatch House (alterations), Tilford; 1891, Munstead Corner (now Munstead Place), Heath Lane; 1892, Red House, Effingham; Surrey, England. 1893, Garden, Woodside, Chenies, Buckinghamshire, England. 1893–1895, Chinthurst Hill, Wonersh; 1894, The Hut (now Munstead Wood Hut), Munstead; 1894, Lodge, Shere Manor House; 1896, Warren Lodge (rebuilding; now Warren Mere), Thursley; 1896–1897, Munstead Wood; 1897–1899, Fulbrook, Elstead; 1897–1899, Hazelhatch, Burrows Cross; 1897–1899, Orchards, Munstead; Surrey, England. 1897–1899, Tower House, Mayfield, Sussex, England. 1897–1899, Wood End, Witley, Surrey, England. 1898, Le Bois des Moutiers, Varengeville-sur-mer, France. 1898, Overstrand Chapel, Norfolk, England. 1898, Roseneath House, Dumbartonshire, Scotland. 1899, Red House, Godalming, Surrey, England. 1899–1901, Overstrand Hall, Cromer, Norfolk, England. 1899–1901, Tigbourne Court, Witley, Surrey, England. 1899–1902, Deanery Garden, Sonning, Berkshire, England. 1900–1901, Grey Walls (bothies 1909), Gullane, Scotland. 1901, Homewood, Knebworth, England. 1901–1904, Marshcourt, Stockbridge, Hamphsire, England. 1902, Little Thakeham, Sussex, England. 1903–1904, Lindisfarne Castle (restoration), Holy Island, Northumberland, England. *1903–1904, Papillon Hall, Leicestershire, England. 1904, Country Life Building, Tavistock Street, London. 1904–1938, Ashby Saint Ledgers (alterations and additions), Northamptonshire, England. 1905–1908, Nashdom (now Nashdom Abbey), Taplow, Buckinghamshire, England. 1905–1912, Lambay Castle, Ireland. 1906, Folly Farm, Sulhampstead, Berkshire, England. 1906, Heathcote, Ilkey, Yorkshire, England. 1906, Hestercombe House (garden), Somerset, England. 1907, Fisher's Hill Cottage, Woking, Surrey, England. 1908, Middlefield, Staplefield, Cambridge. 1908–1910, Hampstead Garden Suburb (Saint Jude's, Free Church, Manse, Institute, houses in North Square and Erskine Hill), London. 1909, Great Maytham, Rolvenden, Kent, England. 1909, Les Communes, Varengeville-sur-mer, France. 1910, Great Dixter, Northiam, Sussex, England. 1910, Mulberry Tree Cottage, Park Lane, Knebworth, Hertfordshire. 1910–1932, Castle Drogo (never completed), Drewsteignton, Devon, England. 1910–1941, Art Gallery (never completed), Johannesburg. 1911, British Pavilion (later the British School), Rome Exhibition. 1911, Rand Regiment's Memorial, Johannesburg. 1911, The Salutation, Sandwich, Kent, England. 1911–1913, Theosophical Society (not completed until 1929 by C. Wontner Smith), Tavistock Square, London. 1912, Number 18, Little College Street, London. 1912–1931, Viceroy's House Complex (now Rashtrapati Bhavan), New Delhi. 1913, Abbey House, Barrow-in-Furness, Lancastershire, Engand. 1913, Numbers 1–6, Chequers Cottages, Chequers Lane, Preston, Hertfordshire, England. 1914, Mausoleum, Golder's Green Crematorium, London. 1916, Saint Edmund's House (chapel), Mount Pleasant, Cambridge. 1918–1924, War Memorial and Cemetery, Etaples, France. 1919, Count de Cimera House, Madrid. 1919–1920, Cenotaph, Whitehall, London. 1920, All India War Memorial Arch, New Delhi. 1920, Leeds War Memorial, England. 1920, Penheale Manor (additions and cottages), Egloskerry, Cornwall, England. 1920–1924, Britannic House, Finsbury Circus, London. 1920–1924, Doll's House (in miniature), Windsor Castle, England. 1921, Colombo War Memorial, Ceylon. 1921–1923, Palace for the Gaekwar of Baroda, New Delhi. 1921–1925, Midland Bank, 126 Picadilly, London. 1922, Barlin Cemetery, France. 1922–1926, Gledstone Hall, Yorkshire, England. 1923, War Memorial, Victoria Park, Leicester, England. 1923–1924, Cemetery, Etaples, France. 1924–1939, Midland Bank, Poultry, London. 1925–1928, Memorial to the Missing of the Royal Air Force, Arras, France. 1926, Palace for the Nizam of Hyderabad, New Delhi. 1927,

Norwich War Memorial, England. 1927–1928, British Embassy, Washington. 1927–1932, Monument to the Missing of the Somme, Thiepval, France. 1928–1929, Apartments, Page and Vincent Streets, London. 1928–1932, Magdalene College (various works), Cambridge. 1929, Number 120 Pall Mall, London. 1930, Irish National Memorial, Dublin. 1931–1939, George V Memorial and Fountains, New Delhi. 1932, Jekyll Family Tomb, Church of Saint John, Busbridge, Surrey, England. 1933, Hampton Court Bridge, London. 1934, Cedar House, Philpott Lane, Chobham, Surrey, England. 1935, Reuters and Press Association, Fleet Street, London. 1935–1942, Campion Hall, Oxford. 1936–1938, Australian National Memorial, Villers-Bretonneux, France. 1937–1939, Admiral Beatty and Admiral Jellicoe Memorial Fountains, Trafalgar Square, London. 1938, Halnaker House, Sussex, England. 1938, Middleton Park (with Robert Lutyens), Oxfordshire, England.

BIBLIOGRAPHY

Compiled with Margaret Richardson.

BROWNE, JANE 1982 *Gardens of a Golden Afternoon—The Story of a Partnership, Edwin Lutyens and Gertrude Jekyll.* Harmondsworth, England: Penguin.

BUTLER, A. S. G. 1950 *The Architecture of Sir Edwin Lutyens.* 3 vols. London: Country Life; New York: Scribner.

BRYON, ROBERT 1931 "New Delhi." *Architectural Review* 69:1–30.

CHIPKIN, C. M. 1958 "New Delhi." *South African Architectural Record* Nov.:21–28.

GEBHARD, DAVID 1972 "The Master Builders: 13." *Sunday Times Magazine* May 14, pp. 18–30.

GHOSH, BIJIT, and SCHOOL OF PLANNING AND ARCHITECTURE, NEW DELHI 1980 *The Making of New Delhi.* New Delhi: The school. Exhibition catalogue.

GOODHART-RENDEL, H. S. 1944 "Sir Edwin Lutyens, O.M., P.R.A.." *Journal of the Royal Institute of British Architects* Jan.:51–52.

GOODHART-RENDEL, H. S. 1945 "The Work of the Late Sir Edwin Lutyens, O.M." *Journal of the Royal Institute of British Architects* Mar.:123–131.

GRADIDGE, R. 1981 *Edwin Lutyens: Architect Laureate.* London: Allen & Unwin.

GREENBERG, A. 1969 "Lutyens's Architecture Restudied." *Perspecta* 12:129–152.

GREIG, DOREEN E. 1978 "The Work of Sir Edwin Lutyens in Johannesburg." *Mafeking Mail* 1, no. 5.

HOMBERGER, ERIC 1976 "The Story of the Cenotaph." *Times Literary Supplement* Nov. 12, p. 1429.

HUSSEY, CHRISTOPHER 1934 "The Cathedral of Christ the King, Liverpool: Sir Edwin Lutyens's Model at the Royal Academy." *Country Life* May:451–454.

HUSSEY, CHRISTOPHER 1924 "A Vision of New London." *Country Life* 92:692–696.

HUSSEY, CHRISTOPHER 1950 *The Life of Sir Edwin Lutyens.* London: Country Life; New York: Scribner.

HUSSEY, CHRISTOPHER 1959 "An Early Lutyens Castle in the Air." *Country Life* 125:148–149.

INSKIP, P. 1979 *Edwin Lutyens.* London: Academy Editions.

JEKYLL, FRANCIS 1934 *Gertrude Jekyll: A Memoir.* London: Cape.

JEKYLL, FRANCIS (1900)1926 *Home and Garden.* London: Longmans, Green.

LUTYENS, EDWIN 1918 "The Work of the Late Philip Webb." *Country Life* 37:619.

LUTYENS, EDWIN 1931 "What I Think of Modern Architecture." *Country Life* 69:775–777.

LUTYENS, MARY 1980 *Edwin Lutyens: A Memoir by His Daughter.* London: J. Murray.

LUTYENS, ROBERT 1942 *Sir Edwin Lutyens: An Appreciation in Perspective.* London: Country Life.

Lutyens. The Work of the English Architect Sir Edwin Lutyens (1869–1944) 1981 London: Arts Council. Exhibition catalogue.

"The New Delhi. The Work of Sir Edwin Lutyens and Sir Herbert Baker." 1926 *Architectural Review* 60:216–225.

"Obituary." 1944 *Architect's Journal* 177:3–9.

O'NEILL, DANIEL (1980) *Edwin Lutyens: Country Houses.* London: Lund-Humphries; New York: Whitney Library of Design.

PEVSNER, NIKOLAUS 1951 "Building with Wit: The Architecture of Sir Edwin Lutyens." *Architectural Review* 109:217–225.

"Reminiscences of Sir Edwin Lutyens." 1959 *Architectural Association Journal* 74:226–236.

RICHARDSON, M. 1981 *Lutyens and the Sea Captain.* London: Scolar.

SHOOSMITH, A. G. 1931 "The Design of New Delhi." *Indian State Railways Magazine* 4, no. 5:423–433.

STAMP, GAVIN 1977 *Silent Cities.* London: Arts Council. Exhibition catalogue.

STAMP, GAVIN 1981 "Lutyens's Unbuilt Masterpiece." *Harpers and Queen* Mar.:140.

STAMP, GAVIN 1981 "The Rise and Fall and Rise of Edwin Lutyens." *Architectural Review* Nov.

VOYSEY, CHARLES F. A. 1931 "1874 and After." With a Foreword by Edwin Lutyens. *Architectural Review* 70:91.

WEAVER, L. (1913)1981 *Houses and Gardens by Edwin Lutyens.* London: Antique Collectors Club.

LUZARCHES, ROBERT DE

See ROBERT DE LUZARCHES.

LYMINGE, ROBERT

Robert Lyminge (?–1628), whose name is also spelled Liminge or Lemyinge, was the principal architect of two of the finest houses of the Jacobean period, Hatfield House, Hertfordshire, and

Blickling Hall, Norfolk, but he is nevertheless a shadowy figure. Nothing is known of him before 1607, when he is recorded working as a carpenter at Theobalds, Hertfordshire. In the same year, he began work at Hatfield. The unusually full documents surviving at the house make it apparent that Lyminge had a dominant role in the building's design and construction, but Simon Basil and INIGO JONES were also consulted, and parts of the present structure are often attributed to the latter. At Blickling, Lyminge was more indisputably in charge; the cypher RL appears in numerous parts of the building, and the local parish burial register records him as "the architect and builder of Blickling Hall." A drawing by Lyminge for a projected garden banqueting house is preserved at Blickling.

IAN CHILVERS

WORKS

1607–1612, Hatfield House, Hertfordshire, England. c.1616–c.1627, Blickling Hall, Norfolk, England.

BIBLIOGRAPHY

HUSSEY, CHRISTOPHER 1930 "Blickling Hall." *Country Life* 67:813–821.

LEES-MILNE, JAMES 1951 *Tudor Renaissance.* London: Batsford.

LEES-MILNE, JAMES 1955 *Blickling Hall.* London: The National Trust.

STONE, LAWRENCE 1973 "The Building of Hatfield House." In *Family and Fortune: Studies in Aristocratic Finance in the Sixteenth and Seventeenth Centuries.* Rev. version. Oxford: Clarendon.

LYNCH, KEVIN

Born in Chicago in 1918, Kevin Lynch is professor of city planning at the Massachusetts Institute of Technology (M.I.T.) and a leading authority in the field. His early training included an apprenticeship with FRANK LLOYD WRIGHT from 1937 to 1939. Lynch received a bachelor's degree in city planning from M.I.T. in 1947, subsequently joining its faculty. With a Ford Fellowship in 1953, he studied the perceptual form of the city in Italy. He has maintained a private practice as consultant with Carr Lynch Associates. In his theoretical investigations of city planning, which were initially influenced by Gyorgy Kepes, Kevin Lynch takes a psychological approach. He defines the urban environment in terms of imageability; its formal characteristics are the criteria for perception of the city as an inhabitable entity.

SOPHIE GOBRAN

BIBLIOGRAPHY

LYNCH, KEVIN (1960)1966 *The Image of the City.* Cambridge, Mass.: M.I.T. Press.

LYNCH, KEVIN (1962)1971 *Site Planning.* Rev. ed. Cambridge, Mass.: M.I.T. Press.

LYNCH, KEVIN 1972 *What Time Is This Place?* Cambridge, Mass.: M.I.T. Press.

LYNCH, KEVIN 1981 *A Theory of Good City Form.* Cambridge, Mass.: M.I.T. Press.

LYNN, JACK

Jack Lynn (1926–), together with IVOR SMITH, assisted the city architect of Sheffield, England, when that city constructed two vast housing megaliths: Park Hill (1957–1961) and Hyde Park (1959–1966). Lynn and Smith were responsible for these high-rise, concrete cliffs overlooking the city center. Although at the time the blocks were received enthusiastically by sociologists and architects alike, twenty years of unending anonymity and unremitting scale have brought the projects a certain notoriety.

CHRISTOPHER FAWCETT

WORKS

1957–1961, Park Hill Housing; 1959–1966, Hyde Park Housing; Sheffield, Yorkshire.

BIBLIOGRAPHY

BANHAM, REYNER 1973 "The Park Hill Victory." *New Society* 26; Oct. 18:154–156.

BANHAM, REYNER 1974 "Park Hill Revisited." *Architecture Plus* 2, no. 3:108–115.

BRYANT, DAVID, and KNOWLES, DICK 1974 "Sociability and Internal Streets." *Architects Journal* 159, May 15:1067.

NICKLIN, TED ET AL. 1976 "Solutions to Energy Conservation in Buildings: House Under Glass." *Journal of the Royal Institute of British Architects* 83, no. 2:51.

LYONS, ERIC

Born in London, Eric Lyons (1912–1978) was articled to Stanley Beard, studying architecture at night. He passed through the doors of many offices, including that of WALTER GROPIUS and EDWIN MAXWELL FRY. The designer of the popular Tecta chair, Lyons joined in private practice with G. P. Townsend (1945). Together, they formed a professional team that would contemporize speculation housing in postwar Great Britain, bringing an imaginative and modern aesthetic to the previously dreary builder-designed speculative housing through the innovative use of space, scale, and landscaping. He proved that the public was receptive to and anxious for attractive speculation housing and that he could provide it at a competitive price.

An outspoken opponent of overly restrictive building regulation codes, he fought and often won numerous court battles with local planning authorities. Lyons felt that architecture should be primarily a social art not overly concerned with the technological aspects and emphasizing the creative process.

LYNDA GREENBERG

WORKS

1959, Blackheath Development, England. 1969–1977, World's End, Chelsea, London. 1970–, New Ash Green, Kent, England.

BIBLIOGRAPHY

FURNEAUX-JORDON, ROBERT 1959 "SPAN., The Spec. Builder as Patron of Modern Architecture." *Architectural Review* 125:102–120.

LYONS, ERIC 1971 "Back to Blackheath." *The Architect* 1, no. 6:36–42.

LYONS, ERIC 1976 "Architecture—The Social Art." *Journal of the Royal Institute of British Architects* 3, no. 1:2–6.

M

MACARTNEY, MERVYN

A pupil of R. NORMAN SHAW, Mervyn Macartney (1853–1932) belongs to the scholarly strand in Edwardian architecture. His reticent buildings; his book, *Later Renaissance Architecture in England* (1901), written with John Belcher; and his editorship of *The Architectural Review* from 1905 to 1920 all reveal the dignity and proportion of English vernacular building, especially in the age of CHRISTOPHER WREN. In his capacity as surveyor to Saint Paul's Cathedral, Macartney's crowning achievement was to protect the dome of Wren's masterpiece by encircling it with stainless steel.

ALAN CRAWFORD

WORKS

1887, Courtstile Cottages, Angley Park, Cranbrook, Kent, England. 1889, 169 Queen's Gate; 1893, 1–6 Egerton Place; London. 1893, Sandhills, Bletchingley, Surrey, England. c.1899, Welders, Chalfont Saint Peters, Buckinghamshire, England. 1900, Frithwood House (now Admiralty House), Watford Road, Northwood, Middlesex, England. 1906, The Court, Woolhampton, Berkshire, England. 1906, Lombarden, Limpsfield, Surrey, England. 1906–1931, Saint Paul's Cathedral (repairs), London. 1907, Bussock Wood (now Phillips Hill House); Winterbourne; 1907, Kennet Orleigh, Woolhampton; Berkshire, England. 1914–1921, South Avenue, Whiteley Village, Surrey, England. 1916, Central Library, Essex Road, London.

BIBLIOGRAPHY

DAVEY, PETER 1980 *Arts and Crafts Architecture.* London: Architectural Press.

MACARTNEY, MERVYN 1907–1927 *The Practical Exemplar of Architecture.* 7 vols. London: Architectural Press.

MACARTNEY, MERVYN 1908 *English Houses and Gardens in the 17th and 18th Centuries.* London: Batsford.

MACARTNEY, MERVYN, and BELCHER, JOHN 1901 *Later Renaissance Architecture in England.* London: Batsford.

MACDONALD, ROBERT HENRY

Robert Henry MacDonald (1875–1942) was born in Melbourne, Australia, and studied there with Richard B. Whitaker, and also with Robert Findlay, Montreal, and with GEORGE BROWNE POST and WELLES BOSWORTH in New York City. As a partner of Ross and Macfarlane, Montreal (Ross and MacDonald after 1913), he designed major hotels, railway stations, and commercial buildings across Canada, as well as the Montreal Forum, the Toronto Maple Leaf Gardens, and the T. Eaton Company stores in both cities. Strongly influenced by early twentieth-century architecture in New York, he developed the first giant architectural practice in Canada.

JOHN BLAND

MACHUCA, PEDRO

Pedro Machuca (1485?–1550) is known to us as an architect only by way of the unfinished palace of Charles V in the Alhambra in Granada, but that extraordinary block-design palace with a round, double-colonnaded courtyard reveals a command of the High Renaissance style that was rare among non-Italian architects in the late 1520s. We know only that he was born in Toledo and that in 1517 he was an accomplished painter in the manner of RAPHAEL, because in that year he signed a large painting of the "Madonna del Suffragio." In 1520, Machuca returned from Italy to Spain in the company of Jacopo Torni L'Indaco, a Florentine painter with a workshop in Rome. As far as we know, Machuca worked exclusively as a painter in Italy and Spain until 1526 when he designed arches and tableaux for the entry of Emperor Charles V into Granada. Apparently, his success in that assignment led to his appointment as architect of the new residence ordered by Charles V shortly before his departure. Although Machuca also designed a wall fountain for the Alhambra (1545) and a catafalque for Mary of Portugal (1549), our idea of him as an architect depends on the palace. Machuca did not have as free a hand in its design as many have assumed; some of his architectural ideas were opposed by the Castilian architects called upon by Charles V for advice. The most disruptive features intruded by the Castilians are the grey marble frames of the main entries (*portadas*), which Machuca designed reluctantly and intruded into the already executed white (now gilded) sandstone façades. For the western front he designed a one-story frontispiece in grey marble with a second story in white sandstone in 1549, but his sober project (like that for the south portal) was elaborated by sculptural additions, and in the 1590s an upper story in grey marble was added. He was also required to angle his originally free-standing residential block into the fire-damaged south end of the Court of Myrtles in order to make space for the forecourts surrounded by stables, office, and guest quarters, which were required by the emperor and then never built. Although he managed to retain his double colonnade in the round courtyard, his son in the 1560s used conglomerate stone rather than white marble for the columns, raised the colonnade to tilt the annular vault back on the corridor wall and used shorter columns on pedestals for the gallery (with the massive parapets added by Juan de Minjares in the 1590s). After these and other qualifications are taken into account, it is evident that Pedro Machuca's architectural repertory was formed in the Tuscan ambience of Rome in 1510–1520 and that many of his motives were derived from the speculative designs rather than the buildings of Tuscan architects. Most notable motives are the round porticoed courtyard, the double colonnade, the rhythmic grouping of three distinctive bays along the corridor to stress the cardinal and intracardinal axes of the courtyard, the monumental staircase composed wholly of winders, and the three-door palatine entry. Whereas the component elements of his designs are surprisingly orthodox, his compositions are often without analogies in Italy until the mid-sixteenth century. Primary examples are the hierarchical stylar façades, scanned by single pilasters with paired pilasters closing the ends and (originally) framing the wider central entry bays, and the Tuscan pilasters that are interlocked with the patterned masonry of the rusticated ground floor of the palace. Excluded from autograph parts of the palace are most of the features characterized as Lombard or Mannerist, and his native tradition is reflected in his receptivity to those Renaissance motives for which there were analogies in Spanish architecture: the surround (*alfiz*), rustication (*almohadillado*), coffered ceilings (*artesonado*), the wide vestibule (*zaguán*), the octagonal chapel, and the vertical unification of a portal and the window above it. Pedro Machuca was surprisingly inventive within the classical mode and resolute in the maintenance of his severe High Renaissance style in the Plateresque ambiance of Spain.

EARL E. ROSENTHAL

Machuca.
Courtyard of the Palace of Charles V (Alhambra).
Granada, Spain.
1526–1537

WORK

1526–1537, Palace of Charles V, Alhambra, Granada, Spain.

BIBLIOGRAPHY

BAYON, DAMIÁN 1967 *L'architecture en Castille au XVIe siècle: Commande et réalisations.* Paris: Editions Klincksieck.

BYNE, ARTHUR, and STAPELY, MILDRED 1917 *Spanish Architecture of the Sixteenth Century.* New York: Putnam.

CAMÓN AZNAR, JOSÉ 1945 *La arquitectura plateresca.* Madrid: Aguirre.

CHUECA GOITIA, FERNANDO 1953 *Arquitectura del sigle XVI.* Madrid: Editorial Plus Ultra.

GÓMEZ-MORENA Y GONZÁLEZ, MANUEL 1885 "Palacio de Carlos V." *Revista de España* 103:191–225.

GÓMEZ-MORENO Y MARTÍNEZ, MANUEL 1941 *Las águilas del renacimiento español.* Madrid: Gráficas Uguina.

JUSTI, KARL 1891 "Anfänge der Renaissance in Granada." *Jahrbuch der königlich-preussischen Kunstsammlungen* 12:186–187.

LOUKOMSKI, GEORGE 1944 "The Palace of Charles V at Granada." *Burlington Magazine* 84:119–124.

ROSENTHAL, EARL EDGAR n.d. "The Palace of Emperor Charles V in Granada and Its Architect: Pedro Machuca." Forthcoming publication.

MACKINTOSH, CHARLES RENNIE

Charles Rennie Mackintosh (1868–1928) was one of the most remarkable architects of his day. He turned his hand with equal facility and uncompromising individuality to architecture, interior design, and furniture; craft work, drawing, and watercolor painting. His buildings—in particular, his masterpiece, the Glasgow School of Art—are notable for the elegance and clarity of their spatial concepts, the skillful exploitation of natural and artificial illumination, and the care lavished on their detailing. In the true Arts and Crafts succession, Mackintosh demonstrated that architecture and the decorative or "minor" arts are, or should be, mutually dependent; each design, whether for a chair, a room, or a building, is visualized as a total work of art to the wholeness of which each part, each carefully contrived detail, contributes. His buildings, therefore, are an endless source of delight to the observer who at every turn will find some unorthodox feature or decorative element, carefully placed for his enjoyment, an aesthetic extension of the basic form and spatial qualities of the building itself.

It seems incongruous that an architect of Mackintosh's stature should emerge from a somewhat remote northern industrial city, apparently out of the mainstream of European artistic development. Yet, although nineteenth-century industrial Glasgow could not aspire to the cultural distinction of its elegant neighbor, Edinburgh, capital of Scotland and "the Athens of the North," it could claim with some justification to be the second city of the British Empire. Wealth from coal, iron, heavy industry, and shipbuilding was reflected in a rapidly expanding population and the creation of ambitious and often fine public and private buildings. Glasgow's Victorian architecture, among the best of its kind in Britain, was predominantly classical in style, which, together with row upon row of solemn, four-story tenement dwellings, produced an urban environment of great dignity and impressive scale, relieved by generous parks and open spaces (Gomme and Walker, 1968). At mid-century, the dominance of the classical revivalists and their Gothic colleagues was challenged by the remarkably innovative work of ALEXANDER "Greek" THOMSON, an important precursor of the modern movement, whose buildings are reminiscent of those of KARL FRIEDRICH SCHINKEL in Germany. Glasgow also had its share of experimental iron-and-glass façades. Moreover, the city could boast a number of architects of considerable stature who, working within the classical or Scottish Baronial tradition, produced imaginative variations on familiar themes; among these, the most important was the Beaux-Arts-trained JOHN J. BURNET. Others were JAMES SELLARS, JOHN HONEYMAN, T. L. Watson, Hugh and David Barclay, and among the Gothicists, the London-based GEORGE GILBERT SCOTT, who designed the University of Glasgow (1866–1872), JAMES SALMON, and James Brown. Of these, Mackintosh greatly admired the Burnets, father and son, and John Honeyman who, with John Keppie, established the firm of HONEYMAN AND KEPPIE, in which Mackintosh became a draftsman and eventually a partner. Smaller domestic work in the Scottish tradition by JAMES MACLAREN, William Dunn, and Robert Watson appealed immensely to Mackintosh and may have inspired his own residential buildings.

Beginnings. Charles Rennie Mackintosh was born in Glasgow. At age sixteen, he was articled for five years to John Hutchison, a competent if undistinguished practitioner, and in 1889 he joined, as draftsman, the new firm of Honeyman and Keppie. Mackintosh also enrolled at the Glasgow School of Art, taking courses in subjects such as building construction and drawing in a variety of media. In 1890, he won the Alexander Thompson Scholarship, which enabled him to spend the summer of 1891 traveling and sketching in Italy.

The Glasgow style. In 1891, two young women, Margaret and Frances Macdonald, enrolled in the School of Art as students in free-hand, plant and model drawing, ornament, and anatomy. They began to produce experimental work which, in spirit, bore a strong resemblance to that of Aubrey Beardsley, Edvard Munch, Jan Toorop, and other European symbolists, then emerging as sig-

Mackintosh. Conversazione Programme. 1894

nificant figures in the art world. Headmaster Francis H. Newbery noticed that the style and imaginative content of the work of the two women was remarkably similar to that of the two architects, and he encouraged the four young people to combine forces. This event was of special significance; over the next few years, they produced a number of remarkably original and evocative works—watercolors, posters, metal, glass, gesso, and fabrics—all of which had in common an unfamiliar, often grotesque, linear conventionalization of plant and human forms, usually with some symbolic meaning. By 1895, they had already established a local reputation as "The Four," or to the cynics "The Mac Group," with Mackintosh indisputably the dominant personality, and the Glasgow School of Art earned the sobriquet "The Spook School."

In 1896, The Four sent work to the Arts and Crafts Exhibition Society's triennial show in London, where they were severely criticized for emulating the despised, continental, new-art style which was soon to be labeled Art Nouveau. However, in 1897 they were given international recognition in an article titled, "Some Glasgow Designers and Their Work" by Gleeson White, editor of *The Studio,* first of the new decorative art publications which had been launched in 1893. White pleaded for tolerance and said prophetically that those who criticized the artists today would probably wish to eulogize them tomorrow. It was through the pages of *The Studio* (an American edition was introduced in 1896) that FRANK LLOYD WRIGHT, the brothers CHARLES S. GREENE and HENRY M. GREENE, and others in the United States became aware of the Scottish designers. By the turn of the century, the so-called Glasgow Style was firmly established.

Professional experience. Although Mackintosh was now attracting attention as a new force in the world of the decorative arts, his progress as an architect was somewhat less spectacular. No evidence remains of his work for John Hutchison, and the only building by the firm to which he contributed was Wylie Hill's Store, Buchanan Street, Glasgow, destroyed by fire in the early 1900s. In 1890, however, he obtained his first private commission for a pair of semidetached, stone houses. Designed for a relative, these were unassuming in character and without signs of marked originality.

As a junior assistant with Honeyman and Keppie, Mackintosh's handiwork first appeared as a draftsman in architectural competitions. The tower of the Glasgow Herald Building (1893), with its bulbous silhouette and great curved angle features, can be claimed with some justification as Mackintosh's first executed design in the office: it was followed by Queen Margaret's Medical College (1894–1896) and Martyrs' Public School (1895). In these buildings the young architect's growing ascendancy may be noted in a number of characteristic features and details of stone and timber which reflect the principles he was beginning to establish in furniture design, craft work, and graphics.

Philosophy. His philosophy was solidly based on AUGUSTUS W. N. PUGIN and JOHN RUSKIN and rooted in the Scottish tradition. He deplored his colleagues' preoccupation with the architecture of Greece and Rome which could not readily be adapted to meet the Scottish climate and functional needs of his own time. In his view, the Scottish Baronial style had successfully absorbed foreign influences and was sternly functional. He stressed the importance of what he described as genuineness in utility and the expression of function (plan) in elevation. He believed that a revival of the Scottish Baronial style, adapted to modern needs, was imminent, and all his buildings demonstrate his determination to contribute to this revival. In his lecture to the Glasgow Architectural Association in 1893 which was based largely on WILLIAM R. LETHABY's *Architecture, Mysticism and Myth,* he repeated Lethaby's statement that "architecture is the synthesis of the fine arts [and] all the crafts"; that modern ideas must be clothed with modern dress; and that it was the duty of the architect to produce "designs by living men for living men" (Lethaby and Sedding both used this expression). In his later lecture to the same association ("Seemliness," undated) he stated that the supreme quality of the artist (for which we must also read "architect") "which characterises him above all else—and determines his vocation—is the exceptional development of the imaginative faculties."

The Glasgow School of Art. The year 1896 marked Mackintosh's emergence as an architect in his own right. Honeyman and Keppie won a limited competition for the new Glasgow School of Art and the competition design was indisputably the work of their young assistant who, with Newbery's enthusiastic support, took personal charge of the entire project.

The design of the school presented particularly difficult problems: not only was the site steeply sloping and closely defined by three streets, two of them falling precipitously north to south, but the budget of £14,000 was totally inadequate. After much protest and debate, the competitors were asked to state what portion of their design could be carried out within the financial limit and to submit an estimate of the final cost. The Board of

Governors rather plaintively declared "it is but a plain building that is required." However, neither the financial limitations nor Newbery's ambitious program and specifications for large studio windows and good lighting deterred Mackintosh; in fact, the rigorous constraints enabled him to produce a design of exceptional functional elegance and simplicity. The resulting structure with its great north-facing studio windows, traditional, fortresslike east end, and towering south side is now universally familiar as, indeed, is the single-bank, E-shaped corridor system with its spectacular central staircase, vast studios, and endless examples of the architect's spatial and decorative ingenuity.

With the money available only the eastern half of the building including the main entrance and staircase could be erected (1897–1899), and even this exceeded the estimated cost. The Board of Governors waited ten years, until 1907, before they were able to build the second and final section, including the library which was redesigned in 1906. Mackintosh personally supervised every phase of construction of the first section of the school and devoted a great deal of time to it. His practice of modifying details as work proceeded in order to obtain the precise effect he desired did not endear him to his clients, but he usually succeeded in getting his way.

While the school was under construction, he was commissioned by Catherine Cranston to design mural decorations and light fittings for the first of her four famous Glasgow tearooms (Buchanan Street), a commission he shared with George Walton, who designed the furniture. This period of intense creative activity saw in rapid succession the design and building of Queen's Cross Church of Scotland (1897–1899), now the headquarters of the Mackintosh Society; furniture for Miss Cranston's Argyle Street tearooms (1896–1897); the competition designs for the Glasgow International Exhibition of 1901, which had to be submitted in 1898 and which included his famous saucer-domed concert hall; Ruchill Street Church Halls (1898), and Windy Hill (1899–1901) for William Davidson, his first important domestic commission. In addition to all this work at the office, he designed furniture and *objets d'art* for private clients. Examples of his furniture were illustrated for the first time in a European periodical, the new *Dekorative Kunst* (1898, 1899).

The fruitful partnership of *The Four* came to an end in 1898 when Herbert McNair was appointed instructor in decorative design in the school of architecture and applied art at Liverpool University. He married Frances Macdonald the following year. Mackintosh and Margaret Macdonald were married in 1900. Before the wedding, they decorated and furnished their first home, 120 Mains Street, Glasgow. The drawing room is one of the most important interiors in modern design history. It represents a complete departure from contemporary practice in its whiteness, elegance, and freedom from superficial decoration. Every piece of furniture, the light fixtures, and other details were designed by the architect and his wife. The furniture, and the chairs in particular, indicate clearly that Mackintosh's distinctive style was now fully developed.

Mackintosh.
Glasgow School of Art.
Scotland.
1896–1899

Interiors and furniture. Although he had experimented from about 1890, Mackintosh's real opportunity came in 1896–1897 when he produced his first unorthodox furniture—including his high-backed chair with the oval top rail—for the Argyle Street tearooms; on this occasion, George Walton designed the mural decorations and light fixtures. At Mains Street, however, he brought together a variety of original pieces, including a heavy, boxlike wing chair in oak; a large, white-painted bookcase with leaded-glass panels; a writing desk; and duplicates of several of the tables and high-backed chairs he had designed for the Argyle Street and Ingram Street tearooms. The Mains Street flat demonstrated that Mackintosh had reached positive conclusions about the nature of interior design and the psychological effect of color, texture, and light. From this time on, he consistently used two main themes in his domestic work according to the function of the spaces involved: white for living rooms and bedrooms; dark for hallways and dining rooms. Walls, floors, and ceilings were virtually devoid of pattern, in contrast not only to popular Victorian and Edwardian taste in Britain but also, with the notable exception of Voysey and M. H. BAILLIE-SCOTT, to the work of many of the followers of WILLIAM MORRIS, the exponents of Art Nouveau, and the Secessionists. For these alternatively pristine and somber settings, he relied for contrast on the sculptural forms of his furniture; small, bright areas of color (often leaded glass, enamel, or ceramics) in fireplaces, woodwork, and furniture; flowers and plants arranged in the then popular Japanese manner, and, of course, framed paintings or prints. All such incidentals were carefully controlled and placed with discrimination. Curtains decorated with simple geometrical patterns, often embroidered by Margaret Macdonald, were usually of muslin to diffuse the light.

Lighting. Mackintosh's skillful manipulation of natural and artificial light is a characteristic of his work. His domestic use of muslin curtains without heavy drapes is a simple example. On a different scale, he often employed roof light to dramatic effect, as in the first section of the School of Art, where he introduced light "funnels" channeling daylight vertically to illuminate an internal corridor, a method used in Renaissance Europe and without doubt observed during his scholarship tour of 1891.

His desire to control artificial light was clearly demonstrated in the Mains Street apartment. Control was a difficult problem in his day when gas was a common source of lighting usually with a fishtail rather than an incandescent mantle burner. Moreover, the principal light source was invariably in the center of the ceiling. At Mains Street, he closed the center outlet with a large square patress from behind which gas piping was led to the four sides of the room, given an elegant twist, and connected, again from behind a square patress, to the corner light fixtures. Each fixture consisted of four square lamps with domed covers, suspended on four piano wires; the lamps were made of silvered tin and had colored leaded glass inserts of heart shape on all four sides. The intensity of the light was adjusted by pulling on cords that varied the gas supply. Thus, the brightness of light could be controlled independently in all four corners of the room, a flexible system that could be equaled with electricity only by using separate rheostats.

Most if not all of the fixtures designed by Mackintosh were later converted to electricity and, of course, many were specifically designed for electrical energy. By modern standards his fixtures would be considered inadequate; light was usually directed downward while the room was softly illuminated by reflected light enriched by subtle hues created by colored glass inserts in the fittings themselves. Wall sconces, on the other hand, often had bare electric lamps with reflectors, sometimes partially screened by suspended leaf-shaped, leaded-glass elements. In later work the light source was frequently a cluster of bulbs enclosed in attractive opaque glass shades. The most brilliant of his lighting concepts was probably that designed for the *Room de Luxe* in The Willow Tearooms of 1903–1905, where the central ceiling fixture consisted of a series of small, wrought-iron hoops, surrounded by a multitude of clear, blown-glass globes suspended on wire, among which were naked electric lamps.

Most of Mackintosh's furniture was built in Glasgow by local cabinetmakers and craftsmen who worked mainly from the drawings provided by the architect which gave a minimum of information. However, he was a frequent visitor to the workshops and supplemented his drawings with precise verbal instructions, often standing by the craftsman until exactly the right detail had evolved. In furniture making, as in building, he believed that the design and working drawings were only an indication of the artist's intentions and that the product should be capable of modification as it was formed. There is no evidence that Mackintosh constructed any furniture himself, and it is regrettable that he did not attempt to found a guild or school of handicrafts in the manner of CHARLES R. ASHBEE or similar to JOSEF HOFFMANN's Wiener Werkstätte.

Like many architects and designers, Mackintosh saw his work first and foremost as a highly personal, artistic creation; he was often prepared to sacrifice convenience, practicality, and even comfort on the altar of visual and sensuous delight. His chairs, especially, represented an incredible outpouring of inventive genius—he produced over four hundred different designs in little more than a decade. The tall, oval-backed chairs which were without doubt the most distinctive of all his designs, represent tree symbols and, like most of his chairs, are structurally weak. The origin of the tall backs and of some of his ladder backs is not easy to determine CHARLES F. A. VOYSEY used chairs of a similar height in his own house, The Orchard (1900), and so did Frank Lloyd Wright in the Dana House, Springfield, Illinois (1903). Wright's were closer in spirit to Mackintosh's chairs but they were very heavily constructed, all the parts being of rectilinear cross-section and straight; by comparison, with Mackintosh's chairs, they were crudely detailed and even more uncomfortable. Plagiarism on the part of either man would seem to be out of the question and in all probability they drew upon a common source, the English Arts and Crafts school. Then again, Mackintosh may have turned for inspiration to seventeenth- or eighteenth-century European models, and Wright to Shaker furniture.

The European phase (*1900–1906*). The Mackintoshes received an invitation in 1900 to exhibit at JOSEPH MARIA OLBRICH's Secession House, Vienna, and they were enthusiastically welcomed by the avant-garde as leaders in the European Modern movement. The Scottish section of the exhibition, dominated by Mackintosh's white rooms, entranced the Viennese. Contemporary exhibition spaces, even by architects of the stature of Hoffmann and Olbrich, tended to be overcrowded and relatively disorderly. Mackintosh's austere and carefully controlled arrangements, therefore, were a revelation. After this exhibition, the Viennese Secessionist style quickly assumed a new elegance and gaiety, due in no small part to Mackintosh's influence, and he, Hoffmann, Fritz Wärndorfer (a wealthy young Viennese banker), and other members of the Secession became firm friends. Hoffmann and Wärndorfer visited Mackintosh in Glasgow in the early 1900s. One of their objectives was to discuss with him the possibility of his working in Vienna and participating in the proposed Wiener Werkstätten program. Correspondence reveals that Hoffmann and his colleagues were hoping to move beyond custom-made furniture and artifacts to the production of reasonably priced, well-designed articles for everyday use. This objective had Mackintosh's wholehearted support, although machine production does not seem to have been discussed. It was left to PETER BEHRENS, the German industrial designer, who knew the Viennese group well, to take that important step. In 1900, Mackintosh submitted, unfortunately late, a design for the German Haus eines Kunstfreundes competition organized by the Zeitschrift für Innendekoration. Baillie-Scott was awarded second prize; since no competitor had produced a design to the liking of the jury, the first prize was withheld. Mackintosh received a special award of D.M. 600, and there can be little doubt that he would have won the competition had his project been received on time; his excellent plans, spatial organization, and dramatic elevational treatments alone would have assured his success, quite apart from his interior schemes and furnishings. His design was published in portfolio form under the title *Meister der Innenkunst* as were those of BAILLIE-SCOTT and LEOPOLD BAUER. Mackintosh's portfolio was prefaced by a critical discourse on his "art principles" by the German architect-critic HERMANN MUTHESIUS, author of *Das Englische Haus* (1904–1905) in which Mackintosh's domestic work was illustrated.

Francis Newbery was invited to supervise the design and installation of the Scottish section at the Turin International Exhibition of Decorative Art in 1902, a project for which he made Mackintosh responsible; both men visited the Italian city at that time. Again, Mackintosh's white, elegant interiors and furniture were widely acclaimed. Furthermore, his drawings for the *Haus eines Kunstfreundes* competition were exhibited in a stand designed by Peter Behrens, and they, too, attracted universal attention.

Regrettably, no major architectural commissions came from his European excursions; apart from some small interior work and furniture, his most widely publicized project was a music salon designed for Fritz Wärndorfer in Vienna (1902). The salon was completely furnished by Mackintosh and included a large frieze of decorative panels depicting Maeterlinck's "Six Princesses" designed jointly with Margaret Mackintosh; the panels were installed later (c.1906). Ludwig Hevesi, the critic, visited the salon in 1905 and described it as "the well-known masterpiece" which "in the time of the Secession caused so much talk." He spoke of the "Mackintosh Group in Glasgow" as "great artists." After eulogizing the furnishings and their setting, he said, "There is new poetry in the world not dreamed of before."

Mackintosh and the Glasgow group had little if any contact with Belgian and French Art Nouveau designers such as VICTOR HORTA, HENRI VAN DE VELDE, and HECTOR GUIMARD, names that were not mentioned at any time by his friends and colleagues nor, for that matter, by the British professional journals. Mary Newbery Sturrock, daughter of Francis Newbery, said in an interview (1973) that Mackintosh did not like Art Nouveau: "he fought against it with the straight lines, against these things you can see for yourself are like melted margerine. . . ." It should be quite evident, however, that Mackintosh did not fit into any mainstream of Art Nouveau: little of his work had the fluid, often eccentric characteristics affected by European advocates of the new style.

The Viennese interlude, and it was little more than an interlude, and his other European triumphs marked the high point of Mackintosh's career. From comparative obscurity in Glasgow he had emerged, in the remarkably short period of two or three years, as one of the most important leaders of the new movement. His work was profusely illustrated in the new, elegantly produced German periodicals *Die Kunst, Dekorative Kunst,* and *Deutsche Kunst und Dekoration;* and he found his name linked with those of Baillie-Scott, PHILIP S. WEBB, Voysey, and other architect-followers of William Morris.

Architectural work in Scotland. At home in

Scotland during these years Mackintosh continued to maintain a high level of creative activity. While preparing the *Haus eines Kunstfreundes* project in 1901, he not only designed the Daily Record Office, Glasgow, a large building situated on an awkward site in a narrow street, but he also began work on the competition for the Church of England Cathedral in Liverpool, a competition won by GILES GILBERT SCOTT. Mackintosh's design, submitted under the name of Honeyman and Keppie, was a bold composition in modernized Gothic with a traditional Latin-cross plan, double transepts, a square east end in the English tradition, twin western towers, and a great central lantern over the crossing. The decorative elements of tracery and carving were beautifully modeled, and kept in control throughout. The drawings, in Mackintosh's own hand, especially the elevations and magnificent perspective with a characteristic linear sky, provided a clear and direct statement of his intentions. It was most unfortunate that his project was unpremiated; had he been given the opportunity of guiding his building through to completion, the story of his life might have been very different. While working on the Cathedral, the Turin Exhibition, and the Wärndorfer Music Salon, Mackintosh continued with the furnishing and decoration of the Ingram Street tearooms for Miss Cranston (1900–1912), the third of the tearoom projects, all of which had necessitated the remodeling of existing buildings. Ingram Street was particularly interesting because here, for the first time, he had a completely free hand and was able to divide and subdivide the space of the uninspiring premises, construct mezzanines, and generally create varied, charming, and intimate spaces for the enjoyment of the owner's clientele.

Mackintosh.
W. W. Blackie House (Hill House).
Helensburgh, Scotland.
1902–1906

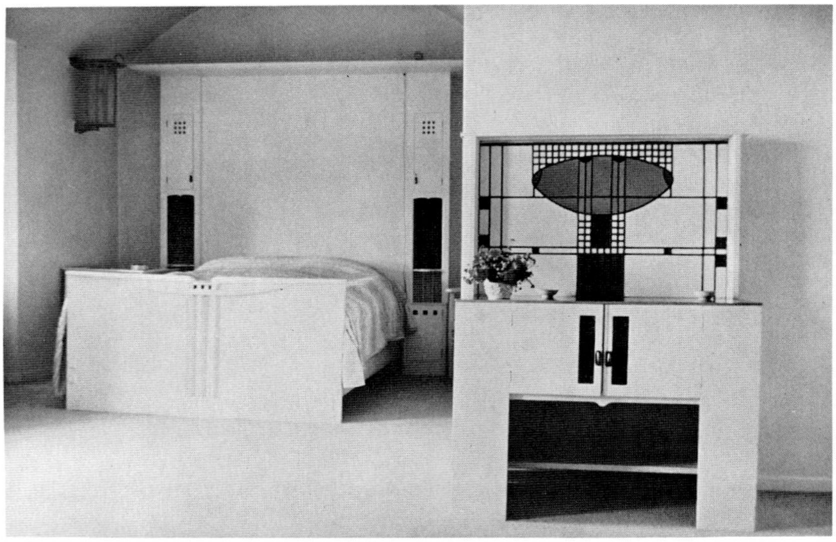

Mackintosh.
W. W. Blackie House (White Bedroom).
Helensburgh, Scotland.
1902–1906

Hill House. At this time, too, Mackintosh was commissioned by the publisher W. W. Blackie to design Hill House, Helensburgh, the best of his domestic projects. Hill House was built very much in the Scottish tradition with stone walls covered externally with rough-cast (harling). Its long gabled roofs and small windows responded to the demands of the cold climate of the Clyde Estuary, and the interior was carefully planned to meet the special needs of an exacting client. Following his usual practice, the hallway and superb staircase bay, the dining room, and the library were lined in wood, mostly oak, finished in a dark stain, but relieved here and there by small areas of color either in tiles or stenciling. These colors, again, were the familiar rose-pinks, greens, and occasional purples. Sometimes, Mackintosh used coarse wrapping paper of neutral color—white, grey, or dark brown—for walls, and occasionally he applied stenciled decoration; he did not use commercial patterned paper, not even that produced by William Morris. At Hill House, the drawing room and bedrooms were white, the former a finely proportioned, L-shaped apartment designed for summer and winter use with an elegant ceramic mosaic fireplace; for entertaining there was an alcove at one end to accommodate the grand piano. The walls were stenciled with an inobtrusive geometrical pattern in silver, with conventionalized floral motifs in pink and green. The ceiling was painted black and the floor, like that in the hall, was covered by a luxurious carpet designed by the architect with patterned borders of squares, a motif that was reflected in the light fittings, furniture, curtains, and elsewhere. The white bedroom at Hill House is one of the architect's most distinguished interiors. It is also L-shaped, with a low-arched ceiling over the bed recess and its ancillary closets. Twin wardrobes, a built-in settee, and a fireplace, together with the exquisitely proportioned dressing table, cheval mirror, and chairs, provide an exotic ensemble which, in its controlled simplicity, continues to astonish and delight the observer.

As at W. W. Davidson's house Windy Hill

(1899), Mackintosh designed not only the building and its contents, but the garden and garden furniture as well, including the garden wall, gates and, at Hill House, the gardener's cottage, which was integrated into the wall itself. He was, in every sense, the complete architect, caring not only for the architectonic qualities of a building, but considering the human value of every aspect of the things he created. Moreover, he still found time for sketching and flower studies, which remained his primary source of inspiration. At Hill House there is evidence that Mackintosh was beginning to discard the flowing lines and organic forms that had distinguished his earlier work in favor of a more formal geometry. This change may be related to his experiences in Europe, particularly in Vienna, where discussions with Hoffmann and his followers may well have caused him to revise some of his earlier ideas.

The Willow Tearooms. Two other notable commissions came in rapid succession, both from his friend and patron, Miss Cranston. The first of these, the Willow Tearooms (1903–1919), opened in 1904, presented a startlingly white, stuccoed façade to traditional Sauchiehall Street, Glasgow, one of the city's busiest thoroughfares. Internally, the long, narrow building was a delight: by introducing a balcony, a bridge, and a fine, open staircase, Mackintosh created spatial magic enhanced by superb wrought-iron work, metal and glass elements, fireplaces, and a great plaster frieze of abstract, geometrical design based upon the willow-tree motif. The ladder-backed chairs and other furniture contributed to the elegance of this interior, but the staircase led to the center and core of the concept, the *Room de Luxe.* This was a relatively small, oval apartment, painted white with as its theme a gesso panel designed by Margaret Macdonald and inspired by Rossetti's sonnet "The Willow Wood." There was a low frieze of mirrors with leaded geometrical and floral emblems which, combined with the high-backed chairs, also painted white, upholstered and stenciled with a floral motif, evoked a dream world far removed from the great industrial city outside. Mackintosh designed everything for The Willow except the china which was of the traditional blue-and-white willow pattern. Glasgow citizens responded with moderate enthusiasm to each of Miss Cranston's successive ventures; visitors from abroad were ecstatic. It is interesting to note that British professional journals paid little attention to Mackintosh and his work at this time, but Hill House and The Willow Tearooms were reviewed in detail and were splendidly illustrated in *Deutsche Kunst und Dekoration* and *Dekorative Kunst* in 1905; the Glasgow School of Art does not appear to have been illustrated in any journal, either at home or abroad, before World War I.

Mackintosh. Willow Tearooms. Glasgow, Scotland. 1903–1919

Hous'hill. In 1903, Miss Cranston and her husband, Major Cochrane, commissioned Mackintosh to decorate and design furniture for their residence, Hous'hill, a very large, old house in the Glasgow suburb of Nitshill. Apart from some excellent fixtures and furniture, Hous'hill was notable mainly for the architect's treatment of the large drawing room whose dual use was defined by a semicircular, open-work wooden screen which continued the curve of a bay window in one end wall, thereby subdividing or, to use LUDWIG MIES VAN DER ROHE's expression, zoning the space for different uses. The screen was a fixture built of narrow laths radiating from the center of the curve and enclosing a grand piano painted by George Walton. The acoustical properties would hardly be affected by this transparent structure, and aesthetically, Mackintosh created the illusion of a room within a room—yet another imaginative, even more subtle variation on his spatial experiments in the tearooms and elsewhere.

Scotland Street School. While working for Miss Cranston, Mackintosh designed Scotland Street Public School (1904), a symmetrical composition based upon the standard Board School plan of the day which required separate entrances for boys and girls. The central, four-story block of classrooms was flanked by powerful staircase towers, enclosed almost entirely in glass with slender stone mullions rising to a decorated upper story, capped by a conical roof. An unusual feature of this building was the treatment of cloakrooms at each floor level; each was stepped back progressively and given a flat roof and a horizontal row of windows. This treatment anticipated later developments in Europe, but here it was used, no doubt, to enhance the appearance of the great staircase bays by freeing them in part from the massive classroom block. Mackintosh's brilliant pen-and-ink perspective drawing of Scotland Street School was published in two British journals in 1906.

The Glasgow School of Art; library wing. In the fall of 1906, the Board of Governors of the Glasgow School of Art decided to proceed with the completion of the building, and Mackintosh was asked to revise the original drawings. This he did. With the exception of the library, the building was constructed more or less in its original form. On the earlier drawing the west façade was unimaginative and the library itself, although two stories high, was expressed in elevation by windows of domestic proportions. As revised, the library section became one of the architect's most daring compositions. Mackintosh introduced another floor and increased the height of this section of the building considerably. With its exciting horizontal rhythms and soaring verticals of glass and metal; its large, plain surfaces of masonry; and its rigid, clean-cut angularity of form the library wing represents a work of uncompromising originality. The west façade itself is modeled in high relief, whereas on the south side, built right to the property line, the windows and other features are cut back into the great wall plane. On the south side, Mackintosh introduced a small, cantilevered conservatory, a glass-walled extension thrust out into space some 80 feet or more above ground level, a daring innovation unparalleled in contemporary work, but having antecedents at Claypotts and other Scottish castles. It is interesting to note that the conservatory appeared on the architect's original drawings and, therefore, was conceived in 1896, a remarkable anticipation of future trends. The 25-feet high library windows were flanked by pairs of roughly hewn blocks of stone which, according to the architect's drawing, were to be

Mackintosh.
Library, Glasgow School of Art.
Scotland.
1906–1909

Mackintosh.
Library, Glasgow School of Art.
Scotland.
1906–1910

sculptured to represent Cellini, ANDREA PALLADIO, Saint Francis, with others unspecified. Had this work been undertaken, it would have been possible to envisage more clearly the effect of the great bands of sculptured figures that the architect proposed in his design for Liverpool Cathedral.

The interior of the library is one of Mackintosh's best known and certainly most accomplished interiors. It is a small room for such an important function—about 35 by 35 feet square—but it seems much larger because of the architect's ingenious spatial treatment. The soaring lines of the west windows were echoed internally by tall, square pillars rising from the floor to the coffered timber ceiling. The front of a narrow gallery was set back some three feet from the pillars on supporting beams, and three square balusters with chamfered angles, brightly colored, were placed in the intervening space. The interior was enriched by the subtle modulation of surfaces and profiles, and a modest amount of carved decoration on pendants extended below the gallery front. The artificial lighting was subdued, and a great cluster of rectilinear brass lampshades with colored glass inserts suspended from the center of the ceiling served as a sculptural element of considerable importance in an otherwise appropriately austere setting. Mackintosh also designed the reading tables, magazine racks, and chairs, the latter of a simple Windsor type of rather fragile construction. Work on the second section of the school started in 1907; it was finished in 1909, including the timber-framed, attic story that ran the full length of the building.

At this time Mackintosh carried out a number of domestic commissions including Mosside, Kilmacolm, and Auchinibert, now named Cloak, Killearn, neither of which are of particular importance; several commissions for furniture; extensions to the Argyle Street and Ingram Street Tearooms; and other minor work. He continued to travel and sketch in England, and in 1908 he spent some time in Portugal.

Decline. There is reason to believe that Mackintosh was made a partner in the firm of Honeyman and Keppie in 1902, but this was not announced publicly until John Honeyman retired in 1904; the firm then became Honeyman, Keppie, and Mackintosh. In 1906, the Mackintoshes moved from their Mains Street apartment to Number 78, South Park Avenue, the end house of a late nineteenth-century terrace adjacent to Glasgow University. This they transformed by bringing furniture, fireplaces, and other effects from Mains Street and by redecorating in their characteristic fashion. Those who remember this period speak of animated conversation, delightful tea parties in the white drawing room, and much laughter.

Despite the security of the domestic scene, however, all was not well with Mackintosh's professional life and, by the time the School of Art was completed in 1909, he had virtually ceased to be an effective contributor to the professional scene in Glasgow. The reasons for his decline are complicated. Although a partner with Honeyman and Keppie, he never took kindly to the constraints of formal architectural practice and office routine, a situation that was exacerbated when either his colleagues or his clients did not see eye to eye with him on design policy. The nature of his early work, akin to Art Nouveau, and his close association with the Spook School alienated him from a conservative Scottish society and from his influential English contemporaries of Arts and Crafts persuasion. Of greater significance, however, was his sustained criticism of his fellow professionals. At the age of twenty-eight, he had the temerity to berate an audience of Glasgow architects, predominantly classicists, with these words: "How absurd it is to see modern churches, theatres, banks etc. . . . made in imitation of Greek temples." And a decade later, "The architect must become an art worker and be content to forego the questionable distinction and pleasure of being respected as the head (perhaps the founder) of a large and successful business." In his view, his colleagues lacked the imagination either to understand or to share his vision of a new architecture, essentially a Scottish architecture, based on native traditions, yet responding to contemporary needs.

The only group with whom he seems to have been in complete accord was the Vienna Secession, who had urged him to live and work in the Austrian capital. In 1904, however, he was profoundly disturbed by news of a serious schism within the Secession itself. As in Scotland, there seemed to be no clear way ahead. Ironically, 1904 was the year in which Hoffmann, financed by Fritz Wärndorfer, founded the Wiener Werkstätten, the imaginative project he had discussed with Mackintosh in Vienna and Glasgow. A Secessionist exhibition planned for that year, to which Charles and Margaret Mackintosh were invited, did not take place, and thereafter, as the impetus of the Secession waned, communications with Vienna became more and more tenuous. Although the Mackintoshes did, in fact, exhibit once more in Vienna, in 1909, the exciting prospect of fruitful collaboration with Hoffmann and the Wiener Werkstätten had by then faded. Tensions at the office, aggravated by Mackintosh's increasingly intemperate habits, reached a point at which, in 1913, he decided to leave the firm and set up his own practice.

He opened an office in Glasgow, but this venture came to nothing, and after a few months it was abandoned.

The London period. In the summer of 1914, the Mackintoshes left Scotland. They stayed for a time at Walberswick, a coastal village in Suffolk, where the Newberys had a cottage, before acquiring two studios in Glebe Place, Chelsea, London (1915). There, they attempted to re-establish themselves in the professional world but, in wartime, architectural work was very difficult to come by. In 1916, Mackintosh was commissioned by W. J. Bassett-Lowke of Northampton, an engineer whose firm was noted for the manufacture of scale-model locomotives and boats, to alter and furnish his newly acquired house, No. 78 Derngate, Northampton. Because of his design background, Bassett-Lowke proved to be an exacting but appreciative client. The plan was typical of the small nineteenth-century English rowhouse; it had a 15-foot frontage with a narrow entrance corridor and a staircase adjacent to a small parlor. Mackintosh demolished the dividing wall, turned the staircase at right angles, and set it back behind an open-work wooden screen of squares. The ceiling, walls, and furniture were painted black, relieved by a deep stenciled frieze of geometrical motifs, mostly triangles, in yellow, blue, purple, green, and red; the carpet was patterned with black and grey squares. The triangular motif, which appeared also in the curtains, in leaded-glass panels in the staircase screen, and as inlay in the furniture, was used extensively by Mackintosh for the first time here, and was borrowed, possibly, from JOSEPH URBAN, the Viennese designer, whose work was well-known to him. The most interesting feature of the Derngate House was a four-story extension to the garden which provided an attractive bay window to the ground floor dining room and balconies to the bedrooms above. The simplicity of the clean-cut rectilinear form and proportions of the openings and the use of flowering plants and sun blinds all suggest contemporary developments in Europe and may, in fact, have been inspired by ADOLF LOOS's early work in Vienna. The guest bedroom on the second floor which, it is now believed, was decorated and furnished by Mackintosh around 1919, was illustrated in *The Ideal Home* in 1920. This was a white room, but the furniture of waxed oak was of simple, rectilinear form, and on a remarkably small scale. The most striking feature of the room was a black and white striped paper applied to the wall behind the twin beds, and carried across the ceiling in the convention of a great canopy. The striped motif was picked up in bedspreads of black and white silk, with ultramarine blue centers.

The Mackintosh collection of drawings housed in the Royal Institute of British Architects, London, contains a series of studies for the redesign of the stenciled triangular decorations in the Derngate hall, prepared in 1920 to meet Bassett-Lowke's request for a simplification of the exotic decorations. The drawings and details of the Derngate project bear a close resemblance to the leaded-glass door and wall panels and electric light fittings designed by Frank Lloyd Wright for the Dana House, Springfield, Illinois, in 1903. The Dana House was illustrated in the portfolio of Wright's work published in Berlin by Ernst Wasmuth in 1911; the introduction was written by Wright's friend Charles R. Ashbee. Mackintosh may have come upon the portfolio either just before leaving Glasgow or upon his arrival in London. Although Wright visited Ashbee in England in 1910, it is unlikely that Mackintosh met him at this time; certainly, there is no record of any such meeting.

Mackintosh's minor work for Bassett-Lowke included several charming clock cases which were inlaid, as was much of the furniture, with newly developed, casein-based plastics which were produced under various trade names—Erinoid, Lactolith, and Galalith. These may have been introduced to him by Bassett-Lowke or he may have come across them during his time in Vienna; one at least was of German origin. Only a single example has come to light so far of an object designed entirely in plastics by Mackintosh: an elegant candlestick some 18 inches high on a circular base. He also designed several colorful, adhesive labels for Bassett-Lowke's firm which were fascinating compositions of industrial and engineering symbols and a highly successful venture into the new world of advertising.

At this time (1917–1920), the Mackintoshes were commissioned by Miss Cranston to design the interior of a basement extension to The Willow Tearooms known as "The Dugout," a name that had particular significance to these involved in trench warfare in Europe. Like the Derngate hallway, it was an exotic interior with a black ceiling and walls enriched by small areas of strong primary color. The triangular motive appeared here also, most notable in the central memorial fireplace, decorated with glass inlay and ceramic mosaics including, to a small scale, flags of the nations involved in the war.

While working on "The Dugout," Mackintosh received a further commission for furniture from Bassett-Lowke and from the latter's brother-in-law, F. Jones of The Drive, Northampton. This was designed for a cottage at Rode near Northampton. Roger Billcliffe (1979) claims, with some justification, that this is "probably the most modern and utilitarian" furniture that Mackintosh ever designed. Mackintosh used oak, stained almost black, inlaid with Ernoid; chair seats were covered with the newly developed leather substitute Rexine. Other furniture for Bassett-Lowke included such modern pieces as a coffee table, a service trolley, and a gramophone cabinet. Mackintosh's work at Northampton seems to have passed unnoticed, except for the illustrated article in *The Ideal Home* (1920) which, although highly complimentary, did not mention his name. Thus, he was denied public recognition at a time when it would have been particularly helpful to him.

Fabric design. While living in Chelsea, the Mackintoshes designed printed fabrics and had work accepted by two well-known textile firms in London, Foxtons and Seftons. Their experiments in this new field achieved some measure of success, and during the year 1920 alone, the only period for which a reliable record exists, they received about £200 in fees, a substantial sum at that time. Unfortunately, all stocks of fabric, together with the firms' records, were destroyed by the German air raids on London during World War II. A number of original drawings have survived in the Glasgow University collection, and they demonstrate that Mackintosh's fertile imagination and command of color, pattern, and texture were unimpaired. Two of the Foxton block prints were illustrated in *The Studio Year of Decorative Art 1917,* which also contained reproductions of two colorful gesso panels, "The Queen of Diamonds" and "The Queen of Spades" from a set of four designed by Margaret Macdonald for the cardroom at Hous'hill, Glasgow. Designs for the fabrics varied from close repeats of flower, bud, or seed forms to vigorously undulating, rhythmic linear patterns inspired by tulips and other flowers combined with triangles and checks. There were also lively combinations of floral and geometrical patterns that seemed to have three-dimensional qualities.

The Mackintoshes extended their Glasgow palette of colors by using a wide range of reds and blues which were given additional vibrancy by the juxtaposition of black and white. The two designs illustrated in the *Studio Year Book of 1917* stand out in sharp contrast to the many other illustrations of traditional character by the William Morris school; they have a simplicity, directness, and clarity that place Mackintosh indisputably in the vanguard of modern textile designers.

Flower studies and landscape. Mackintosh's passion for flowers never diminished: one of his earliest drawings is dated Lamlash, Arran, 1893, and one of the last, Mont Louis, France, 1925. These lovely, translucent studies were executed very rapidly in pencil with a bold, unhesitating line and then delicately colored with transparent washes. It has been stated erroneously that on occasion Margaret added the color washes but neither his wife nor anyone else was allowed to work on his drawings. It was his intention to publish the flower studies in Germany, but the outbreak of World War I made this impossible; when peace came, the cost of publication in Britain was found to be prohibitive.

During the Chelsea period, Mackintosh became more and more interested in cultivated flowers, and some of his most superb, formal watercolors, for example, *Anemones* (1916), *Pinks* (1922–1923) and *The Grey Iris* (1922–1924), belong to this period. In addition, he and Margaret painted highly conventionalized flower studies usually against a black background which, no doubt, were intended for printed fabrics.

In 1920, the Mackintoshes spent a month's vacation in Dorset, where Charles produced several watercolors that indicated a new and more mature approach to landscape, clearly anticipating his later work in France. The interlude in Dorset came while Mackintosh was designing a block of studio flats in Chelsea for the Arts League of Service and a small theater for his friend Margaret Morris. Unfortunately, these and several other small architectural projects came to nothing largely because of difficulties with the local authorities. The surviving drawings show that, in any case, they were probably too ambitious and beyond the financial capacity of the clients. The failure of the Chelsea Studio project, the theater, and more specifically, perhaps, Bassett-Lowke's decision in 1922 to employ Peter Behrens as architect of his new house greatly discouraged Mackintosh, and once again, as in Glasgow, he became deeply depressed. It was at this time that he confided in his friend J. D. Fergusson, the artist, that he intended to give up architecture entirely and devote himself to watercolor painting.

The last phase—France. On the advice of friends, the Mackintoshes decided to take a long vacation abroad. In 1923, they sublet their studios in Glebe Place and, after a short stay at Mont Louis in the Pyrenees, they finally settled at Port Vendres, a tiny hamlet on the Mediterranean side of the Franco-Spanish border. In this environment Mackintosh embarked on his new career as watercolorist with confidence and enthusiasm. The watercolors he produced between 1923 and 1927 are as diverse and full of character, as vigorous and original as his youthful experiments in the field of decoration and craft work. In all this work it is evident that his interest lay primarily in design—as indeed one would expect—, in mass composition, and in the pattern and texture of natural landforms. He made little attempt to achieve depth or atmosphere; instead, he emphasized the geometrical relationship of rocks, fields, and buildings, and these elements are juxtaposed and woven together into fascinating architectural patterns. Mackintosh was a slow worker and during the four years he spent at Port Vendres he completed only about forty pictures. His paintings were exhibited at the Third, Fourth, and Fifth Chicago International Exhibitions in 1923, 1924, and 1925 respectively, at the Duveen Invited Artists Show in Paris in 1927, and at the Leicester Galleries in 1928.

In the autumn of 1927, the year in which he executed many of his best watercolors, he returned to England for medical treatment. For some months he underwent radium treatment for cancer of the tongue and practically lost his power of speech, but he never doubted that he would pull through. From the hospital he was moved to a small furnished house in Hampstead Heath where he was devotedly nursed by his wife and visited constantly by Margaret Morris, who taught him to express himself in sign language and was instrumental in helping him regain his power of speech. Desmond Chapman-Huston, a friend from the Glasgow days, offered the Mackintoshes the use of the two upper floors of his house in Porchester Square, London, where they were able to enjoy for a short time Chapman-Huston's library and garden. However, Mackintosh's health declined and in the autumn of 1928, he was moved into a nursing home in Porchester Square. After a brief illness, he died on December 10, 1928.

After Margaret Mackintosh's death four years later, the contents of the studios were appraised. According to the official assessment, the entire contents of the two studios were "practically of no value." They were exhibited in Glasgow in 1933 but attracted little attention, and only a few pieces were sold. In 1975, a single Mackintosh chair from *Hous'hill,* Glasgow, was auctioned by Sotheby's of London for £9,300 and in 1980 a small table from the Wärndorfer Music Salon brought £30,000—an extraordinary indication of changing values, at least as reflected by the collectors' market.

Quite apart from such mundane evidence, historical perspective and the universal recognition by architects, artists of many persuasions, and critics of Mackintosh's great contribution have indisputably confirmed his position in the forefront of twentieth-century pioneers. In our present materialistic age he is acknowledged as a highly gifted, uncompromising individual with a rare sense of mission; a designer supremely aware of tradition and the indivisibility of architecture, fine art, and the crafts; and an intensely humane person willing to lavish time and creative energy on both large and small things in order to delight the observer.

THOMAS HOWARTH

WORKS

Excellent collections of work by Charles Rennie Mackintosh are permanently housed in the Glasgow School of Art, and the Huntarian Art Gallery, Glasgow University, Scotland. Several pieces are in the United States, notably in the Museum of Modern Art, New York, and the Sidney and Frances Lewis Collection, Virginia.

1890, William Hamilton House (Redclyffe), Springburn; 1893, Glasgow Herald Building Tower (with John Keppie); 1894–1896, Queen Margaret's Medical College (with Keppie); 1895, Martyrs' Public School (with Keppie); *1896, Buchanan Street Tearooms (mural decorations); 1896–1897, Argyle Street Tearooms (furniture); 1896–1899, Glasgow School of Art (eastern section); 1897–1899, Queen's Cross Church of Scotland; Glasgow, Scotland. 1898, Brüchmann Dining Room, Munich. 1898, Ruchill Street Church Halls, Glasgow, Scotland. 1899–1901, William Davidson House (Windy Hill), Kilmacolm, Scotland. *1900, Mackintosh Apartment (furnishings and decoration), 120 Mains Street; 1900–1912, Ingram Street Tearooms (some interiors and furnishings preserved); 1901, Daily Record Offices; Glasgow, Scotland. *1902, Scottish Section, International Exhibition of Modern Decorative Art, Turin, Italy. 1902–1904, W. W. Blackie House (Hill House), Helensburgh, Scotland. *1902–1906, Wärndorfer Music Salon (with Margaret Mackintosh), Vienna. 1903–1910, Cochrane House (Hous'hill), Nitshill, Scotland. *1903–1919, Willow Tearooms (restored without furniture in 1979–1980), Glasgow, Scotland. 1904, Holy Trinity (chancel furniture), Bridge of Allan, Stirlingshire, Scotland. 1904, Scotland Street School, Glasgow, Scotland. 1905, Ball Dining Room, Berlin. 1906, H. B. Collins House (Mosside), Kilmacolm, Scotland. 1906, Mackintosh House (interiors reconstructed in the Huntarian Art Gallery, Glasgow University, in 1979–1980), 78 Southpart Avenue, Glasgow, Scotland. 1906, F. J. Shand House (Auchinibert; now Cloak), Killearn, Scotland. 1906–1909, Glasgow School of Art (redesigned the western section, including the library); 1908, Lady Artists' Club (doorway and furnishings); Glasgow, Scotland. 1916–1920, W. J. Bassett-Lowke House (interiors and furniture), 78 Derngate, Northampton, England. 1917–1920, Dugout (interior), Glasgow, Scotland.

BIBLIOGRAPHY

ALISON, FILIPPO (1974)1978 *Charles Rennie Mackintosh as a Designer of Chairs.* London: Academy Editions.

BILLCLIFFE, ROGER 1977 *Architectural Sketches and Flower Drawings by Charles Rennie Mackintosh.* London: Academy Editions.

BILLCLIFFE, ROGER (1978)1979 *Mackintosh Watercolours.* London: J. Murray.

BILLCLIFFE, ROGER 1979 *Charles Rennie Mackintosh: Furniture and Interiors.* London.

BILLCLIFFE, ROGER, and VERGO, PETER 1977 "Charles Rennie Mackintosh and the Austrian Art

Revival." *Burlington Magazine* 119:739–746.
COOPER, JACKIE (editor) (1978)1980 *Mackintosh Architecture.* With an introduction by Barbara Bernard. New York: Rizzoli.
GOMME, ANDOR, and WALKER, DAVID 1968 *Architecture of Glasgow.* London: Lund Humphries.
HAWDIE, WILLIAM R. 1976 *Scottish Painting: 1837–1939.* London: Studio Vista.
HOWARTH, THOMAS (1953)1977 *Charles Rennie Mackintosh and the Modern Movement.* 2d ed. London: Routledge & Kegan Paul. Includes a comprehensive bibliography.
KOSSATZ, HORST-HERBERT 1971 "The Vienna Secession and Its Early Relations with Great Britain." *Studio International* Jan.:9–20.
MACLEOD, ROBERT 1968 *Charles Rennie Mackintosh.* Feltham, England: Country Life.
PEVSNER, NIKOLAUS 1950 *Charles R. Mackintosh.* Milan: Il Balcone.
SEKLER, EDUARD 1968 "Mackintosh and Vienna." *Architectural Review* 144:455–456.
VERGO, PETER 1975 *Art in Vienna.* London: Phaidon.
WALKER, DAVID 1973 "The Early Works of Mackintosh." In Nikolaus Pevsner and J. M. Richards (editors), *The Anti-Rationalists.* University of Toronto Press.

MACKMURDO, A. H.

Arthur Heygate Mackmurdo (1851–1942), English architect, designer, and socioeconomic theorist, received his architectural training under T. Chatfield Clark and JAMES BROOKS. His first building, 6 Private Road, Enfield, London, designed in 1872 and built in 1876, is dominated by the influence of R. NORMAN SHAW and of JOHN RUSKIN. However, his later buildings, though extremely varied, always display great originality. For example, 8 Private Road, Enfield, London (1886–1887), and 25 Cadogan Gardens, London (1893–1894), are both elegantly simple designs, owing something respectively to the early Italian Renaissance and to the Queen Anne style; while in *Great Ruffins* at Wickham Bishops, Essex (c.1904), simplicity is abandoned in favor of an extravagant baroque inspired by CHRISTOPHER WREN.

In 1882, Mackmurdo founded the Century Guild, an association which aimed to reconcile the fine and applied arts by producing beautiful articles of use, and which publicized its ideals through an artistically produced journal, *The Hobby Horse.*

Mackmurdo's furniture, which influenced C. F. A. VOYSEY and C. R. MACKINTOSH, possesses structural simplicity and clarity. It often incorporates square-sectioned posts rising above the structure and capped by elegant, flat-topped finials. Mackmurdo also designed beautiful patterns in a variety of media, and his swirling plant forms anticipated continental Art Nouveau.

J. E. HESELTINE

WORKS

1872–1876, House, 6 Private Road; 1886–1887, "Brooklyn" House, 8 Private Road; London. c.1890, Gordon Institute for Boys (gymnasium), Saint Helens, England. 1890, House, 16 Redington Road, London. 1891, House, 12 Hans Road; 1893–1894, House, 25 Cadogan Gardens; 1900, Warehouse, 109–113 Charterhouse Street; London. c.1904, *Great Ruffians* House, Wickham Bishops; c.1932, Village Hall, Bradwell; Essex, England.

BIBLIOGRAPHY

"A. H. Mackmurdo." 1942 *Journal of the Royal Institute of British Architects* 49:94–95. With a footnote by Nikolaus Pevsner.
The Eccentric A. H. Mackmurdo 1851–1942. 1979 Introduction by John Doubleday. Catalogue of an exhibition held at the Minories, Colchester, Essex, England, from February 24 to March 25, 1979. Colchester: The Minories.
HASLAM, MALCOLM 1975 "A Pioneer of Art Nouveau: Arthur Heygate Mackmurdo." *Country Life* 157:504–506, 574–579.
PEVSNER, NIKOLAUS 1962 "Mackmurdiana." *Architectural Review* 132, July:59–60.
PEVSNER, NIKOLAUS 1968 "Arthur H. Mackmurdo." Volume 2, pages 132–139 in *Studies in Architecture and Design.* New York: Walker; London: Thames.
POND, EDWARD (1960)1973 "Mackmurdo Gleanings." Pages 111–115 in James M. Richards, and Nikolaus Pevsner (editors) *The Anti-Rationalists.* London: Architectural Press. Reprint of an article originally published in *The Architectural Review* 128:429–431.
VALLANCE, AYMER 1899 "Mr. Arthur H. Mackmurdo and the Century Guild." *The Studio* 16:183–192.

MACLAREN, JAMES M.

James M. MacLaren (1843–1890) was one of the major British architects to pioneer and practice the principles of Arts and Crafts vernacular design.

Born in Stirling, Scotland, and educated locally, MacLaren completed a Beaux-Arts training in Paris and became apprenticed to the Glasgow firm of Campbell Douglas. He formed his own practice in 1886 following a brief spell in the London office of EDWARD WILLIAM GODWIN who, along with MacLaren's fellow architects in the Art Workers' Guild and the American H. H. RICHARDSON, was the major influence on his work.

Following the design of his most successful large building, the Stirling High School (1887–1888), MacLaren produced a series of remarkable works in Perthshire, Scotland, for his patron Sir

MacLaren.
Tenant Farmer's House.
Fortingall, Perthshire, Scotland.
1889–1890

Donald Currie of Glenlyon, notably the Tenant Farmer's House, and Aberfeldy Town Hall, both of 1889–1890. These stone-built and white-washed buildings are remarkably original, while at the same time being geometrically and visually simple and sharing an obvious affinity with the vernacular.

The significance of MacLaren's brief career is best emphasized by his substantial influence on the leading architects of the next generation, in particular CHARLES F. A. VOYSEY and CHARLES RENNIE MACKINTOSH. MacLaren's few buildings display a charm and naturalness unsurpassed by any of his contemporaries.

JOHN MCASLAN

WORKS

1886, Park House, Ledbury, Herefordshire, England. 1887–1888, Stirling High School, Scotland. 1888, 22 Avonmore Road, London. 1889–1890, Cottages (two blocks); 1889–1890, Farm Steading; Fortingall, Perthshire, Scotland. 1889–1890, Santa Catalina Hotel, Las Palmas, Canary Islands. 1889–1890, 10–12 Palace Court, London. 1889–1890, Tenant Farmer's House, Fortingall; 1889–1890, Town Hall, Aberfeldy; Perthshire, Scotland. 1890–1891, Heatherwood, Crawley Down, Sussex, England.

BIBLIOGRAPHY

GOODHART-RENDEL, H. S. 1949 "Rogue Architects of the Victorian Era." *Journal of the Royal Institute of British Architects* 56:251–259.

MCARA, DUNCAN 1970 "An Architect for Connoisseurs." *Scottish Art Review* 12, no. 4:28–33.

SERVICE, ALASTAIR 1973 "James MacLaren and the Godwin Legacy." *Architectural Review* (London) 154:111–118.

SERVICE, ALASTAIR (1975)1977 *Edwardian Architecture.* London: Oxford University Press.

MACLURE, SAMUEL

Samuel Maclure (1860–1929) was probably the single most influential architect in western British Columbia during the rapid development period from 1900 to 1940. Born in New Westminster, British Columbia, Maclure developed an early attachment to British Columbia's rugged wilderness while accompanying his father on surveying expeditions. Demonstrating a natural talent for art from an early age Maclure was encouraged to pursue formal training. The brief period he spent at the Spring Garden Art School in Philadelphia in 1884–1885 provided him with the only formal training which he later applied to the study and practice of architecture.

His early work was undistinguished, consisting mainly of Queen Ann Shingle style residences and a few commercial buildings. In 1892, Maclure moved to the capital city, Victoria, and opened his own practice. Specializing in small-scale residential work, he rapidly developed a large clientele. By 1900, he was capturing the major commissions in the prestigious Rockland area, including the design of Government House (1901), a project he shared with FRANCIS MAWSON RATTENBURY.

Maclure's success was a direct result of his ability to adapt the current American Arts and Crafts style and its timber construction technology to a sophisticated English immigrant society. Wherever possible, he took full advantage of the mountainous topography in siting his many commissions in Victoria and the nearby coastal communities. Through over 350 commissions that passed through his practice, he developed a series of highly individual house types based on the colonial bungalow, the shingled European chalet, and the Tudor Hall house. These, and a very original unbarked slab-wall treatment, he interpreted with a unique sensitivity for native woods, site-quarried masonry, and breathtaking scenic locations. A major feature of many of the houses is a spacious entertainment hall, opening up the interior and containing a dramatic staircase, fireplace, and balconied second floor. Major rooms opened onto this spatial core through wide sliding doors; and at ground level the hall often opened directly out into the gardens, themselves developed from the architect's own designs. His largest commission using these elements was the Edwardian country castle *Hatley Park* (1906–1908) for coal baron James Dunsmuir at Sooke, British Columbia.

Maclure's postwar work experienced a dramatic change as he turned more toward a Lutyenesque (see EDWIN LUTYENS) classicism for inspiration. It was, however, the early works, in particular a very personal interpretation of the Shingle style and half-timber façade treatment, that influenced a generation of British Columbia architects throughout the Province.

MARTIN SEGGER

WORKS

1889, Royal Columbia Hospital (with C. F. Clow), New Westminster, British Columbia. 1893, Temple Building; 1896–1897, A. C. Flumerfeldt House; 1899, A. E. MacPhillips House; 1900, R. Dunsmuir House; 1901, Government House (Carey Castle; with Francis Mawson Rattenbury); 1905–1906, Biggerstaff Wilson House; Victoria. 1906–1908, Hatley Park, Sooke, British Columbia. 1908, G. M. Audain House, Victoria. 1910, W. H. Churchman House, Oak Bay, British Columbia. 1911, C. Phillips Wolley House, Somenos, British Columbia. 1911–1912, Seton Academy for Girls (with Cecil Croker Fox); 1911–1912, Western Residential School for Boys (with Cecil Croker Fox); Vancouver, British Columbia.

BIBLIOGRAPHY

EATON, LEONARD K. 1971 *The Architecture of Samuel Maclure.* Art Gallery of Greater Victoria.

EATON, LEONARD K. 1981 "The Cross-axial Houses of Samuel Maclure." *Revue d'art canadienne/Canadian Art Review* 7, nos. 1–2:49–57.

SEGGER, MARTIN 1981*a* "The Englishness of Samuel Maclure." *West Coast Review* 15, no.4:28–35.

SEGGER, MARTIN 1981*b* "Variety and Decorum: Style and Form in the Work of Samuel Maclure 1860–1929." *Bulletin of the Society for the Study of Architecture in Canada* 7, nos. 1–2:4–12.

MADERNO, CARLO

Carlo Maderno (c.1556–1629) was the outstanding architect in the period just before the full flowering of seventeenth-century architecture in Rome under FRANCESCO BORROMINI, PIETRO BERRETTINI DA CORTONA, and GIOVANNI LORENZO BERNINI. He belongs to a generation contemporary with the painter Annibale Carracci, that is sometimes considered transitional. It can be described as a last flowering of the Italian Renaissance or as the early baroque, depending on definitions and point of view.

Maderno was a member of an architectural dynasty, the nephew of DOMENICO FONTANA, who was architect of Pope Sixtus V (1585–1590); and he was in some sense the uncle of Borromini. In the 1590s, Maderno gradually succeeded the older generation of Roman architects—Fontana, Francesco da Volterra, GIACOMO DELLA PORTA—and gathered all of their patronage into his own hands. He became architect of St. Peter's in 1603 and completed the church with its nave and façade. Toward the end of his life, he was at least the nominal architect of the Palazzo Barberini (1626–1628), which opened a new era in Roman secular architecture.

Maderno was born in Capolago on the southern tip of Lake Lugano in what is now the Canton Ticino of Switzerland, then under Milanese rule. His birthdate is not known from contemporary records; in 1602 he was reported to be about forty, which would put his birthdate around 1562; the conventional date of 1556 was given by the eighteenth-century biographer Giovan Battista Passeri with no known basis in fact. Maderno's mother was the sister of the architects Domenico and Giovanni Fontana. His sister married into the family that produced Borromini, whose grandmother was another Maderno. All of these Roman architects were born within a few miles of each other, and they are only the best known of a whole series of masons and stonecutters who went to Rome in search of work from that general area.

Maderno was surely in Rome by the mid-1570s, working in the Fontana workshop; he quickly became the responsible younger member of the group, often receiving payment for their work and quite possibly designing some of the buildings that we associate with Domenico Fontana: the Villa Montalto on the Quirinal, done for Sixtus V before he became pope; the Cappella Sistina at Santa Maria Maggiore for the same patron, and the Vatican and Lateran palaces.

Maderno's earliest profession was that of master of stucco decoration, and even in later life, he tended to favor that ornament in vaults, stairs, and courtyards. Maderno soon became prominent as an engineer with the re-erection of the ancient Egyptian obelisks at Santa Maria Maggiore, San Giovanni in Laterano, and Santa Maria del Popolo. Domenico Fontana's greatest claim to fame was the removal and re-erection of the Vatican obelisk to the piazza before St. Peter's (1586), and Maderno shared the responsibility for this feat: at the end of his life, when he designed his coat of arms, he put the obelisk on it and his Latin epitaph mentions it first among only three achievements, the others being the completion of St. Peter's and another work of engineering, the transportation of the remaining ancient column of the Basilica of Maxentius and Constantine to Santa Maria Maggiore. If we assume that he dictated the contents of this epitaph, we can also deduce that his own sense of accomplishment was the old-fashioned one of solving engineering problems rather than the more modern one of producing novel or beautiful architectural designs. Although Maderno made real contributions to world architecture that we still admire, the bulk of his activity was practical. Aqueducts, embankments, and other forms of hydraulic control occupied much of his time (he was "architect" of the Tiber river for many years); he often worked on the repair and erection of bridges, as well as the completion of buildings begun and essentially designed by others. Only the

Palazzo Mattei di Giove (1598–1617) was actually begun and finished exclusively by Maderno among the dozens of buildings he worked on over a half-century of practice.

Maderno established a reputation for solid competence during the reign of Sixtus V, when Domenico Fontana, the Pope's favorite, designed a number of relatively styleless buildings, built new streets, piazzas, and fountains, and so transformed Rome that it seemed to one observer like a new city. The credit all went to Fontana, but after the death of his protector he was under attack and was finally exiled in 1594, charged with the embezzlement of papal funds. Maderno emerged from this trial unscathed as the head of a busy firm and soon he was the acknowledged leader of the profession all over Italy.

Maderno's first great achievement, in some ways unsurpassed, was the remodeling of the medieval Church of Santa Susanna (1593–1603) on the Quirinal hill for Cardinal Girolamo Rusticucci, a venerable member of the Curia who was also Vicar General of Rome. Rusticucci presumably engaged Fontana because of his friendship with Sixtus V; Fontana was already working at Rusticucci's palace in the Borgo Nuovo by 1585, and later, Maderno also worked there, but remodeling in the 1930s has made his work impossible to identify. Rusticucci seems to have engaged Maderno to design his projected chapel in the right transept of the Gesù in 1594–1595, for which an elaborate, rather mannerist drawing survives.

Santa Susanna became Rusticucci's titular church in 1570, but it was only in the 1590s that he began to work on it as a result of a change in status of the church. For some time, it had belonged to Cistercian nuns, but only after Sixtus V brought in a new aqueduct, the Acqua Felice, in the 1580s did the Quirinal become an attractive site for residential building. As a consequence of the increased habitation that was projected for that high site, Santa Susanna became a parish church in 1589 and the cloistered nuns were relegated to a rear portion of the property. These changes led to the construction of a new monastery, a nuns' choir, and finally in 1593 the restoration of the main church with Fontana and Maderno as co-architects. Fontana's departure soon put Maderno in sole charge. The new high altar, and the old apse and triumphal arch were lavishly decorated with stucco ornament and paintings, which entailed the destruction of the apse mosaic of Leo III (795–816). Below, the semiannular crypt, probably also Leo's, was refurbished with an altar. Access was given through a pair of curving stairs leading down from the nave and enclosed by a decorative balustrade that also functions as a partial choir-screen for the raised chancel. This crypt is an outstanding example of the rising cult of early Christian martyrs, although Susanna, together with her father and uncle, is no longer considered to be an historical figure. Nevertheless, what seem to be Constantinian walls, together with records of a place of worship on that site going back to 499 and a dedication to Susanna in 595, all make it a truly venerable site of Christian worship.

The church itself was divided with a medieval system of three diaphragm arches; the one before the chancel remains but the two in the nave were truncated and remain only as piers supporting statues. Thus, the nave became an unbroken space to be decorated with a coffered wooden ceiling designed by Maderno, with frescoes on the walls. Most of this was done in 1596–1598.

Maderno's first and perhaps greatest masterpiece is the façade, dated 1603, for which there is a contract of November 1597. Thus, the design was presumably made by that time. Like other façades of the period, it is a separate architectural feature, essentially independent of the building behind and rising high above it. Its material, the local travertine stone, with luxuriant carved details, gives it majestic proportions even though the entire façade is relatively small. Maderno tied it into the side wings, which he built of brick laid in fine courses, which also covers the monastery and other service buildings. Thus, the exuberant composition of the façade itself is framed by sober, one-story elements with pilaster strips. The façade seems to burst up and out of this simple environment, but the balusters on the side wings were carried over the pediment (to the horror of neoclassic critics) in order to unify the composition.

The façade proper, of five bays, continues the wings on a forward plane but quickly breaks forward again and rises to its full two-story height. This break is also signaled by a change from the Corinthian pilasters of the ends to engaged but almost freestanding columns in the center bays below, which broaden to the central portal bay with its own triangular pediment in the middle of the composition. The sequence of pilaster-strips, pilasters, columns, and paired columns as one moves from side to center makes the façade more sculptural, fuller of light-dark contrasts, and ultimately more exciting as an architectural picture than any façade before it. For this reason, it has often been considered to be a decisive break with the past and to be the first baroque façade. Nevertheless, its ties with sixteenth-century tradition are as important as its novelty.

A façade with three similar planes leading to a powerful central portal-bay had been designed for the Gesù by Giacomo Barozzi da Vignola in

Maderno.
Santa Susanna (new façade).
Rome.
1593–1603

1573, although it was broader and less dramatic than Maderno's design; indeed, it was relatively static, with columns framing only the central bay, above and below. Maderno drew both on that design and on della Porta's actual façade for the Gesù, and in addition used the idea of adjoining "palace" bays that may already have been built for San Giacomo degli Incurabili by Francesco da Volterra. Since Maderno actually built the façade of that church with minor modifications of Volterra's designs, we cannot be altogether sure what was added, but the inorganic connection of those wings with the façade makes me believe that Maderno perfected an idea of Volterra's.

The upper story of Santa Susanna continues the sequence found below, but with Composite pilasters. The bays above and below contain elaborately carved frames for statuary niches; in the center, a sturdy window frame with Ionic colonnettes stands above the door, continuing the columnar motif from below. The actual height of the church within can be discerned from the narrow slit of window at the bottom of the arched frame: almost the entire second story rises above the ceiling of the building behind, with a pair of seemingly springy volutes mediating between the unequal widths of the two façade stories.

The novelty of Maderno's façade consisted in

the dramatic adoption of Vignolesque motifs to a relatively narrow site, which he made notably vertical by ignoring the shape of the church. The unity of the whole, with the wings, is affirmed by the novel balustrade climbing up the raking cornices of the pediment. But it is the almost rushing climax of the bays moving inward to the central portal, changing to columns and then to paired columns, on four levels of relief, that makes the design one of the great monuments of Roman architecture, whether one considers it to be the culmination of the later Renaissance or the birth of the baroque. Although Maderno designed related façades for St. Peter's, and for Sant'Andrea della Valle toward the end of his life, he was never able to equal the perfection, balance, and dynamism of this design. Its columnar forms, with their dramatic chiaroscuro, were influential and innovative, and Maderno can be given credit for introducing a north Italian columnar architecture that he disciplined and dramatized in a way that was unknown in the north.

By the time Santa Susanna was finished, Maderno was architect of St. Peter's; after the accession of Pope Paul V Borghese in 1605 he received his greatest commission, the completion of the central church of Roman Catholic Christendom. He had also established himself by then as a leading domestic architect as well. His only wholly autonomous construction is the Palazzo Mattei di Giove, begun for Asdrubale Mattei in 1598 and completed, after interruptions, in 1617. In the first phase of construction (1598–1601), he built the block on the via dei Funari and six bays around the corner on the via Caetani, with a rear loggia but not as yet the court and garden that became a chief feature of the palace. The main entrance on the via dei Funari, leading to the courtyard, was built at this time. The exterior of the palace is essentially conventional, unadorned, and uses finely laid thin bricks without stucco coating for the façade, no doubt in emulation of antique brickwork. After a short break, building continued in 1604 with changes in design and with a new grand portal on the via Caetani. At this time, the vista from that portal to the stairway was presumably created; the main building with its fresco decorations was completed by 1611. The chief features are an ingenious and attractive stairway, framed by a perspective niche, that turns first right then left as one ascends to the main floor. It is decorated with elaborate stucco vaults that must reflect Maderno's own decorative taste. The plan of the palace is usual, with the main portal leading to the court, the subordinate portal to the perspective niche and stair; both vistas seem to be cut into the irregular block at angles to the planes of the façades, and the axis veeers slightly into the court as later construction modified the main entrance enfilade, which orginally ended with a niche-fountain at the rear of the court. There, a one-story bridge provides access on the main story to the opposite wings of the U-shaped palace. The small court was decorated with busts of emperors and with antique reliefs, all in elaborate frameworks of stucco that give a tapestrylike effect. In 1613, Maderno made a new plan for an adjoining wing, of different design outside to preserve the symmetry of the façade on the via Caetani. Here, Mattei constructed a gallery on the *piano nobile,* which was later decorated by da Cortona and others. The garden was furbished with a grotto fountain and other decorative elements now lost.

Maderno. Courtyard, Palazzo Mattei di Giove. Rome. 1598–1617

With the death of Giacomo della Porta in 1602, Maderno inherited the last remaining architectural practice of Rome and took over responsibility for the Aldobrandini buildings begun under Pope Clement VIII, most notably the Villa Belvedere at Frascati, built for the cardinal nephew, Pietro Aldobrandini. Maderno presumably modified the upper features of della Porta's unfinished palace and designed the magnificent water theater, a semicircular construction featuring arched niches with columnar decoration and a huge inscription commemorating the defeat of Ferrara by papal forces in 1598. The water comes down a chain of stepped waterfalls crowned by a pair of symbolic spiral columns from whose capitals water spurted. A series of rustic fountains and grottoes rise high above that point, invisible from the floor of the amphitheater. Such villas were inspired by reports of ancient Roman country life. This one had an elaborate literary and propagandistic program devised by Cardinal Pietro Aldobrandini's artistic adviser, Monsignor Giovan Battista Agucchi. All of this work took considerable time to complete because of a change in Aldobrandini's fortunes brought about by the death of the pope early in 1605. Work was suspended for many years; some fountains as well as the chapel to the left and the

Stanza d'Apollo at the right, were not finished until around 1620.

Among several other important commissions that Maderno inherited from della Porta, the greatest was the completion of San Giovanni dei Fiorentini, whose foundations were begun in 1520 by Antonio da Sangallo (see SANGALLO FAMILY) but soon suspended because of the expense of building adequate supports for a construction on the verge of the Tiber river. The nave and chapels were built by della Porta according to older plans between 1582 and around 1588. Maderno became architect in the late 1590s but the construction of the crossing, dome, and apse according to his design dates from 1608–1615. He changed the older model by erecting broad and high transepts with flat walls almost flush with those of the nave outside; he shortened the apsidal area by ending it with a flat wall, thus avoiding further extension into the Tiber bed. Maderno's designs were cramped through lack of funds from Florence, but the interior of the transept is impressive and simple; the alternating windows and niches in the interior of the drum, with light coming in on axis, are unlike della Porta's design. The round interior drum is articulated with paired pilasters that continue up into the dome as decorative strips. Outside, because of its dramatic site on a bend in the river, the church once seemed to rise directly from the Tiber. Maderno's end with its octagonal drum and high, pointed dome developed from the Cappella Sistina by Fontana at Santa Maria Maggiore, is the main feature as seen from across the river, where it rises as a kind of High Renaissance structure since the nave is essentially invisible behind. Only its insistent verticality labels it a work of its period.

Maderno had freer rein at Sant'Andrea della Valle (1608–c.1628), the Theatine Order's answer to the Jesuit Gesù, which was begun in 1591, perhaps to della Porta's design. Like San Giovanni, it was abandoned around 1600 after the nave was underway. After the death of the first patron, Cardinal Alfonso Gesualdo, confusion reigned for some years. In 1608, Cardinal Alessandro Peretti, a nephew of Pope Sixtus V, agreed to finish the church. He employed the family's old architectural

Maderno. Villa Aldobrandini. Frascati, Italy. 1603–c.1620

Maderno.
Sant'Andrea della Valle.
Rome.
1608–c.1628

firm, now headed by Maderno. The nave was finished, the transepts and chancel were built, and the drum was begun by 1620. In that year, Maderno made a model of the dome, which is more magnificent and more developed than that of San Giovanni dei Fiorentini. Unlike that church, Sant'Andrea is embedded in the midst of the old city and the dome was not meant to be seen simultaneously with the parts below. Rather, it rises as an independent tempietto, an autonomous work of art with a function similar to that of a Renaissance façade: to announce the presence of the church and to dignify it by its splendor, but in no sense to match another part of the design. The dome is second to that of St. Peter's in diameter and is probably the most distinguished and beautiful of Rome's minor domes. It develops Maderno's earlier designs by borrowing from St. Peter's itself, using paired Ionic columns on the corners of the octagon that alternate with windows in the intervening bays. Its sense of serenity in the drum is coupled with a relatively vertical, pointed dome and a high lantern that make the design in some ways an improvement on its exalted model. In designing the dome, Maderno had the benefit of his new assistant, Francesco Borromini, who designed many of the exterior details with freedom and attention to optical effects. This is most notable in the lantern, where the paired columns share a single capital.

Inside, Sant'Andrea is distinguished by a series of noble clustered pilasters that were part of the old design; originally, they were plain, and Maderno continued them through the apse. This area of the vault was decorated with stuccoes and frescoes by Domenichino. The drum was given a paired-pilaster decoration similar to that of San Giovanni dei Fiorentini but the dome itself is painted. All eight windows of the drum admit light, making the church notably brighter. Early in the twentieth century the church was considerably modified with fluting in the pilasters, gilt decoration, and frescoes in the nave vaults. Originally, this church, like San Giovanni, was essentially white with cool tones of travertine and stucco.

Maderno also planned a grandiose travertine façade in the mid-1620s that was begun but soon abandoned and completed with notable modifications by CARLO RAINALDI only in the 1660s, by which time its design was something of an anachronism. Maderno's only other façade, apart from that of Santa Susanna, was for St. Peter's, where he had to follow in great measure the articulation of MICHELANGELO's exterior design.

The early history of new St. Peter's can be followed by consulting the entries under DONATO BRAMANTE, Sangallo, and Michelangelo. In 1588–1590, della Porta built the dome according to a modified, more pointed version of Michelangelo's design. At that time, the final form of the church was still undecided; but the most powerful faction among the cardinals preferred a nave in order to cover the hallowed ground of Constantine's basilica as well as to provide needed room for a sacristy and a choir for the canons. Nevertheless, a vocal group still wanted to preserve the integrity of the Bramante–Michelangelo centralized design; and a few pious souls actually wanted to shore up what remained of the decaying early Christian nave, which stood until 1605–1606. Pope Paul V Borghese, elected in 1605, determined to finish the church and soon took the advice of his newly founded Congregation of Works to build a nave and façade. Although Maderno must have had a model of both ready by this time, he was only one of several competitors for the greatest architectural commission of the age. Even when his façade model was chosen in September of 1607, the nave that was begun was not Maderno's but an older, narrower compromise design that was scrapped in favor of Maderno's project in April–June of 1608. Meanwhile, the façade continued, with work sometimes carried out night and day with over 700 laborers recorded on more than one occasion. Thousands of bricks, and hundreds of cartloads of travertine had to be furnished. Water welled up as they dug the southern end of the foundations; the underground spring that runs through that area caused Maderno great trouble and eventually almost destroyed Bernini's career when he built an ill-advised tower on that end and cracks began to appear below. On May 12, 1611, Paul V was able to give the benediction from the new loggia above

Maderno.
St. Peter's (façade).
Rome.
1607–1612

Maderno.
St. Peter's (engraving of façade).
Rome.
1607–1612

the entrance portal, although the loggia was still unvaulted. The entire façade with its coat of arms, inscription, and some statuary was essentially finished in 1612.

The façade of St. Peter's was originally conceived as a more sculptural version of Michelangelo's design for the flanks of the church, which Maderno continued down the exterior of his new nave. Thus, it was to be two stories high and could not have the dramatic quality of his façade for Santa Susanna. Moreover, because the pope needed a loggia for benedictions above the portal, the whole façade was essentially a screen with a narthex portico within and the loggia above, themselves formidable buildings. Maderno perhaps guided the taste of the cardinals of the *Fabbrica di San Pietro* by promoting a stucco decoration for the vault of the narthex. The five portals leading into the narthex correspond to the five great doors within, echoing Constantine's original five-aisled plan.

In 1612, the pope ordered that Maderno's façade be flanked by two campanili, whose design was an afterthought that tended to spoil the proportions of the original façade. The foundations for the north (right) campanile were begun immediately but the south foundations were begun only in 1618, and with trepidation because of the underground spring or river. When digging was underway there were earthslides that endangered the vast façade already built; "wells" were constructed and piles, tiles, bricks, and sandbags were poured into the foundations in 1619. Nevertheless, construction terminated at the height of the attic; Maderno's actual campanili, known from an engraving by Mattheus Greuter, were never built.

Maderno's huge, three-bay nave (1609–1616) originally was built in brick and stucco with granite columns and travertine details. The brick floor of the nave was lower than the marble pavement of the crossing, just as the vault of the nave was higher than that of the crossing to the west. Maderno presumably sought to differentiate his addition and to preserve some sense of the integrity of the central building that Michelangelo had left. Maderno lighted the nave with six vault windows. It is articulated with paired pilasters, continuing the pairing begun by the earlier architects. Off the first bays attached to the older church, Maderno built a huge choir chapel at the left and a sacrament chapel to the right, which were then decorated with stuccoes and other rich ornaments. Although the nave of St. Peter's is Maderno's most important interior design and one of the largest vaulted spaces built before the nineteenth century, it was largely based on what was already there. The piers and arches follow the previous design in order to achieve a reasonably unified space. Maderno seems to have been eager to preserve the old central design, however, since earlier projects (including one that presumably was in consideration when the façade was begun) show the eastern arm of the unfinished central church partially closed to make it correspond to the apse in the west, which would have decisively broken the interior spatial continuity between the new addition and the sixteenth-century building. Maderno's success can be gauged by the fact that only a tiny fraction of the visitors to St. Peter's have any idea that a decisive change in plan was made at the juncture of the nave with the centralized crossing area.

Maderno's aisles, which are relatively narrow, open upward into high spaces crowned with oval

Maderno.
St. Peter's (nave).
Rome.
1609–1616

domes whose lanterns project high above the roof to bring in light, thus avoiding the dark aisles of contemporary churches like San Giovanni dei Fiorentini or Santa Maria in Vallicella. Since the chapels off the aisles were for different purposes and were of different depths—only the center bay actually has an altar giving directly off the aisle—Maderno gave the larger chapels façades matching the altars of the central chapel. The width of the nave was dictated by the older church, as was its essential height. Because of the large chapels desired for the choir and sacrament, Maderno's aisles were essentially made up of the space left in between; but he disguised their functional quality through the use of impressive oval vaults, columnar tabernacle-niches, and visual tricks that seem to join the architecture of the aisles with the actual altar-tabernacles of the old church.

The rich decoration of pavement, sculpture, marble, gilt, and mosaic was all added later, but the elaborately coffered stucco vault of the nave was part of Maderno's design and is one of his most impressive achievements, avoiding the sometimes niggling detail of his earlier decorative ornament.

In addition to the immense work of design and construction for the nave and façade, Maderno was also in charge of decoration in the crossing that may have had a lasting influence on the appearance of the church, even though its present appearance is essentially the result of Bernini's activities in the 1620s and later. The present pavement is high above the original level of Constantine's basilica. In order to make contact with the site of St. Peter's grave, Maderno designed curving stairs leading down to the lower level, built 1615–1617. The stairs were a version of those that he had designed for Santa Susanna but on a far larger scale, and the balustrade around this space is directly before the high altar with its famous baldachin designed and built by Bernini around 1624–1632. The baldachin seems to have had at least two predecessors designed by Maderno—large but more conventional canopies that seemed to be held up by stucco angels with staves (1606). Maderno may also have proposed a design using twisted columns, based on the "Salomonic" marble columns from old St. Peter's, and with a suspended canopy above. Although that design is lost, it was mentioned by Borromini many years later and presumably influenced the bronze monument that was slowly erected in the 1620s. Borromini, who was prejudiced against Bernini, implied that the new pope, Urban VIII Barberini had his favorite, Bernini, construct Maderno's project. But there is no doubt that the crowning feature of the baldachin as built was a new design of around 1630, and the great monument as it now stands has no relationship to Maderno's style apart from the coats of arms on the bases.

Although Maderno's designs for the piazza were not extensive, he projected a fountain-pool around the obelisk and rebuilt the old fountain at one corner of the inchoate piazza, a design that was so successful that Bernini kept it when he built the actual piazza in the 1650s, moving it up to the cross-axis of the obelisk and building a duplicate to the south, with bigger pools below. Maderno's design (1609) used the old (antique) basin and capped it with a scaled, mushroom-shaped top. The water, fed by a new aqueduct, the Acqua Paola, erupted from the fountain with unprecedented force, splashing down over the domed shape into the old basin and down into the pool below. Informed writers considered it to be the most beautiful fountain in Europe, and it has often been copied and imitated as the most successful, purely architectural fountain in history.

Under Paul V, Maderno was architect of St. Peter's but not the Borghese family architect. From the beginning, they had employed FLAMINIO PONZIO and then the Dutchman Hans van Zanten (GIOVANNI VASANZIO), who was less experienced. As a consequence, Maderno became active in the family building program as an experienced consultant, collaborator, and even as an architect; he seems to have been at least partially responsible for the new long wing of the Borghese family palace with its hanging garden and loggia facing the Ripetta port, built 1612–1614. The wing is a new development in Roman city architecture and reflects the desire of city dwellers to live in a more relaxed, villalike manner. The extension juts out like the prow of a ship toward the Tiber, where it was given a rusticated façade like a villa portal or gate. Above, two stories of arches originally open, gave out to the view and the garden, like the casino of a country villa. Elements normally reserved for a private courtyard-garden now spilled out into the open toward the picturesque port, which was destroyed in the nineteenth century.

An analogous design was built in an actual city garden for Cardinal Borghese next to the Quirinal Palace of the pope, which was the usual summer headquarters of the papacy. There, above the ruins of the Baths of Constantine, a series of gardens and casinos were constructed around a central palace complex. Maderno was presumably responsible for the Casino dell'Aurora (1612), so named after the famous fresco by Guido Reni within. The picturesque red columns and arch together with the stucco-framed reliefs make it a richer, more gracious design than that of the Palazzo Borghese or the Mattei courtyard. Ponzio and Vasansio presumably contributed to the design as well, and the arched motif had been used by the Florentine artist-architect Ludovico Cardi (Il Cigoli), who also worked at the garden after having competed unsuccessfully for the commission to finish St. Peter's. The complex is now known as the Palazzo Rospigliosi-Pallavicini (1611–1613). The Casino looks out at a pool, originally larger, and the whole hanging garden is approached through another version of the double, curved stairs that Maderno used so often.

He also continued and essentially completed the Quirinal Palace itself with its fourth wing on the present via del Quirinale (1613–1617). He built the huge Cappella Paolina there with a coffered, stuccoed barrel vault designed by Martino Ferrabosco, and the Sala dei Corrazzieri, which was decorated with frescoed friezes by Giovanni Lanfranco and others. Under Urban VIII, Maderno continued this work, enlarging the piazza and building a defensive tower where the Datary joined on the west. He presumably also designed fountains in the gardens there as well as in the Vatican gardens, where the decorations have been attributed generically to him; but just what part he played among the large group of designers is not certain.

Maderno's official duties did not prevent him from doing extensive work for other patrons, both ecclesiastical and domestic. He seems to have collaborated with Marchese Vincenzo Giustiniani, himself an architectural amateur, in his Villa at Bassano Romano (formerly Bassano di Sutri) in the years after 1600, and he may also have helped design the centralizing church built there around 1620–1641. Maderno's name has been associated with the small aisleless Church of Sant'Ambrogio della Massima, which has a large central crossing and a concealed dome (1606–1622; finished later). He surely designed and built Santa Maria della Vittoria (c.1608–1612; façade by GIOVANNI BATTISTA SORIA, 1625–1627). The aisleless church is now famous as the site of Bernini's Cornaro Chapel in the left transept.

Maderno's most important work outside of Rome was for San Domenico in Perugia, where he replaced the collapsed Gothic nave vaults and interior after others had failed. A new model was made in 1621; work continued for ten years. He kept the basic system of supports and openings, substituting piers faced with paired Ionic pilasters and facing the existing transept with a version of the same motif. He seems to have lowered the aisles, walling up old windows higher in the outside walls. Despite its odd origins, the interior gives an excellent example of Maderno's plain, Counter-Reformation style of architecture since it has not received later adornment.

Maderno was in demand as a designer of chap-

Maderno. Palazzo Baberini. Rome. 1626–1628 (completed by Bernini)

els. He completed della Porta's project for the Aldobrandini Chapel in Santa Maria sopra Minerva (after 1602), added the high-altar chapel to Santa Maria della Pace in 1611–1614 at the expense of Gaspar Rivaldi, and in 1612–1614 designed and built the large Aldobrandini Chapel off the old Ravenna Cathedral (entrance changed when a new church was constructed in the eighteenth century).

Maderno was evidently proud of his feat of detaching the last colossal monolithic column from the ancient Basilica of Maxentius and Constantine, transporting it to the Piazza di Santa Maria Maggiore in 1613–1614, and re-erecting it on a new base. A statue of the Virgin was placed on top in 1614. The fountain below was also Maderno's design, now altered.

Maderno played large but unspecified parts in the construction or continuation of a number of private palaces, including the enlarged palace (now Chigi) for the Aldobrandini on the Corso at Piazza Colonna (1616 on), remodeled after 1660, and the Palazzo Ludovisi (now Chigi-Odescalchi) in Piazza Santi Apostoli (1622–1623). During the brief reign of Pope Gregory XV Ludovisi (1621–1623), Maderno worked for the family at their villa at Frascati (previously Altemps, later Torlonia), building the long, straight line of wall fountains at the bottom of a pre-existing waterfall, now badly damaged and restored. A long line of spouting vases and tritons in niches made this a spectacular sight, recorded in engravings. He also remodeled the garden buildings and palace of the new Villa Ludovisi (now largely destroyed) on the Pincian Hill, near the present via Vittorio Veneto (1621–1623). The villa palace had an elaborate approach from a hill in front over a hanging entrance court and was faced with a two-story false façade of pilasters and pilaster strips in the center, with projecting wings left relatively unadorned.

Some of these features appear in the most problematic and important of Maderno's late works, the Palazzo Barberini on the Quirinal (1626/1628–), which was completed by Bernini after Maderno's death with the help of Borromini and perhaps of Cortona. Like other papal families, the Barberini set about creating a family palace after the election of Urban VIII in 1623. They purchased an old palace on the outskirts of Rome near the Quirinal Palace, in a garden that had once belonged to Cardinal Rodolfo Pio da Carpi, which had been one of the great collections of antiquities in the mid-sixteenth century. In the 1580s, the Fontana had probably worked on this palace, which then belonged to Marchese Paolo Sforza. The Barberini purchased the property in 1625/1626 and began to plan for its extension. But Urban VIII had long since made it clear that he did not wholly approve of Maderno's projects, and a number of semiprofessional and even dilettantish plans and proposals were submitted. Maderno himself designed a palace that would have risen from the present Piazza del Tritone to join the long palace above. In the end, the new palace used that wing as the north side of an H-shaped palace that in some ways resembles a villa. The façade itself is not on a street but set back in a garden. Moreover, instead of a flat façade, as was customary, the central section is set back from the sides and displays three stories of arcades, open below to allow coaches to enter a covered atrium, closed above. The top arcade is closed down with perspective inserts as in the entrance to the stairs of the Palazzo Mattei.

The plan is as novel as the elevation. The old left wing was attached to the new and was given access through a square stairway with a large central well. On the other side of the central arcade is a spiral stair of oval plan—again, features that seem to belong more to a country villa than to a city palace. The main floor has a huge, two-story *salone* that gives onto a rear room of oval plan. The rear garden façade opens up the short axis of this oval and leads out to the gardens behind over a bridge, as at the Villa Ludovisi nearby. The garden façade itself is a kind of triumphal arch motif set onto the undistinguished long rear façade, but the meaning of that façade was changed later in the century when a carriageway was put through the center of the main block, rising up into the garden behind.

Preliminary drawings in Borromini's hand, one with numerals written by Maderno, prove that planning for the actual palace was done under Maderno's direction, although he was presumably not responsible for all of the novel aspects of the design, which was altered in a number of minor ways after construction began in December 1628. Since Maderno died on January 31, 1629, he was not the supervisor; his successor was Gianlorenzo Bernini, who was not a professional architect, and control seems to have wavered between him and various subordinates, including Borromini, who resigned from all responsibility in 1632 before work was finished. Thus, both the design and the construction reveal divisions of authority, and although the main façade seems like a unified and indeed successful and novel design, other parts of the building, notably the rear and the upper portions, were built with little concern for aesthetic effect.

The Palazzo Barberini, like all of Maderno's architecture, shows both novel and traditional elements. The articulation of the façade (windows, columns) derives essentially from the Palazzo Farnese, the greatest Roman papal palace. Such derivation was both iconographically and stylistically understandable. The arches in the center may at some preliminary stage have been conceived as open, as one anonymous project recommended. As drawn by Borromini and as built, the windows light the *salone*.

The Palazzo Barberini is in one sense related to the Borghese garden-palace built near the Quirinal Palace; unlike it, the Barberini is more palace than villa and has qualities that may even derive from the Quirinal Palace itself since that building for years had an open U-shaped courtyard without a street façade (until Maderno himself added it). In addition, the Palazzo Barberini, by accident or on purpose, faced west toward St. Peter's and the Vatican, establishing a symbolic relationship between the seat of papal power and the family palace across the lower city between.

As built, many features modify the original design and show the personalities of Bernini and Borromini, including the famous top floor windows flanking the west arcade. The oval room may have been suggested by Bernini since he used the form twice in the early 1630s as well as later. In other respects, too, Bernini may have been the real architect of the palace: it was he whom the pope trusted above all others and its was Bernini, not Maderno, who was credited by Filippo Baldinucci as being the architect of the palace.

Maderno's achievements rank him as a great architect, certainly the best of his generation in Italy. It was his fate to be succeeded by men of authentic genius like Bernini and Borromini who made his achievements seem conventional and old-fashioned. Nevertheless, it was Maderno who introduced a novel and powerful columnar architecture into Roman design, first in the façade of Santa Susanna, later in church interiors; and finally he used columns with arches on a city palace façade. His solutions to difficult problems were often ingenious and even inspired, and he continued great projects like St. Peter's with intelligence and mastery.

Maderno's personal life is almost unknown. He seems to have led the life of a distinguished man, living in his own palace near San Giovanni dei Fiorentini. He married three widows over the years but only one daughter survived him. His influence on Borromini was great; but it was perhaps his example and, above all, his encouragement and psychological support that led Borromini to revere the older man to such an extent that he insisted on being buried in his grave in San Giovanni dei Fiorentini.

HOWARD HIBBARD

WORKS

1586, Obelisk (with Domenico Fontana), Vatican City; 1587, Obelisk, San Giovanni in Laterano; 1587, Obelisk, Santa Maria Maggiore; 1589, Obelisk, Santa Maria del Popolo; 1593–1603, Santa Susanna (new façade and remodeling); *c.1595, Palazzo Salviati (completion); 1598–1617, Palazzo Mattei di Giove; 1600, Cappella Salviati, San Gregorio Magno; 1600, Santa Maria in Aquiro; c.1600–c.1608, San Giacomo degli Incurabili (façade); 1603, Santa Lucia in Selci; 1603–c.1605, Cappella Aldobrandini, Santa Maria sopra Minerva (completion); Rome. 1603–c.1620, Villa Aldobrandini, Frascati, Italy. 1606, St. Peter's (first temporary baldachin, choirscreen and wooden ciborium); 1607–1612, St. Peter's (façade); c.1608–c.1612, Santa Maria della Vittoria; 1608–1615, San Giovanni dei Fiorentini (crossing, drum, and dome); 1608–c.1628, Sant'Andrea della Valle (completed nave, began façade and built crossing, drum, and dome); 1609, Fountain, Vatican Belvedere (now changed); 1609–1616, St. Peter's (nave); 1611–1613, Borghese Garden Palace on Quirinal (Palazzo Rospigliosi-Pallavicine; with others); 1611–1614, Cappella Rivaldi, Santa Maria della Pace; Rome. 1612–1614, Aldobrandini Chapel, Ravenna Cathedral, Italy. 1612–1614, Palazzo Borghese (completion); 1613–1617, Quirinal Palace (completion); 1614, Fountain, Piazza di San Pietro; *1617, Convent, Santa Maria Maddalena dei Convertini; Rome. 1617–1624, Palazzo Barberini, Castelgandolfo, Italy. 1618–1625, Palazzo di Monte di Pietà; 1622, Palazzo Aldobrandini (Chigi: construction); Rome. 1622, Villa Ludovisi (water theater), Frascati, Italy. 1622, Villa Lodovisi; 1622–1623, Palazzo Ludovisi (Chigi-Odescalchi; later remodeled); Rome. 1625, Castelgandolfo (new construction), Italy. 1625, Palazzo-Peretti (Fiano-Almagià); *1626, Pantheon (campanili); 1626, Sant 'Ignazio (built by others); 1626–1628, Palazzo Barberini (completed by Gianlorenzo Bernini); Rome.

BIBLIOGRAPHY

BAGLIONE, GIOVANNI (1642)1935 Pages 136–139 in *Le vite de' pittori, scultori, architetti, ed intagliatori.* Reprint. Rome: Calzone.

BERGER, ROBERT W. 1974 "Garden Cascades in Italy and France: 1565–1665." *Journal of the Society of Architectural Historians* 33, no. 4:304–322.

CAFLISH, NINA 1934 *Carlo Maderno.* Munich: Bruckmann.

HIBBARD, HOWARD 1971 *Carlo Maderno and Roman Architecture: 1580–1630.* University Park: Pennsylvania State University Press.
WADDY, PATRICIA 1976 "The Design and Designers of Palazzo Barberini." *Journal of the Society of Architectural Historians* 35, no. 3:151–185.
WHITMAN, NATHAN T. 1970 "Roman Tradition and the Aedicular Façade." *Journal of the Society of Architectural Historians* 29, no. 2:108–123.
KIRWIN, W. CHANDLER 1981 "Bernini's Baldacchino Reconsidered." *Römisches Jahrbuch für Kunstgeschichte* 19:143–171.

MAEKAWA, KUNIO

Born in Niigata, Niigata Prefecture, Japan, Kunio Maekawa (1905–) graduated from Tokyo University, after which he went to France to study and work under LE CORBUSIER. After his return to Japan two years later, he worked for ANTONIN RAYMOND until 1935 when he opened his own office.

When he started to work independently, there was a strong trend of militarism in Japan, while in Europe fascism was coming to the fore. Most architects went with the trend and were looking to express nationalistic feelings in their buildings. In opposition to the trend, Maekawa tried to develop a modern architecture for Japan based on his experience in France. In that way, he had a tremendous influence on young architects; after World War II, KENZŌ TANGE, among others, worked in his office.

In the 1950s, Maekawa advocated a technical approach to architectural design, aiming at the modernization of the building industry and improving basic techniques. He used, for the first time in Japan, the curtain wall system, aluminum door sash, and precast concrete parts for the Main Office of the Nihon Sōgo Bank in Tokyo (1952).

Maekawa.
Tokyo Cultural Hall.
1961

When he designed the Harumi Cooperative Apartment House for Workers in Tokyo (1958), he tried to interpret the traditional scheme of a Japanese house to a modern skyscraper. In the same year, he designed, for the International Exhibition in Brussels, a Japanese pavilion which exposed Europeans to the refined form of modern Japanese architecture.

Two cultural halls, one in Tokyo and the other in Kyoto, are very important to Maekawa; starting from the strong influence of Le Corbusier and trying hard to find some Japanese solution to the International style, he reached the perfect expression in both concrete halls. Another example of this style are the campus buildings of the Gakushū-in College (1963) in Tokyo.

When he designed the Tokyo Kaijō Insurance Company Building in Tokyo (1974), he developed the inset ceramic tile method for the finish. A series of museums he designed recently such as the Prefectural Museums in Ohmiya (1971), Tokyo (1975), and Fukuoka (1979) are set serenely in landscaped surroundings and are finished with tiles set in precast ceramic panels.

As a member of the Japanese Architects Association, he has encouraged every effort to promote the social status of the architect as well as to establish the architect's profession firmly.

SAKA-E OHMI

WORKS

1952, Nihon Sōgo Bank Main Office, Tokyo. 1954, Kanagawa Prefecture Music Hall, Yokohama, Japan. 1958, Harumi Cooperative Apartments, Tokyo. 1960, Kyoto Cultural Hall. 1961, Tokyo Cultural Hall. 1963, Gakushū-in College, Tokyo. 1971, Saitama Prefecture Museum, Ohmiya, Japan. 1974, Tokyo Kaijō Insurance Company.

BIBLIOGRAPHY

FUJIMORI, TERUNOBU (editor) 1981 Volume 10 in *Nihon-no Kenchiku: Meiji, Taishō, Shōwa.* Tokyo.
Kenchiku. 1961 special issue.
MAEKAWA, KUNIO 1968 "My View of Architecture." *Architect: Journal of the Japanese Architects Association* Autumn.
MAEKAWA, KUNIO 1969 "European Civilization and Architecture." *Architect: Journal of the Japanese Architects Association.* Autumn.

MAGINNIS, CHARLES D.

Born in Londonderry, Ireland, Charles Donagh Maginnis (1867–1955) received his first training at the South Kensington Museum School of Art in London. He declined a position in the British Civil

Service and emigrated to America in 1885. His architectural career began in the office of William P. Wentworth, a Boston architect, about 1886. Maginnis joined the staff of EDMUND M. WHEELWRIGHT in 1888 and soon rose to the position of chief draftsman there. He established his own practice as a member of the firm Maginnis, Walsh, and Sullivan in 1898. This practice became known as Maginnis and Walsh in 1908, and, at the time of his death in 1955, was called Maginnis, Walsh, and Kennedy.

Maginnis's Boston firm quickly developed a specialty in ecclesiastical and collegiate architecture. Maginnis's first such commission resulted from his publication of an article critical of American religious architecture in a church magazine. After reading this article, a Whitinsville, Massachusetts, priest gave the young architect the chance to provide constructive criticism through the design of a parish church. Maginnis was thus launched on a long association with the Roman Catholic church; he designed churches, shrines, chapels, seminaries, convents, missions, and colleges in twenty states, Canada, Mexico, and China. He executed these works in a variety of styles—Byzantine, Lombard Gothic, English Collegiate Gothic, Italian Renaissance, and Spanish Mission Revival. His firm won two gold medals from the American Institute of Architects for excellence in ecclesiastical design—the first for the Carmelite Convent in Santa Clara, California (1925), and the second for the Trinity College Chapel in Washington (1926–1927).

Maginnis's abilities as a draftsman led to the publication of his designs in many architectural journals. He taught pen-and-ink drawing at the Cowles Art School in Boston and published a book entitled *Pen Drawing* in 1898. He wrote and lectured extensively on the architectural profession and liturgical arts.

Maginnis was active in a number of professional organizations and art societies. In recognition of his achievements, the American Institute of Architects awarded Maginnis its gold medal in 1948.

MARY N. WOODS

WORKS

1898, Church of Saint Patrick, Whitinsville, Mass. 1906–1907, Cathedral of Saint Vibiana, Los Angeles. 1914, Recitation Building, Boston College. 1922, National Shrine of the Immaculate Conception, Catholic University, Washington. 1925, Carmelite Convent, Santa Clara, Calif. 1926–1927, Trinity College Chapel, Washington. 1942, Saint Patrick's Cathedral (altar and baldacchino), New York. 1952, Chapel of Our Lady of the Airways, Logan Airport, Boston. 1955, Cathedral of Mary Our Queen, Baltimore.

BIBLIOGRAPHY

B., C.H. 1915 "Charles D. Maginnis." *The Brickbuilder* 24:76.

BAXTER, SYLVESTER 1923 "A Selection from the Works of Maginnis and Walsh: Architects." *Architectural Record* 53:93–115.

BYRNE, BARRY 1935 "An Appreciation." *Liturgical Arts* 5:90–104.

PRATT, HENRY T. 1898 "Charles D. Maginnis." *Brochure Series* 4:11–15.

WALSH, ROBERT P., and ROBERTS, ANDREW W. (editors) 1956 *Charles Donagh Maginnis: A Selection of His Essays and Addresses.* New Haven: Yale University.

MAGNANI FAMILY

The most famous member of the Magnani family of painters, sculptors, and architects was Giovan Battista Magnani (1571–1653). He and his teacher, GIOVANNI BATTISTA ALEOTTI, were Parma's leading early baroque architects. Together, they built the severely prismatic Church of Santa Maria del Quartiere (1604–1619), whose form prepares a historical precedent for the later architecture of GUARINO GUARINI. Giovan Battista initially created altars and tombs, as had his father Nicostrato (1532–c.1611), but in 1622 he was named city architect. He is known for his Chiostro della Fontana, San Paolo (1613–1624), the Palazzo del Comune (1627–1629), and the Arco di San Lazzaro (1628), all in Parma. His son and follower Carlo (?–1673) built the octagonal Church of Sant'Elisabetta (1628) in the same city.

GARY M. RADKE

WORKS

1604–1619, Santa Maria del Quartiere; 1613–1624, Chiostro della Fontana, San Paolo; *1627–1629, Palazzo del Comune; 1628, Arco di San Lazarro; 1628, Sant'Elisabetta; Parma. Italy.

BIBLIOGRAPHY

WITTKOWER, RUDOLF (1958)1973 *Art and Architecture in Italy 1600 to 1700.* 3d ed., rev. Harmondsworth, England: Penguin.

MAGNE, AUGUSTE

Serving the City of Paris as inspector general of architectural works, Auguste Magne (1816–1885) developed the *marché* (market) form. His Théâtre de Vaudeville (1873) was the prototype Parisian theater wrapped in the building fabric of the *immeuble.* He published a roofing handbook, *Traité Pratique de Couverture,* which included specifications for all materials and a glossary of technical terms.

ELIZABETH MCLANE

WORKS

1873, Théâtre de Vaudeville; n.d., Church of Saint-Bernard; Paris. n.d., Albert Hospice and Chapel, Cantal, France.

BIBLIOGRAPHY

L'Architecture 1910 23, no. 2:16.

Bauchal, Ch. 1887 Page 695 in *Dictionnaire des Architectes Français.* Paris: André.

"Eglise Saint-Bernard de la Chapelle." 1886 Volume 4, pages 163–192 in *Edifices Religieux.* Paris: Imprimerie Chaix.

Inventaire Général des Oeuvres d'Art, Appartenant à la Ville de Paris. Paris: Imprimerie Chaix.

Mongraphie du Nouveau Théâtre du Vaudeville érigé par la Ville de Paris sous la Direction de M. A. Magne. 1873 Paris: Ducher.

"Théâtre du Vaudeville." 1878 Volume 1, pages 60–66 in *Edifices Civils.* Paris: Imprimerie Chaix.

"Hôtel de Ville." 1889 Volume 2, pages 11–118 in *Edifices Civils.* Paris: Imprimerie Chaix.

MAGNE, LUCIEN

Like his father, AUGUSTE MAGNE, Lucien Magne (1849–1916) served the city of Paris as architect-surveyor and designed markets (*marchés*). His principal activity was research, publication, and teaching of the manufacture and use of antique and traditional building materials. He was a professor at the Ecole des Beaux-Arts and at the Conservatoire des Arts et Métiers in Paris.

ELIZABETH MCLANE

WORKS

1888, House, Rue Etienne Marcel, Paris. n.d., Palais de Justice (restoration), Poitiers, France.

BIBLIOGRAPHY

MAGNE, LUCIEN 1889 *L'Architecture Française du Siècle.* Paris: Firmin-Didot.

MAGNE, LUCIEN 1898 *Conservatoire des Arts et Métiers, créé par le Décret du 10 mars, 1898, Professeur Lucien Magne.* Paris.

Edward and Thomas Mahoney. Pah Homestead. Auckland, New Zealand. 1877

MAGNOCAVALLO, FRANCESCO OTTAVIO

Francesco Ottavio Magnocavallo (1707–1789), noble and architect, was born in Casale Monferrato and died in Moncalvo, Piedmont, Italy. Magnocavallo first studied law in Turin and only came to architecture in his thirties. His works show a knowledge of Lombardy and the Veneto. He wrote a number of works on architecture. His buildings were in sober opposition to the rococo manner of GIOVANNI BATTISTA SCAPITTA, his predecessor in Casale.

HENRY A. MILLON

WORKS

1736, San Vincenzo Martyr, Casorzo, Italy. 1752–?, Assunta, Balzola, Italy. 1756–1758, Madonna delle Grazie, Moncalvo, Italy. 1758, San Croce (unfinished façade), Casale Monferrato, Italy. 1776–1780, San Eusebio, Varengo, Italy.

BIBLIOGRAPHY

BAUDI DI VESME, A. 1966 Volume 2, pages 639–640 in *Schede Vesme.* Turin, Italy: Società piemontese di archeologia e belle arte.

BRAYDA, CARLO; COLI, LAURA; and SESIA, DARIO 1963 *Ingegneri e architetti del sei e settecento in Piemonte.* Turin, Italy: Società Ingegneri e Architetti.

CARBONERI, NINO 1963 Volume 1, pages 75–76 in *Architettura, Mostra del Barocco Piemontese.* Turin, Italy: Catalogo a cura di Vittorio Viale.

OLIVERO, EUGENIO 1940 "Il conte Magnocavalli architetto di Casale Monferrato, 1707–1789." *Palladio* 4:223–234.

TORNIELLI, V. 1957 *Architetture di Otto Secoli del Monferrato.* Casale Monferrato, Italy: the author.

MAHONEY, EDWARD and MAHONEY, THOMAS

Edward Mahoney (1825–1895) was born in Cork, Ireland, and trained there under an architect uncle. He emigrated first to South Australia and then, in 1856, to Auckland, New Zealand, where he practiced as a designer-builder and, from 1870, solely as an architect. His son, Thomas Mahoney (1854–1923), having joined the practice in the mid-1870s, traveled in Europe and the United States of America in 1884. Edward Mahoney designed many churches of different denominations while his son was more notable for houses and commercial buildings, often Italianate in character. Edward

Mahoney's wooden Gothic churches show a fine grasp of structural form.

JOHN STACPOOLE

WORKS

1861, Church of Saint John the Baptist, Parnell, New Zealand. 1866, Saint Mary's Convent Chapel; *1871, Choral Hall; Auckland, New Zealand. 1872, Saint George's Church, Thames, New Zealand. *1875, Theatre Royal; 1877, Pah Homestead, Auckland, New Zealand. 1879, Saint Stephen's Church, Ponsonby, New Zealand. 1880, Church of the Holy Sepulchre; *1881, Kilbryde Homestead; 1884–1885, Saint Patrick's Cathedral (nave); Auckland, New Zealand. 1887, Church of the Assumption, Onehunga, New Zealand. 1888, Government Offices (the customhouse); 1888, Saint Benedict's Church; Auckland, New Zealand. 1890, Dilworth Terrace, Parnell, New Zealand. 1907–1908, Saint Patrick's Cathedral (tower and transepts); 1909, Baradene School; Auckland, New Zealand.

BIBLIOGRAPHY

O'LEARY, GAEL 1978 "St. Mary's Convent Chapel." *Bulletin of New Zealand Art History* 6:18–29.

STACPOOLE, JOHN 1976 *Colonial Architecture in New Zealand.* Wellington: Reed.

MAHONY, MARION

See GRIFFIN, MARION MAHONY.

MAIANO, GIULIANO DA

The second generation of Florentine architects of the Italian Renaissance is distinguished by the relaxation of the architectural principles formulated by FILIPPO BRUNELLESCHI. In the case of Giuliano da Maiano (1432–1490), this takes the form of a highly ornamented and sculpturally rich architectural style in small-scale works. Although his skills do not match those of his near contemporary Giuliano da Sangallo (see SANGALLO FAMILY), his work at Faenza and Naples is of special interest and value as evidence of the spread of Renaissance ideals throughout Italy.

Born near Florence, Giuliano was a carpenter and intarsia worker. He seems to have begun work as an architect when still quite young. The upper floor of the Palazzo Strozzino, Florence (1462), and the Chapel of Santa Fina, San Gimignano (1466), suggest that he had looked carefully at the work of Brunelleschi and MICHELOZZO DI BARTOLOMMEO. Giuliano's taste was drawn to the sculptural. A work like the Palazzo Spannocchi, Siena (1473), recalls LEON BATTISTA ALBERTI's Palazzo Rucellai, Florence, but Giuliano ignored the learned classical quotations of the Rucellai in favor of the charm of the deep-jointed rustication. An interesting revision of the Brunelleschian vocabulary can be seen in the portico he built for Brunelleschi's Pazzi Chapel (1472). The skeletal form of the interior provides the frame for the design of the vault but the texture is dense, lush and deeply cut and quite dissimilar from the interior.

In 1474, Giuliano was invited to Faenza, near Bologna, where he began work on the Cathedral. Giuliano's effort to create a spare, monumental interior in the manner of Brunelleschi presented him with the difficulty of matching his sculptural style to the large-scale composition. The nave elevation with its alternating piers and columns is extremely eccentric but its combination with the sail vaults is bizarre indeed. The vaults may reflect a compromise with the Venetian traditions of northern Italian architecture or an adoption of a favorite Brunelleschian form. In any case, Giuliano seemed unable or unwilling to articulate the nave with a massiveness commensurate with the size of the building. The nave seems spindly and awkward rather than monumental or assured. In this respect we may compare the nave of Faenza to DONATO BRAMANTE's choir and crossing of Santa Maria delle Grazie, Milan, where a similar attempt was made to enlarge the Brunelleschian vocabulary in size.

In 1485, Giuliano was invited to Naples where he worked for Alfonso II. He built a gate, the Porta Capuana, and for Prince Alfonso he began work on the villa of Poggioreale outside Naples. The plan is rectangular with corner pavilions opening onto sumptuous gardens. Along with Giuliano da Sangallo's Poggio a Caiano, it is one of the most important early Renaissance villas. It is based on a careful reading of the classical sources (Pliny) and on careful consultation with other noble families in Italy (the Montefeltro in Urbino, the Gonzaga in Mantua, the Medici in Florence), for whom similar princely residences were then under construction. Other architects, notably FRANCESCO DI GIORGIO MARTINI and FRA GIOCONDO, also contributed to the work. Despite its subsequent neglect and ultimate destruction in the nineteenth century, Poggioreale was most important. Elements of its design were later reused by BALDASSARE PERUZZI in the construction of the Villa Farnesina, Rome (1509–1511). With all the outside advice and discussion concerning Poggioreale it is not surprising that the nature of Giuliano da Maiano's contribution has yet to be made clear. It is suspected that his direct influence on the design was relatively small.

An event that sheds much light on Giuliano's attitude toward the Brunelleschian tradition took place in 1486. Brunelleschi, on his death, had left the Church of Santo Spirito, Florence, incomplete.

His plans had provided for an unusual entrance of four doors that would have given the viewer a series of complex, oblique views down the nave and aisles; the entrance pattern arose from the plan. Giuliano da Maiano, in conjunction with a group of traditional monks, opposed this plan and over the vigorous objections of Giuliano da Sangallo a three-door solution ignoring the form of the plan and providing banal axial views triumphed. This regularization of Brunelleschi's designs suggests the kind of simplification of the work of the first generation practiced by Renaissance masters of the second generation.

Giuliano had two brothers, Giovanni da Maiano (1438–1478) and Benedetto da Maiano (1442–1497), both of whom were sculptors. Benedetto, the more distinguished of the two, was associated with Giuliano on a number of occasions (Faenza, San Gimignano, and Naples). He began his career in the shop of the sculptor Desiderio da Settignano and later worked for Antonio Rossellino. The Mastroguidici Altar, Santa Anna dei Lombardi, Naples (completed 1489), is one of the most noted of his works. The central panel involves an elaborate perspective relief, and richly sculpted architectural ornament is used throughout. Richard Goldthwaite (1973) has convincingly demonstrated that the one architectural work traditionally ascribed to Benedetto da Maiano, the Strozzi Palace, Florence, is largely the work of Simone del Pollaiuolo, known as IL CRONACA.

NICHOLAS ADAMS

WORKS

GIULIANO DA MAIANO

1462, Palazzo Strozzino (upper story), Florence. 1466, Chapel of Santa Fina, Collegista of San Gimignano, Italy. 1470, Church of Santissima Fiore e Lucilla, Arezzo, Italy. 1472, Pazzi Chapel (portico), Church of Santa Croce, Florence. 1473, Palazzo Spannocchi, Siena, Italy. Begun 1474, Faenza Cathedral, Italy. 1481, Santa Maria (largely obliterated), Loreto, Italy. 1485, Porta Capuana; *1487–1492, Villa of Poggioreale; Naples, Italy.

BENEDETTO DA MAIANO

?–1489, Santa Anna dei Lombardi (Mastroguidici Altar), Naples, Italy. Begun 1489, Strozzi Palace (completed 1539 by Il Cronaca), Florence.

BIBLIOGRAPHY

GOLDTHWAITE, RICHARD A. 1973 "The Building of the Strozzi Palace: The Construction Industry in Renaissance Florence." *Studies in Medieval and Renaissance History* 10:94–194.

HEYDENRICH, LUDWIG H. and LOTZ, WOLFGANG 1974 *Architecture in Italy 1400–1600.* Harmondsworth, England: Penguin.

MAILLART, ROBERT

Born in Bern of a Belgian father and Bernese mother, Robert Maillart (1872–1940) graduated in March 1894 from the Federal Polytechnical Institute in Zurich with a degree in civil engineering. There he had studied bridge design under perhaps the greatest teacher of bridge construction in the late nineteenth century, Wilhelm Ritter. From 1894 to 1896 he worked for the Bernese firm of Pümpin and Herzog, laying out rail lines and designing several small bridges. From 1897 to 1899 he worked for the *Tiefbauamt* in Zurich, where he designed, following Ritter's idea, his first major bridge, the Stauffacher, an unreinforced three-hinged concrete arch with a span of 39.6 meters. In 1899, he began working with the Zurich design-construction firm of Froté and Westermann and designed the first reinforced concrete bridge in Zurich over the Hadlaub street (1900) and the first hollow box of concrete for the three-hinged arch bridge over the Inn River at Zuoz (1901). There Maillart met Maria Ronconi, whom he married in 1901 in Bern, one month after the successful load test at Zuoz directed by Ritter. On February 1, 1902, he founded his own design-construction firm, Maillart & Cie., which he directed until the end of World War I. From 1902 until 1914 he built a flourishing business while designing a series of unique bridges and building forms.

In 1908, he carried out tests on beamless floor slabs supported by mushroom-topped columns. Between 1910 and 1912 he entered a series of five major Swiss bridge competitions and, although the juries never awarded his designs a first prize, he eventually got to build three of them because of the high quality of his work and his competitive price. The juries consistently praised the thoroughness of his calculations and the technical excellence of his ideas but they preferred the appearance of more conventional forms. From 1911 to 1914 he taught at the Zurich Federal Polytechnical Institute as a private docent.

In July 1914 he and his three children were forced by the war to go to St. Petersburg. Between 1912 and 1917, Maillart built a series of large industrial buildings in Russia, but the revolution closed his business and he barely escaped in 1918, returning to Geneva penniless and a widower. In Geneva he opened a design office and in 1924 opened branches in Bern and Zurich; by this time he had reestablished himself and was beginning to design new forms of startling originality. After the war he never had a house of his own and during the last decade of his life he lived alone in his Geneva office and created most of the works upon which his reputation is based.

The Salginatobel Bridge (1930) illustrates how Maillart could make a bridge design that won a design-construction competition because it was the least costly and was judged of the highest technical quality. The fact that the bridge has been judged of great beauty only confirms Maillart's goal of striving for all three aspects in each design.

His most significant works from the point of view of the integration of visual and technical excellence are the 1901 Zuoz Bridge (restored 1968), the 1902 Saint Gallen Gas Holders (the largest reinforced concrete tanks when built and the first thin shell concrete structures designed by a complete thin shell theory), the 1905 Tavanasa Bridge (the first open three-hinged, hollow-box form, destroyed by avalanche in 1927), the 1905 Wädenswil factory (completely designed inside and out by Maillart), the 1910 Giesshübel flat slab warehouse in Zurich (the first mushroom slab and two-way reinforced floor without beams), the 1911 Laufenburg Bridge over the Rhine (the first precast concrete block bridge built by Maillart's crenulated method), the 1923 Flienglibach Bridge (the first deck-stiffened arch bridge), the 1924 Chiasso shed roof (the first underslung concrete truss of gabled profile), the 1924 Châtelard aquaduct (a frame with hollow-box girder and tilted splayed columns), the 1925 Valtschielbach Bridge (Maillart's longest spanning deck-stiffened arch), the 1930 Salginatobel Bridge (his first arch bridge to be designed without any reference to masonry ideas), the 1933 Schwandbach Bridge (the first fully integrated curved-plan, deck-stiffened arch), the 1933 Thur River Bridge at Felsegg (the first broken-arch open three-hinged hollow box), the Töss River footbridge (a flat deck-stiffened arch with countercurved profile), the 1936 Arve River Bridge at Vessy (the first use of X-formed columns and one of the least expensive concrete bridges of medium span—56 meters—ever built), the 1939 Cement Hall in Zurich (one of the first roofs of medium span to express visually a concrete thin shell fully without edge members), the 1940 Lachen Bridge (an open three-hinged double hollow-box arch on a sharp skew), and the 1940 Garstatt Bridge (the first open hollow-box arch to be built entirely of a straight-line profile).

Maillart's major new forms, the open three-hinged, hollow-box arch, the mushroom slab, and the deck-stiffened arch illustrate at least three of the fundamentally radical ideas he expressed about twentieth-century structures: first, that mathematical analysis must be as simple as possible and that design should be based primarily on the record of full-scale observation of completed works; second, that design thinking is inseparable from construction practice and that design innovations generally come from designers who are also builders; and third, that even though aesthetic choices are constrained by material efficiency and construction economy, the sensitive designer still has a wide range of freedom. By recognizing this disciplined aesthetic freedom Maillart became one of the greatest engineer artists since the industrial revolution.

David P. Billington

Maillart.
Valtschielbach Bridge.
Donath, Switzerland.
1925

WORKS

1899, Sihl River Bridge (Stauffacher); 1900, Hadlaub Street Bridge; Zurich. 1901, Inn River Bridge, Zuoz, Switzerland. 1902, Saint Gallen Gas Holders, Switzerland. 1904, Thur River Bridge, Billwil-Oberüren, Switzerland. *1905, Rhine River Bridge, Tavanasa, Switzerland. 1905, Wädenswil Factory, Switzerland. 1910, Giesshübel Warehouse, Zurich. 1910, Unterwasser Canal, Wyhlen, Switzerland. 1911, Rhine River Bridge, Laufenburg, Switzerland. 1912, Aare River Bridge, Aarburg, Switzerland. 1912, Rhine River Bridge, Rheinfelden, Switzerland. 1913, Muota River Bridge, Vorder Ibach, Switzerland. 1923, Flienglibach Bridge, Waggital, Switzerland. 1924, Eau-Noire Bridge, Châtelard, Switzerland. 1925, Valtschielbach Bridge, Donath, Switzerland. 1930, Aare River Bridge, Bern, Switzerland. 1930, Landquart River Bridge, Klosters, Switzerland. 1930, Salginatobel Bridge, Schiers, Switzerland. 1932, Rossgraben Bridge, near Schwarzenburg, Switzerland. 1932, Traubach Bridge, Habkern-Bohl, Switzerland. 1933, Schwandbach Bridge, Hinterfultigen, Switzerland. 1933, Thur River Bridge, Felsegg, Switzerland. 1934, Aare River Bridge, Innertkirchen, Switzerland. 1934, Toss River Footbridge, Wulflingen-Winterthur, Switzerland. 1935, Birs River Bridge, Liesberg, Switzerland. 1936, Arve River Bridge, Vessy, Switzerland. 1937, Lutschine River Bridge, Gründlischwand, Switzerland. 1939, Cement Hall, Zurich. 1940, Railroad Overpass, Altendorf, Switzerland. 1940, Railroad Overpass, Lachen, Switzerland. 1940, Simme River Bridge, Garstatt, Switzerland.

BIBLIOGRAPHY

ABEL, JOHN F.; BILLINGTON, DAVID P.; and MARK, ROBERT (editors) 1973 *The Maillart Papers From the Second National Conference on Civil Engineering: History, Heritage and the Humanities.* 2d ed. N.J.: Princeton University Press.

BILL, MAX (1948)1969 *Robert Maillart.* 3d ed. Zurich: Verlag für Architekture.

BILLINGTON, DAVID P. 1979 *Robert Maillart's Bridges: The Art of Engineering.* N.J.: Princeton University Press. Includes a list of most of Robert Maillart's writings as well as all of his known major bridges.

GIEDION, SIGFRIED (1941)1967 *Space, Time and Architecture: The Growth of a New Tradition.* 5th ed. Cambridge, Mass.: Harvard University Press.

MAILLART, ROBERT 1901 "Das Hennebique-System und seine Anwendungen." *SBZ* 37:225–226.

MAILLART, ROBERT 1909 "Die Sicherheit der Eisenbetonbauten." *SBZ* 53:119–120.

MAILLART, ROBERT 1922–1923 "De la construction de galeries sous pression interieure." *Bulletin technique de la suisse romande* 48:256–260, 271–274; 49:41–45, 53–58.

MAILLART, ROBERT 1924 "Der Schubmittelpunkt." *SBZ* 83:109–111.

MAILLART, ROBERT 1926 "Zur Entwicklung der unterzuglosen Decke in der Schweiz und in Amerika." *SBZ* 87:263–265.

MAILLART, ROBERT (1930)1931 "Masse oder Qualität im Betonbau." *SBZ* 98:149–150.

MAILLART, ROBERT 1931*a* "Die Lorraine-Brücke über die Aare in Bern." *SBZ* 97:1–3, 17–20, 23–26, 47–49.

MAILLART, ROBERT 1930*b* "Leichte Eisenbeton-Brücken in der Schweiz." *Der Bauingenieur* 12:165–171.

MAILLART, ROBERT 1934 "Gekrümmte Eisenbeton-Bogenbrücken." *SBZ* 103:132–133.

MAILLART, ROBERT 1935 "The Construction and Aesthetic of Bridges." *The Concrete Way* 7:303–309. Translation with some modifications of an article in *Le Genie civil,* 106:262.

MAILLART, ROBERT 1938*a* "Aktuelle Fragen des Eisenbetonbaues." *SBZ* 111:1–5.

MAILLART, ROBERT 1938*b* "Ueber Eisenbeton-Brücken mit Rippembögen unter Mitwitkung des Aufbaues." *SBZ* 112:287–293.

ROS, M. 1940 "Robert Maillart: Ingenieur, 1872–1940." In *Schweizerischer Verband fur die Materialprufungen der Technik.* Zurich.

MAILLIER, NICOLAS

Apart from the record of his having exhibited a project for an opera house at the 1781 Salon de la Correspondance, Nicolas Maillier (1745?–?) is known only as the author of two treatises written as guides to architectural taste for the nonspecialist. His *L'Architecture* (1781), a didactic poem treating the orders, planning, and architectural history is one of the most original examples of this genre. Maillier's thought in general followed the teachings of the Académie Royale d'Architecture as codified by JACQUES-FRANÇOIS BLONDEL. The Académie reviewed manuscripts of both of Maillier's works, and he may have had a sponsor among the academicians.

RICHARD CLEARY

BIBLIOGRAPHY

Nicolas Maillier's unpublished manuscript, "Architecture raisonneé dans sa théorie: ou, dissertations méthodiques sur la composition de cet art . . . 1770," is in the Avery Architectural Library, Columbia University, New York.

MALLIER, NICOLAS 1781 *L'Architecture, poëme, en trois chants.* Paris: The Author.

MAILLOU, JEAN BAPTISTE

Jean Baptiste Maillou (1668–1753) was a Quebec stonemason who learned architecture under Claude Baillif, a builder-architect in the colony of New France. Jean Baptiste's brother Joseph was his partner, and their library, which contained the works of VITRUVIUS and GIACOMO BAROZZI DA VIGNOLA, instructed them in the classical orders and decoration. Thanks to this knowledge and their practical skills, the Maillou brothers were engaged to build and enlarge the homes of government officials and leading merchants in the colonial capital.

After Joseph's death in 1702, Jean Baptiste became the principal builder-architect in Quebec. He was entrusted with contracts for public works and fortifications, for alterations to the palaces of the governor and intendant, and for church buildings. In 1719, he received the title of king's architect, and in 1728, because of his ability as a surveyor and draftsman, he was made deputy surveyor of highways in the Quebec region. None of his sons followed his trade, but among his six known apprentices was the builder-contractor Girard Guillaume Deguise surnamed Flamand.

PETER N. MOOGK

WORKS

1702, Lower Town Battery (rebuilding), Quebec City. 1702–1708, Saint Laurent Church, Ile d'Orléans, Quebec. 1704, Juchereau Watermill, Saint-Pierre, Quebec. 1705–1707, Saint Louis Bastion; 1711, Fortifications; c.1717, Hôpital-Général; Quebec City. c.1720, Church and Rectory, Saint Nicolas, Quebec. 1726, Intendant's Palace (upper floor), Quebec City. c.1727, Saint Etienne Church, Beaumont, Quebec. 1731, Château Saint Louis (vaults), Quebec City. c.1732, Fort Saint Frédéric, Crown Point, N.Y.

BIBLIOGRAPHY

GOWANS, ALAN 1955 *Church Architecture in New France.* University of Toronto Press.

MOOGK, PETER N. 1974 "Maillou." Volume 3, pages 419–421 in *Dictionary of Canadian Biography.* University of Toronto Press; Quebec City: University of Laval Press.

MAITANI, LORENZO

The life of Lorenzo Maitani (1270?–1330) exemplifies the successful career of an early fourteenth-century architect/engineer. Son of the sculptor Vitale di Lorenzo and first documented in a Sienese tax return of 1290, Maitani received his architectural training at the Cathedral of Siena while Giovanni Pisano (see PISANO FAMILY) was the master of works in 1287–1296. Maitani rose to prominence as *capomaestro* of Orvieto Cathedral in 1310 when he was highly praised for saving the transept walls from collapse. His fifteen-year contract was renewed in 1325 and then cut short by his death in 1330. In a period when head architects often changed frequently, Maitani's long tenure at Orvieto was notable. He enlarged the transepts and constructed the ornately painted wooden roof, but his design for the cathedral's west façade stands as his major contribution to Italian Gothic architecture.

When Maitani began the decoration of Orvieto Cathedral's façade in 1310, no previous façade decoration had been built. Two extant drawings on parchment (Museo dell'Opera, Orvieto), the earliest preliminary sketches for an entire project which have survived in Italian Gothic architecture, present quite different solutions. Nevertheless, a majority of scholars regard both drawings as Maitani's work. One design, showing a single, central gable above the rose and triple portals of equal height, appears more influenced by French Gothic precedents. The other drawing, closer to the existing façade in general proportions and detail, may be the parchment listed as Maitani's in an inventory of 1356. His Sienese heritage is apparent in the triple gable scheme of the façade and the placement of bronze Evangelist symbols on the main piers, similar to those at the Cathedral of Siena, but Maitani's architectural style entirely lacks Giovanni Pisano's sculptural plasticity. With its linearity, fine-scale detail, and unique concave-surfaced piers, Orvieto's façade gives the impression of light, thin planes tautly stretched over a delicate framework. Portal jambs are veiled in rows of myriad, gilt-inlaid geometric patterns, and upper wall surfaces shimmer with mosaic scenes. The narrative reliefs flanking the portals, which remain only partially finished above the halfway mark, and the Virgin and Child with Angels on the central tympanum wre supervised by Maitani. The only documented evidence of his personal work as a sculptor is the bronze symbol of Saint John the Evangelist.

Maitani's reputation as an architect and engineer is documented by his consultations on various other projects, including the repair of aqueducts at Perugia (1317, 1319–1321), repairs at the Castle of Montefalco (1323), and plans for the Castle of Castiglione del Lago (1325). In 1322, he and four other architects provided a detailed written expertise (preserved) on work in progress at Siena Cathedral. In 1327, Maitani was charged with the restoration of Orvieto's Palazzo del Comune and the repair of the city walls, and thus, toward the end of his career, he functioned for all practical purposes as Orvieto's city architect. Maitani's influence is seen in GIOVANNI DI AGOSTINO's work at Orvieto and Siena Cathedrals and in the civic architecture of ANGELO DA ORVIETO.

KATHLEEN GILES ARTHUR

WORK

1310–1330, Orvieto Cathedral, Italy.

BIBLIOGRAPHY

BONELLI, RENATO (1952)1972 *Il Duomo di Orvieto e l'architettura italiana del Duecentro-Trecento.* Reprint. Rome: Officina.

CARLI, ENZO 1965 *Il Duomo di Orvieto.* Rome: Istituto Poligrafico dello Stato, Libreria dello Stato.

GARZELLI, ANNAROSA 1972 *Museo di Orvieto: Museo dell'Opera del Duomo.* Bologna, Italy: Edizioni Calderini.

POPE-HENNESSY, JOHN (1955)1972 *Italian Gothic Sculpture.* London: Phaidon.

WHITE, JOHN 1959 "The Reliefs on the Façade of the Duomo at Orvieto." *Journal of the Warburg and Courtauld Institutes* 22:254–302.

WHITE, JOHN 1966 *Art and Architecture in Italy 1250–1400.* Baltimore: Penguin.

MAKI, FUMIHIKO

Fumihiko Maki (1928–) was born in Tokyo, Japan, and graduated from Tokyo University in 1952. He studied at the Cranbrook Academy of Arts in 1954 and received a master's degree from the Graduate School of Design, Harvard University, in 1956. He worked for SKIDMORE, OWINGS, AND MERRILL in New York for a brief period, after which he taught at the School of Architecture, Washington University, St. Louis, Missouri, from 1956 to 1962. He taught at Harvard University from 1962 to 1965. He opened up his own office of Maki & Associates in Tokyo in 1965. Since 1979,

Maki. Hillside Terrace Apartments. Tokyo. 1967–1977

he has been a professor of architecture at Tokyo University.

His works have expressed simplicity based on the modern rationalism. Forms, however, do not simply follow his theories. Instead, Maki attempts to express space based upon a human physical scale. The Kumagaya Campus, Risshō University, and the Hillside Terrace Apartment in Tokyo all have a clear vision of building ensemble. He has been interested in the traditional character of the urban environment of his own country and has tried to interpret this character in his designs. Maki has received many prizes and awards.

HIROSHI YAMAGUCHI

WORKS

1962, Toyota Memorial Hall, Nagoya University, Japan. 1967–1977, Hillside Terrace Apartments, Tokyo. 1968, Kumagaya Campus, Risshō University, Saitama, Japan. 1971, Kanazawa Ward Office and Community Center, Yokohama, Japan. 1972, Katō Gakuen Primary School, Numazu, Shizuoka Prefecture, Japan. 1974, Austrian Embassy, Tokyo. 1975, National Aquarium, Motobumachi, Okinawa, Japan. 1979, Iwasaki Art Museum, Ibusuki, Kagoshima, Japan.

BIBLIOGRAPHY

Japan Architect 1979 54, no. 265:special issue.

MAKI, FUMIHIKO 1972 *Investigation in Collective Form.* St. Louis, Mo.: School of Architecture, Washington University.

MAKI, FUMIHIKO, ET AL. 1980 *Miegakure suru Toshi.* Tokyo: Kashima-shuppam-Kai.

Space Design 1979 no. 7906:special issue.

MALCOLMSON, REGINALD FRANCIS

Reginald Francis Malcolmson (1912–), a prominent American visionary architect, who was born in Dublin, made his most important contribution to the profession as a teacher of architects. Educated in Ireland and practicing successfully as a Dublin architect, Malcolmson left his homeland for the United States to study specifically with LUDWIG MIES VAN DER ROHE at the Illinois Institute of Technology in 1947, earning an M.S. degree in architecture in 1949. Subsequently he worked with Mies Van der Rohe, LUDWIG KARL HILBERSEIMER and KONRAD WACHSMANN on professional design projects in Chicago between 1949 and 1964.

He joined the faculty of the Department of Architecture and City Planning, Illinois Institute of Technology in 1949, continuing there through 1964. He served as dean of the College of Architecture and Design, University of Michigan, Ann Arbor, from 1964 to 1974, teaching full time until his official retirement in 1981.

His exceptional gift in teaching was the ability to realize, and then, to develop to the fullest his students' potential as young architects. Under his strict tutelage, he skillfully prodded them into high achievement. Malcolmson felt visionary architecture was the vital creative force holding the possibilities for man's future. He insisted that his students know the past and consider the future before designing in order to be responsible in the present. Throughout his articles, lectures, and exhibits, he stressed that visionary work in theory and practice produced architecture of significance. Many of his students joined distinguished firms, such as SKIDMORE, OWINGS, AND MERRILL, later attaining individual distinction.

Emphasis on his outstanding teaching career is not intended to diminish the relevance of his own visionary projects, exemplary of which are MetroLinear (1954–1962), a Theater (1949), and the Expanding Skyscraper (1960). He created precise spatial relationships by reducing elements to their essentials always discarding the unnecessary. Materials and details were elegantly expressed. His fine drawings and models have been exhibited internationally. Malcolmson's style reflects a Miesian vocabulary, but his approach to architecture, particularly with regard to academia, as an admitted 'professional visionary,' is most uncommon.

LINDA L. GRAVES

WORKS

1936–1945, Houses and Community buildings (various locations), Ireland.

BIBLIOGRAPHY

The papers and materials of Reginald F. Malcolmson are being moved to the archives of the Avery Architectural Library, Columbia University, New York.

COLLINS, GEORGE R. 1959 "Linear Planning Throughout the World." *Journal of the Society of Architectural Historians* 17, no. 3.

COLLINS, GEORGE R. 1979 *Visionary Drawings of Ar-*

chitecture and Planning: 20th Century through the 60's. Cambridge, Mass.: M.I.T. Press. Exhibition catalogue.

CHIN, PAO-CHI, and SWENSON, ALFRED 1980 *Architectural Education at I.I.T.* Chicago: Illinois Institute of Technology Press.

HILBERSEIMER, LUDWIG 1955 *The Nature of Cities.* Chicago: Theobald.

MALCOLMSON, REGINALD F. 1980 "Visionary Architecture." *Inland Architect* May.

MALEVICH, KASIMIR

Kasimir Malevich (1878–1935), a painter, was born in Kiev, Russia. He was influenced by Slavic folk art, Paul Cézanne, and Cubism. He was a pioneer of abstract art and founder of suprematism. From 1920 to 1925, he developed architectonic studies of pure form, projects for suprematist satellites orbiting in space, and a "Suprematist Skyscraper" for New York City (1926).

REGINALD MALCOLMSON

BIBLIOGRAPHY

MALEVICH, KASIMIR 1959 *The Non-objective World.* Translated by Howard Dearstyne. Chicago: Theobald.

MALLET-STEVENS, ROBERT

Robert Mallet-Stevens (1886–1945) was born in Paris. He studied there at the Ecole Speciale d'Architecture, but his two years at the Salon d'Automne (1912–1914) were more important to his career. It was there that he met FRANTZ JOURDAIN, PIERRE CHAREAU, and VICTOR BOURGEOIS with whom he later collaborated on different projects. He was in the French Air Force between 1914 and 1918, but by 1920 he had returned to Paris and set up a private practice as an architect and interior designer, becoming one of the most successful of the French rationalist architects of the 1920s and 1930s.

Although Mallet-Stevens worked mainly in Paris, he was very aware of and strongly influenced by other cultures. He had contact with the work of JOSEF HOFFMANN at an early age. He also was influenced in his early career by CHARLES RENNIE MACKINTOSH and by Japanese culture. In later years, he was introduced to and influenced by contemporary Dutch culture. Not only other cultures and artists, but also other arts played a part in his work, especially contemporary music and painting.

Robert Mallet-Stevens was a Renaissance man, and this is evident in his work: the variety of assignments he took, the different influences on his work, and also the way in which he worked and the materials he used. He designed shops and factories, private homes and apartment buildings, public buildings and offices. He designed film sets and furniture. On major commissions, Mallet-Stevens preferred to work in collaboration with other artists. In 1923, for example, he worked with Jourdain and Chareau, among others, on the villa for the comte de Noailles in Hyères, France. Two years later, he worked with Poulène, Honneger, Leger, and Robert Delaunay on the Pavilion of Tourism at the Exposition des Arts Décoratifs, Paris. At the same time, he taught at the Ecole Spéciale d'Architecture. He also was the author of numerous books and articles. Early on, Mallet-Stevens recognized the potential of steel not only as a utilitarian building material in construction but also as a source of beauty. He incorporated steel and other metals into his work even when it was not structurally necessary. Many of his houses were elaborated with metal work, and he designed metal furniture, notably the furniture in his office. In this and his other projects, he sought and attained a unity of architecture and decorative arts.

Although so many factors played a role in Mallet-Stevens's designs, he managed to balance them and achieve a simple elegance and clarity of plan. His play of form versus function which was so contemporary and broad in vision made Mallet-Stevens popular even outside Paris. He exhibited internationally—especially early in his career—in Ghent, London, and San Francisco, besides many cities throughout France.

In 1929, Mallet-Stevens became one of the founders of the Union des Artistes Modernes in Paris, and the years just before World War II were spent trying to create an international architecture.

JUDITH COHEN

WORKS

*1922, Aéro-Club de France Pavilion, Salon d'Automne; 1923, Bookshop; 1923, Cafés du Brésil (façades); Paris. 1923, Vicomte de Noailles Villa, Hyères, France. 1924, Poiret Chateau, Mezy, Seine et Oise, France. 1924, Hôtel des Roches Noires (reconstruction), Trouville, France. 1925, Alfa Romeo Building, rue Marbeuf; *1925, Pavilion of Tourism, Exposition des Arts Décoratifs; Paris. 1926, House, Boulogne-sur-Seine, France. 1926, Houses, rue Mallet-Stevens, Paris. 1926, House, Ville d'Avray, France. 1926, Frères Martel House; 1927, Mallet-Stevens House; Paris. 1928, Casino, Saint Jean de Luz, France. 1929, Apartment Building, rue Mechain; 1929, Bally Shoe Shop, Boulevard de la Madeleine; Paris. 1929, House, Pernambuco, Brazil. 1929, P. F. Department Stores Offices; 1930, Delza Shop, rue de la Paix; Paris. 1930, Government Distillery, Istanbul, Turkey. 1930, Municipal

Theater, Grasse, Alpes Maritimes, France. 1930, Shop Front, rue d'Assas, Paris. 1931, C. House, Roubaix, France. 1930, T. House, Sceaux, France. 1931, House/Studio for Glassmaker, Barillet, Paris. 1934, Houses, Roubaix, France. 1935–1936, Fire Station, rue Mesnil; *1937, Palais d'Electricité, World's Fair; Paris.

BIBLIOGRAPHY

"Architects and Their Offices: Robert Mallet-Stevens." 1928 *Architectural Record* 64:277–279.

DESHOULIÈRES, DOMINIQUE ET AL. 1977 "Mallet-Stevens." *Architecture Mouvement Continuité* no. 41:5–27.

HABASQUE, GUY 1959 "Mallet-Stevens." *L'Oeil* no. 60:100–104.

LUGNIER, MICHEL 1975 "Le Corbusier, Mallet-Stevens, Chareau et quelques autres." *Architecture Française* 36, no. 393:60–65.

MALLET-STEVENS, ROBERT 1922 *A Modern City.* London: Benn.

MALLET-STEVENS, ROBERT 1929 *Grandes Constructions.* 2 vols. Paris: Moreau.

MALLET-STEVENS, ROBERT 1934 *Pour l'Art Moderne; Cadre de la Vie Contemporaine.* Paris.

MALLET-STEVENS, ROBERT 1937 *Vitraux Modernes.* Paris: Moreau.

MALLET-STEVENS, ROBERT 1937 "Union des Artistes Modernes: Introduction." *L'Architecture d'Aujourd'hui* 6, no. 9:73.

MOUSSINAC, LÉON 1931 *Mallet-Stevens.* Paris: Crès.

RAYNAL, MAURICE 1930 *Robert Mallet-Stevens: Dix Années de Réalisations en Architecture et Décoration.* Paris: Massin.

ROBERTSON, HOWARD 1934 "House at Roubaix, France, by Robert Mallet-Stevens." *Architect and Building News* 138:375–379.

SARTORIS, ALBERTO 1930 *Robert Mallet-Stevens: Architecte.* Paris.

"Wohnhäuser an der rue Mallet-Stevens." 1965 *Werk* 52:49–51.

MALMSTEN, CARL

A fervent advocate of the Swedish tradition in furniture and crafts, Stockholm-born Carl Per Hendrik Malmsten (1888–1972) was apprenticed to the cabinetmaker Pelle Jönsson in 1910. In 1916 Malmsten won the furniture competition for RAGNAR ÖSTBERG's new City Hall in Stockholm.

As a teacher and writer, Malmsten emphasized that crafts had an important role in any curriculum. Among the schools devoted to furniture making and handicrafts which he founded are Olofskolan, Stockholm (1928), Malmstens Verkstadtsskola, Stockholm (1930), and Capellagården, Vickelby, Öland (1960).

Backed by some contemporaries, Malmsten opposed the 1930 International Exposition in Stockholm because it was a forum for internationally inspired functionalism. It was against Malmsten and the other opponents of the 1930 exhibition that ERIK GUNNAR ASPLUND, OSVALD ALMQVIST, and others directed their manifesto, "Acceptera." Although Malmsten never opposed mass production or the machine as a tool for efficiency, his unwillingness to allow the machine to wipe out the rich Swedish handicrafts tradition meant the success of Swedish interior design as a compromise between new and old.

Malmsten's furniture won a grand prize at the International Exhibition of 1925 in Paris and was exhibited prominently at the 1939 World's Fair in New York.

JUDITH S. HULL

WORKS

1916–1923, Stockholm City Hall (furniture). 1926, Grand Hotel (furniture); Stockholm. 1926, Stockholm Concert House (furniture). 1934, Council President's Room (furniture), League of Nations, Geneva. 1937, Swedish Trade Bank (furniture); 1939, Swedish Institute (furniture); Rome.

BIBLIOGRAPHY

MALMSTEN, CARL 1916 *Om Svensk karaktär i nom konstkulturen.* Stockholm: Bonnier.

MALMSTEN, CARL 1925 *Skönhet och travnad i hemmet: Det enkla svenska hemmet.* Stockholm: Bokförlaget Natur och Kultur.

MALMSTEN, CARL 1941 *Arbetsritningar till enkla möbeltyper.* Stockholm: Natur och Klutur.

MALMSTEN, CARL 1944 *Från barkbåt till eget hem, en ütstallning in Carl Malmstens regi.* Stockholm: National Museum.

MALMSTEN, CARL 1949 *Mittens rike.* Stockholm: Natur och Kultur.

MALMSTEN, CARL 1954 *Schwedische Möbel.* Basel: Wepf.

MALMSTEN, CARL 1963 *Lärlingar och Mästare.* Kalmar, Sweden: Natur och Kultur.

WENNERHOLM, ERIC 1969 *Carl Malmsten hel och hållen.* Stockholm: Bonnier.

MANETTI CIACCHERI, ANTONIO DI

The son of a debt collector, Antonio di Manetti Ciaccheri (1405–1460) first appeared in 1432 as a carpenter repairing building machines for the Florentine Cathedral works and constructing a full-scale wooden model of the stones for the closing ring of the cupola of Santa Maria del Fiore, for testing purposes. He continued at the cathedral, making intarsia furnishings for the cathedral sacristy, building models for FILIPPO BRUNELLESCHI until the 1440s, and competing, against Brunelleschi, with a lantern model of his own. Controversial and pugnacious, Manetti was the last man in Florence in the 1450s who had acquired technical abilities by direct contact with Brunelleschi. His appointment as chief master of the lantern in August 1452, replacing the disgraced MICHELOZZO DI BARTOLOMMEO, was almost a foregone conclusion. In the 1450s, Manetti rose to important executive positions in numerous projects, among them Santissima Annunziata, Santo Spirito, San Lorenzo, and the Medici Villa in Fiesole. He probably rebuilt the collapsed vault of Michelozzo's San Marco Library around 1457. In 1459–1460, he built a model of the projected chapel of the Cardinal of Portugal in San Miniato (executed by the BERNARDO ROSSELLINO shop). He was in Milan early in 1460, advising Francesco Sforza on fortress construction. His importance lies in his technical abilities with which he brought to successful completion numerous buildings left unfinished by Brunelleschi and Michelozzo.

HOWARD SAALMAN

BIBLIOGRAPHY

GAYE, GIOVANNI (editor) 1839 Volume 1, pages 167–174 in *Carteggio inedito d'artisti dei secoli XIV, XV, XVI.* Florence: Molini.

HARTT, FREDERICK; CORTI, GINO; and KENNEDY, CLARENCE 1964 *The Chapel of the Cardinal of Portugal, 1434–1459 at San Miniato in Florence.* Philadelphia: University of Pennsylvania Press.

MANCINI, GIROLAMO (1882)1967 "I due Antonio Manetti." Pages 324–327 in *Vita di Leon Battista Alberti.* 2d rev. ed. Rome: Bardi

SAALMAN, HOWARD 1966 "Tommaso Spinelli, Michelozzo, Manetti and Rosselino." *Journal of the Society of Architectural Historians* 25, Oct.:151–164.

SAALMAN, HOWARD (editor) 1970 *The Life of Brunelleschi by Antonio di Tuccio Manetti.* University Park: Pennsylvania State University Press.

SAALMAN, HOWARD 1980 *Filippo Brunelleschi: The Cupola of Santa Maria del Fiore.* London: Zwemmer.

MANGIN, JOSEPH FRANÇOIS

Probably related to a family of French architects, Joseph François Mangin (?–after 1818) first appears in New York in 1794 as an engineering adviser for the fortifications of that city. In 1796, he became a city surveyor. Although he was responsible for at least three or four other buildings of note in New York, his most significant contribution was the design of New York City Hall, the competition for which he won in 1802 in collaboration with JOHN MCCOMB, Jr., who actually executed the building.

DAMIE STILLMAN

WORKS

*(A)1795–1789, Park Theatre (with Charles Mangin); *1797, New York State Prison; 1802, New York City Hall design (with John McComb, Jr., who executed it, 1803–1812); *1809–1815, Saint Patrick's Cathedral; *1810, Wall Street Presbyterian Church; New York.

BIBLIOGRAPHY

HAMLIN, TALBOT (1944)1964 *Greek Revival Architecture in America.* New York: Oxford University Press.

STILLMAN, DAMIE 1956 "Artistry and Skill in the Architecture of John McComb, Jr." Unpublished M.A. thesis, University of Delaware, Newark.

STILLMAN, DAMIE 1964 "New York City Hall: Competition and Execution." *Journal of the Society of Architectural Historians* 23:129–142.

MANGONE FAMILY

During the latter part of the sixteenth and early seventeenth centuries, one family of woodcarvers and architects, the Mangone, was to be found working in the Duomo of Milan. Giovanni Battista Mangone (1547–1627) was active there from 1591 on the choir stalls, and one son, Giulio Cesare Mangone (1584–?) continued his work there (1606–1621) and was responsible for the Singer's Gallery. The most distinguished of the Mangone, Giulio Cesare's brother Fabio Mangone (1587–1629), a pupil of Alessandro Bisnanti, was *capomaestro* of the Duomo from 1617 until his death. He was responsible for the doors of the Duomo and for some important, though unexecuted, drawings for the façade. In 1620, he was appointed professor of architecture at the Ambrosiana in Milan. Other works include the rather rigid, classicizing Ambrosiana (1611) and the Collegio Elvetico, now the Archivio di Stato (1608), also in Milan.

NICHOLAS ADAMS

WORKS

GIOVANNI BATTISTA MANGONE

1591–1625, Duomo (choir stalls), Milan.

GIULIO CESARE MANGONE

1606–1620, Duomo (choir stalls), Milan.

FABIO MANGONE

1608, Collegio Elvetico; 1611, Ambrosiana; 1617–1629, Duomo (capomaestro; portals); Milan.

BIBLIOGRAPHY

GATTI PERER (editor) 1969 *Il Duomo di Milano.* 2 vols. Milan: Edizioni la Rete.

MANNING, ELEANOR

Eleanor Manning (1884–1973) was born in Boston and educated at the Massachusetts Institute of

Technology. In 1913, she joined Lois Howe and later Mary Almy to form an architectural firm, specializing in the design of low-cost housing. Among her more important works were residential designs for Mariemont, Ohio (1924), and Old Harbor Village (1937), Boston's first public housing project.

EUGENIE L. BIRCH

WORKS

1924, Residential complex, Mariemont, Ohio. 1937, Old Harbor Village, Boston.

BIBLIOGRAPHY

TORRE, SUSANA (editor) 1977 *Women in American Architecture: A Historic and Contemporary Perspective.* New York: Whitney Library of Design.

MANSART, FRANÇOIS

Trained by his father, a master carpenter, and by relatives—Germain Gaultier, a sculptor, and Marcel Le Roy, a mason and contractor—François Mansart (1598–1666) was an acknowledged architect by the mid-1620s. Although apparently almost unlettered, and without experience outside of France, he was a ranking French classical architect, in some ways the leading one. More than half of his work has been demolished and part of what remains has been altered, but the surviving buildings and fragments, together with drawings preserved in the Bibliothèque Nationale and the Archives Nationales in Paris, guarantee his position as a designer of genius. He successfully translated classical forms into a thoroughly French idiom, especially in his châteaux and hôtels. He was a master of the massing of architectural volumes and of plan solutions for irregular sites, and his sense of precisely correct spacings between openings and classical design elements never deserted him. Working mostly for rich parvenus, financiers and government officials, he created a style whose cool elegance, only now and then dressed with dramatic touches, answered his clients' needs exactly.

Mansart was arrogant, touchy, and unpopular, the object of severe professional and personal attacks. He did not invent the roof form that bears his name (of which there are variant spellings), but he used it often, sometimes in complex elaborations. His career began with commissions for châteaux and churches, sometimes for entire structures, sometimes for additions or alterations. In the mid-1630s, he began to be asked to design grand Parisian townhouses. During the next decade, his style, which had previously drawn somewhat on the work of SAMUEL DE BROSSE and, to a lesser extent, on that of Du Cerceau the Elder (see DU CERCEAU FAMILY), began to reflect an increased interest in the work of the High Italian Renaissance masters and some of their immediate successors. In 1645, he was commissioned by Anne of Austria to design and build the Church of the Val-de-Grâce in Paris, but he was found troublesome and his work was too costly; he was dismissed and the building handed over to JACQUES LEMERCIER, who completed it. Thereafter, Mansart worked chiefly on *hôtels* in Paris, some of which are all his, others only altered or remodeled by him. From about 1660, he began to be passed over in favor of the younger generation, though before his death he built an ingenious staircase in the Hôtel d'Aumont (1665), a small masterpiece. During this last period, he produced an extraordinary series of drawings and sketches for two projects of Jean Baptiste Colbert, first minister to Louis XIV: the court and east wing of the Louvre and a new Bourbon dynastic chapel at Saint Denis. These two designs show the vitality and ingenuity of Mansart's thought in its most advanced state.

Inevitably, Mansart designed churches in the essentially Italianate manner firmly established in France since the middle of the previous century. Visible in Paris were many classicizing works such as those of de Brosse, for example, the façade of Saint Gervais, of 1616, as well as structures influenced by the Jesuits, who had behind them the authority of the Gesù in Rome (see GIACOMO BAROZZI DA VIGNOLA and GIACOMO DELLA PORTA). Ancient Parisian churches were given columniated, scenic façades, such as that for Saint Paul-Saint Louis by François Derand (1634), and in 1635 Lemercier began the Church of the Sorbonne, with a façade reminiscent of the Roman work of CARLO MADERNO and della Porta and a plan and superstructure based on that of Rosato Rosati. Patrons required this show of Italian elements of design, and the problems raised by adapting them to French needs and traditions of building lie close to the heart of the story of postmedieval French architecture. Mansart, after some youthful copying and tentative explorations, soon met these problems successfully.

His first work, the façade of the Church of the Feuillants in Paris (1623), largely repeated the upper two stories of de Brosse's three storied Saint Gervais, although Mansart's version has greater articulation and a more dramatic silhouette. His love of slightly rising, or sinking, flat and undecorated wall panels, outlined with sharp-edged reveals, in a fashion reminiscent of DONATO BRAMANTE, Vignola, and MICHELANGELO, is already in evidence. After designing altars for Paris churches (Saint Martin-du-Champs and Notre

Dame), since destroyed, Mansart's next ecclesiastical commission was for the Church of Sainte Marie de la Visitation, also in Paris (1632). A centralized building of circular plan, it has an entranceway consisting of a temple-fronted doorway flanked by broad, flat vertical members, the whole surmounted by a large semicircular pediment. A fairly shallow entrance bay, its sides toed in toward the center line of the main, cylindrical volume beyond, is balanced by an axially centered sanctuary; round about are chapels and other subsidiary spaces. This plan recalls that by PHILIBERT DELORME for the chapel of the Château at Anet, of 1549–1552. There are uncertainties of scale and composition in the exterior design, but the well-lit interior, with its mixture of more or less High Renaissance and mannerist forms, is more successful.

In the chapel of the Château at Fresnes, of about 1645, a short nave opened out into a large circular space made broader by large, curving transverse apses which, with a somewhat shallower apse, formed a spacious trefoil composition. The Val-de-Grâce plan is somewhat similar, although the building is much larger; both recall ANDREA PALLADIO's Redentore in Venice. Before his dismissal, Mansart had raised the Val-de-Grâce to the impost of the vaulting and had completed the first story of the façade. The latter has a projecting Corinthian portico with two pairs of free-standing Corinthian columns. Inside, the three-bayed nave, with its classically correct pilasters and empaneled spandrels, recalls Vignola and, more distantly, LEON BATTISTA ALBERTI. The effect, both inside and out, is suitably monumental; but the work by Mansart's successors at the church doesn't always fit his, or respect his parti. His last ecclesiastical project was an entranceway for the Church of the Minimes in Paris (1657); only a portion of his design was built and that later demolished. He had proposed a Roman baroque composition with a ribbed dome on a high drum, but with wings pulled foward from the façade rather in the manner of those of a château. Of Mansart's seven ecclesiastical works, only the Visitation and the Val-de-Grâce stand today; the others are known through engravings and drawings. What the sum shows in three dimensions is a progression from a kind of French Mannerism, sometimes unsurely handled, toward a more baroque manner, in which both massing and relationships among parts are better adjusted. Plans, on the other hand, and the resulting spatial characteristics and sequences, are confidently managed from the start.

Important though Mansart's ecclesiastical buildings are, his châteaux and hôtels, in the broad expanse of French architecture, are even more significant. Churches had after all been clothed in classicizing architecture in Italy since the early fifteenth century, and by Mansart's day the mode was firmly established beyond the Alps. This is not to say that French churches were mere versions of Italian designs, but only that by about 1600 classicism was entirely normal for ecclesiastical projects. Domestic and palatial architecture was, however, another matter in France, and it was Mansart more than any other French architect who worked his way toward definitive solutions of the thorny problems involved in bringing purely French tradition together with classicism. These problems had been faced by others, for example by Du Cerceau the Elder (*Livre d'architecture,* 1559), by Jean du Cerceau (Hôtel de Sully, Paris, 1624), and especially by de Brosse (the Luxembourg Palace, 1615 ff., the Château at Blérancourt, 1612, and the Palais de Justice at Rennes, 1618). Fine as many of these projects and buildings are, Mansart's surpassed them. He set standards of site planning, of design solutions and, above all, of a peculiarly French kind of massing expressing an elegance for which many a later architect strived; FRANÇOIS BLONDEL, the late seventeenth-century theorist and teacher, standing before Mansart's splendid Château of Maisons, pronounced him the "God of Architecture."

Only a fragment of his earliest château, that at Berny, survives, and that shows a competent, Vignolaesque classicism. Mansart's perspective contract drawing also exists, revealing a deep rectangular courtyard formed by a main structure joined at right angles by wings projecting toward the open side of the court. The main structure, whose central, three-bayed block rose above the rest of the building, was entered through a columned porch, and the right angles between the main structure and the wings were eased at ground level by shallow, curving arcades. Typically French high-pitched roofs and tall chimneys were used. The symmetry of the design was broken by a single stair pavilion, at the edge of one of the wings, that gave onto the estate offices. Judging from the contract drawing, it was a competent design on the whole, suffering somewhat from a degree of fragmentation among the various parts, a condition emphasized by chimneys that were oversize even by French standards.

Still only in his twenties, Mansart next designed the Château of Balleroy (1626?), south of Bayeux. This is quite a different kind of solution. The wings are reduced to small, single-story pavilions, the main broad block behind them forming almost the entire bulk of the building. The height of this nine-bayed structure, whose central element is almost towerlike, is emphasized by colossal chimneys and a cupola centered atop its truncated, steep pyramidal roof. The lower, flanking roofs beside it do not fully abut its walls but pitch down into them, emphasizing the central, higher structure even more. The bays, the three units of the main block, and the flanking, low pavilions are all outlined in stone quoining, with paneled infilling of red brick (a technique inherited from builders of the time of Henri IV). The effect is one of five clearly stated units neatly fitted together hierarchically under a dramatic, zigzag roofline created by the independently defined superstructures of the five units. The whole is placed on an elevated terrace which, together with the scale effect of the single-story side pavilions and the dominance of the tall central element of the main block, results in a château quite unlike the more familiar, more horizontal kind. Finally, the orders are absent.

The classical French château, then, is quite unlike the Italian Renaissance villa with its self-contained central, massive block and comparative lack of pavilions. The French designs hark back to the castle and the late medieval hunting lodge, and although they became more and more classical as time passed they never lost that sense of blocks and pavilions tightly fitted together—reminiscences of the turrets, towers, keeps, and broad walls of their distant ancestors. It is this characteristic that chiefly gives French châteaux their great architectural interest, and it is this that Mansart, his immediate predecessors, and his contemporary LOUIS LE VAU worked to create. Variety both of form and of skyline is difficult to control, to bring into satisfactory balance, even with symmetrical plans, but they succeeded in doing it. At the same time, they managed to impose a classical discipline on their designs without abandoning the ancient, very French imagery from which their inspiration largely sprang.

Still a young man, Mansart was commissioned in 1635 by Gaston, duc d'Orléans, brother of Louis XIII, to rebuild the Château at Blois. Of this grand project only the southwest portion was built, a stately block alongside the courtyard, with short wings projecting in an I-plan from both ends (on the back, above the town, and inward, alongside the court; the northernmost of these, toward the famous spiral exterior stair, is represented only by a wall by Mansart). This arrangement is, however, not symmetrical; the centerline of the court façade does not coincide with that of the town side because the position and width of the projecting short wings had to be adjusted to existing site conditions. Mansart accommodated this discrepancy by absorbing it in his plan (the only way it can be seen, though it is suggested, from the air, by an ingenious, complex roof design) and by providing each façade with an independently centered, projecting feature. By related means he adjusted to the different levels of the site.

François Mansart.
Orléans Wing, Château de Blois.
France.
1635

The courtyard façade, of three stories throughout, has curved quadrant colonnades with paired columns joining the main body with the short wings at ground level. The projecting element centered in the main body is stepped back up through its three stories. There, as in the rest of the block, paired, unfluted pilasters frame the tall window bays, and the layers of the stories are emphasized by deep cornices. There are only a few, very small dormers, and chimneys appear only at the ends of the projecting wings, giving Blois the huge expanse of unfeatured roof surface that is one of its chief characteristics. The roof proper is of the double-pitched variety known by Mansart's name. If the effect is somewhat massive, it is also quite subtle. The proportions of the bays and their paired pilasters, together with the iteration of this motif throughout the design, gives the building a dignified harmony. The corners are fitted with pilasters sharing a common edge at the building's angles, and the blockiness of the whole and the overriding presence of the great roofs are nicely balanced by the disposition of the smaller features. The building's "grand simplicity" (Anthony Blunt [1954]1973) results as much as anything from Mansart's sure and confident handling of the orders, the set-back windows, and the weight-relieving effect this suggested layering produces.

Had the rest of Mansart's project been completed, the portion just described would have formed about one-third of the whole; the older works were to have been demolished and in their place a largely symmetrical structure would have been erected, enclosing a courtyard of regular form. These works would have contained several chambers of curved plan, and the four façades would have been different. For the main, northwest façade, Mansart proposed a domed entrance pavilion of Italianate character, part of which is faintly reminiscent of Maderno's work at Santa

Susanna in Rome. Little of the interior of the structure actually erected has ever been finished. The staircase leading up to the first floor (in the space that accommodates the offset axes) is, however, substantially complete. The stone work of the walls and vaults is in the best French tradition, supporting a dome and lantern lit in part by second-story windows invisible from below; this entire vertical system is open from the entrance level up to the lantern. The rather mannerist sculptural decoration, never completed, of swags, putti, and military furnishings is deep-cut, firm, and, in its present condition at least, not overstated.

The Château at Maisons (1642), hard by the forest of Saint Germain, was commissioned by René de Longueil, an immensely wealthy official who gave Mansart a free hand. Because the estate was later cut up, Maisons has lost its grand avenues and gardens, but the main block and some of its dependencies still stand, justifying a description of it as "probably the most perfect building ever erected in France" (Braham & Smith, 1973). It is in some ways a smaller, perfected version of the work at Blois, but it also harks back to Mansart's earliest works at Berny and Balleroy. The main block, of broad, U-shaped plan, sits upon a moated terrace. Three of the four main axes were extended by avenues and gardens (the village of Maisons cancels the fourth). The long, main avenue, coming in from the northwest, was marked by two sets of gates and a cross-avenue; it led to a lobed forecourt flanked by stables and a (proposed) orangery, thence to the main court and building. The arrangement of these gates and pavilions emphasized the imposing quality of the approach by requiring one to change direction several times; their architecture was of that peculiarly French kind that is sober and solid in mass but dramatic and articulated in detail, encompassing a variety of orders, rustication, and segmental arches, as well as such features as those truncated, superposed pyramids of the kind so enjoyed by French architects.

The main building may be one of the most satisfactory exercises in massing and balance in western architecture. The three-story centerpiece is related to that at Blois, but it is narrower and proportionately taller. The top story is framed against a roof of truncated pyramidal shape, topped by a small cupola in a manner reminiscent of Balleroy, and the roofs of the three main elements of the U-plan each are given their own, separate existence, also in the manner of Balleroy. But below that, the design is distinctly horizontal, with the ground and first floors divided by an emphatic cornice that helps marry the building to its terrace and moat. The entrance centerpieces and the wings on the garden façade have free-standing columns; elsewhere, the window bays and niches are framed in the fashion of those at Blois by the paired, shallow pilasters that are as much Mansart's hallmark as they were Vignola's. The pilasters appear to be rectangular, without entasis, and if this is the case it may be one of the chief sources of the elegant repose the building achieves. Although there is no hint of severity, because of the many projections and recesses of wall surface, each precisely outlined bay seems as uncompromisingly rectangular as the whole block, creating an effect of assured decorum few buildings achieve. This is complemented exactly by the height and pitch of the roofs which, unlike those at Blois, are satisfying in scale with the whole.

François Mansart. Château de Maisons. Near Paris. 1642

Of his châteaux, only Maisons preserves Mansart's interior décor. In the entrance vestibule and the grand staircase, the stone sculpture achieves an effect of "severe richness" (Blunt) without the use of color. The figural work is classical in nature, and the vaults are divided into panels of curved and rectangular shapes by raised wreath and guilloche moldings. The unusual balustrade of the great stair is formed of ingeniously interwoven stone arcs carrying leaf-capitals supporting the massive stone railings. In other parts of the building the decoration is less austere and more colorful, in some places curiously anticipating the elaborate Louis Seize style of the period just before the Revolution.

Mansart was equally successful with his Parisian hôtels. The first was begun in 1635 for Louis de la Vrillière and was contemporary with the new wing at Blois, with which it shared certain problems of siting such as a lack of alignment between major elements. Engravings show an empaneled entrance wall one story high, giving on to a rectangular courtyard lined on three sides by the *hôtel* proper, the base block having dormers and a higher roof than the wings above the uniform two-story line. Although the building was entirely classical, the architectural and sculptural decoration seems to have been sparse. Beyond the base block, there was a large garden, one side of which was flanked by a gallery block. In general, Mansart's concept of a grand townhouse appears almost fully formed in this first exercise. At the Hôtel de Jars, however, a narrower site caused him to double the ranges of rooms in the main block and in the single wing, pushing the courtyard into one quadrant of the rectangular plan. In remodeling the Hôtel de Carnavalet (1660), toward the end of his career, he placed rooms all around the court, eliminating the traditional one-story gateway wall facing the principal street.

The exteriors of these buildings are on the whole more severe, with less modulations of surface, than those of Blois and Maisons. Exuberance, if any was required, was reserved for the interiors. Where these are preserved, Mansart's originality is obvious, as in the vaulting, volumes, and curves of the staircase of the Hôtel de Guénégaud (des Brosses; 1653?). Another example, the last commission Mansart executed, once existed in the Hôtel d'Aumont, where he inserted an unusual staircase. He increased the sense of the size of the limited space he had to work with by prefacing the cubical stair-cage proper with a vestibule expanded by transverse niches. From there, the stairs proper rose, narrowing toward one wall before they began to turn round the vertical center line of the enclosing volume. No step has the same shape as any other, yet the engravings of the stairs persuade one that the solution was satisfactory both functionally and artistically. Others, in particular Le Vau, contributed to the exaltation and architectural definition of the Parisian townhouse, but none more than Mansart.

Toward the end of his life, Mansart was among those architects asked by Colbert, first minister to Louis XIV, to submit designs for two major projects, the completion of the Louvre and a proposed dynastic funerary chapel for the Bourbons, to be attached to Saint Denis. Mansart's drawings for the latter show two schemes and a variant and include elevations and sections. One is for a huge centralized building, entered through the apse of the church, with eight radiating volumes, four of nearly oval shape alternating with smaller, circular ones. The exterior shapes of this cluster of forms were to have been clearly articulated, in contrast to the uniform, cylindrical continuity of GIOVANNI LORENZO BERNINI's design for the same project. In Mansart's elevations, the main space would have been covered with a high drum and dome, the subsidiary ones with smaller, independent domes clustered around it; additional subsidiary domes appear over the passageway between the old church and the chapel and over an additional chamber Mansart considered adding, on the main axis, beyond the central group. The elevations do not entirely fit the plan on whose sheet they were drawn, for the domes over the oval spaces are too small for the spans shown on the plan; the scheme is probably a preliminary essay, one on perhaps too large a scale for Colbert to swallow. The general concept harks back to drawings by LEONARDO DA VINCI, with overtones of GIOVANNI BATTISTA MONTANO's work (Mansart owned a copy of his book) and of Michelangelo's design for San Giovanni de' Fiorentini. Sections show a two-shelled dome of the kind his great-nephew JULES HARDOUIN MANSART built at the Invalides.

For the Louvre project, a number of drawings have survived; they have been meticulously studied by Braham and Smith (1973). Some are finished, some not; some have flaps attached showing alternative solutions to one part or another of their principal subject. It is said that Mansart showed some of the less tidy ones to Colbert, who asked the architect to choose one proposal and redraw it for submission to Louis XIV. But Mansart refused to do this because he wanted to continue working up his schemes. Colbert seems to have taken this well, but he told Mansart that a building like the Louvre could not be changed while under construction, a reference to Mansart's reputation for dismantling, and then rebuilding, as he went along. The same source (Charles Perrault, *Les hommes illustres* [quoted in Braham & Smith, 1973]) adds that it was then that Colbert summoned Bernini, "qui asseurement n'avoit aucun avantage sur luy [Mansart] du costé de l'Architecture."

The drawings reveal as much about Mansart as any of his surviving construction. He returned again and again to the problems of completing the vast building, of harmonizing new work with old, and of giving the whole, especially the east wing, an appropriately stately and grand appearance. The drawings are all firm and assertive and decidedly not sketchy even when rather messy. As might be expected, the solutions he set out are characterized by bold and strongly stated masses, in contrast to Le Vau's more conventional, linear proposals. And nowhere is there anything like Bernini's austerely monumental (and peculiarly scaled) proposals. Mansart's schemes crackle with excitement, both in plan and elevation, because of his genius for massing and for the organization of the rhythms of his elevations, the command of both of which he had shown so splendidly at Maisons. But the excitement never gets out of hand, and the end result is a series of solutions whose rich stateliness would be hard to match.

Two features of these schemes stand out. One is the way in which Mansart breathes life into what is, after all, in essence a rather simple rectangular scheme, however grand in scale. He does this not only by pavilioning the corners and entranceways, as many architects would, but also by pulling the building out into short wings at the corners and by placing hints of subsidiary, secondary pavilions, projecting slightly from the main blocks, behind the main corner pavilions. Furthermore, he is willing to deal with the right angles involved, especially on proposals for the façade of the east front, by masking the re-entrant ones with diagonals, and by cutting the projecting ones off diagonally. He is never wedded to a presumed need for orthogonal clarity, and he has the confidence to depart from tradition and fashion; for example, he brings the elevated dome from its hallowed position over church buildings to mark the position of the vast hall of the east entrance. The other outstanding feature is in his handling of room shapes. Mansart understands that there are other possibilities in the arrangement of rectangular rooms one by another than simply putting them in symmetrical groups or in line, and he fits them together in staggered galaxies of four and six in plan dispositions of exceptional ingenuity. The principal lines of the wings have, as they had to have, the traditional, aligned enfilades, but the main corners of his plans are original. In some schemes they contain rooms of curving or polygonal plans, groups of which in certain cases are set out not along the controlling rectilinear lines of the whole building, but along diagonal lines bisecting the corner angles, chains of rooms that seem to want to push out from the building along axes oblique to the main façades.

The elevations he proposes are equally satisfactory. The windows and the arcades of the rez-de-chaussée (when they appear) are close together, separated usually by orders standing alone or in pairs. Thus, the vast bulk of the proposed structure is broken up, as the walls of Blois were broken up, by a comprehensible texture of solids and voids, with the result of making the building lighter in appearance than greater expanses of solid masonry would have suggested. These façades are penetrable by the eye, and thus the interior space of the palace is intimated, and connections between it and the surrounding city are established. Here and there in the various projects, a curved portion of façade appears, sometimes of segmental, sometimes of elliptical shape.

Mansart rose from common origins to become an architect of very great ability, and a designer of gardens and an engineer as well. What remains of his buildings (perhaps a third of what once stood), together with the drawings, make it clear that he started in his youth at a high level of ability and then pursued the perfection of his art relentlessly until his death. His immediate predecessors had achieved a lot in adapting classical design to French needs; behind them lay the accomplishments of medieval architects and stonemasons. Mansart carried both traditions forward to a point beyond the reach of his contemporaries, and at his death he left an enduring, superior legacy. He accomplished this without having had much, if any, formal schooling, and it may well be that he could read the drawings in his library books more readily than he could the texts. But his efforts cost him dearly. His quest for perfection required the wealthiest of clients. Royal patronage never materialized, so there is no palace or retreat of his of the kind that might have been preserved when his châteaux and hôtels, their patrons' memory dimmed, were demolished or mutilated. And he was the object of very sharp personal attacks, as in the anonymous *Mansarade* of 1651, an actionable document portraying him as incompetent, of questionable personal character, vain, common, dishonest, and avaricious. After his death, however, when passions had receded, he was defended and roundly praised, for example, by Blondel and CHARLES PERRAULT.

His early training must have been sound. The contract drawing for the Château at Berny (1623) shows him, at the age of twenty-five, in command both of the means of presenting a clear view of the building to the client and, more important, of the principles upon which an adequate solution should be based. He owned, among other works, several versions of VITRUVIUS and a 1635 Vignola (which had been published first in 1562). His work shows that he knew and understood classical Italian architecture better than his Parisian contemporaries, though he never took to copying it, avoided SEBASTIANO SERLIO on the whole, and treated the orders not as sacrosanct but as elements he could deal with very freely (his wide-ranging treatment of the Ionic order at Maisons is a case in point). One aspect of his genius was that he saw clearly what would work successfully and what would not when combining classical design with French requirements and French traditions. This is a notoriously difficult kind of thing to judge, and Europe north of the Alps is littered with misapplications of classicism, but Mansart hardly made a false step in dealing with the problem. His classicism is never obtrusive, put there as a parade of learning, but is always neatly subordinated to his designs overall.

Mansart was equally effective in his handling of

the more purely French aspects of his work. His planning, his sure and elegant touch with the proportions and placing of pavilions, and the secure marriages of his façades with their grand roofs all come out of an exact understanding of his architectural patrimony. From Berny onward, he proved again and again that he thought of architecture not as something made up of views from ground level, but as a problem first conceived always in the round, and this helps to explain why he achieved a cohesion among elements of design and a mastery of massing rarely equaled. That many of his commissions were difficult ones, requiring him, for example, to conjure up symmetries from asymmetries, makes his accomplishments the more remarkable.

Mansart's influence was insured by the passage of his knowledge, and many of his drawings and papers, to his great-nephew Jules Hardouin, whom he favored and who took his great-uncle's name; this was the start of a dynasty of French architects named Mansart, or Hardouin, or Gabriel (see ANGE-JACQUES GABRIEL), or some combination thereof, that lasted until close to the end of the eighteenth century. And although Le Vau for a time seems to have been better regarded, Mansart's reputation soon overtook Le Vau's. For some three centuries now, Blois, Maisons, and the hôtels have been praised by imitations and derivatives. In the past, Mansart and Hardouin Mansart have often been confused, a situation that Blunt and especially Braham and Smith have now brought to an end. Thanks to them, his work is at last accessible and his awkward, perfectionist personality, dogged by reversals and the spectacle of half-built buildings, better understood. Mansart has been compared with FRANCESCO BORROMINI, but this seems more useful with regard to certain similarities of temperament than with respect to their buildings. Borromini's convincing, rarefied theatricality, a kind of fluid, architectural articulation of the emotions, was entirely his own. Mansart's best work, also highly original, is by comparison less idiosyncratic, made up almost always of familiar forms and surfaces belonging to an accepted tradition. He did make designs as different, as successful, and as intricately thought-out as Borromini's, but they were the result of artistic advances along quite different lines.

WILLIAM L. MACDONALD

WORKS

*1623, Château of Berny, France. *1623, Church of the Feuillants (façade); *1624, Church of Saint Martin-du-Champs (altar); Paris. 1626(?), Château of Balleroy, France. *1628, Notre Dame (Altar of the Virgin); 1632, Church of Sainte Marie de la Visitation; Paris. 1635, Orléans Wing, Château of Blois, France. *1635, Hôtel de la Vrillière, Paris. 1642, Château de Maisons, near Paris. 1642, Hôtel de Chavigny; 1645, Church of the Val-de-Grâce; Paris. *c.1645, Château de Fresnes (chapel), France. *1645, Hôtel de Jars; *1648, Hôtel de Guénéguad (remodeling); Paris. *1650s(?)–1660s, Château of Gesvres, France. 1653?, Hôtel de Guénéguad (des Brosses); *1657, Church of the Minimes (portal); 1660, Hôtel de Carnavalet (alterations); *1665, Hôtel d'Aumont (staircase); Paris.

BIBLIOGRAPHY

BLUNT, ANTHONY 1941 *François Mansart and the Origins of French Classical Architecture.* London: Warburg Institute.

BLUNT, ANTHONY (1954)1973 Pages 201–221 in *Art and Architecture in France: 1500–1700.* 2d ed., rev. Harmondsworth, England: Penguin.

BRAHAM, ALLAN, and SMITH, PETER 1973 *François Mansart.* 2 vols. London: Zwemmer. Includes detailed documentation, catalogue, and illustrations.

HAUTECOEUR, LOUIS 1948 Pages 20–76 in *Le règne de Louis XIV.* Volume 2 in *Histoire de l'architecture classique en France.* Paris: Picard.

MANSART, JULES HARDOUIN

See HARDOUIN MANSART, JULES.

MANSART DE SAGONNE, JACQUES HARDOUIN

Jacques Hardouin Mansart de Levi, Comte de Sagonne (1703–1758), born in Trévolles, Bourbonnais, France, was the grandson of JULES HARDOUIN MANSART and the younger brother of Jean Hardouin Mansart de Jouy. Following in the footsteps of his famous grandfather, he was named a member of the Royal Academy in 1735 and an *architecte du roi* in 1742.

Mansart de Sagonne is best known for numerous schemes (never realized) for the Place Louis XV in Paris (1748, 1751), and for his Church of Saint Louis at Versailles (1743–1754). The design of the latter recalls Jules Hardouin Mansart's Church of Notre Dame, also located in Versailles (1684–1686), but displays a greater regard for lightness, elegance, and exuberant decoration. This approach was typical of Mansart de Sagonne's rococo style and that of his frequent collaborator NICOLAS PINEAU.

The domestic designs of this architect, among them a house for the ladies of Saint-Chaumont (Paris, 1734) and his own Hôtel Mansart de Sagonne (Paris, 1743), also included a penchant for rococo excess, rendering him a frequent target for critics such as Cochin who supported a classical approach to architecture.

His personal life was equally excessive. Mansart de Sagonne was known for his reckless living and eventually hid from his creditors in the Temple of the prince of Conti. While there, he wrote to the MARQUIS DE MARIGNY, asking for financial support and permission to go to Portugal and Germany. It is believed that he went to Lisbon to help rebuild the city after an earthquake.

KATHLEEN RUSSO

WORKS

1734, Maison des Dames de Saint-Chaumont; 1735, Maison de Cintray; 1738, Château de Saint-Non-la-Bretêche (work); 1739–1747, Hôtel de Lesdiguières; 1743, Hôtel Bazin de Bezons (work); 1743, Hôtel Mansart de Sagonne; Paris. 1743–1754, Church of Saint Louis, Versailles, France. 1752, Maison Clostrier, Paris. 1753, Hospital, Marsailles, France. 1756, Maison Mansart de Levi, Paris. n.d., Domenican Abbey of Prouilles, Languedoc, France. n.d., Palace of Commerce, Tours, France.

BIBLIOGRAPHY

BAUCHAL, CHARLES 1887 *Nouveau dictionnaire biographique et critique des architectes français.* Paris: Daly.

BLONDEL, JACQUES FRANÇOIS, and PATTE, PIERRE 1771–1777 *Cours d'Architecture, ou Traité de la Décoration, Distribution & Construction des Batiments; Contenant les Leçons Données en 1750, & les Années Suivantes. . . .* 9 vols. Paris: Desaint. Patte prepared the last two volumes of text and one volume of plates for publication following Blondel's death. Although following Blondel's topical plan, Patte rewrote extensively much, but not all, of Blondel's material.

DESHAIRS, LEON 1910 *XVIIIe siècle, époque de Louis XV: Nicolas et Dominique Pineau: 208 dessins.* Paris: Longuet.

GALLET, MICHEL 1972 *Paris Domestic Architecture of the 18th Century.* London: Barry & Jenkins.

GRANET, SOLANGE 1959 "Les origines de la Place de la Concorde à Paris." *Gazette des Beaux Arts* 53:153–166.

HAUTECOEUR, LOUIS 1950 *Première moitié du XVIIIe siècle: Le style Louis XV.* Volume 3 in *Histoire de l'architecture classique en France.* Paris: Picard.

JAL, AUGUSTE (1867)1970 *Dictionnaire critique de biographie et d'histoire.* Reprint of 1872 ed. Geneva: Slotkine.

KALNEIN, WEND GRAF, and LEVEY, MICHAEL 1972 *Art and Architecture of the Eighteenth Century in France.* Baltimore: Penguin.

LACROIX, PAUL 1857–1858 "Un concours d'architecture en 1753." *Revue universelle des arts* 6:123–145.

LANCE, ADOLPHE 1872 *Dictionnaire des architectectes français.* 2 vols. Paris: Morel.

LE ROI, JOSEPH-ADRIAN (1854)1868 *Histoire de Versailles.* Versailles, France: Oswald.

LEROUX DE LINCY, ANTOINE-JEAN-VICTOR 1846 *Histoire de l'Hôtel de Ville de Paris.* Paris: Dumoulin.

Nouvelles archives de l'art français. 1872 Paris: Société de l'histoire de l'art français.

RAMBAUD, MIREILLE 1964 Volume 1 in *Documents du Minutier Central concernant l'histoire de l'art, (1700–1750).* Paris: S.E.V.P.E.N.

WARD, HENRY (1911)1976 *The Architecture of the Renaissance in France: 1495–1830.* Reprint of 1929 ed. New York: Hacker.

MANSFELD, ALFRED

Alfred Mansfeld (1912–) studied at the Technische Hochschule in Berlin (1931–1933) and at the Ecole Spëciale d'Architecture in Paris (1933–1935). He went to Israel in 1935, where he has been practicing and teaching architecture. Mansfeld has abandoned his earlier formalist approach in favor of an open-ended system which allows for organic growth and flexibility in architecture. The best known example of his indeterminate architecture is the Israel Museum in Jerusalem, which employs a system of additive clusters allowing for future expansion. In the design of the museum, Mansfeld also sought to achieve "a genuine, though unconventional monumentality without resorting to formality or pompousness."

MEHRANGIZ NIKOU SEXTON

WORKS

1956, Kiryat Eliahu Housing Development (with Munio Weinraub); 1957, Ramat Hadar Residential Quarter (with Weinraub); Haifa, Israel. 1965, Israel Museum (with Dora Gad), Jerusalem. 1972, Mount Carmel Auditorium (with Dani Havkin); 1978, Shaar Háaliya Housing (with Havkin); Haifa, Israel. 1978, Town Hall and Civic Precinct (with Havkin), Jerusalem.

BIBLIOGRAPHY

HERBERT, GILBERT 1980 "Mansfield, Alfred." Pages 509–511 in Muriel Emanuel (editor), *Contemporary Architects.* New York: St. Martin's.

"Israeli Culture." 1961 *Architectural Forum* 114, no. 2:138.

"Leisure Center and Multi-purpose Auditorium, Mount Carmel." 1976 *Architecture and Urbanism* no. 65:35–44.

PEDIO, RENATO 1965 "Profilo dell' architetto Alfred Mansfeld." *L'Architettura, cronache e storia* 11, no. 1:14–34.

PEVSNER, NIKOLAUS 1976 *A History of Building Types.* London: Thames & Hudson.

SANDBERG, WILLIAM 1966 "The Israel Museum in Jerusalem." *Museum* 19, no. 1:15–30.

MARCH, OTTO

Born into a family of wealthy industrialists in Berlin-Charlottenburg, Otto March (1845–1913) lived and practiced in Berlin most of his life. He studied at the Bauakademie in Berlin, where the continuing influence of KARL FRIEDRICH SCHINKEL was being modified by his teachers RICHARD LUCAE and MARTIN GROPIUS. March also studied at the Vienna Polytechnikum with HEINRICH FERSTEL; here, he imbibed Ferstel's ideas about simplicity in design, together with his love of rich materials and polychromy.

On his return from the Franco-Prussian war, where he served as an officer in the Prussian army, March took up a dual career in government service and private practice. As *Regierungsbaumeister* in Berlin from 1878, March was responsible for a number of important government buildings in Berlin, including a new prison in Berlin-Plötzensee, the remodeling of the Supreme Court Buildings, and additions to the University of Berlin. At the same time, he began to build up an extensive clientele among the Berlin commercial and industrial classes and the Prussian nobility. Unlike most of his contemporaries, March never found it necessary to teach.

Although he was never a professor of architecture, March exerted great influence upon his own generation of architects, and on the younger generation as well, through the innovative character of his buildings, which received a great deal of publicity. The private dwellings which he built in great numbers for the affluent bourgeoisie and nobility—townhouses, suburban villas, and rural castles—contributed to the acceptance in Germany of the idea that the house can be a focus for "high architecture," an idea which had already developed in England and the United States. March's designs were characterized by steep roofs, many projecting bays, and the use of wood siding and decorative elements, along with masonry and tile. In the interiors, a relatively open plan was usually organized around a two-story hall, with a balcony looking down into the hall. These houses resembled in many particulars the late Victorian and Shingle style houses of the United States and may also reflect some of the influence of R. NORMAN SHAW.

The commercial and municipal buildings were also of great significance. The Neue Friedrichstrasse Store (1895), for example, used its three-story bays of iron and glass in a manner which prefigured the Fagus Factory of WALTER GROPIUS. The Municipal Theater in Worms (1889), with its severe, massive, and geometricized forms, set a new and forward-looking standard in monumental building. March pioneered, as well, in the design of race courses and stadiums.

March also exerted wide influence as a writer and activist in city planning. He led the movement to set up the competition of 1909 for a "Greater Berlin Plan" and helped to organize the major exposition on city planning held in Berlin in 1910.

The recipient of many honors, March became, in 1909, a member "ordinarius" of the prestigious Akademie des Bauwesens in Berlin. Among German architects, his was one of the most distinguished careers of the last years before World War I. After the war, March's innovations in the areas of housing, city planning and monumental design were carried forward in new ways, by disciples such as ERNST MAY and WERNER HEGEMANN, and by his son, WERNER MARCH.

BARBARA MILLER LANE

WORKS

1889, Municipal Theater, Worms, Germany. 1891, Landhaus Kolbe, Radebeul, Germany. 1892, Landhaus F. Vörster, Cologne, Germany. 1893–1894, House, Düsseldorf, Germany. 1894, Landhaus Dr. J. F. Holtz, Eisenach, Germany. 1894, Twin House, Villencolonie Grünewald; 1895, Neue Friedrichstrassestore; n.d., German Chemical Society Offices; n.d., Prison, Plötzensee; n.d., Schiller Theater, Charlottenburg; Berlin. n.d., Schloss Jahmen, Jena, Germany. n.d., Schloss Kamenz (remodeling), Prussia, Germany. n.d., Supreme Court (remodeling), Berlin. n.d., University of Berlin (remodeling of Frauenklinik). n.d., Karl von Siemens Residence, Potsdam, Germany.

BIBLIOGRAPHY

FRITSCH, K. E. O. 1893 *Der Kirchenbau des Protestantismus, von der Reformation bis zur Gegenwart.* Berlin: Toeche.

GURLITT, CORNELIUS 1899 *Die Deutsche Kunst des neunzhenten Jahrhunderts, ihre Ziele und Thaten.* Berlin: Bondi.

MUTHESIUS, STEFAN 1974 *Das Englische Vorbild: Eine Studie zu den Reformbewegungen in Architektur, Wohnbau und Kunstgewerbe im späteren 19. Jahrhundert.* Munich: Prestel.

STÜBBEN, J. 1913 "Otto March." *Zentralblatt der Bauverwaltung* 33:199–200.

MARCH, WERNER

Werner March (1894–1976), remembered as one of the prominent architects of the Nazi era in Germany, became famous internationally for a single architectural complex: the stadium, grounds, and ancillary buildings on the Reichssportfeld in Berlin for the 1936 Olympic Games. Yet, this complex was already begun and the style established even before the 1920s.

The son of the prominent German architect OTTO MARCH, Werner March was a student both of his father and of GERMAN BESTELMEYER in Munich. His style was conceived to be what the ancient Greeks would have built had they lived in the twentieth century: awe-inspiring classicism of large, simple shapes, coupled with a frank expression of the material essences of brick, ashlar masonry, and reinforced concrete. The elder March had already built a smaller stadium on the Berlin site in 1913; and Werner's brother, Walther, assisted in designing the Sportforum there in the 1920s and the competition-winning stadium design of 1934. The Olympic Stadium and Gate (still extant) were surrounded by an outdoor amphitheater and a complex of imposing physical education facilities, now headquarters for the British garrison in Berlin. Werner March was professor in Berlin in the 1930s and again after World War II.

RON WIEDENHOEFT

BIBLIOGRAPHY

HEGEMANN, WERNER 1930 "German Bestelmeyer und Werner March." *Wasmuths Monatshefte für Baukunst* 14:13–21.

MARCH, WALTHER 1928 "Die Bauten des deutschen Sportforums zu Berlin. *Wasmuths Monatshefte für Baukunst* 12:187–191.

PETSCH, JOACHIM 1978 *Baukunst und Stadtplanung im Dritten Reich.* Munich and Vienna: Hanser.

RITTICH, WERNER (1938)1944 *Architektur und Bauplastik der Gegenwart.* 3d ed., enl. Berlin: Rembrandt.

MARCHAND, JEAN OMER

Jean Omer Marchand (1872–1936), a Montreal architect, was born and educated there and was apprenticed to the partnership of Maurice Perrault and Albert Mesnard. His later training at the Ecole des Beaux-Arts in Paris from 1893 to 1903 is apparent in his finest Canadian work, which includes Saint Boniface Cathedral, Winnipeg (1907), and, with JOHN A. PEARSON, the reconstruction of the Parliament Buildings, Ottawa (1916–1923).

ROBERT HILL

BIBLIOGRAPHY

MORGAN, HENRY J. (1898)1912 Page 729 in *Canadian Men and Women of the Time.* Toronto: Briggs.

"Obituary." 1936 *Journal of the Royal Architectural Institute of Canada* 13, Jun.:125.

MARCHI, VIRGILIO

Like many of the futurist architects, Virgilio Marchi (1895–1960) wrote manifestoes and books, executed sketches, but realized few actual projects. Recalling ANTONIO SANT'ELIA's theories, Marchi argued for an architecture of dynamism, inspired by the forces of new technology. In his *Manifesto of Futurist Architecture* of 1920, Marchi prescribed "formal exaltation . . . of the mechanical" and "constructive intuition" which would "reconcile practical considerations and the lyricism of dramatic energies." His sketches show why so little of his work was built. Most are highly visionary and fantastic renderings of buildings and cityscapes, expressing his belief in architecture as the manifestation of the creator's state of mind. Structures consist of clashing, curving volumes reflecting Marchi's definition of architecture as "habitable sculpture." Transportation and circulation are integrated into the buildings, and supporting concrete armatures are exposed. In these sketches, expressive deformations and vertiginous perspective suggest the imaginative rather than the implementable.

Marchi's transformation of classical ruins into the futurist center of the Bragaglia Bar and Theater in Rome (1921), however, was perhaps the first completed futurist architectural space. In another of several theater reconstructions, he redesigned the Odelscalchi Theater in Rome (1924–1925). From the late 1920s until his death, he worked mostly on set designs for theater and cinema, often highly Expressionist vehicles for unrealized architectural ideas. Those for whom he produced designs include Guido Salvini, Roberto Rossellini, Vittorio de Sica, and also Pirandello who once described Marchi as "the marvelous builder of my dreams."

GERALD D. SILK

WORKS

1921, Casa d'arte Bragaglia e Teatro degli Indipendenti; 1924–1925, Il Teatro dei Piccoli di Vittoria Prodecca at the Teatro Odelscalchi (reconstruction); Rome.

BIBLIOGRAPHY

CLOUGH, ROSE TRILLO 1961 *Futurism: The Story of a Modern Art Movement.* New York: Philosophical Library.

CRISPOLTI, ENRICO 1969 *Il Mito della Macchina e Altri Temi del Futurismo.* Trapani, Italy: Celebes.

D'AMICO, ALESSANDRO, and DAMESI, SILVIA (editors) 1977 *Virgilio Marchi: Architetto scenografo futurista.* Venice, Italy: Electa Editrice.

"From Futurism to Rationalism: The Origins of Modern Italian Architecture." 1981 *Architectural Design* 51, no. 1–2:entire issue.

"Futurismo architettura." 1971 *Controspazio* 3, nos. 4–5:entire issue.

MARCHI, VIRGILIO 1924 *Architettura Futurista.* Foligno, Italy: Campitelli.

MARCHI, VIRGILIO 1931 *Italia Nuova, Architettura Nuova.* Foligno, Italy: Campitelli.

PEHNT, WOLFGANG 1973 *Expressionist Architecture.* New York: Praeger.

MARCHIONNI, CARLO

Born in Rome, Carlo Marchionni (1702–1786) was an architect, sculptor, engineer, and designer of figurative and other ornamental decoration for churches and palaces, monuments and temporary structures, as well as a sizable number of landscapes and caricatures. Through his versatility, Marchionni is comparable to artists of the Roman High baroque, especially GIOVANNI LORENZO BERNINI, with whom he is indirectly connected by his apprenticeship to Filippo Barigioni: Barigioni had trained under two of Bernini's disciples and followers, first under Mattia de Rossi and after the death of the latter (1695) under CARLO FONTANA.

Marchionni's first known works are two designs for a clock dial decoration for Santa Trinità dei Monti in Rome, which date about 1720 or even slightly earlier; they reveal their Berninian inspiration through the postures of the lateral angels which carry the clock face in the fashion of an altarpiece.

The first work that revealed the fertility of his imagination and ability of planning on a wide urban scale is his prize-winning project for the architectural competition of 1728 at the Accademia di San Luca In Rome, a *Piazza per un porto di mare,* for which he shared the first prize with two other competitors and through which he evidently captivated the attention of the judges and the public by the ingenious manner in which he related the arcaded structures which form a hemicycle at the far end and which are elevated by a belvedere to the foreground of the harbor. The latter, though rather remote in concept from a real port, is conceived in Marchionni's drawing as the space from which the spectator views the imposing structures of the background. This demonstration of his unusual scenographic talents may have earned him, as is easily imaginable, the interest which led to the lifelong patronage of Cardinal Alessandro Albani who soon employed him for his villas in Anzio (finished in 1738) and in Castelgandolfo (early 1740s). His projects for pavilions which are connected with these villas and pay homage to the taste of FRANCESCO BORROMINI through the stepped exterior shape of their domes, were not executed. However, the two unidentified drawings which were considered to be late might be connected with projects for the above-mentioned villas. About 1734, Marchionni furnished the project for the parochial church in Nettuno, of which the drawing for the façade, very conventional in style, has survived.

Marchionni.
Project for Academia di San Luca.
Rome.
1728

Retrospective also are his projects for sculptured works of this period, one for a seated figure of Clement XII of the mid-1730s, not executed, which shows the pope with the traditional gesture of blessing; and the more pretentious, though also very traditional monument to Benedict XIII of about 1739 in Santa Maria Sopra Minerva, for which he furnished the design, assisted by the painter Pietro Bianchi; he participated in its realization by executing the relief of the sarcophagus and the statue of the angel with the Orsini coat of arms himself. Most of his sculptural work falls into the period of the 1740s, beginning with a statue of an unidentified pope to the right of the Holy Virgin on top of FERDINANDO FUGA's façade of Santa Maria Maggiore (c.1741), and followed by a monument to Benedict XIV in Santa Croce in Gerusalemme (1743); the arrangement of busts and inscription tablets to honor the benefactors of the Palazzo di Propaganda Fide in the vestibule of the *piano nobile* (c.1745); a monument to Cardinal Giacomo Milli in San Crisogono (1747); the statue of Sant' Ignazio on a side altar in Sant' Apollinare (1748); and the two low reliefs with representations from the life of the Holy Virgin in the chapel of Saint John in San Rocco in Lisbon (Visitation, 1747); and in the Cappella della Madonna del Voto (Chigi) in the Cathedral in Siena (Birth of the Virgin, 1748). All of these works show Marchionni within the mainstream; they are respectable in concept and execution but without particular distinction. Official recognition came to Marchionni in 1740 when he was accepted by the Accademia di San Luca in Rome.

In 1742, he had decorated the lateral chapels of the Church of San Giovanni at Montecelio, followed by the temporary decoration of the interior of Santa Maria Sopra Minerva for the canonization of Santa Caterina dei Ricci in 1746. Toward the end of the 1740s, he seems to have begun the preparatory drawings of his first major work on a grand scale that was put into execution: the Villa Albani, Rome, for which his patron, Cardinal Alessandro, had begun to acquire the building premises in 1746. The map by Nolli shows the situation of 1748: a deep, rectangular site surrounded by a wall which forms a hemicycle at the far end and is reached by an avenue diagonally to this area through vineyards later transformed into *boschetti.* With the intention to create a home for his extensive collection of antique marbles and other works of art, Cardinal Alessandro Albani is reputed to have developed this project which was executed by Marchionni. The architect, who was evidently inspired by the analogous situation of the loggia at the Villa Mondragone at Frascati, which faces a fountain in the shape of an exedra, and in consideration of the previous situation of this building site, placed a two-storied casino on the straight side of the rectangle (1755–1757). The casino, with a closed tier above an open portico (influenced by MICHELANGELO's Palazzo dei Conservatori), faces across the parterre a semicircular one-storied edifice with statues which opens in the center into a "coffee-house" (1762). Lateral wings (*gallerie*) are appended to the casino in the fashion of Algardi's engraved original project for the Villa Doria Pamphilj, but they terminate in two classicizing though not very orthodox "Greek" temples facing each other; one of them was intended as a shrine for the statue of Diana of Ephesos. The other, using original caryatids instead of Ionic columns, serves merely as a solemn decoration for a doorway leading to the *boschetto* area. It was in these structures that Marchionni attempted to make his contribution to the drawing movement of neoclassicism, initiated in Rome by GIOVANNI BATTISTA PIRANESI, most clearly represented on the site of the Villa Albani in the building of the artificial ruin.

During the years when the planning of the Villa Albani was well advanced, Marchionni had a number of onerous obligations which must have taken a great deal of his time. On January 1, 1754, he followed his former master Filippo Barigioni as *architetto revisore* of the *Fabbrica di San Pietro,* and in 1773, he replaced LUIGI VANVITELLI as *architetto soprastante* of the Basilica of St. Peter's.

In 1756, Marchionni went to Ancona, where, much to the chagrin of Luigi Vanvitelli, he revised the latter's plans and with superior technical skill terminated the Molo Clementino. Whether the storehouse was remodeled to his design is a contentious issue. A fine contribution to the urban embellishment of Ancona is his Church of San Domenico (1763–1786), the façade of which overlooks the Piazza del Plebiscito, once a sloping site, which was structured by Marchionni with the introduction of a central staircase leading to the middle portion of the church front that also served as a

Marchionni.
Casino of Villa Albani.
Rome.
1755–1757/1762

backdrop for Cornacchini's statue of Clement XII (to whom Ancona owed the improvement of its harbor); at the sides, the church is effectively flanked by the ascending ramps remaining from the original slope. In 1765, the Chiesa della Maddalena in Messina was begun according to Marchionni's plans, but it was finished only in the period 1780–1860. The austere façade, the upper half of which is destroyed, recalls as a kind of reelaboration that of San Domenico in Ancona in its widely spaced but shorter columns and the rhythmic articulation of the overall scheme.

There are two projects for a centralized church which were hypothetically connected with Cardinal Alessandro's villas in Nettuno and Castello and dated to the 1750s. The first of these two projects, which also includes a ground plan—a transverse octagon with convex bays on the diagonals and an oval room for the high altar—is indebted not only

Marchionni.
Project for a chapel.

to Bernini and Borromini, whose influence is recognizable in the motif of the forward-curving bays, but also to Carlo Fontana, from whom the low campanili set on the transverse axis have been carried over. The second design leans more toward Bernini and brings to mind not only Sant' Andrea al Quirinale with its motif of the screening walls but also the Assunta at Ariccia with the campaniletti placed at the rear of the church.

Although he was endowed with an especially fertile imagination in matters of scenographic effects, Marchionni's connections with the theater are remarkably unknown to us. Sometime before 1763, he was occupied with enlargement projects for the Teatro Argentina, constructed not long before by GIROLAMO TEODOLI, and there are drawings dated 1770 for the decoration of the Teatro Alibert in commemoration of the Emperor Joseph II, who had visited the theater in the preceding year.

There is a series of designs for temporary structures of another nature: catafalques, among which the most notable are the *castrum doloris* for King Augustus III of Poland and Saxony commissioned by Giovanni Francesco Albani for San Salvatore in Lauro (1764). The sarcophagus with the medallion of the king is held aloft by ribs connected to heavy piers that also support four allegorical statues holding trees, which brings to mind Bernini's Fontana dei Quattro Fiumi. An even stronger profusion of vegetal motifs can be observed on other designs for catafalques which make the connection with fountain decoration ever closer.

More architectural is the catafalque for an unidentified king, a pyramid on a high pedestal with a medallion surrounded by a flying angel and a putto, which is evidently derived from Carlo Fontana's monument for Francesco Erizzo in San Marco of 1700. More restraint in the employment of vegetal decoration can also be observed in the catafalque for King Carlo Emanuele III de Savoya of 1773, where Marchionni seems to rely on FILIPPO JUVARRA's catafalque for Carlo Emanuele II (1732).

The major commission of the final period of Marchionni's career concerned the planning and construction of the New Sacristy for St. Peter's, a building task that had been languishing since the days of the rebuilding of the basilica and that included the erection of a palace for the canons. For this enormously important project only a few preparatory drawings related to the structure have survived. However, these are supplemented by the engraved drawings for the building as it stands now. Marchionni's solution consists of an octagonal structure for the *Sagrestia Comune* in the dimensions of the early Christian Tempietto della Madonna delle Febbre which had served as a sacristy on a temporary basis. Marchionni's centralized structure flanked by the lateral sacristies for the

Marchionni. St. Peter's (sacristy). Rome. 1776–1783

canons and the *benefiziati,* faces the southern front of the basilica with a double-ramped staircase, but the connection with the church, the level of which is higher, is performed by twin corridors which connect the sacristy complex with the Porta di Santa Marta and the passage leading to the Cappella del Coro. In the first of these two corridors, Marchionni repeats Carlo Fontana's experiment with the truncated dome of the Baptismal Chapel in St. Peter's, which also receives its light indirectly through an outer window. On the rear side, the edifice for the living quarters has been added around a court, which is completely opened toward the south above the second floor level. In a masterly compromise, Marchionni succeeded to co-ordinate his structure to that of the basilica without totally omitting to provide it with an accent of its own, which consists of the externally visible dome above the Sagrestia Comune, carefully proportioned so as not to interfere with the lateral front of the basilica, from where Michelangelo's surface articulation was accepted as the inspiring source. This had occurred before analogously with the casino façade of the Villa Albani, which echoed that of the Palazzo dei Conservatori on the Capitol. Not executed was a concavely receding building which would have closed the prospect from the palace of the canons toward the south.

Marchionni's life and career span a long period. From the Roman late baroque, as represented by Bernini's direct followers, his style matured in the period of a revival of the Roman full baroque, represented first of all by Ferdinando Fuga. Most formative for his development were the prototypes provided by Michelangelo. But his flexibility was such that he was able even to participate in the rococo movement of Roman eighteenth-century architecture. A series of fountain designs for the Villa Albani, for example, are perhaps the most playful and ingenious expression of this trend.

Marchionni was least convincing when he tried to conform to the new mode of the neoclassical period, an almost paradoxical situation when one considers that his task—as far as Cardinal Alessandro Albani was concerned—had consisted in providing a setting for a most outstanding collection of ancient classical sculpture. No doubt, Marchionni was one of the most talented architects of the Roman Settecento, though more in terms of his ability to solve the problems related to preconditioned situations than in true originality of architectural design.

Relatively little is known about the independent architectural activity of Marchionni's son, Filippo (1738–1805), whose drawings are almost indistinguishable from those of his father. His best known work is probably the Porta Pia at Ancona which honors Pius VI.

HELLMUT HAGER

WORKS

1734, Collegiate Church, Nettuno, Italy. 1738, Cardinal Alessandro Albani Villa (later altered), Anzio, Italy. 1739, Santa Maria Sopra Minerva (monument to Benedict XIII; execution of sarcophagus relief with representation of Lateran Council; statue of angel with Orsini family coat of arms); 1741, Santa Maria Maggiore (statue of unidentified pope); Rome. 1742, San Giovanni (decoration of lateral chapels), Montecelio, Italy. 1743, Santa Croce in Gerusalemme (monument to Benedict XIV); c.1745, Palazzo di Propaganda (vestibule busts); *1746, Santa Maria Sopra Minerva (temporary interior decoration); 1747, San Crisogono (monument to Cardinal Giacomo Milli); Rome. 1747, San Rocco (relief in the Chapel of Saint John), Lisbon. 1748, Sant'Apollinare (statue of Sant' Ignazio), Rome. 1748, Siena Cathedral (relief in the Cappella della Madonna del Voto), Italy. 1755–1757/1762, Villa Albani (casino; coffeehouse, temples, fountains); Rome. c.1756, Molo Clementino of the Harbor, Ancon, Italy. 1763–1786, Piazza del Plebiscito; 1763–1786, San Domenico; Ancona, Italy. *1764, Catafalque (for King Augustus III of Poland and Saxony). Begun 1765, Chiesa della Maddalena, Messina, Italy. *1773, Catafalque (for King Emanuele III of Savoy). 1776–1783, St. Peter's (sacristy), Rome.

BIBLIOGRAPHY

ACCASINA, MARIA 1964 *Profilo dell' Architettura a Messina dal 1600 al 1800.* Rome: Ateneo.

BELLI BARSALI, ISA 1970 *Ville di Roma: Lazio.* Milan: SISAR.

BERLINER, RUDOLF 1958–1959 "Zeichnungen von Carlo und Filippo Marchionni." *Münchner Jahrbuch der bildenden Kunst* 9–10:267–396.

BLUNT, ANTHONY 1968 *Sicilian Baroque.* London: Nicolson; New York: Macmillan.

BRAHAM, ALLAN, and HAGER, HELLMUT 1977 *Carlo Fontana: The Drawings at Windsor Castle.* London: Zwemmer.

CANCELLIERI, FRANCESCO GIROLAMO 1784 *Sagrestia Vaticana eretta dal Regnante Pontefice Pio Sestoe.* Rome: Casaletti.

CARRERAS, PIETRO 1977 *Studi su Luigi Vanvitelli.* Florence: La nueva Italia.

COUDENHOVE-ERTHAL, EDUARD 1930 *Carlo Fontana und die Architektur des römischen Spätbarocks.* Vienna: Schroll.

COUSINS, WINDSOR F. "The Concorso Clementino of 1728." Architectural Fantasy and Reality. Drawings from the Architectural Competitions of the Accademie di San Luca in Rome. Exhibition catalogue, Pennsylvania State University Museum of Art, 1981–1982.

ELLING, CHRISTIAN (1967)1975 *Rome: The Biography of Her Architecture from Bernini to Thorvaldsen.* Translated from Danish by Bob and Inge Gosney. Boulder, Colo.: Westview.

FERRARI, GIOVANNI 1920 *Le Bellezze Architettoniche*

per le feste della chinea in Roma. Turin, Italy.

GAMBARDELLA, ALFONSO 1979 *Architettura e Committenza nello Stato Pontificio tra Barocco e Rococcò.* Naples: Società editrice napoletana.

GAUS, JOACHIM 1967 *Carlo Marchionni: Ein Beitrag zur römischen Architektur des Settecento.* Cologne, Germany: Böhlau.

HAGER, HELLMUT 1970 *Filippo Juvarra e il Concorso di modelli del 1715 bandito da Clemente XI per la Nuova Sacrestia di S. Pietro.* Rome: De Luca.

HAGER, HELLMUT 1981 "Gian Lorenzo Bernini e la ripresa dell' Alto Barocco nell' architettura del Settecento Romano." In *Atti del Convegno Bernini e il Barocco Europeo.* Rome: Istituto della Enciclopedia Italiana.

JACOB, SABINE 1975 *Italienische Zeichnungen der Kunstbibliotek Berlin: Architektur und Dekoration 16. bis 18. Jahrhundert.* Berlin: Staatliche Museen Preussischer Kulturbesitz.

JUSTI, CARL (1898)1956 *Winckelmann und seine Zeitgenossen.* 3d ed. Cologne, Germany: Phaidon.

LEWIS, LESLEY 1961 *Connoisseurs and Secret Agents in Eighteenth-century Rome.* London: Chalto & Windus.

MANCINI, CLAUDIO M. 1967 *S. Apollinare: La Chiese e il palazzo.* Rome: Marietti.

MARCONI, PAOLO 1964 *Giuseppe Valadier.* Rome: Officina Edizioni.

MATTEUCCI, ANNA MARIA, and LENZI, DEANNA 1977 *Cosimo Morelli e l'architettura delle legazioni pontificie.* Imola, Italy: Bologna University Press.

MITCHELL, HERBERT, and NYBERG, DOROTHY (editors) 1975 *Piranesi: Drawings and Etchings at the Avery Architectural Library, Columbia University.* With an introduction by Adolf K. Placzek. New York: Arthur M. Sackler Foundation.

ORTOLANI, SERGIO (1924)1969 *Santa Croce.* Volume 106 in *Le Chiese di Roma Illustrate.* Updated by C. Pericoli Ridolfini. Rome: Marietti.

PORTOGHESI, PAOLO (1966)1970 *Roma Barocca.* Translated by Barbara Luigia La Penta. Cambridge, Mass.: M.I.T. Press.

RICCOBONI, ALBERTO 1942 *Roma nell' arte: La scultura nell' evo Moderno; dal Quattrocento ad oggi.* Rome: Casa Editrice Mediterranea.

SALERNO, LUIGI 1967 *Piazza di Spagna.* Naples: Di Mauro.

SCHIAVO, ARMANDO 1956 *La Fontana di Trevi e le altre opere di Nicola Salvi.* Rome: Istituto Poligrafico dello Stato.

STAMPFLE, FELICE 1978 *Giovanni Battista Piranesi: Drawings in the Pierpont Morgan Library.* With a Foreword by Charles Ryskamp. New York: Dover.

VANVITELLI, LUIGI, JR. (1975)1976–1977 *Vita di Luigi Vanvitelli a cura di Mario Rotili.* With an introduction by Robert Pane and a preface by Guerriera Guerrieri. Galantina, Italy: Congedo.

VASI, GIUSEPPE (1747–1761)1946 Volume 10, page 25 in Alfredo Petrucci (editor), *Le Magnificenze di Roma.* Rome: Palombi.

WITTKOWER, RUDOLF (1958)1973 *Art and Architecture in Italy: 1600–1750.* 3d ed., rev. Harmondsworth, England: Penguin.

MARCONI FAMILY

The Marconi Family was a Polish-Italian architect family between the eighteenth and twentieth centuries.

Leandro Marconi (1763–1837), architect and painter, was born in Mantua, Italy, and did his studies with Paolo Pozzo in Mantova; he practiced in Rome. He built a country house for the Marquis Bagno di Mantova in Savignano.

Giovanni Battista Marconi, architect and painter, brother of Leandro, born in mid-eighteenth century, was an assistant of Paolo Pozzo from 1783 on in the construction of the Arazzi apartment in Plaza Ducale in Mantova; he also did the ceiling decoration of Sant'Andrea in Mantova.

Enrico (Henryk) Marconi (1792–1863), architect, son of Leandro, was born in Rome and died in Warsaw. He studied in Bologna and settled in Warsaw in 1822 where he was both state and private architect.

Leandro Jan Marconi (1834–1919), architect, son of Enrico, was born in Warsaw and died in Montreux, Switzerland. He was assistant to his father. Leandro Jan built a synagogue and various plazas in Warsaw and churches in Smogoszez and Czyzew.

Leonard Marconi (1836–1899), architect and sculptor and a nephew of Giovanni, was born in Warsaw. He taught at the Academies of Warsaw (1856–1858) and of Rome (1859). Leonard worked in Warsaw (1862–1874) and later was professor in Leopoli.

Wladyslaw Marconi (1848–1915), architect, son of Erīc, was born in Warsaw and studied in St. Petersburg. He practiced in Warsaw, where he built houses and country residences.

FARHAD NIROUMAND-RAD

BIBLIOGRAPHY

ARCO, C. D' 1857–1959 *Delle arti e degli artefici di Mantova.* 2 vols. Mantua, Italy: Agazzi.

ŁOZA, STANISŁAW (1917)1954 *Architekci i budowniczowie w Polsce.* Warsaw: Wende.

MATTEUCCI, VITTORIO 1902 *Le Chiese Artistiche del Mantovano.* Mantua, Italy: Segni.

MARCU, DUILIU

After graduating from the School of Architecture in Bucharest, Duiliu Marcu (1885–1966) studied at the Ecole des Beaux-Arts in Paris (1907–1912). From 1929 to 1957, he taught at the Institute of Architecture in Bucharest.

Marcu made a considerable contribution to modern Rumanian architecture through his involvement in housing programs, administration and education, and urban planning. In his early works, he used an eclectic, neoclassical French style. Later, inspired by traditional Rumanian architecture, he turned his attention to creating a modern Rumanian style. His works influenced an entire generation of younger architects.

CONSTANTIN MARIN MARINESCU

WORKS

1927, Art Pavilion and Restaurant (La Colonnade), Soseaua Kiseleff; 1935, Urban Development Plan; Bucharest. *1937, Rumanian Restaurant, Exposition des Arts Décoratifs, Paris. 1937, Apartment Buildings, 61–63 Calea Victoriei and 14 Boulevard Magheru; 1937–1944, Palace of the Council of Ministers; 1941, Palace of State Planning Committee; Bucharest.

BIBLIOGRAPHY

CEGĂNEANU, SP. 1941 "Urbanism, arhitectură şi artă naţională." *Arhitectura* nos. 3–4: 10–17.

IONESCU, GRIGORE 1965 Volume 2 in *Istoria Arhitecturii in Romania.* Bucharest: Editura Academiei Republicii Romañe.

IONESCU, GRIGORE 1969 *Arhitectura in Romania: Perioda anilor 1944–1969.* Bucharest: Editura Academiei Republicii Socialiste Romañia.

IONESCU, GRIGORE 1972 "Saptezeci si cinci de ani de la infiintarea invatamintului de arhitectura din Romania." *Arhitectura* 20:35–42.

MAMBRIANI, ALBERTO 1969 *L'Architettura Moderna nei Paesi Balcanici.* Bologna, Italy: Capelli.

OPREA, DAMIAN 1975 "Duiliu Marcu." *Arhitectura* 23, no. 6:40–45.

PATRULIUS, RADU 1973–1974 "Contributii Romanesti in Arhitectura Anilor '30." *Arhitectura* 21, no. 6:44–52; 22, no. 1:53–59.

POPESCU-CRIVEANU, Şerban 1972 "Atitudini prospective la urbaniştii noştri din trecut." *Arhitectura* nos. 3–4:159–161.

SASARMAN, GHEORGHE 1972 "Incepturile gindirii teoretice in arhitectura româneasča (1860–1916)." *Arhitectura* 20, no. 6:44–46.

MARIGNY, MARQUIS DE

Abel-François Poisson de Vandières (1727–1781), Marquis de Marigny et de Menars, served as the *directeur-général des bâtiments du roi* to Louis XV from 1751 to 1773. Marigny, the younger brother of Madame de Pompadour, was the only man ever specifically trained to direct the centralized arts establishment in France. Marigny is important as a patron for his reorientation of French royal support for the arts to bring royal policy into line with the values of the French Enlightenment, to revitalize the grand classical tradition in France, and to promote the monarchy by associating the Crown with public-spirited projects and a high moral tone. Although Marigny never promoted the adoption of a uniform architectural style for his administration, there did emerge from his circle, which included JACQUES GERMAIN SOUFFLOT and the engraver Charles Nicolas Cochin the Younger, a re-evaluation of classical forms and imagery for modern usage.

Architectural projects for Paris commissioned during his tenure included work to complete the unfinished Louvre, ANGE JACQUES GABRIEL's Place Louis XV (now Place de la Concorde), Soufflot's Sainte Geneviève (now the Pantheon), the Mint by JACQUES DENIS ANTOINE, the École Militaire by Gabriel, and the Comédie Francaise (now the Théâtre de l'Odéon) by CHARLES DE WAILLY and Marie-Joseph Peyre (see PEYRE FAMILY).

Marigny oversaw numerous projects at the royal châteaux including the construction of Gabriel's Petit Trianon at Versailles and major works at Compiègne, Choisy-le-Roi, and Bellevue.

Marigny's own houses in Paris at Roule, on the Place des Victoires, and at the Château de Menars were objects of active architectural experimentation undertaken by his close friend and associate Soufflot.

ALDEN RAND GORDON

BIBLIOGRAPHY

MARQUISET, ALFRED 1918 *Le Marquis de Marigny: 1727–1781.* Paris: Emile-Paul.

MARKELIUS, SVEN GOTTFRID

The architecture of Sven Gottfrid Markelius (1889–1972) may be described as a happy combination of humane and aesthetic functionalism. In town planning, the content of individual buildings and their relationship to their surroundings were equally important.

Born in Stockholm, he graduated in 1913 from the Technical College and in 1915 from the Fine Arts Academy. Thereafter, he traveled through Europe and worked as a draftsman for RAGNAR ÖSTBERG. Markelius's first noteworthy work was a concert hall at Hälsingborg, for which design he won first prize in a competition in 1925. Though not actually constructed until 1932, the concert hall was still innovative a decade after its design. Markelius established his international reputation as an architect with his Swedish pavilion, a masterpiece of aesthetic integration, at the 1939 New York World's Fair. During the war, Markelius built his own villa at Kevinge which demonstrated his desire for integration between buildings and their surrounding landscape.

From 1939–1944, Markelius was the chief of planning of the Royal Board of Building, and from 1944 to 1954, he was director of the Stockholm Planning Commission. In this capacity he initiated the policy of establishing satellite towns to prevent haphazard city growth. He termed these "town sections" to emphasize their integration with the city. In this manner, Vallingby, near Stockholm, was planned and construction was begun in 1953. Other "sections" included Farsta and Högdalen. Markelius developed the master plan for Stockholm, followed by studies for the redevelopment of its central commercial section and for the development of Hötorget in the 1960s. He was no less concerned with the buildings themselves: "Admitting that our greatest and most difficult problem is the planning of our cities—our external environment and its organization and shaping according to men's material demands and spiritual values—we must not overlook the important and often disregarded problems which concern our closer environment, the planning and shaping of buildings" (Markelius, 1964, pp. 153–164).

Markelius felt that social concern in architecture could be expressed most directly in housing. His scheme for the Ör area of Sundyberg accommodated half its population of 12,000 in single-family dwellings interlocked and built over connecting streets to achieve a much higher density than the more usual rowhouses.

Markelius was a most unbiased and conciliatory member of an international group of consultants for the United Nations Building in New York, of the advisory committee on the UNESCO Building in Paris, and of UNESCO's art committee. He taught at the Technical College in Stockholm and was Visiting Professor at Yale University in 1949. In 1945 he was elected honorary corresponding member of the American Institute of Architects, and in 1962 he was awarded the Gold Medal of the Royal Institute of British Architects.

REGINALD R. ISAACS

WORKS

1925, Hälsingborg Concert Hall, Sweden. 1935, Kollektivhus, Sweden. 1936, Stockholm Building Society. 1939, Swedish Pavilion, New York World's Fair. c.1942, Markelius Villa, Kevinge, Sweden. 1953, 1954, Trades Union Center, Linköping, Sweden. 1955, Trades Union Center, Stockholm. c.1965, Hötorget Development, Sweden. 1965?, Ör (Sundyberg) Housing Project, Sweden.

BIBLIOGRAPHY

HAMLIN, TALBOT F. 1939 "Sven Markelius." *Pencil Points* 20:357–366.

MARKELIUS, SVEN 1949*a* "Local Environment." Council for Planning Action, *Symposium* 1:28–30.

MARKELIUS, SVEN 1949*b* "Town Planning Problems of Stockholm." *Architects Year Book* 3:64–75.

MARKELIUS, SVEN 1952*a* "Relation of Dwelling Type and Plan to Layout of Residential Quarters." Pages 36–40 in *Papers of the International Federation for Housing and Town Planning, 20th Congress, Lisbon.* Amsterdam: Van Munster.

MARKELIUS, SVEN 1952*b* "Swedish Land Policy." *Secretariat* 1952:128–142.

MARKELIUS, SVEN 1956 "Stockholms Struktur." *Byggmästaren* 35, #A3:49–76.

MARKELIUS, SVEN 1964 "Architecture in a Social Context." *Architectural Record* 135, Apr.:153–164.

MARKELIUS, SVEN and SIDENBLADH, GÖRAN 1949 "Town-planning in Stockholm." *Svenska Arkitekters Riksförbund* 1949:62–78.

RAY, STEFANO 1969 *Contributo Svedese all' Architettura Contemporanea.* Rome: Edizioni Officina.

SHEPHEARD, PETER 1953 "Sven Markelius." *Modern Gardens.*

MAROT, DANIEL

Among the many talented Protestant artists, architects, and craftsmen who left France after the revocation of the Edict of Nantes in 1685, Daniel Marot (1661–1752) occupies a place of outstanding importance. It was he who, almost single-handedly, brought the full-blown baroque style of the court of Versailles to England and Holland during the reign of William III. Marot's corpus of over 300 engravings—covering architecture, decorative painting, sculpture, furniture, textiles, ceramics, wrought-ironwork and gardening—offers a more comprehensive statement of the Louis Quatorze style than the work of any of his contemporaries. At the same time, it proposes a more unified system of architectural decoration than that attempted by any other designer before the ADAM FAMILY. Marot's influence in the early eighteenth century can be traced as far away as Denmark and Sweden, Germany and Austria; in England, it was to some extent superseded by the Palladian (see ANDREA PALLADIO) school after 1714, but in Holland, the country of his adoption, it remained paramount until the end of his long life. The staid townhouses of Amsterdam and The Hague continued to be built in the vocabulary of Marot's old-fashioned French baroque long after the rising tide of rococo had engulfed the rest of Europe.

In sharp contrast to the widespread influence of Marot's engravings and the key positions he held both at William III's court and at the center of a web of Huguenot craftsmen (most of them connected by marriage), the details of his life and his known works in architecture are tantalizingly obscure. As a draftsman and designer in the widest sense of the word, he appears to have been seldom involved in the execution of the various projects with which he was concerned. He would thus be paid out of a patron's private purse for an elevation or other drawing, and the details would not necessarily be recorded in the latter's regular building accounts. Further documentary evidence of his activities may yet emerge (particularly from English archives), but until then no account of Marot's life can do full justice to his achievement.

Daniel Marot was born in Paris, the eldest son of the architect and engraver Jean I Marot, designer of the châteaux of Turny and Lavardin, the façade of the Church of the Feuillants, and many private *hôtels* in Paris. Although he was associated with JACQUES LEMERCIER in his celebrated project for the Louvre and was the author of a vast unexecuted scheme for a palace at Mannheim, the elder Marot's chief claim to fame lies in the two collections of topographical engravings which he published: the first, the "Petit Marot," between 1654 and 1660; the second, known as the "Grand Marot" because of its larger quarto format, after 1670. Daniel Marot's early schooling in his father's atelier was to be of great importance for his future development, and it is significant that, for instance, his *Nouveau Livre des Bâtiments,* published in Amsterdam about 1700, contains some designs plundered almost line for line from his father's work of forty years earlier.

The other formative influences over the young Marot were the *ornemanistes* Jean Lepautre and JEAN I BERAIN. The latter, as *chef des menus-plaisirs* —second only to the painter Le Brun in the artistic hierarchy of Versailles—commissioned some of Marot's earliest work, such as the engravings of the Triumphs of Louis XIV (1679), the *porte de l'antichambre du roi,* and the lying-in-state of Maria Theresa of Austria at Notre Dame (1683). Themes taken from Berain, and particularly the latter's grotesques ultimately derived from RAPHAEL, run through the whole of Marot's later work. Nor are these confined only to Berain's early work: when, after 1700, Marot came to engrave designs he had first made a decade or so earlier, he edited them to accord better with the more fluid late style Berain had only recently developed, anticipating the Régence. He evidently kept in touch with his old master after leaving France, if only to the extent of acquiring his latest prints.

At the time of the revocation of the Edict of Nantes, in October 1685, Marot was only twenty-four years old, though his precocity as an engraver had already earned comment in the *Mercure galant.* A Huguenot and member of the congregation at the famous Charenton *temple,* he could still have conformed, like his younger brother Jean II Marot,

Marot. Detail of Plate from Nouveau Livre des Bâtiments.

recorded as *architecte du roi* in Paris from 1688 to 1702, or his cousin, the painter François Marot, a member of the Académie Royale after 1702. Instead, Daniel and his youngest brother Isaac chose to go into exile in Protestant Holland, settling in The Hague. It was there that, in 1694, he married Catherina Maria Gole, daughter of a cabinetmaker and niece of Pierre Gole, one of the most celebrated of all Louis XIV's *ébénistes.*

One of Marot's first important commissions in Holland was to design the staircase and other interiors at the Castle of Zeist, near Utrecht. His patron, William Adrian of Nassau-Odijk, had recently served as ambassador to France, and it was probably he who introduced Marot to his cousin, William of Orange. It was also at Zeist that Marot first encountered the Leiden architect Jacob Roman, with whom he was to collaborate closely throughout the 1690s—notably on William and Mary's Palace of Het Loo, near Apeldoorn, where work continued until 1702, and on the house De Voorst (1697–1700) built for William's favorite, Joost van Keppel, earl of Albemarle. Marot's other major work in Holland at this time was the remodeling of the Binnenhof, the meeting-place of the States-General in The Hague.

Although described on the title pages of his engravings as *architecte de Guillaume III, Roy de la Grande Bretagne* and as "Surveyor to the King and director of the workes of building painting &c . . . in great favour & esteem with that Prince," Marot occupied a position at the Stadholder's court more like that of Berain than JULES HARDOUIN MANSART at Versailles. The form and decoration of interiors, the layout of gardens and designing of garden buildings, even the occasional drawing for an exterior façade, might lie within his province, but he remained a *maître-ornemanistes* rather than a practicing architect in the modern sense. At Hampton Court, for instance, he was employed as early as 1689 to design the great semicircular parterre on the east front and to remodel the interiors of the old Water Gallery for Queen Mary, but CHRISTOPHER WREN and WILLIAM TALMAN between them retained control of the new buildings grouped around the Fountain Court.

Marot's two eldest children were baptized in London in 1695 and 1696, and he is known to have worked for the duke of Montagu, among other English patrons. In the purely architectural field, his name has been associated with a group of three important English houses: Petworth in Sussex, Boughton in Northamptonshire, and Montagu House in London (the last two owned by the duke of Montagu and the first by his stepdaughter, the duchess of Somerset). All three have idiosyncratic features which can be paralleled in Marot's engravings, but not in the work of his English contemporaries.

Daniel Marot's first patent for an edition of engravings was taken out in The Hague in 1687, and over the next fifteen years a spate of prints followed, usually published in a series of six at a time, with titles such as the *Livre d'Ornemens,* the *Nouveau Livre de Placfond,* and the *Livre d'appartement,* many of them representing executed designs both in England and Holland. The first collected edition of 108 plates, the *Oeuvres du Sieur D. Marot,* was published by Pierre Husson in The Hague in 1703, perhaps to re-establish the first copyrights, which had just lapsed. A second edition of 126 plates, published in Amsterdam, followed in 1713; and after that, a two-volume version with Dutch title pages containing a total of 237 plates. A characteristic of Marot's style, established by these engravings, is the recurrence of decorative motifs translated into every medium: the busts on tapered plinths derived from Lepautre, for instance, can be seen in the carved wooden overmantels at De Voorst, in stone on the west front of Petworth, or in the Delft tulip-vases designed for Queen Mary II; the tassled cloth-of-estate, one of Le Brun's favorite devices, can be seen in designs for ceiling paintings, coaches, clocks, even parterres.

Though he may have visited England again after 1697, Marot seems to have resided mainly in The Hague from that date, except for the period from 1705 until about 1713, which he spent in Amsterdam. His pension of 900 guilders a year granted by William III in 1698 was confirmed by the States-General after the king's death, and Marot subsequently worked for the Friesian Stadtholder Johan Willem and his wife Amalia von Anhalt at Oranienstein (now in Germany) and Oranjewoud. He also greatly enlarged the Huis ten Bosch, near The Hague, for William IV. In general, however, Marot's services were called on by a much wider range of rich mercantile and official patrons after 1702, and his role became more purely architectural and less that of an *ornemaniste* outside the court circle. In addition to smaller garden buildings such as the pavilions at Rozendaal, near Arnhem, and at the Huis Fagel in The Hague—two of his finest surviving works—, he was capable of grand townhouse façades like those of the Brants Rushofje on the Heerengracht in Amsterdam, and the Huis Huguetan (now the Royal Library) in The Hague.

Marot.
Palace Het Loo.
Apeldoorn, Netherlands.
c.1687–1702

The most important of such later townhouses was undoubtedly the Huis Wassenaar-Obdam (later known as the Paleis Kneuterdijk) in The Hague. Here, confronted with an exceptionally awkward site, Marot showed that he could, on occasion, produce a plan of great ingenuity: façades full of baroque movement and united by an oval dome, conceal difficult changes of axis and oddly projecting wings. Buildings like this and the drama of some of Marot's architectural interiors, such as the staircase at the Huis Schuylenburch, nearby on the Lange Vijverberg, may well have influenced German architects of the following decades, notably LUCAS VON HILDEBRANDT and JOHANN BERNARD FISCHER VON ERLACH.

Daniel Marot's last known works date from the late 1730s, though he lived on into extreme old age. His eldest son, Daniel Marot the Younger (1695–1769), assisted his father as a draftsman for many years besides purusing his own independent career as a decorative painter, designer, and engraver. A younger son, Jacob, also practiced as an architect.

GERVASE JACKSON-STOPS

WORKS

1686, Slot Zeist (interiors and garden buildings), Utrecht. c.1687–1702, Palace Het Loo (interiors, gardens, and garden buildings), Apeldoorn, Netherlands. (A)c.1689–1694, Boughton House (north front), Northamptonshire, England. (A)c.1689–1694, Montagu House, London. (A)c.1689–1696, Petworth House (west front), Sussex, England. 1689–1698, Hampton Court Palace (interiors of Water Gallery and gardens), Middlesex, England. 1696, *Meer en Berg* (garden and orangery), Heemstede, Netherlands. 1696–1698, Binnenhof (interiors, including *Trèveszaal*), The Hague. 1697–1700, De Voorst (interiors), Zutphen, Netherlands. 1707–1709, Schloss Oranienstein (additions and interiors), Diez an der Lahn, Germany. 1707, Huis Fagel (including garden and pavilion), 138–140 Noordeinde, The Hague. 1707, Slot Oranjewoud (alterations), Heerenveen, Netherlands. 1715, Huis Schuylenburch, 8 Lange Vijverberg; 1716–1717, Huis Wassenaar-Obdam (later Paleis Kneuterdijk); The Hague. 1717, Kasteel Duivenvoorde (Grote Zaa), Voorschoten, Netherlands. (A)c.1724, Kasteel Rozendaal (interiors, garden pavilion, cascade), near Arnhem, Netherlands. 1725–1726, Portuguese Synagogue, The Hague. 1732–1734, Brants Rushofje, 475 Heerengracht, Amsterdam. 1734–1735, Town Hall (new wing); 1734–1737, Huis Huguetan (now Royal Library); 1734–1739, Huis ten Bosch (additions, including new wings); The Hague.

BIBLIOGRAPHY

BÉRART, A. 1865 "Catalogue de toutes les estampes qui forment l'oeuvre de Daniel Marot." *Revue universelle d'arts* 20:289–319, 361–390.

HIJMERSMA, HERBERT JAN, and CORNFORTH, JOHN 1974 "Kasteel Duivenvoorde, Holland." *Country Life* 155:130–133, 186–189.

Marot. Huis Schuylenburch. The Hague. 1715

JACKSON-STOPS, GERVASE 1976 "Slot Zeist, Netherlands." *Country Life* 160:534–537, 594–597.

JACKSON-STOPS, GERVASE 1977*a* "The Building of Petworth." *Apollo* 105:324–333.

JACKSON-STOPS, GERVASE 1977*b* "Huis Schuylenburch, The Hague." *Country Life* 161:722–725, 786–789.

JACKSON-STOPS, GERVASE 1980 "Daniel Marot and the 1st Duke of Montagu." *Nederlands Kunsthistorisch Jaarboek* 31:244–262.

JESSEN, PETER 1892 *Das Ornamentwerk des Daniel Marots.* Berlin: Wasmuth.

LANE, ARTHUR 1949 "Daniel Marot: Designer of Delft Vases and of Gardens at Hampton Court." *Connoisseur* 123:19–24.

LANE, ARTHUR 1959 "Delftse tegels uit Hampton Court en Daniel Marot's werkzaamheid aldaar." *Bulletin van het Rijksmuseum* 7:12–21.

OZINGA, M. D. 1939 *Daniel Marot: De Schepper van den Hollandschen Lodewijk XIV-Stijl.* Amsterdam: Paris.

ROYAARDS, C. W. 1972 *De restauratie van het Koninklijk Paleis Het Loo.* The Hague: Staatsdrukkerij.

MARSHALL, JOSHUA

Joshua Marshall (1629–1678) was a sculptor (mainly of tombs) and mason-contractor. In 1673 he succeeded his father, Edward Marshall, as master mason to the king. He worked at royal palaces and on several important buildings in London, notably Saint Paul's Cathedral, the Monument, Temple Bar, and some of CHRISTOPHER WREN's city churches, but he is not known to have designed any buildings himself. The best-known work from his hand is the pedestal for Hubert Le Sueur's equestrian statue of Charles I at Charing Cross, London.

IAN CHILVERS

BIBLIOGRAPHY

COLVIN, HOWARD (editor) 1976 Volume 5 in *The History of the King's Works: 1660–1782.* London: H.M. Stationery Office.

GUNNIS, RUPERT (1953)1968 *Dictionary of British Sculptors 1660–1851.* Rev. ed. London: Abbey Library.

KNOOP, DOUGLAS, AND JONES, D. P. 1935 *The London Mason in the Seventeenth Century.* Manchester (England) University Press.

WHINNEY, MARGARET 1964 *Sculpture in Britain 1530–1830.* Harmondsworth, England: Penguin.

MARTIN, LESLIE

Sir (John) Leslie Martin (1908–) received his professional education at the Manchester University School of Architecture, obtaining the M.A. and Ph.D. degrees. Between 1930 and 1934, he was assistant lecturer and master of design at that university. Appointed head of the School of Architecture at Hull in 1930, he remained there until 1939.

In 1937, Martin was co-editor with Ben Nicholson and Naum Gabo of *Circle,* an international survey of constructive art. This publication, organized to define the aims of constructive, nonfigurative art enlisted Barbara Hepworth, Piet Mondrian, LE CORBUSIER, MARCEL L. BREUER and WALTER GROPIUS as contributers to present a united front among modern artists and architects. In 1939 Martin became principal assistant architect for the London Midland Scottish Railway. From 1948 to 1953, he was deputy architect for the London County Council, and from 1953 to 1956 he was architect to the Council.

From 1956 to 1972, Martin was professor and head of the University of Cambridge Department of Architecture and concomitantly opened his practice. He served as consultant to the universities of Leicester, Hull, and London to 1978. He held the Slade Professorship of Fine Art at Oxford in 1965–1966, the Gropius Lectureship at Harvard in 1966, and the Bishop Professorship at Yale in 1973–1974.

A Fellow of the Royal Institute of British Architects, he was knighted in 1957. He was awarded the Soane Medal in 1930, the London Architecture Bronze Medal in 1954, and the Royal Institute of British Architects Distinction in Town Planning in 1956. In 1973 he was presented with the R.I.B.A.'s Gold Medal.

Martin's approach to planning is a comprehensive one. The distinctive qualities of his architecture are achieved through his understanding of relationships in programming, selection of construction methods and materials, and by his regard for the context of the buildings. In education, he insisted on consideration of basic architectural concepts, on thorough research, and on recognition of the totality of environment.

REGINALD R. ISAACS

WORKS

1951, Royal Festival Hall (with Robert Matthew, PETER MORO, and Edwin Williams), London. 1956, College Hall (with Trevor Dannatt), University of Leicester, England. 1957–1962, Harvey Court Residential Building (with Colin St. John Wilson and Patrick Hodgkinson), Cambridge University. 1959, Library Buildings (with Wilson); 1964–1970, Zoology/Psychology Building (with Douglas Lanham); Oxford University. 1969, Kettle's Yard Gallery (extensions; with David Owers), Cambridge University. 1970, Government Centre (with Owers), Taif, Saudi Arabia. 1972, Pembroke College Library and Saint Ebbe's Building (with Colin Lumley), Oxford University. 1978, New Music School (with Lumley and Ivor Richards), Cambridge University.

BIBLIOGRAPHY

MARTIN, LESLIE 1937 "The State of Transition." Pages 215–219 in *Circle London.* London: Faber.

MARTIN, LESLIE 1953 "Walter Gropius: 70 Years." *Architects Year Book* 5:27–28.

MARTIN, LESLIE 1957 "Construction and Intuition." In *Gabo.* London: Lund Humphries.

MARTIN, LESLIE 1965 *Whitehall: A Plan for the National and Government Centre.* London: H. M. Stationery Office.

MARTIN, LESLIE 1968 "Education Without Walls." *Journal of the Royal Institute of British Architects* 75:356–361.

MARTIN, LESLIE 1978 "Notes on a Developing Architecture." *Architectural Review* 164:10–17.

MARTIN, LESLIE, and MARCH, LIONEL (editors) 1972 *Urban Space and Structures.* Cambridge University Press.

MARTIN, LESLIE; NICHOLSON, BEN; and GABO, N. (editors) 1956 *High Flats: Report of a Symposium Held on 15 February 1955.* London: Royal Institute of British Architects.

MARTIN, LESLIE, and SPEIGHT, S. 1939 *The Flat Book.* London: Heinemann.

MARTIN, LESLIE, and WILSON, COLIN 1974 "Too Big for Its Site." *Architectural Review* 155:68–70.

MARTINELL BRUNET, CÉSAR

César Martinell Brunet (1888–1973), a Catalan architect, studied at the School of Architecture of

Barcelona, graduating in 1916. During his study years, he met ANTONIO GAUDÍ Y CORNET who was working on the Church of the Holy Family in Barcelona. This contact and his twin vocations of architect and historian of Catalan architecture eventually resulted in his publication of the works of Gaudí.

As an architect, Martinell constructed, between 1918 and 1920, a long list of buildings for agricultural cooperatives as well as stores, grain silos, warehouses, and housing. In constructing these buildings, Martinell frequently employed the parabolic arches used by Gaudí and his circle of followers and developed a repertory of technical solutions and decorations based on the possibilities of traditional materials. Closed arches of brick, storerooms and conveyances, covered roofs, and grand portals were shaped in brilliant constructive solutions starting with economical materials and the exploitation of traditional construction techniques. The cooperative of Roquefort de Queralt (1918), the agricultural syndicates of Nules (1918) and Falset (1919), the large cooperative stores of Pinell de Brai (1919) and Gandesa (1920), and the agricultural syndicates of Cornudella (1919), Montblanc (1919), Barbera (1920), Llorenç del Penedés (1919), and Sant Guim (1920) are some of the most significant works of this period.

Engaged in more traditional works, Martinell specialized in the restoration of historical buildings. Outstanding examples are the monasteries of Poblet and Santes Creus, the Seu Vella de Lleida, the Seu d'Urgell and the churches of Sant Pere de Reus, Santa Maria de Igualada, and the parochial church of Arenys.

Much of this work was accompanied by studies and historical monographs, such as the studies on Seu de Lleida (1923), Poblet (1927), Santes Creus (1919), and Igualada (1944). But his works on baroque art in Catalonia and on Gaudí were the most important. His *Baroque Architecture and Sculpture in Catalonia* (3 vols., 1959–1964) and his monograph on *The Sculptor Bonifàs i Masso 1730–1781* (1948) are the most significant publications on the subject. On Gaudí he published various texts to which belongs his fundamental work, *Gaudí, his life, his theory, his work* (1967), published in several languages. Martinell at the end of his life published an autobiographical book detailing his experience as architect of the agricultural buildings, *Agrarian Constructions in Catalonia* (1975), which contains precious information on his activity and the execution of his plans for rural architecture.

IGNASI DE SOLÀ-MORALES
Translated from Spanish by Judith E. Meighan

WORKS

1918, Agricultural Syndicate, Nules, Spain. 1918, Cooperative, Roquefort de Queralt, Spain. 1919, Agricultural Syndicate, Cornudella, Spain. 1919, Agricultural Syndicate, Falset, Spain. 1919, Agricultural Syndicate, Llorenç de Penedés, Spain. 1919, Agricultural Syndicate, Montblanc, Spain. 1919, Cooperative, Pinell de Brai, Spain. 1919, Santes Creus Monastery (restoration), Spain. 1920, Agricultural Syndicate, Barbera, Spain. 1920, Agricultural Syndicate, Sant Guim, Spain. 1920, Cooperative Store, Gandesa, Spain. 1923, Seu Vella de Lleida (restoration), Spain. 1927, Poblet Monastery (restoration), Spain. 1944, Santa Maria de Igualada (restoration), Spain. 1946, Parochial Church of Arenys (restoration), Spain. 1948, Sant Pere de Reus (restoration), Spain. 1949, Seu d'Urgell (restoration), Spain.

BIBLIOGRAPHY

BOHIGAS, ORIOL 1973 *Reseña y Catalogo de la arquitectura modernista.* Barcelona, Spain: Lumen.

MARTINELL Y BRUNET, CÉSAR 1976 *Construcciones agràrias en Cataluña.* With an introduction and prologue by Ignasi de Solà-Morales. Barcelona, Spain: Gaya Ciencia.

MARTINELLI, DOMENICO

Born in Lucca, Italy, Domenico Martinelli (1650–1718) took clerical vows before entering the studio of CARLO FONTANA in Rome in 1678. He taught perspective at the Roman Academy of Saint Luke in 1683–1689 and 1705–1716, but built little in Rome or elsewhere in Italy. Except for a few modest commissions in his native Lucca, his principal works are located in Vienna and eastern Europe where he was active from 1690–1705. Like another Fontana pupil, JOHANN BERNARD FISCHER VON ERLACH, Martinelli was instrumental in the dissemination of Italian ideas north of the Alps. His town palace for the Prince of Liechtenstein in Vienna (1692–1705) is his most innovative and important work.

JOHN VARRIANO

WORKS

c.1690, Harrach Palace; 1692–1705, Town Palace for the Prince of Liechtenstein; 1694–1711, Suburban Palace for the Prince of Liechtenstein; Vienna. 1698, Liechtenstein Palace, Landskron, Bohemia, Czechoslovakia. 1700–1710, Buchlowitz Palace; n.d., Ausee Palace; Moravia, Czechoslovakia. n.d., Chapel of Saint Ignatius, San Giovanni, Lucca, Italy. n.d., Kaunitz Palace, Austerlitz, Czechoslovakia. n.d., Palazzo Talenti; n.d., San Andrea (high altar); n.d., San Nicolo; Lucca, Italy.

BIBLIOGRAPHY

FRANCESCHINI, GIOVANNI BATTISTA 1772 *Memoria della vita di Domenico Martinelli.* Lucca.

GRIMSCHITZ, BRUNO (1944)1947 *Wiener Barockpaläste.* Vienna: Wiener Verlag.
KUBÁTOVÁ, TAT'ÂNA 1956 "Architekt Domenico Martinelli." *Umĕni* 4:133–144.
"Náčrt činnosti Domenica Martinelliho na Moravĕ." 1963 *Sbornik practi filosoficke fakulty Brnĕnske university* 12:63.
TIETZE, HANS 1919 "Domenico Martinelli und seine tätigkeit für Österreich." *Jahrbuch des Kunsthistorischen Institutes des Staatsdenkmalamts.* 13:1–46.

MARTINEZ, FRANCESCO

Francesco Martinez (1718–1777), sculptor and architect and a relative of FILIPPO JUVARRA, was born in Messina and died in Turin, Italy. He studied in Rome before being called to Turin in 1740 to assist BENEDETTO ALFIERI. Appointed royal architect in 1765, he worked in Novara on the campanile of San Gaudenzio (1760s) and the Hospital (1770–1789); in Cuneo on the façade of the Jesuit College (1776), now Municipio; in Albiano d'Ivrea he designed San Martino (1775); and in Turin, the façade of Santissima Annunziata (1776). The tombs of Carlo Emanuele III and Vittorio Amedeo II in the Basilica at Superga (1773) and the altar of Santi Cosimo and Damiano in San Francesco d'Assisi, Turin survive.

HENRY A. MILLON

WORKS

1760s, San Gaudenzio (campanile); 1770–1789, Hospital; Novara, Italy. 1773, Basilica (tombs of Carlo Emanuele III and Vittorio Amedeo II), Superga, Italy. 1775, San Martino, Albiano d'Ivrea, Italy. 1776, Jesuit College (façade, now Municipio), Cuneo, Italy. 1776, Santissima Annunziata (façade); n.d., San Francesco d'Assisi (altar of Santi Cosimo and Damiano); Turin, Italy.

BIBLIOGRAPHY

BAUDI DI VESME, ALESSANDRO 1966 Volume 2 in *Schede Vesme.* 3 vols. Turin, Italy: Società piemontese di archeologia e belle arte.
CARBONERI, NINO 1963 Volume 1, pages 656–657 in *Architettura, Mostra del Barocco Piemontese.* Turin, Italy: Catalogo a cura di Vittorio Viale.
COLI, LAURA, and SESIA, DARIO 1963 *Ingegneri e architetturi del sei e settecento in Piemonte.* Turin, Italy: Società Ingegneri e Architetti.

MARTINI, FRANCESCO DI GIORGIO

See FRANCESCO DI GIORGIO MARTINI.

MARTORELL, JOAN

Joan Martorell y Montells (1833–1906) is the best-known representative of the Eclectic school of Barcelona. His thorough knowledge of Gothic architecture and other medieval styles had a strong influence on his buildings. He considered himself a disciple of EUGÈNE EMMANUEL VIOLLET-LE DUC and was the first Spanish architect to use graphic statics. Martorell was born in Barcelona. After studying at the School of Master Builders (a body of guild origins), he obtained his degree in architecture in 1876. He was among the first graduates at the Barcelona School of Architecture, having studied with ELIAS ROGENT I AMAT.

A man of deep religious faith, Martorell carried out his professional career mainly in Barcelona and in Comillas, Santander, where he built the Palace of Sobrellano (1878–1888) and a chapel and family vault in a neo-Gothic style for the marquis and marquise of Comillas (1878–1881). He submitted a design for the Pontifical Seminary (1881–1890), which was carried out in collaboration with Cristòfol Cascante i Colom. This design included a church which is considered among the best examples of Spanish Eclecticism. The church's rich trimming reveals the influence of Byzantine architecture.

Martorell took part in a competition to build the façade of the Cathedral of Barcelona which was still uncompleted. His project was welcomed, but it was not carried out in the end. Martorell is the author of a good number of restorations and reconstructions of medieval buildings, among them the remarkable removal and reconstruction (1888) of the Church and Convent of Montsió (built in 1388), which is an exemplary building of Catalan Gothic architecture.

Martorell was influenced by English neo-Gothic architecture, as can be seen in the Saint Ignatius School of the Jesuits (1893–1896). This building, designed in collaboration with CAMIL OLIVERAS GENSANA, is considered a copy of British colleges in Oxford and Cambridge. More specifically, he was influenced by WILLIAM BUTTERFIELD and the *The Ecclesiologist* group with which he agreed as to the use of bricks (*opus latercicium*) as façade trimming. He also adopted enameled pottery inlays and some typological solutions, one of which was the use of belfry foundations as a vestibule, as in the Church of the Salesas (1882–1885), which is undoubtedly his most outstanding work. This church reflects the specific influence of public and religious Catalan Gothic architecture, as well as that of Gothic, Romanesque, and Mudejar styles. All these elements are integrated, in the traditional scheme of a Latin cross plan, by means of new formal solutions that anticipated Catalan modernism; the Church of the Salesas is considered one of its clearest precedents.

In 1900, the Barcelona city council awarded him a prize for his building for the Mercantile Credit Society, for which he drew his inspiration from neo-classical and Academicist architecture.

ANTONIO GAUDÍ Y CORNET stands out among his disciples. Gaudi worked with Martorell during his youth. Martorell used his influence to help Gaudi obtain a concession for the building of the Church of the Holy Family in Barcelona.

MIGUEL PÉREZ I SÀNCHEZ

WORKS

1874–1876, Church and Convent of the Worshippers, Barcelona, Spain. 1878–1881, Chapel and Family Vault of the Marquis and Marquise of Comillas; 1878–1888, Palace of Sobrellano, Comillas; 1881–1890, Pontifical Seminary (with Cristòfol Cascante y Colom); Comillas; Santander, Spain. 1882, Cathedral of Barcelona (façade). 1882, Convent of Villaricos (with Antoni Gaudi y Cornet); 1882–1885, Church and Convent of the Salesas; 1883–1885, Church and Convent of the Jesuit Priests (with Camil Cliveras y Gensana); 1885–1892, Parish of Saint Stephen (with Emili Sala y Cortes), Castellar del Vallès; 1886–1887, Church of Saint Monica (reconstruction); 1888, Church and Convent of Montsió (removal and reconstruction); 1888, Church of the Mercedes (dome); 1893–1896, Saint Ignatius's School of the Jesuit Priests (with Cliveras); 1896–1900, Mercantile Credit Society; 1897, Monastery of Pedralbes; Barcelona, Spain.

BIBLIOGRAPHY

BOHIGAS, ORIOL, and POMÉS, LEOPOLDO 1968 *Arquitectura Modernista.* Barcelona, Spain: Editorial Lumen.

HERNANDEZ-CROS, J. EMILI; MORA, GABRIEL; and POUPLANA, XAVIER 1973 *Arquitectura de Barcelona.* Barcelona, Spain: COACB.

NAVASCUES PALACIO, PEDRO 1978 Volume 5 in *Historia del Arte Hispánico.* Madrid: Alhambra.

PIFERRER, P., and PI Y MARGALL, FCO. Volume 1 in *España, sus monumentos y artes. Su naturaleza e historia.* Barcelona, Spain: Cortazo.

RÁFOLS, JOSE F. (editor) 1951–1954 *Diccionario biográfico de artistas de Cataluña desde la época romana hasta nuestros días.* 3 vols. Barcelona, Spain: Milla.

ROGENT Y PEDROSA, FRANCISCO 1897 *Arquitectura moderna de Barcelona.* Barcelona, Spain: Parera.

MARUSCELLI, PAOLO

Paolo Maruscelli (1596–1649) was a productive baroque architect of the same generation as GIANLORENZO BERNINI, FRANCESCO BORROMINI, and PIETRO DA CORTONA. He was something of a specialist in residential architecture for the religious orders established in Rome, particularly the Filippini, the Dominicans, and the Theatines. It is possible that he received his training in the orbit of GIOVANNI BATTISTA SORIA and GIROLAMO RAINALDI. Unlike the many Tuscans and Lombards who had immigrated to Rome, he is one of the very few native Roman architects of the period; at the end of his rather brief career, he was active as a hydraulic engineer organizing a company to drain the Pontine Marshes. Almost forgotten today, he achieved a respectable reputation among his contemporaries and won some of the most important commissions of the day.

His first patrons appear to have been the Filippini, or followers of San Filippo Neri, who employed him to design the Chiesa Nuova in Perugia (1626–1649) and the definitive projects for their Roman oratory and residence, the Casa dei Filippini (1622–1636). For the latter, he worked in close collaboration with the Oratorian priest and architectural amateur VIRGILIO SPADA, who helped him evolve the final design in 1627 and who oversaw the initial stages of construction in 1629–1634. Maruscelli's project is remarkable chiefly for the way in which it synthesized three earlier sources into a new imagery uniquely suited to the new type of organization which the Oratorians had developed, in particular, ANDREA PALLADIO's Convent of the Carità in Venice, PELLEGRINO TIBALDI's Archepiscopal Palace in Milan, and Giovanni Battista Soria's Palace of the Borghese Retinue in Rome. In 1637, however, Maruscelli lost the commission to Borromini, who transformed his project and added the famous curved façade to the oratory. Maruscelli continued as the architect of several other religious houses, particularly the Theatine House at Sant'Andrea della Valle (1629–?), the sacristy of Santa Maria dell'Anima (1636–1644), and the east convent wing attached to the cloister of Santa Maria sopra Minerva (1638–1642). In addition, he served Cardinal Bernardino Spada as the architect of many minor alterations in the Palazzo Spada-Capodiferro

Maruscelli. Palazzo Medici-Madama (rebuilding and renovation). Rome. 1642

(1633–1649), including a painting gallery and a painted perspectival illusion that was a forerunner of Borromini's perspective colonnade (1652). But his main commission was the renovation and rebuilding of the Palazzo Medici-Madama in Rome (1642), which involved the enlargement of an early Renaissance palace, the construction of several new wings and a grand *salone,* and the design of an imposing façade, loosely modeled on the Palazzo Farnese façade, but enriched with princely motifs including Hercules and the Lion of Leo X. Given the fact that the Medici were at war with Pope Urban VIII at the time the palace was rebuilt, the façade should be interpreted as a statement about Medici power and autonomy vis-à-vis the Papal State.

Maruscelli's erudition and theoretical interests may be deduced from the library of 123 volumes which was inventoried in his house at his death. In addition, about thirty of his architectural drawings have been identified in museums and Roman archives; they show him to have been a skilled, colorful, and impeccably neat draftsman.

JOSEPH CONNORS

WORKS

1622–1636, Sacristy of Santa Maria in Vallicella (with project for oratory and residence), Rome. 1626–1649, Chiesa Nuova (not completed until 1665), Perugia, Italy. 1629–?, Theatine House at Sant'Andrea della Valle; 1633–1649, Palazzo Spada-Capodiferro (alterations); 1635, San Carlo ai Catinari (front left chapel); 1636–1644, Sacristy of Santa Maria dell'Anima; 1638–1642, Santa Maria sopra Minerva (east convent wing); 1642, Palazzo Medici-Madama (rebuilding and renovation); Rome.

BIBLIOGRAPHY

CONNORS, JOSEPH 1980 *Borromini and the Roman Oratory: Style and Society.* Cambridge, Mass.: M.I.T. Press.

GNOLI, DOMENICO 1926 "Il Palazzo del Senato già Madama." *Nuova Antologia* 248:249–264.

POLLAK, OSKAR 1910 "Architektenmärchen." *Kunstgeschichtliches Jahrbuch der k.k. Zentral-Kommission für Erforschung und Erhaltung der Kunst und historischen Denkmale* 4:168–174.

MARVUGLIA, GIUSEPPE VENANZIO

Giuseppe Venanzio Marvuglia (1729–1814) was the most influential early neoclassical architect in Sicily. Born in Palermo, Marvuglia studied architecture in Rome from 1747 to 1759; the neoclassicism of Cardinal Alessandro Albani's circle and the late baroque architecture of LUIGI VANVITELLI had a lasting influence upon him. After his return to Palermo, Marvuglia's first major commission was the Monastery of San Martino delle Scale (1762–1774), which is baroque in its scale and grandeur but neoclassical in its ornamental restraint and severity. From this period also is his Oratory of San Filippo Neri (1769) attached to the Church of the Olivella, a sophisticated admixture of Vanvitellian and Louis XV style. Similar combinations of baroque and classical elements can be seen in his Palermo palaces such as Palazzo Galati (c.1770) and Palazzo Riso-Belmonte (c.1780), while the villas he designed, for example, Villa Villarosa at Bagheria (c.1770), emulated Louis XV style.

In 1789, Marvuglia met LÉON DUFOURNY, who was a scholar of Greek architecture in Sicily. While in Palermo, Dufourny designed the Gymnasium (1789) of Palermo's Botanical Garden, which was a revolutionary building because of its use of the Greek Doric order. Impressed by Dufourny's building, Marvuglia designed two flanking pavilions, the Tepidarium and the Caldarium (1789), in a similar stripped neoclassical style.

In addition to experimenting with the Doric order, as in his Fountain of Hercules at the Villa della Favorita (1814), Marvuglia toward the end of his life also produced chaste versions of Palladianism (see ANDREA PALLADIO), such as his villa Belmonte all'Acquasanta (1806) below Monte Pellegrino, and experimented with chinoiserie in his Palazzina Cinese.

STEPHEN TOBRINER

WORKS

1762–1774, Monastery of San Martino delle Scale; 1769, Oratory of San Filippo Neri all'Olivella; c.1770, Palazzo Galati; Palermo, Italy. c.1770, Villa Villarosa, Bagheria, Italy. 1772, San Francesco di Sales; 1776, Palazzo Coglitore; c.1780, Palazzo Riso-Belmonte; c.1780–c.1880, Palazzo Geraci; c.1785–1788, Palazzo Costantino; 1789, Tepidarium and Caldarium, Botanical Garden; c.1800, Palazzina Cinese; Palermo, Italy. 1803, Hunting lodge for Ferdinand IV, Ficuzza, Italy. 1806, Villa Belmonte all'Acquasanti; 1814 Hercules Fountain, Villa della Favorita; near Palermo, Italy.

BIBLIOGRAPHY

BLUNT, ANTHONY 1968 *Sicilian Baroque.* London: Weidenfeld & Nicolson.

CALCAGNO, ANNALZA MANIGLIO 1967 "Contributo allo studio di Venanzio Marvuglia." *Quaderni della Facoltà di Architettura dell'Università di Palermo.* 10, no.11: 37–93.

CARACCIOLO, EDOARDO 1955 "L'architettura dell'Ottocento in Sicilia." *Atti del Congresso nazionale di Storia dell'Architettura.* Palermo, Italy: The congress.

CARONIA ROBERTI, SALVATORE 1934 *Venanzio Marvuglia (1729–1814).* Palermo, Italy: Priulla.

COMANDÈ, GIOVANNI BATTISTA 1958 *Giuseppe Venanzio Marvuglia.* Palermo, Italy: Edizione "Casa nostra."

MEEKS, CARROLL L. V. 1966 *Italian Architecture: 1750–1914.* New Haven: Yale University Press.

MARX, ROBERTO BURLE

See BURLE MARX, ROBERTO.

MASCHERINO, OTTAVIANO

Ottaviano Mascherino (1536–1606) was born Ottavio dei Nonni in Bologna, Italy. Spanning the second half of the sixteenth century, with the high point of his career in the 1580s and 1590s, Ottaviano's life coincides with the age of transition between the mannerist and baroque periods.

Mascherino spent the first half of his life in Bologna, where he trained as an architect and a painter. Projects such as the 1569 Porta San Isaia, which was destroyed in a twentieth-century expansion of the city, date from this period, as well as fresco commissions in numerous Bolognese palaces.

It was in his capacity as a painter that Mascherino's talents were first recognized outside of Bologna. In 1574, two years after the Bolognese Cardinal Ugo Buoncompagni became Pope Gregory XIII, Ottaviano was summoned to Rome. Here, he painted in the Vatican palace, introducing Rome to the illusionistic style of quadratura painting then popular in Bologna. Mascherino was one of the first channels through which the Bolognese school was brought to sixteenth-century Rome.

From 1574 to 1578, Ottaviano is mentioned in the Vatican archives as a painter, and in 1576 he joined the Roman Academy of Saint Luke as such. He is first listed as an architect in the Vatican documents of 1578, and from that time until 1585, the papal archives list him in connection with a 1574 building campaign in the Vatican Cortile di San Damaso and additions to DONATO BRAMANTE's Cortile di Belvedere, which were built between 1578 and 1580 and 1582 and 1585.

Mascherino's activity in Rome was not limited to the Vatican. He built several churches and palaces in the city, among them the Palazzo dei Commanditore di Santo Spirito (1574–1585), a project commissioned by Gregory XIII, and the Church of San Salvatore in Lauro (1591–1600). As with painting, Mascherino introduced certain traits common to northern Italian architecture into the buildings of Rome. At San Salvatore, he encircled the nave with a colossal order of engaged marble columns. Popular in the north, this motif, which was later developed by seventeenth-century architects such as CARLO RAINALDI, was unfamiliar in Rome in the late sixteenth century. It created a new sense of interior spatial organization in the church. Cinched as it was by columns, the nave became visually separate from the unadorned transept, an effect different from the consistently articulated wall surface common in such churches as GIACOMO BAROZZI DA VIGNOLA's Church of the Gesù (1568).

Mascherino's major project for Gregory XIII was the planning of the Quirinal Palace as a summer residence. This took place between 1583 and 1585, the year of Gregory's death. At that time Ottaviano was replaced by FLAMINIO PONZIO, the choice of Pius V.

In the sixteenth century, the Quirinal Hill was essentially a rural area filled with the summer residences of church officials and upper class Romans. As designed by Mascherino, the palace rose over and incorporated elements of a summer house which had existed on the site since the early sixteenth century. As it is preserved in plan, Mascherino's design for the project shows a squat, rectangular courtyard enclosed on four sides. The main entrance is set on the short, two-storied south end, while a loggia, also of two stories, stands opposite it to the north. Longer wings with rooms and passageways connect these two members, the one on the east being a full story higher than the one on the west. This plan differs substantially from the courtyard as it was finally built: in the end, the connecting wings were lengthened, a clock tower was added over the loggia, and the west wing was built to the same height as the east.

The choice of components in Mascherino's complex is interesting and important, as is the change between the stages of planning and execu-

Mascherino. Palazzo del Quirinale. Rome. 1583–1585

tion. In combining a courtyard with a loggia, Mascherino's palace juxtaposes elements from two hitherto distinct architectural genres, the urban and the suburban. The courtyard springs from the former, the loggia from the latter. The coupling of these elements is interesting in that it shows Mascherino's creative treatment of earlier sixteenth-century architectural forms in response to the needs and wishes of his patron.

The loggia on the courtyard's northern end is the most interesting aspect of Ottaviano's treatment. The façade of the loggia consists of five arcuated bays in two stories with architectural moldings worked in flat, undecorated strips. A clock tower rises over the central bay and a low balustrade runs the length of the upper level, checking any of the vertical impulses suggested by the tower. Inside, a spiral staircase, oval in shape and edged by rows of paired Doric columns, connects the two levels, while the loggia itself is joined to the flanking east and west wings by shallow, projecting pavilions. The voids of the arcades balance neatly with the solids of the pavilions, and bays between pavilion and arcade afford an easy visual passage between the two. This combination of the urban and the suburban resulted from the specific needs of the pope. Although Mascherino was eager to preserve aspects of the rural *vigna* on his design for the summer palace, the ceremonial commitments which the pope needed to honor even in the hottest days of summer demanded that he incorporate more formal, urban elements into his palace design; hence, the courtyard for receiving visitors and the loggia's second-story balcony, which connected with the papal apartments and functioned as a benediction loggia.

This novel combination of different genres shows Mascherino working creatively within the vocabulary of the Renaissance architectural tradition to answer new needs and develop new aesthetic concepts. In the seventeenth century, it became commonplace for elements of suburban architecture to invade the city. Mascherino's project for the Quirinal set the stage for this kind of development.

The changes introduced into the Quirinal project between the final stages of Mascherino's blueprint and the actual building of the courtyard are instructive as to trends in late sixteenth-century architecture. The elongation of the courtyard through the expansion of the connecting wings and the building of those wings to an identical height create a strong axis which focuses unequivocally on the loggia. In the original plan, this axis was ambiguous. The shorter and proportionally broader courtyard made a less insistent vista, and this, in turn, was offset by the fact that the west wing was a story lower than the east, revealing a view of Rome. The viewer was thus drawn away from the loggia by a secondary vista; this ambiguity was characteristic of more fully mannerist designs. This consciously developed aesthetic principle is visible in the courtyard of BALDASSARE PERUZZI's Palazzo Massimi, Rome (1536), where a fountain to the right of the central axis competes with the main axis for attention, and in Mascherino's own design for the Vatican Cortile di San Damaso (1578), where his addition is two stories lower than those previously built. As constructed, however, the courtyard at the Quirinal is without this spatial ambiguity. Rather, the deep, straight plunge to the loggia is emphasized by the expanded length of the courtyard and the even height of its enclosing wings. This sense of direction and framing anticipated a more fully developed baroque aesthetic.

A movement toward the development of the same aesthetic is evident in the design of the loggia façade. In the balance of solid and void and the accent on the horizontal, there is a sense of classical harmony and unity in the façade. It is not, however, the same sense present in the architecture of the High Renaissance. The rhythm of line, void, and mass depends not only on the regularity of repetition, but also on interruption, variation, and stressed movement, as in the switch from single to paired pilasters between the open and closed areas of the façade. This interest in varied articulation of the façade is characteristic of more fully developed baroque architectural schemes such as CARLO MADERNO's façade for the Church of Santa Susana, Rome (1603).

Mascherino's career coincides with one of the more exciting periods in the urban history of Rome. In the late sixteenth century, Europe was in the throes of the Counter Reformation and Rome was the seat of that movement. The memory of the city's sack by the army of Charles in 1527 was fading and Rome was beginning to flourish anew. Eager to ornament their city for its role as the center of the great new Christian Roman Empire, the popes of the last half of the century instigated numerous building campaigns, the most famous of which was Sixtus V's revamping of the city street system under DOMENICO FONTANA. Using traditional forms to develop a new aesthetic, Mascherino's architecture partook of the resurgent and enthusiastic spirit of his age. Although he certainly owed a great debt to the architects of the early Renaissance and mannerist periods, the clarity of direction, focus, and articulation in his final projects places him in the vanguard of the creators of the baroque style.

SARAH E. BASSETT

WORKS

*1569, Porta San Isaia, Bologna, Italy. 1574–1585, Palazzo dei Commanditore di Santo Spirito, Rome. 1575, Villa dell'Opera Pia Cassoli Guastavillani, Bologna, Italy. 1578, Cortile di San Damasco (loggia), Vatican City; 1578, Modern Archive (third story), Vatican City; 1578, Torre dei Venti; Vatican City; 1580, Capella Bandini, Church of San Silvestro al Quirinale; 1582–1585, Cortile di Belvedere (west loggia, upper court), Vatican City; 1583–1585, Palazzo del Quirinale; 1591–1600, Church of San Salvatore in Lauro; 1592, Church of Santa Maria della Scala (façade); 1593, Church of Santo Spirito dei Napoletani (façade); Rome.

BIBLIOGRAPHY

ACKERMAN, JAMES 1954 *The Cortile del Belvedere.* Vatican City, Rome.

BRINCKMANN, A. E. 1915–1919 *Die Baukunst des 17 und 18 Jahrhunderts in den Romanischen Landern.* Berlin: Akademisches Verlagsgesellschaft Athenaion.

CALLARI, LUIGI (1907)1970 *I Palazzi di Roma.* Reprint. Rome: Bardi.

FROMMELL, O. L. 1973 *Die römische Palastbau der Hochrenaissance.* Tübingen, Germany: Wasmuth.

GOLZIO, VINCENZO 1929–1930 "Note su Ottaviano Mascherino architetto in Roma." *Dedalo* 10:164–194.

GUIDI, M. 1941 "Gli architetti del Palazzo del Quirinale da Gregorio XIII a Paolo V." *L'Urbe* 6:2ff.

OJETTI, R. 1913 "Ottaviano Mascherino." *Atti e Memorie della Reala Accademia di San Luca, Annuario* 3:106ff.

RICCI, C. (1882)1968 *Guida di Bologna.* Reprint. Bologna, Italy: Alfa.

WASSERMAN, JACK 1963 "The Quirinal Palace in Rome." *Art Bulletin* 45, no. 3:205–244.

WITTKOWER, RUDOLF (1958)1973 *Art and Architecture in Italy: 1600–1750.* 3d ed., rev. Baltimore: Penguin.

MASÓ I VALENTI, RAFAEL

Graduated from Barcelona's School of Architecture in 1906 and practicing in Girona, Rafael Masó i Valenti (1888–1935) was one of the most representative architects of what can be called the Catalan Secession. Formed in the years of greatest strength of Modernisme, he nevertheless manifested his adherence to those who were renovating that language in the more classical style of Noucentisme as formulated by Eugenii d'Ors and initiated by JOSEF PUIG I CADAFALCH from about 1904. By means of a progressive simplification of Modernista language—in line with Viennese Secessionists like JOSEF HOFFMANN and CHARLES RENNIE MACKINTOSH's Glasgow school—Masó incorporated elements from the Spanish popular baroque tradition, following a modern and flexible style that resulted in one of his best moments: the Masramón House (1914). His later move toward Mediterranean sensibility in his various works in S'Agaró (1929–1935) is of much less interest polemically.

ADOLF MARTÍNEZ I MATAMALA
Translated from Spanish by Judith E. Meighan

WORKS

1907–1910, Mas El Soler, Carretera d'Anglés, Sant Hilari Sacalm; 1908, Masó Pharmacy, 25 Carretera de l'Argentería; 1909–1910, Batelle House, 2 Carretera Fontanilles; 1910–1911, Teixidor Flour Company, 42 Carretera de Santa Eugenia; 1911, Salieti House, 8 Carretera Ciutadans; 1911–1912, Masó House, 29 Carretera de les Ballesterías; 1913, Athenea Building, 30 Carretera J. Anselm Clave; 1913–1915, Ensesa House, 68 Carretera Barcelona; 1914, Masramón House, 6 Carretera Vayreda, Olot; 1916, Casas, Carretera a la Platje de Sant Pol, Sant Feliu de Guíxols; 1921–1923, Gispert-Sauch House, 66 Avenida Jaime I; 1926–1927, La Económica Palafrugellense Cooperative, 18 Carretera de Sant Martí; 1928–1929, Teixidor Urbanization, 1, 3, and 5 Carretera Ibéria; Gerona, Spain. 1929–1930, Houses, S'Agaró, Spain.

BIBLIOGRAPHY

COOPER, A. E. W. 1966 "Gerona Modernista." *Cuadernos de Arquitectura* no. 63:34–40.

PERICAS, JOSEP MARIA 1935 "L'arquitecte Rafael Masó i la ciutat de Girona." *Arquitectura i Urbanisme* no. 7:3–9.

Presència 1977 no. 299: entire issue.

TARRÚS GALTER, JOAN 1971 *Rafael Masó.* Barcelona, Spain: The author.

MASON, GEORGE C. SR.

Born into Newport, Rhode Island's old-line elite, George C. Mason, Sr. (1820–1894), was an artist, antiquarian, writer, some-time real estate agent, civic leader, and self-taught architect. The first architect residing in Newport, he opened his office in 1858. His most interesting buildings date to 1860. In that year, Mason designed four large cottages which established his reputation. His apprentices included DUDLEY NEWTON and GEORGE C. MASON, JR. The latter became his father's partner in 1871, and the office was retitled George C. Mason & Son. From about 1870 on, most of the firm's design work is credited to Mason, Jr.

DAVID CHASE

WORKS

1860, Edward Ogden House; 1860, Edmund Schermerhorn House; 1860, George Tiffany House; *1860–1890, August Belmont Estate; 1862–1863, Long Wharf School; *1863, Leonard Jerome House; *1864–1865, Antonio Iznaga del Valle House; *1865–1867, A. P.

Merrill House; 1867–1869, Kay Chapel; 1873–1874, George C. Mason, Sr. House II; 1874–1875, Redwood Library (addition); *1877–1878, Thomas Dunn House; 1891–1892, Naval War College; Newport, R.I.

BIBLIOGRAPHY

CASE, DAVID 1974 *The Kay Street—Catherine Street—Old Beach Road Neighborhood, Newport, R.I.* Providence: Rhode Island Historical Preservation Commission.

DOWNING, ANTOINETTE F., and SCULLY, VINCENT J., JR. (1952)1967 *The Architectural Heritage of Newport, Rhode Island: 1640–1915* 2d ed., rev. New York: Potter.

JORDY, WILLIAM H., and MONKHOUSE, CHRISTOPHER (editors) 1982 *Rhode Island Buildings on Paper.* Cambridge, Mass.: M.I.T. Press.

MASON, GEORGE C., SR. 1858 *The Application of Art to Manufacturers.* New York: Putnam.

MASON, GEORGE C., SR. 1875 *Newport & Its Cottages.* Boston: Osgood.

MASON, GEORGE C., SR. 1878 *The Old House Altered.* New York: Scribners.

"Necrology." 1895 *Publications of the Rhode Island Historical Society* New Series 3, no. 1:50–55.

Newport Mercury. 1848–1895.

MASON, GEORGE C. JR.

George Champlin Mason, Jr. (1850–1924) entered the Newport, Rhode Island, office of his father, GEORGE C. MASON, SR., in 1865. The firm became George C. Mason & Son in 1871, and Mason, Jr., executed most of the firm's design work after about 1870. During the early 1870s, he created a series of architecturally ambitious and occasionally startling buildings, all in Newport. In 1876, the Mason office produced the Queen Anne style Cranston Street School, and soon Mason, Jr., was designing Queen Anne residential structures marked by an aggressive yet spritely use of Colonial detail. In the late 1880s, Mason, Jr., moved to Philadelphia, opened a branch office, and started designing Dutch and "Flemish Renaissance" style masonry buildings.

After 1895, Mason, Jr., did little work. What he did do largely involved restoration. Indeed, he may be the first American architect to make restoration a specialty: his earliest restoration projects date to the 1870s. Mason, Jr., published widely on architectural subjects, including his restoration projects. He took a keen interest in professional matters, becoming a fellow of the American Institute of Architects upon admission in 1875 and serving as national secretary from 1883 through 1886.

DAVID CHASE

WORKS

*1869–1870, Thomas Cushing House; 1871–1872, Loring Andrews House; *1871–1872, Frederick Sheldon House; 1872, de Ternay Monument (restoration); *1872–1873, Newport Exchange; 1873–1874, George C. Mason, Sr., House II; 1873–1874, Rogers High School; 1873–1876, George Fearing House; *1876–1877, Cranston Street School; *1877–1878, Thomas Dunn House; 1878–1879, Old Stone Mill (restoration); *1882–1883, Fitch Bosworth House; *1882–1883, Gardner Block/A. C. Titus Store; 1884, Sabbatarian Meeting House (restoration); *1886, F. O. French Banquet Hall; 1886–1888, Belmont Chapel; Newport, R.I. 1888, Sarah B. and George C. Mason, Jr., Townhouses, Philadelphia. 1889–1890, Sarah Zabriskie House; 1891–1892, Naval War College, Newport, R.I. 1896, Gloria Dei Church (restoration); 1898, Delancey School; c.1910, Saint James Kinsessing Rectory; Philadelphia.

BIBLIOGRAPHY

The George C. Mason, Jr., manuscript scrapbook is in the Redwood Library, Newport, R.I.

CHASE, DAVID 1974 *The Kay Street—Catherine Street—Old Beach Road Neighborhood, Newport, R.I.* Providence: Rhode Island Historical Preservation Commission.

JORDY, WILLIAM H., and MONKHOUSE, CHRISTOPHER (editors) 1982 *Rhode Island Buildings on Paper.* Cambridge, Mass.: M.I.T. Press.

MASON, GEORGE C., JR. 1907 *Architects & Their Environment: 1850–1907.* Ardmore, Pa.: Privately printed.

Newport Mercury. 1865–1895.

MASON, GEORGE DEWITT

Trained in the office of Detroit architect Henry T. Brush, George D. Mason (1856–1948) practiced in that city with Zacharias Rice from 1878 to 1898, then alone, always keeping pace with the various style changes over the years in his large practice. Active in professional organizations, he was particularly interested in the education and registration of architects.

GWEN W. STEEGE

WORKS

*1882, Joseph H. Berry House, Grosse Pointe, Mich. 1886, Young Men's Christian Association, Detroit, Mich. 1887, Grand Hotel, Mackinac Island, Mich. 1889, First Presbyterian Church, Detroit, Mich. 1892, Hiram Walker and Sons Office Building, Walkerville, Ontario. 1898, Detroit Opera House; 1907–1916, Pontchartrain Hotel; 1922–1926, Masonic Temple; 1931, Central Woodward Christian Church; Detroit, Mich.

BIBLIOGRAPHY

FERRY, W. HAWKINS 1968 *The Buildings of Detroit: A History.* Detroit, Mich.: Wayne State University Press.

MASON, WILLIAM

Born at Ipswich, England, William Mason (1810–1896) entered the London office of EDWARD BLORE. After brief practice in Ipswich, he went to Sydney where he worked with MORTIMER W. LEWIS and then to New Zealand as superintendent of works for Governor Hobson. He practiced independently in Auckland from 1841 to 1862 and in Dunedin from 1862 to 1874. He was mayor of Dunedin and a member of Parliament.

JOHN STACPOOLE

WORKS

1836, Poorhouse, Epsom, England. 1836, Poorhouse, Stroud, England. 1837, Church of Saint James, Brightlingsea, England. 1837, Church of Saint Lawrence, East Donyland, England. 1838, Saint Botolph's Church, Colchester, England. *1841, Saint Paul's Church; 1856, Old Government House; Auckland, New Zealand. *1863, Bank of New Zealand; 1865, All Saints' Church; 1865, Edinburgh House; *1865, Exhibition Buildings; *1865, Post Office (Stock Exchange); 1866, Bank of New South Wales; *1866, Provincial Council Chambers; 1872, Bishopscourt (Columba College); 1873, Saint Matthew's Church; Dunedin, New Zealand.

BIBLIOGRAPHY

STACPOOLE, JOHN 1971 *William Mason: First New Zealand Architect.* New Zealand: Auckland University Press.

MASSARI, GIORGIO

Giorgio Massari (1687–1766) was the most important Venetian architect of the second third of the eighteenth century. Massari's working career spanned some fifty years in which he was involved in a prodigious number of secular and ecclesiastical commissions all over the Venetian state, where he was born. Tradition has it that Massari was a pupil and follower of the architect Andrea Tirali, but it was also through BALDASSARE LONGHENA, the great Venetian baroque architect, that Massari absorbed Palladian (see ANDREA PALLADIO) architectural ideas and motifs as well as the use of plastic decoration.

Nothing is known of Massari's initial training, but many of the parish churches and villas which he designed in the Venetian countryside display certain Palladian motifs both in their façades and in their interiors. One such example is Massari's first documented work, the Villa Tamagnini-Massari-Lattes at Istrana (c.1712). Massari's integration of Palladian motifs is evident in the placement of the two small oculi on either side of the third-floor windows of the façade. Massari's first ecclesiastical commission appears to have been the Parish Church of Vedelago (c.1717), but no precise documents have survived. In 1720, Massari presented his designs for the Church of Santa Maria della Pace, in Brescia, and building was begun in that same year. The church has been compared to GIUSEPPE SARDI's façade for Santa Maria degli Scalzi in Venice (begun 1656), for its façade has the same five-part horizontal division with four massive columns and a two-part vertical design.

Massari's most famous ecclesiastical work is the Chiesa dei Gesuati (1725–1736) located on the Canal della Giudecca in Venice. As in Palladio's San Giorgio Maggiore (as revised by VICENZO SCAMOZZI), Massari's façade is articulated by four engaged Corinthian columns on high pedestals surmounted by a triangular pediment with a central oculus. The portal with two Corinthian columns is reminiscent of Palladio's Church of the Redentore. Yet, if the general disposition recalls Palladio, the individual treatment of detail is much less restrained. In particular the corner grouping of the columns, which has a certain undulating quality, is to be noted. In the interior, Massari retained the elegant Palladian motif of the freestanding columns in the choir which again reflects the Church of the Redentore. The plan as well is derived from that of the Redentore, each church having a single nave with three chapels on each side. But the design of the choir is substantially different in the Gesuati. Perhaps the most significant difference between the two churches lies in the treatment of light. In the Redentore, light comes in through both the side chapel windows and the clearstory windows. In the Gesuati, light enters only through the high windows above the chapels. Highest illumination is thus given to the nave and its wall surfaces while the chapels lie in a much softer shadow.

During the years that Massari was involved in the building of the Gesuati, he was at work as well on the replanning of the church and Hospital of the Catecumeni (1727–1744) and the Scuola di San Giovanni Evangelista (1727–?) Massari's scrupulous attention to detail is evident in his interest in designing the railings, kneelers, and altars for the Catecumeni. In San Giovanni Evangelista, Massari modernized the great salon, raising the ceiling and incorporating typically eighteenth-century decoration.

These were years of intense work for Massari. In 1735, he won the contest for the reconstruction of the Church and Hospital of Santa Maria della Pietà. Work, however, was not begun until 1744 (the hospital was never completed). The church also served as an auditorium for concerts of sacred music with choirs and orchestras, and as such it was known throughout Europe. Massari's elliptical, centrally planned design, with its rounded corners and vault, combined the characteristics of concert hall and church. His concern with every aspect of the architecture is again apparent in his attention to the design of minor architectural features, such as confessionals, pulpits, and iron gratings. Contemporary accounts relate that the church was widely praised, and in his voyage of 1786, Goethe preferred concerts in that church over any other. Construction was still in progress in 1755, when the ceiling was frescoed. The large fresco in the central compartment of the ceiling by Giambattista Tiepolo is one of his most successful mature works.

In 1731, Massari began construction of the façade of Sant'Antonio at Udine, one of his most neoclassical works. Again, four Corinthian columns are placed on high pedestals. A triangular pediment surmounts the whole. It has been said that one finds the same motifs here as in the Church of the Gesuati, but in a more personal manner. From 1738 to 1743, Massari was involved in the reconstruction of the Church and Hospital of the Penitenti, which was never completed. The exterior stone on the façade of the church rises only to the levels of the plinths of the columns.

Two of Massari's best-known secular works are the completion of the Palazzo Rezzonico (1750–1766) and the Palazzo Grassi (1748–1766), both in Venice. The Palazzo Rezzonico is one of the most famous buildings on the Grand Canal, today housing the city's museum of eighteenth-century decorative arts. It was begun in 1667 by Baldassare Longhena, and only the first floor was complete at the time of his death in 1682. In 1748, Massari was hired to complete the second and third stories, following Longhena's designs and the intermediate work of ANTONIO GASPARI. One of Massari's changes was to eliminate the socles on the columns, thus lightening the effect of the entire façade. Massari's touches are noticeable as well in the detail given to doors and to the staircase.

In 1748, Massari was given the commission to build a palace for the Grassi family opposite the zation of the dome of Cividale (begun 1760). Palazzo Rezzonico. The façade is in a restrained neoclassical mode. The ground-floor plan, where a four-columned atrium leads to a square courtyard and on to a handsome grand staircase is beautifully proportioned. These un-Venetian elements have been perfectly integrated into the house.

One of Massari's last projects was the moderni-From surviving drawings we know that Massari's suggestions were followed, although after his death in 1766 notable alterations occurred. Massari's last work in Venice was the redesigning of the façade of the old Scuola della Carità (1756). It is very difficult, however, to discern his part, for the building was substantially altered in the nineteenth century.

As an architect, Giorgio Massari combined many aspects of older styles with contemporary novelties to create a uniquely personal style that made him one of the outstanding architects of the eighteenth century.

CARLA PUPPIN

WORKS

c.1712, Villa Tamagnini-Massari-Lattes, Istrana (Treviso), Italy. *c.1717, Parish Church of Vedelago (Treviso), Italy. 1720–1742, Church of Santa Maria della Pace, Brescia, Italy. 1725–1736, Church of the Gesuati; 1727–1744, Church and Hospital of the Catecumeni; 1727–?, Scuola di San Giovanni Evangelista, Venice, Italy. c.1731, Church of Sant'Antonio, Udine, Italy. 1738–1743, Church and Hospital of the Penitenti; 1744–1760, Church and Hospital of Santa Maria della Pietà; 1748–1766, Palazzo Grassi; 1750–1766, Palazzo Rezzonico; 1756, Scuola della Carità (façade); Venice, Italy. 1760–?, Dome of Cividale, Italy.

BIBLIOGRAPHY

BASSI, ELENA 1962 *Architettura del Sei e Settecento a Venezia.* Naples: Edizioni scientifiche italiane.

MASSARI, ANTONIO 1971 *Giorgio Massari: Architetto Veneziano del Settecento.* Venice: Pozza.

MOSCHINI, VITTORIO 1932 "Giorgio Massari: Architetto Veneto." *Dedalo* 12:198–229.

MATAS, NICCOLO

Niccolo Matas (1798–1872) is best known as the designer of the façade of Santa Croce in Florence, Italy. He was one of several nineteenth-century Italian architects engaged in the renovation of Florence and the completion of its medieval and Renaissance monuments. His projects for Santa Croce reveal a profound understanding of the vocabulary of fourteenth-century Florentine architecture.

CHRISTINE SMITH

WORKS

(A)1854, Cemetery (behind San Miniato al Monte); (A)1857–1863, Santa Croce (façade); Florence.

BIBLIOGRAPHY

BRUES, EVA 1965 "Die Fassade von S. Croce in Florenz, ein Werk des Architekten Matas." *Mitteilungen des Kunsthistorischen Instituten in Florenz* 12:151–170.

MATHIEU DE LAYENS

Mathieu de Layens (?–1483) is recorded in 1445 as town architect of Louvain, Belgium, a post he held until his death. Best known as architect of the Town Hall in Louvain (1447–1463), one of the most important monuments of flamboyant Gothic in the Netherlands, he also designed the Tabernacle of the Passion for Saint-Pierre, Louvain (1450) and the Church of Sainte-Waudru in Mons, Belgium (1458–1469).

ELIZABETH SCHWARTZBAUM

WORKS

1439–1475, Saint-Pierre (transept and reconstruction of belfry after the fire of 1458); 1447–1463, Town Hall; 1450, Tabernacle of the Passion, Saint-Pierre; Before 1453, Saint-Quentin (choir); Louvain, Belgium. 1458–1483, Sainte-Waudru (not completed until 1691), Mons, Belgium. 1467–1483, Saint-Jacques (choir and transept not completed until 1488); *1480–1488, Building, east side of Grand'Place (not completed until 1488); Louvain, Belgium.

BIBLIOGRAPHY

EVEN, EDWARD VAN 1858 *Monographie de l'église de Saint-Pierre à Louvain.* Brussels: Fonteyn.

EVERAERTS, ADOLPHE 1872 *Monographie de l'Hôtel-de-ville de Louvain.* Louvain, Belgium: Icky & Ferdinand.

LEMAIRE, RAYMOND (editor) 1971 *Province de Brabant: Arrondissement de Louvain.* Volume 1 in *Le Patrimoine Monumental de la Belgique.* Liège, Belgium: Solédi.

PIRLOT, CONSTANT (editor) 1975 *Province de Hainaut: Arrondissement de Mons.* Volume 4 in *Le Patrimoint Monumental de la Belgique.* Liège, Belgium: Solédi.

TONDREAU, LUCY 1972 *La collégiale Sainte-Waudru à Mons.* Mons, Belgium: Fédération du tourism de la province de Hainaut.

VAN HAMME, M. 1972 "L'hôtel de ville de Louvain." *Brabant* 1.

MATTE-TRUCCO, GIACOMO

Giacomo Matte-Trucco (1869–1934), born in Trevy, France, graduated from the Politecnico in Turin in 1893. An engineer, he worked primarily for the Fiat Motor Company designing production facilities. His widely illustrated Fiat Lingotto Factory in Turin (1916–1923) was an important early example of modern architecture.

DENNIS DOORDAN

WORK

1916–1923, Fiat Lingotto Factory, Turin, Italy.

BIBLIOGRAPHY

POZZETTO, MARCO 1975 *La Fiat-Lingotto.* Turin, Italy: Centro Studi Piemontesi.

SIGNORELLI, BRUNO 1975 "Architetti della Fiat." In *Studi in onore di Renzo Gandolfo.* Turin, Italy: Centro Studi Piemontesi.

MAUFE, EDWARD BRANTWOOD

Edward Brantwood Maufe (1883–1974) was educated at Wharfedale School, St. John's College, Oxford, and was then articled to W. A. Pite. Throughout the interwar period, his domestic work had a stylish "alternative" modernity reflecting the influence of Sweden. He was noted as a designer of modern churches, and his interwar churches show him developing a style of simplified Gothic. His cathedral at Guildford, won in competition in 1932, carries this simplification still further. He was chief architect to the Commonwealth War Graves Commission (1941–1969). After the war, he rebuilt Gray's Inn and Middle Temple, London, in a scholarly neo-Georgian style. Maufe's work had a rare sensitivity and expressed historicism in its most simplified form.

MARGARET RICHARDSON

WORKS

1912–1914, Kelling Hall, Norfolk, England. 1922–1923, Church of Saint Bede and Institute for the Royal Association in Aid of the Deaf and Dumb, Clapham Road; 1924, Church of Saint Saviour (for the R.A.D.D.), Acton; London. 1926, Shepherd's Hill (alterations), Buxted, Sussex, England. 1928–1929, Far Scar, Grassington, Yorkshire, England. 1929, Yaffle Hill, Water Tower Road, Broadstone, Dorset, England. 1931, Religious Studio, British Broadcasting Corporation, Portland Place; 1932, Church of Saint Thomas, Hanwell; London. 1932–1966, Guildford Cathedral, Surrey, England. 1936, Heal and Company (extensions), Tottenham Court Road, London. 1936, Playhouse Theatre, Oxford. 1937–1938, Church of Saint John the Evangelist, Hook, Hampshire, England. 1937–1939, Chapel Court and North Court, Saint John's College, Cambridge. 1936–1954, Saint John's College (alterations and extensions), Oxford. 1949–1951, Royal Air Force Memorial, Coopers Hill, Runnymede, Surrey, England.

BIBLIOGRAPHY

CORNFORTH, JOHN 1975 "Shepherd's Hill, Sussex." *Country Life* 158, Oct.:906–909.

MAUFE, EDWARD 1946 *Modern Church Architecture.* London: Incorporated Building Society.

"Obituary." 1975 *Architect's Journal* 161, no. 2:67–68.

"Obituary." 1975 *Building* 227, nos. 51–52:27.

"Obituary." 1974 *The Times,* Dec. 14, p. 14.

MAWSON, THOMAS HAYTON

Thomas Hayton Mawson (1861–1933) was a largely self-taught English landscape architect and town planner. A noted orator and writer, he traveled and lectured widely in Europe, the United States, Canada, and Australia. He worked closely with CHARLES F. A. VOYSEY and with the firm of GEORGE AND PETO. Mawson blended architecture with landscaping and advocated a closer liaison among architects, landscape architects, and town planners, following American "City Beautiful" ideals, the grand designs of European cities, and English landscape and colonial city planning traditions. A man with a strong social conscience, he strove to have schools of landscape architecture and town planning established in England, based on those in America. After World War I, he became a founding member of the Royal Fine Arts Commission in London, designed "ideal" towns for the war disabled, and lobbied for the erection of war memorials. His sons studied architecture at the Ecole des Beaux-Arts in Paris before joining their father's firm. The resulting family business still flourishes in Lancaster, England.

E. JOYCE MORROW

WORKS

1889, Graythwaite Hall, Sawrey, Lancashire, England. 1899, Mound Stuart, Isle of Bute, Scotland. 1902, Foots Cray Place, Kent, England. 1905–1912, Thornton Manor, Thornton Hough, Cheshire, England. 1906, The Hill, Hampstead, England. 1908, Huidöre, Copenhagen. 1908–1910, Peace Palace Gardens, The Hague. 1912, Dalhousie University Campus, Nova Scotia. 1912, Houses of Parliament Gardens, Regina, Saskatchewan. 1912, Royal Gardens, Athens. 1912, University of Saskatoon Campus, Saskatchewan. 1913, Royal Palace Gardens, Corfu, Greece. 1922, Stanley Park, Blackpool, England.

BIBLIOGRAPHY

BEARD, GEOFFREY, and WARDMAN, JOAN 1976 *Thomas H. Mawson, 1861–1933: The Life and Work of a Northern Landscape Architect.* England: University of Lancaster Visual Arts Centre.

MAWSON, THOMAS H. (1900) 1926 *The Art and Craft of Garden Making.* 5th ed. London: Batsford.

MAWSON, THOMAS H. 1911 *Civic Art: Studies in Town Planning, Parks, Boulevards and Open Spaces.* London: Batsford.

MAWSON, THOMAS H. 1914 *Borden Park, Ottawa: Report on the Development of the Estate for the Great Eastern Realty Co.* London: Mawson.

MAWSON, THOMAS H. 1914 *The City of Calgary, Past, Present and Future.* London: Batsford.

MAWSON, THOMAS H. 1917 *An Imperial Obligation: Industrial Villages for Partially Disabled Soldiers and Sailors.* London: Grant Richards.

MAWSON, THOMAS H. 1917 *Afforestation for the Partially Disabled.* London: Grant Richards.

MAWSON, THOMAS H. 1927 *The Life and Work of an English Architect.* London: Batsford.

MORROW, E. JOYCE 1979 *Calgary, Many Years Hence.* Calgary, Alberta: Comprint.

MAXWELL, EDWARD, and MAXWELL, W. S.

Edward Maxwell (1867–1923) and William Sutherland Maxwell (1874–1952) designed an outstanding variety of houses for wealthy Montreal clients and were equally skilled in the planning of public and commercial buildings. Edward Maxwell, the eldest son of a successful Montreal lumber merchant, worked for SHEPLEY, RUTAN, AND COOLIDGE in Boston before establishing his own practice in 1892. This experience during his formative years greatly influenced his conception of architecture. Early buildings, especially the H. V. Meredith House (1892–1893) and the Henry Birks and Sons Jewelry Store (1893), display the transitional, half-Romanesque–half-Renaissance style which he developed during his apprenticeship in Boston. He was best known for his series of picturesque railway stations and hotels built for the Canadian Pacific Railway at various locations along its transcontinental line.

W. S. Maxwell, Edward's younger brother, became his partner in 1902. Together they designed palatial buildings in a grand neoclassical manner. The Regina Parliament Buildings (1907–1910), Regina, Saskatchewan; the J. K. L. Ross House (1908), Montreal; and the Montreal Art Association Gallery (1910–1912) reveal the influence of W. S. Maxwell's formal training at the Ecole des Beaux-Arts in Paris. The Tower Block and Saint-Louis Wing of the Château Frontenac Hotel in Quebec City (1920–1924) was their crowning achievement. Their office operated on the atelier system and provided sound training for young draftsmen, including JOHN SMITH ARCHIBALD.

ROBERT LEMIRE

WORKS

EDWARD MAXWELL

1892–1893, H. V. Meredith House; 1893, R. B. Angus and D. McIntyre Houses; 1893, Henry Birks and Sons Jewelry Store; *1893, E. S. Clouston House; 1893, James Crathern House; *1893, Knox Presbyterian Church; 1893, J. B. Learmont House; 1894, H. A. Allan House; Montreal. 1894, G. W. Cook House, Westmount, Quebec. 1895, Selkirk Cross House; 1895, R. A. E. Greenshields House; 1895, Merchants' Bank of Halifax; Montreal. 1896, J. B. Allan House, Senneville, Quebec. 1896, J. M. Elder House, Westmount, Quebec. 1897, Canadian Pacific Railway Station, Moose Jaw,

Northwest Territories. 1897, Canadian Pacific Railway Station, Vancouver, British Columbia. 1897, James Crathern House, Sainte-Agathe-des-Monts, Quebec. 1897, Melville Presbyterian Church, Westmount, Quebec. 1897, Charles Meredith House; 1897, F. L. Wanklyn House; Senneville; Quebec. 1898, J. H. Birks House, Montreal. 1898, B. Hal Brown House, Saint-Bruno, Quebec. 1898, Canadian Pacific Railway Station, McAdam Junction, New Brunswick. 1898, Canadian Pacific Railway Station, Sicamous Junction, British Columbia. 1898, J. Gardner House; 1898, London and Lancashire Life Building; 1898, A. Paterson House; Montreal. 1898, E. L. Pease House, Saint-Bruno, Quebec. 1898, T. G. Shaughnessy House, Saint Andrews, New Brunswick. *1899, R. B. Angus House, Senneville, Quebec. 1899, Canadian Pacific Railway Station, New Westminster, British Columbia. 1899, E. S. Clouston House, Senneville, Quebec. 1899, George Drummond House, Saint-Bruno, Quebec. 1899, L. J. Forget House, Senneville, Quebec. *1899, Montreal Street Railway Building. 1900, Canadian Pacific Railway Station, Ottawa. 1900, C. R. Hosmer House, Montreal. 1900, H. S. McDougall House, Dorval, Quebec. 1900, Royal Bank, Vancouver, British Columbia. 1901, William Hope House, Saint Andrews, New Brunswick. 1901, Dumont Laviolette House, Senneville, Quebec. 1901, Royal Bank, Havana. 1901, W. C. Van Horne House, Selkirk, Manitoba. 1901–1903, W. C. Van Horne House, Ministers Island, Saint Andrews, New Brunswick.

EDWARD MAXWELL AND W. S. MAXWELL

1902, A. Hamilton House; *1902, Edward Maxwell House; Montreal. *1903, Bank of Montreal, Westmount, Quebec. 1903, E. Lafleur House, Montreal. 1903, Royal Bank, Westmount, Quebec. 1903, E. A. Whitehead House, Dorval, Quebec. 1904, J. Galt House; 1904–1906, Canadian Pacific Railway Station and Hotel; Winnipeg, Manitoba. 1905, D. McNicoll House, Westmount, Quebec. 1905, Charles Meredith House; 1905, Royal Victoria Hospital (Nurses Residence); *1906, William Hope House; Montreal. 1907, R. R. Mitchell House, Westmount, Quebec. 1907, Unitarian Church of the Messiah, Montreal. 1907–1910, Regina Parliament Building, Saskatchewan. 1908, J. K. L. Ross House; 1909, J. T. Davis House; 1909, A. Hamilton House; 1909, W. S. Maxwell House; 1909, E. M. Renouf House; 1910, C. C. Ballantyne House; Montreal. 1910, F. Markay House, Saint Andrews, New Brunswick. 1910–1911, Dominion Express Building, Montreal. 1910–1912, Montreal Art Association Gallery. 1911, Saint Charles Country Club, Winnipeg, Manitoba. 1911–1914, Canadian Pacific Railway Hotel, Calgary, Alberta. 1912, E. Lafleur House, Hudson, Quebec. 1912, Saint Giles Presbyterian Church, Outremont, Quebec. 1912–1913, High School of Montreal. 1913, L. T. Cahan House, Outremont, Quebec. 1914, Maxwelton Apartments; 1915, Jacques Cartier Monument; Montreal. 1919, Thomas Tait House, Saint Andrews, New Brunswick. 1920–1924, Château Frontenac Hotel (tower block and Saint-Louis wing), Quebec City.

BIBLIOGRAPHY

ATHERTON, WILLIAM H. (editor) 1914 Volume 3, pages 342–343 in *Montreal: 1535–1914.* Montreal, Vancouver, British Columbia, and Chicago: Clarke.

GOTCH, J. ALFRED 1914 "Residence on Drummond Street, Montreal." *Construction* 7, no. 7:267–274.

KALMAN, HAROLD D. 1968 *The Railway Hotels and the Development of the Château Style in Canada.* University of Victoria, Maltwood Museum.

LUDLOW, THOMAS W. 1915 "The Montreal Art Gallery." *Architectural Record* 37:132–148.

MAXWELL, W. S. 1908 "Architectural Education." *Canadian Architect and Builder* 21, no. 1:21–25.

"Saskatchewan Legislative Buildings, Regina." 1924 *Journal of the Royal Architectural Institute of Canada* 1, no. 2:41–53.

SMITH, J. ROXBURGH 1952 "Obituary: William Sutherland Maxwell." *Journal of the Royal Architectural Institute of Canada* 29, no. 10:311.

WOOD, WILLIAM (editor) 1931 Volume 4, pages 183–184 in *The Storied Province of Quebec: Past and Present.* Toronto: Dominion.

MAY, EDWARD JOHN

Edward John May (1853–1941) was DECIMUS BURTON's last pupil and a student at the Royal Academy Schools of Architecture in London. Afterward he worked for W. EDEN NESFIELD and RICHARD NORMAN SHAW, winning in 1876 the [A. W. N.] PUGIN Studentship. In 1875, Shaw started work on his garden suburb, the Bedford Park Estate, where May, who later went to live there, designed a number of buildings. May was an excellent draftsman, but his practice, which was started in 1881, was not large and entirely domestic. For many years, he was architect to the Church of England Waifs & Strays Society.

GODFREY RUBENS

WORKS

1879, Clubhouse; c.1882, The Vicarage; 1883, Hogg's House, Priory Gardens; 1883, House, South Parade; 1883, House, Newton Grove; 1883, House, The Orchard; 1883, Queen Anne's Grove; Bedford Park, London. 1890, Barnsdale, near Oakham, Rutland, England. 1892–1897, Jardine Hall (alterations and additions), Dumfries, Scotland. c.1900, Honeyhanger and Hilder, Haslemere; c.1900, 4 South Side Common; Wimbledon; Surrey. 1905, Ballindune, Haslemere; 1905, Munster Oaks, Munster; 1907, Waifs & Strays Home, Pyrford; Surrey. 1910–1911, Guildhall (rebuilding and extension), Sandwich, Kent, England.

BIBLIOGRAPHY

The Builder. 1941 160:323.

HITCHCOCK, H. R. 1977 *Architecture: 19th and 20th Century.* Harmondsworth, England: Penguin.

Journal of the Royal Institute of British Architects. 1941 48:124.

MAY, ERNST

Ernst May (1886–1970) was the son of an industrialist in Frankfurt-am-Main. He studied at the Technische Hochschule of Darmstadt and Munich, was a student of FRIEDRICH VON THIERSCH and THEODOR FISCHER, and later attended University College in London. He worked with RAYMOND UNWIN, becoming a strong advocate of garden city idea. From 1918 to 1925, in Breslau, May was technical director of the Silesian Building Department. Between 1925 and 1930, he was *Stadtbaurat* (city building councillor) of Frankfurt. May supervised all municipal projects, headed the city's largest building society, had authority over all project applications, and directed the master plan. He was responsible for the construction of 90 percent of all housing from 1925 to 1933. In 1926–1930, May founded and edited a magazine, *Das neue Frankfurt,* developing ideas about housing designs, city planning, mass transportation, and smoke control. May also published *Wohnungswirtschaft* and *Das neue Berlin.* At the invitation of the Soviet Union, May moved there in 1930 to engage in planning. In 1934, unable to obtain reentry into Germany, he farmed in Kenya. He was interned for over two years in South Africa during World War II. Subsequently, May planned and built in Kenya and Uganda. Returning to Germany in 1945, he became planning adviser for Mainz, Bremerhaven, and Wiesbaden, worked on *Die neue Heimat* in Hamburg, practiced as an architect-planner, and served on numerous civic commissions.

WALTER GROPIUS saluted May as a pioneer in planning, housing, and prefabrication: "His sense of the unity of a culture pervaded all actions under his leadership. . . . This sense for the whole developed over the years Ernst May's most important contribution: a clear concept for the articulation of cities" (Gropius, 1963).

May concentrated on constructing an estate, a district, or a town rather than a single building in his social commitment to improve living conditions.

REGINALD R. ISAACS

WORKS

1919, Housing Development, Klettendorf, Germany. 1920, Housing Development, Haynau, Germany. 1920, Housing Development, Oltaschin, Germany. 1921, City Plan, Breslau, Germany. 1922, Housing Project, Ohlau, Germany. 1925, Single-family Houses; 1926, Römerstadt Housing Development; Frankfurt. 1926–1930, Housing Development, Praunheim, Germany. 1929–1930, Housing Development, Westhausen, Germany. 1930, City Plan, Aftostroy, Russia. 1930, City Plan, Magnitogorsk, Russia. 1930, General Plan, Moscow. 1933, Aga-Khan Maternity Hospital; 1933, Aga-Khan School; Kisumu, Kenya. 1933, Culture Center, Moshi, Tanganyika. 1933, Delamere Housing Project; 1933, Ernst May Residence; Nairobi. 1933, Oceanic Hotel, Mombasa, Kenya. 1933, Schematic Plan, Kampala. 1953, Housing Development, Aachen, Germany. 1953, Housing Development, Aunmuhle, Germany. 1953, Housing Development, Berlin. 1953, Housing Development, Bremen, Germany. 1953, Housing Development, Bremerhaven, Germany. 1953, Housing Development, Düsseldorf, Germany. 1953, Housing Development, Frankfurt. 1953, Housing Development, Hamburg, Germany. 1953, Housing Development, Lubeck, Germany. 1953, Housing Development, Mainz, Germany. 1953, Housing Development, Neu-Altona, Germany. 1953, Housing Development, Rheinhausen, Germany. 1953, Housing Development, Wiesbaden, Germany. 1953, Housing Development, Wolfen, Germany.

BIBLIOGRAPHY

BUEKSCHMITT, JUSTUS 1963 *Ernst May.* Stuttgart, Germany: Alexander Koch.

GROPIUS, WALTER 1963 Introduction in Justus Buekschmitt, *Ernst May: Bauten und Planungen.* Stuttgart, Germany: Verlag Koch.

MAY, ERNST 1930 "Die Wohnung für das Existenzminimum." Pages 10–16 in *Die Wohnung für das Extenzminimum.* Frankfurt: Englert & Schlosser. Acts of the second International Congress for Modern Architecture.

MAY, ERNST (1931)1975 "Der Bau neuer Städte in der U.S.S.R." Pages 357–367 in Giorgio Grassi (editor), *Das neue Frankfurt 1926–1931.* Translated by Sonia Gessner. Bari, Italy: Dadalo.

MAY, ERNST 1948 *Report on the Kampala Extension Scheme.* Nairobi: Government printer.

MAY, ERNST 1957 "Wohnungsbau." Pages 115–221 in *Handbuck Moderner Architektur.* Berlin: Safari.

MAY, ERNST 1962 "Städtebau Heute." *Atlantis, Länder, Völker, Reisen* 34, no. 3:118–128.

MAY, ERNST 1976 "Kranischstein new Town." Pages 43–48 in Dennis Sharp (editor), *Planning and Architecture Essays.* London: Barrie & Rockliff.

MAY, ERNST; BOESLER, FELIX; and LEIBBRAND, KURT 1961 *Das neue Mainz.* Mainz, Germany: Margraf & Fischer.

MAY, HUGH

Hugh May (1621–1684), like Sir ROGER PRATT and Sir BALTHAZAR GERBIER, belongs to a rather mysterious group of architects practicing during the Restoration period. They bridge a notable stylistic gulf between the Palladianism of INIGO JONES and the English baroque associated especially with JOHN VANBURGH and NICHOLAS HAWKSMOOR. Though only a handful of his houses have survived, Eltham Lodge (1664) and the interiors at Cassiobury Park (1677–1684), and Windsor Castle (1675–1684) clearly mark the direction the baroque was to follow in the seventeenth century. It presented a notable fusion of Dutch and French elements that relied much on May's personal circumstances.

Hugh May's career before 1660 seems to have been connected with the duke of Buckingham as some sort of administrator for the Buckingham Collection at York House. He went into exile in 1657 in Holland and also traveled in France. It was during this time that both his architectural style and his court patronage were formed. He returned to England with the monarchy in 1660 and seems to have slipped deftly into architectural practice. In this respect, he was like ROBERT HOOKE and even CHRISTOPHER WREN, and unlike the arch-, but unsuccessful, professional JOHN WEBB.

He rebuilt NICHOLAS STONE's Cornbury House (1663–1668), adding a chapel and stable block. The east front there was repeated on a smaller and less monumental scale at Eltham Lodge the following year. The distinctly Dutch air of Eltham probably came from the use of brick and stone, but its seven-bay façade is remarkably close to that found in PHILIPS VINGBOONS's *Gronden en afbeeldsels der voornaamste gebouwen* (1648). Its "double pile" plan, of a type associated with Roger Pratt (seen in the 1650s at Coleshill and Thorpe Hall) could well be derived from Vingboons.

At Windsor and Cassiobury, May put together a remarkable team of carvers and decorative artists who together created some of the most spectacular rooms of baroque England. Though Cassiobury was destroyed in 1922, Grinling Gibbons's great staircase survives in the Metropolitan Museum in New York. A similar fate overtook May's work at Windsor, where between 1675 and 1684, he remodeled twenty-one rooms in the upper ward of the castle. The Chapel Royal (1680–1684) which he and Antonio Verrio created was as much an expression of the absolutism of Charles II as were the Grands Appartements of Louis XIV at Versailles.

A. A. TAIT

WORKS

1663–1668, Cornbury House (rebuilding and additions), Oxfordshire, England. 1664, Eltham Lodge, Kent, England. 1665, Berkeley House, London. *1675–1684, Windsor Castle (remodeling upper ward; with others), England. *1677–1684, Cassiobury Park (not completed until 1780), England. 1682–1683, Chiswick, Middlesex, England.

BIBLIOGRAPHY

DOWNES, KERRY 1966 *English Baroque Architecture.* London: Zwemmer.

HILL, OLIVER, and CORNFORTH, JOHN 1966 *English Country Houses, Caroline, 1625–1685.* London: Country Life.

MAYBECK, BERNARD R.

Bernard Ralph Maybeck (1862–1957), recipient of the Gold Medal of the American Institute of Architects in 1951, was born in New York City and died in Berkeley, California, his home for sixty years. His work seemed to contain the seeds which flowered a generation later as the modern movement. Yet he never lost touch with the humane element of architecture, which distinguishes his work from the modernists of the International style. To Maybeck, a house could never be a "machine for living"—a house was always a shell and only gained interest from those who would live in it.

Maybeck was neither a revolutionary, nor a pioneer who advocated a complete break with building traditions. He was an eclectic architect in the literal sense; he sought to combine the designs of the past with the techniques and materials of the present to create the form of the architecture of tomorrow. He belongs in that group of architects, including H. H. RICHARDSON, LOUIS H. SULLIVAN and FRANK LLOYD WRIGHT, who made distinctly American contributions to architecture. Maybeck's greatest over-all contribution was in domestic architecture. His early inventive and novel planning of the small house set an example for the generation of California architects, led by WILLIAM WILSON WURSTER, who dominated American residential design for two decades. The San Francisco Bay Region style was based on Maybeck's conviction that each client and architectural problem was unique, demanded individual solution, and had little dependence on stylistic elements.

Maybeck was born in the heart of what is now Greenwich Village. Maybeck's maternal grandfather, Christian Kern, and his father Bernhardt Maybeck, were both emigrants from Germany, victims of the revolutionary events of 1848. They imbued young Bernard with a strong sense of democratic values which resulted in Maybeck's idealism and respect of the individual in society. His father was a professional woodcarver, who taught him cabinetmaking. His mother died when he was three years old.

Maybeck studied architecture at the Ecole des Beaux Arts in Paris, in the atelier of Jules Louis André (see ANDRÉ FAMILY), who carried on the traditions of HENRI LABROUSTE's free atelier. Maybeck developed a great admiration for the teachings of EUGÈNE EMMANUEL VIOLLET-LE-DUC, and his emphasis on inventive structure and ready acceptance of new materials and technological developments, as well as his medievalism, are based in Viollet-le-Duc's theory. In 1886 Maybeck returned to New York to work with John M. CARRÈRE AND Thomas HASTINGS on the Ponce de Leon and Alcazar hotels in St. Augustine, Florida. Maybeck supervised the construction of the buildings but by 1888 he had decided to start an independent practice. He spent an unproductive year in Kansas City, where he married Anne White. He moved to San Francisco in 1890 and eventually found work in the office of A. PAGE BROWN. The young men of Brown's office—WILLIS POLK, A. C. SCHWEINFURTH, and Maybeck—are credited with introducing an unpretentious style of residential architecture directly expressive of its wooden construction.

Maybeck. First Church of Christ Scientist. Berkeley. 1927–1929

Outstanding among Maybeck's work are a large reception pavilion, Hearst Hall (1899), built as a demountable structure employing large laminated wooden arches, and simple residential designs which feature open planning and direct structural expression (G. H. Boke House in Berkeley [1902]) and those using new materials such as reinforced concrete (A. C. Lawson House in Berkeley [1907]), but his treatment of large expensive residences is equally distinctive (L. L. Roos House in San Francisco [1909]; A. E. Bingham House in Santa Barbara [1916]).

The best single example of Maybeck's architecture embodying his beliefs is the First Church of Christ Scientist (1910–1912) in Berkeley, whose design respects tradition and individuality without pretense. Its combination of industrially produced materials and building craftsmanship creates a structure easily appreciated by architects and laymen. Christian Science Church includes a Sunday school and office wing added by Maybeck in association with Henry Gutterson in 1927–1929. The materials of the exterior are surprisingly ordinary; the tracery decoration and the piers are of cast concrete; exterior walls are faced with gray cement-asbestos panels accented by small squares of the same material in brick-red; the window walls of the gallery are industrial steel sash enriched with

Maybeck. First Church of Christ Scientist. Berkeley. 1927–1929

special glass; the roof now covered with tile was originally a standing seam metal roof. The construction is reinforced concrete combined with heavy timber. The main body of the church is a Greek cross inscribed in a square; its central portion is diagonally spanned by intersecting paired trusses in box form constructed of stock lumber and iron ties. The sheathing of the roof is exposed on the interior, common in Maybeck's work, and the purlins are given a decorative spacing. Natural light enters from openings in the clerestory and continuous perimeter of glass at the ground level. There is a symbolic coordination of decoration and structure reminiscent of Gothic architecture. The tracery within the trusses follows the direction of the tension rods; metal plates are marked by stencilled designs; and structural ties that are not visible are indicated by ornament on the surface. The materials alone are testimony to Maybeck's adaptability to the conditions of building in an industrialized economy, rare in romantic architects.

Maybeck was an eclectic architect, but he could use the vocabulary of Gothic, Roman, baroque, or Tudor architecture as inspirations for unique formulation of space, light, and textures in contexts sensitively suited to modern life. Maybeck, unlike his contemporaries raised in the shadow of the Ecole des Beaux-Arts, was able to respect tradition and individuality without shame. He could successfully turn the pomp of his time to winning fantasy in structures such as the Palace of Fine Arts (1913) in San Francisco and the Earle C. Anthony Oakland Packard building (1928). Costly craftsmanship was not essential to Maybeck's work, and his inventiveness in using materials made it possible for him to give individuality to the most economical design. He experimented with low-cost bungalows (1924) sheathed in gunny sacks, dipped in light-weight concrete. In fact, Maybeck's more modest work has proven to be the most significant for architects of succeeding generations, because in his simple house and community projects he demonstrated how the individualism and human scale of the preindustrial age can be preserved without denying the economic and technical imperative of modern society.

KENNETH H. CARDWELL

WORKS

*1899, Hearst Hall; 1902, G. H. Boke House; 1907, A. C. Lawson House; Berkeley. 1909, L. L. Roos House; 1913, Palace of Fine Arts; San Francisco. 1916, A. E. Bingham House, Santa Barbara, Calif. 1910–1912, First Church of Christ Scientist; 1927–1929, First Church of Christ Scientist (Sunday School and additions; with Henry Gutterson); Berkeley. 1928, Earle C. Anthony Oakland Packard Building, Calif.

Maybeck. Palace of Fine Arts. San Francisco. 1913

BIBLIOGRAPHY

BANGS, JOHN MURRAY 1948 "Bernard Ralph Maybeck, Architect, Comes into His Own." *Architectural Record* 103:72–79.

CARDWELL, KENNETH H. 1977 *Bernard Maybeck: Artisan, Architect, Artist.* Santa Barbara, Calif.: Peregrine.

CHENEY, SHELDON 1930 *New World Architecture.* London: Longmans.

HAYS, WILLIAM CHARLES 1906 "Some Interesting Buildings at the University of California: The Work of Bernard Maybeck, Architect." *Indoors and Out* 2:70–75.

MCCOY, ESTHER 1960 *Five California Architects.* New York: Reinhold.

SARGEANT, WINTHROP 1949 *Geniuses, Goddesses and People.* New York: Dutton.

MAYER, ALBERT

Albert Mayer (1897–1981) was an American architect, planner, and civil engineer whose commissions extended from private houses, urban playgrounds, and multistory apartment buildings to new towns and regional plans. In his writing, which was extensive, he addressed national housing and planning policies. He was known particularly for his social concerns and his vigorous commitment to constructive change, both of which permeated his varied activities for five decades.

Mayer was born in New York and graduated in 1919 from the Massachusetts Institute of Technology. During the 1930s, along with planners and architects such as CATHERINE KROUSE BAUER, Lewis Mumford, CLARENCE S. STEIN, and HENRY WRIGHT, he advocated new forms of housing which would provide inhabitants both with a sense of community and with such physical essentials as sunlight, fresh air, and exterior recreation space. The group's advocacy of government sponsored large-scale housing projects led, in 1937, to the establishment of the United States Housing Authority.

Mayer's own buildings stressed these same considerations. He formed a partnership in New York with Julian Whittlesey in 1935, which was later joined by William Glass. The firm designed such advanced apartment houses in New York as 240 Central Park South in 1941; its ingenious layout afforded numerous park views and accommodated a generous variety of apartment types without sacrificing construction economies which might ultimately benefit the tenants. The firm also designed Manhattan House with Skidmore, Owings, and Merrill in 1951.

Mayer served as United States Army engineer during World War II, and his eventual meeting with Jawaharlal Nehru led to numerous important commissions. In 1946, he began work on the Pilot Development Project for rural villages in the district of Etawah, India, which was eventually adapted for 300 villages throughout the country. It called for modern agricultural techniques, small scale manufacturing, and citizen participation in administrative decisions. With MATTHEW NOWICKI, he designed the original scheme for Chandigarh (1949–1950) which incorporated four self-contained residential superblocks, reflecting principles used in Radburn, New Jersey (1929) by Stein and Wright. Many of his ideas were retained in the final scheme produced by LE CORBUSIER, EDWIN MAXWELL FRY, PIERRE JEANNERET, and JANE DREW, in 1951.

Mayer's philosophy received its fullest exposition in *The Urgent Future* (1967*b*). His warning that "trend is not destiny" is an underlying theme. He strenuously denied that the unbridled growth of urban areas observed in recent years was inevitable and he decried the sprawling continuum, which he referred to as "megalopolis," both for its amorphousness and for its inhuman scale. He advocated as an alternative the development of moderately sized cities, along with the decentralization and reorganization of existing overgrown metropolitan areas. As in his planning in India, Mayer was concerned as much with modes of governance—which he felt must be at once efficient and democratic—as with plans themselves; he proposed new levels of administration with jurisdictions both larger and smaller than those of municipal governments, such as agencies with broad regional authority and neighborhood units small enough to invite citizen interest. He illustrated his proposals with existing precedents and throughout urged concern, optimism, and committed action. He planned several new towns, notably that of Kitimat, British Columbia, before retiring from practice in 1961, but he remained extremely active afterward as a planning consultant.

MICHAEL HOLLANDER

WORKS

1936, Plan for Greenbrook, (with Henry S. Churchill, Henry Wright, and Allan Kamstra), N.J. 1941, 240 Central Park South, New York. c.1948, Pilot Development Project, Uttar Pradesh (Etawah district), India. c.1954, Plan for Kitimat (with Clarence Stein), British Columbia. 1957, Allahabad Agricultural Institute, Uttar Pradesh, India. 1960. East Harlem Plaza, New York.

BIBLIOGRAPHY

"Apartment Buildings: 240 Central Park South." 1941 *Architectural Forum* 74, May:311–319.

EMMETT, ROBERT C. 1977 *Guide to the Albert Mayer Papers on India in the University of Chicago Library.* Chicago: Committee on Southern Asian Studies, University of Chicago.

EVENSON, NORMA 1966 *Chandigarh.* Berkeley: University of California Press.

"Industry Builds Kitimat." 1954 *Architectural Forum* 101, no. 1:128–148, no. 2:120–127, no. 4:158–161.

"Manhattan House." 1952 *Architectural Forum* 97, no. 1:140–151.

MARRIOTT, MCKIM, and PARK, RICHARD L. (1959)1973 *The Story of Rural Development at Etawah, Uttar Pradesh.* Reprint. Westport, Conn.: Greenwood.

MAYER, ALBERT 1967*a* "Greenbelt Towns Revisited: In Search of New Directions for New Towns in America." *Journal of Housing* 24, no. 1:12–26, no. 2:80–85, no. 3:151–160.

MAYER, ALBERT 1967*b* *The Urgent Future.* New York: McGraw-Hill.

MAYER, ALBERT 1969–1970 "It's Not Just the Cities." *Architectural Record* 145, no. 7:151–162; 146, no. 3:171–182, no. 5:139–146, no. 6:105–110; 147, no. 7:137–142; 148, no. 1:101–160.

MAYER, ALBERT; WRIGHT, HENRY; and MUMFORD, LEWIS 1934 *New Homes for a New Deal: A Concrete Program for Slum Clearance and Housing Relief.* New York: New Republic.

MUMFORD, LEWIS 1967 "Trend Is Not Destiny." *Architectural Record* 142, no. 6:131–134.

MAYMONT, PAUL

Born in Paris, Paul Maymont (1926–) studied architecture at the Ecole des Beaux-Arts. In 1950, he won a fellowship to the Technical University in Berlin. A pioneer in the field of urban spatialism and floating architecture, Maymont patented a design for a floating city in 1960 while at Kyoto University in Japan.

SUSAN STRAUSS

BIBLIOGRAPHY

"Aventure de la Cité Future." 1966 *Urbanisme* 35:special issue.

BANHAM, REYNER (1976)1977 *Megastructure: Urban Futures of the Recent Past.* New York: Harper.

"Floating City." 1965 *Apxitektonikh* 9, no.38:85–86.

"Paul Maymont: Le fantastique concretise." 1964 *L'Architecture d'aujourd'hui* 34, no.115:30–36.

RAGON, MICHEL 1966 *Les Cités de l'Avenir.* Paris: Planète.

RAGON, MICHEL 1972–1978 Volumes 2 and 3 in *Histoire Mondiale de l'Architecture et de l'Urbanisme Modernes.* Tournai, Belgium: Casterman.

MAYREDER BROTHERS

Karl Mayreder (1856–1935), chief architect of the Viennese planning department from 1894 to 1902 and professor at the Technical University of Vienna from 1893, and his brothers Julius Mayreder (1860–1911) and Rudolf Mayreder (1864–1937), lawyer and civil engineer and municipal councillor of Vienna from 1895 to 1904, exercised a considerable influence upon the development of fin-de-siècle Vienna.

Their success in the major planning competitions in Vienna granted them a strategic position to pursue the interests of the building industry which they represented as the owners of a big, still existing construction company. Integrated into the public planning and private building institutions, they never left the mainstream of contemporary architecture and city planning. As architects they hung on to historicism, and as planners they were influenced by German city planning as represented by Joseph Stübben who had just discovered the ideas of CAMILLO SITTE.

They used their influence in politics and planning to create increased building activities but they used the city's money sparingly. The development plan for the central area of Vienna is the best example: they did not cut streets through built up areas à la GEORGES EUGÈNE HAUSSMANN but enlarged the existing streets, leaving the piecemeal execution to private enterprise and not forcing the city to spend large sums on expropriation. Needless to say, this plan was never fully realized, and thus, some of the most scenic sites of old Vienna were saved.

RENATE BANIK-SCHWEITZER

WORKS

KARL MAYREDER

1894–1911, Development Plans for Jägerndorf, Czechoslovakia. 1894–1911, Development Plans for Karlsbad, Czechoslovakia. 1894–1911, Development Plans, Rovereto, Italy. 1896, Development Plan for the First District; 1900, Palace Isbary; Vienna. 1904, Mausoleum Borgfeldt, Kaltenleutgeben, near Vienna. 1909, Avenue Building, Lemberg, Poland.

JULIUS MAYREDER

c.1895, Hotel Fortino, Grado, Italy. *1897, Schuckertwerke, Vienna. c.1900, Danubius-Textilwerke, Bratislava, Czechoslovakia. 1901, Herrnhuter Building, Vienna.

KARL MAYREDER AND JULIUS MAYREDER

1898, Kreuzherrenhof, Vienna.

BIBLIOGRAPHY

GOLDEMUND, HEINRICH, and MAYREDER, KARL 1903 "Das mit dem zweiten Preise ausgezeichnete Konkurrenzprojekt 'Entwicklung' für einen Generalregulierungsplan der Landeshauptstadt Brünn." *Zeitschrift des Österreichischen Ingenieur- und Architekten-Vereines* 55:337–340.

MAYER, WOLFGANG 1972 "Gebietsänderungen im Raume Wien 1850–1910 und die Debatten um das Entstehen eines Generalregulierungsplanes von Wien." Unpublished Ph.D. dissertation, University of Vienna.

MAYREDER, CARL 1904 "Zur Frage der Umgestaltung des Karlsplatzes in Wien." *Deutsche Bauzeitung* 38:366–368, 477.

MAYREDER, CARL 1905 "Stadtentwicklung." Volume 1, pages 49–79 in Paul Kortz (editor), *Wien am Anfang des XX. Jahrhunderts.* Vienna: Gerlach & Wiedling.

MAYREDER, CARL; MAYREDER, JULIUS; and MAYREDER, RUDOLF 1893 *Bemerkungen zu dem Entwurfe für einen Verbauungsplan über den zwischen dem Donau-Canale, der Rothenthurmstrasse, Wollzeile und der vorderen Zollamtsstrasse gelegenen Theil der Stadt Wien.* Vienna.

MAYREDER, GEBR. 1894 "Besprechung der Entwürfe für einen General-Regulierungsplan für Wien." *Zeitschrift des Österreichischen Ingenieur- und Architekten-Vereines* 46:385-390, 393–395.

MAYREDER, KARL 1894–1895 "Über Wiener Stadtregulierungs-Fragen." *Wiener Bauindustrie-Zeitung* 12:545–549, 567–570.

MAYREDER, KARL 1895 "Das Project der 'Wienzeile' von Schönbrunn bis zum Stadtparke als Theil des General-Regulierungsplanes von Wien." *Zeitschrift des Österreichischen Ingenieur- und Architekten-Vereines* 47:345–349, 360–361.

MAYREDER, KARL 1895–1896 "Motivenbericht zum Antrage des Stadtbauamtes für den Regulierungsplan der Inneren Stadt." *Wiener Bauindustrie-Zeitung* 13:251–256, 268–274.

MAYREDER, KARL 1896 "Mitteilungen über den General-Regulierungsplan von Wien." *Zeitschrift des Österreichischen Ingenieur- und Architekten-Vereines* 48:389–394, 468–471.

MAYREDER, KARL 1897 *Enquete für die Überprüfung der Regulierungsprojekte für den I. Bezirk und den Karlskirchenplatz.* Vienna.

MAYREDER, KARL 1899 "Das Project einer Villencolonie auf der Gutsbesitzung Cobenzl. *Zeitschrift des Österreichischen Ingenieur- und Architekten-Vereines* 51:437–443.

MAYREDER, KARL 1900 "Mitteilungen über die Ausgestaltung des Karlsplatzes." *Zeitschrift des Österreichischen Ingenieur- und Architekten-Vereines* 52:221, 269–271.

MAYREDER, KARL 1903 "Städtische Bauordnungen mit besonderer Berücksichtigung der Wohnungsfrage." *Schriften der Österreichischen Gesellschaft für Arbeiterschutz* 5:1–36.

MAYREDER, KARL 1908 "Der Regulierungsplan für die Altstadt Salzburg." *Zeitschrift des Österreichischen Ingenieur- und Architekten-Vereines.*

MAYREDER, KARL; MAYREDER, JULIUS; and MAYREDER, RUDOLF 1893 *Erläuterungs-Bericht zu dem Concurrenz-Projecte für einen General-Regulierungsplan der k.k. Reichshaupt- und Residenzstadt Wien.* Vienna.

SCHWEITZER, RENATE 1970 "Der Generalregulierungsplan für Wien (1893–1920)." *Berichte zur Raumforschung und Raumplanung* 14:23–41.

SCHWEITZER, RENATE 1972 "Österreichische Bibliographie für Stadtebau und Raumplanung 1850–1918." Volume 17 in *Schriftenreihe des Institutes für Stadtebau, Raumplanung und Raumordnung, Technische Hochschule Wien.* Vienna: Springer.

STÜBBEN, JOSEF 1896 "Der Baulinienplan für die Altstadt Wien." *Deutsche Bauzeitung* 30:501–503, 509–510.

WAETZOLDT, STEPHAN (editor) 1977 *Bibliographie zur Architektur im 19. Jahrhundert: Die Aufsätze in den deutschsprachigen Architekturzeitschriften 1789–1918.* Nendeln, Germany: KTO.

MAZZONI, ANGIOLO

Born in Bologna, Italy, Angiolo Mazzoni (1894–1979) trained at the Scuola di Applicazione per gli Ingegneri (1916–1919) in Rome. There, his teachers instilled in Mazzoni an appreciation of asymmetrical picturesque compositions, that would remain a distinctive feature of his architecture throughout his life. Entering the service of the state railway and postal system in 1921, Mazzoni, a devoted functionary, between 1926 and 1938 designed and built approximately thirty major buildings. After World War II, Mazzoni lived in Bogotá, Colombia (1948–1963), where he taught architecture and entered private practice. Mazzoni returned to Italy in 1963 and lived in Rome until his death in 1979. As the co-director with Mino Somenzi of the Futurist newspaper *Sant'Elia* in 1934–1935, Mazzoni was the most important architect in Filippo Tomaso Marinetti's post-World War I Futurist movement.

Architecture for Mazzoni was a calling. His lyrical understanding of his profession, evident in both his writings and his mature work, made him a prime candidate for Marinetti's attention. Mazzoni's architecture of the 1930s was characterized by a rich contrapuntal movement of contrasting horizontal and vertical volumes, often luxuriously colored with a profusion of contrasting marbles. Mazzoni's style shared the elegance and dynamism of the streamlined look so popular in Europe and America at that time. In his quest for a total architectural synthesis, Mazzoni designed every aspect of his buildings, including lighting fixtures, benches, tables, and so on.

As a functionary, Mazzoni was often obliged to design conservative buildings to please the local authorities. Today he is remembered most vividly for two such designs: the traditionalist project for the Florentine train station Santa Maria Novella (1931), which touched off one of the most famous controversies of the century, and the design for the central train station in Rome (1938), begun in a classical imperial style but halted during the war. Mazzoni's true spirit, however, can be found in a number of his projects: the cylindrical purity of the Post Office in Agrigento (1931–1934); the dramatic antimalarial screens around the Post Office at Littoria (now Latina; 1932); the colorful and rhythmic massing along the beach in the children's resort at Calambrone (now Tirrenia; 1933) with special accents provided by the spiral stairs twisting around the cylindrical water towers; the dynamic lines and asymmetrical massing of the train stations of Siena (1933–1935) and Trento (1934–1936) that frame the mountains behind them; the contrapuntal rhythms of the post office at Ostia (1934) built around a sheltered piazza; and the most Futurist of his works, the Centrale Termica (1934) along the tracks of the Station Santa Maria Novella in Florence with its daring circular stairs and elevated catwalk crowning a dramatic play of contrasting geometric forms. All of these works could be described by Marinetti's praise of "the useful and lyrical play of volumes." During his lifetime, Mazzoni was famous for the skillful resolution of functional problems to which he gave such dynamic architectural forms.

RICHARD A. ETLIN

WORKS

1926–1930, Post Office, Ferrara, Italy. 1927, Post Office, Nuoro, Italy. 1927–1928, Train Station, Bolzano, Italy. 1929–1932, Post Office, Bergamo, Italy. 1929–1934, Post Office, Palermo, Italy. 1930, Dopolavoro Ferroviario (with Efisio Vodret), Rome. 1930–1933, Post Office, La Spezia, Italy. 1930–1933, Post Office, Trento, Italy. 1930–1933, Post Office, Varese, Italy. 1931–1934, Post Office, Agrigento, Italy. 1932, Post Office, Gorizia, Italy. 1932, Post Office, Grosseto, Italy. 1932, Post Office; 1932, Train Station; Littoria, Italy. 1933, Colonia

Marina, Calambrone, Italy. 1933, Post Office, Massa, Italy. 1933–1935, Train Station, Siena, Italy. 1934, Central Terminal, Santa Maria Novella Station, Florence. 1934, Post Office, Abetone, Italy. 1934?, Post Office, Pistoia, Italy. 1934, Post Office, Pola, Italy. 1934, Post Office, Ostia-Lido, Rome. 1934, Post Office, Sabaudia, Italy. 1934–1936, Train Station, Trento, Italy. 1935–1938, Train Station, Reggia Emilia, Italy. 1937, Post Office, Ragusa, Italy. 1937, Train Station, Montecatini Terminal, Italy. 1937?–1938?, Train Station, Reggia Calabria, Italy. *1937–1939, Train and Maritime Station, Messina, Italy. 1938, Rome Terminal (Central Train Station; incomplete).

BIBLIOGRAPHY

FORTI, ALFREDO 1978 *Angiolo Mazzoni: Architetto fra fascismo e libertà.* Florence: Edam.

SEVERATI, CARLO 1973*a* "Cronaca di Santa Maria Novella in margine al concorso per il fabbricato viaggiatori della Stazione di Firenze." *L'Architettura, cronache e storia* 19, no. 211:54–64.

SEVERATI, CARLO 1973*b* "Stazione di Venezia Santa Lucia." *L'Architettura, cronache e storia* 19, no. 216:338–346.

SEVERATI, CARLO 1975*a* "1. Il Caso Mazzoni e le poetiche del '900." *L'Architettura, cronache e storia* 20, no. 231:588–600.

SEVERATI, CARLO 1975*b* "2. Manierismo mazzoniano: Le Poste di Ostia." *L'Architettura, cronache e storia* 20, no. 232:652–659.

SEVERATI, CARLO 1975*c* "3. Angiolo Mazzoni: Dalle poetiche al linguaggio moderno dell'architetture." *L'Architettura, cronache e storia* 20, no. 233:714–723.

SEVERATI, CARLO 1975*d* "4. Siena '33: Un architetto futurista?" *L'Architettura, cronache e storia* 20, no. 234:784–789.

SEVERATI, CARLO, and VIDOTTO, MARCO 1973 "Un progetto inedito del 1936 per la stazione principale di Roma." *L'Architettura, cronache e storia* 18, no. 209:754–764.

MAZZUCHETTI, ALESSANDRO

Alessandro Mazzuchetti (1824–1894) is known principally for the design (with CARLO CEPPI) of the railroad station at Porta Nuova, Turin (1866–1868), which established new standards for urban integration and collaboration between architect and engineer. The great arched central space became the focus for Piazza Carlo Felice (designed by CARLO PROMIS, 1851) with its picturesque English garden. The elimination of wall, the extreme use of glass, the exposed metal structure, the large arched entrances, and the high arched train shed exhibit a happy exploration of structural design.

HENRY A. MILLON

WORKS

1849–1850, Railroad Station, Alessandria, Italy. 1853, Principal Railroad Station, Genoa, Italy. 1860, Ministero di Lavori Pubblici; 1866–1868, Porta Nuova Railroad Station (with Carlo Ceppi); Turin, Italy.

BIBLIOGRAPHY

HITCHCOCK, H. R. (1958)1977 *Architecture: Nineteenth and Twentieth Centuries.* 4th ed., rev. Baltimore: Penguin.

LEVA PISTOI, MILA 1969 *Torino: Mezzo secolo di architettura.* Turin, Italy.

MEEKS, CARROLL L. V. 1956 *The Railroad Station: An Architectural History.* New Haven: Yale University Press.

MEEKS, CARROLL L. V. 1966 *Italian Architecture: 1750–1914.* New Haven: Yale University Press.

MCARTHUR, JOHN JR.

John McArthur, Jr. (1823–1890) was born in Bladenock, Scotland, and was brought to Philadelphia at ten. He was apprenticed to an uncle carpenter and also attended lectures by THOMAS U. WALTER at the Franklin Institute in Philadelphia. He began his architect's career at twenty-five by winning the competition for the House of Refuge. In the 1860s and 1870s, McArthur and ALFRED B. MULLETT were the leading practitioners of the Second Empire style in America. During the Civil War, he built numerous temporary hospitals for the army and the navy.

McArthur is best remembered for his long association with Philadelphia City Hall. He won the competition in 1860, but the war stopped the project. He won another competition in 1869 for "the Public Buildings" (combining City Hall and Courthouse). The construction of these buildings was delayed by site disputes and political controversies; the cost was over $24 million. McArthur died in 1890 when the building was in use but not yet finished. On completion in 1901, the Philadelphia City Hall was the largest ($4\frac{1}{2}$ acres) and tallest (548-foot tower) public building in the United States. Rich sculpture enhances the exterior; the interior spaces include spectacular staircases, the mayor's reception room, and council chambers.

McArthur worked for federal, state, county, and city governments through many scandals, but his integrity was never doubted. His designs, with their simple plans and massive construction, always met Vitruvian (see VITRUVIUS) criteria of utility and firmness; the opinions on their beauty have fluctuated with the general views on the nineteenth century.

JOHN MAASS

WORKS

*1848, House of Refuge, Philadelphia. 1850, Farmer's

Bank, New Castle, Del. *1851–1852, County Almshouse, Wilmington, Del. *1852, Girard House, (hotel); *1853, La Pierre House (hotel); Philadelphia. 1855, Presbyterian Church, Media, Pa. *1858–1860, Continental Hotel; 1859, Frankford Presbyterian Church; 1859, West Spruce Street Presbyterian Church; *1860, Caldwell Jewelry Store; *1860, Franklin Market House (later the Mercantile Library); *1860, Mikveh Israel Synagogue; *1864, John McArthur, Jr., House; 1865, First National Bank; *1865–1866, David Jayne House; *1866, Public Ledger Building; Philadelphia. 1867–1870, County Jail, Wilkes-Barre, Pa. *1869, George W. Childs House; 1872–1901, City Hall; Philadelphia. 1873, State Hospital, Warren, Pa. 1873, Pardee Hall, Lafayette College, Easton, Pa. *1888, Children's Ward, Presbyterian Hospital, Philadelphia.

BIBLIOGRAPHY

FAUST, FREDERICK 1897 *The City Hall, Philadelphia: Its Architecture, Sculpture and History.* Philadelphia: The author.

GILLETTE, HOWARD, JR. 1973 "Philadelphia's City Hall: Monument to a New Political Machine." *Pennsylvania Magazine of History and Biography* Apr.:233–249.

MAASS, JOHN 1965 "Philadelphia City Hall: Monster or Masterpiece?" *Journal of the American Institute of Architects* Feb.:23–30.

The New Public Buildings. 1880 Philadelphia: Commissioners for the Erection of the Public Buildings.

WODEHOUSE, LAWRENCE 1969 "John McArthur, Jr. (1823–1890)." *Journal of the Society of Architectural Historians* 28:271–283.

MCCOMB, JOHN JR.

The son of a mason and builder-architect, John McComb, Jr. (1763–1853) became the leading architect in New York during the first quarter of the nineteenth century. Remaining true to a late colonial-Adamesque (see ROBERT ADAM) style which he developed in the 1790s, McComb was responsible for a substantial number of churches, houses, and semipublic buildings, mostly, though not exclusively, in New York, as well as lighthouses and other engineering activities. His drawings reveal an interest in unusual room shapes and other indications of an awareness of the English neoclassical manner of the latter part of the eighteenth century, but in most of his executed work this was subdued in favor of a more conservative approach, tempered by an enjoyment of neoclassical decoration and proportions.

His most important work was the building, between 1803 and 1812, of New York City Hall on the basis of the winning design submitted jointly in his name and that of JOSEPH FRANÇOIS MANGIN in the competition of 1802. Although the competition drawings and the French neoclassical style they represent were the work of Mangin, McComb modified this in execution, introducing his more English-inspired version in details and especially in the interior treatment, and supervised the work with sensitivity and care. Among his other significant projects were The Grange, the country house of Alexander Hamilton (1801–1802), which included octagonal rooms and Adamesque decorative detailing and is still extant though moved, shorn of its porches, and in a poor state; Washington Hall (1809–1914), the headquarters of the Washington Benevolent Society; and Saint John's Chapel (1803–1807), an imposing chapel of ease for the Episcopal diocese of Trinity Church.

Sufficiently esteemed in 1817 to be considered, jointly with CHARLES BULFINCH of Boston, as a possible successor to BENJAMIN HENRY LATROBE as architect of the United States Capitol, McComb largely retired from practice about 1826.

DAMIE STILLMAN

WORKS

*1790, Government House (provided designs), New York. 1792, Lighthouse (with William Pers), Cape Henry, Va. *c.1793–1795, Tontine City Tavern (provided designs; executed?), New York. *1795, Lighthouse, Montauk Point, N.Y. *1795 Rufus King House, New York. *c.1797, Dominick Lynch House, Clauson's Point, N.Y. *1797–1798, Lighthouse, Eton's Neck, N.Y. *1797–1799, John B. Coles House; 1801–1802, The Grange; 1802–1812, New York City Hall (with Joseph François Mangin); *1803–1807, Saint John's Chapel; *1807–1808, Cedar Street Presbyterian Church; New York. 1808–1811, 1825, Queen's Building, Rutgers University, New Brunswick, New Jersey. *1809–1814, Washington Hall; *(A)1810–1811, Castle Clinton; *1811–1812, Murray Street Presbyterian Church; New York. 1815–1817, Alexander Hall, Princeton Theological Seminary, New Jersey. *1822–1823, American Bible Society; *1822–1823, George Youle's Shot Tower; *(A)1824–1825, The Bank for Savings; *1825–1826, American Tract Society; *1825–1826, Bleecker Street Presbyterian Church; New York.

BIBLIOGRAPHY

GILCHRIST, AGNES ADDISON 1969 "Notes for a Catalogue of the John McComb (1763–1853) Collection of Architectural Drawings at the New-York Historical Society." *Journal of the Society of Architectural Historians* 28:201–210.

GILCHRIST, AGNES ADDISON 1972 "John McComb, Sr. and Jr., in New York, 1784–1799." *Journal of the Society of Architectural Historians* 31:10–21.

STILLMAN, DAMIE 1956 "Artistry and Skill in the Architecture of John McComb, Jr." Unpublished M.A. Thesis, University of Delaware, Newark.

STILLMAN, DAMIE 1964 "New York City Hall: Competition and Execution." *Journal of the Society of Architectural Historians* 23:129–142.

MCELFATRICK, J. B.

John Bailey McElfatrick (1828–1906) was born near Middletown, Pennsylvania, and began practice in Fort Wayne, Indiana, as a carpenter and architect, his father's trades. As his practice grew, he moved first to Louisville, Kentucky, then to St. Louis, Missouri, with his sons, John Morgan McElfatrick and William H. McElfatrick, who worked with him under the name of J. B. McElfatrick and Sons. The firm was well established in the specialty of theater design when it moved to New York in 1884. Locating in Tin Pan Alley, the hub of America's theatrical activity, McElfatrick was able to secure some 228 theater commissions in over ninety cities across the country, including over sixty in New York City. The projects ranged in scale from small-town opera houses to great multi-auditorium facilities like Hammerstein's Olympia (1895) and Proctor's Pleasure Palace (1895) in New York, B. F. Keith's New Theater (1894) in Boston, and the National Theater (1885) in Washington, D.C. His designs were praised in their time for their reasoned approach to stage design, audience sight lines and acoustics, their safety from fire and panic, and their well-considered provisions for performers and audiences.

Upon his father's death, William H. McElfatrick continued the firm until his own death, in 1922.

ANDREW CRAIG MORRISON

WORKS

1873, Central Colored School; *1873, Macauley's Theater, Louisville, Ky. *1880, English's Opera House, Indianapolis, Ind. *1882, Olympic Theater, St. Louis, Mo. 1885, National Theater, Washington. *1886, Grand Opera House, Detroit, Mich. *1887, Theater Vendome, Nashville, Tenn. *1889, Harlem Opera House, New York. *1889, Park Theater, Philadelphia. *1892, Manhattan Opera House, New York. *1893, Abbey's Theater, New York. *1893, DeGive's Grand Theater, Atlanta, Ga. *1893, Dramatic Mirror Building; *1893, Empire Theater; *1893, Metropolitan Opera House, New York. *1894, B. F. Keith's New Theater, Boston. *1895, Hammerstein's Olympia; *1895, Proctor's Pleasure Palace, New York. *1902, Grand Opera House, Cincinnati, Ohio. 1906, Gayety Theater, Baltimore, Md.

BIBLIOGRAPHY

BIRKMIRE, WILLIAM H. (1896)1907 *The Planning and Construction of American Theatres.* New York: Wiley.

BLACKWOOD, DAVID BYRNE 1966 "The Theatres of J. B. McElfatrick and Sons, Architects, 1855–1922." Unpublished Ph.D. dissertation, University of Kansas, Lawrence.

McElfatrick. Hammerstein's Olympia. New York. 1895

KINSILA, EDWARD BERNARD 1917 *Modern Theatre Construction.* New York: Chalmers.

History of Architecture and Building Trades of Greater New York. 1899 New York: Union Historical.

MCGRATH, RAYMOND

With two scholarships from Sydney University, Raymond McGrath (1903–1977) journeyed to England in the late 1920s. A confirmed expatriate, he was nonetheless a counsel and friend to the many young Australian architects who visited him. His writings in the 1930s were influential. He helped introduce central European modernism to England and from 1948 was principal architect of Public Works, Dublin.

DONALD LESLIE JOHNSON

WORKS

1928, Mansfield Forbes House (remodeling), Cambridge. 1930–1934, British Broadcasting Commission Studios (design consultant), London. 1932, Aircraft Interiors for Imperial Airways. 1937, Forognal House, Chertsey, Surrey, England. 1937, Aspro Factory, Buckinghamshire, England. 1940, House, Galby, Leicestershire, England. 1948, President's House (improvements), Dublin.

BIBLIOGRAPHY

HANSON, BRIAN 1977 "Rhapsody in Black Glass." *Architectural Review* 162, July:58–64.

MCGRATH, RAYMOND 1934 *Twentieth Century Houses.* London: Faber.

MCGRATH, RAYMOND, and FROST, A. C. 1937 *Glass*

in Architecture and Decoration. London: Architectural Press.

SAUNDERS, DAVID 1978 "Raymond McGrath 1903–1977." *Architecture Australia* 67, May:72.

MCHARG, IAN

Ian Lennox McHarg (1920–) is an important American landscape architect and regional planner who vigorously espouses ecological goals and systematic procedures for their realization through his teaching, writing, and practice. McHarg was born in Clydebank, Scotland, and received degrees in landscape architecture and city planning from Harvard University in 1950 and 1951. In 1946 he emigrated to the United States and founded the department of landscape architecture in Philadelphia, and regional planning at the University of Pennsylvania forming a multidisciplinary faculty. His book, *Design with Nature* (1969), combines moral philosophy and rational methodology. McHarg suggests that man's survival is threatened by shortsighted economic considerations, rooted in traditional cultural beliefs that mandate the free exploitation of nature; the only recourse is to engage in active cooperation with the environment. To this end, McHarg demonstrates how, by superimposing numerous maps of a given region's natural and social features, planners may synthesize a composite characterization which can guide effective and respectful land use. His proposals are illustrated with examples from the ample work of his firm, Wallace, McHarg, Roberts, and Todd, which he began in 1963 with David A. Wallace.

MICHAEL HOLLANDER

BIBLIOGRAPHY

CLIFF, USSULA 1970 "Ian McHarg: The Designer as Ecologist." *Landscape Architecture* 1, no. 2:28–31.

HOLDEN, CONSTANCE 1977 "Ian McHarg: Champion for Design with Nature." *Landscape Architecture* 67, Mar.:154–156, 180.

MCHARG, IAN 1963 "Man and Environment." Pages 44–58 in Leonard J. Duhl (editor), *The Urban Condition.* New York: Basic.

MCHARG, IAN 1969 *Design with Nature.* New York: Doubleday.

MCHARG, IAN 1971 *Man: A Planetary Disease.* Washington: Government Printing Office.

MCHARG, IAN 1980 "The Garden as a Metaphysical Symbol." *Journal of the Royal Society of Arts* 128, Feb.:132–143.

MCINTIRE, SAMUEL

Many of the lovely streets in Salem, Massachusetts, as seen today are the result of eighteenth-century labors by local carpenters and builders chief among whom was Samuel McIntire (1757–1811). But McIntire was more than a carpenter and builder. Through his special talent and extraordinary manual skill, he gradually attained the level of architect and wood carver; and by middle life he could draw, design, and plan as well as CHARLES BULFINCH, whose work he studied and much admired. It was in the art of woodcarving and architectural decoration that McIntire excelled, and his remarkable talent still graces the façades and interiors of many Salem buildings.

McIntire was born in Salem to Joseph and Sarah (Ruck) McIntire and baptized January 16, 1757. Joseph was a housewright, and his father, John McIntire, was a mariner and housewright. Furthermore, two of his father's brothers were housewrights, and his own brothers, Joseph and Angier, were carpenters and wood carvers. Thus it was inevitable that Samuel would be trained at home and follow the family occupation. Yet there was a difference. Samuel, though always living modestly, raised himself above the average carpenter to become one of the leading architects of his day. He also had more ambition than the rest of his family. Eager to learn more than just carpentry, he became proficient at drawing and increased this ability, and the knowledge of current styles, by studying volumes on English architecture, some of which were certainly in his own collection.

McIntire had married Elizabeth Field in October 1778. By 1786 he was able to buy property and build his own house. It was fittingly modest in size and had no architectural embellishment. On the same property stood his workshop, so that his residence also served as his place of business. Many of his tools, enumerated in the probate inventory, are still preserved at the Essex Institute. The original set included an amazing number of chisels and gouges, moulding planes, and large planes.

The men of Salem for whom McIntire worked were merchants and clever businessmen. They owned well-built ships, with able captains, who protected their vessels from enemies and weather. These ships roamed the world and brought back to Salem wealth unheard of in the previous century. As the merchant owners—Ward, Pickering, Gardner, Peirce, Derby, and others—became rich they spent their money on building large houses, filling them with fine furniture and luxurious household goods, much of which was purchased abroad. Their houses, however, though strongly influenced by British style, necessarily had to be designed and built in Salem where their ships were constructed and their families lived. To meet this demand, and to provide the first-class craftsmanship required, a large number of carpenters, builders, shipwrights, and other craftsmen connected with mercantilism gathered in Salem, and they in turn left their stamp on the city.

The first recorded work of McIntire was in August 1776 when he and his brother Joseph worked on board the schooner *Harlequin* in Salem harbor. The *Harlequin* was a part of Salem's fleet of privateers outfitted to attack British shipping and bring home goods sorely needed during the Revolutionary War. As there is no evidence to show that Samuel McIntire ever went to sea, we can presume that he continued with ship repair work during the war. By 1779, however, he and his brother were doing carpentry work for at least two Salem merchants. Extant receipts fail to show payments for further work until early in 1784, but during the intervening years McIntire did make drawings for the house of his first important patron, Elias Hasket Derby. In 1780 the house was partially built, near Derby's wharf. As completed much later however, it does not resemble McIntire's designs: it is larger and lacks McIntire's typical ornament. The Peirce–Nichols House (1782) was by far the finest of his early efforts. The house was renovated by McIntire in 1801 to conform with contemporary taste, though several of the rooms remain in their original style. Because of the twenty-year interval in McIntire's designs, the house makes a most interesting comparative study of his early and later styles. The decorations of the 1782 work are quite directly inspired by Batty Langley's *City and Country Builder's and Workman's Treasury* (1740). The renovation of 1801 produced ornament smaller in scale and crisply Adamesque. The handsome Georgian exterior, clapboarded, with corner pilasters, a high balustrade, and Doric portico, is as fine as any in New England.

In 1784 the McIntire brothers were again working on board ships and completing various cabinet and joinery work for Elias Hasket Derby, though at substantially reduced wages. Then came McIntire's first civic commission—the new courthouse in Salem (1785–1786). The modest Georgian brick building with a Doric portico stood prominently in Washington Street until 1839. The great merchant, Elias Hasket Derby, frequently sought the services of McIntire no matter how large or small the task might be. In 1786 he bought an old house near the center of town and McIntire was engaged to renovate it. As Mrs. Derby insisted upon living fashionably, the house was brought up to date by adding giant pilasters, a balustrade, and a Doric portico. On the interior he added his own characteristic architectural mouldings and carved ornament.

For the next few years, Elias Hasket Derby seems to have employed McIntire almost constantly, but in 1792 he blossomed out, doing a commercial block and the set of drawings for the United States Capitol competition. The large Capitol drawings (now in the possession of the Maryland Historical Society) are competent, straightforward, Georgian designs meeting the requirements of the commissioner's program, but lacking the monumentality of those submitted by ETIENNE S. HALLET, and later, WILLIAM THORNTON, and McIntire offered no central dominating dome. This is the only public competition McIntire ever entered.

In 1793 McIntire increased his activity by continuing his work for Derby (notably the beautiful little summerhouse at Danvers), and by designing the important Nathan Read (1793) and Lyman (1793-1798) houses. These introduced new architectural features and decorative schemes. The Read House, for instance, has the first of McIntire's curvilinear projecting porticoes. He had previously made detailed drawings of Bulfinch's Joseph Barrell House in Somerville, Massachusetts (1792–1793), evidently attracted by the newly introduced Adam ornament. Fiske Kimball sees this house as the source for the Read House portico, but the Barrell House has no portico. Instead it has a projecting oval room with an open colonnade above. As Bulfinch is known to have based some of his designs on those of JOHN SOANE, it is more likely that McIntire had also seen one of Soane's books in which curvilinear porticoes appear. The Lyman House, a real mansion in its proportions and intent, was the first of McIntire's to use a Palladian system of coupled pilasters on the second level over a first floor base. The most interesting room in the Lyman House is the oval parlor decorated in a delicate Adam manner. Without doubt this elegant room reflects McIntire's visit to the Barrell House and the desire of Theodore Lyman to acquire a fashionable house for his large estate.

McIntire's greatest triumph must have seemed to him the designing and decorating of the enormous Elias Hasket Derby House—the owner's last and most lavish attempt at heading Salem's social order. It was begun in 1795 and only completed at Derby's death four years later. Derby asked several architects to submit plans to him, including the talented and popular Charles Bulfinch. However, McIntire's was chosen even though it may appear to many that the Bulfinch design is superior. The house was to have been in brick, but Derby with all his wealth found the cost prohibitive. The massive, three-storied mansion was finally built of structural wood and covered with clapboards. The façade had tall pilasters of the Ionic order rising through the second and third stories, a balustrade above the eaves, and the whole capped by a cupola from which the town and harbors could be surveyed. The interior was lavishly decorated and furnished, partially with McIntire furniture and architectural decorations as can be ascertained from the bills that survive and from his own drawings. Like the Lyman House, an oval room was the artistic masterpiece. Unfortunately the mansion did not stand for long, as it was too large for the inheriting members of the family to maintain and was torn down in 1815, though not forgotten for many years. Even after Derby died, McIntire continued to work for the Derby family, designing in particular Oak Hall, Peabody (1800–1801), for a Derby daughter, where the mantelpieces are especially noteworthy.

The South Church in Salem (1803–1804) was McIntire's finest religious building. Its plan and general contours were derived from the Congregational meetinghouse at Newburyport. McIntire had been sent by the congregation to study both the Newburyport meetinghouse and that in Exeter, New Hampshire (1801). Old photographs of the Exeter Church (burned in 1903) show how stately and graceful were the tower and spire (166 feet). There was ample opportunity for McIntire's decorative contributions, some of which are saved at the Essex Institute. The new building was completed in time for dedication on New Year's Day 1805.

Having fully established his reputation by 1804 as both designer and decorator, McIntire was commissioned to carry out a considerable number of projects during the next five years. The John Gardner House (1804–1805), now owned by the Essex Institute and open to the public, exemplifies this new group. It was built of brick instead of the customary wood and its other refined walls set an example for numerous elegant houses, both in Salem and elsewhere along the New England coast. The proportions of the house are just right and the entranceway, a version of the curvilinear entrance to the Read House, is strikingly handsome. Corinthian columns and pilasters, and other ornaments are tastefully displayed in McIntire's best manner. In fact this house is an excellent example of the Federal style. The interior contains several fireplace mantels which are enriched with ornament unknown in quality to previous generations in Salem. The lightly hanging swags, bowls of fruit, sheaves of wheat, spiraling vines, and decorative moldings are all typical of McIntire. The Gardner House is perhaps his finest remaining work. Many other houses have been attributed to McIntire in this period on the basis of style, but the Tucker House (now vastly changed [1808–1809]), almost directly across the street from the Gardner House, is confirmed by documentation. It had one of the splendid curvilinear entranceways, which is in the Essex Institute awaiting possible replacement if the Tucker House is renovated.

The most important of McIntire's late public and commercial buildings is Hamilton Hall (1805–1807). It is rather plain and lacks the graceful ornament of his private commissions. Built for the Federalists and named for Alexander Hamilton, it served as an assembly hall for political gatherings,

McIntire.
John Gardner House.
Salem, Massachusetts.
1804–1805

McIntire.
John Gardner House.
Salem, Massachusetts.
1804–1805

dances, etcetera. The floor plans by McIntire still exist, proving his authorship.

On the day of Samuel McIntire's death the Reverend William Bentley wrote in his diary: "This day Salem is deprived of one of the most ingenious men it had in it. He was descended of a family of Carpenters who had no claims on public favor and was educated at a branch of that business. By attention he soon gained a superiority to all of his occupation and the present Court House, the North and South Meeting houses, and indeed all the improvements of Salem for nearly thirty years past have been under his eye. . . . He had a fine person, a majestic appearance, calm countenance, great self command and amiable temper."

Bulfinch in Boston and McIntire in Salem gave New England the high standard in architectural design which would be followed until the coming of the Greek Revival style, but McIntire's influence is particularly noticeable in the many brick mansions built in the decade after his death where his extraordinarily tasteful ornament was widely imitated. Indeed, enthusiasm for his decorative work both in architectural embellishment and furniture design appears to have been greater than for his building designs, and his name still denotes a particularly beautiful variation of the Adam style.

PAUL F. NORTON

WORKS

1780, Elias Hasket Derby House; 1782, 1801, Peirce-Nichols House; (A)1782–1789, F. Boardman House; *1785–1786, Courthouse; 1786, Second Elias Hasket Derby House (renovation); 1793, Nathan Read House; Salem, Mass. 1793–1794, Derby Summer House, Danvers, Mass. 1793–1798, T. Lyman House, Waltham, Mass. (A)1795, William Orne House; *1795–1799, Fourth Elias Hasket Derby House; 1796, Assembly House; Salem, Mass. *(A)1800–1801, Oak Hill, Peabody, Mass. *1803–1804, South Congregational Church; 1804–1805, John Gardner House; (A)1804–1806, C. Crowninshield House; 1805–1807, Hamilton Hall; 1808–1809, G. Tucker House; Salem, Mass.

BIBLIOGRAPHY

ALLEN, GORDAN 1952 "The Vale, Lyman House, Waltham." *Old-Time New England* 42, Apr.:81–87.

BENTLEY, WILLIAM 1905–1914 *The Diary of William Bentley, D. D.* 4 vols. Salem, Mass.: Essex Institute.

COUSINS, FRANK, and RILEY, PHIL M. (1916)1970 *The Wood-Carver of Salem.* Reprint. New York: AMS.

DOWNS, JOSEPH 1947 "Derby and McIntire." *Metropolitan Museum of Art Bulletin* New Series 6, Oct.:73–81.

DYER, WALTER A. 1915 *Early American Craftsmen.* New York: Century.

KIMBALL, FISKE 1930–1931 "Furniture Carvings by Samuel McIntire." *Antiques* 18:388–392, 498–502; 19:30–32, 116–119, 207–210.

KIMBALL, FISKE (1940)1966 *Mr. Samuel McIntire, Carver: The Architect of Salem.* Reprint. Gloucester, Mass.: Peter Smith.

LANGLEY, BATTY (1740)1922 *The City and Country Builder's and Workman's Treasury.* Reprint of 1750 ed. Boston Architectural Club.

LITTLE, NINA FLETCHER 1972 "Corné, McIntire, and the Hersey Derby Farm." *Antiques* 101:226–229.

Samuel McIntire: A Bicentennial Symposium, 1757–1957. 1957 Edited by Benjamin W. Labaree. Salem, Mass.: Essex Institute.

SWAN, MABEL 1931 "A Revised Estimate of McIntire." *Antiques* 20:338–343.

SWAN, MABEL 1932 "McIntire: Check and Countercheck." *Antiques* 21:86–87.

SWAN, MABEL 1934 "McIntire Vindicated." *Antiques* 26:130–132.

WALKER, AMBROSE 1932 "Samuel McIntire—A Sketch." *Essex Institute Historical Collections* 68:97–116.

WARD, GERALD W. R. 1976*a* *The Assembly House.* Salem, Mass.: Essex Institute.

WARD, GERALD W. R. 1976*b* *The Gardner-Pingree House.* Salem, Mass.: Essex Institute.

WARD, GERALD W. R. 1976*c* *The Peirce-Nichols House.* Salem, Mass.: Essex Institute.

MCKENZIE, VOORHEES, and GMELIN

The firm of Andrew C. McKenzie (1861–1926), Stephen Francis Voorhees (1878–1965), and Paul Gmelin (1859–1937) continued the practice that CYRUS L. W. EIDLITZ had established in New York City in the 1880s. In the 1910s (sometimes with the semiretired Eidlitz as consulting architect), the firm frequently reworked the flavor of the Italian Romanesque found in their earlier Times Tower of 1900 with which Voorhees and Gmelin are often associated. The New York Telephone Office Building in Albany (1915) and the Walker-Lispenard Building in New York (1912) are typical examples of this work; the latter building was the largest telephone exchange in the world when completed, with 200 operators. The early 1920s saw more diffuse designs of diminishing character, such as the Brooklyn Municipal Building (opened in 1927 but designed several years earlier) and the New York Telephone exchanges at 235 East 30th Street and 125 West 73rd Street in New York (both 1922). The acclaimed Barclay-Vesey Building of 1926, although technically a work of the firm, was principally the design of young RALPH T. WALKER (soon to be a partner) and represents a new period of design which really began at the end of the McKenzie, Voorhees, and Gmelin partnership. In the 1910s, the work of the firm was estimated to be 80 percent telephone related, and the present successor firm, Haines

Lundberg Waehler, is still prominent in the design of communications and technical buildings.

CHRISTOPHER S. GRAY

WORKS

1912, Walker-Lispenard Building, New York. 1915, New York Telephone Offices, Albany. 1915, Saint Matthew's, Brooklyn, N.Y. 1918, Underwood Service Building; 1922, Telephone Exchanges, 235 East 30 Street, 125 West 73 Street; 1923, Western Electric Warehouse; 1926, Barclay–Vesey Building (with Ralph T. Walker); New York. 1927, Municipal Building, Brooklyn, N.Y.

MCKIM, MEAD, and WHITE

This most important New York architectural partnership, formed at the end of the nineteenth century by Charles Follen McKim (1847–1909), William Rutherford Mead (1846–1928), and STANFORD WHITE (1853–1906), introduced a new freedom of plan in residential design and a new probity of form in public and civic building. By 1882, they were among the leading advocates of a return to classicism as an expression of national architectural character.

For many years the best known firm in the United States, McKim, Mead, and White received over 785 commissions during their active period, 1879 to 1910, but including their earliest work and the commissions undertaken by the junior partners while Mead was in semi-retirement up to 1919, the total number of commissions approached one thousand. Because of the firm's geographically widespread work, its extensive publication, the scores of young architects it trained, and the partners' many private and institutional efforts in support of architectural education, McKim, Mead, and White exerted a strong influence well into the twentieth century, not only across the United States, but in Europe as well, particularly England. The firm's work appeared to CHARLES HERBERT REILLY, English architect and educator, to be "one of the great determining forces in the history of the architecture of our own time" (*McKim, Mead & White,* 1924, p. 7).

Charles Follen McKim, whose father was a leading abolitionist and whose mother was a staunch Quaker, was born and raised in southeastern Pennsylvania, and studied for a year at the Harvard Lawrence Scientific School. During the summer of 1867, he worked in the office of RUSSELL STURGIS, New York, an experience that reinforced his interest in studying JOHN RUSKIN. McKim then spent three years at the Ecole des Beaux-Arts, Paris, in the atelier of Pierre-Gérôme-Honoré Daumet, with periods of travel in France and England. Spurning current Parisian architectural fashions, McKim learned at the Ecole the value of large-scale, comprehensive planning, the expressive power of the integration of the arts, and something of the role of buildings in crystallizing civic aspirations and acting as public symbols. He returned to the United States in 1870 and entered the office of H. H. RICHARDSON, New York, where he worked until about 1873; meanwhile during the years 1871–1872, he began to obtain his own commissions. While in Richardson's office he apparently worked on the drawings for the Brattle Square Church, Boston, the Hampden Country Courthouse, Springfield, Massachusetts, and the first studies for Trinity Church, Boston.

William Rutherford Mead was born and raised in Brattleboro, Vermont, one of a number of children in an artistic family (his brother and later collaborator was Larkin Goldsmith Mead). He was graduated from Amherst College in 1867, worked briefly for an engineer in New York, spent over a year in the office of Russell Sturgis, and then lived with his brother for a year and a half in Florence, Italy, while studying informally. On his return to the United States in 1872, he shared an office with McKim at 57 Broadway, New York, and gradually formed a loose partnership which, after mid-1877, also included William B. Bigelow. Beyond a number of country and summer houses which McKim and Mead designed separately, the principal works of this period were the William Dean Howells House (1877–1878), *Redtop,* Belmont, Massachusetts, and an unsuccessful joint entry in a competition for a new City Hall (1874), Providence, Rhode Island. Bigelow, who had also been a student at the Ecole, was an extremely facile draftsman, but he appears to have had a limited role in design during the short partnership. McKim married Bigelow's sister in 1874, but the marriage ended in divorce in 1878; Bigelow withdrew from the partnership a year later. During the brief time together, the three partners produced several distinguished summer houses (largely through the maturation of McKim's design), including the Prescott Hall Butler House (1878–1880), *Bytharbor,* Saint James, New York, and the Mrs. Anna C. Alden House (1879–1880), *Fort Hill,* on Lloyd's Neck, Long Island, New York.

Stanford White, a native of New York, was the son of noted Shakespearean scholar and critic of art, literature, and music Richard Grant White. Through his father, Stanford came to know the major artists and architects of the city, most notably John La Farge, and received from them encouragement and criticism. He also had at his disposal his father's considerable library on art and architecture, including among the several thousand volumes many by James Jackson Jarves and Ruskin. Though talented as a draftsman, White had no formal training, but in 1872 at the suggestion of his father's close friend, FREDERICK LAW OLMSTED, Stanford was placed in the office of H. H. Richardson. He was given increasingly more responsibility for the interior detailing of Richardson's houses; his incisive renderings of Richardson's buildings frequently appeared in the *New York Sketch Book of Architecture,* of which McKim was the de facto editor. Among his best drawings of the period were the published perspectives of the William Watts Sherman House, Newport, Rhode Island, and the revised tower for Trinity Church, Boston. In the summer of 1877, he joined McKim, Mead, and Bigelow for a sketching trip along the New England coast to study eighteenth-century architecture; the sketches, regrettably, have not survived. In 1878, White left Richardson's office to travel in Europe. On his return in September 1879, he entered into partnership with his friends McKim and Mead, assuming the position just vacated by Bigelow, who continued a separate practice until about 1905.

The quick success of the firm was the result of a fortunate combination of highly complementary but radically different temperaments. McKim worked slowly, endlessly restudying details and proportions, while White worked at a feverish pace, handling as many as fifteen commissions to McKim's one. Mead, a shrewd, quiet, good-humored Yankee, tempered their differences and offered timely criticism; his partners credited him with devising a number of their best plans. Mead was also in charge of the office staff, job management, and construction supervision. Though their staff became exceptionally large for the period—numbering more than 110 in 1892–1893, falling during the depression of the nineties, and rising again to nearly 100 by 1909—the organization was always rather loose, more like an atelier, in contrast to the clearer hierarchy in the office of DANIEL H. BURNHAM. (For a discussion of the operation of the office, see L. M. Roth, *The Architecture of McKim, Mead & White, 1879–1920: A Building List,* New York, xii–xlviii.) The firm was also fortunate to practice during the last two periods of great economic prosperity before enactment of the graduated income tax which sharply reduced the kind of patronage it enjoyed.

The firm's work falls into clearly defined periods: 1879 to 1886, the early years of experimentation; 1887 to 1893, the first masterworks; 1894 to 1899, years of economic depression; and 1900 to 1909, maturity. In addition, the firm from the beginning was interested in the design of building groups or ensembles. This work, too, divided into definite periods: 1879 to 1899, early experiments through the impact of the World's Columbian Exposition; and 1900 to 1909, the application of the lessons of the Exposition.

During the early years, McKim's search for order and clear geometries and White's penchant for picturesque variety in color and texture found expression in the Shingle style houses and country clubs for which the firm first became known in the 1880s. In addition to their studied irregularity and inventiveness, these shingled buildings incorporated many elements derived from the close study of American colonial architecture both in material and detail, from Japanese architecture, and from the texture of slate-covered medieval buildings in rural France. This is seen most clearly in their Newport Casino (1879–1880), Newport, Rhode Island; the Short Hills Music Hall (1879–1880), Short Hills, New Jersey and in the planned informality of such houses as those for H. Victor Newcomb (1880), Elberon, New Jersey, and Isaac Bell (1881–1883), Newport, Rhode Island. Gradually, the geometries became more abstract and formal, as in the Cyrus McCormick House (1880–1883), *Clayton Lodge,* Richfield Springs, New York; this style culminated in the elemental William G. Low House (1886–1887), Bristol, Rhode Island, a house which has achieved international recogni-

McKim, Mead, and White. William G. Low House. Bristol, Rhode Island. 1886–1887

McKim, Mead, and White.
Henry Villard House Group.
New York.
1882–1885

tion since 1955 but which was unpublished and hardly known in its own time.

The years 1882–1883 are significant for the start of three houses, each of which embodied Renaissance forms appropriate to its setting. For the six-house complex commissioned by Henry Villard (1882–1885), New York, McKim and White employed correct Quattrocento Italian details; for the John F. Andrew House (1883–1888), in Boston's Back Bay, the firm used Federalist motifs and a bowed front typical of Beacon Hill; and in Newport they drew upon local sources, even incorporating salvaged eighteenth-century paneling in one room of the large neo-Colonial summer house for H. A. C. Taylor (1882–1886). This decided turn to classical and Colonial sources marked the effect of the sketching trip of 1877 and the firm's growing interest in the national architectural heritage. It is evidence, too, of the probable influence of Joseph Morrill Wells, then the major draftsman in the office, who had become an advocate of the Italian Renaissance; curiously, he refused a partnership shortly before his untimely death in 1890. This individualized adjustment of classical references was also a portent of the way the firm came to use the classical language, carefully adapting the expression of each building to the character of its use and place.

During the 1880s, the firm designed a group of early commercial blocks, many of them for the Goelet brothers of New York, most notably the Goelet Building (1886–1887), New York, which developed the tripartite organization of the exterior. All of these were wall-bearing structures (the first and highly controversial all metal frame building in New York was erected by BRADFORD L. GILBERT in 1888–1889). More important for its long-range implications was the firm's integration of the arts in their work, such as the incorporation of sculpture by Augustus Saint-Gaudens and murals by John La Farge in the Villard House and the dramatic chancel remodeling of the Church of the Ascension (1885–1888), New York, under the general direction of White and with contributions by Louis Saint-Gaudens, D. Maitland Armstrong, and La Farge.

In 1887, the firm began work on three large buildings which marked their emergence as major architects. This was eminently true of McKim's Boston Public Library (1887–1898), with its splendid embellishments by Augustus and Louis Saint-Gaudens, Daniel Chester French, D. Maitland Armstrong, Puvis-de-Chavannes, Edwin Austin Abbey, and John Singer Sargent, among others. The library occupied the block west of Copley Square dominated on the opposite side by Richardson's craggy mass of Trinity Church. Forming a spacious court at the center of the library block, the architects then had to fit and refit various services inside as the library trustees kept changing the program. This was the world's first large public lending library, and being the first of its kind it posed many functional problems. It was also to define a major space, and so McKim conceived the façade as a variation on PIERRE FRANÇOIS HENRI LABROUSTE's Bibliothèque Sainte Geneviève, Paris, long the paradigm of library design among Ecole students. To Labrouste's scheme McKim added greater mass and solidity, moving closer to Renaissance and Roman sources. Just as the Boston Public Library embodied McKim's scholarly correctness, the Madison Square Garden (1887–1891), New York, in its complexity of internal functions, its light-colored terra cotta, profuse ornament, and sparkling electric illumination, epitomized White's ebullience. The massive articulated H-plan of the duplicate New York Life Insurance Company Buildings (1887–1890), Kansas City, Missouri, and Omaha, Nebraska, represented the planning and organizing ability of Mead. The New York Life buildings, however, did not celebrate their great height as ADLER AND SULLIVAN's Wainwright Building was to do so dramatically a few years later; indeed, this experience with skyscraper design (using traditional wall-bearing construction) persuaded the partners to avoid skyscraper commissions when at all possible until just prior to White's death in 1906.

In 1888, McKim gave special significance to the Georgian Revival in his Johnston Gate at Harvard. The gate was to stand between two of the oldest brick buildings at Harvard, exemplary of the Georgian tradition. In deference to them McKim selected reject bricks laid in thick buff-tinted mortar and had the grilles fabricated of hand-hammered wrought iron. In this way he chose to adhere to Harvard's ancestral expression as a way of maintaining identity and a clearer sense of Harvard's history at a time when the campus and curriculum were undergoing sweeping transformation under the leadership of Charles W. Eliot. The brick and stone Georgian idiom was also used for the double Amory-Olney Houses (1890–1892), Boston, and the Bryan Lathrop House (1891–1893), Chicago, but for the Rhode Island State Capitol, won in competition in 1891, the reference was varied. Inspired by the national Capitol in Washington, but designed as a coordinated whole and built entirely of white marble (including the dome), it immediately became the model for CASS GILBERT's Minnesota Capitol. These two, then, initiated a generation of austere classical domed state capitols, embellished internally by the most eminent sculptors and mural painters.

A good demonstration of how architects and artists could work together was the compact brick and stone Walker Art Gallery (1891–1894), Bowdoin College, Brunswick, Maine. Its domed central rotunda was enriched by four lunette murals by Elihu Vedder, Kenyon Cox, Abbott Thayer, and John La Farge. The last major building of the period was a new house for the New York *Herald* (1890–1895), New York. Seeking to change the

McKim, Mead, and White. Boston Public Library. 1887–1898

McKim, Mead, and White. Madison Square Garden. New York. 1887–1891

McKim, Mead, and White. State Capitol. Providence, Rhode Island. 1891–1903

paper's image, owner James Gordon Bennett selected a new site on what became known as Herald Square, in the heart of the city's theater district. For the low building, dictated by Bennett, White translated the fresco decoration of the Renaissance model into white and yellow terra cotta relief. By 1893, the work of the firm was almost entirely classical, ranging from the richly modeled northern Italian and Spanish Renaissance as paraphrased in the Madison Square Garden and the *Herald* Building, or the grave neoclassicism of the Rhode Island Capitol. Of the firm's extensive oeuvre only four buildings were Gothic, all churches done before 1900. With this shift to classicism came an elevation of the palette of materials toward closely coordinated white, cream, yellow, and buff terra cotta. The horizontal line was unquestionably dominant.

During the 1890s, the firm began to use a complete metal frame in commercial buildings and internal metal frames for many large houses, though the frame never became for them the determining force in the design or detailing of the exterior. Perhaps most important, the buildings designed between 1887 and 1893 incorporated a growing sensitivity to their urban settings and to the interaction between the building and its environment, as demonstrated both in the Boston Public Library and its impact on Copley Square and in the *Herald* Building and its relationship to the hustle and bustle of the theater district. Both buildings were shaped by their environments and both attempted to augment and strengthen the character of their settings.

As early as 1879, the partners were involved in the design of buildings in groups, a relatively rare enterprise for architects at that time. The Short Hills Music Hall, for instance, had been the focal point for a newly planned suburban community for which the firm also designed a model house. In 1881–1882, the firm designed a cluster of seven shingled weekend houses at Montauk, on the tip of Long Island, New York, their grounds landscaped by Frederick Law Olmsted. Whereas the Montauk houses were within a few hundred yards of one another, the projects undertaken for the Northern Pacific Railroad in 1882–1884 spanned half a continent, ranging from modest remodeling of company offices in Saint Paul, Minnesota, to expansive hotels for Portland, Oregon, and Tacoma, Washington, and a grand station for Portland (never built), where Villard, then president of the railroad, envisioned the line would terminate.

Even before leaving Richardson, White had begun to collaborate with Augustus Saint-Gaudens, designing for his bronzes bases and settings which went far beyond the customary form of pedestals. It is not accidental that these were also the sculptor's best creations, beginning with the Farragut Monument (1877–1881), Union Square, New York, the landscaped setting for the Chapin Monument (1880–1887), Stearns Park, Springfield, Massachusetts, and reaching a fine balance of creative power and restraint in the holly-sheltered enclosure of the Adams Memorial (1886–1891), Rock Creek Cemetery, Washington. McKim, too, worked with Saint-Gaudens, providing the granite frame for the Shaw Memorial (1881–1897), Boston Common, Boston.

These efforts were but preliminary to the firm's participation in the World's Columbian Exposition (1891–1893), Chicago. Beside designing the large Agriculture Building on the focal Court of Honor and the New York State Building patterned on the Villa Medici, Rome, the firm also built two small pavilions; but perhaps more far-reaching was the assistance McKim gave Daniel Burnham, who came to call McKim his "right hand man." After the fair, both the firm and Burnham became involved in urban design and planning, though Burnham pursued this on a far more comprehensive scale. McKim, Mead, and White concentrated on smaller ensembles, beginning with White's campus plan, library, and classroom buildings for New York University (1892–1901), New York. While this was inspired in part by JOSEPH JACQUES RAMÉE's Union College plan of 1812, McKim's larger and more formal Columbia University plan of 1893–1894 recalled the new Sorbonne in Paris, and, to a lesser extent, THOMAS JEFFERSON's University of Virginia, Charlottesville, Virginia. Both White's and McKim's schemes focused on domed library buildings, as did Jefferson's. Coincidentally, shortly after both

McKim, Mead, and White. Columbia University. New York. 1893–1902

these campuses were started, the firm was engaged to repair Jefferson's Rotunda at Charlottesville after it was gutted by fire; at the instruction of the university trustees, the firm also added three restrained brick classroom buildings at the low end of Jefferson's campus. Much influenced by Jefferson's neoclassicism and by the interposition of the Johnston Gate at Harvard, the firm next devised a compact, centralized plan for Radcliffe College (1897), Cambridge, Massachusetts, though of this only the gymnasium (1898–1899) was completed by the firm. Beside college campus plans, the firm also designed two workers' housing villages at Roanoke Rapids (1894–1895), North Carolina, and *Echota* (1892–1895), Niagara Falls, New York. In both towns, the firm also designed the factories and power plants. Whereas the electrical generating plant at Niagara Falls was of massive, rather Richardsonian masonry, the houses were simplified and traditional, with traces of Colonial detail. In Naugatuck, Connecticut, however, the firm was engaged by John Howard Whittemore during 1885 to 1905 to design a broad range of buildings including two public schools, a public library, bank, church, public fountain, and three houses.

By 1894, the first effect of the economic depression of the 1890s was being felt by the firm, though ironically some of the largest and most elaborate of their country houses were designed in these years. Many are well-illustrated in the *Monograph of the Work of McKim, Mead, & White* (1915–1920). Among the most elaborate are the Frederick W. Vanderbilt House (1895–1899), Hyde Park, New York; the Herman Oelrichs House (1897–1902), *Rosecliff,* Newport, Rhode Island; and the Clarence H. Mackay House (1899–1902), *Harbor Hill,* Roslyn, New York. By this time, all of the firm's work was Georgian or Italian classical, including summer and country houses, though the firm bowed to pressure from the Mackays and modeled *Harbor Hill* on FRANÇOIS MANSART's Château Maisons-Lafitte. Urban houses were either decidedly Roman or Florentine, such as the H. A. C. Taylor House (1892–1896), New York, or Georgian-Federalist, such as the George A. Nickerson House (1895–1897), in the Back Bay, Boston, which recalls ALEXANDER PARRIS's Sears House on Beacon Hill. Georgian was deemed appropriate, too, for collegiate structures such as the Harvard Union (1899–1901), Cambridge, Massachusetts, and the Harvard Club (1893–1916), New York. For the larger University Club (1896–1900), New York, McKim employed a generic Italian Renaissance palazzo type, massively built in pink granite. Budget limitations required that the structure of the Boston Symphony Hall (1892–1901) be rather restrained Georgian, but in an effort to guarantee acoustical

McKim, Mead, and White. Herman Oelrichs House. Newport, Rhode Island. 1897–1902

perfection the firm collaborated with the young physicist Wallace K. Sabine, making this the first American symphonic hall in which acoustical performance was determined in advance. More Roman in scale and character, recalling somewhat the Columbian Exposition, was the master plan for the Brooklyn Institute (Brooklyn Museum) (1893–1915), New York. The austere granite classical Cullum Memorial Hall (1893–1898), West Point, New York, was compared by critic Montgomery Schuyler to *néo-Grec* work in France. The construction of the spacious and lavishly embellished Bowery Savings Bank (1893–1895), New York, contradicted the economic downturn, but the austere white State Savings Bank (1898–1900), Detroit, Michigan, signaled the end of the depression.

Although Saint-Gaudens had begun his Sherman Memorial in the early 1890s, McKim's broad base could not be designed until 1902 when the final orientation and site had been selected in Central Park, New York. Other settings for sculpture followed, including several by White which were not completed until his and Saint-Gaudens's deaths. Far more important was the continuing influence of the Columbian Exposition on McKim, Burnham, and Frederick Law Olmsted, Jr. These three, together with Saint-Gaudens, constituted the Senate Park Commission charged with replanning the government center and the park system of Washington (1901–1902). Their challenge was to restore the sense of order and balance inherent in PIERRE CHARLES L'ENFANT's master plan (1791) which over the years had been broken up by successive administrations and agencies. This the Commission did in a dazzling presentation of drawings, colored perspectives, and models which were so compelling as to have been the conceptual basis of the District's development ever since. No sooner was this plan presented than the firm began to turn to smaller groups, devising the master plan for the U.S. Army War College (1902–1907), Washington. Their proposal (1902) for replanning the U.S. Military Academy at West Point lost in competition to Cram, Ferguson, and Goodhue (see BERTRAM G. GOODHUE). In any case, the next year they developed an expanded master plan for Columbia University and continued building there for another decade. In 1906, the firm prepared a more circumspect plan for the University of Nevada, Reno, which included the Mackay School of Mines (1906–1908). The basic tenet underlying such planning, intimated in the Columbian Exposition, was expressed in the report of the Niagara Falls Commission in which McKim participated in 1907–1908. In advising on how the area around the falls could be restored after many years of industrial use, the Commission insisted that the natural beauty of the rapids, falls, and gorge "should not be despoiled to promote the material welfare of even many individuals." In planning, the Commission implied, the long-term benefits to the community must take precedence over the short-term advantage to individuals or corporations, an admonition that still bears heeding.

With the return of economic prosperity by 1900 came a flood of commissions, including those most often singled out as representative of the work of McKim, Mead, and White. There were, of course, more large urban residences, such as the Venetian palace for Joseph Pulitzer (1900–1903), New York, or the crisply and richly ornamented white Robert Wilson Patterson House (1900–1903), Washington, which incorporated an automobile garage on the ground floor. Most sumptuous of all, inside and out, was the Payne Whitney House (1902–1909), New York. In the William Kissam Vanderbilt, Jr., House (1904–1907), New York, next to William Morris Hunt's epochal French château of 1879, White returned to a delicate François Ier French Renaissance idiom he had not employed since 1885. The Georgian-Federalist houses of this period included the broadly fenestrated Thomas B. Clarke House (1902), New York; the sedate Charles Dana Gibson House (1902–1903), New York; and the finely proportioned Percy Pyne House (1906–1912), New York. This historical sensitivity was expressed most fittingly in the careful restoration of the White House (1902), Washington, in which McKim endeavored to re-establish as closely as possible the character of JAMES HOBAN's Executive Mansion. It was the best, because the least evident, of McKim's reconstructions.

The firm's well-known ability to handle complex planning problems was further demonstrated in the schemes for the expanded Bellevue Hospital (1903–1913), New York, and the additions to the Metropolitan Museum of Art (1904–1916), New York. Particularly notable, too, were the additions made to two nineteenth-century banks—the connecting bridge and horizontal expansion of the Bank of Montreal (1900–1905), Montreal, Quebec, Canada, and the vertical addition above ISAIAH ROGERS's Merchants' Exchange for the National City Bank (1904–1910), New York. McKim meanwhile served two terms as president of the American Institute of Architects, 1902–1903; he also received the Gold Medal from the Royal Institute of British Architects in 1903. Perhaps the most personal of his work, and almost certainly his best studied, was the small library for J. Pierpont Morgan (1902–1907), New York. The

McKim, Mead, and White.
J. Pierpont Morgan Library.
New York.
1902–1907

precision of its dry masonry walls, the marble inlay of its floors, and the muted coloration of its murals were calibrated to augment but not to surpass the library's exquisite contents. White's work after the turn of the century tended toward greater sobriety of form with ornament concentrated in zones. The volume of his work continued unabated, but the results showed more study than before. He designed two tall commercial buildings in New York, for the Gorham Company and Tiffany's (both 1903–1906). He contributed his services in the design of the shell of the mammoth power house for the Interborough Rapid Transit (1901–1904), New York, and developed a scheme for the new Grand Central Terminal (1903), proposing a broad fourteen-story base above which would rise a sixty-story tower. Much admired by Montgomery Schuyler, because of its clear structural expression and its rich but controlled embellishment, was White's templar Knickerbocker Trust (1901–1904), New York, which became the model for a generation of banks. Perhaps White's masterwork, according to John Jay Chapman, was the Madison Square Presbyterian Church (1904–1906), New York, a compact cube fronted by a massive hexastyle Corinthian portico scaled in anticipation of the skyscrapers which were certain to rise around it. Its buff brick walls were complemented by terra cotta ornament with glazes of moss green, yellow, and powder blue, one of the earliest applications of full polychromy in American architectural terra cotta. While all of this was underway, the firm was busy developing plans for the huge Pennsylvania Station (1902–1911), New York. Before later thoughtless modifications, the station functioned, wrote Lewis Mumford, with logical inevitability; the areas of fast movement were small in scale, while areas where one came to rest soared vertically with an abundance of space. Below the street were three levels, with vehicular ramps leading to the ticket and baggage areas for long-distance travelers, while separate passages and stairs on all sides provided easy access for commuters. The granite exterior had minimal detail to reduce maintenance and was also boldly scaled to remain strong in the face of expected development around the station. The vast space of the great waiting room was modeled after the Baths of Caraculla, Rome, but enlarged nearly 25 percent in each direction, while next to it, over the concourse and stairs down to the trains, was an equally vast glass roof, its crystalline vaults both ancient in profile and advanced in material to provide a transition between the trains, the waiting room, and the city beyond. Through

McKim, Mead, and White. Pennsylvania Station. New York. 1902–1911

McKim, Mead, and White. Pennsylvania Station. New York. 1902–1911

the careful manipulation of space and historic reference, Pennsylvania Station was made the gate to a great metropolis.

In the midst of this flurry of work, White was killed on the evening of June 25, 1906, while attending the opening of a musical on the roof-top cabaret of his Madison Square Garden, shot by Harry Kendall Thaw, the crazed husband of Evelyn Nesbit whom White had befriended years before. The yellow press of New York initiated a campaign of vilification, portraying White as one who preyed upon young chorus girls, a cruel device to boost circulation from which McKim never fully recovered. After the Niagara Falls Commission report was made, he quietly withdrew from office affairs and died in Saint James, New York, in 1909. Though Mead remained technically a part of the firm until his official retirement in 1919, he traveled almost incessantly, leaving most of the office work to younger partners who were added in 1906 and 1909. He died while on one such trip in Paris in 1928.

During the decade after 1909, there was only a gradual change in the character of the firm's work as the junior partners carried on. (For a discussion of the junior partners—William Mitchell Kendall, William Symmes Richardson, Bert L. Fenner, Teunis J. Van der Bent, and Lawrence Grant White, Stanford's son—see the new edition of the *Monograph of the Work of McKim, Mead & White,* 1973.) The vibrant tension that had existed between austere McKim and firebrand White was now gone, but a number of the buildings of the decade had something of the spirit of the founders and they have frequently and erroneously been regarded as the work of McKim or White. The towering bulk of the Municipal Building (1907–1916), New York, and the broad sweep of the New York Post Office (1908–1913), behind Pennsylvania Station, were Kendall's, while the restrained luxury of the apartment block at 998 Fifth Avenue (1910–1914), New York, was Richardson's. The firm's largest and costliest building ever was the Hotel Pennsylvania (1915–1920), New York, to the east of Pennsylvania Station, whose intricate structural and functional problems were handled by Van der Bent. The founders' concerns for civic decorum, for an architecture that enhanced the character of the street, and for a just balance of mass and scale, were continued in the Racquet and Tennis Club (1916–1919), New York.

Through the junior partners the work of the founders reached a broad audience, for they undertook the preparation of the 400 plates of the *Monograph,* issued in installments during 1915–1920. Copies quickly reached the most outlying cities of the United States, were studied with delight in

England, and were sent to Japan. By the time the book appeared, however, scores of young architects had established themselves throughout the nation after serving apprenticeships in the office. Prominent among these former assistants were Cass Gilbert, HENRY BACON, JOHN MERVEN CARRÈRE AND THOMAS HASTINGS, EDWARD YORK AND PHILIP SAWYER, and Walter D. Bliss and William B. Faville. Whereas these partnerships started in the office, other assistants formed partnerships later, such as Thomas M. Kellogg who joined John H. Rankin in Philadelphia, or William H. Whidden who joined Ion Lewis in Portland, Oregon. For distant commissions the firm associated with local architects, as with HOLABIRD AND ROCHE for the Bryan Lathrop House, Chicago.

Although in 1902 the founders designed a London hotel for Lewis Sherry, the firm never completed a building in England, but appreciation of the firm's work was strong there by the turn of the century. Charles Herbert Reilly traveled to the United States in 1909 expressly to visit the large McKim, Mead, and White office, writing about its organization in "The Modern Renaissance in American Architecture," *Journal-Royal Institute of British Architects* (1909–1910). Reilly's admiration was manifest in his small but perceptive volume, *McKim, Mead & White* (1924), in which he wrote, "the work of McKim, Mead & White sums up the finest aspirations of a great people at a great epoch" (p. 24). Contemporary American historians and critics such as THOMAS E. TALLMADGE and Fiske Kimball were somewhat more qualified in their praise. Russell Sturgis, however, in his published articles and private correspondence had long before bitterly attacked the firm's work, and the earliest work of Lewis Mumford and Henry-Russell Hitchcock maintained a similar position. In 1936, Hitchcock wrote in his study of H. H. Richardson that when White left his mentor to join McKim and Mead he went from being a one-eyed minister to a king among the blind (*The Architecture of H. H. Richardson and His Times,* 1966, pp. 163–164). Subsequently, however, in *Architecture: Nineteenth and Twentieth Centuries* (1958), Hitchcock took the far more positive position that in their Boston Public Library the firm was continuing in the same direction Richardson took in his last buildings. In the meantime, the nadir of appreciation of McKim, Mead, and White was reached in the late 1940s. In 1948, John Kouwenhoven was convinced that "the work of men like McKim . . . had less relation to the vital contemporary forces of American life . . . than even the crudest, least ingratiating examples of small-town dwellings" (*Made in America,* 1948, p. 95). By the end of the 1950s, however, leading architectural critics and historians such as Mumford, Hitchcock, and Vincent Scully in his *Shingle Style* (1955), had established the importance of the firm. Scully was even more emphatic in his positive estimation of the firm's urban work in *American Architecture and Urbanism* (1969). The cycle of critical perception turned nearly full circle by 1975 on the occasion of the exhibition of Ecole des Beaux-Arts drawings at the Museum of Modern Art, New York. By this time the new annotated edition of the *Monograph* had been published, followed in 1978 by an illustrated catalogue of the firm's work and several articles examining diverse aspects of their architecture.

McKim, Mead, and White held fast to a fervent Ruskinian and Vitruvian idealism to "build well." They wished to bring a measure of order and harmony to the urban American environment at a time when it seemed that the entire culture was in flux. They wanted to reinvigorate the native classical American building tradition. They looked upon architecture and urban design as a concert of all the arts celebrating but not dictated by function. They attempted to mold plans that had an inner inevitability, enabling people to move from space to space as though drawn by an internal force. They believed that every site, rural or urban, was different, and though one might use a universal and national classicism, it was always to be conditioned by the traditions of the place. They believed that to provide merely the most economical solution demeaned first the client and architect and subsequently all of a building's users; it was the architect's responsibility to shape the best design in the best way. They repudiated "minimum standards," not only because they knew all too well that such quickly become the only standards but also because they viewed architecture as a commitment to the future. Growing out of the idealized formalism of nineteenth-century architecture and its symbolic and associational references to the past, the work of McKim, Mead, and White represented a generous realization of Vitruvian commodious planning, sound construction, and visual delight.

LELAND M. ROTH

WORKS

EARLY WORK

1874, Thomas Robinson House (addition by McKim), Newport, R.I. 1877–1878, William Dean Howells House (McKim and Mead), Belmont, Mass. 1877–1881, Base for Farragut Memorial (White), Union Square, New York.

MCKIM, MEAD AND BIGELOW

1877–1879, Edward N. Dickerson House, New York. 1878–1880, Prescott Hall Butler House, Saint James,

N.Y. 1879–1880, Anna C. Alden House, Lloyd's Neck, Long Island, N.Y.

MCKIM, MEAD AND WHITE

1879–1880, Newport Casino, R.I. *1879–1880, Short Hills Music Hall, N.J. *1880, H. Victor Newcomb House, Elberson, N.J. *1880–1883, Cyrus McCormick House, Richfield Springs, N.Y. 1880–1887, Deacon Chapin Monument, Springfield, Mass. 1881–1882, House Group, Montauk, N.Y. 1881–1883, Isaac Bell House, Newport, R.I. 1881–1897, Shaw Memorial, Boston. 1882–1883, Ross R. Winans House, Baltimore. *1882–1884, American Safe Deposit Company Building, New York. *1882–1884, Hotels and Terminal Stations, Northern Pacific Railroad, Portland, Ore., and Tacoma, Wash. *1882–1884, Phillips and Lloyd Phoenix House; *1882–1885, Charles L. Tiffany House Group; 1882–1885, Henry Villard House Group; New York. *1882–1886, H. A. C. Taylor House, Newport, R.I. *1883–1885, Julia and Marian Appleton House, Lenox, Mass. 1883–1885, RusWin Hotel, New Britain, Conn. 1883–1885, Saint Paul's Church, Stockbridge, Mass. 1883–1887, First Methodist (Lovely Lane) Church, Baltimore. 1883–1888, John F. Andrew House, Boston. 1885–1888, Church of the Ascension (chancel remodeling), New York. 1885–1905, Schools, Library, Bank, Church, Fountain, and Three Houses for J. H. Whittemore, Naugatuck, Conn. 1886–1887, Goelet Building, New York. *1886–1887, William G. Low House, Bristol, R.I. 1886–1889, Algonquin Club, Boston. 1886–1890, Saint Peter's Church, Morristown, N.J. 1886–1891, Adams Memorial, Washington. 1887–1890, New York Life Insurance Company Building, Kansas City, Mo. 1887–1890, New York Life Insurance Company Building, Omaha, Neb. *1887–1891, Madison Square Garden, New York. 1887–1898, Boston Public Library. 1888–1890, Johnston Gate, Harvard University, Cambridge, Mass. 1889–1891, Century Club; *1889–1891, Hotel Imperial; 1889–1891, J. Hampden Robb House; New York. 1890–1891, Browne and Meredith Apartment Block; 1890–1892, Amory-Olney Double House; Boston. *1890–1895, Herald Building; 1891–1892, King Model Houses; New York. *1891–1893, Agriculture Building, New York State Pavilion, and other buildings, Columbian Exposition; 1891–1893, Bryan Lathrop House; Chicago. 1891–1894, Metropolitan Club, New York. 1891–1894, Walker Art Gallery, Bowdoin College, Brunswick, Maine. 1891–1903, State Capitol, Providence, R.I. 1892–1895, Power Houses and *Echota* Housing, Niagara Falls, N.Y. *1892–1896, Three Houses for H. A. C. Taylor, New York. 1892–1901, Five Buildings, New York University. 1892–1901, Boston Symphony Hall. 1893–1895, Bowery Savings Bank, New York. 1893–1898, Cullum Memorial Hall, West Point, N.Y. 1893–1902, Seven Buildings, Columbia University; 1893–1915, Brooklyn Institute (now Brooklyn Museum); 1893–1916, Harvard Club; New York. *1894–1895, Factory and Housing, Roanoke Rapids, N.C. 1895–1897, George A. Nickerson House, Boston. 1895–1899, Frederick W. Vanderbilt House, Hyde Park, N.Y. 1896–1900, University Club, New York. 1896–1907, Rotunda (restoration) and Four Buildings, University of Virginia, Charlottesville, Va. 1897–1899, Gymnasium, Radcliffe College, Cambridge, Mass. 1897–1902, Herman Oelrichs House, Newport, R.I. 1898–1900, State Savings Bank, Detroit, Mich. 1899–1901, Union, Harvard University, Cambridge, Mass. *1899–1902, Clarence H. Mackay House, Roslyn, N.Y. 1900–1903, Robert W. Patterson House, Washington. 1900–1903, Joseph Pulitzer House, New York. 1900–1905, Bank of Montreal (additions). *1901–1904, Knickerbocker Trust; 1901–1904, Interborough Rapid Transit Powerhouse; 1902, Thomas B. Clarke House; New York. 1902, White House (restoration), Washington. 1902–1903, Charles D. Gibson House; 1902–1903, Sherman Memorial; 1902–1907, J. Pierpont Morgan Library; New York. 1902–1907, Numerous Buildings, War College, Washington. 1902–1909, Payne Whitney House; *1902–1911, Pennsylvania Station; 1902–1914, Fourteen Branches, New York Public Library; 1903–1906, Gorham Building; 1903–1906, Tiffany's; 1903–1913, Bellevue Hospital (eleven sections); 1903–1914, Ten Buildings, Columbia University; *1904–1906, Madison Square Presbyterian Church; *1904–1907, William Kissam Vanderbilt, Jr., House; 1904–1910, National City Bank (renovation and addition); 1904–1916, Metropolitan Museum of Art (eight sections and additions); New York. 1906–1908, Mackay School of Mines, University of Nevada, Reno. 1906–1912, Percy Pyne House, New York.

SUCCESSOR FIRM: 1910–1919

1907–1916, Municipal Building; 1908–1913, Central Post Office; 1910–1914, 998 Fifth Avenue; 1915–1920, Hotel Pennsylvania; 1916–1919, Racquet and Tennis Club; New York. 1917–1920, Butler Art Gallery, Youngstown, Ohio.

BIBLIOGRAPHY

Archival material on McKim, Mead and White is in the New-York Historical Society; the Avery Architectural Library, Columbia University, New York; and the Manuscript Division, Library of Congress, Washington.

ANDREWS, WAYNE 1951 "McKim, Mead and White: New York's Own Architects." *New-York Historical Society Quarterly* 35:87–96.

BALDWIN, CHARLES C. (1931)1976 *Stanford White.* Reprint. New York: Da Capo.

Brickbuilder 1910 19:entire issue on McKim.

CHAPMAN, JOHN J. 1919 "McKim, Mead & White." *Vanity Fair* 13, Sept.:37, 102, 104.

DAVID, A. C. 1906 "An Architectural Oasis." *Architectural Record* 19:135–144.

DAVIS, Richard H. 1906 "Stanford White." *Collier's Magazine* 37:17.

DESMOND, HARRY W., and CROLY, HERBERT 1906 "The Work of Messrs. McKim, Mead & White." *Architectural Record* 20:153–246.

GRANGER, ALFRED H. (1913)1972 *Charles Follen McKim: A Study of His Life and Work.* Reprint. New York: Arno.

HILL, FREDERICK P. 1950 *Charles F. McKim: The Man.* Francestown, N.H.: M. Jones.

Hitchcock, H. R. (1936)1966 *The Architecture of H. H. Richardson and His Times.* Rev. ed. Cambridge, Mass.: M.I.T. Press.

Kouwenhoven, John 1948 *Made in America.* Garden City, N.Y.: Doubleday.

A Monograph of the Works of McKim, Mead & White, 1879–1915. (1915)1973 With an essay by Leland M. Roth. New ed. New York: Blom.

Moore, Charles (1929)1969 *The Life and Times of Charles Follen McKim.* Reprint. New York: Da Capo.

Moses, Lionel 1922 "McKim, Mead & White: A History." *American Architect* 121:413–424.

Mumford, Lewis 1958 "The Disappearance of Pennsylvania Station." *New Yorker* 34, June 7:106–113.

Ramsey, Stanley C. 1917 "The Work of McKim, Mead and White." *Journal of the Proceedings of the Royal Institute of British Architects* 25, Nov. 5:25–29.

Reilly, Charles H. 1909–1910 "The Modern Renaissance in American Architecture." *Journal of the Proceedings of the Royal Institute of British Architects* 17:630–635.

Reilly, Charles H. (1924)1972 *McKim, Mead & White.* Reprint. New York: Blom.

Roth, Leland M. 1978 *The Architecture of McKim, Mead & White, 1870–1920: A Building List.* New York: Garland.

Roth, Leland M. 1979 "Three Industrial Towns by McKim, Mead and White." *Journal of the Society of Architectural Historians* 38:317–347.

Sully, Vincent 1955 *The Shingle Style.* New Haven: Yale University Press.

Scully, Vincent 1969 *American Architecture and Urbanism: A Historical Essay.* New York: Praeger.

Sturgis, Russell 1895 "The Works of McKim, Mead & White." *Architectural Record:* Great American Architects Series, No. 1.

White, Lawrence Grant 1920 *Sketches and Designs by Stanford White.* New York: Architectural Book Publishing.

Wilson, Richard Guy 1979 "The Early Work of Charles F. McKim: Country House Commissions." *Winterthur Portfolio* 14:235–267.

MEAD, WILLIAM RUTHERFORD

See McKim, Mead, and White.

MEBES, PAUL

Paul Mebes (1872–1938) was one of twentieth-century Germany's most significant housing designers and architectural theorists. After architectural training at the Technische Hochschule in Braunschweig, Mebes established a private practice in Berlin, and, in 1907, was appointed director of one of the city's largest housing cooperatives, the Beamtenwohnungsverein. First alone and then in partnership with Paul Emmerich, Mebes specialized in row housing and apartment housing for three decades, attempting to achieve efficient planning, the maximization of light and air, and the provision of a high standard of amenities, goals which would also inspire the better-known housing designers of the late 1920s, Martin Wagner, Bruno Taut, Ernst May, Otto Haesler, and Walter Gropius.

Even more influential than his housing designs, however, was Mebes's book on Germany's Biedermeyer architecture. *Um 1800: Architektur und Kunsthandwerk im letzten Jahrhundert ihrer traditionellen Entwicklung,* published in two lavish volumes of text and photographs in 1908, immediately set off a storm of controversy in Germany. Mebes argued that the simple cubic forms of German neoclassicism around 1800 were more suited to a modern industrial and urban architecture than were either the *Jugendstil* or the flamboyant eclecticism of many German architects. This view, though resisted by many, confirmed the turn toward simple yet monumental neoclassical forms which was already taking place in the work of such men as Peter Behrens, Paul Bonatz, Paul Ludwig Troost, and Paul Schultze-Naumburg, and reinforced the views of those who sought some standardization in German architecture, such as Hermann Muthesius and Gropius. The second and expanded version of *Um 1800,* which Mebes published in 1918 in collaboration with Walter Curt Behrendt, placed increased emphasis on the importance of monumental neoclassical buildings in ordering the cityscape. This edition, however, was less widely noticed, since the younger generation of architects had already begun to transform Mebes's teachings into a new and antihistorical style.

Barbara Miller Lane

WORKS

1907–1909, Housing Development, Pankow; 1912–1923, Housing Development, Zehlendorf; 1913, Oberrealschule, Zehlendorf; 1913, Offices, Nordsternversicherungsgesellschaft; 1920–1929, Housing Development, Lichterfelde; 1920–1929, Housing Development, Reinickendorf; 1920–1929, Housing Development, Schöneberg; 1920–1929, Housing Development, Steglitz; 1920–1929, Housing Development, Templehof; Berlin. 1929–1931, Neu-Gohlis (with others), Leipzig. 1931, Housing Development. Schöneweide; 1932, Housing Development, Weissensee; Berlin.

BIBLIOGRAPHY

Åman, Anders 1966 "Architektur." Volume 11, pages 170–185 in Rudolf Zeitler (editor), *Die Kunst des 19. Jahrhunderts.* Berlin: Propyläen.

"Dreissig Jahre neuer Wohnbau dargelegt an Bauten von Mebes und Emmerich." 1938 *Monatshefte für Baukunst und Städtebau* 22:233–240.

"Die Feuer- und Rauchlose Siedlung in Berlin-Steglitz." 1932 *Wasmuths Monatshefte für Baukunst und Städtebau* 16:115–122.

LANE, BARBARA MILLER 1968 *Architecture and Politics in Germany, 1918–1945.* Cambridge, Mass.: Harvard University Press.

LANE, BARBARA MILLER 1979 "Changing Attitudes to Monumentality: An Interpretation of European Architecture and Urban Form, 1880–1914." Pages 101–114 in *Growth and Transformation of the Modern City.* University of Stockholm and the Swedish Council for Building Research.

LEITL, ALFONS 1938 "Bauten von Mebes und Emmerich." *Monatshefte für Baukunst und Städtebau* 22:177–184.

MEBES, PAUL, and BEHRENDT, WALTER CURT (1908)1920 *Um 1800. Architektur und Handwerk im letzen Jahrhundert ihrer traditionellen Entwicklung.* 3d ed. Munich: Bruckmann. Mebes was the sole author of the first edition.

MEBES, PAUL 1932 "Die Friedrich-Ebert-Siedlung in Berlin." *Wasmuths Monatshefte für Baukunst und Städtebau* 16:429–435.

MEYER, EDINA 1972 *Paul Mebes: Miethausbau in Berlin, 1906–1938.* Berlin: Seitz.

"Das neue Oberlyzeum in Zoppot." 1932 *Wasmuths Monatshefte für Baukunst und Städtebau* 16:49–56.

PAUL, JACQUES 1972 "German Neo-Classicism and the Modern Movement." *Architectural Review* 152:176–180.

"Die Spreesiedlung in Berlin-Niederschöneweide." 1932 *Wasmuths Monatshefte für Baukunst und Städtebau* 16:515–516.

MEDD, H. A. N.

Henry Alexander Nesbitt Medd (1892–1977) was one of those British architects who established a school of classical architecture in New Delhi under the influence of EDWIN LUTYENS. Born in Gloucestershire, England, Medd was articled to F. C. Eden. In 1915, he worked in London for Lutyens on drawings for New Delhi. In 1919, Medd supervised the erection of HERBERT BAKER's buildings in New Delhi. Medd won the competitions for both the Anglican (1928–1935) and Roman Catholic (1930–1945) churches (now cathedrals) in New Delhi. In Britain from 1931–1935, Medd returned to India as consulting architect to the Government of the Central Provinces. In 1939, he succeeded R. T. RUSSELL as chief architect to the Government of India, although the outbreak of war followed by independence prevented much work coming from this appointment. Medd returned to Britain in 1947.

GAVIN STAMP

WORKS

1928–1935, Church (now Cathedral) of the Redemption; 1930–1945, Roman Catholic Church (now Cathedral) of the Sacred Heart; New Delhi. 1937–1942, High Court, Nagpur, India. c.1940–1950, New Mint, Calcutta.

BIBLIOGRAPHY

STAMP, GAVIN 1976 "Indian Summer." *Architectural Review* 159:365–372.

MEDICI, GIOVANNI DE'

Born in Florence, Italy, the illegitimate son of Grand Duke Cosimo I of Tuscany, Giovanni de' Medici (1567–1621) was a professional soldier, military engineer, and dilettante architect. He is credited with the design (1602) for the Chapel of the Princes at San Lorenzo in Florence (executed by MATTEO NIGETTI) as well as with proposals for projects in Florence, Pisa, Siena, and Livorno.

CHARLES RANDALL MACK

BIBLIOGRAPHY

BORSI, FRANCO 1974 *Firenze del Cinquecento.* Rome: Editalia.

PAATZ, WALTER, and PAATZ, ELISABETH 1952–1955 *Die Kirchen von Florenz.* 4 vols. Frankfurt: Klostermann.

VENTURI, ADOLFO (1939)1975 *Storia dell'arte italiana: Architettura del Cinquecento.* Reprint. Nendeln, Liechtenstein: Kraus-Thomson.

MEDLEY, EDWARD

The Reverend Edward Shuttleworth Medley (1838–1910), born at Exeter, England, came to New Brunswick in British North America when his father, the Most Reverend John Medley, became the first (Anglican) Bishop of Fredericton in 1845. The son must have been directed to architecture by the construction of Fredericton Cathedral, begun in 1845 FRANK WILLS for the father, who was a notable patron and influential "Ecclesiologist" even before becoming bishop. About the time this important Victorian Gothic work in stone was completed in 1853, with designs from WILLIAM BUTTERFIELD, Edward went to England for three years to study with Butterfield. Returning to New Brunswick, Edward Medley carried out a brilliant series of intensely rational and structurally expressive neo-Gothic churches in wood—the logical material in the forest wilderness—in the 1860s and 1870s: Christ Church (1863–1864) in Saint Stephen was the most ambitious of these. Medley also graduated from King's College, Fredericton, in 1862, then studied theology. Controversy followed his ordination as priest in 1864, and he moved to England in 1872, abandoning architecture.

DOUGLAS RICHARDSON

WORKS

1861, All Saints' Church, McKeen's Corner, New Brunswick. 1863–1864, Church of the Virgin, New Maryland, New Brunswick. 1863–1864, Christ Church, Saint Stephen, New Brunswick. 1871–1872, Church of the Ascension, Aphoaqui, New Brunswick.

BIBLIOGRAPHY

HERSEY, GEORGE L. 1972 *High Victorian Gothic: A Study in Associationism* Baltimore: Johns Hopkins Press.

RICHARDSON, DOUGLAS 1972 "Hyperborean Gothic; or, Wilderness Ecclesiology and the Wood Churches of Edward Medley." *Architectura* 2:48–74.

RICHARDSON, DOUGLAS 1975 "The Spirit of the Place: Canadian Architecture in the Victorian Era." *Canadian Collector* 10, no. 5:20–29.

VROOM, WILLIAM FREDERICK 1913 *Christ Church, St. Stephen, N.B., with a Biographical Sketch of the Architect, Rev. Edward S. Medley, B.A.* New York: Thwing.

MEDUNA, GIOVANNI BATTISTA

Giovanni Battista Meduna (1810–1880) was one of the most active and versatile architects in Venice during the nineteenth century.

After studying at the Academy in Venice, Meduna worked in the city's Office of Public Works. He was granted an architect's license by the Venetian government after he had studied architecture and engineering on his own for several years.

In 1836, he was entrusted with the restoration of the north and south façades of the Basilica of San Marco. That same year, Meduna and his brother Tommaso began the restoration of La Fenice Theater. Their work included an exquisite neorococo interior.

The eclectic Meduna also executed some of the earliest neo-Gothic buildings of his time, including a private house of 1846. In addition, he worked confidently in a neoclassical idiom in the Caviola Store of 1859. In his prolific career, Meduna carried out numerous restorations of villas and churches in and around Venice and greatly contributed to the architectural renewal of that city at mid-century.

ELLEN R. SHAPIRO

WORKS

1836, San Marco (restoration of north and south façades of the basilica); 1836–1854, La Fenice Theater (restoration; with others); Venice, Italy. 1840–1852, Alighieri Theater, Ravenna, Italy. 1845–1850, Ca' d'Oro (restoration); 1846, House, Camp San Fantin; 1847, Palazzo Giovanelli (restoration); Venice, Italy. 1852–1855, Palazzo Revedin (restoration), Castelfranco Veneto, Italy. 1852–1856, Villa Balbi-Valier (partial restoration), Pieve di Soligo, Italy. 1853–1858, Church of Santa Lucia (restoration), Carpenedo, Italy. 1853–1858, Church of Santa Lucia (restoration), Piave, Italy. 1859, Caviola Store, Venice, Italy.

BIBLIOGRAPHY

GUBERNATIS, ANGELO DE (editor) 1889 *Dizionario degli artisti italiani viventi.* Florence: Le Monnier.

HOWARD, DEBORAH 1980 *The Architectural History of Venice.* London: Batsford.

MOTHES, OSCAR 1860 Volume 2 in *Geschichte der Baukunst und Bildhauerei Venedigs.* Leipzig: Voight.

MOTHES, OSCAR 1884 *Die Baukunst des Mittelalters in Italien.* 2 vols. Jena, Germany: Costenoble.

ROMANELLI, GIANDOMENICO 1977 *Venezia Ottocento.* Rome: Officina.

SELVATICO, PIETRO 1847 *Sulla architettura e sulla scultura in Venezia.* Venice, Italy: Carpano.

MEHMET TAHIR AĞA

Mehmet Tahir Ağa (18th century) was an Ottoman Turkish architect, active in Istanbul during the second half of the eighteenth century. He was the official royal architect from 1764 to 1767 under Sultan Mahmut III. He was one of the first Turkish architects to adapt to Turkish architecture the European baroque and rococo styles, initially introduced by European architects. This architect's works set the stage for the great nineteenth-century royal commissions along the Bosporus.

BEATRICE ST. LAURENT

WORKS

(A)1741–1742, Fountain, opposite Dolmabahce Cami; (A)1745, Hasan Pasa Complex; (A)1760, Ayazma Cami; (A)1761–1762, Racip Pasa Library; Istanbul. (A)1763, Lâleli Cami, Aksaray, Turkey. (A)1767–1771, Fatih Cami (rebuilding); (A)1769, Zeynep Sultan Cami; Istanbul.

BIBLIOGRAPHY

ALTAN, KEMAL 1937 "Mimar Mehmet Tahir." *Arkitekt* 1937:193–195.

ERDOĞAN, MUZZAFER 1960 "On sekizinci asır sonlarında bir Türk sanatkârı Hassa Bas Mimarı." *Tarih Dergisi* 11:25–46.

GOODWIN, GODFREY 1971 *A History of Ottoman Architecture.* Baltimore: Johns Hopkins University Press.

KUBAN, DOĞAN 1954 *Türk barok mimarıšı hakkında bir deneme.* Istanbul: Pulhan matbassı.

KUMBARACILAR, IZZET 1937 "Türk mimarları." *Arkitekt* 1937:59ff.,88ff.

MAYER, LEO 1956 *Islamic Architects and Their Works.* Geneva: Kundig.

ÖZ, TAHSIN 1962 *Istanbul Camileri.* Ankara: Türk Tarih Kurumu Basimevi.

MEIGS, MONTGOMERY C.

Montgomery C. Meigs (1816–1892), a U.S. army career officer, was an inventive engineer/architect notable for contributions to the architecture of Washington, D.C. Trained at West Point in civil and military engineering, Meigs was supervising engineer for the Washington Aqueduct, for which he designed bridges, pumphouses, tunnels, and reservoirs (1852–1860), and for the Capitol dome and wings where he influenced the design and directed the construction (1852–1860). In a private capacity, Meigs designed his own house (1869), a preliminary plan for the National Museum Building of the Smithsonian (1878–1880), and the Pension Building (1882–1887) in styles which combined classical planning with nineteenth-century advances in materials and structure.

CYNTHIA R. FIELD

WORKS

1841, Fort Delaware, Pea Patch Island, Del. 1841–1849, Fort Wayne, Detroit, Mich. 1850–1852, Fort Montgomery, Lake Champlain, N.Y. 1852–1860, Aqueduct System; 1853–1859, United States Capitol (extension); 1855–1859, United States General Post Office (extension); *1869, Meigs House; 1878–1880, National Museum Building (with Adolph Cluss and Paul Schultz), Smithsonian Institution; 1882–1887, Pension Building; Washington.

BIBLIOGRAPHY

SKRAMSTAD, HAROLD K. 1969–1970 "The Engineer as Architect in Washington: The Contributions of Montgomery Meigs." *Records of the Columbia Historical Society* 69–70:266–284.

WEIGLEY, RUSSELL F. 1959 *Quartermaster General of the Union Army: A Biography of M. C. Meigs.* New York: Columbia University Press.

MEISSONNIER, JUSTE-AURELE

It was said of Juste-Aurèle Meissonnier (1695–1750) a few years after his death in the *Mercure de France* (February 1755) that he destroyed straight lines, invented contrasts, and banished symmetry. Fiske Kimball described Meissonnier's artistic milieu as follows: "Through the hardening established lines of the French interior, about 1730, rustled a fresh breeze, bringing new life and movement. The novelty and import were recognized by contemporaries, who within a generation were to call it the *'goût nouveau'* or the *'genre pittoresque'* and to remark on its most striking characteristic, asymmetry—*'le contraste dans les ornemens'* (Kimball, 1943, p. 152). Meissonnier was one of the most versatile and brilliant practitioners of the *genre pittoresque.*

He was born in Turin, Italy, of French ancestry. He was apprenticed to his father, a sculptor and silversmith, and about 1718, he made his way to Paris. In 1724, he was named *orfèvre du roi* at the Gobelins by Louis XV, and in 1726, he took over the duties of the post made vacant by the death of Jean II Berain of *dessinateur de la chambre et du cabinet du roi,* meaning that he was in charge of designing all court festivals. In addition, through this important position in the court, he was called upon by other members of the nobility for commissions.

The most effective documentation of Meissonnier's career is provided by the series of engravings published in small groups during his lifetime and as a complete bound set, entitled *Oeuvre de Juste-Aurèle Meissonnier,* after his death by the indefatigable Gabriel Huquier. The engravings record Meissonnier's designs for ornamental cartouches and for metalwork, as well as for architectural projects.

Two such projects merit particular attention. The first is for a house for Léon de Bréthous in Bayonne, France, dated 1733. The problem of its site, triangular in outline, was a challenge that Meissonnier met by planning an irregularly shaped house. Many of the rooms are regular in form, but a number have rounded corners, one has two concavely curving walls, and the main salon is octagonal with four short walls concavely curved. Meissonnier's predilection for sweeping, undulating curves rather than right angles is in evidence.

The second architectural design of note is that for Count François Bielinski, the grand marshal at the court of August II of Poland in Dresden, Germany. On the titlepage of the *Oeuvre,* Meissonnier is described as painter, sculptor, architect, and designer to the king. For the Count Bielinski's cabinet, Meissonnier wore all of his hats. Large painted wall panels of allegorical subjects were placed between the central mirrors and curved corners, where sculptured putti push out from the wall. Arched niches below an elaborate and monumental ceiling painting in the style of PIETRO BERRETTINI DA CORTONA contain busts or putti. The room was displayed at the Palace of the Tuileries before being shipped to Dresden, causing some controversial comment in regard to its emphasis on plasticity and unconventional telescoping of window molding and cornice.

The finishing of the Church of Saint Sulpice in Paris enticed Meissonnier as it did many other architects in the 1720s and 1730s. He made a design for the façade, dated 1726 in the *Oeuvre,* one for a chapel dated the following year and another for the altar. None were executed. The façade design is a highly original combination of traditional structure and innovative details. The positioning of the five bays—forward at either side and recessed in the center—creates a feeling of movement and play of light and shadow. The swooping curves of the transept roof and undulating curves of the spire funnel the movement into other directions. The attempt at fluidity on a solid base shows Meissonnier as an architect of contrasts.

ELAINE EVANS DEE

WORKS

1730s, La Baronne de Bézenval Apartment, Paris. 1730s, Saint Aignan, Orléans, France. 1730s, Saint Leu (altar), Paris. 1733, Léon de Bréthous House, Bayonne, France. 1734, Cabinet and furnishings for Count Francois Bielinski, Dresden, Germany. 1745–1750, Church and Palace, Order of the Holy Ghost, Paris.

BIBLIOGRAPHY

BATAILLE, MARIE L. 1930 "Meissonnier, 1695 à 1750." Volume 2, pages 363–378 in Louis Dimier, *Les peintres français du XVIIIe siècle.* Paris and Brussels: Van Oest.

DONNELL, EDNA 1941 "Juste-Aurèle Meissonnier and the Rococo Style." *Bulletin of the Metropolitan Museum of Art* 36, no. 12:254–260.

FITZ-GERALD, DESMOND 1963 *Juste-Aurèle Meissonnier and Others.* New York: Seiferheld Gallery.

GARMS, JÖRG 1967 "Projects for the Pont Neuf and Place Dauphine in the First Half of the Eighteenth Century." *Journal of the Society of Architectural Historians* 26, no. 2:102–113.

HAUTECOEUR, LOUIS 1950 Volume 2 in *Histoire de l'architecture classique en France.* Paris: Picard.

KALNEIN, WEND GRAF, and LEVEY, MICHAEL 1972 *Art and Architecture of the Eighteenth Century in France.* Harmondsworth, England: Penguin.

KIMBALL, FISKE (1943)1980 *The Creation of the Rococo.* Reprint. New York: Dover.

NYBERG, DOROTHEA 1969 *Oeuvre de Juste-Aurèle Meissonnier.* New York: Blom.

MELLOR, TOM

Tom Mellor (1914–) studied at Liverpool University, England, under WILLIAM GRAHAM HOLFORD. He established his practice in 1949 and served on the council of the Royal Institute of British Architects. His designs are eclectic, based on classicism and on LE CORBUSIER. He is a surrealist and romantic painter, exhibiting at the Royal Academy, London.

M. J. TOOLEY

WORKS

1950, War Memorial Housing (Chapel and Clubroom), Lytham Saint Annes, England. 1952, Churchwood House, Lytham, England. 1959, Saint Bernadette's (reredos by John Piper), Lancaster, England. 1960, County Secondary School, Carnforth, England. 1964–1968, Halls of Residence, University of Sheffield, England. 1966–1975, Library, Department of Physics, Chemistry, Biological and Environmental Sciences, University of Lancaster, England. 1967, Commercial Center and Graduate Club, University of Liverpool, England. 1967, Halls of Residence, University of Birmingham, England. 1968, Senate and Administrative Building (sculpture by Barbara Hepworth), University of Liverpool, England.

BIBLIOGRAPHY

ASHWORTH, J. A., and MELLOR, TOM "British Overseas Possessions: A Little Known Outpost of Empire." *Architectural Review* 85:23–28, 54.

MELLOR, TOM 1948 "Within a Victorian Shell." *Ideal Home* 58:36–39.

MELLOR, TOM 1949 "The Designer's Dilemma." *Town Planning Review* 20:150–161.

MELLOR, TOM 1953 "The End of the Beginning: Notes on the Future of Architectural Design in Britain." *Town Planning Review* 24:47–51.

MELLOR, TOM 1955 "The Persistent Suburb." *Town Planning Review* 25:251–254.

MELNIKOV, KONSTANTIN

Konstantin Stepanovich Melnikov (1890–1974) was one of the major innovators of early Soviet architecture. The hard-edged, primary geometric forms of his best work, huge graphics incorporated into their design, expressed succinctly the initial ardor of the Russian revolution. He was born in Moscow in 1890, the grandson of a serf. Thanks to the patronage of an employer, he studied architecture at the prestigious Moscow School of Painting, Sculpture and Architecture, and received his diploma in 1917 among those who, as he later recalled, got up from their student desks during that year of upheaval and sat down in professors' chairs. In 1920 he joined the first faculty of architecture at Vkhutemas, the Soviet parallel to the Bauhaus.

Melnikov's colleagues during these years included VLADIMIR TATLIN, whose influence can be seen in his early projects. For a pavilion at the 1923 Moscow Agricultural Exposition for the Makhorka tobacco combine, he developed an architectural language that drew on rural shed construction, and whose angular profiles recalled those of Tatlin's early reliefs. He allowed its rough timbers to admit proudly their standard sawmill measurements, as he did again in the pavilion he built for the Soviet exhibitions at the Paris Exposition of 1925. There diagonal staircases led to entrances at the very center of the building, effecting dramatic interpenetration of exterior and interior space.

In Paris, Melnikov received international acclaim, and when he returned to Moscow he found ready commissions for new work. Uncomfortable in the polarized world of the Soviet architectural associations, he set himself up as an independent, and in four years had to his credit in Moscow ten completed buildings. In six severely geometric workers' clubs, he experimented with new kinds of spatial versatility and with a dynamic organization of architectural mass, such as in the Rusakov club whose auditorium galleries project dramatically out through the façade. In the house he built for himself, the walls of its two interlocking cylinders are pierced with more than sixty openings to facilitate the flow of air and light. His name, which he wrote boldly across the street front of his house, was, however, never once mentioned in the pages of *Sovremennaia arkhitektura,* the preeminent Soviet architectural journal of the time. Its orientation was functionalist, and Melnikov's work was considered too individual, too incapable of mass production, too expressionistic, even to warrant criticism.

During the increasingly frightening early 1930s, in his attempt to respond to competitions calling for an architecture glorifying collectivization, Melnikov submitted entries marked by a retreat into depersonalized fantasy. When the 1937 All-Union Congress of Soviet Architects accused him of formalism, however, he refused to recant. He was silenced as an architect, put under virtual house arrest, and for a time earned his living building stoves.

For thirty-seven years, until his death in 1974, he continued from time to time to enter competitions, including one for the Soviet Pavilion at the 1964 World's Fair. Some fragmentary recognition was finally accorded him, but the only exhibition of his work, held in Moscow in 1965, was forced to close after only four days, and he did not live to see his name officially cleared.

STEPHEN S. GARMEY

WORKS

*1923, Makhorka Pavilion, First All-Union Agricultural and Cottage Industries Exposition; 1924, Sukharyovka Market bar/administrative building; Moscow. *1925, Soviet Pavilion, International Exposition of Decorative Arts, Paris. 1926, Leyland Bus Garage; 1927, Frunze factory workers' club; 1927, Rubber factory workers' club; 1927, Rusakov factory workers' club; Moscow. 1927–1928, Pravda china factory workers' club, Dulevo. 1927–1928, Svoboda (now Gorkii) factory workers' club; 1927–1929, K. S. Melnikov House; 1929, Stormy Petrel factory workers' club; 1929, Gosplan Parking Garage; 1929, Parking Garage, Novo-Ryazanskaia Street; 1934, Intourist Garage; Moscow.

BIBLIOGRAPHY

BYKOV, V. 1969 "Konstantin Melnikov i Georgii Golts." *Sovetskaia arkhitektura* 18:59–67.

GERCHUK, IURII 1971 "Konstantin Melnikov." In O. A. Shvidkovsky (editor), *Building in the U.S.S.R., 1917–1932.* London: Studio Vista.

STARR, S. FREDERICK 1978 *Melnikov, Solo Architect in a Mass Society.* N.J.: Princeton University Press.

MEMHARDT, JOHANN GREGOR

Born in Linz, Upper Austria, probably in the second decade of the seventeenth century, Johann Gregor Memhardt (?–1678) received his training as an engineer and architect in Holland, where his Protestant parents had fled at the outbreak of the Thirty Years War. He was in the service of Brandenburg-Prussia as a military and fortifications engineer from about 1635 until, in 1650, Frederick William, the Great Elector, called him to the court in Berlin. Here, in the Lustgarten next to the palace, Memhardt built the Lusthaus with grotto and belvedere (1650). In this, his main work, four octagonal rooms were grouped around a square central hall; the south façade had two towers; and an octagonal dome rose over the roof terraces. Memhardt's Dutch style is shown in elongated Ionic pilasters, high windows and niches for statues, heavy garlands, and ashlar-framed brick walls. At the Brandenburg court, connected as it was to the House of Orange, this style came to predominate. Within the Berlin palace itself, Memhardt designed the apartments of the Electress Louisa Henrietta of Orange (1650–1651). Also for the electress, he built the Schloss Oranienburg near Berlin (1651–1655) in the tradition of the Dutch palaces by PIETER POST (later enlarged by JOHANN ARNOLD NERING and Johann Friedrich Eosander) and designed and built the surrounding park (1651–1667). The town of Oranienburg was built according to his plans (1656–1667) as was the Oranienburg Orphanage (1663–1665), a simple brick building with squared-stone pilaster strips and a high roof. His appointment as *electoralis architectus* (1656) gave Memhardt supervision over all electoral buildings. He himself built the Ballhaus in Berlin (1659) and the main gate of the palace in the form of a flat triumphal arch surmounted by a gable (1668). As an engineer he participated in the design and building of Berlin's new fortress and in the layout of the Berlin district of Friedrichswerder (1656–?) which was begun at the same time. He had had his own house there since 1653. In 1669 he became mayor of that quarter. As a hydraulic engineer, he oversaw the installation of the moats and built the sluice near the mills of Friedrichswerder (1657). After the death of Philip de Chiese, he took over the construction of the Potsdam Town Palace (1673–1676). It is thanks to him that, after the Thirty Years War, seventeenth-century baroque classicism as shaped by Dutch Protestantism was introduced into Berlin.

FRITZ-EUGEN KELLER
Translated from German by
Beverley R. Placzek

WORKS

*1650, Lusthaus and Lustgarten; *1650–1651, Apartments of Louisa Henrietta; Berlin Palace. 1651–1655, Oranienburg Palace; 1651–1667, Park of Oranienburg Palace; Brandenburg, Germany. *1653, Memhardt House, Friedrichswerder, Germany. 1656–?, Friedrichswerder district (planning); *1656–1675, Fortification Buildings; 1657, Sluice near Friedrichswerder Mills, *1659, Ballhaus, Berlin. 1663–1665, Orphanage, Oranienburg, Germany. *1668, Berlin Palace (main gate). 1673–1676, Potsdam Town Palace (begun by Philip de Chiese), Germany.

BIBLIOGRAPHY

BOECK, WILHELM 1938 Pages 15–34 in *Oranienburg.* Berlin: Deutscher Verein für Kunstwissenschaft.

BORRMANN, RICHARD 1893 *Bau- und Kunstdenkmäler von Berlin.* Berlin: Springer.

GALLAND, GEORG 1911 Pages 1–40, 191–193 in *Hohenzollern und Oranien.* Strasbourg, France: Heitz.

GEYER, ALBERT 1936 Volume 1, pages 61–63, 75–79 in *Geschichte des Schlosses zu Berlin.* Berlin: Deutscher Kunstverlag.

HEMPEL, EBERHARD 1965 *Baroque Art and Architecture in Central Europe.* Harmondsworth, England: Penguin.

REUTHER, HANS 1969 *Barock in Berlin.* Berlin: Rembrandt.

MENDELSOHN, ERIC

Eric (or Erich) Mendelsohn (1887–1953) contributed as much or more to the emergence of modern architecture in the 1920s as any other German architect. In 1919, along with LUDWIG MIES VAN DER ROHE, WALTER GROPIUS, PETER BEHRENS, ERNST MAY, and others, he organized the Berlin *Novembergruppe* of revolutionary artists and, in 1925, the Ring of architectural activists, to promote the avant-garde. His early work, notably the Einstein Tower in Potsdam (1919–1924), the Schocken department stores in Stuttgart (1926) and Chemnitz (1928–1929), and the Universum cinema (1926–1929) and the Metal Workers Union building (1928–1929) in Berlin, made the new architecture popular in Germany. His architectural imagery unquestionably influenced second-generation modern architects, such as ALVAR AALTO, EERO SAARINEN, PIER LUIGI NERVI, WALTER A. NETSCH, and JØRN UTZON.

Mendelsohn was born in 1887 in East Prussia, one of five children of a businessman of Russian-Polish background. In 1910, he married Louise Maas, a cellist. Working his way through architecture school in Berlin and Munich, where he graduated in 1912, just as the Jugendstil, as the Germans called Art Nouveau, was giving way to Expressionism. When he opened his architectural practice in Berlin, in 1919, after military service in World War I, he was an Expressionist, just as Mies and Gropius had been before they embraced Constructivism, and as LE CORBUSIER was to become thirty-one years after Mendelsohn's Einstein Tower, with his chapel at Ronchamp (1950–1954). Mendelsohn acknowledged his admiration for JOSEPH MARIA OLBRICH long after this flamboyant Austrian Secession architect was thoroughly out of fashion. He was close to the Expressionist Blaue Reiter group of painters which included Wassily Kandinsky, Franz Marc, and Paul Klee. The sculptural free form of the Einstein Tower, an observatory and laboratory for research on the theory of relativity, is, of course, Expressionist architecture par excellence.

After a visit to the Netherlands in 1924, Mendelsohn embarked on what he called his "reconciliatory program" between Expressionism and Constructivism, between J. J. P. OUD's cerebral de Stijl group's style and H. P. BERLAGE's evocative romanticism. That year, he visited the

Mendelsohn. Einstein Tower. Potsdam, Germany. 1919–1924

Mendelsohn. Maimonides Health Center. San Francisco. 1946–1950

United States. He had a cordial meeting with Frank Lloyd Wright at Taliesin, at which Richard Neutra served as interpreter. The exciting volume of photographs, *Amerika* (1926), is one of the fruits of that trip. The following year he visited the Soviet Union.

Mendelsohn created his architecture, as he once put it, in "an ecstasy of vision," committing his ideas to paper in quick, vivid sketches. He drew the first sketches, some no larger than a postage stamp, while on guard duty on the eastern front. The sketches were exhibited in 1919 at the Berlin gallery of Paul Cassirer under the title "Architecture in Steel and Concrete." Numerous buildings designed after Mendelsohn's death echo these visions. Eero Saarinen's Dulles International Airport terminal near Washington (1958–1963), and Netsch's United States Air Force Academy near Denver, Colorado (1954–1962), are particularly striking examples. At the time, neither Mendelsohn nor anyone else had the technical knowledge to construct such forms. Nevertheless, as Mendelsohn remarked, "it was all there"—the dramatic shapes, the sweeping curves emphasized by window ribbons, the tension between round and square, the deep recesses, and the earth-hugging horizontality. Mendelsohn believed that buildings, like good political and social structures, ought to be horizontal and thus give equal value to many facets rather than superimpose one upon the other.

Mendelsohn's Berlin office was one of the busiest and most successful in Germany. His buildings received much publicity. He considered it part of their function to serve their clients as advertisements. Like all early moderns, he was mainly concerned with individual buildings rather than the harmony and continuity of the cityscape.

Mendelsohn was forced to leave Germany in 1933 when Hitler came to power. For a time, he worked with Serge Chermayeff in England. Together they won the competition for the de la Warr Pavilion (1933–1935) in Bexhill-on-Sea. The beach pavilion's circular, glass enclosed staircase, jutting out from the façade, however, is typically Mendelsohnian drama. Before the pavilion was completed, Mendelsohn was invited to Palestine to design a house for Chaim Weizmann, the Zionist leader and, later, Israel's first president. The Weizmann House in Rehovot (1934–1936), the Hadassah University Medical Center on Mount Scopus in Jerusalem (1937–1939), the Agricultural Institute in Rehovot (1939), and his other work have a strong indigenous character—more so perhaps than other modern buildings in Israel. Mendelsohn adapted his style not only to the climate and available building materials, but also to the compelling power of Israel's strange and beautiful landscape and ancient culture.

In 1941, at the age of fifty-four, Mendelsohn moved to San Francisco and returned to the almost unrestrained, sculptural élan of his early sketches. The Maimonides Health Center (1946–1950), unfortunately, suffered severe maltreatment by a new owner soon after its completion. The Russell House (1950–1951), also in San Francisco, remains pure Mendelsohn, rendered in redwood. Mendelsohn seems to have been best understood, however, by America's Jewish community. He designed seven Jewish community centers for as many cities. Four were built—in St. Louis (1946-1950), in Cleveland (1946–1950), in Grand Rapids, Michigan (1948–1952), and in Saint Paul, Minnesota (1950–1954). They are bold affirmations of twentieth-century art and the Jewish faith. In all of them, the sanctuary and the social and administrative spaces are integrated into one unit, serving a total religious purpose.

Mendelsohn was a witty, self-confident man, who managed to combine an exuberant, intuitive creativity with sound business sense. He frequently worked late into the night, accompanied by the music of Bach or Brahms. He took complete charge of his building designs, down to the last detail and doorknob. "God had no associates when He created the world," he once said, "so why should I?" Despite seeming arrogance, he shared an easy, generous camaraderie with his employees and his many friends. As William W. Wurster said at his funeral in 1953, Mendelsohn "stood for freedom, imagination, and creative individual leadership."

Wolf Von Eckardt

WORKS

1919–1924, Einstein Tower, Potsdam, Germany. 1921–1923, Berliner Tageblatt Building, Berlin. 1921–1923, Herman and Company Hat Factory, Luckenwalde, Germany. *1926, Schocken Department Store, Stuttgart, Germany. 1926–1929, Universum cinema; 1928–1929,

Metal Workers Union Building; Berlin. 1928–1929, Schocken Department Store, Chemnitz (Karl-Marx-Stadt), Germany. 1929, Mendelsohn House, Rupenhorn; *1930–1932, Columbus House; Berlin. 1933–1935, De la Warr Pavilion (with Serge Chermayeff), Bexhill-on-Sea, England. 1934–1936, Weizmann House, Rehovot, Palestine (Israel). 1936, Schocken Library, Jerusalem. 1937–1938, Government Hospital, Haifa, Palestine (Israel). 1937–1939, Hadassah University Medical Center, Jerusalem. 1939, Agricultural Institute, Rehovot, Palestine (Israel). 1946–1950, B'nai Amoona Temple and Community Center, St. Louis, Mo. 1946–1950, Maimonides Health Center, San Francisco. 1946–1950, Temple and Community Center, Cleveland, Ohio. 1948–1952, Emanu-El Temple and Community Center, Grand Rapids, Mich. 1950–1951, Russell House, Pacific Heights, San Francisco. 1950–1953, Mount Zion Temple and Community Center (not completed until 1954), St. Paul, Minn.

BIBLIOGRAPHY

L'Archittetura, cronache e storia. 1963 9:290–432. Special issue devoted to Eric Mendelsohn.

BEYER, OSKAR (editor) (1961)1967 *Eric Mendelsohn: Letters of an Architect.* Translated by Geoffrey Strachan. New York and London: Abelard-Schumann. With an introduction by Nikolaus Pevsner.

PEHNT, WOLFGANG (1973)1979 *Expressionist Architecture.* Translated by J. A. Underwood and Edith Kustner. London: Thames and Hudson.

VON ECKARDT, WOLF 1960 *Eric Mendelsohn.* New York: Braziller. Part of the Masters of World Architecture series.

WHITTICK, ARNOLD (1940)1956 *Eric Mendelsohn.* 2d ed. London: Hill; New York: Dodge.

ZEVI, BRUNO (editor) 1970 *Opera completa architetture e immagini architettoniche.* Milan: ETAS Kompass. With biographical notes by Louise Mendelsohn.

MENGONI, GIUSEPPE

Giuseppe Mengoni (1829–1877), born in Fontanelice, Italy, studied at the nearby Academy of Bologna. In 1861 he won the competition for the Galleria Vittorio Emanuele in Milan (1865–1877), his most significant work and one that secured him an international reputation. The finest iron-and-glass covered arcade of the nineteenth century, designed in the local Renaissance style, it is a major achievement of urban design and includes a monumental façade to the Piazza del Duomo. At the age of forty-eight, Mengoni fell to his death from a scaffold while examining the triumphal archway of the Galleria.

JOY M. KESTENBAUM

WORKS

1863–1865, Palazzo Cavezza, Bologna, Italy. 1863–1867, Palazzo Comunale, Malalbergo, Italy. 1865–1877, Galleria Vittorio Emanuele and Piazza del Duomo, Milan. 1868–1876, Palazzo della Cassa di Risparmio, Bologna, Italy. 1869–1874, Mercato Centrale, Florence. n.d. Arcades of Campo Santo, Bologna, Italy. n.d. Palazzo Mengoni, Castel Bolognese; near Bologna, Italy.

BIBLIOGRAPHY

BESSONE-AURELJ, ANTONIETTA MARIA 1947 *Dizionario degli Scultori ed Architetti Italiani.* Genoa: Società Anonima Editrice Dante Alighieri.

GEIFT, JOHANN FRIEDRICH 1979 *Passagen: Ein Bautyp des 19. Jahrhunderts.* Munich: Prestel.

"Giuseppe Mengoni e la Galleria Vittorio Emanuele di Milano." 1914 *Emporium* 39:393–398.

GRANDI, MAURIZIO, and ATTILO PRACCHI 1980 *Milano: Guida all'Architettura Moderna.* Bologna, Italy: Zanichelli.

MEEKS, CARROLL L. V. 1966 *Italian Architecture: 1750–1914.* New Haven: Yale University Press.

"Mengoni, Giuseppe." 1951 Volume 22, page 855 in *Enciclopedia Italiana.* Rome: Istituto della Enciclopedia Italiana.

"Obituary of Giuseppe Mengoni." 1978 *American Architect and Building News* 3, Feb. 2:37.

MERKELBACH, BEN

Together with five friends from the School for Applied Arts in Haarlem, Netherlands, Ben Merkelbach (1901–1961), born in Amsterdam, founded the group of architects "de 8." By means of a manifesto, published in the avant-garde magazine *i 10* they made themselves known as being opposed to the architecture of the Amsterdam school, which they had gotten to know so well in

Merkelbach. AVRO Radio Studio. Hilversum, Netherlands. 1934–1936

the time of their schooling. The members of "de 8" considered this style, because of its expressionistic forms, a building art, whereas they thought that architecture should be a building science that directed itself to the demands of society and studied the requirements of the consumer. From a functional plan would grow a good form. This can be considered the start of the *Nieuwe Zakelijkheid* or functionalism in the Netherlands. At the first meeting of the Congrès Internationaux d'Architecture Moderne (CIAM) in 1928, the members of "de 8" were not yet represented, but one year later in Frankfurt they were, after which, together with the Rotterdam group "Opbouw," they became the Dutch representatives.

Merkelbach and his associate Charles Karsten applied their ideas for the first time in Landlust, a housing development west of Amsterdam (1932–1937). At the insistence of Merkelbach and with the help of CORNELIS VAN EESTEREN, who was main architect of the department of town planning in Amsterdam, the originally closed housing blocks were changed into open strips.

The "de 8" en "Opbouw" had become so close that together they began publishing a magazine with the name *de 8 en Opbouw* (1932) which became the mouthpiece for all progressive Dutch architects. Merkelbach was one of its most important editors until the end of the magazine in 1943. During World War II, Merkelbach was a member of a study group to develop guidelines for high-quality postwar housing. Merkelbach's proposals were mostly turned down because of conflict with more conservative architects.

In spite of this, Merkelbach was able to carry through his ideas in some quarters of Amsterdam, such as in the housing development *Frankendaal* (1951). After World War II, Merkelbach kept his leading position within "de 8 en Opbouw" but the contrast with younger architects became more pronounced. In 1956, "de 8 en Opbouw" was dissolved. His appointment as municipal architect of Amsterdam in 1956 gave Merkelbach official recognition for his ardor to renew housing in Holland.

WIM DE WIT

WORKS

1932–1937, Landlust Housing Development, Amsterdam. 1934–1936, AVRO Radio Studio, Hilversum, Netherlands. 1939, Willem van Rijn Office and Factory; 1951, Frankendaal Housing Development; 1960, Gemeenschappelijk Administratie Kantoor; Amsterdam.

BIBLIOGRAPHY

BLIJSTRA, R. 1962 *Nederlandse Bouwkunst na 1900.* Utrecht: Spectrum.

BLIJSTRA, R. 1968 *B. Merkelbach.* Amsterdam: Meulenhof.

Bouwen '20–'40: De Nederlandse Bijdrage aan het Nieuwe Bouwen 1971 Eindhoven, Netherlands: Van Abbemuseum. Exhibition catalogue.

MIERAS, J. P. 1954 *Na-oorlogse Bouwkunst in Nederland.* Amsterdam: Kosmos.

ROY VAN ZUYDEWIJN, H. F. J. 1969 *Amsterdamse Bouwkunst: 1815–1940.* Amsterdam: De Bussy.

SZÉNÁSSY, ISTVAN L. 1969 *Architectuur in Nederland: 1960–1967.* Amsterdam: Scheltema & Holkema.

VRIEND, J. J. 1957 *Nieuwere Architectuur.* Bussum, Netherlands: Moussault's Uitgeverij.

MERRILL, JOHN O.

See SKIDMORE, OWINGS, and MERRILL.

MESTRES I ESPLUGAS, JOSEP ORIOL

Josep Oriol Mestres i Esplugas (1815–1895) was born in Barcelona, Spain. In 1841, he obtained his professional title from the Royal Academy of San Fernando. His principal works are the plan and construction of the Campos Eliseos (Elysian Fields) in the community of Gracia in Barcelona (1853), the project for the construction of the Grand Theater of the Lyceum (1847), and for its reconstruction after a fire in 1861. With the architect AUGUST FONT I CARRERAS, he planned the neo-Gothic façade for the Cathedral of Barcelona (1887–1895). He was the author of various monographs. His style is eclectic, detailed with applied classic and Gothic elements.

XAVIER GÜELL GUIX
Translated from Spanish by
Judith E. Meighan

WORKS

1847, Grand Theater of the Lyceum; 1853, Campos Eliseos, Gracia; 1861 and later, Grand Theater of the Lyceum (reconstruction); 1887–1895, Cathedral (façade, with August Font i Carreras; not completed until 1913); Barcelona, Spain.

METEZEAU FAMILY

The Métezeau were a distinguished French family of architects, active from the middle of the sixteenth century until the third quarter of the seventeenth century. The two most important architects of the family were Louis (1562–?) and his youngest brother, Jacques Clément (1581–1652). The Métezeau were closely related to Henry IV and his attempts to overall town planning and improvements for Paris.

Henry IV took a very active role in the development of his planning principles, and as a consequence many of the names of architects have become overshadowed by the king himself. Louis Métezeau was one of the architects closest to the regent and instrumental in the conception of the Place des Vosges, the royal palace. In 1563, Catherine de' Medici wished to have a Place de Valois placed on the site of the palace of the Tournelles. Henry IV's idea was to construct a place of assembly and at the same time provide an area for upper class houses. Louis Métezeau was involved with the project from its inception in 1603. The heavy style of the façade is typical of the designs done for Henry IV. A rhythmic pattern of window space attempts to balance the lower story arcade, but the weight of the upper stories essentially becomes more prominent. Although predominantly classical in design, a certain premonition of the early baroque can be traced to the Place des Vosges, particularly in the ascending symmetricality and the rustication, used as linear device. Louis Métezeau was also involved with designing the south façade of the Grande Galerie at the Louvre.

Jacques Clément Métezeau was perhaps the more accomplished of the two brothers. Basically a transitional figure, Clément produced designs that were clearly indicative of the waning style and at the same time foretelling the advancements of LOUIS LE VAU. His façade of the Church of Saint Gervais (traditionally attributed to SALOMON DE BROSSE) in Paris applies the three orders superimposed and reflects the fashionable Roman church façade. The façade was placed on a tall Gothic building, however, and thereby necessitated three floors rather than the more usual two floors in Roman buildings. Marie de' Medici sent Clément to Florence in 1611 to make drawings of the Palazzo Pitti in preparation for the construction of her replication of the palace. In 1615, he worked in connection with de Brosse in directing the work on the Luxembourg Palace in Paris. Clément died in Paris well after his innovations had been assimilated into a baroque framework.

JEFFREY HUGHES

WORKS

LOUIS METEZEAU

1601–1608, Grande Galerie (south façade), Louvre; 1601–1608, Petite Galerie (interior), Louvre; 1603, Place des Vosges; 1610, Hôtel de Jean de Fourcy (interior decoration); Paris.

JACQUES CLEMENT METEZEAU

1610, Place Ducal, Charleville, France. 1615, Luxembourg Palace (with Salomon de Brosse), France. 1616, Saint Gervais (façade); 1617, Orangerie du Louvre; 1630–1632, Hôtel de Brienne; Paris.

BIBLIOGRAPHY

BLUNT, ANTHONY (1953)1970 *Art and Architecture in France 1500 to 1700.* 2d ed. Harmondsworth, England: Penguin.

NORBERG-SCHULZ, CHRISTIAN 1971 *Baroque Architecture.* New York: Abrams.

MEWES, CHARLES

Born in Alsace, Charles Mewès (1860–1914) grew up a Parisian after his family fled the Prussian invasion of 1870. He trained under J. L. PASCAL at the Ecole des Beaux-Arts and, throughout his career, eschewed Art Nouveau and the Modern style for an elegant, meticulous recall of eighteenth-century France: the logical, spatial symmetry of Louis XVI recurs continuously. Mewès's hotels, steamer interiors, clubs, and private residences suited the Edwardians' opulent taste. He designed Ritz Hotels in Paris (1898), London (1905–1906), and Madrid (1908–1910); the London Ritz was one of Britain's earliest steel-framed buildings. Subsequently, he undertook the design of Pall Mall's largest club, the Royal Automobile Club (1910) which featured a "Pompeiian" swimming bath adapted from the earlier l'Etablissement Hydrominéral (1899–1900) at Contréxeville. His first maritime interior, the Hamburg–Amerika Line's *SS Amerika* was completed in 1905; the company so admired it that Mewès became their resident designer. On three German ships he incorporated a Pompeiian pool, although not on his last vessel, Cunard's *Aquitania* (1914).

Although Mewès spoke only French, he opened firms in both London and Cologne, Germany, with ARTHUR JOSEPH DAVIS, and with the Swiss Alphonse Bischoff.

JOHN MAXTONE-GRAHAM

WORKS

1898, Ritz Hotel, Paris. 1900, Carlton House Grill, London. 1900, Palais des Congrès, Paris Exposition. 1902–1903, Luton Hoo (interior renovation), Bedfordshire, England. 1905, *SS Amerika.* 1905–1906, Morning Post Office; 1905–1906, Ritz Hotel; London. 1907–1908, *SS Kaiserin Auguste Victoria.* 1908, Cavalry Club Extension, London. 1908–1910, Ritz Hotel (with Don Luis Landecho), Madrid. 1910, Royal Automobile Club, Pall Mall, London. 1911–1912, *SS Imperator.* 1913, *SS Vaterland.* 1914, *RMS Aquitania.* 1914, *SS Bismarck* (later *RMS Majestic*).

BIBLIOGRAPHY

"The Creator of the Modern Luxury Hotel: Charles

Mewès, Architect, 1860–1914." 1947 *Journal of the Royal Institute of British Architects* 54:603–604.
FLEETWOOD-HESKETH, PETER 1971 "The Royal Automobile Club." *Country Life* 150:966–969.
FORD, GEORGE BURDETT 1907 "The Ritz Hotel, London." *Architectural Review* 14:137–148.
HAMLIN, TALBOT (1940)1953 *Architecture Through the Ages*. Rev. ed. New York: Putnam.
LEES, FREDERIC 1914 "Two Metropolitan London Hotels, the Ritz and the Waldorf." *Architectural Record* 36:462–474.
MAXTONE-GRAHAM, JOHN 1972 *The Only Way to Cross*. New York: Macmillan.
RAMSEY, STANLEY C. 1915 "London Clubs-XI: The Cavalry Club." *Architectural Review* 37:56–58.

MEYER, ADOLF

Adolf Meyer (1881–1929) attended the Düsseldorf Kunstgewerbeschule (arts and crafts school) headed by PETER BEHRENS who, in Berlin in 1907–1908, employed Meyer. Behrens recalled: "[As my pupil] he impressed me as one of the few who showed great promise for a career. This belief was not so much founded on his outstanding artistic competence and his talent for design and good taste but rather for his thoughtful interest, his profound dedication and his devotion to solving a given problem" (Behrens, 1929, p. 177).

His earliest employment, however, was in the office of Dutch architect J. L. M. LAUWERIKS. In 1909 and 1910, he worked in the office of BRUNO PAUL. During 1911–1914 and 1919–1925, he was WALTER GROPIUS's principal assistant. Gropius described Meyer and their association:

> It was Behrens himself and particularly Lauweriks with his theosophic philosophy who were his most profound influences. . . . I was attracted by his passion for modern architecture and his reliable and trustworthy character. . . . When I started my own architectural office he joined me and stayed with me for 14 years, interrupted only by the war years. . . . We complemented each other in our ideas and ability and when I was requested to found the Bauhaus in Weimar, he acted as teacher and as my assistant. . . . He began to discover his own style and gradually developed the urge to be on his own and to take responsibility for his work. (*ibid.*)

With the closing of the Weimar Bauhaus, Meyer continued alone for a short period, working in the Frankfort-am-Main Bauamt (design office) and teaching the building class at the Kunstgewerbeschule. Gropius also stated: "In this new and independent setting his work and energy expanded and he wrote me the following, expressing deep satisfaction: 'The opportunities for work are great, and the set-up unusually favorable, a positive encouragement for new ideas in all phases of architecture.'" (*ibid.*)

Yet, Meyer, in his own work or in the service of the city, was not destined to achieve again such successes or recognition as in the fruitful collaboration with Gropius, although Gropius stated: "His more mature works are proof of great skill and full recognition of the responsibility of the modern architect" (*ibid.*, pp. 178–179). Later, Gropius modified his description: "Adolf Meyer was a very kind and wonderful person. Though not of independent character he was a very good and reliable person. He was not a strong personality, not sure of himself, somewhat reticent and timid. He was always a paid employee and never a partner" (Gropius, interview, 1965).

Ernst Neufert, Meyer's successor in Gropius's Dessau office, said that, "although Adolf Meyer was a man of ideas he could not make decisions with the perception and foresight which Gropius exercised. Gropius was also a great deal more practical" (Neufert, interview, 1964).

In 1929, Meyer drowned by accident in the North Sea.

REGINALD R. ISAACS

WORKS

1910–1911, Fagus Shoe Factory (with Walter Gropius), Alfeld, Germany. 1913–1914, Housing Development (with Gropius), Wittenberg, Germany. 1913–1914, Kleffel Cotton Factory (with Gropius), Dramburg, Germany. 1923–1924, State Theater (renovation; with Gropius), Jena, Germany. 1924, Hanover Paper Mill (with Gropius); 1924–1925, Kappe Shops (with Gropius); Alfeld, Germany. 1925, Military Installations, Praunheim, Germany. 1925, Military Installations; 1925, Nidda River Bridge; Rodelheim, Germany. 1925, Planetarium; 1925, Zeiss Works; Jena, Germany. 1928, Power Plant, Eschersheim, Germany.

BIBLIOGRAPHY

BEHRENS, PETER 1929 "Eulogy." *Das neue Frankfurt* 3, no. 9:177–179.
GROPIUS, WALTER 1929 "Eulogy." *Das neue Frankfurt* 3, no. 9:177–179.
MEYER, ADOLF 1925 *Ein Versuchshaus des Bauhauses in Weimar*. Munich: A. Langen.
MEYER, ADOLF 1928 "Modell und Grundriss für eine katholische Kirche." *Moderne Bauformen* 27, no. 9:362.

MEYER, HANNES

The appointment of Hannes Meyer (1889–1954) as director of the Dessau Bauhaus to succeed WALTER GROPIUS in 1928 became not only the highest distinction that Meyer received in his lifetime but also a most important turning point in his career.

Unfortunately, the impassioned criticism which his selection aroused and the defense offered by Meyer and his supporters obscured his many attributes and intended contributions to education and society. Meyer did not continue Gropius's apolitical policies, and in less than two years his philosophy and programs, offered in a period of political change, hastened the end of the Dessau Bauhaus.

However, even without his appointment to the Bauhaus, Meyer undoubtedly would have had a satisfying professional career. He was already well along in the practice of architecture, following study at the Gewerbeschule in Basel, where he was born, and at the Gewerbeschule in Berlin, in which city he also took courses at the Landwirtschaft-Akademie. Having served his apprenticeships in the several building trades, he worked for construction and architectural concerns. Before World War I, he inspected garden cities and housing developments in England. Following two years in the Swiss army (1914–1916), he assisted Georg Metzendorf in the design of workers' housing for Krupp, thereafter working for the Krupp industry itself. After the war, he opened his own office in Basel where he was joined seven years later by Hans Wittwer. He designed housing and a school of note as well as other projects. Gropius recommended Meyer to Dessau Mayor Fritz Hesse when they were considering prospective leaders for the school, and Meyer was subsequently appointed; he was already a member of its faculty.

During the transitional period, Meyer appeared to be in accord with the school's established directions, and the communal life of the Bauhaus continued among the students even though there was less cohesiveness among the faculty, uncertain as to changes to come. Upon Gropius's departure, Meyer began to stress the exact sciences and working methods at the expense of the abstract painters. He sped the school toward an architectural emphasis, sacrificing basic studies to do so. He introduced city planning, bringing in MART STAM and LUDWIG HILBERSEIMER to teach the courses. Meyer also introduced Marxism and Leninism as a fundamental study, and this and other changes made by him aroused attacks from within and without the Bauhaus, leading to his dismissal in 1930. Meyer did not leave without protest—a protest which is still a basis for argument today as it will be in the future.

So frequently did Gropius have to reply to questions regarding Hannes Meyer, that he prepared a formal statement describing his successor:

> I esteemed Meyer at the beginning on account of his good architectural work, but my change of opinion later on was not on principles, but personal. I erred in my judgment of his character and am to blame that he became my successor—for I did not recognize the mask over his face. When I appointed him, I judged the financial position of the Bauhaus to be relatively assured and its connections with industry to be well established. Meyer's reputation as an architect with strong public interests had attracted me and, during the first period of his work with the Bauhaus, I never doubted his qualifications. I liked his work for the Trade-Union School at Bernau which he had done with the modest and gifted Wittwer. Nevertheless I never made true personal contact with him for he was taciturn and—as turned out later—purposely concealed his personal views and intentions (Gropius, statement, 1964?).

Meyer did not understand Gropius's Bauhaus approach of an all-embracing art and his principle of teamwork. "Meyer's *Kollektiv* ideas were very strongly politically oriented" and, in Gropius's opinion, "led astray from an objective point of view without spelling out what is meant by his *Kollektivarbeit.* Meyer endangered the advancement of his social thoughts by letting party politics disintegrate the school." Gropius expressed the opinion that Meyer's inner downfall was his denial of art as such. "If the rational point of view is made the only factor . . . a fatal excluding instead of including, the field becomes narrowed. Drawing deliberate limitations always leads to a strait jacket."

Soon after Meyer's dismissal, he went to Russia as did so many German professionals, but unlike most of these, he was welcomed with unusual respect and honors. He was appointed chief architect of the Giprovtus Institutes of Technology and Higher Education of the Giprogor Town Planning Institute and held other official positions. Meyer remained in Russia for five years. As he was unsympathetic to Stalinist prescribed architecture, town planning became his major contribution in the Soviet Union. Impatient with bureaucracy, he returned to Switzerland in 1936, practicing there till 1939 when he began a ten-year career in Mexico City, occupying a series of governmental posts and pursuing a private practice. There, he was much appreciated by architects and artists oriented to Mexico's social direction and thus more open-minded toward his ideas. As in the instances of earlier out-of-country stays, Meyer missed the mountains and green valleys of his homeland, and in 1949 he returned to Switzerland where, in his remaining years, he practiced and wrote.

Although Meyer's critics were of opposing views regarding his conduct of the Bauhaus and his politics, few deprecated his professional work. At worst, they minimized Meyer's role, giving greater credit to Wittwer and the planning teams with which Meyer worked in Russia. Meyer's Freidorf Housing Development (1919–1921) and his proposal for a girls' school near Basel (1926) and the Meyer–Wittwer competition entry for the League of Nations Headquarters in Geneva (1926–1927) were admired. Meyer's extension of the Toerten development (1928–1930) and his Trade Union's School in Bernau (1930) were particularly appreciated, the latter serving as a prototype. His planning in Russia provided standards as did his work, built or projected, in Mexico.

REGINALD R. ISAACS

WORKS

1919–1921, Freidorf Cooperative Housing Development; 1926, Saint Peter's School for Girls (with Hans Witter); Basel. 1928–1930, Toertan Housing Development (extension), Dessau, Germany. 1930, Trades Union Federation School, Bernau, Germany. 1938, Children's Home, Solothurn, Switzerland. 1947, Bank, Mexico City.

BIBLIOGRAPHY

BOURGEOIS, VICTOR 1955 "Hannes Meyer." *Ruimte* 2, no. 1:15.

HÜTER, KARL-HEINZ 1966 "Bauhaus Contra Bauhaus." *Deutsche Architektur* 15:54–57.

JUNGHANNS, KURT 1964 "Hannes Meyer und das Bauhaus." *Deutsche Architektur* 13, no. 7:441–442.

MEYER, HANNES (1930)1977 "Mein Hinauswurf aus dem Bauhaus." *Bauwelt* 68:1101–1102.

MEYER, HANNES (1940)1964 "Erfahrungen in der polytechnischen Erziehung." *Deutsche Architektur* 13, no. 7:443–446. Originally published in Spanish.

MEYER, HANNES (1969)1973 *Scritti, 1921–1942; Architettura o Revoluzione.* Edited by Francesco Dal. Padua, Italy: Marsilio.

MÜNZ, WALTER 1961 "Werk und Werken des Architekten und Städtebauers Hannes Meyer (1889–1954)." *Deutsche Bauzeitung* 66, no. 3:191–195.

SCHNAIDT, CLAUDE (editor) 1965 *Hannes Meyer: Bauten, Projekte und Schriften.* Tenfen, Switzerland: Niggli.

WINGLER, HANS M. 1974 "Hannes Meyer." In *Kleine Bauhaus-Fibel; Geschichte und Wirken des Bauhaus 1919–1933.* Berlin: Bauhaus-Archiv.

Michela. Santa Marta. Agliè, Italy. 1739

MICHELA, COSTANZO

Costanzo Michela (1689–1754) was born in Aglie, Italy. The entire activity of his narrow career was restricted to the Canavese area north-west of Turin, and he fell into obscurity soon after his death. In 1729, he was *vice direttore,* a foreman's job, on the construction of the castle at Stupinigi. His work there did not bring him under the influence of FILIPPO JUVARRA, but rather prepared him for the revival of GUARINO GUARINI's architecture after 1737, which he interpreted in an original manner. In 1739, he was referred to as a notary, a profession he may have practiced before turning to architecture. By the end of the 1740s, he was as prominent in the Canavese as BERNARDO ANTONIO VITTONE.

The 1729 contract for the parish church of Barone also proves Michela's authorship of the Barone Castello. This is a trapezoid with concave sides in plan; an outdoor staircase connects the garden to the oval *salone.* The details of its planning are perhaps too polished to be by Michela. The church's Greek-cross plan is inscribed in a rectangle with low cupola and shallow satellite domes, habitual in Michela's work. The lively façade is an exercise in farcical proportions, testifying to Michela's disregard of Juvarra's elegance and to his own cranky individuality. The architect flaunts a taste for the jarring.

Four projects were provided by Michela for San Giacomo in Rivarolo. The least expensive version, which was chosen, was merely a grander and more accomplished version of the Barone church. The reconstruction of Santissima Trinità in Valperga, where he replaced Vittone, has only the rich main altar to recommend it; the façade is a stiff repetition of Rivarolo. The designs done in the same years for the two different sites for the Borgomasino parish church were not realized. Vittone took over that job, but Michela's drawings show some development from rigid to curvilinear and vigorous. Michela's only important work is the confraternity church of Santa Marta in Agliè. It is the only variation south of the Alps on the longitudinal churches of Guarini and one of the few churches adapted to confraternity use. Santa Marta is a small church built in two campaigns and altered in a third one due to increased membership. The bell tower, triangular with concave sides was built in 1785–1787 but it is so well integrated with the plan of the church that it must be by Michela. It is of finer brickwork than the church, and its height is articulated with vigorous cornices. The plan of the church is in three segments: a circle for the two-level choir, a square for the sanctuary, and a triangle with concave sides for the congregation. The independence of the bays is emphasized by the extensive research in the curvature of arches which are used to join and separate bays. Vittone also bent arches inward and outward, creating lens-shaped vaults, and Juvarra experimented with outcurving arches. The entrance is through one of the piers, which are frescoed in imitation of dark marble. The curved profiles of the triangular segment's walls push toward the altar and are carved out with musicians' balconies which before the addition of screens must have seemed even more cavernous. The interior is painted in lively hues, which increases the crude and cramped initial impact of the church. The façade is very thick, of unplastered brick. Columns are notched into the sides; the deep naked arch on the upper level is framed by columns and volutes; and the "pediment shatters the crowning pile of mouldings" (Pommer, 1968). The vivacity of the façade and interior has no source or counterpart in Piedmont, but the churches of the DIENTZENHOFER BROTHERS and BALTHASAR NEUMANN have some analogous qualities.

MARTHA POLLAK

WORKS

1739, Parish Church, Barone, Italy. 1731, Madonna delle Grazie (enlargement), Citano Canavese, Italy. 1731, Nostra Signora della Neve, Piora, Italy. 1733, San Giacomo, Rivarolo Canavese, Italy. 1739, Santa Marta; 1746, Madonna delle Grazie (Bario); Agliè, Italy. 1748, Santissima Trinità (reconstruction), Valperga, Italy.

BIBLIOGRAPHY

BRINCKMANN, ALBERT E. 1931 *Theatrum novum Pedemontii.* Düsseldorf, Germany: Schwann.

CELANO, CESARE 1967 "S. Marta ad Agliè." *L'Architettura* 12:750–759.

POMMER, R. 1968 "Costanzo Michela and Santa Marta in Agliè: A Guarinesque Rarity." *Art Bulletin* 50:169–182.

TELLUCCINI, AUGUSTO 1930–1931 "Il castello di Rivoli torinese." *Bollettino d'art* Series 2 10:145–161, 193–216.

MICHELANGELO

Michelangelo Buonarroti (1475–1564) was born near Arezzo, Italy, but he was soon taken back to his family home in Florence. Although he was apprenticed at the age of thirteen to the painter Domenico Ghirlandaio, a profession of any kind was considered demeaning by his father, who was a poor member of a proud old Florentine family. Michelangelo himself was later persuaded that he was descended from the Counts of Canossa and probably always felt himself to be a member of a social class above that of mere workmen or artists. He became an acknowledged authority on Dante and wrote powerfully expressive poetry, chiefly sonnets.

Thus, in Michelangelo we meet a special kind of artist even among the larger group of unusual Renaissance men. He was an even more unusual architect, an art he never claimed to practice.

Although Michelangelo's lifelong profession was sculpture, we do not know of any apprenticeship he served in that art; he seems to have been self-taught, as he was in architecture. He did not have an architectural practice in the modern sense, but he is nevertheless one of the greatest architects of the entire Renaissance and one of the most original and influential designers of all time.

Michelangelo's career is divided into four unequal parts: (1) early career; (2) Rome, 1505–1515; (3) Florence, 1516–1534; and (4) Rome, 1534–1564. His architecture was produced almost exclusively in the later periods. His first pseudo-architectural design was probably the Tomb for Julius II, which he was commissioned to design early in 1505. This project, which came to an abrupt halt early in 1506, was for a freestanding monument that was essentially a display of marble sculpture. The project was revived, postponed, and successively reduced in size over a period of forty years until it was finally completed as a wall monument in San Pietro in Vincoli in the mid-1540s. Many of the forms and ideas for the first tomb project were transferred to paint in the architectural framework, painted in *trompe l'oeil,* of the Sistine Ceiling (1508–1512).

Michelangelo's true architecture begins only with his return to Florence in 1516, when he sought and gained the commission for the façade of San Lorenzo, which was abandoned in 1520 without anything having been built. His first actual building is the New Sacristy or Medici Chapel attached to the same church, begun in 1519–1520 and finished around 1534. Thus, his architectural career began after he was forty-five years old, and it was never more than a sideline; he was constantly occupied with commissions for sculpture and, for long periods, for fresco decorations as well. Simultaneously with the Medici Chapel, he began to plan a new library for San Lorenzo, the Biblioteca Laurenziana, which was built in spurts between 1524 and 1559, with the artist absent after 1534. His greatest architectural achievements were in Rome, where he spent his final thirty years on great projects, the most important ones being the redesigned Capitol (Piazza del Campidoglio), with designs beginning around 1538 and construction extending well into the next century; and the new designs for St. Peter's, after 1546, which again remained unfinished until the seventeenth century and was completed with notable modification of Michelangelo's plans. Nevertheless, these works are, respectively, the most innovative example of city planning and the most powerfully unified and organic church design of the Renaissance. In addition, Michelangelo made changes in the design of the Palazzo Farnese (1546–1549), the greatest city palace of the period, designed a novel city gate, the Porta Pia (1561–1564), and contributed to a number of other projects of great interest.

Michelangelo's first project for the Tomb of Julius II (1505–1506) was to be built in the so-called Rossellino Choir of Old St. Peter's, a fifteenth-century addition to the Constantinian basilica. The tomb was to be of unusual size, about 23 x 36 feet (7.2 x 10.8 meters) in plan. The lower level was to contain an oval burial chamber, perhaps the first oval planned in Renaissance architecture. The exterior of the tomb was to have been articulated by arched niches with statuary alternating with herm pilasters bearing sculptured figures of fettered prisoners. This was the essentially architectural aspect of the design, which was overwhelmingly sculptural. A revised project of 1513 set one end against a wall, with a high *cappelletta* or tabernacle rising above the tomb, surmounted by an arch. These projects survive in copies after Michelangelo's drawings, and some elements of the early projects are incorporated into the tomb of the 1540s, which has an entirely different flavor in its later parts. The early tomb was to have been covered with relief grotesque decorations, as some of the lower parts of the present tomb still demonstrate.

The Florentine architecture. Michelangelo's fortunes changed with the death of Julius II early in 1513. Julius's successor, Leo X, was a childhood acquaintance of Michelangelo's and second son of Lorenzo il Magnifico. Although Michelangelo had been harbored by Lorenzo in the months before his death in 1492 and had known the Medici children well, Leo's tastes were for a less rigorous art than Michelangelo's, and he seems to have been most comfortable when the artist was out of town: he encouraged him with projects in Florence, not in Rome.

The first of these was for the façade of San Lorenzo, the Medici church begun by FILIPPO BRUNELLESCHI and finished around 1470 with the façade left in the rough. At first, the façade was to have been a work of collaboration, but Michelangelo elbowed out the competition in 1516, when he was also quarrying marble for the Tomb. He began planning a façade of unprecedented size and splendor that would have been richly decorated with sculpture. Its architectural form is known from drawings and a wooden model commissioned in December 1516 and finished only about a year later. His actual contract dates from January 1518 and allowed eight years to complete the façade, but trouble began immediately because of controversies over the source of marble. Michelangelo lost most of four years of his creative life between 1516 and 1520 with abortive projects for the façade, trying to open new Florentine quarries in Pietrasanta and quarrying marble for figures for the Tomb that were never used. The drawings and model of the façade show the bare skeleton of architecture, which must be imagined, like the Tomb, with a rich sculptural incrustation. Even so, the design is powerful and novel architecture.

Early Renaissance façades had been compromises between the classical rules of architectural composition and the irregular, two-story shape of the Christian basilica. Michelangelo solved this problem by avoiding it: he designed a two-story, palacelike façade that did not reflect the building behind. The lower level was to be articulated with four pairs of engaged columns, echoed above in pilasters with an intervening socle area. Its projecting central section was crowned with a pediment. The paired orders at the ends carried up through a broken section of entablature to support a similar terminal section above. Thus, the façade was on two levels, with recessed bays between the central temple front and the ends. The design embodied a full bay around the corners. Compared with the relief of the columns, the other architectural elements were relatively flat: doors, niches, *tondi* over the side doors on the upper story, and a central window between. The façade was essentially a field for sculpture and represents an outgrowth of his ideas for the Tomb of Julius II.

Michelangelo claimed not to know why this great project lapsed early in 1520, but he already had a new project underway: a Medici funeral chapel attached to the right transept of San Lorenzo. The patron was Cardinal Giulio de' Medici, archbishop of Florence. In May 1519, the idea of building a pendant to Brunelleschi's sacristy was already in the air, and work began on the site later that year. It is still not certain whether a building had already been begun according to Brunelleschian principles, for Michelangelo's new sacristy essentially follows the old plan and repeats some of the features of the Quattrocento building, which was the family mausoleum of an earlier generation. The idea evolved rapidly even though plans for the tombs seem to have changed several times before their final form was reached in the mid-1520s. The death of Leo X in 1521 delayed construction, but in 1523, Cardinal Giulio, his illegitimate cousin, was elected pope as Clement VII, and work resumed with definitive plans for two single wall tombs and a double tomb honoring members of the family, which now had no surviving male heirs apart from the pope. The chapel as built uses the contrast of the dark, slippery greenish-gray Florentine stone called *pietra serena* against white plaster, as in Brunelleschi's sacristy, though Brunelleschi's room employs the orders only on the altar wall whereas Michelangelo used them all around. But if this was Michelangelo's model, he made a major change almost immediately: the New Sacristy is a full story higher. Instead of supporting the dome on pendentives reaching down toward the floor, he inserted a mezzanine between the pendentive architecture and dome. The dome, unlike Brunelleschi's, has antique coffering like the Pantheon; the mezzanine story with its small order is also based on that prototype, whereas Brunelleschi's chapel has a dome with umbrellalike ribs. The upper part of Michelangelo's design seems to have undergone changes since at one point he wanted the dome painted by Giovanni da Udine, a specialist in pseudo-antique grotesque paintings. He also had to treat the exterior from a different and independent point of view in order to make it harmonize with the old structures around it.

The most decisive change from the Quattrocento model was Michelangelo's decision to insert marble architectural membering within the thin moldings of *pietra serena.* These marble elements include the tombs themselves, of which only two were completed; it may be supposed that in order to make the tombs seem to be part of the architecture he was led to include other marble elements as well: doors with niches above, carved to his novel designs. These door-niche elements are paired at each of the corners of the room, and because they are large and project strongly, they seem to crowd and jostle the more traditional dark membering of the Brunelleschian order. The tombs themselves are the most important aspect of this marble architecture. They are essentially above our heads and larger than life-size in their figural ornament, wedged into the *pietra serena* framework and even cut off by it: the paired pilasters framing the statues of the Medici have no echo at the ends of the tomb design. Instead, there is a pierlike molding of *pietra serena* that Michelangelo inserted within the architecture borrowed from the old scheme, which squeezes the tombs further. The crowding was Michelangelo's choice.

Michelangelo. Medici Funeral Chapel (dome). Florence. 1519–1534

The details are if anything more novel than the general scheme: fantastic capitals and grotesque, masklike friezes. But the overall impression is one of austerity, of empty marble niches in the tombs and elaborate, unstructural niches over the doors, most of which are themselves blind. We also see the simple use of antique motifs: bosses and swags set into the deliberately complex niches, whose interior moldings seem to deny the validity of the traditional gable. Michelangelo modified traditional capitals here in favor of extreme simplicity, in contrast to those of the tombs.

In the mezzanine story, the windows are framed in *pietra serena* and the design seems more normal. In the pendentive area above, large windows with splayed sides go counter to the normal perspective diminution of sight, and thus look even narrower above than they actually are, making the story seem higher than it is. Michelangelo changed his design for the room several times, in part because of new requirements for the tombs. Since the actual tombs are on the side walls, the chapel today lacks its basic focus, which would have been between the double tomb of the Medici *Magnifici* with the Madonna in the center on one wall, and the elaborately carved altar at the other end. The altar designed so that the priest stood behind it and looked over the altar into the room:

Michelangelo.
Medici Funeral Chapel.
Florence.
1519–1534

the chapel was not for the living but for the salvation of the souls of the dead. Much of this is lost; when Michelangelo left Florence forever in 1534, the figures for the two tombs were still lying on the floor; in 1559, the idea of completing the chapel was finally abandoned.

Although we have to deal with an imperfect room, it is nevertheless one of the most impressive in the world. Michelangelo had a different attitude toward the models of the past—both of antiquity and of his Renaissance predecessors—than other architects. This difference was not merely due to the fact that he was not trained as an architect. Most of the great Renaissance architects were painters or sculptors, and professional architecture as such was in its infancy, its chief representative being the mediocre Antonio da Sangallo (see SANGALLO FAMILY). In the Medici Chapel, however, we feel that the architecture is the work of a sculptor. The tombs is a decorative, sculptor's architecture, and the design of the whole was essentially conceived as a framework for sculptured tombs that were planned with much more decoration than was ever carved. Even the "pure" architectural elements have been, so to speak, carved, as we can see in the powerful drawings he made of profiles for moldings and other details.

Michelangelo seems to have felt that architectural forms should be strange, *alla grottesca,* which is an expression that GIORGIO VASARI used in describing the New Sacristy but that he had also applied to the decorative architecture of Donatello. Michelangelo's contemporaries and followers understood that there was an affinity between the two men's approach to architectural decoration; Vincenzo Borghini, a friend of Michelangelo's in Florence, penned a motto that reads, translated: "Either the spirit of Donatello works in Buonarroti, or that of Buonarroti had worked in Donatello." The novelty of the New Sacristy impressed even Michelangelo's most ardent admirers as being outside of the usual canons of good practice. Vasari specifically wrote that his designs were

extremely novel, and in them he departed a great deal from the kind of architecture regulated by proportion, order, and rule that other artists did according to common usage and following Vitruvius and the works of antiquity but from which Michelangelo wanted to break away. . . .

The license he allowed himself has served as a great encouragement to others to follow his example; and subsequently we have seen the creation of new kinds of fantastic ornamentation containing more of the grotesque than of rule or reason. Thus all artists are under a great and permanent obligation to Michelangelo, seeing that he broke the bonds and chains that had previously confined them to the creation of traditional forms [Vasari, 1966, p. 366].

These words, although written about the Medici Chapel, may seem more appropriate to the final appearance of the Laurentian Library (1524–1534), which stretches out on the other side of San Lorenzo on one side of the second story of the cloister adjacent to the church. There, even more unusual combinations of traditional architectural elements can be found. All of this novelty is to be ultimately explained by the genius of an unusual, solitary, and uniquely gifted artist. But some aspects of his self-education may throw some light on his early approach to architecture, which here enters realms that were unknown to his Renaissance forebears.

At the time of the commission for the façade of San Lorenzo, Michelangelo seems to have set about teaching himself aspects of architectural drafting and thinking by making copies of the drawings after ancient and modern Rome buildings in the so-called Codex Coner of around 1515. He seems to have been concerned with the mastery of details, of parts rather than of wholes: capitals, bases, cornices. The profiles of moldings are repeated and varied in Michelangelo's drawings, but there are no plans or elevations and no sense of concern with structure. It has been asserted that in the Medici Chapel and the Laurenziana, Michelangelo demonstrated the strength of his *disegno* (which might be translated as the art of art) rather than a truly architectural attitude. The results still smack of drawings on a page rather than the product of a spatial imagination. Even the most architectonic elements impress us as sculpture. The setting is superhuman, largely above our heads in the Medici Chapel, and the visitor is dwarfed and even alienated by an architectural world that has not taken him into account.

In the Biblioteca Laurenziana, Michelangelo achieved new heights of expression and even of perversity. Although the idea for the library went back to 1519, nothing was done until 1524. Michelangelo had visited Rome in December of 1523 when Clement VII was newly elected, full of hopes for the future. In January 1524, Michelangelo was asked to send a drawing showing dimensions of separate Greek and Latin libraries with provisions for a well-lighted vestibule. Michelangelo professed surprise and ignorance, saying (as was his wont) that architecture was not his profession, but that he would do his best.

The site eventually chosen was a traditional one, in a cloister and above ground in order to be well lighted and to preserve the books from dampness. The need for such a library was clear since the old Medici collection of manuscripts, notably enriched by Lorenzo il Magnifico, was still housed privately in the Medici Palace in Florence. The new pope, the last of the great Medici of the Quattrocento, felt the need to enshrine this collection in a more suitably public place to honor the family and to serve scholars. Michelangelo rejected a site on the piazza before the church on the grounds that it would impede the view—he still hoped to build the façade. When the actual site off the west cloister was chosen in April 1524, it was obvious that the lower floor of the new library needed to be reinforced with new vaults. In 1525, the building progressed rapidly, but Michelangelo always worked from moment to moment, changing, revising, and substituting details until it was too late to make changes. While the lower floor was being built he was still designing what was to go above. This promising beginning slowed with the pope's decision to favor the Chapel over the Library in 1526 for the sake of economy: the work was costly. After the disastrous Sack of Rome in 1527, the pope was exiled and in disgrace; Florence took up arms against the Medici, and Michelangelo, a staunch Republican who worked actively on the defense of his city, quit working on Medici projects. A little more work was done before Clement died in 1534 and Michelangelo left Florence, but he never saw the Library in anything like the form we know. It was continued by Niccolò Tribolo, Vasari, and BARTOLOMMEO AMMANNATI according to Michelangelo's verbal instructions and was opened only after his death, in 1571.

Michelangelo's plans incorporated a long, unbroken reading room (152 x 35 x 28 feet) with light coming in on both sides, not unlike a modern railroad car. To keep the construction as light as possible, it was designed as a skeletal system with piers, faced with *pietra serena* pilasters, supporting a thin entablature inside, and with two sets of windows, large and small, set vertically within each of the intervening bays. This articulation was kept on the interior end walls as well with the addition of large doors with elaborate cornices. Projecting from the walls were desks with built-in reading stands attached to the seats in front, each one coordinated with a window for light and with a pilaster for aesthetics. This entire bay system was strengthened on the outside wall with buttresses, as in a medieval church.

The floor and ceiling enrich this system of solids and voids. In the letters to and from the pope, it is notable that the pope was the practical and even sometimes the imaginative one in his demands, whereas Michelangelo started, here as elsewhere, with more abstract ideas that he later modified and harnessed to the specific needs of the site and commission. The final design of the Library is delicate and light, rhythmically regular in its succession of bays and enriched by the colorful ceramic design of the floor and its echo in the wooden coffers of the ceiling, which are loosely based on antique "grotesque" decorations: the painted and stuccoed vaults of Imperial Roman Baths and of Nero's Golden House in Rome had been rediscovered in the late fifteenth century. Although Michelangelo's Library does not look like anything that had been built before, the basic color scheme of *pietra serena* set against plaster walls was traditional. However, the walls were reduced to little more than moldings around the frames and architectural members, thus reversing their usual relationship.

The vestibule (*ricetto*) is the most unusual of Michelangelo's Florentine designs. Its most obvious and startling feature is the stairway that occupies most of the floor space, which was the last feature to be built. Many drawings show that Michelangelo toyed with a number of different forms for the stair, and it is obvious that from the beginning he wanted it to be the major feature of the room. In 1525, the pope said that he preferred a single stair, and Michelangelo, who had been experimenting with flights on each of the side walls merging in the center, then began to experiment with prototypes of the stair that was finally built. By the time that it was actually ready to be built in 1558, however, the artist, then in his eighties, claimed that he could not remember what he had planned. In January 1559, Michelangelo sent some kind of model and instructions to Ammannati, who built the stairs out of stone rather than the walnut that Michelangelo had preferred as "more in keeping with the desks, the ceiling, and the door." The stair that was built (which is certainly Michelangelo's design, if not precisely what he was planning in the 1520s) is one of the most famous and controversial in the history of architecture and the first interior stairway of importance. Previous stairways inside buildings had been largely utilitarian, although grand ceremonial stairs were known in many ancient and later cultures. Here, the stair is treated as a feature of design and only secondarily as a means to ascend and descend; indeed, the stair is positively frightening, with two external and even dangerous ramps with odd side projections that must be navigated with extreme care and that eventually join the central flight. The main stairway is also peculiar, with projecting oval risers of irregular size, decreasing in width as they go up, and with side projections in the main sections that make walking a peril. The main flight is divided into separate sets of three, seven, and five steps, which is again a hazard for the thoughtless scholar, delightful and capricious as it may be to contemplate. This strange, freestanding stairway occupies the entire center of the space and becomes, for the first time in the Renaissance, a major feature of architectural design. One would think that such an innovation would have been the work of Michelangelo himself, as in a sense it was; but the fundamental idea actually came from Clement VII, who was quoted in 1525 as wanting a stair "that takes up the whole vestibule." Not surprisingly, the Laurenziana stairway has not exerted much influence on later stairs, which became important features of interior design in the eighteenth century, most obviously in the palaces of JOHANN BALTHASAR NEUMANN.

If the stairway is a strange and late aberration of immense fascination, the vestibule itself is an authentic if unfinished example of Michelangelo's design in the 1520s. In contrast to the Library, the *ricetto* is small (31 x 34 feet) and high (44 feet), making a purposeful contrast to the long, rather monotonous reading room beyond. At first, Michelangelo had the idea of unifying the levels of the rooms by carrying on the height of the reading room into the articulation of the *ricetto* and by vaulting it at the same height as the ceiling of the reading room. For structural reasons the scheme was then changed to one with a wooden ceiling

Michelangelo. Biblioteca Laurenziana. Florence. 1524–1534 (not completed until 1571 by others)

with skylights; the *ricetto* is next to the transept of San Lorenzo, and lighting it was a problem. The solution finally chosen was to raise the walls in order to create a clearstory, changing the proportions of the vestibule to something more like a shaft than a traditional room. The space dwarfs the visitor, who enters and looks upward at an architectural landscape essentially above his head and who is confronted with a strange staircase that allows him a bizarre escape into a calmer environment.

By the end of 1525, Michelangelo settled on the articulation of the walls that has made this part of his design the most controversial and debated aspect of all of his Florentine architecture. The most unusual feature is the use of paired, monolithic Tuscan columns set into the body of the wall on the level of the library, so that the order, instead of lying on the wall or in front of it, is actually in it and forms a disjunctive continuity formed of wall and paired order together. Since the wall is itself punctured by large niches in *pietra serena,* with smaller contrasting niches above of the same material, the wall as a plane tends to disappear, as in the Library. The ceiling originally planned was to rest on the columns not on the walls. Paired brackets lie below the paired columns not as if they support anything but as decorative elements in the lower, basementlike story of the vestibule. Here, we see Michelangelo's tendency to extrapolate the elements of traditional architecture as decorative features of a novel design. In the corners, these brackets meet and merge in an organic way.

Although recessed columns were known in antique decorative architecture and had even been briefly considered by LEONARDO DA VINCI in a drawing, modern critics have focused on the seeming perversity of this motif and have pointed to other inversions of usual architectural form: the pilasters of the tabernacles taper toward the bottom, the capitals rest on the shafts, and so on. Ambiguity, conflict, and restlessness seem to dominate the small room. As a result, the critics of the 1930s, led by Rudolf Wittkower, tried to formulate criteria of Mannerist architecture based in large part on Michelangelo's performance at the Laurenziana. More recently, it has seemed less productive to insist on the *ricetto* as an example of a Mannerist period, and art historians have tried to understand its genesis within Michelangelo's own development: James Ackerman's book on Michelangelo's architecture, which appeared in 1961, never mentions Mannerism.

The Florentine architecture of Michelangelo, though developed from Renaissance principles, exhibits a novel and personal quality that is not paralleled by most of the other architecture of the period and is not easily understood as part of a period style, even though it could not have been produced much earlier in the Renaissance—even by a Michelangelo. It is, among other things, a product of the achievement in Rome of 1505–1515 by DONATO BRAMANTE, BALDASSARE PERUZZI, RAPHAEL, and Sangallo, which Michelangelo had studied in his drawings after those in the Codex Coner. This heritage was enlivened and enriched by his involvement with the requirements of the individual commissions and by his own imagination, which he always considered to be a basic ingredient of art. In this sense his architecture is a highly individual example of a new freedom, a sometimes bizarre quality that can be found in the work of a few other architects, most obviously Raphael's pupil GIULIO ROMANO in his works in Mantua.

Michelangelo's Medicean commissions were interrupted by a political crisis: Pope Clement VII and the Emperor Charles V were enemies; and after a Roman uprising in 1526 the emperor's troops entered and sacked the city in May 1527. Clement escaped to the Castel Sant'Angelo and, when peace was declared, moved to Orvieto; but the authority of the papacy as a secular force was forever shattered and Clement himself was a broken man: the Renaissance papacy was over. In Florence, the citizens rose up against the Medici and declared a new republican regime. Although the pope tried to keep Michelangelo in his service, Clement was bankrupt and his court reduced to a few miserable stragglers. Michelangelo turned his hand to the defense of Florence and devised a series of notable drawings for fortifications: a new alliance of pope and emperor threatened and eventually overcame the republican government. Clement VII wanted above all to get his city back. Late in 1528, Michelangelo was engaged in improving the Florentine defenses, and in January 1529, he was a member of a committee assigned to complete the fortifications begun by the Medici in 1526. In April, he was governor-general of fortification, working on earthworks defending the hill of San Miniato. Michelangelo's drawings for fortifications are exciting simply as abstract patterns. The imaginative, almost zoomorphic plans show artillery fire coming out belligerently at every angle. His desire was not aesthetic, however; the drawings are one of the best examples of Michelangelo's will to formal, expressive beauty; their intent was solely to provide a rational and successful defense, though it has been suggested that his complex, isolated corner bastions were probably too exposed to have been wholly successful. The earthworks he built have not survived.

When the Medici finally took Florence, Michelangelo prudently escaped to Venice in September 1529; but in two months, he was back home. Although the Medici had declared a general amnesty, it was not honored, and an order was issued to seek Michelangelo out and kill him. Clement soon wrote urging that Michelangelo be treated in a friendly manner, however, and by the end of the year he seems to have been at work in the Medici Chapel.

The Roman architecture. Michelangelo grew gradually dissatisfied with Florence after this episode, and for various reasons. One of them was a platonic infatuation with a handsome Roman, Tommaso de' Cavalieri, to whom he wrote impassioned letters and sonnets and for whom he made mythological drawings of previously unknown refinement. Moreover, the reduced program of the Medici Chapel interested him less and less—he was always more engaged by the concept than by execution—and his new project for the Tomb of Julius II had not been satisfactorily finished though some figures were close to completion.

Late in 1533, Clement VII conceived the idea of a new painted decoration for the altar wall of the Sistine Chapel, which so appealed to his successor, Paul III Farnese (1534–1549), that he forbade Michelangelo to do anything else, fobbing off the Della Rovere heirs with promises of a completed tomb in the future. Michelangelo settled permanently in Rome, working chiefly on the *Last Judgment,* which occupied him between 1534 and 1541. Nevertheless, he was gradually enticed to do architectural projects, and by the mid-1540s, they began to take up most of his time and ingenuity. Michelangelo's Roman architecture is almost completely different from the Florentine: the earlier works were private, essentially interior, and based on the old color contrast of the Quattrocento. The Roman architecture is triumphantly public, built in Roman travertine with its richly sober appearance. The scale, too, is wholly different—Rome is an imperial city, and its architecture is often on an imperial scale. Michelangelo's is colossal, using giant orders to unite several stories, and modeled in space and sunlight to achieve a seemingly organic unity out of the diversity of architectural members.

The earliest of these commissions, but the slowest to be realized, was his project for the Capitoline Hill. The scheme began rather innocently when Emperor Charles V made a ceremonial visit to Rome early in 1536. Paul III did his best to set up suitable temporary ornaments in order to greet the emperor in the recently ravaged city, but there was no great central square in which to receive him. The obvious place to have such a ceremony would have been on the Capitol, the focus of ancient Roman triumphs and the seat of Rome's city government. In ancient days, the chief temple of the state religion was there, as were the state archives, the sacred Wolf, and the mint. All of these monuments and symbols had long since crumbled or been buried in their own debris; and the focus of the ancient Capitol toward the Forum Romanum made no sense in the Renaissance, for that old center was wholly outside the settled area and was used chiefly as a cow pasture. A medieval palace for the ceremonial Senator of Rome was begun in the twelfth century over the ruins of the ancient archives (Tabularium), but it now faced the other direction, toward the Tiber, Campus Martius, and the Vatican. A palace for the Conservators of Rome was built into the ruins of the state temple of Jupiter, Juno, and Minerva in the fifteenth century. It stood opposite the church of Santa Maria in Aracoeli, whose long Gothic flank rises above the piazza to the east.

Thus, the Capitol had seen a revival before 1500 associated with the rather amorphous organization of the Roman people (*popolo romano*) and its civic government. Paul III determined to rebuild the Piazza del Campidoglio, as it came to be called, and decided, against Michelangelo's advice, to move the famous equestrian statue of Marcus Aurelius there. This statue was the only monumental bronze statue to survive the Middle Ages in Rome, having escaped destruction through its misidentification as Constantine, the first Christian emperor; even in Paul III's time, it was wrongly identified as Antoninus Pius.

Michelangelo, meanwhile, was made an honorary Roman citizen in a ceremony on the Capitol in December 1537, which apparently helped him to accept the statue. He designed a new base for it when it was set up in 1538 in the center of the amorphous and unpaved piazza before the Palazzo del Senatore, facing the approach from Rome. Perhaps at this time, Michelangelo also made preliminary sketches for a new architectural environment around the statue. We do not really know the date of his projects, and little was built before his death. Details still remained to be designed in the later 1550s, and after his death the new architects made some changes. But Michelangelo's friends saw to it that what they knew of his plans was preserved in engravings; and the scheme was built more or less according to his wishes, though it was finished only in the mid-seventeenth century by Girolamo Rainaldi and Carlo Rainaldi.

The base Michelangelo designed for the statue had oval ends and seems to imply the oval area that he eventually described around it. At the right, facing the statue, he planned a new porticoed façade for the Palazzo dei Conservatori, which rose

Michelangelo. View of Piazza del Campidoglio. Rome. 1540s

at an acute angle to the Palazzo del Senatore. To balance it on the other side of the piazza he projected an identical façade at a similar angle. The perspective engraving makes this look like a rectangular piazza and many visitors may also make that mistake on arrival; it is actually a trapezoid with the short side toward the entrance (the reverse of the impression given in the engraving). What can be thought of as three roughly equal sides of an unfinished triangle are formed by the side palaces and the refurbished Palazzo del Senatore at the rear.

The three buildings, together with the balustrade and the ancient Roman statues and trophies that were eventually set up on it, serve to create an almost enclosed space, open to the sky—something the Italians call a *piazza salone,* an open-air room. The visitor, climbing the ramp leading to the piazza, gradually sees the architectural landscape rising above him, with the gleaming gilt-bronze equestrian statue in the center on a raised mound. Seen in perspective, this oval mound and the trapezoidal space enclosing it tend to be read as a circle and a square, something Michelangelo may have intended. The egg-shaped segment of the oval supporting the statue may symbolize the old idea of the Capitol as the center or head of the world, the *caput totius mundi.* The statue itself stands augustly for Rome's imperial might, and the other relics serve to encrust this symbolism with further accretions of the glorious past, the dignity, power, and beauty of both ancient and modern Rome. Nothing that is visible refers to the Church. Thus, the Capitol is a piece of city planning with unique ties to the most glorious past that any city can boast, and in that respect (as in others) it is unique and uniquely moving to visit—even with the gigantic white monument to King Victor Emmanuel II towering over the entire hill.

The contrast between the narrow entrance, the irregular, pseudo-triangular space, and the central statue creates a dynamic tension between the central focus and the lure of the side palaces with their dark porticoes. The oval, which defines the trapezoid as both a central space and a longitudinal one, attracts the visitor to the center but also sends him to the sides and to the rear. The oval was an unusual form that became increasingly popular after this time. Here, it unites the three buildings on the piazza with brilliant success. Michelangelo planned an elaborate geometrical pavement that seems to be related to ancient cosmological schemata; a modern version was installed only in the mid-twentieth century.

It is surely the conception as a whole that is the most important achievement of this great, if relatively small, piazza design. Nevertheless, it would not be so successful were it not for the imposing and novel façades that Michelangelo planned for the flanking palaces. Since the Palazzo dei Conservatori was begun ony in 1563, the year before Michelangelo died, we cannot be sure that its design was settled much earlier, but presumably the entire scheme was essentially planned in the 1540s when the double stairway in front of the Palazzo del Senatore was begun and loggias were built to the left and the right with stairways ascending to Santa Maria in Aracoeli on one side and up behind the Palazzo dei Conservatori on the other. This scheme of three imposing stairs is symptomatic of a larger plan that may date from the time of Michelangelo's first statue base of 1538. In 1561–1564, the base of the statue was enlarged; funds were now set aside for the restoration of the Palazzo del Senatore by Pope Pius IV (1559–1565). This is the latest possible date for the final project and its individual elements. Tommaso de' Cavalieri, Michelangelo's old friend, was in charge of the Palazzo del Senatore, and working drawings were made for the Palazzo dei Conservatori by Guidetto Guidetti in accordance with Michelangelo's instructions. Michelangelo's projects of this period were preserved more or less accurately in engravings by ETIENNE DUPÉRAC, including a plan dated 1567 and a perspective view of 1569.

The Palazzo del Senatore was given a facing of pilasters on the upper stories that serve to unite both the main floor (*piano nobile*) with its new portal, at the top of Michelangelo's novel double stair, and the lower attic windows. These colossal pilasters support an impressive cornice with a balustrade and statuary. A central bell tower seems to have been part of Michelangelo's plan; as built in 1583 by Martino Longhi il Vecchio (see LONGHI FAMILY), it is a foreign element in the design, but it emphasizes the central axis of the *cordonata,* as the ramp up to the piazza is called, as Michelangelo desired. The high ground floor of the palace was treated as the rusticated base of the colossal pilaster order above; behind, the medieval building is largely preserved—Michelangelo essentially added an aesthetic coating to an older structure. The façade was finished around 1600.

The chief single glory of the Piazza del Campidoglio is the design of the Palazzo dei Conservatori, repeated in its twin, the Palazzo Nuovo, so-called because it had no function apart from the essential one of completing this permanent stage set, which is in a sense what Michelangelo designed. The façade of the Palazzo dei Conservatori was finished in 1584, that of its opposite only between 1603 and 1654. Here, Michelangelo's power as a Roman designer is felt in its full force. The old Quattrocento palace had had an arcaded loggia, echoing ancient stoas and porticoes. Michelangelo preserved that idea while carrying the main pier-pilasters up the full height of the building, creating a system of vertical supports that are crowned by a magnificent cornice scaled to the full height and length of the building, surmounted by balustrade and statuary. As in Florence, Michelangelo cut away the decorative stone wall upon which the pilasters rest, so that the wall becomes only a frame for the brick surface underneath—which we consequently read as the main or real wall surface. The large windows rest in that wall, serving to reduce it to a kind of border. The idea of designing in layers, which may have its origins in Bramante, seems to have appealed to Michelangelo and influenced many of his followers, most particularly GIACOMO BAROZZI DA VIGNOLA and his school.

The walls and sculptural windows of the *piano nobile* make a contrast to the deep shadows of the openings below. The executor, GIACOMO DELLA PORTA, completed the building with an enlarged central window not found in Dupérac's engraving; it gives an emphasis to the cross-axis that Michelangelo probably did not want. The façades facing the city were given two bays instead of the one seen in Dupérac's plan. Nevertheless, the design seems to be remarkably close to what Michelangelo envisaged, even though the façade was completed in 1584, twenty years after his death.

Michelangelo was able to dispense with vaulting over the loggia, providing it with a flat stone ceiling supported by the bulky Ionic columns visible in the openings and by matching ones next to the wall behind. These columns, and the walls of the adjoining rooms, form a skeletal system supporting the façade. The function of each individual element is clear from its size and shape. The nonbearing walls are of brick, again a two-color scheme but different from the contrasting one of Florence. Here, the colors are gray travertine and yellow brick, a softer, less obvious combination of forms and colors that breaks decisively with the decorative, linear appearance of the Florentine works. The forms, like the materials, remind us of ancient Rome. A novel monumental feature, the colossal pilaster, was not precisely antique but rather a modern adaptation that gives harmonious unity and stability to multistoried buildings. In using it, Michelangelo seems to have invented a form that was of enormous significance for architects for over two hundred years.

Michelangelo's piazza with the statue in the center has served as the model for countless squares in later years, but neither in design nor in its evocation of a past era has it ever been equaled. One of the obvious aspects of Michelangelo's plan for the Capitol is its symmetry—not from every point of view but on its chief axis. This symmetry is a constant in his designs, which he himself compared (in a letter written in the 1550s) to the human body, with one hand like the other and one eye like the other.

Michelangelo's other great Roman commissions made him the unwilling successor of Antonio da Sangallo il Giovane, who died in 1546. Sangallo had succeeded Raphael as architect of St. Peter's in 1520 and had also built an unprecedented number of private buildings, including the Palazzo Farnese, which enlarged an older structure for Cardinal Alessandro Farnese before 1530 who then carried it on according to more grandiose plans after he was elected Pope Paul III in 1534. A contract of 1541 called for further demolition and enlargement, with the stipulation that some of the work could not be evaluated because Sangallo still did not know how it was to be made. Even before his death, a competition was set up to provide a cornice more to the pope's liking than the one Sangallo had designed. Michelangelo's entry was tried out *in situ,* a full-size wooden section, ten feet high, set over a corner of the building. Obviously, the concern was for visual effect. His cornice was designed in scale with all three stories of the façade rather than as a crown to the top floor, as Vitruvian (see VITRUVIUS) theory might have dictated. The projection of the massive cornice with its deep shadow below gives meaning to the whole design, which Michelangelo further strengthened with a larger central window and coats of arms above. A view of the newly completed façade was published by Lafreri in 1549, showing a huge piazza in front of the palace with a large, chequered pattern corresponding to the bays of the palace. The houses standing on the site of the piazza had been acquired by that time and the piazza was, in a sense, part of the design. If Michelangelo did not plan the piazza, he almost surely designed the patterned pavement, which was never executed.

An engraving of 1560 seems to show his project for the rear wing of the palace looking from the court, since that part was still inchoate. The purpose of the plan was to open the rear wing as a loggia with a view through the gardens and beyond. Vasari tells us that Michelangelo planned a bridge to unite the palace with gardens on the other side of the Tiber that the Farnese had acquired. The top floor was to be closed, so that the visitor in the court would have looked through the rear wing over the Tiber to the gardens beyond; at the same time, the court would have been visible from the gardens. This part of Michelangelo's plan was not built, but the center rear of the palace was opened up with arches on the lower and upper floors by later architects.

Sangallo built the court in two floors of massive arcades faced with engaged columns; most of the arches were open but some had to be closed. He had not resolved the top floor articulation, because it needed to be wholly enclosed, and thus, if the lower system had been continued, all of the arches would have been walled up with windows in the walls—a contradictory and anomalous system. To avoid this problematic scheme, Michelangelo cut the Gordian knot by scrapping the arches entirely, designing a system of bays divided by clustered pilasters and novel window frames with gables that ride over the window like an eyebrow, unattached. Here, we see some of the perverse or ambiguous devices he used in Florence: capitals without columns, guttae hanging from pilaster shafts, brackets that do not support, moldings that seem to have slid from their places. As built in crisply carved Roman travertine, the top story of the courtyard is newly monumental and solves what seemed to be a hopeless dilemma.

After Sangallo died, every effort was made by his followers to keep Michelangelo from succeeding him at St. Peter's. The Fabbrica di San Pietro, the office of works, had invested all of the available funds for years in a large model for the building's completion, and they did not want to make changes. Accordingly, Giulio Romano was called in to succeed Sangallo, but he died in the same year, 1546. In desperation, Pope Paul III turned to Michelangelo. He was then seventy-one years of age and, as always, considered himself an architectural amateur. He also knew that the members of the Fabbrica were determined to continue the status quo and would fight his every attempt at change. Michelangelo, apparently a reluctant appointee, tried to make his position impregnable by accepting no salary. By doing so, he was able to cancel Sangallo's wastefully extravagent project even though it meant tearing down walls that had already been built, something no patron wants to do.

Sangallo's elaborate and ungainly design was a compromise: it developed the Bramante-Peruzzi-Raphael plans for a central Greek-cross church with ambulatories and corner towers, adding a huge fore-church with enormous twin campanili. Sangallo's misguided Vitruvianism led him to multiply stories and orders, achieving pettiness on a grand scale. Michelangelo reformed this and preceding plans by returning to the basic Greek cross of Bramante, paring off the ambulatories and corner towers. He strengthened the outer walls and simplified the plan at the same time. Although he had been replaced in Pope Julius II's favor by Bramante's project for New St. Peter's in 1506 and felt neurotically aggrieved by Bramante and his followers ever after, Michelangelo fully appreciated Bramante's achievement, writing to a member of the Fabbrica early in 1547 that Bramante had been as great an architect as anyone since antiquity, having established the "first plan of St. Peter's, not full of confusion but clear and neat, with ample light and isolated on all sides . . . and [it] was considered a beautiful thing, as is still clear today, so that any who have deviated from Bramante's plan, as Sangallo did, have deviated from the truth." He then went on to criticize Sangallo's model and concluded by saying that he did not want the commission. That appeal found its mark, and Michelangelo was given a free hand.

He faced a superhuman task and set about it by ordering two new models based on a design totally different from Sangallo's. Only the support of the pope allowed him to succeed; and although Paul III died in 1549, his successors also took Michelangelo's part. Because Michelangelo worked for nothing, he was obviously doing what he thought was best for St. Peter's. Eventually he was paid, but by the papal treasurer rather than by the Fabbrica.

St. Peter's had been underway for forty years. Work had begun with the central crossing piers that Bramante planned to support a dome modeled on that of the Pantheon, and equal to it in diameter. Two arms of the Greek cross were already vaulted; Michelangelo's changes were essentially confined to the outer and upper parts of the building, its perimeter and dome, which he radically revised. The interior also profited, gaining in light and visual coherence. Even Bramante's plan had been complex; Michelangelo simplified the interior while he reduced the peripheral areas to a great square of vaults around the Greek cross already underway, a saving in expense and a clarification in design. The Greek-cross plan itself may have had an anthropomorphic significance for Michelangelo, who seems to have identified it with the body of Christ; and Jesus himself had likened his body to a temple (John 2:19–21).

Michelangelo revolutionized the exterior of St. Peter's by giving it a revetment of travertine based on the colossal order, as at the Capitol. It was already designed by the fall of 1547 when the small wooden model was finished. He designed pairs of Corinthian pilasters that echo the articulation of Bramante's original piers in the crossing. These pairs of pilasters move around the exterior, now on the planes of the square, now on the curve of the apsidal areas, serving to unify elements that would otherwise seem disparate. As at the Capitol, the pilasters rest on a cut-away strip of wall, so that the profiles at the curves and angles multiply and become almost like the pleats in an accordion. In the larger bays between the paired order he put superimposed niche-window combinations; between the pilasters themselves, triple niches. This exterior revetment is below the level of the Vatican Hill toward the rear, but it rises high above the ground toward the eastern façade.

Michelangelo, typically, had not made a model of a façade before he died in 1564, since construction had not reached that point. Nevertheless, a series of engravings by Dupérac give a fair idea of what he planned: a portico supported by freestanding columns carrying on the pilaster order of the flanks, with a central section of four additional columns set in the center as a pedimented temple front. None of this was built.

Michelangelo's most conspicuous contribution to St. Peter's was his design for the drum and dome, which broke radically with Sangallo's

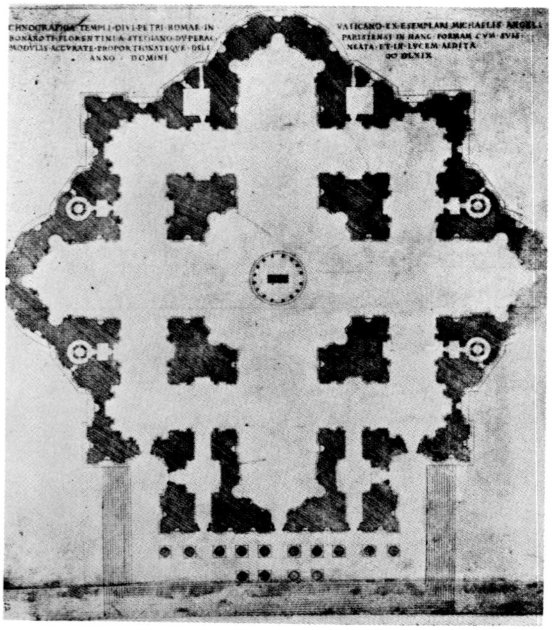

Michelangelo.
Engraving of Ground Plan for St. Peter's.
Rome.

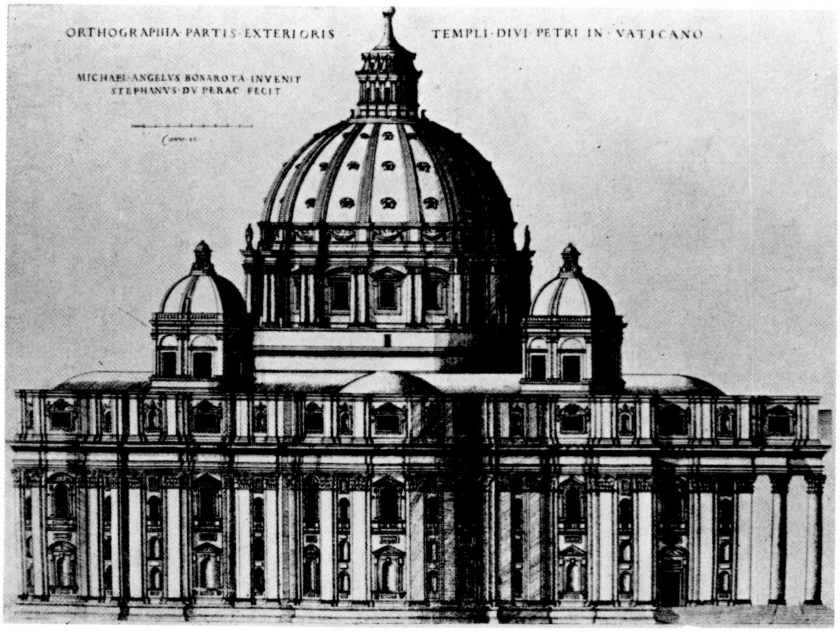

Michelangelo.
Design for façade of St. Peter's.
Rome.

model. Michelangelo built a sixteen-sided drum with paired columns jutting out to help absorb the thrusts of the dome. Over the years, he planned domes of varying profile, some more pointed, with smaller lanterns, others hemispherical with larger lanterns above. The sequence of these designs is not clear and his last thoughts are imperfectly known, but Dupérac's engravings were meant to preserve his project. They show an almost hemispherical dome and a large lantern. As built by Giacomo della Porta in 1588–1590, the dome is more pointed, perhaps following earlier designs by Michelangelo with modifications; the new profile was surely chosen for structural rather than aesthetic reasons. The paired pilaster-buttresses of the drum seem to carry on the rhythm of the paired pilasters of the flanks; these elements continue in the ribs of the dome of Michelangelo's plan, up to a lantern with paired columns and more vertical elements above. Thus, there is an upward quality of the decoration of the dome as built that is partially due to Michelangelo's design.

The dome was built according to a two-shelled design for structural reasons; a wooden half-model, once thought to be Michelangelo's, actually shows only his inner shell; an outer shell was added like that of the dome as built. These projects were first expressed in a clay model of 1557 and in an elaborate wooden model of 1558–1561.

As completed under CARLO MADERNO in the next century, the church has a long nave and an ungainly façade with bases for campanili that could not be built, all of which destroys the crystalline clarity of the earlier design. The interior of the dome was richly decorated, modifying the monochromatic effect Michelangelo had desired; he seems to have wanted a magical or divine light to suffuse the dome from hidden windows in the lantern. Nevertheless, from the flank or rear we can still imagine the building as Michelangelo wanted it. The changes include the two "little domes," actually massive structures surmounting the Gregorian and Clementine Chapels below, which were designed by della Porta. Their prototypes are seen in Dupérac's engraving, where they are also found in the corresponding positions toward the west; but the design for the domes seen in the engraving is obviously not Michelangelo's; we must surmise that they were desired, but not designed when he died. The attic seen on Dupérac's engraving of the elevation (c.1569) is shown as built. Earlier, Michelangelo had begun an unornamented attic that was probably to have been surmounted by an equally smooth dome. These ideas were then superseded by a ribbed dome and a decorated attic in the early 1560s. When Michelangelo died, the building was complete to the top of the drum and enough had been done to the flanks to ensure that they would be continued according to his design.

Michelangelo.
St. Peter's.
Rome.
1558–1564 (dome not completed until 1590 by Porta)

Michelangelo's other Roman works are relatively minor. The most important, designs for San Giovanni dei Fiorentini, were never built but survive in impressive drawings and in engravings after his wooden model. The Florentines had begun their church on the banks of the Tiber opposite St. Peter's in the 1520s, but after constructing an expensive foundation that extended into the banks of the river, money ran out. In 1559, Michelangelo was asked to provide new plans and, old as he was, produced a series of powerful drawings for a centralized, Pantheon-like design that did not take the old foundations into account. The model based on his drawings shows how, in the ten years that had elapsed after his earlier designs for St. Peter's, his ideas had simplified and calmed to a new serenity. The church was built later by Giacomo della Porta on an older plan.

The one project that was actually built more or less according to Michelangelo's plans was the Porta Pia, named after Pope Pius IV (1559–1565), one of Michelangelo's great admirers. The gate ornaments a newly straightened street that connects with one of the great roads into Rome from the north and east. Normally, such a gate would face outward for defense and to impress the visitor. Michelangelo designed a portal for the city, facing inward. He began his project as a kind of garden portal, like others giving onto the same street, and improvised around it to create new designs, a process that can also be followed in his drawings for details of the Palazzo Farnese and for the Capitol. The Porta Pia was a conscious part of a city-planning scheme that depended on new straight streets and vistas, an idea later taken up by Sixtus V (1585–1590). The idea of the city gate as a work of art may even have been the pope's; Michelangelo imagined it as a complex and powerful presence with an elaborate double gable surrounded by ornaments of great originality and surmounted by an aedicula. The present gate is only partially his design, with new additions on the outside.

Pius IV also commissioned Michelangelo to remodel the tepidarium of the Baths of Diocletian into a church, using the ancient vaulting and eight granite columns, 46 feet high, of the old Baths. The idea went back to 1541; in 1561, Pius IV took responsibility for the building, which was also to house his tomb. The church was called Santa Maria degli Angeli, partially corresponding to the pope's Christian name; it lies adjacent to his new street, then named the via Pia, leading to the Porta Pia. Michelangelo placed the high altar on the transverse axis of the antique hall so that it seems to be the transept of the church. It was renovated in the eighteenth century in a different style with new columns at the entrance to the chancel and in front, between the entranceway and the hall, with polychrome decorations applied to the walls, and a stucco entablature added to the old tepidarium hall. Michelangelo's building was white, punctuated by the red granite of the antique columns.

His other late designs were no less novel. He projected a chapel for the Sforza family in Santa Maria Maggiore (c.1560), which was built after his death by della Porta (consecrated 1573). It is our best example of his late conception of an interior space, a kind of truncated Greek-cross design with curving side chapels and powerfully projecting columns set diagonally from the corners. They are of travertine, and because of their height (30 feet) and the vaults above, they seem to stand free in space.

Michelangelo's late designs show his concern for an almost unbroken spatial architecture that uses segments and other curves in plan and in vaults. All of these interiors seem to have been planned as monochromatic, unlike their imperial forerunners. Columns, more or less freestanding, play an important part.

Michelangelo's achievement was personal and immense. His buildings stand outside of the common architectural practice of the Cinquecento just as he himself did as a person. Although it was "not his profession," his architecture is arguably his greatest and most perfect achievement. He was criticized, tacitly and overtly, for having set aside the standard practice of architecture in favor of personal caprice, but it was his intention to depart from the rulebook Vitruvianism that had plagued many Renaissance architects. Michelangelo's achievement is not, finally, an aberration. It is individual even in an age of individualism, but it has stood the test of time. His works meet the Vitruvian standards of firmness, commodity, and delight as well as any other architect's in history.

HOWARD HIBBARD

WORKS

1505/1506–mid-1540s, Monument to Pope Julius II, San Pietro in Vincoli; 1514, Chapel of Pope Leo X (façade), Castel Sant'Angelo; Rome. 1519–1534, Medici Funeral Chapel, San Lorenzo; 1524–1534, Biblioteca Laurenziana (not completed until 1571 by Niccolò Tribolo, Giorgio Vasari, and Bartolommeo Ammannati according to Michelangelo's designs), San Lorenzo; 1525–c.1533, Sant'Apollonia (portal); *1527–1529, Fortifications; Florence. 1539, Base for the Equestrian Statue of Marcus Aurelius, Capitol; 1539–1564, Piazza del Campidoglio (not completed until later by others); 1540s, Palazzo del Senatore (stairway); 1546–c.1549, Palazzo Farnese (cornice design; completion of façade and courtyard); 1546–1564, Palazzo Nuovo (Museo Capitolino); 1547, 1558–1564, St. Peter's (dome not completed until 1590 by Giacomo della Porta and Domenico Fontana from Michelangelo's model; building not completed until 1626 by Carlo Maderno); 1550–1551, Vatican Palace (stairway in the upper garden of the Cortile del Belvedere); c.1560, Cappella Sforza (not completed until 1573 by della Porta), Santa Maria Maggiore; 1561–1564, Porta Pia; 1561–?, Santa Maria degli Angeli (interior); Rome.

BIBLIOGRAPHY

ACKERMAN, JAMES S. (1961)1971 *The Architecture of Michelangelo.* Harmondsworth, England: Penguin. Abridged catalogue based on revised 1964 edition published in London by Zwemmer.

CONDIVI, ASCANIO (1553)1976 In Hellmut Wohl (editor), *The Life of Michelangelo.* Translated by Alice Sedgewick Wohl. Baton Rouge: Louisiana State University Press.

FROMMEL, CHRISTOPH L. 1973 *Der römische Palastbau der Hochrenaissance.* 3 vols. Tübingen, Germany: Wasmuth.

HEYDENREICH, LUDWIG H., and LOTZ, WOLFGANG 1974 *Architecture in Italy: 1400–1600.* Harmondsworth, England: Penguin.

"Michelangelo als Architekt." 1967 Volume 2, pages 3–70 in *Stil und Überlieferung in der Kunst des Abendlandes.* Berlin: Mann.

PORTOGHESI, PAOLO, and ZEVI, BRUNO (editors) 1964 *Michelangiolo architetto.* Turin, Italy: Einaudi.

SAALMAN, HOWARD 1975 "Michelangelo: S. Maria del Fiore and St. Peter's." *Art Bulletin* 7, no. 3:374–409.

SCHWAGER, KLAUS 1973 "Die Porta Pia in Rom." *Münchner Jahrbuch der bildenden Kunst* Series 3 24:33–96.

SUMMERS, DAVID 1972 "Michelangelo on Architecture." *Art Bulletin* 54, no. 2:146–257.

THOENES, CHRISTHOF 1968 "Bemerkungen zur St. Peter-Fassade Michelangelos." Pages 331–341 in

Munuscula Discipulorum. Berlin: Hesshing.

VASARI, GIORGIO 1962 *La vita di Michelangelo nelle redazioni del 1550 e del 1568.* Edited with commentary by Paola Barocchi. Milan and Naples, Italy: Ricciardi. An abridged version of the *Life of 1568* appears in *The Lives of the Artists,* translated by George Bull, and published in Harmondsworth, England by Penguin in 1966.

WILDE, JOHANNES 1978 *Michelangelo.* Oxford: Clarendon.

WITTKOWER, RUDOLF 1964 *La cupola di San Pietro di Michelangelo.* Florence: Sansoni.

WITTKOWER, RUDOLF 1978 "Michelangelo's Biblioteca Laurenzia." Pages 10–71 in *Idea and Image.* London: Thames & Hudson.

MICHELOZZO DI BARTOLOMEO

Michelozzo di Bartolomeo (1396–1472), who is sometimes incorrectly referred to as Michelozzo Michelozzi, was one of the major architects and sculptors of the early Renaissance in Italy. Although his reputation was overshadowed by the genius of FILIPPO BRUNELLESCHI, he was connected with almost every major architectural enterprise in Florence, Italy, of the early and mid-fifteenth century, and became the chief architect and designer for Cosimo de' Medici and his son Piero. His participation is securely documented in only about a half-dozen projects, but the list of attributions to him has been augmented by circumstantial and visual evidence and the testimony of GIORGIO VASARI, the sixteenth-century biographer of Italian artists. His style and personality were popular and easily understood by his patrons, and almost all his commissions were completed.

Born in Florence, Michelozzo began working as a die caster in the Florentine mint at the age of fourteen, and by 1420 he was an assistant of LORENZO GHIBERTI on the North Doors of the Baptistery in Florence. After working as a partner with him on several other commissions (the architecture of the sacristy of Santa Trinità, often connected with Ghiberti, has been attributed to Michelozzo without much justification), Michelozzo established a nine-year partnership with the sculptor Donatello to execute three large architectural-sculptural tombs, the outdoor pulpit on the Prato Cathedral, and other works. Michelozzo seems to have been in charge of bronze casting, creating the architectural frameworks and acting as the organizer and executive director of the shop of the partnership.

About 1422, he became associated with Cosimo de' Medici, building for him the small church and monastery called Bosco ai Frati in the Mugello and remodeling the nearby Medici villas at Trebbio and Careggi. These early projects are characterized by a strong dependence on the medi-

Michelozzo di Bartolomeo. Library, San Marco. Florence. c.1437–1452

eval tradition, merging with the awakening Renaissance ideas of space, light, and the simplicity of wall surfaces, but without the developed classical vocabulary of Brunelleschi.

However, the influence of Brunelleschi and his principles of Renaissance architecture are clearly evident in Michelozzo's designs for the building and reconstruction of the Church and Monastery (cloister, refectory, cells, and public rooms) of San Marco in Florence, undertaken at the expense of Cosimo de' Medici (c.1437–1452). Although his participation is undocumented, critics are nearly unanimous in seeing Michelozzo's personal style in the simple, unadorned mural surfaces subtly articulated with gray *pietra serena* accents, reminiscent of the architectural forms in Fra Angelico's altarpieces of the same period and location. The masterpiece of the monastic complex is the library, which, with its triple-aisled, barrel-vaulted simplicity and the rhythm of the double row of slender columns supporting elegant arcades, became the model for most of the private and public libraries of fifteenth-century Italy.

Michelozzo di Bartolomeo. Medici Palace. Florence. 1444–1459

Michelozzo di Bartolomeo. Medici Palace (courtyard). Florence. 1444–1459

Michelozzo is best known today as the architect of the Medici Palace (1444–1459) and thus for his contributions to the development of the Florentine Renaissance palace type. The Medici Palace is said to be the first designed for the comfort and convenience of the owners. The regularized placement of windows on the façade and in the square cortile, the use of classical motifs (capitals, cornice) and the clear definition of space are new elements in Florentine palaces. Simultaneously, he may have been supervising the construction of the nearby Church of San Lorenzo (c.1442–1457?), another Medici project in which accounting ledgers were shared with the Palace.

Michelozzo is documented as *capomaestro* of a large complex of buildings at Santissima Annunziata in Florence between 1444 and 1455. The tribune of this church was perhaps the most original of all Michelozzo's designs: a huge circular dome supported on massive piers between which opened nine small niche-chapels constituted one of the first centrally planned spaces in Renaissance Italy, later altered by LEON BATTISTA ALBERTI.

At the death of Brunelleschi in 1446, Michelozzo was elected *capomaestro* of the Cathedral of Florence to supervise construction of the lantern of the dome as designed by his predecessor. He was replaced in 1455 and spent the rest of the decade providing plans and designs for churches, buildings, palaces, and three large tabernacles in and around Florence, before leaving for Dubrovnik, Yugoslavia (then called Ragussa), in 1461 where he was employed as city engineer, building fortifications and city walls. Between 1464 and 1467, he held a similar position on the Greek island of Chios and traveled around the Aegean before returning to Florence about 1470 with his son Niccolo Michelozzi, an important Renaissance humanist, scholar, and writer. Michelozzo died in Florence in 1472.

An analysis of Michelozzo's career illuminates the problem of the role of the architect and the meaning of the term in the early Renaissance. His works fall into three general categories. In the first, he was responsible for the design and actively participated in at least certain phases of the execution, closely supervising the workers (San Marco, and

Medici Palace, Santissima Annunziata). In the second group (San Lorenzo, Bosco ai Frati, the Medici villas), his role was limited to that of overseer, occasionally checking on the progress. In the third, he provided only the design, leaving the execution entirely in the hands of others (the Palazzo Pubblico in Montepulciano, 1440; Santa Maria delle Grazie in Pistoia, 1452; and the Hospital of San Paolo dei Convalescenti, Florence, 1459). Only a few of the many projects attributed to him by his contemporaries and by later historians can be verified by the documents, and several must now be rejected as untenable (the Portinari Chapel and the Medici Bank in Milan, for instance), while others seem possible (the façade of Sant'Agostino in Montepulciano, c.1437; San Bartolomeo at Monte Oliveto, 1454; and the cortile of the Palazzo Vecchio, 1454–1458).

Any appraisal of Michelozzo as an architect must return to the point from which he developed: Brunelleschi. Although in his mature style he assimilated the master's elements, he represents a reaction against the linear language of Brunelleschi. Michelozzo is more facile, his spatial sense clearer than the stylistic vigor of his great contemporary. He nevertheless contributed to the diffusion of the humanistic principles enunciated by Brunelleschi and Alberti, applying them to the popular taste and creating a simple, practical, understandable style of his own which assimilated medieval forms into Renaissance architecture.

HARRIET MCNEAL CAPLOW

WORKS

c.1422, Villa at Trebbio; c.1422–1426, Church of Bosco ai Frati; Mugello, Italy. c.1425, San Girolamo, Volterra, Italy. Before 1427, Villa at Careggi, Mugello, Italy. c.1437, Sant'Agostino (façade), Montepulciano, Italy. c.1437–1452, San Marco, Florence. 1440, Palazzo Pubblico, Montepulciano, Italy. c.1442–1457, San Lorenzo; 1444–1455, Santissima Annunziata; 1444–1459, Medici Palace; c.1444–?, Palazzo Vecchio, Dogana; c.1445–?, Santa Croce; Florence. 1446–1452, Cathedral of Florence. 1452, Santa Maria delle Grazie, Pistoia, Italy. c.1452, Villa at Cafaggiolo, Mugello, Italy. 1454, San Bartolomeo at Monte Oliveto; 1454–1458, Palazzo Vecchio, Cortile; Florence. c.1458–1461, Villa Medici, Fiesole, Italy. 1459, San Paolo dei Convalescenti Hospital, Florence. 1461–1464, City Walls and Fortifications, Dubrovnik.

BIBLIOGRAPHY

CAPLOW, HARRIET MCNEAL 1972 "Michelozzo at Ragusa: New Documents and Revaluations." *Journal of the Society of Architectural Historians* 31, no. 2:108–119.

CAPLOW, HARRIET MCNEAL (1970)1977 *Michelozzo.* Reprint. New York: Garland.

FABRICZY, CORNELIUS VON 1904 "Michelozzo di Bartolomeo." *Jahrbuch der Königlich Preussischen Kunstsammlungen* 25:34–110.

GOMBRICH, E. H. 1960 "The Early Medici as Patrons of Art." Pages 279–311 in E. J. Jacob (editor), *Italian Renaissance Studies: A Tribute to the Late Cecilia M. Ady.* London: Faber.

GORI-MONTANELLI, LORENZO 1957 *Brunelleschi e Michelozzo.* Florence: Olschki.

HEYDENREICH, L. H. 1931 "Die Tribuna der SS. Annunziata in Florenz." *Mitteilungen des Kunsthistorischen Institutes* 3:268–285.

HEYDENREICH, L. H. 1938 "Gedanken über Michelozzo di Bartolomeo." Pages 264–290 in *Festschrift Wilhelm Pinder.* Leipzig: Seemann.

HYMAN, ISABELLE 1977 *Fifteenth Century Florentine Studies: The Palazzo Medici and a Ledger for the Church of San Lorenzo.* New York: Garland.

MORISANI, OTTAVIO 1951 *Michelozzo architetto.* Turin: Einaudi.

SAALMAN, HOWARD 1965 "The Palazzo Comunale in Montepulciano." *Zeitschrift für Kunstgeschichte* 28:1–46.

SAALMAN, HOWARD 1966*a* "Michelozzo Studies: I. Michelozzo at Santa Croce." *Burlington Magazine* 108:242–250.

SAALMAN, HOWARD 1966*b* "Tommaso Spinelli, Michelozzo, Manetti and Rossellino." *Journal of the Society of Architectural Historians* 25, no. 3:151–164.

SAALMAN, HOWARD 1968 "Michelozzo Studies: The Florentine Mint." Pages 140–142 in Antje Kosegarten and Peter Tigler (editors), *Zeitschrift Ulrich Middeldorf.* Berlin: De Gruyter.

VASARI, GIORGIO (1568)1973 *Le opere di Giòrgio Vasari, con nuove annotazioni e commenti.* 9 vols. Edited by G. Milanesi. Reprint. Florence: Sansoni. Originally published in 1550 with the title *Le vite de piv eccelenti architetti.* There are many English translations and selections from Vasari's *Lives;* the standard one by G. du C. de Vere was published in ten volumes in London by the Medici Society in 1912–1915.

MICHETTI, NICOLA

Nicola Michetti (c.1675–1758) figures prominently among CARLO FONTANA's pupils, who extended the tradition of Roman baroque architecture into the eighteenth century. Michetti was born in Rome between 1672 and 1681. His architectural practice, extending over a period of more than fifty years (from approximately 1705 to his death in 1758), can be conveniently divided into five periods. In the first of these, roughly between 1704 and 1713, he was involved in projects which were outgrowths of his training in studio. Michetti's earliest known design is an unexecuted project for the Trevi Fountain (1704), which clearly shows the influence of his master. The most significant early commissions he received were chapels for two Roman patrons, the Rospigliosi

(1710-1719) family and Cardinal Giuseppe Sacripante (1712), in which architecture, painting and sculpture are orchestrated to create illusionistic compositions which have their source in the work of GIOVANNI LORENZO BERNINI. Also during this time Michetti furnished designs and supervised work on festival decorations for Cardinal Ottoboni.

In a second period, between 1713 and his departure for Russia in 1718, he was engaged in two large-scale projects: an oval-plan church erected in Zagarolo (1717–1723) and the preparation of a model for his unexecuted design for the Sacristy of Saint Peter's (1715). Both of these designs bear comparison with the work of Michetti's great contemporary, FILIPPO JUVARRA. Between 1718 and 1723 Michetti was in Russia, where he worked for Peter the Great, primarily in the new imperial capital of Saint Petersburg. In the service of the czar, Michetti built two imposing summer palaces at Tallin (1718–1720) in Estonia and Strelna (1720–1723) near Leningrad, and laid out extensive gardens in the French style at Peterhof (1719–1723); other grand but unexecuted projects are known from his drawings in the Hermitage Museum. Michetti played an important role in introducing baroque architecture to Russia and laid the foundation for the accomplishments of BARTOLOMMEO RASTRELLI in the next generation.

The ten years following Michetti's return from Russia, especially those between 1729 and 1733, were his most productive. In recognition of his stature as architect of the czar, Michetti was elected to the Academy of Saint Luke in 1725. Between 1731 and 1732 he built an imposing new façade for the Colonna Palace, perhaps his most successful design. The freestanding corner pavilion of the palace contains one of the finest secular spaces of eighteenth-century Rome. Its airy lightness, scenographic effects of mural transparancy and exquisite stuccoes bear comparison with contemporary designs by Juvarra in Piedmont. At the same time Michetti was also producing ephemeral designs for festivals and the theatre, which were recorded in prints. In 1729 he designed the elaborate sets for a play entitled *Carlo Magno* which was performed in Cardinal Ottoboni's theatre in the Cancelleria, and between 1730 and 1733, as architect of the Colonna family, he was responsible for six large-scale fireworks displays for the *Festa della Chinea.* After 1733, and until his death in 1758, Michetti held two salaried positions as architect of both the *Camera Apostolica* and the Theatine Order, which demanded most of his attention. The spare and utilitarian *Polveriera,* or gunpowder magazine, he built just inside the Porta San Paolo in 1752 characterizes his work for the papal administration, while the monumental staircase of his last building, the Monastery of Sant'Andrea della Valle (1755–1757), is representative of his activity in the service of the Theatines.

Michetti's respect for the classical orders and his predeliction for scenographic compositions remain constant through his career, and constitute the essence of his personal style. At the same time, he showed himself to be unusually receptive to a variety of influences, both native and foreign, and capable of incorporating them into an imaginative synthesis which reveals the richness and complexity of late baroque design. Such a synthesis is evident in an early work like the Rospigliosi Chapel, which betrays his study of Bernini and ANDREA POZZO, as well as in a mature design, like the monumental plan for the gardens at Peterhof, so profoundly influenced by ANDRÉ LE NOSTRE and JEAN BAPTISTE ALEXANDRE LE BLOND. Michetti also actively contributed to the dissemination of the grand Roman tradition of architecture; along with FISCHER VON ERLACH, JAMES GIBBS, LUCAS VON HILDEBRANDT, and other pupils of Carlo Fontana, he played a major role in exporting what might be called an international style of late baroque design to northern Europe.

JOHN PINTO

WORKS

1708–1715, Santi XII Apostoli (completion); 1710–1719, San Francesco a Ripa (Rospigliosi Chapel); 1712, Sant'Ignazio (Sacripante Chapel); *1714, Teatro Pallacorda; 1714–1718, Palazzo Montecitorio (completion); Rome. 1717–1723, San Pietro, Zagarolo, Italy. 1718–1720, Katharinental, Tallin, Estonia. 1719–1723, Peterhof (gardens and fountains), Russia. 1720–1723, Palace and Gardens, Strelna, Russia. 1731–1732, Palazzo Colonna (west façade), Rome. 1732, San Pietro, Castel San Pietro Romano. 1733, Villa Corsini, Anzio, Italy. 1752, Porta San Paolo (gunpowder magazine); 1755–1757, Monastery of Sant'Andrea della Valle, Rome.

BIBLIOGRAPHY

GRABAR', IGOR' EMMANUILOVICH 1909 Volume 3 in *Istoriia russkago iskusstva.* Moscow: Knebel.

LAVAGNINO, EMILIO 1942 "Palazzo Colonna e l'architetto romano Niccolò Michetti." *Capitolium* 17:139–147.

PANSECCHI, FIORELLA 1962 "Il modello della cappella Pallavicini Rospigliosi in S. Francesco a Ripa." *Bollettino dei Musei Comunali di Roma* 9:21–31.

PINTO, JOHN 1977 "An Early Project by Nicola Michetti for the Trevi Fountain." *Burlington Magazine* 119:853–857.

PINTO, JOHN 1979 "An Early Design by Nicola Michetti: The Sacripante Chapel in the Roman Church of S. Ignazio." *Journal of the Society of Architectural Historians* 38:375–381.

PINTO, JOHN 1980 "Nicola Michetti and Ephemeral Design in Eighteenth Century Rome." Pages 289–

322 in Henry A. Millon (editor), *Studies in Italian Art and Architecture, 15th through 18th Centuries.* Cambridge, Mass.: M.I.T. Press.

VORONIKHINA, ANNA NIKOLAEVNA 1972 *Peterburg i ego okrestnosti v chertezhakh i risunkakh arkhitektorov pervoi treti XVIII veka.* St. Petersburg (Leningrad): Avrora.

MICKLETHWAITE, J. T.

John Thomas Micklethwaite (1843–1906) was articled to GEORGE GILBERT SCOTT in 1862. He entered independent practice in 1869 and worked in partnership with Somers Clarke, Junior, from 1876 to 1892 and with Sir Charles Nicholson from 1893 to 1894. A liturgical scholar and antiquary, he designed almost exclusively ecclesiastical buildings. A patron of C. E. Kempe, the glass-painter and church craftsman, he contributed frequently to architectural and antiquarian journals and was a founding member of the Alcuin Club, the Henry Bradshaw Society, and the Saint Paul's Ecclesiological Society. His churches are noble and satisfying, distinguished by qualities of refinement in design and materials and "bald common sense" (W. R. LETHABY), derived from the school of late Gothic historicists led by GEORGE F. BODLEY, of which Micklethwaite and Somers Clark were conspicuous members. He is buried in the west cloister of Westminster Abbey.

ANTHONY SYMONDSON

WORKS

1873–1874, Saint Anne's, Wrenthorpe; 1876–1881, Saint Hilda's, Leeds; 1884, Saint John's (with Somers Clark), Horbury; Yorkshire, England. 1884, Saint John the Divine (with Clarke), Gainsborough, Lincolnshire, England. 1886, Saint Lukes, Sharlston, Yorkshire, England. 1889–1896, Saint Paul's (with Clarke), Wimbledon Park, London. 1890–1898, All Saints, Brixham, Devon, England. 1891–1893, All Saints (with Clarke), Morton, Lincolnshire, England. 1892–1893, Kirkstall Abbey (restoration), Yorkshire, England. 1895–1898, All Saints, Church Streton, Staffordshire, England. 1896–1898, Technical Schools, Wimbledon, Surrey, England. 1901, Saint Saviour's, Scarborough, Yorkshire, England. 1902, Saint Edward the Confessor's Shrine (restoration and copes, high altar frontal, and pall), Westminster Abbey; 1902, Saint Bartholomew's, East Ham; 1902, Saint Mary Magdalene's (furniture), Munster Square; 1906, Westminster Abbey (restoration of north wall, south transept, and west front; with E. D. Caroë); London.

BIBLIOGRAPHY

CLARKE, BASIL F. L. 1938 *Church Builders of the Nineteenth Century.* London: Society for Promoting Christian Knowledge.

FEASEY, H. J. (editor) 1899 *Westminster Abbey Historically Described.* London: George Bell.

LETHABY, W. R. 1906 "John Thomas Micklethwaite." *The Athenaeum* no. 4124:589–610.

MICKLETHWAITE, J. T. 1874 *Modern Parish Churches: Their Plan, Design and Furniture.* London: King.

"Obituary." 1906 *The Builder* 91:516.

MIES VAN DER ROHE, LUDWIG

Ludwig Mies van der Rohe (1886–1969), one of the most influential architects of the twentieth century, owed his early recognition as one of the founders of the Modern movement to a number of visionary projects. Although Mies emerged as one of Germany's leading architects at the end of the 1920s, his worldwide influence postdates World War II. It was then that his fame spread beyond the circles of the initiated and of the students he had taught at the Illinois Institute of Technology, Chicago, since 1938. The increasingly substantial commissions he received in the United States and abroad during the last two decades of his life were both the cause and the effect of his growing reputation. The architectural vocabulary he developed in these late buildings dignified corporate needs in an age of spectacular expansion, and Mies has become, as a consequence, one of the principal targets of current post modernist criticism.

Mies produced some of the most remarkable drawings in architectural history and was, by temperament, more an artist than a practitioner. Once attracted by a project he would pursue it with total absorption, making innumerable sketches to study just one detail. This approach required time, and more than one of his early clients lost their patience. Even in hard times, he preferred to work for others rather than compromise his aspirations, and in those rare years when the right commissions were available Mies still maintained only a small office. Even in his American period, he always shared the execution of his designs with other firms.

In the execution of his buildings, Mies was more a craftsman than a practitioner, a notable exception among his contemporaries whose revolutionary concepts were self-fulfilling prophecies of rapidly declining standards in the building trades. In contrast, Mies had an unwavering preference for substantial materials, which, combined with his exacting standards of execution, placed him within an earlier tradition.

Mies was born in Aachen, Germany, into a family of stonemasons whose principal business was burial monuments. The wide, free-standing slabs of polished stone for which Mies prepared the lettering were to re-emerge in his architecture as the interposed marble-clad wall elements that found their ultimate realization in the Barcelona Pavilion. It is not without irony that Mies, who left the renowned local Roman Catholic Latin school after three years to attend a conventional trade school, found his vocation as an apprentice in an architectural firm specializing in the mass design of pseudo-Renaissance stucco decorations. Aachen was a provincial city that enjoyed a certain patriotic reputation as a former Carolingian capital and Prussian spa, and it was natural for the gifted young draftsman to be persuaded by visiting architects from Berlin to seek his fortune in the capital. A job was arranged there for him in 1905 at a suburban town hall, where the nineteen-year-old Mies, who had learned everything about stone, bricks, and stucco, felt, as he later recalled, totally unprepared to deal with the wood paneling of the council chamber. By coincidence, BRUNO PAUL, the eminent cartoonist of *Simplizissimus* and a consummate designer of interiors, had come to Berlin in the same year to head the school of the Prussian Decorative Arts Museum, an institution that WALTER GROPIUS's granduncle had built and directed. Mies found employment in Paul's architectural office for two years until, in 1907, he secured his first commission from a client who not only mistrusted famous names but also wanted to participate in the education of a young architect, prompting him to see Italy. Mies returned sooner than intended, longing for the cloudy skies of his native latitudes, revealing in this a natural predisposition that is quite the opposite of LE CORBUSIER's Mediterranean perception of light. It explains Mies's subsequent proclivity for dissolving exteriors into glass or giving them a shallow vertical relief treatment responding to a low sun.

The Riehl House (1907), which was to be followed by several in the same Berlin suburb of Neubabelsberg, is a modest one-family affair with a high-pitched roof over a contained rectangular volume. Its most remarkable feature is the siting, perpendicular to a slope above which the house is raised by a long retaining wall that incorporates a basement façade and supports one end of the house with a deep porch. The retaining wall extending beyond the building recurred in many of Mies's later projects, particularly in its expanded version as the classic podium, as did the often ingenious exploitation of sloping sites. As a building type, the Riehl House relates much more to the local late eighteenth-century tradition of *Bürgerhäuser* than to the Anglicized country house style that HERMANN MUTHESIUS popularized at the time, the originals of which Mies may have encountered on a visit to England with the German Garden City Association. The details of the house, especially the interiors, are reminiscent of Paul's attempts at a revival of the Bierdermeier style, while other elements, such as the generous handling of planes, indicate the influence of PETER BEHRENS.

It was another one of those fortuitous coincidences in Mies's early career that Behrens had been appointed chief designer of the Allgemeine Elektrizitäts Gesellschaft (AEG), the giant German electrical concern, in the same year (1907) in which the Deutscher Werkbund, the famous designer association, was founded. Like Paul, Behrens had moved from painting and graphics to applied art and from there into architecture, but what made him a special case was that he had become the first industrial designer, in the current sense of the term, who devoted his efforts to arc lamps as well as turbine factories. In 1908, Mies joined Behrens's office in Neubabelsberg where he found other promising young architects, among them Gropius, ADOLF MEYER, and, though only in a brief guest role, Le Corbusier. The only project Mies claimed to have been responsibly involved in there was the Small Motors Factory, in 1911. The building he later appreciated most was the Assembly Plant for Large Machines (1912) which was, indeed, an exemplary modern structure, although its steel portal frames with glass and brick infill reflected common industrial practice of the time. Following the example of the Fagus buildings (1911) by Gropius, who published his collection of industrial architecture material in the 1913 Werkbund yearbook, the avant-garde of the 1920s adapted the factory vernacular that was so compatible with their reductionist impulses. Mies, however, did not expose the steel in his brick houses of those years, although he revered the Dutch architect H. P. BERLAGE's precepts about the "truth of materials." It was only after his exposure to American methods of steel construction in the late 1930s that he revived this German tradition with unprecedented refinement in his building on the IIT campus.

Of more immediate impact in 1911 was Behren's rediscovery of KARL FRIEDRICH SCHINKEL, the great neoclassicist. Behrens is said to have taken his colleagues on weekly excursions to the many remaining buildings by Schinkel in and around Berlin. The results of this preoccupation were a series of designs, from the Mannesmann Headquarters to the German Embassy, both 1911–1912, which not only pay a general homage to Schinkel but also prove in parts to be literal copies of his work. The extent of Mies's involvement in the embassy, which he maintained was limited to negotiations with the local contractors in St. Petersburg, has still to be ascertained. Even if

Mies van der Rohe.
Project for Kröller-Müller's House.
The Hague.
1912

none of these borrowings is directly attributable to Mies, he must have absorbed the lessons of Schinkel so thoroughly that a decade later he reportedly went through a rather emotional crisis trying to rid himself of this dominant influence. Whether it was then or on another occasion, Mies is known to have destroyed almost entirely the drawings and records of his early work, an act not so uncommon in the history of art. Nevertheless, the knowledge of the neoclassical vocabulary and its rules of composition are evident throughout Mies's entire body of work in his unique sense of proportion.

The last project in which Mies was involved during his association with Behrens was the residence-*cum*-gallery for the Kröller-Müllers in The Hague. There is reason to believe that Mies worked rather independently on the scheme, and not only because of its similarities to his own subsequent version. Persuaded by Mrs. Kröller-Müller, he was probably not too reluctant to undertake an alternative design on his own account even if it meant leaving Behrens's office. In this second, even more palatial scheme of 1912, the exterior appears also to be more classical, and the somewhat archaic compactness of the first proposal had given way to a loose arangement of components reminiscent of such Schinkelesque groupings as the gardener's house and Roman baths at Charlottenhof in Potsdam. However, Mies's project is dominated by a strong horizontal emphasis, which, together with a pronounced serialization of such façade elements as the upper story windows, points to elements of FRANK LLOYD WRIGHT's work. Mies always acknowledged the historical impact of the Wasmuth publication of 1910 and the exhibition of 1911 in which the American architect burst upon his generation of Europeans. Moreover, in the Netherlands he had met the only architect to whom he was ever willing to concede the role of mentor, Berlage, who showed him sketches from his recent visit to America.

The second scheme for the Kröller-Müllers did not meet with the approval of the clients, and the entire project was abandoned. but Mies, having left Behrens's office (which he had left once before for almost a year on account of personal differences with another staff member), must have felt confident enough to establish his own practice, for which he could expect to find a sufficient number of clients in the affluent circles of the upper middle class into which he was about to marry in 1913. Despite the scarcity of personal documents from this period, one can assume that Mies also had access to quite diverse and cosmopolitan circles of young intellectuals and artists such as the dancer Mary Wigman and the psychologist Hans Prinzhorn. His friendship with Wilhelm Lehmbruck, which was to last only a few years until the early death of the sculptor, must have been particularly important to Mies, who throughout his life showed a particular affinity to sculpture and a predilection for Lehmbruck's work.

At the outbreak of World War I, Mies had completed two houses (1913, 1914) and had made plans for his own not insubstantial house (1914) in one of the more distant but not less fashionable suburbs of Berlin. At the age of twenty-eight, he saw the promise of a prosperous career and a stimulating life about to be redeemed when history intervened and relegated him to a period of stagnation, a fate that would repeat itself several times in his life and in the lives of members of his generation. Mies was drafted and served with an engineering unit assigned to maintain railroads on the Balkan front. When he returned to civilian life, he was confronted, like everyone else, with a drastically changed professional and personal situation. He was the father of three daughters born during the war, which his marriage, however, had not survived. Mies stayed by himself in the apartment which was located in an old residential area near the center of Berlin that was to serve him for the next twenty years as both living quarters and office space. Work was no longer to be expected from most of his former clients, but he found at least one undaunted optimist who commissioned a house. Confirming for the architect as well as for the client the rule that people always start where they left off before a catastrophe, the Kempner House (1919) is basically a descendant of Mies's prewar houses despite its flat roof and arched loggia. This allusion to the Italianate classicism of the Schinkelschule is the last identifiable quotation Mies permitted himself before accepting the Modern movement's dogma of historicism as the original sin.

As the political and economic disintegration that followed Germany's defeat spread throughout the entire social structure, the intellectual revolution also gathered momentum, releasing an unprecedented wave of creative talent. Artists grouped and regrouped, following currents of artistic and political ideologies, and maintained the ferment that gave the 1920s their notoriety. Mies seems to have been at first more an observer than a participant, as was his nature, and evolved only gradually into the role of the activist, a role which he performed, however, by the mid-1920s, with remarkable sagacity. His earliest affiliations can be traced to personal contacts that prompted him to assist friends or their deserving causes, ranging from the Liga für Unabhängigen Film (League for Independent Film) to the Gesellschaft für Deutsch-Sowjetische Freundschaft (Society for German-Soviet Friendship). In the case of the Novembergruppe, which he joined in 1922 and whose president he became the following year, there may have been professional reasons as well as personal connections, because this large association of avant-garde artists, which took its name after the month of the 1918 German revolution, more for symbolic than political reasons, not only included many architects but also exhibited their work in its major annual show at the Grosse Berliner Kunstausstellung. Among the architects were BRUNO TAUT and MAX TAUT, HANS AND WASSILI LUCKHARDT, HANS POELZIG, HUGO HÄRING, ERIC MENDELSOHN, Gropius, Adolf Meyer, and LUDWIG HILBERSEIMER, representing the whole range of emerging trends, from so-called Expressionistic to functionalist architecture. What united the various factions were their common propagandistic goals, for at a time when even the most conventional buildings had little chance to be realized, their revolutionary ideas needed, above all, exposure and dissemination.

Mies van der Rohe.
Project for Friedrichstrasse Office Building.
Berlin.
1921

Mies's famous Five Projects (1921–1923) were produced in a format that lent itself to exhibition, specifically in competition with paintings and sculptures, which explains the unusual dimensions of some of the drawings, which exceed eight feet in length, as well as their powerful rendering in charcoal or pastel. The first of the projects, the Friedrichstrasse Office Building (1921), was not as ambitious in its presentation because it was originally an entry for a competition held in January 1922. The program called for a high-rise office building on a specific site adjoining the Friedrichstrasse railroad station in the center of Berlin. The triangular shape of the lot was most congenial to the Expressionistic solutions of many participants, such as Mies's daring and, at the time, hardly realizable concept of a totally glass-enclosed structure which created, with its broken, sharp-edged surfaces, the image of a crystal, a favorite symbol of the Expressionists. It is no coincidence that the project, together with a statement by Mies, was first reproduced in *Frühlicht,* the magazine published by Bruno Taut, whose early involvement in glass architecture and connection with PAUL SCHEERBART, the author of a treatise on glass architecture, may have been the source of Mies's inspiration.

The experimental nature of Mies's ideas is especially apparent in the second project, the Glass Skyscraper (1922), where he tried to explore the refractory potential of vast undulating glass surfaces. Both projects show only scant indications of the supporting structure, except that all vertical members are set back from the glass skin to reinforce its autonomy as well as the appearance of transparency and weightlessness of the entire building. The curvilinear plan of the Glass Skyscraper resembles similar configurations in projects by Häring, the originator of so-called organic architecture, who for some time used office space in Mies's apartment where they were, as Häring later recalled, more occupied with discussions than with commissions. To the followers of the Modern movement, these projects must have appeared as nothing less than manifestoes, proclaiming an irrevocable departure from past tradition and momentum toward a morally better world where architecture would purge itself from the hypocrisy of stucco façades and reveal its innermost structure with honesty. Mies shared these aspirations to the extent that he exploited the contrast between his visionary projects and their dreary surroundings with the help of the photomontage technique; possibly suggested by the work of his Dadaist friends, especially Hannah Höch. The Five Projects should, however, not be taken for a planned series but rather as incidental opportunities for experimentation which Mies succeeded in turning into programmatic statements.

The third project, the Concrete Office Building (1922), is a bold adaptation of a utilitarian building type, the warehouse, to office use. Rows of concrete posts support concrete beams and floor slabs which are enclosed by continuous concrete parapets and glass bands, the first radical formulation of the ribbon window. Unlike the glass skyscrapers, this building conveys solidity. Its elevations are articulated in depth, their dominating horizontality given rhythmic scale. Separation from the ground is achieved by the setback of the basement, and the top is terminated by the recessed roof slab. A detail such as the entrance, barely defined by the flight of steps in the cut-out portion of the long side, illustrates the quintessential Miesian approach: simplicity for the sake of monumentality. Although never realized by himself in any form, the concept was to become one of the most often applied formulas of twentieth-century architecture. Mies's phrase "skin and bone" structures was to become equally popular; he first used it in one of his briefest programmatic statements, accompanying the publication of the Concrete Office Building in G, the *Zeitschrift für elementare Gestaltung* (Magazine for Elementary Creation). The shortlived magazine, which Mies helped edit and finance, included among its editors and authors many of his friends and broadened his contacts with other avant-garde groups. ELEAZAR M. LISSITZKY, who published the Glass Skyscraper alongside a bone section in the special issue of Kurt Schwitters's *Merz* magazine which he edited, was the link to the Russian Constructivists, who held Mies in high esteem. More intimate was Mies's relationship with the Dutch painter THEO VAN DOESBURG during the latter's stay in Germany in 1921–1922. Mies, who by origin and temperament felt an affinity for all things Dutch (when he added his mother's maiden name "Rohe" to his family name he linked it with the Dutch "van der") was certainly attracted by the work of the *De Stijl* group. Although he resisted offers to join it, he accepted van Doesburg's invitation to participate in the exhibition of *De Stijl* architects in Léonce Rosenberg's Galérie de l'Effort Moderne in Paris in 1923.

Of the two last projects, the Brick Country House (1923) has always been cited as the example that shows the strongest *De Stijl* influence in Mies's work; it prompted Alfred Barr of the Museum of Modern Art to a direct comparison with van Doesburg's painting *Rhythms of a Russian Dance* of 1919. The similarity, however intentional, is only superficial because the highly stylized plan does not actually represent the interposed walls and free-flowing space it suggests. As the perspective rendering shows, the Brick Country House is, on the contrary, an intricate composition of cubic volumes, expanding and contracting along the long axis from the living quarters to the service areas. The movement follows, vertically as well as horizontally, the sloping terrain that has been stabilized by long retaining walls which seem to extend beyond the limits of the drawing. On the other hand, the Concrete Country House (1923), more compact by virtue of its material, appears nevertheless looser and more dynamic in the arrangement of its components, which exploit the changing levels of the site in a swastika configuration, forming courts open to different directions. The strong horizontal emphasis in the long cantilevered roofs above the living and entrance areas as well as in the slit windows of the basement level, with the massive chimney acting as the only vertical counterweight, seems to echo Wright's early houses. Although both projects are likely to have been produced in the course of 1923, it remains uncertain whether there was a distinct sequence and whether they were intended for the same site and the same client, the architect himself or the publisher Gustav Kiepenheuer. The Brick Country House relates, by virtue of its material, to the Wolf, Lange, and Esters houses; the Concrete Country House joined the other early projects in the exhibitions of 1923: in Berlin, where Mies exhibited for the first time with the Novembergruppe; in Weimar, where he participated at Gropius's invitation in the International Architecture Exhibition, one of the events of the Bauhaus's Third Anniversary celebrations; and in Paris, at the *De Stijl* architecture exhibition.

As effective as these propagandistic efforts of exhibition and publication were in establishing the profile of the architectural avant-garde, they did not produce the private commissions which the political stabilization and economic improvement of the mid-1920s had seemed to promise. The public institutions, administered by liberals and socialists, who identified their progressive causes with that of the new architecture, appeared to be the more sympathetic clients. Mies, who at that time seriously considered succeeding Bruno Taut as head of the Magdeburg building department, and Häring (who had dissuaded him) decided, instead, to form a politically influential group of the most renowned modern architects in Berlin, which came to be known as the Zehner Ring. The members, who always met in Mies's apartment, included OTTO BARTNING, WALTER CURT BEHRENDT, Häring (who became the secretary of the group after it became a nationwide organization in 1926), Hilberseimer, Mendelsohn, Poelzig, and the Taut brothers. One of their first targets was the city building department of Berlin, which, in 1925, had a new director, MARTIN WAGNER, who shared their aspirations and initiated numerous housing projects with the participation of Ring members. Mies, who designed only one project, four rather plain buildings on the Afrikanische Strasse (1926–1927), never seemed much attracted by low-cost housing developments. In fact, in his policy statement on the Weissenhof exhibition in Stuttgart (1927), he asserted explicitly the prerogatives of architectural design over the technological methods of "standardization and rationalization," which were seen by most of his contemporaries as the only means to combat the housing shortage.

Another target of the Ring was the Werkbund, which, while still recognized as a cultural institution of national importance, had lost much of its luster by the mid-1920s. Confronted with the threat of secession of its younger members, it decided to rejuvenate its executive committee by electing Mies, who had already been chosen artistic director of the Weissenhof exhibition, first vice president in 1926 and other members of the Ring to the committee in the following years. The Werkbund, however, experienced not only rejuvenation but also a reorientation of its program, from the improvement of industrial design and crafts standards to the promotion of the new architecture. The success of the Ring group was based on its members's shared belief in one common politically and culturally reactionary enemy; individually, they represented quite different architectural creeds, although by the mid-1920s the emerging pragmatism known as *Neue Sachlichkeit* had made many converts. Politically, the members displayed a similar diversity, ranging from the architect *engagé,* such as Hilberseimer, Mies's lifelong interlocutor, who for many years wrote for the *Sozialistische Monatshefte* (Socialist Monthly), to the uncommitted sympathizer, like Mies himself.

Even his most political commission, the monument for Karl Liebknecht and Rosa Luxemburg (1926), is not likely to have had any other origin but his personal contact with the chairman of the Communist Party's monument committee, Eduard Fuchs, the eminent collector and art historian, for whom Mies remodeled the house he had built in 1911 for the Perls family. Except for its hammer and sickle emblem, the monument itself was meant to convey a more universal aspect of terrorism—the wall as symbolic of all firing-squad executions. Dissolved into projecting and receding volumes, surfaced with used split bricks, and supported by invisible steel frames, the wall conveys, at the same time, the image of a monumental accumulation of gravestones.

Nothing, however, did more to establish Mies's reputation as the leading figure of the avant-garde than his role as director of the Weissenhof exhibition in Stuttgart. Organized under the auspices of the Deutscher Werkbund, this first full-scale demonstration of the new architecture, which included not only all leading German practitioners but also such major foreign modernists as Le Corbusier, J. J. P. OUD, MARTINUS STAM, VICTOR BOURGEOIS, and JOSEF FRANK, received a great amount of publicity outside the professional press and beyond the borders. The city of Stuttgart, which had been persuaded by the local Werkbund chapter to assign funds to the exhibition project originally allocated a communal housing development, was gratified by the number of visitors and by the official interest shown in the government's evaluation of the experimental construction methods employed by almost all participants. In addition to his organizational role, Mies made two specific contributions. He designed the only apartment building among the thirty-three single or row houses, an elongated slab on the hill crowning the exhibition site, and he also had developed the master plan.

The first site plan shows a distinctly sculptural treatment of the hillside, transforming it into layers of staggered terraces. Restrained by budget limitations, his final plan conforms more to the conventional layout of the villa quarters of German cities, and only the mandatory flat roofs of the executed houses echo the Mediterranean hill-town effect originally intended. Abiding by the norms established for public housing, Mies's apartment building was not an exceptionally innovative solu-

Mies van der Rohe. Werkbund Exposition. Stuttgart, Germany. 1927

tion, although the exhibition budget offered him enough latitude to employ a steel skeleton structure. As a result, he was able to enlarge the window surfaces considerably and to provide an unusual degree of flexibility in the internal wall arrangement. It was this latter aspect that Mies emphasized in his program statement as most relevant to the exhibition's central theme, the "New Dwelling," which he regarded as "spiritual" and part of a continuing "battle for new forms of living."

All the houses were furnished to some extent, and the actual housing was supplemented by exhibitions on new building materials and modern industrial design. Lack of funds and time frustrated many architects who were eager to develop new furniture and to present complete modern interiors. Mies succeeded at least in introducing the first of his famous tubular steel chairs, which, based on ideas by MARCEL BREUER and Stam, was also the first true cantilevered chair. The numerous variations that were to follow as well as the classic chairs for the Barcelona Pavilion (1929) and the Tugendhat House (1928–1930) make Mies one of the most outstanding furniture designers of the Modern movement.

To demonstrate the flexibility of the interior spaces, he also equipped the living rooms in his apartment building with movable veneered partitions, elements he was to develop into the space-defining interposed walls of the Barcelona Pavilion and the Tugendhat House. A prefiguration of the Barcelona Pavilion, not only by the nature of its transparent partitions but also in parts of the plan, appears in the glass industries display, one of the industrial materials presentations he designed for the Weissenhof exhibition. Even the cruciform column of the Barcelona Pavilion had its antecedent in a display element for wallpaper in another section.

The Weissenhof exhibition was also in one other respect an important event in Mies's career as it marked the beginning of his close professional and personal relationship with Lilly Reich, which was to last until his departure for the United States. This period included the most productive years of his practice in Germany. Through her presence (she is said to have been the only person in his office with whom he liked to discuss his work) and her connections which led to various commissions, Reich's contribution to this creative phase can hardly be overestimated. A talented designer herself, with experience at the Wiener Werkstätte under JOSEF HOFFMANN before World War I, she had been active in the Werkbund for many years and was the first woman ever to be elected to its executive board. Reich had proven her organizational skills in the annual design exhibitions that she assembled on behalf of the Werkbund at the Frankfurt fair. Since her interests were fabrics and fashion, she had developed close connections to the textile industry, in particular the silk manufacturers of Krefeld. In 1927, at the *Mode der Dame* exhibition in Berlin, Mies and Reich designed the "Velvet and Silk Cafe," a sumptuous chromatic display of fabric curving around Mies's tubular steel furniture.

The next year, 1928, he built the adjoining houses of the silk manufacturers and brothers-in-law Hermann Lange and Esters in Krefeld. Both are solid residences executed in brick and set in parklike gardens. Although related to the projects of the early 1920s, these houses show much less movement in the play of cubic volumes. In 1930, Mies participated in the competition for the Country Club in Krefeld. He was asked in 1932 to rebuild the dye works of the silk manufacturers, and in 1935 to design a house for Ulrich Lange, a court house scheme that failed to receive the approval of the Nazi authorities. Finally in 1937–1938, he was commissioned to plan the administration building of the silk industries, a project he worked on until his emigration. This four-story, three-wing complex with its regular factory window pattern seems far removed from the transparency of Mies's early skyscrapers, which the commercial projects of 1928 and 1929 such as the Adam department store in Berlin, the bank building near the Stuttgart railroad station, and the second proposal for the Friedrichstrasse Office Building in Berlin still retained. This applies also to the office blocks he suggested in the only urban renewal proposal of those years, the Alexander Platz project in Berlin (1928) which in many aspects, especially in the rows of horizontal slabs, reflects the city planning ideas of his friend Hilberseimer.

However, two buildings were executed on a smaller scale that would become synonymous with Mies's architecture of the 1920s: the Barcelona Pavilion (1929) and the Tugendhat House (1928–1930). Although on the drafting boards simultaneously, these buildings were too different by nature not to have different results: the Tugendhat House is a demonstration of Mies's way of building; the Barcelona Pavilion is a manifestation of the ideas he contributed to the final evolution of modern architecture. The Tugendhat House in Brno, Czechoslovakia, was commissioned by a textile manufacturer and his wife who involved themselves enthusiastically in Mies's proposals and spared no funds for their realization. Thus, Mies had a free hand to design every detail, down to the door handles and curtain rods, which were executed in the best available materials and with the highest standards of workmanship. With his choice of precious materials and rich colors, such as golden onyx for the interposed wall in the living area or the macassar veneer for the semicircular wall around the dining table, Mies did much to alleviate the strict functionality that dominated the design. A particular tribute is paid to modern architecture's preoccupation with health and hygiene through an expensive mechanism that allowed the floor-to-ceiling window panes of the main level to be lowered into the basement, transforming the living area with its white linoleum floor into a sanatorium terrace. Despite the open-plan arrangement of the living, dining, and study areas, the spatial concept is without much complexity, and its main attraction was probably the descent from the entrance on the upper level, which also contained the master and children's bedroms, to the lower level facing a panoramic view of the city and the sloping gardens.

There are few buildings in history about which so much has been written on such scant evidence—a dozen photographs and a schematized plan—as the German Pavilion at the International Exhibition in Barcelona, Spain. The immediate approval it found with the German government and the press confirmed public acceptance of modern architecture by the end of the 1920s, and the place it occupied in the imagination of the succeeding generation of architects attests to the potency of the ideas realized in the Pavilion. Ironically, it was an afterthought prompted by the unexpected appearance of national pavilions by other participants. Originally, the exposition was to follow the nineteenth-century tradition of exhibits by industries rather than nations. Thus, the original task given to Mies as artistic director of the German section, and to Reich, his deputy, was the design of standardized components for 270 German industrial displays and to emphasize their national identity. The Pavilion was designed in an unusually brief period and erected on time despite serious budgetary and logistical difficulties. All materials, the travertine for the podium and the walls in the unroofed area, the Tinian and vert antique marble as well as the onyx for the freestanding walls in the roofed area, the frames and the panes in different colors for the glass partitions, the green and black glass that lined the large and small reflecting pools, and even the steel for the structural members, had to be brought in from Germany.

The Pavilion has generally been regarded as an architectural artifact without real purpose or specific place, yet it was determined by these factors to a decisive extent. Mies selected a particular site at the end of the major transverse axis of the exposition park where the Pavilion was in full view and offered the best view over the grounds and the city. Also, the location provided access to higher terrain in the rear of the Pavilion, which was meant to function as passageway and resting place. In addition to this public role, the Pavilion had to fulfill a representational purpose as an official reception area, for which the roofed section could be closed

Mies van der Rohe. German Pavilion and Industrial Exhibits, International Exhibition. Barcelona, Spain. 1929

Mies van der Rohe. German Pavilion and Industrial Exhibits, International Exhibition. Barcelona, Spain. 1929

off by glass screens. The principal occasion that determined the arrangement of the interior was the inaugural ceremony at which the king and queen of Spain were to sign a golden book on a table placed against the altarlike onyx wall. Perpendicular to the wall facing the reception line stood the two Barcelona chairs with their white kid leather cushions, clearly intended as an evocation of the archetypal royal throne. In the cross-bracing of the chromed furniture supports, the pre-eminence of the podium, and the balance of its proportions, the Pavilion reveals again the neoclassicist undercurrent in Mies's work. More deliberate seems the use of *De Stijl* methods of composition in the plan, with its asymmetrical—parallel or perpendicular—placement of freestanding wall elements. Yet, their ultimate function was to conduct the flow of space, perceived by Mies as a dynamic and universal medium, into and through the field established by the horizontal floor and roof planes. The tension generated by the spatial fluidity and its subtle containment points to Japanese precedents with which the Pavilion shares the contemplative nature of a serene space that seems to tolerate but a solitary viewer.

The Barcelona Pavilion, which was dismantled after the closing of the exposition, has one reduced and domesticated successor in Mies's work, the model house for a childless couple that he showed in the Berlin Building Exposition of 1931. Although the glass enclosure of the house is by necessity tighter, the placement of the walls is freer, extending horizontally beyond the roof to form an open court at the bedroom end. On the other end of the low rectangular house, one long wall joins Reich's model house, and, while both houses were to be understood as a conceptual entity, this link is also symbolic of the close connection of their designers. Mies and Reich together directed the exhibition's central presentation, "Dwelling in Our Time," and contributed designs for various industrial displays. On view in their model houses and apartments were new versions of tubular steel furniture which Mies had produced at Thonet, thus securing a source of income on which he would depend almost entirely in the coming years.

In 1931, when Mies reached the height of public recognition and was elected to the Preussische Akademie der Künste, he had not a single commission. The Depression had already struck the German economy severely, and the political events it would bring about in 1933 would prevent Mies and many other architects from competing for those opportunities that did present themselves. Too prominent in his association with the cultural endeavors of the Weimar period, Mies was unacceptable to the new Nazi regime. His entry in the Reichsbank competition of 1933 and his design for the German Pavilion at the 1934 International Exposition in Brussels must have been submitted without much hope of acceptance. Mies's withdrawal from the public scene during these years is reflected in innumerable sketches for court houses, introversions of the Barcelona Pavilion, where the walls close ever tighter around the house and its interior court as if to shut out the sound of marching boots from a last enclave of civilization.

The origin of this preoccupation goes back to his studio classes at the Bauhaus where he had introduced the court house formula as his principal teaching device both out of the conviction that the one-family house was a student's only legitimate field of experience and in reaction to the so-called scientific design methods of his predecessor at the Bauhaus, HANNES MEYER. Mies, who had been appointed director on Gropius's recommendation after Meyer's dismissal in 1930, not only calmed down the controversies inside the institution and with the city of Dessau but also introduced significant changes in the curriculum. In reducing the commercial activities of the workshops and in subordinating them to or even merging them with the architecture department, he shifted the emphasis from experimentation to instruction with a more clearly defined structure and more consistently imposed standards. Since he divided his time between the office in Berlin and his roles at the Bauhaus as director and teacher, Mies's success owed much to the support of Hilberseimer, who had taught there since 1928, and of Reich, who took over the interior design studio and the weaving workshop in 1932. In the autumn of that year, the Nazi majority in the city council forced the closing of the Bauhaus, to which Mies responded by reopening the school as a private institution in a vacant factory in Berlin. Half a year later, in the spring of 1933, it was raided by the police and threatened with another closing. In negotiations that were not without risk, Mies succeeded in averting this threat so that he and the faculty could close the Bauhaus of their own accord. Mies continued to teach students privately at his Swiss vacation retreat until late in 1934.

In the mid-1930s, Mies received several offers from the United States, among them one from Harvard University for the chair later occupied by Gropius, another from Armour Institute in Chicago for the position of director of architecture, and he was also under consideration, together with J. J. P. Oud, as Alfred Barr's choice for the architect of The Museum of Modern Art. Even though this proposition was withdrawn before it was formally made, one of the Museum's trustees, Mrs. Stanley Resor, became interested enough in Mies's work to invite him, in 1937, to visit the site in Jackson Hole, Wyoming, where she wanted him to build a vacation house. This fortuitous offer provided Mies with the opportunity to resume, in person, negotiations with his admirers in Chicago and to bring them to a conclusion tempting enough to uproot himself despite his age and unfamiliarity with foreign countries and languages.

As director of the architecture department at Armour Institute, which later became IIT, Mies was given a free hand to establish his own educational program and make his own appointments, at least with respect to Hilberseimer and Walter Peterhans, who had been head of the photography department at the Bauhaus, and also to plan the new campus and design its buildings. These arrangements were favorable enough to promise an end to years of enforced professional stagnation, but the outbreak of World War II limited his architectural contribution to the first group of campus buildings. Much of his time was devoted to teaching and especially to the development of the curriculum, which was to give the school a singular place in American architectural education. The curriculum structure is partly based on the famous Bauhaus preliminary course, devoted to the experimental investigation of the visual and tactile fundamentals and to progressive attitudes shared by most modern architects such as systematized analyses of building functions. Yet, the curriculum also reveals Mies's more traditional preferences such as emphasis on the instructional value of exacting drawing techniques and, above all, on his personal philosophies. As stated in the published programs, architecture was to be considered ultimately an art that must transcend its utilitarian foundations and maintain its consanguinity with the other arts; and, further, architecture was authentic only if it genuinely expressed the *Zeitgeist.* In order "to recognize the sustaining and compelling forces of his times" the student was advised to make use of the optional year that had been added to the four-year program. Mies, who closed his inaugural address at Armour Institute by quoting Saint Augustine's dictum, "Beauty is the Splendor of Truth," had always been associated with the philosophy of the Fathers of the Church. Yet, although his interest in and contacts with Roman Catholic thinkers and theologians dates back to the early 1920s, there is no evidence that this predilection was an exclusive and methodical pursuit in itself. What mattered to him was the relevance of the Thomistic reinterpretation of Aristotelian reason to his search for philosophical foundations that would support his ideal of an architecture of order, clarity, and universality.

Mies's deep involvement in architectural education furthered the systematization of his own thoughts, and the process directly influenced the character of the work of his last three decades, as did, indirectly, the collaboration of his former students in his office. Although he believed as much as ever that "God is in the detail," Mies's choice among the commissions he was offered in America indicates a growing preference for large-scale projects. In fact, he declined, with three exceptions, all requests for one-family houses. In his first project for IIT, the campus master plan (1939–1941), Mies responded to the street grid out of which the site had been carved by imposing his own modular grid, which was not only to organize the placement of the individual buildings but also the structural disposition of the buildings themselves. As if in deference to the Anglo-Saxon campus tradition, the central group is laid out in classic axial symmetry, a scarcely modern principle that Mies had dared to employ in projects of the 1930s. Its effect here, however, would have been mitigated by the buildings' differentiations in volume and their distances from each other. The subtle massing and grouping of buildings in and around open spaces which attest to Mies's sculptural sensibilities was brought to perfection in many later projects. By the end of the 1940s, Mies had completed half a dozen IIT buildings, but he was not to be entrusted with most of the others. The most regrettable cancellation was the Library and Administration Building (1944), which would have surpassed its predecessors on the campus not only in size but also in concept. The large spans of its longitudinal bays would have created a vast interior space interrupted only by a mezzanine platform and an atrium court. Its construction, steel frame with brick and glass infill, would have followed the industrial vocabulary Mies had adopted for the campus, but the materials would have been visible as clearly on the inside as on the outside. This ultimate homage to Berlage's "honesty of structure" doctrine showed Mies's immense care for the detail, from the famous corner of the steel frame to the elaborate joints with infill material.

Toward the end of the 1940s, Mies began to receive commissions for apartment buildings from a young developer, Herbert Greenwald, who remained until his early death in 1961 Mies's enthusiastic client, entrusting him with such substantial projects as the Lafayette Park redevelopment scheme in Detroit (1955–1956). The first of the apartment house projects, Promontory Apartments in Chicago (1946–1949), still seems, with its exposed concrete frame and brick spandrels, a somewhat transitional solution in comparison to the second commission, the 860–880 Lake Shore Drive Apartments (1948–1951), which became the prototypical Miesian high-rise structure. The two identical towers, each twenty-six stories high and placed perpendicular to each other, have all the features that would recur in the various apartment and office buildings of the next two decades: the open ground level, revealing the elevator shafts; the flat roof termination of the cubic volume; the flexible arangement of the floor spaces around the utility core; and the external expression of the structure's modular configuration. Much copied and lately maligned, Mies's solution for the curtain wall was an ingenious response to inherent practical problems as well as to Mies's aesthetic intentions: The skin of the Lake Shore Drive Apartment Towers reveals clearly the structural bays, three on one side and five on the other, beneath the curtain of I-beam mullions which subdivide the bays further into four segments and anchor the window frames and the fascia plates of the floors. Admittedly, these somber technological surfaces have little in common with the crystal

Mies van der Rohe. Lake Shore Drive Apartments (with others). Chicago. 1948–1951

images of his early skyscraper projects, but the modular articulation of the skin gave Mies's tall buildings scale, making their configurations readable and thus less overpowering.

The most notable among the over three dozen high-rise apartment and office buildings that were designed in Mies's office during the 1950s and 1960s are the Commonwealth Promenade Apartments in Chicago (1953–1956), in which the solutions for structure and skin were further refined; the Seagram Building in New York (1954–1958), Mies's first and still unsurpassed office building that owes much of its reputation to the noble materials used in its construction, such as the bronze for its skin; and the Toronto-Dominion Center (1965) and the Chicago Federal Center (1959–1973), both of which comprise a group of two high-rise buildings flanking a single-story, clear-span building with a specific function, a banking facility in the first, a post office in the second.

The clear-span hall, the unobstructed space enclosure, is the other major theme that occupied Mies's last two decades. Its origin can be seen in the project of a Museum for a Small City (1942), in which Mies attempted to apply the formula of the Barcelona Pavilion to a much larger roofed area. Whereas the eight columns of the Pavilion could easily be integrated into the spatial composition, the rows of supports in the museum project assumed a rhythmic presence of their own that contravened the flow of space around the freestanding wall elements. The weekend house Mies designed for Edith Farnsworth in Plano, Illinois (1945–1950), pointed to the solution of an external support for the roof, for in the Farnsworth House the supporting I-beams are welded to the

Mies van der Rohe. Seagram Building (with others). New York. 1954–1958

fascias of the roof and floor frames, the latter being raised above the ground. Enclosed for two-thirds of its perimeter by floor-to-ceiling glass panes, the white steel cage appears in its transparency and lightness to hover above its bucolic site.

The next step in Mies's search for a universal enclosure was Crown Hall (1950–1956), where pairs of exterior I-beams are connected at their tops to steel plate girders from which the roof is suspended. Completed in 1956 as one of his last buildings on the IIT campus, Crown Hall houses the schools of architecture, town planning, and design. The large unobstructed glass-enclosed main level, which is divided in half by low partitions at the entrance area, rests on an independent basement structure, a feature that further confirms the enveloping nature of the building's exterior. On an even larger scale, using open roof trusses, the same solution is applied to the 1953 project for the National Theater in Mannheim, Germany. Another point of departure was the roof structure itself, which, given the necessary rigidity, would allow further reduction in the number of support points. In the Fifty-by-Fifty-Foot-Square-House study project (1950–1951), the steel roof consists of an egg-crate grid welded to the underside of a continuous plate, which was considered rigid enough to be supported by one peripheral column at the center of each side. The project for the Chicago Convention Hall (1953–1954) carried this principle to the outer limits in size and material with its thirty-foot-deep two-directional truss that was to span a 720-foot-square space.

Mies developed a variation of the coffered roof in reinforced concrete for the 1957 Bacardi Office Building project in Cuba, which links all previous investigations with Mies's last and only work executed in his native country after his emigration, the New National Gallery in Berlin (1962–1968). In its design one can also detect a return to neoclassicist sources, for what Mies proposed—the horizontal separation of the museum functions of temporary exhibitions and permanent collection—amounted to nothing less than a "temple on a podium scheme. Yet, all classical allusions notwithstanding, the enormous steel structure of the exhibition hall impresses, above all, as a monumental feat of twentieth-century engineering, which one associates with America rather than Europe. Its 213-square-foot roof—a grid of girders welded to a continuous plate and supported at its edges by only two cruciform columns on each side—is the first rigid plate ever executed at that scale in construction history. Inside, behind the recessed glass enclosure, interposed wall elements were again to act as regulators of the space continuum, a role in this case assumed by the exhibition wall panels which, suspended from the roof girders, would offer almost infinite spatial arrangements. Mies himself worked on the proposals made for the first exhibition, but never saw it installed, as he died not long after the inauguration of the New National Gallery.

The architectural language Mies sought to formulate in his American work was, if not by intent then by implication, of universal applicability, and was, in fact, almost immediately adopted by other architects here and abroad. Among them, the firm of SKIDMORE, OWINGS, AND MERRILL produced the most original and successful interpretations of Mies's ideas during the 1950s and 1960s, while some of the more recent projects carried out by former students, notably Myron Goldsmith in the firm's Chicago office, continued to maintain Mies's influence. His impact in Chicago had been the most immediate and also lasted the longest; there, his successor firm, a partnership of his former associates and his grandson, still flourishes under the name Fujikawa, Conterato, Lohan. Other associates have risen to the top of leading firms, such as Jacques Brownson and Gene Summers at C. F. Murphy Associates.

Yet, as so often happens with great men, Mies's posthumous reputation was eclipsed by the shadow of his own fame, leaving his work to be rediscovered and reassessed. With all his drawings and records in the custody of the Mies van der Rohe Archive at The Museum of Modern Art, the evidence is at hand for such future interest.

LUDWIG GLAESER

Mies van der Rohe. New National Gallery. Berlin. 1962–1968

WORKS

1907, Riehl House, Neubabelsberg; 1911, Perls House (later Fuchs House), Zehlendorf; 1913, House, Heerstrasse; 1914, Urbig House, Neubabelsberg; 1919–1921, Kempner House; Berlin. 1925–1926, Wolf House, Guben, Germany. *1926, Monument to Karl Liebknecht and Rosa Luxemburg, Berlin. 1927, Apartment House, Werkbund Exposition, Stuttgart, Germany. 1927, Silk Exhibit (with Reich), Exposition de la Mode, Berlin. 1928, Esters House; 1928, Lange House; Krefeld, Germany. 1928–1930, Tugendhat House, Brno, Czechoslovakia. *1929, German Pavilion and Industrial Exhibits, (International Exhibition), Barcelona, Spain. *1931, Model House and Apartment, Berlin Building Exposition. 1939–1941, Master Plan; 1942–1943, Metals Research Building (with others); 1944–1946, Engineering Research Building (with others); 1945–1946, Alumni Memorial Hall (with others); 1945–1946, Chemistry Building; 1945–1946, Metallurgical and Chemical Engineering Building (with others); 1945–1950, Boiler Plant; Illinois Institute of Technology, Chicago. 1945–1950, Farnsworth House, Plano, Ill. 1946–1949, Promontory Apartments (with others); 1948–1951, 860 and 880 Lake Shore Drive Apartments (with others); 1950–1956, Crown Hall (with others), Illinois Institute of Technology; 1953–1956, Commonwealth Promenade Apartments (with others); Chicago. 1954–1958, Cullinan Hall (with others), Museum of Fine Arts, Houston, Tex. 1954–1958, Seagram Building (with others), New York. 1955–1956, Lafayette Park Housing Development, Detroit, Mich. 1957–1961, Bacardi Office Building, Mexico City. 1959–1973, Chicago Federal Center (with others). 1960–1963, American Federal Savings and Loan Association (with others), Des Moines, Iowa. 1962–1968, New National Gallery, Berlin. 1963–1969 Toronto-Dominion Centre (with others).

BIBLIOGRAPHY

BLASER, WERNER 1977 *Mies van der Rohe: Principles and School.* Basel: Birkhäuser.

CARTER, PETER 1974 *Mies van der Rohe at Work.* New York: Praeger.

DREXLER, ARTHUR 1960 *Ludwig Mies van der Rohe.* New York: Braziller.

GLAESER, LUDWIG 1977 *Ludwig Mies van der Rohe: Furniture and Furniture Drawings.* New York: Museum of Modern Art.

HILBERSEIMER, LUDWIG 1956 *Ludwig Mies van der Rohe.* Chicago: Theobald.

JOHNSON, PHILIP (1947)1978 *Mies van der Rohe.* 3d ed. New York: Museum of Modern Art.

MIGGE, LEBERECHT

A prominent garden architect during the experimental 1920s in Germany, Leberecht Migge's (1881–1935) ideas on the socialization and practical use of urban open spaces stirred much controversy. Born in Danzig in northern Germany, he worked from 1904 to 1913 for the respected landscape architecture firm of Jacob Ochs in Hamburg.

An important theoretical writer, one of his first publications was *Die Gartenkultur des XX. Jahrhunderts* (1913). His book, *Jedermann Selbstversorger* (1918), marks the beginning of his passionate campaign for intensive gardening and even farming within the urban context. In 1920, Migge moved to the famous artists' colony at Worpswede, where his Sonnenhof (sun farm) became the experimental show piece of a school for *Siedlungswesen* (science of settlement). Rationalized intensive gardening as practiced in the Orient, utilizing sewage for fertilization and walls of glass bricks for passive solar heating, formed the core of a program that required active input from all members of a household.

Migge believed that it was dangerously wasteful to devote the vast open spaces of the new housing developments to aesthetic recreational purposes alone, and that if expertly laid out within the total plan, such areas of greenery could encompass private gardens for growing vegetables, fruits, and flowers, large communal recreation areas (*Volksparks*), commercial nurseries, and even small farms. He felt that a scientific approach to planning the smallest plot was in order and that individual gardeners needed firm guidance. In this vein, Migge designed the green areas of many of the large housing developments built in the Weimar Republic, among them Georgsgarten in Celle with OTTO HAESLER.

In the late 1920s, Migge established the Grünpolitik der Stadt Frankfurt am Main with ERNST MAY, and was responsible for landscaping the entire Nidda valley as a setting for the satellite developments planned by May. Migge carefully integrated recreational (bicycle paths, walkways, sport fields) and aesthetic-scenic aspects with productive gardens for which he also utilized the flat roofs of the modern housing.

Shortly before his death, Migge designed the vast, luxurious Reemtsma Estate in Altona, near Hamburg (1931–1933).

CHRISTIANE C. COLLINS

WORKS

1909, Public Park, Dobbengelände, Oldenburg, Germany. 1909, Public Park, Hamburg/Fuhlsbüttel, Germany. 1909, Public Park, Wohldorf, Germany. 1913, Gardens, International Architectural Exhibition, Leipzig. 1920–193?, Sonnenhof, Worpswede, Germany. 1924–1926, Georgsgarten, Celle, Germany. 1926–193?, Nidda Valley, Frankfurt, Germany. 1931–1933, Reemtsma Estate, Altona, near Hamburg, Germany.

BIBLIOGRAPHY

HÜLBUSCH, INGE META 1978 "'Jedermann

Selbstversorger'—Das Koloniale Grün Leberecht Migges: Von der Flucht ins harmonische Landleben zur Konzeption einer sozial engagierten Gartenarchitektur." Pages 66–71 in Lucius Burckhardt (editor), *Der Werkbund in Deutschland, Österreich und der Schweiz: Form ohne Ornament.* Stuttgart, Germany: Deutsche Verlags-Anstalt.

MIGGE, LEBERECHT 1913 *Die Gartenkultur des XX. Jahrhunderts.* Jena, Germany: Eugen Diederichs.

MIGGE, LEBERECHT 1918 *Jedermann Selbstversorger! Eine Lösung der Siedlungsfrage durch neuen Gartenbau.* Jena, Germany: Eugen Diederichs.

MIGGE, LEBERECHT 1926 *Deutsche Binnen-kolonisation: Sachgrundlagen des Siedlungswesens.* Berlin/Friedenau: Deutscher Kommunal-Verlag.

MIGGE, LEBERECHT 1929 "Renaissance des öffentlichen Grüns." *Der Städtebau* 2:37–47.

MULLIN, JOHN ROBERT 1977 "City Planning in Frankfurt, Germany, 1925–1932: A Study in Practical Utopianism." *Journal of Urban History* 4:3–28.

MILANOV, IORDAN

Iordan Popov Milanov (1867–1932) was born in Elena, Bulgaria. In 1892, he obtained an architecture degree in Vienna; upon graduation, he worked for his former professor, Karl König. For forty years, Milanov was a pioneer in professional design and legislative work.

From 1892 until World War I, he worked with PETKO MOMCHILOV on religious and civic buildings, most notably the reconstruction of Saint Sedmochislenitsi Church (1901), the Palace of the Bulgarian Synod (1906–1908), and the Central Mineral Baths (1905–1911), all landmarks of Sofia, and all in Byzantine style. From 1893 until 1921, Milanov was employed at the Board of Works. Together with G. Nenov, he wrote the first Bulgarian Building Code, and he also developed zoning ordinances for over eighty towns and 800 villages in Bulgaria.

Milanov participated in the design and construction of Sofia's University (1912–1932) and of the Shrine-Memorial *Alexander Nevski* (1920–1932) in Sofia, two major landmarks of the city. Milanov bequeathed all of his property to social funds, including the first fellowships for architectural students.

MARIA POPOVA

WORKS

1893–1900, Main Post Office; 1895, Alexandrov's Hospital Complex (several pavilions; with P. I. Momchilov); Sofia. 1901, Saint Sedmochislentitsi (reconstruction; with Momchilov) Sofia.; 1901–1902, High School for Girls (with Momchilov), Varna, Bulgaria. 1905–1911, Central Mineral Baths (with Momchilov); 1906–1908, Palace of the Bulgarian Synod (with Momchilov); Sofia. 1910–1912, Public Housing Complex, Pernik, Bulgaria. 1912, 1920–1932, Sofia University (design and construction; with others); 1920–1932, Alexander Nevsky Shrine-Memorial (with others); Sofia.

BIBLIOGRAPHY

BŬLGARSKA AKADEMIÎA NA NAUKITE 1974 *Entsiklopediîa na Bulgaria.* Sofia: The academy.

BŬLGARSKA AKADEMIÎA NA NAUKITE 1963–1969 *Kratka Bŭlgarska Entsiklopediîa.* Sofia: The academy.

BŬLGARSKA AKADEMIÎA NA NAUKITE 1965 *Kratka Istoriîa na Bŭlgarskata Arkhitektura.* Sofia: The academy.

KOEVA, M. 1975 "Iordan Milanov i Petko Momchilov—Arkhitekti ot Purvata Generatsiia." *Arkhitektura* 3–4:51–54.

MUTANOV, S. 1968 "Arkhitekt Iordan Milanov—Rodnachalnik na Sledosvobozhdenskata ni Arkhitektura." *Arkhitektura* 1:26–28.

MILIUTIN, NIKOLAI ALEKSANDROVICH

Born in Russia, Nikolai Aleksandrovich Miliutin (1889–1942) seems to have been educated only in the field of fine art, which he studied between 1905 and 1912. Aside from his revolutionary activity and brief military career as a Red Guard commandant, little is known of his early formation until 1917 when he assumed his first administrative post as chairman of the accounts department of Petrograd Hospital. His involvement with urbanism dates from 1925, when he became chairman of the New Towns Committee of the Communist Academy, and from this point on he became more and more involved in the formation of socialist planning theory. At the same time, he was appointed Commissar and Member of the Small Commissariat of the Russian Soviet Federated Socialist Republic, a post which he held until 1929.

The 1930 publication of his book *Sotsgorod* (Socialist Towns) and the foundation in 1931 of his magazine *Sovetskaia Arkhitektura* (Soviet Architecture), published by Nokompros, inaugurated Miliutin's career as an urban theorist and polemicist of modern architecture. The argumentative nature of *Sotsgorod* explicity reflects the ideological struggles of the period, with Miliutin's own proposals oscillating between meeting the immediate demands of the society and the construction of an appropriate urban infrastructure for the future. Although Miliutin categorically repudiated the reduction of the habitat to nothing but an agglomeration of individual cells, he was equally repelled by those petty bourgeois elements in the Party who wished to sustain the nuclear family. As far as Miliutin was concerned, the only societal components that had to be changed immediately in order to ensure the progressive transformation of society were the kitchen and the nursery school, since the liberation of women from domestic drudgery, when combined with the collectivization of the life services, would immediately increase the productive capacity of the society and hence raise the standard of living.

Socioeconomic issues permeate the entire body of *Sotsgorod,* from the need to bring about an immediate improvement in the living standard to the determination to evolve, after Ford's industrial methods, the "one best way" for the organization of the urban environment. In the famous Soviet planning dispute of the late 1920s between the Urbanists and the Deurbanists, Miliutin came down decidedly on the side of the latter, but not to the extent of recommending the disestablishment of all existing cities.

Influenced by the linear city model first advanced in 1880 by the Spanish urbanist ARTURO SORIA Y MATA, Miliutin advocated the formation of new linear "agro-industrial" settlements strictly structured in accordance with a six-banded principle comprising a railway band, an industrial band, a green band with an autoroute, a residential band, a park band, and an agricultural band. The biological nature of this model is evident from the various kinds of movement which Miliutin envisaged as passing either along or across these zones: the linear transshipment of surplus production and the transverse movement of excrement from the residential sector to the fields.

It is difficult to reconcile the economic nature of Miliutin's approach with his persistent defense of the architectural avant-garde, which on occasion extended beyond his alignment with YAKOVLEVICH MOISEI GINSBURG's functionalist OSA group. Nothing could have been further removed from the rigors of productive economy than Miliutin's defense of Jacob Chernikov's *Architectural Fantasies,* published in 1933, or the support that both he and Ginsburg gave to the imaginative but "afunctional" projects of IVAN IVANOVICH LEONIDOV. Equally strange, given his standing in the Party, was his criticism of Anatole Lunacharsky's conservative cultural policies, which first came to the fore with Miliutin's public attack on the prize-winning design for the Lenin Library of 1928.

Miliutin was officially criticized for his advocacy of deurbanism in Lazar Kaganovich's Bolshevik Party address of June 1931, and his recantation followed in *Sovetskaia Arkhitektura* in 1932, when he formally disavowed his deurbanist position. In 1934, after the closure of *Sovetskaia Arkhitektura,* Miliutin was given a sinecure as head of Kinofikatsia (Central Board of Film Distribution). In 1939, he was marginally involved in the building of the Palace of the Soviets in Moscow and one year later he was awarded an architectural degree by the Moscow Architectural Institute on the basis of a fly-over design which he submitted as a testimony of study.

KENNETH FRAMPTON

BIBLIOGRAPHY

KHAN-MAHOMEDOV, S. O. 1971 "N. A. Miliutin, 1889–1942." In O. A. Shvidkov (editor), *Building in the U.S.S.R.: 1917–1932.* New York: Praeger.

MILIUTIN, NIKOLAI A. 1974 *The Problem of Building a Socialist City.* Cambridge, Mass.: M.I.T.

MILIZIA, FRANCESCO

Francesco Milizia (1725–1798) was unquestionably the most influential and the most prolific of the Italian Settecento theoreticians whose concepts and opinions, subsumed under the term Illuminismo (enlightenment), are connected with rationalism and particularly with the doctrines of CARLO LODOLI. Milizia's architectural criticism is also the most consistent in its advocacy of the new, antibaroque, and neoclassicist ideals. He used his critique as a way to interpret history and, in addition, attempted to establish a fundamental system of architecture which went far beyond the comparable *Cours d'Architecture civile* (Paris, 1771–1777) of JACQUES FRANÇOIS BLONDEL in consistency and which retained its authority into the first half of the nineteenth century. Unlike the elegant literary promulgation of Lodoli's ideas practiced by FRANCESCO ALGAROTTI, Milizia's approach to architectural theory was marked by a strong commitment and precise, often controversial partisanship. This, in the papal Rome of the late eighteenth century, went hand in hand with undisguised sympathies for French ideas and politics. Unlike Andrea Memmo, Milizia went beyond the impetus provided by Carlo Lodoli's merely theoretical contemplation and aimed at a universal theory of architecture and a system of architectural thought into which architectural criticism could also be integrated.

Milizia was born in 1725 in Oria (Apulia) and received his education on the "axis of enlightenment" between Padua and Naples. In 1761, he settled in Rome where, until his death in 1798, he carried on a mostly controversial activity as a critic and theoretician. Intellectually and economically independent, he declined employment by the king of Naples to supervise the buildings of the Farnese family within the papal state. He was on friendly terms with the painter Anton Raphael Mengs and with the Spanish ambassador Giuseppe Nicola d'Azara. Through his correspondence with TOMMASO TEMANZA, with Count Francesco di Sangiovanni, and with Leopoldo Cicognara, he was connected with the progressive milieu of the Veneto, whose positions he propagated in Rome—even to the point of admiring Canova.

Only in Rome did Milizia first discover his love of architecture, "senza sapere neppur disegnare" (without even knowing how to draw) as he himself confesses (*Notizie,* 1805, p. v). As the first result of this preoccupation, he published—at first anonymously—*Le Vite de' piu celebri Architetti d'ogni Nazione e d'ogni tempo* (Rome, 1768) which contained in the appended *Saggio sopra l'architettura* the kernel of his theoretical views on architecture, later expanded in his *Principj d'Architettura.* An appendix to the former, on the *Meccanismo delle Volte,* testifies to his early interest in the mathematical basis of architecture, in questions of vault construction, and in stonecutting. The standard edition of his works, the *Vite . . . ,* appeared in 1781 in Parma under the title *Memorie degli Architetti antichi e moderni,* and was identified as the *terza edizione* (third edition), having appeared after the French translation with the comments of Pingeron (1771). In it, Milizia presents a great number of monographs, in chronological sequence, on architects from antiquity to his own time. According to the customary historical typology, the listing is divided into three parts: Antiquity; *Dalla Decadenza dell'Architettura fin al suo Ristabilimento* (fourth to fifteenth centuries); and *Dal Ristabilimento dell'Architettura accaduto nel secolo XV fino al secolo XVIII* (fifteenth to eighteenth centuries). Beside the introductory fundamental statements of the *Saggio* (essay), the individual monographs also clearly show the critical and classicist aesthetic of Milizia, which was averse to any infringement.

In addition to being inclined toward the enlightenment in architectural theory, Milizia was open to every increase of knowledge and fundamentals provided by the natural sciences. In 1771, basing himself on de Caille and d'Alembert, he published the *Elementi di Matematiche Pure* which presents mathematics as the fundamental science, to which architecture, too, is subordinate. The work is expressly meant for architects and, according to the *Efemeridi Letterarie di Roma* of March 7, 1772 (no. X, p. 73), was intended, together with further treatises on mechanics and hydrostatics, to form an architectual study course. In demanding that modern mathematics and in particular differential and integral calculus be made usable for the specific needs of architecture, the work is the first of a series of related works (Ermenegildo Pini, Lorenzo Mascheroni, Vincenzo Lamberti). Moreover—citing the spherical trigonometry of Roger J. Boscovich—Milizia defines trigonometry as "una scienza assolutamente necessaria per passare dalla Teoria alla Pratica" (a science which is absolutely necessary for proceeding from theory to practice; *Elementi . . . ,* 1771, p. 248).

The work was twice republished (1775, 1796) and, aside from further publications on natural science and medicine, was followed by *La Storia dell'Astronomi di M. Bailly ridotta in compendio* (Venice, 1791) of similar intent. Finally, a small treatise on *Economia Pubblica* (Rome, 1798) shows how far Milizia's interests reached, also in matters concerning society as a whole. This same broad overview characterizes the description of architecture and its tasks in Milizia's main theoretical work, the *Principj di Architettura Civile* (Finale, 1791; Bassano, 1785; Bassano, 1804). Going beyond VITRUVIUS's claim that architecture is the leading branch of all the arts, Milizia defines architecture as "legame della Società Civile" (bond of civilized society), linking it to economic progress and the representation of public and private prosperity, and ultimately to the preservation of these social achievements. It is also on such ethical considerations that Milizia, in by far the longest section of his book, namely that on Vitruvius's *distributio,* classifies the various building tasks and then applies them to a series of functional building types (university, library, academy, college, courthouse, stock exchange, mint, banks, abattoirs, hospitals, field hospitals, cemeteries), a classification that became largely binding for nineteenth-century Europe. Public architecture, as might be expected, takes up the largest amount of space and is subdivided according to aspects of public safety, usefulness, rationality, opulence, health and cleanliness, self-representation (*magnificenza*), and high solemnity (*sublimità*).

This important practical section of enlightened, open-minded architectural precepts is preceded by a theoretical and aesthetic section which pursues Lodoli's aim of bringing Vitruvian ideas into a logical scientific system. Indeed, this section is regarded by people like, for instance, G. Antolini as the metaphysical core of Milizia's architectural theory. According to Milizia, all architecture must partake of *bellezza* (beauty), *commodità* (convenience), and *solidità* (solidity). The final section of the book was never written; the second was concerned with the classification of building tasks according to *utilità pubblica* (public usefulness) in support of *buona legislazione* (good laws) as described above, while the first, in improved Vitruvian style, discusses the four main components of the Beautiful: the orders and building styles, proportions, aesthetic principles such as order, unity, simplicity, variety, and contrasts, and finally propriety. The latter is emphasized by Milizia as the first principle and thus also leads him back to the contemplation of aesthetic criteria within a social framework. This all-pervasive approach enriches the radicalism of Lodoli by taking the societal context into account. Milizia points to the basic ethical attitude and patriotism, on the threshold of the Revolution, of the "cittadini accesi d'amore per il pubblicobene" (citizens fired by love of the public good). This tenet constitutes the main message of Milizia's architectural theory, anticipating formulations presented in France by CLAUDE NICOLAS LEDOUX and JEAN NICOLAS LOUIS DURAND, and accounts for the high esteem in which—after the initial skepticism of, for instance, Comolli—Milizia was held by L. Cicognara (1808) in the Napoleonic era. This esteem was based not on his purist classicism, for which he was still being reproached by Julius Schlosser in 1924 ([1935]1964 ed., p. 667), but on his basic moral and ethical attitude. In the Rome of the late eighteenth century, to advocate a free society of citizens was tantamount to opting for French ideals, the very ideals that sparked the sharp criticism of Roman architectural history and tradition for which Milizia became far better known than for his theoretical views.

In this connection, Milizia provoked a first scandal with his treatise *Del Teatro,* first published in 1771 (it appeared in its final form as *Trattato completo, formale e materiale del Teatro* in Venice in 1789 and 1794). Making a plea for a theater *all'antica,* he used the occasion to castigate the Romans for their negligent treatment of ancient monuments—the Theater of Marcellus! But Milizia owes his reputation as a sharp critic mainly to two treatises that appeared in the 1780s: *Dell'Arte di vedere nelle Belle Arti del Disegno secondo i principj di Sulzer e Mengs* (Venice, 1781; enlarged edition, Genoa, 1786) that not only introduced new criteria for judging works of art based on the aesthetic views of Sulzer and Mengs, but also changed the whole tenor of art criticism, which up to that time had been benevolent and descriptive. In consequence, any basic discussion of Milizia's ideas was overlaid by the scandal created by his derogatory judgments, particularly of MICHELANGELO's Moses ("a horrible watchdog, dressed like a stoker, badly placed and useless."). Milizia expanded and extended this critical treatise—though, in the later volumes, confining himself to architecture to avoid further annoyance—in his main polemical work, *Roma delle Belle Arti del Disegno: Parte Prima dell'Architettura Civile* (Bassano, 1787). Here, under the banner of a neoclassicist, antibaroque critique which denounced all *abusi,* he describes the *bizzarerie* of Michelangelo, the *cartocci* (paper cones) of Martino Longhi (see LONGHI FAMILY), the *follie* of FRANCESCO BORROMINI. Here, too, is the characterization of the barocchetto-façade of the Maddalena as "the ultimate in twisted taste" as well as the famous criticism of the last great building enterprise of papal architecture in the eighteenth century: "this description of Roman buildings reaches from the Cloaca Massima to the Sacristy of St. Peter's: from the best to the worst" (p. 205).

These sharp criticisms brought Milizia under vehement attack in his own time. Regardless of the consistency between such statements and his theoretical opinions, he was ridiculed as the "day-book of capricious observations" and as the "Don Quixote of the fine ideal". With an equal disregard of his basic theoretical position, Milizia's criticism of the Roman baroque remained the normative influence until the re-evaluation of baroque architecture a hundred years later.

WERNER OECHSLIN
Translated from German by
Beverley R. Placzek

BIBLIOGRAPHY

ANTOLINI, G. 1817 *Osservazioni ed aggiunte ai principi di architettura civile di Francesco Milizia proposte agli studiosi ed amatori dell'architettura.* Milan, Italy: Stella.

BRUSATIN, M. 1980 *Venezia nel Settecento: Stato, architettura, territorio.* Turin, Italy.

CICOGNARA, L. 1808 *Memoria intornoall'indole e agli scritti di F. Milizia e progretto di pubblicare alcune sue lettere inedite.* Pisa, Italy.

COMOLLI, A. 1788–1792 *Bibliografia storico-critica dell'Architettura Civile ed Arti subalterne.* Rome: Stamperia Vaticana.

MILIZIA, FRANCESCO 1826–1828 *Opere complete.* Bologna, Italy.

PROZZILLO, I. 1971 *Francesco Milizia teorico e storico dell'architettura.* Naples: Guida.

SCHLOSSER, JULIUS, and KURZ, OTTO (1935)1964 Pages 667–668, 683 in *La Letteratura artistica.* 3d ed. Rome: Nuova Italia.

ZAMPETTI, P. 1967 "Francesco Milizia, uomo e critico d'arte." Volume 2, pages 675ff. in *Sensibilità e razionalità nel Settecento.* Florence.

MILLER, SANDERSON

Sanderson Miller (1717–1780), an English architect, enjoyed a considerable reputation as an antiquarian among a wide circle of amateurs and is principally responsible for the fashion of erecting battlemented ruins as prospect towers on country estates. His friends also consulted him in effecting alterations in the Gothic style to their domestic and ecclesiastical buildings. However, he was equally adept in the classical styles and he supervised the erection of the Shire Hall, Warwick, Warwickshire (1754–1758), and, in domestic architecture, Hagley Hall, Worcestershire (1754–1760).

MICHAEL MCCARTHY

WORKS

1743–1748, Radway Grange, Warwickshire, England. 1747–1753, Wroxton Abbey and Church, Oxfordshire, England. 1748, Sham Castle, Hagley Park, Worcestershire, England. 1750–1762, Adlestrop Park and Church, Gloucestershire, England. 1752–1757, Belhus (alterations), Essex, England. 1754–1755, Lacock Abbey (additions), Wiltshire, England. 1754–1758, Shire Hall, Warwick, England. 1754–1760, Hagley Hall, Worcestershire, England. 1754–1760, Pomfret House, Arlington Street, London.

BIBLIOGRAPHY

DICKENS, LILLIAN, and STANTON, MARY 1910 *An Eighteenth Century Correspondence.* London: Murray.

MCCARTHY, MICHAEL 1972 "Documents on the Greek Revival in Architecture." *Burlington Magazine* 114, no. 836:760–769.

MCCARTHY, MICHAEL 1976 "The Building of Hagley Hall, Worcestershire." *Burlington Magazine* 118, no. 877:214–225.

MCCARTHY, MICHAEL 1976–1977 "Eighteenth-Century Cathedral Restorations." *Studies: An Irish Quarterly Review* 65:330–343; 66:60–76.

WOOD, ANTHONY C., and HAWKES, WILLIAM 1969 "Sanderson Miller of Radway, His Work at Wroxton." *Cake & Cockhorse* 4, no. 6:79–112.

MILLS, PETER

Born in East Dean, Sussex, Peter Mills (1598–1670) was a builder, surveyor, and architect during the Interregnum and first decade of the Restoration. Apprenticed in 1613 to John Williams as a tyler and bricklayer, he subsequently became in 1643 Bricklayer of the City of London, and Master of the Tyler's and Bricklayer's Company, in 1649–1650 and 1659–1660. First recorded as a surveyor in 1638 in connection with Inigo Jones for the design of the Church of Saint Michael-le-Querne, he is best known for Thorpe Hall, near Peterborough (1653–1656), where he employed the "artisan mannerist" style that he used earlier, c.1640, for houses in Great Queen Street and Lincoln's Inn Field. His later designs evolved toward the new "domestic" style introduced by HUGH MAY and ROGER PRATT.

Appointed a member of the Committee for the City of London Militia in 1648, Mills was on the other hand, commissioned in 1661 to design the triumphal arches erected in London to celebrate the coronation of Charles II. After the Great Fire of London in 1666, he was one of the three city representatives, along with Hooke and Jerman, appointed to serve with the three Royal appointees (CHRISTOPHER WREN, May, and Pratt) on the Commission for Rebuilding the City, and one of the surveyors (together with Hooke, Jerman, and Oliver) to supervise the reconstruction of the city.

MARC DILET

WORKS

c.1640, Great Queen Street Houses (south side); c.1642, Castle Street Houses (now Furnival Street), Holborn; London. 1653–1656, Thorpe Hall, Northamptonshire, England. 1661, Triumphal Arches, London. 1659–1661, Hitcham Building, Pembroke College, Cambridge. 1661–1663, Cobham Hall (remodeling of central block), Kent, England. 1667–1670, Christ's Hospital (additions), London.

BIBLIOGRAPHY

MILLS, PETER, and OLIVER, JOHN (1946–1956)1962–1964 *The Survey of Building Sites after the Great Fire in 1666.* With an introduction by Walter H. Godfrey. Reprint. London Topographical Society. Facsimile of a manuscript.

MILLS, ROBERT

The career of Robert Mills (1781–1855) spanned the first half of the nineteenth century, during which, in his major works, he successfully established his version of the Greek Revival as the style most expressive of the new American political system. His designs met the wide variety of demands made by intense nationalism, mercantile capitalism, burgeoning governmental bureaucracy, expanding population, and urbanization. A strong, determined man, imaginative as well as practical, conscious of being the first native-born and -trained American architect, he helped to define and to shape the public architecture of his rapidly developing country. Whether in monumental classicism or in his occasional practice of stylistic eclecticism, he was a creative designer; but his emphasis on utility, economical construction and sound fire-proofing also vastly enhanced the professionalization of architecture.

Mills was born in Charleston, South Carolina, where he received a classical education at Charleston College and took lessons in drawing. In 1801, he joined JAMES HOBAN who had left Charleston in 1792 for Washington to build the President's House and the Capitol. Here Mills caught the eye of THOMAS JEFFERSON who encouraged him and gave him access to the library at Monticello. For some months in 1802, armed with letters of introduction, including one from Jefferson to CHARLES BULFINCH, he made a tour to study the buildings of the Northern states. In 1803, Jefferson recommended him to BENJAMIN HENRY LATROBE, and for six years Mills assisted Latrobe at the Capitol, in surveying for the Chesapeake & Delaware Canal, and on works in Philadelphia.

Mills's education thus included a cross-section of current theories, styles, and practices that he later applied to the American situation as he perceived it. An initial acquaintance through Hoban with English Georgian and Palladian (see ANDREA PALLADIO) architecture was reinforced by Jefferson's Palladianism and by readings. In an early essay on the Tuscan order as well as in later writings, Mills's emphasis on rational order and utility as the basis of architectural design showed a debt to such authors as Palladio and Sir WILLIAM CHAMBERS. The Adamesque (see ROBERT ADAM) element he saw in Bulfinch's work appeared in forms Mills employed during the first two decades of his practice. Jefferson imparted an awareness of Roman architecture as well as modern French ideas, especially on interior planning for convenience and comfort, both of which are marks of Mills's domestic works. Most important for Mills was Latrobe in both his preference for the Greek orders and his practice of a modern, Soanic (see JOHN SOANE) style; from this rational neoclassicism Mills developed a compositional method for shaping the building mass as a dominant geometric whole articulated by a few smaller stylistic elements. Equally important, Mills acquired from Latrobe an understanding of the range of responsibilities entailed by professionalism, namely, draftsmanship and presentation of a design, superintendence of all aspects of construction, and competence in engineering. He was exposed to some of the best architectural minds of his time and to a variety of styles, which gave him flexibility in meeting the demands of patrons of different tastes and needs.

Latrobe sent Mills to Philadelphia in 1808 to superintend construction of houses and the Bank of Philadelphia (1807–1808), and within a year of his arrival, he had married, cultivated friendships, and established an independent architectural practice. A tentative, searching quality appeared in his Philadelphia works, which included the covering of Louis Wernwag's Upper Ferry Bridge (1813–1814), Washington Hall (1809, 1814–1816), Franklin Row (1809–1810), and probably some speculative housing. He used a Greek Doric order for the bridge entrances, a modern vaulted and screened niche in the Hall, and dispositions of rectangular and arched openings on row housing that evoked Latrobe and Soane. The circular Sansom Street Baptist Church (1811–1812) and the Octagon Unitarian Church (1812–1813) showed a wide range of sources in the centralized church plans, probably based on JAMES GIBBS's published designs, Adamesque arched recesses with tripartite Soanic windows, and a pair of giant Erechtheum-type Ionic columns as a screen on the Baptist Church. This stylistic variety appeared against increasingly large and simple geometric shapes, expanses of bare surfaces, strong horizontal elements, and occasional concentrations of symbolic ornament.

Mills also competed for several major commissions, among which were the Monumental Church (1812–1817) in Richmond, Virginia, and the Washington Monument (1814–1842) in Baltimore. The Monumental Church was his fourth centralized design. He considered this type of plan superior to the customary longitudinal structure because it brought the preacher closer to every member of the congregation and improved seeing and hearing, a contention he repeatedly supported by his experiments in acoustics. For Mills, the first necessity in architecture was utility. A large stuccoed brick octagon with a wooden dome, the Monumental Church has on its street side the masonry memorial porch, a thirty-two-foot cube with wide openings through which is visible the sarcophagus containing the ashes of those victims of a theater fire which the church was built to commemorate. Doric columns, distyle in antis in the porch openings, have fluting at the top and bottom of the shaft, like the unfinished columns of the Temple of Apollo at Delos; similar columns inside the church support the gallery. The channeling at the top of the shaft is a tall necking that evokes the Ionic order developed by Robert Adam

Mills. Monumental Church. Richmond, Virginia. 1812–1817

Mills.
Washington Monument.
Baltimore.
1814–1842

and used by Bulfinch in the Tontine Crescent in Boston. In reaction to this touch of Adamesque eloquence, however, Mills went even further than Latrobe toward a bolder, masculine plain style, a style that was to characterize his work.

Mills's Washington Monument in Baltimore, a major work of the early Greek Revival, is a Delos-type Greek Doric column with fluting just below the capital. It was intended to be ornamented in a manner similar to the Column of Trajan, but the seven bands of bronze figural reliefs, symbolic devices, and inscriptions were not completed for lack of funds. The intricate composition of the base was reduced to a simple cubical block with four entries. The statue at the top, originally intended as an equestrian Washington, became the sixteen-foot togaed figure of the General resigning his commission at Annapolis, a treatment which symbolized the superiority of civilian over military authority in the American political system. Despite the circumstantial elimination of the intended sculpture, the geometry of the massive column and entrance block is an essential aspect of Mills's architectural conception.

To superintend construction of the Monument, Mills took up residence in Baltimore in April 1815, and he established close, long-lasting relationships with its board of managers. As merchants and lawyers, they formed the core of the upper middle class that assumed responsibility for creating a modern city. Many of them commissioned works from Mills, and they referred him to further opportunities. No other architect of the decade received more commissions for public and commercial buildings, churches, houses, and the large and small urban improvements in Baltimore. Several of the managers were also directors of the Baltimore Water Company, of which Mills served as president for three years, beginning in 1816. While directing day-to-day operations, Mills was responsible also for developing the Company's property. He planned the twelve-unit Waterloo Row (1816–1819) and invited artisans and suppliers of materials to participate in the construction, each party to receive a house as compensation.

Virtually his own client, Mills developed Waterloo Row on the basis of his earlier rows in Philadelphia. Here many of the elements of Mills's highly individual style are clearly apparent. White marble and wood horizontals against the brick complemented the wide, recessed arches, two per house, running the length of the block. Vertically, the alignment of tripartite windows from basement to third floor alternated with the lines of simple rectangular openings. The rhythmic movement along the whole block was punctuated by the individual houses, while the network of horizontals and verticals locked every element into its place in the whole. Although Mills never again applied this method, a similar control of large-scale design reappeared two decades later in the Treasury Building in Washington. The number of different forms in Waterloo Row was very small, and although derived from the Federal style, they were purified and simplified with a rigor as strict as the linear pattern.

Drawings and old photographs reveal that the austerity of Waterloo Row gave way to more substantial, richer forms in the residences of other patrons. Both urban and country houses were stuccoed and scored to imitate masonry. Usually, one-story porticoes covered the entrance, and the orders, used with much freedom, had a Federal attenuation as often as the ancient proportions. In part because it shares these late Federal characteristics, the Brockenbrough House (c.1816–1818; now the Museum of the Confederacy) in Richmond, Virginia, is attributed to Mills. Although the plans of the Baltimore houses have been lost, the John Hoffman House (1821–1822) is the only one with a suggestion of anything other than rectangular rooms; its apsidal side entrance suggests a Latrobean plan with two prominent rooms ending in curves, such as Mills was to employ shortly afterward in South Carolina.

Mills's ability to make stylistic adaptations to please his patrons was demonstrated by two contrasting churches designed during his Baltimore period. The First Baptist Church (1816–1818) in Baltimore, his fifth centralized structure, was composed of a broad, low domed rotunda, a rectilinear entrance block, and a projecting hexastyle portico, all abruptly juxtaposed and bound together by a tall frieze and cornice. Arched doorways and rectangular windows were cut into stuccoed surfaces. Unfluted shafts compressed the Roman Ionic capitals and spare bases. The structure had the muscularity and stylistic severity of Waterloo Row. With the First Baptist Church (1817–1822) in Charleston, Mills retreated from early Greek revival austerity to a Georgian composition. A four-columned Doric portico abuts a wider rectangular building, the entrance block marked off from the nave in the manner of Gibbs's Saint Martin-in-the-Fields in London. Two rows of arched windows along the nave walls mark the main floor and gallery levels inside, another Gibbsian touch. The Doric columns are set on Attic bases and distanced so that two metopes occur over the intercolumniation, in the refined Palladian manner of Chambers.

A third church highlights Mills's personal stylistic inventiveness. Unusual for its two façades, the Bethesda Presbyterian Church (1821–1823) in

Camden, South Carolina, is even more Palladian than the Charleston church in its orders and in the Federal simplicity of its white columns and red brick body. The light, open interior, however, belongs to the early Greek revival and suggests the original appearance of the Baltimore church. The arched windows and the doors flanking the high pulpit, all unframed, are typical of Mills's austerity. A cornice separates the wall from coves that rise to a flat ceiling ornamented with a large medallion; the cornice and medallion are close in form to those of Waterloo Row. Mills led his patrons gradually toward a modern taste while respecting the strong Georgian traditions of South Carolina.

In Baltimore, Mills received numerous small commissions: a schoolhouse, store fronts, a book store, house additions and alterations, and tombstones. He was especially in demand for his successful hot air heating system; he installed furnaces in houses, churches, factories, and mills, in the City Hospital, and the Peale Museum. He proposed and executed a method of channeling Jones Falls, the river bisecting the city, to contain floodwaters and improve navigation. To define the site for Waterloo Row, he laid out at least one major street. In many of these works he continued the practice of Latrobe in offering the specialized skills of an engineer as part of an architect's competence. Following the depression of 1819, however, even such commissions, as well as work on the Monument, came to a halt.

By this time Mills had gained a professional reputation that led to an invitation to return to his native state. On reaching Columbia, South Carolina, in mid-December 1820, he was immediately appointed acting commissioner on the Board of Public Works with the responsibility of designing buildings across the state. Later changes by the legislature altered Mills's appointments, so that from December 1823 to 1826 or 1827 his work was confined to Charleston. Occasionally, he gave limited supervision and provided plans beyond his mandate for which he received separate payment.

Mills's early Greek revival work of this decade incorporates Latrobean and Palladian forms and compositional devices, as seen in the County Record Building, called the Fireproof Building (1822–1827; now the South Carolina Historical Society), in Charleston. Its façade, identical on both north and south sides of the block, is five bays wide with a four-column portico projecting from the center on a high basement opened by three arches. The disposition is based on a villa by Palladio, modernized by arched openings derived from Latrobe. Here appears the free attitude toward the orders: giant unfluted Doric columns in Greek proportions support an austere Tuscan entablature.

Mills.
County Record Building (Fireproof Building; now the South Carolina Historical Society).
Charleston, South Carolina.
1821–1827

A proper pediment, shown in Mills's drawing, was replaced following an earthquake in 1886, by the present triangular blocking and high parapet. Thick walls carry brick vaults over rooms and halls of the basement and main story. Only the roof structure and ceiling of the top floor are of wood; iron replaced combustible materials wherever possible. Adapted from Latrobe, these improved methods of fireproofing reappeared in Mills's later public buildings.

Another Palladian design is the Second Ainsley Hall House (1823–1825; now the Robert Mills Historic House) in Columbia, commissioned by one of the wealthiest merchants in the state. Its north façade is adapted from an illustration in OTTAVIO BERTOTTI SCAMOZZI's *Le fabbriche ei disegni di Andrea Palladio* with such Millsian preferences as arched openings and a belt course uniting the window sills of the upper story. On the south side, a seven-arched basement supports a loggia the full width of the house, fronted by a Doric colonnade carrying arches. Windows in this front are all tripartite, and in the center is a semicircular recess with a niche and two flanking doors, identical with the side entry of the Hoffman House in Baltimore. These doors lead into the tangent rounded ends of two rooms connected by a sliding door; opposite the recess is the rounded end of the entrance hall from the north front. These rooms and disposition of the main floor are modeled closely on Latrobe's design (1814) for the Commandant's House at the Pittsburgh Arsenal.

Mills's official assignment in South Carolina was in response to the legislature's authorization in 1819 of the construction of county courthouses and jails across the state as well as an asylum in the capital, Columbia, and the Fireproof Building and a powder magazine (1824–1826) in Charleston. He was well-occupied, designing perhaps a dozen buildings in a year and a half. In 1822, Mills advertised for bids and in some cases construction began immediately. He did not employ standard plans, but the factors of use, state authority and financing, and the concentrated period of time for design and drafting of specifications insured many basic similarities in these buildings. The rectilinear block is emphasized, its smooth wall surfaces broken by shallow recessions or projections and a plain belt course between the upper stories; most are set on a high basement and have a columned portico and simplified entablature. All give the impression of substantial construction with an eye on economy, utility, and austerity. Each building has been individualized, not only according to the size appropriate for its locale and functions, but also in appearance.

The courthouses share many aspects of the Fireproof Building. Most have a prominent entry to vaulted fireproof offices and record storage on the ground floor. Lateral staircases rise to the porticoed landing and entrance to courtroom and related services. Many of the courthouses have been demolished and those surviving have been altered, enlarged, and restored, but some fronts are close to their original form. One had the temple shape with giant orders (Camden, 1825–1830), but on most a pedimented portico on a basement abuts a wider block.

A pressing social problem led to the establishment of an asylum for the mentally ill at Columbia. The original building (1822–1827) comprises a central block of four stories over the basement and two wings of three stories. The wings angle back from the line of the front, and a drawing by Mills plots additional wings at increasing angles to form a semicircle which, enclosed, would provide security as well as privacy for the patients; this plan was not followed in the additions. The main block, with its portico of six giant Doric columns on an arcaded and rusticated basement, can be seen as an enlargement of the Fireproof Building. Intended for enlightened modern care and treatment, the building provided individual rooms for patients. On each floor of the wings a wide corridor faces the front, and along the back is a series of individual rooms. The main block houses services, apartments for caretakers and staff, and areas for therapy; above, high parapets enclose roof gardens for patient use. Furnaces in the basement supplied hot air heating, while extensive use of brick for walls and the spiral stone stairways increased the fire resistance of the building.

Not only fireproofing, but a demonstration of another kind of strength appears in the county jails that Mills designed at the same time. Most have given way to modern facilities and advanced penology, but two survive, at Lancaster and Union (both 1822–1823), and although enlarged and extensively altered inside, they exemplify Mills's primary concern for utility. The broad, astylar rectangular blocks are exceptionally self-contained, and the construction—ashlar at Union, stuccoed rubble with liberal use of stone for corner quoins, archivolts, and belt course at Lancaster—conveys the impression of strength and containment. These small county jails are Mills's closest approach to the *architecture parlante* of the late eighteenth-century French neoclassicists. The only suggestion of how the interior planning related to Mills's concept of penology is found in his brief description of the four-story wing (1822–c.1824) he added to the county jail in Charleston: "It is divided into solitary cells, one for each criminal, and the whole made fireproof" (*Statistics of South Carolina,* 1826, p. 420).

Throughout his lifetime Mills published pamphlets and books on topical matters, arguing for the promotion of canals, railroads, and other internal improvements. From 1824 to 1826, with architectural commissions becoming rare, he assembled the materials for his *Atlas of the State of South Carolina* (1826) and *Statistics.* The former, a milestone in American cartography, still proves useful for its series of large-scale maps of each county; the latter is a massive compilation of historical, economic, geographic, and geological data about the state. He spent much time overseeing the production and sale of these books, and he used them also while seeking employment. He sent a copy, for example, to President Andrew Jackson in the hope of a federal appointment.

The mid- and late-1820s was a slack period for Mills. Friends in Baltimore provided small jobs, and in 1829–1830, he surveyed the route of a canal along the Susquehanna River, from Maryland to Pennsylvania. But he saw his real opportunity in Washington, and by March 5, 1830, he was established in the capital, which remained his home until his death in 1855.

For six years, Mills performed small works: minor alterations in the White House, Capitol, and the Executive Office Buildings, such as rearrangement of rooms, repairs after fire, new furnaces, creating a reliable water supply system, fencing in grounds, and moving the Tripoli Monument. Best known is his improvement of acoustics in the House of Representatives which he achieved by introducing partitions behind the colonnade and by raising the floor.

During this period Mills developed standard plans for two groups of buildings, customs houses and marine hospitals. Four customs houses (1834–1835) were built in Middletown and New London, Connecticut, and Newburyport and New Bedford, Massachusetts. The first three are virtually identical, and indeed the same specifications were used for the Middletown and Newburyport buildings: two stories high and almost square in plan, three bays wide and three deep, of brick and rubble faced with masonry, with tall angle pilasters at the corners carrying the continuous entablature, and a small entrance portico with two Doric columns. Minor differences individualize each structure. Except for the wooden roof structure, all are of brick and stone, contain vaulted rooms and halls inside, and have cast iron doors, windows, shutters, stairs, and railings. The larger custom house in New Bedford is five bays wide and has a tall pedimented portico carried by four giant Doric columns. All are Greek Revival works, with Mills's typical simplifications of the Doric order, such as the plain frieze. On the other hand, areas of smooth masonry against the expanse of quarry-faced stone were in accord with the modern development of granite architecture in New England and the growing taste for textural variation.

Mills then designed the old Marine Hospital (1831–1834; now the City Housing Authority) in Charleston; it proved to be the prototype for many later ones. The two-story rectangular block presents a long side on the street, its façade of seven bays carried on a low arcaded basement. Loggias run the length of the building, with clustered columns of Gothic form and tall pointed arches, the shape used also for windows. Stuccoed brick is lined to simulate masonry; the same material employed inside provides the safety measure of fireproofing, while it imposes a regular subdivision into vaulted wards and offices. The Marine Hospital is one of the rare instances of the Gothic in Mills's work. Like his friend Latrobe, he had little feeling for the style, and the geometric simplicity with which he treats the forms makes the building as much Neoclassical as Gothic.

When a campaign for the construction of several marine hospitals developed in 1837, Mills designed and published uniform plans for 50- and 100-patient hospitals. Although this program is insufficiently studied, it is known that Mills's designs continued in use to the 1870s for structures on the Atlantic and Gulf coasts, the Great Lakes, and the Ohio and Mississippi Rivers. Loggias might have occurred on both long sides of the two-story structures, and enclosed corner pavilions rose another story to become towers. In style there were both classical and Gothic variants, but their superposed Doric columns or compound piers were unusual in the work of Mills, who preferred giant orders. The regular disposition of strong interior walls on either side of the corridor indicates fireproof construction. There were fireplaces and furnaces; Mills's notes record studies of cast-iron beds and treated cloth for greater protection against fire. Nominally under the Treasury Department, the Navy and Army Departments also constructed marine hospitals, so that the standard plans underwent many changes to meet local conditions.

In 1836, Mills won a limited competition for his best known work, the Washington National Monument (designed 1833; built 1848–1884). This design was based on the obelisk form he had used in two earlier monuments (1824–1827) in South Carolina. One, in Columbia, commemorates Dr. Jonathan Maxcy, first president of the state university; the other celebrates Baron de Kalb, who died in the Revolutionary War. Each has an obelisk on a block shaped as a Roman cippus. Since 1830, Mills had considered a memorial to Washington at a site prepared by Bulfinch in the crypt and rotunda of the Capitol. With the definite refusal of the Washington family to allow removal of the General's remains from Mount Vernon, Mills sketched outdoor commemorative monuments, including a huge statue and a triumphal arch. In 1833, the Washington National Monument Committee, a private fund-raising organization, was formed, and three years later it selected his obelisk design. The 550-foot shaft originally was to rise from a building of 250-foot circumference, surrounded by a Doric colonnade. Although the base was never built, the giant obelisk was dramatically placed at the end of the Mall, in line with the dome of the Capitol, and in its pure geometry it is an eloquent memorial to one of the most memorable figures in American history.

After destruction by fire in 1833 of the Executive Building housing the Treasury Department, Mills prepared designs for a new fireproof structure. He was thus ready, when appointed by President Andrew Jackson on July 6, 1836, to go to work at once on a new Treasury Building (1836–1842). From the outset, Mills planned a large structure, of which he built only the first stage. The long front on 15th Street consists of thirty giant Erechtheum-type Ionic columns carried on a full basement and crowned by a tall, planar entablature with balustrade; the stretch of the strong horizontals contains and lightens the regular drumbeat of the persistent verticals. A shallow stoop with lateral stairs leads to the loggia and the entrance hall of the principal story, where stairways rise in open wells. From the entrance, barrel-vaulted corridors run in three directions, punctuated by the doorways to groin-vaulted offices on each side. In spite of severe criticism, Mills drew on his experience of the previous decades, and reduced the mass of the walls by using so-called hydraulic cement and brick, thus achieving economy as well as strong fireproof construction. Although never completely finished by Mills himself, the Treasury Building, as planned, was the largest office build-

Mills.
Treasury Building.
Washington.
1836–1842

ing yet built in the United States, and because it was vaulted throughout it was the first of its kind in which the disposition of interior space was determined by a structural module. The Ionic colonnade, with its origins in ancient Greece, was intended by Mills and understood by his time as an appropriate symbol of democracy, and it marked the culmination of the architect's Greek revival work.

Mills's appointment included a provision for constructing the Patent Office Building according to the plan of William Parker Elliot, who was associated with ITHIEL TOWN and ALEXANDER JACKSON DAVIS. Elliot's design depended on the New Yorkers for both its monumental Doric portico, derived from the Parthenon, and the sequence of tall pilasters along its walls. Mills built the south or F Street wing (1836–1840; now the National Portrait Gallery) and, claiming he never had access to Elliot's drawings, planned the interior in accordance with his customary fireproofing methods. Offices filled the ground floor and much of the principal story, while the top story was an open exhibition hall. Two elements of the principal floor deserve notice, the model gallery and the entrance lobby, areas where the vaults are supported by Delos-type Doric columns with fluting at the necking and base only. Made of granular sandstone, these massive columns display a primitive strength in contrast with the polished marble floor and stairs; the latter has in addition bronze railing panels of the richest Greek revival form.

While these buildings were under construction, Mills designed and built the first part of the Old Post Office (1839–1842; now the International Trade Commission) on E Street, foreseeing its extension northward to F Street opposite the Patent Office. Lowering of the surrounding streets has raised the former basement story of rusticated pilasters and broad rectangular windows. The two upper stories are linked by a tall Corinthian order marking the structural bays, four engaged columns define the central pavilion, the rest are pilasters out to the corners. The Renaissance character of the building, enhanced by the pedimented windows of the second story and the mezzaninelike top story windows, has been recognized from the first. Although the part constructed by Mills extended only seven bays from E Street, its eventual completion as a rectangle around a central court was already contemplated. Internally, the continuous corridor flanked by offices parallels the dispositions of the Treasury and Patent Office Buildings, and it also employs the vaulted modules of his fireproof construction.

While engaged on these three buildings, Mills designed smaller works and in some instances supervised their construction, for example, the Courthouse (1838–1839) in Alexandria, Virginia, and the Washington Jail (1839–1841). The drawing for the latter shows a three-story block, its seven-bay front marked by buttresses rising above the eaves into battlements. With its exterior stuccoed and lined in imitation of granite, it was vaulted in Mills's fireproof construction. Its simplified Norman Gothic is another example of Mills's austere handling of the style. It also helps to explain how he could later be responsive to the

Romanesque forms of JAMES RENWICK's Smithsonian Institution (1846–1849), for which he served as supervising architect.

Mills's position and the title he used, Architect of the Public Buildings, were abolished in 1842. For several years, he performed a number of minor design and supervisory functions until he was appointed in June 1849 to enlarge the Patent Office by constructing the east and west wings. At this time, he offered designs for enlargement of the Capitol. In July 1851, he was dismissed from both projects, and the works were taken up by THOMAS U. WALTER and others of the younger generation who could equal his ability to carry through large masonry construction. Except for a brief period (1850–1852) when he built the pedestal for Thomas Crawford's Washington Monument in Richmond, Virginia, Mills's public career was finished, though his mind still teemed with projects.

Mills customarily worked hard and rapidly, and he employed a problem-solving approach; in his notebooks he often posed a specific query, then proceeded to a solution. These practices underlay his ability as an administrator in coordinating the efforts of many people, whether in an architectural or engineering enterprise, or in assembling the materials for his *Atlas* and *Statistics*. He preferred solutions based on what he considered "science"; his improvements in acoustics and fireproofing rested, he said, on experiments and observations made in a search for principles. He turned these inquiries to such problems as the harnessing of river currents and tidal power for clearing harbors or, as early as 1816, the development of the railroad. Such investigations showed him a man of his times in his concern for rapid communication and transportation of merchandise, the economic basis for the prosperity of the country.

These were concerns and interests he shared with his upper middle class and governmental clientele. Grand, but practical architecture, rational as well as classical, was to express and serve the spirit of the new republic, and Mills, more than any of his contemporaries, was its architect.

ROBERT L. ALEXANDER

WORKS

*1804–1806, Circular Church, Charleston, S.C. 1807–1812, First Presbyterian Church, Augusta, Ga. 1808–1810, Prison (now the Historical Burlington County Prison Museum), Mount Holly, N.J. *1809–1810, Franklin Row; *1809–1812, State House (wings); *1809–1816, Washington Hall; *1811–1812, Sansom Street Baptist Church; *1812–1813, Octagon Unitarian Church; Philadelphia. 1812–1817, Monumental Church, Richmond, Va. *1813–1814, Upper Ferry Bridge (cover), Philadelphia. 1814–1842, Washington Monument, Baltimore. c.1816–1818, Brokenbrough House (now the Museum of the Confederacy), Richmond, Va. *1816–1818, First Baptist Church; *1816–1819, Waterloo Row; Baltimore. 1817–1822, First Baptist Church, Charleston, S.C. c.1818–1820, Potts House, Frederick, Md. *1821–1822, Hoffman House, Baltimore. 1821–1823, Bethesda Presbyterian Church, Camden, S.C. 1821–1823, Jail, Lancaster, S.C. 1821–1823, Jail, Union, S.C. 1821–1825, Courthouse, Winnsboro, S.C. *1821–1826, Powder Magazine, Charleston, S.C. 1821–1827, Asylum, Columbia, S.C. 1821–1827, County Record Building (Fireproof Building; now the South Carolina Historical Society), Charleston, S.C. 1822–1824, Courthouse, Georgetown, S.C. *1822–1824, Jail wing, Charleston, S.C. 1822–1825, Courthouse, Kingstree, S.C. 1823–1825, Second Ainsley Hall House (now the Robert Mills Historic House), Columbia, S.C. 1823–1825, Courthouse, Conway, S.C. 1824–1827, de Kalb Monument, Camden, S.C. 1824–1827, Maxcy Monument, Columbia, S.C. 1825–1830, Courthouse, Camden, S.C. *c.1830–1835, Customs House, Mobile, Ala. 1831–1834, Marine Hospital (now the City Housing Authority), Charleston, S.C. 1833–1855, Washington National Monument (not completed until 1884). 1834–1835, Customs House, Middletown, Conn. 1834–1835, Customs House, New Bedford, Mass. 1834–1835, Customs House, Newburyport, Mass. 1834–1835, Customs House, New London, Conn. *1834–1839, Appraisors Stores, Baltimore. 1836–1840, Patent Office Building (now the National Portrait Gallery); 1836–1842, Treasury Building; Washington. *1838–1839, Courthouse, Alexandria, Va. 1838–1940, South Carolina Library, Columbia, S.C. *1839–1841, Jail; 1839–1842, Post Office Building (now the International Trade Commission); Washington.

BIBLIOGRAPHY

ALEXANDER, ROBERT L. 1975 "Baltimore Row Houses of the Nineteenth Century." *American Studies* 16:65–76.

AMES, KENNETH 1968 "Robert Mills and the Philadelphia Story." *Journal of the Society of Architectural Historians* 27:140–146.

BROWN, GLENN 1900–1903 *History of the United States Capitol.* 2 vols. Washington: Government Printing Office.

BRYAN, JOHN MORRILL 1976 *Robert Mills, Architect, 1781–1855.* Columbia, S.C.: Columbia Museum of Art.

BRYAN, JOHN MORRILL, and JOHNSON, JULIE M. 1979 "Robert Mills' Sources for the South Carolina Lunatic Asylum, 1822." *Journal of the South Carolina Medical Association* 75, no. 6:264–268.

DAVIES, JANE B. 1965 "A. J. Davis' Projects for a Patent Office Building." *Journal of the Society of Architectural Historians* 24:229–251.

ELDER, WILLIAM VOSS, 3D 1971 *Robert Mills' Waterloo Row—Baltimore 1816.* Baltimore: Baltimore Museum of Art.

GALLAGHER, HELEN MAR PIERCE 1935 *Robert Mills.* New York: Columbia University Press.

HALL, LOUISE 1947 "Mills, Strickland, and Walter: Their Adventures in a World of Science." *Magazine of Art* 40:266–271.

HAMLIN, TALBOT 1944 *Greek Revival Architecture in America.* New York: Oxford University Press.

HOYT, WILLIAM D., JR. 1939–1940 "Robert Mills and the Washington Monument in Baltimore." *Maryland Historical Magazine* 34:144–160; 35:178–189.

MASSEY, JAMES C. 1963 "Robert Mills Documents, 1823: A House for Ainsley Hall in Columbia, S.C." *Journal of the Society of Architectural Historians* 28:228–232.

MILLER, J. JEFFERSON, 2D 1964 "The Designs for the Washington Monument in Baltimore." *Journal of the Society of Architectural Historians* 23:19–28.

MILLS, ROBERT 1935 "The Daily Journals of Robert Mills. Baltimore, 1816." *Maryland Historical Magazine* 30:257–271.

MILLS, ROBERT 1938*a* "Letters from Robert Mills." *South Carolina Historical and Genealogical Magazine* 39:110–124.

MILLS, ROBERT 1938*b* *Some Letters of Robert Mills, Engineer and Architect.* Edited by Bess Glenn. Columbia, S.C.: Historical Commission of South Carolina.

MILLS, ROBERT 1951–1952 "The Journal of Robert Mills, 1828–1830." Edited by Hennig Cohen. *South Carolina Historical and Genealogical Magazine* 52:133–139, 218–224; 53:31–36, 90–100.

PIERSON, WILLIAM H., JR. 1970 *American Buildings and Their Architects: The Colonial and Neo-Classical Styles.* Garden City, N.Y.: Doubleday.

RAVENEL, BEATRICE ST. JULIEN 1945 *Architects of Charleston.* Charleston, S.C.: Carolina Art Association.

WADDELL, GENE 1979 "Robert Mills' Fireproof Building." *South Carolina Historical Magazine* 80:105–135.

WADDELL, GENE, and LISCOMBE, R. WINDSOR 1982 *Robert Mills's Courthouses and Jails.* Easley, S.C.: Southern Historical Press.

WASHBURN, W. E. 1969 "Temple of the Arts; National Collection of Fine Arts and National Portrait Gallery." *American Institute of Architects Journal* 51:54–61.

WILLIAMS, GEORGE W. 1953 "Robert Mills' *Contemplated Addition to St. Michael's Church* and *Doctrine of Sound.*" *Journal of the Society of Architectural Historians* 12, no. 1:23–31.

ZUKOWSKY, JOHN 1976 "Monumental American Obelisks: Centennial Vistas." *Art Bulletin* 58, no. 4:574–581.

MINNUCCI, GAETANNO

Gaetanno Minnucci (1896–) was born in Macerata, Italy. He graduated from the Facolta di Ingegneria in Rome in 1920. A founding member of the Gruppo Urbanisti Romani (1926) and the Rationalist movement, he was active in town planning. From 1937 until 1966, he taught in the Facolta di Architettura in Rome.

DENNIS DOORDAN

WORK

1962–1964, Gemelli Polyclinic, Rome.

BIBLIOGRAPHY

CENNAMO, MICHELE 1973 *La Prima Esposizione Italiana di Architettura Razionale.* Naples Italy: Fausto Fiorentino.

DE'SETA, CESARE 1972 *La cultura architettonica in Italia tra le due guerre.* Bari, Italy: Laterza.

MIQUE, RICHARD

Richard Mique (1728–1794) probably did not make a trip to Rome, yet he, with JACQUES GERMAIN SOUFFLOT, NICHOLAS MARIE POTAIN, JEAN FRANÇOIS CHALGRIN, Marie Joseph Peyre (see PEYRE FAMILY), and JACQUES GONDOUIN, was one of the creators of a new style in France.

Mique came from a family of architect-contractors established in Nancy. His father had built the left wing of the Château of Lunéville. After having received his initial training from a relative, who was the inspector of fortifications in Alsace, and on the construction sites of his father, Mique studied with JACQUES FRANÇOIS BLONDEL in Paris. At Lunéville, King Stanislas ennobled him in 1761 and named him chief engineer of the Ponts et Chaussées of Lorraine and Barrois in 1762. He received the title of *académicien* in 1775 and headed the French Académie Royale d'Architecture from 1782 to 1792. By 1761, he had realized the Portes Stanislas and Sainte-Catherine as well as the Sainte-Catherine barracks in Nancy.

After the death of King Stanislas, Queen Marie Leszcynska called her father's architect to Versailles and charged him with building the convent of the Ursulines, today the Lycée Hoche. Construction began in 1767. Madame Adelaide allowed Richard Mique to continue the work after her mother's death. Completed in 1772, the building successfully blends French tradition with the lessons of antiquity. Mique also built the Church of the Carmelites, today a museum, in Saint-Denis in 1775, and the chapel of the Hospice de Saint-Cloud in 1788.

Mesdames, the daughters of Louis XV, recommended their protégé to their niece, Queen Marie Antoinette. In 1775, Richard Mique succeeded ANGE JACQUES GABRIEL as *premier architecte du roi.*

Trianon was to be developed in "the English taste" for Queen Marie Antoinette. After consulting with the gardener and the painter HUBERT ROBERT, Mique presented a master plan in February 1777. He built successfully the Temple de l'Amour, the Theater, the Grotto with its cascade, and the Belvedere. After 1783, the new park of the Hameau du Trianon was begun.

While executing this work, Richard Mique had undertaken in 1779 at Versailles the decoration of the *petits appartements* of the queen: the Méridienne, the two libraries, and the Cabinet Intérieur or Petit Salon de Marie Antoinette. Assisted by the Rousseau brothers, Mique created a work clearly announcing the style of the end of the century. He also decorated the Châteaux of Saint-Cloud and Fontainebleau.

GÉRARD ROUSSET-CHARNY
Translated from French by Richard Cleary

BIBLIOGRAPHY

MOREY, PROSPER 1868 *Richard Mique.* Nancy, France: Raybois.

MITCHELL, ROBERT

Robert Mitchell, thought to have been from Aberdeen, began practicing in London before 1782. Three years later he may have published a book entitled *Designs for Rural Villas on Economical Principles,* although no copy has been traced. His *Plans* of his own works appeared in 1801. Apart from country houses with good Adamesque interiors, his fame rests on his Nelson Column (1808–1809), Montreal, the proportions of which were unfortunately spoiled in execution.

PIERRE DE LA RUFFINIÈRE DU PREY

WORKS

1777–1779, Moore Place, Much Hadham, Hertfordshire, England. *1793–1794, The Rotunda, Leicester Square, London. 1794, Preston Hall, Midlothian, Scotland. 1796, Silwood Park, Berkshire, England. 1808–1809, Nelson Column, Montreal.

BIBLIOGRAPHY

COLLARD, ELIZABETH 1969 "Nelson in Old Montreal: A Coade Memorial." *Country Life* 146:210–211.

MITCHELL, ROBERT 1801 *Plans, and Views in Perspective, with Descriptions, of Buildings Erected in England and Scotland: and also an Essay, to Elucidate the Grecian, Roman, and Gothic Architecture, Accompanied with Designs.* London: Wilson.

NARES, GORDON 1956 "Moor Place, Hertfordshire." *Country Life* 119:156–159, 204–207.

MITCHELL/GIURGOLA

Ehrman B. Mitchell (1924–), a Philadelphian trained at the University of Pennsylvania, and Romaldo Giurgola (1920–), native of Italy, educated at the University of Rome and Columbia University, formed their partnership in Philadelphia in 1958; they also have an office in New York City. Mitchell is distinguished for his participation in the American Institute of Architects, serving as its national president; Giurgola has taught at Cornell University, the University of Pennsylvania, and Columbia University, where he served as chairman of architecture and is Ware Professor of Architecture. He received the Gold Medal of the American Institute of Architects in 1981.

The firm's projects range from small houses to large urban office buildings, institutions, and plans for urban areas. The work is distinguished by considered response to the urban context and the natural environment, and by an intent to create a sense of place that will, as Mitchell and Giurgola profess, "give form and accommodation to the family of man." "A building," Giurgola has said, "is a fragment of the larger environment which includes other continuously growing structures and the natural landscape. As a meaningful fragment, it should have its own inner order to be able to relate to others."

LEE COPELAND

WORKS

1958, Crockett House, Corning, N.Y. 1959, Stine House, Bryan, Ohio. 1960, Wright Brothers Memorial Visitors Center, Kill Devil Hills, Evansville, Ill. 1963, White House, Chestnut Hill, Pa. 1965, Myrick Pavilion, The American College, Bryn Mawr, Pa. 1970, Dayton House, Wayzata, Minn. 1971, Public Library (South End Branch), Boston. 1971, Subway Concourse Entrance, Market and 8th Street; 1971, United Fund Headquarters; Philadelphia. 1972, Bok Tower, Mountain Lake Sanctuary, Lake Wales, Fla. 1972, Mission Park Residential Houses, Williams College, Williamstown, Mass. 1973, Columbus High School, Ind. 1973, Worship Assembly Building, Benedictine Society of Saint Bede, Peru, Ill. 1974, Student Union, State University College of New York, Plattsburgh. 1975, Penn Mutual Tower; 1975, William Penn High School; Two INA Plaza (office building); Philadelphia. 1978, Harbor Plaza, Stamford, Conn. 1979, Newman House, Bedford, N.Y. 1979, Physical Activities Building, Swarthmore College, Pa. 1980, Graduate Studies Center, The American College, Bryn Mawr, Pa. 1980, Wainwright State Office Complex (with Hastings and Chivetta), St. Louis, Mo. 1981, Student Housing, San Pietro al Natisone, Italy. 1981, Technical High School, Maniago, Italy.

BIBLIOGRAPHY

DEAN, ANDREA 1976 "Profile of the Firm Award Recipient: Mitchell/Giurgola." *Journal of the American Institute of Architects* 65:58–61.

GIURGOLA, ROMALDO, and MEHTA, JAIMINI 1975 *Louis I. Kahn.* Boulder, Colo.: Westview.

MARLIN, WILLIAM 1976 "Mitchell/Giurgola Associates: Three Bench Mark Buildings." *Architectural Record* 159:107–118.

MARLIN, WILLIAM 1977 "Structures with a Social Value." *Christian Science Monitor* 21:23.

MIX, EDWARD T.

Born in New Haven, Connecticut, Edward Townsend Mix (1831–1890) completed an architectural apprenticeship in New England and in 1856 went to Milwaukee, Wisconsin. Early in his practice, he associated with WILLIAM W. BOYINGTON, a Chicago architect, and during the 1880s, he worked with Walter A. Holbrook. Mix was state architect of Wisconsin from 1874 to 1879. His Kansas State Capitol design was rejected (1866), his Mitchell Building (1876–1878) and Chamber of Commerce Building (1879–1880) in Milwaukee were of recognized early architectural importance, and his twelve-story Guaranty Loan Building (1888–1889) in Minneapolis, with its full-height glass-roofed court, was a landmark there.

WESLEY I. SHANK

WORKS

1873–1875, Immanuel Presbyterian Church, Milwaukee, Wis. 1874, Montauk (Governor William Larrabee House), Clermont, Iowa. 1876–1878, Mitchell Building; 1879–1880, Chamber of Commerce (Mackie) Building; Milwaukee, Wis. *1888–1889, Guaranty Loan (Metropolitan) Building, Minneapolis, Minn.

BIBLIOGRAPHY

PERRIN, RICHARD W. E. 1968 *Milwaukee Landmarks: An Architectural Heritage, 1850–1950.* Wisc.: Milwaukee Public Museum.

TORBERT, DONALD R. 1958 *A Century of Minnesota Architecture.* Minn.: Minneapolis Society of Fine Arts.

WIGHT, PETER B. 1916 "Milwaukee Revisited: The Northwestern Mutual Life Insurance Company's Last New Building." *Architectural Record* 40:129–144.

MIZNER, ADDISON

Addison Mizner (1872–1933) is best known as the originator of the Revival of Spanish-style architecture in Florida. Born in Benicia, California, Addison attended the University of Salamanca in Spain. Returning to San Francisco after several months, Addison expressed a desire to pursue a career as an artist. His parents, hoping that he would continue the family's three-generation tradition of diplomatic service, sent him to China, but Addison returned intent on a career in architecture. He joined the office of WILLIS POLK and became a partner in 1893. In 1897, after accumulating heavy debts, Mizner was forced to leave San Francisco. He worked as a goldminer in northern California and then joined three of his brothers in the Klondike gold rush.

Mizner returned to San Francisco in late 1899 with enough money to pay his debts and retain a modest fortune but he departed promptly for a two-year tour of the Orient. Eventually reaching Guatemala, Mizner began trading in antiques and religious artifacts. In 1904, he returned to New York and, under the patronage of Mrs. Hermann Oelrichs and Mrs. William K. Vanderbilt, opened a Fifth Avenue antiques business. Mizner received a few minor architectural commissions through his social connections and Mrs. Oelrichs' friendship with STANFORD WHITE. These commissions led to others, and Mizner established himself as a Long Island estate architect. He purchased the Baxter Homestead (c.1775) on the waterfront in Port Washington, Long Island, and remodeled it into a home and private museum.

Mizner practiced in an eclectic palette of styles. Realized projects from this period include a Spanish house for I. Townsend Burden near Rosyln, a Chinese teahouse for Mrs. O. H. P. Belmont at Sands Point, and an exact reproduction of an English inn, all on Long Island.

World War I brought a dramatic reduction in estate construction, and in 1918, Mizner, in poor health and finances, moved to Palm Beach, Florida. There, Mizner met Paris Singer, heir to part of the Singer Sewing Machine fortune. With Singer's patronage, Mizner built the exclusive Everglades Club and was soon deluged with commissions to design estates for postwar millionaires who, unable to reach the war-stricken Riviera, had chosen to winter on the Florida coast. With Klondike panache, Mizner lionized the Palm Beach social scene and received hundreds of commissions from clients including Harold Vanderbilt, John S. Phipps, A. J. Drexel Biddle, and Rodman Wanamaker. These were almost without exception designed in Mizner's Saracenic-Spanish style; they were not literal copies of Spanish buildings but festive and airy American suburban villas of Spanish inspiration.

Taking a keen interest in the craft of building, Mizner established business interests for the fabrication of wrought iron, terra-cotta roof tiles, and cast-stone ornament. His buildings were often executed with only sketchy or incomplete designed drawings and Mizner made frequent alterations on the site.

The successful completion of Palm Beach and the continuing Florida land boom encouraged Mizner to purchase land twenty-six miles south of

Palm Beach at Boca Raton. With financing by T. Coleman Du Pont and Jesse Livermore, Boca Raton was an immediate success. In six months, $30 million worth of lots were sold and many of the town's canals, yacht basins, polo fields, country clubs, and hotels were completed before the Florida bubble burst in the spring of 1926. By 1927, the Florida land collapse had left Mizner bankrupt; the final six years of his life were spent writing *The Many Mizners,* the first volume of which was published in 1932.

Mizner's buildings are picturesque and theatrical; he shunned architectural academicism and never participated in the American Beaux-Arts movement or in the Colonial Revival, which dominated domestic architecture of the Northeast during the 1920s. Instead, he was keenly observant and dedicated to an architecture that combined comfort and convenience with a system of architectural symbols which came to represent the domestic and social structure of the Florida boom years. Although CARRÈRE AND HASTINGS's 1887 Spanish-style design for the Ponce de Leon Hotel at Saint Augustine predates Mizner's Florida work by thirty years, Mizner was, nonetheless, the father of the Florida Renaissance. He, more than any other architect of the time, promoted the extravagant revival architecture which remains today an expression of the fanciful exuberance of America's pre-Depression prosperity.

GRAHAM S. WYATT

WORKS

Exact dates are not available for the works listed below, but all were built between 1916 and 1930.

n.d., A. J. Drexel Biddle, Jr., House; n.d., Arthur B. Claflin House; Palm Beach, Fla. n.d., The Cloister, Boca Raton, Fla. n.d., Mrs. Hugh Sillman House, Palm Beach, Fla. n.d., Riverside Baptist Church, Jacksonville, Fla. n.d., Preston Hope Satterwhite House; n.d., Edward T. Stotesbury House; n.d., Harold Vanderbilt House; n.d., Rodman Wanamaker House; n.d., William Gray Warden House; Palm Beach, Fla.

BIBLIOGRAPHY

"Addison Mizner Dies in Florida of Heart Attack." 1933 *New York Herald Tribune* Feb. 6, p. 15.

JOHNSTON, ALVA 1953 *The Legendary Mizners.* New York: Farrar, Straus.

KINNEY, HENRY 1966 *Once Upon a Time.* Boca Raton, Fla.

MIZNER, ADDISON (1902)1918 *The Cynics Catalogue of Revised Wisdom.* San Francisco: Elder & Shepard.

MIZNER, ADDISON 1932 *The Many Mizners.* New York: Sears.

MIZNER, ADDISON and TARBELL, IDA M. 1928 *The Florida Architecture of Addison Mizner.* New York: Helburn.

ORR, CHRISTINA n.d. *Addison Mizner (1872–1933): Architect of Dreams and Realities.* Exhibition catalogue. Includes a bibliography.

ROBERTS, KENNETH L. 1926 *Florida.* New York: Harper.

SULLIVAN, EDWARD DEAN 1935 *The Fabulous Wilson Mizner.* New York: Henkle.

SULLIVAN, EDWARD DEAN 1936 "Palm Beach." *Fortune* 13:54–62.

MNESIKLES

Mnesikles, the author of the celebrated gateway to the Athenian Akropolis and one of the most talented architects of the classical world, is known to us by name only from two short literary references, both dating considerably after his lifetime. Philochorus, a late-fourth-century B.C. historian from Athens, records that the construction of the Propylaea began during the archonship of Euthymenes (437–436 B.C.) with Mnesikles as the architect (Harpocration, IV). Plutarch (A.D. 50–120), the well-known Greek biographer, is equally succinct: "The Propylaea of the acropolis were brought to completion in the space of five years, Mnesicles being their architect" (*Pericles,* XIII). A partially preserved marble stele from the Akropolis inscribed with the accounts of the five years of building has a lacuna of exactly the right amount of letter spaces on the prominent second line for the insertion of the architect's name. It has been suggested with good reason that this official document may have served as the source of information for the two literary accounts from later periods (Dinsmoor, 1913, pp. 371–398).

This is the extent of direct information about Mnesikles; neither the architect himself nor any of his contemporaries left a biographical account of his life or works. His birth and death dates are not known, but he was active during the second half of the fifth century B.C. We have no particular knowledge of his social background or professional training. Unlike for some of his colleagues, no architectural treatise or other theoretical writing is attributed to Mnesikles. It is evident, however, that along with IKTINOS and KALLIKRATES, the architects of the Parthenon, Mnesikles was recognized as one of the leading architects of his generation and entrusted, by Perikles personally, with important commissions on the Akropolis. Our understanding and appreciation of his artistic personality must depend, predominantly, on the Propylaea (437–432 B.C.), the only building that can be firmly attributed to him although a few others have been associated with his name on stylistic grounds. Despite considerable variety in the interpretations and analyses of the Propylaea, most modern scholars concur in recognizing the progressive nature of his work and the genius of his design solutions.

The first architectural organization of the west entrance to the Akropolis dates to the sixth century B.C., a response to the establishment of the Greater Panathenaic festival in 556 B.C. This was probably when the first straight ramp for the procession was put up replacing the old zigzag footpath. The ramp, 80-meters long, had a total rise of 25 meters from one end to the other, producing, certainly, a very steep gradient but one not impossible to negotiate especially if steps were introduced intermittently. A few stretches of the polygonal retaining wall for the Archaic ramp have been recovered. At about the same time, a monumental gate structure must have replaced an earlier military gate which had given access to the Mycenaean fortress.

The immediate predecessor to Mnesikles's Propylaea was the Old Propylon, constructed sometime between 490–480 B.C., contemporary with the older Parthenon and destroyed by the Persians in 480 B.C. It appears to have been designed along the lines of a traditional propylon: a rectangular, pedimented structure with front and back porches and, probably, four Doric columns in antis. At its southwest corner, it bordered on the thick Mycenaean fortification wall at a 120° angle and created a recessed, courtlike space with several steps which gave access to the sanctuary of Athena Nike. A section of the foundation wall in marble at this corner is the only substantial portion left from the building. In this position, the alignment of the Old Propylon was some 23 degrees askew (northeast/southwest) from the direction of the straight ramp. The sense of enclosure in front of the gate was augmented by a late-sixth-century apsidal structure situated northwest of the entrance. This small edifice (Building B), oriented north–south, had a back room and a porch with three columns in antis. It is believed to have served as a kind of lounge for the refreshment and relaxation of the pilgrims on their way to the Akropolis and can be compared to a number of buildings of similar purpose in many other sanctuaries (Travlos, 1971, p. 482; Weller, 1904, pp. 35–37).

Mnesikles's new gate for the Akropolis is a complex structure which attempts to unify the disparate and independent elements of the old scheme into one, formally conceived architectural whole. The project was interrupted by the Peloponnesian Wars and was never quite completed. Built entirely in Pentellic marble (with some details in Eleusinian dark stone), the Propylaea is composed of a prominent central gate-building, flanked on the west side by wings placed at right angles to it. Before the addition of these wings, during the first three years of its construction, the structure was called a propylon, in the singular. Mnesikles turned the entire composition clockwise 23 degrees to match the alignment of the straight ramp; the new alignment also coincided with that of the Parthenon (447–438 B.C.) and the long axis of the Akropolis and brought the group into direct visual axis with the colossal statue of Athena Promachos. The length of the old ramp was retained but its width was nearly doubled from 11 meters to 21 meters which precisely equaled the width of the central gate. A section of the retaining wall for this ramp built in blocks of poros has been uncovered north of the old polygonal wall.

The east and west porches of the central gate are modeled after the fashion of a Doric temple front, six prostyle columns carrying individual pediments. Yet, the nature of the building as a monumental gate is clearly revealed by the unusually wide central intercolumniation (5.43-meters axial spacing with double metopes) which allows an uninterrupted stretch of the ramp as the main roadway. The difference in level between the two porches due to rising ground (the east porch is higher by 1.40 meters) was partially accommodated by introducing five steps inside the gate structure leading to a cross-wall placed at two-thirds of the distance from the west front and expressed by a separate gable on the roof. Further adjustment to the difference in level was made possible by elevating the columns of the west porch on a platform of four steps while the east porch columns were set on a single stylobate and are shorter by about 0.30 meter (height of western columns: 8.81 meters; height of eastern columns: 8.53 meters; the columns of both sides have a bottom diameter of 1.56 meters; axial spacing with double contraction: 3.63 meters, 5.43 meters central, and 3.38 meters at corners).

The cross-wall, pierced by five doors diminishing in size from the center outward, creates on the outer, western side, a large room. Judged by the stone benches placed against the side walls it might have been used as a waiting or resting area for the visitors. Flanking the processional ramp in the center are two rows of three slender Ionic columns which reach to the full height of the room and support the coffered marble ceiling. (The columns, 10.13 meters high, are nearly 1.50 meters taller than the Doric columns.) The marble beams of the aisles span a clear 5.40 meters and weigh nearly 11 tons each including their share of the coffer load. The double-member architraves of the Ionic colonnade which carry these beams (loaded one over each column and one at mid-span) are fortified by iron bars embedded inside channels cut into their top surfaces. Although modern investigations show that the use of these bars was quite unnecessary and even incorrect (the iron is overloaded and the bearing capacity of marble underestimated), Mnesikles's interest in progressive building technology is laudable. In the excessively wide central spans of the east and west porches, he displays an excellent understanding of the double-cantilever principle. The Doric frieze over the central opening is built as two long monolithic beams (instead of the usual separate blocks of triglyphs and metopes) which rest on the columns at mid-length and cantilever out almost an equal distance on both sides, thus relieving the stress on the architrave. Furthermore, the excessive weight of the taller, central block of the pediment is hollowed out at the back in order to insure an evenly distributed loading over the critical span (Dinsmoor, 1947; Coulton, 1977, pp. 148–152).

The northwest wing, known as the Pinakotheke (picture gallery), is connected to the central gate at right angles and projects beyond the columns of the west porch by some 7 meters; the blank western face of the structure is elevated on a tall terrace wall of ashlar and reaches down to the level of the terrace which contains the base of the so-called Agrippa Monument. A porch with three Doric columns in antis precedes the small, rectangular chamber lit by two windows on either side of a door which is placed off-axis in the wall; consequently, all openings are shifted eastward from the axis of symmetry. In the past, the explanation for this irregularity was sought in elaborate aesthetic theories establishing a number of ideal vantage points on the approach ramp (erroneously believed to be zigzag) which offered optimum angles of vision and made the openings "appear" symmetrical through the intervening row of columns. Consequently, these imaginary viewing stations and optical lines were used to determine the course of the zigzag ramp (Stevens, 1946; Elderkin, 1912, pp. 1–6). The asymmetry was also explained on functional and structural grounds, as providing the optimum lighting conditions for the room (Franco, 1930–1931, pp. 9–25). However, based on an acceptance of the function of the space as a dining room (following the tradition of its predecessor, Building B), the current interpretation is practical and refreshingly straightforward: the door of the Pinakotheke was shifted off-axis for the best possible arrangement of the dining couches inside (Travlos, 1971, p. 482).

In Pausanias's account of his visit to the Akropolis in the second century A.D., the northwest wing of the Propylaea is referred to as "a chamber containing pictures" (I.22.6). Although we cannot be sure if this was among the original functions of the room, the quasireligious nature of a ritual dining space is quite compatible with the display of art. Pausanias gives a fairly lengthy description of the pictures themselves but he does not make it clear whether they were easel or wall paintings, or how they were displayed in the room. Dinsmoor (1950, p. 203) points out that the upper parts of the interior marble walls were never finished and suggests that they could have been intended to receive a smooth layer of stucco for wall paintings which was never applied.

The southwest wing of the building presents a more complicated appearance. Simply an open porch giving access to the terrace of the sanctuary of Athena Nike, it has a false front of three columns in antis, mirroring the façade of the Pinakotheke. Although the position of the western anta corresponds to that of the northwest wing, there is no wall behind it. The anta is a double-faced, free-standing element, an isolated pier against which the colonnade terminates. The roof, the true building line of the porch, is set back in alignment with the westernmost Doric column and leaves sufficient space for the altar in front of the temple of Athena Nike. The west façade of the southwest wing is open with the exception of a slender pier between the antae supporting an entablature as unorthodox as the design of the wing itself: triglyphs are omitted from what is supposed to be a Doric frieze. The over-all appearance recalls the smooth, continuous lines of the Ionic Temple of Nike which faces the west porch of the wing at a short distance. The wing is only 6-meters wide, stopping against the Mycenaean wall which must have risen more than 13 meters above the floor of the Propylaea.

Both wings are covered by simple hip roofs rather than the pediments that are shown in some of the earlier reconstruction drawings of the building. The columns of the wings are smaller than those of the central gate by one-third, but a sense of continuity is achieved by the alignment of the easternmost wing columns with the larger end columns of the west porch. The unity of the façade, despite the difference in scale, is further enhanced by the U-shaped platform of four steps which continues unbroken under all columns, except in the middle where it is interrupted by the roadway.

The outlook of the Propylaea began to change in the mid-third century A.D. when the Akropolis was converted back to a fortress and became a part of the new circuit of city walls. The building was more firmly enmeshed in the defense system in the following centuries and suffered much damage, the most serious of which probably occurred during the Venetian siege of Athens in 1687. By the end of the seventeenth century, most of the upper structure had already collapsed. Thanks to preservation and reconstruction efforts in the twentieth century by N. Balanos and A. Orlandos, the Propylaea presents a reasonably complete appearance today.

Like the other projects of the classical period of the Akropolis, the Propylaea is a building of precision and exquisite workmanship in marble. Contemporaries and political opponents of Perikles criticized and condemned the extraordinary costliness of the building; writers and travelers of later years appeared to be particularly impressed by its enormous expense and rapid construction.

Among the subtleties which must have contributed to the cost is the entablature of the east porch which displays an upward curvature of 0.019 meters, confirmed by the actual variations in column heights, and not by any settlement of foundations. The Doric hexastyles of the east and west porches have double contractions. The Ionic columns of the western vestibule introduce an imperceptible *entasis* (hitherto a Doric feature) of 0.0063 meters for a height of more than 10.13 meters. Their capitals are considered to be among the most exquisitely formed and articulated Ionic capitals ever made and were later imitated in the Erechtheion (421–406 B.C.). The impeccable order and the daring span of the ceiling beams and marble coffering of the same room elicit praise from the critics of today as they did from Pausanias, who wrote that "the Propylaea has a ceiling of white marble which in size and beauty of the blocks remains supreme even to my time" (I.22.4). In his time, Pausanias could, undoubtedly, see and admire the painted decoration of the coffers with a gilt star or palmette in the center of each, still largely visible as late as 1846 when Penrose studied the building and produced a set of restoration drawings of the polychrome ornament (Penrose, 1851, pp. 58–59, plates 24, 25; Lawrence, 1957, p. 162, plates 61, 62).

Pausanias also mentions a number of statues displayed in the Propylaea: a Hermes ("Hermes of the Portal") and a representation of the Graces were exhibited somewhere in the west porch, probably inside the recesses created by the antae; the base of the statue of Athena Hygieia is still *in situ* just outside the southernmost column of the east porch; several others, a Leaena ("lioness"), an Aphrodite, and a Diitrephes, have been hypothetically positioned inside the east porch (I.22.8; I.23.1–5; Stevens, 1936, pp. 446–458).

Quite apart from the superb craftsmanship, the architectural ornament and detailing of the Propylaea admit features that were quite uncommon and even revolutionary at a time when Athenian architecture was enjoying its most experimental and creative period. Among the noteworthy additions to the repertoire of the Doric is the cyma reversa bed molding for the horizontal cornice of the Propylaea's main entablature. The introduction of an ovolo molding to crown the Doric frieze as well as the choice of the ovolo profile for the sima of the cornice were, on the other hand, clearly influenced by the recently completed Parthenon. But unlike the Parthenon which retains the traditional palmette-and-anthemion decoration for the sima, the sima of the Propylaea adheres to the Ionic convention of decorating the ovolo with egg and dart, an unprecedented step in the development of the Doric order. Equally unprecedented is Mnesikles's use of the cyma recta profile in the sima of his minor order, the cornice of the southwest wing. This particular combination of Ionic profiling of a Doric sima crops up during the fourth century B.C. in a rather sporadic fashion. Its more immediate employment in the Erechtheion and in Iktinos's temple of Apollo at Bassae (c.450 B.C.) suggests the direct influence of the Propylaea. In the case of the temple at Bassae, it may even be conceived as a kind of compliment returned by Iktinos to his (younger?) colleague who had previously borrowed from his work on the Parthenon. Finally, in the Caryatid Porch of the Erechtheion, the detail of substituting triangular openings in the interstices between the eggs and darts of the sima instead of the usual lion-headed spouts to eject the rain water must have been modeled after the side cornices of the Propylaea's main gate, where this unique motif had already been employed by Mnesikles, perhaps for the first time.

The use of the dark, Eleusinian stone mixed with white marble, an ostensibly insignificant and ornamental feature of the Propylaea, reveals upon closer examination the workings of a sensitive and sophisticated purpose. Applied as a string course under the windows of the Pinakotheke and continued along its inner walls, the dark band emphasizes the structure of the windows and literally underscores them as special elements, a justifiable distinction since windows were not common in Greek public buildings. Furthermore, the firm, horizontal line occurring at 2.40 meters above the floor works as a space modulator or an element of scale to which the occupants of this exceptionally tall room could relate. It might also have served as a base above which the paintings were displayed, thus separating the dining couches, the zone of practical usage, from that of art. A similar sense of visual and functional separation of space is achieved by the row of dark orthostats in the western vestibule of the gate building; the color change also hints at the structural significance of the socle traditionally emphasized in wall con-

Mnesikles.
The Propylaea, Akropolis.
Athens.
437–432 B.C.

struction. In the same room, the dark threshold of the five doors at the top of the steps calls attention to the major change of level inside the building and marks the spatial transition between the vestibule and the east porch, the outer and the inner gates.

But the most cogent and effective use of the Eleusinian stone in the Propylaea is in the four-stepped platform which runs continuously under the columns of the west porch and the wings and unites the diverse elements of the plan into one architectural whole. This ingenious decision of Mnesikles, however, created its own drawback. The scale of columns in the Doric order ideally bears a certain proportionate relationship to the height of the stylobate and its steps. Here, the columns of the west porch, though substantially larger in size, were made to share the same stylobate. The architect's solution to this difficult problem, inherent in the inflexible canon, was equally ingenious in its attempt to subordinate physical size of the object to its visual perception by the eye. All four steps were built in marble except at the wings where the bottom step is of dark stone. So, although the total composition is pulled together by the continuous four-stepped platform, the columns of the central porch and the flanks can be accepted, perhaps as much intellectually as optically, to maintain an appropriate scale to their respective stylobates (Shoe, 1949, pp. 342–347; Coulton, 1977, pp. 120–121).

Although Mnesikles was not the first architect to introduce dark stone for polychromatic effects in Greek architecture, he appears to have been the first one to realize and fully exploit the architectonic potential of the combination beyond its usual employment for decorative purposes.

The progressive and creative spirit displayed in the architectural ornament and details of the Propylaea is reflected in larger dimensions, in the over-all design and spatial organization of the building which takes maximum advantage of the sloping site and transforms the entire west end of the Akropolis into a man-made harbor. The composition is deliberate and complex, collecting and boldly juxtaposing elements of diverse function and scale. Although the separateness of the units tends to be emphasized by their individual roofs, the unity of the group is assured by the positive and dynamic relationship established between the masses and voids. Seen at eye level, instead of from aerial perspective, the isolation of the solids would have been even less conspicuous. Until the emergence of the elaborately laid out sanctuaries of the Hellenistic era, the planning of the Propylaea had no real precedents or followers in the Greek world.

Mnesikles's source of inspiration, as J. A. Bundgaard (1957) maintains, could have been the informal group of elements around the Old Propylon; indeed, he may have been given the same or a similar kind of program to follow. But there the similarity ends. In Mnesikles's Propylaea, the disparate parts of the old scheme, including the monumental ramp, have been pulled together into a formally organized whole and integrated into the hill side. Even the traditional form of the Old Propylon with its columns between heavy antae has been effectively altered by moving the columns in front of the structure and surmounting them with proper pediments. Whereas the temple form reasserts the authority of the unique and indisputed position of the Athenian Akropolis among the other sanctuary sites, the projecting wings continue the rhythm of the main colonnade at a minor and somewhat informal scale and welcome the visitor like a pair of arms outstretched in a grand gesture of reception. The capacity of these colonnaded wings and their terraced, solid extensions to anchor the powerful thrust of the processional ramp, and to capture and enclose space from the great expanse of sky stretching out in front of the steep Akropolis cliffs and beyond to the sea, is a remarkable and truly revolutionary achievement.

Equally remarkable is the impression of space created inside the west vestibule of the gate building. At the outset, the nature and the intensity of this experience are underlined by the contrast between the compact Doric of the exterior and the light and airy Ionic of the interior. The static sense of volume established by the generous dimensions and the cubical proportions of the room seems to be stirred and stretched by the tense energy of the slender Ionic columns soaring up to meet the severe outline of the marble-beamed ceiling. The extraordinary breadth of the interior, unique in the design of gate structures, finds an invigorating counterpoint in the long axis established by the processional way. In terms of usage, the room is defined at its western and eastern ends by flights of five steps each, while its hollow center, uninterrupted by changes in level, is the port of arrival, the last spatial terminal at which to pause and linger before the holy ground of the Akropolis is gained. The religious and spiritual content of arrival and passage was not invented by Mnesikles, it was inherent in the act and in the ritual; but Mnesikles recognized its full meaning and gave it a new symbolic and emotional depth through the sensitive articulation of the shape of space and the manipulation of the purposeful human movement through it. Ascending the flight of steps pushed against the cross-wall of the gate, the last physical barrier between the outside and the inside is crossed, and the visitor finds himself in the shallow east porch, a platform of vantage offering a momentary shelter from the awesome emptiness of the hill-top sanctuary which seems to echo the palpitating realization of being there. In the words of Vincent Scully ([1962]1969, p. 180), "the great fact of the Propylaia is that it is an interior space which leads from one kind of exterior to another and makes the human being who passes through it a different man entering and leaving it."

We may never know the original or "ideal" design Mnesikles had in mind for the Propylaea. The question of whether the present building is "merely the relic of a much more grandiose project" (Dinsmoor, 1950, p. 204) or whether it is fairly close to what the architect had intended it to be is as much a methodological problem, obscured by our own inconsistency to define what exactly is meant by "original design," as it is an archaeological one stemming from lack of sufficient evidence.

However, the evidence we do have—antae projecting from the northeast and southeast corners of the main building and preparations for a roof (beam holes left on the east walls of the northwest and southwest wings)—indicates that a pair of halls of equal height were planned to flank the east porch of the gate. It is also evident that the project never got much beyond planning or preparatory stages since no foundations were laid for their outer walls or for the hypothetical, but necessary, inner row of columns to support the sloping rafters of a hip roof. It is difficult, even impossible, to determine how far north and south these halls were intended to extend, although the short stump of a wall on the northeast corner of the Pinakotheke suggests that the northeast hall might have been planned to be taken all the way to the edge of the Akropolis cliff. The complications imposed by the restricting nature of the topography, the existence of a major portion of the Mycenaean Wall, and the well-established presence of the sanctuaries of Athena Nike to the west and Artemis Brauronia to the east make any extension in the southern direction problematic and give rise to a number of historical controversies about the nature of Mnesikles's original intentions and design for the southeast and southwest wings of the Propylaea.

Swayed primarily by Wilhelm Dörpfeld's extensive studies of the building, many late nineteenth- and early twentieth-century scholars were anxious to accept a fully and rigidly symmetrical scheme for the Propylaea covering the entire west end of the Akropolis. Dörpfeld's reconstruction (1885) proposed two stoas of equal length flanking the east porch and extending out on both sides to the Akropolis walls; in fact, the stoa on the south is shown running slightly over the wall. On the west side, the southwest wing was supposed to have been a full wing, mirroring the Pinakotheke. The west front of this wing was believed to have been arranged as a colonnade of four columns between antae in order to provide access to the sanctuary of Nike. Although modified significantly as a result of the archaeological work which the American School in Athens and the Greek Archaeological Service carried on intermittently into the middle of the twentieth century, Dörpfeld's symmetrical scheme still served as the basis for Dinsmoor's restoration, in which the long sides of the east halls facing the Akropolis are shown with solid walls except for a pair of doors at their ends (the unfinished "antae" are interpreted to be door jambs). The west side of the southwest wing is also restored as a solid wall like that of the Pinakotheke instead of an open colonnade as proposed by Dörpfeld (Dörpfeld, 1885, pp. 38–56, pls. 2–5; Dinsmoor, 1950, 204–205). B. Schweitzer (1950, pp. 116–125) also believes that the southwest wing was conceived as a full-sized unit open to the sanctuary of Nike on the west by a colonnade.

All of these studies are grounded on the presumption that Mnesikles started out from a totally symmetrical scheme for the Propylaea which was frustrated by the opposition of the conservative priesthood of Athena Nike and Artemis Brauronia whose sanctuaries were seriously encroached upon by the projected south wing of the complex. Consequently, the abandonment of the southeast hall and the amputation of the southwest wing are considered to be reluctant but clever design adjustments on the part of the architect who could not realize his original and ideal conception. The construction of the northeast hall, on the other hand, on land free from similar restrictions, progressed to include beam and rafter holes in its south and west walls but had to be stopped before further work could be undertaken due to the outbreak of the Peloponnesian Wars.

Recent scholarship finds the theory of symmetrical design insupportable on archeological and architectural grounds. According to Bundgaard (1957, pp. 77–83), Mnesikles excluded, or postponed indefinitely, the two east halls from the start and left their execution to others; the southeast wing, at any rate, was never meant to be anything more than an access corridor some 4 meters in width. Others, among them, L. Guerrini (1963, p. 130); Claudio Tiberi (1964, p. 47); J. J. Coulton (1977, p. 120); and John Travlos (1971, p. 482), maintain that Mnesikles never intended to make the south wings absolutely symmetrical to the north ones; the lack of space and the difference in functions would have prevented such an approach from the inception of the project. They contend, however, that he obviously did want to create the *appearance* of a symmetrical west façade and found a solution by inventing the false front for the southwest wing which successfully hides the irregularity of the porch behind it.

The argument for Mnesikles's original design for the Propylaea is a vague and elusive concept that needs clarification. Do we mean by it an abstract and ideal project that can exist only in the mind of the architect quite irrespective of real conditions such as the demands of topography and usage that ordinarily contribute to the shaping of a design—what one might call a predesign stage? Or are we considering a project which takes into account these restrictions but which has to be further modified and curtailed during the planning or construction stage due to additional and unforeseeable impositions? The former, without hard, written evidence, poses an intangible condition whose consideration lies largely in the realm of speculation, though informed to a degree by our knowledge of the artistic personality of the man and the architectural sensibilities of the period. Could Mnesikles's design sense gravitate toward a perfectly symmetrical layout—one that would also cover the entire west end of the Akropolis and obliterate a large part of the highly esteemed sacred ground? Would the general development of the mid-fifth century B.C. architecture in Greece favor, even allow, complete and rigid symmetry in the planning of a complex building group?

The answers to these questions should be broad and tentative. Although it is unwise to make sweeping generalizations about the theory and application of symmetry in Greek architecture (only a couple of generations ago, the zigzag approach way to the Propylaea, then thought to be Mnesiklean, was admired for its subtlety and informality, whereas the "rigid and insensitive axiality" of the straight ramp was simply tolerated for being characteristically Roman), it would not be unjustifiable to assert that a strict, drafting-board mentality was alien to Greek design in this period. Even if the site had not imposed certain restrictions, complete symmetry and axiality in a scheme composed of so many independent elements as the Propylaea would be highly unlikely. Furthermore, there are no precedents for that kind of planning in the fifth century B.C. It seems unfair and injudicious to associate Mnesikles, whose work shows—quite apart from questions of over-all planning—sensitivity and skill at all levels, with a scheme that seeks easy solutions in the mechanical applications of blueprint symmetry.

Mnesikles must have been perfectly familiar with the profusion and the venerable nature of the cults and shrines that existed on the prehistoric bastion of Athena Nike, including the poros *naiskos* and the altar of the goddess and the colossal Mycenaen Wall that occupied a substantial amount of space at the east end of the terrace. These were the existing conditions he had to face as real and important a part of his design as the program he was expected to fulfill. Neither the argument for Mnesikles's desire to remove the shrines in order to build over the holy ground nor the one about hostile priestly opposition against this wish are based on hard evidence and must remain assumptions. On the contrary, it is perfectly possible that both Mnesikles and Perikles bore a reverential attitude toward these shrines and sought from the outset for an arrangement that would include them with honorable recognition. (Interestingly, the only information on the Propylaea in Plutarch, other than the sentence about Mnesikles, is an anecdote testifying to Perikles's sense of piety in connection to this building: Perikles, who was much dismayed about an injured workman from the Propylaea, was visited in a dream by Athena herself who prescribed a fast and effective cure for the invalid—an event which Plutarch describes as "a wonderful thing . . . which indicated that the goddess was not holding herself aloof, but was a helper in both the inception and the completion of the work" [I.22.7–8]).

An inscription of 448 B.C., well before any work had started on the Propylaea, informs us of the decision to erect the present marble temple and altar to Athena Nike and names Kallikrates as the architect. An amendment to the inscription records that a committee, consisting of three members of the *boule* (counsel), was to review the plans with the architect and give its final approval before anything could be built. Further epigraphical evidence indicates that the actual work on the temple did not start until 427/426 B.C. and was completed in 424 B.C. with the dedication of the cult statue. The twenty-year delay in construction suggests that the committee remained long undecided in its assessment of the proposed project(s), political as well as design considerations playing a role in the delay. Meanwhile, the Propylaea had been finished in its present form.

It is highly improbable, in fact, quite impossible that the development of these overlapping projects progressed without recognition of each other. We cannot know how many design stages the Propylaea went through, how many proposals were brought before the committee (if it still existed), and how each design was modified and curtailed to meet the complex and reciprocating requirements of the cult centers and shrines in existence. Mnesikles might have had some ideas that had to be altered and discarded; these are the normal steps in the development of any design. But the final form of the southwest wing should be judged as a positive and intelligent response to those conditions and considered as a permanent and finished state as it is. Indeed, the architectural relationship between the southwest wing of the Propylaea and the temple terrace of Athena Nike is too cogent to ignore.

The rebuilding and reorganization of the Nike terrace and the old Propylon are both Periklean projects of the same civic and religious concern. Originally, the prehistoric bastion was some 4 to 5 meters higher than its present level and served as a tower guarding the military gate. The upper part of the bastion might have been demolished as early as the seventh century B.C., bringing the top to 1.40 meters below today's level. The earliest date recorded for cult activity on the bastion is 556 B.C. The construction of the poros *naiskos* and altar for the goddess is believed to have been undertaken between 490–480 B.C., contemporary to the building of the old Propylon and the older Parthenon. All were destroyed by the Persians in 480 B.C. The Periklean work on the Nike terrace constituted the following: the Mycenaean bastion was enlarged by building a poros, ashlar wall which sheathed the old, irregularly shaped core of polygonal masonry; the level was raised by 1.40 meters to match the level of the Propylaea; the north wall of the new terrace was aligned with the main axis of the Propylaea and became an extension of the stepped podium of the southwest wing, thus presenting a solid, uniform flank for the approach ramp; a direct entrance into the sanctuary of Nike from the north, by way of a short stairway at the junction of the southwest wing podium and the bastion, was introduced or a similar arrangement from an earlier period was remodeled; an alternative scheme which retained the lower level of the bastion might have been considered at this time because the marble pillar (or door post as it leans slightly toward west) flanking the entrance seems to have been designed for a different stairway, one which was planned to start at a lower level and reach exactly the old level of the terrace top. All this preparatory work either followed the completion of the Propylaea immediately or progressed concurrently with it (Travlos, 1971, pp. 148–149; Bundgaard, 1957, pp. 70, 180ff.; Schweitzer, 1950, pp. 116–125; Wrede, 1932, pp. 74–91; Schleif, 1933, pp. 177–184).

The construction of Kallikrates's Temple of Nike and its altar which occupies nearly all available space on the newly created top of the bastion must have taken place soon after the terracing work was finished. The L-shaped west porch of the southwest wing of the Propylaea provides easy access to the sanctuary and at the same time creates a miniature private court and an architectural backdrop for the temple and the altar. The "wing" made by the projecting double-anta establishes a dynamic architectonic relationship between the porch and the obliquely positioned temple; the sense of space and enclosure suggested by the wing motif, here on a minor scale, reflects and recalls the use of the same motif in the larger frame of the Propylaea's west front. Mnesikles's Propylaea is not only a gate to the Akropolis, but also a gate to the sanctuary of Athena Nike on a suitably diminished scale.

It is also possible to argue for the existence of a conscious affinity between the Ionic order of the Nike temple and the Doric of the Propylaea, which seem to have taken on each other's characteristics in an effort to tone down their differences. The columns of the temple exhibit stockier proportions than usual for Ionic, while their Doric neighbors of the southwest wing are uncommonly slender. The incorporation of the cyma recta motif in the sima of the latter building can be interpreted as a visual response to the profiling of the Ionic temple. The closest parallels to Kallikrates's Ionic capitals are those from the interior of the Propylaea; the same is true for the three-fascia architrave of the temple, a detail which is more typical of Asia Minor than mainland Greece, but already used by Mnesikles inside the Propylaea.

Seen in this light, the idea of the Propylaea and the terrace of Athena Nike with all of its monuments as the product of a single design conception—rather than schemes developed separately and grafted onto each other—becomes extremely attractive and prompts the question as to who was the architect predominantly responsible for the project, Mnesikles or Kallikrates? Undoubtedly, both of these men had the official sanction and professional qualifications to contribute toward the shaping of the project. An objective analysis of the final design overwhelmingly suggests a close and intelligent collaboration between them. Based on what we know about the Propylaea—the larger, inherently more complex and sophisticated, and the earlier (at least, in construction) of the two buildings—it would not be unreasonable to imagine that it was Mnesikles who occupied a more vigorous and leading position in the proposed partnership (Tiberi, 1964, pp. 154–161; Shear, 1963, pp. 376–387; Bundgaard, 1957, pp. 177–184).

A new and even larger notion of Mnesikles's authority and architectural responsibilities on the Akropolis emerges as a result of two fortuitously preserved decrees of Kallias, the wealthy Athenian statesman and patron. After a thorough discussion, Dinsmoor dates the inscriptions to 438–437 B.C., the year in which the Parthenon was completed and the Propylaea was ready to be started. With the exception of Dinsmoor's, almost all of the scholarship on these well-known documents has restricted itself to problems of dating and to the evidently significant issues taken up in the second decree, such as the final authorization for the pedimental sculpture of the Parthenon, the making of two golden Nikes, and the commencement of the work on the Propylaea, and has overlooked the full import and implications for Mnesiklean studies of the section which reads that "the whole Akropolis, apart from the work hitherto provided for, is to be tidied up and reorganized at a cost not to exceed 10 talents per year under the joint supervision of the treasurers of Athena and the architect of the Propylaia, the specifications being drawn up by the latter 'just as in the case of the Propylaia' " (Dinsmoor, 1947, p. 132). Although we do not know what exactly is meant by "tidying up and reorganization" or to what extent the actual work followed the precepts outlined in the inscription, the appearance twice in the annual expense records of the Propylaea provisions for payments for works on the Akropolis "other than those in the Propylaia" may be interpreted as allusions to the reorganization activity mentioned in the Kallias decrees. Furthermore, the lack of any record of payment for site work in the fully preserved expense accounts of the Parthenon suggests that this was, indeed, the same item included annually at the end of the Propylaea accounts and hence credited to Mnesikles.

If we take the document at face value, as Dinsmoor does, the attribution of the design for the setting of the Parthenon—the approach ramp, the west terraces and terrace walls, the steps, and the positioning of some of the minor monuments—must go to Mnesikles rather than Iktinos. It also follows that Mnesikles must have been responsible for much of the over-all organization of the Chalkotheke and the sanctuary of Artemis Brauronia, especially their terracing and the fixing of their northern boundaries by a wall parallel to the main axis of the Propylaea. Even the plan of the Stoa of Artemis Brauronia, with its projecting wings, might owe something to Mnesikles (Dinsmoor, 1947, p. 127ff.; Tiberi, 1964, p. 162; Stevens, 1936, p. 472ff.; Travlos, 1971, p. 124).

The important decrees of Kallias do not furnish conclusive evidence but certainly point to the strong possibility that the design of the entire Akropolis west of the Parthenon, including the Propylaea and the sanctuary of Athena Nike, was part of a single, grandiose master plan in which the complex and often conflicting needs of various cults and shrines were welded into a realistic and workable solution; if this is true, the person who was entrusted with the master plan was Mnesikles, the architect of the Propylaea.

Notwithstanding the highly plausible hypothesis that Mnesikles might have collaborated with Kallikrates on the design of the Nike sanctuary, there is no record illuminating the architect's professional training and background or his relationship with his colleagues and students. Gottfried Gruben (Berve & Gruben, 1963, pp. 380–382) suggests that Iktinos might have been Mnesikles's teacher without necessarily implying that the latter worked in the Parthenon project as an apprentice. His judgment is based on the well-known affinity between the Doric order of the Parthenon and its less monumental application in the hexastyle façades of the Propylaea, and particularly on the observation of a number of specific similarities of proportion and ornament between the two buildings. A part of this should be attributed to the very strong likelihood that the craftsmen who had just finished the work on the Parthenon were employed on the Propylaea. Yet, the similarities are sufficiently numerous and close to lend credibility to Gruben's theory: the width of the Propylaea's west vestibule is almost equal to the width of the Parthenon's cella and the depth is very close to that of its west room; the diameter-to-height ratio of the Propylaea's Doric columns is $1/_{5.47}$ meters versus $1/_{5.48}$ meters of the Parthenon; the ratio of the entablature height to bottom diameter is $1/_{1.74}$ meters for the Propylaea and $1/_{1.73}$ meters for the Parthenon; the ovolo molding crowning the Propylaea's Doric frieze as well as the ovolo profile of the sima were used in the Parthenon's frieze and cornice.

Although Iktinos's earlier and prestigious work might have supplied immediate models for Mnesikles and although both the Propylaea and the Parthenon represent highly innovative and original conceptions in design and decoration, they are at the same time buildings of their own time and place, quite in step with the over-all development of the Doric order during this period. The interest in combining Ionic features with the Doric, experimenting with novel arrangements using traditional elements, and a general propensity toward additional decoration in the orders are among the more distinct and important characteristics of the fifth-century Attic style. Mnesikles's spirit of search and creativity gains its true meaning and depth only when it is framed by this broad understanding of tradition and development. This is not to suggest that his role as an architect must be reduced to that of a technician or a job coordinator who followed custom and usage without much thought or responsibility for aesthetic problems. This last view of the Greek architect, and in particular of Mnesikles, was advanced by Bundgaard (1957) who held that innovation and progress in Greek architecture was bound by the slow and time-honored laws of unself-conscious evolution in craftsmanly traditions. Bundgaard also rejected the idea that the Greek architect used drawings, plans, or elevations and that the design of buildings was recorded by detailed word descriptions whose implementation was largely left to the job site habits and sensibilities of master masons. In the case of the Propylaea, the theory was effective to explain a number of alleged incongruities and errors in construction. Not surprisingly, Bundgaard's thesis has not found much support among scholars. There is good evidence that indicates the use of drawings and models for buildings, and the position of the Greek architect as a true professional seems to be unassailable (Tiberi, 1964, pp. 71–72; Kostof, 1977, pp. 11–16).

The Propylaea is the only building that can be attributed to Mnesikles with certainty; his name, however, has been connected with the Erechtheion (421–405 B.C.) on the Akropolis and the Stoa of Zeus Eleutherios (c.430 B.C.) in the agora. The theory that Mnesikles was the designer of the Erechtheion is based on the observation that the irregularities of this complex structure (described as a "temple-telesterion") were the result of difficult site and programmatic conditions comparable to those of the Propylaea—primarily the necessity of accommodating a wide variety of earlier cults and shrines. The creative and flexible manner in which these problems were solved in both buildings led first Dörpfeld, then Dinsmoor to suggest that they were the works of the same master. (Dörpfeld, 1911, pp. 39–72; Dinsmoor, 1947, p. 135).

More recent scholarship, however, decided to look at the problem from a different angle and is reluctant to accept this view. I. M. Shear (1963, pp. 375–424) and Tiberi (1964, pp. 168–170) both recognize certain similarities of composition, ornament, and detail between the Propylaea and the Erechtheion, but they judge the differences to be more profound. The Propylaea is a severe and dramatic building invoking something of the austere stability of the old order, the aristocratic reserve, and the lofty ideals of the Periklean Age; the Erechtheion represents the turbulence of the new, post-Classical era. The masses and the voids of the Propylaea are expressed individually; in contrast, a uniform, horizontal roofline conceals the level differences in the main building of the Erechtheion, while its north and south porches, though elegant, appear as somewhat decorative appendages. Shear goes one more step in maintaining that more meaningful similarities are to be found between the temple of Athena Nike and the Erechtheion and proposes that the architect of the latter was also Kallikrates.

Opinion is more united in accepting the strong possibility that the architect of the Stoa of Zeus Eleutherios, situated in the northwest corner of the Athenian Agora, was Mnesikles. This unusually planned Doric stoa, datable to c.430 B.C., is perhaps the earliest of a type in which the ends of a simple, row-type colonnade have been elaborated by projecting wings—the unique design feature that establishes its primary stylistic connection with the Propylaea. There are also remarkable similarities in proportions and details of the architectural orders: the combination of white and blue marble decoration in both and an over-all sobriety of ornament. Like the Propylaea, the stoa is elevated at a four-step crepidoma. Homer A. Thompson (1937, p. 53), the excavator of the building, wrote: "One is tempted to suppose that the design of the building in the market place, if it was not directly due to Mnesicles, was at any rate influenced by the free and ingenious spirit evident in the works of that master on the hill above."

The direct and indirect influences of Mnesikles's masterpiece can be felt in a number of Doric propylaea and stoas in following centuries. These were, by and large, simplified schemes which retained only a few of the salient motifs of the original: the interior cross-wall, the ramped approach or the widened central intercolumniation, in the case of the gate structures; projecting wings, in the case of the stoas. Among the examples, one can include the propylon of the Sanctuary of Demeter in Selinus (third century B.C.), with six steps leading up to the distyle façade and an interior change of level, and the elaborate gate for the precinct of Poseidon in Sounion (fourth century B.C.) whose central gate, flanked by Doric porticoes, was approached by a ramp. The propylon for one of the minor sanctuaries on Mount Kynthos in Delos is a late Hellenistic structure with a pedimented porch of four prostyle Doric columns (c.95 B.C.). More ambitious is the greater Propylaea of the sanctuary of Demeter at Eleusis which is almost an exact copy of the central building of its Athenian prototype. Dated in the Antonine period (c.170 A.D.), the imposing marble structure represents Roman academicism at its best.

It was academicism of a similar sort that must have inspired C. G. LANGHANS's interpretation of the Athenian Propylaea in the Brandenburg Gate (1789–1794) in Berlin. Langhans's knowledge of Greek architecture was derived mainly from archeological publications which were becoming quite numerous and available by the end of the eighteenth century; the Propylaea, in particular, had been included in the second volume of JAMES STUART and NICHOLAS REVETT's *Antiquities,* published in 1787. Among the countless neoclassical schemes that hint at aspects of the Propylaea's design, the most sensitive and convincing appears to be LEO VON KLENZE's Propylaeum in Munich (1846–1860). Klenze's acquaintance with Greek architecture was firsthand. He had visited Greece in 1834 and was even entrusted with the responsibility of the preservation and restoration of the Akropolis monuments, including the Propylaea, then being freed of its encumbrances. Klenze's early studies for the Munich Propylaeum are closer to the original; in the final project, he replaced the wings with solid towers, retaining, perhaps, as much a visual echo of the Nike bastion as he did of the austere and functional classical style of FRIEDRICH GILLY and KARL FRIEDRICH SCHINKEL.

Mnesikles.
Porch of Maidens, The Erechtheion.
Athens.
421–405 B.C.

But the true and natural followers of the Propylaea are the great Hellenistic sanctuaries with their multiterraced, symmetrical layouts, in which, if not the direct influence, the principles of Mnesikles's masterpiece live on. In the sanctuary of Athena in Lindos (late fourth–early third centuries B.C.), with its monumental stairs flanked by the projecting wings of the propylaeum and preceded by symmetrical extensions of stoas, or in the sanctuary of Aesklepios at Kos (second century B.C.), where the main temple is surrounded by a U-shaped stoa facing the axial, ramped approach, or in the Roman Imperial fora, something of the underlying order and the revolutionary nature of the Propylaea's planning is reflected. These are, like the Propylaea, schemes composed of a number of formally integrated elements conceived within an environmental matrix.

In the ingenuity of his design solutions and in the boldness of his structural and ornamental experiments, Mnesikles was part of the progressive spirit and even of the traditions of his time; in his enlarged vision for a synthetic and compositional order of architecture, he was centuries ahead.

FIKRET K. YEGÜL

WORKS

437–432 B.C., The Propylaea, Akropolis; (A)c.430 B.C., Stoa of Zeus Eleutherios; Athens.

BIBLIOGRAPHY

Translations of the classical texts can be found in the Loeb Classical Library series, published by Harvard University Press and Heinemann.

BERVE, HELMUT, and GRUBEN, GOTTFRIED 1963 *Greek Temples, Theatres and Shrines.* New York: Abrams.

BEULÉ, ERNEST 1853–1854 *L'Acropole d'Athène.* 2 vols. Paris: Didot.

BOHN, RICHARD 1882 *Die Propyläen der Akropolis zu Athen.* Berlin: Spemann.

BUNDGAARD, J. A. 1957 *Mnesicles: A Greek Architect at Work.* Copenhagen: Scandinavian University Books.

COULTON, J. J. 1977 *Greek Architects at Work.* London: Elek.

DINSMOOR, B. W., SR. 1910 "The Gables of the Propylaea at Athens." *American Journal of Archaeology* Series 2 14:143–184.

DINSMOOR, B. W., SR. 1913 "Attic Building Accounts. III: The Propylaea." *American Journal of Archaeology* Series 2 17:371–398.

DINSMOOR, B. W., SR. 1922 "Structural Iron in Greek Architecture." *American Journal of Archaeology* Series 2 26:148–158.

DINSMOOR, B. W., SR. 1947 "The Hekatompedon on the Athenian Acropolis." *American Journal of Archaeology* Series 2 51:109–151.

DINSMOOR, B. W., SR. (1950)1975 *The Architecture of Ancient Greece.* 3d ed. Reprint. London: Batsford. Originally published as a third edition of W. J. Anderson and R. P. Spiers, *The Architecture of Ancient Greece and Rome.* London: Batsford, 1902.

DINSMOOR, B. W., JR. 1980 *The Predecessors.* Volume 1 in *The Propylaia to the Athenian Acropolis.* Princeton, N.J.: American School of Classical Studies at Athens.

DÖRPFELD, WILHELM 1885 "Die Propyläen der Akropolis von Athen." *Athenische Mitteilungen* 10:38–56, 131–144.

DÖRPFELD, WILHELM 1911 "Zu den Bauwerken Athens." *Athenische Mitteilungen* 36:39–72.

ELDERKIN, GEORGE W. (1912)1973 *Problems in Periclean Buildings.* Reprint. Washington: McGrath.

FRANCO, FAUSTO 1930–1931 "Le asimmetrie della Pinacoteca dei Propilei sull'Acropoli d'Atene." *Annuario, Scuolo Archeologia Italiana* 13–14:9–25.

GUERRINI, L. 1963 "Mnesikles." Volume 5, pages 128–130 in *Enciclopedia dell'Arte Antica.* Rome: Enciclopedia Italiana.

IVANOFF, SERGIO 1861 "Sulla grande scalinata de'Propilei dell'Acropoli d'Atene." *Annali dell'instituto di Corrispondenza Archeologica* 33:275–293.

KOSTOF, SPIRO (editor) 1977 *The Architect.* New York: Oxford University Press.

LAWRENCE, ARNOLD W. (1957)1967 *Greek Architecture.* 2d ed. Baltimore: Penguin.

PENROSE, FRANCIS C. (1851)1973 *The Principles of Athenian Architecture.* Reprint of 1888 ed. Washington: McGrath.

SCHLEIF, HANS 1933 "Der Nikepyrgos und Mnesikles." *Jahrbuch des deutschen archäologischen Instituts* 48:177–184.

SCHWEITZER, B. 1950 "Mnesikles und die perikleische Planung des Westaufganges zum Akropolis." Pages 116–125 in *Aus Antike und Orient.* Edited by Siegfried Morenz. Lipsia, Germany: Harrassowitz.

SCULLY, VINCENT (1962)1969 *The Earth, the Temple and the Gods.* Rev. ed. New York: Praeger.

SHEAR, IONE M. 1963 "Kallikrates." *Hesperia* 32:375–424.

SHOE, LUEY T. 1949 "Dark Stone in Greek Architecture." *Hesperia* 8 (supplement):341–352.

STEVENS, GORHAM P. 1936 "The Periclean Entrance Court of the Acropolis of Athens." *Hesperia* 5:443–520.

STEVENS, GORHAM P. 1946 "Architectural Studies Concerning the Acropolis of Athens." *Hesperia* 15:73–106.

STUART, JAMES, and REVETT, NICHOLAS (1762–1838)1968 *The Antiquities of Athens.* 5 vols. Reprint. New York: Blom.

THOMPSON, HOMER A. 1937 "Buildings on the West Side of the Agora." *Hesperia* 6:1–226.

TIBERI, CLAUDIO 1964 *Mnesicle: L'architetto dei Propilei.* Rome: Officina Edizioni.

TRAVLOS, JOHN 1971 *Pictorial Dictionary of Ancient Athens.* New York: Praeger.

WELLER, CHARLES H. 1904 "The Pre-Periclean Propylon." *American Journal of Archaeology* Series 2 8:35–70.

WREDE, WALTER 1932 "Mnesikles und der Nikepyrgos." *Athenische Mitteilungen* 57:74–91.

MOFFATT, WILLIAM B.

William Bonython Moffatt (1812–1887) was the son of a builder in Cornwall, England. Trained as a joiner, Moffatt undertook an architectural apprenticeship in London with James Edmeston in 1829 where he met his future partner, GEORGE GILBERT SCOTT. Scott and Moffatt (1835–1846) competed for workhouse commissions, securing over fifty during the years of their association. Moffatt was given to extravagance and was imprisoned for debt in 1860.

MOSETTE GLASER BRODERICK

WORKS

1853, Royal Earlswood Asylum (later Hospital), near

Redhill, Surrey, England. 1855–1858, Shire Hall, Taunton, Somerset, England. 1857, Crystal Palace Hotel, Sydenham, London. n.d., Manor Villa, South Norwood, England. n.d., Charles Russell House, 19 (later 23) Park Lane, London. n.d., Somerset Lunatic Asylum, England. n.d., Surrey Lunatic Asylum, England.

BIBLIOGRAPHY

COLE, DAVID 1980 *The Work of Sir Gilbert Scott.* London: Architectural Press.

SCOTT, GEORGE GILBERT (1879)1977 *Personal and Professional Recollections.* Reprint. New York: Da Capo.

STAMP, GAVIN M. 1976 "Sir Gilbert Scott's Recollections." *Architectural History* 19:54–73.

STRANGE, CHARLES HILBERT n.d. "Charles Matthew Strange: 1838–1925." Unpublished manuscript, Library, Royal Institute of British Architects, London.

MOHOLY-NAGY, LÁSZLÓ

László Moholy-Nagy (1895–1946), born in Hungary, inscribed his name in the history of art as a painter, an art photographer, an experimenting constructor, a model designer, a writer on arts, and a pedagogue. Giving up the study of law, he became a painter, exhibiting in Budapest as early as 1918.

After a short stay in Vienna in 1920, he went to Berlin, where as an artist and a writer he worked for Dutch, French, and other journals. He cooperated with the group *Gestaltung* and participated in the Constructivist Congress in Düsseldorf. He got acquainted with the members of the Dutch group *De Stijl* and with the Russian Constructivist artist ELEAZAR LISSITZKY. In Berlin, WALTER GROPIUS took notice of his works and invited him among the masters of the Bauhaus.

Moholy-Nagy was master and professor of the Bauhaus from 1923 to 1928. He became director of the preparatory class and leader of the metal workshop. He continued his experiments in the field of painting, photography, and polychromatic mobiles, which can be regarded as the starting point of kinetic art. He participated in the reform of the teaching method of the Bauhaus, closely cooperating with Walter Gropius. On the occasion of the transfer of the Bauhaus to Dessau in 1925 he had a significant role in the designing of the new buildings.

In 1928, he left the Bauhaus. Back in Berlin, he participated in several exhibitions and continued his experiments in industrial models, typography, and so on. He started to apply synthetic materials and aluminum in his painting at this time. His "light-space modulator" was displayed in 1930.

After several years in the Netherlands and England, Moholy-Nagy moved to the United States in 1937. He was one of the founders of the New Bauhaus in Chicago. A year later, Moholy-Nagy established his own school, the Institute of Design.

Moholy-Nagy summarized his pedagogical ideas in a book that was published after his death in 1946.

JUDITH KOÓS

BIBLIOGRAPHY

BRENDEL, JANOS 1971 "László Moholy-Nagy. Twórczocs artysty do 1923. roku." *Studia Muzealne* 9:70–81.

DENEGRI, JESA 1977 "László Moholy-Nagy." *Umetnost* 54:66–71.

HAUS, ANDREAS 1978 *Moholy-Nagy. Fotos und Fotogramme.* Munich: Schimer Mosel.

KALIVODA, FRANTISEK, and GIEDION, SIEGFRIED 1936 "Sondernummer über Moholy." *Telehor* 1936: nos. 1–2.

KALLAI, ERNST 1924 "Jahrbuch der jungen Kunst." *Ladislaus Moholy-Nagy* 5:181–189.

KEPES, GYORGY 1969 "László Moholy-Nagy and the Bauhaus Tradition." *Print* 23:35–39.

KOÓS, JUDITH 1980 "Moholy-Nagy László és a Bauhaus" ("László Moholy-Nagy and the Bauhaus"). *Magyar Hirek* 23, no. 22:24–25.

KOPPE, RICHARD 1969 "László Moholy-Nagy and His Visions." *Art International* 23, no. 10:43–46.

KOSTALANETZ, RICHARD 1970 *Moholy-Nagy.* New York: Praeger.

MATYAS, PETER 1921 "Moholy-Nagy." *Ma* 6:119.

MOHOLY, LUCIA 1972 *Marginalien zu Moholy-Nagy.* Krefeld, Germany: Scherpe.

MOHOLY-NAGY, SYBIL (1950)1969 *Moholy-Nagy: Experiment in Totality.* 2d ed. Cambridge, Mass.: M.I.T. Press.

MOHOLY-NAGY, SYBIL 1966 "Constructivism from Malevitch to Moholy-Nagy." *Art and Architecture* June: 24–28.

OLBRICH, M. N. 1976 "Moholy-Nagy und der Konstruktivismus in 50 Jahre Bauhaus Dessau Kolloquium 1976." *Wissenschaftliche Zeitschrift der Hochschule für Architektur und Bauwesen* 23: nos. 5–6.

PÉTER, LÁSZLÓ 1972 "The Young Years of Moholy-Nagy." *The New Hungarian Quarterly* 13, no. 46:62–72.

SINKOVITS, PETER 1976 "Moholy-Nagy Exhibition in Buda Castle." *The New Hungarian Quarterly* 17, no. 62:172–178.

SOUCEK, LADISLAW 1965 *László Moholy-Nagy.* Bratislava, Czechoslovakia.

WEITMEIER, HANNAH 1972 *Licht-visionen; Ein Experiment von Moholy-Nagy.* Berlin: Bauhausarchiv.

MÖHRING, BRUNO

Architect, influential author, editor, and city planner, Bruno Möhring (1863–1929) was a leading figure in German professional circles before and after World War I. Born in Königsberg, East Prussia (now Soviet Union), he studied in Berlin and first attracted attention through his artistic designs for bridges (for example, the Rhine Bridge at Bonn and U-Bahn Station Bühlowstrasse in Berlin). He also established his name through designs for international expositions (Milan, Paris, St. Petersburg, San Francisco, Turin), especially the World's Fair in St. Louis, 1904, where he headed the German team.

Möhring was an enthusiast for CAMILLO SITTE's concepts of city planning and became a leader of the young profession in Germany. In 1910, he joined with the economist Rudolf Eberstadt and the traffic engineer Richard Peterson in submitting a design for the Greater Berlin planning competition, winning second place. From then on, Möhring was recognized as a planning authority. Collaborating with CORNELIUS GURLITT, he founded the periodical *Stadtbaukunst alter und neuer Zeit* in 1919 and the German Academy of City Planning (*Deutsche Akademie des Städtebaues*) in 1922. His writing, editing, and three-year presidency of the academy gave him influence and recognition among colleagues which augmented the impact of his designs. Illness caused him to withdraw from public life in the mid-1920s.

RON WIEDENHOEFT

BIBLIOGRAPHY

EBERSTADT, RUDOLF; MÖHRING, BRUNO; and PETERSON, RICHARD 1910 *Ein Program für die Planung einer neuzeitlichen Gross-Stadt.* Berlin.

LEHWESS, WALTER 1924 "Zu Bruno Möhrings 60. Geburtstage." *Stadtbaukunst alter und neuer Zeit* 5:7–8.

LEHWESS, WALTER 1929 "Zum Gedächtnis Bruno Möhrings." *Stadtbaukunst alter und neuer Zeit* 10:1–4.

MOLINOS, AUGUSTE ISIDORE

Auguste Isidore Molinos (1795–1850), a Parisian, studied architecture with his father, Jacques Molinos, at the Ecole des Beaux-Arts and followed him as a municipal architect for Paris and as a teacher. Auguste built several fountains in Paris, but his major works are his two austere, neoclassical churches in Neuilly and Batignolles.

RICHARD CLEARY

WORKS

1827–1831, Church of Saint Jean Baptiste, Neuilly-sur-Seine, France. 1828–1829, Church of Sainte Marie, Batignolles, France.

BIBLIOGRAPHY

BAUCHAL, CHARLES 1887 "Auguste Isidore Molinos." Page 700 in *Nouveau dictionnaire biographique et critique des architectes français.* Paris: André, Daly.

DELAIRE, EDMOND 1907 *Les architectes élèves de l'école des Beaux-Arts (1793–1907).* Paris: Librairie de la Construction Moderne.

HAUTECOEUR, LOUIS 1955 *La Restauration et le gouvernement de Juillet.* Volume 6 in *Histoire de l'architecture classique en France.* Paris: Picard.

MOLINOS, JACQUES

Architect to the city of Paris during the Empire, Jacques Molinos (1743–1831) became a member of the Institut de France in 1829.

Between 1780 and 1785, he built the château of Puisieux, near Villers-Cotterets, for the marquis de Vasan. Collaborating with J. C. LEGRAND, he designed the Julien garden at Epinay. He also built the Orangerie du Muséum.

During the Empire, he was the designer of decorations for festivals held by the city of Paris. He was the architect of the Fontaine Valhubert. In 1809, he erected the Marché Saint-Honoré, and from 1808 to 1811, the rag market in the Enclos du Temple.

In 1826, he built the Barrière de Rochechouart and from 1829 to 1831 the Marché Popincourt, both in Paris.

GÉRARD ROUSSET-CHARNY

Translated from French by
Richard Cleary

BIBLIOGRAPHY

GALLET, MICHEL 1972 *Paris Domestic Architecture of the 18th Century.* Translated by James C. Palmes. London: Barrie & Jenkins.

MØLLER, C. F.

Christian Frederik Møller (1898–) entered the Royal Academy in Copenhagen in 1920 and graduated in 1925. He was in partnership with KAY FISKER from 1928 to 1943. Møller is a pupil of the Klint school (see KAARE KLINT), and his favorite building materials are brick and tile. He has exerted a great influence on architecture in Jutland and on the Århus school of architecture. Among his most outstanding buildings are Århus University (1938–1974) and the two museums in Herning, Denmark (1963–1965 and 1973).

LISBET BALSLEV JØRGENSEN

WORKS

1929, Vodroffsvej 2 (housing; with Kay Fisker), Copenhagen. 1931–1974, Århus University (with Fisker and Povl Stegmann), Denmark. 1935–1939, Vestershus (housing; with Fisker), Copenhagen. 1949–1950, Dormitory, Århus University, Denmark. 1963–1965, Angli Shirt Factory (with C. T. Sørensen and Carl-Henning Pedersen; now the Museum of Modern Art), Herning, Denmark. 1969–1974, Radio and Television House, Århus, Denmark. 1973, Carl-Henning Pedersen Museum, Herning, Denmark.

BIBLIOGRAPHY

LANGKILDE, HANS ERLING 1949 Volume 2, pages 418–419 in *Weilbachs Kunstnerleksikon.* Copenhagen: Aschehoug Dansk Forlag.

LANGKILDE, HANS ERLING 1960 *Arkitekten Kay Fisker.* Copenhagen: Arkitektens Forlag.

MØLLER, CHRISTIAN FREDERIK 1978 *Arhus Universitets Bygninger.* Århus (Denmark) University Press.

MOLLER, GEORG

Training under FRIEDRICH WEINBRENNER in the building of ducal Karlsruhe, Germany, prepared Georg Moller (1784–1852) ideally for his career in Darmstadt, Germany, where, after 1810, he shaped the neoclassical town center and rose to the directorship of architecture in Hessen. Although Moller's discovery of the medieval plan of Cologne Cathedral and his pioneering studies of German medieval architecture, especially the *Denkmäler der deutschen Baukunst* begun in 1815, gave considerable impetus to the early Gothic Revival in Germany, he considered Gothic an unsuitable model for contemporary architecture. His buildings are severely treated and monumentally conceived classical designs such as the Pantheon-inspired Ludwigskirche (1822–1827). In the Theater at Mainz (1829–1833), Moller employed a Renaissance vocabulary and a bold juxtaposition of circular auditorium and square stagehouse, clearly expressed in the exterior massing, an idea suggested by FRIEDRICH GILLY's designs (1799) for Berlin. Moller's technical expertise found influential expression in his writings and in his restorations, such as that of Mainz Cathedral, where he built an iron crossing dome.

BARRY BERGDOLL

WORKS

1811–1814, Houses, Rheinstrasse; *1812, Main and Neckar Gates; 1813–1825, Houses, Neckarstrasse; Darmstadt, Germany. 1816, Church, Gräfenhausen, near Darmstadt, Germany. 1816, Protestant Church, Birkenau, near Weinheim, Germany. c.1816, Rhine Gate; *1817, Casino; *1817–1818, Freemasons Lodge (portico survives); 1819–1820, Court Theater; Darmstadt, Germany. 1819–1821, Church, Giessen, Germany. 1822–1827, Ludwigskirche (never completed; simplified in restoration after 1944 bombing), Darmstadt, Germany. 1823–1825, Gothic House, Homburg, Germany. 1825, Schloss Meisenheim (remodeling), Germany. 1825–1826, New Chancellory Building; 1827–1831, Mausoleum, Rösenhöhe; Darmstadt, Germany. 1828, Cathedral (dome); 1829–1833, Municipal Theater, Mainz, Germany. 1833, House (with J. Baryer), Mathildenhöhe; *1834, Palace of Prince Carl; Darmstadt, Germany. 1835–1837, Ducal Palace (remodeling), Wiesbaden, Germany. 1840, Flotow Villa; *1841–1842, Old Palace (remodeling); 1841–1844, Ludwig I Monument; Darmstadt, Germany.

BIBLIOGRAPHY

Alt-Darmstadt und Georg Moller 1911 Darmstadt, Germany: Denkmalarchiv für das Grossherzogtum Hessen. Exhibition catalogue.

FRÖHLICH, MARIE, and SPERLICH, HANS-GÜNTHER 1959 *Georg Moller: Baumeister der Romantik.* Darmstadt, Germany: Roether.

HAUPT, GEORG 1952–1954 *Die Bau- und Kunstdenkmäler der Stadt Darmstadt.* 2 vols. Darmstadt, Germany: Roether.

HERMANN, WOLFGANG (1932)1977 Volume 1 in *Deutsche Baukunst des 19. und 20. Jahrhunderts.* Reprint. Basel: Birkhäuser.

KRIMMEL, BERND (editor) 1978 *Darmstadt in der Zeit des Klassizismus und der Romantik.* Darmstadt, Germany: Magistrat der Stadt Darmstadt.

MOLLER, GEORG 1815–1844 *Denkmäler der deutschen Baukunst.* 3 vols. Darmstadt, Germany: Leske.

MOLLER, GEORG 1818 *Bemerkungen über die aufgefundene Originalzeichnungen des Domes zu Köln.* Darmstadt, Germany: Heyer.

MOLLER, GEORG 1832–1844 *Beiträge zu der Lehre von den Construktionen.* Darmstadt, Germany: Leske.

MOLLER, GEORG, and HEGER, FRANZ 1825–1826 *Entwürfe ausgeführter und zur Ausführung bestimmter Gebäude.* Darmstadt: Leske.

MOLLET FAMILY

The Mollet family represents seven generations of important French royal gardeners, garden designers, and architects. In 1582, Jacques Mollet and his son Claude, working under the architect ETIENNE DUPÉRAC, planted the first Italian embroidery parterre in France at Anet. At the royal gardens, Claude (d.1643?) established the basic design elements, unity, scale, and house-garden interrelationship of the *jardin français* subsequently developed by JACQUES BOYCEAU and ANDRÉ LE NOSTRE. Claude's son André (d.1665) transplanted these ideas to royal courts in England, the Netherlands, and Sweden. Armand-Claude (d.1742), great-grandson of Claude Mollet, was *contrôleur général* of the king's buildings, a leading member of the Académie de l'Architecture, and architect of several Parisian *hôtels* in a baroque-rococo transition style.

RICHARD O. SWAIN

WORKS

The dates listed below for each garden are the founding dates.

CLAUDE MOLLET

c.1582, Anet, France. c.1595, Fontainebleau Lake Garden, France. c.1595, Saint Germain-en-Laye, France. c.1595, Tuileries, Paris.

ANDRÉ MOLLET

1633, Honselaarsdijk, Netherlands. c.1642, Wimbledon Manor House, England. 1648–1653, Humlegården; 1648–1653, Kunsträdgården; 1648–1653, Royal Palace Garden; Stockholm. c.1662, Saint James's Palace Garden, London.

ARMAND-CLAUDE MOLLET

c.1720, Hôtel d'Evreux (now the Palais de l'Elysée); c.1720, Hôtel d'Humières; Paris.

BIBLIOGRAPHY

HAZLEHURST, F. HAMILTON 1966 *Jacques Boyceau and the French Formal Garden.* Athens: University of Georgia Press.

KARLING, STEN 1931 *Trädgårdskonstens historia i Sverige.* Stockholm.

KARLING, STEN 1974 "The Importance of André Mollet and His Family for the Development of the French Formal Garden." In F. Hamilton Hazlehurst (editor), *The French Formal Garden.* Washington: Dumbarton Oaks.

KIMBALL, FISKE 1964 *The Creation of the Rococo.* Philadelphia: Norton.

MOLLET, ANDRÉ 1651 *Le jardin de plaisir.* Stockholm.

MOLLET, CLAUDE 1652 *Le théâtre des plans et jardinages.* Paris.

MOLTON, JOHN

John Molton (?–1547) was one of the leading masons of Henry VIII's reign. He is first recorded working at Westminster Abbey in 1524, became master of the works at Bath Abbey in 1527, and in 1528 succeeded HENRY REDMAN in the offices of master mason to the king and to Westminster Abbey. John Harvey describes him as "the last great English architect of the old [Gothic] school" and attributes several buildings to him, but very little work is securely documented as his.

IAN CHILVERS

WORKS

1531–1532, York Place (extensions; later the Palace of Whitehall), London. 1532–1536, Hampton Court Palace (extensions, including the Great Hall), Middlesex, England.

BIBLIOGRAPHY

HARVEY, JOHN 1954 *English Mediaeval Architects: A Biographical Dictionary down to 1550.* London: Batsford.

MOMCHILOV, PETKO

Born in Gorna Oriakhovitsa, Bulgaria, Petko Ivanov Momchilov (1864–1923) studied architecture in Prague, Czechoslovakia. Until World War I, he worked with IORDAN MILANOV on religious and civic buildings, such as the reconstruction of Saint Sedmochislenitsi Church (1901), the Palace of the Bulgarian Synod (1906–1908), and the Central Mineral Baths (1905–1911), all in Sofia and all designed in Byzantine forms in an attempt to create a new monumental Bulgarian style.

In his numerous residences, however, Momchilov incorporated Renaissance and baroque forms, as appropriate for secular buildings. Most of these Sofia residences are now used for civic purposes.

MARIA POPOVA

WORKS

1893–1894, High School, Ruse, Bulgaria. 1895, Alexandrov's Hospital Complex (several pavilions; with I. P. Milanov), Sofia. 1901, Saint Sedmochislenitsi (reconstruction; with Milanov); 1905–1911, Central Mineral Baths (with Milanov); 1906–1908, Palace of the Bulgarian Synod (with Milanov), Sofia. 1910–1923, Hot Spring Spa Resort, Sliven, Bulgaria. 1910–1923, Maichin Dom Hospital; 1910–1923, Petko Momchilov Residence (now the Dobraudzha Restaurant); Sofia.

BIBLIOGRAPHY

BŬLGARSKA AKADEMIIA NA NAUKITE 1963–1969 *Kratka Bŭlgarska Entsiklopediia.* Sofia: The academy.

BŬLGARSKA AKADEMIIA NA NAUKITE 1965 *Kratka Istoriia na Bŭlgarskata Arkhitektura.* Sofia: The academy.

BŬLGARSKA AKADEMIIA NA NAUKITE 1974 *Entsiklopediia na Bulgaria.* Sofia: The academy.

KOEVA, M. 1975 "Iordan Milanov i Petko Momchilov-Arkhitekti ot Purvata Generatsiia." *Arkhitektura* 3–4:51–54.

MONEYPENNY, GEORGE

George Moneypenny (1768–?) was primarily a designer of prisons and bridges in south and west England in the late eighteenth and early nineteenth centuries. He was the son of a Derby sculptor of the same name. Moneypenny's training is unclear, but his executed buildings probably are best understood in the context of Enlightenment fascination with social reform and "visionary" complexes found in the works of GEORGE DANCE THE YOUNGER, BENJAMIN H. LATROBE, CLAUDE NICOLAS LEDOUX, GIOVANNI BATTISTA PIRANESI, and JOHN SOANE. Moneypenny evidently succeeded WILLIAM BLACKBURN as the major English prison designer of the period. He practiced until the 1820s.

GERALD L. CARR

WORKS

*1790–1792, County Jail, Leicester, England. 1799, Northam Bridge, Southampton, England. *1805, County Jail, Winchester, England. *1807–1809, County House of Correction, Exeter, England. 1817–1819, Sessions House and House of Correction, Knutsford, Cheshire, England.

BIBLIOGRAPHY

DUGDALE, JAMES 1819 *The New British Traveller; or, Modern Panorama of England and Wales.* 4 vols. London: Robins.

PAPWORTH, WYATT (editor) 1852–1892 *The Dictionary of Architecture.* 8 vols. London: Architectural Publication Society.

MONTANO, GIOVANNI BATTISTA

Giovanni Battista Montano (1534–1621) was a carpenter, wood sculptor, and architect who moved from Milan to Rome during the pontificate of Gregory XIII. His teacher was apparently Bernardo Radi da Cortona, whose engraved altar and tomb designs influenced Montano's own work in this field; according to Giovanni Baglione (see BAGLIONI FAMILY), he imitated the sculptor-goldsmith Prospero Bresciano in the vivacity of his designs and knew how to work wood with all the liveliness and fluidity of wax. All of his known architectural works are connected with his trade as a carpenter. In 1589–1591, he signed a joint contract with Stefano Possenti for the coffered ceiling of the oratory of the Arciconfraternità dei Convalescenti e Peregrini in Rome. In 1597–1599, he executed the elaborate organ on the north inner façade of the transept of San Giovanni in Laterano in Rome as part of Clement VIII's restoration program; at some uncertain date, he executed the organ above the side door of the church of Santa Maria di Loreto in Rome, along with the *choretti* figures opposite. In August 1597, he drew up plans for the façade of the Church of San Giuseppe dei Falegnami, which had been rebuilt on the plans of GIACOMO DELLA PORTA. Montano's façade features capitals with inverted volutes that look forward to a favorite device of baroque architects, as well as extraordinary aediculae at the sides of the upper story and decorative volutes manipulated with the malleability of clay or wax. In 1598–1600, he prepared a wooden model of Giacomo della Porta's design for the Medici funeral chapel, but the Medici failed to be won over.

By far his most important legacy to the history of architecture was Montano's drawings after ancient ruins in the Roman countryside; the drawings themselves are preserved in museums in London, Oxford, Berlin, and Milan, but they were also engraved and published in the decades following Montano's death by his pupil GIOVANNI BATTISTA SORIA and by Calisto Ferrante. In the preface to the first volume (1624), Soria described Montano's working methods: he often measured out the ruins on the site, descending into grottoes and caverns when necessary, but then would supplement the actual ruins with elevations and sections drawn from his "exquisite imagination." It seems that he also corrected plans in the interests of regularity and axial symmetry. Montano also drew heavily on the antiquarian tradition, reproducing plans from SEBASTIANO SERLIO, ANDREA PALLADIO, ETIENNE DUPÉRAC, PIRRO LIGORIO, and Sallustio Peruzzi, sometimes without acknowledgment. Often he failed to convey the grandeur of the originals; on the other hand, he shows some feeling for the complexities of structure in Roman concrete architecture, particularly in his renderings of superimposed concrete vaults and complex systems of staircases. In some plates he foreshadows the haunting archeological visions of GIOVANNI BATTISTA PIRANESI.

Although Montano is remembered as the teacher of only two archtiects of the next generation, Soria and VINCENZO DELLA GRECA, his real influence was much broader. His antiquarian researches influenced the plan of PIETRO BERETTINI DA CORTONA's Church of Santi Luca e Martina, as

Montano. Plate from Scielta di varii tempietti antichi.

well as the façade of GIOVANNI LORENZO BERNINI's Church of Sant'Andrea al Quirinale. His publication of altar designs seems to have influenced some of the altars of GUARINO GAURINI, particularly that in the Church of San Nicolò in Verona. And most important, he was a formative influence on the great baroque architect FRANCESCO BORROMINI, who arrived in Rome before Montano's death. Many of Borromini's buildings show a close study of Montano's renderings after the antique.

JOSEPH CONNORS

WORKS

1589–1591, Arciconfraternità dei Convalescenti e Peregrini (oratory ceiling); 1597–?, San Giuseppe dei Falegnami (façade); 1597–1599, San Giovanni in Laterano (organ on the north transept wall); n.d., Santa Maria di Loreto (organ above side door); Rome.

BIBLIOGRAPHY

BAGLIONE, GIOVANNI (1642)1935 *Le vite de' pittori, scultori, et architetti.* Reprint. Rome: Calzone.

BLUNT, ANTHONY 1963 "Introduction." Volume 3, pages 3–11 in *Studies in Western Art.* N.J.: Princeton University Press.

HENNEBERG, JOSEPHINE VON 1977 "Emilio dei Cavalieri, Giacomo della Porta, and G. B. Montano." *Journal of the Society of Architectural Historians* 36:252–255.

MONTANO, GIOVANNI BATTISTA 1624 *Scielta di varii tempietti antichi.* Edited by G. B. Soria. Rome.

MONTANO, GIOVANNI BATTISTA 1625 *Diversi ornamenti capricciosi per depositi o altari.* Edited by G. B. Soria. Rome.

MONTANO, GIOVANNI BATTISTA 1628 *Tabernacoli diversi.* Edited by G. B. Soria. Rome.

MONTANO, GIOVANNI BATTISTA 1636 *Architettura con diversi ornamenti cavati dall'antico.* Edited by G. B. Soria. Rome.

NOEHLES, KARL 1970 *La Chiesa dei SS. Luca e Martina nell'opera di Pietro da Cortona.* Rome: Bozzi.

ZANDER, GIUSEPPE 1958, 1962 "Le invenzioni architettoniche di Giovanni Battista Montano milanese (1534–1621)." *Quaderni dell'Istituto di Storia dell' Architettura dell'Università di Roma* 30:1–21; 49/50:1–32.

MONTEREAU, PIERRE DE

See MONTREUIL, PIERRE DE, and MONTREUIL, EUDES DE.

MONTFERRAND, AUGUSTE RICARD DE

Auguste Ricard de Montferrand (1786–1858) was born in Chaillot, France, and studied under Charles Percier (see PERCIER AND FONTAINE). He worked on the Madeleine and settled in Russia in 1816 where he somehow was commissioned to design the new Saint Isaac's Cathedral, St. Petersburg, a project which he greatly modified from 1818 until 1853. Its golden dome, inspired by Saint Paul's in London, is its most successful feature.

THOMAS J. MCCORMICK

WORKS

1818–1858, Saint Isaac's Cathedral; 1830–1834, Alexander Column; St. Petersburg, Russia.

BIBLIOGRAPHY

BERCKENHAGEN, EKHART 1979 *Architektenzeichnungen: 1479–1979.* Berlin: Kunstbibliothek. Exhibition catalogue.

BUTIKOV, GEORGY 1980 *St. Isaac's Cathedral.* Leningrad: Aurora Art Publishers.

GRABAR, IGOR, LAZAREV, V. N.; and KEMENOV, V. S. (editors) 1963 Volume 8, part 1 in *Istoriya russkogo iskusstva.* Moscow: Knebel.

HAMILTON, GEORGE H. (1954)1975 *The Art and Architecture of Russia.* 2d ed. Harmondsworth, England: Penguin.

HOFER, PHILIP 1944 "Montferrand and the *Alexanderine Column* at Leningrad." *Gazette des Beaux Arts* 6, per. 26:333–348.

MONTFERRAND, AUGUSTE RICARD DE 1845 *L'Eglise cathédrale de Saint-Isaac: Description architecturale, pittoresque, et historique de ce monument.* St. Petersburg, Russia: Belizard.

NIKITIN, N. P. 1939 *Ogiust Monferran.* Leningrad: Lundberg.

REAU, LOUIS (editor) 1932 "Lettres inédites de l'architecte Ricard de Montferrand à son ami Favart (1834–1843)." *Archives de l'art français* per. 17:207–223.

MONTREUIL, PIERRE DE, and MONTREUIL, EUDES DE

Pierre de Montreuil (active c.1235–1267) was one of the chief architects in Paris in the mid-thirteenth century. Probably from Montreuil-sur-Bois near Vinciennes, he was influenced by the work at Amiens Cathedral and was possibly trained there. His earliest documented works, both in Paris, are a refectory (1239) and a Virgin Chapel (1245) for the Abbey of Saint-Germain-des-Prés, now both destroyed. He is mentioned in a text of 1247 as *cementarius* (mason) at Saint-Denis, and on this basis is believed by some to have been the master of Saint-Denis in the 1230s and 1240s, but this claim has been challenged by others. A tradition going back to the sixteenth century attributes the Sainte-Chapelle in Paris (1239?–1244?) to Pierre, but this cannot be confirmed. Pierre's sole surviving work is the upper part of the south arm terminal of the transept of the Cathedral of Notre-Dame in Paris (1258/1267). He assumed responsibility for this project after the death of Je(h)an de Celles in February 1258 and was employed at Notre-Dame as late as 1265 when he is termed *magister operum* (master of works) there. Pierre was greatly honored in Paris. He owned houses and quarries, and in (October?) 1260 served king Louis IX the Saint in arbitrating a dispute. He died in 1267 and was buried in the chapel he built at Saint-Germain-des-Prés. His tombstone (destroyed) honored him as *doctor lathomorum* (doctor of masons).

Eudes de Montreuil (active c.1250–1287), possibly a son of Pierre, is cited in a text of September 1285 as *magister cementarius operum domini regis* (master of the king's [Philippe III le Hardi] works), but no specific buildings can be attributed to him. As early as the sixteenth century it was reported that Eudes accompanied Louis IX the Saint on crusade and built, c.1250, the fortifications at Jaffa, Palestine, but no contemporary source confirms this. Undocumented attributions of buildings as early as 1219 and as late as 1314 (after his death!) have been made to him, including the curtain walls of Aigues-Mortes and the Cathedral of Beauvais. Eudes died in 1287 and was buried in the Church of the Cordeliers (Franciscans) in Paris where his tomb bore his portrait until a fire in 1580.

CARL F. BARNES, JR.

WORKS

(A)1231–1267, Abbey Church of Saint-Denis (upper part of choir, transept, and nave), France. *1239, Abbey of Saint-Germain-des-Prés (refectory); (A)1239?–1244?, Sainte-Chapelle; *1245, Chapel of the Virgin, Abbey of Saint-Germain-des-Prés; 1258/1267, Cathedral of Notre-Dame (upper part of the south arm terminal of the transept); Paris.

BIBLIOGRAPHY

The earliest association of Pierre de Montreuil with the Sainte-Chapelle is Paris, Bibl. Nat., Ms fr. 16886. The earliest association of Eudes de Montreuil with Louis IX the Saint and Jaffa is in André Thevet, Les vrais portraits et vies des hommes illustres. *Paris: I. Keruert & Guillaume Chaudiere, 1584.*

BRANNER, ROBERT 1965 *St. Louis and the Court Style in Gothic Architecture.* London: Zwemmer.

BRIGGS, MARTIN S. (1927)1974 *The Architect in History.* Reprint. New York: Da Capo.

Pierre and Eudes de Montreuil. Cathedral of Notre-Dame (upper part of the south arm terminal of the transept). Paris. 1258/1267

MOORE, CHARLES W.

Charles Willard Moore (1925–) affirms the values of pluralism in architecture, and this is everywhere apparent in his work. Bound neither ethically nor aesthetically to one architectural tradition, Moore considers himself an inclusivist in contradistinction to exclusivist Modernists.

Moore was born in Benton Harbor, Michigan. Between receiving a B.Arch. degree from the University of Michigan in 1947 and being appointed associate professor of architecture at the University of California at Berkeley in 1959, Moore practiced architecture in San Francisco, served two years in the Army Corps of Engineers, received a Ph.D. in architectural history in 1957 from Princeton University, and taught. Instruction by Enrico Peresutti, JEAN LABATUT, and LOUIS I. KAHN at Princeton University and interaction with fellow students Donlyn Lyndon and William Turnbull (who, with Moore and Richard Whitaker, would form the partnership "MLTW" in 1962) were instrumental in Moore's developing a humanist position, according to which architecture is defined as "the making of places" and its excellence resides, to a great extent, in its ability to communicate and to engage the individual's mind in making connections through time and space. Moore depends on the unexpected juxtaposition of decontextualized forms to effect a unique and exciting synthesis.

MLTW's eight-year association resulted in several of Moore's better known works, including the Sea Ranch residential resort (1964–1965) north of San Francisco. In its unified image, the design is reminiscent of ALVAR AALTO's work; in detail, it

Moore.
Sea Ranch Residential Resort (with MLTW Associates).
North of San Francisco.
1964–1965

takes its cues from vernacular architecture, specifically a weather-beaten barn with a shed roof adjacent to the site.

During Moore's tenure at Yale University from 1966 to 1975 (until 1971 as chairman of the architecture department), the emphasis of the department shifted from a concern with the formal elaboration of space to a re-examination of the nature and function of architecture in an increasingly complex world. Illustrative of the way in which Moore's sensibilities respecting social and political ideals have stimulated his creativity are: Church Street South, a New Haven housing project for the poor (1966–1968), and Kresge College at Santa Cruz (1965–1974), a complex in which the essences of seemingly antithetical references—Italian hill towns and Disneyland's Main Street—are distilled and integrated into a unified composition.

In 1975, Moore accepted a position at the University of California at Los Angeles. Notwithstanding his relocation, Moore maintains an office in Essex, Connecticut, under the name of Moore Grover Harper; in addition, he is a partner in two Los Angeles-based firms: Moore Ruble Yudell and the Urban Innovations Group. Moore's most interesting projects of recent years are the Piazza d'Italia (1975–1978) in New Orleans, Louisiana, which allowed him to explore the use of historical and cultural references in the creation of a public place, and the House near New York (1973–1976), which embodies the idea expressed by Kent Bloomer and Moore in *Body, Memory, and Architecture* (1977) that ideally architecture must elicit response from all the senses, not only the visual.

SUSAN STRAUSS

WORKS

1962, Moore House, Orinda, Calif. 1964–1965, Sea Ranch Residential Resort (with MLTW Associates), north of San Francisco. 1965–1974, Kresge College (with MLTW/Turnbull Associates), University of California, Santa Cruz. 1966, Faculty Club, University of California, Santa Barbara. 1966–1968, Church Street South Housing (with MLTW Associates), New Haven. 1970, Housing Project, Orono, Maine. 1973–1976, House (with Richard Oliver), near New York. 1975–1978, Piazza d'Italia (with August Perez Associates), New Orleans, La.

BIBLIOGRAPHY

BLOOMER, KENT, and MOORE, CHARLES 1977 *Body, Memory, and Architecture.* New Haven: Yale University Press.

COOK, JOHN W., and KLOTZ, HEINRICH 1973 "Charles Moore." In *Conversations with Architects.* New York: Praeger.

"Dossier: Charles W. Moore." 1976 *L'Architecture d'aujourd'hui* 184, March–April:1–64.

FILLER, MARTIN 1980 "Charles Moore: House Vernacular." *Art in America* Oct.:105–112.

MISAWA, HIROSHI; EHIRA, KANJI; and SUGAWARA, MICHIO 1965 "Charles Moore and his Partners." *Japan Architect* 112, Sept.:75–86.

MOORE, CHARLES 1965*a* "Architecture—Art and Science." *Journal of Architectural Education* 19, no.4:53–56.

MOORE, CHARLES 1965*b* "You Have to Pay for the Public Life." *Perspecta* 9–10:57–97.

MOORE, CHARLES 1967 "Plug It In, Rameses, and See If It Lights Up, Because We Aren't Going to Keep It Unless It Works." *Perspecta* 11:32–43.

MOORE, CHARLES 1973 "In Similar States of Undress." *Architectural Forum* 138, May:53–54.

MOORE, CHARLES 1977 "On Post-Modernism: Review of *The Language of Post-Modern Architecture* by Charles Jencks." *Architectural Design* 47:255.

SCHULZE, FRANZ 1970 "Chaos as Architecture." *Art in America* 58: no.4:88–96.

SCOTT BROWN, DENISE 1967 "Team 10, Perspecta 10, and the Present State of Architectural Theory." *American Institute of Planners Journal* 33, no.1:42–50.

STERN, ROBERT A. M. (1969)1977 *New Directions in American Architecture.* Rev. ed. New York: Braziller.

MOORE, TEMPLE

Temple Lushington Moore (1856–1920) was one of the most important English late Victorian church architects, whose work combined scholarly revival of Gothic precedent with subtle originality. The son of a soldier, born in Ulster, Moore was articled in 1875–1878 to GEORGE GILBERT SCOTT, JR., who had great influence on his style. Moore set up in practice in 1879 but continued to work with Scott and finished several of his buildings after Scott's mental breakdown. Moore's wife came from Yorkshire, where he did much work. His practice was largely ecclesiastical.

GAVIN STAMP

WORKS

1881, Saint Aidan's Church, Calton, Helmsley, Yorkshire, England. 1885–1903, All Saints' Church, Peterborough, Northamptonshire, England. *1892, Saint Augustine's Church (with G. G. Scott, Jr.), Hull, England. 1894–1896, Saint John's Church, Hendon, London. 1893–1911, Saint Peter's Church, Barnsley, Yorkshire, England. 1896–1897, Saint Mark's Church, Mansfield, Nottinghamshire, England. 1897–1898, Saint Mary's Church, Sledmere; 1900–1902, Saint Cuthbert's Church, Middlesborough; 1902, Saint Columba's Church, Middlesborough; Yorkshire, England. 1902–1908, Hexham Abbey (restoration and new nave), Northumberland, England. 1904–1906, All Saints' Church, Tooting, London. 1905–1914, Saint Wilfrid's, Horrogate; 1906, Saint Mary's Church, Rievaulx; Yorkshire, England. 1908–1910, All Saints' Church, Uplands, Stroud, Gloucestershire, England. 1907, Saint Luke's Church, Well Hall, Eltham, London. 1913, Saint James's Church, Clacton, Essex, England. 1911–1914, Pusey House, Oxford, England. 1914, Saint Mary's Church, Sculcoates, Hull, Yorkshire. 1915–1934, All Saints' Church (incomplete), Nairobi.

BIBLIOGRAPHY

GOODHART-RENDEL, H. S. 1926 "The Churches of Temple Moore." *Architectural Review* 59:12–17.

GOODHART-RENDEL, H. S. 1928 "The Work of Temple Moore." *Journal of the Royal Institute of British Architects* 35:470–492.

MOOSBRUGGER, CASPAR

Caspar Moosbrugger (1656–1723) was, along with Franz Beer, the most important representative of that group of architects and craftsmen, active for four generations, known as the "Vorarlberg Baroque architects" because they all came from the Bregenzerwald region at the east end of Lake Constance. A continuity in types of commissions, building methods, and building style derived also from close familial ties within a few families and from their guild organization, which was grounded in the medieval *Bauhütte* (mason's guild) tradition. Architectural development in the southwestern German-speaking region outside the centers of artistic and cultural renewal (Salzburg and Munich) was determined essentially by the Vorarlberg Baroque school. After the triumph of the Counter Reformation and especially after the Thirty Year's War their work spread throughout Swabia, Switzerland, the Jura mountains, and into parts of modern-day Baden-Württemberg. This development was fostered and directed by ecclesiastical patronage, especially during the late seventeenth century flowering of the monasteries. In contrast to the urban situation, where increasingly into the early eighteenth century architects were imported from Italy, an autochtonous architectural development characterized the Vorarlberg region from early on. This style drew relentlessly on the "post-rinascimentalen" [late Renaissance] northern Italian ecclesiastical design tradition and its south German counterparts in Salzburg and Munich, which were continually elaborated by Vorarlberg architects. Within this general development from chiefly Italian models to independent solutions, the Vorarlberg architects realized an ecclesiastical architecture, the significance of which should not be underestimated. This development continued until c.1710–1720 when a radical reaction strove to surpass their achievements, culminating in the works of Domenikus Zimmermann (see ZIMMERMAN BROTHERS) and JOHANN MICHAEL FISCHER in Swabia and Bavaria.

At this decisive juncture Beer and Moosbrugger were still at least peripherally involved: it was manifested in the culmination as well as surpassing of the long experiments with the wall-pier system of articulation, in richer solutions using complicated, curvilinear elements; in the involvement with central plan types; and finally in the timely reaction to the convex façade of JOHANN BERNHARD FISCHER VON ERLACH's Kollegienkirche in Salzburg. This process was especially characteristic of Moosbrugger's principal work: the monastery church of Einsiedeln (1674–1723), which matured in design during the protracted course of its planning.

Moosbrugger was born (with the given name Andreas) in 1656 in Au in Bregenzerwald and began his training as a stone mason in the guild there in 1670. In 1673 he was declared an independent practitioner by Christian Thumb (see THUMB FAMILY). From 1674 he was active as a stone mason at Einsiedeln and thus took part in the first phase of the Baroque renovations of the Benedictine monastery: including the new choir (1674–1676), and the sacristy, the confessional chapel, and chapel of the Magdalene (1676–1678/1680–1684) under the direction of the architect JOHANN GEORG KUEN from Bregenz. From this first activity a lifetime's work was to develop. In 1681, still as a stone mason, Moosbrugger solicited admission to the monastery, which he entered as Brother Caspar in 1682. Evidently his training as an architect took place during this same period. In 1691 he replaced Kuen as architect just as the new projects for the Upper Minster were being considered. Testimony to his "training," which took the form of a guided attention to historically comparable solutions to those required by the monastery, are his copies, careful to the smallest detail, after SEBASTIANO SERLIO's Fifth Book on temples. The "Auer Lehrgänge" (Au training courses), known in two different versions, are derived principally from Moosbrugger. These are handwritten treatises and pattern books, which, in addition to depictions of the orders taken from GIACOMO BAROZZI DA VIGNOLA, in the edition by Davilier and Sturn, and the simplest rules of perspective drawn from ANDREA POZZO, contain a number of model plans after Italian and Vorarlberg buildings and projects. All told this "study material" reveals the confluence of native experience and foreign models and finally, novel compositions as well, which derive from these sources. The drawing with a (varied) wall-pier system and an attached oval-plan space is an example.

The intended complete rebuilding of the Einsiedeln monastery offered sufficient provocation to remain on the lookout for new possibilities of this sort. Yet after Moosbrugger's designs of c.1691 for the upper choir, the undertaking was postponed until the chapter's vote in 1702. Nonetheless in the interim Moosbrugger was active for the first time as a consulting and planning architect for a number of neighboring and associated monasteries. From 1684 he was repeatedly occupied with work for the Benedictines at Muri. The remodeling of their medieval church, a nave flanked by side aisles, into a baroque octagon by eliminating the dividing walls is most probably based on plans by Moosbrugger, although execution (1695–1697) was entrusted to others. Likewise he gave advice and designs in the 1680s and 1690s to the Benedictine monastery at Disentis. The same is true of Fischingen, where his involvement beyond consultation cannot be ascertained with certainty. Planning and construction of the monastery and church at Seedorf began in 1695. In 1697–1698 followed the Etzelkapelle, a property of Einsiedeln, which is a free reworking of Solari's Gnadenkapelle (confessional chapel) at Einsiedeln. This already reveals clearly Moosbrugger's study of Roman architecture—perhaps that of DOMENICO FONTANA—as well as his skillful accommodation and reduction in the face of limited economic and technical means. Thus in all the most important Swiss building projects touched by Vorarlberg hands during the first decades of the eighteenth century. Moosbrugger's suggestions and designs are encountered: in Rheinau (1702), Lachen (1703), Solothurn (1711) and Saint Gallen (1721). On the other hand his early contact with Weingarten (1684) remained without consequence, in contradiction to earlier scholarly opinion, in the planning history of that most important church of the Vorarlberg school next to Einsiedeln.

The Rheinau project, with its combination of a drumed dome and a wall-pier system anticipates Moosbrugger's central problem at Einsiedeln after 1702. It was a problem which would occupy him intensively and force him to confront external impulses as well. After the chapter's decision to rebuild in 1702, and the groundstone laying of the new monastery in 1704, the decisive impetus came from the 1705 meeting of the Abbot of Einsiedeln with the Bolognese scholar Luigi Ferdinando Marsigli. Marsigli, who appealed to a "Bernini-pupil," specified the central problems of the new building with particular attention to its role as a pilgrimage church. He thereby inspired a rich series of projects including Moosbrugger's, which surpassed the customary wall-pier system and, broadened the typologically rich variants of domed spaces and pilgrim's space (octagon), by reworking the sanctuary of the Gnadenkapelle. The realization of Marsigli's third suggestion, the creation of a square before the building, was left for later architects, whose projects remained distantly indebted to GIOVANNI LORENZO BERNINI's Piazza di San Pietro (St. Peter's Square).

The new buildings of the monastery followed, principally in the years 1705 to 1713. In 1713 a change in plan, with a setback of the west front, resulted in a new series of church projects. Only in 1713 was building finally decided. In 1721 the ground stone of the new church building was laid; but already in 1723 plans were modified following the chapter's vote for an abbreviated drum for the dome. Moosbrugger died soon thereafter. His chief work was later altered still further in decorative additions, especially the stuccoing and frescoing by the ASAM brothers, Egid Quirin and Cosmas Damian between 1724 and 1726.

For all the richness in the planning of the Einsiedeln monastery church, the end result remains, in the final analysis, disunified despite the "Great Design". The difficulties of inserting a complicated monastic program into the traditional form of the monastic cloistered square is evident in all too many junctures. The juncture of the narrow choir of traditional Vorarlberg type with an orderly series of wall-piers is only mildly successful, all the less since the adjacent range of the cloister does not permit either a side entry or even lighting in the transept to compensate for the lack of the intended drumed dome. The entrance section, cramped at the west end by the "Gnadenkapelle" and likewise flanked by the western range of the cloister, was also subject to a solution of "irregular means". Thus it is only the middle section which features a "normal" composition of wall-piers, galleries, and clearly articulated and generously fenestrated side elevations. This section, especially, represents a mature moment of Vorarlberg architecture with its vast and massive free-standing piers, the lofty arches carrying vaulting compartments and the similarly simple and monumental composition of the side walls, pierced by large windows. These derive ultimately from the thermal window motif of Venice and ANDREA PALLADIO, which was transmitted to the Vorarlberg via Herkomer.

Compared with the rich façade projects, which themselves sought to compete with St. Peter's in Rome and with Milanese models, the realized form of the exterior is restrained and meagre. The formal language is—in total contrast to Franz Beer's work at Weingarten—ecclectic in comparison; a sufficiently prominent portal motif is lacking, while the monumental colossal order is weakly handled. The monumental gesture of the convex, protruding façade reads, nonetheless, most convincingly. Derived from Fischer von Erlach's Kollegienkirche in Salzburg, the motive reached Einsiedeln via Weingarten and documents just how, even in his last years, Moosbrugger continued to compete with the new possibilities. The series of projects he prepared demonstrates in the richness and difference of the variants, and even in a change in style (the same project is offered with and without rustication), the scope of Moosbrugger's training, including the precise adoption of roman motives (eg. Domenico Fontana's Portal of the Lateran Palace). The "Great Design" however lacks in its execution inner homogeneity and repose. The difficulty of uniting the cult and functions of a monastery church and a pilgrimage shrine made it impossible to adopt the mature standard solution, such as Franz Beer had employed in his contemporary Basilica at Weingarten. On the other hand it lead to such original solutions as the spacious octagon. Einsiedln depends more on the earlier series of fertile experiments of Moosbrugger himself, who was constantly developing; but these experiments in the end did not exclude a dependence on Weingarten.

It was indeed Moosbrugger who first introduced the radical alternative of groundplan types with central plan-like elements, after decades of more or less consistent development of the wall-pier type church. He also enriched with Italianisms the all but rudimentary formal vocabulary of the Vorarlberg school to the point of excess, at least in his projects. On the other hand, he remained a monk and a monastic architect, limited in possibilities. Only a very few illustrated books were available to him. A direct experience of "modern Italian architecture" was, of course, excluded and explains a certain unsureness in his treatment of sources. Nonetheless—and as this situation is hardly atypical of later architecture in Germany and Switzerland—Moosbrugger's innovative achievements stimulated a fuller elaboration of the highest value, even if his own chief work, the monastery church at Einsiedeln, in its completed form reflects only incompletely (or only partially) Moosbrugger's conception of architecture.

WERNER OECHSLIN
Translated from German by
Barry Bergdoll

WORKS

1674–1723, Benedictine Monastery (various projects and complete rebuilding from 1702; not completed until 1735 by others), Einsiedeln, Switzerland. 1683–1699, Benedictine Monastery and Church (design), Disentis, Switzerland. 1684/1695–1697, Benedictine Monastery (renovation of nave), Muri, Switzerland. 1690–1711, Saint Ulrich Kapelle (not completed until later by others), Saint Urbain, Switzerland. 1695 and later, Benedictine Convent and Church, Seedorf, Switzerland.

BIBLIOGRAPHY

KUHN, P. ALBERT (1880–1881)1913 *Der jetzige Stiftsbau Maria-Einsiedeln.* Einsiedeln, Switzerland.
BIRCHLER, L. 1924 *Einsiedeln und sein Architekt Bruder Caspar Moosbrugger.* Augsburg, Germany.
BIRCHLER, L. 1927 *Die Kunstdenkmäler der Schweiz (KDM), Kanton Schwyz I.* Basel.
LIEB, N., and DIETH, F. (1960)1976 *Die Vorarlberger Barockbaumeister.* Munich: Schnell & Steiner.
OECHSLIN, WERNER (editor) 1973 *Die Vorarlberger Barockbaumeister: Katalog der Austellung in Einsiedeln und Bregenz.* Einsiedeln, Switzerland.
REINLE, A. 1950–1951 "Ein Fund barocker Kirchen- und Klosterpläne." *Zeitschrift für Schweizerische Archäologie und Kunstgeschichte* 11:261ff.; 12:1ff.
REINLE, ADOLF 1966 "Die Doppelturmfassaden der Vorarlberger Meister." *Montfort* 2:342ff.
SANDNER, OSCAR 1962 *Die Kuen—Bregenzer Baumeister des Barock.* Konstanz, Germany.
SAUERMOST, H. J. 1969 "Schema und Eigenbrödler: Eine Analyse der Vorarlberger-Forschung." *Unsere Kunstdenkmäler* 20:310ff.

MORANDI, RICCARDO

Born in Rome, Riccardo Morandi (1902–) is the most representative civil engineer of Italian modern architecture. He has a predilection for big structures of precompressed reinforced concrete; as such, he looks for the same challenges as PIER LUIGI NERVI, but he distinguishes himself from Nervi by a very different attitude toward modern architecture.

Graduated in 1927 from the *Scuola di applicazione* for engineers, he started his professional work in Rome in 1931. After World War II, he extended his activity outside Italy and even outside Europe, testing new techniques on big structures and spaces such as cinemas, bridges, factories, exhibition halls, and hangars. In 1949–1950, Morandi built his first work in precompressed concrete, the bridge over the Elsa in Siena, Italy. In 1950–1951, he built the first example of a precompressed concrete portal in the Di Tommaso barracks, Rome.

After these works, he distinguished himself more and more because of his ability to overcome the technical difficulties encountered by engineers on big structures. Morandi continued the great tradition of the nineteenth-century engineers by applying himself to the problems of integral design methodology. He reached a personal synthesis of technical, formal, and executive themes expressed in an individual architectonic style in tune with the Modern movement. Morandi has been interested in the individuality of each work as well as in the possibility of repetition of models or prototypes. His most famous international work, the bridge over the Maracaibo's Lagoon in Venezuela (1957–1962) represents the invention of a new structural model (the *strallato* bridge, a type of suspension bridge with oblique connecting rods which guide loads on few pillars) as well as the prototype of various later applications, such as the bridge over the Polcevera (1960–1967), his most important work in Italy.

ANTONINO TERRANOVA

WORKS

1949–1950, Bridge, Elsa River, Siena, Italy. 1950–1951, Di Tommaso Barracks (portal), Rome. 1957–1962, Bridge, Maracaibo Lagoon, Venezuela. 1960–1967, Bridge, Polcevera River, Italy.

BIBLIOGRAPHY

BOAGA, GIORGIO, and BONI, BENITO (editors) (1962)1965 *The Concrete Architecture of Riccardo Morandi.* Rev. & enl. ed. New York: Praeger.

MASINI, LAURA VINCA (editor) 1974 *Riccardo Morandi.* Rome: De Luca.

MORANDI, RICCARDO 1954 *Strutture di calcestruzzo armato e di calcestruzzo precompreso.* Rome: Dedalo.

MORANDI, RICCARDO 1959 *Forma e struttura dei ponti.* Florence.

MOREAU, KARL VON

Born in Paris, where he also studied, Karl von Moreau (1758–1840) worked in Austria from 1801 on, first as an architect, later as interior decorator and painter. In his architecture, he developed a clean, nondecorative cubic style—derived from *Revolutionsklassizismus*—which had an essential influence on Viennese neoclassicism and contributed to the development of Vienna's architecture in the Biedermeier period.

ECKART VANCSA

WORKS

1795–1805, Castle in Eisenstadt (remodeling), Austria. *1807, Apollosaal; 1809–1813, Palais Palffy; *1812, Palais Erdödy; 1821–1823, k.k. Nationalbank; Vienna.

BIBLIOGRAPHY

KASTNER, RICHARD H. 1967 "Das Werk des Architekten Karl Moreau: Die Konstruktionsgebundenheit als Wesensmerkmal der Baukunst." *Alte und moderne Kunst* 12, no. 92:8–15.

WAGNER-RIEGER, RENATE 1970 *Wiens Architektur im 19. Jahrhundert.* Vienna: Österreichischer Bundesverlag.

MOREAU-DESPROUX, PIERRE-LOUIS

Pierre-Louis Moreau-Desproux (18th century) sojourned to the French Academy in Rome in the company of his friend CHARLES DE WAILLY.

Returning to Paris, he built the house of Monsieur de Chavannes at the corner of al Porte du Temple. He likewise constructed the *hôtel* of baron de Saint Julien on rue d'Artois and that of the marquise de Gontaut on rue Louis-le-Grand, and he decorated the Hôtel de Luynes. Related to the Beausire, Moreau-Desproux was the last holder of the position of *maître des bâtiments* for the city of Paris from 1763 to 1787.

From 1763 to 1770, he rebuit the hall of the Palais Royal for the opera company. Around 1773, he designed a series of projects for the Théâtre Français. Certain baroque elements are associated with the repertoire of forms which combine to define neoclassical taste, such as the rigidity of the general lines and the dryness of angles. He completed the portal and executed diverse other works on the Church of Saint-Eustache.

For the ceremonies organized by the city of Paris on the occasion of the birth of the Dauphin in 1782, Moreau-Desproux decorated the court of the Hôtel de Ville and, in order to enlarge this building, erected perpendicular to the façade a wooden structure containing a banquet hall in the tradition of brilliant festival architecture. The façade was given rhythm by Corinthian columns enclosing boxes intended for spectators. Opposite this structure, next to the Seine on the newly enlarged quay, Moreau-Desproux erected the Temple of Hymen, a work of Palladian (see ANDREA PALLADIO) inspiration that encircled high rocks, jets of water, and cascades. This composition was framed by two gigantic columns provided with interior staircases and surmounted by dolphins holding the crown of France.

In 1764, he erected the Fontaine des Haudriettes in Paris. In 1769, he submitted a general plan for the expansion of Paris to the king. He had realized only a slight portion of this program when he retired from his positions in 1787.

GÉRARD ROUSSET-CHARNY
Translated from French by
Richard Cleary

BIBLIOGRAPHY

GALLET, MICHEL 1961 "Dessins de Pierre-Louis Moreau-Desproux. pour des édifices parisiens." *Bulletin du Musée Carnavalet* 14, no. 2:6–15.

GRUBER, ALAIN-CHARLES 1972 *Les grandes fêtes et leurs décors à l'époque de Louis XVI.* Geneva:Droz.

MOREIRA, JORGE

As a pioneer of twentieth-century architecture in Brazil, Jorge Moreira (1904–) has been true to the orthodox principles of functionalism throughout his career. An outstanding graduate of Rio de Janeiro's National School of Fine Arts in 1932, Moreira was asked to join LÚCIO COSTA's architectural team in 1936 to design the Ministry of Education Building with LE CORBUSIER as a consultant.

In 1949, Moreira was appointed chief planner and architect of the Federal University of Brazil in Rio de Janeiro. Having abandoned Le Corbusier's 1936 plan, but not his spirit, Moreira linked thirteen islands with reclaimed land forming 147 acres and outlined a campus of high-rise classrooms reminiscent of Le Corbusier's initial idea. He devoted full time to the project until 1964 when he was seriously injured in a car accident.

The university's award-winning Institute of Child Welfare (1953) displays Le Corbusier's structural grammar with *pilotis, brise soleil,* and open planning, marking Moreira's rationalistic approach which he has methodically applied to each of his commissions, giving special attention to details. As director of architecture and planning at the university and recently as an architectural consultant, Moreira has encouraged young architects to create architecture that is both plastic and utilitarian.

ELIZABETH D. HARRIS

WORKS

1934, White House; 1937–1945, Ministry of Education and Health (now the Palácio da Cultura; with Lúcio Costa, Carlos Leão, Oscar Niemeyer, Eduardo Affonso Reidy, Ernani Vasconcellos, and Le Corbusier as consultant); Rio de Janeiro. 1942, Clinics Hospital, Pôrto Alegre, Brazil. 1949–1964, Federal University of Brazil (chief planner and architect); 1952–1958, Ceppas Apartment Building; 1953, Institute for Child Welfare; 1955, Department of Architecture, University City; 1957, São Correia da Costa Apartment Building; 1958, Ceppas House; 1963, Graphic Arts Building, University City; Rio de Janeiro.

BIBLIOGRAPHY

BRUAND, YVES 1981 *Arquitectura Contemporânea no Brasil.* São Paulo: Editora Perspectiva.

MINDLIN, HENRIQUE 1956 *Modern Architecture in Brazil.* New York: Reinhold.

MOREL, JEAN-MARIE

Architect and garden theorist, Jean-Marie Morel (1728–1810) is best known for his book on garden theory (1776), which echoes the views of Thomas Whately and the MARQUIS DE GIRARDIN. Little is known of his garden designs: his chief work, at Ermenonville, despite his claims to total design responsibility, seems to be limited to several garden structures.

DORA WIEBENSON

WORK

Before 1776, Ermenonville Garden, France.

BIBLIOGRAPHY

FORTAIR, S. DE 1813 *Discours sur la vie et les oeuvres de Jean-Marie Morel.* Paris: Colas.

MOREL, JEAN-MARIE (1776)1802 *Théorie des jardins.* 2d ed., rev. Paris: Panckoucke.

WIEBENSON, DORA 1978 Pages 75–76 in *The Picturesque Garden in France.* Princeton, N.J.: Princeton University Press.

MORELLI, COSIMO

A prolific and long-lived architect, Cosimo Morelli (1732–1812) was chiefly active in the region around Imola (Bologna), the town of his birth and death. His father Domenico Maria, a master mason, and his great-uncle Domenico Trifogli, a minor architect, introduced him to the building trade, and by the mid-1750s he had already embarked on an independent career. In 1759, on the first of several trips to Rome, he met Giovanni Angelo Braschi, a countryman and the future Pope Pius VI. When Braschi acceded to the Holy Office in 1775, he made Morelli a cavalier of the Golden Spur and named him architect of the papal legations of Ferrara, Bologna, and Romagna. In his official and unofficial capacities, Morelli received more than one hundred commissions, mostly, but not exclusively in the pontifical territories.

Ecclesiastical works comprised half of Morelli's activity, with civic, private, and theater commissions constituting the other half. His principal churches are all longitudinal in plan and are impressive in the varied treatment of their nave elevations. San Francesco in Lugo (1762–1772), for example, employs piers faced with broadly spaced pilasters; San Cassiano in Imola (1775–1782), piers with paired pilasters; San Maurenzio in Fossombrone (1769–1780), the Roman arch order; San Giuliano in Macerata (1771–1790), paired columns with arcade; and San Petronio in Castelbolognese (1783–1786), paired columns with entablature. The façades of these churches tend to be quite conservative with variations on Palladian (see ANDREA PALLADIO) and other Cinquecento themes being most common.

Among Morelli's private commissions, two works stand out: the Palazzo Anguissola in Piacenza (1774–1777) and the better known Palazzo Braschi in Rome (1790–1804). The severe retrogressive character of the façades of these palaces hardly prepares one for the grandiloquent and typically eighteenth-century open stairways that lie within. Morelli's ability to mold interior space is equally evident in his theater auditoriums, a building type of which he made a specialty.

Morelli's stylistic development is remarkably constant. His churches, palaces, and theaters all show a steady progression from a sculptural late baroque manner in the 1760s and early 1770s to an increasingly severe neoclassic style in his later years. Such a development is not surprising for an architect born between the generation of late baroque classicists like LUIGI VANVITELLI or CARLO MARCHIONNI and that of true neoclassicists like GIUSEPPE VALADIER. The Italian spokesman for Morelli's generation was FRANCESCO MILIZIA, a critic whose refutation of the picturesque baroque in favor of reductive classicism closely corresponds to the stages of Morelli's own creative progress.

JOHN VARRIANO

WORKS

1762–1772, San Francesco, Lugo, Italy. 1769–1779, Lauro Rossi Theater, Macerata, Italy. 1769–1780, San Maurenzio, Fossombrone, Italy. 1771–1790, San Giuliano, Macerata, Italy. 1774–1777, Palazzo Anguissola, Piacenza, Italy. 1775–1781, San Cassiano; 1775–1782, Theater of the Cavalieri Associates; Imola, Italy. 1777–1781, Santi Nicolò ed Agata, Zola Predosa, Italy. *1777–1785, Villa all'Orto Vaina, Italy. 1781–1789, San Maria Assunta, Fermo, Italy. 1783–1786, San Petronio, Castelbolognese, Italy. 1790–1798, Communal Theater, Ferrara, Italy. 1790–1804, Palazzo Braschi, Rome. 1792–1798, Pergolesi Theater, Iesi, Italy.

BIBLIOGRAPHY

"Cenni biografici dell'architetto Cav. Cosimo Morelli." n.d. Unpublished manuscript, Biblioteca Comunale, Imola, Italy.

FISCHER, MANFRED 1969 "Studien zur Planungs- und Baugeschichte des Palazzo Braschi in Rom." *Römisches Jahrbuch für Kunstgeschichte* 12:95–136.

GAMBETTI, GUIDO 1926 *Cosimo Morelli: Architetto imolese (1732–1812).* Imola, Italy: Galeati.

MATTEUCCI, ANNA MARIA, and LENZI, DEANNA 1977 *Cosimo Morelli e l'architettura delle legazioni pontificie.* Bologna (Italy) University Press.

MILIZIA, FRANCESCO (1768)1826–1828 *Memorie degli architetti antichi e moderni.* Volumes 4 and 5 in *Opere complete di Francesco Milizia.* Bologna, Italy: Stamperia Cardinali e Frulli. Originally published with the title *Le vite de' più celebri architetti.*

MORETTI, GAETANO

Born in Milan, Gaetano Moretti (1860–1930) was a lively and original interpreter of eclecticism. The Renaissance Revival which he adopted in 1889 in the competition design for the Parliament House in Rome, was soon abandoned for a vocabulary based on the Romanesque, which he often combined with Oriental forms as in the Crespi Mausoleum of 1896. At the turn of the century, the contact with Art Nouveau enriched his style with a new vivacity, witnessed in his major work, the neo-Romanesque Electric Power Station of Trezzo d'Adda (1906) and in his own house (1911) in Milan. In 1897, he became a member of the editorial board of the journal *Edifizia Moderna,* and in 1908, he replaced his master, CAMILLO BOITO, in the chair of architecture at the Academy of Brera, Italy.

MANFREDI G. NICOLETTI

WORKS

1894, Cemetery of Chiavari, Italy. 1896, Crespi Mausoleum, Capriate d'Adda, Italy. 1897, Polvara Chapel, Cemetery of Annone, Italy. 1903, Pacchetti House, via Legnano, Milan. 1906, Electric Power Station, Trezzo d'Adda, Italy. 1906, Pacchetti Villa, Ghiffa, Italy. 1911, Moretti House, via Maino, Milan.

BIBLIOGRAPHY

ANNONI, AMBROGIO 1952 *Un maestro dell'architettura fra l'Ottocento e il Novecento: Gaetano Moretti.* Milan.

BELTRAMI, LUCA 1912 *Gaetano Moretti: Costruzioni, concorsi, schizzi.* Milan.

CALZAVARA, MAURIZIO 1958 "L'architetto Gaetano Moretti." *Casabella continuita* no. 218:69–83.

MEEKS, CARROLL L. V. 1966 *Italian Architecture: 1750–1914.* New Haven: Yale University Press.

NICOLETTI, MANFREDI 1978 *L'Architettura Liberty in Italia.* Rome and Bari, Italy: Laterza.

PEROGALLI, CARLO 1956 *La centrale elettrica di Trezzo sull'Adda.* Milan.

MORETTI, LUIGI

Luigi Moretti (1907–1973) was a significant exponent of modern architecture in Italy, both during the tormented years of the fascist regime and during the postwar period. He was born in Rome, where he received his diploma in architecture in 1930. He was a member of the faculty of architecture in Rome during the years 1931–1934 and taught courses in the history of architecture and in the restoration of monuments. Although he remained a close disciple of the rationalist architecture, he never accepted totally its rigorous vocabulary and never participated in the heated polemic, largely political, that caused the young adherents of the new architecture to oppose fiercely MARCELLO PIACENTINI, Ugo Ojetti, and the academics. Already with the first works constructed in Rome, the Youth House of the Littorio of 1933 and the Casa delle Armi in the Forum of Mussolini of 1934, Moretti became known for his personal artistic style, which is characterized by the accentuation of the plastic and volumetric elements of the building. Although his architectural style was clearly modern, with full marble façades and elegant monumentality, his style is nonetheless founded on the continuation of the classical tradition. The references to Greek architecture became more evident in his projects of 1938 for the Piazza Imperiale of the E. 42 in Rome, where columns dominate, adopted more for their capacity to create a rhythm of light and shadows (as in the Pittura Metafisica) than for their adherence to the official monumentalism of the fascist regime. After the war, Moretti founded the periodical *Spazio,* which he edited between 1950 and 1952, and in which he developed the theme of the relationship between architecture and the figurative arts and numerous analyses on baroque space, classical modeling, and the color values of the surfaces of buildings.

Between 1947 and 1951, Moretti worked in Milan, where he built several residences and commercial buildings on the Via Corridoni, on the Via Lazzaretto and on the Corso Italia, buildings that show a violent stereometry marked by very strong plastic features, vertical openings, horizontal lines, distinct juxtapositions between the lower parts along the street level and the upper portion, freely developed. These buildings, with their daring accentuation of dynamic effects and independent volumetric form, place themselves in sharp contrast to the texture of traditional Milan. Moretti's tendency to juxtapose to the surrounding reality an architectural object strongly characterized by a formal individuality is most evident in the buildings he constructed in Rome, such as the house of the Astrea of Via Jenner (1949), the house of the Girasole (1950), and the Villa La Saracena at Santa Marinella (1952).

The introduction of diagonal and curved surfaces, of slanted corners, of a precise differentiation between lower level, upper body, and roof line, and the frequent interruption of the external mass, reveal a neoplastic treatment of volumes and a scenographic rapport with the surrounding space. In 1957, Moretti founded the National Institute for Mathematical Research and for Urban Planning, forming the principles of parametric architecture, introduced also at the Triennale of Milan in 1960. The method of parametric architecture is based on the concept of determining architectural forms, their dimensions and their relationship, and their functional dependency through the use of quantitative parameters, as evident in mathematical prototypes.

Probably the most successful result of his aspirations toward an architectural expression, rich in proportional and visual values, and dynamic and fluid spaciality is the Watergate complex in Washington (1960–1963). Situated on a triangular site opening toward the Potomac, Moretti's building, excluding rectilinear schemes and ortogonal placements, is modeled after a concave core on three exedra opening on the river. The various curvatures and the slimming of the terminal elements, the oblique slant of the top, the variety of the balconies, of the projections, and of the roof here reach an authentic virtuosity. This is a work of full maturity and in full possession of expressive means, as well as occasion for full creative freedom, never again seen in Moretti's work, neither in the seat of the Esso Society in EUR in Rome (1964) nor in the Stock Exchange Tower in Montreal, built in 1967 together with PIER LUIGI NERVI.

LUCIANO PATETTA
Translated from Italian by
Shara Wasserman

WORKS

1949, House of the Astrea, Via Jenner; 1950, House of the Girasole; Milan. 1952, Villa la Saracena, Santa Marinella, Italy. 1960–1963, Watergate Complex, Washington. 1964, Esso Society Headquarters, EUR, Rome. 1967, Stock Exchange Tower (with Pier Luigi Nervi), Montreal.

BIBLIOGRAPHY

COLLINS, PETER 1966 "Stock-Exchange Tower, Montreal." *Architectural Review* 139, no. 832:432–438.

MOREY, MATHIEU PROSPER

Born in Nancy, a plasterer's son, Mathieu Prosper Morey (1805–1886) enrolled at the Ecole des Beaux-Arts in 1825, the pupil of ACHILLE LECLÈRE. He won the Grand Prix of Rome in

1831. After six years in Rome, he embarked with Desiré Raoul-Rochette to find the site of Troy. His student drawings during these years are in the Bibliothèque Municipale in Nancy. Morey returned to Paris, working under FÉLIX DUBAN and serving as an adviser at law, before returning in 1850 to Nancy as *architecte de la ville.*

R. D. MIDDLETON

WORKS

1849–1852, Covered Market, Place Henri Mengin and rue Saint Dizier; 1855–1857, Saint-Vincent-Saint-Fiacre, rue de Metz; 1858–1870, Palais de l'Université (Palais des Facultés), Place Carnot; *1862, Hôtel de Ville (entrance stairway), rue Pierre Fourier; 1864–1875, Saint Epvre, Place-Joseph Malval; 1873–1875, Palais Ducal (rebuilding and restoration; with Emile Boeswillwald), Grande-Rue; 1874–1880, Saint-Nicholas, rue Charles III; 1877, Lycée Henri Poincaré, rue de la Visitation; 1882–1883, Hôpital Civil, Avenue de Strasbourg; Nancy, Meurthe et Moselle, France.

BIBLIOGRAPHY

ELIE, HUBERT 1964 *Un architecte nancéien: Prosper Morey, 1805–1886.* Nancy, France: Thomas.

EUGÈNE, P. 1890 *Monographie de la basilique Saint-Epvre à Nancy.* Nancy, France: Desclée, Lefebvre.

MOREY, MATHIEU P. 1841 *Charpente de la cathédrale de Messine.* Paris: Firmin-Didot.

MOREY, MATHIEU P. 1854 *Recherches archéologiques dans la Troade, ou fragment d'un voyage fait dans le cours de l'année 1838.* Nancy, France: Grimblot & Raybois.

MOREY, MATHIEU P. 1863 *Notice sur le vie et les oeuvres d'Emmanuel Héré de Corny, premier architecte de S. M. Stanislas.* Nancy, France: Raybois.

MOREY, MATHIEU P. 1866 *Notice sur la vie et les oeuvres de Germain Boffrand, premier architecte de Léopold.* Nancy, France: Raybois.

MOREY, MATHIEU P. 1868*a* *Notice sur la vie et les oeuvres du R. P. François Derand, architecte lorrain.* Nancy, France: Raybois.

MOREY, MATHIEU P. 1868*b* *Richard Mique: Architecte de Stanislas, roi de Pologne, et de la reine Marie-Antoinette.* Nancy, France: Raybois.

VAPEREAU, LOUIS GUSTAVE (1858)1893 *Dictionnaire universel des contemporains.* 6th ed. Paris: Hachette.

MORGAN, JULIA

Julia Morgan (1872–1957) was California's first licensed woman architect. Born in San Francisco, she graduated from the University of California at Berkeley with an engineering degree. She was encouraged to become an architect by BERNARD MAYBECK and by her cousin, Pierre Lebrun. In 1896, she went to Paris, where she struggled successfully for two years to be the first woman accepted in the architecture section of the Ecole des Beaux-Arts.

Morgan's career as an architect began with collaborations with Maybeck on buildings in Berkeley. After her return from Paris, she worked for JOHN GALEN HOWARD on the Mining Building and the Greek Theater at the university. Her first independent commissions, for Mills College, included a 72-foot campanile (1903–1904) of reinforced concrete (the earliest college bell tower in the West), the library (1905–1906), the gymnasium (1907–1908), and the Social Center (1916).

In the architectural boom following the San Francisco earthquake of 1906, Morgan's career flourished. Her commissions included hundreds of houses throughout the Bay Area and many new institutions resulting from the changes in women's status. More than seven hundred buildings attested to her skills. The residences are distinguished by her client-centered approach to design, her use of locally available materials, and her integration of the varied architectural traditions of the West with the sophisticated vocabulary of her Beaux-Arts training. For these reasons, Morgan buildings cannot be said to reflect one definitive style. Nevertheless, they are all distinguished by the fine attention to detail and the craftsmanlike quality of construction, whether of redwood shingle, Mediterranean stucco, or reinforced concrete.

Morgan's institutions included churches, clubs, banks, schools, hospitals, and stores. A principal client was the Young Women's Christian Association, for which she built residences and recreation centers in California, Utah, and Hawaii. Asilomar (1913–1928) is now a state monument and national conference center.

Her popularity as an architect can be attributed to her reputation for meticulous craftsmanship, her dramatic indoor and outdoor swimming pools, and her ability to mold a project to the emotional and budgetary needs of the client. Morgan's most celebrated clients were the Hearst family. At his mother's death, William Randolph Hearst turned to Morgan to fulfill his own dreams. This led to a twenty-five-year collaboration including projects in Mexico, the Grand Canyon (1925), Wyntoon (1930–1945), and San Simeon (1919–1940). That grand estate, designed to be both a celebrities' playground and a museum for Hearst's collections, is now a state monument.

Julia Morgan's final project, a design for a medieval museum in San Francisco's Golden Gate Park, remains unrealized. After forty-five years in practice, during which she shared all her profits with her atelierlike staff, she closed her office and had her records destroyed. She insisted that the buildings should speak for her, adding that "architecture is a visual, not a verbal art."

SARA HOLMES BOUTELLE

WORKS

1903–1904, Bell Tower, Mills College, Oakland, Calif. 1903–1910, Phoebe Apperson Hearst Hacienda (alterations and additions), Pleasanton, Calif. 1905–1906, Library; 1907–1908, Gymnasium; Mills College, Oakland, Calif. 1908–1910, Saint John's Presbyterian Church (now Julia Morgan Center for Performing Arts), Berkeley. 1909, Kapiolani Rest Cottage, Mills College, Oakland, Calif. 1913–1915, Young Women's Christian Association, Oakland, Calif. 1913–1915, Young Women's Christian Association, San Jose, Calif. 1913–1928, Young Women's Christian Association Conference Center, Asilomar-Pacific Grove, Calif. *1915, Panama-Pacific International Exposition Women's Building, San Francisco. 1916, Social Center, Mills College, Oakland, Calif. 1919–1940, San Simeon Buildings, Calif. *1925, Hearst Cottage, Grand Canyon, Ariz. 1926–1927, Phoebe Apperson Hearst Memorial Gymnasium (with Bernard Maybeck), University of California, Berkeley. 1926–1927, Young Women's Christian Association, Honolulu, Hawaii. 1926–1927, Young Women's Christian Association, Salt Lake City, Utah. 1930, Berkeley Women's City Club (now Berkeley City Club). 1930–1945, Hearst Estate, Wyntoon, McCloud, Calif.

BIBLIOGRAPHY

BEACH, JOHN 1976 *Julia Morgan—An Architect from Oakland.* Oakland, Calif.: The Museum. Catalogue from an exhibition held at the Oakland Museum in 1976.

BOUTELLE, SARA 1976 "The Woman Who Built San Simeon." *California Monthly* 86, no. 6 April: 12–14 and cover.

BOUTELLE, SARA 1981 "Women's Networks: Julia Morgan and Her Clients." *Heresies* 11, no. 3:91–94.

LONGSTRETH, RICHARD 1977 *Julia Morgan, Architect.* Berkeley (Calif.) Architectural Heritage Association.

MURRAY, KEN 1971 *The Golden Days of San Simeon.* Garden City, N.Y.: Doubleday.

RIESS, SUZANNE (editor) 1976 "The Julia Morgan Architectural History Project." 2 vols. Regional Oral History, Bancroft Library, University of California, Berkeley.

STEILBERG, WALTER 1918 "Some Examples of the Work of Julia Morgan." *Architect and Engineer of California* 55:39–107.

TORRE, SUSANA (editor) 1977 *Women in American Architecture.* New York: Watson-Guptil. Section on Julia Morgan by Sara Boutelle.

WINSLOW, CARLETON 1980 *The Enchanted Hill.* Milbrae, Calif.: Celestial Arts.

MORGAN, WILLIAM

Practicing in his native Jacksonville, Florida, since 1961 after studying under JOSEP LLUIS SERT at Harvard, William Newton Morgan (1930–) has developed "architecture as landscape" employing natural elements in a formalized architectural vocabulary. Following a series of rectilinear glass-walled houses, platforms for observing nature, Morgan's subsequent buildings have incorporated expansive terraces and berms, coincident with his studies of prehistoric American earth structures. Broad horizontal layerings characterize the Florida State Museum, Gainesville (1969–1971), and the pyramidal Hilltop House (1974–1975); the Dunehouse Apartments, Atlantic Beach (1975), less successfully interpret curvilinear contours. The Federal Building, Fort Lauderdale (1977–1979), creates a new terraced landscape in an urban environment, a theme developed in many of Morgan's recent public and commercial structures.

THOMAS G. BEDDALL

WORKS

1962–1963, Rawls House; 1965–1966, Hatcher House; Jacksonville, Fla. 1970–1971, Florida State Museum, Gainesville. 1971–1973, William Morgan House, Atlantic Beach, Fla. 1974–1975, Hilltop House, Central Florida. 1974–1975, Oceanfront Condominium, Ocean City, Md. 1975, Dunehouse Apartments, Atlantic Beach, Fla. 1975–1977, Police Memorial Building, Jacksonville, Fla. 1977–1978, Federal Building/United States Court House, Fort Lauderdale, Fla. 1978–1979, Forest House, Central Florida. 1978–1979, State Office Building, Jacksonville, Fla. 1981–1982, Westinghouse Headquarters, Orlando, Fla.

BIBLIOGRAPHY

"Breaking Down the Battlements." 1978 *Architectural Record* 163, no. 1:117–124.

"Buildings as Landscape: Five Current Projects." 1972 *Architectural Record* 152, no. 3:129–136.

DEAN, ANDREA O. 1978 "Underground Architecture." *Journal of the American Institute of Architects* 67, no. 4:34–51.

"Florida State Museum Uses Earth Forms Boldly." 1971 *Architectural Record* 150, no. 3:121–126.

HOYT, CHARLES 1979 "Celebration of Justice." *Architectural Record* 166, no. 5:81–86.

MORGAN, WILLIAM N. 1979 "Up to Earth: Earth Architecture." *Progressive Architecture* 160, no. 4:84–87.

MORGAN, WILLIAM N. 1980 *Prehistoric Architecture in the Eastern United States.* Cambridge, Mass.: M.I.T. Press.

"Starting a Successful Practice." 1965 *Architectural Record* 138, no. 1:133–142.

ZEITSCHMANN, ERNST 1965 "Rawls House, Jacksonville, Fla." *Bauen und Wohnen* 19, no. 12:472–476.

MORIYAMA, RAYMOND

Raymond Moriyama (1929–) is a Canadian architect of Japanese descent, born in Vancouver, British Columbia. Educated at Toronto and McGill Universities, he established his own practice in Toronto in 1958. His first building to receive widespread attention was the Ontario Science Centre (1969). Since then his work has gained popular success rather than critical acclaim. Eclectic in their sources and derived more from intuition than from an objective theory of architecture, his buildings achieve their significance through their force of imagery and interesting design effects. Most notable for the quality of their interior spaces are the Scarborough Civic Centre (1973) and the Metropolitan Toronto Library (1977).

ANTHONY JACKSON

WORKS

1969, Ontario Science Centre, Toronto. 1973, Scarborough Civic Centre, Ontario. 1977, Metropolitan Toronto Library.

BIBLIOGRAPHY

VASTOKAS, JOAN M. 1978 "Architecture, Meaning and Values: Raymond Moriyama and the New Metropolitan Toronto Library," *Artscanada* 35, Feb.–Mar.:18–31.

MORRIS, ROBERT

Robert Morris (c.1702–1754) is the acknowledged theorist of the neo-Palladian movement in England by virtue of his publications, although as an architect he is of little consequence in the general picture of Palladian England. *An Essay in Defence of Ancient Architecture* (1728) aligns Morris with the EARL OF BURLINGTON, the EARL OF PEMBROKE, and Andrew Fountaine, and basically provides the architecture inspired by ANDREA PALLADIO and INIGO JONES with an aesthetic theory. His *Lectures on Architecture* (1734–1736) is one of the first books to consider the appropriateness of types of houses to their situations. A pattern book, *The Architectural Remembrancer* (1751), contained Jonesian and Kentian (see WILLIAM KENT) designs. He was kinsman of ROGER MORRIS, whose architecture may be seen as complementary to Robert's writings.

JOHN HARRIS

BIBLIOGRAPHY

MORRIS, ROBERT 1728 *An Essay in Defence of Ancient Architecture: Or a Parallel of the Ancient Buildings with the Modern.* London: Browne.

MORRIS, ROBERT 1734–1736 *Lectures on Architecture, Consisting of Rules Founded Upon Harmonick and Arithmetical Proportion, in Building.* London: Brindley.

MORRIS, ROBERT 1751 *The Architectural Remembrancer: Being a Collection of New and Useful Designs, of Ornamental Buildings and Decorations, for Parks, Gardens, Woods, etc.* London: The author.

MORRIS, ROBERT SCHOFIELD

Robert Schofield Morris (1898–1964) was born and educated in Ontario, Canada. Commissioned in the Royal Field Artillery (1917), he served in France and Belgium and was wounded at Ypres. Graduating from the school of architecture of McGill University in 1923, he worked with CARRÈRE AND HASTINGS in New York before becoming a partner in the firm of Marani, Lawson, and Morris, Toronto, in 1929. During the Great Depression, the firm's most notable building was perhaps the Bank of Canada, Ottawa (1938), designed in a modest Art Deco style. After World War II, the partnership, now Marani and Morris, rapidly became one of the most active in Canada, producing many governmental, commercial, professional, and hospital buildings notable for their restrained neoclassicism and excellent detailing.

THOMAS HOWARTH

WORKS

1930, Abitibi Power and Paper Company Head Office Building, Toronto. 1938, Bank of Canada Head Office Building; 1943, Bank of Canada War Savings Certificate Building; Ottawa. 1948, Grandstand, Canadian National Exhibition, Toronto. 1950, Guelph General Hospital, Ontario. 1956, Groves Memorial Hospital, Fergus, Ontario.

BIBLIOGRAPHY

"Presentation of The Royal Gold Medal for 1958 to Robert Schofield Morris, F.R.A.I.C." 1958 *Journal of the Royal Institute of British Architects* 65, no. 7:220–222.

"The Royal Gold Medal for Architecture." 1958 *Journal of the Royal Institute of British Architects* 65, no. 4:111–114.

MORRIS, ROGER

Roger Morris (1695–1749) emerged out of the COLEN CAMPBELL stable, but soon allied himself with the EARL OF PEMBROKE, for whom he acted as an amanuensis and transmitter of designs. Morris's other great patronizing family were the Campbells, dukes of Argyll, notably the second duke, for whom he altered Adderbury, Oxfordshire (1731), and the third duke, for whom he built Whitton Place, Middlesex (1732). Morris's Palladianism (see ANDREA PALLADIO) is highly individual and he is the master of the neo-Palladian villa, whose model he permutated in a series of exquisite houses, including Combe Bank, Kent (c.1725) and Westcombe House, Kent (c.1730). With Clearwell Castle, Gloucestershire (c.1728) and Inverary Castle, Argyllshire (1745), he demonstrated his flair for the massing of castles and Gothic buildings in an unparalleled way.

JOHN HARRIS

WORKS

1724, Marble Hill (with the Earl of Pembroke), Middlesex, England. c.1725, Combe Bank, Kent, England. 1727, White Lodge (with Pembroke), Richmond, England. c.1728, Clearwell Castle, Gloucestershire, England. 1729, Castle Hill (with Pembroke), Devon, England. 1730, Westcombe House, Kent, England. 1731, Adderbury (alterations), Oxfordshire, England. 1732, Whitton Place, Middlesex, England. 1732, Wimbledon House (with Pembroke), Surrey, England. 1745, Inverary Castle, Argyllshire, England.

MORRIS, WILLIAM

For William Morris (1834–1896), artist, craftsman, poet, merchant, socialist, medievalist, and printer, architecture was connected with all the other arts as a "tangible expression of all . . . order" (Mackail, 1899, vol. 1, p. 78). Born in Walthamstow, then outside of London, he gained in boyhood a deep love of nature and Gothic architecture as he rode about the Essex countryside and visited its churches. On first seeing Canterbury Cathedral, he thought "that the gates of heaven had been open to me" (Blunt, 1932, p. 229). He attended Marlborough School and in 1853 entered Exeter College, Oxford, where he developed strong interests in literature, history, the arts, and the Middle Ages. He subscribed to *The Builder* and in JOHN RUSKIN's chapter, "The Nature of Gothic" from *The Stones of Venice,* he found his creed: art as the expression of joy in one's work. Morris's visits in the summers of 1854 and 1855 to the cathedrals and churches of northern France led him to choose a career in architecture. Early in 1856, he entered the office of GEORGE E. STREET, the Gothic Revival architect, where he formed a lasting friendship with PHILIP WEBB. However, Morris found office detail irksome, so by the end of the year he left Street to try his hand at painting with his close friend Ned Jones, later Sir Edward Burne-Jones, under the guidance of Dante Gabriel Rossetti. During this year, among several contributions to the short-lived *Oxford and Cambridge Magazine,* he wrote "The Story of an Unknown Church," told by a French master mason of the thirteenth century, and "Shadows of Amiens," a fervent appreciation of the cathedral. In 1857, he joined Rossetti, Burne-Jones, and others in decorating the upper wall of the debating hall (now the library) of the Oxford Union Society Building with scenes from the *Morte d'Arthur* of which little survived on the unprepared surface. Morris's decoration of the open timber roof and its supports, as redone by his firm in 1875, remains.

Morris married Jane Burden in 1859 and engaged Philip Webb, now an independent architect, to build them a home in Bexleyheath, Kent. Red House (1859–1860) was named for its exposed brick walls. It was L-shaped with a cone-roofed brick and oak wellhouse in the angle. Morris and his friends decorated the interior with stained glass, paintings on walls and cabinets, furniture, embroidered hangings and other furnishings of their own design. This cooperative artistry, springing from Morris's distaste for the design and quality of contemporary products of the mechanical revolution, led to the artistic-commercial venture of Morris, Marshall, Faulkner & Co. (later Morris & Co.), "Fine Art Workmen in Painting, Carving, Furniture and the Metals." The firm opened in London in 1861, stating: "The Growth of Decorative Art in this country, owing to the efforts of English Architects, has now reached a point at which it seems desirable that Artists of reputation should devote their time to it" (Mackail, 1899, vol. 1, p. 150). Stained glass, mural decoration, embroidery, painted tiles, and furniture were among their early products, followed by wallpapers and printed and woven fabrics. Morris did not create the "Morris chair" but contributed most of the firm's flat design, particularly for wallpapers and fabrics. The taste and high standards maintained by Morris & Co. had a distinct effect on interior decoration and the design of objects for use. Morris's stress on the need for artists to contribute their talents to the "useful arts" helped to stimulate the Arts and Crafts movement. Through the firm, Nikolaus Pevsner maintains, "Morris laid the foundation of the modern style" and thus began "a new era in Western Art" (Pevsner, 1965, pp. 39, 22).

Ill health caused Morris to sell Red House and return to London in 1865. In the following years, besides administering his business, he wrote *The Earthly Paradise*, a series of long narrative poems that made him famous; translated Icelandic sagas and visited Iceland twice (1871 and 1873); produced decorated calligraphic manuscripts as "Sunday work"; and discovered Kelmscott Manor, an Elizabethan house on the upper Thames, which was his country home for many years. The old house seemed to Morris to have "grown up out of the soil"; its charm consisted in its combination of the attractive domestic architecture of its period with the continuity of its use and the beauty of "meadow and acre and wood and river" (Morris, 1936, vol. 1, p. 371).

Morris was instrumental in founding the Society for the Protection of Ancient Buildings in

1877, a pioneer effort at preservation. For Morris, pre-Renaissance buildings constituted a precious heritage for the nation and he protested their destruction by demolition or by the restoration that had been visited on cathedrals and churches by GEORGE GILBERT SCOTT and others.

About this time, Morris began to take an interest in public affairs and to lecture on art and on social concerns. The grim condition of the lower classes and his vision of a better state of society based on communal living in tasteful habitations made him an active socialist in 1883. He pictured his utopia in *News from Nowhere* (1891): London about 2090 has been rebuilt with buildings inspired by, but not in imitation of, medieval models.

The first exhibition of the Arts and Crafts Exhibition Society took place in November 1888. A lecture there by Emery Walker—printer and photoengraver and a friend of Morris—on historical printing and type faces inspired Morris to design a new font of type. This led to the founding of the Kelmscott Press for which Morris designed two type faces, which show the influence of incunabula type design, and over six hundred decorative borders, initials, title pages, and so on. The pages of the fifty-three titles that were produced on the hand presses of the Kelmscott Press between 1891 and 1898 embody his insistence on good materials and intelligent typography. His principles influenced subsequent improvement in typography and book design.

JOSEPH R. DUNLAP

BIBLIOGRAPHY

BLUNT, WILFRID S. (1919)1932 *My Diaries.* New York: Knopf.

FAULKNER, PETER 1980 *Against the Age.* London: Allen & Unwin.

HENDERSON, PHILIP 1967 *William Morris: His Life, Work, and Friends.* New York: McGraw-Hill.

LETHABY, WILLIAM (1935)1979 *Philip Webb and His Work.* Rev. ed. London: Haven Oak Press.

MACKAIL, JOHN W. 1899 *The Life of William Morris.* 2 vols. London: Longmans.

MORRIS, MAY 1936 Volume 1, pages 106–192, 266–286, 364–371 in *William Morris: Artist, Writer, Socialist.* Oxford: Blackwell.

MORRIS, WILLIAM 1950 *The Letters of William Morris to His Family and Friends.* Edited by Philip Henderson. London: Longmans.

MORRIS, WILLIAM (1910–1915)1966 *Collected Works.* 24 vols. Reprint. New York: Russell.

MORRIS, WILLIAM 1969 *The Unpublished Lectures of William Morris.* Edited by Eugene LeMire. Detroit, Mich.: Wayne State University.

PEVSNER, NIKOLAUS (1936)1965 *Pioneers of Modern Design.* Harmondsworth, England: Penguin. Originally published as *Pioneers of the Modern Movement.*

PEVSNER, NIKOLAUS 1956 "William Morris, C. R. Ashbee and the Twentieth Century." *Manchester Review* 7:437–458.

PEVSNER, NIKOLAUS (1957)1968 "William Morris and Architecture." Volume 2, pages 108–117 in *Studies in Art, Architecture and Design.* London: Thames & Hudson.

THOMPSON, PAUL 1967 Chapter 2 in *The Work of William Morris.* London: Heinemann.

MOSER, KARL

Karl Moser (1860–1936) has always been highly respected by the pioneers of modern architecture in Switzerland as one of the movement's early teachers and mentors. Since the 1920s, Moser favored the new ideas in his capacity as juror at important competitions. That he tried together with H. P. BERLAGE and others (but against the vote of VICTOR HORTA), to help LE CORBUSIER and PIERRE JEANNERET get the first prize for their project of the Palace of the League of Nations in Geneva (1927) is well known. As a sign of gratitude, the Congrès Internationaux d'Architecture Moderne (CIAM) elected him as their first president in 1928. Moser himself adopted the new style in the course of his career as professor at the Technische Hochschule (ETH) in Zurich (1915–1928) partly under the impression of recent developments in the Netherlands (he especially admired WILLIAM MARINUS DUDOK) and to a certain degree also in response to the avant-garde positions held by some of his students. His late buildings—especially the Antonius-Kirche in Basel, the first concrete church in Switzerland (1925–1931)—represent early peaks of International style architecture in this country.

His earlier work, although of extraordinary bulk and richness, is less known. Son of an architect who had studied with LUDWIG EISENLOHR in Karlsruhe, Germany, and who had realized important public buildings in his canton, Karl Moser studied in Zurich (1878–1882) and entered the studio of his former teacher, ALFRED FRIEDRICH BLUNTSCHLI. From 1883 to 1884, he attended classes at the Ecole des Beaux-Arts in Paris; thereafter, he did practical work in Baden, Switzerland, and Wiesbaden, Germany. After a trip to Italy, from where he returned with a large number of landscape watercolors, he settled down in a rather successful practice both in Southwest Germany and in Switzerland. The firm rapidly became well known for its numerous office buildings, private houses, and churches, both Roman Catholic and Protestant.

As a member of what Karl Werner has called the *moderne Karlsruher Architektenschule,* Moser

Karl Moser. Saint Anton's. Basel. 1925–1931

Karl Moser. University of Zurich (main building). 1911–1914

represented, together with a few other Karlsruhe architects such as HERMANN BILLING, a middle line between the formal exuberance of both Art Nouveau and Viennese Secessionism (of which nearby Darmstadt with its Mathildenhöhe had become a center) and more traditional approaches, which favored the use of historic styles. Well aware of EUGÈNE EMMANUEL VIOLLET-LE-DUC, Moser started off with a clear preference for Gothic forms. Around 1900, however, he developed a special inclination toward the Romanesque. Although under the rule of the German emperors the Romanesque style had acquired unmistakable imperialist overtones, symbolizing as it does a tradition of power reaching back to the Hohenstaufen, the Karlsruhe architects seem to have been primarily interested in the unorthodox handling of space, proportion, and architectural detail which this style makes possible. No doubt, Moser was impressed by the work of H. H. RICHARDSON and his followers, who had proposed a similarly empirical rather than ideological use of Romanesque forms and whose work had been publicized extensively by Karl Hinckendeyn and Julius Becker in their volume on *Neubauten in Nordamerika* (1897). If one compares the Bankhaus Homburger in Karlsruhe, Germany (1898–1901), with Richardson's Ames Building in Boston (1881–1883), or Saint Paul's Church in Basel (1897–1901) with Trinity Church, Boston (1872–1877), the stylistic analogies are striking. Yet, in the buildings of Moser—most of which he designed in collaboration with Hans Curjel—the emphasis lies more clearly on the unity of the overall form. Architectural members and sculptural decoration are subordinate to an organic conception of the whole, and in later works half-columns, pilasters, and arches articulating façades often seem to be stretched by the boldly swelling spaces inside.

Around 1907, the Romanesque dropped out of Moser's work, and elements of classical and baroque traditions seen with Secessionist eyes came to the fore. The Museum of Fine Arts in Zurich (1907–1910) combines the outlines of a classical temple with grossly inflated Doric metopes. The main building of Zurich University (1911–1914) brings together the roof form of an eighteenth-century palace, the vertical façade articulation of ALFRED MESSEL's Wertheim Store in Berlin, and the interior of a Carolingian palatial chapel à la Aachen transformed into a large rectangular hall.

In his lectures at ETH, Moser emphasized organic treatment of space as the *raison d'être* of architectural design. Furthermore, the idea of a close partnership of the architect with sculptors and painters was of primary importance to him, as can be seen in all his works.

The powerful handling of space functions as an organizing principle in his buildings, not only in that it effectively unifies their often diverse formal elements but also in that it secures a coherence of style among buildings emphatically different in their stylistic references. Moser was an eclectic able to practice a wide range of styles without ever betraying his strong authenticity as an artist.

STANISLAUS VON MOOS

WORKS

1891–1893, Saint John's, Berne. 1896–1897, Villa Boveri; 1898–1899, Villa Römerberg; Baden, Switzerland. 1898–1901, Saint Paul's, Basel. c.1900, Christ Church, Karlsruhe, Germany. 1902–1905, Saint Paul's, Berne. 1905, Saint John's, Mannheim, Germany. 1906, Luther Church, Karlsruhe, Germany. 1907–1910, Museum of Fine Arts; 1908, Saint Anton's; Zurich. 1909–1911, Protestant Church, Flawil, Switzerland. 1911–1912, Saint Paul's, Lucerne, Switzerland. 1911–1914, University of Zurich (main building). 1912, Savings Bank, Aarau, Switzerland. 1912–1913, Badischer Bahnhof, Basel. 1918–1920, Fluntern Church; 1925–1926, Museum of Fine Arts (addition); Zurich. 1925–1931, Saint Anton's, Basel.

BIBLIOGRAPHY

BIRCHLER, LINUS 1936 "Karl Moser und moderne katholische Kirchenbau." *Schweizer Rundschau* 36, no. 8:633–639.

CURJEL, HANS 1958 "Karl Cölestin Moser." Pages 549–554 in *Biographisches Lexikon des Kantons Aargau.* Aarau, Switzerland.

CURJEL, HANS, and MOSER, KARL 1962 *Die Pauluskirche in Basel.* Basel.

EESTEREN, CORNELIUS VAN; GIEDION, SIEGFRIED; LE CORBUSIER; and SCHMIDT, GEORG 1936 "Karl Moser + 28 February 1936." *De 8 en opbouw* 7, no. 8:85–96.

GANTNER, JOSEPH, and REINLE, ADOLF 1962 Volume 4 in *Kunstgeschichte der Schweiz.* Frauenfeld, Switzerland: Huber.

MOSER, KARL 1922 "Neue holländische Architektur: Bauten von W. M. Dudok, Hilversum." *Werk* 9:205–214.

KIENZLE, HERMANN 1937 *Karl Moser: 1860–1936.* Zurich: Zürcher Kunstgesellschaft.

PLATZ, GUSTAV 1930 "Architekt K. Moser in der baukünstlerischen Entwicklung seiner Zeit." *Schweizerische Bauzeitung.*

LESCAZE, WILLIAM 1942 *On Being an Architect.* New York: Putnam.

MOSER, KOLOMAN

Koloman Moser (1868–1918) studied painting and the graphic arts, first at the Academy and later at the School of Applied Arts in Vienna. As one of the founders of the Vienna Secession, he had early contacts with the architect members of this group, and for a number of years he was a close friend and collaborator of JOSEF HOFFMANN. Hoffmann valued Moser highly as a stimulating and inspiring influence well acquainted with international art movements. In 1899, both were appointed to teach at the School of Applied Arts, and in 1903, with the financial aid of Fritz Wärndorfer, they founded the *Wiener Werkstätte* which Moser left in 1907 to devote himself more intensively to painting.

As a designer, Moser was most versatile; in addition to every kind of illustration and graphic design including posters, stamps, and money, he designed glassware and ceramics, stained glass, patterns for fabrics (often with striking figure-ground effects), costumes, jewelry and objects in metal, exhibitions and stage sets, as well as interiors and furniture. During the years of their collaboration, the furniture designs of Moser and Hoffmann were very close though Moser's tended to be more sumptuous in their decoration. Gustav Klimt once observed that in an exhibition Moser's designs attracted all ladies; Hoffmann's, the male visitors. In recent years, the interest in and appreciation of Moser has increased.

EDUARD F. SEKLER

WORKS

1899, Secession Building (stucco decoration; now partly destroyed); 1900–1904, Designs for the Sixth, Thirteenth, Eighteenth, Nineteenth, and Twentieth Exhibitions of the Vienna Secession; *1903, Wiener Werkstätte (interiors; with Josef Hoffmann); *1904, Flöge Sisters Fashion Studio (with Hoffmann); Vienna. *1904, Purkersdorf Sanatorium (some interiors; with Hoffmann), Austria. *1904, Wiener Werkstätte Exhibition (with Hoffmann), Hohenzollern-Kunstgewerbehaus, Berlin. 1904–1905, Saint Leopold's Church (stained-glass windows), Vienna. *1905, Stoneborough Apartment (with Hoffmann); *1906, J. and J. Kohn Shop (salesroom, shop front, and interior; with Hoffmann); Berlin.

BIBLIOGRAPHY

ABELS, LUDWIG 1901 "Koloman Moser." *Dekorative Kunst* 7:227–233.

FENZ, WERNER 1976 *Kolo Moser.* Salzburg, Austria: Residenz Verlag.

MOSER, KOLO 1916–1917 "Mein Werdegang." *Velhagen und Klasings Monatshefte* 31:254–262.

OBERHUBER, OSWALD, and HUMMEL, JULIUS 1979 *Koloman Moser.* Vienna: Hochschule für angewandte Kunst. Exhibition catalogue.

ZUCKERKANDL, BERTA 1904 "Koloman Moser." *Dekorative Kunst* 12:329–344.

MOSER, WERNER M.

Grandson of Robert Moser, son of KARL MOSER, and father of Lorenz Moser, Werner M. Moser (1896–1970) is third in line of an extraordinary Swiss architectural dynasty. He lived his youth in Karlsruhe, Germany; after studying under his father in Zurich, he went to Rotterdam, Netherlands, where he worked with M. J. GRANPRÉ-MOLIÈRE, the head of the romantic regionalist movement called the Delft school (1922–1923). Later, he moved to the United States, where he

Werner M. Moser. Public Bath Allenmoos (with Haefeli). Zurich. 1938–1939

Werner M. Moser. Congress Building (with Haefeli and Steiger). Zurich. 1937–1939

worked for FRANK LLOYD WRIGHT, among others. While there, he designed a project for a 26-story office building in Chicago.

After settling again in Switzerland, he joined the local avant-garde of the *Neues Bauen,* participated in the foundation of the Congrès Internationaux d'Architecture-Moderne (CIAM) at La Sarraz (1928), and realized, together with Ferdinand Kramer and MARTINUS STAM, the Old People's Home of the Budge-Stiftung in Frankfurt, a much publicized highlight of ERNST MAY's *Neues Frankfurt.* At the same time, he participated, in partnership with Emil Roth, in the design of the Eglisee housing development in Basel (1930), and in that of the even more important Werkbundsiedlung Neubühl in Zurich (1930–1931) with MAX HAEFELI, CARL HUBACHER, RUDOLF STEIGER, Emil Roth, PAUL ARTARIA, and HANS SCHMIDT. However, after 1934, the Swiss stopped their public housing programs, so that Neubühl turned out to be the conclusion rather than the beginning of a new tradition of progressive housing in Switzerland.

Moser, like many of his Swiss friends from the CIAM group, concentrated on the masterly design of individual houses for an enlightened elite. At the same time, he channeled his vision of a better society into the careful study and design of schools—as expressed in his book, *Das Kind und sein Schulhaus* (1933)—and of public baths. His Allenmoos-Bad (1939) in Zurich, realized together with Max Haefeli, is an example of a modern architectural empiricism that works with local materials and tries to re-establish links with regional building traditions. The Protestant Church in Zurich Altstetten (1937–1941) goes even further in this direction and reaches a fragile equilibrium between a modern conception of space and a discretely regionalist handling of detail.

From 1937 on, many of Moser's major works were realized in collaboration with Haefeli and Steiger. The most important among these are the Congress Building—realized in the context of the Swiss National Exhibition, 1939—and the Cantonal Hospital in Zurich (both 1937–1939), and after World War II, he designed the Hohenbühl Apartments in Zurich (1951–1953), the Office Building Zur Palme in Zurich (1960–1964)—an interesting synthesis of Wright, Italianate Brutalism, and Team 10 ideals—, and the elegant Bally Building on Zurich's Bahnhofstrasse (1962–1968). To many architects and former students, the best among these buildings will continue to reflect the precious mixture of poetic tenderness and visionary fervor that characterized Moser as a man.

STANISLAUS VON MOOS

WORKS

1928–1930, Hagmann House, Zurich. 1929–1930, Old People's Home (Budge-Stiftung; with Martinus Stam and Ferdinand Kramer), Frankfurt. 1930, Moser-Guggenbühl House, Zurich. 1930–1932, Neubühl Housing Development (with Max Haefeli, Carl Hubacher, Rudolf Steiger, Emil Roth, Paul Artaria, and Hans Schmidt), Switzerland. 1937, Von Schulthess House, Zollikon, Switzerland. 1937–1939, Congress Building (with Haefeli and Steiger); 1938–1939, Public Bath Allenmoos (with Haefeli); Zurich. 1938–1941, Protestant Church, Altstetten, Switzerland. 1942–1951, Cantonal Hospital Complex (with Haefeli, Steiger, Hermann Fietz, Josef Schütz, and Hermann Weideli), Zurich. 1949, Neo-Apostolic Church, Geneva. 1951–1953, Eternit Administration Building (with Haefeli and F. A. van Kuyk), Niederurnen, Switzerland. 1960–1964, Office Building Zur Palme (with Haefeli, Steiger, and André Studer); 1962–1968, Bally Building (with Haefeli and Steiger); 1967, ASM Administration Building (with Haefeli and Steiger); Zurich.

BIBLIOGRAPHY

CARLONI, TITA 1980 "Notes sur l'architecture organique en Suisse." *Archithèse* 2:54–57.

MEYER, PETER 1937 "Zur Architektur des Zürcher Kongressgebäudes." *Schweizerische Bauzeitung* 7:80–82.

MOSER, WERNER M. 1949 "Das vielgeschossige Mietshaus im neuen städtischen Wohnquartier." *Werk* 36, no. 1:306.

MOSER, WERNER M. (editor) 1952 *Frank Lloyd Wright: Sechzig Jahre lebendige Architektur.* Winterthur, Switzerland: Buckdruckerei Winterthur.

MOSER, WERNER M. 1956 "Das Verhalten des Laien zur heutigen Baukunst." *Schweizerische Technische Zeitschrift* 46.

MOSER, WERNER M. 1959 "Die Bedeuting Frank Lloyd Wrights für die Entwicklung der Gegenwartsarchitektur." *Werk* 46, no. 12:423–428.

MOSER, WERNER M. 1965 "Zur Diskussion über Unterrichts- und Schulbaufragen." *Schweizerische Bauzeitung* 83, no. 14:217–218.

MOSER, WERNER M., and GONZENBACH, W. 1933 *Das Kind und sein Schulhaus.* Zurich.

STEINMANN, MARTIN 1980 "Das Allenmoos-Bad: Bedeutung der Formen—Formen der Bedeutung." *Archithèse* 2:31–36.

VOGT, ADOLF MAX 1980 "Werner M. Mosers fünf Punkte zum 'Bauen im Kontext'." *Archithèse* 2:45–47.

MOULD, JACOB WREY

Jacob Wrey Mould (1825–1886) was born in Chislehurst, Kent, England, and was educated at King's College in London. A pupil of OWEN JONES, Mould is said to have assisted him with the polychrome decoration of the London Crystal Palace (1851) and with the illustrations of several of Jones's publications. Mould received further training in the office of LEWIS VULLIAMY, Jones's teacher and associate, and is credited with the design for the grand staircase of Vulliamy's Dorchester House (1848–1856), which he is said to have designed following an injury of the architect. In 1848, Mould exhibited a design for a stone barn at the Royal Academy and until 1852, he maintained an office of his own.

In 1852, Mould settled in New York, where he continued his varied career as an architect, designer, songwriter, and opera translator. His first major New York commission was All Soul's Unitarian Church and Parsonage (1853–1855), a work he obtained with the help of Moses Hicks Grinnell, a prominent churchman who is said to have brought Mould to New York. Designed in an Anglo-Italianate Romanesque style with alternating bands of red brick and Caen stone and thus nicknamed "Church of the Holy Zebra," All Souls' introduced constructional polychromy to American architecture. By the late 1850s, in his unexecuted project for Plymouth Church (1859), Brooklyn, New York, and the Trinity Church Parish School (1860) and West Presbyterian Church (1863–1865) in New York, Mould adopted the English High Victorian Gothic style of which he was one of the earliest and most creative practitioners in the United States. His work was an important influence on the American architects who practiced in this style in the following years. Mould's later design for the First Presbyterian Church (1874–1877) in Bath, New York, shows the influence of EUGÈNE EMMANUEL VIOLLET-LE-DUC.

In addition to his ecclesiastic designs, Mould built a number of noteworthy residences. The New York townhouse of Runyon W. Martin (1865–1869), the first dwelling erected on Fifth Avenue across from Central Park, was one of the few residences designed in a Ruskinian (see JOHN RUSKIN) Gothic style. Mould's other domestic work included the Hudson Valley home (c.1865–1867) of Albert Bierstadt, the painter, in Irvington, N.Y., the palatial and lavishly ornamented Swiss chalet-style country residence (c.1866) of Thomas Kennard, the English-born railway engineer, in Glen Cove, New York, and the High Victorian stone mansion (1868) of Thomas Clapham in Roslyn Harbor, New York, the only still standing, though greatly altered.

As an ornamental designer in the tradition of Jones, Mould executed numerous designs for interior polychrome decoration. Soon after his arrival in New York, he prepared unexecuted designs for the New York Crystal Palace, which received the praise of architects. His polychrome scheme for the interior of All Souls' was never executed. His decorative work for the interior of the townhouse of John A. C. Gray (1858), as well as that for Mould's own residence (1859) do not survive.

Much of Mould's career was devoted to New York's Central Park. As the assistant architect to FREDERICK LAW OLMSTED and CALVERT VAUX beginning in December 1858, Mould designed the architectural detail of many of the park structures. His naturalistic designs for the stone carving of the Terrace (1858–1871) are a major achievement of Ruskinian Gothic ornament. Mould's sense for polychrome decoration was best applied to the Music Stand (1862) and the designs for the encaustic tiles of the Terrace.

From 1870 to 1871, Mould served as architect-in-chief of the Department of Public Parks as reorganized under Boss Tweed. He planned new park structures for Central Park that were foreign to the original *Greensward* plan of Olmsted and Vaux. In addition, he executed decorative work for other city parks and squares. As associate architect (1871–1874), he designed, in association with

Vaux, the initial plans for the Metropolitan Museum of Art (1874–1880) and the Museum of Natural History (1874–1877). Only one wing of each museum was built according to their plans. From 1875–1879, Mould was employed by Henry Meiggs, railroad contractor, as the architect-in-chief of the Department of Public Works of Lima, Peru. In this capacity, he was responsible for the design of Lima's parks. Mould was also the architect of the polychrome brick-and-stone mansion of E. C. Dubois (c. 1879) in Lima, thus bringing his Anglo-American style to South America. Mould returned to New York and from 1880 to 1882 was engaged to design the architectural features of Morningside Park. From 1885 until his death in 1886, he served as architectural draftsman to the Department of Public Parks. His last work was the temporary tomb for President Ulysses S. Grant erected in Riverside Park, New York (1886).

Despite his great talent as a draftsman and designer, he never achieved great success in his profession. Eccentric, ill-mannered, and lacking any business sense, Mould received few commissions in his later years.

DENNIS STEADMAN FRANCIS
and JOY M. KESTENBAUM

WORKS

*1853–1855, All Souls' Unitarian Church and Parsonage; *1856?, Matthew Morgan Bank; New York. *1857–1858, Second Unitarian Church, Brooklyn, N.Y. *1858, John A. C. Gray House (interior decoration), New York. 1858–1860, Unitarian Congregational Church, Yonkers, N.Y. 1858–1871, Terrace, Central Park (with Calvert Vaux); *1859, Mould House (interior decoration); 1860, Trinity Church Parish School; New York. *1862, Central Park Music Stand; *1863–1865, West Presbyterian Church; *1864–1865, Church of the Holy Trinity; *1865–1869, Runyon W. Martin House; New York. *c.1865–1867, Albert Bierstadt House, Irvington, N.Y. *c.1866, Thomas W. Kennard Residence, Glen Cove, N.Y. 1868, Thomas Clapham House, Roslyn Harbor, N.Y. *1870–1871, Central Park Boathouse (with Calvert Vaux); 1870–1871, Central Park Sheepfold (now Tavern-on-the-Green); 1870–1871, Central Park Stable (with Calvert Vaux); *1871, Central Park Casino; New York. 1873–1880, Saint Mary's Episcopal Church, Luzerne, N.Y. 1874–1877, First Presbyterian Church, Bath, N.Y. 1874–1877, Museum of Natural History (with Calvert Vaux); 1874–1880, Metropolitan Museum of Art (with Calvert Vaux); New York. c.1875–1879, Parque de la Reserva; c.1879, E. C. Dubois House; Lima. 1880–1882, Morningside Park (retaining wall); *1886, Temporary Tomb for Ulysses S. Grant; New York.

BIBLIOGRAPHY

COOK, CLARENCE C. 1972 *A Description of the New York Central Park.* Reprint. New York: Blom.

HITCHCOCK, H.R. 1968 "Ruskin and American Architecture, or Regeneration Long Delayed." In John Summerson (editor), *Concerning Architecture: Essays on Architectural Writers and Writing Presented to Nikolaus Pevsner.* London: Allen Lane.

"Jacob Wrey Mould." 1886 *The Studio* 1886:14–16.

KOWSKY, FRANCIS R. 1980 *The Architecture of Frederick Clarke Withers and the Progress of the Gothic Revival in America after 1850.* Middleton, Conn.: Wesleyan University Press.

VAN ZANTEN, DAVID T. 1969 "Jacob Wrey Mould: Echoes of Owen Jones and the High Victorian Styles in New York 1853–1865." *Journal of the Society of Architectural Historians* 28:41–57.

MOUNTFORT, B. W.

Benjamin Woolfield Mountfort (1824–1898) was born in England but emigrated to New Zealand in 1850. In London, he had been articled to RICHARD CARPENTER. In New Zealand, practicing in Christchurch, he designed many fine churches, houses, and public buildings, nearly all in the Gothic Revival style. He was Canterbury Provincial Architect from 1855 to 1865.

JOHN STACPOOLE

WORKS

1855, Saint Bartholomew's Church, Kaiapoi, New Zealand. 1856, Englefield House, Christchurch, New Zealand. 1858, Saint John's Church, Waikouaiti, New Zealand. 1858–1865, Provincial Council Chambers; 1859–1862, Christchurch Club; 1869–1877, Canterbury Museum; 1871–1893, Sunnyside Mental Hospital; 1872, Church of Saint Michael and All Angels; Christchurch, New Zealand. 1875, 1882, Church of Saint John the Baptist, Rangiora, New Zealand. 1875, Trinity Congregational Church, Christchurch, New Zealand. 1876, Saint Paul's Church, Papanui, New Zealand. 1877, Canterbury College Clocktower Block; 1882, Canterbury College Hall; Christchurch, New Zealand. *1886, Christ Church, Nelson, New Zealand. 1886, New School, Christ's College, Christchurch, New Zealand. *1886–1888, Napier Cathedral, New Zealand. 1886–1896, St. Mary's Church, Parnell, New Zealand.

BIBLIOGRAPHY

STACPOOLE, JOHN 1976 *Colonial Architecture in New Zealand.* Wellington, New Zealand: Reed.

STACPOOLE, JOHN, and BEAVEN, PETER 1972 *New Zealand Art: Architecture, 1820–1970.* Wellington, New Zealand: Reed.

MOYA, JOHN HIDALGO

See POWELL and MOYA.

MUḤAMMAD B. AL-ḤUSAYN and ḤĀJJĪ B. AL-ḤUSAYN AL-DĀMGHĀNĪ

Muḥammad b. al-Ḥusayn and Ḥājjī b. al-Ḥusayn were brothers who, together with their father Ḥusayn b. Abī Ṭālib al-Dāmghānī, signed various buildings in Basṭām and Dāmghān in the first two decades of the fourteenth century. Muḥammad signed five works at Basṭām, dating between 1302 and 1313; Ḥājjī signed the same 1302 band in the cell at Basṭām as well as an undated band in the ruins of a mosque in Dāmghān. Their father, Ḥusayn, collaborated with Muḥammad on the 1308 tomb tower inscription at Basṭām and signed the lower register of the interlaced Kufic inscription, the work (*ᶜamal*) of Ḥusayn b. Abī Ṭālib, the engineer (*al-muhandis*) of Dāmghān.

This wealth of signatures is extremely important in understanding the organization and activities of craftsmen in the Mongol period in Iran. First, it underscores the familial organization of artisans, for a father and two sons collaborated on the same large-scale project at Basṭām. Second, it illustrates the movement of artisans: the family *nisba,* al-Dāmghānī, and Ḥājjī's signature in a locally commissioned mosque at Dāmghān suggest that the family base was the town of Dāmghān, but the signatures of three members in an imperially commissioned complex at Basṭām, some 75 kilometers away, show that artisans were relatively mobile in the Ilkhanid period and were often recruited to work on special projects. Third, these signatures indicate that artisans were not as specialized as their epithets might indicate. The father signed his work as the engineer (*al-muhandis*); Ḥājjī either used no title or called himself the builder (*al-bannā'*); Muḥammad at various times used both of these titles as well as a third one, stucco worker (*al-jaṣṣāṣ*). In sum, these signatures are important not only as one of the earliest examples of multiple buildings signed by the same craftsmen, but also as evidence of the role and increased social position of architects in the Mongol period in Iran.

Sheila S. Blair

WORKS

MUḤAMMAD B. AL-ḤUSAYN

1302–1303, Bāyazīd Basṭāmī Shrine (cell band); 1308–1309, Tomb Tower of Öljeitü's Son (upper bank of tomb tower and upper band around portal recess connecting the tomb tower with the mosque); 1313–1314, Bāyazīd Basṭāmī Shrine (stucco band around entrance corridor); n.d., Arch of the Mihrab, Mosque, adjacent to the tomb of Bāyazīd Basṭāmī; Basṭām, Iran.

ḤĀJJĪ B. AL-ḤUSAYN AL-DĀMGHĀNĪ

1302–1303, Bāyazīd Basṭāmī Shrine (cell band), Basṭām, Iran. n.d., Mosque (stucco inscription), near Pīr-i ᶜAlāmdār Tomb, Dāmghān, Iran.

BIBLIOGRAPHY

Blair, Sheila n.d. "The Interlaced Kufic Inscription of the Tomb Tower at Basṭām." In Ch. Adle (editor), *Le Monde Iranien et l'Islam.* Forthcoming publication.

Mayer, L. A. 1956 Pages 63, 96 in *Islamic Architects and Their Works.* Geneva: Kundig.

Combe, Et.; Sauvaget, J.; and Wiet, G. (editors) 1944–1954 Volume 13, numbers 5124, 5155, 5156, and Volume 14, numbers 5328, 5329 in *Repertoire Chronologique d'Épigraphie Arabe.* Cairo: Institute Français d'archéologie Orientale.

Wilber, Donald (1955)1969 *Architecture of Islamic Iran: The Il khānid Period.* Reprint. Westport, Conn.: Greenwood.

Wilber, Donald 1976 "Builders and Craftsmen of Islamic Iran: The Earlier Periods." *Art and Archaeology Research Papers* 10:31–39.

MUHAMMAD B. ATSIZ

Muhammad b. Atsiz (12th century) completed the mausoleum of Sultan Sanjar at Merv (c.1150–1160), one of the key monuments in Persian dome construction. It is a large cube covered by a double dome. The exterior one, originally decorated with blue tiles, rises above a gallery pierced with alternating bays. The inner dome, spanned with clusters of projecting ribs, rises from a sixteen-sided polygon. The structure was connected to a mosque, now gone, and its interior was primarily decorated with stucco.

Massumeh Farhad

WORK

c.1150–1160, Sultan Sanjar Mausoleum, Merv, Russia.

BIBLIOGRAPHY

Cohn-Wiener, E. 1925 "Die Ruinen von der Seldschuken-Stadt von Merw und das Mausoleum Sultan Sandschars." *Jahrbuch Asiatischer Kunst* 1925:114–122.

Mayer, L. A. 1956 *Islamic Architects and Their Work.* Geneva: Kundig.

Pope, Arthur U. 1965 *Persian Architecture: The Triumph of Form and Color.* New York: Braziller.

MUHAMMAD B. MAHMUD AL-ISFAHANI

Muhammad b. Mahmud al-Isfahani (14th–15th centuries) completed the mausoleum of Gur-i Amir in 1404 at Samarkand, in present-day Uzbek, Union of Soviet Socialist Republics. It was commissioned for Timur's grandson, Muhammad Sultan. The tomb consists of an octagonal exterior and a cruciform inner chamber. The crypt is located directly below. A high, ribbed double dome crowns the mausoleum. In 1405, Timur was also buried here.

MASSUMEH FARHAD

WORK

1404–1405, Gur-i Amir (completion), Samarkand.

MUJICA, FRANCISCO

Francisco Mujica (20th century), born in Peru, spent most of his professional career in Mexico. He received architectural degrees from the University of Chile and the University of Mexico and studied city planning at the Sorbonne in Paris.

In 1929, Mujica published *The History of the Skyscraper,* dealing with the architects whose innovations contributed to skyscraper style and technology. He researched the archeological ruins of Mexico and Central America for many years and evolved the theory that modern building technology must respond to the forms and motifs of ancient Meso-American construction. His Neo-American style sought a unique continental identity through the terraced and pyramidal shapes of indigenous architecture.

PATRICIA C. PHILLIPS

BIBLIOGRAPHY

MUJICA, FRANCISCO (1929)1977 *The History of the Skyscraper.* Reprint. New York: Da Capo.

SKY, ALISON, and STONE, MICHELLE 1976 *Unbuilt America.* New York: McGraw-Hill.

MULHOLLAND, ROGER

Roger Mulholland (1740–1818) was one of the most distinguished Belfast architects in the later eighteenth century. Born in the diocese of Derry, Ireland, he was a major entrepreneur in building and designed all of his own speculative properties. His best buildings are among the finest examples of Georgian Irish architecture.

JAMES STEVENS CURL

WORKS

1779, First Presbyterian Church, Dunmurry, County Antrim, Ireland. 1782, First Presbyterian Church, Rosemary Street. *1780–1790, Housing on Donegall Street, Academy Street, William Street, Church Street, Dunbar Street, Gordon Street, Robert Street, Hill Street; *1783–1785, White Linen Hall; *1787, Belfast Castle (coach house); *1790, Houses on Linenhall Street (now Donegall Place); *1796, Bridge over Reed's Strand (repairs); *1805, House of Correction; Belfast.

BIBLIOGRAPHY

BRETT, C. E. B. 1967 *Buildings of Belfast 1700–1914.* London: Weidenfeld & Nicolson.

BRETT, C. E. B. 1976 *Roger Mulholland, Architect, of Belfast, 1740–1818.* Belfast: Ulster Architectural Heritage Society.

MULLETT, ALFRED B.

Alfred Bult Mullett (1834–1890) had two careers in architecture in post-Civil War America, and both ended tragically. They were marked by brevity as well as the architect's sense of enterprise, flair for innovation, and untiring energy. Even his enemies praised his unflagging industry and confessed grudging admiration for his honesty in the Gilded Age.

In his first career, Mullett was the Treasury's supervising architect from 1866 through 1874. Designs of imposing magnificence were among the fruits of his tenure, forty-two structures in all. The exemplar was the State, War, and Navy Building (1871–1889) in Washington, now the Old Executive Office building, which attested to Mullett's mastery of the Second Empire style. Spurred by an undiagnosed psychiatric disorder, he ended his career with an unheralded resignation and deserted his profession. On his return in 1884, he began a private practice in Washington which ended in suicide in October 1890. An innovative design of his second career was the Sun Building (1885–1886) in Washington, a skyscraper in the infancy of skyscrapers. Now the American Bank Building, it may be the oldest elevator building to survive from the days when skyscrapers were becoming the marvel of American architecture.

Born in England, Mullett moved with his family to Glendale, Ohio, on the fringe of Cincinnati, in 1845. He was buried there despite having lived the last half of his life in Washington. Historians to the contrary, Mullett had no college training. He was apprenticed to his profession in his teens. A pilgrimage to the Old World's architectural wonders capped his training. In 1857, his first appearance in Cincinnati directories identified him as an architect in the firm headed by ISAIAH ROGERS. The 1860 volume lifted Mullett to a partnership, but his name vanished from the 1861 listings.

Family lore has it that the young man answered Lincoln's call for 75,000 men. His regiment was disbanded on reaching Washington, however, because Ohio's quota had been exceeded. Mullett then found a job with Treasury's Register, a handy spot for moving to the supervising architect's office. He competed for the post of supervising architect from which AMMI B. YOUNG was dismissed in 1862, but Treasury Secretary Salmon P. Chase had offered it to Rogers. Early in 1863, Mullett joined the staff. By June, he was assistant supervising architect. Before the year closed, a quarrel erupted between Rogers and Mullett, and in the end Rogers resigned. Mullett gained the post on June 1, 1866.

The task of reversing the wartime ebb in constructing public buildings fell to Mullett. Before settling to the job he took a role no Treasury architect had ever performed—de facto architect of the White House. He replaced the east wing with a colonnaded entrance (1865–1867) and put a huge fountain on the grounds opposite Treasury's west wing (1856–1864), the first of two to embellish the Treasury. He set the second north of the building. By 1910, they had become foliage-draped pools. The stonework was carted off in the 1940s.

Before 1866 ended, Mullett started two buildings, initiating work which would ultimately embrace forty others. One was a prototype of many Mullett designs, a courthouse and post office in Springfield, Illinois (1866–1869). A lofty mansard topped by an eagle in flight accentuated its height and helped identify Mullett with the Second Empire idiom, but Italianate influences harmonized in a composition in which neither derivative detracted from the other. Similar combinations reappeared many times in the next eight years in medium-sized buildings. Undiluted Second Empire styling was visible in more monumental structures, companions to the State, War, and Navy Building, the prime example. Along with the St. Louis Customhouse (1873–1884), it survives to avouch Mullett's predilection for resplendent monuments.

In an eclectic age he evinced a mastery of styles, eschewing only the Gothic. He varied from historicism to prepare designs of utilitarian character, often lightening their starkness with Italianate touches. Although the Greek Revival age had ended, he used the style to finish buildings begun in its heyday. Twice he turned to the Greek by his own choice. The San Francisco Mint (1869–1874) has stirred historians to wonder at his decision, but the dating could be enlightening. He began the mint when he was finishing Treasury's Greek Revival north wing (1867–1869). Significantly similar drawings suggest that a hard-pressed architect kept a crew of draftsmen at work in a style which they understood.

The mint drew to completion in 1874, the year of Mullett's breakdown. Half his buildings, twenty-two in all, were well-developed, making it his busiest year. An altercation in November with Treasury Secretary Benjamin H. Bristow evoked the architect's resignation, but letters they exchanged ignored the dispute, citing instead Mullett's broken health. At Bristow's request, he stayed on till a successor was recruited.

The departure thrust Mullett into a chaotic world darkened by financial stress. Twice, perhaps three times, he tried to regain the office without success. Once he was given the sop of appointment as superintending architect of six buildings, a unique post manufactured for him. But a successor, James G. Hill, undercut Mullett by warning the construction superintendents that he had no authority to give them any directions whatever. Shocked, Mullett appealed to Treasury Secretary John Sherman not only for Hill's dismissal, but also for reappointment. The letter's twenty-nine pages, dated March 20, 1877, indicted Hill for corruption and waste. Revelations that paranoiac fears of misrepresentation and hostility gripped the writer dotted every other page. Sherman took no action, but Hill's resignation in 1882 in the heat of an investigation of similar charges vindicated Mullett.

His role also changed in 1882 when the Washington directory identified him as "USN." Earlier directories had ceased calling him an architect, presumably at his option. An appointment to a commission to study the navy yards, the only member from civil life, brought him to the Navy Department. Before his duties ceased on March 1, 1884, Mullett ended a decade's absence from his profession by setting up an architectural office.

Over his remaining years, Mullett cultivated an active practice, forming A. B. Mullett and Co. in 1889, which survived him by nearly fifty years. The eminent character of his clientele ranked him among the foremost local architects. How many structures he designed is unknown. His obituary listed about a dozen, all with the cachet of prestige. An incomplete count of permits issued on his plans runs to about forty.

One of the first clients was the *Baltimore Sun.* For its Washington office Mullett designed a building which soars 116 feet above F Street, NW, where it fills a narrow plot. The dimensions undoubtedly encouraged Mullett to design a skyscraper when tall buildings were a rarity. The permit was dated July 23, 1885, the year WILLIAM LEBARON JENNEY completed Chicago's ten-story Home Insurance Building, often acclaimed the first skyscraper. Varied figures have been given for the floors in Mullett's building, from eight and a half to eleven, but an actual count comes to nine even though the permit said eight below a story-and-a-half tower, removed in the 1940s because it rose above the stated height.

Strikingly handsome, the white marble façade has mellowed, but the three-bayed building gains its charm from two parallel tiers of oriel windows which rise five floors—the third through the seventh—accentuating verticality. The tiers terminate in a mansard, akin to the Second Empire masterworks of the 1870s, which cloaks the eighth and ninth floors. Large Romanesque arches flank a narrow arched doorway, making the first two floors a base. Apparently, Mullett was the first architect to devise the tripartite design for tall buildings. Whether GEORGE B. POST borrowed from Mullett in designing New York's Union Trust Company Building (1889–1890), considered a tripartite first, will never be known. But the conical caps which Post poised on the rounded corner towers of Newark's Prudential Life Insurance Building (1890) echoed the twin towers of the Central National Bank (1887–1888) in Washington, Mullett's most piquant landmark. The latter rises six stories at Seventh Street and Pennsylvania Avenue.

Mullett's houses ran about $12,000, according to building permits. At least three were far more costly, ranging from $25,000 to $100,000. The latter, a palatial elevator-equipped residence for Dr. William A. Hammond (1888–1889), was probably the most costly ever built in the city.

By 1890, Mullett had sued Dr. Hammond for $29,000. The suit deepened the disappointments the architect suffered that summer. His wife, Pacific Pearl Myrick, whom he had married twenty-five years earlier, was under a doctor's care. He had been unable to sell three houses he had built adjoining his home. The harshest blow was the loss of a suit in the Court of Claims. *A. B. Mullett* vs. *the United States* was the vehicle by which Mullett sought professional fees of $158,450.91 for designing and superintending the State, War, and Navy Building. His counsel, George S. Boutwell, had been treasury secretary when the architect accepted the task and, indeed, had done so at Boutwell's direction. This weighed against the claim that the building fell outside the treasury architect's sphere. The decision went against him; he collected nothing. But Mullett's practice appeared to be going smoothly. W. B. Moses had retained him to design an addition to Moses's Great Store (1886–1887), a seven-story furniture emporium of Mullett's design. Mullett had reviewed the plans with a building inspector on the afternoon of October 20 and gone home to rest. Later that day, Mullett shot himself.

The suicide ended a fractured but fruitful life. In his second career, his exploration of the design of tall buildings displayed enterprise, pointing to a promising future. Mullett will be long remembered for his work for the Department of the Treasury. He was a rarity in his profession, an architect whose name came easily to people's lips: witness "Mullett's Monstrosity," New York's nickname for its Courthouse and Post Office (1869–1880) and "Mullett's Masterpiece," Washington's tag on State, War, and Navy. Buildings erected in private practice have survived less well than his public buildings. One certain to survive is the Logan Mausoleum (1888) in Soldiers' Home National Cemetery. Although twenty-four of his public designs have been destroyed, eighteen are in use or in private hands—all in the National Register of Historic Places. Four also have a higher rating—National Historic Landmark.

DONALD J. LEHMAN

WORKS

1850–1879, Customhouse, Charleston, S.C. *1865–1867, White House (alterations), Washington. *1866–1869, Courthouse and Post Office, Springfield, Ill. 1866–1870, State Museum (Mint), Carson City, Nev. *1866–1869, Treasury Building (fountains); 1867–1869, Post Office, Ogdensburg, N.Y. 1867–1869, Treasury Building (north wing extension), Washington. *1867–1871, Appraisers' Stores, Philadelphia. *1867–1871, Courthouse and Post Office, Des Moines, Iowa. *1867–1871, Courthouse and Post Office, Madison, Wis. 1867–1872, City Hall (Customhouse and Post Office), Cairo, Ill. *1867–1872, Courthouse and Post Office, Portland, Maine. *1867–1873, Customhouse, Saint Paul, Minn. *1867–1873, Marine Hospital, Chicago. 1868–1872, Customhouse, Portland, Maine. 1868–1872, Old Customhouse, Wiscasset, Maine. *1869–1873, Customhouse, Astoria, Ore. 1869–1874, Mint, San Francisco. *1869–1874, Post Office and Subtreasury, Boston. 1869–1875, Pioneer Courthouse, Portland, Ore. *1869–1880, Courthouse and Post Office, New York. 1870–1871, Assay Office, Boise, Idaho. *1870–1875, Courthouse and Post Office, Omaha, Neb. 1871–1872, Community Services Administration (Customhouse and Post Office), Machias, Maine. 1871–1874, City Hall (Courthouse and Post Office), Columbia, S.C. 1871–1874, East Tennessee Historical Center (Courthouse and Post Office), Knoxville. 1871–1889, Old Executive Office Building (State, War, and Navy Building), Washington. *1873–1877, Federal Building, Port Huron, Mich. *1873–1878, Courthouse and Post Office, Trenton, N.J. 1873–1879, Customhouse, Courthouse, and Post Office, Chicago. *1873–1882, Customhouse and Post Office, Hartford, Conn. 1873–1884, Customhouse and Post Office, Saint Louis, Mo. 1874–1879, City Hall (Courthouse and Post Office), Lincoln, Neb. *1874–1879, Courthouse and Post Office, Parkersburg, W. Va. 1874–1879, Century Station Post Office, Raleigh, N.C. *1874–1881, Appraisers' Stores, San Francisco. *1874–1884, Post Office and Courthouse, Philadelphia. *1874–1885, Customhouse and Post Office, Cincinnati, Ohio. 1885–1886, Sun Building (now American Bank Building); *1886–1887, Moses's Great Store; 1887–1888, Central National Bank; 1888, Logan Mausoleum; *1888–1889, William A. Hammond House; Washington.

BIBLIOGRAPHY

CONDIT, CARL W. 1968 *American Building.* University of Chicago Press.

FITCH, JAMES MARSTON (1966)1973 *American Building: The Historical Forces That Shaped It.* 2d ed. New York: Schocken.

HILLS, W. H., and SUTHERLAND, T. A. (compilers) 1901 *A History of Public Buildings under the Control of the Treasury Department.* Washington: Government Printing Office.

HINES, THOMAS S. (1974)1979 *Burnham of Chicago.* University of Chicago Press.

HOPKINS, GRIFFITH MORGAN 1887 *A Complete Set of Surveys and Plats of Properties in the City of Washington, District of Columbia.* Philadelphia.

HOPKINS, GRIFFITH MORGAN 1892–1896 *Real Estate Plat-book of Washington, D.C., Comprising the Entire North-west Section from the Original Plats of Squares and Subdivisions.* Philadelphia.

Illustrated Washington: Our Capital. 1890 New York: American Publishing.

JENNINGS, J. L. SIBLEY, JR. 1975 Volume 2 in *Massachusetts Avenue Architecture.* Washington: Government Printing Office.

JORDY, WILLIAM H. (1972)1976 Volume 3 in *American Buildings and Their Architects.* Garden City, N.Y.: Anchor.

MADDEX, DIANE 1973 *Historic Buildings of Washington, D.C.* Pittsburgh: Ober Park Associates.

MYERS, DENYS PETER (compiler) 1974 *Maine Catalog: Historic American Buildings Survey.* Augusta, Maine: State Museum.

National Register of Historic Places. 1976 2 vols. Washington: Government Printing Office.

NEVINS, ALLAN, and THOMAS, MILTON HALSEY (editors), (1952)1974 *The Diary of George Templeton Strong: Post-war Years, 1865–1875.* New York: Octagon.

PECK, RALPH BRAZLETON 1948 *History of Building Foundations in Chicago.* Urbana: University of Illinois Engineering Experiment Station.

SCHWARTZ, NANCY B. (compiler) 1976 *District of Columbia Catalog, 1974.* Charlottesville: University of Virginia Press.

TATUM, GEORGE B. 1961 *Penn's Great Town: 250 Years of Philadelphia Architecture.* Philadelphia: University of Pennsylvania Press.

U.S. CONGRESS, HOUSE, COMMITTEE ON EXPENDITURES ON PUBLIC BUILDINGS 1862 *House Report 137.* 37th Cong., 2d sess., July 10. Washington: Government Printing Office.

U.S. CONGRESS, HOUSE 1870 *Post Office Buildings, House Report 58.* 41st Cong., 2d sess., April 14. Washington: Government Printing Office.

U.S. CONGRESS, SENATE, PUBLIC BUILDINGS COMMISSION 1918 *Public Buildings in the District of Columbia, Senate Document 155.* 65th Cong., 2d sess., Dec. 18, 1917. Washington: Government Printing Office.

WEISMAN, WINSTON 1972 "The Commercial Architecture of George B. Post." *Journal of the Society of Architectural Historians* 31, no. 3:22–37.

WODEHOUSE, LAWRENCE 1967 "Alfred B. Mullett's Court Room and Post Office at Raleigh, North Carolina." *Journal of the Society of Architectural Historians* 26, no. 4:301–306.

WODEHOUSE, LAWRENCE 1969 "John McArthur, Jr. (1823–1890)." *Journal of the Society of Architectural Historians* 28, no. 4:271–283.

WODEHOUSE, LAWRENCE 1972 "Alfred B. Mullett and his French Style Government Buildings." *The Journal of the Society of Architectural Historians* 31, no. 1:22–37.

WODEHOUSE, LAWRENCE 1973 "William Appleton Potter, Principal Pasticheur of Henry Hobson Richardson." *The Journal of the Society of Architectural Historians* 32, no. 2:175–192.

MULLGARDT, LOUIS CHRISTIAN

Louis Christian Mullgardt (1866–1942) was a native of the Midwest. Although his career unfolded from London to Honolulu, his most important works were in the San Francisco Bay Area, where he was a major influence in the development of the California house in the early years of this century. During the following decade, he turned to an inventive neohistoricism and then was overwhelmed by events of the 1920s.

Mullgardt was born in Washington, Missouri, the son of immigrants from Prussia and Schleswig-Holstein. At the age of fifteen, he began an apprenticeship first with Wilhelmi and Janssen and then with James Stewart and Company, both in St. Louis. Six years later, he was hired by SHEPLEY, RUTAN, and COOLIDGE, who had inherited the practice of H. H. RICHARDSON in Brookline, Massachusetts. There, while working on plans for the campus of Stanford University, Mullgardt first encountered the idea of creating an architecture that was expressly Californian. After brief employment with PEABODY AND STEARNS, and also with Brigham and Spofford, he enrolled as a special student at Harvard College in the fall of 1889. This exposure to formal training was cut short by illness, however, and he returned to Missouri.

By 1891, Mullgardt was working in the Chicago office of HENRY IVES COBB, where he was soon recognized as a versatile designer in many styles. Responsible for the Romanesque exterior of the Newberry Library (1891), as well as the Venetian façade of the Chicago Athletic Club (1892), he also helped plan the first Gothic Revival buildings of the University of Chicago (1891–1893). His most remarkable work for Cobb was the detailing of the Fisheries Building at the World's Columbian Exposition of 1893. In droll anticipation of the palace's exhibits, he enlivened the Romanesque columns, capitals, and balustrades with turtles, frogs, and fishes.

Before leaving Chicago, Mullgardt entered his first partnership: Stewart, McClure, and Mullgardt (1892–1894). The most ambitious undertaking of this St. Louis firm was the Arlington Hotel in Hot Springs, Arkansas (1892–1894), which was one of the largest Colonial Revival structures of its day. A European tour followed in 1894–1895 and then a short-lived partnership with John M. Dunham in 1899. Few of Mullgardt's projects of the late 1890s were built, although the Charles R. Blake House in St. Louis (1898) still stands to demonstrate the prodigious, albeit somewhat undisciplined talent of its designer.

Mullgardt participated in early discussions regarding the Louisiana Purchase International Exposition of 1904. However, the official planners ignored his advice to locate it on the St. Louis riverfront instead of in Forest Park, and awarded him no commission for its buildings. The years 1903–1904 were spent as a structural consultant in England. Contact there with the architecture of the Arts and Crafts movement was a major turning point in his career.

Mullgardt suddenly arrived in San Francisco in the late spring of 1905, where he opened his own office by early 1906. After failing to realize several ambitious schemes in Carmel and Montecito, Mullgardt built his first California works in the hills of Oakland and Piedmont during 1907. They were speculative houses of frame construction, clad with bulky clapboards, stucco, and suggestions of half-timbering. Making dramatic use of sloping sites, Mullgardt placed the rooms along extended axes of stairs and glazed hallways, opening them with bands of casement windows and French doors. Interiors were finished with boards and battens of redwood.

Mullgardt.
Ernest A. Evans House.
Mill Valley, California.
1907

A house in Mill Valley for Ernest A. Evans (1907) differed from the architect's distended compositions of the previous months in its compact plan organized around the brick core of a massive fireplace. There was a hint of the Alpine chalet in the lines of the roof; the service porch was enclosed by a wooden grille that was all but Japanese. Such wooden imagery, however, was soon discarded. During the next five years, the houses that made Mullgardt famous had walls rendered in roughcast stucco, usually painted white. The heavily bracketed roofs were sometimes covered with a mosaic of terra-cotta "cobblestones." Large, buttressed chimneys punctuated the forms and gestured toward the sky.

The most ambitious expression of this new style was the Henry W. Taylor House (1908–1910), which was an imposing landmark in the Berkeley foothills until its destruction in 1935. Mullgardt combined aspects of the work of CHARLES F. A. VOYSEY, whose houses he knew from his sojourn

Mullgardt.
Henry W. Taylor House.
Berkeley.
1908–1910

in England, with the massive, white-washed walls and tiled roofs of the California missions. Some observers also noted an affinity with the architecture of Tibet, which had been extensively published at the time of the British expedition in 1903–1904. Such a complicated synthesis was considered appropriate in California, a place so rich in juxtapositions of the East and the West.

These houses were soon adapted by developers and builders throughout the Bay Area. By then, however, Mullgardt had begun to turn his attention to other building types. In 1912–1913, he designed the Durant School in Oakland, spreading it around three sides of a playground. Classrooms were opened from floor to ceiling with glass panels in a decorative grid of terra cotta. Across the bay, he planned the San Francisco Juvenile Court and Detention Home (1914–1916), a nine-story structure of reinforced concrete that was set back above the third level in an elegant slab. Articulated by mullions that run the length of the shank and become brackets for the gabled roof, it still offers a striking profile in the cityscape.

This later period of Mullgardt's career, marked by a renewed interest in historicism, began with his appointment in 1912 to the architectural board of the Panama-Pacific International Exposition of 1915. His assignment was the courtyard at the eastern end of the grounds. Calling it the Court of the Ages, he surrounded the garden with a giant arcade encrusted with Manuelinesque details of plant and animal life. A triumphant "altar tower" rose from the north side. Mullgardt intended the court to be a fervent sermon in lath and plaster about the evolution of mankind and the progress of culture and intelligence. Social Darwinism was made architectural to celebrate California's coming of age.

The courtyard and tower occupied Mullgardt's energies for over three years. This intense involvement with sculptural decoration and impermanent materials affected most of his subsequent oeuvre. Light and shadow became crucial raw materials; color and texture were now obsessions. When commissioned to design the President's House for Stanford University (1915–1918), Mullgardt embraced a grassy knoll at the rear of the campus with an ornate central pavilion and obtuse wings. The combed stucco of the exterior was tinted a tawny pink; windows and doorways were bordered with complicated configurations of precast concrete. Sometimes, the architect relied on inadequate materials to achieve such effects. The M. H. de Young Memorial Museum in Golden Gate Park (1916–1921), for example, emulated more than anything else the Court of the Ages, and it was almost as temporary. Disintegrating finials plunged through skylights or threatened passers-by until the exterior was finally scraped clean in the late 1940s.

Of all the opportunities that came to Mullgardt as a result of his postexposition fame, none was potentially greater than his scheme for a business center in Honolulu. It was a most unusual response to the City Beautiful idea—and it was for the commercial rather than the civic realm. Seven buildings were included in the initial plans of 1917. Mullgardt evoked an "architecture of the mid-Pacific, the Hawaiian Renaissance style . . .

Mullgardt.
Court of the Ages,
Panama-Pacific International Exposition.
San Francisco.
1912–1915

Mullgardt.
Theo H. Davies Building.
Honolulu, Hawaii.
1917–1921

the spirit of the Far West." Recalling the Marshall Field Wholesale Store in Chicago (which was completed in 1887 while he worked for Richardson's successors), he adapted the Italian Renaissance palazzo as the basic theme. Each building was to be varied in plan, height, fenestration, and surface details.

Only the Theodore H. Davies Building was executed according to Mullgardt's designs (1917–1921). Covering an entire city block, the vast concrete structure was primarily a wholesale warehouse. The exterior was faced with terra cotta—not in conventional simulation of stonework, but glazed in mottled shades of green and ochre. Unfortunately, the "Hawaiian Renaissance" was diverted by war and by Mullgardt's difficult personality. The remaining clients eventually went to other architects, and he was left with little work in the 1920s.

Returning to San Francisco after a 1922–1923 world tour, Mullgardt found the city alive with controversy about bridging the bay. He offered an unsolicited proposal in December 1924. Combining two preoccupations of the decade, the skyscraper and the bridge, he envisioned a sequence of habitable piers that were to be hotels, office buildings, and factories. These were connected by steel trusses supporting a three-tiered roadway with twenty-four lanes of traffic! Mullgardt was ignored as a hopeless fantasist. His reputation suffered further when he ventured into spiritualism after the tragic death of his second son in 1928.

Typical of his generation, Louis Mullgardt hardly survived World War I professionally. He had helped to shape the architecture of California, and few doubted the importance of his early houses there. But his mature work, full of historical allusions and eccentric details, was too unorthodox for the afterglow of the American Renaissance and was antithetical to the rise of heroic modernism. Frustrated and disillusioned, Mullgardt died in a state hospital in Stockton, California. Most of his drawings and personal effects were destroyed soon afterward.

ROBERT JUDSON CLARK

WORKS

*1892–1894, Arlington Hotel, Hot Springs, Ark. *1896–1901, J. C. Strauss Studio; 1898, Charles R. Blake House; 1900, Budweiser Building; St. Louis, Mo. 1907, House, Dormidera Avenue, Piedmont, Calif. 1907, Ernest A. Evans House, Mill Valley, Calif. 1908–1909, Samuel Orie Johnson House; *1908–1910, Henry W. Taylor House; Berkeley. 1908–1910, Robert J. Tyson House, Piedmont, Calif. 1909, Louis W. Wolcott House, Berkeley. 1909–1910, Charles W. Fore House; *1909–1910, Delia Moffitt House; Piedmont, Calif. 1910, Arthur G. Nason House, Oakland, Calif. 1910, Alexander Sclater House, Berkeley. 1911, Everett Grimes House, San Francisco. 1911–1912, Charles B. Colby House, Bakersfield, Calif. 1912, Horatio T. Harper House; *1912–1913, Durant School; Oakland, Calif. *1912–1915, Court of the Ages, Panama-Pacific International Exposition; 1913, House in St. Francis Wood; *1914–1915, Home of Redwood, Panama-Pacific International Exposition; 1914–1916, Juvenile Court and Detention Home; San Francisco. 1915–1918, President's House, Stanford University, Calif. 1916–1917, Ansel Mills Easton House, Diablo, Calif. 1916–1921, M. H. de Young Memorial Museum, San Francisco. *1917–1921, Theo H. Davies Building; Honolulu, Hawaii. 1926, Charles D. Stevens House, San Jose, Calif. 1928–1929, Infant Shelter Building, San Francisco. 1930, Artists' Studio, Bohemian Grove, Monte Rio, Calif.

BIBLIOGRAPHY

CLARK, ROBERT JUDSON 1962 "Louis Christian Mullgardt and the Court of the Ages." *Journal of the Society of Architectural Historians* 21, Dec.:171–178.

CLARK, ROBERT JUDSON 1966 *Louis Christian Mullgardt: 1866–1942.* Santa Barbara: University of California, Art Gallery.

CROLY, HERBERT D. 1911 "An Architectural Innovator." *Architectural Record* 30, Aug.:117–134.

CROLY, HERBERT D. 1914 "Some of the California Work of Louis C. Mullgardt." *Architect and Engineer* 36, Mar.:47–87.

MORROW, IRVING F. 1917 "Recent Work of Louis Christian Mullgardt." *Architect and Engineer* 51, Dec.:39–103.

MULLGARDT, LOUIS CHRISTIAN ET AL. 1915 *The Architecture and Landscape Gardening of the Exposition.* San Francisco: Elder.

PHILLIPS, WALTER BELLEVILLE 1911 "Recent Work of Louis Christian Mullgardt." *American Architect and Building News* 100, Aug.:49–53.

SWALES, FRANCIS S. 1924 "Master Draftsmen, IV: Louis Christian Mullgardt." *Pencil Points* 5, Aug.:51–57, 65.

MUNDAY, RICHARD

Little is known about Richard Munday (?–1739) and nothing of how or where he learned his craft. Essentially an architect-builder in the sense typical of the seventeenth and eighteenth centuries not only in America but also in England, he worked in Newport, Rhode Island, in the 1720s and 1730s when the baroque forms of CHRISTOPHER WREN's day put a stamp on the town's early building style. Munday has been identified as the man responsible for Trinity Church (1726), the Colony House (1739–1740), and (with Benjamin Wyatt) the Stephen Ayrault House (1739) on Thames Street, Newport. His name has also been linked with the Sabbatarian Meeting House (1729) and several pri-

Munday.
Colony House.
Newport, Rhode Island.
1739–1740

vate mansions, including Godfrey Malbone's town (1728) and country (1739) houses, all in Newport.

Munday, who listed himself as a carpenter, belonged to a remarkable group of artisans whose work was then transforming seventeenth-century Newport into a handsome port town rivaling Boston, Charlestown, Philadelphia, and New York. Tools and craftsmen went from new building to new building so that it becomes almost impossible to isolate the key builder-designer without positive identification.

Munday's name first appears in Newport records in 1713 when he married Martha Simons. He owned pew No. 10 in Old Trinity Church in 1719 and he was listed as an innkeeper in the same year. In 1721, he was a house carpenter and in 1722 he became a freeman. Proof for his role as architect for Trinity Church is derived from the frequency and kind of references in the church records. By 1731, he was living in Bristol, Rhode Island, where he presumably went to build the new galleries for Saint Michael's Church. His wife died in that same year and he remarried in 1732. He was back in Newport in 1738, where he died a year later. In 1743, his widow petitioned the General Assembly for payment for a draft of a plan for the Colony House and for "directing and forwarding the building until a few days before his death."

By 1725, the First Trinity Church of 1702 had been outgrown. The new church, a rectangular pitch-roofed wood structure with a square fore tower, designed on a classic church plan, proved Munday's mastery of his art. It also exemplified fully the close liaison between the Anglican churches in the Colonies and those of London. Immediate inspiration came from the newly built Christ Church (1725) in Boston, the design for which has been credited to WILLIAM PRICE, a print seller. But the brick Christ Church and the wooden Trinity show such specific knowledge of Wren's work that NORMAN M. ISHAM, in his carefully analytical *Trinity Church,* concluded that the plans may have been from a Wren design "in some way secured" for a church "perhaps never built" after the London Fire of 1666. The interior of Trinity, with its vaulting system and its balconies supported by superimposed piers relates to Saint Andrew's Holborn, Saint James Piccadilly, and Saint Andrew's-by-the-Wardrobe, all in London. The steeple is similar to that of Christ Church, Boston, and derives ultimately from Wren's Saint Lawrence Jewry. Designed in 1726, it was not built until 1741; after having been taken down in 1760, it was rebuilt along its original lines by CHARLES BULFINCH in 1807. It stands today as one of the best remaining Wren-inspired steeples in America.

On the interior, the raised bolection paneling and all the woodwork harks back to Wren's time, although the system of proportion with its combination of parts for piers, pilasters, pediments, entablatures, and cornices varied enough from Wren's work to make a system of its own, at once archaic and fresh, entirely suited to wood construction. The church was lengthened by two bays in 1762 but the triple-deck wine-glass pulpit has always been located in the center aisle and the structure has basically been little altered.

The Sabbatarian Meeting House was built on the meeting house plan, with entrance on the long side of the plain pitch-roofed houselike clapboard building, but the handling of the fine interior detail bears the hallmark of other Newport work of the period and was certainly by the workman who built Trinity Church.

The Colony House, a rectangular brick building set on a high rusticated sandstone basement and covered with an almost brusque truncated gable roof, is somewhat domestic in scale, and has a Dutch feeling that was common to a number of seventeenth-century English country houses. Its strong, central emphasis is established by the central cupola and a richly detailed balcony with foliated pedimented doorways under a gable of the same truncated form as the roof. One of the few pre-Revolutionary brick structures in this predominantly wooden town, it is the last of Newport's public buildings to display the baroque character of Wren's time.

On the interior, the splendid great hall was refinished in 1784 to repair damages incurred in the Revolutionary War. At that time, the original solid tree trunk columns were cased; otherwise the room is little changed. The second-floor plan has been altered from its original three-room layout and in 1840 to 1850 took its present form of two rooms—the Senate Chamber and the Representatives Room, the latter of which was designed by RUSSELL WARREN. The Council Chamber, enlarged by one bay from its original eighteenth-century form, still contains magnificent floor-to-ceiling bolection paneling finished with Corinthian pilasters set on high pedestals and doubled and mitered at the corners. This room, containing the best eighteenth-century work in the state, has now been painted the "stone color" ordered during the repairs made in 1784.

The two Malbone houses associated with Munday's name were typical early eighteenth-century gambrel-roofed structures similar to the Thomas Hancock House (1737) in Boston and in the genre of the Newport Colony House. Descriptions and a surviving marble mantel and an elaborately carved Corinthian capital together with a foliated door hood from the Stephen Ayrault House (now installed as the rear entrance of the Sabbatarian Meeting House) further illustrate the free baroque character of Newport work of Munday's time.

ANTOINETTE F. DOWNING

WORKS

1726, Trinity Church (spire not built until 1741); *(A)1728, Godfrey Malbone Town House; (A)1729, Sabbatarian Meetinghouse; Newport, R.I. (A)By 1731, Saint Michael's Church (galleries), Bristol, R.I. *(A)1739, Malbone Country House; *1739, Daniel Ayrault House (with BENJAMIN D. WYATT); 1739–1740, Colony House; Newport, R.I.

BIBLIOGRAPHY

DOWNING, ANTOINETTE F. 1937 *Early Homes of Rhode Island.* Richmond, Va.: Garrett and Massie.

DOWNING, ANTOINETTE F., and SCULLY, VINCENT J., JR. (1952)1967 *The Architectural Heritage of Newport, Rhode Island.* Reprint. New York: Bramhill House.

GREENE, JOHN H., JR. n.d. *The Building of the Old Colony House at Newport, Rhode Island.* The Old Colony House Association of Newport, Rhode Island.

GULBRANSON, P. C. 1895 "The Principal Entrance to the State House at Newport, R.I." *American Architect and Building News* 48:plate is unnumbered.

HITCHCOCK, H. R. (1939)1968 *Rhode Island Architecture.* Reprint. New York: Da Capo.

ISHAM, NORMAN MORRISON 1917 "Special Number Devoted to the Colony House or Old State House, Newport, R.I." *Old-Time New England* 8:entire issue.

ISHAM, NORMAN MORRISON 1936 *Trinity Church in Newport, Rhode Island.* Boston: Privately printed.

MASON, GEORGE CHAMPLIN 1890–1894 *Annals of Trinity Church.* 2 vols. Newport, R.I.: V. Mott Francis.

MASON, GEORGE C., JR. 1881 "Colonial Architecture." *American Architect and Building News* 10:71–74, 83–85.

MASON, GEORGE C., JR. (1898–1900)1923 "The Seventh-Day Baptist Church at Newport, R.I." Volume 1, pages 31–33 in *The Georgian Period.* Rev. ed. New York: U.P.C.

PLACE, CHARLES A. 1922–1923 "From Meeting House to Church in New England." *Old-Time New England* 13:68–77, 110–123, 148–164; 14:2–20.

TERRY, RODERICK 1927 "History of the Old Colony House at Newport." *Bulletin of the Newport Historical Society* 63:1–36.

WARE, WILLIAM ROTCH (editor) (1898–1901)1923 *The Georgian Period.* Rev. ed. by Charles Keefe. New York: U.P.C.

AL-MUNĪF FAMILY

The al-Munīf family practiced during the seventeenth and eighteenth centuries in Sfax, Tunisia. They are known through inscriptions recording the reconstruction of the city's fortifications. Master (*muᶜallim*) ᶜAṭiyya al-Munīf and Master Aḥmad al-Munīf, the sons of Master Ibrāhīm al-Munīf, rebuilt a tower in the southern wall in 1630/1631. Master Aḥmad, Master ᶜUmar al-Munīf, and Master ᶜAbd al-Laṭīf al-Munīf reconstructed a gate in 1646. Master Aḥmad and Master al-Darīf al-Sifaqsī (from Sfax) restored the Qaṣba of Gafsa, Tunisia, in the middle of the seventeenth century. Ṭāhir, the son of the late Master Aḥmad al-Munīf, along with his brothers and cousins, restored another gate in the city walls of Sfax in 1748. Despite the reoccurrence of the name Aḥmad, the genealogical tree of this family has yet to be established.

JONATHAN M. BLOOM

BIBLIOGRAPHY

MAYER, LEO ARY 1956 *Islamic Architects and Their Works.* Geneva: Albert Kundig.

MÜNTZ, JOHANN HEINRICH

Johann Heinrich Müntz (1727–1798) was born in Mülhausen (then in Germany, but now Mulhouse, France) and had traveled widely before his arrival in England in 1755. He was patronized by HORACE WALPOLE until the end of 1759, but his principal architectural designs were made for Richard Bateman at Old Windsor (1760), and for WILLIAM CHAMBERS at Kew and at Marino (1768), Ireland.

MICHAEL MCCARTHY

WORKS

1756–1759, Strawberry Hill (decorative features); Middlesex, England. 1759, Gothic Cathedral, Kew Gardens, Surrey, England. 1759, Gothic Room (for Mr. Hudson), Twickenham, Middlesex, England. 1760, Gothic Room (for Mr. Bateman), Old Windsor, Berkshire, England. 1762, Egyptian Room (for Lord Charlemont); 1768, Gothic Building (for Lord Charlemont); Marino, Dublin.

BIBLIOGRAPHY

HARRIS, JOHN 1971 *A Catalogue of British Drawings for Architecture, Decoration, Sculpture and Landscape Gardening, 1550–1900, in American Collections.* Upper Saddle River, N.J.: Gregg.

MCCARTHY, MICHAEL 1977 "Johann Heinrich Müntz: The Roman Drawings (1749–76)." *Burlington Magazine* 119:335–340.

MURANO, TŌGO

Tōgo Murano (1891–) is one of the most remarkable Japanese architects of this century. Born in Karatsu, Saga Prefecture, he graduated from Waseda University in 1918 and entered the office of Setsu Watanabe in Osaka. Watanabe had the largest and most prominent architect's office in Japan before World War II, and Murano soon became chief designer there. In those days, he was influenced by American works such as those designed by the office of MCKIM, MEAD, AND WHITE. Many of his buildings met modern functional needs, yet they all featured stylized decorations.

His independent activities began in 1929, when he established his own office in Osaka. His works in the 1930s were greatly influenced by the Congrès Internationaux d'Architecture Moderne (CIAM). A careful observation of his works, however, would reveal that his design methods, particularly that of dealing with details, was not learned from the theory of Modernism but rather from a modernization of traditional techniques learned at the Watanabe office. This approach is evident in his early works such as the Sogo Department Store (1935) and Ube Public Hall (1937).

In an article he wrote in 1919, Murano stated that he saw himself as a "presentist" rather than a futurist or one concerned with the past. He would be neither a traditionalist who values the level of perfection reached in previous styles nor a futurist who dreams of rationalistic architecture. Throughout his life, he has concentrated on finding the best and most realistic solution, always taking into account the "present" social condition of Japan. In that sense, he is a thorough realist. He has warned younger architects repeatedly that architecture belongs to society and cannot be the object of experiment to try out an architect's principle or theory.

Murano. Hakone Prince Hotel. Kanagawa Prefecture, Japan. 1978

In 1949, his office was reorganized as Murano, Mori, and Associates and as such has designed a number of notable public buildings. Murano has also designed attractive houses of high quality. It should be noted that Murano adopted the space composition and details of the traditional Japanese architecture in his works of timber. His teahouses, restaurants, hotels, and houses, while living in the present, are deeply rooted in the historical continuity of Japanese architecture. One of the most attractive aspects of his designs is the ingenious unity of the structure and the garden. Exterior and interior spaces are profoundly united, creating soft shades and variations in the architectural space. Murano's architecture can be characterized not by a strong, masculine bone structure and muscles but by its fascinating expression and fine texture of femininity. His works possess the qualities of modesty and gentleness which have always characterized the ideal Japanese woman.

TAKASHI HASEGAWA

WORKS

1935, Sogo Department Store, Japan. 1937, Ube Public Hall, Japan. 1956, World Peace Memorial Cathedral, Hiroshima, Japan. 1959, Shigetsu-tei House; 1963, Nissei Theater; 1966, Chiyoda Life Insurance Office; 1970, Japan Lutheran Theological Seminary; Tokyo. 1978, Hakone Prince Hotel, Kanagawa Prefecture, Japan.

BIBLIOGRAPHY

Architectural Design in the Traditional Style by Tōgo Murano. 1978 Tokyo.

MURANO, TŌGO 1964 *Works.* Tokyo.

MURATORI, SAVERIO

Architect, town planner, historian, professor and philosopher, Saverio Muratori (1910–1973) was an outstanding figure in twentieth-century Italian culture.

His commitment to the resolution of modern architecture's unresolved questions is expressed in his theoretical concepts and teachings and in his work as an architect. This gradually led him to work out a vast and articulated philosophical system, in which one of the principal questions of contemporary thought—the self-conscious relationship between man's civilization and the natural reality—found a congruent solution and a reference model in architecture and in the environment.

His initial formative period before World War II was characterized by an experimental approach to the various demands expressed by the Modern movement (Expressionism, Functionalism, Rationalism), demands that he was to attempt to satisfy by recomposing his solution in a unitary way. There followed his engagement in Italy's postwar reconstruction, when various INA-CASA housing neighborhoods in Rome were designed, partly inspired by Scandinavian examples. This accelerated in him a process of reassessment already outlined in his 1950 essay "Vita e storia delle città."

From then on, his research about cities as living organisms was to be scientifically formulated for his university courses held in Venice (1950–1955) and in Rome (from 1956). His concepts were systematically organized following novel and experimental criteria.

At the same time he tested the validity of his research on architectural works (churches for Pisa and Rome, the ENPAS Head Office (1952–1953) in Bologna, and Rome's Christian Democrat Headquarters (1956–1960)). He also proposed an urban development scheme for Venice's mainland. All these works testified to a substantial will to renovate methodically the architecture's linguistic heritage and to a noteworthy effort to blend his buildings into their physical and cultural environment.

During the last decade of his life, he progressively broadened his theoretical inquiry by evaluating the crisis in architecture as a crisis of civilization. His continual analysis gradually encompassed the relationships between man and his environment and the fundamental principles of ecumenical civilizations (Chinese, Indian, and Western). His proposals stress how a self-consciousness of the transformation processes of reality can bring about a substantial cultural change to overcome the present world crisis.

GIANCARLO CATALDI

WORKS

1933–1935, Rome University Student House (with others). 1947–1948, Amenity Building, Railway Men's Cooperative Society, Via Cilicia; 1948–1949, INA-CASA Housing Scheme (with others), Stella Polare; Ostia, Italy. 1949–1950, INA-CASA Housing Scheme (with others), Valco Saint Paolo; 1951–1953, INA-CASA Housing Scheme (with others), Ruscolano II; 1952–1953, Low Cost Housing Scheme (with others), Villa dei Gordiani; Rome. 1952–1957, ENPAS Head Office, Bologna, Italy. 1956–1960, Christian Democrat Party Headquarters, Rome.

BIBLIOGRAPHY

BACIGALUPI, VINCENZO; BOAGA, GIORGIO; and BONI, BENITO 1965 *Guida dell'architettura contemporanea in Roma. Guide to Contemporary Architecture in Rome.* Bilingual. Rome: Associazione Nazionale Ingegneri ed Architetti Italiani.

MURATORI, SAVERIO 1950 "Vita e storia delle città." *Rassegna critica di Architettura* 11–12:3–52.

MURATORI, SAVERIO 1960 "Il problema critico dell'età gotica." Preface in Paolo Maretto, *L'edilizia gotica veneziana.* Rome: Istituto Poligrafico dello Stato.

MURATORI, SAVERIO 1963 *Architettura e civiltà in crisi.* Rome: Centro Studi di Storia Urbanistica.

MURATORI, SAVERIO 1967 *Civiltà e territorio.* Rome: Centro di Storia Urbanistica.

PORTOGHESI, PAOLO 1980 *Dopo l'architettura moderna.* Bari, Italy: Laterza.

SERMONTI, GIUSEPPE 1977 "Ricordo di Saverio Muratori: L'ultimo figlio del Rinascimento." *Il Tempo* 266:3.

TAVELLA, PATRIZIO 1978–1979 "Il tipo nel rapporto analisi progetto." Unpublished Ph.D. dissertation, University of Florence.

MURPHY, D. X.

Dennis X. Murphy (1854–1933) was a leading designer of commercial and institutional buildings in Louisville, Kentucky. Murphy was born in Louisville and was probably trained in the office of local architect, HENRY WHITESTONE, whose practice he took over in 1880. In partnership with his brothers James and Peter, he designed hospitals, schools, libraries, factories, and residences, as well as many Roman Catholic churches. D. X. Murphy & Brothers best-known work is the Clubhouse at Churchill Downs (1894–1896), but the Jefferson County Jail (1902–1905), a combination of the Richardsonian and Chicago school styles, is Murphy's masterpiece.

WILLIAM MORGAN

WORKS

1890–1893, Saint Boniface; 1893, Presentation Academy; 1894–1896, Clubhouse, Churchill Downs, Louisville, Ky. 1901, Mother House, Sisters of the Charity of Nazareth, Bardstown, Ky. 1902–1905, Jefferson County Jail; 1907, Bourbon Stockyards; 1910, Snead Manufacturing Building; 1911, General Hospital; 1912–1913, Jefferson Branch, Louisville Free Public Library, Louisville, Ky.

MUSMECI, SERGIO

Sergio Musmeci (1926–1981) was an engineer in the tradition of PIER LUIGI NERVI and RICCARDO MORANDI, deeply involved in the architectural values of structures. He proposed a three-kilometer-span bridge over the Straits of Messina. His best work is the viaduct over the Basento river in Potenza, Italy, whose bulging arcades display a daring sculptural rhythm.

RENATO PEDIO

WORKS

1975, Viaduct over the Basento river (with Aldo Livadiotti), Potenza, Italy.

BIBLIOGRAPHY

PEDIO, RENATO 1976 "Pontee sulla Basento e sulla zona industriale a Potenza." *L'Architettura, cronache e storia* 22, no. 247:6–13.

"Sergio Musmeci o delle tensioni cognite." 1979 *Parametro* 10, no. 80:special issue.

MUTHESIUS, HERMANN

In 1896, Hermann Muthesius (1861–1927) was appointed attaché to the German Embassy in London, his assignment to study and record English architecture and design. His findings were reported in a series of folios; the first two, devoted to *Die englische Baukunst der Gegenwart,* were published in 1900 and 1902, and a third, *Die neuere kirchliche Baukunst in England* was published in 1903 by Wasmuth, the German company that was to publish the influential monograph on FRANK LLOYD WRIGHT. Muthesius's most important work, *Das englische Haus,* was published after his return to Germany in 1903.

In this three-volume study, Muthesius traced not only the style and form of the English house but also its history and typological origins. He praised the principles espoused by the English Arts and Crafts movement, eulogizing craftsmanship and economy in design. His writings had a specific influence on the style of German design, prompting an "English style" in domestic architecture. More important, however, was their ideological and pedagogical impact on German design theory.

Above all else, Muthesius admired the qualities of suitability and functionality in English domestic design, qualities which he sought to promote in German work. As a leader of the *Sachlichkeit* movement (Muthesius introduced the term in articles he wrote for *Dekorative Kunst* while in England), Muthesius extolled the virtues of utilitarian and functional design. In 1907, Muthesius, then superintendent of the Prussian Board of Trade for Schools of Arts and Crafts, delivered a public address in which he chastized German crafts and industry for their inability to adhere to such standards. Out of the furor his remarks provoked, the Deutscher Werkbund was born. Together with Friedrich Naumann and Karl Schmidt, Muthesius set up a school dedicated to quality in industrial work, honesty of materials, and organic design.

The Werkbund itself, however, lacked a clear consensus. Muthesius's own opinions, aired in a speech on the occasion of the Deutscher Werkbund Exhibition in Cologne in 1914, touched off a famous debate with HENRY VAN DE VELDE. The argument divided along classic lines with Muthesius preaching standardization and Van de Velde defending individuality in art. Muthesius called for the development of normative industrial types (Typisierung) similar to LE CORBUSIER's *objet-types.* He urged artists to move beyond handicrafts into machine art and to study methods of mass production. The reactionary contingent, led by Van de Velde, forced Muthesius to withdraw his program. But the debate did not die, surfacing again in the Bauhaus discussions until the war stifled all such theoretical concerns.

DARALICE DONKERVOET BOLES

BIBLIOGRAPHY

FRAMPTON, KENNETH 1980 *Modern Architecture: A Critical History.* London: Oxford University Press.

HITCHCOCK, H. R. (1958)1977 *Architecture: Nineteenth and Twentieth Centuries.* Baltimore: Penguin.

MUTHESIUS, HERMANN 1901–1902 *Die englische Baukunst der Gegenwart.* 2 vols. Berlin: Wasmuth.

MUTHESIUS, HERMANN 1903 *Die neuere kirchliche Baukunst.* Berlin: Wasmuth.

MUTHESIUS, HERMANN (1904)1979 *The English House.* Edited by Dennis Sharp. Translated by Janet Seligman, with a preface by Julius Posener. New York: Rizzoli. Originally published with the title *Das englische Haus.*

PEVSNER, NIKOLAUS (1936)1960 *Pioneers of Modern Design: From William Morris to Walter Gropius.* Rev. ed. Harmondsworth, England: Penguin.

MUTTONI, FRANCESCO

Born at La Cima on Lake Lugano, Francesco Muttoni (1669–1747) enrolled in the stonemasons' guild in Vicenza in 1696. He is the greatest Vicentine master of the transition from a robust and elaborate late baroque to Palladian neoclassicism: in addition to a large oeuvre of palaces, villas, public buildings, and churches, Muttoni was the anonymous author ("N.N.") of a fundamental treatise of the revival movement, the *Architettura di Andrea Palladio.* Eight volumes of this beautifully researched and illustrated work were published in 1740–1748, and a ninth was issued by Muttoni's collaborator Giorgio Fossati in 1760; manuscript portions of the unpublished tenth volume are divided between the Palladian Center in Vicenza and the Library of Congress in Washington. In 1708, Muttoni drew antiquities in Rome for the English "grand tourist" Sir Thomas Twisden, whose example may have influenced LORD BURLINGTON to acquire the Muttoni drawings now at Chatsworth. Another influence on northern neoclassicism was his presentation to the king of Denmark of the project for a huge square palace, enclosing a round court ringed by quadrant staircases (1708–1709).

DOUGLAS LEWIS

WORKS

1701–1711, Palazzo Repeta; Vicenza, Italy. 1702–1703, Villa Valmarana-Morosini (stable; villa completed 1724), Altavilla Vicentina, Italy. 1703, Biblioteca Bertoliana; 1704–1706, San Vincenzo (chancel); 1706–1707, Palazzo Velo; Vicenza, Italy. 1708–1710, Villa Fracanzan, Orgiano, Italy. 1714–1715, Villa Da Porto (La Favorita), Monticello di Fara, Italy. 1717–1722, Villa Trissino (garden stairs, avenues, and gates), Trissino, Italy. 1718, Palazzo Trento-Valmarana, Vicenza, Italy. 1718–1728, Villa Americo-Capra (La Rotonda; completion of attic rooms and other works), near Vicenza, Italy. 1719?–1746, Parish Church, Rossano, Italy. 1720s?, Villa Piovene (colonnaded wings and garden stair), Lonedo, Italy. Before 1740, Villa Poiana (addition of north wing), Poiana Maggiore, Italy. 1720s–1747, Parish Church (completed 1707; façade 1834), Leffe in Val Seriana, Bergamo, Italy. Before 1740, Villa Thiene (addition with south façade), Quinto Vicentino, Italy. 1741–1747, Monte Berico (portico-stair to sanctuary), Vicenza, Italy.

BIBLIOGRAPHY

BARBIERI, FRANCO 1980 "I disegni di Francesco Muttoni a Chatsworth." *Arte Lombarda* 55–57:219–235.

BARBIERI, FRANCESCO; CEVESE, RENATO; MAGAGNATO, LICISCO (1953)1956 *Guida di Vicenza.* 2d ed. Vicenza, Italy: Eretenia.

BRUSATIN, MANLIO 1980 *Venezia nel Settecento: Stato, architettura, territorio.* Turin, Italy: Einaudi.

CEVESE, RENATO 1971 *Ville della Provincia di Vicenza* (*Ville Italiane, Veneto 2*). 2 vols. Milan: SISAR.

LEWIS, DOUGLAS 1976 "A New Book of Drawings by Francesco Muttoni." *Arte Veneto* 30:132–146.

PUPPI, LIONELLO 1980 "Alle origine del Neopalladianesimo: Il contributo comasco di Francesco Muttoni." *Arte Lombarda* 55–57:236–242.

MUZIO, GIOVANNI

The name of Giovanni Muzio (1893–) is inseparable from "metaphysical" architecture. Indeed, the work of his early years is by now accepted as synonomous with a cultural world woven by scenographers, sculptors, painters, writers, and musicians rather than by architects. The assonance with Giorgio de Chirico, the "metaphysical" painter par excellence, is immediate. Muzio's work is metaphysical to the extent that there is a difference between building—constructing an artifact according to certain traditional or modern techniques—and architecture—adopting techniques in light of a certain spirit, so that a structure, rather than being a narrowly functional shelter, becomes something larger, a creative act of the kind found in a painting or a piece of music.

Muzio was born in Milan of a family from Bergamo. He received his degree in 1915 from the Milan Polytechnic Institute and served in the Italian army from 1915 to 1919. Almost from the beginning, the tenor of his work was that of an architect who sought to affirm the Italian traditions handed down to him by his family and the larger culture, but this did not lead him into a narrow parochialism. On the contrary, he knew the Europe of the Great War, especially France and Paris, and he sought to confront other cultures without imitating them and without abandoning the architectural traditions of his homeland. Within these broad limits he explored, sometimes with exasperating fullness, the discipline of architecture, producing what might be called one of the last "local" products that yet managed to transcend its time.

In his best-known early work, the Ca'bruta (1923) in Milan, Muzio expressed his debt to the Bergomasque tradition of Italian culture. However, his was always an autonomous position, dissociated even from the emerging Italian Rationalism, from Art Nouveau, and from late nineteenth-century eclecticism. In subsequent work, for example, at the Exhibit of Decorative Art in Monza (1930), Muzio clarified his particular style. He demonstrated once again that it was possible to maintain an autonomous and entirely original position and still create an architecture that was sensitive to the debates which swirled around modern art in Italy during the Fascist period.

EDOARDO PERSICO's assessment of Muzio is

Muzio. Plan for Ca'bruta. Milan. 1923

worth noting. Although Persico did not view Muzio as an ally in the battle for the European Modern movement, he recognized that the answers to Muzio's art had to be sought more in the artist's psychology and cultural background than in the work itself.

Muzio taught at the Milan Polytechnic Institute from 1935 to 1963. When the tumult quieted down after World War II, Muzio's work stabilized, another indication that although his position was independent, he was nonetheless influenced by the interwar culture. His subsequent work has included urban projects in Bergamo, Milan, Portugal, and elsewhere, in addition to a large number of churches and apartment and office buildings in the Lombard region of Italy.

RICCARDO MARIANI

WORKS

*1923, Ca'bruta, via Turati and via Moscova; 1926–1936, Catholic University of Milan; 1932, Palazzo de l'Arte; Milan. 1935, Palazzo del Governo, Sondrio, Italy. 1936, Church of San Antonio, Cremona, Italy. 1938, Palazzo della Casa di Risparmio; 1956, Colleges at the University of Bocconi, Milan. 1957, Sanctuary of San Antonio, Varese, Italy. 1967, Church of Colognola, Bologna, Italy. 1968, House, via Borgonovo, via dei Giardini, Milan. 1969, Basilica dell'Annunciazione, Nazareth, Israel.

BIBLIOGRAPHY

DE'SETA, CESARE (1972)1978 *La cultura architettonica in Italia tra le due guerre.* 2d ed. Bari, Italy: Laterza.

GREGOTTI, VITTORIO 1976 "Milano e la cultura architettonica tra le due guerre." Pages 16–21 in Silvia Danesi (editor), *Il Razionalismo e l'architettura in Italia durante il fascismo.* Venice, Italy: Edizioni la Biennale di Venezia.

MELOGRANI, CARLO 1969 "Passato e presente nell'architettura italiana contemporanea." *Rassegna dell'Istituto di Architettura e Urbanistica* 5, Apr.–Aug.:13–14.

MYERS, ELIJAH E.

Elijah E. Myers (1832–1909), architect of three major state capitols and SAMUEL SLOAN's friend and probable student, was born to a working class Philadelphia family. A $55,000 fee for his first courthouse provided the wherewithall to enter numerous competitions and win many governmental commissions.

ROXANNE WILLIAMSON

WORKS

1872–1879, Michigan Capitol Building, Lansing. 1883–1888, Texas Capitol Building, Austin. 1890–1894, Colorado State Capitol, Denver.

BIBLIOGRAPHY

HITCHCOCK, H. R., and SEALE, WILLIAM 1976 *Temples of Democracy: The State Capitols of the U.S.A.* New York: Harcourt.

WEBB, WALTER PRESCOTT (editor) 1952 *The Handbook of Texas.* Austin: The Texas State Historical Association.

MYLNE, ROBERT and FAMILY

The pedigree established by the Reverend Robert Scott Mylne for his monumental family history *The Master Masons to the Crown of Scotland* (1893) illustrates the dynastic sway of this outstanding Scottish family of masons, architects, and engineers.

With the exception of Alexander Mylne (?–1548), there is little documentary evidence for the careers of the earlier Mylnes before John Mylne (?–1621). Family tradition was strong enough to enable Robert Mylne (1633–1710) to claim in a petition of 1708 that the office of master mason to the Crown of Scotland "hath been given and continueth to my ancestours in blood from the time of King James the Third, and for now more than two hundred years."

During the 1580s, John Mylne was in Dundee engaged on public works, particularly the repair of the harbor, and designed the market cross. In 1604, he was in Perth to undertake the construction of a new bridge of eleven arches across the River Tay which was completed in 1617, but destroyed by floods in 1621. John Mylne was also engaged on private houses; in 1587, with a fellow mason, George Thomson, he contracted to build Bannatyne House, Newtyle, for Lord Bannatyne, and he is said to have built The Drum, near Edinburgh, for Lord Somerville in 1584. Mylne subsequently settled at Perth where he died in 1621 and was buried in the Greyfriars Churchyard.

His son, John Mylne (?–1657), who had assisted his father with the Tay Bridge, succeeded him as master of the Masons Lodge at Scone. In 1616, he was summoned to Edinburgh to complete the statue of King James I & VI on the Netherbow Port. In 1620, he contracted to rebuild Falkland Church, and in 1622, he was in Aberdeen supervising the new Tolbooth steeple. In 1629, he contracted to form a pond at Holyrood for Charles I, and after the death of WILLIAM WALLACE he was made principal master mason to the Crown in 1631. Mylne's royal works at Edinburgh included in 1633 a sundial at Holyrood, in which he was assisted by his sons John and Alexander. In 1636, he resigned his office in favor of his son John and returned to Dundee where he was engaged on various public works between 1643 and 1651.

John Mylne (1611–1667) was born in Perth but was established in Edinburgh during the 1630s, becoming a burgess in 1633 and the town's master mason in 1637; he represented Edinburgh in the Scottish Parliament in 1662. His numerous works there include the Tron Kirk (finished 1647), one of two new churches projected to take congregations displaced from Saint Giles when Charles I raised the latter to cathedral status; work on Heriot's Hospital where he succeeded William Aytoun as master mason in 1643; additions to the College; the rebuilding of the crown steeple of Saint Giles in 1648; the fortification of Leith in 1650; and the division of Greyfriars Church to take two congregations in 1655. These large undertakings and his success drew him into political life. Outside Edinburgh, he designed Cowane's Hospital, Stirling (1637), and reported on Jedburgh Abbey in 1642; he prepared the designs for Panmure House in 1666 and for Linlithgow Tolbooth in 1667 (unexecuted) shortly before his death. After the Restoration, as master mason to Charles II he drew up designs for the repair of Holyrood, but this work was not begun until after his death when his nephew Robert—John had no surviving male heirs—succeeded him as master mason to the Crown.

Robert Mylne (1633–1710), son of Alexander Mylne the sculptor, was apprenticed to his uncle in 1653. He inherited several incomplete commissions from his uncle including the design of the Perth Market Cross (1668) and alterations at Leslie House. As the king's master mason of the time, he undertook the rebuilding of Holyrood which finally began in 1671 to the designs of WILLIAM BRUCE and which was completed in 1679. At the same time, with Bruce, he was involved in private commissions for the duke of Lauderdale, the king's Scottish Secretary, at Thirlestane Castle, and he made gatepiers to Bruce's designs for the Lauderdale house at Ham outside London.

In Edinburgh, he repaired the Castle fortifications and continued his uncle's public works, including a new water supply whose cisterns were designed by Bruce from 1674, and built the cupola of Heriot's Hospital (1693). His other works include the west tower of South Leith Parish Church and a bridge over the Clyde at Ram's Horn Pool.

Mylne was active as both builder and private speculator in the large-scale replacement of Edinburgh's timber buildings with stone tenements, of which the principal were Mylne's Court (1684) and Mylne's Square (1690). Earlier in 1678, he had built a block of tenements on reclaimed land on the Shore of Leith. His successful professional career and these speculations enabled him to acquire two estates. Balfargie in Fife and another at Inveresk to the east of Edinburgh where he died in 1710. Mylne's daughter married JAMES SMITH, and his son William and grandson Thomas succeeded him as mason architects in Edinburgh, although their careers are overshadowed by Robert Mylne (1733–1811) whose early training the latter oversaw and whose outstanding success brought the family name back into the forefront of British architecture and engineering.

IAN GOW

WORKS

JOHN MYLNE (?–1621)

1580s, Public Works (including harbor repair and design of market cross), Dundee, Scotland. 1584, The Drum, near Edinburgh. 1587, Bannatyne House (with George Thompson), Newtyle, Scotland. *1604–1617, Bridge (with John Mylne), River Tay, Perth, Scotland.

JOHN MYLNE (?–1657)

1616, Statue of King James I and IV (completion), Netherbow Port, Edinburgh. *Completed 1617, Bridge (with John Mylne), River Tay, Perth, Scotland. 1620, Falkland Church (rebuilding), Scotland. 1622, Tolbooth Steeple, Aberdeen, Scotland. 1629, Pond; 1633, Sundial (with John and Alexander Mylne); Holyrood Castle, Edinburgh. 1643–1651, Public Works, Dundee, Scotland.

JOHN MYLNE (1611–1667)

1637, Cowanes Hospital, Stirling, Scotland. Completed 1647, Tron Kirk Church, 1648, Saint Giles (rebuilding of Crown Steeple); 1650, Fortification of Leith; 1655, Greyfriars Church (remodeling); n.d., Edinburgh University (additions to College); n.d., Heriot Hospital (various works); Edinburgh.

ROBERT MYLNE (1633–1710)

1668, Perth Market Cross (designs by John Mylne), Scotland. 1671–1679, Holyrood Castle (rebuilding; designs by William Bruce); Begun 1674, Water Supply System (cistern design by Bruce); 1678, Tenement Block, Shore of Leith; 1684, Mylne's Court; 1690, Mylne's Square; 1693, Heriot's Hospital (cupola); n.d., South Leith Parish Church (west tower); n.d., Bridge, Ram's Horn Pool, River Clyde; Edinburgh.

BIBLIOGRAPHY

ARCHITECTURAL PUBLICATION SOCIETY 1853–1892 *The Dictionary of Architecture.* London: Richards.

DUNBAR, JOHN G. 1970 *Sir William Bruce.* Edinburgh: Scottish Arts Council. Exhibition catalogue.

DUNBAR, JOHN G. 1975 "The Building Activities of the Duke and Duchess of Lauderdale: 1670–82." *Archaeological Journal* 132:202–230.

MACGIBBON, DAVID, and ROSS, THOMAS 1887 *The Castellated and Domestic Architecture of Scotland.* Edinburgh.

MYLNE, ROBERT SCOTT 1893 *The Master Masons to the Crown of Scotland.* Edinburgh.

N

NAISSANT, CLAUDE

Born in Paris, Claude Naissant (1801–1879) entered the Ecole des Beaux-Arts in 1828, where he studied under Jean François Julien Mesnager. By 1843, he was architect to Sceaux (incorporated into Paris in 1860) and retained that position until 1866. His work was not much admired in France, although the spare Romanesque style of his churches gained the approval of *The Ecclesiologist* (1855).

R. D. MIDDLETON

WORKS

1844–1845, Saint Hermeland (restoration), Bagneux; 1848–1856, Saint Lambert, rue Bausset, Vaugirard; 1855–1864, Notre Dame de la Gare, Place Jeanne d'Arc, Gobelins; 1855–1866, Sous-préfecture (later Mairie du XIVe; enlarged and built over by Elie François Alexandre Emile Auburtin 1882–1889), Sceaux; 1856–1866, Saint Charles Borromée, Joinville-le-Pont; 1857–1859, Saint Pierre, Place de l'Eglise, Charenton-le-Pont; 1857–1866, Saint Geneviève, Place Carnot, Rousny-sous-Bois; 1861, Notre-Dame de la Médaille Miraculeuse, 80 Avenue Pierre Larousse, Malakoff; 1863–?, Mairie, Issy-sur-Seine; Paris.

NASH, JOHN

John Nash (1752–1837) was the planner of Regent Street and Regents Park, London, and the architect of many of the buildings in the street (all demolished) and most of those in the park (nearly all preserved). This vast operation, with its many extensions, he successfully completed between his sixtieth and seventy-fifth year. The earlier part of his career is hardly less memorable. He was the leading architect of the Picturesque school, building country houses either in the "castle" style or in a Tuscan vernacular inspired by the landscapes of Claude Lorrain, and, in addition, creating a type of cottage architecture depending on the traditional buildings of the English countryside. A third aspect of his career, as the personal architect of George IV, is also important. For him he remodeled the Royal Pavilion, Brighton, in an "Indian" style and rebuilt Buckingham House as Buckingham Palace.

Although probably born in London, Nash was of Welsh descent and had strong Welsh loyalties. His father, who died when he was six, had been a millwright in Lambeth. In or about 1766, Nash was apprenticed to one of the leading London architects, Sir ROBERT TAYLOR, in whose office he showed himself a somewhat raffish youth with a prodigious if erratic capacity for work. Leaving Taylor in 1774, he married and at once plunged into speculative development in London. Houses in Bloomsbury Square and Great Russell Street, built by him in 1777, survive; they reflect Taylor's style but are finished in stucco, a material not yet in common use but which Nash was later to render almost universal in the street architecture of fashionable London.

This first speculative venture failed and in 1783 Nash was bankrupt. His marriage was also in trouble and he had even taken the first steps toward obtaining an Act of Divorce. The process now had to be postponed. He retired to Carmarthen in South Wales, leading, according to his own account, a profligate life, neglecting architecture but conducting various business enterprises and contracting to build a new roof for Carmarthen church. When a former fellow pupil in Taylor's office, SAMUEL PEPYS COCKERELL, visited Carmarthen, figuring as a brilliant young architect in a good way of business, Nash's interest in the profession was suddenly reanimated; and when a wealthy local landowner invited him to design a bathhouse on his estate, he accepted and received his first professional fee.

By this time, he had become well-known as a *bon viveur* among the squires of south Wales, and the disclosure that he was also a professionally trained architect soon brought him commissions. In 1789–1792, he built a new jail and house of correction for the county of Carmarthen. This was followed by a jail at Cardigan (1792–1793) and another at Hereford (1795–1798). He rebuilt the west front of Saint David's Cathedral (1791–1793) in a Gothic style and built several bridges and a market house at Abergavenny. He was in request also as a designer of small country villas of a more sophisticated kind than had previously been seen in Wales.

By 1796, Nash had established himself as a west country architect of considerable fame and was preparing to seek his fortune again in London, where the bankruptcy episode was by now presumably forgotten. The divorce proceedings, abandoned in 1783, had been resumed but proved abortive. It must be assumed, however, that his wife died before 1798, in which year he married again and built a house of considerable pretensions in Dover Street, London.

Nash. Southgate Grove. Middlesex, England. 1797

Nash's immediate success as a country house architect, working from London, was mainly the consequence of his association with the landscape gardener HUMPHRY REPTON. He was a man of Nash's own age who had gained a reputation as the successor of the famous CAPABILITY BROWN, who had died in 1783. Repton had a practice extending all over the country, and in the conduct of this he needed the collaboration of a sympathetic architect whom he could introduce to those of his clients who desired to have their houses altered or rebuilt to accord with the landscape improvements proposed by Repton. In Nash, Repton found an enthusiastic ally.

Nash and Repton had a common interest in the movement known as the Picturesque. Adumbrated by William Gilpin in his books of *Observations* on landscape and developed on more philosophical lines by RICHARD PAYNE KNIGHT and Sir UVEDALE PRICE in their own printed works, it was a philosophy of landscape and not of architecture. The style and character of buildings within landscape were, however, necessarily involved. The paintings of Claude Lorrain and Gaspar Poussin, which Knight and Price regarded as basic documents of the Picturesque, showed buildings of irregular form as points of interest in their landscapes and it was in the spirit of these that Knight designed his own house, Downton Castle, Herefordshire, in 1774–1778. This was, externally, a towered and turreted building of wildly irregular silhouette; it was the first essay of its kind and was to be the model upon which Nash's own ideas of castle architecture were to be shaped.

Nash's partnership with Repton, formed about 1796, developed fruitfully for some six years, during which Nash built at least eight houses and many cottages and lodges as a result of introductions by Repton. When, in 1797, Repton was summoned by the Prince of Wales to advise him on his estate at Brighton, he almost certainly introduced Nash who, in the following year, exhibited "A Conservatory for the Prince of Wales" at the Royal Academy. There is no evidence that it was built, however, and Nash was to wait for fourteen years before receiving effective royal patronage.

By 1802, the partnership had broken up, Nash having, it seems, become too self-assertive and less than generous in his acknowledgment of his partner's talents. By this date, however, Nash was well afloat as an architect with a reputation for social amiability and architectural invention. Between 1802 and 1812, he built, rebuilt, or substantially altered between twenty and thirty houses in England and Ireland. Of these, twelve were in the castle style. Others were in an Italian vernacular derived probably from landscape paintings and engravings. Others again were in Tudor or Elizabethan or in the neoclassical fashion of the day. Many of these houses have been destroyed. Among the castles, Luscombe, Devonshire (1800–1804), Killymoon (1801–1803) and Lough Cutra (1811), both in Ireland, and Caerhayes, Cornwall (c.1808), are the only survivors. Of those in the Italian style Cronkhill near Shrewsbury (1802), and Sandridge Park, Devonshire (1805), are the best of those still standing.

Nash's Picturesque house plans were of two main kinds. One was an "explosion" of the conventional villa plan, producing a balanced irregularity in perspective and silhouette. The other was a plan in which the main rooms were placed irregularly, on either side of a long gallery, open from the ground floor to the roof and with continuous balconies projecting at first floor level. This type of plan, unique to Nash, occurs in more regular form in the Brighton Pavilion (1815–1821) and even in Buckingham Palace (1824–1830). In the ornamental detail of his houses Nash showed very little interest. His Gothic is naively crude and the interiors of his houses are repetitive and perfunctory. He staked everything on striking exterior arrangements of mass and silhouette.

An important part of Nash's participation in Repton's practice had been the building of lodges, cottages, and farm buildings on the estates which Repton was improving. These types appealed to Nash as an architectural problem capable of an infinite variety of solutions based on the vernacular of the English countryside. Many of these small buildings survive and at Blaise Castle, near Bristol, Nash built on the estate a group of cottages for pensioners, picturesquely assembled in a field and representing an anthology of his cottage types. Blaise Hamlet (1810–1811), as the group is called, is now the property of the National Trust.

In 1806, Nash was appointed architect to the Office of Woods and Forests. The appointment was not lucrative but there was a special reason why it should be held at this time by an architect of experience and ability. This was because in 1811 the five hundred acres of Marylebone Park, then on lease from the Crown to the duke of Portland, would revert to the Crown. Situated on the northern fringe of expanding London it would be essential for the Crown to develop the park as a residential area. Reports on such a development had already been submitted to the government; the Office of Woods and Forests would be the appropriate agency to promote the development and

Nash.
Luscombe Castle.
Dawlish, Devonshire, England.
1800–1804

their architect would, in all likelihood, be the man to make the plans.

Although as far back as 1793 a premium of £1000 had been offered by the government for proposals for Marylebone Park, nothing had resulted from this. By 1810, the matter had become urgent. In that year, the Office of Woods and Forests was united with the Office of Land Revenue. As the latter office retained a salaried surveyor, two official planners were involved. The commissioners of the united offices now instructed both the Woods and Forests architect, John Nash, and the Land Revenues surveyor, THOMAS LEVERTON, to prepare plans, thus obtaining for comparison the ideas of a fashionable country house architect and a London surveyor of acknowledged competence.

An important factor in the development of the park was accessibility. It had long been realized that this could be secured only if a new street were constructed providing easy communication between the park and the parliamentary and legal centers around Charing Cross and Whitehall. The architects were advised therefore to submit proposals for such a street with their plans for the park. The plans and reports were delivered in 1811 and in due course Nash's plans for both park and street were accepted by the Treasury.

Nash's plan for the park was strikingly original, especially when compared with Leverton's which offered little more than an extension of the checkerboard pattern of west London northward across the Marylebone fields. Nash introduced as a major element a gigantic double circus joined by three arms to a periphery of streets, squares, and crescents. He nevertheless preserved a large area as open parkland, with individual residences scattered among groves of trees. The plan as a whole showed the influence of John Wood's planning of Bath but introduced a new element of semirural picturesqueness. It was in effect a garden city.

Nash's proposal for the new street was no less original. A shrewd analysis of the social and economic factors suggested a line where the chaotic pattern of the Soho area met the more regular pat-

Nash.
The Quadrant (façades), Regent Street.
London.
1815–1830

Nash.
Waterloo Place (façades), Regent Street.
London.
1815–1830

tern of the West End estate developments, enabling the commissioners to buy reasonably cheap, run-down property on the east but to open up the street to the more fashionable area on the west. This line, however, involved a sudden eastward switch in the lower part of the street to reach a new line which would bring the street down to Pall Mall without disturbing the aristocratic area of Saint James's Square. This change of direction Nash achieved by introducing the quarter-circle known as the Quadrant. This joined Piccadilly at Piccadilly Circus, whence there was a straight run downhill to the colonnaded screen of the Prince Regent's residence in Pall Mall, Carlton House.

The conduct of the street was the responsibility of the commissioners of Woods and Forests, under the New Street Act of 1813, with Nash as their professional adviser. In that capacity he acted as planner, architect, engineer, financial adviser, valuer, and estate agent. When the sites for the new street had been cleared and compensation settlements reached, it was open to the building community to apply for building leases. Nash controlled the designs of the builders' street fronts but did not impose an overall design except in Waterloo Place, the Quadrant, and Oxford and Piccadilly circuses. He persuaded the builders to take blocks of sites which would be pictorially effective and supplied each builder with an elevation for his block. In the case of the Quadrant, where none of the big builders would undertake the long curving units, he undertook them himself, assembling a team of building tradesmen willing to operate on a "work against work" basis, and giving them the opportunity to take leaseholds instead of cash payments. This was not successful financially, but it pulled the street through a difficult period and opened up the straight northern stretch where plots were more readily taken. The street was named Regent Street in 1819 and was completed in 1826.

An extension of the scheme was immediately put in hand, the Charing Cross Act of 1826 empowering the commissioners to form an open square on the site of the ancient Royal Mews at the north end of Whitehall and to replan the western parts of the Strand. The square, eventually named Trafalgar Square, was intended by Nash as a center for cultural buildings of monumental character, and the National Gallery, designed by William Wilkins, was built on the north side in 1834–1838. No buildings in the square are by Nash, but the exposure of James Gibbs's Saint Martin-in-the-Fields and the effective realignment of streets between the church, the square, and the Strand are due to him.

The development of Marylebone Park (Regents Park from 1819) started in 1812, but its dependence on the completion of the new street delayed further building for nearly ten years. A special difficulty arose over the adoption of Portland Place as the connection between the new street and the park. Built by James Adam in 1773–1775 as an exclusive residential enclosure, Portland Place belonged to the duke of Portland. Hostile to interference with his private road, the duke planned to obstruct the scheme by acquiring a property which would effectively block the southern outlet. He made a handsome offer to the owner. Nash, hearing of this, stepped in with an exorbitantly improved offer and secured the property for his own disposal. Here, as in the Quadrant,

Nash.
Harmonic Institution, Regent Street.
London.
1819

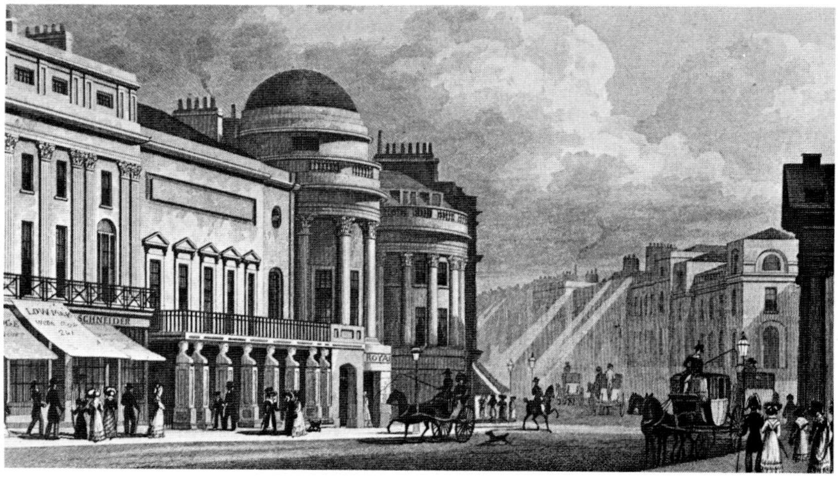

he exerted his own initiative and financial ability to save the street. "The new street," he observed, with reference to this occasion, "was an object very near my heart."

When building in the park did eventually proceed, it did so on a plan substantially revised from that which Nash had submitted to the commissioners in 1811. Prime Minister Spencer Perceval had insisted on a reduction in the amount of land to be devoted to buildings and a corresponding increase in open parkland. Nash accepted the situation with reluctance but eventually produced a more open plan with which he declared himself entirely satisfied. The number of villas was reduced from fifty to twenty-six and two of these were built in 1818–1820. The terraces of houses on the perimeter of the park followed in 1821 to 1827.

There are twelve of these terraces, each containing from twelve to thirty houses built by speculative builders with façades designed by Nash or (in two cases) by DECIMUS BURTON with Nash's approbation. They are symmetrical classical compositions with varying arrangements of columns and pilasters, all in stucco. As in Regent Street, the façades are designed for broad scenic effect rather than detailed appreciation. The most ambitious is Cumberland Terrace (1826–1827), on the east side of the park, a three-part composition 230 meters long, with a central portico of ten Ionic columns, above and behind which rises a giant pediment filled with sculpture; the Ionic order is carried through to pavilions in supporting wings which are connected to the center block by triumphal arches. The monumental character of this terrace appears to be due to its siting opposite a piece of ground on which the prince regent proposed to build a *guinguette* or pleasure pavilion. The *guinguette* was never built and no designs for it are known, but the site was still reserved for it at George IV's death in 1830.

The great double circus which forms such a conspicuous element in the early plans was never built, and in 1826, it was decided to eliminate the terraces planned along the northern boundary. The park as it stands today is thus a mere shadow of the densely built garden city which Nash originally planned.

An element shown in the original project which did come to fruition was the Regents Canal. The idea of forming a canal through the north London suburbs to connect the Paddington basin of the old Grand Junction Canal with a new dock on the Thames at Limehouse was under discussion before Nash's arrival on the scene. It was Nash, however, who took the lead in forming a company and raising capital for the enterprise. The reason for his interest was twofold. First, he envisaged a

Nash. Cumberland Terrace, Regents Park. London. 1812–1827

branch canal or "commercial cut," leading southward from the main canal to serve a series of marketplaces in the park. Second, he saw the possibility of using the canal water to feed an arabesque of ornamental water as one of the amenities of the park landscape. Both these ideas took effect. A marketing area was formed on the east side of the park consisting of three connected squares. These still show on the map but have been entirely rebuilt and the whole of the commercial cut was filled in soon after 1945. The ornamental water, however, is still a conspicuous feature of the park.

Nash invested heavily in the Regents Canal and made himself responsible for the wharfs of Regents Canal Basin. He also took for himself, in 1824, two narrow strips of property on either side of the commercial cut. On these he laid out, more for amusement than for profit, the two Park Villages. These consist of small houses of Picturesque design and varying style recalling some of the small houses and cottages of his earlier years. Park Village West survives, nearly intact; Park Village East was half destroyed by railway developments of the 1880s.

In his work for Regent Street and Regents Park, Nash worked under contract with the Commissioners of Woods, Forests, and Land Revenues. Simultaneously, from 1815, he was one of the three architects attached to the Board of Works, his colleagues being JOHN SOANE and ROBERT SMIRKE. From 1813, he was also employed by the prince regent as his private architect. His relation with the prince went some way beyond the purely professional, for in 1812 we find him acting as the prince's emissary in a political crisis involving the prince's relations with his German wife, while in the same year he prepared to stand for election as a member of Parliament with the object of promoting the prince's interests in the House of Commons. The opportunity passed, however.

His first architectural work for the prince was the enlargement of a cottage (1813–1816) in Windsor Great Park to provide a residence for him pending his accession to his father's throne and the occupancy of Windsor Castle itself. This was followed, in 1813–1814, by a suite of new rooms at Carlton House and by an extravagant pyrotechnic display, involving a Chinese pagoda mounted on a bridge in Saint James's Park, to celebrate the visit of Louis XVIII of France and the Czar of Russia after the Treaty of Paris.

In 1815, the prince instructed Nash to consider improvements at his marine residence at Brighton, called the Royal Pavilion. This had been mostly built in 1787 by HENRY HOLLAND in a modest neoclassical style, while in 1804, WILLIAM PORDEN had added a huge domed stable building, purporting to be in an Indian style. The prince now decided to resolve the stylistic conflict by adopting this style in further extensions to the main building. The work proceeded from 1815 to 1821 and took the form of a somewhat bizarre but highly picturesque improvisation. Nash added a music-room to one end of the building and a banqueting room at the other, with a connecting gallery alongside the main body of the old building. The old building itself he transformed through the addition of Indian colonnades and verandas and a series of five onion domes on the skyline, the "Indian" details being mainly borrowed from the work of the topographical artists and travelers, William and THOMAS DANIELL. The interior decorations are not Indian but Chinese and mainly the work of Frederick Crace. The Pavilion is original not only in style but in structure. The central onion dome is iron framed and covered with iron sheeting, finished with Hamlin's patent mastic; the two staircases are wholly of cast iron with brass ornaments.

In 1820, the prince regent succeeded to the throne as George IV and it was not long before the question arose of building a new royal palace. The British sovereigns had never been adequately housed in their capital since the burning of Whitehall in 1698 and in the years of euphoria after Waterloo the notion of a palace symbolizing the nation's new status in Europe and the world received much support. Soane had a design ready by 1821 and probably hoped for the commission but, inevitably, Nash, as the prince's favored architect, took precedence. He was now seventy and by no means eager to undertake so onerous a commission but, pressed by the king, he had no choice. Parliament was not overgenerous. The first estimates were for a reconstruction of Buckingham House, a mansion of 1715, magnificently sited at the southwest end of Saint James's Park. Nash, however, preserved nothing of the old house except the brick carcass. Work started in 1824.

Following on the decision to rebuild Buckingham House as Buckingham Palace came a series of highly important moves affecting Regent Street and Saint James's Park. In 1825, Carlton House, which had originally been adopted as the terminal feature of the new street, was demolished and its site and grounds laid out for development. The street now terminated in a flight of steps leading down from Waterloo Place to Saint James's Park, while to the east and west of the steps the two rows of houses known as the Carlton House Terraces were formed. Nash replanned and replanted the park as a suitable foreground to the new palace and recreated the mall as a formal avenue on the palace axis. The success of this rearrangement was sealed by the erection of a column commemorating the king's brother, the duke of York, at the head of the steps (hence called the Duke of York's Steps) in 1831–1834. Though not designed by Nash, it

Nash. The Royal Pavilion (remodeling and extension). Brighton, England. 1815–1821

followed an earlier proposal by him for a column standing before Carlton House.

If the Carlton House Terraces, the steps, and the column can be counted among Nash's conspicuous successes, the same cannot be said for Buckingham Palace. Designed in haste, under pressure from the aging king, it presented such an unhappy appearance when half-finished that Nash himself tried to obtain authority for partial demolition. A compromise was reached and the building was virtually complete when George IV died in 1830. By that time, however, Nash was in deep trouble, though less now in the matter of design than of expenditure. His loyalty to the king on the one hand and his obligation to submit to Treasury control on the other had led him into subterfuges which could only too readily be interpreted (by the Treasury) as gross professional misconduct. Immediately after the king's death, he was challenged to explain the reasons for excessive expenditure. He failed to do so and in October 1830 the palace works were stopped and Nash was dismissed from his office as architect to the Board of Works.

A parliamentary inquiry into the palace affairs, its architect's conduct, and even the structural stability of the fabric somewhat mitigated the architect's culpability, but there could be no question of rehabilitation. The palace was put into other hands, a new frontal block facing the park was erected (1847–1850), to be in turn replaced by the present façade of 1911. Nothing can now be seen of Nash's work, except from the garden side and in some of the staterooms. Of the latter it must be said that they achieve a regal splendor and stylistic variety somewhat unexpected at the hands of a septuagenarian architect whose specialty had never been creations of this kind.

From 1829, Nash was a sick man suffering, probably, from the effects of a mild stroke. In 1834, he gave up the magnificent house which he had built for himself in Lower Regent Street and retired to the estate at East Cowes in the Isle of Wight which he had acquired at the time of his second marriage and where he had built a house in the castle style, now demolished. His last years were not without anxiety, partly because of a recession in the real estate market, where he had invested so heavily and partly because of a transaction involving the defalcation of a banker friend. He died at East Cowes in 1835 and was buried at the base of the tower of the modest Gothic church which he had built on his estate.

At his death, Nash's reputation as an architect had sunk very low. His shallow stylistic eclecticism, indiscriminate use of stucco and iron, and ill-considered detailing made him a proper target for abuse by a rising generation bent on purity and vigor of detail and truth to materials. It was never possible, however, to ignore his masterly conduct of the metropolitan improvements of his time. He had given London a vital new artery, created a magnificent sequence of broad streets and picturesque parks and, in the process, liquidated many acres of squalid obsolescence.

Physically a little man and by no means handsome, with a bullet head and snub nose, Nash was endowed with extraordinary courage and resilience. Devious and ruthless on occasion, his fundamental integrity was never successfully assailed. He could be humorous and humane. Above all, he possessed a faculty of invention which enabled him to create opportunities out of seemingly impossible situations. He was the first man since CHRISTOPHER WREN to propose a major replanning of London. Wren's proposal failed; Nash's succeeded.

JOHN SUMMERSON

WORKS

1789–1792, Jail and House of Correction, Carmarthen, England. 1791–1793, Saint David's Cathedral (rebuilding of west front), Abergavenny, England. 1792–1793, Jail, Cardigan, England. 1795–1798, Jail, Hereford, England. *1797, Casina, Dulwich, England. 1797, Southgate Grove, Middlesex, England. *1798–?, East Cowes Castle, Isle of Wight, England. 1800–1804, Luscombe Castle, Dawlish, Devonshire, England. c.1801–1803, Killymoon Castle, County Tyrone, Ireland. c.1802, Cronkhill, near Shrewsbury, England. c.1805, Longner Hall, Shropshire, England. 1805, Sandridge Park, Stoke Gabriel, Devonshire, England. *c.1806, Garnstone Castle, Herefordshire, England. *1806–1813, Childwall Hall, Lancashire, England. *1808, Aqualate Hall, Staffordshire, England. c.1808, Caerhayes Castle, Cornwall, England. *c.1808, Ravensworth Castle, County Durham, England. *c.1809, Knepp Castle, West Grinstead, Sussex, England. *1810, Rockingham House, County Roscommon, Ireland. 1810–1811, Blaise Hamlet, Bristol, England. 1811, Lough Cutra Castle, County Galway, Ireland. 1812–1827, Terrace Façades and Lodges, Regents Park; *1813–1814, Carlton House (suite of rooms on lower ground floor); *1813–1815, Langham House; London. *1813–1816, The Royal Lodge, Windsor, England. 1815–1821, The Royal Pavilion (remodeling and extension), Brighton, England. *1815–1830, Façades, Regent Street, London. *1818–1819, Shanbally Castle, County Tipperary, Ireland. *1819, Harmonic Institution, Regent Street; *1820–1821, Nash House, 14 Regent Street; 1822–1824, The Royal Mews, Pimlico; 1823, Suffolk Street Gallery; 1822–1825, All Souls Church, Langham Place; begun 1824, Park Village West and *Park Village East, Regents Park; 1824–1830, Buckingham Palace (rebuilding); *1826–1827, Saint Mary's Haggerston; 1826–1828, United Services Club, Pall Mall; 1827–1833, Carlton House Terrace and Carlton Gardens; London.

BIBLIOGRAPHY

COLVIN, HOWARD (editor) 1973 Volume 6 in *The History of the King's Works.* London: H. M. Stationery Office.

DAVIS, TERENCE (1966)1973 *John Nash, the Prince Regent's Architect.* Newton Abbot, England: David and Charles.

HOBHOUSE, HERMIONE 1975 *A History of Regent Street.* London: Macdonald & Jane's in association with Queen Anne Press.

MUSGRAVE, CLIFFORD 1959 *Royal Pavilion: An Episode in the Romantic.* London: Leonard Hill.

ROBERTS, HENRY D. 1939 *A History of the Royal Pavilion, Brighton.* London: Country Life.

SMITH, H. CLIFFORD 1931 *Buckingham Palace: Its Furniture, Decoration and History.* Introductory chapters on the building and site by Christopher Hussey. London: Country Life; New York: Scribner.

SUMMERSON, JOHN 1980 *The Life and Work of John Nash.* London: Allen.

TEMPLE, NIGEL 1979 *John Nash and the Village Picturesque.* Gloucester, England: Alan Sutton.

NEBELONG, J. H.

Johan Henrik Nebelong (1817–1872) was trained at the Academy in Copenhagen. From 1840 to 1853, he lived in Norway, where he was commissioned to build several public and private buildings such as the Customs Warehouse and Oscarshallen in Oslo. After his return to Denmark, he became a collaborator of MICHAEL G. B. BINDESBØLL in the building of the mental hospital at Oringe. He subsequently ran his own office in Copenhagen.

VILLADS VILLADSEN

NEDEHAM, JAMES

James Nedeham (?–1544) was a carpenter who in 1532 became the first craftsman to be appointed surveyor of the King's Works, a post previously held by clerics. In this position, Nedeham was an important administrator in Henry VIII's building works, and he also worked privately for Cardinal Wolsey and Thomas Cromwell, but his status as an architect is uncertain. He is, however, documented as making "platts" and "moulds" (designs and templates) for the magnificent hammerbeam roof of JOHN MOLTON's Great Hall at Hampton Court.

IAN CHILVERS

WORK

1532–1536, Great Hall (roof), Hampton Court Palace, Middlesex, England.

BIBLIOGRAPHY

COLVIN, HOWARD (editor) 1975– Volumes 3 and 4 in *The History of the King's Works.* London: H.M. Stationery Office.

HARVEY, JOHN (1947)1948 *Gothic England: A Survey of National Culture, 1300–1550.* 2d ed., rev. London: Batsford.

HARVEY, JOHN 1954 *English Mediaeval Architects: A Biographical Dictionary down to 1550.* London: Batsford.

SALZMAN, L. F. (1952)1967 *Building in England down to 1540: A Documentary History.* Corrected Reprint. Oxford: Clarendon.

NEGRO DI SANFRONT, ERCOLE

Ercole Negro di Sanfront (1541–1622), count, architect, engineer, and general, was born in Centrallo and died in Savigliano, Italy. He served in the army of Henry III of France before entering the service of Carlo Emanuele I of Savoy. Ennobled in 1589, he was appointed general of artillery in 1604 and later superintendent of fortresses. He served as governor of Savigliano in 1600–1604 and again from 1619 to 1622.

He built many fortifications but also designed churches and palaces. His most admired work is the Palazzo Cravetta (1620) in Savigliano. Sanfront's design for a large sanctuary, oval in plan, at Mondovi was selected, but later, Carlo Emanuele, who intended to use the building as a Savoy mausoleum, replaced it with a design by ASCANIO VITOZZI. The paucity of work by Sanfront and uncertainty of attribution makes a characterization of his ability difficult.

HENRY A. MILLON

WORKS

1606, Madonna dell'Olmo, Cuneo, Italy. (A)1620, Palazzo Cravetta, Savigliano, Italy. 1621, Chapels of Suffragio and Corpus Domini, Madonna della Pieve, Cuneo, Italy.

BIBLIOGRAPHY

BIANCO DI S. SECONDO, E. 1930 "E. Negro di Sanfront architetto e generale di Carlo Emanuele I." *Bolletino della Società Piemontese di Archeologia e Belle Arte* 14:18–32.

BRAYDA, CARLO; COLI, LAURA; and SESIA, DARIO 1963 *Ingegneri e architetti del sei e settecento in Piemonte.* Turin, Italy: Società Ingeneri e Architetti.

CARBONERI, NINO 1963 Volume 1, pages 24–25 in *Architettura, Mostra del Barocco Piemontese.* Turin, Italy: Catalogo a cura di Vittorio Viale.

PROMIS, C. 1871 "Gli ingegneri militare che operarono o scrissero in Piemonte dal 1300 al 1650." *Miscellanea di Storia Italiana* 12:591–602.

RODOLFO, G. 1930 "Lettere dell'architetto Ercole Negro Marchese di Sanfront." *Bolletino della Societa Piemontese di Archeologia e Bella Arti* 4:36–38.
ROSSO, G. 1935 "Il progetto archetipo del Santuario di Mondovi e la sua rielaborazione." *Comunicazione della Reale Deputazione Subalpina di Storia Patria, Sezione di Cuneo.*

NELSON, PAUL

Paul Nelson (1895–) was born in Chicago and was educated at Princeton University. He went to Paris as an art student before World War I, volunteered as an aviator in the Lafayette Escadrille during the war, and later worked in the atelier of AUGUST PERRET. Practicing as an architect in France between the wars, he was appointed chief architect of hospital design and construction at Lille in the 1930s, where he pioneered research in hospital design. Associated with Fernand Léger, Hans Arp, and Joan Miró in Paris, he designed the "Suspended House" in 1937–1938 which was widely exhibited in Europe and the United States.

REGINALD MALCOLMSON

NENCIULESCU, NICOLAE

Nicolae Nenciulescu (1879–1973), a Rumanian architect, graduated from the Ecole des Beaux-Arts in Paris in 1910. For a short while, he worked for VICTOR A. F. LALOUX who, together with AUGUSTE PERRET, influenced his early work. He was also influenced, as was an entire generation of architects, by the architecture of the 1906 International Exhibition in Bucharest.

Nenciulescu taught at the Institute of Architecture in Bucharest from 1931 to 1946. His early works were mostly an interpretation of neoclassical architecture and French eclecticism. In the 1930s, he was concerned with finding a synthesis of the current architectural trends. His later buildings exhibit a new plasticity free of any stylistic coercion from the past. His most important achievement in monumental architecture is the Royal Palace (1928–1937; now Palace of the Republic) in Bucharest.

CONSTANTIN MARIN MARINESCU

WORKS

1914, Administration Building and Houses, Paper Factory Betea, Bacău, Rumania. 1916, Sărindar Theater, C. Mille Street; 1921, Apartment Building, 50 Boulevard Republicii; 1925, Palace of Agricultural Ministry (extension); 1928–1937, Royal Palace (now Palace of the Republic); 1930, Office Building Generala; 1936, National Bank of Rumania; Bucharest. 1936, Maritime Sanatorium, Eforie, Rumania.

BIBLIOGRAPHY

IONESCU, GRIGORE 1965 Volume 2 in *Istoria Arhitecturii in Romania.* Bucharest: Editura Academiei Republicii Romaîne.
IONESCU, GRIGORE 1969 *Arhitectura in Romania; Perioda anilor 1944–1969.* Bucharest: Editura Academiei Republicii Socialiste Romaîia.
IONESCU, GRIGORE 1972 "Saptezeci si cinci de ani de la infiintarea invatamintului de arhitectura din Romania." *Arhitectura* 20:35–42.
LUPU, NICOLAE GH. 1975 "Nicolae Gr. Nenciulescu (1879–1973)." *Arhitectura* 23, no. 1:49–55.
MAMBRIANI, ALBERTO 1969 *L'Architettura Moderna nei Paesi Balcanici.* Bologna, Italy: Capelli.
PATRULIUS, RADU 1973–1974 "Contributii Romanesti in Arhitectura Anilor '30." *Arhitectura* 21, no. 6:44–52; 22, no. 1:53–59.
PICA, DOMENICO 1938 *Nuova Architettura nel Mondo.* Milan: Hoepli.
SASARMAN, GHEORGHE 1972 "Inceputurile gindirii teoretice in arhitectura româneasča (1860–1916)." *Arhitectura* 20, no. 6:44–46.

NENOT, HENRI-PAUL

Henri-Paul Nénot (1853–1934) studied at the Ecole des Beaux-Arts and was a student of C. A. QUESTEL and CHARLES GARNIER. He was the architect of new buildings for the Sorbonne, restoring and expanding the existing seventeenth-century structures. It is the eclectic master's largest and finest work. Nénot is also the architect of the League of Nations complex in Geneva (1927–1937).

JAMES WARD

WORKS

1878, Architectural Restorations, Delos, Greece. 1882–1901, La Nouvelle Sorbonne; 1911, L'Institute Oceanographique; Paris. 1927–1937, Palace of the League of Nations (with others), Geneva.

BIBLIOGRAPHY

FAVIER, JEAN 1937 "Le Palais de la Société des Nations à Genève, par MM. Nénot, Broggi, Flégenheimer, LeFèvre et Vago, architectes." *Construction Moderne* 52:26–38.
FAVIER, JEAN 1938 "Salon 1938: La Rétrospective Paul-Henri Nénot (1853–1934)." *Construction Moderne* 53:527–530.
"Henri-Paul Nénot, Royal Gold Medalist, 1917." 1917 *Architectural Review* 42:5–10.
LANCHESTER, H. V. 1934 "Henri-Paul Nénot." *Architect and Building News* 140:351.
"Les Maîtres de l'Architecture Française." 1895 *Construction Moderne* 11:325–328.

LOUVET, A. 1935 "Paul-Henri Nénot (1853–1934)." *L'Architecture* 48:241–244.

NÉNOT, HENRI-PAUL 1895 *La Nouvelle Sorbonne.* Paris: Colin.

NÉNOT, HENRI-PAUL 1903 *Monographie de La Nouvelle Sorbonne.* With an introduction by C. Gréard. Paris: Imprimerie Nationale.

ROBERTSON, HOWARD 1937 "The League of Nations Buildings, Geneva. . . ." *Architect and Building News* 149:118–121.

NERING, JOHANN ARNOLD

Johann Arnold Nering (1659–1695) was born of a Dutch family in Wesel, Germany. In 1676, he was granted a scholarship to study military engineering in Berlin, and from 1677 to 1679 he traveled at government expense to continue his studies, spending a considerable time in Italy. In 1678, he became an engineer, in 1685 an engineer-colonel on the Brandenburg (Prussian) General Staff, and, in 1691, chief building director for the elector of Brandenburg, a position which gave him almost exclusive control over architecture in Berlin until his death.

His first work as an engineer was building sluices and fortifications, mainly in Berlin, where he erected the Leipziger Tor (Leipzig Gate), a monumental conclusion to the fortifications begun by JOHANN GREGOR MEMHARDT. Beginning in 1679, he worked continuously on the Berlin Stadtschloss (town palace). Notable are the sumptuous festival hall (*Alabastersaal*) built in the fashion of a Palladian (see ANDREA PALLADIO) Corinthian hall with rhythmical pilaster orders formed à la FRANCESCO BORROMINI, and the gallery (1685–1690) with its multistoried pillar-arcades, set between the apartment of the elector and that of his wife, as well as the two story pillar-arcade overlaid by a colossal half-column order in the courtyard. Nering was involved in both the first building phase (1688–1690) and, most probably, the second, re-building phase (1691–1695), a correction of the first to adjust it to Borromini's Oratory courtyard. (The ascription of the second phase to Nicodemus Tessin the Younger [see TESSIN FAMILY] is dubious.)

In 1684–1685, for the Elector Frederick III, he built the chapel of Köpenick Castle, near Berlin, and expanded Oranienburg Castle (Brandenburg) to a three-wing structure with an arcaded gallery enclosing the court. In 1688, the elector entrusted him with the planning and building of the Berlin district of Friedrichstadt, which was intended for the accommodation of the Huguenots who, in 1685, had started moving into Brandenburg. Built on a rectangular street grid, Friedrichstadt lay outside the fortifications, south of the Boulevard Unter den Linden and west of Friedrichswerder. Nering supervised the erection of over 300 two-story dwellings and also, for the nobility, built several palaces in a restrained Palladian style after his own plans (for example, the Palais Danckelmann [1689–1690]). He also created urbanistic accents: the Lange Brücke (1692–1694), a stone bridge connecting the old town with the electoral residence district, on which an equestrian statue of Friedrich Wilhelm, the Great Elector, was to be erected; and the French Merchants' House near the Münzturm (Tower of the Mint [1689–1690]). In 1695, he began the first monumental secular building of the Berlin baroque, the Zeughaus (arsenal), on plans he had developed from a design by FRANÇOIS BLONDEL. His sudden death in 1695 interrupted the work; it was continued by ANDREAS SCHLÜTER and completed in 1710 by JEAN DE BODT. Also in 1695, Nering began work on the Lützenburg Castle (later called Charlottenburg) for the wife of the elector. Built as a country house, it combined an organization derived from the French—oval, domed main hall projecting from the central façade, and side wings forming a court—with Palladian façade ornamentation—large Corinthian half-columns set on high pedestals—and with a motif from Borromini—concave walls in the spaces between. Also in that same year, Nering's designs for the Parochial Church were ready for building. In 1696–1703, it was erected after reduced and altered plans by Martin Grünberg. Nering had planned a wide rectangular center surrounded by a four-conch design, with domed roofs, a high central lantern, and an entrance hall surmounted by a pediment. In this design, the ideal type of Protestant church architecture—a centralized interior space flooded with light—was created with monumental forms that combined Palladian motifs (the entrance hall) with others derived from Borromini (the concave walls inset on the conch façades, the lantern) and from Rome (the attic) in a masterly solution; it is the most mature work in Nering's oeuvre. The art-historical appraisal of this architect remains a matter of dispute; overshadowed by Schlüter, he is frequently underestimated. With his origins in the Dutch tradition, he converted French and Palladian, as well as Roman-Borrominesque elements into an independent style. Though he did not possess extraordinary artistic talent, his excellent training enabled him to create monumental architecture in a sober baroque-classicist style well suited to the royal ambitions of the elector.

FRITZ-EUGEN KELLER
Translated from German by
Beverley R. Placzek

WORKS

*1679–1681, Elector's Apartments, Berlin Castle. *1681–1685, Alabastersaal, Berlin Castle. *1683, Leipzig Gate, Berlin. 1684–1685, Chapel, Köpenick Castle, near Berlin. *1685, Orangery, Berlin Castle. 1687, Barby Castle (executed by Giovanni Simonetti), Saxony, Germany. *1687–1689, Mews, Dorotheenstadt, Berlin. *1687–1690, Castle Church, Königsberg, East Prussia (now Kalingrad, Russia). *1687–1695, Courtyard (remodeling), Berlin Castle. 1688–1695, Friedrichstadt Master Plan; *1689–1690, Danckelmann Palace; Berlin. 1689–1695, Oranienburg Castle (expansion), Brandenburg, Germany. 1692–1694, Lange Brücke (later Kurfürstenbrücke), Berlin. *1692–1695, Friedrichsthal Castle, near Oranienburg, Germany. *1693, Gross-Hollstein Castle (executed by Georg Heinrich Kranichfeld), East Prussia. 1695, Arsenal (executed after altered plans by Martin Grünberg, Andreas Schlüter, and Jean de Bodt), Berlin. 1695, Lützenburg Castle (altered and expanded by JOHANN FRIEDRICH EOSANDER), near Berlin.

BIBLIOGRAPHY

BOECK, WILHELM 1938 *Oranienburg.* Berlin: Deutscher verein für Kunstwissenschaft.

BORRMANN, RICHARD 1893 *Die Bau- und Kunstdenkmäler von Berlin.* Berlin: Springer.

FRITSCH, GEORG 1930 *Die Burgkirche zu Königsberg in Preussen und ihre Beziehungen zu Holland: Ein Beitrag zur Neringforschung.* Konigsberg, Germany: Leupold.

GEYER, ALBERT 1936 Volume 1, pages 59–60, 66–75, 77–79 in *Geschichte des Schlosses zu Berlin.* Berlin: Deutscher Kunstverlag.

HEMPEL, EBERHARD 1965 Pages 207–209 in *Baroque Art and Architecture in Central Europe.* Harmondsworth, England: Penguin.

KELLER, FRITZ-EUGEN 1980 "Zur Datierung der Planvorschläage Nicodemus Tessins des Jungeren für das Schloss Lützenburg." Pages 39–65 in Wolfgang Ribbe (editor), *Von der Residenz zur City, 275 Jahre Charlottenburg.* Berlin: Colloquium.

KUHN, MARGARETE 1955 *Schloss Charlottenburg.* Berlin: Deutscher Verein für Kunstwissenschaft.

LADENDORF, HEINZ 1935 *Der Bildhauer und Baumeister Andreas Schlüter.* Berlin: Deutscher Verein für Kunstwissenschaft.

REUTHER, HANS 1969 *Barock in Berlin.* Berlin: Rembrandt.

SCHLIEDLAUSKY, GÜNTER 1942 *Martin Grünberg.* Burg bei Magdeburg, Germany: Hopfer.

NERVI, PIER LUIGI

Pier Luigi Nervi (1891–1979) was one of the great master builders of the twentieth century. His vision of an integrated design and construction process, his extraordinary "static intuition," his physical understanding of the behavior of reinforced concrete, and his inventive use of a material he practically created, ferrocemento, led him to the conception and realization of some of the most important architectural monuments of our time.

Born in Sondrio, Italy, Nervi graduated in civil engineering from the University of Bologna, Italy, in 1913. His ten year apprenticeship in the design office of the "Societa' per Costruzioni Cementizie" of Bologna was interrupted by three years service as an officer in the Corps of Engineers of the Italian army (1915–1918). In 1920 he established the "Societa' Ingg. Nervi e Nebbiosi" in Rome, which in 1932 became the "Impresa di Costruzioni Ingg. Nervi e Bártoli" and eventually the present "Studio Nervi, S.p.A." Three of his four sons joined his firm in the 1950s and were his faithful and inspired collaborators until his death.

The first work of Nervi to call international attention to his originality as a designer and a builder was the Municipal Stadium in Florence, Italy (1929–1932). The 24-feet cantilevered roof over its stands and its daring helicoidal stairs, together with the exposure of its entire structure, expressed a new conception of concrete aesthetic based on the correct interpretation of static spatial requirements and on an almost ethical concern with the optimal use of materials. Nervi eloquently explains his approach to structure in his writings. He dealt with the problems of structure from an intuitive viewpoint, based on years of reflection and practice. He considered concrete not as a dead material, but as the sinews of a human body. Nervi was aware of the influence of time and temperature on concrete and of the potentialities of its monolithic action, but preferred to interpret the monolithicity of statically indeterminate structures through simplified statically determinate models that allowed him to grasp the working of his structures on a purely physical basis.

The evolution of Nervi's structural thought and practice is exemplified by the eight hangars he designed and built between 1935 and 1942 for the Italian Air Force. The first two, at Orvieto, Italy, are covered by curved "lamella" roofs, 366 feet by 147 feet, of poured-in-place concrete, consisting of two series of arches meeting at 90 degree angles. The remaining six hangars at Orvieto, Orbetello, and Torre del Lago Puccini, Italy, consisted of the same framework of intersecting arches, but each arch consisted of short lengths of prefabricated trusses, with reinforcing steel dowels sticking out at the ends. The dowels of the four trussed elements meeting at a joint were welded in place and the joints were then grouted with a cement mortar to make the entire structure monolithic. When at the end of World War II, the Germans dynamited the hangars' buttresses, the "lamella" roofs crashed to the ground from a height of 35 feet, but most of the joints were undamaged.

The prefabricated hangars lead directly to the

Nervi.
Palazzeto dello Sport (with Annibale Vitellozzi).
Rome.
1956–1957

Nervi.
Palazzo dello Sport (interior with Marcello Piacentini).
Rome.
1958–1959

Great Hall B of the Exhibition Hall at Torino, Italy (1947–1949), where for the first time Nervi used ferrocemento structurally. Ferrocemento is a reinforced concrete type material consisting of a number of superimposed steel meshes surrounded by concrete mortar. The diffusion of the steel in the mortar gives this material a behavior analogous to that of steel, a tensile capacity far superior to that of reinforced concrete, and the capability of prefabrication of curved elements of very small thickness. The Torino hall is covered by a cylindrical, corrugated roof of ferrocemento elements, rigidly connected by poured-in-place concrete at their valleys and ridges. The buttresses supporting the roof, which fan out to the corrugations, have made this structure one of Nervi's best known works.

Nervi used similar prefabrication techniques—variously shaped elements poured in molds of ferrocemento—in what many engineers and architects consider his masterpiece, the Palazzetto dello Sport in Rome (1956–1957), which is covered by a circular dome 164 feet in diameter, supported by radial buttresses restrained by a prestressed concrete underground ring. The Palazzo dello Sport (1958–1959), covered by a dome 328 feet in diameter, was prefabricated with the same technique, but in addition exhibits the sculpted columns and the floor slabs stiffened by curved ribs, which became Nervi's signature and introduced in concrete construction new aesthetic elements entirely justified by structural requirements.

A different type of building with large span was designed by Nervi for the Conference Hall of UNESCO in Paris (1953–1958), in which the end walls consist of a continuous "folded plate" and the roof's floor slab waves up and down the main beams according to structural requirements. The adjoining Secretariat Building is supported on stilts, shaped by hyperbolic paraboloidal surfaces, which give them an extraordinary appearance.

Although Nervi is rightly famous for his prefabricated domes, he has shown his original thinking in all types of structures. Two of the three skyscrapers he designed—the Pirelli Tower (1955–1959) in Milan and the Place Victoria Tower (1962–1966) in Montreal—have unusual reinforced concrete skeletons. The Pirelli Tower is supported by four enormous shear walls, with free floor spans of 79 feet and 47 feet, while the structure of the Place Victoria Tower consists of a massive concrete core connected at the three mechanical floors to four external concrete buttresses by deep diagonal trusses supporting the intermediate floors. His only bridge—at Verona, Italy—repeats the concept of the roof of the UNESCO Conference Hall, leading to a continuous structure of great beauty. His outstanding building in the United States, (one of only four in America), Saint Mary's Cathedral in San Francisco (1966–1971), has a 144-foot roof that consists of four almost vertical, reticulated hyperbolic paraboloids, covered with travertine slabs. When confronted with the problem of creating a single room 98 feet by 820 feet for a paper manufacturing plant in Mantua (1961–1963), Italy, Nervi resorted to a roof hanging from the cables of a suspension bridge, whose towers, in the shape of the Greek letter lambda, were poured into forms of prefabricated slabs of ferrocemento that constitute the permanent surface of the buttresses. He used reinforced concrete during World War II to build a 400-ton cargo boat and later ferrocemento for the hull of a sailing ketch for his family.

If Nervi's beginnings were hard (each of his structures was built because he won a competitive bid), starting in 1950 the world gave him wide recognition. At his death in 1979, he had received eight honorary degrees, ten honorary memberships in institutes and academies, and ten awards, among them the Gold Medals of the American Institute of Architects, of the Royal Institute of British Architects, of the Institute of Structural Engineers in London, and of the Académie d'Architecture in Paris. A reserved and modest man, he basked in the thought of what his sons would achieve in continuing his work. His credo was clear and simple. He wrote in his lectures as Charles Eliot Norton Professor of Poetry at Harvard University in 1961–1962: "A technically perfect work can be aesthetically expressive, but there does not exist, either in the present or in the past, a work of art which is accepted and recognized as excellent from an aesthetic point of view, which is not excellent from a technical point of view. Good technology seems to be a necessary, although not a sufficient condition for good architecture."

MARIO G. SALVADORI

WORKS

*1929–1932, Municipal Stadium, Florence. *1935, Geodesic hangars, Orvieto, Italy. *1939–1942, Prefabricated hangars, Orvieto, Orbetello, Torre del Lago Puccini, Italy. 1942–1943, Cargo Boat. 1947–1949, Great Hall B, Exhibition Hall; 1949–1950, Hall C, Exhibition Hall; Torino, Italy. 1953–1958, UNESCO Secretariat Building and Conference Hall (with BERNARD ZEHRFUSS and MARCEL BREUER), Paris. 1955–1959, Pirelli Tower (with GIO PONTI and others), Milan. 1956–1957, Palazzeto dello Sport (with Annibale Vitellozzi); 1957–1959, Flaminio Stadium (with Antonio Nervi); 1958–1959, Palazzo dello Sport (with MARCELLO PIACENTINI); 1958–1960, Corso Francia elevated road; Rome. 1958–1961, Railway station, Savona, Italy. 1960–1961, Palace of Labor, Torino, Italy. 1960–1962, Bus Terminal, New York. 1961–1963, Burgo paper manufacturing plant, Mantua, Italy. 1961–1967, Australia Square Tower, Sydney. 1962–1966, Place Victoria Tower, Montreal. 1963–1968, Risorgimento Bridge, Verona, Italy. 1966–1971, Saint Mary's Cathedral, San Francisco. 1966–1971, Papal Audience Hall, Vatican City.

BIBLIOGRAPHY

DESIDERI, PAOLO; NERVI, PIER LUIGI, JR.; and POSITANO, GIUSEPPE 1979 *Pier Luigi Nervi.* Bologna, Italy: Zanichelli Editore.

HUXTABLE, ADA LOUISE 1960 *Masters of World Architecture: Pier Luigi Nervi.* New York: Braziller.

NERVI, PIER LUIGI 1945 *Scienza o arte del construire?* Rome: Edizioni della Bussola.

NERVI, PIER LUIGI (1955)1956 *Structures.* New York: F. W. Dodge. First published as *Construire correttamente.*

NERVI, PIER LUIGI 1965 *Aesthetics and Technology in Building: The Charles Eliot Norton Lectures, 1961–1962.* Translated by Robert Einaudi. Cambridge, Mass.: Harvard University Press.

NESFIELD, W. EDEN

One of the cleverest of English domestic architects, William Eden Nesfield (1835–1888) was the son of W. A. Nesfield, successively soldier, watercolorist, and landscape gardener of many early Victorian country houses. After schooling at Eton, the younger Nesfield was articled in 1851 to his father's friend WILLIAM BURN, the country house architect. Here he worked with many young Scots including his future partner R. NORMAN SHAW. They became close friends and in their spare time studied the architecture of A. W. N. PUGIN and the emerging Gothic Revival. In 1853, Nesfield left Burn and transferred to the office of his uncle ANTHONY SALVIN. This was followed in 1857–1858 by a prolonged tour in Europe.

On return, Nesfield set up on his own but for some time his practice was desultory. He spent the summers of 1859–1861 in France; the fruits of these visits were published as *Specimens of Mediaeval Architecture* (1862), one of the handsomest architectural books of the day. In 1863, he rejoined Shaw and began work in earnest, soon gaining sizable commissions through his father's and his own connections. His early buildings were refined, original, exuberantly decorative and extremely eclectic; they were also costly. Together Shaw and he evolved a gamut of domestic styles ranging around what were later to be known as Old English and Queen Anne. Between 1866 and 1869, Nesfield and Shaw were formally partners, but they never did a joint work and they drifted apart after 1870. Nesfield's architecture of the 1870s is as accomplished as ever, but it shows some falling off toward the end of the decade. He retired prematurely in 1880, married in 1885, and died in 1888.

Bohemian in his habits and friendships and manic-depressive by temperament, Nesfield was a brilliant draftsman, designer, and decorator of advanced aesthetic persuasions. He was dedicated to his craft but ill-fitted to the tedium of regular prac-

Nesfield. Bodrhyddan. Flintshire, Wales. 1872–1874

tice. Being well-off, he accepted jobs only if they interested him, shunned publicity, and regarded his work as a purely personal affair. He insisted on being accepted on equal terms by his clients at a time that this was rare. Though Nesfield never had close imitators, his importance in the development of the English vernacular revival is considerable. The playful inventiveness of his buildings has consistently attracted discerning admirers of architecture.

ANDREW SAINT

WORKS

1860–1861, Shipley Hall (farm buildings), Derbyshire, England. 1861–1862, Croxteth Hall (cottages), Lancashire, England. 1863, Sproughton Manor, Suffolk, England. *1863–1865, Combe Abbey, Warwickshire, England. *1864–1865, Regents Park (lodge), London. *1866–1868, Cloverley Hall, Shropshire, England. 1866–1874, Plas Kinmel and Kinmel Park, Denbighshire, Wales. 1867, Kew Gardens (lodge), London. 1872–1874, Bodrhyddan, Flintshire, Wales. 1872–1874, Plas Dinam, Montgomeryshire, Wales. 1872–1875, Barclays Bank, Saffron Walden; 1875, Newport Grammar School; Essex, England. 1877–1878, Babbacombe Cliff, Devonshire, England. 1877–1880, Gwernyfed Park, Breconshire, Wales. 1878, Loughton Park, Essex, England.

BIBLIOGRAPHY

BRYDON, J. M. 1896–1897 "William Eden Nesfield." *Architectural Review* 1:235–247, 283–295. Reprinted in Alistair Service (editor), *Edwardian Architecture and its Origins.* London: Architectural Press, 1975.

CRESWELL, H. B. 1897 "William Eden Nesfield, 1835–1888: An Impression and a Contrast." *Architectural Review* 2:23–32.

FORSYTH, JAMES 1901 "William Eden Nesfield." *Architectural Association Notes* 16, Aug.:109–111.

HEBB, JOHN 1903 "William Eden Nesfield." *Journal of the Royal Institute of British Architects* Series 3 10:396–400.

NESFIELD, W. EDEN 1862 *Specimens of Mediaeval Architecture.* London: Day.

SPIERS, R. P. 1898 "Development of Modern Architecture." *Magazine of Art* 21:83–88.

SAINT, ANDREW 1976 *Richard Norman Shaw.* New Haven: Yale University Press.

NEUFFORGE, JEAN FRANÇOIS DE

The architectural engraver Jean François de Neufforge (?–1791) was born near Liège, Belgium, and settled in Paris in 1738, studying with Pierre Edmé Babel, woodcarver and engraver of rococo ornament. His mid-century work on the measured architectural engravings of the ruins of Greece for JULIEN DAVID LE ROY's pioneering book nourished the archeological classicism that informed much of de Neufforge's own multivolume *Recueil élémentaire* (1757–1780), published with the MARQUIS DE MARIGNY's encouragement and Academy sanction. The nine hundred plates range from the exaggerated rustication of Serlian (see SEBASTIANO SERLIO) models in the first volume through the giant pilasters of Palladianism (see ANDREA PALLADIO) to the insistent freestanding columns of the French *goût grec.* This pattern book of façades and plans earned him the chronologically inaccurate epithet of the "Vignola (see GIACOMO BAROZZI DAVIGNOLA) of Louis XVI."

MYRA DICKMAN ORTH

BIBLIOGRAPHY

BRAHAM, ALLAN 1980 *The Architecture of the French Enlightenment.* London: Thames & Hudson.

ERICKSEN, SVEN 1974 *Early Neo-Classicism in France.* London: Faber.

HAUTECOEUR, LOUIS 1952 *Seconde moitié du XVIIIe siecle: Le style Louis XVI.*

GUILMARD, DÉSIRÉ 1880 *Les Maîtres ornémanistes.* Paris: Plon.

KALNEIN, WEND GRAF, and LEVEY, MICHAEL 1972 *Art and Architecture of the Eighteenth Century in France.* Harmondsworth, England: Penguin.

NEUFFORGE, JEAN FRANÇOIS DE 1747 *Nouveaux livres de plusieurs projets d'Autels et de Baldaquins inventés et dessinés par Neufforge, gravés par Babel. Livre I.* Paris: Chereau.

NEUFFORGE, JEAN FRANÇOIS DE (1757–1780)1967 *Recueil Elémentaire d'Architecture, Contenant Plusieurs Etudes des Ordres d'Architecture d'après l'Opinion des Anciens et le Sentiment des Modernes.* 3 vols. Farnborough, England: Gregg.

NEUMANN, F. I. M.

Franz Ignaz Michael (von) Neumann (1733–1788) was the son of the great JOHANN BALTHASAR NEUMANN whose assistant he became. Born in Würzburg, he had attained the position of engineering officer when he died there. Influenced by his study trips to France and probably also to Italy, he developed into an architect with a talent for construction. His plan of 1755 for the vaulting of his father's abbey church in Neresheim (Württemberg) already shows a novel technique that anticipates ideas of reinforced concrete construction. In Mainz, he erected private houses with massively built roofs as a protection against fire. His style combines French baroque classicism with *Zopf* forms (the German version of rococo-classicism). In the restorations of the cathedrals at Mainz

(1767–1774) and Speyer (1772–1778), there emerges a pseudomedieval spirit, rich in ideas.

HANS REUTHER
Translated from German by
Beverley R. Placzek

WORKS

1767–1774, Cathedral of Mainz (restoration), Germany. *1772–1778, Cathedral of Speyer (restoration), Germany. 1777–1779, Paradieshäuser, Mainz, Germany.

BIBLIOGRAPHY

HAAS, WALTER 1961 "Romanische Bauformen im 18. Jahrhundert: Zum Wiederaufbau des Speyerer Domes." *Pfälzer Heimat* 12:103ff.

HOFFMAN, ILSE 1938 *Der süddeutsche Kirchenbau am Ausgang des Barock.* Munich: Filser.

WEILER, CLEMENS 1937 "Franz Ignaz Michael von Neumann." *Mainzer Zeitschrift* 32:1–45.

NEUMANN, JOHANN BALTHASAR

Johann Balthasar Neumann (1687–1753) created some of the most commanding, complex, and impressive architecture in the West, designs conceived as compositions of architectural space. In them, walls and supporting structures are diminished, dissolved, or disguised. Space, no longer captured within solid matter, is articulated by open frameworks honed to a minimum and by vault shells arranged above them with elegant precision. Space becomes transparent and lucid, charged with direction and counterpoint, enriched by complexities, the unexpected, the startling. A plenitude of huge windows permits daylight to deluge the interior, and this radiance is orchestrated with dramatic certainty in relation to the space. Neumann promoted the ebullient integration of other artistic media—painting, statuary, stucco, color, gilding, metalwork, carving—to amplify the spatial resonance of the interior, to intensify its splendor and richness, and to specify its meaning.

This conception of design contrasted with traditional practice. Commonly in Western architecture, the continuous surface of wall had been employed to define the configuration of the interior. Only on occasion before Neumann's time, at moments during the Byzantine and medieval periods and again in the seventeenth century, had the relationship between mass and space departed from this norm. This alternative approach can be found in Byzantine churches such as Hagia Sophia and Hosios Loukos, in some Gothic cathedrals of the medieval era, and in several projects by FRANCESCO BORROMINI and FRANÇOIS MANSART, seventeenth-century contemporaries from Italy and France respectively.

Happily, Neumann lived during an age of intense building activity in central Europe, a time when, according to calculations by some, more construction relative to population size was being undertaken than at any period before or since. He enjoyed the active support of a family of great patrons, the Schönborns, who were lavish with commissions and funds. Neumann offered them his brilliance as a designer and a high level competence in completing tasks responsibly and with dispatch. As a result, in a career fully active from 1719 to 1753, he produced several score churches, almost two dozen palaces, and an imposing array of other buildings, utilitarian structures, and urban constructions. Ability and opportunity meshed for Neumann as they rarely do.

Neumann's architectural career—his training, patronage, and commissions—was tightly connected to his adopted city of Würzburg, at that time the seat of a prince-bishop. We have no indication that he initially traveled to Würzburg with architecture in mind. The seventh of eight children, he was born at Eger (now Cheb), located on the western fringe of Bohemia. Hans Christoph Neumann, his father, eked out a meager living as a weaver. At thirteen, Balthasar was settled in the founder's trade. But the youngster appears to have been ambitious, and he involved himself as well with hydraulics and the then fashionable art of fireworks display.

In 1711, Neumann settled in Würzburg in order to work as an apprentice in the huge foundry of Ignaz Kopp, where, among other commissions, the artillery for the Franconian military was produced. Kopp was an obvious place of employment for a fledgling founder, and since Neumann's mother, Rosina Grassold, had come from Würzburg, he may have had family connections to recommend him to the foundry. This trade did not hold him long, however, and within a year Neumann was learning architecture, geometry, and surveying. Soon he quit his job at Kopp in order to devote himself completely, with loans from the city of Eger, to his architectural studies. His mentor during these years was Andreas Müller, a captain in the corps of engineers; Neumann also would practice architecture as a career officer. This coupling of professions was not uncommon at the time, since military training provided instruction in drawing and surveying, in geometry and mathematics, disciplines basic to the study of architecture.

Already by 1713 Neumann was demonstrating an independent turn of mind in architectural matters. He invented an *instrumentum architecturae,* a device that provided the different diameters for Tuscan, Doric, and Ionic orders at given heights. This method of relating width to height contrasted with the standard practice of establishing a set diameter as the generator of various column heights. Neumann subordinated received theory about column proportions to pragmatic concerns: once he had established an appropriate floor height relative to a building's purpose, he could apply a properly proportioned order.

The following year, 1714, Neumann began his thesis project, a detailed map of Würzburg, which he completed in 1715. By this time he had taken up work with Josef Greising, the major builder within the Würzburg area during the first two decades of the eighteenth century, but a modest and unadventurous designer. Neumann traveled with Greising to various undertakings throughout Franconia and in this way must have experienced much of the architectural legacy of the region.

Neumann's architectural career was interrupted for two years when he participated in the 1717 Belgrade campaign of Prince Eugene; afterward he undertook extensive travel to Vienna, through Austria and Bohemia, and within northern Italy. Upon his return to Würzburg in 1718, his career as a military officer commenced when he was commissioned Captain of the Engineers; he advanced rapidly during the next years, and by 1744 attained the rank of full colonel. After his return, he also initiated an independent architectural practice, constructing a group of row houses in Würzburg. In 1725 he married Eva Maria Schild; they had eight children, one of whom, Franz Ignaz Michael Neumann (1733–1785), worked as an architect, although not with the spectacular success of his father. But in 1719 a series of events began to take place that would enable Neumann to develop and realize his potential as a designer.

In that year, Johann Philipp Franz Graf Schönborn was elected prince-bishop of Würzburg. As both secular and ecclesiastical head of the Würzburg territory, he immediately initiated the planning of a palace on a grand scale for himself. He appointed Neumann his architect for this operation, introduced him to other members of the extensive Schönborn clan, including his uncle, the patriarchal Lothar Franz, Archbishop and Elector of Mainz, and brought him into association with the Bohemian-trained architect, Johann Dientzenhofer (see DIENTZENHOFER BROTHERS), who had completed both Fulda Cathedral and the monastery church at Banz within the decade. Two years later, both Müller and Greising died, leaving Neumann as the only local architect of stature. Neumann quickly capitalized on this situation by promoting legislation that required his approval of all construction undertaken in the city. The student of five years earlier had now established himself legally as final architectural authority within the municipality. The jurisdiction of this position was extended in 1729, when Neumann was named Baudirektor responsible for all military, ecclesiastical, and civil building in the bishoprics of Würzburg and Bamberg, and for the private palaces of Friedrich Karl, prince-bishop of Würzburg and Bamberg. In 1733, Neumann was named consultant of the entire military and civil building in the important city of Trier, further broadening his architectural authority.

Of greater significance for Neumann's achievement as architect was his involvement with the Schönborn family. Their patronage and connections enriched his education and provided him with an extensive list of imposing commissions. He in turn possessed the creative and managerial ability to master this range of work.

Schönborn patronage was similar in scope and quality to that of the Medici in an earlier time. The Schönborns' political, spiritual, and cultural dominance of much of Franconia, Baden-Württemberg, and the Pfalz had already by the 1740s given rise to the term *Schönbornzeit* to denote the best of times. Lothar Franz, whose infectious enthusiasm for architecture spurred on similar involvements in his nephews Johann Philipp Franz and Friedrich Karl, passionately pursued any building enterprise with which he could in some way involve himself. But it was the nephews who created the working context for Neumann. Johann Philipp Franz started him on his largest single commission, the Residenz (1719–1753) in Würzburg, and Friedrich Karl was directly or indirectly responsible for most of Neumann's ecclesiastic projects. Neumann was first and foremost a Schönborn architect, and the architecture sponsored by the Schönborns excelled because of Neumann.

Neumann's initial association with the Schönborns was as architect of what was to become one of the largest, most glorious palaces in Europe. During the seventeenth and eighteenth centuries, many imposing residences were erected by rulers of small territories. In Würzburg, as elsewhere, building intensified the economy of the entire principality, developed political and financial power, and permitted the systematic build-up of an orderly bureaucracy. The palace promoted political prestige within a context of competition with rivals, and it satisfied the compulsion for impressive representation: symbol of the absolute, well-organized, well-off state. Court and government became closely meshed within the program of a palace, which included a dwelling for the sovereign, offices for officials, and apartments for bureaucrats and civil servants. Since state and church were united in the person of the prince-bishop, the palace chapel was large and luxuriously finished. Often, though not inevitably, palace construction imposed compulsory labor and additional taxation on the citizens.

In 1720, after a year of planning the Würzburg Residenz, Neumann supervised the start of construction. He remained in charge of the undertaking, at times together with, at times in spite of, other architects who were involved over the years: Johann Dientzenhofer (until 1723), JOHANN MAXIMILIAN VON WELSCH (until 1729), and JOHANN LUCAS VON HILDEBRANDT (until 1738). After completion of the structural shell in 1744, Neumann supervised decoration of the interior, which was still in progress when he died. The scale of the palace seemed out of all proportion to the size of the bishopric supporting it, and Lothar Franz lamented that the enterprise would ruin the Schönborn family. But Johann Philipp Franz was obsessed with the undertaking and would not be cajoled into reducing its size. His quest for building funds was continuous and unending, and he rented a house on the edge of the palace site to follow the daily progress of construction.

At the Residenz, as at other palace projects, design and construction proceeded hand in glove. Moreover, the process of design was a collective undertaking that included the patrons and several architects. In the initial stages of planning, Neumann had to prepare designs according to Johann Philipp Franz's ideas, accommodate proposals by Lothar Franz and Friedrich Karl, integrate contributions from the architects Maximilian von Welsch, Lucas von Hildebrandt, Johann Dientzenhofer, ROBERT DE COTTE, and GERMAIN BOFFRAND, and acknowledge material on palaces sent to Johann Philipp Franz from ten different European cities.

At the outset, Lothar Franz questioned Neumann's maturity as an architect and pushed to have him travel and broaden his architectural education. With Neumann deeply involved in his palace undertaking, Johann Philipp Franz resisted. In 1721, he did permit Neumann some study time with the book and print collections of the Uffenbachs in Frankfurt (the collection contained almost every work on architecture published by that time and large numbers of *vedute* from France, Holland, England, and Italy), and two years later Neumann spent several months in Paris and vicinity consulting about the Residenz, noting the latest in French taste, hiring specialists to work on the Residenz, and buying great amounts of merchandise, from coaches to doorlocks.

Neumann. Residenz. Würzburg, Germany. 1719–1753

In August 1724, the egoistic, impulsive Johann Philipp Franz was poisoned while on the hunt, and the competing family of the Huttens assumed the political and religious leadership of Würzburg. Work on the Schönborn enterprise of the Residenz was virtually brought to a halt. In 1729, with the election of Friedrich Karl as prince-bishop of Würzburg and Bamberg, the Schönborn hegemony reasserted itself in the bishopric, and work on the Residenz was resumed.

The Residenz has a U-shaped plan with four interior courts. Neumann marked centers and corners of the entrance, garden, and flank elevations with projecting polygonal, oval, and rectangular pavilions, some domed, some carrying pediments. Doric columns frame the many entrances, the order of the second story, where used, is composite. Elaborately carved frames surround the windows, and their pediments, whether triangular or broken, are filled with sculpture. Originally, the surface of the building was painted a warm yellow ocher, the architectural elements stood out in silver gray, and the sculpture and carving were of a luminous white, with parts gilded and multicolored. Together with an elaborate, curved gate that defined the entry court, this color combination gave the exterior a spectacularly festive appearance.

Inside, for the major public areas, Neumann created one of the grandest sequences of space known in the West. Coaches were driven directly into a somber, heavily vaulted hall supported by sturdy Doric columns and powerful herms. The visitor demounted and could proceed to the garden through an oval Gartensaal, covered by a flat, low-set vault supported by widely spaced columns, and ringed by an ambulatory. From this point one can also ascend the stairs to the Kaisersaal. The grandiose, freestanding stair lifts to an intermediate landing, from which two flights return in the

Neumann. Residenz (stair). Würzburg, Germany. 1719–1753

opposite direction to the main level. As the stairs rise, they leave the darker, columned ground floor and lift into a completely open, light-flooded space approximately 20 by 30 meters, spanned by the sweep of a single vault. On this enormous surface, Tiepolo later painted a magnificent representation of Europe, Asia, Africa, and America. A broad walkway permits the visitor to perambulate the entire perimeter of the hall at the stair's top, offering many views of the fresco. Skeptics at the time maintained that Neumann would never be able to construct a single vault of this enormous size and to support it by walls carved away by vast windows. He succeeded with characteristic brilliance. By employing blocks of a light volcanic tuff for the vault, locking the stones together with iron clamps, and placing the whole in a thick bed of mortar, he created a primitive form of reinforced concrete shell, producing a remarkably stable vault.

From the dramatic sweep and overwhelming spectacle of this space, the visitor is led into a smaller, rectangular hall (the area above the vestibule) as extraordinary in its way as was the stair. In a room illuminated by only three windows placed along one of its short walls, Antonio Bossi created a composition of richly plastic stucco on the walls and coved ceiling. Realized in white on white alone, the Weissersaal with its startling but abstract character forms a vivid contrast both with the stair and with the Kaisersaal to which it is the immediate prelude.

The visitor must change direction 90 degrees in order to enter the Kaisersaal. This domed, oval space, the culmination of the imposing sequence, overpowers with its brilliance and splendor. Walls are dissolved by windows and mirrors, above them lunettes arch generously into the vault. Columns are transformed by patterns of colored, shimmering marble, and the sweep of gilded stucco is picked up by crystal chandeliers. Three Tiepolo paintings are arranged on the long axis of the vault, and porcelain-white, larger than lifesized sculpture is located in wall niches. The floor is a composition of colored tiles. Architecture and the other arts are brought together in the radiance of direct, reflected, and refracted light.

Of the other, almost two dozen palaces that Neumann worked on in whole or in part, alone or with other architects, as new designs or as remodelings, those that were built and those that remained projects, none can match the scale, grandeur, and completeness of the Residenz. Several of these undertakings, however, are imposing interpretations in their own right. The elevations for Werneck (1733–1745) and Schönbornlust (1748–1752), for example, are spirited, decorative ensembles, in which windows, orders, and sculpture are joined in prominent display, reducing the surface of the wall to an aesthetically neutral plane. And the internal spatial sequences in several projects were extraordinary. Neumann's unexecuted designs for both Stuttgart (1747–1750) and the Hofburg (1746–1747) in Vienna locate multitiered, free-standing stairs in open, light-saturated spaces. The movement of the spectator is choreographed through and up into and within variously formed, layered spaces, spaces slotted into spaces within light.

The most unusual of these other palace projects, however, was the Residenz Saint Damiansburg (1728–1750) at Bruchsal. Neumann was not involved when construction began in 1722, but four years later client and the first architect met an impasse. Unable to agree on an appropriate design for the main stair, the architect was dismissed, and Neumann brought to Bruchsal in early January 1728 as supervising architect, a position he held until his death. According to the already established design parameters, the stairs were to be located within an oval unit located in a court in the center of the palace. Attached to the flanks of the oval were rectangular spaces for the vestibule and Gartensaal. Working with these existing elements, Neumann inserted cylindrical walls into the oval and drew a double flight of stairs up around them. He then carved away the walls of the cylinder with large, arched openings, mirroring the huge windows that dissolve the oval walls. The top of the cylinder became a free-standing platform connected by bridges to the stairs and to rectangular rooms located along either flank. As the visitor approaches, the spaces above are fragments partially seen. As one ascends the stairs, somber light from the court windows becomes brighter, the mass of the architecture less, until the stairs reach a bridge and the oval platform. Here, suspended on bridges and platform, in an arena free of supports, without mass, and flooded by light, the visitor seems released within the space, the equivalent of weightless levitation through the medium of architecture.

Over this area, a dome frescoed by Johannes Zick with representations from the history of the bishopric elegantly caps the space. Beyond the bridges in each direction are the formal reception rooms richly adorned with patterned orders, stucco, gilt, frescoes, festive paneling, and crystal chandeliers.

On ground level, a severe Doric order and deeply carved vault mark the rectangular vestibule. A tunnel leads from the vestibule into the center of the cylinder and from there through a second tunnel into a space made grottolike by fountains, sea shells, and a low-slung vault. The architectural elements in the tunnel intentionally are left rough-carved, as if abandoned incomplete. The character of these rectangular areas contrast with the elaboration of the formal rooms located above them.

Neumann's central spaces at Bruchsal, like those of the Residenz, although on a different scale and by other means, are stunningly composed. The various themes of architectural severity, rusticity, and sophistication, of the partially seen and the completely revealed, of the closed and the open, the heavy and the airy, the dark and the light, are made wonderful, complex, compelling, and resplendent.

Throughout his career, Neumann was involved with palace projects. His churches, however, are greater in number and design variety. Where the limitations of patrons' demands and programmatic considerations were minimal, the epic power of Neumann's architectural language is boldest, clearest, and richest. In church after church, employing a great number of different design strategies, he achieved extraordinary spatial

Neumann. Augustusburg Palace (main stair). Brühl, Germany. 1741–1750

Neumann. Saint Damiansburg Palace. Bruchsal, Germany. 1728–1750

compositions. He explored the relation between spatial figures, their arrangement within a differently shaped outer shell, and the lucid transparency of the whole. He choreographed movement in the architecture and for the user, orchestrated light, and promoted the elaboration of all this by means of other artistic media, such as painting, sculpture, stucco, and gilding.

Schönborn intervention in the church projects, unlike that in the palaces, concerned details, not the larger dispositions of plan, elevation, and space. As clients, the Schönborns determined to a great extent the nature of decoration: how much painting, sculpture, stucco; according to what theme; placed where. Technical questions, such as the ingredients of plaster or the manufacture of porcelain, were of interest to them. But the Schönborns never attempted to establish the basics of church design nor did they suggest reworking a design that had been presented. With amused irony, they referred to their architects as godly directors of construction. Proposals were accepted or rejected whole. Rather than attempting to manipulate the elements of one master's design, they would express dissatisfactions or uncertainties by requesting alternatives from other masters, both before and during the planning stage, at times even after construction had begun. The Schönborns then selected what appeared to them to be the more successful solution.

Neumann's first church, the Schönborn chapel (1721–1736) attached to Würzburg Cathedral, demonstrates his decisively independent design abilities within the context of another architect's work. Maximilian von Welsch had started the building as a circular domed structure with rectangular chapels located on the cross axis, but shortly before April 1721, Neumann proposed a modification of this project. This reorganization reveals his commitment to the primacy of architectural space and introduces the three architectural components which he would continue to use in order to achieve and articulate his spatial compositions: the free-standing, load-bearing column, the three-dimensionally curved arch, and the continuous vault shell.

Accepting von Welsch's circular configuration, Neumann placed paired columns in front of the wall, connected them with three-dimensionally curved arches, and located a dome on pendentives above them. The curved outer wall was kept separate from these elements, so that the circular domed unit seemed inserted into a cylinder, one form within another, like a bolt slid into its casing. By changing the side chapels from rectangles to ovals, Neumann augmented and intensified the spatial, curvilinear implications of the central area. His modifications of von Welsch's project were minimal, the consequences decisively different. As a first design, at the outset of his career and within the context of an established master's work, the achievement is all the more striking.

Neumann's next major commission, the huge Benedictine monastery church at Münsterschwarzach (1727–1743), shows the ease and effectiveness with which he could work on a monumental scale. He began with a traditional church type, the Latin-cross basilica with crossing dome and two-tower façade. But inside he translated the standard architectural elements of this type—piers faced with pilasters, entablature, barrel vault with cross arches—into a massive, sculptural framework that defined the enormous, vertical spaces of chapels and vault lunettes. Huge windows extensively eliminated any solid, exterior surface, filling the depth of the wall with light. Nave and two-bay choir became spaces of deep, luminous relief realized on a monumental scale. Within this setting, the crossing was treated as a powerful spatial center of the interior. Derived from the free-standing, domed unit of the Schönborn chapel, Neumann's design raised the paired columns on tall pedestals and located a steep dome illuminated by oculi above. The towering cylindrical forms created a magnificent crescendo within this imposing interior. Church and attached monastery were razed in the early nineteenth century, victims of the secularization imposed by Napoleon.

At Gössweinstein (1729–1739), Neumann used a similar shell for a local parish and pilgrimage church. Inside he abandoned his Münsterschwarzach interpretation and, by means of layerings and frames, translated the internal elevation into a space-impregnated wall. The nave vault is made into a flat surface that possesses the papery quality of folded, bent, and embossed cardboard.

Neumann. Benedictine Abbey Church. Münsterschwarzach, Germany. 1727–1743

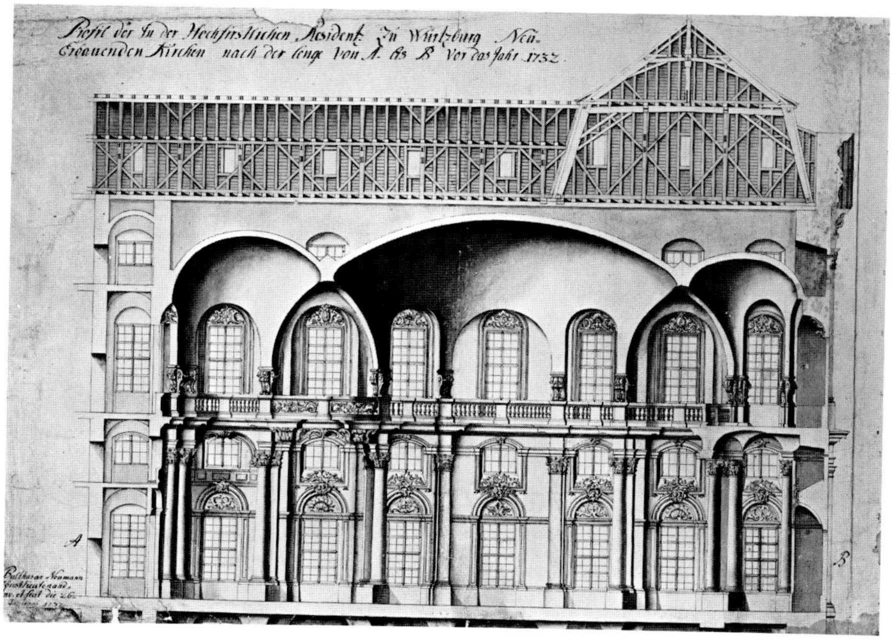

Neumann.
Palace Church, Residenz.
Würzburg, Germany.
1730–1743

Neumann.
Palace Church, Residenz.
Würzburg, Germany.
1730–1743

In crossing, transept, and choir the vaults are treated as partial surfaces that reveal a second continuous layer above. These disparate elements are formed in such a way that they refer to and complement one another: diversity and unity in balance. The decorative scheme—cool, quiet, and unassuming—confirms the understated architecture of the interior. Not a place of exuberance and spectacle, Gössweinstein urges introspection and silent contemplation, an unusual pilgrimage goal within the context of the jubilant architecture of south Germany.

Neumann's most demanding interpretation of the 1720s and 1730s was the church for the Würzburg Residenz (1730–1743). He placed a longitudinal oval, with cross ovals attached to either end, in a rectangular shell. In elevation, these curved units consist of columns, pilasters, balcony, and deep vaults opened by lunettes. Their concave shapes hollow out the wall where they sweep to it and create sculptural frames for the huge windows that extensively supplant the wall with sheets of glass. The edges of the vaults are not arches or ribs but literally the thickness of the unit put on display. Here for the first time, Neumann reveals the vault as a shell, as he would do in the later churches of Kitzingen, Forchheim, Vierzehnheiligen, Vienna, and Neresheim. This vault shell, propped up on the point supports of the elevation framework, mirrors the plan below. The flat plane on which the visitor stands contrasts with the voluminous, space-filled zone above—a three-dimensional development of a two-dimensional geometry, in which space as form swells into shadow and light beyond.

This 1732 design is a colossal performance, combining seemingly contradictory elements into a complex unity. Ovoid forms are placed within a rectangular box. These forms are established absolutely by the ellipsoid vaults, yet are opened almost entirely to the exterior rectangle in elevation. The outer surface of the box consists of a glass plane, but masonry links that surface with the dynamically curvilinear interior. Light constitutes a major factor in the dematerialization of internal mass while presenting the final outer boundary. The longitudinal axis of the interior, culminating in the more somber altar ensemble, produces a directional thrust that is as imperative as the centralizing effect of the oval shapes. In short, a series of paradoxes is vigorously resolved, creating a design of dynamic balance. Neumann was forced to compromise the clarity of this project in the built church, due to the influence of von Hildebrandt and the desires of the client, yet its impact remains in this splendidly compelling space.

Neumann's other projects of these years, though not as complex, sophisticated, or demanding as those discussed, explore in more modest ways the creation of open, light-saturated space articulated by free-standing units. In each, he pursues this intention by different means: at Holzkirchen (1726–1730), a circular plan, an elevation assembled from discrete components, a hemispherical dome; at Bamberg (1730), a circle and Greek cross combined, using a free-standing cylindrical unit; at Trier (1734–1754), a longitudinal arrangement of nave and choir, a skeletal elevation of piers and frames, and an undulating barrel vault; at Werneck (1733–1745), an open-work oval cage established by piers and supporting a deep ovoid vault, the whole a compact version of the Residenz church; at Bruchsal (1738–1753), a Greek-cross plan, paper-thin walls, and a floating dome; at Heusenstamm (1739), a Latin-cross plan with wall piers employed in a conventional manner and a vaulting system that is a bland version of Gössweinstein; at Kitzingen (1740), a Greek cross with unequal arms, an elevation consisting of neutral walls and a free-standing, open unit, and a crossing marked by a bold circular vault on columns. At Würzburg, the Dominican Church (1741–1753), consisting of nave, aisles, and a choir without a transept was designed to appear like a medieval structure done in baroque. The Käppele (1740) and Gaibach (1740) are longitudinal churches containing detachable crossing units that support shallow pendentive domes. But whereas the Gaibach dome is ovoid and carried by square piers, the Käppele dome is circular and rests on paired columns. Weight and mass complement the static nature of the former, whereas the latter is treated as open and light, and is distinguished from the external fabric by a spatial layer, conveying the impression that it could be rotated on its axis. The Gaibach nave elevation has wall piers molded to concave frames; the Käppele also employs wall piers, but here they are related to a free-standing oval unit.

Between 1742 and 1747, Neumann designed five of his greatest churches. Three of them—Mainz, Langheim, and Vierzehnheiligen—were begun in 1742, although the last underwent several transformations until 1744. Vienna was designed in 1746, and planning for Neresheim began the following year. These commissions, representing some of Neumann's finest work, require closer attention.

For the Latin-cross plan of the Jesuit church at Mainz (1742–1746), Neumann composed an interior elevation consisting of three levels: a plain ground story, an elaborate main story, and a tall clearstory. In the nave, these three parts are treated as a slender grid standing before an unfigured wall opened by large windows. The cylinder of the crossing is realized as an attenuated set of supports below a steep dome, and the entire unit in turn is snugly fitted within an extensively opened cylindrical shell. Choir walls and vault are drawn in more closely around the altar. Space in the nave is vertical, open, and saturated with light, the longitudinal direction tempered by a suggestion of centralization in the coves and bays. The towering crossing and bold cross axis of the transept creates a strong caesura. From here, the visitor could enter the first bay of the choir but not further: beyond, the heavier mass of the elevation sheltered the altar. Procession from entrance to altar was measured and rhythmic; though the raised altar would have been clearly visible from the moment one entered, the interior unfolded with a calculated awareness of movement, each unit demanding its own attention.

Mainz was demolished in 1805–1811 following a destructive fire; the Cistercian abbey church at Langheim, designed in 1742, was never built. Neumann's Langheim project was for an immense church. The aerial spaces of the nave, created by means of a delicate vault and paired columns set on the cross axis, were bordered by more solidly realized aisles. The crossing, contained within massive piers, was interpreted as two cylinders, one within the other; rectangular transept arms bracketed its flanks. Space contracted in the choir, wall and vault became more massive, with more projecting and recessed solid parts and with considerable stucco decoration. Windows were smaller and fewer. The expansive, spatial drama of the long, richly contrasted and cavernous nave and crossing was drawn in to the more intimate, more solidly plastic choir, an area of relatively small dimensions. The festive nature of the choir was marked by its sculptural elaboration, its solemnity by the restricted light.

When Neumann designed Vierzehnheiligen (1742–1753) as a Latin-cross basilica similar to Langheim, he also produced a second project for his personal satisfaction. In this design, an oval unit partially engaged with the outer walls dominates the nave, the crossing is a free-standing cylinder established by four pairs of columns and a dome, and the choir consists of a cross oval partially embedded in the outer walls. Apse and transept arms are also given a circular form.

In 1744, Neumann was forced to change the design of Vierzehnheiligen. The local supervising architect had placed the choir too far to the east, so that the sacred ground of the fourteen helper saints would wind up in the nave rather than in the choir as intended. Neumann now developed a plan containing oval and circular units derived from his personal design in order to produce a church that would appropriately coincide with the holy area in the nave. A sequence of three ovals, smaller–larger–smaller, was arranged from entrance to choir. The ends of the smaller ovals push out the end walls, the larger unit is freestanding. To the west, a minor cross axis is established by altars set within oval spaces, a major axis in the east is created by means of substantial circular transepts. The free-standing forms consist of imposing frameworks of columns, balconies, and arches and are open to an extensively perforated outer wall. Oval and circular forms produce a compelling dynamic in their interaction with one another and with the outer wall, heightening the dramatic integration of a longitudinal and centralized interior.

The heart-shaped shrine of the fourteen helper saints, designed by Neumann's assistant Johann Jakob Michael Küchel, occupies the center of the central oval. Vibrant and lively, it intensifies the space, elaborating upon an already demanding multiplicity of readings. The interior is everywhere open to a flood of light, which reduces the substance of the framework elevation, emphasizing its delicate quality. Complementing this brilliant illumination is the treatment of surface. Gilding, silver, and pastel are arranged within the pervasive white of the interior. Though realized only after Neumann's death, these elements are integral to the whole, magnificently complementing his architecture.

Neumann's unexecuted project for the palace church of the Hofburg in Vienna (1746–1747) is one of his most spectacular performances. A large oval on the cross axis occupies the center, a circular unit is imposed on the entrance rectangle, a smaller one on the choir rectangle. Each of these areas is defined by a triple layer in elevation, the distinct planes being arranged concentrically in depth. Movement animates the open space: the contrast of choir and entrance within the symmetrical unity of the interior, the opposition of rectangular and curved units, and the tension between the static and contained qualities of choir and entrance and the expansive crescents of the oval. The luminous shading in Neumann's drawings demonstrates the importance of light. The dematerializing effect of light on the internal frameworks may be understood as analogous to the Residenz church or Vierzehnheiligen. The spectator would look toward the light through the openness of one layer to the next. Distinct in placement, each layer is informed with a specific rhythm as well. Yet in their articulation, these layers complement one another, so that a decisive definition of interior space is established by open borders. Neumann's ability to resolve conflict and paradox in a seemingly effortless manner is demonstrated by the creation of spaces with space, the drama of movement within symmetry, the complexity of elevations, and the brilliance of light.

At Neresheim, a Benedictine monastery church (1747–1753), Neumann composed a drama of motion, color, light, and surprise within the stately measure of an ordered whole. In an arena of sober purpose, he exhilarated the beholder with the elegant force of his architecture, matching human scale with monumentality, the pleasure of familiar things with grandeur.

Neresheim contains two cross ovals in the nave, the crossing and transept are made up of three longitudinal ovals, and two circular units constitute the choir. Undulating frames of columns, pilasters, arches, and piers supporting the oval and circular vaults are arranged free-standing within the enormous rectangle of outer walls. The interior is so lucid and open, the solid parts so reduced, that the whole space is visible from any spot in the church. Despite this transparency, the visitor experiences new impressions with every step: the relationships of parts shift and change, spaces are defined, lead to other areas, are in turn recalled. Direction, counterpoint, and focus are handled with dramatic certainty.

Light deluges the interior, becoming a complement of the space. Spilling into the church through enormous windows, clear light dematerializes substance by means of highlight and shadow, backlighting and raking light. On gray days, the interior collects light like a gigantic lens, appearing brighter inside than the day outside. The dominant white tonality and reduced amount of decoration reinforce a sense of severe elegance. But movement is also vital to the interior and is realized both by the spectator entering and using the church and within the architecture itself—in the relation of the internal units to the wall, in the sinuous curves of the three-dimensional arches, and in the dramatic contrast between the immense crossing dome and the other vaults.

Neumann's church commissions after Neresheim were modest by comparison. Both the Käppele (1747–1750) and Forchheim (1748) are based on Greek-cross plans with a dome over the crossing. That at the Käppele is a more conventional pendentive dome with lantern; a hemisphere largely dissolved by huge arches marks Forchheim. Elevation and lighting range from the sculptural accentuating shadows of Forchheim to the massiveness and direct illumination of the

Neumann.
Pilgrimage Church of the Assumption of Mary.
Vierzehnheiligen, Germany.
1742–1753 (not completed until 1772)

Neumann.
Benedictine Abbey Church of the Holy Cross.
Neresheim, Germany.
1747–1753 (not completed until the 1790s)

Käppele. Limbach (1751–1753) is a longitudinal church in which nave and crossing are directly joined. A framework consisting of flat piers, flat pilasters, shallow arches, and straight balconies runs parallel to the walls. The fabric is opened regularly about the entire building, filling the interior with a uniform, bright illumination that matter-of-factly records the dispassionately clear articulation. From the 1730s on, Neumann was also active as a builder of small parish churches located in country villages. The highly consistent formula for these is an aisleless, two-bay nave articulated by wall piers and terminated by a narrower one-bay choir with polygonal apse. The exterior is plain, with some design attention paid to the façade, which is marked either by a slightly projecting tower or a pediment. Records survive for more than thirty of these country churches, most of them built and still standing.

Closely related to Neumann's church architecture are his many designs for altars. Some are constructions set into niches and as a result minimally responsive to the surroundings (Holzkirchen; Schönborn chapel). Others are located on raised platforms and include monumental, free-standing sculptural pieces (Kitzkingen; Heusenstamm). But the type of altar Neumann designed most frequently consisted of columns with a baldachinlike central unit and spreading wings. This approach was first fully developed in the Cathedral of Worms, with forerunners at Münsterschwarzach, the church in the Würzburg Residenz, and Gössweinstein, and with major variations for Altspeyer, Vierzehnheiligen, Brühl, Trier, Bruchsal, and Neresheim. Conceived as open, framework structures, the altars are designed to reiterate and synthesize the surrounding architecture in a manner that makes them a focus for prayer and contemplation. Neumann's interest lay in the architectonic concept of the altar. To complete each, he let others design the required sculpture, painting, and decoration. Consequently, altars subscribing to very similar concepts, such as those for Brühl and Trier, may possess very different qualities. Johann Wolfgang van der Auvera's completion makes the former jaunty and pointed, whereas for the latter Ferdinand Tietz employed languid and rounded forms.

Neumann was involved throughout his life with other commissions as well. These include a variety of building types such as houses, monasteries, hospitals, a hotel, a city hall, and a court house, and miscellaneous religious structures. He undertook various urban design projects for Würzburg, which concerned laying out streets and a square. Military commissions included the fortifications for several towns and the building of barracks. He constructed bridges, laid out gardens and designed garden structures such as pavilions and orangeries, put in municipal water systems, and arranged huge fireworks displays. In addition to these undertakings, he ran a glass factory, a mirror polishing workshop, and served as a consultant for several restorations. Details for many of these efforts are sketchy, yet the catalogue alone reveals the enormous body of work he produced.

Neumann's architecture is, at one and the same time, traditional and unique. A lineage extending back to the fifteenth century informs the over-all disposition of his palaces as well as his general approach to the longitudinal and centralized churches. He followed standard practice in the basic compositional devices of his façades. Emphasis on the grand staircase and the frequent use of oval and circular configurations for plan and vaults were common coinage. And like many others, he promoted various artistic media—such as paintings, sculpture, stucco, woodwork, and metalwork—as integral components of architectural design. Nor was architecture based on space composition a recent phenomenon. Introduced during the mid-seventeenth century, it had become de rigueur among Neumann's central European contemporaries, such as the ASAM BROTHERS and DOMINIKUS ZIMMERMANN, JOHANN MICHAEL FISCHER, the Vorarlberg masters, and the Dientzenhofers. But Neumann accepted this common ground only as a point of departure for explorations of architectural space that reveal an astonishing range and brilliance. The discussions of individual projects document this achievement. With consummate authority he combined clarity with complexity in plan and section. He boldly charged the interior with light and dematerialized mass, and thrust both into a powerful encounter with space. He orchestrated the experience of space for the beholder in ways that were at once striking, lucid, and imposing, gradually revealed, demanding, and human. With adroit skill, Neumann transformed standard architectural assemblages into unique and bold statements.

No particular persons, places, or publications appear specifically to have assisted Neumann in this achievement. He was well-versed in a broad range of European architecture as a result of his travels throughout Franconia and Bohemia, within France and Holland, to Vienna and Milan. He had contact with many other architects, including Josef Greising, Johann Dientzenhofer, Maximilian von Welsch, Johann Lucas von Hildebrandt, Robert de Cotte, and Germain Boffrand. The enthusiasms of his patrons directed him often to things French and Italian. His library included many subject areas in addition to architecture: dictionaries and grammars, poetry and fiction, theology, law, medicine, natural science, philosophy, history, geographies and maps, mathematics, optics, perspective, considerations of painting, sculpture, drawing, and engraving, publications about functional structures, especially waterworks, and material on the science and history of war, fortifications, and artillery science. Publications specifically on architecture included standard materials from Italy, France, and England, as well as an imposing collection of German treatises. This array of contacts suggests that Neumann possessed a general humanist orientation and specifically an acquaintance with the architecture of the past as well as with the parameters of contemporary practice. But it provides no suggestion that his designs were extrapolated from specific building prototypes or from specific approaches of other architects any more than it indicates that they were based on a body of theory or a set of principles. His vast correspondence, mostly with the Schönborns, reports in detail on the progress of various commissions and remains devoid of references to his purposes, theoretical positions, and architectural ideals. In short, the particulars of Neumann's background and career do not explain the unique quality of his work nor do they provide insight into it.

His architecture does, however, collect meaning from the context of its production. The religious and political persuasions alive within the various social groups for which he built were heightened during these decades by a surge of religiosity that swept the arts and politics along with it. This is seen in an outpouring of devotional tracts, in masses of people moved to follow the pilgrimage, in a growing enthusiasm for religious festivals, in the ever more splendidly arranged practice of Roman Catholic ritual. The ideal type of worldly leader was the churchman as prince, such as many of the Schönborns were prince-bishops. Political absolutism reflected the dynamic and polemical theology rife in the universities of the time. This characterized God as the "highest good," asserting that the goal of belief was the quest for *unio mystica.* In their variety, exuberance, and individuality, Neumann's churches are part and parcel of this religious sensibility. The transparent spatial unity of each interior reveals the *unio mystica.* Meanings are emotional, not intellectual constructs. Analogous purposes, slanted toward political representation, inform the palace designs.

This architecture excited popular enthusiasm during its time. When Neumann died, he left an imposing architectural legacy, some of it still under construction, and the shock of his death reverberated among the Würzburg citizenry. As the funeral procession passed through the city to his burial place in the Marienkapelle, the streets and houses along the route were filled with mourners.

CHRISTIAN F. OTTO

WORKS

1719–1753, Residenz (not completed until 1776); 1721–1736, Schönborn Chapel; 1726, Inn "Zum Hirschen" (now Dresdner Bank); Würzburg, Germany. 1726–1730, Benedictine Priory Church (roof incorrectly replaced), Holzkirchen, Germany. *1727–1743, Benedictine Abbey Church, Münsterschwarzach, Germany. *1728–1750, Saint Damiansburg Palace, Bruchsal, Germany. 1729–1739, Pilgrimage and Parish Church of the Holy Trinity, Gössweinstein, Germany. 1730–1733, Chapter House, Bamberg, Germany. 1730 (and later), Fortifications in Forchheim, Königshofen, Kronach, Germany. 1730 (and later), Water Supply System; 1730–1743, Palace Church, Residenz; Würzburg, Germany. 1731–1733, Seminary (now City Hall), Bamberg, Germany. 1733–1745, Schönborn Summer Palace, Werneck, Germany. 1734–1753, Collegiate Church Saint Paulin (not completed until 1754), Trier, Germany. 1737?–1745, Palace Church of the Guardian Angel, Schönborn Summer Palace, Werneck, Germany. 1737–1753, Market Place, Stores, Theaterstrasse, Würzburg, Germany. 1738–1740/1741, Cathedral (high altar), Worms, Germany. 1738–1740, Rombach Palace, Würzburg, Germany. 1738–1753, Parish Church of Saint Peter (not completed until the 1770s), Bruchsal, Germany. 1739–1753, Parish and Mortuary Church of Saints Cecilia and Barbara (not completed until 1756), Heusenstamm, Germany. 1740–1745, Parish Church of the Holy Cross, Gaibach, Germany. 1740–1745, Parish Church of the Holy Cross, Kitzingen, Germany. 1740–1752, Pilgrimage Church of the Visitation of Mary (called the Käppele; later additions 1761–1781); 1741–1753, Dominican (now Augustinian) Church (not completed until 1771); Würzburg, Germany. 1741–1750, Augustusburg Palace (main stair), Brühl, Germany. *1742–1746, Jesuit Church of Saint Ignatius, Mainz, Germany. 1742–1753, Pilgrimage Church of the Assumption of Mary (not completed until 1772), Vierzehnheiligen, Germany. 1742–1753, Premonstratensian Monastery (facade, convent; stair, completed 1760), Oberzell, Germany. 1745–1751, Holy Stairs, Bonn, Germany. 1747–1753, Benedictine Abbey Church of the Holy Cross (not completed until the 1790s), Neresheim, Germany. *1748–1752, Schönbornlust Palace, near Koblenz, Germany. 1749, Cathedral (choir floor lowered and sacristies added), Würzburg, Germany. 1751–1753, Pilgrimage and Parish Church of the Visitation of Mary (not completed until the 1760s), Limbach am Main, Germany. 1752, Monastery (front wings; constructed by J. J. M. Küchel), Banz, Germany. 1753, Palace (additions and stair), Veitshöchheim, Germany.

BIBLIOGRAPHY

ANDERSEN, LISELOTTE 1966 "Studien zu Profanbauformen Balthasar Neumanns: Die grossen Residenzprojekte für Wien, Stuttgart und Karlsruhe." Un-

published Ph.D. dissertation, University of Munich.
Balthasar Neumann in Baden-Württemberg. 1975 Stuttgart, Germany: Staatsgalerie. Catalogue of an exhibition from September 28 to November 30, 1975, at the Staatsgalerie, Stuttgart, Germany.
Balthasar Neumann, Leben und Werk: Gedächtnisschau zum 200. Todestage. 1953 Catalogue of an exhibition from June 21 to October 18, 1953, at Würzburg Residenz. Catalogue prepared under the supervision of Max Herrmann von Freeden. Würzburg, Germany: Universitätsdruckerei H. Sturtz AG.
BOLL, WALTER 1925 *Die Schönbornkapelle am Würzburger Dom: Ein Beitrag zur Kunstgeschichte des XVIII. Jahrhunderts.* Munich: Müller.
FREEDEN, MAX HERRMANN VON (1937)1978 *Balthasar Neumann als Stadtbaumeister.* Reprint. Würzburg, Germany: Freunde Mainfränkischer Kunst und Geschichte.
FREEDEN, MAX HERRMANN VON (1953)1963 *Balthasar Neumann: Leben und Werk.* 2d ed. Munich and Berlin: Deutscher Kunstverlag.
HEGEMANN, HANS WERNER 1937 "Die Altarbaukunst Balthasar Neumanns." Ph.D. dissertation, University of Marburg, Germany.
HIRSCH, FRITZ (1912)1978 *Das sogenannte Skizzenbuch Balthasar Neumanns: Ein Beitrag zur Charakteristik des Meisters und zur Philosophie der Baukunst.* Nendeln, Germany: Kraus. Reprint of *Zeitschrift für Geschichte der Architektur*, Beiheft 8, 1912.
HOTZ, JOACHIM 1965 *Katalog der Sammlung Eckert aus dem Nachlass Balthasar Neumanns im Mainfränkischen Museum Würzburg.* Würzburg, Germany: Schöningh.
KELLER, JOSEPH 1896 *Balthasar Neumann: Eine Studie zur Kunstgeschichte des 18. Jahrhunderts.* Würzburg, Germany: E. Bauer.
KNAPP, FRITZ 1937 *Balthasar Neumann—Der grosse Architekt seiner Zeit.* Bielefeld, Germany: Velhagen; Leipzig: Klasing.
LOHMEYER, KARL 1911 *Die Briefe Balthasar Neumanns von seiner Pariser Studienreise 1723.* Düsseldorf, Germany: Schwann.
LOHMEYER, KARL 1921 *Die Briefe Balthasar Neumanns an Friedrich Karl von Schönborn, Fürstbischof von Würzburg und Bamberg, und Dokumente aus den ersten Baujahren der Würzburger Residenz.* Saarbrücken, Germany; Berlin; Leipzig; and Stuttgart: Hofer.
NEUMANN, GÜNTHER 1947 *Neresheim.* Munich: Filser.
OTTO, CHRISTIAN F. 1979 *Space Into Light: The Churches of Balthasar Neumann.* New York: Architectural History Foundation.
REUTHER, HANS 1953*a* "Die Landkirchen Balthasar Neumanns." *Zeitschrift für Kunstgeschichte* 16:154–170.
REUTHER, HANS 1953*b* "Neues Schriftum über Balthasar Neumann." *Kunstchronik* 6:209–221.
REUTHER, HANS 1954 "Nachtrag zum Balthasar Neumann-Jubiläumsjahr 1953." *Kunstchronik* 7:35–37.
REUTHER, HANS 1960 *Die Kirchenbauten Balthasar Neumanns.* Berlin: Hessling.
SCHENK, CLEMENS 1939 *Balthasar Neumanns Kirchenbaukunst.* Würzburg, Germany.
SEDLMAIER, RICHARD, and PFISTER, RUDOLF 1923 *Die fürstbischöfliche Residenz zu Würzburg.* 2 vols. Munich: Müller.
TEUFEL, RICHARD (1936)1957 *Vierzehnheiligen.* 2d ed. Lichtenfels, Germany: Schulze. Originally published with the title *Die Wallfahrtskirche Vierzehnheiligen.*
TEUFEL, RICHARD 1953 *Balthasar Neumann: Sein Werk in Oberfranken.* Lichtenfels, Germany: Schulze.
Verzeichnis der Bücher, Kupperstiche und Handzeichnugnen aus der Verlassenschaft. 1804 Würzburg, Germany: Stahel. List of books, prints, and drawings auctioned off at the tavern "zum Eichhorn" in Würzburg, Germany, on June 18 and following days.

NEUTRA, RICHARD

Few architects were as zealously messianic about the practical and aesthetic values of modernism as Richard Joseph Neutra (1892–1970). He championed the architectural implications of such machine age phenomena as assembly line production and the interchangeability of prefabricated parts. His artistic temperament and his sure eye for form and proportion gave a fine aesthetic balance to his commitment to practicality and replicability of design.

Born in imperial Vienna to a family of middle-class Jewish secular agnostics, his early heroes included Gustav Mahler, Arnold Schönberg, Arthur Schnitzler, and Hugo von Hofmannsthal.

Neutra's greatest heroes, however, were OTTO WAGNER and ADOLF LOOS, and after *Gymnasium,* he studied architecture at the Technischehochschule. He frequented Loos's studio-salon, where he met RUDOLF SCHINDLER. He heard Loos extol the virtues of modern machine prefabrication, excoriate the use of needless ornament, and proclaim the virtues of American civilization, which was confirmed and heightened for Neutra by the 1910 German publication of the work of FRANK LLOYD WRIGHT. Neutra decided to see such work firsthand, but was delayed by the outbreak of World War I. Following the war, Neutra worked briefly in Switzerland for the landscape gardener Gustav Ammann, learning much about botany and garden design. Unable to get a visa until 1923, Neutra served briefly as city architect in the North German town of Luckenwalde and then joined ERIC MENDELSOHN's Berlin office.

In 1923, Neutra emigrated to America, working for nearly a year in the large Chicago office of HOLABIRD AND ROCHE, where he gained much of the material for his book on American architecture, *Wie Baut Amerika?* (1927). In Chicago he visited LOUIS H. SULLIVAN. At Sullivan's funeral, he met Frank Lloyd Wright, who invited him to work with him at Taliesen during the fall of 1924. Wright had little work, and in January 1925, Neutra moved to Los Angeles, where he formed a loose partnership with Schindler, the Architectural Group for Industry and Commerce. The most fruitful result was the Neutra designed Jardinette Apartments, Los Angeles (1927). Built of stern, reinforced concrete, with cantilevered balconies and long rows of metal framed window bands, the Jardinette was one of the first major examples in America of the International style. The two collaborated on a design for the League of Nations Headquarters competition (1926), which was won by LE CORBUSIER. Due to personal and professional differences, Schindler and Neutra dissolved their AGIC relationship in the early 1930s.

The Lovell "Health House," Los Angeles (1927–1929) catapulted Neutra to fame. Resting on a light steel frame, the three-story house of concrete, glass, and metal panels epitomized the ethic and aesthetic of mechanical assemblage. It was a poetic and elegant homage to *Sweet's Catalogue,* the architect's building supply manual. Perched over a canyon in the Hollywood Hills, a terrace leads from the street into an entry hall on the top floor. The hall is also a balcony, framing and overlooking one of the finest stairways in all modern architecture, wherein the stair lights beneath the railing are headlights from the Model-T Ford. Between the stair and the central fireplace is an inglenook banquette. Connected to the main cube, via patios, trellises, and garden walls is a large garage with rooms underneath. Philip Lovell's elaborate gymnastic equipment served as outdoor sculpture on the lushly landscaped terraces.

After the Lovell achievement, Neutra traveled around the world, stopping first in Japan. He was a visiting critic at the Bauhaus and later served as the American delegate to the Brussels meeting of the Congrès Internationaux des Architectes Modernes.

Neutra's work in the 1930s and 1940s, his most productive years, confirmed the promise of his earlier work. Important commissions came from film industry figures. The building for Carl Laemmle, of Universal-International, at the corner of Hollywood and Vine, Los Angeles (1931), housed a restaurant and chic stores on the ground level with offices on the second floor, topped by large, integrally built-in bill boards. The rear service yard was an especially elegant exercise in minimalist composition. Los Angeles houses for the actress Anna Sten (1934), and the directors Josef von Sternberg (1935) and Albert Lewin (1938) juxtaposed dramatic curving elements to the otherwise rectilinear geometry. The von Sternberg house was all of aluminum while the Sten and Lewin stucco structures made effective use of industrial imaginery and technics.

In the 1920s, Neutra designed a "Ring Plan School" in his ideal metropolis, Rush City Reformed, but only with the Corona Avenue School, Los Angeles (1934), was he able to demonstrate his ideas. The sliding glass window walls, expanding the classrooms outdoors, seemed radical and "other-worldly," but the school soon became a Los Angeles prototype. Neutra's Strathmore Apartments, Los Angeles (1937), stacked back into the hillside, revealed his continuing skill with multiple unit buildings and his admiration for the southwest Indian Pueblo aesthetic. Strathmore also predicted his acclaimed Channel Heights Housing (1942) for shipyard workers, near the Los Angeles harbor, San Pedro.

The scarcity of industrial materials during World War II led to such superb wooden buildings as the Nesbit House, Los Angeles (1942). The building code now demanded pitched roofs, and for the rest of his career, Neutra alternated wood with harder materials and pitched roofs with flat. The Kaufmann House, Palm Springs (1946), a

Neutra.
Lovell House.
Los Angeles.
1927–1929

Neutra.
Kaufmann House.
Palm Springs, California.
1946

superb pavilion recalling his style of the 1930s, reflected the influence of LUDWIG MIES VAN DER ROHE's Barcelona Pavilion (1929). The Tremaine House (1948), Montecito, was an important transition to his more lyrically relaxed houses of the 1950s and 1960s—buildings which no longer seemed startlingly avant garde, but pleasantly suitable for the popular "shelter magazines."

By 1949, Neutra reached the pinnacle of his success, and was the first architect on the cover of *Time* magazine. He enlarged his practice via a partnership with planner Robert Alexander which resulted in large commissions in Sacramento, Tulsa, and Guam. It also led to such large public buildings as the United States Embassy, Karachi, Pakistan (1959), the Lincoln Memorial, Gettysburg (1959), and the Los Angeles Hall of Records (1961). These buildings lacked the taut, stylish, *élan* of his earlier, smaller work. In the late 1950s, this partnership dissolved and Neutra spent most of his last decade in partnership with his son, Dion. From the 1930s through the 1960s, Neutra's office was staffed with numerous gifted architects, many of whom went on to distinguished careers.

Neutra was perhaps, of all twentieth century architects, the best informed and immersed in the physical and behavioral sciences. His *Survival Through Design* (1954) had an especially wide influence. While some of Neutra's later work reflected the fatigue and the growing identity problems of the late modern movement, his best work reflected its happier, sturdier phase. Celebrating the machine and its place in modern life, Neutra was ever the romantic engineer, searching for the nexus of art, technology, and life.

THOMAS S. HINES

WORKS

1927, Jardinette Apartments; 1927–1929, Lovell "Health House"; 1931, Office Building for Universal-International; 1934, Corona Avenue School; 1934, Sten House; Los Angeles. *1935, Von Sternberg House, San Fernando Valley, Calif. 1937, Brown House, Fisher's Island, N.Y. 1937, Kraigher House, Brownsville, Tex. 1937, Kun House, Los Angeles. 1937, Miller House, Palm Springs, Calif. 1937, Strathmore Apartments; 1938, Lewin House; Los Angeles. 1940, Evans Plywood Building, Lebanon, Ore. 1942, Channel Heights Housing, San Pedro, Calif; 1942, Nesbit House, Los Angeles. 1946, Kaufmann House, Palm Springs, Calif. 1948, Tremaine House, Montecito, Calif. 1951, Hinds House, Los Angeles. 1951, Price House, Bayport, N.Y. 1952, Moore House, Ojai, Calif. 1957, Slavin House, Santa Barbara, Calif. 1959, Lincoln Memorial Museum, Gettysburg, Penn. 1959, United States Embassy, Karachi, Pakistan. 1961, Glen House, Stamford, Conn. 1961, Hall of Records, Los Angeles. 1964, Rentsch House, Wenger, Switzerland. 1968, Brown House, Washington.

BIBLIOGRAPHY

BOESIGER, WILLY (editor) (1951–1966)1966 *Richard Neutra, Buildings and Projects (1923–1966)*. 3 vols. New York: Praeger.

GEBHARD, DAVID 1972 *Schindler*. New York: Viking.

HINES, THOMAS S. 1981 *Richard Neutra and the Search for Modern Architecture: A Biography and History*. New York: Oxford University Press.

MCCOY, ESTHER 1960 *Richard Neutra*. New York: Braziller.

NEUTRA, RICHARD 1954 *Survival Through Design*. New York: Oxford University Press.

NEUTRA, RICHARD 1962 *Life and Shape*. New York: Appleton.

NEWSOM, SAMUEL, and NEWSOM, JOSEPH CATHER

In nineteenth- and early twentieth-century America most domestic architecture was designed and produced by builders or self-trained architects rather than by major figures. A case in point is that of the late nineteenth-century architecture of the brothers Samuel Newsom (1854–1908) and Joseph Cather Newsom (1858–1930). Their most famous design, the William Carson House (1884–1885) at Eureka, California, has often been mentioned and used as illustration, but little attention has been directed to the two brothers who produced this acknowledged masterpiece of Victorian architecture. Later, when their names came to be associated with the design of the Carson House, little was said about their architectural practice and how it fitted into the late nineteenth-century scene in California.

Although one may offer a number of explanations for the relative obscurity of Samuel and Joseph Cather Newsom, the fundamental reason is that in the teaching of the history of architecture only the work of high-art practitioners is discussed. It could be argued that one can form a much more thorough understanding and a more comprehensive picture of late nineteenth-century American architecture by looking into the practice of architects such as the Newsom brothers rather than by concentrating exclusively on the work of a few acknowledged major figures. This is especially the case when one considers domestic architecture, for the streets of America's small towns and cities were and still are dominated by single- and multiple-family houses designed by builders/carpenters and self-trained architects like the Newsom brothers.

Since the office records of the Newsom brothers no longer exist, we will probably never know for how many buildings they were directly or indirectly responsible. In California alone, they designed well over six hundred buildings between 1878, when their partnership was formed, and 1908, when Samuel Newsom died. In addition, they designed houses, commercial buildings, and churches in Texas, Indiana, Pennsylvania, New Jersey, and upper New York State. They also claimed to have designed residences in Mexico, South America, Europe, Japan, and New Zealand, and there is no reason to think that this was not the case.

Added to this direct production of their own were the numerous built structures that were based upon designs contained in one or another of their eleven popular pattern books. Like other producers of pattern books, the Newsoms advertised that the readers of their books could purchase inexpensive stock plans for any of these published designs. How many houses, stores, or churches were built from their designs remains unknown, but a casual look into street scenes of California's towns and cities shows that many cottages and houses reveal a strong Newsomian look. The principal sources for the architecture of the Newsoms are the drawings and photographs contained in the eleven pattern books which were published between the years 1884–1885 and 1900.

Both Samuel Newsom and Joseph Cather Newsom were born in southern Ontario Province in Canada. Around 1860, their eldest brother, John J. Newsom, went to San Francisco, and the following year the rest of the family went. Their father, Lavens Newsom, who on occasion was involved in speculative building activities, worked as a nurseryman and florist in Oakland, where the family established itself. Sometime in the early 1870s the two older brothers, John J. and Thomas D. Newsom, set themselves up as architect/builders. John J. Newsom had, it appears, some formal training in Canada, and he had worked with his father on speculative housing in and around Montreal before coming to California. Both Samuel and Joseph Cather Newsom received their architectural training in their elder brothers' office. Samuel entered their office in 1874 and Joseph Cather began his apprenticeship around 1876. In 1878, Samuel and Joseph Cather established their partnership, a partnership which lasted until 1888. Between these dates they had offices simultaneously in San Francisco and Oakland, and in 1886 Joseph Cather went south to establish another office in Los Angeles, so that they could participate in the land and speculative boom of the 1880s in southern California. Samuel and Joseph Cather Newsom quickly built up a successful practice. By 1879 they were designing upper middle class residences in Oakland and a courthouse and opera

Newsom Brothers. William Carson House. Eureka, California. 1884–1885

Newsom Brothers. William Carson House. Eureka, California. 1884–1885

house in Napa. At the beginning of the 1880s they had broken into the upper middle class, middle class, and speculative housing world of San Francisco, and their designs were being published in the *California Architect and Building News.* By 1884 they were producing buildings for a good number of northern California communities, including their most publicized building, the William Carson House (1884–1885) at Eureka. Also at this time, they published the first of their pattern books, *Picturesque California Homes* (1884–1885).

With Samuel in San Francisco and Oakland and Joseph Cather in Los Angeles, the firm was still able to design and realize many buildings during these years. Sought out by investors in the Bay, the Newsoms worked on the plans for many of these new towns created by land speculators; in numerous instances they designed hotels, business blocks, and speculative housing. In and around Los Angeles and to a lesser extent in the San Francisco Bay area, the brothers designed, constructed, and sold speculative single- and multiple-family housing on their own.

In Los Angeles the Newsoms designed the

Newsom Brothers.
L. L. Bradbury House.
Los Angeles.
1887

six-story Bryson-Bonebrake Block (1888), one of the city's largest and most elaborate interior-court-lighted buildings. During 1887–1888, they designed additional commercial blocks in downtown Los Angeles, schools, college buildings, churches, public buildings, and one- and two-story commercial blocks in southern California. In both San Francisco and Los Angeles they obtained commissions for several of their largest residences, the O. H. Baldwin House in San Francisco (1887) and the L. L. Bradbury House in Los Angeles (1887).

The aggressive, flamboyant personality of Joseph Cather was in marked contrast to the middle class staidness of his older brother Samuel. Joseph Cather had a tendency to credit himself alone for various projects, so it should not have been a surprise that their partnership dissolved in January 1888. Joseph Cather took over the Los Angeles office and Samuel their San Francisco and Oakland practice. During the partnership most of the work in southern California was probably handled by Joseph Cather, but even of this we cannot be sure.

With the sudden collapse of the speculative boom of the 1880s Joseph Cather found it increasingly difficult to obtain new commissions. His principal work of these years, the David C. Cook House at Piru (1888–1891), the J. F. Cosby House in Los Angeles (1888–1890), and the Chauvin Block in Los Angeles (1890), were all commissioned before the collapse of the boom. Sometime at the end of 1889 or very early in 1890 Joseph Cather returned to San Francisco and he established his own office. Northern California had been less hard hit by the depression at the end of the 1880s, and Samuel's practice was little diminished. Samuel's most widely acclaimed buildings of the early 1890s were the Horticultural and Agricultural Building at the Mid-Winter International Exposition in Golden Gate Park (1893) and the Carson Block in Eureka (1891). He also submitted well-publicized designs for a proposed "Château en Espagne," a mansion for the governor of California in Sacramento (1890), the invitational competition for the California Building at the World Columbian Exposition in Chicago (1892), the competition for the Oakland High School Building (1894), and for a large-scale hotel near Golden Gate Park in San Francisco (1895).

In 1893, Samuel's eldest son Sidney came into his father's office, and in 1904 he became a full partner. Sidney's younger brother Noble also became a member of the firm and a partner in 1905, the firm name changing to Newsom and Newsom. Previously, between 1898 and 1900, Samuel had entered into partnership with Frederick H. Meyer under the firm name of Newsom and Meyer. The predominance of commissions obtained by Samuel Newsom from the mid-1890s until his death in 1908 were, as before, residential with the notable exception of a number of designs for churches. Most of the houses were middle class single-family dwellings, with a smattering of speculative housing and upper middle class residences. The largest of the latter was the Rudolph Spreckels House in San Francisco (1897–1899) and the Parker House outside of San Rafael.

Joseph Cather Newsom's smaller-scale practice in San Francisco and Oakland continued until 1896. Through what may have been church connections he moved to Philadelphia where he opened an office under the title of The Up-to-Date Architectural Association. The full extent of his work in and around Philadelphia is not known. He began publishing a new architectural periodical, *Up-to-Date Architecture.* He also began to associate once again, albeit at a distance, with his brother Samuel. While in the east, Joseph Cather designed at least four churches, some speculative housing, and upper middle class single-family residences in Pennsylvania, New Jersey, and New York State.

Although Joseph Cather seemed to have established a reasonably productive practice in Philadelphia, he returned to the Bay Area in 1900, before he moved to Los Angeles in 1903. In his three-and-a-half years in Los Angeles, Joseph Cather concentrated on a score or more upper middle class dwellings, bathhouses, and rental multiple housing. By 1906 he was back in San Francisco and Oakland.

This move may have been prompted by his having been accused of bribing to obtain the commission for the Long Beach Pier and Public Recreation Hall (1904) at Long Beach, California, or perhaps there was a lack of commissions. Then too, San Francisco after the 1906 earthquake must have seemed a fertile ground for an architect. But Joseph Cather's resumption of a really successful practice did not materialize. While he continued to design modest-sized houses for individual clients, his principal activities were in speculative housing in and around Oakland. In 1910, he formed a very brief partnership with I. E. Frary of Chicago. During the 1910s Joseph Cather divided his time between architecture and real estate. In 1923 he retired from practice, and died in Oakland in 1930.

The chronicle of the architectural practice of Samuel and Joseph Cather Newsom is significant within the history of late nineteenth-century American architecture not only for the insight it provides into the everyday world of the business of design and construction but also for the fascinating glimpse it allows into the rapidly shifting world of architectural imagery as well as the highly individual and at times outrageous interpretations of images of that time.

The Newsoms viewed the task of an architect as one of creating fashionable images. In fact, for the Newsoms the two fundamental responsibilities of the architect were modernity of images and the requirement that their designs should be highly recognizable in the sense that they would be "striking and commanding."

Like other late nineteenth-century American architects, the Newsoms assumed that their buildings would satisfactorily fulfill the utilitarian demands placed upon them and that they would entail the latest technological innovations. Central heating, modern bathrooms and kitchens, electric lights and alarm systems, and well-organized ventilating systems were common features in their dwellings and other buildings. In these utilitarian matters the Newsoms kept closely abreast of improvements and changes, but these matters of utility were taken for granted in their architectural practice. Like all architects (or almost all) from Vitruvius on, they loved to throw up a verbal smoke screen of utility, practicality, and cost, behind which they partially hid their primary interest—the creation of images.

As their buildings so beautifully attest, the Newsoms were fully committed to the theme of up-to-dateness in their use of images. Both were adroit at keeping up with the latest. At the beginning of their practice in 1878, they took up the then popular Eastlake (Stick) style; by the early 1880s they were fully committed to the American version of the Queen Anne. This imagery was quickly supplemented by the Richardsonian (see H. H. RICHARDSON) Romanesque and the early Colonial Revival (Shingle style). On occasion, their rendering of the Richardsonian Romanesque was almost correct, but generally they distorted one or another aspects of their design so that the building ended up as a personal interpretation. In the early 1890s they went on to the Châteauesque, the Georgian Colonial Revival and the classical Beaux-Arts. The two brothers were among the earliest advocates of the regional Mission Revival, and later of the Mediterranean and Spanish Colonial Revival. Just before the turn of the century they were caught up in the Arts and Crafts movement with its image of the California bungalow, and they produced a wide variety of medieval designs, based upon both English and French precedence.

In looking over this wild array of images, it is obvious that the Newsoms always followed the latest; they never originated it. Yet, no one could ever accuse the Newsoms of being restrained. The continual imprint of their personality on their buildings was a result not of the conventional massing, surfaces, and details which they used but of how they rearranged and in most cases distorted the traditional vocabularies they employed. The ability of architecture to create artifacts of fantasy was one of their prime concerns, whether it was the illusion of a Victorian castle, or the sense of a rural cottage, as in Joseph Cather's R. George Zahn House in Oakland of 1893.

Newsom Brothers. Coleman Residence. Near Santa Cruz, California. c.1907

Whatever the style image employed, it always tended to be exuberant, flamboyant, and anything but pure. From 1878 through 1885 the two brothers designed a number of upper middle class houses which they called Eastlake or Swiss. These houses, exemplified by the Allison House (c.1883) in San Francisco, tend to read as compressed and vertically strung-out compositions. At the same time the brothers were beginning to mix the Eastlake with the newly arrived Queen Anne. The William Carson House in Eureka sums up this mixture. Its basic verticality, its tall thin tower are Eastlake, but much of its interior and exterior details are Queen Anne—ranging from the squat paired turned columns of the principal porch to the interior moon gate arches and windows.

A forceful example of their up-to-dateness can be seen in their published design for a "Dwelling of 11 Rooms, Picturesque," first published around 1884. This is a pure example of American Queen Anne in elevations and plan. The veranda is not just a porch but a semienclosed living space of real dimensions. Within the divisions of space are few, and the large openings between rooms fully express the open plan. The Moon Hall of this house with its fireplace is a living hall and the platform and staircase provides a vertical, picturesque flow of space between the first and second floors.

Like other late nineteenth-century American architects, the Newsoms employed a dual set of images when they were designing commercial and institutional buildings. In the case of a number of their smaller buildings and hotels, they employed whatever was the then current domestic image; for other nondomestic designs they adopted the traditional monumental masonry approach. Their largest realized building, Joseph Cather's six-story Bryson-Bonebrake Block (1888) in Los Angeles is, one would guess, an exercise in the Richardsonian Romanesque. There are Romanesque arches, horizontal bands of coupled columns, appropriate heavy rusticated masonry, and so on, but the total effect of the design defies any stylistic designation.

Before and immediately after the two brothers dissolved their partnership in 1888, they placed on the landscape a number of the wildest versions of the Queen Anne Revival style in America. The L. L. Bradbury House (1887) on Bunker Hill in Los Angeles displays a superabundance of details, which amazingly were held in place within the overall composition of the building. Though Joseph Cather labeled the Cosby House (1888–1890) in Los Angeles as "American Renaissance," its vocabulary, like that of the large and sumptuous Glendale Villa Hotel (1887) or the small cottage at San Rafael (c.1887), was American Queen Anne. If the project and its budget was large enough, such as in the Cosby House or the Glendale Villa Hotel, the Newsoms often introduced a central vertical space dominated by a skylight. In the Cosby House the Rotunda Hall had an

> inner dome of jeweled art glass just under the outside dome and lit on the inside by a suspended cluster of gold calla lillies, from each of which there springs a light, while just below hangs a rose-colored globe. . . . The dome is lit by electricity and at dusk its heraldic design, emblazoned in the national colors, begins to glow, reminding the pedestrian of some fairy witch tower [*Los Angeles Evening Express,* October 7, 1890, p. 15].

The first inklings of a regional interest in California's Mission past surfaced first in the literature of the 1880s, and by 1889–1890 this interest began to appear in projected and realized buildings. Though Samuel Newsom did not win the competition for the California Building (1892) at the World Columbian Exposition in Chicago, his design is in fact in many ways a more original one than that of the winning design of A. PAGE BROWN. Newsom posed the façade of the four missions as a series of billboards behind which was the low, tentlike pavilion. The semirustic provincial scale of his design for the California Building was realized in his Agricultural and Horticultural Building at the California Mid-Winter International Exposition in Golden Gate Park in San Francisco.

The theme of the missions was a recurring one through the 1890s and early 1900s in the work of the two brothers. Sometimes the rendition was pure Mission Revival with scalloped parapets, low arcades, stucco walls, and quatrefoil windows; on other occasions, such as Samuel's projected Hotel near Golden Gate Park (1895) in San Francisco, the Newsoms anticipated the later Spanish Colonial Revival of the 1910s and 1920s. By the early 1900s they, like other designers, had taken the Mission motif and made it part of the Craftsman Bungalow.

One might think that by the end of the century Samuel and Joseph Cather would have become more conventional and reserved in their personal dictionary of styles, but this was not the case. In the first volume of his *Up-to-Date Architecture,* Joseph Cather indicated that his menu of styles included Picturesque Rambling order, Mexican-American style, Old English Framework order, Old Dutch and English Combination styles, Picturesque Florentine style, Suburban style, Spanish-Florentine style, and the Ann Hathaway style. Added to these were other offerings. Samuel Newsom's O. D. Baldwin House (1893) in San Francisco was Dutch Renaissance, his projected Clubhouse for San Francisco (?) (c.1897) and his

Cottage for Oakland (c.1897) were in the French style, that is, Châteauesque.

Equally pervasive in their work at the time were shingled Colonial Revival houses that closely followed the regional versions of this style developed in the Bay Area by ERNEST COXHEAD, WILLIS J. POLK, and Brown. Samuel's Eugene J. Bates House (c.1896) in San Francisco aptly demonstrates how in plan and elevation the Newsoms were capable of distorting and individualizing any design regardless of its source. It is easy to point out specific aggrandizement of details in all of the designs of the Newsoms, but their principal device of distortion was scale. Joseph Cather accomplished a major distortion of scale in his proposed Beaux Arts-styled Business Block for Market Street in San Francisco (c.1895), where the orders and the suggested attic of the first three floors are of such size that the upper nine floors present themselves as another building in the distance. Newsom and Meyer's Marin County Bank Building (1897) in San Rafael produced similar results with its heavy roof and broad entablature which appear to have pressed the remaining part of the building deeply into the ground.

While Samuel and Joseph Cather's churches of the 1890s and early 1900s were all medieval of a sort, the brothers were never pure in their style borrowings, never used a vocabulary correctly, and inevitably maneuvered scale in some perverse way. The scale and tiny entrances of Samuel's First Presbyterian Church (1897) at Berkeley seem destined to receive nymphs, fairies, and brownies. Joseph Cather's Broadway Methodist Episcopal Church (1897–1898) in Camden, New Jersey, has all the appearances of a cut-out doll house that at the stroke of a magic wand had suddenly been enlarged.

The play between the real and make-believe world which scale can provide continued to dominate the work of the two brothers after 1900. For the Louisiana Purchase Exposition at St. Louis, Samuel and Joseph together designed the San Francisco City Building (1904), and Samuel produced the California State Building (1904). The latter corrected the original provincial "errors" of the Santa Barbara Mission (and in the process introduced some new errors), while the San Francisco City Building sported a towerlike shaft that seemed to have been plunged into the heart of a Beaux-Arts temple. Even the innocent California bungalow was rescaled so that it too could externally and internally read as picturesque.

The extensive projected and unrealized work of the Newsoms forces us to reexamine carefully a number of questions relating to architecture in general and specifically American architecture. The designs of low-art firms such as the Newsoms' are in many ways a more accurate mirror of the ideals of their age than much of the work of their high-art contemporaries. The strength and vigor of their designs should prompt us to pause and look again at how we form judgments in architecture. The element of memorability, so important to the Newsoms and their clients, is a factor rarely touched upon in discussion of the architecture of the past or present.

DAVID GEBHARD

WORKS

SAMUEL AND JOSEPH CATHER NEWSOM

1879, Beach House, Oakland, Calif. c.1883, Allison House, San Francisco. 1884, D. H. Boyd House; 1884–1885, William Carson House; Eureka, Calif. 1886, A. M. Starr House, San Francisco. 1887, O. D. Baldwin House; 1887, L. L. Bradbury House; Los Angeles. c.1887, Cottage, San Rafael, Calif. 1887, Glendale Villa Hotel, Calif. 1888, Bryson-Bonebrake Block (completed by J. Cather Newsom); 1888–1890, J. F. Cosby House (completed by J. Cather Newsom); Los Angeles. 1904, San Francisco City Building, Louisiana Purchase Exposition, St. Louis, Mo.

SAMUEL NEWSOM

1891, Carson Block, Eureka, Calif. 1893, Horticultural and Agricultural Building, Mid-winter International Exposition, San Francisco. 1893, O. D. Baldwin House; c.1896, Eugene J. Bates House; San Francisco. 1897, Cottage, Oakland, Calif. 1897, First Presbyterian Church, Berkeley. 1897, Marin County Bank Building (with Meyer); 1897, Parker House (with Sidney Newsom); San Rafael, Calif. 1897–1899, Rudolph Spreckels House (with Sidney Newsom), San Francisco. 1904, California State Building, Louisiana Purchase Exposition, St. Louis, Mo.

JOSEPH CATHER NEWSOM

1890, Chauvin Block, Los Angeles. (A)1888?–1891, David C. Cook House, Piru, Calif. 1893, R. George Zahn House, Oakland, Calif. c.1896, Eugene J. Bates House, San Francisco. 1896, Four Speculative Houses, Longport, N.J. 1896, Presbyterian Church, Narberth, Pa. 1896, United Methodist Church, Hightstown, N.J. 1897, Baptist Church, Coudersport, Pa. 1897–1898, Broadway Methodist Episcopal Church, Camden, N.J. 1904, Long Beach Pier and Public Recreation Hall, Calif.

BIBLIOGRAPHY

BAIRD, JOSEPH A. 1962 *Time's Wondrous Changes: San Francisco Architecture, 1776–1915.* San Francisco: California Historical Society.

GEBHARD, DAVID; VON BRETON, HARIETTE; and WINTER, ROBERT 1979 *Samuel and Joseph Cather Newsom: Victorian Architectural Imagery in California 1878–1909.* Santa Barbara, Calif.: University of California, Santa Barbara Art Museum.

KIRKER, HAROLD 1973 *California's Architectural Frontier.* Santa Barbara, Calif.: Peregrine Smith.

NEWSOM, JOSEPH CATHER (1888*a*)1981 *Artistic Buildings and Homes of Los Angeles.* With an introduction by Jeanne C. Bennett. Reprint. Los Angeles: Calliope Press.

NEWSOM, JOSEPH CATHER 1888*b* *California Low Priced Cottages.* San Francisco.

NEWSOM, JOSEPH CATHER 1890 *Picturesque and Artistic Homes and Buildings of California.* San Francisco.

NEWSOM, JOSEPH CATHER 1893 *Modern Homes of California.* San Francisco.

NEWSOM, JOSEPH CATHER c.1895*a* *Artistic City Buildings, Flats and Residences.* San Francisco.

NEWSOM, JOSEPH CATHER c.1895*b* *Artistic Country Homes.* San Francisco.

NEWSOM, JOSEPH CATHER (editor) 1897–1899 *Up-To-Date Architecture.* San Francisco.

NEWSOM, JOSEPH CATHER c.1898 *New Booklet on Churches.* Philadelphia.

NEWSOM, SAMUEL 1890 *Some City and Suburban Homes.* San Francisco: Bancroft.

NEWSOM, SAMUEL, and NEWSOM, JOSEPH CATHER (1884–1885)1978 *Picturesque California Homes.* Reprint. Los Angeles: Hennessey & Ingalls.

NEWSOM, SAMUEL, and NEWSOM, JOSEPH CATHER 1887 *Picturesque California Homes: No. 2.* San Francisco.

OLMSTED, ROGER, and WATKINS, T. H. 1968 *Here Today.* With photographs by Morley Baer. San Francisco: Chronicle Books.

SACKS, BENJAMIN 1979 *Carson Mansion and Ingomar Theatre.* Fresno, Calif.: Valley Publishers.

WALDHORN, JUDITH LYNCH, and WOODBRIDGE, WALLY B. 1978 *Victorian Legacy: Tours of San Francisco Bay Architecture.* San Francisco: 101 Productions.

WOODBRIDGE, SALLY (editor) 1976 *Bay Area Houses.* New York: Oxford University Press.

NEWTON, DUDLEY

Born in Newport, Rhode Island, Dudley Newton (1845–1907) trained during the early 1860s with the city's first resident architect, GEORGE C. MASON, SR., launching his own Newport career in 1866. The bulk of Newton's work involved summer cottage design, augmented occasionally by a commission for a commercial block. He took little interest in professional matters, writing, or having his buildings published. Newton made one foray into the commercial realms of the building industry in 1871 when he patented the "Newton Roof," an improved form of mansard.

A man of only local renown in his own lifetime, Dudley Newton was all but forgotten in the early twentieth century. It is due to the writings of Henry-Russell Hitchcock and Vincent Scully that Newton now has a substantial reputation. Scully in particular promoted Newton's fame, citing the architect's work of the mid-1870s as the epitome of what Scully has labeled the Stick style—a style known during the 1870s as modern Gothic. Scully and subsequent critics have lamented Newton's historicizing later work, especially the Colonial Revival Weaver House in Newport of 1898, for "non-progressive" eclecticism.

DAVID CHASE

WORKS

*1866–1867, Police Station; 1870, George H. Norman Estate (improvements); 1872, King-Birkhead House; 1873, Clarence Rathbone House; *1873–1874, Newport Gas Company Building; 1875, George H. Norman (stable and gate lodge); Newport, R.I. 1875–1876, Mrs. George C. Cram House, Middletown, R.I. 1875–1876, Henry Swinburne House; 1881–1882, Charles F. Chickering House; 1882, Mrs. Julia Eldridge House; 1882, Mrs. Seymour House; 1883–1884, Major T. K. Gibbs House; 1883–1884, William G. Weld House; 1884–1888, J. J. Van Alen House, Wakehurst; with C. E. Kempe); 1891–1893, Aquidneck Bank/Kinsley Block; Newport, R.I. *1892, Levi P. Morton Barn, Rhinecliff-on-Hudson, N.Y. 1894–1895, Harold Brown House; 1897–1898, Stuyvesant Fish House (Crossways); 1898, Susan B. Weaver House; Newport, R.I.

BIBLIOGRAPHY

For additional information on Dudley Newton, see the Robert Curry manuscript building contracts collection in the Newport Historical Society, R.I.

DOWNING, ANTOINETTE, F., and SCULLY, VINCENT J., JR. (1952)1967 *The Architectural Heritage of Newport, Rhode Island: 1640–1915.* 2d ed., rev. New York: Potter.

HITCHCOCK, H. R. (1957)1963 *Architecture: Nineteenth and Twentieth Centuries.* 2d ed. Baltimore: Penguin.

JORDY, WILLIAM H., and MONKHOUSE, CHRISTOPHER (editors) 1982 *Rhode Island Buildings on Paper.* Cambridge, Mass.: M.I.T. Press.

Newport Mercury. 1860–1900.

RHOADS, WILLIAM B. 1977 *The Colonial Revival.* New York: Garland.

SCULLY, VINCENT J., JR. (1955)1971 *The Shingle Style and the Stick Style.* Rev. ed. New Haven: Yale University Press.

NEWTON, ERNEST

Born in London, Ernest Newton (1856–1922) was articled to RICHARD NORMAN SHAW in 1873. He stayed there until he set up in practice in 1897. He specialized in the design of both suburban and country houses. In 1919, he became a Royal Academician after receiving the Royal Institute of British Architects Gold Medal in 1918. His practice was continued after his death by his son W. G. Newton.

GODFREY RUBENS

WORKS

*1881, Church of the Good Shepherd, Handen Road; 1883–1892, House of the Retreat, Lloyds Square; London. c.1886, Beechcroft, Bickley Park Road, Bromley, Kent, England. 1891, Banstead School, Banstead, Surrey, England. 1894–1895, Red Court, Scotland Lane, south of Haslemere, Surrey, England. 1897, Glebelands, Glebelands Road, Wokingham, Berkshire, England. 1897–1898, Martin's Bank; 1897–1898, Royal Bell Hotel; Bromley, Kent, England. c.1900, Steep Hill, near Saint Hellier, Jersey, England. 1902–1903, Newbies, Bauhurst, Hampshire, England. 1907, Luckley, Wokingham, England. 1908, Scotman's Field, Burway Hill, Church Stretton, Shropshire, England. 1911, Saint Gregory and Saint Augustine, 322 Woodstock Road, Oxford.

BIBLIOGRAPHY

NEWTON, ERNEST 1883 *Sketches for Country Residences.* London: Batsford.

NEWTON, ERNEST 1890 *A Book of Houses.* London: Sprague.

NEWTON, ERNEST 1903 *A Book of Country Houses.* London: Batsford.

NEWTON, WILLIAM GODFREY 1925 *The Work of Ernest Newton, R.A.* London: Architectural Press.

NEWTON, WILLIAM

William Newton (1735–1790), son of a London cabinetmaker, was educated at Christ's Hospital in London (1743–1750), apprenticed to William Jones, and worked under MATTHEW BRETTINGHAM. Visiting Rome in 1766, he published the first English translation of VITRUVIUS (1771). Despite his learning and accomplishment, he remained a relatively minor architect following the neoclassical style associated with JAMES Stuart and ROBERT ADAM. With commissions for private houses, major projects for the most part eluded him. In 1782, he became clerk of the works at Greenwich Hospital, assisting Stuart in the rehabilitation of the chapel, burnt in 1779. He helped edit the second volume of Stuart's *Antiquities of Athens* (1788).

LESLEY LEWIS

WORKS

1764–1768, Durdans, Epsom, Surrey, England. *1765–1768, The Londern Tavern. 1768, Highams, Woodford Green, Walthamstow, Essex, England. *1768, Hungerford Park, Berkshire, England. 1782–1783, Greenwich Hospital (Boys' School); 1782–1788, Greenwich Hospital (chapel; with James Stuart); England.

BIBLIOGRAPHY

LEWIS, LESLEY 1947 "The Architects of the Chapel at Greenwich Hospital." *Art Bulletin* 29:260–267.

LEWIS, LESLEY 1951 "Greece and Rome at Greenwich." *The Architectural Review* 109:16–24.

NICHOLS, WILLIAM

William Nichols (1777?–1854) was the principal architect in the American South before the Civil War, serving successively, in name or function, as state architect or engineer in North Carolina (1817–1826), Alabama (1827–1833), Louisiana (1834–1835), and Mississippi (1836–1848). During more than fifty years of practice, Nichols confronted the entire range of building needs presented by a developing frontier, from law offices to courthouses and capitols, academies to universities, cottages to plantation houses, jails to penitentiaries, and sidewalks to canals and railroads, providing answers that were economical, elegant, and influential. He was versed in Federal, Gothic, Egyptian, and Italianate forms, but those of the Greek Revival proved his mainstay.

Born in Bath, England, where he received his training in a family of builders, Nichols left in 1800 for New Bern, North Carolina. His role in North Carolina's architecture in the first quarter of the century was central. From the fine Federal architecture of New Bern to, beginning in 1815, essays in the Gothic and Greek Revivals, his works throughout that state provided lasting models. Patterns of patronage and wide-ranging practice established in North Carolina were repeated during seven years in Alabama, two years in Louisiana, and a final eighteen in Mississippi. Government appointments put Nichols in contact with each state's leading political figures, jurists, lawyers, clergymen, educators, businessmen, and planters, resulting in commissions diverse in type and location. Nichols's influence was spread not only by executed works and drawings but also by his apprentices and associates, including William Nichols, Jr. (his son), Asa King, Benjamin Boulton, Cornelius Leary, Nimrod West, James Reed, James Riggs, Giles Johnston, John Berry, John Robb, and Reuben Clark.

C. FORD PEATROSS

WORKS

1806–1809, New Bern Academy, N.C. 1806–1809, Saint Paul's Church; 1815, Joseph Blount Skinner House Law Office; Edenton, N.C. *1817, Cape Fear Bank; 1820, Bank of the United States Branch; Fayetteville, N.C. *1820–1822, 1833, State Capitol; *1820–1824, Government House; Raleigh, N.C. 1822–1826, University of North Carolina at Chapel Hill. 1823–1825, Masonic Lodge, Hillsborough, N.C. *1824, Wake County Jail, Raleigh, N.C. *1825, Davidson County Courthouse, Lexington, N.C. *1827–1830, Guilford County Courthouse, Greensboro, N.C. *1828–1831, University of Alabama; *1829–1831, Christ Church; Tuscaloosa, Ala. *1833, Muscle Shoals Canal, Ala. *1834–1835, State Penitentiary, Baton Rouge, La. *1835, State House, New Orleans, La. 1836–1840, State Capitol; *1836–1847, State Penitentiary; 1839–1842, Executive Mansion; *1843–1846, First Presbyterian Church; Jackson, Miss. 1845–1848, University of Mississippi, Oxford. *1849–1850, Yazoo County Courthouse, Yazoo City, Miss. *1853, Lexington Male and Female Academy, Miss.

BIBLIOGRAPHY

CRAIG, JAMES H. 1965 *The Arts and Crafts of North Carolina: 1699–1840.* Winston-Salem, N.C.: Old Salem.

DECELL, HARRIET, and PRITCHARD, JOANNE 1976 *Yazoo: Its Legends and Legacies.* Yazoo City, Miss.: Yazoo Delta Press.

ELLIOT, CECIL D., and SCHUMACHER, ROSS 1958 "The North Carolina State Capitol." *Southern Architect* May:19–22; June:23–26; July:23–27.

HAMLIN, TALBOT F. (1944)1964 *Greek Revival Architecture in America.* Reprint. New York: Dover.

MCCAIN, WILLIAM D. 1953 *The Story of Jackson: A History of the Capital of Mississippi, 1821–1951.* 2 vols. Jackson, Miss.: Hyer.

PEATROSS, C. FORD, and MELLOWN, ROBERT 1979 *William Nichols: Architect.* University: University of Alabama Art Gallery.

SWAIM, DAVID L. 1867 *Early Times in Raleigh.* Raleigh, N.C.: Walters.

NICHOLSON, PETER

Born at Prestonkirk, East Lothian, Scotland, Peter Nicholson (1765–1844), a stonemason's son, was apprenticed to a cabinetmaker, but his unusual gift for mathematics led him into architecture. He established a school of carpentry and joinery in London in the 1780s and in 1792 published the first of twenty-four books on mathematics, masonry construction, stairbuilding, and other refinements of construction that revealed the complexities inherent in these endeavors and contributed significantly to the separation of architecture from engineering during the nineteenth century. Nicholson's architectural works are known primarily as they were published in his books.

JACK QUINAN

WORKS

1802–1818, Carlton Place, Laurieston, Glasgow, Scotland. c.1805, Buchanan Cottage, near Glasgow, Scotland. c.1805, Coffee House, Paisley, Renfrewshire, Scotland. c.1805, Grey House, Glasgow, Scotland. c.1805, Timber Bridge, River Clyde, near Glasgow, Scotland. 1806, Fulton Alexander House (Yorkshire Ho), Partick, Lanarkshire, Scotland. 1811, Robert Mousey House (Castletown), Rockliff, Cumberland, Scotland. 1811–1813, Hamilton Building, Old College, Glasgow, Scotland. 1812–1817, Corby Castle (remodeled for Henry Holland), Cumberland, Scotland.

BIBLIOGRAPHY

NICHOLSON, PETER (1792*a*)1815 *The Carpenter's and Joiner's Assistant.* 4th ed., rev. London: Taylor.

NICHOLSON, PETER (1792*b*)1871 *The Carpenter's New Guide.* Philadelphia: Lippincott.

NICHOLSON, PETER (1795–1798)1848 *Principles of Architecture.* 3 vols. 6th ed., rev. London: Bohn.

NICHOLSON, PETER (1820)1847 *Treatise on the Construction of Staircases and Handrails.* New ed. London: Taylor.

NICHOLSON, PETER (1822)1838 *A Key to Nicholson's Popular Course of the Pure and Mixed Mathematics.* London: Sherwood.

NICHOLSON, PETER (1823)1860 *New and Improved Practical Builder and Workman's Companion.* 3 vols. London: Kelly.

NICHOLSON, PETER 1824 "Memoir of Mr. Peter Nicholson." In *The Builder and Workman's New Director.* London: Compton.

NICHOLSON, PETER (1826)1838 *The Practical Cabinet Maker, Upholsterer, and Complete Decorator.* London.

NICHOLSON, PETER (1827)1835 *A Practical Treatise on the Art of Masonry and Stone-cutting.* 3d ed. London: Maynard.

NICHOLSON, PETER 1828 *The School of Architecture and Engineering.* London: The author.

NICOLE, NICOLAS

Born in Besançon, France, the son of a high official in the Mint, Nicolas Nicole (1702–1784) trained first as an engraver. In 1737, he went to Paris to study under JACQUES FRANÇOIS BLONDEL, returning after two years to begin a noteworthy career as an ecclesiastical architect, in time evolving a neat geometric style. Between 1770 and 1778, he supervised the building of VICTOR LOUIS's Intendance in Besançon. He also invented a revolver.

R. D. MIDDLETON

WORKS

1739–1745, Eglise du Refuge, 14 rue de L'Orme de Chamars; 1746–1766, Sainte Madeleine (not completed until 1830); Besançon, France. 1749–1759, Saint Pierre (completed by Petitjean), Jussey, Haute Saône, France. 1755, Maison Nicole, 5 rue Charles Nedier, Besançon, France. 1758–1780, Abbey, Baume-les-Dames, Doubs, France. c.1768–1772, Château de Choye, Haute Saône, France. 1774–1776, Apartment Block, 138 Grande rue, Besançon, France. 1774–1779, Eglise de l'Assomption, Voray-sur-l'Ognon, Haute Saône, France. 1779–1784, Church (not completed until 1789 by Louis Beuque), Percey-le-Grand, Haute Saône, France.

BIBLIOGRAPHY

ESTAVOYER, LYONEL; GRISEL, DENIS; and LANGROGNET, JEAN LOUIS 1980 *Architectures en Franche-Comte au XVIIIe siècle.* Besançon, France: Archives Départementales du Doubs et de la Haute-Saône.

TOURNIER, RENÉ 1937 "L'Architecte Nicolas Nicole (1702–1784)." Pages 112–136 in *Académie des Science, Belles-Lettres et Arts de Besançon. Proces-verbaux et mémoires. Année 1938.* Besançon, France: Jacques & Demontrond.

TOURNIER, RENÉ 1970 *Maisons et hôtels privés du XVIIIe siècle à Besançon.* Paris: Belles Lettres.

NICOLETTI, MANFREDI G.

Born in Rieti, Italy, Manfredi G. Nicoletti (1930–) studied with GIACOMO BALLA and PIER LUIGI NERVI. He graduated from the Massachusetts Institute of Architects, after which he worked with MINORU YAMASAKI. An initiator of megastructural conceptions, he designed the Law Court Buildings of Rome and the satellite town of Monaco for 22,000 people distributed in four amphitheaterlike macrobuildings. His bold design of the Helicoidal Skyscraper (1968–1973) in New York embodies new aerodynamic and structural principles with dynamical elegance.

RENATO PEDIO

WORKS

1958–1964, Law Court Buildings (with G. Perugini and S. de Feo), Rome. 1974–1979, Catania Airport (control tower, freight station, and fire station), Sicily, Italy. 1974–1979, Trapani Airport (passenger station), Sicily, Italy.

BIBLIOGRAPHY

BANHAM, REYNER 1976 *Megastructure.* London: Thames & Hudson.

BURNS, JAMES T. 1965 "Venetian Transportation Island." *Progressive Architecture* 46:200–203.

BURNS, JAMES T. 1966 "Monegasque Hanging Gardens." *Progressive Architecture* 47:154–157.

CRISPOLTI, ENRICO 1979 "Nicoletti Manfredi." In *Immaginazione Megastrutturale dal Futurismo a oggi.* Venice, Italy: Biennale.

KEPES, GYORGY 1972 *Arts of the Environment.* New York: Braziller.

KOENIG, GIOVANNI K. 1970 "L'Es'ecutivo dell'utopia: Attività progettuale di Manfredi G. Nicoletti." *Casabella* 34, no. 347:16–27.

LARSON, LESLIE 1964 *Lighting and Its Design.* New York: Whitney Museum.

NICOLETTI, MANFREDI G. 1978 *Continuity Evolution Architecture.* Bari, Italy: Dedalo.

RAGON, MICHEL 1978 Volume 3 in *Histoire Mondiale de l'Architecture et de l'Urbanisme modernes.* Tournai, France: Casterman.

VILLECCO, MARGUERITE 1973 "Nicoletti's Tower." *Architecture Plus* 1, no. 10:28–37.

ZEVI, BRUNO (1950)1975 *Storia dell'Architettura Moderna.* 5th ed. Turin, Italy: Einaudi.

NIEMEYER, OSCAR

Brazil's best known architect, Oscar Niemeyer (1907–) has created a unique form of modern architecture that audaciously combines modern technology with the love of curves and freedom of form representative of Brazilian baroque. Son of a well-to-do Rio de Janeiro family, Niemeyer entered the National School of Fine Arts in 1930 just as its antiquated nineteenth-century Beaux Arts curriculum was being updated by LÚCIO COSTA to reflect the progressive architectural theories of LE CORBUSIER and the Bauhaus. Only a year later, Costa was forced to resign. Niemeyer soon petitioned Costa for a job in order to continue his education of modern architectural techniques.

In 1936, when the Brazilian government invited Le Corbusier to give lectures and advise Costa on his designs for the Ministry of Education Building and university city, Niemeyer insisted on becoming part of the group of young architects selected to work with him. During the brief visit, Niemeyer became Le Corbusier's personal draftsman and later chief architect for the construction of the Ministry Building.

Gustavo Capanema, Minister of Education, introduced Niemeyer to his most important patron, Juscelino Kubitschek. In 1942, when they met, Kubitschek was the mayor of Belo Horizonte, the capital of Brazil's wealthiest central state, Minas Gerais. A friendship ensued between these two young ambitious Brazilians, which led to Niemeyer's commission of Pampulha, a suburban area of Belo Horizonte. Niemeyer designed five different recreational facilities (1942–1947) that hug the edges of an artificial lake, responding to Kubitschek's desire to enhance community life of the area. Pampulha's cruciform Church of Saint Francis of Assisi (1943) is contained in a series of irregular barrel vaults enclosed on one end with Candido Portinari's colorful ceramic mural, depicting the life of Saint Francis. Niemeyer also designed a casino, a restaurant, and a yacht club that effectively used Le Corbusier's butterfly roof and *brise-soleils.* At Pampulha, Niemeyer began to develop a style that was lighter and more lyrical than Le Corbusier's and involved undulating forms.

Following Pampulha, Niemeyer's architectural career was firmly established in Brazil, and he was asked to serve on the advisory committee of the United Nations Building in New York. He worked closely with Le Corbusier on it, and a combination of their designs, Project 23–32 (23 being Le Corbusier's and 32 Niemeyer's) was chosen for actual execution.

In 1956, the competition for Brazil's new capital was won by Lúcio Costa, and Kubitschek, now president of Brazil, appointed Niemeyer as technical adviser to Novacap (the authority of the new capital of Brazil), making him responsible for the design of the most important federal buildings of the new capital including the cathedral, the president's home, a residential housing complex, the university, and other major structures. Joaquim Cardoso, Brasília's chief structural engineer, worked closely with Niemeyer, giving form to Niemeyer's imaginative symbolism in the concave dome that enclosed the Senate chambers and the convex bowl that housed the Congress. Dramatically forceful, the government palaces escaped stagnation. This was not true of the repetitious series of ministries that line either side of the city's monumental esplanade. Niemeyer continued to elaborate designs for Brasília until 1964 when the government fell in a right-wing coup and he moved his office to France in a self-imposed exile.

A new phase of his career began as he became more accessible to international commissions. Before this move, Niemeyer's intense fear of flying had made it difficult for him to accept work outside Brazil. With an established reputation, he could pick and choose projects according to his architectural and political convictions. Niemeyer never lacked commissions. Niemeyer considers the Mondadori Headquarters (1968–1975) in Milan and the Communist Party Headquarters (1967–1972) in Paris to be his best works.

In the early 1960s, Giorgio Mondadori decided to build a new complex for his publishing house that would be a monument to his father and went to Niemeyer because of his work in Brasília. The project necessitated offices for administrative work and the editorial staff, plus a staff amenity area. Three separate structures make up the complex, the main building an abstracted variation of Itamarati (Ministry of Foreign Relations) in Brasília—a glass box hung from a cage of reinforced concrete arches set in a pond of water. Niemeyer has often lightened his buildings by surrounding them with water or by using minimal ground supports, evoking a sense of calm and structural weightlessness.

A communist since 1945 and winner of the Lenin Peace Prize in 1962, Niemeyer felt honored to design the Communist Headquarters in Paris, producing a serpentine glass box surmounting a hill of concrete. In front of the structure a domed protrusion emerges from the concrete that outlines the roof of an underground auditorium. Furnished with Niemeyer's leather and steel furniture, the structure remains one of his most finely finished buildings.

In terms of modernity, Niemeyer's design for the University of Constantine in Algeria (1978) extends the tensile strength of reinforced concrete to its limits. A 100-meter-long building houses most of the classrooms and has a 50-meter span between ground supports. From afar, the building appears to float above the ground.

An extraordinarily dedicated architect, Niemeyer still works a ten-hour day receiving young architects from all over the world, elaborating designs, and often refusing compensation for his community-oriented projects. As a young architect, Niemeyer quickly absorbed Le Corbusier's sensitivity to architectural aesthetics which above all inspired Niemeyer to strive for beauty through the manipulation of form.

ELIZABETH D. HARRIS

WORKS

1936–1945, Ministry of Education and Health (with Lúcio Costa, Ernani Vasconcellos, Carlos Leão, JORGE MOREIRA, AFFONSO EDUARDO REIDY, and Le Corbusier as consultant; now the Palâcio da Cultura), Rio de Janeiro, Brazil. 1942–1947, Pampulha Recreation Facilities, Belo Horizonte, Brazil. 1953, Niemeyer House, Rio de Janeiro, Brazil. 1957–1964, Brasília (all major government buildings, the cathedral, the university, the National Theater, and a housing complex; project completed in 1970 by others). 1962, New Pampulha Yacht Club, Belo Horizonte, Brazil. 1966, Manchete Headquarters, Rio de Janeiro, Brazil. 1967–1972, Communist Party Headquarters, Paris. 1968–1975, Mondadori Headquarters, Milan. 1969–1978, University of Constantine, Algeria. 1972, Gomes House, Rio de Janeiro, Brazil.

BIBLIOGRAPHY

L'Architecture d'Aujourd'hui. 1974 171, Jan.–Feb.: entire issue.

NIEMEYER, OSCAR 1975 *Oscar Niemeyer.* Milan: Mondadori.

NIEMEYER, OSCAR 1978 *A forma na architectura.* Rio de Janeiro, Brazil: Avenir.

PAPADAKI, STAMO (1950)1954 *The Work of Oscar Niemeyer.* 2d ed., rev. & enl. New York: Reinhold.

PAPADAKI, STAMO 1956 *Oscar Niemeyer: Works in Progress.* New York: Reinhold.

PAPADAKI, STAMO 1960 *Oscar Niemeyer.* New York: Braziller.

SPADE, RUPERT (1969)1971 *Oscar Niemeyer.* New York: Simon & Schuster.

NIGETTI, MATTEO

The son of an obscure Florentine artist, Matteo Nigetti (1580?–1649) is noted mostly as the collaborator and assistant of BERNARDO BUONTALENTI. On the death of Buontalenti in 1608, Nigetti succeeded him as clerk of the works of the Cappella dei Principi at the Church of San Lorenzo, Florence. During the next forty years, Nigetti became the major interpreter of the branch of Florentine architecture that led ultimately to the baroque. Although Nigetti has been given little place in histories of architecture, overshadowed as he is by the earlier mannerist phase of Florentine architecture, he has recently been the object of further study and is reckoned one of the most important architects of the early seventeenth century in Florence.

In addition to his work on the Chapel, Nigetti was responsible for a number of small churches in Florence. The Church of San Francesco Vanchetoni (1602–1603), dedicated to the Blessed Ippolito Galantini, recalls the work of BARTOLOMEO AMMANNATI in its decorative work. A later work is Nigetti's façade for the Church of the Ognissanti (1637). In comparison with an earlier façade of similar composition, the Church of San Stefano dei Cavalieri in Pisa by GIORGIO VASARI, G. Kauffmann notes that Nigetti's work is denser in texture and more sculptural. The opposing pediments recall Buontalenti's Porta delle Suppliche at the Uffizi.

Nigetti's major work is the Cappella dei Principi, a tomb chapel for the Medici princes. The first model of this structure was prepared in 1561 by Giorgio Vasari. Thereafter, other architects, including Buontalenti and GIOVANNI DE' MEDICI, revised the plan so that by the time Nigetti took over, the basic outline of the structure had been determined. Nigetti's specific contribution to the design still has to be clarified. He was certainly responsible for placing much of the decoration and he made many design decisions to vary the initial plans. The result—in its formal, grandiose, highly learned style—is as much the result of Nigetti as of the earlier masters.

The phase of architecture in Florence represented by Nigetti has no real comparison in Rome or elsewhere in Italy. It is, for all intents and purposes, the result of Medici rule. Stylistically, Nigetti derives from the late sixteenth-century Vasari-Ammannati-Buontalenti group, but as a result of his patrons he learned to master a monumental style that is neither mannerist nor baroque but a grander, enriched, enlarged example of the earlier Florentine renaissance of FILIPPO BRUNELLESCHI.

NICHOLAS ADAMS

WORKS

1602–1603, San Francesco Vanchetoni; 1608–1649, Cappella dei Principi, San Lorenzo; 1637, Church of the Ognissanti (façade); *1638, San Pier Maggiore (façade still extant) Florence.

BIBLIOGRAPHY

BERTI, LUCIANO 1950 "Matteo Nigetti, I." *Rivista d' Arte* 26:157–184.

BERTI, LUCIANO 1951–1953 "Matteo Nigetti, II." *Rivista d' Arte* 27:93–106.

BORSI, FRANCO (editor) 1980 *Firenze e la Toscana dei Medici nell' Europa del Cinquecento: Il potere e lo spazio: La scena del Principe.* Florence: Edizioni Medice.

DADDI-GIOVANNOZZI, VERA 1937–1940 "Untersuchungen über Don Giovanni de' Medici und Alessandro Pieroni." *Mitteilungen des Kunsthistorischen Instituts Florenz* 5:58–75.

KAUFFMANN, GEORG (1962)1971 *Florence: Art Treasures and Buildings.* London: Phaidon.

NIZZOLI, MARCELLO

Marcello Nizzoli (1887–1968) was one of the most versatile Italian designers of the twentieth century. Born in Boretto, near Reggio Emilia, Nizzoli first exhibited his paintings with the Futurist group in 1914, and after World War I became active in the Italian Modern movement. A frequent collaborator of EDOARDO PERSICO and GIUSEPPE TERRAGNI, Nizzoli achieved his most important works in exhibits and industrial design objects. He designed many typewriters and calculators for Olivetti, including the famous Lettera 22, as well as the Necchi Mirella sewing machine. His architectural works possess a similar elegance, and the façade of the Olivetti Building (1954) in Milan ranks among the most refined exercises in steel and glass construction.

THOMAS L. SCHUMACHER

WORKS

1932, Room dedicated to the year 1919, Tenth Anniversary Exhibit of the Fascist Revolution; 1934, Parker Store (with Edoardo Persico); 1934, Publicity Stand (with Persico), Victor Emmanuel Gallery; 1934, Room of the Golden Medals (with Persico), Aeronautics Exhibit; 1936, Victory Room (with Persico), Vi Triennale; Milan. 1938, Olivetti Store, Venice, Italy. 1940, Summa Adding Machine; 1948, Lexicon 80 Typewriter; 1950, Lettera 22 Typewriter; for Olivetti. 1950–1953, Residential Quarter (for Olivetti workers; with A. Fiocchi); 1953, Housing (for Olivetti dependents; with G. M. Oliveri); Ivrea, Italy. 1954, Olivetti Office Building (with Bernasconi and Fiocchi); Milan. 1956–1958, ENI Building (with Oliveri), San Donato Milanese, Italy.

BIBLIOGRAPHY

AMBASZ, EMILIO 1971 *Italy: The New Domestic Frontier.* New York: Museum of Modern Art.

CELANT, GERMANO 1968 *Marcello Nizzoli.* Milan, Italy: Edizioni di Communità.

DREXLER, ARTHUR, and DANIEL, GRETA 1959 *Introduction to Twentieth Century Design.* Garden City, N.Y.: Doubleday.

GALARDI, ALBERTO 1967 *New Italian Architecture.* New York: Praeger.

GHIRARDO, DIANE 1980 "Politics of a Masterpiece: The Vicenda of the Decoration of the Façade of the Casa del Fascio, Como, 1936–1939." *Art Bulletin* 62:462–478.

GREGOTTI, VITTORIO 1968 *New Directions in Italian Architecture.* New York: Braziller.

MOSS, R. 1961 "The Anatomy of an Image." *Industrial Design* 11.

SARTORIS, ALBERTO (1948)1954–1957 Page 114 in *Encyclopédie de l'Architecture Nouvelle.* Milan: Hoepli.

NOBBS, PERCY ERSKINE

A leader in Canadian architectural and planning circles, Percy Erskine Nobbs (1875–1964) went to Canada in 1903 to become the second director of the McGill School of Architecture (established in 1896). Born in Haddington, Scotland, but raised in St. Petersburg, Russia, Nobbs received a master's degree from the University of Edinburgh in 1896 and then spent four years as an early articled pupil of ROBERT S. LORIMER. Winner of the Royal Institute of British Architects' Tite Prize (1900) and the Owen Jones Studentship (1902), Nobbs worked for some months in 1901 for the London County Council Architect's Department, Fire Brigade branch. As the designing partner in the firm of Nobbs and Hyde (1910–1945), Nobb's works, mainly in the Montreal region, skillfully demonstrate the ideals of the Arts and Crafts movement. A man of many interests and talents, Nobbs wrote extensively, won a silver medal for fencing in the 1908 Olympic Games, and in 1948 founded the Atlantic Salmon Association to ensure the species' survival.

SUSAN WAGG

WORKS

1904–1906, McGill University Union; 1907–1909, Macdonald Engineering Building, McGill University; 1911–1912, New Birks Building; Montreal. 1911–1913, John L. Todd House, Senneville, Quebec. 1912, University of Alberta General Plan (with Frank Darling), Edmonton. 1912–1913, University Club; 1913–1916, Percy E. Nobbs House, Montreal. 1913–1915, Arts Building; 1919–1920, Provincial College of Medicine; University of Alberta, Edmonton. 1921, McGill University Library Extension, Montreal. 1922, Naval Memorial, Halifax, Nova Scotia. 1922–1923, A. H. Scott House, Dorval, Quebec. 1922–1924, Pathological Institute, McGill University; 1924–1930?, Grove Park Estate; 1926–1928, Pulp and Paper Research Institute, McGill University; 1928–1930, R. Reid Dobell House; 1929–1930, Drummond Medical Building; 1930–1931, Royal Victoria College Extension, McGill University; Montreal.

BIBLIOGRAPHY

NOBBS, PERCY E. 1905 "On the Value of the Study of Old Work." *Canadian Architect and Builder* 18, May:74–75.

NOBBS, PERCY E. 1906 "The Official Architecture of European Capitals." *Canadian Architect and Builder* 19, Mar.:38–40.

NOBBS, PERCY E. 1923*a* "Daylight in Buildings." *American Architect* 124, July:1–6; Aug.:99–106.

NOBBS, PERCY E. 1923*b* "Wall Textures." *American Architect* 124, Sept.:244–250.

NOBBS, PERCY E. 1924 "Architecture in Canada." *Journal of the Royal Institute of British Architects* 31:199–211, 238–250.

NOBBS, PERCY E. 1925*a* "University Education in Architecture." *Journal of the Royal Architectural Institute of Canada* 2:68–71, 106–109.

NOBBS, PERCY E. 1925*b* "The General Scheme for the University of Alberta." *Journal of the Royal Architectural Institute of Canada* 2:159–164.

NOBBS, PERCY E. 1926 "The Subdivision of Residential Suburban Property." *Journal of the Town Planning Institute of Canada* 5:10–16.

NOBBS, PERCY E. 1934 *Salmon Tactics.* London: Philip Allan.

NOBBS, PERCY E. 1935 "Architectural Economics: Design." *Journal of the Royal Architectural Institute of Canada* 12:30–32.

NOBBS, PERCY E. 1936 *Fencing Tactics.* London: Philip Allan.

NOBBS, PERCY E. 1937 *Design: A Treatise on the Discovery of Form.* Toronto: Oxford University Press.

SAVAGE, PETER 1980 *Lorimer and the Edinburgh Craft Designers.* Edinburgh: Paul Harris.

WAGG, SUSAN W. 1982 "Two Buildings by Percy Erskine Nobbs." *Selected Papers from the Society for the Study of Architecture in Canada Annual Meetings 1977 & 1978.* Ottawa: The society.

NOEL, MARTÍN

Martín Noel (1888–1963) was the most important Argentine architect of the "Nationalist Restoration," an ideological movement that proposed the Spanish colonial style as the source of inspiration for Latin-American architecture.

Noel graduated in Paris as an academic architect but, after returning to Buenos Aires, he built outstanding neocolonial buildings. His most lasting influence—to give a place of real value to the Hispanic art of the Americas—was made through his teachings, his books, and his active life as a politician and as president of the Academia Nacional de Bellas Artes for more than twenty years.

ALBERTO NICOLINI

WORKS

1919, City Hall (restoration), Luján; 1920, Charles and Martín Noel House (now the Fernández Blanco Museum); 1922, Enrique Larreta Country House; 1923, Yrurtia House; Buenos Aires. 1930, Argentine Pavilion, Ibero-American Exposition, Seville, Spain.

BIBLIOGRAPHY

GUTIÉRREZ, RAMÓN 1971 "Presencia y Continuidad de España en la Arquitectura Rioplatense." *Hogar y Arquitectura* 97:17–92.

NOEL, MARTÍN 1921 *Contribución a la Historia de la Arquitectura Hispano-Americana.* Buenos Aires: Talleres Peuser.

NOEL, MARTÍN 1926 *Fundamentos para una estética nacional.* Buenos Aires: Talleres Rodriguez Giles.

NOEL, MARTÍN 1929 *España vista otra vez.* Madrid: Editorial España.

NOEL, MARTÍN 1932 *Teoría histórica de la Arquitectura Virreinal.* Buenos Aires: Editorial Peuser.

NOEL, MARTÍN 1939–1942 Volumes 1–3, 4, 8, 14–15 in *Documentos de Arte Argentino.* Buenos Aires: Academia Nacional de Bellas Artes.

NOEL, MARTÍN 1943–1960 Volumes 1–5, 7–9, 11–12 in *Documentos de Arte Colonial Sudamericano.* Buenos Aires: Academia Nacional de Bellas Artes.

NOLLI, GIOVANNI BATTISTA

Giovanni Battista Nolli (1701–1756) is less well known as an architect than as the master topographer responsible for the famous Rome plan of 1748. Born in Montronio, near Como, Nolli was active as a surveyor first in Milan (1722–1724) and then in Piedmont (1729–1731). By 1736, he was in Rome, already at work on the great Rome plan, which involved the most accurate and thorough survey of Roman monuments, ancient and modern, that had ever been attempted. The base drawing of his survey was completed in 1742, and the plan was issued in printed form six years later. In every respect, Nolli's ichnographic plan is the worthy successor of the *Forma Urbis*, the marble plan of ancient Rome (which he restored in 1742), for it records with precision the form of the city at the time when the expansions of the Renaissance and baroque periods had reached their fullest extent.

The only certain testimony of Nolli's architectural skill is the modest Roman church of Santa Dorotea in Trastevere (1751–1756). Nolli's edifice occupies the site of an earlier church belonging to a Franciscan monastery, which had no architectural pretensions. It is hardly surprising, granted the sensitivity to the city's urban fabric displayed

Nolli. Santa Dorotea in Trastevere. Rome. 1751–1756

in Nolli's Rome plan, that his solution for the insertion of Santa Dorotea into the pre-existing street plan of the area is extremely subtle and effective. The concave plan of Santa Dorotea's façade echoes and amplifies the curving street on which it is situated; likewise, the spare but monumental forms of the exterior elevation respond to the site, for they are intended to be scanned obliquely, at a distance. Indeed, it is impossible to take in the façade in its entirety from an axial viewpoint, so narrow is the street on which it fronts.

The interior of Santa Dorotea is centered on an octagonal space, with a decided emphasis on the longitudinal axis. As in the façade, spareness and clarity characterize the interior. There is a smooth, uninterrupted flow of space from the entrance to the sanctuary, but each part of the plan is clearly defined and compartmentalized. Moreover, Nolli's design embodies a direct expression of relationships between load and support—particularly evident in the broad diagonal ribs resting on the piers supporting the cupola—and a calculated use of light to differentiate the spatial units. The plan and the cupola of Santa Dorotea especially appear to have been influenced by Nolli's great contemporaries, LUIGI VANVITELLI and NICOLA SALVI.

It would be a mistake to interpret the pared-down simplicity of Santa Dorotea as pointing toward the more severe architectural vocabulary of neoclassicism. Rather, this unique example of Nolli's architecture should be viewed as a particular response to the austere rule and limited financial means of his clients. Nolli's respect for the urban context of Santa Dorotea recalls a long line of baroque precedents (of which PIETRO BERRETTINI DA CORTONA's Santa Maria della Pace is perhaps the most outstanding example) as well as his position as Rome's most accomplished topographer.

JOHN PINTO

WORK

1751–1756, Santa Dorotea in Trastevere, Rome.

BIBLIOGRAPHY

EHRLE, FRANCESCO (editor) 1932 *Roma al tempo di Benedetto XIV: La pianta di Roma di Giambattista Nolli del 1748.* Vatican City: Vatican Press.

FACCIOLI, CLEMENTE 1966 "Gio. Battista Nolli (1701–1756) e la sua gran 'Pianta di Roma' del 1748." *Studi Romani* 14:415–442.

"S. Dorotea in Rom und verwandte Kitchenbauten." 1974 *Architectura* 4:165–180.

ZANKER, JURGEN 1973 "Die 'Nuova Pianta di Roma' von Giovanni Battista Nolli (1748)." *Wallraf-Richartz* 35:309–342.

NOTMAN, JOHN

Born in Scotland, John Notman (1810–1865) became one of America's most innovative architects of the mid-nineteenth century. Like other emigrés, he introduced to his adopted country not only new styles and sophisticated approaches to design and program, but also a sense of professionalism in the practice of architecture.

Raised near Edinburgh, Notman was apprenticed to a builder and then worked in the office of William Henry Playfair (see JAMES PLAYFAIR AND WILLIAM HENRY PLAYFAIR). In 1831, during a period of economic depression, Notman emigrated to Philadelphia.

Notman. Prospect Villa. Princeton, New Jersey. 1851–1852

He supported himself as a carpenter until receiving his first important commission, the design of Laurel Hill Cemetery (1836–1839) on the outskirts of Philadelphia. The concept of the picturesque rural cemetery had been introduced to the United States at Mount Auburn Cemetery (1831) in Cambridge, Massachusetts, which was designed by gentlemen amateurs. Laurel Hill, the first architect-designed cemetery, exhibits far more control of form. Laurel Hill received extensive publicity, establishing Notman's reputation. He was subsequently awarded commissions for other rural cemeteries, the most important of which was Hollywood Cemetery (1848) in Richmond, Virginia. In addition he designed Capitol Square (1850–c.1860), also in Richmond, the country's first major picturesque urban park.

Through the backers of Laurel Hill, Notman met the patrons for his first two important houses, Nathan Dunn's Cottage (1837–1838) at Mount Holly, New Jersey, and Riverside (1839) at Burlington, New Jersey. Both projects were published in the first edition of ANDREW JACKSON DOWNING's *A Treatise on the Theory and Practice of Landscape Gardening* (1841). The former, now altered beyond recognition, was described as "semi-oriental." Despite its exotic applied decoration, it was clearly derived from Regency villas, like those illustrated in English pattern books of the preceding two decades. Riverside, demolished in 1961, introduced the full-blown robust Tuscan villa style to the United States. Notman undoubtedly became familiar with the style in Playfair's office. The Scottish architect was producing accomplished Italianate country houses during Notman's apprenticeship, a few years before CHARLES BARRY's first tentative exercises in the style.

Notman would return to an Italianate vocabulary and other American architects would later adopt it. However, what was more important than the style of Riverside was that it embodied a new approach in the United States to the organization of space in domestic buildings. Eschewing symmetry, Notman conceived Riverside as a series of outflung pavilions, controlled and held together by a central core rising the full height of the house. The result was a picturesque silhouette on the exterior, and an interior characterized by the interplay of forms, materials, and light, articulated in elevation as well as plan. This theme was expanded and refined in Notman's later villas, such as Prospect (1851–1852) and Fieldwood (1853?–1855), now known as Guernsey Hall, both in Princeton, New Jersey.

Although Notman's reputation was established by 1840, the first years of the decade were lean ones because of the depression that followed the Panic of 1837. In 1842, however, Downing included one of his houses as Design IX in *Cottage Residences.* Also Italianate, but far simpler than Riverside, the design has been identified as the prototype for several houses in North Carolina.

The second half of the decade was Notman's most productive period. In the spring of 1845 he worked simultaneously on two major commissions, the redesign and enlargement of the New Jersey State House in Trenton (1845–1846), and a new building for the Athenaeum of Philadelphia (1845–1847). The former, now engulfed by later additions, was an exercise in picturesque classicism. Impressed state officials promptly awarded Notman the commission for the New Jersey State Lunatic Asylum (1845–1848), now known as Trenton Psychiatric Hospital. This was the first major mental hospital based on Dr. Thomas S. Kirkbride's theories of treatment.

For The Athenaeum, Notman produced a Renaissance Revival building in the form of a Florentine palazzo. Influenced by such English prototypes as Barry's Travellers' and Reform Clubs, the Athenaeum introduced to the United States the fashion for gentlemen's clubs in the Renaissance mode that was followed for generations.

In 1845 Notman also designed his first church. The Chapel of the Holy Innocents (1845–1847) in Burlington, New Jersey, was a modest building, but it adopted medieval forms in a manner prescribed by English ecclesiologists, who urged a return to pre-Reformation ritual and the revival of English medieval architecture. Notman's masterpiece in the Gothic Revival style is Saint Mark's Church (1847–1852) in Philadelphia. In addition to "correct" detailing, it reflects Notman's expressed aim of achieving excellence primarily through form and proportion. Among Notman's other major Gothic Revival churches are Saint Peter's (1851–1852) in Pittsburgh and the cathedral of Saint John (1857–1858) in Wilmington, Delaware.

For clients who were not High Anglicans, Notman designed in other styles. The façade of the cathedral of Saint Peter and Saint Paul (1851–1857) in Philadelphia reflects Italian prototypes. His last two major Philadelphia churches, Holy Trinity (1856–1859) and Saint Clement's (1855–1859), are Romanesque, the latter a composition of great power and force.

Throughout his career Notman took advantage of advances in technology. His earliest houses were equipped with central heating, indoor plumbing, and sophisticated ventilating systems. In rebuilding Princeton's Nassau Hall (1855–1859) after a fire, he used rolled iron joists; the building was among the first half dozen in the country utilizing this construction technique.

Little is known about the architects trained in Notman's office, except that George W. Hewitt, later a partner of FRANK FURNESS, worked there as a draftsman. Notman was a committed professional, zealous in guarding his responsibility for and control of his work. With THOMAS U. WALTER, he was one of two Philadelphians invited to be a founding member of the American Institute of Architects. His professional attitudes, together with a somewhat contentious personality, sometimes led to difficulties with clients. His death, in 1865, is said to have been hastened by a fondness for strong drink.

CONSTANCE M. GREIFF

WORKS

1836–1839, Laurel Hill Cemetery, Philadelphia. *1837–1838, Nathan Dunn's Cottage, Mount Holly, N.J. *1839, Riverside, Burlington, N. J. *1839–1840, Academy of Natural Sciences, Philadelphia. 1845–1846, New Jersey State House (redesign and enlargement), Trenton. 1845–1847, The Athenaeum of Philadelphia. 1845–1847, Chapel of the Holy Innocents, Burlington, N.J. 1845–1848, New Jersey State Lunatic Asylum (now Trenton Psychiatric Hospital). 1847–1852, Saint Mark's Church, Philadelphia. 1848, Hollywood Cemetery; 1850–c.1860, Capitol Square; Richmond, Va. 1851–1852, Prospect Villa, Princeton, N.J. 1851–1852, Saint Peter's Church, Pittsburgh. 1851–1857, Cathedral of Saint Peter and Saint Paul (façade), Philadelphia. 1853?–1855, Fieldwood Villa (now Guernsey Hall); 1855–1859, Nassau Hall; Princeton, N.J. 1855–1859, Saint Clement's Church; 1856–1859, Holy Trinity Church; Philadelphia. 1857–1858, Cathedral of Saint John, Wilmington, Del.

BIBLIOGRAPHY

DALLETT, FRANCIS JAMES 1959 "John Notman, Architect." *Princeton University Library Chronicle* 20, no. 3:127–139.

DOWING, ANDREW JACKSON 1841 *A Treatise on the Theory and Practice of Landscape Gardening Adapted to North America.* New York and London: Wiley & Putnam.

DOWNING, ANDREW JACKSON 1842 *Cottage Residences.* New York and London: Wiley & Putnam.

FAIRBANKS, JOHNATHAN 1961 "John Notman: Church Architect." Unpublished M.A. thesis, University of Delaware, Newark.

GREIFF, CONSTANCE M. 1979 *John Notman, Architect.* The Athenaeum of Philadelphia.

GREIFF, CONSTANCE M.; GIBBONS, MARY W.; and MENZIES, ELIZABETH, G. C. 1967 *Princeton Architecture.* Princeton, N.J.: Princeton University Press.

JACKSON, JOSEPH 1923 *Early Philadelphia Architects*

and Engineers. Philadelphia: Privately printed.
SMITH, ROBERT C. 1951 "John Notman and the Athenaeum Building." In *Athenaeum Addresses.* The Athenaeum of Philadelphia.
SMITH, ROBERT C. 1953 "John Notman's Nassau Hall." *Princeton University Library Chronicle* 14, no. 3:109–134.
TATUM, GEORGE B. 1961 *Penn's Great Town.* Philadelphia: University of Pennsylvania Press.

NOVOTNÝ, OTAKAR

Otakar Novotný (1880–1959) actively contributed to all phases of modern Czech architecture, from the Modern style (Secession), through rationalistic and civilistic trends, to cubism and functionalism. The most fruitful period was between 1909 and 1914 when he introduced to Bohemia, under the influence of H. P. BERLAGE and the Dutch school, a modern rationalist style represented by several houses made of red brick (particularly the Jan Štenc Publishing House in Prague). Of great importance also was his theoretical and educational work.

VLADIMÍR ŠLAPETA

WORKS

1908–1909, J. Otto House, Zbraslav, Prague. 1908–1911, Gymnasium, Holice, Czechoslovakia. 1909–1911, Jan Štenc Publishing House, Prague. 1911–1912, Zemánek House, Holice; 1912, Gymnasium, Rakovník; Bohemia, Czechoslovakia. 1914, Czech Werkbund Pavilion, Werkbund Exhibition, Cologne, Germany. 1919, Cooperative Teacher's House; 1927–1930, S.V.U. Mánes Art Association Building; 1930, Václav Špála Residence; Prague.

BIBLIOGRAPHY

NOVOTNÝ, OTAKAR 1958 *Jan Kotěra a jeho doba.* Prague: Státní nakl. krásné literatury, hudby a umění.
NOVOTNÝ, OTAKAR 1959 *O architektuře.* Prague: Nakladatelství československých výtvarných umělců.
PEČÍRKA, JAROMÍR 1931 *Otakar Novotný.* Geneva: Verlag Meister der Baukunst.
ŠLAPETA, VLADIMÍR 1980 *Otakar Novotný 1880–1959.* Prague and Olomouc, Czechoslovakia. Exhibition catalogue, with a complete list of architectural and theoretical works.

NOWICKI, MATTHEW

Born in Poland, Matthew Nowicki (1910–1951) studied first in Chicago at the Art Institute and then at the Warsaw Polytechnic where he sharpened his innate talent in drawing and furthered his skills in both engineering and architecture. Through a comprehensive, self-styled course of study and extensive travel, he grouted the historical gaps left by his earlier education. This rare combination of native ability, educational variety, and a dogged quest for professional excellence would have catapulted him to the forefront of his generation's architectural frontier if it had not been for the plane crash that abruptly ended his life. At first acutely influenced by LE CORBUSIER, he was not content to parrot the architectural phraseology of the exalted leader of Formalism and soon retraced his steps to search for what might have been too hastily pared away. He found a new mentor in AUGUSTE PERRET.

Nowicki's early works show hints of genius. While acting as head of the School of Design in North Carolina, he quietly revolutionized its curriculum and set the pace for future architectural programs throughout the country. It was at this time that he designed the Dorten Arena for the State Fair in Raleigh, North Carolina, a dramatic creation using two hyperbolic parabolas that intersect at the base of the structure. Other noteworthy projects on which he collaborated were the master plan for Brandeis University (with EERO SAARINEN) and the New York Columbus Circle project. He was also part of an international team that scouted the location for the future United Nations. It was, however, the project for Chandigarh New Capitol City in Punjab, India, to which he would have made his greatest contribution. His drawings reveal a joyful balance of the seemingly battling themes of "order and variety, logic and emotion, and the universal and the local." The realization of his plans would have been the final stage in his emancipating flight from the chrysalis of rigid dictums that had tightly wound and stifled the general architectural movements of his generation.

LYNDA GREENBERG

WORKS

*1938, Polish Pavilion, World's Fair, New York. 1948–1953, Dorton Arena, North Carolina State Fair, Raleigh. 1949, Building for Brandeis University, Waltham, Mass.

BIBLIOGRAPHY

MUMFORD, LEWIS (editor) 1952 *Roots of Contemporary American Architecture.* New York: Reinhold.
MUMFORD, LEWIS 1954 "The Life, Teaching, and the Architecture of Matthew Nowicki." *Architectural Record* 115:139–149; 116:128–135, 153–159, 169–175.
NOWICKI, MATTHEW (1951)1973 "Origins and Trends in Modern Architecture." In *The Writings and Sketches of Matthew Nowicki.* Edited by H. B. Schafer. Charlottesville: University of Virginia Press.
SHAFER, BRUCE 1975 "The Writings and Sketches of Matthew Nowicki." *Design* 19, no. 2:27–30.

NOYES, ELIOT

Eliot Fette Noyes (1910–1977) was an American architect and industrial designer whose work was uniformly simple and unpretentious, often elegant, and whose considerable versatility was reflected in the broad scope of his commissions. He was a leading advocate of the integration of product, architectural, display, and graphic design in business and industry. Born in Boston, Noyes graduated with an architectural degree from Harvard University in 1938. He worked in the office of WALTER GROPIUS and MARCEL BREUER the next two years. On Gropius's recommendation, he became director of the department of industrial design at the Museum of Modern Art in New York in 1940.

In 1947, after having served as design director for NORMAN BEL GEDDES in New York, he began his private practice, Eliot Noyes and Associates, in New Canaan, Connecticut. In addition to houses, schools, and exhibition pavilions, Noyes designed numerous office buildings, interiors, and products for large corporations. He is particularly known for the IBM Selectric typewriter and the Mobil service station prototype with its cylindrical pumps, designed in 1965. An influential consultant to IBM, Westinghouse, and Mobil Oil, he advocated enduring design criteria rather than transitory promotional considerations. The forms of his buildings and products, alike, are conspicuously simple, the subdivisions in their smooth flat surfaces suppressed through studied detail. The crisp spaces and focal stone partitions and fireplaces in his residences suggest the influence of Marcel Breuer.

MICHAEL HOLLANDER

WORKS

1953, Bubble Houses, Hobe Sound, Fla. 1955, Noyes House, New Canaan, Conn. 1965, Mobil Service Station Prototype. 1967, United Nations Pavilion, *Expo '67*, Montreal. 1970, Graham House, Greenwich, Conn. 1971, Mobil Stonybrook Center Engineering Building and Customer Service Laboratory, Hopewell Township, N.J. 1980, IBM Management Development Center, Armonk, N.Y.

BIBLIOGRAPHY

"Eliot F. Noyes (1910–1977)" 1977 *Industrial Design* 24, Sept.-Oct.:42–43.

KELLY, SCOTT 1966 "Curator of Corporate Character: Eliot Noyes and Associates." *Industrial Design* June:36–43.

MORGAN, JIM 1973 "Mobil." *Architecture Plus* 1 July:50–57.

NOYES, ELIOT 1941 *Organic Design in Home Furnishing.* New York: Museum of Modern Art.

NYDELE, ANN 1975 "Design for the Corporation." *Progressive Architecture* 56, no. 10:80–85.

NYRÉN, CARL

Carl Nyrén (1917–) graduated from the Royal Institute of Technology in Stockholm in 1942 and has been in private practice since 1948. Originally mainly occupied with school buildings, he has designed several office structures of considerable interest during the two latest decades. Characteristic of his early projects is the façade material of dark red brick and a remarkable simplicity in plan and expression combined with a striking care for details. He has also shown beautiful examples of Brutalist architecture, as in the Västerort Church at Vällingby outside Stockholm (for the Swedish Missionary Society, 1956). The Arrhenius Laboratory of Stockholm University (1972–1975) and the Savings Bank at Hamngatan 31 in Stockholm (1973–1975) are both expressive buildings characterized by visible construction elements in concrete or steel, referring to the structuralist trend in late modern architecture. Nyrén has also designed beautiful additions to old environments, such as the annex to the von Fersen Palace at Blasieholmstorg in Stockholm (1973–1976) and the light-colored wooden church of the Swedish Missionary Society at Jönköping (1975).

FREDRIC BEDOIRE

WORKS

1948–1952, School of Economy, Götenburg, Sweden. 1956, Västerort Church, Vällingby outside Stockholm. 1961–1964, School of Education, Malmö, Sweden. 1963–1965, Trygg-Fylgia Insurance Office, Helsingborg, Sweden. 1967–1973, 1980, Pharmacy, Office, and Laboratory, Uppsala, Sweden. 1972–1975, Arrhenius Laboratory, Stockholm University. Completed 1973, Värnamo Town Hall, Sweden. 1973–1974, Ålidshem Church, Umeå, Sweden. 1973–1975, Savings Bank, 31 Hamngatan; 1973–1976, von Fersen Palace (annex), Blasieholmstorg; Stockholm. 1975, Swedish Missionary Society Church, Jönköping, Sweden.

NYROP, MARTIN

Working in the tradition of simple and highly geometricized brick buildings established in Denmark by J. D. HERHOLDT and inspired also by late medieval Italian styles, Martin Nyrop (1849–1921) led Danish architecture away from neoclassicism at the end of the nineteenth century. Nyrop was trained first as a carpenter and then studied at the Academy of Art under J. V. Dahlerup. In 1880, he received the Academy's highest honors, the Grand Gold Medal and the chief traveling fellowship. After three years of foreign travel to Italy, Greece, France, and several other countries, Nyrop returned to Copenhagen to join the teaching staff of the Academy as assistant to HANS JØRGEN HOLM. Here he rose rapidly, becoming professor in 1906 and director in 1908. Thus, for almost forty years, Nyrop exerted a dominant influence upon Danish architects and architecture. He also remained in close touch with developments abroad.

Nyrop's most important work was the Copenhagen Town Hall (1892–1905), which he began designing in 1888. This was a plain-looking rectangular building executed in dark red brick, with some medieval detailing on the exterior and a slender central tower. Set in a shell-shaped plaza, the Town Hall significantly resembled the Palazzo Publico in Siena. The interior spaces were arranged around two courtyards, one of which, covered by a glass roof, served as an arena for major ceremonies. Interior decoration was elaborate, colorful, and innovative: bands of brick and stone in geometric patterns and extensive stone carving were combined with mosaics and murals in a flat and two-dimensional style which was related to late medieval art and prefigured some kinds of Art Nouveau work. The Copenhagen Town Hall antedated the famous Amsterdam Stock Exchange by H. P. BERLAGE and may have influenced it; for European architecture before World War I, Nyrop's was by far the more important building. Nyrop's work influenced the National Romantic movements in Sweden and Finland, and some aspects of continental expressionism. Among his Danish disciples were ANTON S. ROSEN and, at one generation's remove, KAY FISKER.

BARBARA MILLER LANE

WORKS

1879, Villas; 1884, Gymnastics Building, Volkshochschule, Vallekilde; Själland, Denmark. 1888, Agriculture and Art Buildings, Exposition of Industry, Copenhagen. 1889, Frants Henningsen House, Hellebäk, Själland, Denmark. 1891–1892, Landesarchive; 1892–1905, City Hall; 1899–1900, Bridge, Fredericksholm Canal; Copenhagen. 1903–1904, Church, South Jutland, Denmark. 1903–1904, Church, Stenderup, Denmark. 1903–1904, Church, Sundeved, Denmark. 1905–1906, Lyngebäksgaard, near Nivaa, Själland, Denmark. 1905–1908, Elias Church, Copenhagen. 1907, Volkshochschule (remodeling and additions), Vallekilde, Denmark. 1908–1913, Bispebjerg Hospital; 1914–1918, Luther Church (with J. Smith); 1916–1918, Bispebjerg Hospital (additions); Copenhagen. 1918–1919, Martin Nyrop House, near Gentofte, Själland, Denmark. 1919–1921, Villa Bjerrelide, Ordrup; 1920, Landsarchiv (additions); Copenhagen.

BIBLIOGRAPHY

BECKETT, FRANCIS ET AL. 1919 *Arkitekten Martin Nyrop.* Copenhagen.

BECKETT, FRANCIS, and HENDRIKSEN, FRANCIS 1908 *Københavns Raadhus.* Copenhagen: Bangs.

CERVIN, OLOF Z. 1905 "The City Hall at Copenhagen." *Architectural Record* 18:283–299.

FABER, TOBIAS (1963)1977 *Dansk Arkitektur* 2d ed. Copenhagen: Arkitektens Forlag.

"Københavns raadhus, opført 1894–1905." 1948 *Arkitekten* 50:5–10.

LANDBERG, HARALD, and LANGKILDE, HANS ERLING 1942 *Dansk Byggesaet omkring 1792 og 1942.* Copenhagen: Den almindelige brandforsikring for landbygninger.

LUND, HAKON, and MILLECH, KNUD 1963 *Danmarks Bygningskunst fra Oltid til Nutid.* Copenhagen: Hirschsprungs.

MILLECH, KNUD 1951 *Danske Arkitekturstrømninger 1850–1950.* Copenhagen: Udgivet af Østifternes kreditforening.

RASMUSSEN, STEEN EILER 1930 "Dansk Bygningskunst: Nutiden." Pages 63–100 in *De Danske Byggefag.* Berlin.

RASMUSSEN, STEEN EILER 1940 *Nordische Baukunst.* Berlin: Wasmuth.

NYSTRÖM, CARL GUSTAF

Although Carl Gustaf Nyström (1856–1917) continued the neoclassical and neo-Renaissance tradition in Finland, he used internal steel frames, as in the State Archives (1890). A long-time teacher at the Polytechnic Institute in Helsinki, he introduced modern construction methods to his students. His Union Bank (1896–1898), Helsinki, was a pioneer work of granite architecture, further developed in Turku Art Museum (1901–1904) in the National Romantic style and strongly influenced by H. H. RICHARDSON.

PIRKKO-LIISA LOUHENJOKI

WORKS

1886, Institute of Medical Chemistry, Helsinki University; 1888, Market Hall; 1889, Greenhouse, Helsinki University Botanical Gardens; 1890, State Archives; 1891, House of Estates; Helsinki. 1896, Market Hall, Turku, Finland. 1896–1898, Union Bank; 1900, Customs House; Helsinki. 1901, Union Bank, Tampere, Finland. 1901–1904, Turku Art Museum, Finland. 1906, Bank of Finland, Kotka. 1906, Helsinki University Library Extension.

BIBLIOGRAPHY

BOLTON SMITH, JOHN 1976 *The Golden Age of Finnish Art.* Helsinki: Otava.

EATON, LEONARD K. 1972 *American Architecture Come of Age.* Cambridge, Mass.: M.I.T. Press.

RICHARDS, JAMES M. 1978 *800 Years of Finnish Architecture.* Newton Abbot, England: David & Charles.

SALOKORPI, ASKO 1970 *Modern Architecture in Finland.* London: Weidenfeld & Nicholson.

WICKBERG, NILS ERIK 1959 *Finnish Architecture.* Helsinki: Otava.

OBRIST, HERMANN

A Swiss sculptor, Arts and Crafts designer, and teacher active in Germany, Hermann Obrist (1862–1927) was enormously influential in inspiring a new approach to all art and particularly to architecture in the years before World War I. Having never received commissions for buildings, Obrist explored his architectural ideas in models and in his famous fountains and funerary monuments. His works and writings were based on aspects of the perceptual psychological theory of empathy propounded by Theodor Lipps and reveal Obrist's intent to open new aesthetic experiences. In architecture, Obrist believed in the "possibilities of new shapings of space, new static effects, new constructions, new forms, new methods and new ornamentations."

Obrist was born in Kilchberg outside Zurich, the son of a physician. In 1885, he entered the university in Heidelberg to study medicine and the natural sciences, but he left for Berlin the next year and traveled to England and Scotland (his mother's country of origin) in 1887. In the fall of that year, he enrolled in the school of applied arts in Karlsruhe, Germany, to study ceramics only to find greater satisfaction as an apprentice in a rural pottery works. His design talents were first recognized at the 1889 Paris Exposition where his ceramics and furniture won a gold medal. He subsequently moved to Paris where he worked at the Académie Julian and studied sculpture. By 1892, he had established a studio for embroidery in Florence which he transferred to Munich in 1894. He lectured widely on reform in the arts and crafts and on art education and was the prime force in the founding in 1897 of the Vereinigte Werkstätten für Kunst im Handwerk in Munich. Not only had Obrist by this time gained an international reputation for his exquisite embroidery designs, but he had also gained recognition within Germany as an inspired teacher. In 1902, he and Wilhelm von Debschitz opened in Munich their Lehr und Versuch-Ateliers für angewandte und freie Kunst (Teaching and Experimental Studios for the Applied and Fine Arts) which became known for its innovative methods that stressed a perceptual-psychological approach to problems of artistic form. Obrist's writings on art and education first appeared in the periodical *Dekorative Kunst* and were collected into a book of essays, *Neue Möglichkeiten in der bildenden Kunst* (1903). His ideas influenced numerous artists and designers working in Munich around 1900, including PETER BEHRENS, AUGUST ENDELL, and Wassily Kandinsky.

Obrist was one of a number of artists active in the first two decades of the century whose work was instrumental in fostering an Expressionist architecture. Two civic projects, the spiral monument and the column monument or "arch pillar," both dated around 1898/1900, illustrate the diversity of forms which Obrist explored to achieve heightened expressions. The purpose in these and other of Obrist's works was to transcend mundane bourgeois concerns and through form to evoke sensations and something of life's inner spiritual essence, much as poetry does through words and music does through sounds. His pursuit of empathetic and symbolic expression was inspired by both the organic and the inorganic products of nature and was made manifest in forms rough-textured and smooth, curvilinear and cubistic. Further testimony to the range of Obrist's inventiveness and to the architectural relevance of his work are a fountain design of 1902 for the Bavarian town of Kempten, the Karl Oertel tomb monument in 1903 in Munich, and an imaginary project for a vast domed building on a mountain (c.1908). Similar to later Expressionists, Obrist employed natural forms both sensuous and harsh in an effort to turn architecture into a higher entity embodying universal laws of nature.

Contemporary artists and critics lauded Obrist's work for its fantasy and its personal, rhythmic language. As one influential critic, Karl Scheffler, noted, "his apparent abstractions are bursting with sensuality; in the chaos of his form there is an embryonic higher architectural order." Obrist was delighted by the 1919 exhibit of utopian Expressionist projects by members of the Arbeitsrat für Kunst. He sensed in their visionary schemes a kinship with his own desire to extend the poetic range and emotive associations of art and architecture in an effort to transform our lives. Obrist did not participate in the postwar phase of Expressionism, having preferred instead to withdraw into his own private world.

EUGENE A. SANTOMASSO

BIBLIOGRAPHY

BREDT, E. W. 1902 "Verkünden und Handeln." *Die Kunst* 9:218–226. Discusses Obrist's theories and early designs.

BREDT, E. W. 1904–1905 "Ein neues Grabmal von Hermann Obrist." *Die Kunst* 12:118–121. Discusses the Karl Oertel monument.

FRANK, WILLY 1904–1905 "Ein neues Grabmal von Hermann Obrist." *Deutsche Kunst und Dekoration* 15:166–168. Discusses the Karl Oertel monument.

HAENEL, ERICH 1902 "Konkurrenz für ein Brunnendenkmal in Kempten." *Die Kunst* 10, Apr.–Sept.:362–364.

HALM, PH. M. 1903 "Wettbewerb um einen Monumentalbrunnen für Kempten." *Kunst und Handwerk* 53:33–38.

LAMPE-VON BENNIGSEN, SILVIE n.d. *Hermann Obrist: Erinnerungen.* Munich: Post.

OBRIST, HERMANN 1903*a* "Erläuterungen zu Obrist Modell vom Künstler selbst." *Kunst und Handwerk* 53:39–40. Obrist's remarks on the Kempten fountain design.

OBRIST, HERMANN 1903*b* *Neue Möglichkeiten in der bildenden Kunst-Aufsätze von 1896–1900.* Leipzig: Diederichs. Includes material published in *Dekorative Kunst* up to 1901.

OBRIST, HERMANN 1904 "Die erste öffentliche Austellung der Lehr- und Versuch-Ateliers für angewandte und freie Kunst." *Dekorative Kunst* 12, no. 6:228–237.

OBRIST, HERMANN 1907 "Der 'Fall Muthesius' und die Künstler." *Dekorative Kunst* 16, no. 1-42–44.

SCHEFFLER, KARL 1910 "Hermann Obrist." *Kunst und Künstler* 8:555–559.

STEIGERER, H. 1913–1914 "Zu den Arbeiten Hermann Obrists." *Die Kunst* 30:84–86.

VAN DE VELDE, HENRY 1914 "Ein Brunnen von Hermann Obrist." *Kunst und Künstler* 12:38–42. On the fountain in the courtyard of the Kunstgewerbehaus, Munich.

WEISS, PEG 1979 Pages 28–34 in *Kandinsky in Munich: The Formative Jugendstil Years.* N.J.: Princeton University Press.

WICHMANN, SIEGFRIED (editor) 1968 *Hermann Obrist: Wegbereiter der Moderne.* Munich: Stuck Villa. Exhibition catalogue.

O'DONNELL, JAMES

James O'Donnell (1774–1830) was born in Ireland, where he worked in the late Georgian manner before emigrating around 1812 to the United States. In New York, O'Donnell designed several Federal-style houses; the Bloomingdale Asylum (1817–1821); the renovated Columbia College (1817–1820); the Fulton Street Market (1821–1822); and several churches.

His masterwork is the Gothic Revival Church of Notre-Dame in Montreal (1823–1829), a building of enormous size and of lasting impact on the architecture of French Canada.

FRANKLIN TOKER

BIBLIOGRAPHY

TOKER, FRANKLIN 1970*a* *The Church of Notre-Dame in Montreal.* Montreal: McGill-Queen's University Press.

TOKER, FRANKLIN 1970*b* "James O'Donnell: An Irish Georgian in America." *Journal of the Society of Architectural Historians* 29:132–143.

O'GORMAN, JUAN

A Mexican, Juan O'Gorman (1905–) studied at the National University of Mexico and later worked in the office of José Villagrán García. Influenced by Le Corbusier and other vanguard European designers of the 1920s, O'Gorman produced early in his career a number of houses and schools that were among the first specimens of architectural functionalism to be constructed in North America. In critical and theoretical writings of the 1930s he expounded the commitment to progressive socialism which underlay his philosophy of architectural production. But by World War II, and attendant upon a decided shift in his ideological position, O'Gorman had become disenchanted with functionalism and temporarily abandoned architectural practice altogether in order to devote himself to painting. In the early 1950s, he re-emerged as an outstanding Mexican architect, now advocating an "organic architecture" inspired in part by the thought and achievements of Frank Lloyd Wright. In this second phase of his career, O'Gorman integrated pre-Columbian and vernacular architectonic and decorative motifs (often in the form of murals and mosaics of his own design) with modern structural and spatial arrangements, so as to achieve a locally significant architecture expressive of the cultural, social, and environmental realities of Mexico.

Alfred Willis

WORKS

1929–1930, Juan O'Gorman House I; 1929–1930, Rivera House and Studio; 1931, Tomás O'Gorman House; 1932–1934, Technical School; 1934, Castellaños House; 1936, Electricians' Union Building; 1952–1953, National Library, State University of Mexico; *1953–1956, Juan O'Gorman House II; Mexico City.

BIBLIOGRAPHY

Bullrich, Francisco 1969 *New Directions in Latin American Architecture.* New York: Braziller.

Cetto, Max 1961 *Modern Architecture in Mexico.* Translated by G. Stephenson. New York: Praeger.

Cetto, Max 1980 "O'Gorman, Juan." In Muriel Emmanuel (editor), *Contemporary Architects.* New York: St. Martin's.

Damaz, Paul F. 1963 *Art in Latin American Architecture.* New York: Reinhold.

Goeritz, Matthias 1980 "Juan O'Gorman." *Arquitectura* 16:232–233, 236.

O'Gorman, Juan 1937 "Contenido politico de la arquitectura." *Edificación* no. 5:10–12.

O'Gorman, Juan 1953 "Que significa socialmente: La arquitectura moderna en Mexico?" *Espacios* no. 15:3–10.

"O'Gorman Cave House Disappears." 1970 *Progressive Architecture* 51:40.

"O'Gorman House." 1970 *Architectural Design* 40:429.

Smith, Olive Bamford 1967 *Builders in the Sun: Five Mexican Architects.* New York: Architectural Book Publishing Company.

O'Gorman.
National Library, State University of Mexico.
Mexico City.
1952–1953

OHE, HIROSHI

Born in Akita, Japan, and graduated from Tokyo University, Hiroshi Ohe (1913–) first worked for the Ministry of Education. After World War II, he opened his own office, he started to teach at Hōsei University in 1958. His work on the Hōsei University campus won prizes from the Architectural Institute of Japan, the Ministry of Education, and the Building Contractors' Society. His campus buildings express the modern rationalism which he learned as a university student. The fact that his father was an architect and had a thorough understanding of traditional architecture gave his son certain influence. It is not surprising, therefore, that he could design the Nogi Shinto Temple in a traditional style. His own unique philosophy, however, which is a blend of modernism and tradition, is revealed in a series of buildings such as the Furendo School (1968) in Tokyo and the Kakunodate Traditional Craft Center (1980). For the latter, he received the prize of the Japan Academy of Art in 1981.

Hiroshi Yamaguchi

WORKS

1953–1958, Hōsei University Campus; 1955, Tōyō-eiwa Primary School; Tokyo. 1966, Kagawa Prefecture Cultural Hall, Takamatsu, Japan. 1968, Furendo School, Tokyo. 1973, Marugame Hall of Martial Arts, Kagawa Prefecture, Japan. 1980, Kakunodate Traditional Crafts Center, Akita Prefecture, Japan.

BIBLIOGRAPHY

Kurita, Isamu (editor) 1973 *Gendainihon Kenchikuka Zenshū.* Volume 12. Tokyo: Sanichi Shobō.

OHMANN, FRIEDRICH

The architect Friedrich Ohmann (1858–1927) was born in Lemberg (now Lvov in the Ukraine) and died in Vienna. He received his training at the Technical University and at the Academy of Fine

Arts in Vienna with the historicists Max Ferstel, Karl König, and Friedrich von Schmidt, and he himself remained a historicist. He became König's assistant and then went to Prague to teach at the State School of Arts and Crafts. In 1899, he was called back to Vienna to superintend the building of the new wing of the Hofburg, the imperial residence. In 1907, he resigned because of differences with the Archduke Francis Ferdinand, heir to the throne, over a proposed alteration in GOTTFRIED SEMPER's design for the Kaiserforum, a triumphal gateway to the park (the Volksgarten). Under the influence of the Vienna Secession, his historicizing architecture gained in versatility by incorporating Secessionist elements. This enabled him—who was probably the most accomplished draftsman of his generation—to adapt himself to existing ensembles and to create buildings of intense evocative feeling. From 1904 on, he led a master class in architecture at the Vienna Academy.

The buildings erected in connection with the regulation of the river Wien are a felicitous mixture of neobaroque and the style of the Secession; the Empress Elisabeth Monument (in the Volksgarten) is an impressive *Gesamtkunstwerk* of garden design, architecture, and sculpture. Ohmann provided the design for the Kurhaus (casino) in Merano (1912) and a Secessionist hothouse of glass and iron for the Imperial Garden in Vienna.

SOKRATIS DIMITRIOU
Translated from German by
Beverley R. Placzek

WORKS

1899–1907, Hofburg (expansion), Vienna. 1899–1907, Museum of Arts and Crafts, Magdeburg, Germany. 1903–?, Buildings in the Stadtpark; 1907, Empress Elisabeth Memorial, Volksgarten; Vienna. 1912, Kurhaus (casino), Merano, Italy.

BIBLIOGRAPHY

Arbeiten aus der Ohmann-Schule. 1910 Vienna: Schroll.

FELLNER, FERDINAND 1906–1914 *Friedrich Ohmann's Entwürfe und ausgeführte Bauten.* Vienna: Schroll.

HEVESI, LAJOS 1906 *Acht Jahre Sezession.* Vienna: Konegen.

OHTAKA, MASATO

Born in Miharu, Fukushima Prefecture, Japan, Masato Ohtaka (1923–) graduated from Tokyo University in 1947 and started to work for the Maekawa office in 1948. He left the office and opened his own in 1961. In the 1960s, he was a member of the group called "Metabolism" with KIYONORI KIKUTAKE and FUMIHIKO MAKI, attempting to develop a new design philosophy. In the 1970s, his main concern was in creating free space by using precast concrete building parts. Works from this period are the Main Library of Chiba Prefecture (1968) and the Assembly Hall of the Tochigi Prefecture (1969). He was awarded a prize from the Ministry of Education for the former and one from the Architectural Institute of Japan for the latter. He is primarily interested in urban planning, and one of his works in this line is the urban renewal on the artificial ground in Saka-ide, Kagawa Prefecture, for which he received a prize from the City Planning Institute of Japan in 1967.

HIROSHI YAMAGUCHI
Translated from Japanese by
Bunji Kobayashi

WORKS

1965–1968, Urban Renewal on the Artificial Ground, Saka-ide, Kagawa Prefecture, Japan. 1968, Prefectural Main Library, Chiba, Japan. 1969, Prefectural Hall of Tochigi Prefecture, Utsunomiya, Japan. 1971, Center for Agricultural Cooperative Association of Shizuoka, Japan. 1973, Chōju-en High Rise Apartment House, Hiroshima, Japan. 1980, Gumma Prefectural Museum, Takasaki, Japan.

BIBLIOGRAPHY

KURITA, ISAMU (editor) 1970 *Gendainihon Kenchikuka Zenshū.* Volume 18. Tokyo: Samichi Shobō.

OKADA, SHIN-ICHIRŌ

Born in Tokyo, Japan, and graduated from Tokyo University, Shin-Ichirō Okada (1883–1932) taught at the Tokyo Art Academy and at Waseda University. When he was twenty-nine, he won the first prize in the design competition for the Osaka Central Auditorium. He had a thorough knowledge of architectural styles of Europe and was very skillful in designing buildings of eclectic styles. The main office of the Meiji Life Insurance Company in Tokyo (1934) which he designed in the Renaissance style is the finest example of buildings in an eclectic style designed by Japanese architects. He wrote many articles introducing new trends outside of Japan that had a tremendous influence on young architects.

SAKA-E OHMI
Translated from Japanese by
Bunji Kobayashi

WORKS

*1922, Takashimaya Dry Goods Store; 1925, Kabuki; *1926, Tokyo Prefectural Art Museum; *1932, Toraya Store; 1934, Meiji Life Insurance Main Office; Tokyo.

BIBLIOGRAPHY

"A Funeral Address to Mr. Shin-ichirō Okada." 1932 *Journal of the Architectural Institute of Japan* May.

OKADA, S. 1910 "Architecture and Current Ideas." *Journal of the Architectural Institute of Japan* May.

OKADA, S. 1914 "Meaning of Modern Architecture." *Journal of the Architectural Institute of Japan* July.

OKADA, S. 1915 "Architect as a Social Reformer." *Journal of the Architectural Institute of Japan* Sept.

Okada. Meiji Life Insurance Main Office. Tokyo. 1934

OKHITOVITCH, M.

M. Okhitovitch (20th century) was born and worked in Russia. His major field of activity was the sociology of housing and physical planning. He is known through his researches conducted in collaboration with the Union of Contemporary Architects, a major actor in the discussions in the Soviet Union about housing and town planning between 1929 and 1931. Okhitovitch was the leader of the Deurbanist orientation, opposed to the Urbanists whose leader was L. M. SABSOVITCH. The Deurbanists believed that the existing towns should disappear altogether and be replaced by a "New Socialist Resettlement of Mankind" which implied total decentralization. The new industries created within the framework of the first Five Year Plan (and of the following ones) were to be located on virgin land near the sources of raw material. Housing was to be built in the form of individual cells organized in ribbon form along the main Russian roads. The central idea was to give all points of the territory identical possibilities through an even distribution of the new energy: electricity. Despite the individual cells, life was to be collective according to the prevailing ideas of the 1920s. "Collective Bases" were provided for that purpose. The resolution of the Central Committee of the Bolshevik Party (May 29, 1930) denouncing as "utopical" the ideas of social change of the Deurbanists (as well as of the Urbanists) put an end to Okhitovitch's known activity.

ANATOLE KOPP

BIBLIOGRAPHY

Okhitovitch contributed many articles to two periodicals, Sovremennaia Arkhitektura *and* Planovoie Hosiaistvo.

OLBRICH, JOSEPH MARIA

Joseph Maria Olbrich (1867–1908) came from a remote province of the Austro-Hungarian empire to be educated in Vienna. Most of his professional life, however, was spent in Darmstadt, Germany. Shortly before his untimely death in 1908, he had begun to establish himself in Düsseldorf and Cologne. Self-confident and irrepressibly charming, Olbrich left an oeuvre remarkable for its decorative inventiveness and breadth of imagery. His short career characterized the spirited search for architectural form in the Germanic world at the turn of the century.

Born in Troppau, Austrian Silesia, Olbrich enrolled at the State School of Applied Arts, Vienna, at the age of fourteen. One of his teachers was the architect and theorist CAMILLO SITTE, from whom he acquired a broad interest in the fine, applied, and performing arts, as well as a respect for indigenous traditions. After four years of practical experience back in his native city, Olbrich returned to Vienna in the fall of 1890 and entered the Academy of Fine Arts as a student of KARL VON HASENAUER. The last of the great generation of Ringstrasse architects, Hasenauer lauded Olbrich's facile draftsmanship and inspired a predilection for colorful materials and decoration.

Olbrich won most of the intramural competitions during his three years at the academy. For his final project—an immense neobaroque theater—he was awarded the Rome Prize. He departed in November 1893 for an intended full year in Italy, but he was soon bored by the ancient ruins and Renaissance palaces of Rome. "What seems to me most important for our own time I have not found here even in embryo," Olbrich reported, and began wandering about southern Italy, Sicily, and northern Africa. It is evident from surviving letters and drawings that the objects of his greatest fascination were the simple, whitewashed houses that he found in the sun-drenched villages along the way.

Before leaving Vienna, Olbrich had been hired as a draftsman by OTTO WAGNER. In May 1894, he suddenly returned to resume this association, which was to continue until 1898. Wagner admired the young architect's buoyant spirit and his talent at the drafting table; Olbrich soon became the chief assistant and surrogate son. He contributed significantly to the activity in Wagner's office,

Olbrich. Secession Building. Vienna. 1897–1898

including designs for several stations of the Viennese Stadtbahn.

Wagner encouraged his assistants to take on extra work of their own, and in the mid-1890s Olbrich entered many architectural competitions, the most important of which was for the North Bohemian Museum of Applied Arts in Reichenberg (1895). His project revealed a superb mastery of the Wagnerian idiom: an abstracted, severe classicism with quickly drawn details of a semitraditional configuration. By 1897, however, a newer kind of decoration was visible. In place of the freely contrived classical references, there appeared a jovial vocabulary of botanical motifs in consistent geometries. This came to be known as Viennese *Jugendstil*—or more specifically *Sezessionsstil,* named after the organization of painters, sculptors, and architects for which Olbrich designed the clubhouse and exhibition gallery.

The Secession Building (1897–1898) was the first work to be constructed under Olbrich's own name. Although this startling "temple of art" had a certain adolescent awkwardness, its novel details radiated the boundless enthusiasm of their designer and the exuberance of the Secessionists' cause. The most prominent aspect of the exterior was the spherical dome of wrought-iron laurel leaves that embodied the idea of *Ver Sacrum,* or sacred spring, the new era of avant-garde art that the Secessionists sought to bring to their homeland. The interior was even more unusual. Interrupted only by six columnar supports, the gallery could be completely rearranged for each exhibition. Such adaptability of space and the accompanying preoccupation with custom installations became a major legacy of the Secession.

This extraordinary building caused a minor scandal in the Habsburg capital. Yet, it also attracted many of Olbrich's initial clients. Opening an office in 1898, he began to design houses, interiors, and furnishings for wealthy businessmen and friends of the Secessionists. The most ambitious of these early jobs was the completion of a half-constructed villa in Hinterbrühl for Max Friedmann (1898–1899). Olbrich designed all of the contents, including wallpapers, textiles, and lighting fixtures. The Austrian response to the English Arts and Crafts movement had, at last, appeared—fully formed and, at this point, largely curvilinear.

In the fall of 1899, just as he was being recognized as Wagner's heir apparent, Olbrich left the Danube for the Rhine. Invited to join the artists' colony in Darmstadt by Ernst Ludwig, the grand duke of Hesse, Olbrich was settled in time to begin the new century with his German colleagues. His primary task was to design a communal studio building, the Ernst Ludwig House (1899–1901). A longitudinal structure lighted by an expansive northern skylight, it was his first real masterpiece, the development of a strong, clearly formulated idea without obvious historical precedent. The bold arch of the entrance, which was bracketed by monumental sculptures of Man and Woman, emphasized the cultlike overtones of this "temple of work." It also gave axial focus to the forum of private houses on the hillside.

Olbrich's own residence (1900–1901), with its jerkin-head roof and asymmetrical eaves, was based on the Austro-German farmhouse. Such rural inspiration was considered a sign of modernity; in Vienna, Ludwig Hevesi had argued that "peasant styles were always secessionistic, for they know nothing about academic theory." Olbrich dressed the elevations with a band of blue and white tiles—the quadrat motif that he and JOSEF HOFFMANN had borrowed from CHARLES RENNIE MACKINTOSH and had made a signature of Viennese *Jugendstil* in its more rectilinear phase.

Seven houses by Olbrich—and one by his antagonist PETER BEHRENS—were opened to the public in the summer of 1901 for the colony's first public gesture. Called a "Document of German Art," this exhibition was intended to introduce the artistic experiment to Hessian patrons and craftsmen and to raise the general level of taste in the grand duchy. Olbrich's labors were greeted with mixed reactions, usually negative. He was scolded by critics for conjuring up the place with too much haste and effervescence; some felt that his Viennese *Liebenswürdigkeit* was inappropriate for this more Teutonic realm.

Nevertheless, Olbrich found success in his new land. Beginning in June 1901 and continuing posthumously until 1914, there appeared the

Olbrich.
Ernst Ludwig House.
Darmstadt, Germany.
1899–1901

Olbrich.
J.M. Olbrich House.
Darmstadt, Germany.
1900–1901

handsomely published series of drawings and photographs, *Architektur von Olbrich,* published by Ernst Wasmuth in Berlin. These large folios helped to spread the architect's fame and influence; commissions now came from all over Europe.

During 1902–1904, many of Olbrich's works revealed a cloying mannerism, a parody of forms that had been invented for the Mathildenhöhe or were contrived in pursuit of more novelty thereafter. For example, when the second exhibition of the colony was planned for 1904, he designed a group of three semidetached houses with a bewildering variety of materials, colors, and details. From letters written to Claire Morawe, whom Olbrich married in April 1903, we learn that he was not always satisfied with the results in these years.

True to his Secessionist background, Olbrich constantly focused his energies on the decorative arts. He designed silverware, ceramics, textiles, and jewelry for Hessian manufacturers, thus fulfilling one of the major intentions of the grand duke and anticipating the goals of the Deutscher Werkbund, of which he was a founding member in 1907. Despite this concern for the minor arts, and perhaps partly in reaction against his post-1901 lapses, there emerged in Olbrich's architecture a new monumentality and a revived interest in historicism. This was first seen in his project for the Basel Railroad Station (1903), whose large gable front was articulated with engaged columns supporting swag-bearing maidens.

A projected house for Eduard Schwarzmann in Strasbourg (1905) not only had the most interesting plan Olbrich ever devised, but also its drawings suggested the generous volumes of a late-eighteenth-century villa. Other designs of 1906–1908 revealed his growing interest in the architecture of one hundred years earlier. Many others in the profession shared this fascination. As elsewhere in the Western world, increasing nationalism was fostering the revival of a recent classical past. Symptomatic of the German story was the publication in 1908 of PAUL MEBES's *Um 1800,* which served as a textbook of forms gleaned from that age of discipline and repose.

Olbrich's late works became increasingly architectonic, many of them more classical. The Wedding Tower and Exhibition Building (1905–1908) in Darmstadt have an intriguing duality: the tower recalls the north German medieval tradition of stepped gables, whereas the adjacent galleries are more formal, even though picturesquely arranged atop the municipal reservoir. This complex was completed in time for the third exhibition on the

Olbrich.
Wedding Tower and Exhibition Building.
Darmstadt, Germany.
1905–1908

Mathildenhöhe, held in the summer of 1908. For that event Olbrich also designed a simple worker's dwelling and the elaborate Upper-Hessian House. He also redecorated several rooms in his Julius Glückert House of 1900–1901, revealing how the new interest in German domesticity of an earlier generation was bringing about a Biedermeier Revival.

In the final two years of his life, Olbrich began working for another cast of clients—families and firms of the merchant barons on the lower Rhine. For example, in conjunction with a 1906 exhibition of Rhenish art, he designed the Frauenrosenhof (1905–1906), built on the edge of a pond in the Flora Park, Cologne. It was a romantic, cloister-like pavilion, filled with elegant objects that he had conceived for wealthy women of Cologne's society. His vocabulary of forms seemed to be inexhaustible; so did his new business connections.

More important was the competition that Olbrich won for the Leonhard Tietz Department Store in Düsseldorf (1906–1909). (It was because of this assignment that he opened a subsidiary office there in June 1907.) He showed a remarkable ability to handle large architectural problems, for the building was given a convincing architectural presence that loomed beyond Olbrich's penchant for details. It was a logical step in the tradition of department stores that had developed in Germany since the 1890s—with much debt to ALFRED MESSEL's Wertheim in Berlin. The Tietz, in its turn, established an influential pattern in the Rhineland that continued until after World War II.

Olbrich.
Leonhard Tietz Department Store.
Düsseldorf, Germany.
1906–1909

Olbrich.
Joseph Feinhals House.
Cologne, Germany.
1908 (not completed until 1909)

Olbrich's last major work was a house for Joseph Feinhals in Cologne (1908–1909). The client and his architect intended that it be "a gesture toward the future, a testament of artistic longing amid years guided by a different persuasion." Borrowing from antiquity, the Italian Renaissance, and eighteenth- and nineteenth-century Cologne and Munich, the design revived the past to serve the present as a way forward. The blocky forms, German mansard roof, and six Doric columns in the garden loggia were clues to the architect's coming maturity. But Olbrich died of leukemia just as the walls were beginning to rise.

Wagner had taught his students that their best work could not be expected until after their fortieth year. Olbrich was not yet forty-one years old. Yet, in the decade of his independent practice he helped invent the forms of Viennese *Jugendstil,* brought that style to Germany, and then helped lead the move toward a renewed Germanic classicism.

Olbrich must be regarded in the context of the designers born in the 1860s. He, like most of them, was primarily an Arts and Crafts architect. But he was one of the few who had an impressive academic education, and this was partially responsible for the ambivalence of his oeuvre. At the beginning of his career, and again at the end, he designed classical buildings with a craftsman's sensitivity to materials and details. Meanwhile, he participated in the heroic but short-lived attempt to establish a historical style. At its 1914 exposition in Cologne, the Deutscher Werkbund honored the late Olbrich as one of its "twelve apostles," along with such contemporaries as Peter Behrens, RICHARD RIEMERSCHMID, Josef Hoffmann, and HENRY VAN DE VELDE. They had brought German architecture and design across the threshold of the new century. The next chapter belonged to a younger generation.

ROBERT JUDSON CLARK

WORKS

1897–1898, Secession Building, Vienna. 1898–1899, Max Friedmann House, Hinterbrühl, Austria. 1899–1900, Hermann Bahr House, Vienna. 1899–1900, Hermann Stöhr House, Saint Pölten, Austria. 1899–1901, Ernst Ludwig House; 1900–1901, J. M. Olbrich House; 1900–1901, Artists' Houses and Private Villas; *1900–1901, Exhibition Buildings; *1901–1902, Joseph and Gustav Stade Houses; Darmstadt, Germany. 1901–1903, Albert Hochstrasser House, Kronberg im Taunus, Germany. *1902, Carl Kuntze House, Berlin. 1902, Playhouse for Princess Elizabeth of Hesse, Wolfsgarten Castle, Germany. 1903–1904, Triple House Group, Darmstadt, Germany. *1903–1904, Fountain Court, Louisiana Purchase International Exposition, St. Louis, Mo. *1904, Edmund Olbrich House (façade), Troppau, Austrian Silesia. *1905, Color Gardens, Darmstadt, Germany. 1905–1906, Der Frauenrosenhof, Cologne, Germany. 1905–1908, Wedding Tower and Exhibition Building, Darmstadt, Germany. 1906–1907, Erwin Silber House, Bad Soden bei Salmünster, Germany. *1906–1908, Old Castle (interiors), Giessen, Germany. 1906–1909, Leonhard Tietz Department Store, Düsseldorf, Germany. 1907–1908, Luisplatz Fountains; *1907–1908, Opel Worker's House; 1907–1908, Upper-Hessian House; Darmstadt, Germany. *1907–1908, Hugo Kruska Houses (not completed until 1909), Cologne, Germany. 1908, Max Clarenbach House, Wittlaer, Germany. *1908 Theodor Althoff Store (not completed until 1909), Gladbeck, Germany. *1908, Walter Banzhaf House (not completed until 1909); *1908, Joseph Feinhals House (not completed until 1909); Cologne, Germany.

BIBLIOGRAPHY

CLARK, ROBERT JUDSON 1967 "J. M. Olbrich: 1867–1908." *Architectural Design* 37, Dec.:565–572.

CLARK, ROBERT JUDSON 1973 "Joseph Maria Olbrich and Vienna." Unpublished Ph.D. dissertation, Princeton University.

CREUTZ, MAX 1909 *Das Warenhaus Tietz in Düsseldorf.* Berlin: Wasmuth.

DARMSTADT, HESSISCHES LANDESMUSEUM 1967 *Joseph M. Olbrich, 1867–1908: Das Werk des Architekten.* Darmstadt, Germany: The museum.

DARMSTADT, HESSICHES LANDESMUSEUM ET AL. 1976 Volumes 4 and 5 in *Ein Dokument Deutscher Kunst: Darmstadt, 1901–1976.* Darmstadt, Germany: The museum.

Kunst in Hessen und am Mittelrhein 1967 7: entire issue.

LATHAM, IAN 1980 *Joseph Maria Olbrich.* London: Academy.

LUX, JOSEPH AUGUST 1919 *Joseph M. Olbrich: Eine Monographie.* Berlin: Wasmuth.

OLBRICH, JOSEPH MARIA 1899 *Ideen von Olbrich.* Vienna: Gerlach & Schenk.

OLBRICH, JOSEPH MARIA 1904 *Architektur von Olbrich.* 4 vols. Berlin: Wasmuth.

SCHREYL, KARL HEINZ 1972 *Joseph Maria Olbrich: Die Zeichnungen in der Kunstbibliothek Berlin.* Berlin: Mann.

SPERLICH, HANS GÜNTHER 1965 *Versuch über Joseph Maria Olbrich.* Darmstadt, Germany: Liebig.

VERONESI, GIULIA 1948 *Joseph Maria Olbrich.* Milan: Balcone.

OLIVERAS GENSANA, CAMIL

Along with LUIS DOMENÉCH I MONTANER and ANTONIO GALLISSA, Camil Oliveras Gensana (1840–1898) belongs to the first generation of modernist Catalan architects. Among his works, the most important are La Casa Provincial de Maternidad in Las Corts, Barcelona (1883–1902), the new Church of Santa Ana (1886), the façade for the Jesuit Convent at 27 Calle Caspe in Barcelona (1883–1885), and several constructions in Comillas, Santander. His work in design is important, especially in the field of labels, stamps, covers, and title pages, and ornamental borders and headpieces of books and periodicals.

XAVIER GÜELL GUIX
Translated from Spanish by
Judith E. Meighan

OLMSTED, FREDERICK LAW

Frederick Law Olmsted (1822–1903), born in Hartford, Connecticut, was one of the foremost landscape architects of the nineteenth century. He adapted the informal eighteenth-century English landscape garden style to American needs. He felt free to use either pastoral, picturesque scenery or a more formal architectural design as appropriate to the site and the requirements of his client.

Until he was thirty-five years old, the intense and highly intelligent Olmsted had no inkling that he would become a landscape architect. To be sure, his father, a wealthy Hartford merchant, had encouraged his love of natural scenery on their long rides and family excursions, but Olmsted had a long struggle to find a congenial occupation, made the more difficult because of haphazard schooling and losing a chance to go to college when his eyes were threatened by sumac poisoning. Instead, he tried surveying, then eighteen months of clerking in a New York dry goods firm, seafaring on a voyage to China in 1843, the life of a gentleman farmer in Connecticut and on Staten Island from 1847 to 1855, and a concurrent writing and publishing career which started in 1850.

In late 1850 he wrote his first book, *Walks and Talks of an American Farmer in England* (1852). It recounted a walking tour he had taken the spring before. The book, full of enthusiasm for English countryside and landscape gardening, foreshadowed his later devotion to public park design in its praise of JOSEPH PAXTON's Birkenhead Park (1847) outside of Liverpool, one of the first publicly owned parks in England. Olmsted found its pastoral vistas delightful and wished that Americans had such a "People's Park" to enjoy.

The success of *Walks and Talks* encouraged Olmsted to go through the southern slave states as a roving correspondent for the *New York Times* and he observed that slavery prevented a true civilization from developing there. He used his letters to write *A Journey in the Seaboard Slave States* (1856), *A Journey through Texas* (1857), and *A Journey in the Back Country* (1860). These much esteemed books were in turn used to write *The Cotton Kingdom* (1861).

Olmsted's literary ambitions led him into a disastrous partnership with Dix, Edwards and Company, publishers of his books and of *Putnam's Monthly,* from which he had to withdraw when their financial difficulties multiplied in 1857. Charles W. Elliott, one of the commissioners of New York's recently acquired Central Park, suggested that Olmsted try for the position of superintendent, under the chief engineer, Egbert Viele, who had done a topographical survey and made a plan for it. Olmsted won the job in September and recruited his work force from New York's unemployed. The same day Olmsted was hired, the Park Commission voted to abandon Viele's plan and to institute a competition for a new design. CALVERT VAUX, an English architect who had inherited A. J. DOWNING's clients when the latter died in 1852, sought out Olmsted to collaborate with him on a design to be submitted for the prize and to fulfill his former partner's dream. Downing, like William Cullen Bryant, editor of the *New York Post,* had started agitation for the park in the 1840s.

Olmsted and Vaux worked on their plan at night because Olmsted's days were filled with the gigantic task of putting more than a thousand laborers to work clearing the park site. Competing with thirty-three other entries, Olmsted and Vaux's "Greensward" won the first prize in the spring of 1858. The Park Board made Olmsted architect in chief, displacing Viele, and appointed Vaux consulting landscape architect to carry out its plan for a country park with a variety of scenery ranging from the pastoral effects of open meadows and water framed with deciduous foliage to picturesque rocky landscapes with cascades, plantings of evergreens, and luxuriant undergrowth. Vaux and Olmsted also designed a formal setting for gatherings of people in a holiday mood to enjoy fine weather and concerts in the Mall and Bethesda Terrace overlooking the lake.

The Central Park Board stipulated that the competition plans provide four roads across the park for city traffic. The Vaux and Olmsted design was the only one which kept these transverse roads from disturbing the enjoyment of the park by designing them to run below grade hidden from view. To further the undisturbed enjoyment of the park, the designers devised a path, bridle path, and carriage road system with no intersections at grade. Instead, horseback riders, pedestrians, and those in carriages crossed only at over- and underpasses formed by Vaux's elegant bridges.

Olmsted had thrown himself into the work of designing and constructing Central Park with more than ordinary intensity, partly to assuage his grief for the death of his brother and close friend, John, who died of tuberculosis in November 1857. Olmsted married John's widow, Mary Olmsted, in 1859, thereby acquiring the responsibility for her and her three young children at the very time he was supervising a force of two thousand workers on the park.

The outbreak of the Civil War interrupted Olmsted's Central Park work. With a leave of absence he accepted the post of general secretary of the United States Sanitary Commission in June 1861. He moved to Washington, to supervise this voluntary organization's medical assistance and distribution of supplies to the Union armies on a thirteen-hundred-mile-long front. The strains of supervising a force of nurses, medical inspectors, and doctors to assist the greatly overburdened Army Medical Bureau broke down his health by the summer of 1863, and exacerbated his relations with the commission. He left his post exhausted but with much accomplished.

Out of a job, Olmsted could not return to work on Central Park because he and Vaux had resigned in May 1863 over irreconcilable differences with the commissioners. Instead, he agreed to manage the gold mines of the Mariposa Estate in the Sierra Nevada of California for their New York owners. Two years in California were enough to convince Olmsted and the New York owners that the mines were not going to be profitable. Before returning east, Olmsted accepted commissions to design a campus and village for the College of California at Berkeley, Mountain View Cemetery (1864) in Oakland, and a park and parkway plan for San Francisco. He also wrote a remarkable report for the governor on a scenic reservation for the Yosemite Valley and Mariposa Big Tree Grove which anticipated the future goals of the national parks movement.

Olmsted finished his California commissions after he returned to New York in the fall of 1865 to join Vaux carrying out his design of Prospect Park (1866) in Brooklyn and to work again on Central Park. Olmsted's formal, axial design for Mountain View Cemetery using plant materials that could survive the dry season was carried out. His informal campus and suburban plan for the college was lost when the University of California took it over. Unfortunately, San Francisco consid-

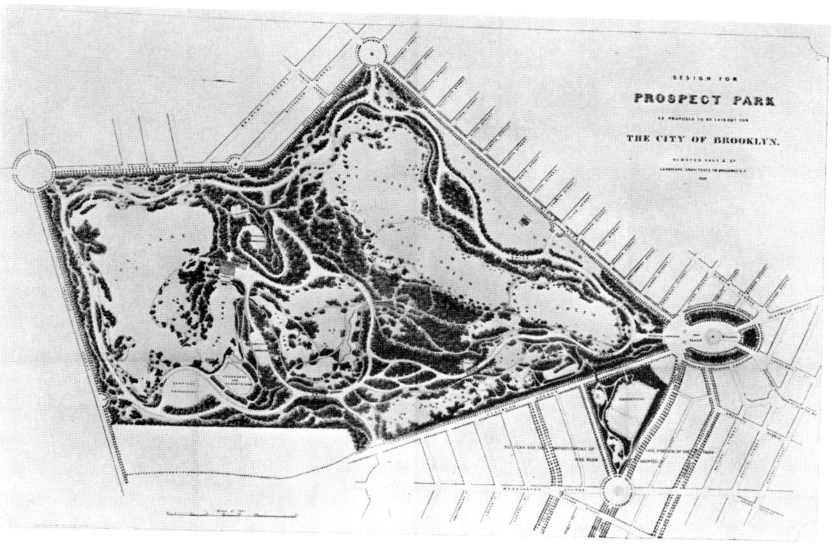

Olmsted.
Plan for Prospect Park (with Vaux).
Brooklyn, New York.
1866

ered his small park and sunken parkway plan, which was also a firebreak along the line of Van Ness Avenue, as too expensive. Olmsted's eloquent Yosemite report argument that the government should be responsible for preserving uniquely beautiful scenery to promote the general welfare was suppressed because it called for funds that other interests coveted for themselves.

In Prospect Park with a far more attractive rolling and well-wooded site than that of Central Park, Olmsted and Vaux had ample scope for broad vistas of meadow and water as well as for the picturesque and formal elements they planned. The park was to connect to a ring of parks by means of two parkways, eventually followed by the present Ocean and Eastern Parkways. Olmsted and Vaux's parkways, though, were not built as designed. They were to be much like the Avenue de L'Impératrice then being built in Paris, with a central pleasure drive flanked on either side by pedestrian ways, service roads, and sidewalks in front of the villas lining them. Although not realized in Brooklyn, Olmsted and Vaux's parkway proposals anticipated their own later work.

In the late 1860s and early 1870s, Vaux and Olmsted found clients outside of New York. In 1868, Emery E. Childs commissioned them to lay out Riverside, a model suburban village on sixteen hundred acres along the Des Plaines River nine miles west of Chicago. They designed a landscape to suggest domesticity, seclusion, and community rather than to give a parklike illusion of unlimited countryside. The village was to have a curvilinear street system for single-family dwellings screened with masses of trees centered on a village common, a park along the river, and a commercial area around the railroad station. The designers proposed a parkway to Chicago so that commuters could drive or ride horseback to work, but that portion of the scheme could not be carried out.

For the Buffalo Park System (1868), Olmsted and Vaux proposed a large country park, Delaware Park, to the north to give the visitor a refreshing sweep of meadow and water vista to ease the pressures of urban life. Humboldt, Lincoln, Bidwell, and Chapin Parkways would connect Delaware Park with other squares and pleasure grounds around the city, including a highly imaginative lake beach and lagoon park proposed in 1888 for the south side of the city. This last was rejected as too expensive. Two smaller south parks with connecting parkways were built, however. Delaware Park is now bisected by a large freeway.

In 1871, the firm of Olmsted and Vaux proposed park land for Chicago running west for three miles from the shore of Lake Michigan on the south side of the city to the flat prairie. Jackson Park, the flat, swampy land along the lake would be dredged out to form a series of lagoons, peninsulas, and islands for a water park of 559 acres with a pier like that at Brighton for steamers bringing people from Chicago. The rectangular Midway Plaisance, about 750-feet wide and a mile long, connected Jackson Park to the 300-acre Washington Park inland. Olmsted and Vaux proposed a canal down the Midway to give the intrepid boater access to Washington Park from Lake Michigan. Work on Washington Park was finished in 1890, but Jackson Park had to wait until after the Chicago World's Fair of 1893. The canal was not built.

Olmsted and Vaux broke up their partnership in 1872 for reasons of mutual convenience, but they continued to hold positions in the Department of Public Parks until the hostile commissioners fired Olmsted in 1878. They collaborated on designs for Morningside Park (1873) and Riverside Park (1875), both in New York City, and finally on Downing Park (1889) in Newburgh, New York. Olmsted went on to do his first major designs on his own starting in 1877 with Mount Royal in Montreal and Belle Isle Park in Detroit, which he began in 1882.

The frustrations of working in New York grew in intensity for Olmsted during the 1870s. Both Andrew Haswell Green, the economy-minded treasurer of the Parks Department, and his political rivals prevented Olmsted from carrying out his curvilinear street system with a steam rapid transit loop below grade (like Central Park's transverse roads) for the Bronx proposed in 1877. H. H. Richardson was one of those who persuaded Olmsted to move his practice to Brookline, Massachusetts, in 1881. Close friends since 1867, Olmsted and Richardson collaborated on plans for the Buffalo State Asylum for the Insane (1871) and on a remarkable proposal, unfortunately rejected, for the development of Staten Island including housing, transportation, public health, water supply, and open space. Together they designed, among other projects, the Oakes Ames Estate (1880–1881), the Ames Memorial Town Hall (1879–1881) both in North Easton, and the Crane Memorial Library (1880–1883) in Quincy, Massachusetts, as well as several railroad stations for the Boston and Albany Railroad.

Olmsted had started his work for the Boston parks in 1878 when the commissioners wanted his advice about ways to abate the peril and stench of the polluted water gathering in the Back Bay and to provide more access to Boston from the surrounding towns. Olmsted suggested they could meet both objectives and extend the park system if they built the necessary causeways, bridges, interceptor sewers, basins, tidal gates, and dams to form a green necklace of pleasure drives, parks, and connected ponds along an artfully shaped and planted Muddy River. This system of links known as the Fenway, Jamaicaway, and Arborway running from the Charles River connected Commonwealth Avenue, the Arnold Arboretum, and Franklin Park. To realize this brilliant scheme and design components like Franklin Park begun in 1879, Olmsted came to rely on the help of his stepson, John C. Olmsted, whom he made a partner in 1884. His stepson also worked with him on Beardsley Park in Bridgeport (1884) and a plan for a park in Pawtucket (1888). Other proposals for park systems the firm did were those for Rochester (1888), Milwaukee (1889), and Louisville (1891).

Olmsted's plan for the United States Capitol grounds (1874) is a good example of his ability to subordinate landscape design to architecture. To this end, he opened up vistas of the Capitol with its great cast-iron dome completed in 1865 and its enormous new Senate and House wings from the foot of Capitol Hill and designed a formal plaza for state occasions on the East Front. To keep the grounds attractive and cool during Washington's sticky summer heat, he shaded the walks and carriageways with low, thickly branching trees which shut out the sun but allowed a good view of the building from all sides. To make a handsome transition from the grounds to the West Front of the Capitol on the slope of the hill, he proposed an architectural terrace and fountain framed with two staircases with a parapet wrapped around the Senate and House wings. The work was completed in the 1890s. He saw the Capitol grounds as a part of a unified setting for the federal city, connected with the Mall, the White House grounds, and parks built along the Anacostia and Potomac rivers and Rock Creek. That vision was realized by Frederick Law Olmsted, Jr., in the 1920s.

While working on the Capitol grounds, Olmsted met Senator Leland Stanford who asked him to design the campus of Stanford University in Palo Alto, California, with Richardson's successor firm, Shepley, Rutan, and Coolidge, beginning in 1886. They proposed a campus with two-story tile-roofed buildings arranged in arcaded quadrangles around paved courts, with large islands planted with low shrubbery and palms. The design, they argued, provided shade and planting appropriate to a semiarid climate. Around the line of interconnected quadrangles, they grouped the faculty houses and student dormitories. A mile-long drive planted informally and surrounded by an arboretum extending into the hills to the west would connect the campus to Palo Alto. The Stanford family made such serious changes in the design as it was being carried out that the Olmsted firm had little to do with it after 1890. Only the central quadrangles were built. The drive was planted with palms and no arboretum was established.

Among the many private estates Olmsted's firm designed one of the largest was Biltmore (1888) with more than two thousand acres for

Olmsted
Plan of Park System.
Boston.
1878

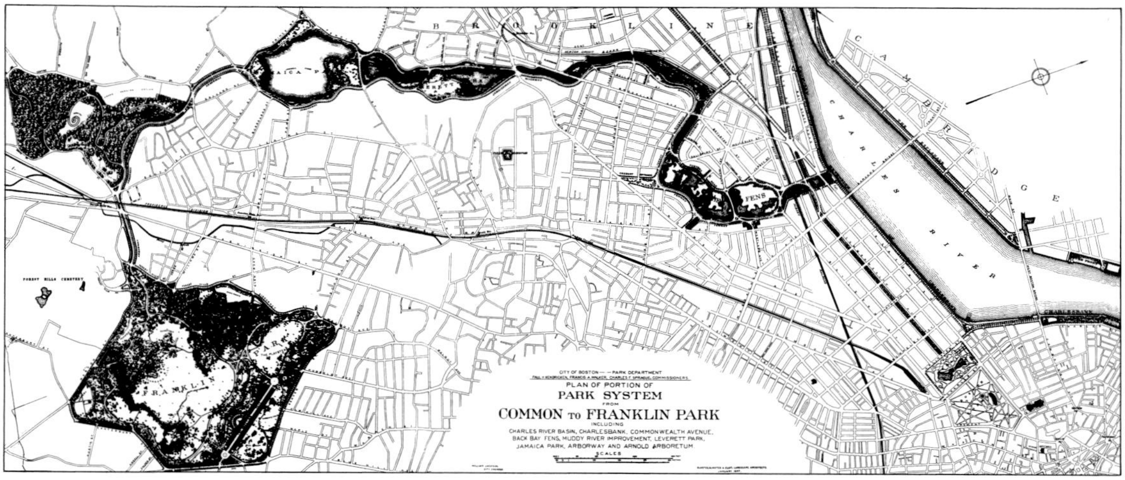

George Washington Vanderbilt in the mountain and river valley scenery near Asheville, North Carolina. Olmsted, consulted first in 1888, accommodated RICHARD MORRIS HUNT's French Renaissance château in a design for the grounds with a formal *rampe douce* and terraces close to the building and a shrub garden leading to a valley, pond, and waterfall below. Olmsted advised Vanderbilt that the river bottom lands below should be farmed and that the rest of the estate should be managed as an arboretum and forest. Olmsted saw the beginnings of scientific forest management at Biltmore under the guidance of Gifford Pinchot, the first American forester. The Biltmore plan was a culmination of Olmsted's interest in scenic preservation and conservation begun with Yosemite. With Charles Eliot Norton of Harvard and others, he led an eighteen-year fight starting in 1869 to save Niagara Falls from uncontrolled industrial and commercial development. In 1887, he and Vaux designed the Niagara Falls Reservation, a scenic reserve with paths and carriageways to give visitors access to vistas of the rapids and falls framed in the indigenous foliage and plant materials flourishing in the spray along the shore and on Goat Island. Their work has been partially obliterated by the Robert Moses Freeway on the American side.

Olmsted's last major design was for the World's Columbian Exposition of 1893, built on the swampy site of Jackson Park south of Chicago on the lake. He reconciled the islands and lagoons of the future park with the fair by making them the foundations of a white city built upon balustraded platforms facing canals and basins. The Wooded Isle was to be an oasis of green in the white neoclassic city of Richard Morris Hunt; MCKIM, MEAD, AND WHITE; DANIEL H. BURNHAM; and others. Olmsted's plan was a masterpiece of transportation and city planning to accommodate the millions who came by steamer and train directly to the fair.

By 1895, Olmsted retired from his firm. Starting in the 1880s, the methodical and hard-working John C. Olmsted had taken over the day-to-day management of the business and carried through the details of the new commissions. For a brief time, the firm had the benefit of the talents of two brilliant young men who had had part of their training in the office. Henry Codman was a partner from 1889 to his tragic young death in 1893. He had been invaluable in the design of the Chicago World's Fair. Charles Eliot was a partner from 1893 to his early death in 1897 and among other things laid the ground work for Boston's Metropolitan Park System. Frederick Law Olmsted, Jr. learned much in the 1890s working on projects like Biltmore and the Chicago Fair. He joined the firm after his father's retirement. With John C. Olmsted he developed a practice many times larger than before.

After having driven himself for years, Olmsted's frail constitution gave way and he died senile in McLean Hospital outside of Boston, the grounds for which he had planned. He was a rare combination of brilliant administrator and imaginative artist who created a new profession. He was mentor to other landscape architects such as H. W. S. CLEVELAND, Jacob Weidenmann, and William Hammond Hall. Olmsted led a new profession and left an immense, though often sadly neglected legacy of twenty parks, seven park systems, twenty-one colleges, six schools, twenty suburban plans, and 175 estates. They look so natural and inevitable in place that it is hard to realize the artistic skill, imagination, and dogged administration that went into their accomplishment.

CHARLES C. MCLAUGHLIN

WORKS

1858, Central Park (with Calvert Vaux), New York. 1864, Mountain View Cemetery, Oakland, Calif. 1866, Prospect Park (with Vaux), Brooklyn, N.Y. 1868, Buffalo Park System (with Vaux), N.Y. 1868, Riverside community (with Vaux), Ill. 1871, State Asylum for the Insane (with H. H. Richardson), Buffalo N.Y. 1873, Morningside Park (with Vaux), New York. 1874, United States Capitol Grounds, Washington. 1875, Riverside Park (with Vaux), New York. 1878, Boston Park System. 1879–1881, Ames Memorial Town Hall (with Richardson); 1880–1881, Oakes Ames Estate (with Richardson); North Easton, Mass. 1880–1883, Crane Memorial Library (with Richardson), Quincy, Mass. 1884, Beardsley Park (with John C. Olmsted), Bridgeport, Conn. 1886, Stanford University (with Shepley, Rutan, and Cooledge), Palo Alto, Calif. 1887, Niagara Falls Reservation (with Vaux), N.Y. 1888, Biltmore Estate (with Richard Morris Hunt), Asheville, N.C. 1888, Rochester Park System, N.Y. 1889, Downing Park (with Vaux), Newburgh, N.Y. 1889, Milwaukee Park System, Wisc. 1891, Louisville Park System, Ky. 1893, World's Columbian Exposition (with others), Chicago.

BIBLIOGRAPHY

BEVERIDGE, CHARLES E. 1977 "Frederick Law Olmsted's Theory of Landscape Design." *Nineteenth Century* 3, no. 2:38–43.

FEIN, ALBERT (editor) 1968 *Landscape into Cityscape: Frederick Law Olmsted's Plans for a Greater New York City.* Ithaca, N.Y.: Cornell University Press.

MCLAUGHLIN, CHARLES C. (editor) 1977– *The Papers of Frederick Law Olmsted.* 12 vols. to date. Baltimore: Johns Hopkins University Press.

Olmsted, FREDERICK LAW (1852)1967 *Walks and Talks of an American Farmer in England.* Reprint. Ann Arbor: University of Michigan Press.

OLMSTED, FREDERICK LAW (1856)1968 *A Journey in the Seaboard Slave States, With Remarks on Their Economy.* Reprint. Westport, Conn.: Negro Universities Press.

OLMSTED, FREDERICK LAW (1857)1969 *A Journey Through Texas: Or a Saddle Trip on the Southwestern Frontier.* Reprint. New York: Franklin.

OLMSTED, FREDERICK LAW (1860)1970 *A Journey in the Back Country.* Reprint. New York: Schocken.

OLMSTED, FREDERICK LAW 1861 *The Cotton Kingdom.* New York: Dix, Edwards and Company.

OLMSTED, FREDERICK LAW, JR., and HUBBARD, THEODORE KIMBALL (editors) (1922)1973 *Frederick Law Olmsted, Landscape Architect, 1822–1903.* 2 vols. Cambridge, Mass.: M.I.T. Press.

ROPER, LAURA WOOD 1973 *F. L. O.: A Biography of Frederick Law Olmsted.* Baltimore: Johns Hopkins University Press.

SUTTON, S. B. (editor) (1971)1979 *Civilizing American Cities: A Selection of Frederick Law Olmsted's Writings on City Landscapes.* Reprint. Cambridge, Mass.: M.I.T. Press.

O'NEILL, GERARD

Professor of Physics at Princeton University, Gerard O'Neill (1927–) has devoted himself to the design of manufacturing facilities in outer space from lunar materials, in particular, a space colony at point Lagrange 5 which is always illuminated by the sun and moon and has stable orbits under the gravitational effects of earth, moon, and sun. Designed in collaboration with his colleague Brian O'Leary, formerly of the National Aeronautics and Space Administration, it has been much published and studied in special seminars.

PATRICIA C. PHILLIPS

BIBLIOGRAPHY

O'NEILL, GERARD KITCHEN 1974 "The Colonization of Space." *Physics Today* 27:32–40.

O'NEILL, GERARD KITCHEN 1975 "Space Colonies and Energy Supply to the Earth." *Science* 190, no. 4218:943–947.

O'NEILL, GERARD KITCHEN 1976 "Colonies in Orbit." *New York Times Magazine* Jan. 18, pp. 10, 11, 25–29.

SKY, ALISON, and STONE, MICHELLE 1976 *Unbuilt America.* New York: McGraw-Hill.

OPPENORD, GILLES-MARIE

Gilles-Marie Oppenord (1672–1742) played a leading role in the field of architecture and decoration during the French Regency and was an important contributor to the development of the rococo style in Europe. He was born in Paris, the son of a Dutch craftsman who had settled in France. In 1684, Oppenord senior is listed as lodging in the ateliers of the Louvre, where he was employed as *ébéniste ordinaire* to the king. Undoubtedly through Gilles-Marie's proximity to the extensive bureaucracy of architects, artists, and artisans that supported the king's many establishments and lively cultural interests, it was his good fortune to become a protégé of the Surintendant des Batiments, Edouard Colbert, the marquis de Villacerf. Through Villacerf's intervention, the twenty-year-old Oppenord was privileged to be attached to the French Academy in Rome without actually living there or having competed for the prize. After two years, in 1694, Oppenord's status as a pensioner became official and the correspondence between the director of the Academy, La Teulière, and Villacerf is filled with praises of Oppenord's engaging personality and talents as a draftsman. In one of the final letters before Oppenord's return to Paris in 1699, La Teulière describes him as having "much talent, accompanied by a fecundity of imagination and a vivacity that are extraordinary, supported by the facility and competence of a superior hand. He has also taste and discernment, formed while drawing the best of everything he found in Italy in the most beautiful works of architects who are distinguished in their profession." There is no doubt that Oppenord's style was formulated during the seven years in Italy. He drew constantly, a habit that he was never to abandon, following Villacerf's directive, on the one hand, to draw "the figure" (meaning antique sculpture) along with making measured drawings of antique monuments, and La Teulière's admonition, on the other, to copy the moderns—specifically GIOVANNI LORENZO BERNINI and FRANCESCO BORROMINI. It should be pointed out that there was no particular course for architects at the Academy at this time; the apportioning of prizes and differentiation of painters', sculptors', and architects' training was to come later. The six surviving sketchbooks and albums of varying sizes and numerous single sheets from Oppenord's Italian sojourn reveal that his interest was not in understanding a building from its plan, but in studying the ornaments and plastic forms. While dutifully making notations of the proportions of a molding, he drew it, habitually, in profile to capture its shape in isolation.

It was Oppenord's digestion of Italian baroque, his rich use of sculptural and figural motives, his free-flowing line, and above all his insistence on movement and variety throughout the ornament that singularizes his part in the evolution of the French rococo.

On his return to Paris, Oppenord, somewhat strangely, was not absorbed into the royal works. His patron, Villacerf, had been succeeded a few months previously by JULES HARDOUIN MANSART and appointments to official posts were already closed. That there was no personal enmity between Mansart and Oppenord seems clear as Mansart and ROBERT DE COTTE, his brother-in-law and assistant, were witnesses at Oppenord's wedding in 1701.

Oppenord seems to have occupied himself by making engravings for book illustrations and continuing to exercise his talents as a draftsman. A design for the altar of Notre Dame was rejected, but in 1704, the altar of Saint Germain-des-Prés was executed from his design. Six different versions for the project are known from Oppenord's facile hand and fertile design resources. One has twisted columns and a superstructure reflecting Bernini's baldachin in St. Peter's; the final version has plain columns, but there are Italian baroque-inspired elements, in particular the two angels on volutes holding the medieval reliquary. Other ecclesiastical commissions followed: a design for an altar for the Abbey of Saint Victor in 1706 (known through an engraving), several tomb monuments, the Altar of Saint Jean in a side chapel in the Cathedral of Amiens in 1709, and the high altar of Saint Jacques de la Boucherie in 1712. The altar of Saint Jean at Amiens still exists; it shows Oppenord's ability to fuse Italian baroque with French traditions of ornamentation. The basic shape of the altar recalls Borromini's altar in Sant'Agnese in Agone in Rome in the manner in which the entablature protrudes at either side, supported by columns with composite capitals. The central portion at Amiens, formerly housing a painting and now a bas-relief, is, however, enclosed in a frame that is characteristically French, with laurel sprays and garlands trailing over the concave curving upper corners.

Oppenord continued to perform commissions for churches throughout his career, including an elaborate choir screen and altars for the cathedral at Meaux in 1729. An undated series of drawings (probably 1732–1740) conserved at the Ecole des Beaux-Arts in Paris for the façade, tribune, and altar of the Eglise d'Oratoire on the rue St. Honoré, Paris, indicates that he hoped for the commission but was rejected. His most important ecclesiastical efforts, however, were for the Church of Saint Sulpice in Paris, where he was chief architect from 1725 to 1731 and for which he continued to supply designs until 1740. From numerous existing drawings it is known that Oppenord submitted several ideas for the west façade, carried out work on the nave, furnished the choir, designed an

Oppenord. Page from a Roman Sketchbook.

altar, and projected a circular communion chapel. His success was dimmed, however, when in 1731 the wooden lantern he had built had to be removed because its weight posed a threat to the underlying structure.

When at the end of Louis XIV's reign some members of the court began to shift their main establishments from Versailles to Paris, a surge in building and redecorating of private residences brought commissions to a number of architects and ornamentalists, including Oppenord. One such was for the Hôtel de Pompone, Place des Victoires, built for Michael Bonnier in 1714. Through the paneling that has survived and through drawings, Oppenord's combination of naturalistically carved elements of trees and animals with fanciful arabesques and trophies can be fully appreciated for its graceful juxtaposition of sculptural and graphic conceptions.

In 1715, both Louis XIV and Oppenord's father died. In a document connected with his father's death, Oppenord is called "premier architecte du Duc d'Orléans." This title was the turning point in Oppenord's career. Louis XV was only five years old at the time of his accession, so his uncle, the duc d'Orléans, was appointed regent of France until 1723 when the young king's majority was established. Not only did Oppenord enter upon a period of heightened activity as a designer for the regent, but commissions from other sources now were diverted to him.

Paris became the seat of government, and the

Oppenord. Design for Altar of Saint Jean, Cathedral of Amiens. France. 1709

Oppenord. Design for the Salon d'Angle, Palais Royale. Paris. 1716–1720

duc d'Orléans's Palais Royal was Oppenord's first major task for his royal patron. The remodeling campaign is known only through drawings and documents as Oppenord's work was swept away when the palace became a theater. Beginning in 1716, Oppenord worked on the duchesse's apartments on the ground floor and the regent's apartment in the left wing. The following year, he rebuilt the end wall of the picture gallery with a magnificently ornamented oval hemicycle. A great central chimneypiece, pilasters, consoles, an immense mirror, groups of cherubs, Victories pulling aside heavy curtains (inspired by Borromini), pyramids, trophies, and a cartouche with a crown of shell, all gilded, gave a splendid dramatic effect. Further changes at the Palais Royal included two cabinets to house part of the regent's painting collection, one called the Cabinet en Lantern or Salon à l'Italienne, and the Salon d'Angle (1719–1720), planned to connect the Grand Appartement with the gallery. This daring scheme involved constructing a room, elliptical at the ends, which overhung the rue de Richelieu. The bedroom of the Grand Appartement was enlarged and redecorated (1719–1720), and in the same year Oppenord submitted designs for a garden pavilion and for stables for the Palais Royal. Besides taking on various architectural projects for the duc d'Orléans and for members of his family, Oppenord's popularity at this time was acknowledged as far away as in a palace in Bonn, Germany, for the elector of Cologne, for whom Oppenord designed a chimneypiece, doors, paneling, and a grotto. It is probable that during this period Oppenord reached the peak of his activity as a furniture designer; many examples of tables, clocks, frames, candelabra, and chimneypieces are known through drawings and engravings.

In France, the demand for his services multiplied. Oppenord was hired by Pierre Crozat, the notable art collector, to remodel the gallery of his *hôtel* on the rue de Richelieu. It had been built beginning in 1704 by one of Oppenord's fellow pensioners at the Academy in Rome, JEAN SILVAIN CARTAUD. Aspersions have been cast on Oppenord's reputation as an architect because a balcony in the gallery collapsed in 1721 causing the deaths of several workmen, but according to a contemporary journalist, the accident occurred before Oppenord's employment. In any event, Crozat continued to use Oppenord's talents in the 1730s for additions to the Hôtel Crozat and for an orangery at his château at Montmorency. From 1731 until his death, Oppenord lived in an apartment which he rented at the Hôtel Crozat. It was undoubtedly there that he met and became friends with Rosalba Carrière and Antoine Watteau.

A commission that may never have been executed but was carefully prepared as evidenced by a series of fifteen elaborately detailed drawings and plans in the Musée des Arts Décoratifs, Paris, was for the Hôtel Gaudion in the Marais in Paris. An inscription alluding to Pierre-Nicolas Gaudion's post as *garde du trésor royal* which he held from 1731 to 1749, provides the possible dates for the designs. An even more speculative and richly ornamented structure known through a group of refined, elegantly rendered drawings at the Ecole des Beaux-Arts in Paris describes a lyric theater that existed only in Oppenord's imagination. It seems to symbolize Oppenord's career: an architect who knew more about making drawings than engineering and constructing buildings, but one whose skills and imagination enriched and influenced eighteenth-century taste. In the total analysis, he was employed less as an architect of buildings from the ground up than as a designer of interiors. The Hôtel Gaudion and the lyric theater drawings may have been Oppenord's attempt to prove conclusively that his capabilities were all-inclusive.

Following his death, some 2,000 of Oppenord's drawings were purchased by the engraver and publisher Gabriel Huquier. Three volumes of engravings (the *Petit, Moyen,* and *Grand Oppenord*) were published by him in the late 1740s, insuring Oppenord's immortality and making possible the dissemination of his aesthetic throughout Europe.

ELAINE EVANS DEE

WORKS

1704, Saint-Germain-des-Prés (altar); 1706, Abbey of Saint Victor (choir); Paris. 1709, Cathedral of Amiens (Altar of Saint Jean), France. 1712, Saint Jacques de la Boucherie (altar); 1714, Hôtel de Pomponne (interior); Paris. 1716, Château de Bonn (interior). 1716–1720, Palais Royal; 1719–1729, Hôtel d'Assy (interior); 1720–1721, Hôtel du Grand Prieur du Temple; 1721–1730, Hôtel Crozat; 1723–1724, Hôtel de Saint Albin; 1725–1740, Saint Sulpice; Paris. 1729, Cathedral of Meaux (choir screen and altars), France. 1731–1749, Hôtel Gaudion; 1732–1740, Eglise de l'Oratoire, Paris.

BIBLIOGRAPHY

BERCKENHAGEN, EKHART 1970 *Die französischen Zeichnungen der Kunstbibliothek.* Berlin: Hessling.

COUSY, HÉLÈNE 1972 "Projets d'Oppenord pour l'achèvement de l'Oratoire Saint-Honoré." *Gazette des Beaux-Arts* Series 6 80:97–107.

DUCLAUX, LISE 1975 *Inventaire général des dessins, école française XII: Musée du Louvre, Cabinet des Dessins.* Paris: Musées Nationaux.

GALLET, MICHEL 1966 "Quelques étapes du rococo dans l'architecture Parisienne." *Gazette des Beaux-Arts* Series 6 67:145–168.

GALLET, MICHEL 1972 *Paris Domestic Architecture of the 18th Century.* Translated by James C. Palmes. London: Barrie & Jenkins.

HAUTECOEUR, LOUIS 1948 Volume 2 in *Histoire de l'architecture classique en France.* Paris: Picard.

HUARD, GEORGES 1928 "Oppenord." Volume 1, pages 311–329 in Louis Dimier (editor), *Les peintres français du XVIIIe siecle.* Paris and Brussels: Van Oest.

KALNEIN, WEND GRAF, and LEVEY, MICHAEL 1972 *Art and Architecture of the Eighteenth Century in France.* Harmondsworth, England: Penguin.

KIMBALL, FISKE (1943)1980 *The Creation of the Rococo.* Reprint. New York: Dover.

MALBOIS, EMILE 1928 "Oppenord et l'église Saint Sulpice." *Gazette des Beaux Arts* Series 6 9:34–46.

MONTAIGLON, ANATOLE 1887–1888 Volumes 1 and 2 in *Correspondance des directeurs de l'académie de France à Rome.* Paris: Charavay.

SYDHOFF, BEATE 1963 "Un édifice religieux: L'église Saint Sulpice." *Information d'histoire de l'art* 8, no. 2:85–90.

ORCAGNA

Andrea di Cione (1308?–1368), nicknamed "Orcagna," was described by GIORGIO VASARI in his *Lives of Seventy Painters, Sculptors, and Architects* (1568) as almost a Gothic archetype of the Renaissance Universal Man. He was skilled in many arts—painting, sculpture, mosaic decoration, and architecture—and in addition, Vasari claims, he was an excellent poet. Orcagna's supposed literary talents and the breadth of his artistic activities set him apart from other Florentine Gothic architects and make his career of particular interest.

Orcagna was enrolled in the Florentine Stonemason's Guild in 1352, a decade after he matriculated in the *Arte dei Medici e Speziali* as a painter in 1343. Vasari states that Orcagna was trained by Andrea Pisano (see PISANO FAMILY), also active as both a sculptor and architect, but he was supported for membership in the Stonemason's Guild by Neri di Fioravanti, who in the late 1340s was employed building the Saint Anne Chapel in Or San Michele. If Andrea received practical architectural training in the five-year period before his matriculation as an independent master, it was probably in Neri di Fioravanti's workshop. This paved the way for his appointment as *capomaestro,* or chief architect, of the oratory of Or San Michele in 1355.

Orcagna's only undisputed, extant architectural work is the Tabernacle of Or San Michele (1352?–1359). This tabernacle was designed to shelter a miracle-working image of the Virgin and Child which had been repainted in 1346 after a fire destroyed the original relic. It assumed even greater religious and social significance after the Black Death of 1348 when funds for the tabernacle were swelled by numerous bequests from victims of the bubonic plague. Conceived in the tradition of ARNOLFO DI CAMBIO's Roman ciboria, Orcagna's tabernacle is a late Gothic version of this architectural type. Four massive piers, punctuated by pinnacles and spires with miniature gargoyles, support a rib-vaulted superstructure with four gables and crowned by a central segmented dome on a drum. Some scholars have suggested that the dome constitutes Orcagna's model for the finished cupola of the Florentine Cathedral, but it also has iconographic significance for the shrine's dedication to the Virgin. However, the cupola's visual effect is outweighed by the dense interweaving of marbles, polychrome enamels, mosaic inlay, gilding, and sculptured reliefs. Typical of Orcagna's inventive, anticlassical vocabulary are the spiral columns complete with capitals which masquerade as ribs in the tabernacle's central groin vault. The shimmering decorative details add tension and ambiguity to the heavy structure. Northern Gothic sources may have influenced Orcagna through the medium of Italian Gothic metalwork. Orcagna's contribution to the architecture of the church of Or San Michele is still debated.

If it had not been for a sudden reversal of opinion by the Florence Cathedral *Opera del Duomo* in 1357, Orcagna would have designed the piers of Santa Maria del Fiore. Orcagna's model was accepted in a six-to-two vote by the Duomo commission and by the arbitrator Piero del Migliore on July 19, 1357. Ten days later, a new set of models

Orcagna. Or San Michele (tabernacle). Florence. 1352?–1359

was abruptly ordered without explanation, and on August 3, 1357, the *capomaestro* of the Duomo, Francesco Talenti (see TALENTI FAMILY) won the competition. The *Opera del Duomo* had suggested to Orcagna that he remove the "tabernacles" from the pier capitals and strengthen the bases of his pier model. It appears from the documents that the artist either refused or neglected to modify his design and thus lost this important commission.

In 1358, just as the tabernacle of Or San Michele was being completed, Orcagna was appointed *capomaestro* of the Cathedral of Orvieto, where he remained until 1362. His major architectural task was directing the construction of the façade's rose window following a design by LORENZO MAITANI, though this was not entirely accomplished during his term. Orcagna is known to have drawn designs for façade mosaics (with his brother Matteo di Cione), but none are preserved. An extant drawing of a never realized pulpit and the design (but not execution) of the tabernacle of the Corporale (1358–1361) have been tentatively attributed to him. As chief architect, Orcagna acted primarily as administrator of the building works and designer of façade decoration. His term as *capomaestro* was too brief to allow Orcagna to leave a personal imprint on the Cathedral of Orvieto.

After his return to Florence in 1362 until his death in 1368, Orcagna headed one of the largest painting workshops in Florence, but he still managed to be active in the *Opera del Duomo* (1364–1367) when debate centered upon the completion of the nave and the proposed form of the Cathedral's east end. It is significant that in Duomo documents he is often referred to as a "master architect" and only occasionally as a painter. Persistent traditions attributing the Loggia dei Lanzi and the oratory of the Bigallo to Orcagna have proven unfounded. Orcagna's reputation thus rests on a single, brilliantly innovative architectural design, the Tabernacle of Or San Michele, which may have been too radical for its own time and still arouses violent and contradictory opinions among architectural critics.

KATHLEEN GILES ARTHUR

WORK

1352?–1359, Or San Michele (tabernacle), Florence.

BIBLIOGRAPHY

POPE-HENNESSY, JOHN (1955)1972 *Italian Gothic Sculpture.* 2d ed. London: Phaidon.

STEINWEG, KLARA 1929 *Andrea Orcagna: Quellengeschichtliche und stilkritische Untersuchung.* Strasbourg, France: Heitz.

TOSI, LUIGI A. MARIA 1933–1934 "Andrea Orcagna architetto." *Bollettino d'Arte* Series 3 27:512–526.

VASARI, GIORGIO (1896)1923 *Lives of Seventy of the Most Eminent Painters, Sculptors and Architects.* Edited by E. H. Blashfield, E. W. Blashfield, and A. A. Hopkins. Translated by Mrs. Jonathan Foster. New York: Scribner.

WHITE, JOHN 1966 *Art and Architecture in Italy: 1250–1400.* Baltimore: Penguin.

ORDISH, ROWLAND M.

Rowland Mason Ordish (1824–1886) was a Victorian structural engineer of great ability and originality. He was born at Melbourne, near Derby, the son of a land agent and surveyor. He had no special education as an engineer, but from an early age he worked in an engineering office. He assisted Sir Charles Fox with the design and erection of the Crystal Palace in Hyde Park and its re-erection at Sydenham. He worked with various architects including OWEN JONES and Sir GEORGE GILBERT SCOTT. In 1858, he patented his straight chain suspension system of bridge construction and later designed a number of bridges using this system.

ROGER DIXON

WORKS

1863, Dutch-Rhenish Railway Station (roof), Amsterdam. 1863–1869, Farringdon Street Bridge, Holborn Viaduct; 1866, Chapter House (concealed metal roof), Westminster Abbey; 1866–1868, Saint Pancras Station (roof; with W. H. Barlow); 1867–1871, Albert Hall (roof); London. 1868, Franz-Josef Suspension Bridge over the Moldau, Prague. 1868, Leeds Infirmary (iron-and-glass winter garden), England. 1872–1873, Albert Bridge, Chelsea, London. 1875, Saint Enoch's Station (roof), Glasgow.

BIBLIOGRAPHY

LETHABY, WILLIAM R. 1925 *Westminster Abbey Re-examined.* London: Duckworth.

ORDISH, ROWLAND M., and MATHESON, E. 1885 *Proposed Bridge over the Thames by the Tower.* London.

PEVSNER, NIKOLAUS 1952 Volume 2 in *London.* Harmondsworth, England: Penguin.

SIMMONS, J. 1965 *St. Pancras Station.* London: Allen & Unwin.

ORSOLINI FAMILY

Active in both Lombardy and Genoa, Italy, members of the Orsolini family worked on the expansion of the Palazzo San Giorgio, Genoa, in the mid-fifteenth century. By the sixteenth century, they had become largely concerned with decorative complexes of sculpture and architecture, as evidenced by the work of Giovanni II (?–1597), Taddeo, and Giacomo on the façade of the Certosa of Pavia. Tommaso Orsolini (1587–1675) later provided two relief altars inside the church, as well as the highly carved altar of San Siro in the Duomo of Pavia (1652). In Genoa, Giovanni Battista Orsolini (?–1646) executed tombs, fountains, and marble-decorated chapels, which were followed by Tommaso Orsolini's carved choir lofts in the cathedral (1655) and the Spinola Chapel in the Church of the Gesù (1667).

GARY M. RADKE

WORKS

1652, Duomo (altar of San Siro), Pavia, Italy. 1655, Cathedral (choir lofts); 1667, Spinola Chapel, Il Gesù; n.d., Palazzo San Giorgio (façade decorations); Genoa, Italy.

O'SHEA BROTHERS

The Irish stonecarvers James and John O'Shea (19th century) and their nephew Edward Whellan (or Whelland) who worked for the architectural firm of DEANE AND WOODWARD in the 1850s, were responsible for the naturalistic and richly associational carving that is one of the identifying characteristics of the Ruskinian (see JOHN RUSKIN) Gothic style associated with that firm's work. From Ballyhooly, County Cork, the O'Sheas were trained and first employed by THOMAS DEANE in Cork in the 1840s. They later followed the firm to Dublin, Oxford, and London, where they executed the carving for Trinity College Museum (1852–1857) and the Kildare Street Club (1858–1861) in Dublin, the Oxford Museum (1855–1861), and the Crown Life Assurance Company Office (1855–1857) in London. Following Ruskin's dicta the O'Sheas, with a minimum of supervision, were left to determine the subjects and to design the details of the carved ornament themselves, often working directly from plants and animals brought into the stone yard.

After Woodward's death, the O'Sheas worked in England and Wales, until they gradually disappeared from record in the early 1860s.

EVE M. BLAU

WORKS

1846–1849, Queen's College (carving), Cork, Ireland. 1852–1857, Trinity College Museum (carving), Dublin. *1855–1857, Crown Life Assurance Company Office (carving), London. 1855–1861, Oxford Museum (carving). *1856–1858, Llys Dulas (carving), Anglesey, Wales. 1857, Oxford Hall (carving); 1857–1859, Middleton Hall (carving); Oxford. 1858–1861, Kildare Street Club (carving), Dublin. 1861, Assize Courts (carving), Manchester, England. 1861, Corn Exchange (carving); 1861, Credence Shelf Exeter College Chapel (carving); Oxford. 1861, Thomas Woolner Studio (carving), Welbeck Street, London. 1862, Cowley House (carving), Oxford. 1863, Catholic Church (carving), Rhyll, Wales

BIBLIOGRAPHY

ACLAND, HENRY, and RUSKIN, JOHN 1859 *The Oxford Museum.* London: Smith, Elder.

BLAU, EVE 1981 *Ruskinian Gothic: The Architecture of Deane and Woodward, 1845–1961.* N.J.: Princeton University Press.

CURRAN, C. P. 1940 "Benjamin Woodward, Ruskin, and the O'Sheas." *Studies* 29:255–268.

FERRIDAY, PETER 1962 "The Oxford Museum." *Architectural Review* 132:409–416.

HANDLEY-READ, CHARLES 1964 "Sculpture in High Victorian Architecture." Pages 26–27 in *The High Victorian Achievement.* Victorian Society, Conference Report no. 2. London: The society.

ÖSTBERG, RAGNAR

From the beginning of the twentieth century up to the end of the 1920s, Ragnar Östberg (1866–1945) occupied a prominent and influential position among Swedish architects, and no Swedish architect—except perhaps ERIK GUNNAR ASPLUND—enjoyed a comparable international reputation.

Educated at the Royal Institute of Technology (1885–1888) and at the Royal Academy of Arts (1888–1891), both in Stockholm, he assisted his senior colleague ISAK GUSTAF CLASON, whose main task of the 1890s was the Nordic Museum, Stockholm. Östberg studied the vernacular architecture of Sweden, went to the United States in 1893, and made his grand tour in 1896–1899, covering France, Italy, Greece, England, and Spain.

At the turn of the century, Östberg and some colleague architects—CARL WESTMAN, LARS ISRAEL WAHLMAN, Torben Grut, and ERIK LALLERSTEDT—promulgated the need for a modern, national architecture, and during the decades to come they all made their contributions to this national movement, an equivalent of the corresponding and better known development in Finland.

Östberg started his architectural practice as a designer of private houses, influenced by English as well as Swedish traditions. His first major work was a school building in Stockholm, Östermalms Läroverk (1910), characterized by heavy volumes, plain walls of dark, red brick, and excellent craftsmanship. Östberg's most important building is the Stockholm City Hall. When he received this commission in 1908, he was well prepared, having made for that very demanding site, since 1901, various projects for a new law courts building. Building started in 1911, but Östberg's project was

Östberg. Stockholm City Hall. 1911–1923

gradually altered and changed. Most important was the change from granite to red brick for the façades, from tiles to sheet copper for the roofing, from heavy to more elegant forms, from Art Nouveau to classicism. In spite of this continual development of the project and of all the influences from various historical periods and from various countries, (the influence from Swedish architecture of the Vasa period) the building (completed in 1923) has a striking architectural unity, a convincing setting in the Stockholm urban scene, and interiors of an unusual quality. Östberg's masterpiece is much more than a city hall in the usual sense of the word. It is a national monument, and a full understanding requires many references to the Swedish cultural background. The fame of the building spread rapidly, and in 1926 Östberg was awarded the gold medal of the Royal Institute of British Architects.

Östberg's second most important work was the Swedish Patent and Registration Office in Stockholm (1921), whose classicist brick walls offered a more practicable pattern than the City Hall. In his Center for Minor Industries (1930), Östberg, according to the purpose of the building, seemingly approached functionalism. But as other late works show (the School in Kalmar, the Maritime Museum), he never gave up the idea of a national architecture (in his old days mostly based upon the tradition of Tessin [see TESSIN FAMILY] and CARL HÅRLEMAN).

Although to some extent an eclecticist himself, Östberg like so many of his generation totally despised the architecture of the nineteenth century. He always looked upon architecture as an art, created by highly talented individuals like himself. Needless to say, his reputation declined in the heyday of functionalism, but obviously not for good.

ANDERS ÅMAN

WORKS

1904, Jungfruberget (Eva Bonnier House), Dalarö, Sweden. 1905, Ebbagården, Tureberg, Sweden. 1905, Ekarne House, Djurgården; 1910, High School (Östermalms Läroverk); 1911–1923, Stockholm City Hall; Stockholm. 1913, Old Fellow Building, Nyköping, Sweden. 1921, Swedish Patent and Registration Office; 1930, Minor Industries' Center; Stockholm. 1930, Students' Club, Uppsala, Sweden. 1933, High School (Kalmar Läroverk), Kalmar, Sweden. 1936, National Maritime Museum, Stockholm. 1939, Museum of Anders Zorn, Mora, Dalecarlia, Sweden.

BIBLIOGRAPHY

CORNELL, ELIAS 1965 *Ragnar Östberg Svensk arkitekt.* Stockholm: Byggmästarens förlag. An English summary is on pages 247–248.

ÖSTBERG, RAGNAR (1926)1956 *The Stockholm City Hall: A Guide.* 3d ed., rev. Stockholm: Generalstabens litografiska anstalts förlag.

ÖSTBERG, RAGNAR 1928 *En arkitekts anteckningar.* Stockholm: Natur och Kultur.

STAVENOW-HIDEMARK, ELISABET 1971 *Villabebyggelse i Sveriga 1900–1925.* Stockholm: Nordiska museet.

Stockholms stadshus 1923 Stockholm: Tisells. An English summary is on pages 333–351.

OSTELL, JOHN

Like many of Montreal's early Victorian architects, John Ostell (1813–1892) was an immigrant to the city. British-born and trained, he arrived in 1834, and set up an architectural practice that was to flourish over the next twenty-five years. As the architect for the Customs House, the Court House, and the McGill University Arts Building, Ostell helped to bring a sense of grandeur to the civic architecture of his adopted city. He is best remembered for these austere and finely detailed classical buildings.

JULIA GERSOVITZ

WORKS

1836, Customhouse, Place Royale; 1839–1843, McGill University Arts Building; *1842, L'Aisle de la Providence; 1842, Notre Dame Church (towers); *1845, McGill Normal School, Belmont Street; *1848, Protestant Orphan Asylum, Saint Catherine Street; *1849, Episcopal Palace; (A)1849, Vieux Séminaire; Montreal. 1850, Church of the Visitation (façade), Sault-au-Récollet, Quebec. 1850–1856, Courthouse (with Henri-Maurice Perrault), 155 Notre-Dame Street East; 1891, Church of Notre-Dame-de-Toures-Graces; Montreal. *1851, Toll Collector's Office, Lachine Canal, Quebec.

BIBLIOGRAPHY

JAMES, ELLEN 1981 "The Civil Architecture of John Ostell." Unpublished Ph.D. dissertation, McGill University, Montreal.

KING, JOHN S. 1975 "The Building of McGill College: An Historical Account." Unpublished manuscript, Montreal.

OSTROWSKI, WACŁAW

Wacław Ostrowski (1907–) studied at the Technical University of Gdansk, Poland, and graduated in 1929. Throughout his many years of teaching and research, he has contributed toward the development of a contemporary planning theory. Characteristic of his approach is a deep concern for the harmonious development of residential areas in accord with the heritage of the past. He has taught history of town planning and urban design at the Technical University in Warsaw since 1952. Since 1962, he has been a member of the International Federation of Housing and Physical Planning. Ostrowski has written numerous articles and several books on the history of town planning.

LECH KŁOSIEWICZ

WORK

1930–1939, Housing Estate, Łodz, Poland.

BIBLIOGRAPHY

L'ECOLE SPECIALE D'ARCHITECTURE 1981 *Avant-Garde Polonais: 1918–1939.* Paris: Moniteur.

OTIS, ELISHA GRAVES

Elisha Graves Otis (1811–1861) developed a safe elevator and increased the practicality of constructing tall buildings, thus becoming a major factor in the evolution of the skyscraper. In 1852, in a factory in Yonkers, New York, Otis installed an elevator with an automatic pin device that prevented the hoisting platform from falling should the lifting chain or rope break. Otis formed an elevator company in 1853, but sales were at first slow, even after he himself publicly demonstrated his invention at the Crystal Palace Exposition in New York in 1854. The first safe passenger elevator with an automatic brake was installed by Otis in JOHN P. GAYNOR and William Badger's Haoghwout Building in New York in March 1857.

GWEN W. STEEGE

BIBLIOGRAPHY

ARNAUD, LEOPOLD 1952 "The Tall Building in New York in the Twentieth Century." *Journal of the Society of Architectural Historians* 11:15–18.

GIEDION, SIEGFRIED (1941)1967 *Space, Time and Architecture.* 5th ed., rev. & enl. Cambridge, Mass.: Harvard University Press.

ORWIG, BENTON B. 1936 "Builders of America: Elisha G. Otis." *Architecture* 73:320–321.

OTIS ELEVATOR COMPANY 1953? *The First One Hundred Years.* New York: The company.

OTTO, FREI

Frei Otto (1925–) is a German architect and engineer who has pioneered the fields of lightweight construction, developing design systems for tent, tensile, and pneumatic structures.

The son and grandson of sculptors, Otto displayed an early interest in construction when as a child he spent many hours building model airplanes. Later, he took up gliding, a hobby that forced him to become acutely attuned to the laws of aerodynamics and the principles of stretched membranes over light frameworks. Another experience that helped shape Otto's interests was his early training as a stonemason.

After leaving school in 1943, Otto joined the German air force, serving as a pilot until he was captured by the Allies in 1945 and spending the next two years in a prisoner-of-war camp near Chartres, France. There, he was put in charge of building and repair crews that had to cope with severe shortages of materials. It was this experience that prompted Otto to think of construction in terms of building the most with the least possible material.

After the war, Otto enrolled in the Technological University in Berlin and spent the year 1950–1951 on a study tour in the United States, during which he met EERO SAARINEN and the civic engineer Fred Severud. At the time, Severud was working with MATTHEW NOWICKI on the Raleigh, North Carolina, State Fair Arena, which had the first great suspended roof and which greatly influenced Otto's doctoral thesis on that type of construction. During the next few years, Otto expanded the scope of his investigations from load-stabilized suspension structures—such as the Raleigh roof—to the prestressed tensile systems of construction that have made him famous.

The first step along this route was the development of radically new tent designs in association with the Stromeyer Company, one of the world's largest tent-making firms. After coming to the attention of Peter Stromeyer in 1954, Otto established what would be a long and fruitful relationship with a company that could offer him the research facilities and the construction opportunities he required to investigate lightweight and tensile structures. Important tent structures designed by (or in consultation with) Otto include: the bandstand at the 1955 Federal Garden Exhibition in Kassel, Germany (one of the first structures to have a prestressed membrane between edge cables); the entrance arch at the same exhibition in Cologne in 1957 (an arch-supported saddle structure); the "Snow and Rocks" pavilion at the Swiss national exhibition in Lausanne in 1964 (a group

Otto.
Olympic Stadium (roof),
Olympic Park.
Munich.
1972

of five sharply peaked tents); and a mobile theater that toured Europe in 1968 (a star-shaped tent stretched over a circular stage).

Having trained himself in the science of tent design, Otto next focused on the problems of cable network structures, which resemble tents in many ways. In both types of structures, a flexible membrane (such as fabric or canvas for tents and a net of metal cables for cable networks) is stabilized by tensile forces. Compressive forces are concentrated on only a few elements such as masts or poles. Such structures can be much lighter and can span much greater distances than conventional buildings. They can also result in dramatic shapes such as hyperbolic paraboloids and anticlastic (or saddlelike) curves. Otto's most famous cable network projects were the West German pavilion at the Montreal Exposition in 1967 and the roofs over several of the sports structures at the 1972 Olympic Park in Munich.

Work in the field of lightweight structures has also led Otto to design retractable roofs for athletic facilities and swimming pools as well as pneumatic enclosures (structures held up by air pressure) for giant greenhouses and arctic shelters. Like R. BUCKMINSTER FULLER, with whom he is often compared, Otto has developed many visionary schemes for enclosing harbors, grain storage facilities, and even whole cities.

To encourage research in both theoretical and practical applications of these structures, Otto in 1957 founded the Development Center for Lightweight Construction in Berlin. In 1964, this institution was incorporated into an Institute for Light Surface Structures set up by the University of Stuttgart's department of civil engineering and Otto was made an honorary professor. To concentrate on research and allow himself to work on as many types of projects as possible, Otto retired from the practice of architecture in 1970 and has worked as a consultant ever since.

In addition to creating some strikingly beautiful structures and exploring new systems of construction, Frei Otto is famous for his methodology, which involves painstakingly extensive analysis and intensive use of soap-film and other types of models. His concern with function and minimalist structure links him to Bauhaus and International style designers, while his analysis of natural forms and the way modern technology can imitate them ties him to the post-World War II generation of architects. This ability to bridge the gap in German architecture history created by the Nazi years and to advance the frontier of structural design has made Otto one of the most important German architects working today.

CLIFF PEARSON

WORKS

*1955, Bandstand, Federal Garden Exhibition, Kassel, Germany. *1957, Entrance Arch and Dance Pavilion, Federal Garden Exhibition, Cologne, Germany. *1963, Wave Hall, International Horticultural Exhibition, Hamburg, Germany. *1964, Snow and Rocks Pavilion, Swiss National Exhibition, Lausanne, Switzerland. *1967, West German Pavilion, World Exposition, Montreal. 1972, Hotel and Conference Center, Mecca, Saudi Arabia. 1972, Olympic Stadium roof, Olympic Park, Munich.

BIBLIOGRAPHY

DREW, PHILIP 1976 *Frei Otto: Form and Structure.* Boulder, Colo.: Westview.

GLAESER, LUDWIG 1972 *The Work of Frei Otto.* New York: Museum of Modern Art.

OTTO, FREI 1961 *Structures: Traditional and Lightweight.* New Haven: Yale University Press.

OTTO, FREI 1963 *Lightweight Structures.* Berkeley: University of California Press.

ROLAND, CONRAD 1970 *Frei Otto: Tension Structures.* New York: Praeger.

OTZEN, JOHANNES

Johannes Otzen (1839–1911) was a leading German architect of churches in a neo-Gothic style during the last quarter of the nineteenth century. Born near the Danish border, he studied at the Baugewerbeschule in Eckernförde and at the Polytechnikum in Hannover before becoming assistant to CONRAD WILHELM HASE in 1864. His most important project was the Johanniskirche in Hamburg-Altona (1869–1883), which established a Gothic hybrid plan for Protestant churches that he applied to similar projects across northern Germany from Wiesbaden to Hamburg, Berlin, and Leipzig. He was appointed professor of architecture at the Technische Hochschule in Charlottenburg (Berlin), where he also taught form language for engineers.

RON WIEDENHOEFT

WORKS

1877, Bergkirche, Wiesbaden, Germany. 1883, Johanniskirche, Hamburg-Altona, Germany. 1885, Gertrudkirche, Hamburg, Germany. 1886, Jakobikirche, Kiel, Germany. 1887, Heilandskirche, Leipzig. 1888, Heiligkreuzkirche, Berlin. 1892, Evangelische Kirche, Dresden, Germany. 1893, Lutherkirche, Berlin.

BIBLIOGRAPHY

BAHNS, JÖRN 1971 *Johannes Otzen.* Munich: Prestel.
VOLLMER 1911 "Johannes Otzen." *Zentralblatt der Bauverwaltung* 31:321.

OUD, J. J. P.

Jacobus Johannes Pieter Oud (1890–1963) has long been considered the foremost Dutch representative of modern functionalism. His low-cost but elegant housing complexes of the 1920s remain for many critics the quintessential examples of the International style as well as an engaging evocation of the Dutch identification of beautiful with clean and pure (*schoon*). One of only four Europeans at the seminal exhibition on modern architecture held in 1932 at the Museum of Modern Art, New York, he was among the first to articulate the goals associated with the *neue Sachlichkeit* (new objectivity), stating in 1918 that "the development of architecture is largely determined by social and technological factors" and calling for "the application on a pure foundation of mass production . . . and standardization" to architecture (*De Stijl*, vol. 1, no. 7). Yet Oud never denied that architecture was an art expressive of the human spirit, noting in 1925 that "I bow my knee to the wonders of technology but I do not believe that a liner can be compared to the Parthenon." Oud's *oeuvre,* furthermore, is far more complex than has generally been acknowledged. The historical reappraisals currently under way, which take into account his early designs as well as later buildings that show a break with orthodox modernism, are sorely needed for a just appreciation of his many-sided contributions.

Born in the small town of Purmerend north of Amsterdam, Oud studied first at arts and crafts schools in the Dutch capital, then at the Technical University in Delft, the chief architectural school in the Netherlands. A brief stint with THEODOR FISCHER in Munich brought him important contacts with German architects. He blossomed quickly, building his first house in Purmerend (1906) at age sixteen; further modest works in the local brick vernacular soon followed. In 1914, Oud moved to Leiden, designing there, with W. M. DUDOK, the workers' housing complex of Leiderdorp (1914–1916). The straightforward solutions put forth here and in other realized works of the Leiden period typify the reductionist strain in Oud's approach, but they are in sharp contrast to three unexecuted designs of 1915. These monumental, elaborate, and deliberately modish projects reveal alternative proclivities and are particularly interesting in showing his debt to H. P. BERLAGE. The choice and treatment of material (heavy brick walls dressed with stone trim kept flush with the wall plane); the employment of a geometric system to compose the elevations; and the medievalizing allusions suggested by the massing, the proportion of solid to void, and the placement of ornamental motifs are all features deriving from Berlage's style. Oud would turn to Berlagian models also when he conceived the housing blocks at Spangen in Rotterdam (1918–1920) and again in the late 1930s and early 1940s. Throughout his career, Oud was guided by Berlage's emphasis on social content in his search for a style that was honest in terms of construction and sufficiently general and objective in formal terms for all situations and audiences.

Simultaneously, however, competing ideologies claimed Oud's allegiance, for 1915 saw a growing absorption also in such avant-garde movements as Cubism and Futurism. This led to a momentous acquaintance with that charismatic iconoclast, THEO VAN DOESBURG, which resulted in Oud's association in 1917 with *De Stijl,* a loose grouping of artists and designers organized around van Doesburg's periodical of the same name. *De Stijl* was dedicated to propagating a universally valid art and architecture purged of subjective sentimentality that spiritually and materially would express the new realities of the Machine Age.

Two collaborations in 1917 heralded a turning point in Oud's style. The vacation retreat for workers *De Vonk*, Noordwijkerhout, designed with van Doesburg, provides an early example of *De Stijl* interior decoration created through flat planes of colors, while the renovation of the Villa Allegonda, Katwijkaan-Zee, decorated by van Doesburg, for M. Kamerlingh Onnes, is Oud's first constructed essay using stripped cubic volumes arranged asymmetrically. Still more prophetic of his celebrated mature manner, however, is the proposal of 1917 for the Ocean Boulevard Apartments, which illustrates Oud's call, published in the first issue of *De Stijl* (October 1917), for an architecture of abstract, machine-produced prismatic forms whose carefully calibrated repetition provides the major aesthetic excitement. Oud's project for a factory at Purmerend, of 1919, with its interlocking horizontal and vertical planes, demonstrates his fascination with the work of FRANK LLOYD WRIGHT.

When Oud moved to Rotterdam to become municipal architect in 1918, a post he retained until 1933, he detached himself from *De Stijl*. Functionalism had not been of much concern to the aesthetically oriented group, and Oud's obligations to solve the housing shortage in Rotterdam required the tempering of any esoteric preoccupations. These had not been, in any case, a major part of his researches; for example, geometry did not hold for him the mystical connotations it had for such former colleagues as van Doesburg and Piet Mondrian, but rather was seen as an expedient means compatible with machine production to achieve clarity and order. Nevertheless, his brief association with the group was not without impact. Although the organization and materials of the housing blocks at Spangen (1918–1920) and Tusschendijken (1922–1923) in Rotterdam are Berlagian, the play of planes achieved in the chimneys and entryways reflect the compositional methods of *De Stijl*. Rectilinearity of form and extension of planes into space are even more evident in the garden village of Oud-Mathenesse, Rotterdam (1922–1923), where the white walls and blue and yellow doors and sash obey the movement's coloristic dictates. Most *De Stijl*-like of all were two little masterpieces that unhappily are no longer extant: the building superintendent's office at Oud-Mathenesse (1923), where cubic volumes painted in primary colors explode centrifugally from a central core, and the Café De Unie in Rotterdam (1924), the façade of which resembled the three-dimensional equivalent of a painting by Mondrian.

Oud's best-known works are three housing developments where the formal goals of *De Stijl* have been assimilated within the broader and more practical idiom of the International style. The two-story rows of dwellings at Hook of Holland (1924–1927) and at Kiefhoek, Rotterdam (1925–1929), embody in their smooth white planar surfaces and strip windows the pervasive modern conception of the exterior wall as an enclosing membrane rather than a structural support. The unusual curved corners endow the focal points of the housing projects with a soaring lyricism. In 1927, Oud participated in the demonstration housing exhibition at the Weissenhofsiedlung in Stuttgart. His contribution was a row of five terrace houses which convincingly justify his belief in the powerful beauty of carefully proportioned, syncopated geometric forms. Through incredibly simple, inexpensive means, he raised the minimal dwelling to the level of an exquisite work of art.

Oud.
Shell Office.
The Hague.
1938–1942

When seen in close proximity—actually at Stuttgart, photographically in New York in 1932—to designs by the other masters of the International style, LUDWIG MIES VAN DER ROHE, LE CORBUSIER, and WALTER GROPIUS, Oud's work holds its own. H. R. Hitchcock, one of the organizers of the MOMA show, considered Oud "the most conscientious of modern architects. . . . In any period he would have been a very great architect, in our own he is of all great architects the most sound" (Barr et al., 1932, p. 97). Such preeminence brought Oud a number of invitations from the United States to lecture and teach. Oud never paid a visit, but he did design a house to be built for the parents of PHILIP JOHNSON in Pinehurst, North Carolina (1930–1931). This was exhibited in model form throughout the United States in 1932, and those who viewed the poised equilibrium of discrete circular and rectilinear volumes and planes must have concurred with Hitchcock's judgment. Like most of his other projects of the 1930s, however, the house was not executed and when Oud next completed a major work, it appeared to constitute a radical refutation of all that had brought him critical acclaim.

The commission that met with such shocked hostility was the Shell (originally Bataafsche Import Maatschappij) Office Building in The Hague (1938–1942). Evidently looking back nostalgically to his own projects of 1915, Oud has restored ornament and monumentality. The composition is academically symmetrical, and over a reinforced-concrete skeleton has been woven—disapproving commentators said "embroidered"—a mantle of wheat-colored, hand-fired bricks and of sandstone carved in novel decorative patterns. Although the building reflects Oud's own search for a way to humanize modernist severity, it was not an isolated phenomenon. Other disenchanted Functionalists in the Netherlands were making similar explorations at the time, and the Shell Building may be regarded as a precocious manifestation of that movement of the 1940s dubbed the "New Empiricism," which enriched modern structures with pattern and traditional references.

Oud's project for the Hofplein in Rotterdam (1942–1943) moves even further toward romantic plasticity and historical allusion, but the executed works of his final years show a rapprochement with the International style as it had been reconstituted after World War II in the direction of greater luxury to appeal thereby to large commercial and institutional patrons. Ambitious in scope, these last buildings seem less personal but nevertheless are fine examples of the genre—bold volumes devoid of decoration yet carefully detailed in highly finished modern materials. The fact that Oud's final design, the Convention Center for The Hague (1957–1963), was executed posthumously makes it less than a perfect ultimate statement, but the model shows Oud's intentions and his skill in renewing certain *De Stijl* ideas while making them compatible for an extensive project. In 1955, Oud received an honorary doctorate from the Technical University in Delft. His executed output is relatively small but it more than makes up in quality for what is lacking quantitatively.

HELEN SEARING

WORKS

1906, Alida Hartog-Oud House; 1911, Vooruit Cooperative (houses and meeting hall); 1912, Schinkel Cinema; Purmerend, Netherlands. 1914, Van Bakel House, Heemstede, Netherlands. 1914–1916, Leiderdorp Housing Estate (with W. M. Dudok), Netherlands. 1915, Van Essen-Vincker House, Blaricum, Netherlands. 1917, Villa Allegonda (renovation with M. Kamerlingh Onnes and Theo van Doesburg), Katwijk-aan-Zee, Netherlands. 1917–1919, De Vonk Vacation Retreat (with van Doesburg), Noordwijkerhout, Netherlands. 1918–1920, Spangen Housing Estate (blocks 1, 5, 8, and 9); 1920, Tusschendijken Housing Estate; 1922–1923, Oud-Mathenesse Housing Estate and Building Superintendent's Office; *1924, Café De Unie; Rotterdam, Netherlands. 1924–1927, Housing Estate, Hook of Holland, Netherlands. 1925–1929, Kiefhoek Housing Estate, Rotterdam, Netherlands. 1927, Terraced Housing, Weissenhofsiedlung, Stuttgart, Germany. 1928–1929, Church, Kiefhoek Housing Estate, Rotterdam, Netherlands. 1937, *SS Nieuw Amsterdam* (interiors). 1938–1942, Shell (originally Bataafsche Import Maatschappij) Office Building, The Hague. 1943, Central Savings Bank; 1947–1950, Esveha Office Building; Rotterdam, Netherlands. 1948, Dutch Soldiers' Monument, Grebbeberg Cemetery, near Rhenen, Netherlands. 1949, War Memorial (sculpture by John and Han Raedecker), Amsterdam. 1950–1956, Lyceum, The Hague. 1952–1960, Bio Convalescent Resort for Children, Arnhem, Netherlands. 1954–1961, Utrecht Life Insurance Company Building, Rotterdam, Netherlands. 1957–1963, Convention Center (completed posthumously), The Hague.

BIBLIOGRAPHY

Many articles written by J. J. P. Oud were published in De Stijl, The Studio, Das neue Frankfurt, Forum, The Architectural Record, *and* Europa-Almanach.

BANHAM, REYNER (1960)1967 *Theory and Design in the First Machine Age*. 2d ed. New York: Praeger.

BARR, ALFRED H., JR.; HITCHCOCK, H. R.; JOHNSON, PHILIP; and MUMFORD, LEWIS 1932 *Modern Architects*. New York: Museum of Modern Art.

BENEVOLO, LEONARDO (1960)1977 *The Modern Movement*. Volume 2 in *History of Modern Architecture*. Translated by H. J. Landry from the third revised Italian edition. Cambridge, Mass.: M.I.T. Press.

FANELLI, GIOVANNI (1968)1978 *Moderne architectuur in Nederland 1900–1940*. Translated from the Italian. The Hague: Staatsuitgeverij.

GRUYTER, W. JOS. DE 1951 *J. J. P. Oud*. Rotterdam, Netherlands: Museum Boymans.

HITCHCOCK, H. R. 1931 *J. J. P. Oud*. Paris: Editions Cahiers d'Art.

HITCHCOCK, H. R., and JOHNSON, PHILIP (1932)1966 *The International Style*. New York: Norton.

JAFFE, H. L. C. 1956 *De Stijl: 1917–1931*. Amsterdam: Meulenhoff.

OUD, J. J. P. (1926)1976 *Holländische Architektur*. Reprint. Mainz, Germany: Kupferberg.

OUD, J. J. P. 1952 "L'edificio della Shell Olandese." *Metron* 45:12–15.

OUD, J. J. P. 1959 *Zijn er nog architecten?* The Hague: Boucher.

OUD, J. J. P. 1961 *Mein Weg in 'De Stijl.'* The Hague: Nijgh & van Ditmar.

OUD, J. J. P. 1962 *Ter wille van een levende bouwkunst*. The Hague: Nijgh & van Ditmar.

OUD, J. J. P. 1963 *Architecturalia voor bouwheren en architecten*. The Hague: Mouton.

POLANO, SERGIO 1977 "Notes on Oud." *Lotus International* 16:42–54. Including translations of three of J. J. P. Oud's articles appearing originally in *De Stijl*.

STAMM, GUNTHER 1978 *The Architecture of J. J. P. Oud, 1906–1963*. Tallahassee: University Press of Florida.

VERONESI, GIULIA 1953 *J. J. Pieter Oud*. Milan: Il Balcone.

WIEKART, K. 1965 J. J. P. Oud. Translated from the Dutch by C. de Dood. Amsterdam: Meulenhoff.

ZEVI, BRUNO (1953)1974 *Poetica dell'Architettura Neo-Plastica*. Reprint. Turin, Italy: Einaudi.

OUELLET, JOSEPH-PIERRE

Joseph-Pierre Ouellet (1871–1959), a prolific church architect of Quebec City, trained under the partnership of Georges E. Tanguay and Alfred Vallee. He commenced his own practice in 1895; his best work includes Saint Felicien Church at Lake St. John, Quebec (1913), and Saint Charles-de-Limoilou Church, Quebec City (1917).

ROBERT HILL

BIBLIOGRAPHY

"The New President of the P.Q.A.A." 1904 *Canadian Architect and Builder* 17, Feb.:42.

NOPPEN, LUC 1973 *La Fin d'une époque.* Quebec City: Ministère des affaires culturelles.

OUTSHOORN, CORNELIS

Cornelis Outshoorn (1810–1875), born in Nieuwveen, Netherlands, is especially famous for his design for the Paleis van Volksvlijt (Palace of People's Industry) in Amsterdam (1857–1864), the Dutch counterpart of the London Crystal Palace. Before receiving this commission, he worked from 1838 to 1857 for the Dutch Iron Railway Company in Amsterdam. Because of his experience in building stations, he received the commission for the Palace of People's Industry. At the same time, he was commissioned to design several buildings in the neighborhood of the Palace to give the whole a metropolitan air. The most important of these works was the Amstel Hotel (1863–1867). As a result of these buildings, he made a name for himself as an architect of monumental structures in the Second Empire style and he received several commissions for hotels, clubs, and so on.

WIM DE WIT

WORKS

*1857–1864, Palace of People's Industry; 1863–1867, Amstel Hotel; Amsterdam. 1869, De Witte Clubhouse, The Hague. *1869, Oranje Hotel, Scheveningen, Netherlands. *1871, Hotel Groot Berg en Dal, Beek bij Nijmegen, Netherlands. 1873, De Buitensociëteit Clubhouse, Arnhem, Netherlands.

BIBLIOGRAPHY

GUGEL, EUGEN (1886)1916–1918 *Geschiedenis van de bouwstijlen in de hoofdtijdperken der architectuur.* 2d ed. Rotterdam, Netherlands: Bolle.

Nederland Bouwt in Baksteen: 1800–1940. 1941 Rotterdam, Netherlands: Museum Boymans-van Beuningen.

ROY VAN ZUYDEWIJN, H. J. F. DE 1969 *Amsterdamse Bouwkunst: 1815–1940.* Amsterdam: De Bussy.

OVCHAROV, GEORGI RADEV

Born in Silistra, Bulgaria, Georgi Radev Ovcharov (1889–1953) graduated from the Polytechnic Institute in Munich in 1911. During forty years of professional practice, Ovcharov developed a personal approach to interpreting the classical heritage and transforming it into a contemporary Bulgarian monumentalism. A talented painter and sculptor, he approached design as an art, creating clear compositions of well-proportioned spaces and façades carefully detailed with simplified classical ornaments and sometimes with forceful colonnades.

Ovcharov created memorable civic buildings such as Burgas City Hall (1939–1942), in Burgas, Bulgaria, the Ministries of Interior Affairs (1935–1939) and of Finances (1941), in Sofia, all monuments of admiration and inspiration for his associates and followers, including IVAN POPOV.

For the design, with Ivan Danchov (see BELKOVSKI AND DANCHOV) and Racho Ribarov, of Dimitrov's Mausoleum (1949) in Sofia, Ovcharov received the Dimitrov's Award in 1951.

MARIA POPOVA

WORKS

1924–1930, Saint Constantin Resort, Varna, Bulgaria. 1929, Bulgarian Agricultural Bank, Sofia. 1930–1935, Worker's Hospital, Plovdiv, Bulgaria. 1935–1939, Ministry of Interior Affairs, Sofia. 1938, Plovdiv Stock Exchange, Bulgaria. 1939–1942, Burgas City Hall, Bulgaria. 1940–1944, Agriculture Cooperative Bank (now the Military Publishing Company); 1942, Ministry of Finances; 1948, State Musical Theater; 1949, Dimitrov's Mausoleum (with Ivan Danchov and Racho Ribarov); Sofia.

BIBLIOGRAPHY

"Arkhitekt Georgi Ovcharov." 1960 *Arkhitektura* 1:36.

BŬLGARSKA AKADEMIÎA NA NAUKITE 1965 *Kratka istoriîa na Bŭlgarskata, arkhitektura.* Sofia: The academy.

BŬLGARSKA AKADEMIÎA NA NAUKITE 1974 in *Entsiklopediîa na Bulgaria.* Sofia: The academy.

MOMIROV, E. 1953 "Arkhitekt G. R. Ovcharov." *Teknichesko Delo* 1953:116.

OWINGS, NATHANIEL

See SKIDMORE, OWINGS, and MERRILL.

OZENFANT, AMEDEE

Amédée Ozenfant (1886–1966) met LE CORBUSIER in 1918. Under Ozenfant's initial leadership, they founded Purism, a style that insisted on the geometric order and clarity associated with urban industrial technology and on the classical ideals of harmony, order, and proportion. They founded *L'Esprit Nouveau* (1920–1925), "the first periodical in the world dedicated to the aesthetic of our times in all its manifestations." Ozenfant contributed photographs to jointly signed articles later published by Le Corbusier as *Vers une Architecture* (1923). Their partnership dissolved in 1926. Ozenfant and Le Corbusier abandoned Purism in painting around 1927, but Le Corbusier continued Purist principles in architecture. In 1930, Ozenfant was commissioned by architect ERIC MENDELSOHN to paint murals for his house in Berlin. From 1939 to 1955 he ran the Ozenfant School of Fine Arts, New York.

Ozenfant designed no buildings but claimed to have played a significant role in Le Corbusier's design for the Ozenfant Studio, Paris (1923).

SUSAN BALL

BIBLIOGRAPHY

BALL, SUSAN 1978 "Ozenfant and Purism: The Evolution of a Style, 1915–1930." Unpublished Ph.D. dissertation, Yale University, New Haven.

BANHAM, REYNER (1960)1967 *Theory and Design in the First Machine Age.* 2d ed. New York: Praeger.

CAMPBELL, LAWRENCE 1973 "Ozenfant: Painter of the 'Absolute Object.'" *Art News* 72, Apr.:27–28.

CASSOU, JEAN 1928 "Amédée Ozenfant." *Cahiers d'art* 3:437–441.

GEORGE, WALDEMAR 1931 "Ozenfant: From Purism to Magic Realism." *Formes* 16:104.

GOLDING, JOHN 1973 *Ozenfant.* New York: Knoedler.

GOLDING, JOHN, and GREEN, CHRISTOPHER (1971)1977 *Léger and Purist Paris.* Woodbury, N.Y.: Barron.

GREEN, CHRISTOPHER 1976 *Léger and the Avant-Garde.* New Haven: Yale University Press.

GUEGUEN, PIERRE 1930 "Réflexions sur l'oeuvre d'Ozenfant." *Cahiers d'art* 5:537–540.

OZENFANT, AMÉDÉE (1925)1979 *Foundations of Modern Art.* Translated by John Rodker. Reprint. Darby, Pa.: Arden Library. Originally published with the title *L'Art.*

OZENFANT, AMÉDÉE 1939 *Journey Through Life.* Translated by Helen Beauclerk and Violet Macdonald. New York: Macmillan.

OZENFANT, AMÉDÉE 1968 *Mémoires, 1886–1962.* Paris: Seghers.

OZENFANT, AMÉDÉE, and JEANNERET, CHARLES-EDOUARD (Le Corbusier) 1918 *Après le Cubisme.* Paris: Editions des Commentaire.

OZENFANT, AMÉDÉE, and JEANNERET, CHARLES-EDOUARD (Le Corbusier) 1925 *La Peinture Moderne.* Paris: Crès.

NIERENDORF, KARL 1931 *Amédée Ozenfant.* Berlin: Nierendorf.

RAYNAL, MAURICE 1921 "Ozenfant et Jeanneret." *L'Esprit Nouveau* 7:807–832.

SILVER, KENNETH 1977 "Purism: Straightening Up After the Great War." *Artforum* 15, March:56–63.

WILL-LEVAILLANT, FRANÇOISE 1975 "Norme et Forme à travers l'Esprit Nouveau." Pages 241–265 in *Le Retour à l'ordre dans les arts plastiques et l'architecture, 1919–1925.* Saint-Etienne, France: Centre interdisciplinaire d'études et de recherche sur l'expression contemporaine.

P

PACCHIONI FAMILY

Beginning with Leonardo the Elder, who was active between 1509 and 1537, the Pacchioni family received a large number of architectural and sculptural commissions in their native city of Reggio Emilia, Italy. The bulk of their work consisted of altars and chapels, but Leonardo the Younger was responsible for the cloister of San Pietro, Reggio Emilia (begun 1513). Leonardo the Elder's other sons, Alberto the Elder and Roberto, are documented to have been active from 1514 to 1572 and 1537 to 1540 respectively. Francesco Pacchioni, son of Prospero, was active between 1588 and 1626, producing the epitaph and bust of his teacher Prospero Sogari, decorations for the presbytery of Reggio Emilia's cathedral, and the cupola and plaster decorations of the Church of the Beata Vergine della Ghiaja (1597), where Francesco's son, Alberto the Younger, was responsible for the altar of Saints George and Catherine.

GARY M. RADKE

WORKS

1513, Cathedral (decoration of presbytery); Begun 1513, San Pietro (cloister); 1597, Beata Vergine della Ghiaja (plaster decorations and the altar of Saints George and Catherine); Reggio Emilia, Italy.

PACIOLI, LUCA

The noted mathematician Fra Luca Pacioli (c.1445–1509?) was born in Borgo Sansepolcro, Italy, where the theoretical writings of Piero della Francesca deeply impressed him. Pacioli's own training in mathematics, however, was in Venice with Domenico Bragadino. Pacioli was not the villainous plagiarizer of Piero that GIORGIO VASARI styles him to be; rather, the classes he taught in Naples, Zara, Rome, Perugia, Urbino, Milan, and Venice, along with the publication of his *Summa de arithmetica, geometria, proportioni et proportionalità* (Venice, 1494; second edition 1523) and his treatise on *Divina proportione* (written 1496; published Venice, 1503) confirmed the mathematical foundation of art and architecture that had been espoused by Piero and LEON BATTISTA ALBERTI in the fifteenth century.

GARY M. RADKE

PACIOTTI, FRANCESCO

Francesco Paciotti (1521–1591), architect and engineer, was born and died in Urbino, Italy. He studied with GIROLAMO GENGA, and worked for the Farnese in Rome and Parma. In Rome, he measured the Baths of Caracalla. In Parma, he designed the fortresses of Montecchio, Correggio, Guastalla, and Scandio, and began the Cittadella of Piacenza (1558). He designed roads and fortifications as well as buildings. He worked in Flanders for Philip II, in Nice on fortifications for the port (1560–1561) for the duke of Savoy, in Spain on fortifications and the Escorial (1561–1562), in Turin on the Cittadella (with Francesco Orologi of Vicenza) for the duke of Savoy (1564–1568), and in Antwerp on the Cittadella (1569).

HENRY A. MILLON

WORKS

1558, Cittadella (continued by GIACOMO BAROZZI DA VIGNOLA), Parma, Italy. 1564–1568, Cittadella (with Francesco Orologi), Turin, Italy. 1569, Cittadella, Antwerp, Belgium.

BIBLIOGRAPHY

KUBLER, G. 1964 "F. Paciotto, Architect." *Essays in Memory of Karl Lehmann*. New York: Institute of Fine Arts.

PROMIS, C. 1863 "Francesco Paciotto." *Miscellanea di Storia Italiana* 4.

PAGANO, GIUSEPPE

Giuseppe Pagano Pogatschnig (1896–1945) was one of the major protagonists in the battles and polemics for the renovation of Italian architecture during the 1930s, not only because of his architectural work but also because of his work as journalist and director of *Casabella,* the magazine that hosted the most vivacious Italian intellectual work of the time.

Pagano was born in Parenzo, Istria, in a humanistic cultural climate that was mixed with vivid Irredentism. When World War I broke out, Pagano volunteered in the Italian army. After the war, he joined the early Fascist movement and was involved in the occupation of Fiume led by Gabriele D'Annunzio. In 1924, he received his degree in architecture at the Turin Royal Polytechnic Institute. His early works in Turin, including the Vittorio Emanuele III and Principe di Piemonte bridges (1925–1928) and some pavilions at the Turin International Exposition (1928), echoed themes of the Viennese Secession, AUGUSTE PERRET, and the early PETER BEHRENS, as well as certain themes that foreshadowed his more mature work. With the Turin exposition, Pagano initiated his activities in journalism as well as his collaboration with GINO LEVI-MONTALCINI, with whom Pagano produced one of the first Rationalist buildings in Italy, the Gualino Office Building (1928–1929). The project for the urban redesign of via Roma in Turin (1931), prepared with the Turin branch of the MIAR (Movimento Italiano Architettura Razionalista). The design aroused considerable debate, but when exhibited in Rome in 1931, it obtained Mussolini's approval, and in effect, it represented the high point of the regime's support for the new architecture. In 1931, Pagano transferred to Milan to direct *Casabella* with EDOARDO PERSICO. Pagano conducted his polemics against the monumentalism and academic rhetoric of the regime in the pages of *Casabella,* and he declared that a new urban policy that would impede speculation was necessary. He also addressed the problem of a "house for everyone," suggesting a design and political solution based upon industrialization of the building industry.

He did not neglect his professional activity during the 1930s, conceiving of it as a militant critique, presenting projects that were themselves prototypes for a new architecture. They included the Steel Structure House for the Fifth Triennale (1933), a complete, standardized system for collective housing; and the plan for Milano Verde (1938), which became a reference point for Italian Rationalism. In Milan, Pagano was intensely involved in numerous activities, often in collaboration with younger architects. At the Milan Triennale in 1936, he designed the Exhibit of Rural Architecture, with extensive photographic documentation which he himself prepared. The exhibit sought to characterize a close relationship between rural building and modern taste by means of their shared logic and functionalism. During this period, he also completed his best-known work, the Istituto di Fisica at the University of Rome (1932–1935). Nonetheless, his best architectural work was the Università Commerciale Bocconi (1938–1941); in the application of proportional schemes in plan and elevation, it testifies to a study of the discipline of architecture founded less upon empirical than upon scientific rules. In 1941, he enrolled in the army and fought in Albania, and after his discharge, he set to work again. By now, however, aware of the failure of his battle and of the involution which Italian architecture had undergone with the support of the regime, he decided to resign from the Fascist party. In December 1942, he was recalled to the army, but at the same time he established his first contacts with clandestine anti-Fascist organizations. He was arrested in November 1943 as a result of his active participation in the resistance, and after being deported to Germany, he died in Mauthausen, Austria.

Pagano's work as architect and critic reflects a conception of architecture as a social service and the basis of a struggle for the political, moral, and aesthetic renewal of the country. In addition to having spread the message of the European avant-garde in Italy, Pagano anticipated urban problems and solutions that are still with us today.

CESARE DE' SETA
Translated from Italian by
Diane Ghirardo

WORKS

*1925–1928, Vittorio Emanuele III and Principe di Piemonte Bridges, Italy. *1928, Fashion Pavilion (with Gino Levi-Montalcini); Chemistry Pavilion; Hunting and Fishing Pavilion; Mining and Ceramics Pavilion (with Paolo Perona); Army, Navy, and Air Force Pavilion (with Levi-Montalcini and Ettore Pittini); Turin International Exposition, Italy. *1928, Gualino Office Building (with Levi-Montalcini); *1931, Design for the urban redesign of via Roma (with Levi-Montalcini, Umberto Cuzzi, Ottorino Aloisio, Ettore Sottsass); Turin, Italy. *1932–1935, Istituto di Fisica, University of Rome. *1933, Steel Structure House (with others), V Triennal; *1936, Exhibition of Rural Architecture, VI Triennal; Milan. 1937, Master Plan for the Rome Universal Exposition of 1942 (with others). *1937–1941, Università Commerciale Bocconi (with others). *1938, Milano Verde (proposal for the Master Plan of the Sempione-fiera zone; with others), Milan.

BIBLIOGRAPHY

DE'SETA, CESARE (editor) 1976 *Architettura e città durante il fascismo: Giuseppe Pagano.* Bari, Italy: Laterza.

DE'SETA, CESARE 1979 *Giuseppe Pagano Fotografo.* Milan: Electa.

MELOGRANI, CARLO 1955 *Giuseppe Pagano.* Milan: Il Balcone.

VERONESI, GIULIA 1953 *Difficoltà politiche dell' architettura in Italia: 1920–1940,* Milan: Libreria Editrice Politecnica Tamburini.

PAIN, WILLIAM

Little is known of the English builder-architect William Pain (c.1730–c.1804) beyond the contents of the eight architectural handbooks that he published between 1758 and 1804. The early books are baroque, but with the publication of *The Carpenter's and Joiner's Repository* in 1778, Pain adopted the "Adam style" (see ROBERT ADAM) and became its principal popularizer in both England and America.

JACK QUINAN

BIBLIOGRAPHY

ESDAILE, KATHERINE A. 1917–1919 "The Small House and its Amenities in the Architectural Hand-Books of 1749–1827." *Transactions of the Bibliographical Society* 15:115–132.

PAIN, WILLIAM (1758)1769 *The Builder's Companion and Workman's General Assistant.* London: Sayer.

PAIN, WILLIAM (1763)1785 *The Builder's Pocket Treasure or, Palladio Delineated and Explained.* Rev. ed. London: Owen.

PAIN, WILLIAM (1774)1804 *The Practical Builder.* 7th rev. ed. London: Taylor.

PAIN, WILLIAM (1778)1792 *The Carpenter's and Joiner's Repository.* New ed. London: Taylor.

PAIN, WILLIAM (1781*a*)1803 *The Builder's Golden Rule.* 3d ed. London.

PAIN, WILLIAM (1781*b*)1803 *The Carpenter's Pocket Directory.* London: Taylor.

PAIN, WILLIAM (1786)1793 *Pain's British Palladio.* London: Taylor.

PAIN, WILLIAM (1788)1815 *The Practical House Carpenter.* 8th ed. London: Taylor.

PAIN, WILLIAM 1793 *The Builder's Sketch Book.* London: The author.

RICHARDSON, A. E. 1946 *Decorative Details of the Eighteenth Century by William and James Pain.* London: Tiranti.

PAINE, JAMES

James Paine (1717–1789) was born at Andover in Hampshire, England, the son of a carpenter. He studied in London at the Saint Martin's Lane Academy and appears to have begun his career through contact with the circle of LORD BURLINGTON. His first commission was to supervise the erection of Nostell Priory, Yorkshire (1737–1750), a large country house designed by James Moyser, a friend and follower of Lord Burlington. From this beginning he established an extensive country house practice in the north of England which he augmented during the 1750s by taking over the North Country practice of DANIEL GARRETT. As early as 1746, however, he returned to live in London. His work was not confined to the North. The large extent of his work prompted THOMAS HARDWICK's comment that Paine and Sir ROBERT TAYLOR "nearly divided the practice of the profession between them, for they had few competitors until Mr. ROBERT ADAM entered the lists" (Chambers, 1825, xlviii–xlix).

In 1755–1756, Paine visited Italy but the journey did not play an important part in his artistic development. He was later to criticize the fashion for foreign travel among architects and he had little sympathy for the emergent interest in the architecture of antiquity, emphasizing the importance of practical convenience rather than the pursuit of "inconsistent antiquated modes." His own considerable originality as an architect was achieved entirely within the framework of English Palladianism (see ANDREA PALLADIO). He was a pioneer of the Palladian villa as a country house form and he developed a lively and highly individual elevational style based on the "staccato" manner of Lord Burlington and WILLIAM KENT. These qualities are illustrated in such houses as Serlby Hall, Nottinghamshire (1754–1773), Belford Hall, Northumberland (1755–1756), and Stockeld Park, Yorkshire (1758–1763), while at Wardour Castle, Wiltshire (1770–1776), he used the villa form for a house of the largest size. In his early years he also adopted the rococo style of interior decoration which had been pioneered in circles close to the Saint Martin's Lane Academy.

Throughout his career, Paine held various posts in the Office of Works but it was only in 1780 that he achieved a relatively senior position, as one of the Architects of the Works, and that was abolished two years later. He was, however, a prominent member of the Society of Artists of Great Britain, the predecessor of the Royal Academy, serving as president in 1770–1772 and designing its Exhibition Room in London (1771–1772). In 1767, he published a selection of his designs, following it with a second volume in 1783. He died in France, having retired there some months previously. John Woolfe served as his assistant in the 1750s and JOHN EVELEIGH was one of his pupils.

PETER LEACH

WORKS

1737–1750, Nostell Priory (supervision of construction and interior decoration), Yorkshire, England. 1744–1745, Heath House, Wakefield, England. 1745–1748, The Mansion House; 1749–1750, Wadworth Hall; Doncaster, England. 1750–1756, South Ormsby Hall, Lincolnshire, England. *1754, 76 Saint Martin's Lane, London. *1754–1757, Hardwick Hall (garden buildings), County Durham, England. 1754–1758, Matthew Fetherstonhaugh House (now Dover House), Whitehall, London. *1754–1768, Alnwick Castle (reconstruction), Northumberland, England. 1754–1773, Serlby Hall, Nottinghamshire, England. 1755–1756, Belford Hall, Northumberland, England. 1755–1764, Gosforth Hall, Newcastle, England. *1755–1778, Middlesex Hospital, London. 1756–1764, Chatsworth (stables, bridge, etc.), Derbyshire, England. 1758, Axwell Park, County Durham, England. *1758–1760, Cavendish Bridge, Derbyshire, England. 1758–1763, Stockeld Park; *1759, Saint Ives; Yorkshire, England. 1760, Bywell Hall, Northumberland, England. 1760–1766, Gibside Chapel, County Durham, England. 1760–1775, Brocket Hall, Hertfordshire, England. *1763–1767, Worksop Manor, Nottinghamshire, England. 1763–1768, Sandbeck Park, Yorkshire, England. 1764–1770, Thorndon Hall, Essex, England. 1765–1770, Weston Park (temple and bridge), Staffordshire, England. *1765–1773, Salisbury Street; *1766–1770, Lord Petre's House, Park Lane; London. 1768–1770, Hare Hall, Essex, England. *1769–1771, 79 Pall Mall, London. 1769–1772, Shrubland Hall, Suffolk, England. 1770–1776, Wardour Castle, Wiltshire, England. *1771–1772, Society of Artists of Great Britain Exhibition Room, Strand; 1773–1774, 37 King Street, Covent Garden; London. 1774–1777, Richmond Bridge; 1779–1785, Chertsey Bridge; *1783, Walton Bridge; *1783–1789, Kew Bridge; Surrey, England.

BIBLIOGRAPHY

BINNEY, MARCUS 1969 "The Villas of James Paine." *Country Life* 145:406–410, 466–470, 522–526.

CHAMBERS, WILLIAM 1825 *A Treatise on the Decorative Part of Civil Architecture.* Edited by Joseph Gwilt. London.

LEACH, PETER 1975 "The Life and Work of James Paine." Unpublished Ph.D. dissertation, Oxford University.

PAINE, JAMES (1767)1783 *Plans, Elevations and Sections of Noblemen and Gentlemen's Houses.* London.

PAIONIOS OF EPHESOS

Together with Demetrios, the slave of Artemis, Paionios of Ephesos (?–310 B.C.) was the architect of the (fifth) colossal Ionic temple of Artemis at Ephesos. The fourth temple (by CHERSIPHRON) was burned down in 356 B.C.; the rebuilding was begun immediately afterward, on the original plan, with yet greater splendor, so that it was rated one of the seven wonders of the ancient world. It was so huge that it was not completed until 236 B.C. Paionios was associated also with the colossal Ionic temple of Apollo at Didyma (begun c.313 B.C.).

B. M. BOYLE

WORKS

*Begun c.355 B.C., Fifth Temple of Artemis (with Demetrios), Ephesos, Greece. *Begun c.313 B.C., Temple of Apollo (with Daphnis of Miletos), Didyma, Greece.

BIBLIOGRAPHY

English translations of the ancient texts can be found in the volumes of the Loeb Classical Library series, published by Harvard University Press and Heinemann.

DINSMOOR, WILLIAM B. (1902)1975 *The Architecture of Ancient Greece.* Reprint of 1950 ed. New York: Norton. Originally published with the title *The Architecture of Ancient Greece and Rome.*

LAWRENCE, ARNOLD W. (1957)1975 *Greek Architecture.* Harmondsworth, England: Penguin.

PLINY, *Historia naturalis,* Book 36.95.

VITRUVIUS, *De architectura,* Book 7.Praef.16.

PALACIO Y ELISSAGUE, ALBERTO DEL

Martín Alberto del Palacio y Elissague (1856–1939), architect and engineer, was born in Bilbao, Spain, and graduated as an architect in Barcelona in 1882. A designer of bridges and large industrial buildings, he is the author of the transfer bridge of Vizcaya, between Portugalete and Las Arenas (1890–1893) and of the train station of Atocha, Madrid (1888–1892). Among his unexecuted projects are a revolving bridge, submarine bridge, and an aerial streetcar.

HELENA IGLESIAS
Translated from Spanish by
Judith E. Meighan

WORKS

1888–1892, Train Station, Atocha, Madrid. 1890–1893, Transfer Bridge, Vizcaya, between Portugalete and Las Arenas, Spain. n.d., Hotel, Calle Miguel Angel, Madrid.

BIBLIOGRAPHY

FULLAONDO, DANIEL 1969 Volume 1 in *La Arquitectura y los Arquitectos de la región y el entorno de Bilbao.* Madrid and Barcelona, Spain: Alfaguara.

NAVASCUES, PEDRO 1973 *Arquitectura y Arquitectos madrileños del siglo XIX.* Madrid: Instituto de Estudios Madrileños.

PUEYO, LUIS 1966 "Alberto de Palacio y una Época." *Arquitectura* 8, no. 87:7–20.

PALACIOS Y RAMILO, ANTONIO

Antonio Palacios y Ramilo (1876–1945) was born in Porriño, a Galician village in the province of Pontevedra, Spain. He studied architecture in Madrid and graduated in 1900. He worked principally in Madrid and in Galicia.

Palacios quickly became famous, along with Joaquín Otamendi, for the winning entry in the competition for the Postal and Telegraph Building in Madrid (1904). The building, completed in 1918, was a novelty in Spain for its monumental form and symbolic richness, based on a free elaboration of Gothic and Plateresque themes. The Four Roads Workers' Hospital in Madrid (1909–1916), one of his most original works, continued the same nationalist trend, but the ornamentation was simplified and the stone construction was given a Brutalist expression. In a series of works built in his home region of Galicia, culminating in the churches of Panjón (1932–1937) and Carballino (1943–1945), Palacios experimented with the application of rustic construction with material of barely dressed stone, arriving at a violent material expression.

ADOLFO G. AMEZQUETA
Translated from Spanish by
Judith E. Meighan

WORK

1909–1916, Four Roads Workers' Hospital.

BIBLIOGRAPHY

AMEZQUETA, ADOLFO G. 1967 "La Arquitectura de Antonio Palacios." *Arquitectura* 106.

PALACIOS Y RAMILO, ANTONIO 1945 *Ante una Moderna Arquitectura.* Madrid: Magisterio Español.

PALADINI, VINICIO

Vinicio Paladini (1902–1971) was a painter, architect, and cinematic set designer, who worked primarily in Rome and New York City. During the 1920s, he was associated with the Futurist movement. He signed the 1922 Futurist manifesto *Arte Meccanica* with Ivo Panaggi and ENRICO PRAMPOLINI. A member of the Movimento Italiano per l'Architettura Razionale, he was graduated from the Scuola Superiore di Architettura in Rome in 1931. From 1935 to 1937 and from 1939 to 1953, he lived in New York City, where he designed mostly interiors for retail spaces.

DENNIS DOORDAN

WORKS

*1937, Pavilion, Textile Exhibition, Rome. *1945, Spinnerin Yarn Company Show Room, New York. 1955, Via Cassia Motel, Rome.

BIBLIOGRAPHY

CENNAMO, MICHELE (compiler) 1973 *Materiali per l'analisi dell'architettura moderna: La Prima Esposizione di Architettura Razionale.* Naples: Fausto Fiorentino.

PALAGI, PELAGIO

Pelagio Palagi (1775–1860), Italian architect, painter, and author, born in Bologna, was one of the most accomplished designers of the neoclassic–neo-Gothic for architecture, interiors, furniture, and decorative arts. His abilities as an artist were recognized while he was still a child by Count Aldrovanti, who received him in his household and who, in 1806, sent Palagi to Rome for further study. Palagi remained in Rome until 1815 when he went to Milan to begin teaching and painting. Called to Turin by King Carlo Alberto in 1832 to be architect, decorator, and inspector of schools of art, he was put to work renovating the Royal Palace in Turin.

His work in Piedmont demonstrates the fertility and versatility of his mind. At the Palazzo Reale, Palagi designed the splendid Ball Room, a white and gold masterpiece of unified architecture and decoration (1835–1842); decorated the Coun-

Palagi. Palazzo Reale (ballroom). Turin, Italy. 1835–1842

cil Chamber (1836) and the Throne Room (1837–1838), designing the bulky neo-Egyptian furniture as well; and built the cast-iron fence for the Piazzetta Reale (1845). For Carlo Alberto at the Castello at Racconigi, Palagi redesigned (from 1832) several rooms including, at the main level, the reception hall, the Etruscan room, and the bathroom at the ground level, one of the finest in the early nineteenth century. In the gardens, with Ernesto Melano, Palagi designed the hunting palace and the margherie with its chapel in crisp, assertive neo-Gothic. Neo-Gothic was used as well for other rural sites (also with Melano) at Desio, Villa Traversi (1838–1844) and at the Castello of Pollenza (date uncertain). A design for a neo-Gothic church commissioned by Carlo Alberto for Turin came to naught. One of Turin's finest nineteenth-century monuments, the Conte Verde in Piazza Palazzo di Città, was done by Palagi in 1853. With Palagi's work, Turin and Piedmont regained their place among the forerunners of European architecture that it had held during the years when FILIPPO JUVARRA was first architect to the king of Savoy.

HENRY A. MILLON

WORKS

1832 and later, Racconigi Castle (reception hall, Etruscan Room, and Carlo Alberto's bathroom); 1835, Margherie; Racconigi, Italy. 1835–1842, Palazzo Reale (ballroom, Council Hall decoration, and throne room); 1845, Piazzetta Reale (cast iron fence); Turin, Italy. 1838–1844, Villa Traversi (neo-Gothic tower), Desio, Italy. n.d., Castle (neo-Gothic additions), Pollenza, Italy.

BIBLIOGRAPHY

The Age of Neoclassicism. 1972 London: Arts Council of Great Britain. Exhibition catalogue.

BOIDI, ADRIANA 1965 "Pelagio Palagi e il neo-gotico in Piemonte." *Bolletino Società Piemontese di Archeologia e di Belle Arti* 19:49–67.

DALMASSO, F. 1969 "Architettura neogotica del primo periodo albertino." *Piemonte vivo* 6:3–12.

GREGORI, LUISA BANDERA 1973 "Filippo Pelagio Palagi: An Artist between Neo-classicism and Romanticism." *Apollo* 97, no. 5:500–509.

GABRIELLI, NAOMI 1972 *Racconigi.* Turin, Italy: Istituto bancario San Paolo.

GRISERI, ANDREINA 1971 "L'architettura del neoclassico a Torino." *Bolletino del Centro Internazionale di Studi di architettura Andrea Palladio* 13:195–207.

GRISERI, ANDREINA, and GABETTI, ROBERTO 1973 *Architettura del eclettissimo.* Turin, Italy: Einaudi.

MALLÈ, LUIGI (1962)1972 *Figurative Art in Piedmont.* Turin, Italy: RIV-SKF.

MATTEUCI, A. M. 1974 "L'attivita giovanile di Pelagio Palagi nei disegni dell'Archiginnasio di Bologna." *Annali della scuola normale superiore di Pisa* Series 3 4, no. 2:461–478.

MEZZANOTTE, GIANNI 1966 Pages 384–391 in *Architettura neoclassica in Lombardia.* Naples: Scientifiche Italiane.

Pelagio Palagi artista e collezionista. 1976 Bologna, Italy: Grafis.

PESCARMONA, D. 1974–1975 "Pelagio Palagi. Contributi alla reconstruzione del corpus delle opere." Unpublished Ph.D. dissertation, University of Turin, Italy.

PALANTI, GIANCARLO

Born in Milan, Giancarlo Palanti (1906–) was a representative architect of northern Italian Rationalism in the group close to GIUSEPPE PAGANO. He was involved in several projects of prewar experimentation and postwar reconstruction, collaborating with others on residential and urban problems. He was part of the Italian delegation to the Congrès Internationaux d'Architecture Moderne (CIAM) in 1947. He served on the editorial staff of the journals *Domus* and *Casabella* and taught architecture at the Polytechnic Institute of Milan from 1935 to 1946. After World War II, he emigrated to Brazil where he designed low-cost apartment buildings.

ANTONINO TERRANOVA

WORKS

1937, Tavani Villa, Leghorn, Italy. 1938–1939, Costanzo Ciano Housing Estate (with others); 1938–1939, Ettore Ponti Housing Estate (with others); 1938–1939, Gabrielle D'Annunzio Housing Estate (with others); Milan. 1945–1947, Quartiere degli Angeli Urban Redevelopment Plan, Genoa, Italy. n.d., Apartment Buildings, São Paulo, Brazil.

BIBLIOGRAPHY

ACCASTO, GIANNI; FRATICELLI, VANNA; and NICOLINI, RENATO 1971 *L'architettura di Roma capitale; 1870–1970.* Rome: Golem.

DE' SETA, CESARE 1972 *La cultura architettonica in Italia tra le due guerre.* Bari, Italy: Laterza.

Gregotti, Vittorio 1968 *New Directions in Italian Architecture.* New York: Braziller.

Istituto Nazionale di Urbanistica, Rome (1952)1954 *Urbanisti italiana.* 2d ed. Rome: The institute.

Pagano, Giuseppe 1976 *Architettura e città durante il fascismo.* Rome and Bari, Italy: Laterza.

PALEARO FAMILY

Giacomo and Giorgio Palearo (Pallearío, Paliari, Fratino, Jacome and Jorge Fratin) were military engineers active in the second half of the sixteenth century in Italy and Spain. They were brothers who came from Morcote, near Lugano, Italy, and seem, for the most part, to have worked together. They began their careers as wandering professional soldiers and eventually entered the service of the Spanish kings Philip II and Philip III, whom they are said to have served for sixty years. During their tenure with these kings, they began to design fortifications. The combined career of professional soldier and military architect became common in the second half of the sixteenth century. At this time, the practical experience of the military specialist began to be valued more highly in the design of such structures than the general artistic and theoretical training of the artist-architect of the first half of the century.

The brothers are known more from the few surviving documents and sources referring to them than from their actual fortifications, for most of these have been destroyed or were changed in the attempt to keep up with the developments in military technology. Giorgio may have been the most well-known, for he even received a letter from the Spanish king.

In 1565, Giacomo requested payment for inspecting the fortifications for the duchy of Milan, and a year later, Giorgio received funds for his work on the castle in Milan. In Spain, the brothers worked on the fortifications of Gibraltar and on a church in Melilla. Giorgio designed the military defenses for Palma on Majorca and was there until at least 1582. In the same decade, Giacomo fortified Pamplona. In 1586, Giorgio was chosen by the Spanish court to visit and inspect all the cities and fortresses controlled by the Spanish in Italy. The record of his inspection was published in *Bollettino storico della Svizzera italiana* ("Nuovi. . .," 1898, 116–124). Finally, in 1588, Giorgio designed the fortress of Casale for the duke of Mantua.

Priscilla Albright

BIBLIOGRAPHY

"Architetti Luganesi dei secoli XV–XVI." 1893 *Bollettino storico della Svizzera italiana* 15:181–185.

"Arte ed Artisti." 1888 *Bollettino storico della Svizzera italiana* 10:257–262.

"Arte ed Artisti Luganesi." 1899 *Bollettino storico della Svizzera italiana* 21:119–123.

"Arte ed Artista nei secoli XIII–XIX." 1906 *Bollettino storico della Svizzera italiana* 28:14–18.

"Artisti Svizzeri in Roma nei secoli XV, XVI, XVII." 1885 *Bollettino storico della Svizzera italiana* 7:105–112.

Bianchi, Giuseppe 1900 *Gli artisti ticinesi.* Lugano, Italy: Libreria Bianchi.

"Di alcuni architetti militari Luganesi dei secoli XV e XVI." 1881 *Bollettino storico della Svizzera italiana* 3:293–295.

"I Sudditi Dei Baliaggi Italiani el servizio militare estero." 1879 *Bollettino storico della Svizzera italiana* 1:276–285.

Llaguno y Amirola, Eugenio 1829 *Noticias de los Arquitectos y Arquitectura de España.* 4 vols. Madrid: Imprenta Real.

"Nuovi documenti intorno agli architetti militari del casato Palcari di Morcate." 1898 *Bollettino storico della Svizzera italiana* 20:116–124, 190–193.

"Il palazzo municipale di Bellinzona in documenti del trecento." 1915 *Bollettino storico della Svizzera italiana* 35:1–4.

Weber, Siegfried (1905–1917)1967 "Gebrüder Giacomo und Giorgio Paleari." In Carl Brun (editor), *Schweizerisches Künstler-lexikon.* Reprint. Nendeln, Germany: Kraus.

PALLADIO, ANDREA

Probably the most influential figure in the history of Western architecture, the genius who was later to be named Palladio (1508–1580) was born in the ancient university town of Padua, in the mainland territories of the Republic of Venice. His parents, a miller named Pietro (sometimes nicknamed "della Gondola") and his lame wife Marta, christened the boy Andrea. Already by the turn of the seventeenth century, it was construed that the choice of his name might indicate his having been born on the feast-day of Saint Andrew (November 30), but the supposition has no backing save that of an early tradition. Palladio died on August 19, 1580, almost certainly while working on a memorial chapel at Maser in the province of Treviso, at the villa of his long-standing friend Marc'Antonio Barbaro. He was buried in his adopted city of Vicenza, in the Church of Santa Corona; nearly three centuries later (August 19, 1845), his supposed remains were moved to a new chapel in the Vicenza cemetery. Only one authentic portrait of Palladio survives, a modest painting of 1576 by his friend Giovanni Battista Maganza, now in the Vicenza collection of Counts Angelo and Paolo di Valmarana (Lewis, 1981, frontispiece). On or shortly after April 14, 1534, Andrea married Allegradonna, the daughter of a carpenter, and the couple had five children: a daughter, Zenobia, and four sons—the architect Leonida, Marc'Antonio (a sculptor, who also assisted Palladio as a draftsman), Orazio (Doctor of Civil Law); and Silla (an assisting architect, who completed his father's building for the Teatro Olimpico in 1580–1583).

Andrea grew up in close touch with the artistic communities of both Padua and Vicenza. The Vicentine sculptor Vincenzo de' Grandi was godfather at his christening, and on October 31, 1521, the thirteen-year-old Andrea was apprenticed (probably at Grandi's suggestion, and after a certain amount of informal training by him) to the Paduan stonemason Bartolomeo Cavazza, from Sossano in the Vicentino. His articles specified an apprenticeship of six years, but after only eighteen months Andrea attempted to move with his father to Vicenza, the native town of both his teachers, where Vincenzo's brother Gian Maria de' Grandi was then working. From that city Andrea was legally constrained on April 28, 1523, to return to Cavazza's shop in Padua—for a reduced tenure, however, of only three more years. Even this compromise failed, and by April 1524, just one year later and with Andrea probably not yet sixteen, he was formally inscribed as an assistant in the Vicenza guild of masons and stonecutters. His sponsors for this enrollment (which was to prove permanent) were the partners of Vicenza's most prominent firm of architectural stonemasons, Giovanni da Porlezza (or di Pedemuro, from his address in Via Pedemuro) and Girolamo Pittoni, whose shop was to be Andrea's home for at least the next decade and his locus of activity for a full quarter-century. Indeed, he was so thoroughly adopted by his Pedemuro shop masters that from this time he effectively became a native of Vicenza. Within the next few years, his own father died, and Andrea thereafter enjoyed an almost filial relationship with Giovanni da Porlezza, to the extent of being designated his executor, with Girolamo Pittoni, at Giovanni's death in 1550. But Andrea's second or "repatriation" contract with Bartolomeo Cavazza in 1523 had promised a continuation of the similarly close relationship ("as if he were his own son") that obtained between the apprentice and his former master as well. We now know that Palladio, far from harboring any ill feeling after the second departure from his Paduan teacher, continued in such close contact as to employ Cavazza's partner Agostino Zoppo, for example, in carving the stonework at his earliest mature villa, for Zorzon Cornaro at Piombino (1551–1553). These mutually supportive attitudes suggest that Andrea must already have been recognized by his mid-teens to be such a highly talented mason and stonecarver as to encourage the best masters in both Padua and Vicenza repeatedly to seek his enrollment and retention in their shops. His own consistent preference for Vicenza was a recognition of its more expansive economy and social structure, and he was rewarded there by more than half a century of successful architectural practice.

The Vicenza to which Andrea moved in 1523 and 1524 was just recovering from the disorders and privations of the lengthy Wars of the League of Cambrai which had involved the whole Venetian state from 1508 into the mid-1520s and had suspended, for example, the urgently necessary rebuilding of its derelict town hall. With the return of peace, the city council recommenced a process of inviting distinguished architects from Venice and other major centers to advise on its reconstruction; and the first of those to arrive, simultaneously with the beginning of Andrea's apprenticeship, was ANTONIO DI PIETRO ABBONDI, the distinguished protomagister of Saint Mark's in Venice. This competent and widely respected artist had already visited Vicenza in 1521, when he had collaborated with Andrea's new masters of the Pedemuro shop in embellishing the civic loggia of the Venetian governor. The advantage of such metropolitan connections, in fact, may have been a determining factor in Andrea's preference for work with this particular firm in Vicenza. When Abbondi returned for consultations on the town hall and governor's palace in May 1525 and May 1532, therefore, we may be confident that the youthful Andrea would have been particularly receptive to both pragmatic and aesthetic influences from this most accomplished representative of the purely local classicism that characterized Venice's native Renaissance style.

The productions of Andrea's first decade with the Pedemuro shop, from the mid-1520s to the mid-1530s, thus display the same decorative applications of small-scale classical elements, usually restricted to the carved stone moldings of portals, altars, and tombs, as we find more comprehensively integrated into an architectural whole, for example, in Abbondi's great Scuola di San Rocco of 1527–1549 in Venice. Even so, such beautiful collaborative achievements as the high altar (1534–1536) and Schio tomb (1537–1538) in Vicenza Cathedral display sufficient architectural sophistication and sculptural refinement to demonstrate the high level of quality at which Andrea was being trained during the years of his artistic development. Still registered as an apprentice upon his matriculation into the Vicenza guild in 1524, he is described as a journeyman stoneworker in

1528 and as an associated master by 1530 and 1532. We are therefore justified, in view of his evolution as a junior partner in the Pedemuro shop, in attributing to him the one significant full building on which we find him associated during this initial decade. This is a large colonnaded barn and service building inscribed MCCCCCXXXIII (1533) at the Villa of Enrico Antonio Godi in Lonedo, which Palladio later incorporated into a unified design for the whole site when Godi's sons Girolamo and Pietro commissioned a new residence there. The Godi family had already been responsible for the three earliest Pedemuro projects on which Andrea seems to have been involved as a collaborative designer, at Santa Maria dei Servi (1531) and the Monastery of San Michele (1532–1533). The comprehensive plan of the Villa Godi at Lonedo (c.1537–1542) was to be Andrea's first autonomous work, and the encouragement of these earliest patrons was crucial for his emergence into independent practice. Indeed, it was during his work on their villa that Pietro Godi first made a payment to him on August 26, 1540, with the designation of his full professional title, "Master Andrea, Architect." A far more profound change than this gradual achievement of seniority within the Pedemuro shop, however, occurred in the architect's life during the same years in which the Villa Godi was rising; and its effect was to inspire his achievement of a new style, radically different from the provincial, artisan-based simplicity of the house at Lonedo.

By April 1537, the most ambitious attempt to create an example of High Renaissance architecture in Vicenza had been begun, and by mid-July, it had progressed to the point of roofing, having involved "many thousands of ducats" to support "more than three months' activity" by "a large number of workmen": the latter, though not documented, are assumed to have been provided by the Pedemuro shop and to have included Master Andrea. The project was the remodeling of an old-fashioned manor house with four corner towers at Cricoli, just north of the city gates; and the patron was Vicenza's most celebrated humanist, Count Gian Giorgio Trissino, an amateur architect who had carefully studied the classical text of VITRUVIUS and had developed the plans for Cricoli himself. In the design of its central frontispiece, however, a two-story loggia connecting the towers on the city façade, he was assisted by the great Bolognese architect and theorist SEBASTIANO SERLIO whom Trissino had known in Rome during the years preceding the Sack of 1527, and probably also in Bologna during its immediate aftermath, before they both took up residence in the Veneto. While in Rome, Trissino had especially admired his friend Pope Clement VII's superb villa by RAPHAEL on Monte Mario (c. 1516–1523), which had passed in 1536 to the imperial princess from whom it takes its name, Madama Margherita of Parma. Gian Giorgio's obsessive identification with her father Charles V (at whose coronation, indeed, Trissino managed to carry the emperor's train) almost certainly provided the motivation, just as Margherita's occupancy of the Villa Madama similarly provides the date (1536–1537), for Serlio's redrafting of Raphael's garden façade for its re-use on the villa at Cricoli. This fascination with Rome and the re-creation of empire is paralleled both in Trissino's writing and in the great achievement of his career. His vast epic poem *L'Italia liberata dei Goti* (begun in 1526/1527) is dedicated to Charles V, and its celestial protagonist is a guardian angel named Palladio. In the symbolic rebuilding of his manor at Cricoli a decade later, Trissino's long life acquired its most significant focus when he came into close association with Master Andrea of the Pedemuro shop—whom he may have known, however, since 1531—and presciently recognized in the accomplished young stonemason a willing instrument for the renewal of Roman grandeur, the potential creator of a new imperial architecture. Andrea's emblematic ordination to this high calling was consummated by his rebaptism (under the sponsorship, we may assume, of Serlio, and at the font maintained for these humanist conversions in the Trissinian academy at Cricoli) with the name of the angelic intermediary invented by his "spiritual father," Gian Giorgio himself.

The whole of this extraordinary episode seems imminently vulnerable, as if destined for an immediate collapse into absurdity; yet, the truly astonishing thing is that Trissino, in making this leap of faith, was right. By February and March 1540, even the public notaries in Vicenza were becoming accustomed to using the form of "Master Andrea Palladio," which the fame of four and a half centuries has indeed made synonymous with the revival of antique classicism, not only in the Venetian nor yet the Holy Roman Empire but in fact throughout the world. In order to avoid an oversimplified assumption that the "real" Palladio was intentionally engendered (as the culminating event of Trissino's life) by an inspired fusion of Master Andrea's precocious talent with the ancient loyalty and global ideal of the divine emissary from *L'Italia liberata,* we should balance our assessment by considering the situation from the architect's point of view. In the campaign of 1537 at Cricoli, Andrea would have been twenty-nine years old, with half of his life already devoted to professional sculpture and architecture in Vicenza. He was doubtless in charge of the project for the Villa

Trissino, as the member of the Pedemuro shop most specialized in full-scale building (thanks to his work for the Godi family, which was clearly bringing him to considerable prominence). He had acquired other powerful patrons, such as Cavaliere Aurelio Dall'Acqua, through his commission for the Cathedral altar, and evidently had even discharged his first public work in a portal of 1536 leading from the Palazzo del Podestà into the Basilica. What could an elderly humanist, devoted to the academic education of young Vicentine nobles, offer him?

The answer is fourfold. In the first place, Andrea was naturally drawn to architectural history and theory and urgently needed skills in reading as well as the requisite languages for elucidating not only Vitruvius and other classics, but also LEON BATTISTA ALBERTI and other modern writers. Second, he was enough of a pragmatist to be drawn equally to the specific study of successful buildings, both ancient and modern. For this purpose, he badly needed a wider experience of existing monuments, preferably within a frame of reference that would embrace both antiquity and its Roman Renaissance, and he could also use instruction in unfamiliar measures, drafting techniques, and writing. Third, he needed a dramatic expansion of his private and especially his public practice in order to support his own ambition as well as a growing family; this required contacts at every level of society and in all fields of humane interest in good building. Fourth, he may even have had his own programmatic identification with a classical namesake, developed from his systematic integration of the rural complex at Lonedo: his friend Pietro Godi not only was one of his patrons there, but he was also a doctoral student at the University of Padua who might well have introduced him to the useful treatise on husbandry by an antique theorist also named Palladio—a personality perhaps more sympathetic to his own nature, either as an initial alternative to or in later substitution of Trissino's angel. Whatever the combination of these influences, whether predominantly idealistic and transcendental on Trissino's side or pragmatic and professional on Palladio's, the bond of symbolic rebaptism held firm. From the first explicit document of their presence together in Trissino's townhouse in Vicenza (February 19, 1538), through the twelve years until the humanist's death in 1550, he and Palladio were constant companions in Vicenza, in Padua, and in Venice, as well as in travels and foreign residences, including three long sojourns in Rome.

The importance of Trissino's adoption of Palladio is strikingly demonstrated by the results of their first four years of study, travel, and experiment. At the beginning of 1538, the unlettered Master Andrea—who evidently did not know how to draw—had one villa barn to his credit (albeit one with Doric columns and a Roman inscription, which might indicate a certain influence from Trissino earlier in his career), and one commission to complete that same complex at Lonedo with a new house. By the end of 1541, Palladio, as an accomplished master of architectural and figural draftsmanship, had an impressive corpus of drawings after buildings of antiquity and the High Renaissance; he had designed and begun two more villas and two townhouses for Vicentine patrons; and he had completed the planning of a great villa complex for Vettor Pisani, a prominent Venetian commission that was to secure his reputation among the architectural avant-garde of the capital. He had also become intimate with two of the most celebrated architects in northern Italy, Serlio and MICHELE SANMICHELI, who had helped him respectively to develop graphic and structural skills. This astonishing transformation can be ascribed in large measure to Trissino's influence, although Andrea's own native gifts of personal attractiveness, high intelligence, aesthetic inventiveness, and conceptual brilliance must be acknowledged to have been at their finest flower during this four-year *curriculum classicum*.

The Villa Trissino at Cricoli was completed by April 1538, and in the same month, the greatest architect then working in Venetian dominions, JACOPO SANSOVINO, had returned to Vicenza from his post as protomagister of Saint Mark's at Venice—after an initial visit in January—to consult on the perennial problem of rebuilding the town hall. Andrea must have profited from the opportunity of meeting him (Sansovino was a close friend of Serlio's, who can be counted upon to have effected the introduction), since some of Palladio's own designs for the Basilica demonstrate a close awareness of Sansovino's Venetian buildings. By mid-May Trissino was in Ferrara, perhaps accompanied by Andrea; by the first of June, Andrea had taken up residence for an approximately two-year sojourn (late spring 1538 to early spring 1540) in the university city of Padua, though not without interruptions: in August and September 1538, he visited Venice and Vicenza respectively, and he returned to the latter city for Serlio's great theatrical production of February 16, 1539, in the Gothic courtyard of Palazzo Porto, which was outfitted for the occasion with a spectacular wooden theater that made a profound impression upon Andrea. In the early spring of 1540 (25 February and 10 March), the architect is first called Palladio in two documents that he witnessed for the family of Nicolino Trissino in Vicenza (in which he was probably acting as proxy for Gian Giorgio, then in Venice), and on August 26, 1540, we have already noticed Pietro Godi's first assigning him the title of "architect" during his supervision of the works at Lonedo. That task seems to have been the reason for not accompanying Trissino—or at least not remaining throughout the latter's entire stay—in Venice during 1540; but this is the only evidence for any separation of the two during these four years. By the summer of 1541, they had made their first pilgrimage to Rome, and Palladio's surviving drawings indicate that they stopped en route at Ravenna, then took the road to Florence, Arezzo, and Perugia, and visited Assisi, the valley of the Clitumnus, and Spoleto. They spent enough time in the Eternal City to enable Andrea to draw several of its modern works as well its most famous antiquities, possibly to get as far afield as Porto on the lower Tiber, and probably to meet the antiquarian architect PIRRO LIGORIO in addition to survivors of DONATO BRAMANTE's shop, from whom he acquired and copied certain drawings. His extensive immersion in the Roman world of classical antiquity was paralleled throughout these four years by expeditions to measure and study the ancient remains in Venetian dominions, above all those in Pola (on the Istrian peninsula in the Gulf of Venice) and in Verona. Palladio's intimate acquaintance with the theater, amphitheater, and triumphal arches of that best-preserved classical city in northern Italy attests to the assiduity of his, Trissino's and Serlio's architectural study tours, but it also suggests (on the analogy of his close investigation of Roman Renaissance works) his thorough knowledge of the art of Michele Sanmicheli, the Roman-trained architect of Renaissance Verona. Sanmicheli soon paid two visits to Vicenza in his own capacity as consultant on the town hall, in November 1541 and again in January 1542. He was lodged at the Pedemuro shop; and even if Palladio no longer lived there—he was well embarked on forty years of happily married life, and by then at least two of his sons had been born—he certainly would have been in close touch with his former masters, especially during the visit of so distinguished a colleague. As incidents that put him in contact with internationally significant architects at the beginning and end of his "learning years," Andrea's collaborations with Serlio at Cricoli and with Sanmicheli in Vicenza would have been the two most important events, from a purely architectural standpoint, on either side of his Paduan and Roman sojourns.

Palladio must already have met Sanmicheli during his and Trissino's residence of 1538–1540 in Padua, where their experiences were to prove central for Palladio's more broadly based humanist training. Foremost among the influences which helped to shape Andrea's artistic character was his introduction, less directly through Trissino than through Serlio (whose first-published *Book of Architecture* in 1537 already carried a dedication expressing his indebtedness) to the principal figure in contemporary Paduan art, ALVISE CORNARO. Author of a famous *Treatise on the Sober Life* and one of the most significant north Italian architectural theorists before Palladio as well as Padua's most prominent patron of modern architecture (of which he was also a gentleman practitioner), Cornaro had had a relationship with the important Veronese painter-architect GIOVANNI MARIA FALCONETTO—who had lived in Alvise's house and even traveled with him to Rome—which exactly prefigured Trissino's relationship with Palladio. For his patron, Falconetto had built the first example of "correct" Renaissance architecture in the whole of the Veneto, a beautifully sculptured and painted loggia (signed and dated 1524) at the end of the garden behind the Casa Cornaro. The structure functioned as a permanent stage for theatrical presentations in the open court, organized by another intimate of the house, the great comic playwright Angelo Beolco, called Ruzante. When Palladio, Trissino, and Serlio frequented Alvise's circle in the late 1530s, the garden was being further embellished by a second splendid fabric intended for chamber music, called the Odeon, evidently designed by Cornaro and executed by Andrea da Valle. Its densely articulated plan, with a niched central octagon surrounded by an arrangement of regularly proportioned rooms, was based on a Giuliano da Sangallo (see SANGALLO FAMILY) drawing purporting to depict the ancient villa of Marcus Terentius Varro at Cassino. With the help of further descriptions of classical villas from the texts of Pliny, Vitruvius, and Alberti, the lavish stucco reliefs and fresco paintings within (by Tiziano Minio and Gualtiero Padovano) were intended to re-create both the rich variety and the exact forms of Roman domestic interiors. The fact that such a spatially complex and decoratively elaborated structure was assuming its final aspect during Palladio's presence in this very garden (1538, 1539, 1540) makes the Odeon Cornaro a definitive influence on his aesthetic development. Its centralized plan and boldly sculptural vaulting shapes had a telling effect on his own designs for villas. Actual images of it, as well as many derivative variants, are as plentiful in Serlio's pages as their more creative parallels are frequent in Palladio's early drawings and mature achievements; and we must imagine the interest of these closely associated masters as being mutually reinforced by their common study of its plan. But its spectacular sculptural and pictorial decoration, applied with the authority of classical precedent over all the vaults and in landscape scenes on the lower walls, has perhaps not adequately been understood as definitively persuading the young Palladio, at the very outset of his career, of the strong desirability of such lavish internal embellishment. As we shall see, he remained remarkably loyal to this richly developed classical paradigm. He had the leisure and the intimate associations to watch it carefully as it took form. With Serlio, Trissino, Cornaro, and even Cardinal Pietro Bembo at his elbow to guarantee its fidelity not only to antique but also to High Renaissance prototypes, he would quickly have been confirmed in his persuasion of its classical accuracy and importance during his subsequent Roman studies of Raphael's Palatine excavations and Villa Madama interiors.

Alvise Cornaro served as administrator and architectural adviser to the cardinal-bishop of Padua, Francesco Pisani, and in this capacity he created a plan himself, or adapted a very late Falconetto design—executed in these same years (1534/1535–1542) by Falconetto's successor, Andrea da Valle—for an immense and impressive villa for the cardinal-bishop near the hillside village of Luvigliano, just south of Padua. This second, deeply influential work was stuccoed again by Tiziano Minio (1542) and frescoed by his collaborator from the Odeon, Gualtiero Padovano (1543), as well as by the Flemish artist Lambert Sustris. In addition to exerting once more a long-range effect on Palladio's conception of villa planning and decoration, this project brought him into contact with Padua-based members of the Pisani family, of whom the youthful Vettor was to commission Palladio's first Venetian villa (at Bagnolo, 1542–1544). But even before that (and as a determining influence on its design), the Venetian commander in Padua, Girolamo Cornaro, a distant cousin of Alvise's and a brother-in-law of the cardinal-bishop, is certain to have introduced into this avant-garde and Roman-oriented circle at the Casa Cornaro the architect of his newly planned bulwark for the Paduan city walls (1539–1540) as well as of his own villa at Piombino (1539–1542), Michele Sanmicheli. Indeed, Palladio's Paduan contact with this branch of the Cornaro family and with their current architect is proven by his later commission to build a second villa at Piombino (1551–1553) for the Venetian commander's younger son, Zorzon Cornaro. Other future patrons then living in Padua were the young Vettor Pisani and his cousin, Daniel Barbaro of Maser.

The context which united these architectural enthusiasts (in addition, that is, to the Giardino Cornaro) was the University. Daniele Barbaro, for example, delivered his oration as a Doctor of Arts on September 19, 1540, to a vast concourse of the nobility and intelligentsia, presided over by the Venetian governor; two weeks later, Trissino's grandson Francesco (he too a future Palladio patron, for a villa in 1553 and a palace later in that decade) took his degree, as did Palladio's current patron and friend, Pietro Godi, in 1542. They had been preceded in 1538 by Antonio Valmarana, who may thus be intelligibly connected with Palladio at a moment appropriate for the very early commission of his own and his cousin Giuseppe's villa at Vigardolo, whose projects were drafted at Padua in 1539–1541 (and which was apparently begun in Palladio's absence from the Veneto during the latter year).

The scope and fruitfulness of these connections indicate the crucial importance of Palladio's early association, in the ambiance of the University, with such a substantial number of patrons whose personal commissions are documented within the first phase of his emerging maturity. Godi, Valmarana, and Trissino as fellow Vicentines all had direct channels of acquaintance with the architect, which were guaranteed as well through the intimate patronage of Trissino's grandfather. But the three wealthy and prominent young noblemen from Venice—Zorzon Cornaro, Vettor Pisani, and Daniele Barbaro—required much more unusual and more persuasive introductions, which cannot adequately be understood save in an atmosphere of mutual enthusiasm for the revival of antiquity, both literary and architectural, such as we know to have been provided by the University.

Gian Giorgio Trissino's main purpose in transferring his residence to Padua, on the heels of his costly remodeling of the villa at Cricoli, must have been in fact to bring his protégé into this indispensable orbit of the University. But indeed, not a single one of Trissino's frequent moves between 1538 and 1541 can be considered as independent of his primary program of completing his young disciple's education, bringing him into personal contact with monuments of antiquity and extending his field of acquaintance as broadly as possible among Venetian as well as mainland leaders of the military, mercantile, ecclesiastical, and intellectual avant-garde. That the elderly humanist actually succeeded beyond his most ambitious expectations in realizing this goal is an outcome that should be attributed not only to the diligent involvement of his international circle of friends, but also to Palladio's own brilliance and persuasiveness, and perhaps above all to the uniquely exalted intellectual and aristocratic cachet conferred upon them through the enthusiastic support of the great Daniele Barbaro. Already in his late twenties, over a residence of ten years in Padua (1535–1545), Daniele had become acknowledged as one of the most original scholars of antiquity and the visual arts in the Venetian Republic. His and Palladio's nine-year collaboration on the famous Vitruvius commentary which they began in 1547 must clearly have been inspired by a program conceived substantially earlier, for they were at that point inconveniently separated by the fifty miles between Vicenza and Venice. Since both Daniele's and Andrea's lifelong absorptions in Vitruvius can probably be traced to Trissino's fascination with that sole architectural theorist of antiquity, it seems most plausible that they would both have been initiated into the mysteries of his arcane text during their joint residencies in the humanist ambiance of Padua. It was providential that these abstractly philological and idealized explications of antique architecture would have been balanced, at the crucial period of Palladio's development, by the radically opposed common-sense practicality of Alvise Cornaro and by the equally pragmatic, down-to-earth literalism of Serlio's interest in the actuality of architecture.

Two sharply divergent attitudes toward antique and modern architecture thus came together in Palladio's training in Padua, and both represented the highest level of analysis which either approach achieved in sixteenth-century Italy. On the one hand, a linguistically oriented attention to antique precedent, brilliantly championed by Trissino and Barbaro, inculcated in Palladio an ideal of creative interpretation of ancient texts that characterized his own significant literary output—including the first modern guides to antiquities and churches in Rome, of 1554; his graphic reconstructions for Barbaro's *Vitruvius* of 1556; his immensely celebrated treatise, *I Quattro Libri dell'Architettura* (*The Four Books of Architecture*), published in 1570; his fully illustrated *Commentaries of Julius Caesar,* of 1574/1575; and his unpublished work on Polybius, now lost save for its dedication of 1579. On the other hand, a totally disparate tradition of straightforward practical empiricism, garrulously developed by Serlio and raised to the level of a moral commitment by Cornaro, instilled in Andrea a lifelong preference for solutions engendered by successful experience—a habit of mind which of course worked in a deeply sympathetic resonance with his previous twenty years of careful, high-quality craftsmanship. His unpretentious early life as an artisan thus made him profoundly receptive to the pragmatic directness of Serlio and the moral candor of Cornaro, and he remained a remarkably clear-headed builder throughout a long career of intensely practical activity. But in his consciously forged second identity as a humanist architect, archeologist, and theorist, converted to loftier ideals through the neo-imperial ambitions of Trissino and Barbaro's subtle elucidations of antique harmony, he encapsulated in his mature works a vision of universality that epitomized architecture as a vehicle of virtue and opened the philosophic doors of his later literary studies. These two halves of his life were probably always in near-perfect balance, even when he lacked the pretensions of ancient culture and relied rather on the intuition of Rome's greatness that was immanent in its monuments. Only in Padua did they come together as a unified whole, precipitating a crystallization of genius that was the real fruit of his spiritual rebaptism as Palladio.

The last ineluctible handicap that had separated the artisan from the architect, namely, a skill in drawing, was also overcome in the transition from Cricoli to Padua, with the astonishing suddenness that bespeaks an immense unpracticed talent. In the sixteen years of his professional activity through 1537, there is not a single surviving sheet to indicate that Andrea had even tried his hand at draftsmanship. But from the first year of his studies in Padua, 1538–1539, come several tentative drawings whose numbers he was to multiply and whose quality he was to improve with such speed that Palladio's graphic corpus—today numbering more than 330 sheets—is certainly one of the largest, and perhaps indeed the finest, of any Renaissance architect. A suspicion that he or a follower might consciously have edited it to preserve only the most beautiful specimens is belied by the character of the survivals (which include preliminary sketches, repetitive drafts, unfinished studies, rejected proposals, and rough notes) as well as by the tell-tale evidence of his first attempts. The earliest of these, now housed at the Royal Institute of British Architects in London as Palladio collection, box XVI, sheet 6 (hereafter to be cited as RIBA, XVI/6), is an extraordinarily heavy-handed and even clumsy plan of a small townhouse whose ground floor opens behind the arcaded portico of a covered sidewalk into a narrow hall flanked by pairs of single rooms, then gives onto a deep garden with a five-bay loggia on axis at the end. Every one of these elements is exactly paralleled by Alvise Cornaro's house and garden in Padua (to which Andrea would have had access only around the middle of 1538), of which this earliest graphic experiment may therefore be taken as a tentative image, probably preserved as a memento of his arrival at the Cornaran "academy," and perhaps set for him as a first exercise by his graphics tutor.

Who Palladio's instructor in draftsmanship may have been is not recorded. Certainly it was not

Trissino, whose rudimentary surviving sketches preclude any possibility of his having inspired Andrea to achieve (as that emerging young genius did almost immediately) a supremely sensitive, articulate, and flexible graphic style. The only other plausible candidate is Serlio, and Palladio's intimate awareness of a great number of his designs, frequently in advance of their publication and as decisive influences on his own earliest projects, not only confirms the relationship but establishes its date. Andrea's elementary plan on RIBA XVI/6 is carefully rendered with the painstaking effort of a neophyte studiously replicating an unfamiliar mode; but several of its architectural forms (especially those most unlike the realities of Casa Cornaro) and most of its graphic techniques are precisely paralleled in Serlio's surviving drawings, as for example in the manuscript versions of his Sixth Book, copies of which are in Munich (Staatsbibliothek) and New York (Columbia University). Two things are striking about this tutelage: one is how suddenly it began—Palladio has left us not a single drawing of the Serlian loggia at Cricoli, emphasizing once more how self-conscious and programmatic was his immediate Paduan commencement under the same master—and the other is how quickly Serlio's influence was superseded. Andrea's two earliest elevations of palace façades (RIBA XVII/26 and XVII/23, for Palazzo Da Monte) display a few isolated quotations from Serlio, with faint reminiscences of Abbondi and Sansovino; but their principal motifs are an eclectic assemblage of design elements from early sixteenth-century masters in Padua itself, such as Lorenzo da Bologna, Biagio di Bigoio, Annibale de' Maggi, and above all Falconetto. Once more we have the impression of an accomplished teacher recommending to an unusual pupil, after the initial mastery of a few essentials, that he should forge his own stylistic amalgam from the living laboratory of the architectural environment—an expression, in other words, of that pragmatic empiricism that was Palladio's principal Serlian inheritance. Already in a much more coherent design from this earliest period, of a two-storied Tuscan and Ionic façade (RIBA, Chiswick no. 27) which may probably be understood as a critical revision of the Odeon Cornaro then in progress, Palladio combines the grace and elegance of Serlio at Cricoli with the massive gravity of Sanmicheli at the Porta Nuova in Verona, in a convincing unity that goes far beyond his Vicentine or Paduan prototypes.

Nevertheless, Serlio's direct responsibility for Andrea's mastery of draftsmanship should not be underestimated. Falconetto's example as an architect (and Palladio's artistic personality was literally formed in his shadow) brings into perspective the relative importance of his and Serlio's influence on Palladio as a draftsman, and here GIORGIO VASARI's testimony is revealing. Falconetto was a native of Verona who had been trained as a painter under Melozzo da Forlì and artists of the school of Mantegna, but who as an architect had worked especially under Alvise Cornaro's patronage in Padua. A significant area of contact between his two modes of activity had been constituted by his corpus of measured perspectival renderings after the antiquities of Verona, Pola, and Rome, which Vasari says were published by others after his death. Recent critics have tended to concur that the publisher was Serlio (in his *Third Book,* printed in March 1540), but Serlio's access to many of these drawings may well have come through his friendship with Falconetto's patron, Alvise Cornaro. By 1538–1540, we may thus postulate the existence of a veritable studio for the development of up-to-date archeological draftsmanship in the Giardino Cornaro (or indeed in Verona or Pola, whither Serlio and Andrea may have repaired for access to other Falconetto drawings or to the monuments themselves). Falconetto's original measured renderings, then, were evidently being adapted by Serlio for his imminent publication at the same time that they were demonstrably being copied as learning models by the young Palladio (who learned much, incidentally, from their figural style). As if to document this process, Serlio himself describes, in his text to accompany the revised Falconetto images of the Pola theater, how the antiquities of that town in particular "have been surveyed by a better draftsman, who is an expert in numbers and measures" (1540, p. 52). This may plausibly be construed as the first published reference to Palladio (it can hardly refer to Falconetto, since the comparison is to Falconetto-based images alongside) as well as the first tribute to the fledgling architect's superb graphic skills—couched, perhaps, in the gruff style of a proud teacher. It should also be noted that the presence of Michele Sanmicheli in the Paduan circles of Girolamo and Alvise Cornaro at this same moment must clearly have involved some transmittal of his drafting technique to Palladio as well. Such a relationship is hard to demonstrate, however, since only one drawing probably by Sanmicheli has yet been found (Lewis, 1981, pp. 23–24); it too is so close to Serlio's mode of draftsmanship as to have had its attribution questioned in favor of the latter. It may thus be possible to suggest that Serlio's graphic style was his most important legacy in the Veneto and that its persuasive example would have been emulated equally by a great professional architect such as Sanmicheli and by a student such as Palladio who by 1541 was already moving decisively toward a blend of Serlian and Sanmichelian vocabularies in the first architectural projects of his independent career.

In 1541, Serlio emigrated permanently to France, and by October, Palladio and Trissino had returned to Vicenza from their first archeological expedition to Rome. Even during the latter part of their stay in Padua, however, Palladio had produced several startlingly beautiful drawings for early domestic projects, whose almost unheralded apparition demonstrates the suddenness of his achievement of competence as a classical designer. On March 13, 1539, Andrea's former Cathedral patron Aurelio Dell'Acqua died, and shortly afterward the Civena family purchased his palace site, for which Palladio prepared a sequence of designs. While even some later ones of these are mere paraphrases of Serlio (RIBA XVII/14), a bold and impressive façade project from the first year of this campaign (RIBA XIII/10, 1539) refers creatively to Sanmicheli in such a prototype as Palazzo Lavezola-Pompei in Verona. An approximately coeval project was Palladio's small palace for Monte Da Monte, a building undocumented save through another remarkably fine façade drawing (RIBA XVII/19) in which Andrea adroitly fused "pure" Sanmichelian motifs from recent works by that master with certain of their Raphaelesque prototypes, possibly studied through drawings that Sanmicheli, Falconetto, or Serlio may have brought from Rome. The commencement of one further project can definitely be assigned to Palladio's Paduan years, namely, his planning for the villa of Vettor Pisani at Bagnolo (built after the architect's return from Rome, in 1542–1544). His earliest proposal (RIBA XVII/16, 1539–1540) is preserved in both elevation and plan, and the latter displays an almost exact replication of the room arrangement at Cricoli. The façade presents a monumental resolution of those disparate Paduan Renaissance motifs that were quoted in the early Da Monte projects, but with a festive confidence and breadth of handling that bespeaks an increasing control of the classical idiom.

The highly detailed draftsmanship of these earliest projects as well as the preciosity of their thinly applied small-scale architectural elements undergo striking changes in a series of designs made on the eve of Palladio's first trip to Rome. In a group of studies whose graphic and architectural styles are so much cleaner as to be almost stark (1540–1541), Palladio evokes both the simplified draftsmanship and the sharply reduced classical ornament of Serlio. These numerous designs refer to his continuing gestation of villa plans for Vettor Pisani at Bagnolo, as well as to a closely related pair of projects for small villas commissioned by Giuseppe and Antonio Valmarana at Vigardolo (c.1541–1543?) and by Taddeo Gazoto at Bertesina (1541–1547). The latter is a timid transitional work whose paper-thin pilasters and window frames still strongly recall Falconetto. Its physical realization, which is closely paralleled by the contemporaneous fabrics of the Civena and Da Monte palaces in Vicenza, is thus less interesting than the inventive vigor of its drawings, especially those for the plan. Several of the most "purified" of its elevation studies refer as well to the shocking abstraction of the Villa Valmarana at Vigardolo, whose undecorated prismatic geometry makes it a real novelty in the history of architecture, though one that was germinal to Palladio's personal synthesis of "functional" simplicity and classical allusiveness. Its latest project drawing (RIBA XVII/2) suggests window frames more elaborate than those executed—the latter so reticent as to leave its vast wall planes essentially unembellished—of the shape known after its popularizer as a Serlian opening, with three apertures crowned by a wide central arch, flanked by narrower lintels. That same motif (miscalled a "Palladian window" through reference to eighteenth-century British examples) recurs in series on a preliminary project for the Vicenza town hall (RIBA XVII/22), where again it is highly diagnostic of this brief phase of straightforward Serlian borrowings.

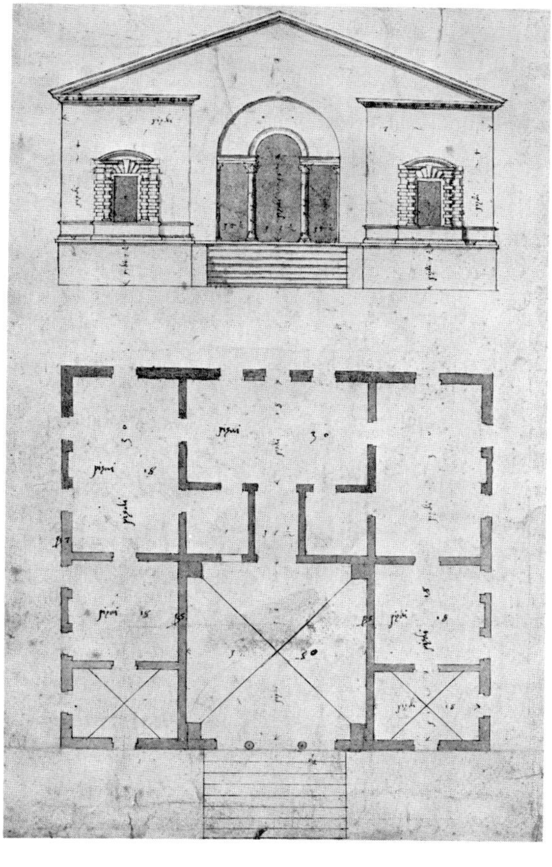

Palladio. Drawing of Villa of Giuseppe and Antonio Valmarana. Vigardolo, Italy. c.1541–1543?

Palladio.
Villa of Vettor Pisani.
Bagnolo, Italy.
1542–1544

Palladio.
Palace of Marc'Antonio Thiene.
Vicenza, Italy.
1542/1546–1551/1558

The effect on Palladio's architecture of his first direct experience of Rome is dramatically exemplified in his sequence of drawings for Vettor Pisani's villa at Bagnolo. From Paduan Early Renaissance through Falconettan and Serlian reminiscences in fussily detailed earlier designs, the frame of reference suddenly changes to a much simpler and grander invocation of Bramante and his classical antecedents, with a great entrance hemicycle borrowed from the latter's Belvedere court and elaborate room shapes with semicircular or "thermal" windows based on ancient Roman baths (RIBA XVII/17). Whereas Andrea's earliest Bagnolo project (RIBA XVII/16) simply repeated Cricoli's and Vigardolo's identical plan of interrelated three-room suites flanking a central axis of loggia, stairs, and hall, his most thoughtfully resolved version (RIBA XVI/7) wraps the suites in L-shaped configurations around a narrower hall, with their re-entrant angles accommodating the stairs. Both systems (as earlier at Cricoli and Vigardolo, and originally [?] in a plan of the mid-1530s by Trissino) employed geometric interrelationships of shapes and dimensions, for example, a large room 30 by 18 feet, adjoined by a chamber 18 feet square, followed by a cabinet or studio of 18 by 12 feet. Using 6 feet as a module, such a series could be expressed in the simple ratios of 5:3, 3:3, and 3:2, the common dimension of 18 feet recurred (in usual practice if not always in theory, in beamed rooms, or in those with vaults) in the ceiling height of the large and middle rooms, with an appropriate reduction in the *camerino,* to create the perfected sequence of a cube-and-two-thirds, a related cube, and a proportionally reduced cube-and-a-half. This extraordinarily brilliant device, whether invented independently by Trissino or developed in an early collaboration with Palladio, became symbolic as a paradigm of rational order and spatial clarity in Andrea's architecture. In three-dimensional experience it is uncannily effective as a frame for ennobling human perception by suggesting a macrocosm of parallel perfection—or, as Palladio would have it, of unchanging virtue. It is one of the principal keys to the universality of his art, and its endlessly creative variations (especially those for the subtle adjustment of vaulting heights, according to laws of harmonic proportion) are an impressive index of his genius.

In contrast to what might seem to be an arid or crystalline ideal of interior space, Palladio's increasingly robust sculptural expressiveness in his façades and structural elements such as loggias, vestibules, and courtyards of the early 1540s is actually paralleled by an elaboration of room and vaulting shapes and by a profusion of interior decoration in both two and three dimensions, which set his work in a decisive new channel. The change once more is prefigured in the Villa Pisani at Bagnolo (1542–1544), whose execution extended over most of the time between Palladio's first return from Rome in the fall of 1541 and his second departure for the papal capital in 1545. As it was finally constructed, the portico of the Villa Pisani lost the sweeping but rather delicate Bramantesque hemicycle that Palladio had projected throughout the sequence of its drawings in favor of a sculpturally massive Sanmichelian composition of three great arches, flanked by heavily rusticated Doric pilasters of "cyclopean" masonry. Similar motifs appear in the drawings (from 1542) and construction (from 1546) of one of the architect's most ambitious works, his immense palace for Marc'Antonio Thiene in the center of Vicenza, which was executed only as the colossal fragment of an exterior corner, with two associated wings embracing one angle of a vast interior court (dated in inscriptions 1551 and 1558). The spectacularly rusticated vestibule of Palazzo Thiene, where whole column shafts are left in the "raw" state of huge uncut blocks, together with its boldly sculptural windows whose framing tabernacles alternate smoothly carved with roughly blocked stones, have made the palace so strange a maverick in Palladio's production that it has periodically been attributed to GIULIO ROMANO. That great exponent of central Italian mannerism did travel from Mantua to Vicenza (for inevitable consultations on the rebuilding of the town hall) in December 1542, just after the signing of a contract for Palazzo Thiene in which Palladio is mentioned only cursorily. The building's notorious window frames, moreover, almost exactly repeat a celebrated prototype on Giulio's own house in Rome, of c.1523–1524; but drawings of that curious prodigy circulated in substantial numbers, and of course Palladio could have seen it himself in 1541. Many other elements in the designs of Palazzo Thiene derive from specific sources in Sanmicheli

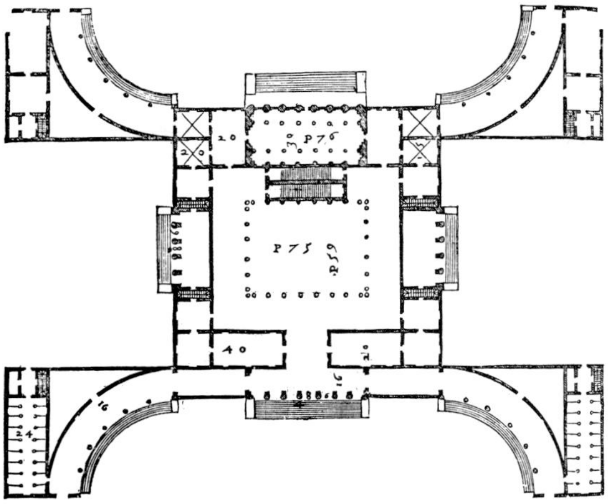

Palladio. Final project for Villa of Leonardo Mocenigo. River Brenta, Dolo, Italy. 1544–1554, 1561–1564

(Palazzo Canossa, Villa Soranzo) or antiquity (for instance, Claudianum) and thus indicate a wide range of Palladian eclecticism rather than a single borrowing from Giulio in the evolution of its design. Even more interesting, the richly modeled stuccoes which ALESSANDRO VITTORIA executed from 1552 in almost all the interiors, in addition to the cycles of fresco paintings extensively associated with them, give the palace an impressive stylistic coherence both inside and out. This unity of intent makes it a worthy successor to such a demonstrable prototype for Palladio as Cornaro's Odeon, where a comparable integration of architecture, sculpture, and painting was first achieved in the Veneto.

A pair of equally ambitious but truncated villa projects coincide with the planning of Palazzo Thiene. For the same patrons, Palladio executed part of a grandiose rural complex at Quinto Vicentino, whose surviving site plan (Worcester College, Oxford—1542–1546) is one of a tiny number of designs to depict the complete environmental context for a Palladian country house. In his treatise of 1570, the architect shows its forms as being doubled in a symmetrical mirror image; but this concept is almost certainly wishful thinking and indicates how untrustworthy that famous book is as a guide to Palladio's original conceptions. An analogous situation is reflected in a sequence of four projects for Leonardo Mocenigo's villa at Dolo on the River Brenta, intended like Quinto to re-create the image of a Roman villa as described by Vitruvius. Between 1544 and 1554, Palladio proposed successively grander (and more impractical) classical schemas, but only a reduced version of the first design was actually built, in 1561–1564; it was totally reconstructed by the patron's heir in 1581–1582 and was demolished in the nineteenth century. Its spectacular memorial, though, is the great woodcut of 1570 in Palladio's treatise, once more a wished-for aggrandizement of its restricted realization: it appears as a huge hollow square set off by four curving wings that embrace the front and back courts like welcoming arms, in an image that proved irresistible to baroque and neoclassical architects around the world.

In September 1545, Palladio and Trissino set off for a second sojourn of six months in Rome. The visit has plausibly been construed as a conscious effort by the aged humanist to infuse in his protégé a still deeper comprehension of classical style, with the specific aim of preparing him for the central and most obvious challenge of his life: a Palladian proposal for the rebuilding of the Vicenza town hall. Andrea indeed returned home for a brief stay in the early spring of 1546 for the purpose of presenting such a project to the town council, under the sponsorship of his former colleague Giovanni di Pedemuro. The councillors were persuaded to authorize the expensive step of erecting a trial bay in wood (March 6, 1546), by which we may sense that the real maneuvering for acceptance of the design must have been accomplished well in advance; shortly afterward, Palladio had an influential group of devoted partisans on the council who lobbied consistently in his behalf. He himself departed once more for Rome, and from mid-March 1546 to mid-July 1547 he enjoyed his longest and most productive stay in Trissino's Roman lodgings. Probably as a result of the latter's extended absence from Vicenza, nothing happened on the pending civic proposal until three commissioners for the rebuilding project were elected in September 1548 and asked Palladio to present more drawings; these again were translated into wooden models, together with the best of the fifteenth-century and early sixteenth-century proposals. After another long delay, the respective submissions were debated in a final council session on April 11, 1549: the two crucial defenses of Palladio's project were delivered by Girolamo Chiericati and Gian Alvise Valmarana, and after fifty years of disagreement his proposal was overwhelmingly adopted. Work began at once, and for the remaining thirty years of his life Palladio regularly supervised the enormous task of encircling the whole Gothic structure with an immense two-story ring of stone loggias, conceived as open screens with superimposed rows of Serlian motifs. The effect of Trissino's support over the long years in which Palladio was able to absorb the spirit of Roman art at the source is nowhere better exemplified than in this neo-antique "Basilica" (as Palladio proudly called it), for the building does in fact function as one of the most successful modern metaphors of ancient splendor and *virtù*. It was completed in 1617, and ever since those impassioned speeches of 1549 it has been recognized as Palladio's masterpiece. It quickly assured his repu-

Palladio. Basilica. Vicenza, Italy. 1549–1580 (not completed until 1617)

tation and brought him scores of commissions throughout the Veneto and even abroad. His consultations in Trent and Innsbruck (1552), in Piedmont (1566), and his invitation to the imperial court in Vienna (1568), however, resulted in no actual building. His work in Vicenza was predictably focused on those patrons who had helped him to achieve the Basilica commission, but he did expand his circles of patronage substantially in the provinces of Venice (together with Udine, Treviso, and Padua) to the east, and Verona to the west. Palladio is still represented in the Veneto by some forty more or less intact structures, and he has left records of many others in his treatise.

While the Basilica project was still in doubt, in the fall of 1546, Girolamo Chiericati and his brother Giovanni had begun to consider Palladian plans for a city palace and villa respectively; with designs completed probably soon after Andrea's return from Rome in 1547, Giovanni's villa at Vancimuglio began to rise almost immediately (1547/1548–1554), and Girolamo's great palace on the "Isola" in Vicenza soon followed (1546/1549–1557), with its splendidly original solution of an antique colonnaded stoa running as an open gallery across the whole length of the façade. An equally important palace for another long-standing Palladian enthusiast was the beautiful structure for Giuseppe Porto (1547/1549–1552); that nobleman had married a sister of the Thiene brothers in 1542, and the unusually extensive series of its project drawings may actually have been begun almost simultaneously with Palladio's designs for Palazzo Thiene.

Palladio. Palace of Giuseppe Porto. Vicenza, Italy. 1547/1549–1552

Two similar cases of projects from the early 1540s that were constructed only later in the decade are the wonderful villa of Bonifacio Poiana (plan 1544/1545, completed 1555), with mainly unmolded apertures so severely abstracted as to be most closely comparable with the stripped style of Vigardolo and Lonedo, and the delicate little villa of Biagio Saraceno at Finale (c.1545–1548?). The latter inaugurates a group of single-story houses characterized by slightly projecting pedimented frontispieces with triple apertures, flanked by plain walls with single window bays on the sides. A solution almost identical with Finale, though with rusticated masonry around the three entrance arches, is the Villa Caldogno (1548/1549–1552, decorated two decades later); another, with the entrance arcade complemented by unmolded round-headed windows, is the Villa Zen at Cessalto (1548/1549?–1553?).

This attractive group of small country houses begins to emphasize an element crucial to the mature Palladian vocabulary, namely, the full classical pediment applied to the front of a private house. The earliest Renaissance example that actually forms part of the roof (as a direct prototype for Palladio's treatments, rather than being applied as a relief decoration to a lower wall) is immediately north of Venice, on the Villa Giustinian at Roncade (c.1511–1513), attributed to Tullio Lombardo. Palladio himself had experimented with approximations of his mature form at Bertesina and Bagnolo, but the pediment of the former corresponds with no projecting frontispiece (standing instead rather ambiguously across the otherwise undifferentiated middle of the façade), while the low pediment at Bagnolo is squeezed uncomfortably between taller towers. Vigardolo and Poiana have gable fronts not devel-

oped as full pediments, and thus Finale, Caldogno, and Cessalto present Palladio's developed form of the motif as applied essentially on the façade plane of single-story house. An early variant of momentous significance is introduced on Giovanni Chiericati's villa at Vancimuglio (1547/1548), where the whole frontispiece breaks forward as a freestanding colonnaded portico with a much more three-dimensional pediment; it required a greater vertical development and is here applied to a tall story-and-a-half. Its plan drawing (showing projecting walls at the sides of the portico) was used again as the plan of the very similar but even taller Villa Foscari at Malcontenta (c.1549), with the modification of lateral files of columns inserted in place of the walls along the sides of the projecting portico. A final step, in order to accommodate a full two stories, was to superimpose *two* colonnaded loggias, with a pediment over the whole. This was the intended scheme at Palazzo Antonini in Udine (c.1550), with one such frontispiece applied as a relief ornament to the street façade, and another, recessed into the block of the house, on the garden front; its pediments were never executed, although a simplified replica of this scheme was fully achieved in Francesco Pisani's villa at Montagnana (1552/1553). At the same time, the most grandiose of these elaborate systems was produced for Zorzon Cornaro's villa at Piombino (1551), where the recessed, superimposed, and pedimented loggias on the garden front are answered by a fully projecting pedimented portico of two stories on the street façade—the only such ambitious form to be executed by Palladio, in direct emulation of Tullio Lombardo's double-storied portico at Roncade of forty years earlier.

A final, related image among Palladio's fertile inventions for the differentiation of aristocratic residence types was the treatment of the entire façade as a full temple front, with an encompassing pediment over the whole. Although suggested periodically in the *Quattro Libri,* the only executed example is the triumphant masterpiece of the villa for Palladio's intimate friends and collaborators Daniele and Marc'Antonio Barbaro, at Maser (projected 1549/1551, constructed 1554–1558, chapel begun 1579/1580). This miraculous building, though certainly incorporating many elements suggested by the Barbaro brothers, is unquestionably Palladio's domestic masterpiece. Its remarkable three-dimensional planning subtly incorporates a change in ground level of a full story as it backs against a hill, and the fountain grotto behind the upper garden represents a sublime conjunction of equal talents by the three designers: Daniele developed the concept of siting and invented the iconographic program, Marc'Antonio is reliably said by contemporaries to have modeled the lavish stucco sculptures, and Palladio achieved the imaginative architectural frame. The three friends were joined in the grotto's decoration by the great fresco painter Paolo Veronese, who also frescoed the whole interior of the palace, making it the principal work of architectural painting in Venetian dominions during the Renaissance.

Palladio's subsequent private houses (which have always been recognized as his most inventive contribution) eschewed these extravagant marvels and returned to a calmly equilibrated mode in his later years. This development is prefigured—with a

Palladio.
Villa of Zorzon Cornaro.
Piombino Dese, Italy.
1551–1553

Palladio.
Villa of Daniele and Marc'Antonio Barbaro.
Maser, Italy.
1549/1551, 1554–1558

slight awkwardness of proportion—in his villa for Francesco Badoer at Fratta (1556/1557–1563) and is raised to a perfect purity in his subsequent design for Leonardo Emo's celebrated villa at Fanzolo (1559/1565–1567). This same impression of distilled refinement is unforgettably conveyed by Palladio's most famous structure, the universally admired Villa Almerico called *La Rotonda* (1565/1566–1569) in Vicenza.

There are mavericks in this sequence. One example is the extraordinary fragment of a villa for the Sarego family, who owned large stone quarries near Verona and thus commissioned a courtyard of colossal rusticated columns two stories high. Its date has been misconstrued, even after recent thermoluminescent tests of the bricks, to the 1530s when in fact the father of Palladio's patron Marc' Antonio Sarego took control of the property (and the partially finished enclosing wings of the house) only in 1552/1553, when he began installing some fountains in the gardens. Palladio's project for the courtyard thus dates at the earliest from these years, and it was actually constructed in 1565–1569. Its grandiose woodcut hastily prepared for the *Quattro Libri* in 1570, as was so often the case, represents an ideally expanded scheme based only loosely on the actual commission.

Three celebrated city palaces, executed for three of his most consistently supportive Vicentine families, close the parabola of Palladio's domestic works. Gian Alvise Valmarana commissioned a palace project which was not built in his lifetime, but was constructed by his widow and son (1565/1566–1571). Its façade notoriously intermingles large and small orders of pilasters and even stucco figures as architectonic elements in ways that have earned for it the dubious reputation of mannerist inversions. In fact, its underlying ordonnance is regular and logical and uses the flanking figures at the edges of the structure to set off a dramatically aggrandized central composition. Palladio's palace for Montano Barbaran (first projects, 1550–1551; second, late 1560s; construction, 1570–1575) was originally intended to have a façade with a similar colossal order, but the patron finally acquired an adjoining property that allowed the scheme to be expanded in breadth. Palladio then reduced the scale of the façade elements to superimposed stories of engaged columns, containing a rich sculptural decoration. A magnificent atrium with groin vaults carried on a double file of Composite columns opens into an unfinished court with superimposed Ionic and Corinthian loggias of extraordinary grace and beauty; the interiors are richly decorated with elaborate stucco reliefs and make the palace one of the most representative ensembles of Palladio's late years. The problematical fragment of Palazzo Porto-Breganze was executed by Palladio's unsympathetic follower VINCENZO SCAMOZZI (by 1615, to a Palladian project of the 1570s?); its colossal order could accord well with other works of Palladio's last decade, but it is raised on the excessively high pedestals preferred by Scamozzi.

Palladio's association with the theater was long and productive and culminated in one of his most famous works, the great Teatro Olimpico, designed and largely built in the last six months of his life (1580). It was preceded by his elaborate temporary theaters of 1558 (and perhaps even 1557) for the earliest site of the Accademia Olimpica, his still more lavish constructions of 1561 for Piccolomini's *Amor Costante* and of 1562 for Trissino's *Sofonisba* (both in the Basilica), and his celebrated tour de force of 1565 for the *Antigone* of 1565 in Venice, now proven conclusively to have been staged in the courtyard of Palazzo Foscari. His final creation for the Accademia Olimpica was the permanent archeological reconstruction of an ancient theater, with a curving cavea and a fixed scaena frons. This had also been the form of his temporary wooden prototypes and of his splendid woodcut plates for Daniele Barbaro's Vitruvius edition of 1556. Although Andrea's youngest son, Silla Palladio, completed the Teatro Olimpico (1580–1583), once more it was modified at the insensitive hand of Scamozzi (1584–1585) in preparation for its inauguration with Sophocles's *Oedipus Rex*. For this occasion, Scamozzi enlarged the portals of the stage front and constructed behind them miniature avenues which diminish in sharp perspectival recession. From drawings by INIGO JONES of a few years later, it seems most likely that Palladio intended the stage portals to have been filled only with *painted* scenery (as in his Vitruvius reconstructions) that would have been changeable according to the production. Such a conclusion might absolve the Teatro Olimpico, at least partially, from an allegation of marginality in the development of the European theater. As the oldest surviving theater building since antiquity, it has in any event a distinguished place in the history of the Western stage.

Apart from the Basilica and the great magnificence of his interior remodelings of the Venetian Ducal Palace after its successive fires of the 1570s, Palladio's public buildings include only one other masterwork, the spectacular late Loggia del Capitaniato for the Venetian governor of Vicenza (1565/1571–1572), whose huge upper hall and elaborate lower lobby are fronted by one of the richest and grandest façades of his career. Four colossal Corinthian column shafts are engaged into a

wall that is almost dissolved in lower arcades, upper windows, and an enframing embroidery of stucco and stone detail which achieves an almost pictorial exuberance. As the perfect exterior counterpart to the lavishness of the Ducal Palace interiors, it expresses a plastic and coloristic vigor, in Palladio's late style, which is still informed by an unerring sense of structural clarity.

Palladio's religious buildings deserve a special word in conclusion, for they appear at first glance to be sharply different from this consistent effort to balance classical harmony with plastic and pictorial richness, a principle that informed Andrea's activity from his days at the Odeon Cornaro to those at the Ducal Palace. His simultaneous commissions in 1560 from the Venetian monasteries of the Benedictines at San Giorgio and the Lateran Canons at Santa Maria della Carità first brought him into the realm of religious building. At the Carità, he was able to execute only one wing (1560–1570) of an enlarged re-creation of a city residence from antiquity, as he reconstructed the concept from Vitruvius. Its exterior face is severely plain, as are all its interiors save one beautiful double-apsed tablinium; the one elaboration in the complex is the superb three-storied courtyard wall, with su-

Palladio.
Teatro Olimpico.
Vicenza, Italy.
1580 (not completed until 1580–1583 by Silla Palladio)

Palladio.
Loggia del Capitaniato.
Vicenza, Italy.
1565/1571–1572

Palladio.
Monastery of San Giorgio Maggiore.
Venice, Italy.
1560–1580

perimposed engaged orders separating arcades, all in brick. The warmth and delicacy of this composition is, as Goethe observed, supremely moving even in its reticence of monochromatic detail. The same tendency toward large forms discreetly handled is apparent in the majestic Refectory at San Giorgio (1560–1563), the breathtaking solemnity of his church interiors there (1565/1566–1580), and, after the plague of 1575—for deliverance from which he was commissioned to design a votive temple—at the Redentore, or Church of the Redeemer (1576/1577–1580). These are sublime concatenations of an apparently infinite number of classical moldings and ornaments, all rendered on pure white plaster surfaces in pale cut stone. Their forms, however, are grand and bold and register as rich nuggets of sculptural density even at the farthest distances. Their effect is a celebration of divine harmony through an acknowledgment of the ordered complexity of the world, and as such these two great works epitomize once more the creative tension that underlay Palladio's lifelong balance of idealized ratiocination and empirical tolerance. Their famous façades, together with Palladio's earlier one at San Francesco della Vigna (c.1565–1570?), together achieve the most original Renaissance solutions to the ancient problem of applying a horizontal classical order to a pyramidal Christian temple. The drawings documenting their genesis, however, demonstrate that their inspiration may have come from the concept of a delicately "winged" triumphal arch than from the interpenetration of two differently sized pedimented temple fronts: such a solution is mainly post-Palladian and depends above all on Scamozzi's revision of the façade for San Giorgio Maggiore. That most conspicuous of all Palladio's works, overlooking the center of Venice across the Bacino di San Marco, was intended by him to display a colossal projecting pedimented portico, as his drawings of 1576/1579 with free-standing columns make clear (RIBA XIV/12; State Archives, Venice, MM 857). This was one of the plans he had contemplated for the Redentore as well (RIBA XIV/13–15), though he revised that design into a planar configuration—without pedestals—in the three years before his death. He returned to it as his favored solution, however, in his two last and most splendid designs in this idiom. His final proposal for the unbuilt façade of San Petronio in Bologna (January 1579; Worcester College, Oxford) recommended exactly such a giant portico, eight columns wide, in what would certainly have been the greatest Renaissance reflection of the Pantheon. That central monument of his architectural credo again inspired the design he was working on when he died, his magnificent centralized Chapel of the Redeemer for Marc'Antonio Barbaro at Maser (1579–1580). Its distilled perfection affords a fitting image of his life: the encompassing single shape is intellectually ordered through antique measure and proportion and thus bespeaks the philosophic confidence of Christian humanism; but the festive exuberance of its naturalistic sculpture more joyously proclaims the miracle of a world redeemed.

Douglas Lewis

WORKS

(A)1531, Santa Maria dei Servi (portal; with Giovanni da Porlezza and Girolamo Pittoni); *1532–1533, San Michele (chapel and tomb of Enrico Antonio Godi; with Pedemuro shop); Vicenza, Italy. 1533, Villa of Enrico Antonio Godi (service building; with Pedemuro shop), Lonedo, Italy. (A)1534–1538, Cathedral of Santa Maria Maggiore (high altar, and tomb of Bishop Girolamo Bencucci da Schio; with Pedemuro shop); (A)1536, Portal between Basilica and Palazzo del Podestà; Vicenza, Italy. (A)1537–1538, Villa Trissino (with Gian Giorgio Trissino and Sebastiano Serlio), Cricoli (Vicenza), Italy. c.1537–1542, Villa of Girolamo and Pietro Godi, Lonedo, Italy. 1539/1540–1542, Palace of Giovanni Giacomo and Pier Antonio Civena; 1540?–1545?, Palace of Monte Da Monte, Vicenza, Italy; c.1541–1543?, Villa of Giuseppe and Antonio Valmarana, Vigardolo, Italy. 1541–1547, 1550–1555, Villa of Taddeo Gazoto (after 1550 of Girolamo Grimani), Bertesina, Italy. 1542–1544, Villa of Vettor Pisani, Bagnolo, Italy. 1542/1546–1547/1548, Villa of Marc'Antonio and Adriano Thiene, Quinto Vicentino, Italy. 1542/1546–1551/1558, Palace of Marc'Antonio Thiene; *1543, Festival structures for entrance of Cardinal Bishop Nicolò Ridolfi; Vicenza, Italy. *1544–1554, 1561–1564, Villa of Leonardo Mocenigo, River Brenta, Dolo, Italy. 1544/1545–1555, Villa of Bonifacio Poiana, Poiana Maggiore, Italy. c.1545–1548?, Villa of Biagio Saraceno, Finale di Agugliaro, Italy. *(A)1546–1547, Santo Spirito in Sassia (baldachin for high altar), Rome. 1546/1549–1557, Palace of Girolamo Chiericati (not completed until c.1680), Vicenza, Italy. *(A)1546/1556–1559, Villa of Paolo Contarini, Piazzola sul Brenta, Italy. 1547–1550, 1565, Villa of Vincenzo Arnaldi (partially preserved), Meledo Alto, Italy. 1547/1548–1554, 1574–1584, Villa of Giovanni Chiericati, Vancimuglio, Italy. 1547/1549–1552, Palace of Giuseppe Porto, Vicenza, Italy. 1548, Villa of Giacomo Angarano (service wings), Angarano (Bassano), Italy. 1548/1549–1552, 1569–1570, Villa of Michele and Lodovico Caldogno, Caldogno, Italy. 1548/1549?–1553?, Villa of Marco Zen, Cessalto, Italy. 1549/1551, 1554–1558, Villa of Daniele and Marc'Antonio Barbaro, Maser, Italy. c.1549–1553, Villa of Nicolò and Alvise Foscari, Malcontenta (Gambarare), Italy. c.1549–1563, Palace of Giovanni Battista Della Torre, Verona, Italy. 1549–1580, Basilica (not completed until 1617), Vicenza, Italy. (A)1540s?, Villa of Girolamo Forni (?), Montecchio Precalcino, Italy. *1550–1552, Wooden bridge on River Cismone, Cismon del Grappa, Italy. c.1550–1552?, Palace of Floriano Antonini, Udine, Italy. 1551–1553, Villa of Zorzon Cornaro, Piombino Dese, Italy. 1552/1553–1555, Villa of Francesco Pisani, Montagnana, Italy. 1552/1553(?), 1565–1569, Villa of Marc'Antonio Sarego, Santa Sofia di Pedemonte (Verona), Italy. 1553–1576, Villa of Francesco and Lodovico Trissino, Meledo di Sarego, Italy. 1554?–1556, Villa of Francesco Thiene (only service building completed), Cicogna di Villafranca Padovana, Italy. *1555–1558, San Pantaleone (high altar), Venice, Italy. 1556, 1563, Arch in honor of Domenico Bollani, Udine, Italy. *1556?–1566, Villa of Francesco Ripeta, Campiglia, Italy. 1556/1557–1563, Villa of Francesco Badoer, Fratta Polesine, Italy. *(A)1557, *1558, Theatrical settings, Accademia Olimpica, Vicenza, Italy. (A)1557–1558, Palazzo Municipale (ground arcade), Feltre, Italy. 1557–1559, 1564–1574, Cathedral of Santa Maria Maggiore (drum and dome of apse), Vicenza, Italy. 1558–1561, House of Leonardo Mocenigo, Padua, Italy. 1559, 1569–1580, Stone bridge on River Tesina, Torri di Quartesolo, Italy. *1559–1561, Wooden bridge on River Bacchiglione, at Porta Santa Croce; 1559–1562, House of Pietro Cogollo; Vicenza, Italy; c.1559/1565–1567, Villa of Leonardo Emo, Fanzolo, Italy. 1560, 1563–1565, Almerico portal, Cathedral of Santa Maria Maggiore, Vicenza, Italy. *c.1560–1562, Villa of Leonardo Mocenigo, Marocco, Italy. 1560–1570, 1574, Monastery of Santa Maria della Carità; 1560–1580, Monastery of San Giorgio Maggiore, Venice, Italy. *1560/1561–1562, Theatrical settings, Basilica, Vicenza, Italy. *c.1560/1565, Santa Lucia (Mocenigo Chapel, not completed until 1592; nave built to Palladio's design 1609–1611), Venice, Italy. 1561/1562–1566/1569, Villa of Vettor Pisani, Bagnolo, Italy. 1561/1565–1566, Palace of Bernardo Schio (façade), Vicenza, Italy; 1562, 1564, Palazzo Municipale (windows), Brescia, Italy. *1562–1567/1569, Villa of Annibale Sarego, Miega di Cologna Veneta, Italy. c.1563–1566, Villa of Gian Francesco Valmarana (not completed until 1615), Lisiera di Bolzano Vicentino, Italy. 1564–1567, Villa of Federico and Antonio Maria Sarego (service court), Cucca (Veronella), Italy. 1564/1565, Palazzo Pretorio (executed by others 1565–1573, 1583–1586), Cividale del Friuli, Italy. *1565, Festival structures for entrance of Bishop Matteo Priuli, Vicenza, Italy. c.1565–1570?, San Francesco della Vigna (façade), Venice, Italy. 1565/1566–1569, Villa of Paolo Almerico (*La Rotonda;* not completed until after Palladio's death); 1565/1566–1571, Valmarana Palace; c.1565/1571–1572, Loggia del Capitaniato; Vicenza, Italy. 1568/1569–1570, Wooden bridge on River Brenta (since rebuilt), Bassano, Italy. *(A)1569/1570–1572/1575, Palace of Giulio and Guido Piovene, Vicenza, Italy. (A)1570–1572, Scuola dei Mercanti, Venice, Italy. 1570–1575, Palace of Montano Barbaran, Vicenza, Italy. 1571, Santa Maria della Celestia (cloister; executed by others), Venice, Italy. *1572, Harbor at Piazza dell'Isola, River Bacchiglione, Vicenza, Italy. 1572, Villa of Giuseppe Porto (unfinished), Molina di Malo, Italy. (A)1572–1577, Palace for Orazio and/or Francesco Thiene (completed in 1593 by Vicenzo Scamozzi), Vicenza, Italy. *1574, Arch and loggia for entrance of King Henry III of France; *1574/1575–1580, Ospedaletto di Santi Giovanni e Paolo; 1574–1580, Ducal Palace (reconstruction and interior decoration); Venice, Italy. 1575–1580?, Tomb of Brunoro Volpe, Santa Corona, Vicenza, Italy. 1575–1580, Stone bridge on River Guà, Montebello Vicentino, Italy. 1576–1580, Valmarana Tomb Chapel, Santa Corona (not completed until 1597); *1576, Wooden Circus (amphitheater) in Campo di Marte; Vicenza, Italy. 1576/1577–1580, Church of the Redeemer (not completed until 1591), Venice, Italy. *1578–1579, Sanctuary of the Madonna di Monte Berico (Altar for College of Notaries), Vicenza, Italy. 1579, Gemona Portal, San Daniele del Friuli, Italy. 1579/1580, Chapel of the Redeemer (Tempietto Barbaro, not completed until 1580–1584), Villa of Marc'Antonio Barbaro, Maser, Italy. 1580, Teatro Olimpico (not completed until 1580–1583 by Silla Palladio), Vicenza, Italy.

BIBLIOGRAPHY

ACKERMAN, JAMES S. (1966)1977 *Palladio.* 2d ed. Harmondsworth, England: Penguin.

BURNS, HOWARD (editor) 1975 *Andrea Palladio 1508–1580; The portico and the farmyard.* London:

Arts Council of Great Britain.

CEVESE, RENATO (editor) 1968– *Corpus Palladianum.* 20 vols. University Park: Pennsylvania State University Press.

HOWARD, DEBORAH 1980 "Four Centuries of Literature on Palladio." *Journal of the Society of Architectural Historians* 39, no. 3:224–241.

LEWIS, DOUGLAS 1981 *The Drawings of Andrea Palladio.* Washington: International Exhibitions Foundation.

LEWIS, DOUGLAS 1983? *The Villa Cornaro at Piombino Dese.* University Park: Pennsylvania State University Press. Forthcoming volume 9 in Cevese (1968–).

PALLADIO, ANDREA (1570)1965 *The Four Books of Andrea Palladio's Architecture.* With an introduction by Adolf K. Placzek. New York: Dover. Facsimile of the 1738 English edition.

PUPPI, LIONELLO (1973)1975 *Andrea Palladio.* Translated by Pearl Sanders. London and New York: Phaidon.

ZORZI, GIAN GIORGIO 1959 *I Disegne delle Antichità di Andrea Palladio.* Venice, Italy: Pozzi.

ZORZI, GIAN GIORGIO 1965 *Le Opere Pubbliche e i Palazzi Privati di Andrea Palladio.* Venice, Italy: Pozzi.

ZORZI, GIAN GIORGIO 1967 *Le Chiese e i Ponti di Andrea Palladio.* Venice, Italy: Pozzi.

ZORZI, GIAN GIORGIO 1969 *Le Ville e i Teatri di Andrea Palladio.* Venice, Italy: Pozzi.

PALLADIUS

Palladius Rutilius Taurus Aemilianus (4th century) was the author of a work on rural economy, including remarks on farm buildings, building materials, etcetera. Drawing extensively on the works of earlier authors, especially Varro, Columella, and to some extent VITRUVIUS, Palladius was one of those responsible for transmitting to later centuries the accumulated knowledge of antiquity, albeit in abridged form. His work was a characteristic product of those late antique circles which strove to maintain the attitudes of a prior age.

B. M. BOYLE

BIBLIOGRAPHY

PLOMMER, WILLIAM HUGH 1973 *Vitruvius and Later Roman Building Manuals.* Cambridge University Press.

SCHNEIDER, J. G. (editor) 1794–1797 *Scriptorum rei rusticae veterum Latinorum.* Leipzig: Fritsch.

PALMA, ANDREA

Andrea Palma (1664–1730) was born in Trapani, Italy. He worked as an architect and painter, and was closely associated with the architect GIACOMO AMATO some of whose designs Palma may have executed.

Palma's major extant works are the interior decoration of Santa Caterina in Palermo and the façade of the Syracuse cathedral (Santa Maria del Piliero o delle Colonne), both in Sicily. At Santa Caterina, Palma was specifically responsible for the decoration of the transept chapels and the lateral chapels, three on each side of the nave, and the splendid right transept altar. This decoration is in polychrome marbles and stucco whose richness and brilliance are outstanding yet not garish. The pilasters stand on high pedestals embellished with high reliefs in white and colored marbles. The arches leading to the chapels are decorated with stucco reliefs illustrating the life of Santa Caterina. The architecture, which is clearly visible, imposes order on the exuberant carving and color.

The new façade of the Syracuse cathedral was built between 1728 and 1754. It replaced the Norman front added to the cathedral, a Greek Doric temple of the fifth century B.C., which had been ruined in the 1693 earthquake. Blunt calls it "by far the most splendid piece of ecclesiastical architecture of the period in Syracuse" and "as an example of the Baroque use of broken masses to create depth and chiaroscuro . . . without equal in Sicily" (Blunt, 1968). While as entry to the simple interior it may be peculiar, the design is a good solution to the problem of combining the bell tower and the façade. The upper story, much taller than the roof of the nave, is a square belfry. The effect would have been more pleasant if the sides of the tower were covered by the façade decoration, as they seem naked at the present. This important elevation is of two orders of detached Corinthian columns which endow it with a great sense of movement.

MARTHA POLLAK

WORKS

1728–1754, Syracuse Cathedral (façade), Italy. n.d., Palazzo del Municipio (design of inscription recording coronation of Carlos III); n.d., Santa Caterina (altar of right transcept; decoration of lateral and transcept chapels); Palermo, Italy.

BIBLIOGRAPHY

ALAJMO, GIULIANA ALESSANDRO 1949 *Andrea Palma e la sconosciuta opera nella barocchia di S. Antonio Abate.* Palermo, Italy.

BLUNT, ANTHONY 1968 *Sicilian Baroque.* New York: Macmillan.

GANGI, GAETANO 1964 *Il Barocco nella Sicilia orientale.* Rome: DeLuca.

GOLZIO, VINCENZO (1950)1960 *Il Seicento e il Settecento.* 2d ed. Turin, Italy: Unione tipografico editrice torinese.

PALMER, JOHN

John Palmer (1785–1846) received his early training as a mason and later studied with WILLIAM ATKINSON. In 1813, he established a reputable practice in Manchester, England. As a leading ecclesiastical architect, Palmer was an exponent of the Gothic Revival. His antiquarian and archeological interests in English medieval architecture were evidenced by his work as a historian and restorer of the Collegiate Church of Manchester.

BRIAN LUKACHER

WORKS

1816–1818, Saints Mary and John, Pleasington; 1820, Saint Augustine's Chapel; 1820–1826, Saint Mary, Blackburn; Lancashire, England.

PANI, MARIO

The prolific career of Mario Pani (1911–) has been responsible for integrating twentieth-century principles of architecture and urbanism into the Mexican architectural heritage. Born in Mexico City, Pani studied in France and received a degree in architecture from the Ecole des Beaux-Arts in 1934. Returning to Mexico, he soon abandoned the Beaux-Arts approach for Bauhaus functionalism combined with the Mexican muralist movement, but Pani advocated the interaction of architecture with the visual arts instead of their integration. He teamed with the painter José Clemente Orozco to exemplify his idea in the design of the National Teacher's School (1945).

Housing Mexico's rising population has always been a major concern for Pani, and he introduced the reinforced concrete highrise as an answer to the high-density housing needs of Mexico City's marshy subsoil characteristics. In 1949, he designed Aleman, the first large multifamily apartment in Mexico, and in 1956 he innovated the co-ownership building "Reforma 369." The success of his housing projects, which stressed variety and durable materials, led to similar commissions throughout Mexico and Central America as well as the master plan for Mexico's university city.

Founder of the prestigious architectural magazine, *Arquitectura,* Pani remains one of the distinguished pioneers of modern Mexican architecture.

ELIZABETH D. HARRIS

WORKS

1936, Reforma Hotel; 1945, National Teacher's School; 1946, National Conservatory of Music; 1949, Aleman Housing Project; 1950, Department of Water Supplies; 1954, Satellite City; 1956, "Reforma 369" Condominium; Mexico City. 1970, Condesa del Mar Hotel, Acapulco, Mexico.

BIBLIOGRAPHY

Arquitectura Mexico. 1959 67, Sept.:entire issue.
CETTO, MAX L. 1967 *Modern Architecture in Mexico.* New York: Praeger. Originally published in German.

PAPPOS

Pappos of Alexandria (3rd–4th centuries), the last of the great ancient geometers, wrote a large collection on mathematical topics, including a book on mechanics. His compilation repeated much of the work of HERON of Alexandria, among others, along with the Hellenistic bias toward the formulation of mechanical and statical problems in geometrical terms. Although many of Pappos's writings were borrowed, sometimes verbatim, from earlier sources, the influence of his approach was felt for the next twelve hundred years of Western building history, much as the Ptolemaic system dominated Western astronomy during the same period.

B. M. BOYLE

BIBLIOGRAPHY

DRACHMANN, AAGE G. 1963 *The Mechanical Technology of Greek and Roman Antiquity.* Copenhagen: Munksgaard; London: Hafner; Madison: University of Wisconsin Press.

PAPWORTH, JOHN B.

John Buonarotti Papworth (1775–1847) was born in London, the son of a plasterer and builder. He himself arrived at architecture by way of drawing lessons from a sculptor and a topographical artist, a couple of years in the office of JOHN PLAW, a three-year apprenticeship to a builder, and a year with a firm of decorators. His "first efficient and active patron" was Sir James Wright, but most of his patrons and friends were ambitious self-made men or tradesmen and artists. Papworth himself was no mean artist, and from 1808 to 1810 he served as honorary secretary to the Associated Artists in Water-Colours. He contributed to the works of some of his artist friends and wrote a number of books of his own. By 1803, he was well enough established to take on his first pupil.

Papworth was a prolific architect, extensively employed also as a landscape gardener and town planner, and in these spheres his work is generally well within the mainstream of romantic classicism.

His inventiveness and amazing versatility are better seen in his many designs for art manufactures in which as early as 1805 he had shown an interest by becoming a member of the Society for the Encouragement of Arts, Manufactures and Commerce. He was early in the use of new materials and technologies and was considered something of an expert on shop fronts. In 1836, he was appointed part-time director of the short-lived Government School of Design.

A keen advocate of professionalism in his art, Papworth was a man of unflinching integrity, much sought after as an arbitrator. He was one of the twelve architects who attended the meeting held on July 2, 1834 that inaugurated the Royal Institute of British Architects to whose council he was appointed in 1835, 1836, and 1837 and whose vice-president he was in 1844 and 1845.

GEORGE MCHARDY

WORKS

1803–1840, Laleham House (works), Surrey, England. *1820–1846, Leigham Court (works), Streatham, London. 1825–1828, Lansdown Estate; 1825–1830, Montpellier Spa; Chelthenham, Gloucestershire, England. *1825–1830, Saint Bride's Avenue, London. *1828–1846, Little Grove (works), East Barnet, Hertfordshire, England. 1832, Church of All Saints, Chicklade, Wiltshire, England. 1839–1844, Basildon Park (works), Berkshire, England.

BIBLIOGRAPHY

PAPWORTH, JOHN BUONAROTTI 1803 *Essay on the Causes of the Dry Rot in Buildings.* London: The author.

PAPWORTH, JOHN BUONAROTTI (1818)1832 *Rural Residences, Consisting of a Series of Designs for Cottages, Decorated Cottages, Small Villas, and Other Ornamental Buildings.* 2d ed. London: Sedding & Tuttle.

PAPWORTH, JOHN BUONAROTTI 1823 *Hints on Ornamental Gardening: Consisting of a Series of Designs for Garden Buildings.* London: Ackermann.

PAPWORTH, JOHN BUONAROTTI 1835 "On the Benefits Resulting to the Manufactures of a Country from a Well Directed Cultivation of Architecture, and of the Art of Ornamental Design." *Transactions of the Royal Institute of British Architects* 1:111–114.

PAPWORTH, WYATT 1879 *J. B. Papworth, Architect to the King of Wurtemburg: A Brief Record of His Life and Works.* Privately printed.

PARENT, CLAUDE

Claude Parent (1923–) of France received his education in architecture as a function of his work with LE CORBUSIER, his encounters with artists in the 1950s, and his work on the journal *l'Architecture d'aujourd'hui.* His contact with Paul Virilio in 1964 resulted in the hypothesis of the *Fonction Oblique,* which became the dominant theme in Parent's work.

SUSAN STRAUSS

WORKS

1961–1968, Maison de l'Iran, France. 1963, Sainte Bernadette, Nevers, France. 1966, Commercial Center, Ris-Orangis, France. 1970, Commercial Center, Sens, France.

BIBLIOGRAPHY

COLLINS, GEORGE R. 1979 *Visionary Drawings of Architecture and Planning: 20th Century Through the 1960s.* Cambridge, Mass.: M.I.T. Press.

"C. Parent." 1966 *Aujourd'hui Art et Architecture* 10, no.54:33–46.

PARENT, CLAUDE 1970 *Vivre à l'Oblique, L'Aventure Urbaine.* Neuilly, France: The author.

PARENT, CLAUDE 1972 *Cinq Réflexions sur l'Architecture.* Nevers, France: Maison de la Culture.

RAGON, MICHEL 1978 Volume 3 in the *Histoire Mondiale de l'Architecture et de l'Urbanisme.* Tournai, Belgium: Casterman.

PARIGI, GIULIO, and PARIGI, ALFONSO

Giulio Parigi (1571–1635) and his eldest son, Alfonso Parigi (1606–1656), were Florentine architects and engineers to the Medici court during the first half of the *seicento.* Giulio studied with his great-uncle, BARTOLOMMEO AMMANNATI; his father, Alfonso di Santi Parigi; and the grand-ducal architect BERNARDO BUONTALENTI, whom Giulio succeeded in 1608. He headed the *Fabbriche* of Florence Cathedral (1621–1635), projecting a model for the façade (1630–1633).

Before becoming court architect, Giulio's fame derived from his landscape sketches, his Uffizi frescoes (1599), and his "academy" on Via Maggio, where he taught (c.1598–c.1629) geometry, perspective, draftsmanship, mechanics, and civil and military architecture to celebrated students, including Cosimo II. When Cosimo became grand duke, he engaged Parigi in numerous court theatricals and festivals. Parigi is best known today for his scenography and festival designs and for his influence on INIGO JONES, Jacques Callot, and Stefano della Bella.

Theatrical aspects can be seen in the few extant examples of his permanent architecture. His best known work, the side extensions to the Pitti Palace (1618–1635, probably on designs of Buontalenti), reflects his stage constructions. The Boboli Gardens, Isolotto (1617–1618), and Amphitheater (1630 and later) give evidence of his theatrical involvement; the Loggia del Grano (1619–1620) reveals scenographic qualities, as does the portico for the hospital of Santa Maria Nuova (1612–1618). Palazzo dell'Antella (1619–1620) in Piazza Santa Croce recalls temporary festival architecture with its frescoed façade (decorated by twelve artists in twenty days under Giovanni di San Giovanni). Parigi designed Villa Poggio Imperiale (and the Viale, 1622–1624) for Grand Duchess Maria Magdalena; not only was it used as a theatrical site (1625), its wings and fictive attic suggest perspective flats. Giulio restored San Lorenzo (1621) and numerous palazzi (including apartments in Palazzo Medici, 1632), building tenements, aqueducts, fountains, and so on, throughout Florence.

Alfonso executed many of Giulio's projects from 1625 to 1635; after Giulio's death, Alfonso completed the Pitti enlargement, the Boboli Gardens, the Amphitheater expansion (1652), and the façade of San Giovannino degli Scolopi (1656). The Parigis' architecture largely followed Buontalenti's late mannerist mode, never fully expressing the baroque.

Arthur R. Blumenthal

WORKS

c.1590–1595, former Convento delle Murate (*cloister and main chapel); 1593–1656, San Giovannino degli Scolopi (courtyard, convent, staircase, etc.; begun by Bartolomeo Ammannati; façade completed by Alfonso Parigi in 1656); c.1606, 1633, Cloister of Santo Spirito (portal and staircase?); 1612–1618, 1619–1624, Ospedale di Santa Maria Nuova (portico on the designs of Bernardo Buontalenti); 1617–1618 (and later), Boboli Gardens and Piazzale dell'Isolotto (with Alfonso Parigi later), Palazzo Pitti; 1618–1635, Palazzo Pitti (lateral additions [with Alfonso Parigi later] and piazza); 1619–1620, Loggia del Grano; 1619–1620, Palazzo dell'Antella (façade); 1621–1622 (and later), former Convento (Ospedale) dei Mendicanti; c.1622–?, *Convento della Crocetta and Palazzo della Crocetta (now the Museo Archeologico); 1622–1624 (and later), Villa Poggio Imperiale, and Viale (with Alfonso Parigi); 1630–1634 (and later), Amphitheater (with Alfonso Parigi), Palazzo Pitti; c.1635–1639 (and later), Cappella dei Parigi in San Felice in Piazza (by Alfonso Parigi on Giulio Parigi's designs); Florence.

BIBLIOGRAPHY

Baldinucci, Filippo (1681)1845–1847 Volume 3, pages 122–145; Volume 5, pages 52–56 in *Notizie dei professori del disegno da Cimbaue in qua. . . .* Edited by F. Ranalli. 5 vols. Florence: Batelli.

Berti, Luciano 1951 "Giulio e Alfonso Parigi." *Palladio* New Series 1:161–164.

Blumenthal, Arthur R. 1979 "Giulio Parigi and Baroque Stage Design." In volume 5 in *Acts of the XXIV International Congress of Art History.* Bologna, Italy: The congress.

Fanelli, Giovanni 1973 *Firenze: Architettura e città.* 2 vols. Florence: Valecchi.

Linnenkamp, Rolf 1958 "Giulio Parigi architetto." *Rivista d'arte* Series 3 8:51–63.

Povoledo, Elena 1960 "Parigi, Giulio; Parigi, Alfonso." Volume 7, columns 1675–1678 in *Enciclopedia dello Spettacolo.* Rome: Casa Editrice Le Maschere.

PÂRIS, PIERRE ADRIEN

Pierre Adrien Pâris (1745–1819), born in Besançon, moved to Paris in 1760 and studied architecture with Louis François Trouard. He won several competitions held by the Académie d'Architecture, and although he did not win the first prize, he traveled to Rome, where he lived for five years cultivating his taste through contact with the monuments of ancient and modern architecture. Charles de Wailly and the Abbé de Saint-Non employed him to draw views of southern Italy. Upon his return to Paris, he received such praise from the academicians for his drawings of Roman palaces and villas that he immediately received the commission for decorating the present Hôtel Crillon. Pâris was sent to Bordeaux to inspect the Grand Théâtre designed by his friend Victor Louis; this building inspired his never realized project for the prince-bishop of Basel in Porrentruy. One of his specialties was garden design, which was characterized by his use of English, French, and Roman styles. Pâris built the hospital in Bourg-en-Bresse, the Hôtel de Ville of Neuchâtel, Switzerland, and other works in the provinces. He was an intimate of Jean-Jacques Rousseau, with whom he shared ideas about nature.

As *dessinateur de la chambre et du cabinet du roi* (1778–1793), Pâris was associated with some of the last creations at Versailles, including a grand project for enlarging the château (1785), temporary structures for festivals and balls (1784–1787), meeting rooms for the notables and the Etats-Généraux (1787 and 1789), and decorations for royal theatricals. He experimented with a variety of styles for stage designs and brought out a taste for historicism and the exotic typical of the nineteenth century. In this, he anticipated his students Charles Percier and Pierre Fontaine, Jacques Ignace Hittorff, and even Eugène-Emmanuel Viollet-le-Duc. After having spent the years of the Empire in Rome, Pâris returned to Besançon, where he died in 1819 bequeathing his collections and drawings to the municipal library.

Alain Gruber

WORKS

1774, Hôtel Crillon, Paris. 1783, Hôtel de Ville, Neuchâtel, Switzerland. 1784–1789, Palais de Versailles (additions, temporary structures, meeting rooms, stage sets), France. 1785, Hospital, Bourg-en-Presse, France.

PARKER, BARRY

Born near Chesterfield, Derbyshire, England, R. Barry Parker (1867–1947) attended the South Kensington Art School in London (1886–1887). Following his apprenticeship to G. Faulkner Armitage, a Manchester architect, Parker moved to Buxton in 1895, where he started a practice with his half-cousin and brother-in-law RAYMOND UNWIN.

Designing houses in the tradition of WILLIAM MORRIS and CHARLES F. A. VOYSEY, Parker and Unwin obtained their first planning commission for the model village of New Earswick, which embodied the progressive ideas of EBENEZER HOWARD. In 1903, they won a competition to build the first Garden City at Letchworth, and in 1907 they undertook the development of Hamstead Garden Suburb, using octagonal and curvilinear planning layouts with cul-de-sacs and pedestrian parkways between buildings. Partners until 1914, they jointly published writings on design process and planning. Parker was the architectural designer preoccupied with the art of building small, nonuniform grouped houses while Unwin was the man of large-scale ideas. In 1918–1920, Parker oversaw the development of Pacaembu, a New Town near São Paulo, Brazil, and upon his return he was commissioned to plan Withershawe, a satellite city of 35,000 people near Manchester.

MARC DILET

WORKS

1895, Campbell Hyslop House, Church Stretton, Shropshire, England. 1902, New Earswick (master plan), near York, England. 1903, Center of Habitation, Letchworth Garden City, Hertfordshire, England. 1903, Homestead House, Chesterfield, Hertfordshire, England. 1903–1904, Goodfellow House (with Raymond Unwin), Clayton near Stoke, Stratfordshire, England. 1903–1904, Rockside Hydropathic Hotel, Matlock, Derbyshire, England. 1903–1904, Woodhead House (with Unwin), Chesterfield, Derbyshire, England. 1907–1908, W. E. Steers Home Hilltop, Whitehill, Caterham, Kent, England. 1907–1910, Hamstead Garden, near London. 1908, Stanley Parker Cottage; 1914, Aitken House (with Unwin); Letchworth, Hertfordshire, England. 1914–1916, Clock House Estate, West Grinstead, Sussex, England. 1920s–1941, Withershawe Estate, near Manchester, England. 1917, Pacaembu (urban planning), near São Paulo, Brazil.

BIBLIOGRAPHY

"Horizontality and Verticality in the Architectural Treatment of Town Planning Schemes." 1916 *Town Planning Journal* 7:136.

PARKER, BARRY, and UNWIN, RAYMOND 1901 *The Art of Building a Home.* London, New York, and Bombay: Longmans, Green.

PARKER, CHARLES

Charles Parker (1799–1881) was a pupil of Sir JEFFRY WYATVILLE and attended the drawing school of George Maddox. He then spent several years in Italy, setting up practice in London by 1826. He was steward and surveyor to the Bedford Estate in London (1859–1869). His few buildings were not important, but he had a great influence on the development of the Italianate style in England through his publication *Villa Rustica* in 1832. A second edition appeared in 1848. It contained ninety-three plates, "selected from Buildings and Scenes in the Vicinity of Rome and Florence and arranged for Lodges and Domestic Dwellings, with Plans and Details" and thus provided practical guidance on the adaptation of Italian forms for English use.

JILL FRANKLIN

WORKS

1829–1833, Hoare's Bank, Fleet Street, London. 1837–1838, Kimpton Church (west tower), Hampshire, England. c.1840, Stourhead House (portico added), Wiltshire, England. 1846–1847, Saint Raphael Roman Catholic Church, Kingston upon Thames, Surrey, England. 1850–1851, Christ Church and Vicarage, Saint Alban's, Hertfordshire, England.

BIBLIOGRAPHY

HUSSEY, CHRISTOPHER 1958 "Hoare's Bank, Fleet Street, E.C.4." *Country Life* 123:450–453.

"New Roman Catholic Church at Surbiton, Surrey." 1847 *The Builder* 5:602–603.

PARKER, CHARLES (1832)1848 *Villa Rustica.* 2d ed. London: Weale.

PARKER, JAMIESON KIRKWOOD

Born in Portland, Oregon, Jamieson Kirkwood Parker (1895–1939) was educated at Portland Academy and the University of Pennsylvania. Following service in World War I, he opened his architectural office in Portland. A talented, eclectic designer, he designed largely residential buildings except for two notable churches. In 1934, he became director of the Historic American Buildings Survey for the states of Oregon and Washington.

MARION DEAN ROSS

WORKS

1924, First Unitarian Church; 1924–1925, Saint Mark's Episcopal Church; Portland, Ore.

BIBLIOGRAPHY

VAUGHAN, THOMAS, and FERRIDAY, VIRGINIA GUEST

(editors) 1974 *Space, Style and Structure.* 2 vols. Portland: Oregon Historical Society.

Parker and Unwin. Design for a Hamlet from The Art of Building a Home.

PARKER and UNWIN

R. BARRY PARKER (1867–1947) and Raymond Unwin (1863–1940) made important and influential contributions to the design and layout of the small dwelling. Both were born in the North of England, and both obtained an early education in the South. They were second cousins, and in 1893 they became brothers-in-law. Both were Christian Socialists, involved with WILLIAM MORRIS's Socialist League—Unwin worked for a time for the League in Sheffield—and both were later members of the Fabian Society. Parker was a friend of the Manchester architect Edgar Wood, whose broad stylistic base had an important influence on the early development of the partners' work. Another influence appears to have been M. H. BAILLIE-SCOTT, whose use of the Shingle style device of the open central living area is repeated in Parker and Unwin's early houses. In their view, the working class cottage was not a shrunken house; it could have rooms that were spacious, though few, but they did introduce into it some of the luxuries of the larger house, such as the inglenook, to subdivide the larger spaces. Unwin had heard JOHN RUSKIN lecture, and he was fond of quoting him on his ideal of the clean, healthy cottage, with its own garden.

Unwin's architectural work began in the early 1890s with a design for a church in the village of Barrow Hill near Staveley, Derbyshire, for the Staveley Coal and Iron Company, to whom he had been apprenticed as an engineer. Parker designed the principal internal fittings. Unwin then went on to design miners' cottages, schools, and the other adjuncts of mining communities. In 1896, he left Staveley to join Parker in his new office at Buxton, Derbyshire. Their ensuing practice benefited from the setting up in the same year of the Northern Art Workers' Guild, through which they were able to obtain a variety of domestic craftwork. In their early years, apart from individual dwellings, they produced projects for cooperative dwellings for the northern cities of Bradford, York, and elsewhere, where they were able to turn their attention to the planned environment. In 1901, they published an illustrated book of lectures called *The Art of Building a Home,* in which some of the results are set forth. These early plans appear in part to have been interpretations of the village green traditions of the northeast of England. In 1901, they were given their first opportunity to design an actual village, at New Earswick, near York, for the Rowntrees. In 1903, they were invited to submit plans for Letchworth Garden City, Hertsfordshire, in a restricted competition, and their plans were adopted in 1904. They were ideally suited to realize EBENEZER HOWARD's diagrammatic visions for the Garden City. For their Hampstead Garden Suburb plan of 1905–1907, in order to incorporate such features as large front gardens and culs-de-sac, special exemptions from restrictive by-laws were obtained from Parliament. To Parker and Unwin, the cottage layout had priority over the road plan.

In 1906, Unwin moved to Hampstead near London, and the Buxton office was closed. Parker remained to oversee building in Letchworth, but the partners continued to undertake numerous domestic commissions. The partnership was formally dissolved in 1914 when Unwin became chief town planning inspector at the local government board. He was thus able to move in government circles at a time when important decisions were being made about the nature of postwar housing. Unwin's preferred low-density cottage development characterized a great deal of the housing of the interwar period. Parker continued in private practice and, like Unwin, gained an international reputation as a planner.

BRIAN HANSON

WORKS

R. BARRY PARKER

1895, Campbell Hyslop House, Church Stretton, Shropshire, England. 1903, Kildare Lodge, Minehead, Sommerset, England. 1913–1914, Clock House, Cowfold, Sussex, England.

RAYMOND UNWIN

1905–1907, Folk Hall; 1911–1912, Primary School; New Earswick, near York, England.

PARKER AND UNWIN

Completed 1895, Saint Andrew's Church, Barrow Hill,

near Staveley, Derbyshire, England. 1896, Macnair House, Hill Crest, Marple, Chesire, England. 1899–1902, C. F. Goodfellow House, Northwood, Staffordshire, England. 1903, E. R. Woodhead House, near Chesterfield, Derbyshire, England. 1903–1906, Cooperative Housing, Saint Botolph's Avenue, Sevenoaks, Kent, England. 1904, H. Vause House, Rugby, England. 1907, Oakdene, Rotherfield, Sussex, England. 1907–1909, Whirriestone, Rochdale, Lancashire, England. 1914, Aitken House, Letchworth, England.

BIBLIOGRAPHY

BATCHELOR, PETER 1969 "The Origin of the Garden City Concept of Urban Form." *Journal of the Society of Architectural Historians* 28:184–200.

CREESE, WALTER 1963 "Parker and Unwin: Architects of Totality." *Journal of the Society of Architectural Historians* 22:161–170.

CREESE, WALTER 1966 *The Search for Environment: The Garden City Before and After.* New Haven: Yale University Press.

CREESE, WALTER (editor) 1967 *The Legacy of Raymond Unwin: A Human Pattern for Planning.* Cambridge, Mass.: M.I.T. Press.

EVANS, PAUL 1976 "Raymond Unwin and the Municipalisation of the Garden City." Volume 1, pages 251–274 in *Transactions of the Martin Centre for Architectural and Urban Studies, University of Cambridge.* Cambridge: Wodehead-Faulkner.

HAWKES, DEAN 1976 "Garden Cities and New Methods of Construction: Raymond Unwin's Influence on English Housing Practice." Volume 1, pages 275–296 in *Transactions of the Martin Centre for Architectural and Urban Studies, University of Cambridge.* Cambridge: Wodehead-Faulkner.

HAWKES, DEAN 1978 "The Garden City Idea." *Architectural Review* 163, no. 976:325–332.

HAWKES, DEAN, and TAYLOR, NICHOLAS 1978 *Barry Parker and Raymond Unwin: Architects.* London: Architectural Association. Exhibition catalogue.

MINISTRY OF HEALTH 1918 *Housing Manual.* London.

PARKER, BARRY 1910–1912 "Modern Country Homes in England." *The Craftsman.* Series of 29 articles.

PARKER, BARRY 1940 "Sir Raymond Unwin." *Journal of the Royal Institute of British Architects* 47, no. 9:208–210.

PARKER, BARRY, and UNWIN, RAYMOND 1901 *The Art of Building a Home: A Collection of Lectures and Illustrations.* London: Longmans.

PEPPER, SIMON, and SWENARTON, MARK 1978 "Home Front: Garden Suburbs for Munitions Workers." *Architectural Review* 163, no. 796:366–375.

UNWIN, RAYMOND 1902 *Cottage Plans and Common Sense.* London: Fabian Society.

UNWIN, RAYMOND 1909 "Planning a Suburb and a Town." Pages 89–90 in *Town Planning and Modern Architecture at the Hampstead Garden Suburb.* London: T. Fisher Unwin.

UNWIN, RAYMOND (1909)1932 *Town Planning in Practice: An Introduction to the Art of Designing Cities and Suburbs.* 2d ed. New York: Century.

UNWIN, RAYMOND (1912*a*)1918 *Nothing Gained by Overcrowding: How the Garden City Type of Development May Benefit Both Owner and Occupier.* London: Garden Cities and Town Planning Association.

UNWIN, RAYMOND 1912*b* "The Town Extension Plan." Lecture 14 in *Warburton Lectures.* Manchester (England) University Press.

UNWIN, RAYMOND (1915)1919 *The Nations' New Houses.* London: Daily News.

UNWIN, RAYMOND 1924 "Higher Building in Relation to Town Planning." *Journal of the Royal Institute of British Architects* 31, no. 5:125–150.

UNWIN, RAYMOND 1925 *Methods of Decentralisation.* London.

PARLER FAMILY

The Parler family, which had its roots in Schwäbisch-Gmünd in Swabia, is typical of several closely related clans of masons whose dynamic building and consulting activities and far-flung networks of connections and communication influenced whole areas of Gothic architecture. Family-operated lodges were no rarity.

Throughout the fourteenth century the Parler (Parlerius, Parlercz, von Gmünd) family formed a tightly knit group of innovative masons working under the culturally very active Luxemburg dynasty. Their influence in architecture, sculpture, and the minor arts ranged from Basel to Prague and was felt to such an extent that the Parler family became legendary. In 1486, Matthäus Roriczer (see RORICZER FAMILY), Hanns Schmuttermeyer, and others mention the "Junker von Prag" as their ultimate authority. As late as 1565, the Parler brothers were shown as three riders on a medal whose face shows the famous north tower of the Minster in Strasbourg where Michael of Gmünd had worked for a few years after 1383.

Whereas in France gigantic architectural experiments had come to a close with the collapse of Beauvais in 1284, the great flowering of Gothic architecture within the German empire had just begun. From Kutna Hora to Vienna, Freiburg, Ulm, and even Milan, the sophisticated hall concept and the use of stairs and other necessary elements as potent decorative devices became identified with the Parler family. The angle hook template, which originally may have been Heinrich's mason's mark, indeed appears from the 1330s into the early fifteenth century on buildings, tombs, statuary, the Parler monstrance of 1512 in Prague, and seals, and it became synonymous with inventive quality.

The exemplary early studies of Neuwirth (1890*a*, 1890*b*, 1891) and Kletzl (1930–1931,

1931–1932, 1934) have recently been summarized in the massive five-volume catalogue of the 1978 Cologne exhibition *Die Parler und der Schöne Stil 1350–1400* (Legner, 1978–1980), in which B. Schock-Werner simplified and revised the complex family genealogy followed here with some readjustments. Johann, for instance, was almost certainly Peter's older brother and is listed first. We also added a new solution to the "Ulm group."

Heinrich Parler

Heinrich (c.1300–) was born possibly in Cologne where he worked at the cathedral as parlier (ballier, paleir, poleyr), that is as foreman in charge of the lodge and its equipment. The cathedral choir was completed in 1322 and the construction of other portions was pursued somewhat hesitantly. He therefore settled in Schwäbisch-Gmünd, where from around 1330 the nave of the large church of the Holy Cross was being replaced. In 1351 he is mentioned as "Magister hainricus architector"; he was in charge of construction and planning and his mason's mark is found in the nave. He may have planned the spacious hall choir, a concept foreign to France. Slender and widely spaced round piers let the room flow into the side aisles and ambulatory, and the total interior can therefore be grasped at a glance. This singular concept of space and especially the bold treatment of the internal choir buttresses, which double as thin chapel walls and permit the presentation of a taut external skin, indicate the authorship of a major talent. In spite of the fact that the choir was not completed until 1410–1414 and was ornamented with complex net vaults as late as 1521, Parler's diffusion of space still transfers an airy feeling of an ample prayer hall (78 meters) destined less for the clergy than for enlightened burghers. The choir served as a model for several churches and probably influenced Milan cathedral. Additionally, Heinrich may have helped to restructure the eastern choir of Augsburg Cathedral and probably provided designs for the Frauenkirche in Nuremberg and the Minster in Ulm. The open immediacy of his interiors, his engineering skills, his precision, and the dynamic "slurring" of usually rigid window tracery patterns through geometric fusion became the Parler hallmark and set high standards for competitors and successors.

Peter Parler

Peter (1330/1335–1399) was the most famous member of the family. Apprenticed by his father, he worked on the choir of the church of the Holy Cross in Schwäbisch-Gmünd. He probably worked in Cologne where he married the daughter of a mason. He also may have constructed the west

Heinrich Parler. Church of the Holy Cross (choir). Schwäbisch-Gmünd, Swabia. 1351?

wall and (parts of?) the nave of the Frauenkirche in Nuremberg in collaboration with his father. Called to Prague by Charles IV around 1350, he joined the lodge of Saint Vitus Cathedral whose architect, Matthias of Arras, died in 1352. He most likely took over construction in 1353; still under thirty, he was made master of the works between 1356–1358. Begun in 1344, the choir was somewhat antiquated French Gothic. Peter Parler completed the upper parts and the two western bays, giving the piers an oval section so as to give the arcades a wider appearance. He completed the triforium and window zone with a steely precision in 1386. A year earlier he had designed the famous, now destroyed, choir stalls. The triforium contains the celebrated busts showing, among the elite, *"Petrus henrici parleri de colonia (?) magister de Gemundem in Suevia secundus."* By that time he owned houses in both sections of Prague, was a juror, and had remarried. In all, he fathered five sons and two daughters. In 1370, he had undertaken the construction of the Church of All Saints on the Hračani, which echoed the Sainte Chapelle in Paris and was ornamented with semiprecious stones. He also was in charge of the choir of Saint Bartholomew's church at Kolin on the Elbe, which was completed in 1378 and is an expanded and more sophisticated version of the Schwäbisch-Gmünd solution. As an architect-engineer Peter constructed the Charles Bridge over the Moldavia river, which was begun in 1357 and was considered a marvel of technology. The massive tower entrance with its sophisticated net vault contains reliefs of Charles IV, Saint Vitus, and Wenceslas IV that were produced in his workshop. His chapel

PARLER FAMILY

- Heinrich
  Master
  Schwäbisch-Gmünd
  - Peter von Gmünd
    Master
    Saint Vitus, Prague
    - m. Elizabeth Agnes von Bur (second wife)
      - Janco
        Master
        Saint Mark, Zagreb
      - Daughter
        m.
        Michael of Cologne
        Mason
        Prague
        Son of Architect
        of Cologne Cathedral
      - Daughter
        m.
        Goldsmith
        Prague
    - m. Gertrud (first wife)
      - John the Younger
        Master
        Saint Vitus, Prague
        m.
        Catherine, daughter of
        Jesco of Kutná Hora
        - John III
          Mason
          Prague
      - Wenceslaus
        Master
        Cathedrals of
        Prague & Vienna
      - Nicolas
        Canon
        Prague
  - Michael Parler
    Mason
    Prague & Zlatá Koruna
  - Johann von Gmünd
    Master
    Freiburg & Basel
    - Henry II of
      Gmünd & Freiburg
      Architect,
      Marggrave of Mähren
      m.
      Drutginis, daughter of
      Michael of Savoy,
      Architect of
      Cologne Cathedral
    - Michael II of Gmünd
      Master
      Strasbourg

"Ulm Group"

- John the Younger
  Master
  Schwabisch-Gmünd
- Heinrich Vealiem
  Master
  Ulm Cathedral
  Son of John Sr.(?)
- Michael the Younger
  Master
  Ulm Cathedral
  Peter's brother or
  son of John Sr.(?)

of Saint Wenceslas, which flanks the south entrance of Saint Vitus and was completed in 1366, seems like a colossal cube and is covered by a vaulting system which, like none other, explains the Gothic quadrature. The decoration of the walls with highly polished, semiprecious stones that were supposed to replace the effect of stained glass, gives instead the impression of barbaric wealth. His technological genius became most apparent in the hanging keystone of the sacristy, completed in 1362, and in the clockwise and counterclockwise solution of the receding spiraling staircases over the south portal, which were completed in 1372 and which inspired the unequaled Strasbourg Cathedral spire design. As a sculptor Peter was responsible for the tomb of Pržemysl Ottokar I, possibly also that of Ottokar II, a tower reliquary in Saint Vitus, and perhaps a statue of Saint Zacharias in the Nuremberg Frauenkirche. He died on August 13, 1399, leaving a testament attesting to his wealth.

Johann von Gmünd

Johann, who used the Parler seal, was Heinrich's first son. He grew up in Prague where he was a respected juror. In the mid-fourteenth century he moved to Freiburg-im-Breisgau where in 1359 he became master of the works of the cathedral for life, proving that the Parlers had maintained close ties with southern Germany. In 1363, six years after the earthquake of Basel, he repaired the tower, choir, and vaults of the cathedral (consecrated 1363). He may also have worked as a consultant for the Cistercian abbey of Heiligenkreuz (after 1351).

Michael Parler the Elder

Heinrich's second son was a mason in Prague where he owned two houses. In 1359, he is mentioned in connection with the Cistercian abbey in Zlatá Koruna (Goldenkron) where he may have been responsible for the south portal and the fountain house. He may be the master of works who appears in Ulm in 1383.

Michael II of Gmünd

Michael was the son of Johann the Elder, was born in Freiburg, and used the Parler seal. Little is known of his early life. He became master of the works at the Minster in Strasbourg from at least June 18, 1383, until his death in 1387 or 1388. There he restored parts of the church damaged by fire in 1384. He may have changed ERWIN VON STEINBACH's plan of the façade, introducing strong horizontal elements. Most likely he also built the cantilevered floor of the great organ. He

Peter Parler. Charles Bridge. Prague. Begun 1357

may also have been a consultant for Freiburg and Ulm Cathedrals.

Henry II of Gmünd, also of Freiburg

Henry, the second son of Johann the Elder, probably worked in Augsburg and Vienna, and on the portal of Saint Peter of Cologne Cathedral. He owned a rente in Cologne and married Drutginis, daughter of the architect of Cologne Cathedral, Michael of Savoy. In 1373, he completed the refined and highly detailed figure of Saint Wenceslas for Saint Vitus in Prague, which bears the Parler emblem on its sockle. He was probably also responsible for two monumental tombs there.

In July 1381 Jodok, margrave of Mähren, hired him as his architect and probably also sculptor. From 1387–1391 he may have replaced his brother Michael II as master of Ulm Cathedral. If so, he was in Milan from November 1391 to May 1392 to advise the fabric on buttressing and over-all proportions. He must have died the same year.

The Sons of Peter Parler

Nicolas. Of Peter Parler's five sons, Nicolas is recorded as a canon of the cathedral in Prague in 1383. He died either in 1392 or 1397.

Wenceslaus. Wenceslaus (Wenzel, Wazlav), Peter Parler's second son, was born around 1360 and joined the cathedral lodge at a young age. He is mentioned as lathomus in 1375, and as lapicide in 1384 and 1388. He probably supervised work on the south tower of Saint Vitus and as temporary(?) *magister operis ecclesie pragensis* donated a chalice to the cathedral. In 1392 and 1397, he is again recorded as the architect in charge, only to be replaced by his younger brother John in 1398. It seems that both sons replaced their aging father whenever necessary. After his father's death in 1399, Wenceslaus probably left to work at Saint Stephen in Vienna where he is mentioned as master of the works in 1404. He most likely enlarged and began to rebuild the south tower. He is mentioned as a consultant for Gaming Cathedral in lower Austria, and in letters addressed to the *"Ingegnere de Praga Venceslao"* was invited by the cathedral administration of Milan as a consultant. He answered in 1403 listing his conditions, but the trip did not take place as he died a year later. He also had a reputation as a goldsmith.

John the Younger of Prague. John, Peter's third son, replaced his brother Wenceslaus and his ailing father as master of the works of Saint Vitus in 1398. He owned several houses in Prague, and in 1383 or 1389 married Catherine, daughter of Jesco of Kutná Hora. She gave him three sons, Wenzel, Benedict, and John. He continued construction of the south tower of Saint Vitus above the chapel level and completed parts of the south transept and pillars of the nave. In addition, he most likely participated in the second building campaign, which led to an enlargement of the extraordinary miners' church Saint Barbara in Kutná Hora, whose choir solution is related to that of Saint Batholomew in Kolin. He died in 1405 or 1406.

John III, son of John, and great-grandson of the venerable Heinrich, is recorded as a mason in Prague.

Janco Parler. Janco, the second son from Peter's second marriage to Agnes von Bur, was born in Prague in 1383. In 1415, he destined as one of his heirs Peter von Prachatitz, architect of Vienna Cathedral from 1404–1429. For this reason Janco has been connected with Vienna. It is more likely and in keeping with family policy of masons that his wife was related to the Vienna architect. In fact, Janco had moved to Zagreb, where he owned a house and sold a vineyard in 1431 and is mentioned as *"Janzlini lapidice dicti Parler, filius Petri de Praga"* (1430). He almost certainly was in charge of the construction of the church of Saint Mark. In 1442, Janco is mentioned together with a Wolfgangus Parler about whom nothing is known.

Peter's Two Daughters

Peter's first daughter married a goldsmith from Prague, and his second daughter married Michael of Cologne, who had worked as a mason in Prague since 1373 and may have been the son of Michael of Savoy, the architect of Cologne cathedral. Henry the Younger having married Drutginis, daughter of Michael of Savoy, the marriage of Peter's daughter with Michael's son would have strenghtened the ties to one of the centers of Gothic architecture. These professional marriages, which are just as common in other families of Gothic architects, clearly point to a conscious desire toward the formation of regular "masonic dynasties, the peripatetic nature of a mason's occupation and more generally, the close contact between families of builders."

The "Ulm Branch" of the Parler Family

B. Schock-Werner (Legner, 1978–1980) has postulated an Ulm branch of the Parlers. This is based on a tomb found under the northeast portal of the minster, which shows two masons' hammers and a large cross over the Parler coat of arms, and on a document of 1386–1387 which states *"von meister heinrich unseres werkmanns seligen wegen von meister michels und von meister hainrichs wegen der nu* [*nun?*] *bestellt worden ist zu dem werk."* Her Heinrich-Michael sequence has to be reversed. For Michael the Younger worked in Ulm from 1383 to 1387 followed by Heinrich von Ulm (1387 to 1391) who was succeeded by Ulrich von Ensingèn in 1392.

The identity of the Parlers of the Ulm branch can be resolved if we assume that Michael von Gmünd, alias von Freiburg, was the son of Johannes Parler the Elder who began his duties in Freiburg in 1383. He acted as consultant in several locations among them probably the nearby Ulm from 1383 when the choir had been provided with an emergency roof, to 1387 or 1388. Work in Ulm continued to procede slowly under Henricus de Gamonda who was Johannes the Elder's second son. He may have returned from Mähren to replace his brother. He thus would be identical with Henricus de Ulma who was called to Milan to check the proportions and the buttressing system of the cathedral from November 1391 through May 1392. He probably died shortly thereafter since he was replaced by Ulrich von Ensingèn the same year. The important west tower and the exceptional sculptural program in the nave which have been compared with other works of the Parlers would therefore be another important contribution of the ubiquitous clan.

François Bucher

BIBLIOGRAPHY

Hausherr, Reiner 1971 "Zu Auftrag, Programm und Büstenzyklus des Prager Domchores." *Zeitschrift für Kunstgeschichte* 34:21–46.

KLETZL, O. 1930–1931 "Die Grabsteine der Dombaumeister von Prag." *Zeitschrift für bildende Kunst* 64:175ff.

KLETZL, O. 1931–1932 "Die Wenzelstatue mit einem Parlerzeichen." *Zeitschrift für bildende Kunst* 65:136–155.

KLETZL, O. 1934 "Zur Identität der Dombaumeister Wenzel Parler von Prag und Wenzel von Wien." *Wiener Jahrbuch für Kunstgeschichte* 9:43ff.

KOTRBA, V. 1974 "Der Dom zu St. Veit in Prag." Pages 511–578 in F. Seibt (editor), *Bohemia Sacra: Das Christentum in Böhmen, 973–1973.* Düsseldorf, Germany: Pädagogischer Verlag Schwann.

LEGNER, ANTON (editor) 1978–1980 *Die Parler und der schöne Stil 1350–1400: Europäische Kunst unter den Luxemburgern.* 5 vols. Cologne, Germany: Museen der Stadt Köln. A superb work that renders most of the previous literature on the Parler family superfluous. Includes essays by B. Schock-Werner, H. Appuhn, Jaromír Homolka, G. Fehr, H. Kissling, Ulrike Jenni, and W. Müller.

MÁDL, K. B. 1898 "Der politische Bezirk Kolin." *Böhmische Topographie* 1:49ff.

NEUWIRTH, JOSEF 1890*a* "Die Prager Karlsbrücke und ihr Einsturz am 4. September 1890." *Repertorium für Kunstwissenschaft* 14:463–471.

NEUWIRTH, JOSEF 1890*b* *Die Wochenrechnungen und der Betrieb des Prager Dombaues in den Jahren 1372–1378.* Prague: Calve.

NEUWIRTH, JOSEF 1891 *Peter Parler von Gmünd.* Prague: Calve.

REINHARDT, H. 1941 "Johannes von Gmünd, Baumeister an den Münstern von Basel und Freiburg und sein Sohn Michael von Freiburg, Werkmeister am Strasburger Münster." *Zeitschrift für Schweizerische Archaeologie und Kunstgeschichte.* 3:138ff.

SWOBODE, KARL MARIA (1941)1943 *Peter Parler.* Vienna: Schroll.

PARNELL, CHARLES OCTAVIUS

Charles Octavius Parnell (?–1865/1866), about whose life very little is known, was architect to the London and County Banking Company, building their London office in 1860–1861 and using steel girder construction on the upper floors. Otherwise, he specialized in club buildings, winning the second competition for the Army and Navy Club, Pall Mall, in 1847 in partnership with Alfred Smith. The bank and clubs were in a so-called florid Italian palazzo style that owed much to sixteenth-century Venetian architecture, especially that of JACOPO SANSOVINO.

JILL FRANKLIN

WORKS

*1848–1851, Army and Navy Club (with Alfred Smith), Pall Mall, London. c.1854, Palatine Club, 7 Bold Street, Liverpool, England. *1860–1861, London and County Bank, 21–23 Lombard Street; 1863–1864, Victoria Sporting Club, Endell Street; 1864–1866, Whitehall Club (completed by Charles Jocelyn Parker after his father's death), 47 Parliament Street; London.

BIBLIOGRAPHY

"The Army and Navy Club House, Pall Mall." 1851 *The Builder* 9:153–155.

"Ceiling Decorations: Army and Navy Club-house." 1851 *The Builder* 9:250.

Civil Engineer and Architects Journal 1851 14:373, plate 13.

"London and County Bank, Lombard Street." 1862 *The Builder* 20:604–605.

"Panel, Army and Navy Club." 1851 *The Builder* 9:298.

The Parish of Saint James, Westminster. 1960 Volumes 29–30 in F. H. W. Sheppard (editor), *The Survey of London.* London: Athlone.

"Proposed Army and Navy Club-house." 1847 *The Builder* 5:518–520.

"The Whitehall Club, Parliament Street, Westminster." 1866 *The Builder* 24:742–743.

PARRIS, ALEXANDER

A builder-architect, Alexander Parris (1780–1852) began in the Adamesque tradition and matured in neoclassicism. Skillful adaptation of a building to particular requirements and the use of massive masonry characterize his work.

Shortly after Parris's birth, November 24, 1780, in Hebron, Maine, his family moved to Pembroke, Massachusetts, where he was educated and apprenticed to a carpenter. He died there on June 15, 1852. A notebook of drawings, begun in 1805 in Portland, Maine, shows his early repertoire of Federal building types in designs for houses, a bank, and a church. The notebook also includes drawings of the Governor's Residence (1811–1812) in Richmond, Virginia, its broad proportions of a southern taste contrasting with the taller New England blocks with their attenuated orders.

During the War of 1812, Parris served with engineers and after the war, in 1815, he settled in Boston where among his first commissions was the David Sears House (1816). Built of Chelmsford granite and later given a third story and doubled in length, this house is composed of neoclassical forms in its smooth-surfaced block with a large semicylindrical projection on the façade. To take advantage of the site, Parris set the entrance on the east side, stretched the hall across the house, and lined the main rooms along the south, or street front.

Parris did major work in masonry as construction supervisor of CHARLES BULFINCH's Massachu-

Parris.
Faneuil Hall (Quincy) Market.
Boston.
1823–1826

setts General Hospital (1818–1823). With Saint Paul's Church (1819–1821), Boston, and the Stone Temple (1828), Quincy, Massachusetts, however, Parris moved to a full neoclassical idiom, in the former employing an Ionic temple front and in the latter translating the WREN–GIBBS–BULFINCH formula into simple geometric shapes in granite.

Classic Revival forms joined monumental masonry in the Quincy Market (1823–1826), Boston, as part of an important urban development. Located east of John Smibert's brick Faneuil Hall (1740–1742); enlarged 1805–1806 by Bulfinch), the 535-foot long building has a tetrastyle Doric front at either end and a large central dome; a rhythmic articulation of the two-story wall surfaces derives from the unframed openings created by monolithic posts and lintels of Quincy granite. The novel employment on the interior of cast iron for fireproof support is one of the earliest examples of its kind in the country. Parallel to Quincy Market and separated by broad avenues, Parris's North and South Market Buildings (1827–1840s) show similar uniform, undecorated fronts.

Parris's extensive professional activity included participation in the first efforts to organize in 1836 the American Institution of Architects (later the American Institute of Architects). He worked closely with SOLOMON WILLARD and ISAIAH ROGERS, all three proponents of construction in granite. Other associates included RICHARD UPJOHN and AMMI B. YOUNG. Unstudied tradition attributes to Parris many works of an engineering nature, such as the dry dock and sea walls (1819–1829) of the Charlestown Navy Yard and Harbor, in Boston, done with Loammi Baldwin. In 1848 he was appointed civil engineer in charge of the Navy Yard in Portsmouth, New Hampshire.

Parris was a member of the generation faced with the demands of a rapidly growing country for structures of greater size, economical yet durable construction, and increasing complexity in functional requirements.

ROBERT L. ALEXANDER

WORKS

1805, Hunnewell-Shepley House; 1807–1808, W. P. Preble House; before 1812, McClellan-Sweat House (now part of the Portland Museum of Art); Portland, Maine. 1811–1812, Governor's Residence, Richmond, Va. 1816, David Sears House (now enlarged as the Somerset Club); 1819–1821, Saint Paul's Church (now Episcopal Cathedral); 1819–1829, Charlestown Navy Yard and Harbor (dry dock and sea walls); 1823–1826, Faneuil Hall (Quincy) Market; 1827–1840s, North and South Market Buildings; Boston. 1828, Unitarian Church (Stone Temple), Quincy, Mass.

BIBLIOGRAPHY

A manuscript notebook, begun by Parris in 1805 in Portland, Maine, is available in the library of the Boston Athenæum.

BRYAN, JOHN MORRILL 1972 "Boston's Granite Architecture, c.1810–1860." Unpublished Ph.D. dissertation, Boston University.

HAMLIN, TALBOT 1944 *Greek Revival Architecture in America.* New York: Oxford University Press.

HUXTABLE, ADA LOUISE 1958 "Quincy Market—1825–1826." *Progressive Architecture* 39:149–152.

KILHAM, WALTER H., JR. 1946 *Boston After Bulfinch: An Account of Its Architecture, 1800–1900.* Cambridge, Mass.: Harvard University Press.

KIMBALL, FISKE (1922)1966 *Domestic Architecture of the American Colonies and of the Early Republic.* Re-

print. New York: Dover.
KIRKER, HAROLD 1969 *The Architecture of Charles Bulfinch.* Cambridge, Mass.: Harvard University Press.
PIERSON, WILLIAM H., JR. 1970 *The Colonial and Neoclassical Styles.* Volume 1 of *American Buildings and Their Architects.* Garden City, N.Y.: Doubleday.
QUINCY, JOSIAH 1852 *A Municipal History of the Town and City of Boston.* Boston: Little Brown.

PASCAL, JEAN LOUIS

Born in Paris, Jean Louis Pascal (1837–1920) entered the Ecole des Beaux-Arts in 1855, where he studied under E. Gilbert and CHARLES AUGUSTE QUESTEL, winning the Grand Prix in 1866. He worked for three years for CHARLES GARNIER on the Opera, and, in 1870, for HENRI LABROUSTE. He took over Questel's atelier in 1872, and taught until his death, a favorite for students from England where he was awarded the Gold Medal of the Royal Institute of British Architects in 1914.

R. D. MIDDLETON

WORKS

1868, A. W. Bouguereau House and Studio, 75 rue Notre Dame des Champs; 1876–1877, Monument to Henri Regnault (with Ernest Georges Coquart, H. M. A. Chapu and C. J. M. Degeorge), Cour du Mûrier, Ecole des Beaux-Arts, rue Bonaparte; *1877, Pavillon des Colonies Portugaises, Exposition Universelle 1878; 1878–1881, Bibliothèque Nationale (manuscript and periodical stack rooms on the rue Colbert); 1879–1881, Hôtel Königswarter, 12 rue de Prony; 1880–1882, Apartment Block, 105 rue Notre Dame des Champs; Paris. 1880–1888, Faculté de Medicine et de Pharmacie, Place de la Victorire, Bordeaux, Gironde, France. 1881–1882, Jules Michelet Tomb, Père Lachaise Cemetery, Paris. 1882, Mairie and School, Ablon, Seine et Oise, France. 1882, Chapelle de la Vierge (decoration with A. W. Bouguereau), Saint Louis, La Rochelle, Charente Maritime, France. 1883–1884, Apartment Block, 197 Boulevard Saint Germain; 1883–1884, Konigswater Tomb, Nord Cemetery; 1883–1884, House (at rear), 14 rue de l'Université; 1888, House, 20 rue de la Petite Voie, Porte de Vanves; 1889, Hôtel Bureau, 76 or 78 Boulevard de Courcelles; 1902, Monument to Charles Garnier (with Jules Thomas), rue Auber; 1902, Monument to E. M. L. and R. M. Y. Hatte de Chevilly, Nôtre Dame de Consolation; 1906–1917, Bibliothèque Nationale (periodicals and manuscript stack rooms on the rue Vivienne; periodicals reading room; with Alfred H. Recoura); Paris. Before 1908, Château du Doux, Altilliac near Beaulieu-sur-Ménoire, Corrèze, France. n.d., Banque de France (refurbishing of the Salle Ventadour), Paris. n.d., Cathedral (extensions and restoration), Avignon, Vaucluse, France. n.d., Château de Maubisson, Clairefontaine, Yvelines, France. n.d., Estragnat Tomb, Montparnasse Cemetery; House, Boulevard Flandrin; Paris. n.d., Monument to Colonel d'Argy, San Luigi dei Francesi, Rome. n.d., Léon Bazile Perrault House, 43 Boulevard de la Croisette, Cannes, Alpes Maritimes, France. n.d., Theater, Place de la Liberté, Valence, Drome, France. n.d., Villa Renouard, Pau, Basse Pyrénees, France.

BIBLIOGRAPHY

BLOMFIELD, REGINALD; BURNET, JOHN; and PASCAL, JEAN LOUIS 1914 "The Royal Gold Medal 1914." *Journal of the Royal Institute of British Architects* 21:543–544.
BURNET, JOHN J. 1920 "Jean-Louis Pascal." *Journal of 1920 Institut de France. Académie des Beaux-Arts:*
FLAMENG, FRANÇOIS, and LALOUX, VICTOR A. F. 1920 *Institute de France. Académie des Beaux-Arts: Funérailles de M. J. L. Pascal.* Paris: Firmin-Didot.
FORMIGÉ, JEAN 1921 *Institut de France. Académie des Beaux-Arts: Notice sur la vie et les travaux de M. Jean-Louis Pascal. 4 Juin 1837–16 Mai 1920.* Paris: Firmin-Didot.
WIDOR, CHARLES MARIE 1920 *Institut de France. Académie des Beaux-Arts: Notice sur la vie et les travaux de M. Jean-Louis Pascal. 4 Juin 1837–16 Mai 1920.* Paris: Firmin-Didot.

PASSANTI, MARIO

Mario Passanti (1901–1975), architect and architectural historian, was born in Argentina and died in Turin, Italy. Passanti's architecture is modest, direct, and simple, disclosing an awareness of the tenets of Italian rationalism but also an appreciation of the quality of materials, subtlety of light, and potential of technology. He was an influential teacher and persuasive historian, focusing on the architecture of the seventeenth and eighteenth centuries, GUARINO GUARINI, and the urban development of Turin. In 1968, he was asked to determine the criteria for building in the historic center of Turin.

HENRY A. MILLON

WORKS

1935, Piedmont Pavilion, Italia '61 Exposition, Turin, Italy. 1947, Café, Sestriere, Italy. 1948, School (with Perona), Moncalieri, Italy. 1952, Housing (with Giovanni Astengo, Molli, Nello Renacco, and Rizzotti), Torino-Falchera, Turin, Italy. 1955, Electric Power Plant (with Ceresa and Gino Levi-Montalcini), Chivasso, Italy. 1955–1961, Provincial Administration Building (with G. Schiavinato), Asti, Italy. 1957, Technical Offices of Turin (with Perona and Barbaccio), Italy.

BIBLIOGRAPHY

PASSANTI, MARIO 1945 *Architettura in Piemonte.* Turin, Italy: Libreria Tecnica.
PASSANTI, MARIO 1963 *Nel Mondo Magico di Guarino Guarini.* Turin, Italy: Toso.

PASSANTI, MARIO 1966 *Genesi e comprensione dell'opera architettomia.* Turin, Italy.
PASSANTI, MARIO (1966)1970 *Lo Sviluppo urbanistico di Torino.* Turin, Italy: Quaderni di studio.
North Carolina State Capitol. Raleigh, N.C.: Uzzell.
SANDERS, JOHN L. 1979 "David Paton." In W. S. Powell (editor), *Dictionary of North Carolina Biography.* Chapel Hill: University of North Carolina Press.

PASTERNAK, A.

A. Pasternak (20th century), brother of the author Boris Pasternak, was born and worked in Russia. He belonged to the Union of Contemporary Architects, the Constructivists who promoted Modern architecture in the Soviet Union. The Constructivists thought of architecture as a "social condenser" favoring new forms of collective living. Pasternak is known for his participation in the competition for a resort city near Moscow, the Green Town (1929), in association with MOISEI YAKOVLEVICH GINSBURG. This project was an illustration of the theories of the "Deurbanists" who stood for a total decentralization of industry and housing. He also belonged to the team which in 1928 studied new housing forms for the Committee for Construction of the Soviet Union.

ANATOLE KOPP

WORKS

1928–1929, Sovnarkom Apartment Building, Sverdlovsk, Russia. 1929, Communal House, Gogol Boulevard (with M. BARCHTCH), Moscow.

BIBLIOGRAPHY

KOPP, ANATOLE (1967) 1970 *Town and Revolution.* Translated by Thomas Burton. New York: Braziller.

PATON, DAVID

David Paton (1801–1882) was born in Edinburgh and was trained by his father, John Paton, and by Sir JOHN SOANE (1829–1830). He came to America in 1833 and in 1834 became clerk of the works on the Greek Revival North Carolina State Capitol at Raleigh (1833–1840) under TOWN AND DAVIS, whom he succeeded as supervising architect (1835–1840). Paton returned to Edinburgh, then came back to the United States in 1849, and spent the rest of his active life teaching architectural drafting in Brooklyn, New York. The North Carolina State Capitol is his only known surviving American architectural work.

JOHN L. SANDERS

WORK

1833–1840, State Capitol (with Town and Davis), Raleigh, N.C.

BIBLIOGRAPHY

ASHE, SAMUEL A. 1909 *David Paton, Architect of the*

PATTE, PIERRE

Irascible, arrogant, and often right, Pierre Patte (1723–1814) fashioned a career based not on distinguished buildings or membership in the Academy of Architecture, but rather on his professional activity as a writer, editor, compiler, and technical critic. He had a strong attachment to order, precision, and honesty. Born in Paris, he studied at the Academy of Architecture, in the atelier of M. Camus, from 1745 to 1749. He traveled in Italy, England, throughout France, and presumably in the German Rhineland as the architect for the duke of Zweibrücken. His built work is not extensive, but it includes a church at Bolbec, France (1776–1784); work for his patron, Zweibrücken, in Paris and in Germany, including a hunting lodge, Schloss Jägersberg (1767), at Petersheim. The appearance of the work is adequate, reinforcing Patte's own admission of greater interest in structure, material, and technical matters other than decoration.

His writing extended over many years and topics. As an editor, he completed the *Cours d'architecture* by JACQUES FRANÇOIS BLONDEL following his friend's death, contributing most of the text of the final two volumes on materials and techniques, as well as most of the accompanying volume of plates. As a compiler, his most important work was the *Monuments érigés en France à la gloire de Louis XV* (1765), which included a plate illustrating the proposals for a royal square in Paris in which the various solutions are imposed on the plan of the city, suggesting a high level of urban design and embellishment. This tactic of compiling a series of similar projects and buildings and then analyzing them was also used in his *Essai sur l'architecture théâtrale* (1782). Beyond objectifying his criteria more than was usually the case, Patte also provided his readers with an opportunity to study a wide range of solutions to develop their own judgments through comparative analysis. As a critic he attacked plagiarism, duplicity, unsound structural proposals, and bad taste. Patte divided architecture into components and purposely sought to study those problems which would provide rationally correct solutions. Questions of ornament and proportion were rejected because they were, he believed, ultimately based on taste, which was not liable to rational resolution.

His career demonstrated the growing possibilities other than building open to architects. He had an important impact on architectural development in Paris through the influence of the printed word. His critical and analytical skills enabled him to identify defects and propose correct solutions to difficult technical problems.

KEVIN HARRINGTON

WORKS

1763, Hôtel de Ville (decoration of Salon), Grenoble, France. c.1764, Duc de Charost House (now the British Embassy); 1767, Duke of Zweibrücken House (decoration), Rue Saint Augustin; Paris. 1767, Schloss Jägersberg, Petersheim, Germany. 1776–1784, Church, Bolbec, Normandy, France.

BIBLIOGRAPHY

BOFFRAND, GERMAIN 1753 *Oeuvres d'architecture.* Edited by Pierre Patte. Paris: The editor.

BLONDEL, JACQUES FRANÇOIS 1777 *Cours d'architecture.* Edited and completed by Pierre Patte. Paris: Desaint.

GALLET, MICHEL 1972 *Stately Mansions: Eighteenth Century Paris Architecture.* Translated by James Palmes. New York: Praeger.

MATHIEU, MAE 1940 *Pierre Patte: Sa vie et son oeuvre.* Paris: Presses universitaires de France.

PATTE, PIERRE 1754*a* *Abrégé de la vie de Boffrand.* Paris: Quillan.

PATTE, PIERRE 1754*b* *Discours sur l'architecture.* Paris: Quillan.

PATTE, PIERRE 1755*a* *Etudes d'architecture.* Paris: The author.

PATTE, PIERRE 1755*b* "Observations sur la manière dont sont décorés les extérieurs de nos églises." *Mercure de France* May:135–143.

PATTE, PIERRE (editor) 1759 *Mémoires de Charles Perrault.* Avignon, France.

PATTE, PIERRE 1760 "Lettre . . . à M. Fréron." *L'Année Littéraire* 1:246–257.

PATTE, PIERRE (1765)1767 *Monuments érigés en France à la gloire de Louis XV.* 2d ed. Paris: Rozet.

PATTE, PIERRE 1766 *De la manière la plus advantageuse d'éclairer les rues.* Amsterdam.

PATTE, PIERRE 1767 *Mémoire sur l'achèvement du grand portail de Sainte Sulpice.* Paris: Gueffire.

PATTE, PIERRE 1769 *Mémoires sur les objets les plus important de l'architecture.* Paris: Rozet.

PATTE, PIERRE 1770 *Mémoires sur la construction de la coupole projetée pour couronner la nouvelle église de Sainte Geneviève.* Amsterdam: Gheffler.

PATTE, PIERRE 1772 "Lettre . . . sur la poussée des voûtes." *Mercure de France* Apr.:183.

PATTE, PIERRE 1780 *Description du théâtre de la ville de Vicence en Italie chef d'oeuvre d'André Palladio.* Paris: The author.

PATTE, PIERRE 1782 *Essai sur l'architecture théâtrale.* Paris: Moutard.

PATTE, PIERRE 1801 *Mémoires qui intéressent particulièrement Paris.* Paris: Bertrand.

PATTE, PIERRE (1801–1802)1802–1803 *Veritables jouissances d'un être raisonnable vers son déclin.* 2d ed., rev. Paris: Langlois.

RIBART, CHARLES F. 1758 *Architecture singulaire, l'éléphant triomphal, grand kiosque à la gloire du roi.* Edited by Pierre Patte. Paris: The editor.

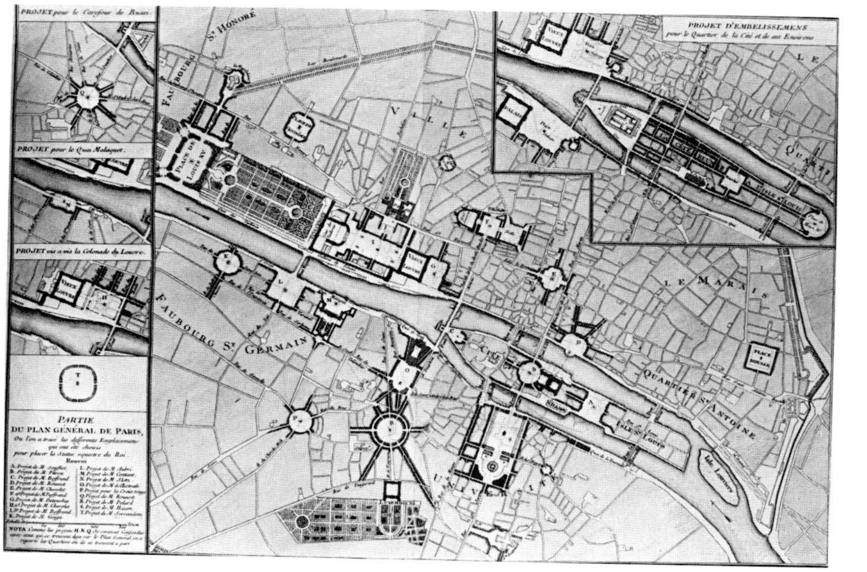

Patte.
Plan of Paris from Monuments érigés en France à la gloire de Louis XV.

PATY, THOMAS

Thomas Paty (1712/1713–1789) was the most talented of a family that dominated Bristol architecture throughout the eighteenth century, and a superlative carver in wood and stone. He planned and designed Park Street (1761–c.1790), which led to the development of Clifton and was responsible for the reordering of the city center. Paty was an able provincial with the tact and knowledge to use JAMES GIBBS's and ISAAC WARE's pattern books intelligently and enough freshness to give the national style a local flavor.

ANDOR GOMME

WORKS

1740, Redland Chapel (carving); 1743, The Exchange (carving); 1761, The Royal Fort (carving); 1761–c.1790, Park Street; 1762–1763, Albemarle Row; 1763–1769, Saint Nicholas' Church (steeple); 1764–1766, Theatre Royal; *1766–c.1775, Bridge Street, Dolphin Street, Union Street; 1766–1786, Brunswick Square; *1775, Saint James' Market; 1775–1777, Saint Michael's Church; Bristol, England. 1776–1780, Town Hall, Wells, England. 1784–1788, Royal Infirmary; 1787–1789, Berkeley Square (not completed until c.1795); Bristol, England.

BIBLIOGRAPHY

GOMME, ANDOR; JENNER, MICHAEL; and LITTLE, BRYAN 1979 *Bristol: An Architectural History.* London: Lund Humphries.

ISON, WALTER WILLIAM 1952 *The Georgian Buildings of Bristol.* London: Faber.

PAUL, BRUNO

Bruno Paul (1874–1968) was an important designer member of the German *Werkbund,* organized in 1907 to raise the standards of architecture and applied design. Paul made a great contribution with his *Typen-Möbel,* furniture that embodied the most elegant style possible through machine production. LE CORBUSIER's own concept of the *objet type* no doubt reflects his contact with Paul and the *Werkbund* in 1910 and his enthusiasm about the German achievement in standardization. Paul's furniture style can be called both "neo-Biedermeyer" because it is historicizing, and "modern" because historical antecedents are formally reduced. Paul directed the Berlin Kunstgewerbeschule in 1906. His architecture developed from a pastiche of Italian Renaissance, moderate *Jugendstil,* Art Deco, and the International style.

JAMES WARD

WORKS

1900, Jugenstil Hunting Room, Paris Exposition Universelle. 1907, Lloyd-Dampfer *S.S. Kronprinzessin Cecelie* (interiors). Before 1909, Hainerberg House, near Konigstein am Taunus, Germany. Before 1909, Pützschen Sanitorium, near Bonn. 1914, Asiatische Museum (later altered), Dahlem, Berlin. 1914, German *Werkbund* Exhibition Buildings, Cologne, Germany. 1925, Das Plattenhaus, Hellerau, Germany. 1929–1930, Kathereinerhochhaus, Kleistpark, Berlin. 1935, Traub House, near Prague.

BIBLIOGRAPHY

"Bruno Paul 19-1-1874—17-8-1968." 1974 *Bauwelt* 65, no. 4:138.

CAMPBELL, JOAN 1978 *The German Werkbund: The Politics of Reform in the Applied Arts.* N.J.: Princeton University Press.

Der Verkehr: Jahrbuch des Deutschen Werkbundes. 1914 Jena, Germany: Diederichs.

GÜNTHER, SONJA 1971 *Interieurs um 1900: Bernhard Pankok, Bruno Paul, und Richard Riemerschmid als Mitarbeiter der Vereinigten Werkstätten für Kunst im Handwerk.* Munich: W. Fink.

KALKSCHMIDT, EUGEN 1925 "Die deutsche Verkehrs-Ausstellung München und die Jahresschau deutscher Arbeit Dresden, 1925." *Der Baumeister* 23, no. 9:73–81.

PAULSEN, FRIEDRICH 1916 "Die unglückliche Liebe der Architekten." *Der Baumeister* 14, no. 12:89–96.

PLATZ, GUSTAV ADOLF (1927)1930 *Die Baukunst der Neuesten Zeit.* 2d ed. Berlin: Propyläen.

POPP, JOSEPH 1916 *Bruno Paul.* Munich: Bruckmann.

STAHL, FRITZ 1914–1915 "Die Architektur der Werkbund-Ausstellung." *Wasmuths Monatschefte für Baukunst* 1:153–204.

"Verwaltungsgebäude Kathreiner A.-G., am Kleistpark." 1931 *Die Bauwelt* 22, no. 19:5.

PAXTON, JOSEPH

Joseph Paxton (1803–1865), best known as the designer of the Crystal Palace, was born into a farming family in Milton Bryan near Woburn, England. At fifteen, he was hired as a garden-boy at Battlesden, Bedfordshire. By 1823, he was working in the gardens at Chiswick, which were then leased by the Horticultural Society from the duke of Devonshire. While at Chiswick, Paxton made the acquaintance of the duke, who brought him to Chatsworth as head gardener in 1826. Paxton remained at Chatsworth for over thirty years, working in horticulture, forestry, and architecture.

As a self-educated landscape designer and botanist, Paxton was influenced by late eighteenth-century writers, notably John Claudius Loudon and RICHARD PAYNE KNIGHT. He published several periodicals, including *The Horticultural Register* (1831–1835) and *Paxton's Magazine of Botany and Flowering Plants* (1834–1849), and was an avid writer on a variety of scientific subjects.

At Chatsworth, Paxton constructed a number of picturesque novelties for the duke's pleasure garden, including an aqueduct and a waterfall. In 1831, he also began building greenhouses. The earliest were conventional in construction, but Paxton soon adopted the use of the ridge-and-furrow roof, a structural system which had been illustrated by Loudon in 1817 but had never been executed. In the zig-zag configuration of this roof type, the long glass panes were "fixed in angles" and thus took best advantage of the sun's shifting rays. Paxton was able to patent his improved version of the system in 1850.

Paxton's greenhouse innovations reached public notice with the building of the Great Conservatory at Chatsworth (1836–1840). The "Great Stove" was constructed to house the duke's collection of large exotic plants; at 277 feet long, 123 feet wide, and 67 feet high, it was the largest glazed building in Europe at the time. Its curvilinear ridge-and-furrow roof was supported by laminated wooden ribs and slender iron columns. The hundreds of thin wooden sash-bars used for glazing were mass-produced on a machine which Paxton devised.

Paxton's reputation as a horticulturalist and builder was further enhanced by his successful cultivation and housing of the *Victoria regia* lily, which he acquired from Kew Gardens in 1849.

The design of this greenhouse was in part inspired by the strong, weblike structure of the giant leaves of the South American water lily. In this carefully heated and ventilated environment, the plant flowered for the first time in England.

The famous design which Paxton submitted to the Building Committee of the Commissioners of the Great Exhibition of the Works of Industry of All Nations in 1850 grew from the technical advancements made in the Victoria regia House. The commissioners accepted Paxton's iron, wood, and glass Crystal Palace proposal after rejecting 245 other designs. Essentially a hybrid of a greenhouse and a train shed, Paxton's Palace was the only scheme which not only provided an exciting and expansive exhibition space but could also be completely disassembled after the fair was over. Contractors Fox and Henderson and glaziers Chance and Company, erected the three-tiered structure in just over six months using prefabricated modular elements. In its final form, the Crystal Palace was 1848 feet long and 456 feet wide; the central vaulted transept, a feature added to the design to accommodate a row of elm trees dear to Prince Albert, rose 108 feet. Elaborate scaffolding and "glazing wagons" were used to install nearly one million square feet of glass. In all, six million people passed through the Crystal Palace in Hyde Park. It was recognized in its day as a stunning technological achievement, one for which Paxton was knighted in 1851. One visitor termed the seemingly weightless structure "a revolution in architecture from which a new style will date" (Giedion, 1967, p. 252). Indeed, the Crystal Palace has long been appreciated for the extent to which it prefigured the structural and aesthetic developments of the twentieth century: "the finished building was as lean and functional as a greyhound, revealing only in its smallest details . . . the imprint of Victorian taste" (Fitch, 1947, p. 91).

After the 1851 Exhibition, Paxton continued to design large glass buildings, but a number of his more innovative proposals were never realized. One of these was the Great Victorian Way in London (1855), an immense urban arcade; another was the domed Exhibition Building for Saint Cloud, Paris (1861).

Paxton was, however, able to capitalize on the popularity of the Crystal Palace. In 1852, he bought and reassembled the building parts on an estate at Sydenham. The Palace was substantially enlarged and became the focus of extensive "Italian style" formal gardens, which were planned and executed by Paxton and his son-in-law, George Henry Stokes. As a railway promoter and investor, Paxton was careful to make his tourist attraction accessible by train from London.

Paxton formally identified himself as an architect after 1851. But his architectural works, other than the glass buildings, were generally unremarkable and very much in keeping with the prevailing Victorian taste for eclecticism. Before 1850, he was primarily engaged in works for Chatsworth and its neighboring villages. During this period, he was assisted by John Robertson, a draftsman; together, they built Paxton's own house, Barbrook, in an Italianate style (1842–1847).

Paxton's two most significant architectural commissions came from the Rothschild family. In 1850, he and G. H. Stokes designed Mentmore in Buckinghamshire in a Jacobean style, but with a central hall covered with a ridge-and-furrow roof. At Ferrières, begun in 1853 just outside of Paris, Paxton was guided by the plan of Mentmore, but he chose a style of decoration more French in tone.

After the death of the duke of Devonshire in 1858, Paxton shifted his attentions from Chatsworth to Sydenham and London. In 1865, he retired from Parliament after serving for ten years.

Lisa B. Reitzes

WORKS

1826–1844, Chatsworth Gardens, England. 1836–1839, Farm Buildings; *1836–1840, Great Conservatory; Chatsworth, England. 1838–1842, Village Cottages, Edensor, near Chatsworth, England. 1842–1843, Upton Park, Slough, England. 1842–1844, Prince's Park, Liverpool, England. 1843–1847, Birkenhead Park, England. 1846, Burton Closes (completed by A. W. N. Pugin), Bakewell, England. 1849–1850, Victoria regia House, Chatsworth, England. *1850–1851, Crystal Palace, Hyde Park, London. 1850–1855, Mentmore (with G. H. Stokes), Buckinghamshire, England. 1850–1858, Lismore Castle, County Waterford, Ireland. *1852–1854, Crystal Palace; 1852–1856, Crystal Palace Park; Sydenham, England. 1853–1859, Ferrières, near Paris. 1854–1863, Park and Grounds, Mentmore, Buckinghamshire, England. 1855–1859, Ferrières (gardens), near Paris. 1864, Battlesden House, Bedfordshire, England.

BIBLIOGRAPHY

Chadwick, G. F. 1961*a* "Paxton and the Great Stove." *Architectural History* 4:77–92.

Chadwick, G. F. 1961*b* *The Works of Sir Joseph Paxton: 1803–1865.* London: Architectural Press.

Fitch, James M. 1947 "The Palace, the Bridge and the Tower." *Architectural Forum* 87, Oct.:88–95.

Giedion, Sigfried (1941)1967 *Space, Time and Architecture.* 5th ed. Cambridge, Mass.: Harvard University Press.

Girouard, Mark 1965 "The Genius of Sir Joseph Paxton." *Country Life* 138, Dec. 9:1606–1608.

Hitchcock, H. R. (1958)1977 *Architecture: Nineteenth and Twentieth Centuries.* New York: Penguin.

Hollister, Paul 1974 "The Glazing of the Crystal Palace." *Journal of Glass Studies* 16:95–110.

PAYSSÉ REYES, MARIO

Mario Payssé Reyes (1913–) is, along with the engineer ELADIO DIESTE, the figure of greatest significance in today's Uruguayan architecture. He was born in Montevideo, where he pursued his studies, receiving the title of architect in 1937, and where he has maintained his professional studio. To date, he has won about twenty first prizes in national contests. He was a disciple and occasional collaborator of JULIO VILAMAJÓ, the chief figure of Uruguayan architecture during the first half of the century. This link proved to be as fundamental in his formation as the contact with Joaquín Torres García and the latter's studio of painting and "constructive art." From these two men Payssé assimilated a solid structural conception and rigorous sense of proportion.

In his work, he makes frequent use of clear tile and also frequently incorporates the visual arts, as is evidenced for example in the Archdiocesal Seminary (1954–1958), partially altered since its transformation into the Military School (1973). Still more outstanding are his preoccupation with adapting modern architecture to local circumstances, particularly in reference to climate, and the integration with the natural locale or with the specific urban setting for each finished work. In this regard, the Banco de Previsión Social (1957–1975) and especially his own home (1954–1955) should be mentioned.

As a rule, Payssé has worked in collaboration with some of his many students at the School of Architecture in Montevideo, where he taught between 1943 and 1957.

MARIANO ARANA
Translated from Spanish by
Florette Rechnitz Koffler

WORKS

1954–1955, Mario Payssé Reyes House; 1954–1958, Archdiocesal Seminary (now the Military School); 1957–1975, Banco de Previsión Social (first stage); Montevideo. 1960–1962, Banco de la Republica (branch), Punto del Este, Uruguay. 1974–1980, Uruguayan Embassy (chancellery), Brasilia. 1978–1981, Uruguayan Embassy (chancellery), Buenos Aires.

BIBLIOGRAPHY

BULLRICH, FRANCESCO 1969 *New Directions in Latin American Architecture.* New York: Braziller.

PAYSSÉ REYES, MARIO 1968 *Where Are We in Architecture?* Montevideo: Arca Editorial.

PEABODY and STEARNS

Although highly successful from the start, Robert Swain Peabody (1845–1917) and John Goddard Stearns, Jr., (1843–1917) were recognized as the most important architectural office in Boston from the death of H. H. RICHARDSON in 1886 until World War I. Their impact was enormous because of the number, variety, and national importance of their commissions and the quality of architects, virtually a dynasty, who emerged from their offices to become leaders of the profession.

Peabody, born in New Bedford, graduated from Harvard University in 1866. After several months in the office of GRIDLEY J. F. BRYANT, he then joined WARE AND VAN BRUNT. Late in 1867, Peabody sailed for England, then entered the atelier Daumet at the Ecole des Beaux-Arts with his lifelong friends Francis Chandler and Charles McKim (see MCKIM, MEAD, AND WHITE). Returning to Boston in 1870, he established a partnership with Stearns, an engineer and graduate of Lawrence Scientific School, who had meanwhile risen to be chief draftsman for Ware and Van Brunt. Their association continued until the death of both partners, within a week, in 1917.

In 1871, Peabody married Annie Putnam of Boston, who in 1876 joined him on a five-month tour of England, France, and Italy. Returning to Boston, he designed their home on Edgehill Road in Brookline, a town which was the site of many later commissions. EDWARD C. CABOT, H. H. Richardson, FREDERICK LAW OLMSTED, and JOHN HUBBARD STURGIS all resided nearby. The precocious Peabody was liaison for the Boston Society of Architects at the 1876 Philadelphia Centennial and already had begun publication of his many written works. By 1877, he was established as spokesman for the American Colonial Revival. In 1882, he again visited England with an architect friend and during the next decade, particularly when Julius Schweinfurth was his head draftsman, many of his architectural masterpieces were produced. As its prime architect, Peabody represented Boston at the World's Columbian Exposition in Chicago in 1893 with his famed Machinery Building and the influential Massachusetts State Building, a free transcription of the Hancock House on Beacon Hill (1737–1863). He was a jurist for the Paris Exposition (1900), winning a silver medal, and supervising architect for the Pan-American Exposition at Buffalo the following year. As president of the American Institute of Architects he designed his home at 22 The Fenway in 1901 in Boston's Back Bay, where he had already built more than eighty residences. In later life, he augmented a continuing architectural career with increased publication and chairmanship of the Boston Parks Commission from 1909 to 1917. His first wife having died several years before, he married Helen Lee of Washington in 1913.

The successful working relationship and complementary talents of Peabody and Stearns produced more than one thousand commissions nationwide. But it was Peabody's genius as manager, teacher, and leader that established the character of their work. Designing for him was a challenging, practical adventure, for he was both businessman and artist. He habitually produced the original sketch for each commission, yet allowed his staff full run in developing detail. Thus, while sharing a certain vigorous massing of forms, a common relation of these to ornament, and a sense of breadth, the oeuvre of Peabody and Stearns lacks the stylistic stamp of a single designer. Peabody's charismatic personality and design philosophy, however, were the magnet that drew the best talent of the time to his drafting tables.

The office occupied in Boston a position similar to that of McKim, Mead, and White in New York. From the Massachusetts Institute of Technology came the best students, who continued on to independent practice and soon formed a network from coast to coast. Theophilus Chandler in Philadelphia and George Newton, Timothy Walsh, and Charles Collens in Boston and New York were primarily ecclesiastical architects. Spahr and MacClure in Pittsburgh, George Fuller and Charles Frost in Chicago, Henry Ives Cobb and Joseph Morrill Wells in New York. Colonialism was propounded from Boston by Arthur Little and from New York by Frank Wallis. In Missouri Aldrich and Eckel worked in St. Joseph and Ames and Young in St. Louis where Pierce Furber, western partner for Peabody and Stearns, served clients from there to Colorado Springs. Lewis and Whidden practiced in Portland and A. C. Schweinfurth in Colorado and San Francisco. Meanwhile in Boston Clarence Blackall, the great theater architect, City Architect Edmund Wheelwright and many others were onetime members of the Peabody and Stearns' "parade team." The varied character of this group can only suggest the vitality which, without specialization, maintained an evolving approach to style and kept Peabody and Stearns in demand for more than four decades. Although much of Peabody's work is uneven, the best in each of the stylistic epochs of his long career has become legendary. Few designs can challenge the Park Square Station (1872–1874) in Boston, the Hemenway Gym (1878) at Harvard, or the First Breakers (1877) at Newport, Rhode Island, as Peabody, fresh from his English trips, developed the High Victorian Gothic and the Queen Anne Revival modes, with closely articulated ornament. Kragsyde (1883), Vinland (1882–1884), and Rough Point (1889) are paragons of the seaside cottage of the 1880s, while the blocky forms of the Second Bleak House (1890) and Shamrock Cliff (1895) anticipate modernism. From the Denny House (1878) to the Massachusetts State Building, Chicago (1893), and the red-brick Groton School (1886–1901), Peabody led the Colonial Revival, while the organic medievalism of the bouldered First Parish, Weston, Massachusetts (1886), anticipated the designs of RALPH ADAMS CRAM. In commercial design the simple power of the R. H. White Warehouse, Boston (1883), was both a landmark and a prototype, while the great Exchange, Cunard, India, Monks, and Russia Buildings gave the financial district Beaux-Arts panache. The Newell and Weld Boathouses (1899, 1905) stand at Harvard on the Charles River where Peabody once rowed, and the Custom House Tower (1909–1911) remains the landmark of Boston Harbor.

MARGARET HENDERSON FLOYD and WHEATON HOLDEN

Peabody and Stearns. George Nixon Black House (Kragsyde). Manchester-by-the-Sea, Massachusetts. 1883–1884

WORKS

*1871–1872, Glen Eyrie Lodge, Colorado Spring. *1872–1874, Providence (Park Square) Railroad Station, Boston. 1873–1875, College Hall, Smith College, Northampton, Mass. *1874–1875, Brunswick Hotel; *1874–1875, Mutual Life Insurance Company Building of New York; Boston. *1875, William A. Appleton House, Milton, Mass. *1877–1878, Pierre Lorillard House (First Breakers), Newport, R. I. *1877–1878, John C. Phillips House, Boston. *1878–1879, Hemenway Gymnasium, Harvard College, Cambridge, Mass. *1879–1880, Union League Club Clubhouse, New York. *1879–1881, Wayman Crow, Jr., Museum of Fine Arts; 1880–1881, Church of the Messiah; St. Louis, Mo. 1880–1881, Easthampton Public Library, Mass. *1880–1881, United Bank Building, New York. *1882–1883, Antlers Hotel, Colorado Springs. *1882–1883, Turner Building, St. Louis, Mo. 1882–1884, Catherine Lorillard Wolfe House (Vinland), Newport, R. I. 1883, National Bank of Commerce, New Bedford, Mass. *1883–1884,

Peabody and Stearns. Mutual Life Insurance Company of New York. Boston. 1874–1875

George Nixon Black House (Kragsyde), Manchester-by-the-Sea, Mass. *1883–1884, R. H. White Warehouse, Boston. 1884–1885, Memorial Hall, Lawrenceville School, N.J. *1884–1885, St. Louis Club Clubhouse, Mo. *1886–1887, Easton Beach Pavilion, Newport, R.I. 1886–1888, First Parish Church, Weston, Mass. 1887–1888, James J. Hill House, Saint Paul, Minn. 1887–1891, Exchange Building; 1888–1889, Fiske Building; Boston. 1889, Union Church, Northeast Harbor, Maine. 1889–1890, Jersey City Railroad Station for the Central Railroad of New Jersey, Jersey City. 1889–1890, Frederick W. Vanderbilt House (Rough Point), Newport, R.I. *1890–1891, Central Railroad of New Jersey Building, New York. 1890–1891, Security Building, St. Louis, Mo. 1890–1891, Union Station, Duluth, Minn. *1892–1893, Machinery Hall; *1892–1893, Massachusetts State Building; Columbian Exposition, Chicago. 1893, John T. Davis House, St. Louis, Mo. 1893, Society for Savings Bank, Hartford, Conn. 1894, John Sloane House (Wyndhurst), Lenox, Mass. 1886–1901, Groton School, Mass. 1896–1898, Worcester City Hall, Mass. *1897–1899, Chamber of Commerce Building, Cleveland, Ohio. 1901, Peabody House (The Fenway); 1902–1904, India Building, Boston. *1902–1904, Percival Roberts House (Penshurst), Narberth, Pa. 1903–1905, 1908, Simmons College, Boston. 1905–1907, Weld Boat Club Boathouse, Cambridge, Mass. 1908–1909, Clinton Town Hall, Mass. 1909–1915, United States Customhouse (extension), Boston. 1911–1914, Bangor Public Library, Maine. 1914–1915, Worcester Academy Gymnasium, Mass.

BIBLIOGRAPHY

Bond, Anthony 1974 "The Commercial Architecture of Peabody and Stearns in Boston." Unpublished M.A. thesis, Pennsylvania State University, Philadelphia.

Damrell, Charles S. 1895 *A Half Century of Boston's Building.* Boston: Hager.

Downing, Antoinette F., and Scully, Vincent J., Jr. (1952)1967 *The Architectural Heritage of Newport, Rhode Island.* 2d ed., rev. New York: Potter.

Floyd, Margaret Henderson 1979 "Measured Drawings of the Hancock House by John Hubbard Sturgis: A Legacy of the Colonial Revival." Volume 51 in *Architecture in Colonial Massachusetts.* Charlottesville: University Press of Virginia.

Goudy, Marvin E., and Walsh, Robert P. (editors) 1967 *Boston Society of Architects: The First Hundred Years, 1867–1967.* Boston.

Herndon, Richard (editor) 1892 *Boston of To-day.* Boston: Post.

Holden, Wheaton A. 1973 "The Peabody Touch: Peabody and Stearns of Boston, 1870–1917." *Journal of the Society of Architectural Historians* 32, no. 2:114–131.

Holden, Wheaton A. 1984 *Robert Swain Peabody of Peabody and Stearns in Boston.* Boston: Northeastern University Press. Forthcoming publication.

Hoyt, Edwin P. 1968 *The Peabody Influence.* New York: Dodd.

Mason, George C. 1875 *Newport and Its Cottages.* Boston: Osgood.

Meeks, Carroll L. V. (1956)1964 *The Railroad Station: An Architectural History.* New Haven: Yale University Press.

Moore, Charles (1929)1969 *The Life and Times of Charles Follen McKim.* Reprint. New York: Da Capo.

Schuyler, Montgomery 1891 "The Romanesque Revival in America." *Architectural Record* 1:151–198.

Schweinfurth, Julius A. 1926 "Robert Swain Peabody: Tower Builder." *American Architect* 130:181–191.

Scully, Vincent J., Jr. (1955)1971 *The Shingle Style.* Rev. ed. New Haven: Yale University Press.

Sheldon, George W. 1886–1887 *Artistic Country Seats.* New York: Appleton.

Sturgis, Russell (1896)1971 *A Critique of the Work of Peabody and Stearns.* Reprint. New York: Da Capo.

PEACOCK, JAMES

James Peacock (1738?–1814) was from 1771 until his death the invaluable assistant to George Dance the Younger, clerk of works to the City of London. He built only one important independent work and is best remembered as the author of the pseudonymously published *Nutshells* (1785). He also addressed himself in several small treatises to social and economic questions.

John Bold

WORK

*1801–1802 Stock Exchange, Capel Court, London.

BIBLIOGRAPHY

Stroud, Dorothy 1971 *George Dance, Architect: 1741–1825.* London: Faber.

PEACOCK, JOSEPH

Information concerning Joseph Peacock's (1821–1893) early life is notably vague. He apprenticed in Worthing, England, and surveyed for railway lines and several large estates around London. His designs are mildly monumental and his works display colored stone and wood ceilings. His structures include some of the best examples of the "Low Church style" of the High Victorian Gothic.

John H. Wilson

WORKS

1859, Saint Simon Zelotes, Chelsea; 1865, Saint Stephen, South Kensington; London. 1869, Saint Andrew, Perth, Scotland. 1887, Holy Cross; 1887, Saint Pancras; London.

BIBLIOGRAPHY

Goodhart-Rendel, H. S. 1949 "Rogue Architects

of the Victorian Era." *Journal of the Royal Institute of British Architects* Series 3 56:251–259.

"Obituary of Joseph Peacock, Fellow." 1893 *Journal of the Royal Institute of British Architects* New Series 9:204.

PEARCE, EDWARD LOVETT

Edward Lovett Pearce (c.1699–1733) was born probably in Ireland or England, the son of Major-General Edward Pearce who was first cousin to Sir JOHN VANBRUGH. Aged sixteen or seventeen, he became a cornet of dragoons and later attained the rank of captain. There is much indirect, but no direct evidence for his architectural education under the tutelage of his cousin Vanbrugh (who also had a military background). During 1723 and 1724, he traveled in France, Italy, and Switzerland, and his annotated copy of ANDREA PALLADIO, taken on the journey, has survived. How long he stayed in England is not known, but by October 1726 he was in Dublin, where his connections rapidly procured him several important commissions, of which the first, perhaps, was the interior and wings of Castletown, County Kildare, begun by his associate ALESSANDRO GALILEI. In 1727, he became a member of parliament for Ratoath in the Irish Parliament. Though THOMAS BURGH was still Surveyor-General, it was Pearce who designed and supervised till his death the new Parliament House, his most important building. In March 1732, he was knighted in the still unfinished Parliament House, having in 1730 succeeded Burgh as Surveyor-General on the latter's death. The Act of 1729 to regulate the building industry and the sizes of bricks was carried through by him, and he built a theater (1733–1734) in Aungier Street, Dublin. His extensive country house practice passed to his assistant RICHARD CASTLE. Pearce married his cousin Anne Pearce and had four daughters. He died suddenly and was buried at Donnybrook. He is one of the earliest and most important Irish Palladian architects.

MAURICE CRAIG

WORKS

(A)After 1726, Castletown (entrance hall, curved colonnades, and wings), County Kildare, Ireland. 1727, Drumcondra House, County Dublin. Before 1729, Cashel Palace, County Tipperary, Ireland. 1729–, The Parliament House (completed posthumously by Arthur Dobbs); c.1730, 9 and 10 Henrietta Street; 1733–1734, Aungier Street Theatre; Dublin. n.d., Bellamont Forest, County Cavan, Ireland. (A)n.d., Castle (upper castle yard, south-east block), Dublin. (A)n.d., Domes Saloon, 12 North Audley Street, London. (A)n.d., Gloster, County Offaly, Ireland. *n.d., Stillorgan (garden layout, underground grotto, mausoleum-obelisk; only partially surviving), County Dublin. (A)n.d., Summerhill, County Meath, Ireland.

BIBLIOGRAPHY

COLVIN, H. M., and CRAIG, MAURICE 1964 *Architectural Drawings in the Library of Elton Hall by Sir John Vanbrugh and Sir Edward Lovett Pearce.* Oxford University Press.

CRAIG, MAURICE 1969 "Castletown, Co. Kildare." *Country Life* 145:722–726; 798–802; 882–885.

CRAIG, MAURICE 1974 "Sir Edward Lovett Pearce." *Quarterly Bulletin of the Irish Georgian Society* 17:10–14.

CURRAN, CONSTANTINE P. 1949 In *The Bank of Ireland, 1783–1946.* Edited by F. G. Hall. Dublin: Hodges, Figgis.

SADLEIR, R. U. 1927 "Sir Edward Lovett Pearce." *Journal of the Kildare Archaeological Society* 10:231.

PEARSON, J. L.

John Loughborough Pearson (1817–1897) trained under Ignatius Bonomi in Durham, England. In London from 1842, he worked briefly for ANTHONY SALVIN and PHILIP C. HARDWICK. His early Gothic churches were indebted to A. W. N. PUGIN.

In the 1850s, JOHN RUSKIN's influence and travel in France and Germany broadened his style, exemplified at Scorborough (1857–1859) and Appleton-le-Moors in Yorkshire (1862–1866). In London, his Vauxhall Church (1859–1864), vaulted and using the Golden Section, is the model for masterpieces at Kilburn (1870–1897), Holborn (1874–1878), and Croydon (1876–1881), where spatial complexity and classical repose combine with an assured use of Early English and French Gothic forms.

Pearson achieved wide recognition with Truro Cathedral, Cornwall (1878–1897), and for controversial restorations. He was a Fellow of the Royal Institute of British Architects, receiving their Gold Medal in 1880, and a Royal Academician. He worked continuously until his death in London. His son Frank Loughborough Pearson was also an architect.

A. P. QUINEY

WORKS

1843–1844, Saint Ann's Chapel, Ellerker, Humberside, England. 1848–1852, Treberfydd House, Llangasty Talyllyn, Powys, Wales. *1849–1852, Holy Trinity Church, Bessborough Gardens, London. 1856–1859, Quar Wood House, Stow-on-the-Wold, Gloucestershire, England. 1857–1859, Saint Leonard's Church, Scorborough, Humberside, England. 1859–1864, Saint Peter's Church, Vauxhall, London. 1862–1866, Christ

Church, Appleton-le-Moors, North Yorkshire, England. 1870–1897, Saint Augustine's Church, Kilburn; 1874–1878, Saint John's Church, Holborn; 1876–1881, Saint Michael's Church, Croydon; London. 1878–1897, Truro Cathedral (not completed until 1910), Cornwall, England. 1882–1885, Saint Agnes's Church, Sefton Park, Liverpool, England. 1887–?, Brisbane Cathedral (with Frank Loughborough Pearson), Queensland, Australia. 1892–1895, 2 Temple Place (former Astor Estate Office), Westminster, London.

BIBLIOGRAPHY

"The Late Mr. J. L. Pearson, R. A., and his Work." 1897 *The Builder* 73:514.

"The Late Mr. John L. Pearson, R. A." 1897 *Building News* 73:866.

"The Late John Loughborough Pearson, R. A." 1897–1898 *Journal of the Royal Institute of British Architects* Series 3 5:113–121.

NEWBERRY, J. ERNEST 1897 "The Work of John L. Pearson R. A." *Architectural Review* 1:1–11, 69–82.

QUINEY, ANTHONY 1979 *John Loughborough Pearson.* New Haven and London: Yale University Press.

PEARSON, JOHN ANDREW

John Andrew Pearson (1867–1940) was born and educated in England. He came to Toronto in 1888 and trained under FRANK DARLING, whose partner he became in 1892. His commissions include rebuilding the Centre Block of the Parliament Buildings, Ottawa (1916–1924), and the Bank of Commerce Head Office, Toronto (1929–1931).

ROBERT HILL

BIBLIOGRAPHY

SULLIVAN, ALAN 1913 "John A. Pearson, Master Builder." *Year Book of Canadian Art* 1:255–262.

PEI, I. M.

Ieoh Ming Pei (1917–) was born in Canton, China. Before emigrating to the United States, he was educated in Shanghai. In 1938, he entered the Massachusetts Institute of Technology and graduated in 1940; six years later, he received a master's degree in architecture from the Harvard School of Design where he studied with WALTER GROPIUS. Between 1942 and 1945, he worked as a concrete designer for Stone and Webster, and in 1946 he began work in the office of HUGH ASHER STUBBINS, in Boston. During the war years, he served on the National Defense Research Committee in Princeton. He was also appointed to the faculty of the Harvard Graduate School of Design (1945–1948), where he was a Wheelwright Fellow.

In 1948, Pei was hired by the real estate developer William Zeckendorf to work for the architectural division of his contracting firm, Webb and Knapp, Inc. As Zeckendorf's architect, Pei had the opportunity, unusual for many young architects, to design buildings both on a large scale and with a large budget. Besides providing Pei with the opportunity and funds to build on a large scale as well as to meet others important in the world of building and architecture, Zeckendorf had other lessons to offer. Two of Pei's early works, Mile High Center, Denver, Colorado, and the Hyde Park Redevelopment, Chicago, exemplify Zeckendorf's method. The former illustrates the successful application of the principle of converting peaceful rural land into valuable commercial property. The latter shows Zeckendorf's lucrative procedure of buying run-down second-rate urban land, renewing it, and realizing enormous profits from its sale. In fact, Zeckendorf's office was devoted to revitalizing urban space through the planning of large-scale, multipurpose urban areas to attract new business, new residents, and new activity. Furthermore, as an entrepreneurial speculator, Zeckendorf was skilled in the art of forging compromises with representatives of many interest groups—commercial, community, and governmental. This approach to planning, which saw revitalization as the key to commercial as well as urban vitality, has characterized Pei's work independent of Zeckendorf. For example, it was fundamental to his proposals for the Government Center (1961), the John Hancock Building (1973), and the Christian Science Center (1973), all in Boston.

Pei worked as the head of the architectural division of Webb and Knapp, Inc. until 1960, when he resigned to found his own architectural office, but he continued to work for Zeckendorf on a contractual basis. In this capacity, he built Kips Bay Plaza, New York, and Town Center Plaza, stage I, 3rd-6th Streets, N.W., Washington,

In terms of style, Pei has been considered a disciple of Walter Gropius. Due to his reliance on abstract form and "cold" materials such as stone, concrete, glass, and steel, I. M. Pei's forms do appear to be a further development of his master's. His theatrical effects, however, evident as early as the office which he built for William Zeckendorf on top of 383–385 Madison Avenue, New York, are distinctive as is his steady departure from the self-contained silhouettes of the International style for a complex arrangement of masses and rich contrast of materials, forms, and spaces.

This penchant for drama is evident in the siting and vistas of many recent buildings: for example, the Herbert F. Johnson Museum of Art (1973), Cornell University, Ithaca, New York; the

East Wing of the National Gallery (1978), Washington, D.C., and the John F. Kennedy Library (1979), Boston. All are sited with a relationship to the surroundings that might well be called romantic. In the case of the Johnson museum, the best epithet might even be sublime; for the East Wing, grand; and for the Kennedy Library, picturesque. Inside these three buildings, there are the views to the outside that are typical of Pei's work, making maximum use of the exterior landscape to afford pleasure and to enrich the interior with added color, pattern, and space. The interest generated by these views augments that provided by the curiously broken up interior spaces and intricate interior plan. Heightening these effects is the expressive and lavish use of materials, of which Pei has a firm grasp. Despite the fiasco of the window panes on the Hancock Tower in Boston, Pei has been praised for his understanding of materials, especially concrete and curtain glass.

Pei departs from the tradition of Gropius in that he does not have a polemical bent nor is he concerned with theory. Furthermore, he does not share Gropius's sense of the exclusive mission of the architect to find forms to express the age and to act in isolation from prevailing commercial forces. Instead, Pei expresses ideas through building and through collaborative efforts with clients, varied interest groups, and members of his own office. It may well be that Zeckendorf's lessons were seeds that fell on fertile ground.

Yet, the question of influence is complicated. Early in his career, Pei worked with WILLIAM LESCAZE in building the offices of Zeckendorf on Madison Avenue, and Lescaze's inclination for bold forms may well have had its effect. In his office, Pei collaborates in a total way with other architects, and designs produced by I. M. Pei and Partners may have as easily been produced by Pei and one of the other general partners as by Pei alone.

Pei's ability to design buildings suitable to their context was noted at the beginning of his career. Walter Gropius himself commented on it in conjunction with Pei's project for a Museum for Chinese Art in Shanghai (c.1948). Gropius (1948) wrote: "This project . . . clearly illustrates that an able designer can very well hold on to basic traditional features—which he has found are still alive—without sacrificing a progressive, conception of design. . . . Mr. Pei . . . was anxious to avoid having Chinese motifs added to public buildings in a rather superficial way as was done for many public buildings in Shanghai [and] . . . to find out how the character of Chinese architecture could be expressed without imitating such form motifs of former periods."

This contextualism and his feeling for Chinese architecture are evident both in this project and in another early, independent work, the Henry Luce Chapel (1963), Taunghai University, Taida, Taiwan. The original intention to use brick, the curving roof (although not its angle), and the copper-colored tiles of the roofs are comments on indigenous styles. Because Pei is now an American citizen and active in the United States, his connections with his native culture are not often noticed. Yet, besides the two works just discussed, he was a consultant for Chung Chi University, Hong Kong, and designed a hotel for Peking. His knowledge of traditional Chinese architecture is revealed in public lectures, and it would be most interesting to know how this knowledge has affected the designs and attitudes of one of America's most prolific architects.

JUDITH S. HULL

WORKS

1954–1959, Mile High Center, Denver, Colo. 1956–1965, Place Ville Marie (with RAYMOND AFFLECK), Montreal. 1961, Government Center, Boston. 1959–1963, Kips Bay Plaza, New York. 1962, Slayton House, Ordway Street, N.W.; 1962, Town Center Plaza (stage I), 3rd-6th Streets, N.W.; Washington. 1963, Henry R. Luce Chapel, Taunghai University, Taida, Taiwan. 1964, Green Center for the Earth Sciences, Massachusetts Institute of Technology, Cambridge. 1964, School of Journalism, Newhouse Communications Center, Syracuse University, N.Y. 1964, Washington Square East/Society Hill, Philadelphia. 1965, L'Enfant Plaza (stage I), Washington. 1966–1967, Area renewal plan (with David A. Crane), Brooklyn, N.Y. 1967, Hoffman Hall, University of Southern California, Los Angeles. 1967, National Center for Atmospheric Research, Boulder, Colo. 1967, University Plaza, New York University. 1967–1970, Air Traffic Control Tower, Federal Aviation Agency (standardized model). 1968, Des Moines Art Center (addition), Iowa. 1968, Everson Museum of Art, Syracuse, N.Y. 1968, Polaroid Corporation, Waltham, Mass. 1969, Bedford-Stuyvesant Superblock, Brooklyn, N.Y. 1970, Dreyfus Chemistry Building, Massachusetts Institute of Technology, Cambridge. 1970, Columbia University Master Plan, New York. 1970, National Airlines Terminal, Kennedy International Airport, New York. 1970, Wilmington Tower, Del. 1971, Celo Rogers Memorial Library, Columbus, Ohio. 1972, Canadian Imperial Bank of Commerce Complex, Toronto. 1972, Mellon Art Center, Choate School, Wallingford, Conn. 1972, Third Church of Christ Scientist and Christian Science Monitor Building, Washington. 1973, Christian Science Church Center (with Arnaldo Cossutta); 1973, John Hancock Tower; 1973, Harbor Tower; Boston. 1973, Herbert F. Johnson Museum of Art, Cornell University, Ithaca, N.Y. 1975, Ralph Landau Building, Massachusetts Institute of Technology, Cambridge. 1976, Chinese Banking Corporation Headquarters, Singapore. 1976, Wilson Commons Building, University of Rochester, N.Y.

Pei.
John Hancock Tower.
Boston.
1973

1977, Dallas Municipal Center, Tex. 1978, National Gallery of Art (east wing), Washington. 1979, Industrial Credit Bank, Teheran. 1979, John Fitzgerald Kennedy Library, Boston. 1979, Museum, Indiana University, Bloomington. 1980, Akzona, Inc., Corporate Headquarters, Asheville, N.C. 1980, Museum of Fine Arts (west wing), Boston. 1981, Nestlé Corporate Headquarters, Purchase, N.Y. 1981, El Paso Tower, Texas Commerce Plaza, Houston.

BIBLIOGRAPHY

BLAKE, PETER 1973 "I. M. Pei and Partners." *Architecture Plus* 1, no. 1:52–59; no. 2:20–77.

FUTAGAWA, YUKIO (editor) 1976 *National Center for Atmospheric Research, Boulder, Colorado.* Boston: Christian Science Church Center.

GOLDBERGER, PAUL 1979 "Winning Ways of I. M. Pei." *New York Times,* May 20, sec. 6, p. 24.

GROPIUS, WALTER 1948 "Museum for Chinese Art, Shanghai China." *Progressive Architecture* 29, Feb.:50–51.

PEI, I. M. 1942 "Standardized Propaganda Units for the Chinese Government." *Task* 1, no. 2:13–16.

PELLEGRIN, LUIGI

Deeply impressed by BRUNO ZEVI's *History,* Luigi Pellegrin (1925–) studied the Chicago school and FRANK LLOYD WRIGHT, whose influence is to be felt in his early works. He has devoted himself to low-cost and prefabricated building, developing a high-tech competence he shares with few other architects.

RENATO PEDIO

WORKS

1956, Post Office, Saronno, Italy. 1959, Pellegrin House, Rome. 1959, Post Office, Suzzara, Italy. 1969, Secondary School, Piacenza, Italy. 1974, Secondary School, Arezzo, Italy. 1977, Vocational School, Pisa, Italy.

BIBLIOGRAPHY

PEDIO, RENATO 1960 "Opere dell-architetto Luigi Pellegrin." *L'Architettura, cronache e storia* 6, no. 59:295–315.

PEDIO, RENATO 1980 "Luigi Pellegrin poli e itinerari della materia nello spazio." *L'Architettura, cronache e storia* 26, no. 300:550–602.

PEDIO, RENATO 1981 "Fabbrica di spazio e spazio fabbricato." *L'Architettura, cronache e storia* no. 309:390–410.

PEVSNER, NIKOLAUS H. (1966)1975 *A Dictionary of Architecture.* London: Allen Lane.

PELLI, CESAR

Among the architects to emerge from the office of EERO SAARINEN, Cesar Pelli (1926–) is one of the most important. Known as a minimalist for his slick detailing and clean, crisp surfaces, Pelli is admired for his exquisite use of glass as an outer skin for his buildings.

Born in Argentina and educated at the Universidad Nacional in Buenos Aires, he came to the United States in 1952 to attend the University of Illinois. From 1954 to 1964, he worked for Saarinen. In 1964, he moved to Los Angeles to work as director of design for Daniel, Mann, Johnson, and Mendenhall and, from 1968 to 1977, for Gruen Associates. In 1977, he became dean of the School of Architecture at Yale University, New Haven, and opened his own architectural practice there.

One work in particular, the Pacific Design Center in Los Angeles, brought Pelli's name to prominence. Built in the tradition of the great glass exhibition halls of the nineteenth century, such as JOSEPH PAXTON's Crystal Palace, the work is astounding not only for its size but also for its unusual dark blue color. It is often referred to as "The Blue Whale." The nickname belies its sleek form and its subtle character; the glass skin takes on the changing colors of the sky so that in effect the building becomes a living phenomenon on the landscape.

In Pelli's most recent work, the renovation of and addition to the Museum of Modern Art, New York, his minimalist character specifically recalls LUDWIG MIES VAN DER ROHE's early drawing experiments with glass skyscrapers.

NICHOLAS ADAMS

WORKS

1965, Sunset Mountain Park Urban Nucleus, Santa Monica, Calif. 1970, Commons Courthouse Center, Columbus, Ind. 1971, Pacific Design Center, Los Angeles. 1977–, Museum of Modern Art (renovation and tower); 1981–, Battery Park City; New York.

BIBLIOGRAPHY

FRAMPTON, KENNETH 1981 *Cesar Pelli/Gruen Associates.* Edited by Yukio Futagawa. Tokyo.

PEMBROKE, EARL OF

Henry Herbert, the ninth earl of Pembroke (c.1689–1750), was thought by Horace Walpole to be a purer architect than either WILLIAM KENT or LORD BURLINGTON, but quite how he operated is unclear. He was early connected with COLEN CAMPBELL, but was later a collaborator with ROGER MORRIS, who acted as his amanuensis. Between them they designed Marble Hill, Middlesex (1724), White Lodge, Richmond (1727), Castle

Hill, Devon (1729), Wimbledon House, Surrey (1732), as well as many others. Pembroke's most exquisite work is the Palladian Bridge at Wilton, Wiltshire (1736), one of the masterpieces of neo-Palladianism.

JOHN HARRIS

WORKS

1724, Marble Hill (with Roger Morris), Middlesex, England. 1727, White Lodge (with Morris), Richmond, England. 1729, Castle Hill (with Morris), Devon, England. 1730, Column of Victory, Blenheim Palace, Oxfordshire, England. 1732, Wimbledon House (with Morris), Surrey, England. 1736, Palladian Bridge, Wilton, England.

PENCHAUD, MICHEL ROBERT

Born in Poitiers, France, Michel Robert Penchaud (1772–1832) was a student of Charles PERCIER AND Pierre Leonard FONTAINE. As official architect for Marseille after 1803, his works included a Protestant Church (1816) and a triumphal arch (1823–1832). Penchaud was also conservator and architect for the Provence. His style often recalled the austere neoclassicism of CLAUDE NICOLAS LEDOUX.

LISA B. REITZES

WORKS

1813–1821, Jail, Aix-en-Provence, France. 1816, Protestant Church; 1820–1823, Constabulary and Jail; 1822–1832, Palais de Justice; Marseille, France. 1822–1826, Hospital, Island of Ratoneau, France. 1823–1832, Arc de Triomphe; 1842, Bourse; Marseille, France.

BIBLIOGRAPHY

HAUTECOEUR, LOUIS 1943–1957 *Histoire de l'Architecture classique en France.* 7 vols. Paris: Picard.

PENNETHORNE, JAMES

Sir James Pennethorne (1801–1871) was an English architect and planner who worked mainly for the British government. Although he designed in the Gothic style, most of his work was classical, ranging from Greek to Renaissance.

He was born in Worcester and died in Malden, Surrey. He was said to be the son of Thomas Pennethorne, a cousin of Mary Ann Nash, the second wife of JOHN NASH. However, he was brought up by Mrs. Nash, who was believed to have been a mistress of the Prince Regent. In 1820, Pennethorne entered the office of Nash who placed him under the charge of Augustus C. Pugin.

From 1824 to 1826, he completed his architectural education with travel in France, Italy, and Sicily. On his return he went back into Nash's office. In 1832, he was first employed by the Commissioners of Woods and Forests and in 1843 he became their sole architect. He carried out various schemes of road improvement including New Oxford Street, Endell Street, Buckingham Gate, Kensington Palace Gardens, and Commercial Road, Stepney. He also designed the layout of Victoria, Kennington, and Battersea Parks.

Pennethorne was widely respected in the architectural profession. In 1865, he received the Gold Medal of the Royal Institute of British Architects. He was knighted in 1870.

ROGER DIXON

WORKS

1834, Swithland Hall, Leicestershire, England. 1836–1837, Christ Church, Albany Street; 1847–1848, Museum of Economic Geology; 1851–1866, Public Record Office (not completed until 1891–1896 by John Taylor); 1852–1856, Somerset House (west wing); 1853–1855, State Ball Room, Buckingham Palace; 1854–1855, Duchy of Cornwall Offices, Buckingham Gate; 1866–1870, University of London (Burlington Gardens; now Museum of Mankind); London.

BIBLIOGRAPHY

CATES, ARTHUR 1871–1872 "A Biographical Notice of the Late Sir James Pennethorne." *Transactions of the Royal Institute of British Architects* 22:53–69.
CATES, ARTHUR 1921–1922 "Sir James Pennethorne." Volume 15, pages 773–774 in Leslie Stephen and Sidney Lee (editors), *Dictionary of National Biography.* Oxford University Press.
"James Pennethorne." 1852–1892 Volume 6, page 81 in *Dictionary of Architecture.* London: Richards.
"Public Improvements in Paris and London: Sir James Pennethorne." 1872 *The Builder* 30:22–24.
"Sir James Pennethorne." 1871 *The Builder* 29:717–718.

PERCIER and FONTAINE

Pierre Fontaine (1762–1853) was born at Pontoise, near Paris. He came from a family in which the profession of architect was almost hereditary. Enrolled at a young age at the small Collège de Pontoise, he withdrew at the age of sixteen, and his father decided to send him to L'Isle-Adam, where he worked on the large estate of the prince of Conti. There, the young man received a practical education which left a profound and long-lasting impression.

Some time later, Fontaine's father, realizing that his son was not satisfied with the lessons he received at L'Isle-Adam, sent the young Pierre to

Paris and introduced him to Antoine-Joseph Peyre, (see PEYRE FAMILY) *architecte des bâtiments du roi,* whose school of architecture was celebrated. In the studio of Jean-François Heurtier, Fontaine met Charles Percier (1764–1838).

In 1779, Fontaine narrowly lost the competition for the Prix de Rome. Nevertheless, he left for Italy. In 1786, admitted to the French Academy in Rome, he and Percier together studied antique Rome and the palaces of modern Rome and surveyed the famous Roman Campagna.

Fontaine returned to France after the Revolution, but because work was hard to find, he left for England, where neoclassic art was in full flower. After several years, he returned to Paris, where he joined Percier in painting theater scenery at the Opéra and the Palais-Bourbon under the direction of Guy de Gisors (see GISORS FAMILY) and ETIENNE CHÉRUBIN LECONTE.

Revolutionary Year VIII (1799–1800) was an eventful one for the two friends, who were charged with restoring the Paris residence of M. de Chauvelin, near that of Mme. Bonaparte, who was looking for a new architect. Percier and Fontaine transformed her small, run-down château, *Malmaison,* into a ravishing *residence consulaire* (its official title), filled with the most graceful art of the era. This château became the favorite home of the future Empress Josephine. The garden, enlarged by the acquisition of several neighboring properties and gardens, was replanted in the English style (*à l'anglaise*).

Abandoning the Luxembourg Palace, the First Consul established himself in the Tuileries Palace, the ancient royal residence which had been pillaged during the revolution. Its interior was completely redone. Unhappy with Leconte, Bonaparte named Fontaine *architecte du governement* in 1801. Josephine, present at the scene and "sensitive to Percier and Fontaine's friendship, insists that the names of the two collaborators not be separated." In his own hand on the decree already signed, Bonaparte adds the name of Percier. Henceforth, all the work in the Tuileries was the collaboration of the two friends.

Percier and Fontaine. Arc du Carousel. Paris. 1806–1808

This was also the case at Saint-Cloud, the First Consul's second official residence. The autumn and winter of 1801 were spent making structural repairs to the magnificent château. The floor boards were rotted. "The First Consul has come several times to learn about the styles of different epochs. He has seen the bad condition of the flooring. He himself has prescribed the layout of the rooms. . . . We notice that he is impatient to make his residence habitable." He took pleasure in being able to pass from his study to the terrace and gardens without being observed. The view was superb and the trees were known as the most beautiful in the Paris region. By the summer of 1802 the château was ready to be furnished.

In 1804, the young architects were engaged in the demolition required to clear the area around the Tuileries. Within the palace, the suite of reception rooms was superb. "The principal portion of the building, overlooking the court of honor, comprising the Salon of Mars, the Gallery of Apollo, and the Salon of Diana, has been set aside for official state affairs. The royal *appartements* have been preserved and repaired. The rooms facing the parterre of the Orangery have become the office of the First Consul. The new *appartements* are the models for contemporary design." Josephine's salon had curtains of white satin embroidered with gold and bordered by a pattern of colored flowers, green palmettes, and swans. Some critics reproached these rooms for their apparent simplicity which created too marked a contrast with the "bronze and guilding used by the seventeenth-century architects in the *grands appartements*."

In 1804, Fontaine wrote: "Everything has made an about-face. The First Consul today is recognized as the Emperor of France." The throne of the Emperor is placed in the principal reception room. It was necessary to arrange and furnish in haste the château at Fontainebleau, to prepare the Pavillon de Flore at the Tuileries, where the Pope will stay, and to transform Notre Dame for the coronation ceremony.

At the end of that year, Percier and Fontaine were named *architectes du Louvre et des Tuileries.* "His Majesty wishes to complete the two palaces and to join them into a single monument devoted to housing the Sovereign. He has given these orders: 'A triumphal arch shall be erected between the two palaces.'" This was the Arc du Carousel, which one can still admire today for its perfect proportions and its rose marble columns. It is the masterpiece of Percier and Fontaine (1806–1808).

It was a time of great building campaigns, in Paris as well as outside the city. A priority was the restoration of the château of Versailles, the legacy of Louis XIV, which, miraculously, survived the Revolution without too much damage. The two Trianons were to be made habitable again, as well as the château in Compiègne, which became the home of Marie Louise, the new Empress.

The greatest ambition of the regime was to erect a grandiose palace on the hill of Chaillot with terraces descending to the Seine and gardens extending to the Bois de Boulogne. The plans were magnificent, but gradually the enthusiasm for building dissipated and credit tightened. This was the end of a dream and the end of a regime. Tardily, as if suffering a twinge of remorse, Napoleon named Fontaine his *premier architecte.* For quite a while, Fontaine enjoyed a free hand in all that he did, not only in and outside of Paris, but also in Italy. On December 18, 1813 he had his last conversation with Napoleon: "The order is given to suspend all work. From now on, all but the war is suspended."

When the Bourbons returned to power, they showed little interest in their palaces. Percier and Fontaine retained the position of *Architectes du Louvre et des Tuileries,* but the post of *premier architecte* was abolished. On order of the king, Fontaine also built a *chapelle expiatoire* in memory of Louis XVI and Marie Antoinette. During the reign of Charles X, the Arc du Carrousel, severely damaged by the Austrian soldiers, was restored.

Under the July Monarchy, extensive work was undertaken at the palace in Versailles, which Louis-Philippe intended to make the *Musée de l'histoire de France.* Fontainebleau, Saint-Cloud, and the Tuileries were all in turn restored. After Percier's death in 1838, Fontaine continued the work alone, fulfilling his responsibilities as architect of the Louvre and the Tuileries.

In 1848, he ended his official career with a letter: "After serving without interruption for a half century under the Consulate, the Empire, Louis XVIII, Charles X, Louis-Philippe, and finally the Republic of 1848, I have finally decided to tender my resignation."

Fontaine led a pleasant life for the next five years in his Hôtel de la Muette, only going out to attend meetings of the Institut de France.

Of the work of Percier and Fontaine, only the beautiful Arc du Carrousel recalls their memory in Paris. One must go to *Malmaison* to evoke the spirit of the two friends.

MARIE LOUISE BIVER
Translated from French by
Richard Cleary

Fontaine.
Chappelle Expiatoire.
Paris.
1815–1826

BIBLIOGRAPHY

BAUSSET, LOUIS FRANÇOIS JOSEPH 1827–1829 *Mémoires anecdotiques sur l'intérieur du palais et sur quelques événemens de l'Empire depuis 1805 jusqu'au Ier mai 1814 (–1816) pour servir à l'histoire de Napoléon.* 4 vols. Paris: Baudouin.

BIVER, MARIE-LOUISE (1963)1964 *Pierre Fontaine: Premier Architecte de l'Empereur.* Paris: Plon.

DUPORTAL, JEANNE 1931 *Charles Percier.* Paris: Rousseau.

PERCIER, CHARLES, and FONTAINE, PIERRE 1798 *Palais, maisons et autres édifices modernes dessinés à Rome.* Paris: Ducamp.

PERCIER, CHARLES, and FONTAINE, PIERRE 1801 *Recueil de décorations intérieures, comprenant tout ce qui a rapport à l'ameublement.* Paris: The authors.

PERCIER, CHARLES, and FONTAINE, PIERRE 1808 *Description des cérémonies, et des fêtes, qui on eu lieu pour le couronnement de L. L. MM Napoléon, empereur des Français et roi d'Italie, Joséphine, son auguste épousse.* Paris: Leblanc.

PERCIER, CHARLES, and FONTAINE, PIERRE 1810 *Description des cérémonies, et des fêtes, qui ont eu lieu pour le mariage de S. M. l'empereur Napoléon avec S. A. L. Mme. l'archiduchesse Marie-Louise d'Autriche.* Paris: Didot.

PERCIER, CHARLES, and FONTAINE, PIERRE 1833 *Parallèle entre plusieurs résidences, de souverain, de France, d'Allemagne, de Suède, de Russie, d'Espagne et d'Italie.* Paris: The authors.

PERCY, GEORGE WASHINGTON

Architectural scholar, leader in professional activities, and exponent of the Richardsonian (see H. H. RICHARDSON) Romanesque, George Washington Percy (1847–1900) was most important as an advocate of reinforced concrete in architecture. He supervised construction of the Stanford University buildings for SHEPLEY, RUTAN, AND COOLIDGE and collaborated with ERNEST L. RANSOME on several of the first reinforced-concrete buildings in the United States. Born in Bath, Maine, Percy worked with F. H. Fassett in Portland, Maine, Bradlee and Winslow in Boston, and JOHN M. VAN OSDELL in Chicago. After a stint in Stockton, California, he was in partnership with Frederick F. Hamilton in San Francisco from 1879 to 1900 and with WILLIS J. POLK briefly in 1900.

MICHAEL R. CORBETT

WORKS

PERCY AND FREDERICK F. HAMILTON

*1880, State Insane Asylum; *1883, Masonic Hall Association Building; Stockton, Calif. 1887–1889, First Unitarian Church; 1887–1898, Sharon Play House, Golden Gate Park; San Francisco. *1888, Sperry Flour Mill, Stockton, Calif. 1888–1889, Bourn and Wise Wine Cellar, Saint Helena, Calif. *1889, Academy of Sciences Building, San Francisco. 1890–1891, Leland Stanford, Jr., Museum; *1891, Roble Hall; Stanford University, Calif. 1891, Trinity United Methodist Church; *1892, Watson House; San Francisco. 1894, City Hall, Alameda, Calif. *1894, Hobart Building, San Francisco. 1895, Boys' Dormitory; 1896, Girl's Cottage; Reno, Nev. 1896, Howard Presbyterian Church; 1897, Wells Fargo Building; San Francisco.

PERCY AND WILLIS J. POLK

1900–1901, Alvinza Hayward Building, San Francisco.

BIBLIOGRAPHY

BABSON, SETH 1900 "G. W. Percy, A.A.I.A." In *Proceedings of the 34th Annual Convention of the American Institute of Architects, 1900.* Washington: The institute.

"George W. Percy." 1901 *American Architect and Building News* 72, no. 1322:31.

KIRKER, HAROLD (1960)1973 *California's Architectural Frontier: Style and Tradition in the Nineteenth Century.* Rev. ed. Santa Barbara, Calif., and Salt Lake City, Utah: Peregrine Smith.

"Percy and Hamilton." 1889 *California Architect and Building News* 10, no. 9: unnumbered page.

PERCY, GEORGE WASHINGTON 1888 "Practical Applications of Iron and Concrete to Resist Transverse Strains." *Transactions of the Technical Society of the Pacific Coast* 5:1–18.

PERCY, GEORGE WASHINGTON 1894 "Concrete Construction." *California Architect and Building News* 15, no. 2:14–17.

RANSOME, ERNEST L., and SAURBREY, ALEXIS 1912 *Reinforced Concrete Buildings.* New York: McGraw.

SNYDER, JOHN WILLIAM 1975 "Index to San Francisco Building 1879–1900." Unpublished M.A. thesis, University of California, Davis.

PÉREZ PALACIOS, AUGUSTO

Augusto Pérez Palacios (1909–) symbolizes the great force of a new generation of architects who forged a new style of building in Mexico after the revolution of 1910–1929.

Among his most notable works is the Stadium of the University City which he designed together with the architects JORGE BRAVO and Raul Salinas for 80,000 spectators; it has a great functionality, excellent visibility, and an enormous aesthetic efficiency. MAX CETTO said of this work: "It is the most important building and the major architectural achievement of the University City."

Pérez Palacios also distinguished himself in the planning and the design of office complexes, industrial buildings, and hospitals.

SALVADOR PINOCELLY
Translated from Spanish by
Judith E. Meighan

WORK

n.d., Stadium (with Jorge Bravo and Raul Salinas), University City, Mexico City.

PERKINS, LAWRENCE B.

Lawrence Bradford Perkins (1907–) was born in Evanston, Illinois, and attended Cornell University College of Architecture. He was a founding partner, with PHILIP WILL, JR., and E. T. Wheeler, of Perkins, Wheeler, and Will in Chicago (1935–1946), later Perkins and Will (1946–1964) and The Perkins and Will Partnership (1964–1970), with offices in New York (since 1951) and Washington (since 1962). He was also director of the Adlai Stevenson Institute of International Affairs, Chicago (1965–1975).

MARY D. EDWARDS

WORKS

1939–1940, Crow Island Elementary School (with ELIEL SAARINEN and EERO SAARINEN), Winnetka, Ill. 1942, Rugen Elementary School, Glenview, Ill. 1948, Greenbriar School, Northbrook, Ill. 1949, Westwood Elementary School, Woodstock, Ill. 1952, Heathcote Elementary School, Scarsdale, N.Y. 1953, Washington School, Evanston, Ill. 1956, Linton High School, Schenectady, N.Y. 1958, Richard E. Byrd School, Chicago. 1960, Rockford College, Ill. 1963, United States Gypsum Building; 1966, First National Bank Building (with C. F. Murphy Associates); Chicago. 1976, Chapel (with A. Egner), Ithaca College, N.Y.

BIBLIOGRAPHY

PERKINS, LAWRENCE B. 1957 *Workplace for Learning.* New York: Reinhold.

PERKINS, LAWRENCE B. 1971 "Must We Live in Unlovely Cities?" *School Administrator.*

PERKINS, LAWRENCE B., and COCKING, WALTER D. 1949 *Schools.* New York: Reinhold.

PERKINS, LAWRENCE B., and WILL, PHILIP JR. 1969 "The Perkins and Will Partnership." *Building Construction.*

PERRAULT, CLAUDE

Claude Perrault (1613–1688) was by profession a physician. Having passed his doctorate in 1642, he followed for many years the course normal for a *docteur régent* of Paris: attending to his patients as well as to the affairs of the medical faculty, where at one time he held the chair of physiology and anatomy. A decisive change came when, in 1666, he was elected to the newly formed Académie des Sciences. From then on he was almost exclusively engaged in scientific research, foremost on dissections of animals performed by a team of scientists among whom he soon became the leader. Being interested in a wide range of subjects, he took an active part in the weekly conferences, read several papers, and published the result of his often original studies in his *Essais de Physique* (1680–1688).

Although it seems that before his entrance into the Academy his interests did not extend to the practical side of architecture, the fact that at about this date he was commissioned with the translation of VITRUVIUS indicates that he brought to it at least a fair knowledge of its theoretical aspect. His *Vitruvius* (1673) was generally acclaimed as a work of outstanding quality that remained a standard work throughout the next century and is still respected and referred to.

In some of the numerous annotations to the Vitruvian text, Perrault advanced his view on classical doctrine which he developed a few years later in the preface to the *Ordonnance* (1683). His unorthodox belief that proportions were not the cause of beauty and could—and should—be arbitrarily fixed, was refuted by the members of the Académie d'Architecture, notably by its director, FRANÇOIS BLONDEL, who attacked Perrault's position with counterarguments which he published in his *Cours* (1683). The controversy was often referred to in the next century, with French writers almost unanimously siding with Blondel, whereas English architects, among them CHRISTOPHER WREN, WILLIAM CHAMBERS, and ISAAC WARE, took serious notice of Perrault's ideas without however adopting them. Perrault's fame rested to a much greater extent on his supposed authorship of the eastern façade of the Louvre.

Perrault's claim to be solely responsible for the design of the Colonnade was disputed even in his lifetime, and these doubts were substantiated when modern scholarship tried to disentangle the intricate history of the Louvre. As a result of these studies, it is now widely believed that Perrault had no part in the conception of the façade, but was responsible for modifications that led to the final design.

As for another building, the Observatoire

Claude Perrault. Frontispiece to Vitruve, Les dix livres d'architecture.

(1667–1669), a research institute of the Académie des Sciences, it is certain that it was executed according to his design, outstanding in its thoughtful restraint and the sparing application of classical features. A design for another monument, an Arc de Triomphe (1669–?) to be erected on the Place du Throne, was accepted, but building operations ceased a few feet above ground.

Apart from the work connected with these three important buildings, Perrault's architectural activity was limited to occasionally submitted designs. The surviving ones are listed below, the last one being dated 1678. Thereafter, until his death ten years later, he was engaged in scientific research, in particular a project planned by the Académie des Sciences, the description of all machines then in use. When this plan came to nothing, Perrault prepared his own treatise which his brother Charles published posthumously under the title *Recueil de plusieurs machines* (1700).

WOLFGANG HERRMANN

WORKS

1667–1669, Observatoire; *1669–?, Arc de Triomphe (design only partially executed); Paris.

BIBLIOGRAPHY

BERGER, ROBERT W. 1970 "Charles Le Brun and the Louvre Colonnade." *Art Bulletin* 52:394–403.

BRAHAM, ALLAN, and WHITELEY, MARY 1964 "Louis le Vau's Projects for the Louvre and the Colonnade." *Gazette des Beaux-Arts* Series 6 64:285–296, 347–362.

BRÖNNER, WOLFGANG D. 1972 "Blondel-Perrault." Unpublished Ph.D. dissertation, Rheinische Friedrich-Wilhelms-Universität, Bonn.

DAMISH, HUBERT 1969 "La Colonnade de Perrault et les fonctions de l'ordre classique." In Pierre Francastel (editor), *L'Urbanisme de Paris et l'Europe: 1600–1680.* Paris: Klincksieck

FICHET, FRANÇOISE (editor) 1979 *La théorie architecturale à l'age classique.* Brussels: Mardaga.

GERMANN, GEORG 1980 *Einführung in die Geschichte der Architekturtheorie.* Darmstadt, Germany: Wissenschaftliche Buchgesellschaft.

HALLAYS, ANDRÉ 1926 *Les Perrault.* Paris: Perrin.

HAUTECOEUR, LOUIS 1927 *L'histoire des châteaux du Louvre et des Tuileries.* Paris: Van Oest.

HAUTECOEUR, LOUIS 1948 *Le règne de Louis XIV.* Volume 2 in *Histoire de l'Architecture classique en France.* Paris: Picard.

HERRMANN, WOLFGANG 1967 "Unknown Designs for the 'Temple of Jerusalem' by Claude Perrault." In Douglas Fraser, Howard Hibbard, and Milton L. Lewine (editors), *Essays in the History of Architecture Presented to Rudolf Wittkower.* London: Phaidon.

HERRMANN, WOLFGANG 1973 *The Theory of Claude Perrault.* London: Zwemmer.

JOSEPHSON, RAGNAR 1927 "Quelques dessins de Claude Perrault pour le Louvre." *Gazette des Beaux-Arts* 2:171–192.

KAMBARTEL, WALTER 1972 *Symmetrie und Schönheit: Über mögliche Voraussetzungen des neueren Kunstbewusstseins in der Architekturtheorie Claude Perraults.* Munich: Fink.

LANGE, LILIANE 1961 "La grotte de Thetis." *Art de France* 1:133–148.

LAPRADE, ALBERT 1960 *François D'Orbay.* Paris: Vincent, Fréal.

MIDDLETON, R. D., and WATKIN, DAVID 1980 *Neoclassical and 19th Century Architecture.* New York: Abrams.

PERRAULT, CLAUDE (1673)1979 *Vitruve, Les dix livres d'architecture. Traduction intégrée de Claude Perrault 1673 . . . présentée par André Dalmas.* Reprint. Paris: Balland.

PERRAULT, CLAUDE 1680–1688 *Essais de Physique, ou recueil de plusieurs traitez touchant les choses naturelles.* 4 vols. Paris: Colgnard.

PERRAULT, CLAUDE 1683 *Ordonnance des cinq espèces de colonnes selon la méthode des anciens.* Paris: Coignard.

PERRAULT, CLAUDE 1700 *Recueil de plusieurs machines de nouvelle invention.* Paris: Coignard.

PETZET, MICHAEL 1957 "Un projet des Perrault pour l'église Sainte-Geneviève à Paris." *Bulletin Monumental* 115:81–96.

PETZET, MICHAEL 1961 *Soufflots Sainte-Geneviève.* Berlin: de Gruyter.

PETZET, MICHAEL 1967*a* "Claude Perrault als Architekt des Pariser Observatoriums." *Zeitschrift für Kunstgeschichte* 30:1–54.

PETZET, MICHAEL 1967*b* "Entwürfe zur Louvrefaçade." *Akten des 21. Internationalen Kongresses fur Kunstgeschichte in Bonn 1964* 3:159ff.

RYKWERT, JOSEPH 1980 *The First Moderns.* Cambridge, Mass.: M.I.T. Press.

SAUVEL, TONY 1964 "Les auteurs de la Colonnade du Louvre." *Bulletin Monumental* 122:323–347.

SIGWALT, ARMAND 1948 *Une mystification de Charles Perrault: La colonnade du Louvre.* Paris: Les éditions nationales.

SORIANO, MARC 1972 *Le dossier Charles Perrault.* Paris: Hachette.

TATARKIEWICZ, WLADYSLAW 1974 Volume 3. pages 416ff and 421ff in *History of Aesthetics.* The Hague.

TEYSSÈDRE, BERNARD 1967 *L'art français au siècle de Louis XIV.* Paris: Le Livre de Pochi.

WEND, GRAF KALNEIN 1962 Review of Albert Laprade, *François d'Orbay. Zeitschrift für Kunstgeschichte* 25:184–190.

PERRAULT FAMILY

Henri-Maurice Perrault (1828–1903), born in Montreal, is believed to have been trained in standard Palladian (see ANDREA PALLADIO) and Gothic manners by JOHN OSTELL, his uncle, with whom he occasionally worked. In the early 1870s, he developed an elaborate Second Empire style, likely derived from the United States, in which he designed the Montreal City Hall (1871) and the Montreal Post Office (1872), his best known works. Later, in partnership with S. Lesage, he was responsible for numerous religious and commercial buildings.

Maurice Perrault (1857–1909) was the eldest son of Henri-Maurice Perrault and likely trained by him; he joined his father's practice in 1877. He was responsible for several major churches and other buildings in exotic styles. The Monument National (1894), a French-Canadian patriotic society hall in Montreal, and the south transept of Saint-Jacques (1891) which has since been incorporated into the façade of the main building of the University of Quebec at Montreal, are his best remembered works.

Joseph Perrault (1866–1923) was the second son of Henri-Maurice Perrault and likely trained by him. He continued the practice with S. Lesage in 1903; his son Jean-Julien Perrault (1893–1970) continued the work into the third quarter of the twentieth century.

JOHN BLAND

PERREAL, JEAN

Jean Perréal (1455?–1530) worked in Lyons, France, from 1485 until his death, advising the city on the construction of bridges, fortifications, and *quais,* and planning decorations for the ceremonial entries of royalty. Also called Jean de Paris, he served Kings Charles VIII, Louis XII, and François I as *valet de chambre* and royal painter. Perréal was acclaimed by his contemporaries for miniature portraits, but few surviving paintings have been definitively attributed to him. For Queen Anne of Brittany he designed the tomb of her parents (1501) and supervised its execution by Michel Colombe. He was retained by Marguerite of Austria (1509–1512) for work on the funerary monument to her husband Philibert, duke of Savoy, at Brou.

HILARY BALLON

WORK

1501, Tomb of François II and Marguerite of Foix, Cathedral, Nantes, France.

BIBLIOGRAPHY

BANCEL, E. M. (1885)1970 *Jehan Perréal dit Jehan de Paris.* Reprint. Geneva: Slatkine.

HAUTECOEUR, LOUIS (1943)1963 "La Première Renaissance." Volume 1, part 1 in *Histoire de l'Architecture classique en France.* Rev. ed. Paris: Picard.

HUILLET D'ISTRIA, MADELEINE 1949 "Jean Perréal." *Gazette des Beaux-Arts* Series 6 35:313–344, 377–386.

MAULDE LA CLAVIÈRE, RENÉ DE 1896 *Jean Perréal dit Jean de Paris.* Paris: Leroux.

PRADEL, PIERRE 1963 "Les autographes de Jean Perréal." *Bibliothèque de l'Ecole des Chartres* 121:132–186.

RING, GRETE 1950 "An Attempt to Reconstruct Perréal." *Burlington Magazine* 92:255–261.

WESCHER, PAUL R. 1948 "Jean Perréal: The 'Master of Charles VIII.'" *Art Quarterly* 11:352–357.

PERRET, AUGUSTE

Auguste Perret (1874–1954), one of the fathers of modern French architecture, was the first architect to give full architectural expression to the reinforced concrete frame: a structural system first patented by FRANÇOIS HENNEBIQUE in 1892. Perret's first multistory reinforced concrete apartment building was constructed in Paris in 1903 (25b rue Franklin). For the next twenty-five years he and his brother Gustave experimented with the new structural system by working as building contractors. Their firm, Perret Frères, constructeurs en béton armé, was inherited from their father Claude Perret, who was a prosperous building contractor in masonry construction. Under their guidance the firm soon established a reputation as the leading French building contractor in this new material; a reputation most triumphantly made manifest in their construction of the Théâtre des Champs Elysées (1911–1913), based on preliminary designs by Roger Bouvard and HENRI VAN DE VELDE.

Auguste Perret was born at Ixelles, near Brussels, where his father had been exiled for participating in the Commune uprising of 1871. But the amnesty of 1881 permitted the family to return to Paris, where the children were educated. After completing his schooling at the Ecole Alsacienne, Perret began studying for the *Concours d'Admission* to the famous Ecole des Beaux-Arts. Once admitted, he studied with JULIEN GUADET, proved an exceptionally gifted student, and won five *premières médailles* in the first class (i.e. the highest level of studies). But he never submitted a *projet de diplôme,* since the diploma would have precluded him, by law, from being a building contractor.

For the first three decades after Hennebique's invention, reinforced concrete was usually covered with a facing material such as brick, faience, stone, or plaster, because the bare surfaces were not merely uneven and unattractive, but were insufficiently compact to protect the reinforcing bars from rust. To create an architecture of reinforced concrete, it was therefore necessary to correct these inadequacies and to find the most effective way of giving visual expression to the new structural system. For technical advice, Perret relied on his consultant engineer, Louis Gellusseau; and since the designs to which he was building usually stipulated traditional facing materials, he and his craftsmen could pursue their own experiments with total freedom. The architects who had designed the buildings were unconcerned with the configuration of the structural core, provided they got the façades and spaces shown on their drawings.

The first manifestation of Perret's success in these experiments was the widely-publicized church of Notre Dame du Raincy (1922–1924). It was to be a war memorial to the soldiers who fell at the battle of the Ourcq—one of the most dramatic

Perret. Apartment Building, 25b rue Franklin. Paris. 1903–1904

Perret. Notre Dame. Le Raincy, France. 1922–1924

and tragic battles of World War I. Though the funds available were quite inadequate, Perret perceived that this was the ideal opportunity to demonstrate the monumental qualities of reinforced concrete devoid of any facing materials whatsoever, and he produced what is generally regarded as his masterpiece. Its continuing glass walls with concrete grilles and its slim columns carrying low-arching vaults achieve an interior of unusual lightness and grace. The stepped-up concrete steeple is of almost Gothic power, although the spirit of the whole building is clearly classic. The high technical accomplishment and innovative qualities of this building tend to attract more attention than its architectural merits; but it rapidly established Auguste Perret as the leading exponent of this architectural system, even though his architectural doctrine was then being eclipsed by LE CORBUSIER's publications and those emanating from WALTER GROPIUS and the Bauhaus, and elsewhere.

Perret's next most important building was the apartment building he constructed at 51–55 rue Raynouard, Paris (1930–1932). Like that at 25b rue Franklin, it was a speculative enterprise on a site which would have been financially unprofitable if built of traditional building materials. On the triangular lot formed by the junction of the rue Raynouard with the narrow, steeply sloping rue Berton, he built nine stories above the level of the former, and twelve above the level of the latter, taking the fullest advantage of all the deviations permitted by the building laws.

The entrance numbered 51 gives access to the multistory apartments. One luxury apartment is on each floor, and Perret himself occupied the apartment at the top. The other entrance (numbered 55) led to the offices of Perret Frères by means of an impressive spiral stairway descending directly to the lower level. Its character has been changed in recent years, but it was originally a single uninterrupted space with a continuous glass façade looking south from the heights of Passy across the Seine. Beneath the office were the servants' rooms, traditionally located in the timber roof-space. The lowest floor, level with the rue Berton at its lowest point adjoining the site, gave access to the garage.

In plan and general conception, it differed little from Hennebique's offices and apartment building in the rue Danton (1898), designed by Edouard Arnaud. But structurally and visually, it constituted a radical and epoch-making innovation in the history of reinforced concrete architecture. All the elements of the structural frame (i.e. the posts and beams) were poured in place and left uncovered, whilst the infilling elements (windows and wall surfaces) were also of bare concrete, but precast.

To achieve these effects, Perret relied on two technical processes which had been developed and perfected during the preceding decade. The first consisted of vibrating the concrete to achieve maximum compactness; the second consisted of removing the thin film of mortar on the surface to disclose the stone aggregate which is the basis of concrete's structural strength.

The vibration of concrete involves technical difficulties more relevant to civil engineering than to architecture, and so will not be discussed here. But the removal of the mortar film is of considerable architectural interest since Le Corbusier, who had worked in Perret's studio, was to claim in 1952 that the retention of this mortar film, or *béton brut de décoffrage,* was a device he had invented for the Unité d'habitation at Marseilles (1946–1952).

Whether or not *béton brut* is more attractive or a more correct expression of reinforced concrete, is a matter of taste and judgement. But the facts of the issue should be stated in order to understand what Perret was trying to achieve, and what he regarded as his more important accomplishments.

In building the church at Le Raincy, Perret used *béton brut* to minimize the costs, and also because he had not yet developed a reliable way to remove the mortar film without endangering the durability of the structure. After World War II, when he rebuilt Le Havre, he also used *béton brut* for much the same reasons as those which motivated Le Corbusier, namely the lack of funds. But when he built his own apartment building in the rue Raynouard (1930-1932), he applied to the vibrated concrete a technique for removing the cement film known as *bouchardage* or bush-hammering. It matters little whether he was the first architect to apply to rough concrete surfaces this masonry technique for cleaning roughly-quarried stone. What matters is that for Perret, the visual expression of the structural material was as important as the visual expression of the constructional system. Far from "lacking a sense of detail" (Scruton, 1979, p. 24), he became obsessed with the desire to achieve it in profiling and coloration. He obtained the former by modulations in the timber formwork. He obtained the latter by using aggregates of varying size and color.

The culmination of Perret's research, and the best expression of his doctrine, was the Mobilier National (1934–1935) built near the Gobelins factory in Paris. This building contains all the antique furniture (including tapestries, carpets, etc.) owned by the French State, and its purpose is the storage, display, repair, and supervision of this priceless collection, which is used to furnish offi-

Perret.
Mobilier National.
Paris.
1934–1935

Perret.
Saint Joseph.
Le Havre, France.
1952

cial government premises. The most difficult problem confronting the architect was the harmonious correlation of disparate and exacting functions within a single edifice; a problem rendered even more complex by the awkward shape of the steeply sloping site.

Perret selected a structural module of $1\frac{1}{2}$ meters, and an axial spacing between the columns of 6 meters. In the final stage of design, the interaxial spacing of the columns was reduced to 5.84 meters, and the module to 1.46. Within this standardized structural frame or *charpente,* the functional spaces gradually increased in scale and monumentality from that of the residential quarters of the curators, at the entrance, to that of the two-story top-lit exhibition gallery crowning the rear façade of the interior courtyard. The floor of the courtyard is in fact the flat roof of a wide-span hall required for the storage of carpets. The main floor at courtyard level consists essentially of loading bays and workshops. Above are the numerous administrative offices for those who control the complex activities of this establishment.

In 1936, when this building was illustrated and described in French periodicals, the international avant-garde generally considered it unworthy of serious attention. Its carefully proportioned structural pilasters and beams were too reminiscent of seventeenth century classicism; its carefully profiled precast windows, and its bush-hammered infill panels, were totally at variance with the flat plastered walls punctured by continuous horizontal windows then in vogue. Eventually, however, it will surely be acknowledged as a great masterpiece.

The last monumental building Perret designed before the outbreak of World War II was the Musée des Travaux Publics, a museum for models of large engineering schemes such as dams, bridges, etc. It was designed in 1936, but was not finished until after his death when it was modified to serve as the headquarters of the commonwealth constituted by former French colonies.

Built on a large triangular site near the Palais de Chaillot, the apex of the triangle was on the Place d'Iena. The only major constraint was that it had to accommodate scale models of enormous size and weight. This its internal columns had to be minimal. Perret's solution was to have the main entrance hall and auditorium adjoining the Place d'Iena, and to span each of the two vast exhibition halls with a concrete slab measuring 65 feet by 250 feet. Thus the upper floors of the exhibition halls had no intermediate supports, but their ground floors were articulated by four rows of columns at approximately 20 feet axial spacing.

To support the roof slabs of these exhibition halls, Perret used freestanding columns, which tapered downward (since their rigidity was maintained by the upper joint as in the case of tables and chairs) from 1.03 meters to 80 centimeters. This diminution was also given entasis: a relatively simple procedure when the formwork is composed of timber staves assembled polygonally, and maintained in position by external timber templates secured at regular intervals. After the removal of this formwork, the joints of the twenty-four staves were left *brut de décoffrage,* but the surfaces between were bush-hammered to display the pebble aggregate. They not only gave the appearance of classical columns; they bore a marked affinity with those of the colonnades facing the Place de la Concorde, both in scale and disposition.

It is doubtful whether anyone—even Perret's most fervent admirers—would claim that the building was architecturally successful. But it is significant in the history of Perret's career as a sort of manifesto against the International style, which for the previous ten years had controlled the professional media and had become the new orthodoxy in German, British, and American schools. The Musée was a dramatic assertion concerning the effects of novel technological skills: that the resulting architectural truths do not necessarily produce unprecedented compositions and details, and that the quality of an environment is more important than any assertions of personal originality.

Four years later, when architectural registration became legally obligatory in France, Perret was named the first president of the newly formed Ordre des Architectes. After World War II, he was elected to the Institut de France, and received numerous tokens of distinction from outside his own country. He was also named president of the International Union of Architects. His final architectural achievement was the rebuilding of Le Havre (1949–1956), which had been demolished during the war. He and a team of his disciples developed the masterplan, but Perret designed the plaza round the new city hall and the church of Saint Joseph (1952).

Perret died in 1954 in the apartment on the rue Raynouard which was not only one of the most striking monuments to his creative ability, but a witness to his sense of place: to the fact that he always built for a particular urban context.

PETER COLLINS

WORKS

1903–1904, Apartment building, 25b rue Franklin; *1905, Garage Marboeuf, 51 rue de Ponthieu; 1911–1913, Théâtre des Champs Elysées; Paris. 1915, Docks of Casablanca, Morocco. 1922–1924, Church of Nôtre Dame, Le Raincy, France. 1926, Church of Sainte Thérèse, Montmagny, France. 1929, Ecole Normale de Musique; 1930–1932, Apartment building, 51 rue Raynouard; 1934–1935, Mobilier National; 1936, Musée des Travaux Publics (now the Conseil Economique; completed after Perret's death); Paris. 1949–1956, Plan of Le Havre; 1952, Church of Saint Joseph; Le Havre, France.

BIBLIOGRAPHY

CHAMPIGNEULLE, BERNARD 1959 *Perret.* Paris: Arts et métiers graphiques.

COLLINS, PETER 1959 *Concrete: The Vision of a New Architecture; A Study of Auguste Perret and His Precursors.* London: Faber.

JAMOT, PAUL 1927 *A. G. Perret et l'Architecture du béton armé.* Paris: Vanoest.

MAYER, MARCEL 1928 "A. & G. Perret: 24 phototypies." *Les albums d'Art Druet,* vol. 16. Paris: Librairie de France.

PARIS, CONSERVATOIRE NATIONAL DES ARTS ET METIERS 1959 *Perret: Catalogue de l'exposition organisée à l'occasion de la remise au Conservatoire du fonds A. G. Perret.* Paris: Conservatoire.

ROGERS, E. 1955 "Auguste Perret." *Il Balcone: Architetti del movimento moderno,* no. 13. Milan: Il Balcone.

SCRUTON, ROGER 1979 *The Aesthetics of Architecture.* N.J.: Princeton University Press.

ZAHAR, MARCEL 1959 *D'Une doctrine d'architecture: Auguste Perret.* Paris: Vincent, Freal.

PERRIAND, CHARLOTTE

Charlotte Perriand (20th century) joined the atelier of LE CORBUSIER in 1927. In the two years that followed, she collaborated with Le Corbusier and PIERRE JEANNERET on the furniture classics exhibited in the 1929 Salon d'Automne.

Although Perriand studied with other major artists—Fernand Leger, George Candilis, and JOSEP LLUIS SERT—her early association with Le Corbusier remained a strong influence on her interior and architectural designs. Her work in the 1950s with JEAN PROUVÉ on "serial" furniture (for example, modular wall cabinets) illustrates her continuing interest in the machine aesthetic—the clean, streamlined design Le Corbusier associated with mass production.

An equally important theme in Perriand's career was her interest in the traditions of different cultures. She traveled widely and incorporated the materials and methods of local crafts into her own distinctively contemporary design (exhibit for a Tokyo department store, 1941; chalet, Méribel les Allues, Savoie, 1963). Perriand's particular achievement was the harmonious synthesis of traditional design elements with the aesthetic of the International style.

CAROL L. CORDEN

WORKS

1929, Salon d'Automne (furniture; with Le Corbusier and Pierre Jeanneret), Paris. *1935, Young Man's Apartment, Brussels International Exhibit. *1941, Department Store Exhibit, Tokyo. 1948, Hotel (interior; with C. Durupt), Méribel les Allues, Savoie, France. 1958, Air-France Agency (with P. Bradock and A. Salomon), London. 1960, Air-France Agency (with J. Sakakura and R. Suzuki), Tokyo. 1960, French Government Tourist Office (with Ernö Goldinger), Haymarket, London. 1963, Chalet, Méribel les Allues, Savoie, France.

BIBLIOGRAPHY

ALISON, FILIPPO 1979 "I Mobili di Le Corbusier à Parigi, the Cassina Production on Show in Paris." *Domus* no.593:30–33.

"Chalet à Méribel les Allues, Savoie." 1963 *Aujourd'*

hui: Arts et Architecture 7, no. 41:70–71.
"Charlotte Perriand." 1964 *L'Architecture d'Aujourd'hui* 35, nos. 113–114:60–61.
"Charlotte Perriand in Giappone." 1947 *Domus* no. 219:23–27.
DIOLÉ, PHILIPPE 1939 "La fonction crée la ligne: Un bureau de Charlotte Perriand." *Art et Décoration* 69:51–53.
"Elementi d'arredamento per la serie." 1953 *Domus* no. 283:22–25.
"French Government Tourist Office." 1963 *Architectural Design* 33:601–603.
"Furniture by Le Corbusier and Charlotte Perriand." 1966 *Architectural Design* 36:361.
PERRIAND, CHARLOTTE 1965 "Temoignage à Le Corbusier." *Aujourd'hui: Arts et Architecture* 9, no. 51:110–111.
PERRIAND, CHARLOTTE 1966 "Pour une prise de conscience de nos responsabilités." *L'Architecture d'Aujourd'hui* 36, no. 126:10.
"Travel Agency." 1960 *Architectural Review* 127:268–269.
"Une habitation au Japon." 1946 *Techniques et Architecture* 6, nos. 7–8:370–373.

PERRONET, JEAN RODOLPHE

Born in Suresnes, France, the son of a Swiss soldier, Jean Rodolphe Perronet (1708–1794) himself started out as a soldier, but in 1725 he entered J. B. A. Beausire's office (see BEAUSIRE FAMILY) in Paris, working on embankments and sewers. He enrolled in the Corps des Ponts et Chaussées in 1735 and was posted to Alençon where he was made an engineer of the *Généralité* in 1737. When Daniel Trudaine initiated the Ecole des Ponts et Chaussées in 1747, Perronet was called to Paris as director, a post he held for forty-seven years. In 1750, he was promoted to *inspecteur général.* His largest undertaking was the Canal de Bourgogne (1775–1832). His bridge-building career, which was to establish him as the most daring and successful engineer in Europe, began in 1763. Perronet's revolution was to reject the idea that each arch of a bridge should be stable in itself. Instead, he designed them to act as counterthrusts to one another and was thus able to increase their spans greatly and to flatten their curves. His aim was to reduce the masonry mass to the utmost degree, a goal also pursued by JACQUES GERMAIN SOUFFLOT at the Church of Sainte Geneviève, and Perronet early became Soufflot's defender and adviser.

R. D. MIDDLETON

WORKS

1745–1753, Notre Dame (tower), Alençon, Orne, France. 1757–1765, Pont de Mantes, over the Seine, Seine et Marne, France. 1765–1786, Pont de Château-Thierry, over the Marne, Aisne, France. 1768–1774, Pont de Neuilly (with Antoine de Chézy and Pierre Antoine Demoustier), over the Seine, Paris. 1770–1771, Pont des Fontaines, Chantilly; *1771–1786, Pont de Sainte Maxence (with Demoustier), over the Oise; Oise, France. 1775, Château d'Etrey, near Claye-Souilly; 1775, Pont Biais, near Lagny, over the Bicheret; Seine et Marne, France. 1785–1787, Pont de Brunoy, over the Yères, Pyramide, France. 1786–1787, Pont de Rozoy, over the Yères, Seine et Marne, France. 1787–1791, Pont de la Concorde (with Demoustier), over the Seine, Paris. 1794, Pont de Nemours (built by Dherbelot and Louis-Charles Boistard 1795–1804), over the Loing, Seine et Marne, France.

BIBLIOGRAPHY

DARTEIN, FERNARD DE (1906)1907 "La vie et les travaux de Jean-Rodolphe Perronet." Volume 2, pages 1–66 in *Etudes sur les ponts en pierre remarquables par leur décoration antérieur au XIXe siècle.* Paris: Béranger.
LESAGE, PIERRE CHARLES 1805 *Notice pour servir à l'éloge de M. Perronet.* Paris: Bernard.
LESAGE, PIERRE CHARLES 1806 "Observations sur les rues, égouts, ponts, places publiques de Londres, routes, chemins, et divers ports de l'Angleterre." Pages 79–116 in *Recueil de divers mémoires extraits de la bibliothèque des Ponts et Chausées.* Paris: Bernard.
PERRONET, JEAN RODOLPHE 1782–1789 *Description des projets et de la construction des ponts de Neuilly, de Mantes, d'Orléans et autres.* 2 vols and supplement. Paris: Imprimerie Royale.
RICHE DE PRONY, GASPARD CLAIR FRANÇOIS MARIE 1829 *Notice historique sur Jean-Rodolphe Perronet, lue à la séance publique des quatre Académies de l'Institut de France, le 24 Avril 1829.* Paris: Firmin-Didot.

PERRY, ISAAC G.

Isaac Gale Perry (1822–1904), the son and apprentice of a carpenter-joiner, was a self-trained architect whose career focused on the design of large public buildings. Beginning as a builder in Keeseville, New York, he moved to New York in 1852 to work in the architectural office of Thomas R. Jackson. Five years later, he received his first major commission, the design and construction of the Gothic Revival New York State Inebriate Asylum (1857–1866) in Binghamton, where he settled in 1872. His work included several churches and municipal buildings, the Second Empire Sherman Phelps Residence (1870), his own cast-iron Perry Block (1876), and the Lackawanna County Courthouse (1881) in Scranton, Pennsylvania. Under one of the civil service reforms initiated by Governor Grover Cleveland, Perry was appointed architect and commissioner in charge of completing the controversial New York State Capitol building in Albany, succeeding the design team of LEOPOLD EIDLITZ, H. H. RICHARDSON, and FREDERICK LAW OLMSTED on the project. Perry's work at the Capitol was Richardsonian in spirit, best represented by the monumental exterior staircase called the Eastern Approach (1889–1897). Perry's office established the prototype of the New York State Architect, his work extending beyond the Capitol to include many state armories, an extensive renovation of the Executive Mansion (1887), and the Saint Lawrence State Hospital complex (1887–1899) in Ogdensburg.

WESLEY HAYNES

WORKS

1852, Rembrandt Hall, Keeseville, N.Y. 1857–1866, New York State Inebriate Asylum; 1866–1868, Centenary Methodist Episcopal Church; Binghamton, N.Y. 1868, First Presbyterian Church, Ossining, N.Y. 1868–1869, Dutch Reformed Church, Port Jervis, N.Y. 1869, First Congregational Church; 1870, First National Bank; 1870, Sherman Phelps Residence, Binghamton, N.Y. 1870–1871, Scranton Second National Bank; 1870–1871, Scranton Trust Company; Pa. 1870–1872, First Baptist Church, Binghamton, N.Y. 1871, First Congregational Church, Wallkill, N.Y. 1871, Phelps Building; 1871–1872, Binghamton Central High School; 1876, Perry Block; Binghamton, N.Y. 1881, Lackawanna County Courthouse, Scranton, Pa. 1883–1899, New York State Capitol; 1887, Executive Mansion; Albany, N.Y. 1887–1899, Saint Lawrence State Hospital, Ogdensburg, N.Y.

BIBLIOGRAPHY

HAYNES, WESLEY 1981 "Isaac G. Perry: Craftsman-Architect." Unpublished manuscript, New York State Capitol Symposium, Albany, N.Y.

LAWYER, WILLIAM (editor) 1900 *Binghamton: Its Settlement, Growth and Development.* Boston: Century.

ZUKOWSKY, JOHN 1978 "The New York State Inebriate Asylum, Binghamton." In *Apocrypha III.* State University of New York at Binghamton.

PERSICO, EDOARDO

Edoardo Persico (1900–1936) never took academic courses in architecture but his role among architects of the 1930s and more generally, in the Italian architectural culture, was and continues to be fundamental.

Persico was born in Naples, where he studied law. He became involved with architecture only after he arrived in Milan in 1929. For several years before that, he had been in Turin, occupied with various things but especially with art criticism, particularly painting. Critical judgment of his work in this respect is divided, but certainly for him it was a highly useful experience which marked the passing of his cultural interests from the field of literature to that of architecture. During his Turin years, Persico managed to fashion a group out of several painters, including Jessie Boswell, Gigi Chessi, Carlo Levi, Francesco Monzio, and Enrico Paulucci, which for a brief time brought life to the cultural and political ambience of the city. Certainly, Persico's presence did not pass unnoticed and, amid contradictory reactions, he was able to provoke situations which brought him to the attention of others. This is of particular importance if one considers the atmosphere of demoralization and opportunism which Fascism's by now undisputed victory provoked.

In the early months of 1929, when he had transferred to Milan, Persico worked first at Pier Maria Bardi's art gallery and then at the Galleria del Milione for some time. Tired of the difficult relationship with painters, he joined the editorial staff of the magazine *La Casa Bella* at the invitation of GIUSEPPE PAGANO. In working as an editor within the cultural and professional ambience which developed around this magazine, Persico finally managed to bring into focus a long series of intuitions and afterthoughts which had accumulated throughout years of wasteful efforts. One of Persico's first objectives in this new activity was the radical transformation of the magazine, including its graphics; with him, *Casabella* stopped being a decorous magazine and soon became one of the most important cultural landmarks in Italy and elsewhere. This does not mean that *Casabella* was his personal tribune. Because of the delicate balance in the editorial staff and above all given Pagano's strong presence, Persico's most important statements appeared in other periodicals, such as GIO PONTI's *Domus,* or at conferences.

Persico's influence on the young who initiated their professional activities during those foreshortened years of the 1930s consisted in suggesting further cultural, or expressive, possibilities so as to overcome the clash which was underway and had by then crystallized around two absolutely irreconcilable and, as demonstrated after the war, decidedly sterile positions. In the polemics of the time, on the one side were the "traditionalist" intellectuals, who were permeated with a post-Risorgimento hybrid culture, and on the other, the younger generation which accumulated a long series of various kinds of claims under the banner of Rationalism. Although the two groups were in opposition, they also shared a common identity which cannot be ignored: their long and substantial adherence to Fascism. Persico was conspicuous for his independent position as a declared Roman Catholic, and as such, he derived every consideration from moral presuppositions of an entirely different source. By virtue of this, he did not accept the political and cultural hegemony of the state as the principle in every situation as did the others. He did his utmost to see to it that the culture in its entirety was permeated with a European spirit, but at the same time he accused Italian Rationalist architects of having scant indigenous expressiveness, of wanting to involve the fortunes of culture with the politics of Fascism, and that was to recognize that in the end architecture was a "state art." In particular, he accused the many polemicists of the time, especially the Rationalists, of "getting along with both God and the Devil," accumulating ambiguities, obvious contradictions, and extemporaneous opportunism on a massive scale.

His major charge concerned their adoption of a program which in his view had been espoused by Charles Fourier a century earlier. Persico vehemently criticized the Rationalists' desire to imagine a new world beginning with an architectural system without first clarifying the meaning and spirit of liberty itself, and this could not be sought in the production of standards or a pre-established reality. Inspired by Jacques Maritain, Persico recalled that the way of looking at art in its practical and moral aspects together is a sign of crisis, the index of an unresolved Romantic problem. He therefore had a clear aversion to "social art," a concept which ultimately pushes artists in all directions indiscriminately. Was there a remedy for all this? Persico indicated it in the search for a superior order which can derive neither from a universal architectural style nor from a more or less Fourieristic system. The order of which he spoke and which was the exultant and tormented tendency of his brief life is beyond architecture and thus cannot be exhausted in a polemical formalism, without substance and above all without faith. "Modern architecture," said Persico, "is not what Americans cynically think it is: 'the engineering solution of the building problem'; it is not LE CORBUSIER's standard nor [BRUNO] TAUT's 'sozialen Fragen' [socially motivated architecture]. Its destiny, its prophecy, is to vindicate the fundamental liberty of the spirit."

RICCARDO MARIANI
Translated from Italian by
Diane Ghirardo

WORKS

1934, Galleria Vittorio Emanuele (publicity construction; with Marcello Nizzoli); 1934, Medaglie d'Oro Room (with Nizzoli), Italian Aeronautical Exhibition; 1934, Parker Store (with Nizzoli), Largo Santa Margherita; 1935, Honor Court (with Nizzoli and Giancarlo Palanti, completed posthumously in 1936); 1935, Parker Store (with Nizzoli), Corso Vittorio Emanuele; Milan.

BIBLIOGRAPHY

GHIRARDO, DIANE 1980 "Italian Architects and Fascist Politics: An Evaluation of the Rationalists' Role in Regime Building" *Journal of the Society of Architectural Historians* 39, no. 2:109–127.

MARIANI, RICCARDO (editor) 1977 *Oltre l'architettura: Scritti scelti e lettere.* Milan: Feltrinelli.

VERONESI, GIULIA 1953 *Difficoltà politiche dell'architettura in Italia: 1920–1940.* Milan: Libreria Editrice Politecnica Tamburini.

VERONESI, GIULIA (editor) 1964 *Tutte le opere: 1923–1935.* Milan: Edizione di Comunità.

PERSIUS, LUDWIG

The closest and most talented of KARL FRIEDRICH SCHINKEL's many pupils, Friedrich Ludwig Persius (1803–1845), a native of Potsdam, Germany, began his brief career as supervising architect under Schinkel at Prince Karl's Schloss Glienicke (1824–1826). There, and at Charlottenhof (1826–1827) at Sanssouci, Persius was introduced to the transformation of older structures into asymmetrically massed compositions carefully integrated with their natural settings. Although his villa style was inspired by Schinkel's use of rural vernacular Italian models, Persius made the genre his own. The exterior massing of his villas is always expressive of the plan, but his primary concern was to treat each building as a problem in abstract cubic composition. Unlike other specialists in the villa style, such as LUDWIG FERDINAND HESSE, FRIEDRICH HITZIG VON ARNIM, and EDUARD KNOBLAUCH who relied upon historical ornament for plastic effect, Persius modeled his villas severely in stucco; their crisp edges lend a clean silhouette. In 1841, Persius succeeded Schinkel as court architect in Potsdam, and in the four years before his death he collaborated with Friedrich Wilhelm IV, newly ascended to the throne, in the transformation of the whole Potsdam region into a panoramic landscape around the Havel River. The riverside churches at Sakrow and Sanssouci, both combining early Christian basilicas with the Lombardic brick and terra cotta style, were major elements in that grand scheme.

BARRY BERGDOLL

WORKS

1833–1834, Handmann House; 1834–1835, Roman Baths (designed by Karl Friedrich Schinkel), Charlottenhof, Potsdam, Germany. 1836–1838, Steam Engine House and Gardener's House, Klein Glienicke, Berlin. 1837–1838, Villa Persius; 1839, Villa Jacobs; 1841, Civil Cabinet Building; 1841–1842, Sanssouci (extensions); 1841–1842, Sello House; 1841–1842, Wildpark Buildings; 1841–1843, Steam Engine House, Sanssouci; Potsdam, Germany. 1841–1844, Heilandskirche (finished in the 1850s by FRIEDRICH AUGUST STÜLER, Ludwig Ferdinand Hesse, and von Arnim), Sakrow, Germany. 1842–1844, Fassanerie, Sanssouci; 1843, Villa Stolberg; 1843, Villa Turm; 1843–1844, Villa Brandt (altered); 1843–1844, Villa Schöningen, Glienicke Bridge; 1843–1850, Nikolaikirche (dome and turrets added); 1844, Meierei in New Garden, Sanssouci; 1844, Steam Engine House, Schloss Babelsberg; 1844, Supply Depot (remodeling), Leipzigerstrasse; 1844–1845, Villa Tiedke; 1844–1846, Kleines Kabinettschaus (Villa Illaire); Potsdam, Germany.

BIBLIOGRAPHY

BORRMANN, RICHARD 1926 "Zeichnungen und Entwürfe von Ludwig Persius im Architektur Museum der Technischen Hochschule zu Berlin." *Zeitschrift für Bauwesen* 76:1–9.

BÖRSCH-SUPAN, EVA 1977 *Berliner Baukunst nach Schinkel, 1840–1870.* Munich: Prestel.

BÖRSCH-SUPAN, EVA (editor) 1980 *Ludwig Persius: Das Tagebuch des Architekten Friedrich Wilhelms IV, 1840–1845.* Munich: Deutscher Kunstverlag.

DEHIO, LUDWIG 1961 *Friedrich Wilhelm IV. von Preussen: Ein Baukünstler der Romantik.* Munich: Deutscher Kunstverlag.

FLEETWOOD-HESKETH, R., and FLEETWOOD-HESKETH, P. 1928 "Ludwig Persius of Potsdam." *Architect's Journal* 68:77–87, 113–120.

GIESE, LEOPOLD 1925 "Ludwig Persius als Architekt." *Kunstchronik* 35:561–565.

HITCHCOCK, H. R. 1931 "The Romantic Architecture of Potsdam." *International Studio* 99:46–49.

KANIA, HANS 1939 *Potsdam: Staats- und Bürgerbauten.* Berlin: Deutsche Kunstverlag.

PERSIUS, FRIEDRICH LUDWIG 1843–1849 *Architektonische Entwürfe für den Umbau vorhandener Gebäude.* Potsdam: Riegel.

POENSGEN, GEORG 1930 *Die Bauten Friedrich Wilhelms IV. in Potsdam.* Berlin: Deutscher Kunstverlag.

POENSGEN, GEORG 1931 "Ludwig Persius." Pages 39–44 in *Schinkel Almanach des Architekten- und Ingenieur Vereins.* Berlin: Architekten- und Ingenieur Vereins.

SIEVERS, JOHANNES 1942 *Bauten für den Prinzen Karl von Preussen.* Berlin: Deutsche Kunstverlag.

PERUZZI, BALDASSARRE

Baldassarre Peruzzi (1481–1536) was born in Siena, Italy. He was buried with great honor and ceremony in the Pantheon in Rome, next to RAPHAEL.

Even in the advanced sixteenth century, Peruzzi still represented the *uomo universale,* that is, the artist of universal and masterly ability interested in both practice and theory, whose works range from the arts to engineering. His oeuvre included works of draftsmanship and painting as well as architecture. Even gravestone statuary can be traced to him (Frommel, 1967–1968).

By the end of his life he had become the leading architect both in Siena and in Rome. His position in sixteenth-century architecture is based on the High Renaissance Palazzo della Farnesina and the mannerist Palazzo Massimo (both in Rome) and furthermore on his conceptual and theoretical contributions to architecture, which, through the publications of his disciple SEBASTIANO SERLIO became known throughout Europe.

In Siena, where Peruzzi was trained and was first active as a painter, he may have been influenced by FRANCESCO DI GIORGIO MARTINI, which may also explain his initial attitude as an architect. This attitude can be discerned in the Villa le Volte (?–1505) which was built near Siena for Sigismondo Chigi and is generally attributed to him. In it some essential aspects of the Roman Palazzo Farnesina were anticipated, as for instance the façade with its two side wings framing a central loggia. This same connection is also apparent in the architectural details.

Some time in the middle of the first decade of the sixteenth century, Peruzzi moved to Rome. For an architect at the beginning of his career, Rome was at this time without question by far the best place for his further education. Not only were there the remains of the exemplary architecture of antiquity, but also, under the dynamic patronage of Pope Julius II, DONATO BRAMANTE and Raphael, with their Vatican church and villa buildings and Roman palaces, were creating the architectural style which, as the Roman High Renaissance, became a model for the whole world. Peruzzi took part in this development, and his compatriot Agostino Chigi, an enormously rich banker and a relative of the owner of the Villa le Volte, soon awarded him with one of the most renowned architectural commissions of the Roman Cinquecento, namely, the commission for what today is known as the Palazzo della Farnesina.

Among the Roman artists who at that time were generating a new basis of understanding for the architecture of antiquity, Peruzzi—not least for his work as a painter and in the decorative arts—held a high but certainly not a leading position. He was open to the influence of Bramante, Raphael, and GIULIO ROMANO. Only in 1520 did he acquire an important post, as "coadjutor" (assistant) to Antonio da Sangallo the Younger (see SANGALLO FAMILY) on the construction of St. Peter's in Rome. With that he also became an autonomous personality. At the untimely end of his life, he had come to be considered an exemplary architect as well as a leading teacher and architectural authority.

The Farnesina (1505/1506–1511) was not

Peruzzi's only work for Agostino Chigi, for whom he also worked outside Rome (Frommel, 1961), but it was his first masterpiece. With the participation of Raphael and his workshop in the decorative work it became a *Gesamtkunstwerk* of the Roman High Renaissance, comprising all the artistic disciplines. In it, Peruzzi appeared not only as the creator of the architectural design but also as the decorative painter of the interior and of the façades and as a master of illusionist perspective (Sala delle Prospettive).

GIORGIO VASARI describes the building as "non murato ma veramente nato" (not built but truly born), but this aperçu must not divert us from noting that what we have here is an integration of Tuscan prototypes (Villa le Volte) with contemporary Roman models, such as the Belvedere of Pope Innocent VIII in the Vatican. These contemporary impressions are also reflected in the organization of the Farnesina's façades, which, with two equal pilastered stories and rectangular window aediculae, represents a quintessential résumé of façade development since LEON BATTISTA ALBERTI's Rucellai Palace in Florence and the window structures of the Roman Palazzo della Cancelleria. The result has been described as "the only achievement equal in genius" to the palaces of Bramante, and this not so much because of any lasting influence as on grounds of artistic quality.

Due to its entirely free-standing "suburban" location in the middle of a garden, the building has a special typological position in the Roman context. Indeed, the question has been discussed whether this is a villa rather than a palace, finally to be decided in favor of a palace. A concomitant of the functional complexity of this structure is that the platform between the two wings represents the court of a theater. Today, a crucial element in the building's exterior appearance is lacking: the decoration of the façades, which were completely painted, can be imagined only from the very few traces now remaining and from the sketches made at the time (the frieze over the south portal is from the nineteenth century). The total impression derives less from a dramatic composition or the articulation of masses than from the balanced harmony of the proportions and a sensitive organization of the surfaces. The whole is a pre-Bramantesque masterpiece in Rome, a sixteenth-century work using the forms of the fifteenth.

Alberto Pio, the imperial ambassador and count of Carpi, was living in Rome next door to the Farnesina during the time Peruzzi was employed by him to develop the city of Carpi into a princely residence. Peruzzi may have traveled to Carpi for the first time in 1514, then again in 1515 when he accompanied Pope Julius II to Bologna.

Peruzzi.
Palazzo della Farnesina.
Rome.
1505–1511

The first structure was a façade for the ancient Duomo of Carpi (*La Sagra*), for which a contract was signed on February 15, 1515, on the basis of a design by Peruzzi. His concept for the façade followed a Bramante prototype, the parish church of Roccaverano, although Peruzzi was more consistent in the articulation of the intersection of the large and small orders. After the Farnesina, this was a new approach to the Bramantesque style.

The model he designed for the new Duomo of Carpi arrived there in 1515 and the building itself was soon executed. (The present building has been reduced by one bay, altered on the façade, and restored.) Peruzzi's plan reflects in reduced form the then current plans for St. Peter's in Rome and bears witness once again to the influence of Bramante. This is, however, valid only in the most fundamental sense; it must be taken into account that the construction was carried out by North Italian workmen and was interrupted by the death of Alberto Pio in 1530. Probably the most characteristic elements are the forms of the piers supporting the dome which echo those of St. Peter's but show an individual variation by being placed diagonally.

The Church of San Nicolò had been founded by Alberto Pio in 1493 and, with the construction of the dome and the spaces surrounding it, was already far advanced. When in the years between 1518 and 1522, because of revived interest, the work was to be pushed forward, Peruzzi's ideas could be applied to the design, requiring remodeling only of the three-bay nave. Even there, given the form language of the older structure already existing, this could affect only general issues of scale and proportion. Besides this, Peruzzi was also active at the palace of the count, as can be seen from the detailing of the forms.

In the second decade of the sixteenth century, Peruzzi's work as a painter-decorator took precedence over his architectural work, and consequently he drew closer to Raphael in his orientation. His painted illusionist decoration of the Sala delle Prospettive in the Farnesina palace can, however, also be interpreted in architectural terms. The illusionist character of the perspective in these decorations is hardly imaginable without Raphael's work in the Vatican loggie, and the rhythmic colonnade that supplies the over-all decorative scheme of the *sala* shows a close connection with Raphael's plans for the ambulatories of St. Peter's.

In spite of literary documentation, the part Peruzzi may have played in Todi (Santa Maria della Consolazione) cannot be verified. However, his projects, submitted in the competition for the building of San Giovanni dei Fiorentini in Rome (1519–1520) give clear evidence of his commitment to the monumental rotunda with strong three-dimensional articulation. After Raphael's death (1520), Peruzzi was put in charge of the work at St. Peter's in Rome.

An invitation to Bologna (1521–1523) provided Peruzzi with new architectural and painting commissions in northern Italy. The projects for the façade of the Cathedral of San Petronio in Bologna that have been preserved still show Raphael's impact in their figural elements while at the same time giving impressive evidence of a Gothic survival in the sixteenth century (Bologna, Museo di San Petronio). Peruzzi's portal of San Michele in Bosco (1522) is a piece of classical architecture, and the captions to the designs for remodeling the courtyard of the Lambertini Palace for the first time give some insight into his opinions on architectural theory (Florence, Cabinetto dei Disegni e Stampe degli Uffizi). The architecture in the design for the so-called Gonzaga Organ (Windsor Castle, Inv.-Nr.5495) belongs within this same stylistic realm. The connection with Bologna was not broken off; the later Ghislardi Chapel for San Domenico is also based on a design by Peruzzi.

Peruzzi's work in the early 1520s, after his return to Rome, is characterized by a definite turn towards Mannerism, as may be seen in the decorative elements of the façade and courtyard of the Fusconi-Pighini Palace (1521/1522–1525/1527), in the Villa Trivulzi-Borromeo on the Salone River near Rome (?–1525), and in the architectural background of his painting of the *Presentation of Mary in the Temple* in Santa Maria della Pace (1523/1524). In these works the composition of the façades and their details suggest the architectural language of Giulio Romano. The extent of Peruzzi's mannerist caprices is shown by the columnar orders in the courtyard of the Fusconi-Pighini Palace, where, in a reversal of the usual sequence, the Doric appears above the Ionic, or again in the complete abstraction of the system of orders. During this period, he was also working with the Sangallos, for instance, on the remodeling of the Castle of Caprarola or the fortifications of Piacenza. Here, too, the upper story of the alter-house in St. Peter's should be mentioned. The connection with the Sangallos did not, however, deal with matters of style, based as it was on their cooperation in practical building and archeological investigation.

For Peruzzi, the Sack of Rome (1527) meant both a personal catastrophe and the start of a new career. He was captured and held hostage by the imperial troops of Charles V and had to go heavily into debt to buy his freedom. He left a devastated Rome to return to his native Siena. On his way, he was again—according to Vasari—attacked and robbed of all his possessions. On July 10, 1527, he became official architect to the then independent Republic of Siena, as well as architect of the Duomo, responsible for all building, ranging from the new altar for the Duomo to the iron industry.

His first and most urgent task was to bring the fortifications up to contemporary standards. This was started in the autumn of 1527 and pushed forward until 1529. In the years 1529–1530, available finances had to be concentrated on monumental decorations for a ceremonial entry of Emperor Charles V; the fortifications were completed around 1531–1532.

Peruzzi's over-all concept for the fortifications was "republican," in the sense that defense would not proceed from a dominating fortress; the citizens would defend their whole city, on all sides. Covered galleries on top of the walls around the city would permit quick changes of position. The city gates themselves were fortified with bastions. It has recently been proved (Adams, 1978) that these bastions were adapted to contemporary artillery technique and would have allowed the whole strategic area around the city to be raked by artillery fire. As can be seen from the Fortino (small fortress) at Porta San Viene, these military constructions do have architectural appeal.

Peruzzi's activities covered the whole Sienese territory. Accordingly, he traveled to the Tuscan towns of Buonconvento (1527), Montorio/Castel'Ottieri (1528), Asciano (1528), Chiusi (1529/1532/1533), Monte Follonica, Sarteano, Cetona, and Chianciano (all 1529), Port'Ercole/Orbetello (1530/1532), and Monticiano (1533). He even went to Florence as a spy (1529) and also to Pisa to investigate the fortifications of the enemy (particularly Poggio Imperiale). His involvement in engineering projects and his designs for a minting machine in 1530, or his almost didactic series of projects for a dam on the Bruna River (1532–1534, Maremma Grossetana) add to the picture of his manifold activities, as do the report of the ceremonial decorations for the entry of Charles V into Siena and his appraisals of the work of other artists.

Among the many buildings in Siena attributed to him with more or less justification, only the Villa Belcaro, for which a plan by Peruzzi exists and the Palazzo Vescovo-Pollini (?–1535), with its elegant proportions and its refined brick masonry, should be mentioned. The painted decorations in both these works also suggest their connection to Peruzzi.

The remodeling of the Gothic Church of San Domenico in Siena (1532/1533) was made necessary by a fire in the church on December 3, 1531, in which the greatest destruction was to the roof. Although Peruzzi had to cope with the walls of the existing structure, his various plans resulted in an exemplary survey of his ideas about Latin-cross church building and, moreover, provide a rare comprehensive demonstration of his mature style. Peruzzi envisioned sequences of domed spaces as well as barrel-vaulted halls, and, finally, a group of cap vaults. The curvilinear geometry of the plans, the powerful three-dimensional articulation of the walls and the rhythmic expansion and compression of the space constitute his last significant statement on the practice of church architecture—comparable in rank to the Palazzo Massimo.

Even before his official appointment, Peruzzi had already made some designs for the Duomo of Siena. These were now to be followed up by decorative schemes for chapels, pulpits, and choirs. Peruzzi, however, set himself to reconsider the (still uncompleted) form of the whole building and to apply to the nave and particularly to the domed space his experience with ancient basilicas and with the planning of St. Peter's. Though his designs are not available in final form, they nevertheless go far beyond the immediate local Sienese problem and touch on his fundamental ideas about architecture. Frey (1915) offers an attempt, heretofore unrivaled, to create a bridge over the uncertainties of Peruzzi's specific plans or commissions and his (not completely preserved) theoretical concepts. The value of such theoretical designs cannot be appraised in terms of feasibility; fantastic and Utopian planning is a basic element of architectural thinking. When Peruzzi indicates a span of 134 or even 182 meters as the diameter of a domed space in his plan, it is not so much his reveling in space as the precision of these measurements that amazes one in these "specific Utopias." To have combined the concepts of the Pantheon, Santa Costanza, and the Basilica of Constantine represents an intellectual contribution to sixteenth-century thinking: ANDREA PALLADIO did just that and even carried it out in part.

The designs for the Palazzo Ricci (1533–1536) in Montepulciano (southern Tuscany) bear witness to Peruzzi's efforts to put together a regular site adequate for the requirements of a modern palace, as well as for the variety of his ideas about palace building. He submitted a series of alternative projects, "A", "B", and "C," finally arriving at the width of the façade as it was actually built by Nanni di Baccio Bigio. The way in which he organized the spaces in sequence or surrounding the main *sala,* or tried to create a courtyard of ideal geometric shape on irregular terrain is characteristic of his ideas about palace architecture in general.

Even after the Sack of Rome, Peruzzi maintained close relations with Rome. There was scarcely a year in which he failed to return for a visit. Starting in 1531, he was again paid for his duties at St. Peter's. As of December 1, 1534, Pope Paul III installed him in a new capacity, as architect of St. Peter's. His employment in Siena came to an end in 1535.

Peruzzi's work on and for St. Peter's may even have come about through Bramante and thus go back to the first decade of the sixteenth century, but not until 1520 was he given an official appointment. How far his activity as coadjutor of Antonio da Sangallo went, beyond the measurements he made of the existing structures, is difficult to say, although it does at least show his formal rank in the succession to Raphael. Some of the plans for St. Peter's may well have originated before 1527.

At this point the issue was to reduce Raphael's ideas to meet the approval of Antonio da Sangallo the Younger and to fit the reduced finances of the papal court. It is also quite possible that the majority of the plans for St. Peter's were developed in the early 1530s in Siena, at a time when important commissions were lacking and Peruzzi was able to prepare himself for the resumption of the work on St. Peter's. In their extraordinary variety of concept, these plans are characteristic of him in several ways, for instance, in the erudite allusions to ancient prototypes. Then there is the almost didactic deployment of all imaginable variations on the theme, starting with the demonstration of the problem shown in perspective which was probably intended to serve for publication purposes, to the

Peruzzi.
San Domenico (rebuilding).
Siena, Italy.
1531–1533

bold anticipation of architectural ideas that would come to be dominant in the future.

The decoration of monuments and theaters provided constant work throughout Peruzzi's life, as did painting commissions, and it is from the former that his earliest architectural drawings are preserved. The façade of a house belonging to Francesco Buzio which he decorated in 1511 is similar to that of the Farnesina and to the one for Ulisse da Fano which he provided in 1513–1514. In 1513, he prepared the pageantry for Pope Leo X as well as a stage set for a theater that was built on the Capitoline Hill in honor of Giuliano and Lorenzo de' Medici. Finally, with his 1515 stage set for the *Calandria* by Bibiena, his success in this field was so firmly established that in 1515 he was asked to accompany Pope Leo X to Bologna to provide the setting for the ceremonial meeting the pope wanted with King Francis I of France.

The preparations for the entry of Charles V

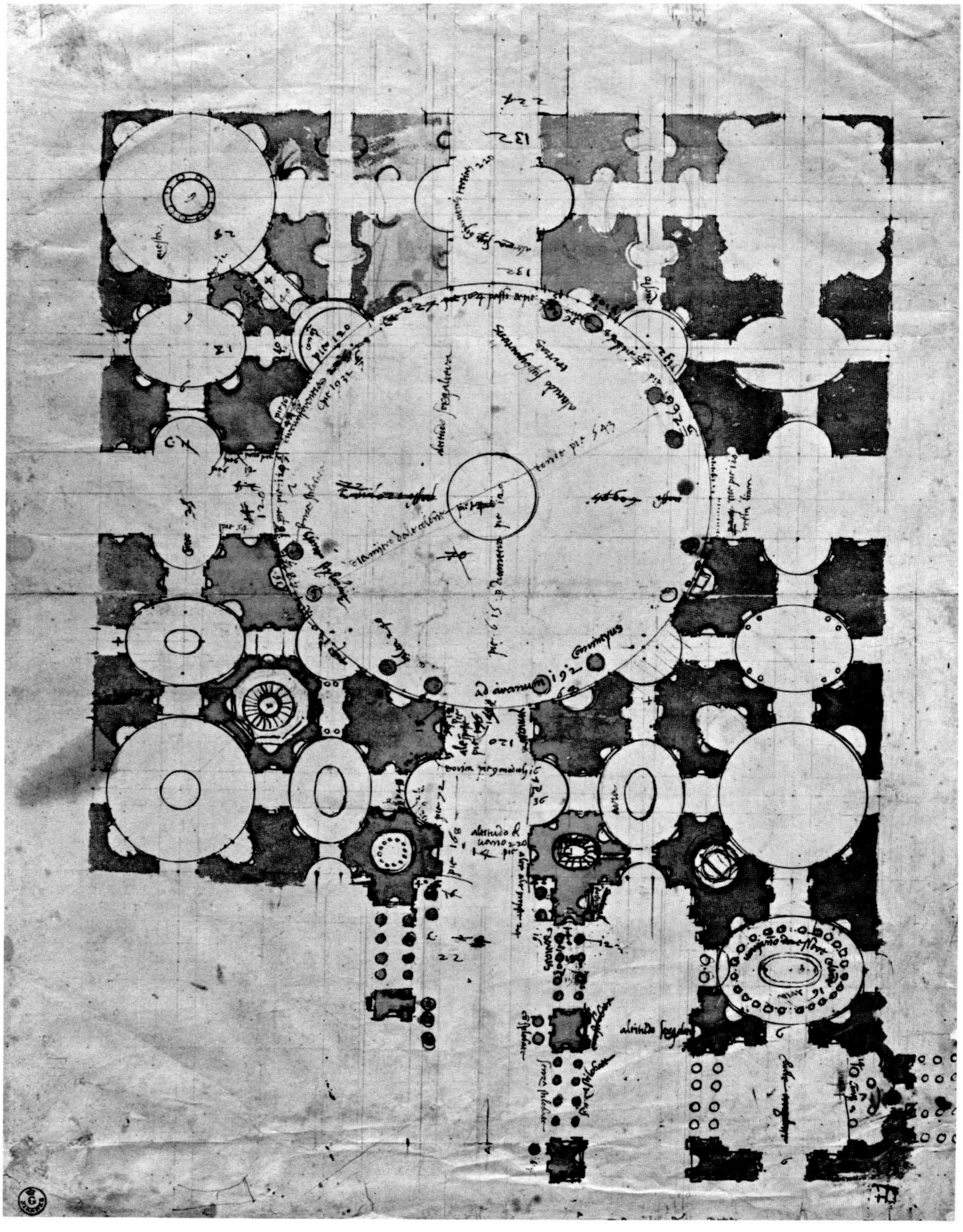

Peruzzi.
Ideal plan for a church.

into Siena provided Peruzzi with new commissions of this kind in 1529/1530. In Rome, in May of 1531, he designed the stage set for the *Bachides* of Plautus. The end of his life came at the time of the preparations for the entry of Charles V, returning in triumph as the conqueror of Tunis into Rome.

An examination of the genesis of the geometric rules of design in his architectural drawings shows that Peruzzi (as well as Serlio, incidentally) was linked to the tradition of medieval mason-guild secrets and also to the revived neo-Platonic interest in geometric and arithmetic proportions. This emerges from the measurements and captions of his projects. As was the disposition of the time, a humanistic comprehension of ancient architecture and art in general was for him a lifelong striving, which applied not only to the Roman ruins but also to works of literature, especially those of VITRUVIUS.

To date it is not possible to describe precisely the progressive stages in his preoccupation with antiquity. If we limit the inquiry to architecture, we find that the earliest of his preserved drawings after examples from antiquity date from the end of the second decade of the century. As far as we can see, we are dealing with a development of only some two decades which may not essentially have been interrupted by the move to Siena. It is certain that in the course of the years his understanding of certain monuments was changing, that in much of what he did he was not working alone but jointly with the Sangallos. Furthermore, in the choices he made between *palmo, braccio,* and *piede,* with all their variants, he also clearly adopted changing systems of measurement. That these drawings range from free-hand sketches to presentation designs is, in this connection, merely a superficial matter. Nor did Peruzzi hesitate to make sweeping judgments: "opera corinthia barbarissima."

The autonomous position he finally adopted may be indicated by the fact that, as Cellini reports, he expressed certain reservations about Vitruvius. According to Peruzzi, Vitruvius had not known all the possibilities of ancient architecture and, since he was not—as was Peruzzi—also a painter, he did not have the full range of artistic expression at his command. Peruzzi's own interests went far beyond architecture, from descriptive geometry all the way to astrology.

Peruzzi was engaged in preparing an architectural treatise. Several motives may have prompted this: his role as a teacher which was part of his official duties; the general theoretical interest of contemporary architects who were trying to establish their profession as one of the liberal arts; and finally, the tendency of the period to didactic presentations. Vasari speaks of a commentary on Vitruvius and a book about antiquity. This whole issue can be examined on the basis of the rich legacy of Peruzzi's drawings preserved in the Uffizi collection (c.500 papers). However, this legacy is fragmentary insofar as the totality of his drawings is concerned and hence is not conclusive in terms of a theory or a publication. It does contain some obvious beginnings and some designs ready for publication, but there is no comprehensive organization; this, however, does not denote inconsistency. In his later years, Peruzzi obviously relied on the writings of Francesco di Giorgio. Nevertheless, even without himself having published, Peruzzi came to have the widest imaginable impact through Sebastiano Serlio. Serlio, who probably became Peruzzi's disciple in Bologna, himself declared his devoted dependence on Peruzzi at the start of his own publications in which he reproduced a large number of Peruzzi's drawings. However, the evident connection of his own to the drawings of Peruzzi requires clarification drawing by drawing. In general, it is unquestionable that Peruzzi's ideas became known all over Europe through Serlio's books.

Although the painters in his workshop may have been more numerous, Peruzzi also had architectural disciples, among whom were his son Salustio, Jacopo Melighino, and PHILIBERT DELORME. What makes the Sienese sketchbooks a problem is the issue of the legacy versus the circle of disciples. The physical production of the drawings—as Egger (1902) has proved—has nothing to do with Peruzzi, as the hand is of the mid-sixteenth century. However, the architectural forms represented may actually be based on Peruzzi drawings and contain Peruzzi ideas. If and to what extent this is true, must be demonstrated individually for each of the 238 drawings in the collection.

Peruzzi's use of the oval as a basic form in his plans is characteristic of his historically momentous treatment of architectural ideas. It is first seen in subordinate spaces in the plan for San Giovanni dei Fiorentini. In the design for the garden of the Trivulzi-Borromeo villa it becomes the basic unifying form, and with this project Peruzzi assumed a leading position as a landscape architect. In the plan for a hospital near San Giacomo in Augusta the oval was used for a monumental church building. Finally, in a single design, he combined fundamental architectural ideas of antiquity—Pantheon, Santa Costanza—in an oval plan that is a bold anticipation of the future architecture of GIACOMO BAROZZI DA VIGNOLA, Delorme, and the baroque.

Peruzzi's final masterpiece was the Palazzo Massimo alle Colonne in Rome (1533–?) which he did not live to see completed. The building has one of the most original palace façades in all of

Peruzzi.
Oval church plan.

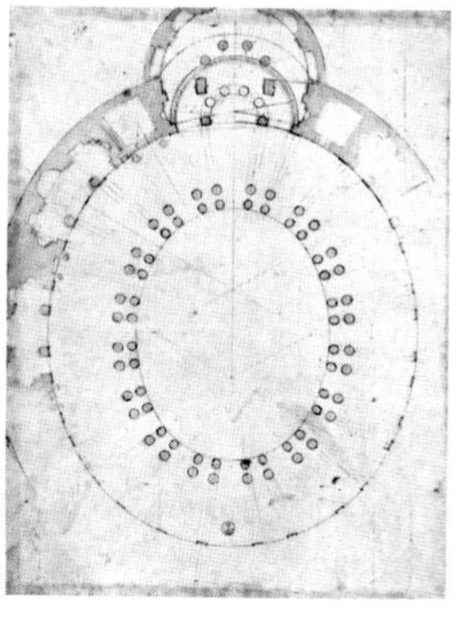

Peruzzi.
Palazzo Massimo alle Colonne (completed after his death).
Rome.
1533–1536

Italian architecture. In spite of changing points of view, its rank has always been fully recognized. It embodies the sum of a lifetime of work with the buildings of antiquity and the theory of architecture—in the specific interpretation of Peruzzi's time: there is the allusion to the plan of a house of antiquity, the integration of ancient prototypes for a modern palace façade, and—seen from the theoretical point of view—a "Doric" façade. Moreover, the façade differs both in type and in style from the Roman tradition, as it does from the whole mannerist development. If the creation of the composition from geometrical fragments is a characteristic of the architect in his last years, the differentiated play of light on the surfaces of façade and courtyard and the powerful contrasts of light and shade reveal the ability of this *peintre-architecte.* Together they are the hallmark of Peruzzi's mature style.

Peruzzi was known for his unvarying open friendliness. His inability, despite all his accomplishments, to further his material interests in a period when successful artists were building palaces for themselves was seen by his biographer, Vasari, as a warning example of incompetence in everyday affairs. In fact, Peruzzi was neither a competitive professional nor an intriguing courtier. Essentially, he was an artist of genius and a learned humanist.

HEINRICH WURM

Translated from German by the author and Beverley R. Placzek

WORKS

(A)?–1505, Villa le Volte, near Siena, Italy. 1505–1511, Palazzo della Farnesina, Rome. 1513–1515, Ancient Duomo (façade); 1513–1515, San Nicolò (nave); Carpi, Italy. 1520–1527, St. Peter's (nave), Rome. 1522, San Michele in Bosco (portal), Bologna, Italy. 1520–1527, Palazzo Fusconi-Pighini (aediculae of façade, courtyard), Rome. ?–1525, Villa Trivulzi-Borromeo, Salone River, near Rome. 1527–1529, 1531–1532, Fortifications (including bastions at city gates); 1531–1533, San Domenico (rebuilding); (A)?–1535, Palazzo Vescovo-Pollini; Siena, Italy. 1531–1536, St. Peter's (plans for completion); 1533–1536, Palazzo Massimo alle Colonne (completed after his death); Rome. 1533–1536, Palazzo Ricci, Montepulciano (southern Tuscany), Italy.

Peruzzi.
Palazzo Massimo alle Colonne (eastern portico).
Rome.
1533–1536

Peruzzi.
Palazzo Massimo alle Colonne (courtyard).
Rome.
1533–1536

BIBLIOGRAPHY

ADAMS, ROBERT NICHOLAS 1977 "Baldassarre Peruzzi, Architect to Republic of Siena." Unpublished Ph.D. dissertation, New York University.

ADAMS, ROBERT NICHOLAS 1978 "Baldassarre Peruzzi and the Siege of Florence, Archival Notes and Undated Drawings." *Art Bulletin* 60:475–482.

ADAMS, ROBERT NICHOLAS 1978 "Baldassarre Peruzzi and a Tour of Inspection in the Val di Chiana. 1528–1529." *RACAR* 5:25–36.

ADAMS, ROBERT NICHOLAS ET AL. 1982 "Rilievi di Fabbriche senesi di attribuzione peruzziana." Siena, Italy: Soprintendenza Siena-Grosseto. Forthcoming exhibition catalogue.

BARTOLI, ALFONSO 1915 Volume 2 in *I monumenti antichi di Roma nei disegni degli Uffizi di Firenze.* Florence.

BURNS, HOWARD 1966 "A Peruzzi Drawing in Ferrara." *Mitteilungen des kunsthistorischen Instituts in Florenz* 12:245–270.

EGGER, HERMANN 1902 "Entwürfe Baldassarre Peruzzis für den Einzug Karls V. in Rom, eine Studie zur Frage uber die Echtheit des sienesischen Skizzenbuches." *Jahrbuch der Kunsthistorischen Sammlungen des Allerhöchsten Kaiserhauses* 23:1–44.

FREY, DAGOBERT 1915 *Bramantes St. Peter-Entwurf und seine Apokryphen: Bramante-Studien.* Vienna.

FROMMEL, CHRISTOPH L. 1961 *Die Farnesina und Peruzzis arkchitektonisches Frühwerk.* Berlin.

FROMMEL, CHRISTOPH L. 1967–1968 "Baldassarre Peruzzi als Maler und Zeichner." *Römischen Jahrbuch für Kunstgeschichte* 11.

FROMMEL, CHRISTOPH L. 1973 *Der römische Palastbau der Hochrenaissance.* 3 vols. Tübingen, Germany.

HEYDENREICH, LUDWIG H., and LOTZ, WOLFGANG (1954)1974 *Architecture in Italy 1400–1600.* Translated by Mary Hottinger. Harmondsworth, England: Penguin.

KENT, WILLIAM WINTHROP 1929 *The Life and the Works of Baldassarre Peruzzi of Siena.* New York.

LOTZ, WOLFGANG 1955 "Die ovalen Kirchenräume des Cinquecento." *Römisches Jahrbuch für Kunstgeschichte* 7:7–100.

LOTZ, WOLFGANG 1956 "Das Raumbild in der italienischen Architekturzeichnung der Renaissance." *Mitteilungen des Kunsthistorischen Instituts Florenz* 7:193–226.

VASARI, GIORGIO (1568)1973 *Le opere di Giorgio Vasari, con nuove annotazione e commenti.* 9 vols. Edited by G. Milanese. Reprint. Florence: Sansoni. Originally published with title *Le vite de piu eccelenti architetti.* There are many English translations and selections from Vasari's *Lives,* the standard one by G. du C. de Vere was published in London by the Medici Society in 1912–1915.

PETERS, C. H.

At an early age, Cornelis Hendrik Peters (1847–1932), born in Groningen, the Netherlands, became interested in the work of P. J. H. CUYPERS and moved to Amsterdam about 1866 to work at Cuypers's office. He was active there until his appointment in 1876 as architect of the finance department. In this capacity, he built the Department of Justice in The Hague (1876–1883). This is Peters's only building in the neo-Renaissance style. In all his other buildings after 1884, he preferred the neo-Gothic style. Although at Cuypers's office, Peters had become acquainted with the Gothic as a medium to give expression to the construction of the building, in his own work he always appeared to be more interested in the Gothic form: he realized this form with all sorts of technical aids without paying attention to the purity of construction. This can be seen clearly in the post offices he built in several towns. Peters kept his position as government architect until 1916. In addition to his architectural activities, Peters also made himself a name as author of publications about the history of Dutch town planning.

WIM DE WIT

WORKS

1876–1883, Department of Justice, The Hague. 1888–1889, Post Office, Arnhem, Netherlands. 1890, East India House, Amsterdam. 1892–1894, Railway Station, Nijmegen, Netherlands. 1894, Museum voor Stad en Lande, Groningen, Netherlands. 1895–1899, Head Post Office, Amsterdam.

BIBLIOGRAPHY

BRUGMANS, HAJO, and PETERS, C. H. 1909–1911 *Oud-Nederlandsche steden in haar ontstaan, groei en ontwikkeling.* 3 vols. Leiden, Netherlands: Sijthoff.

EVERS, HENRI (1905–1911)1916–1918 *De architectuur in hare hooftijdperken.* 2d ed. Amsterdam: Veen.

GUGEL, EUGEN (1886)1916–1918 *Geschiedenis van de bouwstijlen in de hooftijdperken der architectuur.* 2d ed. Rotterdam, Netherlands: Bolle.

Nederland bouwt in baksteen: 1800–1940. 1941 Rotterdam, Netherlands: Museum Boymans-van Beuningen.

ROY VAN ZUYDEWIJN, H. J. F. DE 1969 *Amsterdamse Bouwkunst 1915–1940.* Amsterdam: De Bussy.

ROY VAN ZUYDEWIJN, H. J. F. DE *Haagse huizen en gebouwen.* Amsterdam: De Bussy.

PETERSEN, CARL

Carl Petersen (1874–1924), a Danish architect, was the most influential figure among a group of young architects who about 1910 introduced a new classicistic trend in Danish architecture. In 1912, he was commissioned to build the Faaborg Museum for fysnk Malerkunst; because of its original display of forms and plans, the little art museum became a chief work of the time.

VILLADS VILLADSEN

PETERSEN, VILHELM

Vilhelm Petersen (1830–1913), a Danish architect, was deeply rooted in a sober late classicism, in which style he designed a number of distinguished but modest buildings. In his later works, he assumed the more splendid style of his contemporary Ferdinand Meldahl. Among his works are De Gamles By (old peoples homes), and the building of the Academy of Science, Copenhagen.

VILLADS VILLADSEN

PETITOT DI LIONE, ENNEMONDO ALESSANDRO

Ennemondo Alessandro Petitot di Lione (1727–1801) began studying architecture under JACQUES GERMAIN SOUFFLOT. He attended the Academy of Architecture in Paris and in 1746, as a recipient of the *Grand Prix,* went to the French Academy in Rome. There, he furthered his education studying the monuments of the past as well as contemporary architecture. While in Rome, he also developed a very useful friendship with GIOVANNI BATTISTA PIRANESI. After his return to Paris in 1750, he collaborated with the count of Caylus designing several illustrations of the *Recueil d'Antiquités,* and furthermore planned a chapel for Notre Dame. Di Lione became court architect to the Bourbons of Parma (where he remained until his death) and assumed the duties of principal architect of the ducal enterprises and instructor at the Academy of Fine Arts; he was also active in many other areas. He worked as urban planner, inventor of decorative displays, technician of hydraulic engineering, engraver, and planner of festivals. His first commissions were in Colorno (gardens, stables, chapel, and Great Hall of the ducal palace) and in the Parma Gardens. In 1758, he became a citizen of Parma and published the *Ragionamento sopra la prospettiva.* Between 1759 and 1760, di Lione remodeled the Piazza Grande of Parma, redoing the façade of the Church of San Pietro and the Town Hall. In 1760, the king of France knighted him with the order of Saint Michael and two years later he was elected a member of the Academy of Architecture of Paris. He later worked on the façade of the *Casino di giuoco* (1765), on an aqueduct (1765), and on the Palatine Library (1766), and he also designed for the engraver B. Bossi the Suite de Vases. From 1766, he concentrated on the planning of a new ducal palace; he also redesigned the Palazzo del Giardino and the Palace of the Ministry. In 1769, he planned the festivities for the wedding of Ferdinand of Bourbon, recording the event in an elaborate book with many engravings. In 1771, di Lione designed the lovely Masquerade à la Grecque which was engraved by the same B. Bossi. From this time on, there is little information about him, though he does appear in the rostrum of architecture both in Parma and in Colorno, and as an instructor at the Academy. Di Lione was an important figure in the architectural life of the period, blending in an almost personal style neoclassical, baroque, and Renaissance forms.

MARCO PELLEGRI
Translated from Italian by Richard Koffler

WORKS

1753–1755, Ducal Palace (gardens, stables, chapel, and great hall), Colorno, Italy. 1759–1760, Piazza Grande (remodeling); 1759–1760, San Pietro (façade); 1759–1760, Town Hall; 1765, Aqueduct; 1765, Casino di giuoco (façade); 1766, Palatine Library; 1767–1771, Palazzo del Giardino (redesigned); 1768, Botanical Gardens; 1769, Ara amicitiae Monument, Piazza Grande; Parma, Italy. 1771–1791, Royal Chapel, San Liborio, Colorno, Italy. 1778, San Ambrogio (façade), Parma, Italy.

BIBLIOGRAPHY

ACADEMIE DE FRANCE À ROME 1976 *Piranèse et les Français: 1740–1790.* Rome: The academy.

BEDARIDA, HENRY 1928 *Parme et la France de 1748 à 1789.* Paris.

BEDARIDA, HENRY n.d. *Les premiers Bourbons de Parme et l'Espagne (1781–1802).* Paris.

DUSSIEUX, LEON ETIENNE 1876 *Les artistes français à l'étranger.* Paris.

MEZZANOTTE, GIANNI 1966 *Architettura neoclassica in Lombardia.* Naples.

MONTI, EMMA 1924 *L'architetto Petitot: Uno spiraglio d'arte francese a Parma.* Rome.

PACIAUD, PAOLO MARIA 1769 *Descrizione delle feste celebrate in Parma, l'anne MDCCCLXIX.* Parma, Italy: Stamperia reale.

PELLEGRI, MARCO 1965 *Ennemondo Alessandro Petitot: 1727–1801.* Parma, Italy: Tipografia Già Cooperative.

PELLEGRI, MARCO 1977 *Vita e opere dell'architetto E. A. Petitot nel periodo romano.* Parma, Italy.

PELLEGRI, MARCO 1979 *L'Accademia parmense di Belle Arti, Parma.* Parma, Italy: The academy

REAUX, LOUIS 1933 *Histoire de l'expansion de l'art français: Le monde latin.* Paris.

TASSI, ROBERTO 1979 Pages 250–261 in *L'arte a Parma dai Fannesi al Borboni.* Bologna, Italy.

PETIT-RADEL, LOUIS FRANÇOIS

A student of CHARLES DE WAILLY, Louis François Petit-Radel (1740–1818) won the third prize in the French Académie d'Architecture's competition of 1763. He went to Italy to study the monuments of antiquity. On his return to France, he published a collection of engravings, "Fragments d'architecture." His illustrations of theater decorations in the *Encyclopédie* reveal all the resources of his talent as a designer and an engraver.

He became architect of the royal treasury and of the Palais Bourbon and later an *architecte expert du roi.*

In 1784, he remodeled the choir of the Church of Saint Médard in Paris in the style of Paestum and built an apsidal chapel in cyclopean style. He also built the Talaru tenements in the Faubourg Poissonnière in 1785.

He participated actively in the French Revolution and published his memoirs describing the construction of the Assemblée Nationale and the restoration of the Panthéon in Paris.

During the Empire, as inspector to the Bâtiments Civils, he built the slaughterhouse at Le Roule.

GÉRARD ROUSSET-CHARNY
Translated from French by
Richard Cleary

BIBLIOGRAPHY

ACADÉMIE DE FRANCE À ROME 1976 *Piranèse et les français: 1740–1790.* Rome: Edizioni dell'Elefante.

BRAHAM, ALLAN 1980 *The Architecture of the French Enlightenment.* Berkeley: University of California Press.

PETRE, F. W.

Francis William Petre (1847–1918) was born in New Zealand but educated in England and France. In practice in Dunedin, New Zealand, he designed more than seventy churches, often of domed basilican form. He was a pioneer in the use of concrete construction and served as president of the New Zealand Institute of Architects.

JOHN STACPOOLE

WORKS

Late 1870s, Phoenix House; late 1870s, Royal Exchange House; 1876, Chapman House (Woodside); 1877, Saint Dominic's Priory; 1886, Saint Joseph's Cathedral; 1893, Saint Patrick's Church; Dunedin, New Zealand. 1893–1894, Saint Patrick's Basilica, Oamaru, New Zealand. 1901, Hill Street Basilica, Wellington. 1905, Cathedral of the Blessed Sacrament, Christchurch, New Zealand. 1905, Saint Mary's Basilica, Invercargill, New Zealand. 1906, Saint Patrick's Church, Greymouth, New Zealand. 1910, Church of the Sacred Heart, Timaru, New Zealand.

BIBLIOGRAPHY

FURKERT, F. W. 1953 *Early New Zealand Engineers.* Wellington: Reed.

PEYRE FAMILY

The Peyre were a family of celebrated French architects from the reign of Louis XV (1715–1774) to the July Monarchy (1830–1848). The most important among them is Marie-Joseph Peyre (18th century), also called Peyre the Elder, friend of CHARLES DE WAILLY and brother-in-law of PIERRE LOUIS MOREAU-DESPROUX, two great architects with whom he lived in Italy after receiving his first architecture prize in 1751. His work in archeology (Roman baths, Hadrian's villa) and on ancient architecture, along with that of JULIEN DAVID LEROY, was one of the essential sources of inspiration for neoclassicism during the second half of the eighteenth century. His famous *Livre d'Architecture* (*Book on Architecture*), published in 1765, contains numerous engraved projects, all grandiose. The symbolic and functional role of the colonnade is defined in his writings in a skillful way. Peyre the Elder built little; his major work, the Odeon Theater (1768–1782) in Paris, owes much to his collaboration with De Wailly.

His younger brother, Antoine-François Peyre (18th century), called Peyre the Younger, obtained the grand prize for architecture in 1762. An academician by 1777, he was later in the service of the Elector of Koblenz; still later, he was architect of the Palace at Fontainebleau. Painter and decorator as much as architect, he exhibited in the salons of 1791, 1799, and 1800.

Antoine-Marie Peyre (18th–19th century), son of Marie-Joseph, began a military career as aide-de-camp to General Lafayette during the French Revolution. His career as architect was later quite productive, notably in the service of the Council of Civil Buildings, Paris.

DANIEL RABREAU
Translated from French by
Shara Wasserman

WORKS

MARIE-JOSEPH PEYRE

1760–1765, Villa Neubourg; 1767, Church of the Convent of the Visitation; 1768–1782, Odeon Theater (with Charles de Wailly); n.d., Hôtel de Nivernais, Rue de Tournon; Paris.

ANTOINE-FRANÇOIS PEYRE

1780, Palace and Chapel of the Elector, Koblenz, Germany. 1784, Chapel of the Hospice of Charity and Chapel of the Women of Saint-Thomas, Saint-Germain-en-Laye, France.

ANTOINE-MARIE PEYRE

1795, Museum of French Monuments (remodeling); 1800, Theater of Gayity; 1812, Market of Saint-Martin; 1822–1828, Palais de Justice (additions); 1823, Hospice of the Deaf-mutes; 1832, Amphitheater, Conservatory of Arts and Crafts; Paris.

PHEIDIAS

Pheidias (5th century B.C.) was the most famous artist of his time. His great works in bronze, the Athena Promachos (463–454 B.C.) and the Lemnian Athena (c.450 B.C.), stood upon the Acropolis of Athens; his huge chryselephantine Zeus Olympios (454–448 B.C.) was placed within the temple of Zeus at Olympia and became one of the ancient world's seven wonders. Pheidias's greatest opportunity came when he was appointed supervisor of all works, sculpture and architecture, of the Periclean program on the Athenian Acropolis. Under his direction was produced all the exterior sculpture of the Parthenon, and to his design alone was owed the chryselephantine statue of Athena Parthenos, 42 feet high, which adorned the interior of her temple. Although much of the building and its decoration have survived, of Pheidias's own great works only the renown is preserved today.

B. M. BOYLE

WORKS

*463–454 B.C., Statue of Athena Promachos, Athens. *454–448 B.C., Statue of Zeus Olympios, Olympia, Greece. *c.450 B.C., Statue of Lemnian Athena; *438–432 B.C., Statue of Athena Parthenos; Athens.

BIBLIOGRAPHY

English translations of the ancient texts can be found in the volumes of the Loeb Classical Library series, published by Harvard University Press and Heinemann.

ASHMOLE, BERNARD 1972 *Architect and Sculptor in Ancient Greece.* New York: New York University Press.

DINSMOOR, WILLIAM B. (1902)1975 *The Architecture of Ancient Greece.* Reprint of 1950 ed. New York: Norton. Originally published with the title *The Architecture of Ancient Greece and Rome.*

LAWRENCE, ARNOLD W. (1957)1975 *Greek Architecture.* Harmondsworth, England: Penguin.

PAUSANIAS, *Graeciae descriptio,* Book 5.11.

PLINY, *Historia naturalis,* Books 24.54 and 36.18.

PHILANDER, GUILLAUME

Born in Chatillon-sur-Seine, France, Guillaume Philander (1505–?) was an architect and theoretician who espoused fundamentally humanistic notions. Although no buildings of his are known to exist, his translation and commentaries on the treatises of VITRUVIUS were highly regarded at the time. First published in 1543 in Strasbourg, Philander's writings appeared all over Europe including Italy where, in 1544, a Roman edition bore a dedication to King François I of France.

PETER L. DONHAUSER

BIBLIOGRAPHY

HAUTECOEUR, LOUIS 1948 Volume 1 in *Histoire de l'Architecture Classique en France.* Paris: Picard.

PHILOKLES

The name of Philokles (?–400 B.C.) appears only once, in an inscription of 409 B.C. relating to work on the Erechtheion in Athens, where he is described as architect. However, Philokles was not the designer of the building, but one of a commission appointed to certify contract performance. The interest in this lone reference is that it helps to suggest the variety of duties undertaken by the architect in antiquity. In this instance, Philokles was an outside consultant; on the rest of his architectural career, the record is silent.

B. M. BOYLE

BIBLIOGRAPHY

English translations of the ancient texts can be found in the volumes of the Loeb Classical Library series, published by Harvard University Press and Heinemann.

DINSMOOR, WILLIAM B. (1902)1975 *The Architecture of Ancient Greece.* Reprint of 1950 ed. New York: Norton. Originally published with title *The Architecture of Ancient Greece and Ancient Rome.*

PATON, JAMES M. (editor) (1927)1976 *The Erechtheum.* Reprint. Ann Arbor, Mich.: University Microfilms.

PHILON OF ELEUSIS

Philon of Eleusis (?–310 B.C.) was the architect of the Arsenal of the Peiraeus, near Athens, begun in 340 B.C.. This simple, functional building is of great historical interest because its original specifications have been preserved, carved in stone, providing valuable information on contemporary building practices. Philon wrote a book about the Arsenal, now lost. He was the designer also of the façade of the Hall of the Mysteries (Telesterion) at Eleusis (c.330–310 B.C.), completing the project begun by IKTINOS and others in the preceding century. Neither of these buildings stands today.

B. M. BOYLE

WORKS

*340–330 B.C., Arsenal, Peiraeus, Greece. *c.330–310 B.C., Hall of Mysteries (façade), Eleusis, Greece.

BIBLIOGRAPHY

English translations of the ancient texts by Pliny and Strabo can be found in the volumes of the Loeb Classical Library series, published by Harvard University Press and Heinemann.

COULTON, J. J. *Ancient Greek Architects at Work.* Ithaca, N.Y.: Cornell University Press.

DINSMOOR, WILLIAM B. (1902)1975 *The Architecture of Ancient Greece.* Reprint of 1950 ed. New York: Norton. Originally published with the title *The Architecture of Ancient Greece and Rome.*

LAWRENCE, ARNOLD W. (1957)1975 *Greek Architecture.* Harmondsworth, England: Penguin.

PLINY, *Historia naturalis,* Book 7.125.

STRABO, *Geographikon,* Book 9.1.15.

VITRUVIUS, *De architectura,* Book 7, Praef.12, 16–17.

PHIPPS, CHARLES JAMES

Charles James Phipps (1835–1897) was born in Bath, England, and in the early 1850s was articled to the local architects, Wilson and Fuller. He set up his own practice in 1857 but did not make his mark until he won the competition to rebuild the Bath Theatre (1863). Phipps was then commissioned to design the Theatre Royal in Nottingham in 1865. He also designed a new theater for South Shields (1865–1866). Phipps quickly established himself in London where he had moved in 1866 and immediately undertook the complete reconstruction of the Theatre Royal in Brighton. Later that year, he submitted four perspective drawings of his theater interiors to the Paris Exhibition. Thereafter, commissions, mainly in theater design, came quickly; the variety of his other buildings was limited.

JOHN O'CALLAGHAN

WORKS

1862–1863, Cemetery Chapel, Oewsey, Wiltshire, England. 1863, Bath Theatre (reconstruction), England. 1865, Theatre Royal, Nottingham, England. 1865–1866, South Shields Theatre (with Clemence), England. 1866, Theatre Royal (reconstruction), Brighton; 1870–1875, Devonshire Club (alterations), Saint James's Street; London. 1871, Gaity Theatre, Dublin. 1875, Theatre Royal, Worcester, England. 1876, Theatre Royal, Edinburgh. 1876–1877, Theatre Royal and Opera House, Cork, Ireland. 1879, Haymarket Theatre (alterations); 1880, Princess' Theatre, Oxford Street; London. 1881, Theatre Royal, Belfast, Ireland. 1882, Strand Theatre (remodeled), London. 1883, Royal Lyceum Theatre, Edinburgh. 1884, Prince's Theatre, Coventry Street; 1887, Vaudeville Theatre, Strand; 1888, Lyric Theatre, Shaftsbury Avenue; 1891, Her Majesty's Theatre, Haymarket; 1891, Queen's Hall (with T. E. Knightly); Langham Place; Begun 1897, Carlton Hotel (not completed until 1899); London.

BIBLIOGRAPHY

"Concert Hall, Langham Place." 1891 *The Builder* 60:153. Letter from Charles Phipps and T. E. Knightly disputing the authorship of the design for the concert hall.

"Contemporary British Architects." 1890 *Building News* 58:547. Including a list of Phipps's works.

MONKHOUSE, CHRISTOPHER 1974 *The Connoisseur* 187, Sept.:14–21.

"Obituary." 1897 *Building News* 72:773.

PIACENTINI, MARCELLO

More than any single twentieth-century architect, Marcello Piacentini (1881–1961) changed the face of Rome during his sixty years of professional practice. Born in Rome, the son of PIO PIACENTINI, he opened his professional career with exhibition pavilions in Brussels (1910) and Rome (1911). The first building to gain wide recognition was his Cinema al Corso in Rome (1915–1917), a bold and successful effort to design accommodations for a new art form. By the time he completed the magnificent Palace of Justice in Messina (1912–1928) and the nucleus of the Garden City Garbatella in Rome (1920), Piacentini had established himself as an important and capable architect. The neoclassical Palace of Justice may indeed be his finest work.

Piacentini did not limit his activities to designing buildings. In 1920, he became a professor of architecture in Rome, and in 1921 he and GUSTAVO GIOVANNONI founded the premier Italian architectural magazine, *Architettura ed Arti Decorative.* Piacentini also began to receive major urban commissions, including the planning of new town centers in Bergamo (1917) and Brescia (1927–1931). The power he wielded as both editor and architect soon doubled as he began to sit on the juries of major competitions and as he exerted influence over many smaller commissions. He served, at Mussolini's pleasure, on three of the most significant commissions in Rome during the 1930s: the Master Plan of 1931, the University of Rome (1932–1933), and the Esposizione Universale di Roma, or EUR (1937–1943). Although the latter two projects were team designs, Piacentini's hand is by far the most evident, not because he railroaded his ideas through, but because he was gifted with a compelling personality and a magnetic charm which rallied the enthusiasm and respect of the other architects.

Piacentini. Administration Building. University of Rome (with others). 1932–1933

Like the young Italian Rationalists, Piacentini polemicized against banal imitations of historical styles and the use of unnecessary decorative elements, but he could not embrace modern architecture with the wholehearted ardor common to the Rationalists. In his little book, *Architettura d'oggi* (1930), Piacentini praised the work of the Modernists, but cautioned against its wholesale adoption in Italy. His main objections to the thin-walled, white, and extensively glazed architecture of the north were that it offered no protection against the annual six months of searing Italian sun, and, anticipating the postwar contextualist arguments, that with the richness and diversity of the Italian architectural ambience, one had to move with extreme caution in introducing something as strikingly different as Modern movement architecture. To Piacentini, the Modern movement was principally a style, as indeed it largely was in Italy, rather than a social or political program.

Despite his reservations, Piacentini played a crucial role in helping the Rationalists gain respectability and commissions by recommending their designs when he served on juries, by publishing their work in his magazine, and by inviting them to collaborate on major projects. At the same time, his own blend of classical and modern architecture slowly became the dominant style of fascist buildings, a stripped classicism which lent itself with facility to monumentalization.

Historians have given Piacentini a bad press since his death, far worse treatment than they have accorded dedicated fascists such as GIUSEPPE TERRAGNI and GIUSEPPE PAGANO. Piacentini's problem was that he was not a Rationalist, though he mediated on their behalf and pragmatically used his power to influence architecture in fascist Italy. Piacentini by temperament was neither an architectural nor a political revolutionary nor a dedicated fascist; he was a talented architect who failed to embrace the principles of the Modern movement.

DIANE GHIRARDO

WORKS

*1910, Italian Pavilion, International Exposition, Brussels. *1911, Plans, National Exposition, Rome. 1912, Hotel Roma, Bengasi. 1912–1928, Palace of Justice, Messina, Italy. 1914–1923, Banca d'Italia, Rome. *1915, Italian Pavilion, San Francisco World Exposition. 1915–1917, Cinema al Corso; 1920, Garden City Garbatella (first stage complete; with Gustavo Giovannoni); Rome. 1922, Palace of Justice, Bergamo, Italy. 1923–1930, Triumphal Arch, Genoa, Italy. 1924–1934, Church of Cristo Re; 1924–1938, Casa Madre dei Mutilati; 1927, Ambassador Hotel (with G. Vaccaro); 1928–1931, Ministry of Corporations (with Vaccaro); Rome. 1931, Master plan of Rome. 1932–1933, University of Rome (with others). 1932–1940, Palace of Justice, Milan. 1934–1936, Banca Nazionale del Lavoro, Rome. *1937, Italian Pavilion (with Giuseppi Pagano and C. Valle), Paris Exposition. 1937–1943, Esposizione Universale di Roma (with others), Rome. 1940–1941, Banco di Napoli, Naples. 1950–1951, Chapel, University of Rome. 1950–1951, Cinema Sistina; 1955–1960, Palazzo dello Sport at EUR (with PIER LUIGI NERVI); Rome. 1956, Palazzo della Ragione, Ferrara, Italy. 1957, Palace of Justice, Palermo, Italy.

BIBLIOGRAPHY

ACCASTO, GIANNI; FRATICELLI, VANNA; and NICCOLINI, RENATO 1971 *L'architettura di Roma Capitale: 1870–1970.* Rome: Golem.

CALZINI, RAFFAELE 1942 *Il Palazzo di Giustizia di Milano.* Milan: Garzanti.

DE' SETA, CESARE 1972 *La cultura architettonica in Italia tra le due guerre.* Bari, Italy: Laterza.

INSOLERA, ITALO (1962)1976 *Roma Moderna: Un secolo di storia urbanistica.* Rev. ed. Torino, Italy: Einaudi.

MONTESI, PIO (editor) 1959 *La Casa* 6:entire issue. Special issue on twentieth-century architecture entitled, *l'Architettura Moderna in Italia.*

NEBBIA, UGO 1928 *La Casa Madre dei Mutilati in Roma.* Milan: Alfieri.

PAPINI, ROBERTO 1929 *Bergamo Rinnovata.* Bergamo, Italy: Istituto Italiano d'Arti Grafiche.

PATETTA, LUCIANO 1972 *L'architettura in Italia, 1919–1943: Le Polemiche.* Milan: Clup.

PIACENTINI, MARCELLO 1930 *Architettura d'oggi.* Rome: Cremonesi.

PICA, AGNOLDOMENICO 1936 *Nuova architettura italiana.* Milan: Hoepli.

ZEVI, BRUNO (1950)1975 *Storia dell'architettura moderna.* 5th ed. Torino, Italy: Einaudi.

PIACENTINI, PIO

Less well known than his son, MARCELLO PIACENTINI, Pio Piacentini (1846–1928) was one of the most respected and influential of Roman architects in the first half century after Italian unification. A student at the Accademia di San Luca in Rome and of the great restoration architect VERGILIO VESPIGNANI, Piacentini later became president of the Academy.

He designed and built the first major museum in Rome after unification, the Palazzo delle Esposizioni (1880–1882) on the new Via Nazionale. Relatively small in size but set back from the street and approached by a monumental flight of steps, designed in a Beaux-Arts manner overlaid with Italian rhetorical flourishes, the museum was a flamboyant and arresting building, with few analogues in Italian architecture. Piacentini's major later works, such as the Palazzo Sforza Cesarini (1886–1888) and the Ministero di Grazia e Giustizia (1913–1920) were both more original and more Roman. Inspired by the Renaissance palazzo on the one hand and by Roman brick patterns on the other, these large and blocky buildings were executed in stucco, travertine, and a rosy brick, with sharply molded cornices and string-courses, and, in the case of the earlier buildings, geometricized floral decoration. These mature buildings were colorful, modest in scale, elegant, and well-suited to their setting in central Rome. Although Piacentini was one of the architects who helped to complete the monument to Vittorio Emanuele II designed by GIUSEPPE SACCONI, it is unlikely that he was responsible for the changes in scale and detailing which made the "Vittoriano" so out of keeping with its surroundings.

BARBARA MILLER LANE

WORKS

1880–1882, Palazzo delle Esposizioni, via Nazionale; 1886–1888, Palazzo Sforza Cesarini; 1892–1894, Flats, via Ancona; 1895–1896, Collegio Germanico Chapel, via del Falcone; 1905, Quirinal Tunnel (south façade with GIULIO PODESTI); 1909, Villino Allievi, via A. Farnese; 1913–1920, Ministero di Grazia e Giustizia (with Marcello Piacentini); 1914–1915, Villa Berlingieri, viale Regina Margherita (with Piacentini); Rome.

BIBLIOGRAPHY

ACCASTO, GIANNI; FRATICELLI, VANNA; and NICOLINI, RENATO 1971 *L'architettura di Roma capitale: 1890–1970.* Rome: Golem.

GUTTRY, IRENE DE 1978 *Guida di Roma moderna: Architettura dal 1870 ad oggi.* Rome: De Luca.

MEEKS, CARROLL L. V. 1966 *Italian Architecture: 1750–1914.* New Haven: Yale University Press.

PAOLIS, SAVERIO DE, and RAVAGLIOLI, ARMANDO 1971 *La Terza Roma.* Rome: Palombi.

PIACENTINI, MARCELLO 1952 *Le vicende edilizie di Roma dal 1870 ad oggi.* Rome: Palombi.

PORTOGHESI, PAOLO 1968 *L'eclettismo a Roma: 1870–1922.* Rome: De Luca.

PICCHIATI, FRANCESCO ANTONIO

Among architects of the baroque period in Naples, Francesco Antonio Picchiati (1619–1694) occupies a place behind COSIMO FANZAGO, the most distinguished baroque architect in that city. Typical of Picchiati's work is an octagonal church that he built for the Monte of the Misericordia in Naples (1658–1678). In style, the work seems to hark back to early Renaissance models in Florence although some of the decoration is highly elaborate and typically Neapolitan. Another work is the staircase for the Palazzo Reale (1661), noted by Anthony Blunt (1975) as the first example of the Imperial staircase in Italy; its single short flight splits into two long flights that rise up the side of the entry hall. This type of staircase had been used previously in Spain (Alcazar, Toledo).

Picchiati was a noted collector of antiquities and an amateur archeologist.

NICHOLAS ADAMS

WORKS

1658–1678, Monte della Misericordia Church and Palace; 1661, Palazzo Reale (staircase); 1673–1683, San Giovanni Battista delle Monache; Naples.

BIBLIOGRAPHY

BLUNT, ANTHONY 1975 *Neapolitan Baroque and Rococo Architecture.* London: Zwemmer.

PICCINATO, LUIGI

Luigi Piccinato (1899–) was born in Legnago, Italy. He graduated from the Scuola Superiore di Architettura in Rome in 1923. A founding member of the Gruppo Urbanisti Romani (1926), he also was active in the Rationalist movement in Italy. He is responsible for dozens of town plans for Italian cities, including the plan of Sabaudia, the most important Italian new town of the interwar period. He held numerous important teaching positions with universities in Naples, Rome, and Venice and has lectured extensively outside of Italy. Between 1948 and 1958, he edited the magazine *Metron.* He currently resides in Rome.

DENNIS DOORDAN

WORKS

1933, Town Plan (with G. Cancellotti, E. Montuori, A. Scalpelli), Sabaudia, Italy. 1938, Apartment Building, Rome. 1962, Town Plan, Catania, Italy.

BIBLIOGRAPHY

CENNAMO, MICHELE 1973 *La Prima Esposizione Italiana di Architettura Razionale.* Naples: Fausto Fiorentino.

PIERFRANCESCO DA VITERBO

Pierfrancesco Fiorenzuoli (Florensolius, Renzuoli) da Viterbo (c.1470–1534) was one of several military architects who became famous in the sixteenth century when the Italians were attempting to deal with the changes brought about by the development of the movable cannon and underground powder mines. He was highly praised by his contemporaries, yet he is seldom mentioned today.

Born in Viterbo about 1470, Pierfrancesco spent his early years in the military, fought several Italian wars, and eventually became commander of Cività Castellana. At this time, most fortifications were designed by architects who had been trained in other fields of art, and his early practical experience may have recommended him to Antonio da Sangallo the Younger (see SANGALLO FAMILY).

Pierfrancesco was sent to Piacenza by Pope Clement VII in order to begin the new fortifications for this city in March 1525. This large project, which had nine bastions and was finished only in 1540, was, according to Promis, the earliest example in Italy to use fascines to strengthen the earthen ramparts. A year later, Pierfrancesco toured the Romagna with Antonio da Sangallo the Younger and MICHELE SANMICHELI to inspect fortifications for Clement VII. He also advised the duke of Urbino on the defensive preparations for Pesaro. After the Medici returned to Florence in 1531, Pierfrancesco was called there to assist Antonio da Sangallo the Younger on the designs for the new citadel, the Fortezza da Basso. He died in 1534 while working on this well-known project.

PRISCILLA ALBRIGHT

WORKS

1525–1526, Fortifications (not completed until c.1540 by others), Piacenza, Italy. 1533–1534, Fortezza da Basso (with Antonio da Sangallo the Younger), Florence.

BIBLIOGRAPHY

BANCHI, LUCIANO, and SCIPIONE BORGHESI i 1898 *Documenti (Nuovi) per la storia dell'arte senese.* Siena, Italy: Torrini.

BELTRAMI, LUCA 1902 *Relazione sullo stato delle rocche di Romagna.* Bice Belgisiso, Italy.

GIOVANNONI, GUSTAVO 1959 *Antonio da Sangallo il Giovane.* 2 vols. Rome: Tipografia Regionale.

MAGHERINI-GRAZIANI, GIOVANNI 1897 *L'arte a Città di Castello.* Città di Castello, Italy: Lapi.

PROMIS, CARLO 1874 "Biografie di ingegneri militari italiani del secolo XIV alla metà del secolo XVIII." *Miscellanea di storia italiana* 14:326–330.

RAVIOLO, CAMILLO n.d. *Pierfrancesco da Viterbo.* Rome.

VASARI, GIORGIO (1568)1973 *Le opere di Giorgio Vasari, con nuove annotazioni e commenti.* 9 vols. Edited by G. Milanesi. Reprint. Florence: Sansoni. Originally published in 1550 with the title *Le vite de più eccelenti architetti.* There are many English translations and selections from Vasari's *Lives;* the standard one by G. du C. de Vere was published in ten volumes in London by the Medici Society in 1912–1915.

PIERMARINI, GIUSEPPE

Giuseppe Piermarini (1734–1808) was born in Foligno, Italy. In his youth, Piermarini studied with LUIGI VANVITELLI in Naples. He soon established himself in Milan, where he became that city's principal architect until the close of the eighteenth century. His position as *architetto del stato* brought numerous important commissions his way, both public and private. Piermarini's first major work was the new façade for the Palazzo Reale in Milan (1769–1778), notable for the quiet restraint of its classicizing design. Piermarini's best known work is the Teatro alla Scala, or La Scala (1776–1779), Milan's celebrated opera house. Its ceremonial façade is marked by the grace and simplicity of a mature and accomplished neoclassicist. Other major commissions include the Villa Ducale (1776–1780) and Villa Reale (1777–1780) at Monza, both essentially neo-Palladian (see ANDREA PALLADIO) designs; the Palazzo Belgioioso, Milan (1772–1781); and the Palazzo del Genio Militare, Milan (1782–1783). For many years Piermarini's works were publicly criticized, particularly by the rigorist FRANCESCO MILIZIA, who considered Piermarini's classicizing manner to be overly opulent. Piermarini was nevertheless one of the most accomplished architects of the generation following BERNARDO ANTONIO VITTONE.

ELIZABETH GREENE

WORKS

1769–1778, Palazzo Reale; 1770–1772, Palazzo Bigli in Via Borgonuovo; 1772–1778, Palazzo Greppi; 1772–1781, Palazzo Belgioioso; 1773–1778, Palazzo Ducale; 1775, Palazzo Moriggia in Via Borgonuovo; 1776, Casa Casnedi; 1776–1779, Teatro alla Scala, Milan. 1776–1780, Villa Ducale; 1777–1780, Villa Reale; Monza, Italy. 1777–1780, Teatro della Canobbia; 1782–1783, Palazzo del Genio Militare; Milan.

BIBLIOGRAPHY

FUMAGALLI, I. 1837 *Elogio dell'architetto Giuseppe Piermarini.* Milan: Accademia delle Belle Arti.

MEEKS, CARROLL L. V. 1966 *Architecture in Italy: 1750–1914.* New Haven: Yale University Press.

MEZZANOTTE, GIANNI (1966)1975 *Architettura neoclassica in Lombardia.* Naples, Italy: Scientifiche Italiane.

MORETTI, G. (1837)1909 *In memoria di Giuseppe Piermarini: Parole pronunziate nel Teatro di Foligno il XVII sett. MCMVIII dall'architetto Gaetano Moretti.* Reprint. Foligno, Italy: Campitelli.

PIERMARINI, GIUSEPPE (1789)1970 *Teatro della Scala in Milano, architettura del Regio Professore Piermarini.* Perugia, Italy: Volumnia.

PIETILÄ, REIMA

Reima Pietilä (1923–) is unique among contemporary Finnish architects in that his idiosyncratic, expressive, and seemingly intuitive approach differs sharply from the predominantly rationalistic—at present "high-tech"—architecture in Finland. Furthermore, he is unusual as an architect in basing his design on theoretical studies by thinking, writing, and sketching: for him the design is not an end in itself. Pietilä early became attached to the expressionistic architecture of HUGO HÄRING, HANS SCHAROUN, and BRUNO TAUT. His career began late, and until recently, he had not built much. He was already thirty when he graduated from Helsinki University of Technology. Having received his first commission, he established his own practice in 1957. His first internationally known project was the Finnish Pavilion for the Brussels World's Fair (1958).

Since 1960, he has had a joint office with Raili Paatelainen, his wife, a common practice in Finland, resulting in a strong and fruitful collaboration. The first projects of their partnership were the Kaleva Church in Tampere, Finland (1964–1966), and the Dipoli Congress and Student Center at Helsinki University of Technology in Otaniemi, Finland (1964–1966). The Kaleva Church, made of curved concrete surfaces and lit through narrow vertical bands of windows, rises powerfully on an open hill. The Dipoli, a "nonbuilding," a "poem of Nordic mythology," created a new vocabulary of organic architecture: the external rocks and trees emerge within as materials, the exterior space penetrating the building. After the Suvikumpu Housing Area in the Tapiola Garden City, Finland (1967–1969), the Pietiläs did not have any major commissions. Reima Pietilä was awarded a Finnish State professorship of arts in 1971–1972 and served as a professor of architecture at Oulu University, Finland (1973–1979). In 1975, the Pietiläs won the competition for a Cultural Services Master Plan for Hervanta New Town in Tampere, Finland, and designed the major buildings: the Leisure Time and Congregational Center and the Market Hall (1978–1979). They also won the competition for the Tampere Main Library (1981–1982). These projects seem to be alternatives to the current pragmatic architecture, an attempt to search for an architecture based upon metaphor, association, poetic allusion, and imagery—here with Tampere's past, as contrasted to the Pietiläs' earlier organic and expressionistic architecture. Reima Pietilä calls this style "a humanist form of cultural regionalism" accommodating itself to local conditions, so that "as a work of art, the building can become part of the region where it will stand." The Pietiläs have secured their international fame with the extension of the Sief Palace Area in Kuwait (1981) for a different cultural environment.

PIRKKO-LIISA LOUHENJOKI

WORKS

REIMA PIETILÄ

*1958, Finnish pavilion, World's Fair, Brussels.

REIMA PIETILÄ AND RAILI PAATELAINEN

1966, Kaleva Church, Tampere, Finland. 1966, Dipoli, Congress and Student Center, Otaniemi; 1966–1969, Suvikumpu Housing Area, Tapiola; Espoo, Finland. 1972, Särestöniemi Art Gallery, Kittilä, Finland. 1972, Sauna, Hvitträsk Museum, Kirkkonummi, Finland. 1975, Master Plan for Cultural Services, Hervanta; 1978–1979, Leisure Time and Congregational Center and Market Hall, Hervanta; 1978–1982, Main Library; Tampere, Finland. 1979–1981, Church, Lieksa, Finland. 1980–1982, Finnish Embassy, New Delhi. 1981, Council of Ministers Building; 1981, Ministry of Foreign Affairs Building; 1981, Reception Hall (extension); Sief Palace Area, Kuwait City.

BIBLIOGRAPHY

BORRAS, MARIA LUISA 1967 *Arquitectura Finlandesa en Otaniemi.* Barcelona, Spain: Poligrafa.

DONAT, JOHN (editor) 1964 *World Architecture Today.* New York: Viking.

Finnish Architecture. 1975 The Hague: Museum of Finnish Architecture and the Netherlands Congress Center. Exhibition catalogue.

NORBERG-SCHULZ, CHRISTIAN (1975)1980 *Meaning in Western Architecture.* New York: Rizzoli.

QUANTRIL, MALCOLM 1980 "Pietilä, Reima." Page 629 in Muriel Emanuel (editor), *Contemporary Architects.* New York: St. Martin's.

RICHARDS, J. M. 1978 *800 Years of Finnish Architecture.* Newton Abbot, England: David & Charles.

SALOKORPI, ASKO 1970 *Modern Architecture in Finland.* London: Weidenfeld & Nicolson.

"The Student's Clubhouse in Otaniemi and the Kalevala Church in Tampere." 1963 *Perspecta* 8:27–36.

TEMPEL, EGON 1968 *New Finnish Architecture.* Translated by James C. Palmes. London: Architectural Press.

PIETRASANTA, JACOPO DA

Jacopo da Pietrasanta (?–c.1495) was an architect who participated in the rebuilding of Rome upon the return of the papacy. He was master architect of San Agostino, Rome (1479–1483)—the earliest design of a space on a monumental scale in Quattrocento Rome. He also worked on the Palazzo Venezia, Rome (begun 1455), and was *capomaestro* of the Benediction Loggia, Rome (1461–1462).

HOWARD SHUBERT

BIBLIOGRAPHY

HEYDENREICH, LUDWIG H., and LOTZ, WOLFGANG 1974 *Architecture in Italy: 1400–1600.* Translated by Mary Hottinger. Harmondsworth, England: Penguin.

ROMANIS, ALFONSO CAMILLO DE 1921 *La Chiesa di S. Agostino a Roma.* Rome.

URBAN, GÜNTER 1961–1962 "Die Kirchenbaukunst des Quattrocento in Rom." *Römisches Jahrbuch für Kunstgeschichte* 9–10:73–287.

PIETRE, HENRI

Henri Piètre (c.1725–c.1790) was *inspecteur des bâtiments* for the duke of Orléans at the Palais Royal in Paris in 1749 where he worked with PIERRE CONTANT D'IVRY and his teacher, JEAN SILVAIN CARTAUD, on the large Cour des Fontaines. He worked for the duke on other Parisian projects and on the châteaux of Bagnolet and Raincy. Appointed first architect to the duke in 1776, he carried out major interior transformations at the Palais Royal, soon destroyed by the building of VICTOR LOUIS's Theater (1786–1790). Piètre's project drawings of interiors (Carnavalet) show him to have been in tune with the simple and elegant classical taste of the period. Replaced at the Palais Royal by Louis in 1781, he remained until 1785 *contrôleur des bâtiments.*

MYRA DICKMAN ORTH

WORKS

*1749–1751, Palais Royal (interior remodeling; with Jean Silvain Cartaud and Pierre Contant d'Ivry); *1766, Hôtel Mélusine (façade); *1769, Library, Gallery, Ducal Apartments, Madame Blot's Apartment, Palais Royal; Paris. *c.1770, Château de Villers-Cotterets (outbuildings and gardens), Aisne, France. *c.1773, Château of Raincy (chapel, "salon des glaces," and dining room), France. *1773, Duchess of Chartres's apartment, Palais Royal; 1775, Hôtel de Montesson; 1775, Madame de Valence's apartment; 1775, Stables; 1775, Observatory on Fountain Court; 1777, Salle de Bal; Palais Royal; *1784, Salon Pavilion d'Orléans, Hôtel d'Orléans, Paris.

BIBLIOGRAPHY

Henri Piètre's manuscript memoir, dated 1789, is ms. 51 in the Bibliothèque d'Art et Archéologie, Paris.

BRAHAM, ALLAN 1980 *The Architecture of the French Enlightenment.* London: Thames & Hudson.

CHAMPIER, VICTOR, and SANDOZ, G. ROGER 1900 *Le Palais Royal d'après les documents inédits (1629–1900).* 2 vols. Paris: Société de Propagation des livres d'art.

DALLY, PHILIPPE 1913 "L'Architecte Henri Piètre et la Galerie d'Enée au Palais Royal." *Le Centre de Paris* 1:23–28.

GALLET, MICHEL 1960 "Les Dessins de l'architecte Henri Piètre pour la décoration du Palais Royal." *Bulletin du Musée Carnavalet* 13:8–15.

GALLET, MICHEL 1964 *Les Demeures parisiennes: L'Epoque Louis XVIe.* Paris: Le Temps.

OLIVIER, SARAH 1979 "Le Mécénat architectural de Louis-Philippe, duc d'Orléans (1743–1785)." *Positions des thèses de l'Ecole Nationale des Chartres* 1979:89–95.

PIGAGE, NICOLAS DE

Nicolas de Pigage (1723–1796), born in Lunéville, France, had studied at the Académie d'Architecture in Paris and traveled in Italy and possibly England before being called to the court of the Elector Palatine in 1749 as a landscape architect. Succeeding Guillaume d'Hauberat as chief architect in 1752, Pigage dominated architecture in the Palatine until his death. His early interior decorations are fully rococo, but his later work is characterized by the more restrained classicism of his masterpiece, the Château of Benrath (1755–1765).

RICHARD CLEARY

WORKS

1752, Palace Theater; 1753–1795, Gardens; Schwetzingen, Germany. 1755–1758, Elector's Palace (decoration of the library and other interiors; rebuilt after World War II, Mannheim, Germany. 1755–1765, Château and Gardens on Benrath, near Düsseldorf, Germany. 1769, Gardens of the Jägerhof, Düsseldorf, Germany. 1773, Karlstor, Heidelberg, Germany. *1788–1792, Francesco Schweitzer-Alessina Residence, Frankfurt, West Germany.

BIBLIOGRAPHY

COLOMBIER, PIERRE DU 1956 *L'Architecture française en Allemagne au XVIIIe siècle.* 2 vols. Paris: Presses Universitaires de France.

DE SAGER, WALTER 1966 "Nicolas de Pigage and Schloss Benrath: Its Place in the History of Düsseldorf." *Connoisseur* 163: 212–219.

PIGAGE, NICOLAS DE (1778)1805 *La galerie électorale de Dusseldorf; ou, catalogue raisonné et figuré de ses tableaux.* Rev. ed. 2 vols. Düsseldorf, Germany: Daenzer.

SCHLUMBERGER, EVELINE 1970 "Monuments: Revoir Benrath." *Connoissance des Arts* 215:36–45.

PIKIONIS, D. A.

Dimitrios A. Pikionis (1887–1968) was a prominent Greek architect, a professor at the Polytechnic School in Athens for over thirty years, and a member of the Academy of Athens since 1966. Born in Piraeus to a family of islanders from Chios, he studied architecture and painting in Athens, Munich, and Paris. Pikionis worked in the spirit of Greece's recent architectural tradition.

VASSILIA PH. PETSAS

WORKS

1933–1935, Experimental School of the University of Thessaloniki, Greece. 1951–1954, Xenia Hotel, Delphi, Greece. 1961, Town Hall, Volos, Greece. 1961–1965, Philothei Playgrounds, Athens.

BIBLIOGRAPHY

ANTONIADES, ANTHONY C. 1976 "Poems with Stone: The Enduring Spirit of Dimitrios Pikionis." *Architecture and Urbanism* 72, Dec.:17–22.

ANTONIADES, ANTHONY C. 1977 "Dimitrios Pikionis: His Work Lies Underfoot on Athens' Hills." *Landscape Architecture* 67, Mar.:150–153.

ANTONIADES, ANTONIS K. 1979 Pages 45–58 in *Synchrone Hellenike Architektonike.* Athens: Anthropos-Choros.

PIKIONIS, DIMITRIOS 1968 *Aphieroma tou Syllogou Architektonon ste mneme tou architektonos-kathegetou Dimitri Pikioni.* Athens: Dekembrios.

TZILALIS, CHRISTOS 1970 "He zoe ke to ergo tou Dimitri Pikioni." *Epistemonike Epeteris Polytechnikes Scholes Panepistemiou Thessalonikis* 4:318–379.

Zygos. 1958 27–28: entire issue.

PILCHER, LEWIS F.

Lewis F. Pilcher (1871–1941) attended Wesleyan University in 1889–1890, graduated from the Columbia University School of Architecture in 1895, and apprenticed in the office of Merelin Thomas. While serving as professor of art at Vassar College between 1900 and 1911, Pilcher entered a partnership with W. G. Tachau, and the firm submitted the winning entry in the competition for Troop C Armory (1906) in Brooklyn. Pilcher and Tachau specialized in armories, but their work also included the design of several buildings at Vassar (1906–1907). Appointed New York State architect by Governor William Sulzer in 1913, Pilcher completed the reconstruction of the New York State Capitol following a fire. His work as state architect included an extensive addition to Sing Sing Prison (1919–1920) in Ossining, New York. Upon retirement from state service in 1923, Pilcher served as consulting architect on several projects and returned to teaching, at the University of Pennsylvania from 1926 to 1929 and at Pennsylvania State College from 1929 to 1937.

WESLEY HAYNES

WORKS

1906, Troop C Armory, Brooklyn, N.Y. 1906–1907, Faculty Houses and Dormitory, Vassar College, Poughkeepsie, N.Y. 1912, Kingsbridge Armory, Bronx, N.Y. 1919–1920, Sing Sing Prison (extension), Ossining, N.Y.

BIBLIOGRAPHY

HAMLIN, A. D. F. 1923 "The State Architect and His Works." *Architectural Record* 53:26–43; 54:265–277.

"Lewis F. Pilcher." 1941 *New York Times,* June 16, p. 15.

PILCHER, LEWIS F. 1920 "Psychiatric Classification in Prison." *American Architect and Building News* 117, no. 2301:97–106.

PILCHER, LEWIS F. 1920 "The Wingdale Prison Site." *American Architect and Building News* 117, no. 2301:113–115.

PILCHER, LEWIS F. 1932 "Institutions for the Mentally Affected: A Program of Planning Requirements." *Architectural Record* 71:131, 133–137.

PILGRAM, ANTON

Anton Pilgram (c.1455–1515) is best known as the sculptor of the organ gallery and the pulpit in the Church of Saint Stephan's, Vienna, each decorated with a self-portrait. That he also was an architect of rank has been observed only recently. Born between 1450 and 1460, most likely in Brünn, he obtained his first training in Vienna where he was attracted by the architecture of the Vienna Cathedral architect Hanns Buchsbaum. He must have been familiar with Buchsbaum's work outside of Vienna as well, either from direct knowledge or through Buchsbaum's drawings as is evident from Pilgram's first known architectural work, the choir of the Church of Saint Kilian in Heilbronn (c.1482–1490), South Germany, based on Buchsbaum's plan for Steyr. Pilgram remained there from 1481 or 1482 to the end of the 1480s, executing also some sculptural works for the church. Thereafter, we find him in Wimpfen, where he was involved in the rebuilding of the parish church. His master mark and the dates 1493 and 1497 are found in the masonry of the nave. When Pilgram left Wimpfen, the vaulting of the nave had not yet been begun and was executed after Pilgram's design (preserved among his drawings in the Akademie in Vienna) by Bernhard Sporer from 1512 onward. The commissions for Heilbronn and Wimpfen were most likely awarded by or obtained through the services of

Heilbronn's mayor Hans Eger. By 1502, Pilgram was back in Brünn. His master mark and the date 1502 are found on the walls of Saint James Church in Brünn. He designed the Judentor (one of Brünn's city gates) and the staircase to the Saint James's School. Both works were destroyed during the nineteenth century, but their appearances are known through illustrations. The lintel of the Judentor with Pilgram's signature and the date 1508 is preserved in the Mährisches Museum, Brünn. According to a nineteenth-century drawing, the staircase displayed Pilgram's master mark and the date 1510. A drawing by Pilgram for the ceiling pattern of the staircase is preserved in the Akademie in Vienna. In 1511, he completed the entrance gate to the city hall in Brünn. During that same year, he was also listed as master of the Viennese Cathedral workshop where he succeeded Jörg Oechsl. His work for the Cathedral of Saint Stephan's in Vienna is mainly sculptural. Between 1513 and 1515, he designed rooms in the Niederösterreichisches Landhaus. Plans in the Akademie, Vienna, document his authorship of the ceilings for the former passage way (now chapel) and the guard's room; the design for the passage shows a continuation of design patterns already used in Wimpfen. These rooms are the only surviving examples of secular architecture designed by Pilgram, yet his many plans indicate that other secular commissions must have been awarded to him during these years. The attribution of the churches in Wever and Freistadt to Pilgram is based on his designs in the Akademie in Vienna.

Pilgram's greatest contributions as architect were his many plans for ceilings. During the fifteenth century, the traditional structural design of Gothic vaults gave way to a more ornamental design which at times could even appear to be unstructural. The ceiling was no longer considered the continuation of the walls but assumed a life of its own. The exploration of these features fascinated Pilgram the most and they are also found in his sculptural works.

About Pilgram's life only a few facts are known. Most important is his controversy with the Viennese guild of masons which reveals Pilgram as a ruthless and egotistic person who did not tolerate others but subjected them to the fiercest and, by fifteenth-century standards, unprofessional competition.

EGON VERHEYEN

WORKS

c.1482–1490, Saint Kilian's, Heilbronn, Germany. 1493–1497, Paris Church, Wimpfen, Germany. 1502, Saint James; *1508, Judentor; Brünn, Austria. c.1510, Parish Church, Aschbach, Austria. 1510, Saint James's School (staircase); 1511, City Hall (entrance portal); Brünn, Austria. c.1512, Church, Sindelburg, Austria. 1513, Saint Sebastian, Weyer, Austria. 1513–1515, Nederosterreichisches Landhaus, Vienna. c.1515, Parish Church (choir), Freistadt, Austria.

BIBLIOGRAPHY

CAPRA, MARIA 1953–1954 "Wann und wo starb Anton Pilgram." *Mitteilungen der Gesellschaft für vergleichende Kunstforschung Wien* 6, no. 2:101–102.

FEUCHTMÜLLER, RUPERT 1951 *Die spätgotische Architektur und Anton Pilgram.* Vienna: Österreichische Staatsdruckerei.

GRIMSCHITZ, BRUNO 1953 "Die Risse von Anton Pilgram." *Wiener Jahrbuch für Kunstgeschichte* 15:101–118.

KOEPF, HANS 1953 "Neuentdeckte Bauwerke des Meisters Anton Pilgram." *Wiener Jahrbuch für Kunstgeschichte* 15:119–135.

OETTINGER, KARL 1951 *Anton Pilgram und die Bildhauer von St. Stephan.* Vienna: Herold.

PERGER, RICHARD 1970 "Die Baumeister des Wiener Stephansdomes im Spätmittelalter." *Wiener Jahrbuch für Kunstgeschichte* 23:66–107.

PILKINGTON, F. T.

Frederick Thomas Pilkington (1832–1898), a pupil of his father, was a Scottish High Victorian "Rogue" architect. He built mostly churches and institutional buildings in Scotland. Typical of his work is the Barclay Church in Edinburgh, a polychrome stone structure with early French Gothic details. Bewilderingly roofed with gables, distinct pitches, and a spire, the plan owes nothing to medieval arrangements.

RODERICK O'DONNELL

WORKS

1861–1863, Church of the Trinity, Irvine, Ayrshire, Scotland. 1861–1870, Children's Home, Larbert, Stirlingshire, Scotland. 1862–1863, Barclay Church, Edinburgh. 1867, Saint John's, Edenside, Kelso, Scotland. *1875–1877, Hydropathic Hospital, Moffat, Dumfrieshire, Scotland. *1881–1883, Windsor Hotel, Victoria Street, London.

BIBLIOGRAPHY

DIXON, ROGER, and MUTHESIUS, STEFAN 1978 *Victorian Architecture.* London: Oxford University Press.

PILKINGTON, WILLIAM

William Pilkington (1758–1848), born in Hatfield, England, became a pupil, then assistant (1776?–1788) to Sir ROBERT TAYLOR. Competent in the neoclassical and Tudor styles, he secured various official posts, including surveyor to the

Board of Customs (1781–1810) and to the earl of Radnor.

R. WINDSOR LISCOMBE

WORKS

*1785, Custom House, Portsmouth, England. 1788–1795, Council House (as designed by Robert Taylor), Salisbury, England. *1800, Chilton Lodge, Berkshire, England. 1802, Otterden Place, Kent, England. *1803, Big School, The Charterhouse, London. 1809–1811, Royal Naval Hospital (also attributed to Edward Holl), Great Yarmouth, England. 1812, Clermont Hall, Little Cressingham, Norfolk, England. *1816, Transport Office (later the India Board of Control), Whitehall, London. 1818–1824, Calverton Church, near Stony Stratford, Buckinghamshire, England.

BIBLIOGRAPHY

LEES-MILNE, JAMES 1970 "Otterden Place, Kent." *Country Life* 148:510–514.

PINCH, JOHN

The primary architect working in Bath, England, in the early nineteenth century, John Pinch (c.1770–1827) was a competent designer in late Georgian neoclassical and neo-Gothic styles. Like many of his speculator predecessors in Bath and elsewhere in provincial eighteenth-century Britain, Pinch began as a builder, but bankruptcy in 1804 forced a change of profession—fortunately for the better. He soon emerged as a successful surveyor and architect, and his refined, elegant terraces at once augmented the vigorous local tradition and heralded a renewed society interest in the city itself. But it was as a church architect that Pinch gained a measure of national fame. Saint Mary, Bathwick (1814–1820), evidently undertaken with help from his son, John Pinch, Junior, was highly regarded as a model Gothic-style edifice at the start of the Commissioners era of English church building. Influence of Saint Mary's can be seen in his own church at Hungerford (1814–1816), his son's Saint Saviour, Larkhill, Bath (1829–1831), JAMES SAVAGE's Saint Luke, Chelsea, London (1820–1825), and—through Savage's Saint Luke's—THOMAS U. WALTER's Saint James, Wilmington, North Carolina (1839).

GERALD L. CARR

WORKS

1807–1808, New Sydney Place; 1808–1815, Cavendish Place; 1810, Daniel Street; Bath, England. 1814–1816, Saint Lawrence, Hungerford, Berkshire, England. 1814–1820, Saint Mary, Bathwick, England. 1817–1820, Sion Hill Place, Bath, England. 1817–1821, Bishopstow House, Wiltshire, England. 1817–1830, Cavendish Crescent; 1824–1826, The Royal Hospital; 1825, Raby Place; Bath, England.

BIBLIOGRAPHY

HUNT, J. M. 1962 "A Little-Known Architect of Bath." *Country Life* 131:1448–1451.

ISON, WALTER W. 1948 *The Georgian Buildings of Bath.* London: Faber.

SUMMERSON, JOHN 1969 *Architecture in Britain: 1530–1830.* Harmondsworth, England: Penguin.

PINEAU, NICOLAS

The son of a carver employed at the royal manufactory at the Gobelins, Nicolas Pineau (1684–1754) appears to have trained at the Gobelins, studying mainly under JULES HARDOUIN MANSART.

In 1716, Nicolas signed a five-year contract, along with several other French artists headed by JEAN BAPTISTE ALEXANDRE LE BLOND, to work in Russia for Peter the Great. After Le Blond's death in 1719, Pineau, being the most accomplished member of the group, took over Le Blond's role as architect. Pineau supplied the Russian court with designs for paneling, chimneypieces, doors, tables, frames, and the like. He designed Peter the Great's tomb in 1725, and there also exist drawings for an unexecuted arsenal, a palace, and a church. His most celebrated achievement in Russia, however, was the building in 1721 of a cabinet for Peter the Great in the grand palace at Peterhof. The carving of the panels with military trophies and with attributes of the arts and sciences is brilliantly and perfectly executed. The individual elements seem almost to tumble down the panels in rich profusion, the beaded moldings adding to the elegance of the design.

Pineau was persuaded to stay in Russia beyond his contract, finally returning to Paris sometime between 1727 and 1730 where his superior talents as designer were quickly recognized. A number of architects, such as JEAN BAPTISTE LEROUX, called upon him to collaborate on interior decoration.

The delicacy of Pineau's line and surface pattern, the beauty of curving tendrils and interlacing natural forms in graceful combination with his favorite motif of the sculptured head in a cartouche produced a decoration that was fresh but not excessive. Little is left of Pineau's executed work, but a rich store of drawings by him (as well as by his son and successor, Dominique) in the Musée des Arts Décoratifs in Paris bears witness to his importance as a practitioner of the *genre pittoresque.*

ELAINE EVANS DEE

WORKS

1721, Peterhof (cabinet); 1725, Tomb of Peter the

Great; St. Petersburg, Russia. 1732, Hôtel d'Orrouer; 1732, Hôtel de Rouille; 1733, Hôtel de Roquelaure; 1733, Hôtel Villars; 1735?, Hôtel Varengeville; 1736, Hôtel de Bethune; 1736, Hôtel de Feuquieres; 1738, Hôtel Boutin; 1738, Hôtel de Marcilly; 1740, Hôtel Mazarin; 1740, Michel Tannevot House; Paris. 1743–1745, Chapel, Saint Louis, Versailles, France. 1743–1745, Chartreuse de Lugny, France. 1743–1745, Château Isenghien, Suresnes, France. 1744, Hôtel Bouret; 1749, Hôtel Montmorency-Luxembourg; Paris. 1750–1751, Château de la Voyer d'Argenson, Asnières, France. 1752, Claustrier House, Paris.

BIBLIOGRAPHY

BIAIS, EMILE 1892 *Les Pineau.* Paris: Société des bibliophiles français.

DESHAIRS, LEON 1914 *Dessins Originaux des Maîtres Décorateurs: Nicolas et Dominique Pineau.* Paris: Longuet.

GALLET, MICHEL 1972 *Paris Domestic Architecture of the 18th Century.* Translated by James C. Palmes. London: Barrie & Jenkins.

HAUTECOEUR, LOUIS 1950 Volume 3 in *Histoire de l'architecture classique en France.* Paris: Picard.

HUARD, GEORGES 1928 "Pineau père." Volume 1, pages 331–350 in Louis Dimier (editor), *Les peintres français du XVIIIe siècle.* Paris and Brussels: Van Oest.

KALNEIN, WEND GRAF, and LEVEY, MICHAEL 1972 *Art and Architecture of the Eighteenth Century in France.* Harmondsworth, England: Penguin.

KIMBALL, FISKE (1943)1980 *The Creation of the Rococo.* Reprint. New York: Dover.

PARKER, JAMES 1969 "The Hotel de Varengeville Room . . . A Magnificent Donation." *Bulletin of the Metropolitan Museum of Art* 28, Nov.:129–146.

PINGUSSON, GEORGES HENRI

Georges Henri Pingusson (1894–?) was a French architect and city planner who was trained at the Ecole des Beaux-Arts in Paris and also took degrees in mechanical and electrical engineering. He worked with LE CORBUSIER and in Boulogne practiced what is called *le style Paquebot* under the influence, presumably, of Corbu who had likened architecture to the oceanliner in his *Radiant City* of 1933, calling such a liner a "floating apartment house" and leading to much modern design of the time being nautical and streamlined in appearance.

After World War II, Pingusson was active in reconstruction of the Moselle, Lorraine, and Saar areas, laying out workers' towns. The French government issued a postage stamp in his honor.

GEORGE R. COLLINS

WORKS

1931–1932, Hôtel Latitude 43, Saint-Tropez, France. *1937, Pavillon des Artistes Modernes, Exposition Internationale, Paris. 1945–1950, City Plan, Saarbrücken, Germany. 1953–1959, Satellite Town (with Le Corbusier), Briey-en-Forêt, France.

BIBLIOGRAPHY

PINGUSSON, GEORGES HENRI 1948 "Urbanisme en Sarre." *L'Architecture d'aujourd'hui* 19, Dec.

PINGUSSON, GEORGES HENRI 1951 "Problems de l'equipment sanitaire." *Techniques et architecture* 11, nos. 1–2.

PINGUSSON, GEORGES HENRI 1966 "Hommage a Le Corbusier." *Urbanisme: Revue Française* 35, no. 92.

PRESSMAN, NORMAN 1970(1971) "Georges-Henri Pingusson: Architect of the Humanized Environment." *Architectural Forum* 34, June.

SCHYUT, MICHAEL; ELFFERS, JOOST; and COLLINS, GEORGE R. 1980 Pages 20, 21, 98 in *Fantastic Architecture.* New York: Abrams.

PIPER, FREDRIK MAGNUS

Fredrik Magnus Piper (1746–1824) introduced English landscape gardening to Sweden. After studies in mathematics at the University of Uppsala, Sweden, and fine arts at the Royal Academy of Arts in Stockholm, he received a scholarship to learn landscape gardening in England, Italy, and France. He was strongly inspired by the mannerist sixteenth-century country villas outside Rome and especially by the modern English gardens such as the banker Henry Hoare's plant at Stourhead near Bristol and Kew Gardens. Back in Sweden in 1780, he became the surveyor of the royal household of King Gustav III. Piper now received commissions to create landscape gardens at the royal summer palaces of Drottningholm and Haga outside Stockholm, a work occupying him for the rest of his life. The pattern which he had learned from the new English capitalists was usurped by the Swedish king. This type of gardening soon spread to other country houses. With high artistic quality Piper also designed buildings such as exotic pavilions for the gardens and some villas, which show a heavy reliance on ANDREA PALLADIO.

FREDRIC BEDOIRE

PIPER, WILLIAM W.

Born in New Hampshire, William W. Piper (c.1827–1886) went to Portland, Oregon, in 1863. A builder-architect, he practiced alone and with E. M. Burton. His buildings were Italianate or Second Empire (he probably introduced the mansard roof to Oregon). At times, he was farmer and bridge builder. He died after falling from a train crossing Wyoming.

MARION DEAN ROSS

WORKS

*1864–1866, Multnomah County Courthouse, Portland, Ore. *1870, Chemeketa Hotel, Salem, Ore. *1871–1872, Masonic Building; 1871–1872, New Market Building; Portland, Ore. *1871–1873, Marion County Courthouse; *1872–1874, Sacred Heart Academy; Salem, Ore. 1873–1876, Deady Hall, University of Oregon, Eugene.

BIBLIOGRAPHY

HAWKINS, WILLIAM JOHN, III 1976 *The Grand Era of Cast-iron Architecture in Portland.* Portland, Ore.: Binford & Mort.

NELSON, LEE H. 1959 "Architects of Oregon: Piper and Williams." *The Call Number* (University of Oregon) 20, no. 2:4–15.

VAUGHAN, THOMAS, and FERRIDAY, VIRGINIA GUEST (editors) 1974 *Space, Style and Structure.* 2 vols. Portland: Oregon Historical Society.

WALTON, ELISABETH 1973 "A Note on William W. Piper and Academy Architecture in Oregon in the Nineteenth Century." *Journal of the Society of Architectural Historians* 32, no. 3:231–238.

PIRANESI, FRANCESCO

Although he lacked the imaginative genius and technical brilliance of his father, GIOVANNI BATTISTA PIRANESI, Francesco Piranesi, (1758–1810) fulfilled a crucial role in completing his father's late works and continuing the family business into the nineteenth century. He was born in Rome, the eldest son of six surviving children, and received his initial training from his father. He later studied at the French Academy in Rome.

Francesco seems to have begun his main contributions to his father's printmaking from 1775, when he was seventeen years old. Apart from signs of his contribution to the later plates of the *Vedute di Roma,* he was to play a leading part in the three folios on the Trajan and Antonine Columns as well as in the series of engraved antiquities, *Vasi, Candelabri, Cippi, Sarcofagi,* all characterized by a somewhat hard and mechanical handling of the medium. Most involved of all these collaborations was the production of the twenty plates featuring the Doric temples at Paestum, based on a joint survey made around 1777/1778. Apart from Francesco's signature on the frontispiece and on plates XIX and XX, the fifteen preparatory drawings (later acquired by JOHN SOANE, probably from Francesco himself, in Rome), show considerable intervention by him, especially in the figures.

After his father's death in 1778, Francesco finished several archeological works including a six-plate map of Hadrian's Villa, Tivoli (1781), and a double-plate illustrating aspects of the Emissarium of Lake Fucino (1791). He also added further plates to the existing *Archi Trionfali, Trofei, Vedute di Roma,* and *Antichità Romane.* As a supplement to the latter, he issued the two volumes of the *Tempi Antichi* in 1780 and 1790, the second being devoted to a fully measured survey of the Pantheon. Other new works included *Il Teatro di Ercolano* (1783), *Monumenti degli Scipioni* (1785), and a group of vedute from the Naples region etched from drawings by Desprez. Francesco also issued an anthology of sculpture in the *Collection des plus belles statues de Rome* (1786). To consolidate these achievements, he produced in 1792 a complete catalogue of the Piranesi firm's productions and classified all the plates with Roman numerals.

His career became less dependent on his father's reputation when Gustav III of Sweden purchased the remainder of Giambattista's collection for Stockholm in 1783. The following year, he appointed Francesco royal agent for the fine arts in Italy, and in 1794, Francesco became Swedish consul in Naples. In the meantime, Francesco had become involved in revolutionary politics and while in Naples conducted counterespionage for the French. In 1798, he returned to Rome where he became, with the Jacobin Pietro, an official in the short-lived Republic. However, with the arrival of the British and Neapolitan forces there in 1800, they fled with the rest of the family to Paris where they set up business as the Calcographie des Piranesi Frères.

Besides establishing in 1803 a manufactory of terra-cotta replicas of antiquities from his father's collection, Francesco issued the bulk of the firm's graphic works in a handsome new edition of

Francesco Piranesi. Vue de la Taverne de Pompeia. From Antiquités de la Grande Grèce.

twenty-seven volumes between 1800 and 1807. During the same years, he also published the three-volumed *Antiquités de la Grande Grèce,* containing plates etched from his father's drawings of Pompeii made in the 1770s, together with a map of the excavations, revised in 1795. In the illustrations, the last traces of Giambattista's rococo delicacy of line are replaced by the bolder and more direct expression of Romanticism and the Sublime. After Francesco's death, the entire stock of Piranesi plates was acquired by the publishers Firmin Didot which continued to issue prints in Paris until 1839 when the plates were purchased for Pope Gregory XVI and returned to Rome to enhance the Calcografia Camerale.

JOHN WILTON-ELY

BIBLIOGRAPHY

CALVESI, MAURIZIO (editor) 1967 *Giovanni Battista e Francesco Piranesi.* Rome: Calcographia Nazionale. Exhibition catalogue.

FOCILLON, HENRI 1967 *Giovanni Battista Piranesi.* Edited by M. Calvesi and A. Monferini. Bologna, Italy: Alfa.

GEOFFROY, A. 1896 "Essai sur la formation des collection d'antiques de la Suède." *Revue Archéologique* Series 3 29:1–35.

KJELLBERG, E. 1920 "Piranesis antiksamling i Nationalmuseum." *Nationalmusei Arskbok* 2:115ff.

SCOTT, IAN JONATHAN 1975 *Piranesi.* London: Academy; New York: St. Martin's.

WILTON-ELY, JOHN 1978 *The Mind and Art of Giovanni Battista Piranesi.* London: Thames & Hudson.

PIRANESI, GIOVANNI BATTISTA

Although Giovanni Battista Piranesi (1720–1778) is today far better known as the supreme exponent of topographical etching, his early training and lifelong concerns as an architect were essential to his protean genius. Despite the few executed works, his personal contacts in Rome during three decades and a prolific output of over a thousand plates enabled him to exert a seminal influence on the course of European neoclassicism. His capacity for outstanding flights of imagination was accompanied by a strongly practical grasp of technical skills and an acute business sense. He was a *vedutista* and archeologist; a designer of temporary festival structures, interior schemes, and furniture; a polemicist, restorer, and art dealer. The interrelation of these rarely combined activities, moreover, led him to highly original concepts in design which were developed further by more single-minded practitioners. Almost equally unrecognized are the importance and extent of his theoretical writings published throughout his career, which advocated an unconventional and eclectic use of the past for contemporary architects and designers.

Piranesi's origins in Venice, where he spent his first twenty years, were to prove of lasting significance for his later career. He was born at Mogliano, near Mestre, the son of Angelo Piranesi who, although recorded as a *tagliapietra* or stonemason, appears to have been a master builder. Destined for an architectural career, Giambattista was apprenticed to his maternal uncle, Matteo Lucchesi, a leading architect and hydraulic engineer in the Magistrato delle Acque, the organization responsible for the republic's harbor installations and sea defenses. After certain vigorous disagreements with Lucchesi, Giambattista continued his training in the deeply rooted idiom of Palladian (see ANDREA PALLADIO) design of Venice under Giovanni Scalfurotto, Lucchesi's senior colleague in the Magistrato. The young Piranesi may have assisted in the final stages of his new master's chief building, the Chuch of Santi Simeone e Giuda, constructed overlooking the Grand Canal between 1718 and 1738.

Piranesi is also likely to have assisted Scalfurotto's nephew, the radical architect and theorist TOMMASO TEMANZA, whose survey and restoration of the Roman arch and bridge at Rimini in 1735 may have initiated Giambattista's sense of a future vocation. A taste for controversy and archeological inquiry would also have been gained from the Lucchesi circle during its heated discussions over the Etruscans as the originators of Greek architecture. This polemical atmosphere was intensified by the current teachings in Venice of the Dominican priest CARLO LODOLI, who questioned and entire validity of classical canons of design using the criterion of function.

In contrast to these utilitarian and theoretical impressions, Piranesi's outstanding imaginative faculties were also formed in a variety of ways. He is known to have received training in stage design from the Valeriani brothers, and he was instructed in the elaborate systems of perspective composition by the engraver Carlo Zucchi. Moreover, the densely urban character of Venice itself provided Piranesi with a theater of architectural experiences which he was later to exploit in the topographical *veduta,* an art form then being developed in the city by Heinz, Van Wittel, Carlevarjis and, above all, by Canaletto. Certainly, the most potent of these Venetian influences in Piranesi's formative years was the combination of the baroque stage and the topographical view in the architectural fantasy, or *capriccio,* perfected earlier in the century by Marco Ricci and to be extended stylistically in Canaletto's etched *vedute ideali.* The visual potential of the *capriccio,* however, achieved its full effect on Piranesi's architectural imagination when he entered Rome for the first time in 1740 as a draftsman in the retinue of the Venetian ambassador Marco Foscarini.

Rome, by then the goal of the Grand Tour, was swiftly becoming the intellectual capital of Europe, and Piranesi was to encounter there the ferment of new ideas and the radical questioning of the past that characterized the Enlightenment. However, for an imaginative designer in 1740 the initial experiences of the Eternal City were not only exhilarating but extremely frustrating. On the one hand, there was the visual stimulus of a townscape with violent contrasts of scale produced by the ruins of antiquity and with the spatial drama of baroque planning; on the other, the opportunities for new commissions were at a particularly low ebb after the recent building boom which had involved a number of leading architects such as FERDINANDO FUGA, ALESSANDRA GALILEI, NICOLA SALVI, and LUIGI VANVITELLI. Besides, it soon became clear that the general character of contemporary Roman architecture could offer little inspiration to Piranesi. He therefore decided to acquire a means of livelihood by producing souvenir views for the growing quantity of visitors then being served by the painter Gian Paolo Panini and the engraver Giuseppe Vasi. He spent a brief apprenticeship in Vasi's studio acquiring the rudiments of etching before a quarrel ended their relationship. While there, Piranesi may have collaborated on certain plates in Vasi's methodical survey of the city, issued as *Le Magnificenze di Roma* from 1747 onward, as well as on the full-scale preparatory drawing for the monumental etched panorama of the city seen from the Janiculum, eventually published in 1765.

During these early years in Rome, Piranesi's main creative energies found a ready outlet in devising a variety of architectural fantasies, primarily as a means of exploring new concepts of design. Although Piranesi owed much to Panini's heroic *capricci* on canvas, many of these exercises were strongly inspired by earlier attempts in archeological reconstruction by PIRRO LIGORIO, GIOVANNI BATTISTA MONTANO, and, in particular, JOHANN BERNHARD FISCHER VON ERLACH whose published works he studied in the library of his patron, the Venetian builder Nicola Giobbe. The latter helped his young compatriot to acquire a close familiarity with the principal remains of antiquity and introduced him to leading members of the profession such as Salvi and Vanvitelli. By way of a tribute to this help, Piranesi published in 1743 a selection of his fantasy compositions in the twelve plates of a work ambitiously entitled *Prima Parte di Architetture e Prospettive.* According to the dedication to Giobbe, these visions of grandiose public buildings and awesome ruined structures from the imperial past were intended to reprove the mediocrity of contemporary architects by revealing glimpses of the creative possibilities suggested by the monuments surrounding them. As he expressed it,

> These speaking ruins have filled my spirit with images that accurate drawings, even such as those of the immortal Palladio, could never have succeeded in conveying, though I always kept them before my eyes. Therefore, having the idea of presenting to the world some of these images, but not hoping for an architect of these times who could effectively execute some of them . . . there seems to be no recourse than for me or some other modern architect to explain his ideas through his drawings and so to take away from sculpture and painting the advantage, as the great [FILIPPO] JUVARRA has said, they now have here over architecture.

This speculative activity soon involved Piranesi with a group of art and architectural students at Palazzo Mancini, headquarters of the French Academy and then a lively center of progressive thought and research in Rome. Among their various enterprises, the group was involved in the production of scenery painting, temporary structures, and decorative schemes for ceremonies and public entertainments in the city. As elsewhere in Europe, the improvised nature of these commissions and the ephemeral materials used made it possible for the circle at Palazzo Mancini to experiment freely with original forms and concepts. Piranesi appears to have assisted regularly in these projects and is recorded in 1746 as being responsible for a festival decoration with fireworks to celebrate the recovery from illness of the student sculptor Jacques Saly. Initially, the influences were reciprocal but soon Piranesi's conceptions began to dominate the imagination of the *pensionnaires,* as evident in the festival designs of LOUIS LE LORRAIN and the fantasy compositions of Challe, Dumont, NICOLAS HENRI JARDIN, JEAN LAURENT LEGEAY, and ENNEMONDO A. PETITOT. With the subsequent dispersal of these able designers throughout Europe during the 1740s and 1750s, Piranesi's catalytic ideas were to enter the mainstream of neoclassical architecture.

Toward the mid-1740s, Piranesi decided to travel south to Naples in order to investigate the challenging possibilities being revealed to designers by the current excavations at Herculaneum. Once there, he was quick to realize the need to publicize such archeological discoveries by means of informative and arresting images. In fact, he seems to have received specific encouragement to undertake this mission by the curator of the finds, Camillo Paderni.

However, by May 1744, financial difficulties had forced Piranesi back to Venice where he now came under the crucial influence of one of the greatest artists of the age, Giambattista Tiepolo. Whether or not he actually worked in Tiepolo's studio, as some early sources suggest, the impact is striking both in the dramatic transformation of Piranesi's draftsmanship and etching from a tight, linear style to a richer, painterly manner, and in the unprecedented breadth of imagination in his new fantasies. This change in his etched works is particularly apparent not only in a small group of ruin *capricci* but to a far greater extent in the suite of fourteen imaginary prisons, issued as *Invenzioni Capric di Carceri* in a limited edition around 1745. These arcane images—part Venetian, part Roman—were rapidly sketched on the plate with a daring economy of line. Although ultimately derived from contemporary stage designs, in Piranesi's hands these compositions were transformed into what amounted to an experimental field of architectural inquiry. Whatever symbolic or iconographic meanings can be read into these complex visions, it is clear that they represented to Piranesi himself a means of creative release for the frustrated imagination reflected in the dedication to the *Prima Parte.* Contrary to certain modern interpretations, the *Carceri* cannot be explained away as the products of a hallucinating mind. Careful study, aided by a few related drawings, reveals a highly controlled discipline at work, exploiting the mechanics of baroque illusionism through perspective and lighting to explore new concepts of architectural expression.

Also belonging to the Venetian period were Piranesi's first essays as a designer of interior decoration and applied art in the current idiom of the rococo. Evidence is provided by a group of studies, mainly in pen and ink with chalk and washes, in the Pierpont Morgan Library, New York. Besides an exuberant design for a ceremonial gondola, a set of designs for wall panels and items of furniture may well be connected with decorative schemes he is said to have undertaken in various palaces during these years. However, Venice could no longer hold Piranesi and, around 1745, with promised financial support as an agent for the printseller Giuseppe Wagner, he returned to Rome where he set up business opposite the French Academy in the Via del Corso.

Now permanently established in his adopted city, Piranesi embarked on what was to prove a lifelong mission to record the Roman achievement in all its aspects. Already during his first visit he had begun a topographical record of the city with a series of small plates, produced in collaboration with some of the French *pensionnaires.* These small works, later collected as the *Varie Vedute di Roma* and repeatedly used for various guidebooks, contain some of Piranesi's first tentative steps to enlarge the range and possibilities of the *veduta* as a means of architectural communication beyond its mundane role as a momento of the Grand Tour. This development was rapid, and with the issue in 1748 of his own complete publication of *vedute,* later entitled *Archi Trionfali,* he soon reached a more sophisticated level of image. In these works he exploited the full dramatic range of perspective, lighting, and tone in combination with a now unrivaled understanding of ancient building methods.

A few years later, Piranesi's precarious financial situation was much improved by a dowry in 1753 when he married Angela Pasquini, daughter of Prince Corsoni's gardener, after a precipitous courtship in the Forum Romanum. This enabled him to change over completely to the larger format of copper plate which was to be used for his celebrated series, *Vedute di Roma.* These 135 magisterial plates, issued individually or in small groups throughout the rest of his career were to reflect almost every phase in Piranesi's stylistic evolution and intellectual history. At the end of his life, the *veduta* had become a descriptive aid to architects and archeologists alike. Piranesi invested it with new powers to convey sentiment as well as to record facts with a new accuracy and range of technical information. These plates, moreover, through their carefully controlled production and wide dissemination, were to determine the imaginative conception of Roman antiquity for generations of European artists, designers, and writers.

At the same time, in what might be described as acts of speculative archeology, Piranesi's study of the ruins inspired him to explore new approaches to design in a further set of fantasies of the greatest originality. Several of these mature works, issued in the *Opere Varie* of 1750, such as the "Monumental Roman Harbor" and the "Plan for a Magnificent College," were to have a particularly strong impact on the new intake at the French Academy, which included CHARLES DE WAILLY and A. F. Peyre (see PEYRE FAMILY); they may also have contributed to the development of JACQUES GERMAIN SOUFFLOT, then making his study tour of Italy.

Piranesi's physical appearance at this time is recorded in the etched portrait by his Venetian colleague Felice Polanzani—the earliest image known of him—which was used as the frontispiece to the *Opere Varie.* Almost certainly based on an idea by

Giovanni Battista Piranesi. Monumental Roman Harbor.
Plate from Opere Varie.

Giovanni Battista Piranesi. Section of a crematorium entrance by the Via Appia.
Plate from Antichità Romane.

Giambattista himself, its deliberate ambivalence—part antique fragment, part modern man—symbolizes his chosen role as a creative intermediary between past and present, with the proud inscription *architetto veneziano.*

Archeology was becoming more and more important to Piranesi by the early 1750s during which period he appears to have gradually relinquished his French contacts in favor of those with visiting British artists and architects. Among the first encountered was the young WILLIAM CHAMBERS who arrived in Rome in 1750 after training in the Parisian atelier of JACQUES FRANÇOIS BLONDEL. Despite his resistance to Piranesi's more extreme visions (characterized by a weighty censure on such license many years later in the 1791 edition of his *Treatise on Civil Architecture*), Chambers learned much from the Venetian in terms of Roman monumental composition and the powerful expression of columnar forms, as exploited in the river front to Somerset House, London, built during the 1770s.

The Scottish architect and engineer ROBERT MYLNE, working in Rome between 1755 and 1758, was understandably more affected by Piranesi's current researches in ancient technology. Mylne's investigations into the Roman water system were probably carried out with the Venetian's assistance; strong debts occur in his winning design for Blackfriar's Bridge, erected over the River Thames from 1760. Piranesi, flattered by Mylne's use of certain ancient principles learned from him, such as the application of elliptical arches and the reinforcement of attached columns, published an etching of the bridge in 1769, as under construction, from a drawing supplied at his request.

However, by far the most sympathetic and productive of these relationships was between Piranesi and ROBERT ADAM who studied in Rome between 1755 and 1757 after several years' experience in continuing his father's practice in Scotland. In Adam, the Venetian found a kindred spirit with a perceptive understanding of the exceptional value of his speculative uses of antiquity and a designer who shared something of the same ambitions for the reform of contemporary architecture and design through a creative application of the past. The means toward educating Adam's view of ancient Rome were to be partly achieved through sketching expeditions, shared with CHARLES LOUIS CLÉRISSEAU—himself already greatly affected by Piranesi—as well as through the stimulus of Giambattista's visionary drawings. (Two especially devised for Adam are now in Sir John Soane's Museum, London.) The resulting process was to constitute one of the key influences on the formation of the Adam style in Britain during the 1760s.

The results of Piranesi's extensive antiquarian studies during these years were finally presented in 1756 through the four volumes of the *Antichità Romane.* According to its preface, this work set out to provide an innovative system of archeological inquiry for the education of modern architects and their patrons as much as for scholars. Piranesi brought the mind of a trained architect and engineer to bear upon studies which had previously been dominated by literary evidence and attitudes. He thereby stressed a new concern with constructional techniques and the properties of various building materials, and highlighted the originality of planning forms and the sheer range of the Roman ornamental vocabulary. Perhaps most significant of all, however, was the manner in which Piranesi's intimate knowledge of local topography enabled him to coordinate all the diverse remains and aspects of antiquity within the broader context of Rome as an urban phenomenon. By means of numbered maps and elaborate cross-referencing in the text of the *Antichità,* he was able to demonstrate the interrelation of the defensive and hydraulic systems of the ancient city. Moreover, many of the more original insights of this work were primarily conveyed by means of some 250 plates employing particularly ingenious methods of illustration and often successfully combining a formidable quantity of data with the greatest degree of visual impact.

The publication of the *Antichità* soon established Piranesi's reputation in European scholarship, notably recognized in his election to an Honorary Fellowship of the Society of Antiquaries of London in 1757. In the same year, he issued a strongly critical pamphlet against his erring patron, the young Irish peer Lord Charlemont, who had failed to honor his promised financial support for the expensive plates of the *Antichità.* In the *Lettere di Giustificazione . . . a Milord Charlemont,* Piranesi's eloquent defense of his dignity as a practicing artist and architect reveals how closely he had come to identify his career with the fortunes of Rome. It is hardly surprising, therefore, that he was soon caught up in the opening exchanges of the Greco-Roman controversy and that, by the end of the decade, he had assumed leadership of his cause against the pro-Greek Johann Joachim Winckelmann, established in Rome by 1755 as Cardinal Albani's librarian.

Actively provoked by a series of mounting attacks on the originality and achievements of Rome, chiefly in the publications of JULIEN DAVID LEROY and MARC ANTOINE LAUGIER, Piranesi eventually launched his opening salvo in 1761 with the treatise *Della Magnificenza ed Architettura de' Romani.* In this book, which was dedicated to the new, Venetian, Pope Clement XIII, he used a particularly striking sequence of illustrations, backed by a ponderously erudite text, to defend Roman civilization and its architecture. The basis of Piranesi's argument was the utilitarian and functional austerity of the Etruscans as a highly inventive race and as the original mentors of the Romans. This strongly rationalistic defense, in specific response to Laugier, was oddly combined with a celebration of the decorative riches of late Imperial ornament, represented with visual wit and rhetoric (at Leroy's expense) in a series of large fold-out plates of architectural details.

This manifesto was closely followed during the early 1760s by a sequence of lavishly produced archeological folios, also possessing a strongly polemical bias and largely sponsored by the pope and his family, the Rezzonicos. The *Lapides Capitolini* of 1761 set out to demonstrate the extent and complexity of Rome's early history by means of inscriptions and sculptural fragments. In the *Rovine del Castello dell'Acqua Giulia,* also of 1761, Piranesi included a series of highly ingenious technical reconstructions to expound on the hydraulic science behind the aqueduct system of Rome. A similar approach was adopted in the *Disegno e Descrizione dell'Emissario del Lago Albano,* which appeared the following year, featuring the fourth-century B.C. drainage outlet of Lake Albano. This study conveyed the findings of an exceptionally thorough piece of fieldwork in a sequence of multiple diagrams, several involving reconstructions as well as plans, sections, and elevations. Other Roman as well as Etruscan remains south of Rome were considered in two further publications—*Antichità d'Albano e di Castel Gandolfo* (1762) and *Antichità di Cora* (1764)—also combining the use of dramatic *vedute* together with exemplary technical illustrations.

Above all, it was the folio *Il Campo Marzio dell'Antica Roma* of 1762 which most clearly reflected the evolution of Piranesi's theoretical ideas at this climactic point in his career. Dedicated to Robert Adam, who had been closely involved in its preparation during the late 1750s, this particular work was devoted to the Roman genius for urban design. Its argument was based on an extensive study of the surviving remains of the Campus Martius area of the imperial city, currently embedded in the accretions of medieval townscape, in conjunction with documents and other sources such as the fragmentary Severan Marble Plan. As before, the introductory text defended the author's unorthodox approach to classical archeology on the grounds of its value to modern designers. As he observes in the dedication to Adam,

> I am rather afraid that parts of the Campus which I describe should seem figments of my imagination and not based on any evidence: certainly if anyone compares them with the architectural theory of the ancients he will see that they differ greatly from it and are actually closer to the usage of our own times. But before anyone accuses me of falsehood, he should, I beg, examine the ancient [marble] plan of the city . . . he should examine the villas of Latium and that of Hadrian at Tivoli, the baths, the tombs and other ruins outside the Porta Capena and he will find that the ancients transgressed the strict rules of architecture just as much as the moderns.

The climax to the work was an extravagantly complex planning fantasy, the *Ichnographia,* which, although claiming to show Rome under Constantine, embodied both an apotheosis and an anthology of planning forms, ancient and modern. This tendentious reconstruction was contrived to stir up the imagination of the contemporary architectural profession, and its subsequent influence

Giovanni Battista Piranesi. Plan of the Campus Martius or Ichnographia. *Plate from* Il Campo Marzio dell'Antica Roma.

can be traced among the ideas of a variety of designers from Adam, de Wailly, and JEAN FRANÇOIS DE NEUFFORGE, to ETIENNE LOUIS BOULLÉE, CLAUDE NICOLAS LEDOUX, and JOHN SOANE.

The reissue around 1760 of the fourteen *Carceri* plates—most of them heavily reworked with the addition of two further scenes—significantly marked the climax of another period of creative tension in Piranesi's career as a designer. This situation was brought about by the pressures of the Greco-Roman debate and was particularly related to Piranesi's defense of his free-ranging imagination against the austere and extremely restrictive ethic of the pro-Hellenic theorists. The earlier state of the *Carceri* had gone comparatively unnoticed in the mid-1740s and was in many respects a private act of self-analysis, but the definitive version now appearing in the heat of controversy constituted a public gesture of defiance. The influence of these macabre compositions, moreover, was predictably strongest on those designers who shared Piranesi's increasingly unorthodox attitude toward antiquity and the creative role of architectural fantasy. Such was the case of the English designer GEORGE DANCE THE YOUNGER who studied in Italy for seven years from 1758 onward and whose personal contact with Piranesi powerfully conditioned his formal approach to the design of Newgate Prison, London, constructed between 1769 and 1778. Whatever stylistic motifs may be traced to the mannerism of GIULIO ROMANO or MICHELE SANMICHELI on the façade of Newgate, a far profounder debt is owed to the *Carceri* which introduced Dance to the expressive potential of monumental masonry, involving a novel use of classical forms amplified by exaggerated scale and texture.

It was during the initial years of the polemical 1760s that Piranesi began to formulate the theoretical standpoint which was to determine his work as an architect and designer for the remainder of his career. Following an attack by the French critic Mariette on the provocative arguments of *Della Magnificenza,* Piranesi in 1765 issued a three-part publication having as its main element the *Parere su l'Architettura.* This consisted of a debate between two architects representing the opposing camps of the current controversy—the rigorist Protopiro, a firm supporter of Laugier, and Didascolo who voiced Piranesi's belief in the essential value to designers of free experiment and formal variety. In certain respects, the *Parere* may be seen as the confrontation between the baroque world Piranesi identified with (GIOVANNI LORENZO BERNINI and FRANCESCO BORROMINI are cited in defense of innovative freedom) and the growing restraint of neoclassical theory. The exchange is brief and decisive in favor of Piranesi's convictions which are illustrated by a group of challenging vignettes and, after 1767, by some additional plates of a highly rhetorical nature. These bizarre images, taking the form of complete or partial architectural compositions, involve a remarkably bold eclecticism of motifs drawn from Egyptian and Greek as well as Roman and Etruscan sources.

Set against the background of this imaginative and theoretical turmoil, the 1760s were to prove the most fertile period in Piranesi's career as a practicing architect and designer. With growing prosperity he set up his own print-making business and showrooms in Palazzo Tomati on the Via Sistina, a few hundred yards from the top of the Spanish Steps. The enlightened patronage of Clement XIII and the Rezzonicos now gave him opportunities

Giovanni Battista Piranesi. Imaginary architectural composition. *Plate from* Parere su l'Architettura.

Giovanni Battista Piranesi. Design for projected Lateran Tribune.

to apply his novel aesthetic principles of design to an impressive range of projects and executed works.

In 1763, the pope commissioned him to design a new high altar for San Giovanni in Laterano, and this soon developed into a major scheme for replacing the entire structure to the west of the transepts by a monumental tribune. The architect, given this unparalleled scope for Roman magnificence, rose to the occasion with a scheme involving lavish stucco decoration and featuring a majestic papal altar with baldachin. In addition to some surviving sketch designs in the Morgan Library, at least five distinct solutions are represented in an exceptionally handsome set of finished drawings, now in the Avery Library, Columbia University, which were presented in 1767 to Cardinal Giovanni Battista Rezzonico, nephew of the pope, shortly after the scheme was abandoned.

Among the alternative schemes in the Avery set, Piranesi's ideal project is represented by at least seven drawings. This conception involves a powerful blend of Venetian scenic design—here indebted to BALDASSARE LONGHENA as much as Palladio—and a richness of textural effect with north Italian decorative motifs, deployed according to the compositional principles defended in the *Parere su l'Architettura.* The dominant feature of this scheme (also represented by a very large sectional elevation in the Morgan Library) is an apsidal screen of giant columns enclosing the high altar, with light directed onto it from a clearstory, hidden in the arch between the ante choir and the sanctuary. Further light filters laterally through side windows in the walls of the ambulatory. Although the wide repertoire of detail shows a neoclassical fidelity to antique sources, the total cohesion of this intensely ornamental interior is baroque, and Piranesi can be seen as the conscious heir to Borromini's intentions to complete the modernization of the ancient basilica.

While developing the Lateran designs, Piranesi was invited in 1764 to renovate the church and headquarters of the Knights of Malta on the Aventine by Cardinal Rezzonico as grand prior of the order. In this commission, which was to be Piranesi's only major executed work as an architect, he skillfully applied his unusual mode of composition within the narrow limits of the funds available. Apart from a key group of drawings in the Morgan Library, which include several meticulous working sheets, an extremely detailed account book covering the period from November 1764 to October 1766 (probably compiled by the *capomaestro muratore* Giuseppe Pelosini) records the structural renovations of the sixteenth-century Santa Maria Aventina, extensive work on a group of related buildings, and the execution of an elaborate scheme of decoration throughout the complex.

Piranesi enlarged the nearby Via di Santa Sabina to create a ceremonial piazza with an entrance screen leading to the priory grounds. This was embellished with rich passages of relief in the spirit of mannerist designers such as Ligorio and BALDASSARE PERUZZI whom Piranesi especially admired. Along the opposite wall of the piazza, he set a group of evocative *stelae,* or commemorative pillars, bearing further reliefs. In the sophisticated iconographic scheme, Piranesi the archeologist combined Rezzonico heraldry with antique objects representing the order's military achievements, together with Etruscan symbols relating to the Aventine's early associations with Roman history. The artist in him organized these diverse images within a compositional system that itself consciously emulated the eclectic character of Roman art.

Similarly, the modest church, situated on the south-western corner of the Aventine overlooking the Tiber, was transformed by Piranesi's vision into an imposing memorial to the order. He added an ornamental attic story to the simple pilastered west front and continued over its surface the intricate thematic program from the piazza. Further symbols of the knights' military and naval exploits were augmented by polemical references to the Italic ornamental vocabulary, mixing Etruscan tomb patterns with late Imperial motifs.

Inside the church, Piranesi introduced scenographic ideas from his Lateran tribune whereby an apsidal screen of attached columns and contrived lighting effects were used to set off a particularly elaborate altar—a strange amalgam consisting of a baroque sculptural group representing *The Apotheosis of Saint Basil* and a neoclassical *capriccio* of interlocking sarcophagi. Something of the stylistic and thematic complexity of the altar, which was executed faithfully to Piranesi's designs by the *stuccatore* Tommaso Righi, was extended to the nave. Here, the simple pattern of four bays was enriched by the incorporation of various medieval monuments of the order within a decorative scheme of wall trophies and cartouches, partly inspired by Borromini's similar *capricci* in the aisle bays of the Lateran. Above this area in the church was set a richly decorated vault, including a large relief panel celebrating the Knights of Malta and their naval history, thus completing the iconographic sequence begun on the piazza reliefs.

On the completion of the Aventine commission in 1766, the pope, while visiting the church, conferred on Piranesi the title of *Cavaliere di Sperone d'oro,* which he was to inscribe on all his plates from the following year onward. Another mark of recognition during this decade was his election to the Accademia di San Luca, where he was soon caught up in a controversy over the proposed Balestra Monument in Santi Martina e Luca.

During the 1760s, Piranesi's executed works as a designer of interiors and furniture included schemes undertaken for the pope at Castel Gandolfo, for Cardinal Rezzonico at Palazzo Quirinale, and for Senator Abondio Rezzonico at Palazzo Senatorio on the Campidoglio. Although virtually nothing of these interiors remains, apart from some traces at the latter, an identical pair of side tables for the Quirinal commission have come to light and are now in the Minneapolis Institute of Arts and the Rijksmuseum, Amsterdam, respectively. Also in these years, Piranesi's eclectic approach toward design led him to explore the potential value of Egyptian material in Rome. This resulted in one of the first substantial contributions to the Egyptian Revival when he devised a complete painted interior for the Caffé degli Inglesi in the Piazza di Spagna. The fact that this scheme, carried out during the early 1760s, has vanished with little record is probably connected with the unfavorable reactions expressed almost universally at the time. The only visual information of its appearance is provided by the etched plates of two walls published by the designer at the end of the decade. Piranesi's name is also connected with another fanciful interior, carried out for the Maltese ambassador in this period. It seems to have involved painted ruins and is possibly reflected in the surviving Ruin Room decorated by Clérisseau at the Trinità dei Monti shortly before 1767. Piranesi also turned his ingenuity to providing designs for the carriage work of coaches, one being mentioned in a letter by the Earl of Carlisle who purchased it from the artist in 1768. Virtually all these multifarious activities were to be represented among the illustrations to Piranesi's final theoretical publication, *Diverse maniere d'adornare i cammini ed ogni altra parte degli edifizi,* issued in

Giovanni Battista Piranesi. Santa Maria Aventina (façade). Rome. 1764–1766

1769 with a dedication to his model patron, Cardinal Rezzonico.

The *Diverse Maniere* was to prove the most influential of all Piranesi's works in the architecturally related fields of interior design and the applied arts. Its impact was to be of particular importance on the later designs of ROBERT ADAM, notably in the development of his chimneypieces, his novel types of furniture, and the remarkably imaginative group of Etruscan Rooms of the 1770s. Moreover, the Adam brothers were to adopt many of Piranesi's chief concepts in the theoretical prefaces to their *Works in Architecture* of the same decade. (Four plates etched by Piranesi from Robert Adam's designs for the interiors of the entrance hall and ante-room of Syon House, Middlesex, appeared in the second volume of the *Works* in 1778.) To a lesser extent, the originality of the ideas of the *Diverse Maniere* also made an impression on the more individualistic designers of the Louis XVI Style, such as FRANÇOIS JOSEPH BÉLANGER and JEAN CHARLES DELAFOSSE, in the form of specific borrowings rather than in similar modes of composition.

The substantial text of the *Diverse Maniere*—its English title being given as "An Apologetical Essay in Defence of the Egyptian and Tuscan Architecture"—represented Piranesi's most fully considered philosophy of design, namely in terms of creating a contemporary style through a highly imaginative eclecticism. The essay, consisting of three parallel texts in Italian, French, and English, was addressed specifically to an international audience of architects, designers, and patrons. Although by now Piranesi had largely abandoned the pedestrian exchanges of the Greco-Roman debate, the opening section of the essay expanded his daring claims for the originality of the Etruscans as founders of the Italic genius for invention. Moving on to defend the importance of and variety in Egyptian architecture and its decorative vocabulary, he offered a strikingly advanced justification of formal abstraction, based on a conflation of nature and antiquity. He concluded with a plea for the value of a creative license which transcended the sterile limitations of functionalist and rationalist ideals and which encompassed the sheer wealth of visual inspiration provided by antiquity. Although Piranesi's adoption of eclecticism as the basis for invention was common to many other theorists of the time, certainly no other designer was prepared to risk censure by pushing the practical exercise to such extremes as he did. Fully aware of his unique position, he triumphantly asserted,

Giovanni Battista Piranesi. Design for a chimneypiece in the Egyptian Style. Plate from Diverse Maniere.

> Let us at last shake off this shameful yoke, and if the Egyptians and Tuscans present to us, in their monuments, beauty, grace and elegance, let us borrow from their stock, not servilely copying from others, for this would reduce architecture and the noble arts [to] a pitiful mechanism, and would deserve blame instead of praise from the public, who seek for novelty, and who would not form the most advantageous idea of the artist, as was perhaps the opinion some years ago. No, an artist who would do himself honour, and acquire a name, must not content himself with copying faithfully the ancients, but studying their works he ought to show himself of an inventive, and I had almost said, of a Creating Genius; and by prudently combining the Graecan, the Tuscan, and the Egyptian together, he ought to open himself a road to the finding out of new ornaments and new manners. The human understanding is not so short and limited, as to be able to add new graces and embellishments to the works of architecture, if to an attentive and profound study of nature one would likewise join that of the ancient monuments.

As with Piranesi's previous writings, the theoretical text relied for its full impact on a corpus of illustrations. In this instance, the wealth of original designs offered in the *Diverse Maniere* plates resulted from extensive experiment over little more than a decade. The principal theme was the treatment of the chimneypiece as a peculiarly modern architectural element to which Piranesi applied his unusual mode of composition. The sixty-one examples depicted (including thirteen in the Egyptian taste) are the end products of an involved series of inquiries represented by over eighty surviving sketches and more detailed studies, mainly in the Morgan Library and the Berlin Kunstbibliothek. They range from polemically exaggerated compositions in the manner of the *Parere* plates to far more restrained designs involving easily adopted motifs on the stiles and lintels, which were to prove particularly attractive to Robert Adam and his contemporaries. Included in this latter category are three chimneypieces which Piranesi indicates in the accompanying captions as having already been executed; one for the earl of Exeter and still at Burghley House, Northamptonshire; another for the Dutch merchant banker John Hope (now in the Rijksmuseum, Amsterdam); and one, since disappeared, for Senator Abondio Rezzonico's apartments on the Campidoglio.

Many of the chimneypiece designs are shown to be integral parts of complete interior schemes in the same vogue. In fact, two later plates in the *Diverse Maniere* are those representing the painted interiors of the Caffè degli Inglesi. Moreover, many of the chimneypiece illustrations also include chairs, mirrors, and sconces, and the larger proportion of the remaining plates feature designs for over one hundred separate items of furniture and decorative elements. These depict four commodes, eleven tables, four chairs, two pairs of doors, three tripod stands, two candelabra, two candlestands, eight candlesticks, two sconces, twenty-two clocks (including a particularly extravagant timepiece which is stated to have been executed also for the senator's rooms), eleven vases or urns, ten tea or coffee pots, along with various portions of beading and moldings. For good measure, Piranesi also illustrated the carriage work for six coaches and twelve sedan chairs.

Toward the close of the *Diverse Maniere,* Piranesi referred to his extensive collection of architectural and decorative fragments as an immediate source of stimulus for these novel designs. This characteristic process of transposing ideas from the past into modern situations led him naturally to the reuse of actual decorative fragments in two interrelated fields of activity—the creation of ornamental chimneypieces *all'antica* and the restoration of classical antiquities. Both areas were to prove of considerable importance in his influence on neoclassical architecture and interior design.

With the death of Clement XIII in 1769 and the resulting decline of Rezzonico patronage, Piranesi began to find a ready market in the increasing numbers of foreign clients in Rome, especially the British on their Grand Tour who stayed near his establishment and showrooms above the Piazza di Spagna. In this enterprise he was helped by a team of specialist assistants, joined during the early 1770s by his son, FRANCESCO PIRANESI. To facilitate this lucrative business, Piranesi also collaborated with other dealers and entrepreneurs, such as the Britons Thomas Jenkins, Gavin Hamilton, and the architect James Byers. He also profited from the aid of leading restorers and sculptors.

Piranesi's production of monumental chimneypieces, which had begun with the Exeter and Hope examples in the 1760s, was greatly encouraged by the quantity of antique fragments uncovered by Hamilton's excavations in the Pantanello area of Hadrian's Villa, Tivoli, from 1769 onward. A pair of elaborate chimneypieces incorporating antique reliefs as well as some modern pastiches, was produced for the designer's clients Edward and Harriet Walter of Berry Hill, Surrey, around 1769–1771. (These were transferred to Gorhambury House, Hertfordshire, sometime after 1774.) Another was acquired in 1774 by the Scottish landowner Patrick Home for Wedderburn Castle, Berwickshire, then being refashioned externally by the Adam brothers, and other examples from Piranesi's workshops are known to have been provided for Lord Temple at Stowe, Buckinghamshire (this work has recently been traced to a Spanish collection) and for two other clients in Scotland and Russia. With the publicity given by the *Diverse Maniere,* the production of these architectural features became a thriving industry in Rome by the 1770s, constituting the most immediate source of Piranesi's influence on European interior design in his lifetime.

The considerable output of Piranesi's business and his ingenuity as a restorer was effectively advertised and documented through the issue of 118 individual etchings of classical antiquities, subsequently brought together in the publication *Vasi, Candelabri, Cippi, Sarcofagi* of 1778. This anthology of antique ornamental forms, with its wealth of imaginative transcriptions of various architectural features, had almost as extensive an influence on neoclassical furniture and interiors as did the *Diverse Maniere,* particularly on the later generation of designers of the Regency and Empire periods. The plates of the *Vasi,* largely engraved with studio assistance, reproduced works not only in Piranesi's possession but also in other Italian collections and in some twenty-five British houses, ranging from modest cinerary urns to the spectacular Warwick Vase, reassembled in Piranesi's workshop after its discovery at Tivoli in 1771.

In the case of those works requiring extensive restoration, Piranesi's skill in decorative synthesis prompted him to take increasing liberties, especially in the reconstruction of large marble candelabra. Particularly outstanding examples of these productions are the pair sold to Sir Roger Newdigate by Piranesi in 1775 and given by this client to the University of Oxford. These works were installed in James Gibbs's Radcliffe Camera (later transferred to the Ashmolean Museum) where they represented, in the words of a contemporary observer, "a perfect school in themselves of Sculpture and Architecture." Other imaginatively restored candelabra were later acquired by the designer Thomas Hope for his collection at the Deepdene in Sussex where they served to provide ideas for innovative furniture designs as similar examples had influenced Adam during the 1770s. Significantly, the most ambitious and complex of all these three-dimensional *capricci* was to be the giant candelabrum intended by Piranesi for his own funerary monument and now among the antiquities in the Louvre.

In addition to these manifold activities as a restorer and dealer during the 1770s, Piranesi's architectural energies were also involved in the recording and interpretation of monuments and archeological sites. Throughout the final years of his life he continued a detailed survey of Hadrian's Villa at Tivoli. A number of view studies survive, and the comprehensive site plan of known structures, which was probably begun in the 1750s, was published posthumously by Francesco in 1781. Giambattista also carried out the fieldwork on another feat of Roman hydraulic engineering, the *emissarium* or drainage outlet of Lake Fucino, also published by his son. With considerable studio assistance, Piranesi issued a truly monumental record of Trajan's Column, involving a complete elevation in six contiguous plates, probably finished around 1774; these were subsequently combined with further sets of plates devoted to the other two giant relief columns of Marcus Aurelius and those of Antoninus and Faustina.

Meanwhile, the excavations at Herculaneum and particularly the more recent discoveries at Pompeii attracted Piranesi's interest again. From 1770, he made a number of expeditions there to prepare a plan and views of the latter site. These, again, were realized by Francesco considerably later. The plan of Pompeii first appeared in 1785 and the views were included in *Les Antiquités de la Grande Grèce,* issued between 1804 and 1807. The surviving sketches of Pompeii by Giambattista are unexpectedly bleak and roughly executed when compared with the contemporary studies for Tivoli. However, their coarse lines and rudimentary hints of textures and lighting may well reflect the dearth of inspiration for him in a dead site, devoid of the enlivening forms of foliage and human activity. Besides, the modest scale of the remains then uncovered gave far less scope than those of Hadrian's Villa for expressing a sense of indomitable grandeur and *terribilità.*

In still greater contrast to these Pompeian studies is the surviving group of highly finished drawings of the three Doric temples at Paestum which Piranesi explored with Francesco and his assistant Benedetto Mori during 1777 and 1778. These gaunt structures in their remote setting on the Gulf of Salerno had been rediscovered by adventurous travelers during the middle of the century, and their gradual acceptance by the architectural world plots the evolution of neoclassical taste toward an acceptance of the expressive language of primitive forms. One of the earliest publications on the temples was Dumont's treatise, partly based on his visit to Paestum in 1750, and Thomas Major produced a more accurate if prosaic record in 1768. But Piranesi's twenty plates when they finally appeared, with Francesco's substantial intervention, shortly after Giambattista's death in 1778, provided a decisive act in transforming an archeological interest into an emotional understanding. Although for Piranesi himself the temples of Paestum represented the monumental values of an architecture nurtured on Italian soil, regardless of foreign authorship, the *Différentes vues . . . de Pesto* was decisive in promoting the heavyweight aesthetic of the later Greek Revival, especially in Britain and Germany. The impact of Piranesi's graphic interpretation of Paestum can be found in the works of Thomas Harrison, Sidney Smirke, and Alexander Thomson in Britain, while in Germany its influence can be discerned in a range of monumental buildings by Karl Friedrich Schinkel and Leo von Klenze, as well as earlier influencing projects by Friedrich Gilly.

While at Paestum, Piranesi was already suffering from the advanced stages of a particularly malignant bladder ailment which his strenuous activities aggravated. The unusually finished nature of the preparatory drawings (now in Sir John Soane's Museum, London), which show no decline in his powers to evoke the richly poignant qualities of decay, suggests that the artist was keenly aware of the need to achieve this final project. Shortly after returning to Rome, he died and was buried in his local church, Sant'Andrea della Fratte. At the wishes of his greatest patron, Cardinal Rezzonico, Piranesi's body was shortly transferred to a place of honor on the Aventine. His tomb in Santa Maria Aventina was first marked by the impressive candelabrum as he wished. The following year, however, at the request of his widow Angela and members of the family, this highly appropriate if unconventional work was replaced by Angelini's statue of the architect, dressed *al antica* and bearing various drawing instruments together with the plan of the Temple of Neptune at Paestum.

In opposition to this sober tribute is the animated portrait of Piranesi in contemporary dress, painted by Pietro Labruzzi shortly after the artist's death and now in the Museo di Roma, Palazzo Braschi. He is shown wearing the Order of the *Sperone d'Oro* and in a polemical gesture holds his dividers and crayons, along with a preparatory study for the frontispiece to the *Différentes vues . . . de Pesto.* This portrayal was much influenced by the vigorous marble bust of Piranesi by Joseph Nollekens, executed shortly before 1770 for the Accademia di San Luca where it can still be seen.

Apart from interior design and the applied arts, Piranesi's limited influence on contemporary architecture in the last decades of the eighteenth century can be chiefly explained by the fact that he had lived into an unsympathetic era in which his baroque imagination was increasingly at variance with the austere taste and theories of later neoclassicism. Some indication of professional reactions to his notoriously idiosyncratic vision is found in the writings of one of the leading architectural critics and apologists of the age, FRANCESCO MILIZIA, who classified the Aventine buildings of Piranesi among those works which provoked such disgust "that their designers are not worthy of mention" (*Roma nelle belle arti del disegno,* 1787). However, a contrary attitude is found in those designers, such as Boullée and Ledoux, who shared the Venetian's belief in the prerogative of the designer's imagination to create new forms through pictorial means. Even though neither Frenchman had enjoyed a personal contact with Piranesi, each in his respective way deeply benefited from Giambattista's fantasy plans, particularly the *Ichnographia* of the *Campo Marzio* and his theatrical devices of amplification in developing their visionary designs. Moreover, the brilliant formal repertoire of Ledoux's executed Parisian *barrières* of the 1780s unquestioningly gained from certain eclectic passages among Piranesi's etched fantasy compositions.

Perhaps, Piranesi's most profound impression in the years following his death was exercised on a designer who by 1800 was among the most original minds in Europe—John Soane. As with Robert Adam, Piranesi's conceptions of architectural composition awakened a deep response in the English designer, if less consciously absorbed. Apart from an indirect influence through his master, Dance the Younger, Soane had briefly encountered Piranesi in person during his student visit to Rome in 1778 and had subsequently acquired a quantity of the Venetian's engraved works and publications, along with the preparatory studies for the Paestum etchings. Soane also included certain of Piranesi's restored antiquities in his prodigious collection at Lincoln's Inn Fields, London, which itself closely resembled one of the artist's eclectic fantasies in the extremely original arrangement and setting. Despite the harsh criticism of Piranesi in Soane's professorial lectures to the Royal Academy students later, during the forty-five years spent reconstructing and enlarging the Bank of England from 1788 onward he developed a style as personal as that advocated in the *Parere su l'Architettura.* It was a style comparable to Piranesi's, uninhibited by classical conventions and ingenious in structure and lighting, that made the Bank the most original work of its time.

These exceptional instances apart, many of Piranesi's ideas were developed more extensively in the era of Romanticism, chiefly in four areas—topographical art, stage design, the architectural fantasy, and the symbolic imagery of literature. Common to all these fields of activity was the unprecedented role of architecture as a highly charged medium of emotional expression. It may be claimed that few topographical artists before Piranesi had invested inanimate structures with such profundity; indeed, one of his earliest biographers, Bianconi, was moved to call him the "Rembrandt of the Ruins."

Piranesi's influence on the amplification of architectural mood through the spread of his etchings over Europe and further afield was as extensive as it is elusive to trace in specific instances. It is sufficient to say that all the greatest interpreters of architecture in painting and engraving derived important concepts or approaches from the innovations of Piranesi's forty years as a topographical artist.

Piranesi's language of architectural fantasy, never far from the more sublime heights of topographical art, was to find its most direct expression, both in form and content, in Romantic stage design. Among the more deeply affected were Francesco Fontanesi, Pietro Gonzaga, Pietro Basoli and Giuseppe Badiali, as well as the great Schinkel in his opera designs. Of far greater range was the painted architectural *capriccio,* translated from Piranesi's drawings and etchings into the exhibition canvases of his close friend Hubert Robert. The Venetian's true heir in this field of composition during the Romantic era was Soane's assistant JOSEPH GANDY whose architectural fantasies possess an intensity similar to Piranesi's, also born of frustrated ambitions in the practical field of design. Such works are all the more authentic in their understanding of architectural mood when compared with the visual bombast of Gandy's contemporary John Mart—a painter who exploited the superficial rather than the more fundamental qualities of Piranesi's vision.

Most far-reaching of all was the inspiration of

Piranesi's imagery on the imagination of a host of writers from the early Romantics such as Samuel Taylor Coleridge, through a succession of French authors including Honoré de Balzac and Victor Hugo, to Marcel Proust. In the United States, similar debts are found in the writings of Edgar Allen Poe and Herman Melville. For all these minds, the architecture of the *Carceri d'invenzione* in particular offered a wide range of visual analogies for the phenomenon of disturbing imaginative experiences—a theme brought into the present era with the psychological interpretations of these plates by Aldous Huxley. In this respect, the *Carceri* provide a profound insight into the central mystery of Piranesi's imaginative processes as an architectural thinker of seminal importance in which the exercise of fantasy was not merely a pictorial indulgence but a continuous struggle in search of fresh levels of expression. As Piranesi once exclaimed, "I need to produce great ideas and I believe that were I given the planning of a new universe, I would be mad enough to undertake it."

JOHN WILTON-ELY

WORK

1764–1766, Santa Maria Aventina (reconstruction of the priory church of the Order of Malta and related buildings with additional structures), Rome.

BIBLIOGRAPHY

BRUNEL, GEORGES (editor) 1978 *Piranèse et les Français: Colloque tenu à la Villa Médicis 12–14 Mai 1976.* Rome: Académie de France à Rome.

NYBERG, DOROTHEA, and MITCHELL, HERBERT (editors) 1975 *Piranesi Drawings and Etchings at the Avery Architectural Library, Columbia University, New York: The Arthur M. Sackler Collection.* New York: Columbia University.

REUDENBACH, BRUNO 1979 *G. B. Piranesi: Architecture als Bild.* Munich: Prestel.

RIEDER, WILLIAM 1973 "Piranesi's 'Diverse Maniere'." *Burlington Magazine* 115:309–317.

SCOTT, JONATHAN 1975 *Piranesi.* New York: Academy Editions.

STAMPFLE, FELICE 1978 *Giovanni Battista Piranesi: Drawings in the Pierpont Morgan Library.* New York: Dover.

STILLMAN, DAMIE 1967 "Robert Adam and Piranesi." Pages 197–206 in D. Fraser (editor), *Essays in the History of Architecture presented to Rudolf Wittkower.* New York: Phaidon.

VOGT-GÖKNIL, ULYA 1958 *Giovanni Battista Piranesi: Carceri.* Zurich.

WILTON-ELY, JOHN 1972 *Giovanni Battista Piranesi: The Polemical Works.* Farnsborough, England: Gregg.

WILTON-ELY, JOHN 1976 "Piranesian Symbols on the Aventine." *Apollo* 113:214–227.

WILTON-ELY, JOHN 1978 *The Mind and Art of Piranesi.* London: Thames & Hudson.

WILTON-ELY, JOHN 1978 *Piranesi.* London: Arts Council of Great Britain.

WILTON-ELY, JOHN 1979 "Piranesi and Vanvitelli." Volume 2, pages 83–89 in *Luigi Vanvitelli e il '700 Europeo: Congreso Internazionale di Studi 1976.* Naples: Istituto di Storia dell Architettura, Università di Napoli.

WITTKOWER, RUDOLF 1975 *Studies in the Italian Baroque.* London: Thames & Hudson.

PISANO FAMILY

Nicola Pisano (1225?–c.1280) and his son, Giovanni Pisano (1248?–1314?), were first and foremost innovators in Tuscan thirteenth-century sculpture, but their style had a significant impact on the development of Italian Gothic architecture. Nicola's initial experiments with the relationship between the architectural structure and sculptural decoration of his pulpits led eventually to Giovanni's conception of the Gothic church façade as a stage animated by sculpted figures, a radical change from the Romanesque approach to decoration. Nicola and especially Giovanni, through their sculptural designs for architecture, helped to define a vital new interdependence of the two arts in Gothic Tuscany.

Nicola's earliest known work, the Pisa Baptistery pulpit (1255–1259), was built on a hexagonal plan which departed from the traditional Tuscan *paliotto*-type rectangular pulpit. This innovation raises the question of Nicola's origins and early influences on his style. Its plan and freestanding archivolted structure is related to south Italian pulpits, which corroborates two documentary references to Nicola as "de Apulia." The sculptor created a harmonious balance of sculptural decoration and structure by using contrasting red marble to frame the reliefs. The overall classical aspect of the design, with its possible allusions to Roman triumphal arches in the form of the attic story and spandrel figures, is modulated by Cistercian Gothic details. His synthesis of a variety of sources indicates that Nicola was already a mature artist who must have executed other works, now lost or unidentified, before 1255.

In the late 1260s, Nicola headed an active workshop which produced a second, larger octagonal pulpit for Siena Cathedral (1265–1268). Caryatid groups separate the reliefs instead of the triple columns of contrasting marble used at Pisa, and architectural elements such as moldings and cornices are more ornate so that the plastic and luministic effects outweigh the architectonic framework. A highly sacred Dominican monument, the *Arca* of Saint Dominic (1264–1267), was also designed in Nicola's workshop but executed almost entirely by assistants. It originally consisted of a simple rectangular sarcophagus decorated by reliefs and elevated in mid-air by caryatids, a design which displays little architectural sophistication.

Throughout the decade 1260–1270, Nicola participated in building projects but his precise role is not well understood. The Siena pulpit contract allowed Nicola an absence of fifteen days four times a year to return to Pisa to advise on the work of the cathedral and baptistery *operas* yet he was never designated chief of works. The Pisa Baptistery's exterior second-story arcade which was decorated with console heads and half-length figures by Nicola and his son Giovanni from 1260 to 1285 shares certain classicistic motifs with both the Pisa and Siena pulpits, and may well have been designed by Nicola. Incorporating sculpture in-the-round into the arcade was a radically new idea used here for the first time. As part of the renovation of the Duomo façade (1260–1270), Nicola's workshop produced some capitals that reveal his earlier stylistic ties to Guido da Como and the Lucchese school.

GIORGIO VASARI credits Nicola with numerous churches (most notably Santa Trinità in Florence), bell towers, castles, palaces, and a new method of constructing arched foundations which were exceptionally stable even in shifting Pisan soil. Since these buildings are undocumented, scholars have remained skeptical of Nicola's architectural achievements. Santa Trinità retains little of its thirteenth-century character. Although recent studies confirm the existence of a third church dating around 1257, scholars disagree on the interpretation of Nicolesque console heads presently found in a fourteenth-century vaulting system. Other attributions currently under discussion include San Paola Ripa d'Arno in Pisa, San Pier Somaldi in Lucca, the fortress of Prato, and the Baptistery of Volterra.

Nicola's last major work was the Fontana Maggiore at Perugia, completed in 1278. The architectural conception of the two polygonal basins, with triple columns dividing the sculptured faces of the lower basin and caryatid figures separating those on the upper level is more likely by Nicola rather than by Giovanni, Arnolfo di Cambio, or the overseer of the works, Fra Bevignate. Much of the sculptural execution was left to Giovanni who is warmly praised by Nicola in the fountain's inscription. In 1284, a document refers to Giovanni with terminology indicating that Nicola is dead.

After apprenticing with his father during the fabrication of the Siena pulpit, Giovanni rapidly developed an individual style, still classicizing but more specifically reflecting the influence of French Gothic art. Stylistic evidence suggests that he visited France, probably sometime between 1270 and 1275, and studied Notre Dame de Paris and Reims cathedrals firsthand. From 1284, when the simple brick façade of Siena Cathedral was completed, Giovanni worked on the decoration of this first great Italian Gothic church façade, though only the lower section was built under his direction (1287–1296). The three recessed portals dominate the façade against a background of Tuscan Romanesque marble incrustation. Their jambs are richly articulated by spiral and foliate columns with in-

Nicola Pisano.
Pisa Baptistery (second story arcade).
Italy.
1260

Giovanni Pisano.
Siena Cathedral (façade).
Italy.
1284–1296

habited scrolls, the latter inspired by antique Roman (Flavian or later) models. Instead of the jamb figures customary in French Gothic cathedrals, Giovanni placed an unprecedented number of freestanding figures of prophets, dramatically posed in coordination with each other and their architectural context, in tabernacles on the pier buttresses above the portals. In this revolutionary design, Giovanni freed the sculpture from its subordinate, decorative function without sacrificing a complementary relationship between sculpture and architecture.

While Giovanni was chief architect of Siena, he also worked at the Cathedral of Massa Marittima (1287) and, perhaps as a result, was fined in 1290 and required to remain in Siena until he completed certain half-finished works. In 1296, when the Sienese first contemplated building the new Baptistery behind the cathedral's apse, Giovanni received the commission but apparently never drew up a design. A scandal alleging his mismanagement of the Siena *Opera del Duomo* in 1297 drove him to return to Pisa where he had been working on the Campanile periodically (1295, 1297, 1298), after which he then served briefly as *capomaestro* of Pisa Cathedral in 1299.

In his later career, Giovanni was occupied with the construction of two monumental pulpits which rivaled his father's designs. The hexagonal pulpit of Sant'Andrea in Pistoia was completed in 1301, its general shape derived from Nicola's Pisa Baptistery pulpit. Giovanni used acute trefoil arches in the vault and a staggered rhythm of figural and columnar supports. From an architectural point of view, Giovanni's last and most ornate pulpit for Pisa Cathedral, executed 1302–1311, is more interesting. Although dismantled in the sixteenth century, it was faithfully reconstructed in 1926. The unique circular plan necessitated convex panels for the reliefs which flow together continuously without any architectural breaks and form a massive, unified attic level resting on pairs of foliate corbels. The artist seems to have shifted his focus to the potential of the pulpit's base: a raised circular platform creates a canopied space for freestanding caryatids and columns carved densely with multiple figures. In this final work, which the artist may have regarded as a magnum opus, two long, extraordinary inscriptions concerning his personal feelings give a vivid, if enigmatic, insight into Giovanni's artistic pride and emotional turmoil in later life.

KATHLEEN GILES ARTHUR

WORKS

NICOLA PISANO

1255–1259, Pisa Baptistery (pulpit); 1260–1270, Pisa Cathedral (façade renovation); 1260–1285, Pisa Baptistery (second story arcade); Italy. 1265–1268, Siena Cathedral (pulpit), Italy. 1278, Fontana Maggiore, Perugia, Italy.

GIOVANNI PISANO

1284–1296, Siena Cathedral (façade), Italy. 1287, Cathedral of Massa Marittima (unspecified work), Italy. 1299–1301, Sant'Andrea (pulpit), Pistoia, Italy. 1302–1311, Pisa Cathedral (pulpit), Italy.

BIBLIOGRAPHY

AYRTON, MICHAEL 1969 *Giovanni Pisano.* New York: Waybright & Talley.

CRICHTON, G. H., and CRICHTON, E. R. 1938 *Nicola Pisano and the Revival of Sculpture in Italy.* Cambridge University Press.

CHRISTIANA TESTI, MARIA LAURA 1979 "Itinerari toscani di Niccola Pisano." *Studi per Enrico Fiumi.* Pisa, Italy: Pacini.

FASOLA, GIUSTA NICCO 1938 "Induzioni su Nicolo Pisano architetto." *L'Arte* 41, no. 9:315–343.

KOSEGARTEN, ANTIJE 1968 "Die Skulpturen der Pisani am Baptisterium von Pisa: Zum Werk von Nicola und Giovanni Pisano." *Jarhbuch der Berliner Museen* 10:14–100.

KRÖNIG, WOLFGANG 1953 "Toscana und Apulien: Beiträge zum Problemkreis der Herkunft des Nicolo Pisano." *Zeitschrift für Kunstgeschichte* 16:101–144.

PAATZ, WALTER 1937 *Werden und Wesen der Trecento-architektur.* Burg, Germany: Hopfer.

POPE-HENNESSY, JOHN (1955)1972 *Italian Gothic Sculpture.* 2d ed. London: Phaidon.

SAALMAN HOWARD 1966 *The Church of Santa Trinità in Florence.* New York: College Art Association.

SMITH, CHRISTINE 1978 *The Baptistery of Pisa.* New York: Garland.

SMITH, CHRISTINE 1980 "The Date and Authorship of the Pisa Duomo Facade." *Gesta* 19 no. 2:95–108.

VASARI, GIORGIO (1568)1973 *Le opere di Giorgio Vasari, con nuove annotazioni e commenti.* 9 vols. Edited by G. Milanesi. Reprint. Florence: Sansoni. Originally published in 1550 with the title *Le vite de più eccelenti architetti.* There are many English translations and selections from Vasari's *Lives;* the standard one by G. du C. de Vere was published in ten volumes in London by the Medici Society in 1912–1915.

WEINBERGER, MARTIN 1960 "Nicolo Pisano and the Tradition of Tuscan Pulpits." *Gazette des Beaux Arts* Series 6 15:129–146.

WHITE, JOHN 1966 *Art and Architecture in Italy: 1250–1400.* Baltimore: Penguin.

WHITE, JOHN 1970 "The Reconstruction of Nicola Pisano's Perugia Fountain." *Journal of the Warburg and Courtauld Institutes* 33:70–83.

PISSIS, ALBERT

Albert Pissis (1852–1914) was born in Guaymas, Mexico, to French parents and moved to San Francisco as a child. He attended the Ecole des Beaux-

Arts in Paris (Atelier JULIEN GUADET) from 1872 to 1876. Pissis worked for William Mooser, Sr., from 1879 to 1880 and was in partnership with William P. Moore from 1886 to 1898. Pissis was perhaps the most influential architect in the city from around 1890 to 1910; his bold monumental classicism, embodied in the forward-looking Hibernia Bank (1889–1892) and in a large number of structures, after the earthquake and fire of 1906, provided a vision of urban grandeur which was widely emulated.

MICHAEL R. CORBETT

WORKS

ALBERT PISSIS AND WILLIAM P. MOORE

1889–1892, Hibernia Bank; *1890–1891, Mercantile Library Association Building; *1892–1893, Wenban Building; *1894, J. Zenon Posadas Residence; *1898, Wenceslao Loaiza Residence; San Francisco.

ALBERT PISSIS

*1899, Saint Matthew's Roman Catholic Church, San Mateo, Calif. 1900–1901, University House, Berkeley. *1902, Mercantile Trust Company Building; *1902–1904, Home of the Little Sisters of the Poor; 1904, Sherith Israel Synagogue; 1904–1905, James Flood Building; 1907–1908, The White House; 1908, Anton Borel and Company Bank; 1908–1909, Mechanic's Institute; 1908–1910, Anglo and London Paris National Bank; 1909, Rochat-Cordes Building; 1912, Lane Medical Library; San Francisco.

BIBLIOGRAPHY

"Albert Pissis, F.A.I.A." *Architect and Planner* 37, no. 3:94–95.

BRECHIN, GREY 1981 "The Monumental Albert Pissis." *Heritage Newsletter* (The Foundation for San Francisco's Architectural Heritage) 9, no. 2:10.

CHAILL, B. J. S. 1906 "The Works of Albert Pissis." *American Builder's Review* 3, no. 1:1–37.

CAHILL, B.J.S. 1909 "The Work of Albert Pissis, Architect." *Architect and Engineer* 17, no. 3:35–65.

CORBETT, MICHAEL R. 1979 *Splendid Survivors: San Francisco's Downtown Architectural Heritage.* San Francisco: California Living Books.

"The Hibernia Bank Competition." 1889 *California Architect and Building News* 10, no. 3:31.

KIRKER, HAROLD (1960)1973 *California's Architectural Frontier: Style and Tradition in the Nineteenth Century.* Rev. ed. Santa Barbara, Calif., and Salt Lake City, Utah: Peregrine Smith.

SNYDER, JOHN WILLIAM 1975 "Index to San Francisco Building: 1879–1900." Unpublished M.A. thesis, University of California, Davis.

PITE, ARTHUR BERESFORD

Born in London, Arthur Beresford Pite (1861–1934) was articled to his father's firm of Habershon and Pite. He studied at University College London, the Normal School of Art, South Kensington, and the Royal Academy Architectural Schools. In 1881, he went into JOHN BELCHER's office, where he remained until about 1897 when he set up on his own account. His output was small but always interesting. He was the first professor of architecture at the Royal College of Art (1900–1923) and the architectural director of the London County Council's School of Building.

GODFREY RUBENS

WORKS

1893, 82 Mortimer Street; 1896, Church Home, 46–54 Gt. Titchfield Street; *c.1897, Saint Marylebone General Dispensary, Welbeck Street; 1897–1898, Christ Church (church hall), Mowll Street; 1897–1899, Christ Church, Brixton Street; 1898, 126 Gt. Portland Street; 1899, 37 Harley Street; 1902, Holy Trinity Church (chancel), Clapham Common; 1904, Ames House; *1906–1907, Methodist Church and Cottage, Agincourt Road; 1906–1908, Carnegie Library, Thornhill Square; 1906–1919, London, Edinburgh and Glasgow Assurance Company, Euston Square; 1911–1930, Burlington Arcade (new entrance), Piccadilly; London. 1913–1918, Namirembe Anglican Cathedral, Kampala.

BIBLIOGRAPHY

The Builder 1934 147:925,969.

GOODHART-RENDEL, H. S. 1935 "The Work of Beresford Pite and Halsey Ricardo." *Journal of the Royal Institute of British Architects* 42:117–128.

SERVICE, ALASTAIR 1970 "Belcher and Joass." *Architectural Review* 148:282–290.

PITT, WILLIAM

William Pitt (1855–1918) was born in Melbourne, Australia. He began a private practice after completing his articles in 1879. Pitt immediately distinguished himself by winning first prizes for the design of the Melbourne Coffee Palace (1881), the Queens Bridge over the Yarra, Melbourne (1881), and the Premier Permanent Building Society Offices, Melbourne (1882).

His reputation as an expert designer of sumptuous interiors brought him many major commissions for theater buildings in Australia and New Zealand. However, his most popular designs are the Commercial Gothic buildings in Collins Street, Melbourne. In these, as well as in the Federal Coffee Palace, Melbourne (1887–1888), Pitt captured the mood of Melbourne in the 1880s, when wealth and prosperity convinced Melbournians that their city would soon be the equal of the capital cities of Europe. It is to Pitt's credit that almost all of his designs for public and commercial buildings were and are still much loved by the citizens of Melbourne.

After his death, his practice was continued by his only partner, Albion H. Walkley, who had joined Pitt only a few months earlier. Although he had no governmental or ecclesiastical commissions, Pitt was one of the most successful and the most prolific architects in Australia in the latter part of the nineteeth century.

PETER NAVARETTI

WORKS

1880, Beaconsfield Hotel, Saint Kilda, Victoria, Australia. *1881, Melbourne Coffee Palace; 1881, Queens Bridge; *1882, Premier Permanent Building Society Offices; 1886, Princess Theater; 1887–1888, Federal Coffee Palace (with W. H. Ellerker and E. G. Kilburn); 1889–1890, Safe Deposit Building; 1889–1891, The Stock Exchange; 1890–1891, The Rialto; 1890–1891, Olderfleet Building; 1902–1903, His Majesty's Theater; Auckland, New Zealand. *1908, King's Theater, Melbourne. 1909, Bryant and May, and R. Bell Company Match Factory, Richmond, Victoria, Australia. 1911, Theater Royal, Hobart, Tasmania. 1913–1914, Wellington Grand Opera House, New Zealand.

BIBLIOGRAPHY

FREELAND, JOHN MAXWELL 1971 *The Making of a Profession.* Sydney: Angus & Robertson.

LEAVITT, THADDEUS W. H. (editor) 1888 *Jubilee History of Victoria and Melbourne.* Melbourne: Wells & Leavitt.

NAVARETTI, PETER Y. 1971 "Architects of Melbourne and Their Work, 1900–1940." Unpublished B. Arch., Leighton Irwin Memorial Library, University of Melbourne.

SELBY, ISAAC 1924 *The Old Pioneer's Memorial History of Melbourne.* Melbourne: McCarron, Bird.

SHAW, MARY TURNER 1972 *Builders of Melbourne.* Melbourne: Cypress.

SUTHERLAND, ALEXANDER (1888)1977 Volume 2 in *Victoria and Its Metropolis Past and Present.* Reprint. Melbourne: Today's Heritage.

PLANTERY, GIAN GIACOMO

Gian Giacomo Plantery (1680–1756), uncle of BERNARDO ANTONIO VITTONE, was born in Turin, Italy. Active before the arrival in Turin of FILIPPO JUVARRA, Plantery showed in his early work an appreciation for both GUARINO GUARINI and AMEDEO DI CASTELLAMONTE. His later work, while retaining an unusual fascination for vaulting patterns, reflected the presence of Juvarra well after his death. Although Plantery received a number of religious commissions, he is best known for his palaces which established a new standard of size and disposition for the eighteenth century, but with an appeal to a growing upper middle class.

Plantery's masterpiece, the Palazzo Saluzzo di Paesan (1715–1718), exhibits in its vaults the graceful intersecting and accentuated curving rib patterns that became influential in domestic architecture in Piedmont in the first half of the eighteenth century. The palace, prized for its convenient planning with multiple entries and witty service stairs, is often also praised for its scenographic quality.

Less stimulating, and more Juvarresque, are Plantery's other major works, the Palazzo Cavour (1729), the Palazzo Capris di Ciglié (1730), and the Palazzo Fontana di Cravanzana (1753–1756). Each, however, boasts a large, vaulted, gracefully buoyant atrium enhanced by carefully executed stucco decoration. Plantery's interior decoration of the 1730s and 1740s is somewhat flat and spidery when compared with work by the late Juvarra and the early BENEDETTO ALFIERI. Of special note in the 1750s is Plantery's experimentation with façade articulation in which windows on four levels are joined head to sill producing a series of continuous verticals.

HENRY A. MILLON

WORKS

1715–1718, Palazzo Saluzzo di Paesana; 1729, Palazzo Cavour; 1730, Palazzo Capris di Ciglié; 1753–1756, Palazzo Fontana di Cravanzana; Turin, Italy.

BIBLIOGRAPHY

BAUDI DI VESME 1963 "Planetary, Gian Giacomo." Volume 3, pages 839–840 in *Schede Vesme.* Turin, Italy: Stamperia Artistica Nazionale.

BRAYDA, CARLO; COLI, LAURA; and SESIA, DARIO 1963 Page 56 in *Ingegnere e architetti del sei e settecento in Piemonte.* Turin, Italy: Società degli ingegneri e degli architetti.

CAVALLARI-MURAT, AUGUSTO 1942 "Alcune architetture piemontese del settecento in una raccolta di disegni del Plantery, del Vittone, e del Guarini." *Torino* 20.

CAVALLARI-MURAT, AUGUSTO 1957 "Gian Giacomo Plantery, architetto barocco." *Atti e Rassegna technica . . .* 40:313–346.

MALLÈ, LUIGI 1961 Pages 281–284 in *Le Arti Figurative in Piemonte.* Turin, Italy: Casanova.

PLATT, CHARLES ADAMS

Charles Adams Platt (1861–1933) was born in New York City. He briefly attended the National Academy of Design and the Art Students League, and went to Europe in 1882 etching and painting. He remained there five years. Back in New York in 1887, he became a member of the Society of American Artists and continued etching and painting. In 1890, he designed his first garden for the painter Henry Oliver Walker. In 1892, he traveled in Italy with his brother, William Barnes Platt, who had studied with FREDERICK LAW OLMSTED, and wrote articles on the Italian garden for *Harper's Magazine* which were published in book form in 1894 under the title, *Italian Gardens.*

He received his first architectural commission in 1893 for a house for Annie Lazarus, the sister of the poet Emma Lazarus. Commissions for gardens in the Italian manner came his way first, then some for houses. His career flourished mostly with residential work, but he also handled commissions for apartment houses, schools buildings, and plans for buildings at the Urbana campus of the University of Illinois. He was consultant to the campuses of Dartmouth, Johns Hopkins, and the University of Rochester. He also designed a museum, the Freer Gallery (1913–1918), in Washington. Among his better known clients were Charles F. Freer of Detroit, Michigan, Vincent Astor of New York, Eugene Meyer, Jr., of Washington, Harold F. McCormick of Chicago, and Mrs. James Roosevelt of New York.

Throughout his career, he remained loyal to the classical tradition. His earliest residences, like his gardens, leaned to the Italian, as did several of his office and apartment buildings as well as the Freer Gallery. In later years, he turned more and more to the Georgian style, possibly best exemplified by the John T. Pratt House (1910–1913). Restrained by comparison with other classical work of the time, Platt's buildings reveal a sureness and a mastery of style which placed him in the forefront of the American Renaissance.

HENRY HOPE REED

WORKS

1896–1897, Garden, Brandegee Estate; 1900, Garden, Larz Anderson Estate; Brookline, Mass. 1901, Frank Cheney, Jr., House, South Manchester, Conn. 1901–1904, Winston Churchill House and Garden, Cornish, N.H. 1902, Maxwell Public Library, Rockville, Conn. 1904, John Jay Chapman House and Garden, Barrytown, N.Y. 1904, Herbert Croly House and Garden, Cornish, N.H. 1905–1906, Studio Building, 131–135 East 66 Street; 1907, Mrs. James Roosevelt Twin Houses; New York. 1907–1909, William G. Mather House and Garden, Cleveland, Ohio. 1908–1917, Harold F. McCormick House and Garden, Lake Forest, Ill. 1909, Josephine Shaw Lowell Fountain, Bryant Park, New York. 1910–1913, Russell A. Alger, Jr., House and Garden, Grosse Pointe, Mich. 1910–1913, John T. Pratt House and Garden, Glen Cove, N.Y. 1911–1912, Leader Building, Cleveland, Ohio. 1913–1918, Freer Gallery, Washington. 1914, Astor Court Apartment Building, New York. 1915, Eugene Meyer, Jr., House, Mount Kisco, N.Y. 1919, Hanna Building, Cleveland, Ohio. 1919–1930, University of Illinois Campus and Buildings, Urbana, Ill. 1922, William Fahnestock House, 457 Madison Avenue, New York. 1922, Palmer Library, Connecticut College for Women, New London. 1922–1933, Phillips Academy Buildings, Andover, Mass. 1925, Coolidge Auditorium, Library of Congress; 1926–1927, Corcoran Gallery of Art (addition); Washington. 1928–1929, Apartment Buildings, New York. 1929, Lyman Allyn Gallery of Art, New London, Conn. 1930–1932, Deerfield Academy (buildings and grounds), Conn.

BIBLIOGRAPHY

CROLY, HERBERT 1904 "The Architectural Work of Charles A. Platt." *Architectural Record* 15:181–244.

EMBURY, AYMAR 1912 "Charles A. Platt, His Work." *Architecture* 26:130–162.

ISHAM, SAMUEL (1905)1927 *The History of American Painting.* With supplemental chapters by Royal Cortissoz. New ed. New York: Macmillan.

PLATT, CHARLES A. 1913 *Monograph of the Work of Charles A. Platt.* Introduction by Roal Cortissoz. New York: Architectural Book.

VAN RENSSELAER, MARIANA GRISWOLD 1886 *American Etchers.* New York: Keppel.

PLATT FAMILY

The Platts were architects and builders active in the Rotherham area of Yorkshire during the eighteenth century. The family had originated at Lyme Park, Cheshire, where the brothers Edmund, John I, and George were engaged in rebuilding the house (c.1727–1730) to the design of GIACOMO LEONI; the connection with Yorkshire was first made by John I (?–1730), who designed Saint Paul's Church, Sheffield (1720–1721), and George (1700–1743) established himself in the neighborhood of nearby Rotherham shortly afterward. After the latter's death, his son John II (1728–1810) continued and expanded the business, also engaging in marble quarrying and the manufacture of monuments and chimneypieces.

PETER LEACH

WORKS

JOHN PLATT I

*1720–1721, Saint Paul's Church, Sheffield, England.

GEORGE PLATT

1740–1741, Cusworth Hall, Doncaster, England.

JOHN PLATT II

1747–1748, Summerhouse, Gate Burton Hall, Lincolnshire, England. *1756, Market Cross and Shambles, Doncaster, England. 1767, Canklow House, Rotherham, England. 1768, Cloth Hall and Shambles, Penistone, Yorkshire, England. *1768, Masbrough Hall, Rotherham, England. 1775, Page Hall; 1777, Mount Pleasant; 1777–1778, Thundercliffe Grange; Sheffield, England. *1780–1781, Market House, Rotherham, England. 1784–1788, Wortley Hall (north and west wings),

Yorkshire, England. 1787, Ferham House, Rotherham, England.

BIBLIOGRAPHY

GUNNIS, RUPERT (1953)1968 *Dictionary of British Sculptors: 1660–1851.* Rev. ed. London: Murray's Book Sales.

POTTS, J. D. 1959 *Platt of Rotherham, Mason-Architects, 1700–1810.* Sheffield, England: Northend.

PLAW, JOHN

John Plaw (c.1745–1820) was an architect and master builder in Westminster in 1763, and was a member of the Incorporated Society of Artists until its dissolution in 1791. He exhibited at the Royal Academy from 1775 onward. His reputation and influence derive mainly from his three immensely popular books. *Ferme Ornée* (1795) was an important prototype for the coming wave of British cottage and villa design books. In all three books, he included designs in a pseudovernacular cottage style for middle class clients, and emphasized the integration of architectural forms with surrounding topography.

JOHN ARCHER

WORKS

1774–1775, Belle Isle, Lake Windermere, England. 1781, Villa, near Vauxhall, London. *1781, Wootton Court (alterations), near Canterbury, England. By 1785, Selsdon House (additions), near Croydon, England. *1787, Haresfoot, near Berkhamstead, England. 1788–1791, Saint Mary's Church, Paddington Green, London. By 1795, Brockenhurst House (bathhouse and fishing lodge), Hampshire, England. By 1795, Thornville Royal (farm buildings), near Knaresborough, England. By 1800, House, near Lymington, England. 1806, The Barracks, Southampton, England.

BIBLIOGRAPHY

BLUTMAN, SANDRA 1968 "Books of Designs for Country Houses, 1780–1815." *Architectural History* 11:25–33.

DARLEY, GILLIAN 1975 *Villages of Vision.* London: Architectural Press.

DOBAI, JOHANNES 1977 Volume 3 in *Die Kunstliteratur des Klassizismus und der Romantik in England.* Bern: Benteli.

HODGE, E. W. 1940 "Belle Isle, Westmoreland. . . ." *Country Life* 88:98–101, 120–124.

"John Plaw." 1848–1892 In the Architectural Publication Society, *The Dictionary of Architecture.* 8 vols. London: Richards.

LYALL, SUTHERLAND 1974 "Minor Domestic Architecture in England and Pattern Books 1790–1840." Unpublished Ph.D. dissertation, University of London.

MCMORDIE, MICHAEL 1975 "Picturesque Pattern Books and Pre-Victorian Designers." *Architectural History* 18:43–59.

NACHMANI, CYNTHIA WOLK 1968–1969 "The Early English Cottage Book." *Marsyas* 14:67–76.

PILCHER, DONALD 1947 *The Regency Style, 1800–1830.* London: Batsford.

PLAW, JOHN (1785)1802 *Rural Architecture.* London: J. Taylor.

PLAW, JOHN (1795)1823 *Ferme Ornée; or Rural Improvements.* London: J. Taylor.

PLAW, JOHN (1800)1823 *Sketches for Country Houses, Villas, and Rural Dwellings.* New ed. London: J. Taylor.

TEYSSOT, GEORGES 1974 "Cottages et pittoresque: Les origines du logement ouvrier en Angleterre, 1781–1818." *Architecture, mouvement, continuité* 34, July:26–37.

PLAYFAIR, JAMES

James Playfair (1755–1794) was born near Dundee, Angus. He practiced in London, returning to Scotland annually to supervise progress on his commissions. In 1873, he published *A Method of Constructing Vapour Baths.* He traveled to France in 1787 and to Italy in 1792–1793. He died in Edinburgh.

Playfair's significant works are in Scotland. At Melville Castle, Midlothian (1785–1789), the castellated silhouette is borrowed from Inveraray Castle, Argyll, by ROGER MORRIS. His remodeling of Kinnaird Castle, Angus (1786–1790), was in a more fashionable Gothic; it was removed by DAVID BRYCE after 1855. The nearby Farnell Church, Angus (1788–1789), has even more recondite Gothic detailing.

Playfair is an important neoclassicist. The Graham Mausoleum, Methven Church, Perthshire (1793), has a Greek temple form. More eclectic is Cairness, Aberdeenshire (1791–1797), with interiors reminiscent of JOHN SOANE and an Egyptian billiard room. The attached semicircular offices display Ledoux-like (see CLAUDE NICOLAS LEDOUX) features. Similar advanced ideas are found in the theoretical studies now in the drawings collection of the Royal Institute of British Architects.

JAMES MACAULAY

WORKS

1785–1789, Melville Castle, Midlothian, Scotland. 1786–1788, Town and County Hall, Forfar, Scotland. *1786–1790, Kinnaird Castle (remodeling), Angus, Scotland. *1787–1789, Bothwell House, Lanarkshire, Scotland. 1788–1789, Farnell Church, Angus, Scotland. 1791–1797, Cairness, Aberdeenshire, Scotland. 1793, Graham Mausoleum, Methven Church, Perthshire, Scotland.

BIBLIOGRAPHY

ARCHITECTURAL PUBLICATION SOCIETY 1852–1892 *The*

Dictionary of Architecture. 8 vols. London: Richards.
CROOK, J. MORDAUNT 1972 *The Greek Revival.* London: Murray.
DUNBAR, JOHN G. (1966)1978 *Architecture of Scotland.* Rev. ed. London: Batsford.
MACAULAY, JAMES 1975 *The Gothic Revival, 1745–1845.* Glasgow: Blackie.
MCWILLIAM, COLIN 1970 "James Playfair's Designs for Ardkinglas." In Howard Colvin and John Harris (editors), *The Country Seat.* London: Lane.
WALKER, DAVID, and MCWILLIAM, COLIN 1971 "Cairness, Aberdeenshire." *Country Life* 149:184–187, 248–251.
WATKIN, DAVID 1968 *Thomas Hope, 1769–1831 and the Neo-Classical Idea.* London: Murray.

PLAYFAIR, W. H.

William Henry Playfair (1790–1857) was the son of JAMES PLAYFAIR. Born in London, he was brought up in Edinburgh by his uncle, John Playfair, after his father died in 1794. William Playfair trained under WILLIAM STARK and also, it is said, with JAMES WYATT and Sir ROBERT SMIRKE.

In 1817, Playfair won the competition to complete Edinburgh University, begun by ROBERT ADAM in 1789, which established his reputation. With CHARLES R. COCKERELL, he designed the National Monument on the Calton Hill (1819–?), Edinburgh, as a replica of the Parthenon, but only twelve columns were erected. The Doric peripteral Royal Institution, now the Royal Scottish Academy (1822–1826, extended 1832–1835), is surpassed by the restrained Ionic and subtle modeling of the adjacent National Gallery (1850–1857), but the hexagonal Saint Stephen's Church (1827–1828) is more ingenious both in plan and style. Such works confirmed Edinburgh, architecturally, as the Athens of the North.

Playfair recast Floors Castle, Roxburghshire (1838–1845), in exuberant Tudor. He also used Tudor at Donaldson's Hospital, Edinburgh (1842–1850), which he considered his finest work.

JAMES MACAULAY

WORKS

1817–1824, Edinburgh University (completion). 1818–1820, Dollar Academy, Clackmannanshire, Scotland. 1819–?, Calton Hill Development (with Charles R. Cockerell); 1820–1823, Royal Circus; 1822–1826, 1832–1835, Royal Institution (now the Royal Scottish Academy); 1826–1829, National Monument; 1827–1828, Saint Stephen's Church; 1829–1832, Royal College of Surgeons; Edinburgh. 1838–1845, Floors Castle, Roxburghshire, Scotland. 1842–1850, Donaldson's Hospital; 1846–1850, Free Church College; 1850–1857, National Gallery; Edinburgh.

BIBLIOGRAPHY

ARCHITECTURAL PUBLICATION SOCIETY 1852–1892 *The Dictionary of Architecture.* 8 vols. London: Richards.
CROOK, J. MORDAUNT 1972 *The Greek Revival.* London: Murray.
DUNBAR, JOHN G. (1966)1978 *Architecture of Scotland.* Rev. ed. London: Batsford.
HITCHCOCK, H. R. (1954)1972 *Early Victorian Architecture in Britain.* 2 vols. Reprint. New York: Da Capo.
LINDSAY, IAN G. (1948)1973 *Georgian Edinburgh.* 2d ed. Revised by David Walker. Edinburgh: Scottish Academic Press.
MACAULAY, JAMES 1975 *The Gothic Revival, 1745–1845.* Glasgow: Blackie.
YOUNGSON, A. J. 1966 *The Making of Classical Edinburgh, 1750–1840.* Edinburgh University Press.

PLEČNIK, JOŽE

Jože (Josef) Plečnik (1872–1957) is one of a group of architects who eschewed the international functionalist aesthetic. He once said, "What [AUGUSTE] PERRET does, I cannot do but what I do, Perret cannot." Plečnik's artistic training took place mainly in *fin-de-siècle* Vienna. Although not ignoring modern trends, he was convinced of the inspiring language of classical architecture. At a time when architecture became more and more preoccupied with the logical requirements of human needs, Plečnik remained a humanist who preferred the simplicity of human dignity. Mediterranean forms were of particular national significance for him, frequently occurring in his work. A deeply pious man and an ascetic, he remained content with his humble university stipend.

Born in Ljubljana, Yugoslavia, Plečnik attended the State School of Craftsmanship in Graz, Austria, before going into furniture design in Vienna. In 1894, OTTO WAGNER was so impressed by his draftsmanship that the young Plečnik was offered a place in his atelier. The following year, he joined Wagner's class in the Vienna Academy. From 1898 to 1899, he traveled through Italy and France after winning the celebrated Prix de Rome. Between the years 1903 and 1905, he designed an office and residential building in the centre of Vienna for the industrial magnate Johannes Zacherl. The building distinguished itself through its creative, disciplined series of original answers to the formal questions posed by Wagner. Later, his Church of the Holy Spirit (1910–1913) in Vienna pioneered the use of reinforced concrete in monumental architecture. In 1911, he was invited to take up the post of professor at the Prague School of Applied Arts. In 1921, he gave up this job to

Plečnik. Zacherl House. Vienna. 1903–1905

teach architecture at the newly founded University of Ljubljana.

For the Czech president Thomas G. Masaryk, a friend and patron, he restored and adapted the presidential residence of Prague Castle. In Ljubljana, Plečnik constructed a series of funerary chapels (1938–1940), a market (1939–1942), the National and University Library (1935–1941), and several churches and civic buildings.

DAMJAN PRELOVŠEK

WORKS

1900, Villa Langer; 1901–1902, Residential Apartments, Hamburgerstrasse; 1903–1905, Zacherl House; 1910–1913, Holy Spirit Church; Vienna. 1920–1930, Prague Castle (restoration). 1920–1930, Presidential Villa, Lány, Czechoslovakia. 1923–1927, Bogojine Church, Slovenia, Yugoslavia. 1925–1927, Chamber of Commerce (interiors); 1926–1927, Saint Francis Church; 1928–1930, Insurance Company Building; Ljubljana, Yugoslavia. 1928–1931, Sacred Heart Church, Prague. 1931, Shoemakers Bridge; 1931, Three Bridges; 1931–1933, Villa Prelovšek (restoration); Ljubljana, Yugoslavia. 1932–1957, Saint Anthony Church, Belgrade, Yugoslavia. 1933–1934, Peglezen House; 1935–1941, National and University Library; 1937–1940 Saint Michael in Barje Church; 1938–1940, Funerary Chapels Ensemble; 1939–1942, Market; 1952–1953, Monastery of the German Knights (restoration); Ljubljana, Yugoslavia.

BIBLIOGRAPHY

Architekt Jože Plečnik 1968 Ljubljana, Yugoslavia: Mladinska knjiga. Exhibition catalogue.

Novosti Pražského hradu a Lán. 1928 Prague: Stavební spravá Pražského hradu.

POZZETTO, MARCO 1968 *Jože Plečnik e la scuola di Otto Wagner.* Turin, Italy: Alba.

PRELOVŠEK, DAMJAN 1979 *Josef Plečnik: Wiener Arbeiten 1896–1914.* Vienna: Tusch.

STELE, FRANCE, and PLEČNIK, JOŽE 1955 *Napori.* Ljubljana, Yugoslavia: Slovenska akademija znanosti in umetnosti.

STELE, FRANCE; TRSTENJAK, ANTON; and PLEČNIK, JOŽE 1941 *Architectura perennis.* Ljubljana, Yugoslavia: Mestna občina ljubljanska.

STRAJNIĆ, KOSTA 1920 *Josip Plečnik.* Zagreb, Yugoslavia: Ćelap i Popovac.

PLUMB, GEORGE

Formerly a carpenter, George Plumb (20th century) built his home and adjacent buildings (1963–?) in Duncan, British Columbia, out of bottles given him by neighbors, visitors and industry. Including those used for jam, pop, milk, coke, beer, liquor, and medicine, the bottles are of every kind, color, and shape. Among the buildings stand animals Plumb has carved from concrete.

JANET KAPLAN

BIBLIOGRAPHY

WAMPLER, JAN 1977 Pages 160–165 in *All Their Own: People and the Places They Build.* Cambridge, Mass.: Schenkman.

PLUMET, CHARLES

Generally known as an Art Nouveau architect, Charles Plumet (1861–1928) developed the free-flowing curvilinear forms (breaking from neo-Gothic flamboyant) only in his furniture and shop interior designs, often done in collaboration with TONY SELMERSHEIM. At the turn of the century, he built small apartment buildings and houses for bourgeois clients in Paris where land speculation forced invention in spatial planning. His forms there are abstracted from medieval or early Renaissance French construction. The loggia gallery at attic height and bow-windows in unadorned façades expressed the interior volumes of his buildings. A restrained polychromy and the depressed arc of his openings and traceries became artistic trademarks.

It was the epoch when public exhibitions and publications directed trends in artistic production. Plumet's greatest influence in his time may have been in his roles as protagonist of *l'art dans tout* and as secretary-vice president of the Salon d'Automne. His career was capped when he became chief architect of the 1925 Exposition des Arts Décoratifs et Industriels in Paris.

ELIZABETH MCLANE

WORKS

1895, Apartment House, 67 Avenue Malakoff; 1900, Apartment House, 50 Avenue Victor Hugo; Paris. 1901, Château de Chênemoireau, Loire et Cher, France. 1906, Apartment Buildings, 15 and 21 Boulevard Lannes, Paris. *1911, Pavilion of French Decorative Art, Exhibition, Turin, Italy. 1913–1914, Office Building, 33 Rue du Louvre, Paris.

BIBLIOGRAPHY

ALFASSA, P. 1911 "Le Pavilion de l'Art Décoratif Français à l'Exposition de Turin." *Art et Décoration* 30:317–322.

BADOVICI, JEAN 1923 *Maisons de Rapport de Charles Plumet.* Paris: Morancé.

BOILEAU, L. C. 1907 "Société Nationale des Beaux-Arts." *L'Architecture* 19:152–158.

BORSI, FRANCO, and GODOLI, EZIO 1976 *Paris, 1900.* Brussels: Vokaer.

FORTHUNY, PASCAL 1899 "Un Maître d'Oeuvre: Charles Plumet." *Revue des Arts Décoratifs* 19, no. 6:179–191.

FORD, GEORGE BURDETT 1907 "Further Work of Charles Plumet." *American Architect and Building News* 91, part 2:247–248.

KOECHLIN, RAYMOND 1911 "L'Art Décoratif à L'Exposition de Turin." *L'Art Décoratif* October:129–136.

VITRY, PAUL 1925 "L'Exposition des Arts Décoratifs Modernes." *Gazette des Beaux Arts* 2:1–18, 287–300.

POELAERT, JOSEPH

Joseph Poelaert (1817–1879) was born in Brussels, where he lived for most of his life. He resided for several years in Paris studying with JEAN NICOLAS HUYOT and Louis Visconti. He also studied the works of KARL FRIEDRICH SCHINKEL, whose rationalism influenced many of Poelaert's designs.

He was named city architect of Brussels in 1856, and in 1862, after an international competition failed to produce an acceptable design, he was given the commission for his most important work: the Brussels Palais de Justice. The building, a megalomaniacal structure harmoniously combining elements from numerous cultures, was finished after Poelaert's death.

JOHN H. WILSON

WORKS

1850–1859, Colonne du Congrès; 1852, School building, Rue de Schaerbeek; 1855, Saint Catherine; 1855, Théâtre Royal de la Monnaie (restoration); 1862, Notre-Dame de Laeken, Avenue de la Reine; 1862–1883, Palais de Justice; Brussels, Belgium.

BIBLIOGRAPHY

"Dead with Their Works Unfinished." 1883 *Building* 2:34.

HITCHCOCK, H. R. (1958)1977 *Architecture: Nineteenth and Twentieth Centuries.* Rev. ed. Harmondsworth, England: Penguin.

OZINGA 1933 "Poelaert, Joseph." Volume 27, pages 177–178 in *Allgemeines Lexikon der bildenden Künstler von der Antike bis zur Gegenwart.* Leipzig: Seemann.

POELZIG, HANS

A Berliner by birth, Hans Poelzig (1869–1936) attended school in Potsdam. In 1888 and 1889, he studied architecture at the Technische Hochschule in Charlottenburg, Berlin. After passing his State Board Examination in 1899, he worked in the Technical Office of the Ministry of Public Works. He was assistant to HUGO HÄRING in the Berlin Building Office between 1893 and 1894 and served in the military in 1894–1895.

Poelzig became the director of the Royal Art and Craft Academy of Breslau in 1903 and remained in this position until 1916. In that year, Dresden invited him to teach at their Technische Hochschule and from 1916 to 1920 he also was city architect. Older in years than most of his colleagues in the professions, he was nevertheless active in every progressive effort; in 1918, he became a member of the *Novembergruppe,* and of the *Arbeitsrat für Kunst.* A few years later, he was an active participant of *Der Ring* and by 1924, he was an outspoken member of the "Circle of Friends of the Bauhaus." Respected by both conservatives and progressives alike, he became chairman of the Deutscher *Werkbund* in 1919; in 1926, he was elected chairman of the *Bund Deutscher Architekten.*

Poelzig's private practice began with the turn of the century; for several years the mainstay of his office was church work. In the few years before World War I, Poelzig was known for a watertower at Posen (1911), an office building in Breslau (1912), and a factory in Luban (1912). During the war, few of his many proposals were built. Perhaps it was that long period of relative inactivity which led to Poelzig's Grosses Schauspielhaus (1919), Berlin, his best-known work. Opening his office in Berlin in 1920, he was again more occupied with proposed projects than with realized works. From 1920 to 1924, Poelzig directed the architectural studies at the Berlin Kunstakademie, thereafter becoming professor at the Technische Hochschule of Charlottenburg, a post he held until 1933. By that time, Poelzig had created additional buildings distinguished for their innovative features. Unfortunately, his appointment in 1933 as head of the Associated State Schools of Architecture, Free, and

Applied Art incited objections by the Nazi Kampfbund, forcing him to resign.

Although he had received an honorary doctorate from the Technische Hochschule of Stuttgart on the occasion of his sixtieth birthday in 1929 and had become an associate of the Fine Arts Academy in 1933, Poelzig's problems mounted; for reason of his friendships, his architecture, and his stated principles, the Nazis harried him out of his professional responsibilities as teacher and architect. In late 1935, the Reichskammer für bildende Künste demanded that he prove the purity of the lineage of his English father. Though this was obtained by WALTER GROPIUS, then in England, it did not help Poelzig and he quit Germany for Turkey in May 1936. There, he placed first in a competition for an academy of music and theater in Istanbul. The Turkish government commissioned him with all the public works directed by the Ministry for Public Instruction and offered him a professorship at the School of Architecture in Ankara. However, he suffered complications of pneumonia and heart disease and returned to Germany where he died in June. Gropius's note to MARTIN WAGNER was an epitaph: "Poelzig was not young enough to start again. The poverty of spirit in Germany could not be shown more clearly as in his person if work or honor for a man like him were not provided."

REGINALD R. ISAACS

WORKS

1911, Water Tower, Posen, Germany. 1912, Chemical Factory and Workers' Housing, Luban, Germany. 1912, Housing Development; 1912, Office Building, Junkernstrasse; Breslau, Germany. 1916, Gasworks, Dresden, Germany. 1919, Grosses Schauspielhaus; 1925, Capitol Cinema Building; Berlin. 1927, Sigmund Goeritz Factory, Chemnitz, Germany. 1927, Single-family House, Werkbund Exhibition, Weissenhof Estate, Stuttgart, Germany. 1929, Cassirer Cableworks, Spandau, Berlin. 1929, Single-family Housing, Gafgah, Zehlendorf, Germany. 1930, Broadcasting House, Berlin. 1930, I. G. Farben Administration Building, Frankfurt.

BIBLIOGRAPHY

HEUSS, THEODOR (1955)1966 *Hans Poelzig: Lebensbild eines Baumeister.* Tübingen, Germany: Wunderlich.

POELZIG, HANS 1919 "Rede gehouden ter gelegenheid van de herleving van den Werkbund." *Wendingen* 2, no. 11:4–14.

POELZIG, HANS (1931)1954 *Der Architekt.* Reprint. Tübingen, Germany: Wasmuth.

POSENER, JULIUS 1963 "Poelzig." *Architectural Review* 133:401–405.

SCHEFFAUER, H. G. 1923 "Hans Poelzig." *Architectural Review* 54:122–127.

SHARP, DENNIS 1966 *Modern Architecture and Expressionism.* London: Longmans.

POGGI, GIUSEPPE

Giuseppe Poggi (1811–1901) was an Italian urban planner and architect noted particularly for the laying out of a series of boulevards and avenues on three sides of Florence, Italy, along the route of the old city walls (1865–1877). He was the pupil and son-in-law of the neoclassical architect PASQUALE POCCIANTI and worked largely in a modified sixteenth-century Renaissance style.

Between 1865 and 1870, Florence was the capital of Italy. Poggi's wide, straight, tree-lined streets were designed to bring a European grandeur to Florence, to put it on the scale of Napoleon III's Paris or Franz Joseph's Vienna, both recently remodeled. Poggi also built the elegant ramps leading to the Piazzale Michelangelo and San Miniato al Monte on the south side of Florence. Together with Mariano Fabrini, Poggi destroyed the Mercato Vecchio in the center of the city and built the Piazza delle Repubblica in the 1880s.

NICHOLAS ADAMS

WORKS

1857, Villa Favard (now the Facoltà di Scienze Economiche e Commerciali, Università degli Studi); 1865–1877, Viale Rosselli, Viale Filippo Strozzi, Viale Spartaco Lavagnini, Viale G. Matteotti, and Viale Antonio Gramsci (resystematization of peripheral avenues); 1874, Palazzo Gondi (restoration and addition to left flank); 1887, Piazza della Republica; Florence.

BIBLIOGRAPHY

MEEKS, CARROLL L. V. 1966 *Italian Architecture: 1750–1914.* New Haven: Yale University Press.

POISSON DE VANDIÈRES, ABEL-FRANÇOIS

See MARIGNY, MARQUIS DE.

POLK, WILLIS

Willis Jefferson Polk (1867–1924) was born in Jacksonville, Illinois, the son of an itinerant carpenter. He was apprenticed to a St. Louis contractor at age eight. By 1885, a father–son architectural firm was established in Kansas City, Missouri, with Willis designing some of the projects in-house. Subsequently he worked for a number of architects across the country, including HENRY VAN BRUNT (Kansas City) and A. PAGE BROWN (New York). Polk moved with Brown to San Francisco in 1889, opening his own office there the next year.

Polk did not seek to develop a distinct regional

idiom, as has often been thought. Rather he was instrumental in redirecting the course of architecture in the San Francisco region according to the ideals of the academic movement as championed by McKim, Mead, and White. At the same time, Polk expressed the tenets of that movement in a highly individual manner. During the 1890s, his work was unusually diverse in its use of form, space, scale, and imagery. He designed a number of rustic houses, drawing from postmedieval vernacular sources, and also produced grand, exuberant classical schemes, exemplified by the Bourn House in San Francisco (1895–1896).

At the turn of the century, Polk found a hero, Daniel H. Burnham, whom he sought to emulate in every way. Polk was employed as a designer for Burnham in Chicago (1902–1903) and assisted Burnham in preparing his master plan for San Francisco (1904–1905). After the 1906 fire, he was given charge of Burnham's newly created west coast office. The association lasted until 1910; thereafter, the office continued under Polk's name. Much of his work during the 1900s and 1910s was for large commercial buildings, fashioned in Burnham's suave classical style, yet considerably less original than earlier schemes. A notable exception is the glass curtain wall Hallidie Building in San Francisco (1917–1918). Financial mismanagement led to a steady decrease in commissions after World War I. Little of consequence was in the office when Polk died in 1924.

Richard W. Longstreth

WORKS

1892–1893, Williams-Polk House, San Francisco. 1893, Rey House, Belvedere, Calif. 1895–1896, Bourn House, San Francisco. 1897–1898, Bourn House, Grass Valley, Calif. 1898–1899, Wheeler House, McCloud, Calif. 1907–1909, First National (Crocker) Bank; 1908–1910, Pacific Union Club, San Francisco. 1916–1917, Blaney House, Saratoga, Calif. 1914–1916, Bourn House (Filoli), San Mateo, Calif. 1917–1918, Hallidie Building, San Francisco.

BIBLIOGRAPHY

Dills, Keith W. 1971 "The Hallidie Building." *Journal of the Society of Architectural Historians* 30:323–329.

Hamilton, Frederick 1911 "The Work of Willis Polk & Company." *Architect and Engineer* 24:34–73.

Longstreth, Richard W. 1977 "Architects on the Edge of the World: Ernest Coxhead and Willis Polk in San Francisco During the 1890's." Unpublished Ph.D. dissertation, University of California, Berkeley.

Longstreth, Richard W. 1979 *A Matter of Taste: Willis Polk's Writings on Architecture in the Wave.* San Francisco: Book Club of California.

Price, C. Matlack 1913 "Notes on the Varied Work of Willis Polk." *Architectural Record* 34:566–583.

Woodbridge, Sally (editor) 1976 *Bay Area Houses.* New York: Oxford University Press.

POLLAIULO, SIMONE DEL

See Il Cronaca.

POLSHEK, JAMES STEWART

James Stewart Polshek (1930) was born in Akron, Ohio, and received a Master of Architecture degree from Yale University (1955), where he studied with Eugene Nalle and Louis I. Kahn. He worked for I. M. Pei, Ulrich Franzen, and Westermann and Miller before establishing his own practice in 1962. Since 1972, Polshek has served as dean of the Graduate School of Architecture and Planning, Columbia University.

Susan Strauss

WORKS

1959, Oster House, Stony Point, N.Y. 1964, Teijin Central Research Institute, Tokyo. 1965, Teijin Textile Processing Research Institute, Osaka, Japan. 1968, Donovan House, Port Washington, N.Y. 1969, Bronfman Recreational Structure, Purchase, N.Y. 1970, Clinton Youth and Family Center, Young Men's Christian Association, New York. 1971, New York State Bar Association Center, Albany. 1971, Rosemary Hall Dormitory and Academic Buildings, Wallingford, Conn. 1971, Wesleyan University Central Plant, Middletown, Conn. 1972, Allied Chemical Corporation Materials Research Center, Morristown, N.J. 1972, Twin Parks East, Bronx, N.Y. 1973, Intermediate School 197, New York. 1975, Helen Owen Carey Playhouse, Brooklyn Academy of Music, N.Y. 1975, Health and Physical Education Building, State University of New York, Old Westbury. 1977, Public Works Building, Englewood, N.J. 1977, Simon and Schuster Corporate Offices, New York. 1978, Trancas Associates Medical Center (with Peter Gluck), Napa, Calif.

BIBLIOGRAPHY

Diamonstein, Barbaralee 1980 "James Stewart Polshek." Pages 183–205 in *American Architecture Now.* New York: Rizzoli.

"Functional Grid in Japan." 1964 *Architectural Forum* 119, Aug.–Sept.:130–135.

Gangneux, Marie-Christine 1976 "Derrière le Miroir." *L'Architecture d'Aujourd'hui* 46, no. 186:2–14.

"The Industrial Esthetic: Two Buildings by James Stewart Polshek and Associates." 1978 *Architectural Record* 163, no. 2:95–102.

"James S. Polshek and Associates." 1976 *Architecture and Urbanism* 64, Apr.:27–44.

"A New York Studio di Architettura al Quarantesettesimo Piano." 1966 *Domus* no. 435:17–21.

"Progressive Architecture Sixteenth Annual Design Awards Program." 1969 *Progressive Architecture* 50, Jan.:101–146.

"Research Laboratory in Japan." 1964 *Arts and Architecture* 81, Dec.:30–33.

"Schulen." 1975 *Baumeister* 72, Mar.:185–222.

"The Teijin Central Research Institute." 1964 *Japan Architect* 39, Sept.:11–24.

POLYKLEITOS THE YOUNGER

Polykleitos the Younger (?–350 B.C.), a renowned sculptor, was architect of the Tholos at Epidauros, begun around c.365 B.C. The finest of all ancient *Tholoi,* it was marked by the elaborateness of all its details, especially the splendid Corinthian capitals of its interior columns, which were to influence all later designs in that order. In addition, Polykleitos was said to have been the designer of the great Theater (c.360 B.C.), also at Epidauros. Typical of theaters of the fourth century B.C., it seated more than twelve thousand spectators; much of its original form is preserved today.

B. M. BOYLE

WORKS

*Begun c.365 B.C., Tholos; (A)*begun c.360 B.C., Theater; Epidauros, Greece.

BIBLIOGRAPHY

English translations of the ancient texts can be found in the volumes of the Loeb Classical Library series published by Harvard University Press and Heinemann.

BURFORD, ALISON 1969 *The Greek Temple Builders at Epidauros.* Toronto: University of Toronto Press.

DINSMOOR, WILLIAM B. (1902)1975 *The Architecture of Ancient Greece.* Reprint of 1950 ed. New York: Norton. Originally published with the title *The Architecture of Ancient Greece and Rome.*

LAWRENCE, ARNOLD W. (1957)1975 *Greek Architecture.* Harmondsworth, England: Penguin.

PAUSANIAS, *Graeciae descriptio,* Book 2.27.5.

Polykleitos the Younger. Theater. Epidauros, Greece. Begun c.360 B.C.

POMPE, ANTOINE

Born in Brussels, Antoine Pompe (1873–1980) was educated there at the Académie des Beaux-Arts and at the Kunstgewerbeschule in Munich where he studied art and design. Returning to Brussels in 1893, he worked as a designer of useful objects, furniture, and interiors. He became an architectural draftsman in 1899 and only in 1910 did he build his first independently produced architectural composition, the Van Neck Orthopedic Clinic in Brussels. In this design, Pompe synthesized Belgian Art Nouveau and contemporary German design trends yet also surpassed them to achieve a totally fresh and personal effect. Pompe devoted the remainder of his long career mostly to relatively small-scale domestic work.

ALFRED WILLIS

WORKS

1904–1908, Palace Hotel (with Leener), Brussels. 1910, Van Neck Orthopedic Clinic; 1912, Ghende House (with Fernand Bodson); Ixelles, Belgium. 1919, Batavia Garden Housing (with Bodson and Raphael Verwilghen), Roulers, Belgium. 1921, La Roue Housing, Anderlecht, Belgium 1922–1926, Kapelleveld Garden City Housing and Shops (with LOUIS VAN DER SWAELMEN and others), Woluwé-Saint-Lamber, Belgium. 1926, Grunenwald Villa; *1927, House, avenue de la Floride; Uccle, Belgium. 1928, Row Houses (with Paul Rubbers), Rhode-Saint-Genèse, Belgium. 1934, Villa, avenue Hellevelt, Uccle, Belgium. 1947, Van Neck House, Ganshoren, Belgium. 1953, Pompe House, Wezembeek-Oppem, Belgium.

BIBLIOGRAPHY

Antoine Pompe ou l'architecture du sentiment. 1973 Ixelles, Belgium: Musée d'Ixelles. Exhibition catalogue.

Belgian Art: 1880–1914. 1980 New York: Brooklyn Museum. Exhibition catalogue.

BORSI, FRANCO (1974)1977 *Bruxelles 1900.* New York: Rizzoli.

CULOT, MAURICE, and TERLINDEN, FRANÇOIS 1969 *Antoine Pompe et l'effort moderne en Belgique: 1890–1940.* Ixelles, Belgium: Musée d'Ixelles.

PUTTEMANS, PIERRE 1976 *Modern Architecture in Belgium.* Volume 5 in *History of Architecture in Belgium.* Brussels: Vokaer.

Rythme. 1935 no. 41:entire issue.

SHARP, DENNIS 1972 *A Visual History of Twentieth-Century Architecture.* Greenwich, Conn.: New York Graphic Society.

SMETS, MARCEL 1977 *L'avènement de la Cité-jardin en Belgique.* Brussels: Mardaga.

STYNEN, HERMAN 1979 *Urbanisme et société: Louis Van der Swaelmen, 1883–1929, animateur du mouvement moderne en Belgique.* Brussels: Mardaga.

TAFURI, MAFREDO, and DAL CO, FRANCESCO 1979 *Modern Architecture.* Translated from the Italian by Robert Erich Wolf. New York: Abrams.

POMPEI, ALESSANDRO

Conte Alessandro Pompei (1705–1772) was an amateur painter as well as an eminent architect who played an important role in the resurgence of neoclassicism in eighteenth-century Italy. He was born in Verona and was educated in Parma at the College for Nobility. He studied painting under Clementa Ruta and Antonio Balestra but never pursued it as a career. He was completely self-taught in architecture, though, and learned only by looking at the architecture around him and by studying architects themselves; he was greatly influenced by Scipione Maffei.

Alessandro Pompei was opposed to the baroque flamboyance and wanted to establish a stricter classicism. This is apparent in all his work. At the age of twenty-six, he designed for himself the Villa Illasi in Verona (1731–1737). In 1735, he published *I cinque ordini dell'architettura civile di M. San Michele* (with plates by Pompei and his teacher, Balestra) which contained descriptions of the five orders of architecture as used by MICHELE SANMICHELI and compared each of them to the orders employed by VITRUVIUS, LEON BATTISTA ALBERTI, SEBASTIANO SERLIO, ANDREA PALLADIO, VINCENZO SCAMOZZI, and GIACOMO BAROZZI DA VIGNOLA. Besides his own palazzo, he designed other palazzi around Italy: for the Spolverini family in Verona (1740), for the Marquess Pindemonte in Vo (1742), and for the Conte Giuliari in Sessino (1742). He also designed the Chiesa della tre vie (1742) in Sanguinetto, which was round on the exterior but octagonal within; a dormitory for the monks of San Michele at Campagna and, later in his career, a library for the Franciscan Fathers at Bergamo. Most of his work, though, was done in Verona. He designed the dogana (1744–1753), which was built to resemble a stoa in a Greek marketplace. He also designed the portico of the Accademia Filarmonica (1745) which was to contain the marbles and inscriptions of Maffei, the Museo Lapidario (1739–c.1746) and the façades of the Churches of San Giacomo and San Paolo di Campo Marzo (c.1763). After his brother's death in 1746, he took over the running of the family estate which curtailed his architectural work.

JUDITH COHEN

WORKS

1731–1737, Villa Illasi; 1740, Palazzo for Spolverini Family; Verona, Italy. 1742, Chiesa delle tre vie, Sanquinetto, Italy. 1742, Palazzo for Marquess Pindemonti, Vo, Italy. 1742, Villa for Count Giuliano, Sessino, Italy. 1739–c.1746, Museo Lapidario; 1744–1754, Dogana; 1745, Accademia Filarmonida (portico); 1763, San Giacomo (façade); 1763, San Paolo di Campo Marzo (façade and interior alterations); Verona, Italy.

BIBLIOGRAPHY

POMPEI, ALESSANDRO 1735 *Li cinque ordini dell'architettura civile di Michele Sanmicheli.* Verona, Italy: Vallarsi.

SEMENZATO, CAMILLO 1961 "Un architetto illuminista: Alessandro Pompei." *Arte veneta* 15:192–200.

PONTELLI, BACCIO

Baccio Pontelli (1450–1492) was an architect-sculptor-engineer of the Italian Renaissance. Born in Florence (his father was a carpenter), he is particularly noted for his fine fortification plans which reflect the beginnings of the age of artillery.

Pontelli was trained in the workshop of FRANCIONE, the distinguished Florentine architect-carpenter and intarsia master who also taught the architect Giuliano da Sangallo (see SANGALLO FAMILY) and GIULIANO DA MAIANO. Pontelli may have transferred to Pisa with his father in 1471; in any case, there is a record of payments for intarsia work by him in the Pisa Duomo in 1475. In 1479, Pontelli moved to Urbino, where he worked under FRANCESCO DI GIORGIO MARTINI and LUCIANO DA LAURANA on the construction of the Ducal Palace. Pontelli was by then sufficiently prominent to be asked by Lorenzo de' Medici to send him drawings of the Palace. Unfortunately, these drawings have been lost.

Shortly after 1481, Pontelli transferred to

Pontelli. Fortress. Ostia, Italy. 1483–1486

Rome. His career there has yet to be systematically studied. GIORGIO VASARI, in his life of Pontelli, attributed an enormous body of work to him there, but subsequent scholarship has stripped all of this from him. There remain now only a few tentative attributions such as San Pietro in Montorio (1480–1494) and parts of the Hospital of Santo Spirito (1484) that may be by Pontelli. More important, however, is the fact that Pontelli seems to represent the incursion into Rome at this time of strong Urbinate influence as can be seen in the Palazzo del Cancellaria. One of the future tasks of scholarship will be to define Pontelli's Roman work.

From 1483 onward, it seems that Pontelli's major activity was in the field of fortifications. At Ostia (1483–1486), he built a fortress for Giuliano delle Rovere and reorganized the small Renaissance *borgo* around the Church of Sant'Aurea which he also built. Ostia is a key work in the history of Renaissance fortifications: "The high *mastio,* or keep, is a medieval remnant, as are the machicoulis gallery, which had lost their purpose by this time, but which proved to be an extremely tenacious feature. But the main structure is relatively low, the towers have been cut off at curtain level, and fully casemated gun emplacements (among the first of their kind) have been placed near the bases of the walls to permit a sweeping defence of the ditch with horizontal fire" (de la Croix, 1972, p. 40). Thus, the fortress at Ostia has both the characteristics of the older medieval curtain wall defense and the new flanking coverage and low profile of the Renaissance angle bastion.

Just before his death in Urbino in 1492, Pontelli was hired as inspector general of fortifications for the Marches. As such he was responsible for additions and renovations to the fortresses at Jesi, Offida, and Osimo.

NICHOLAS ADAMS

WORKS

1483–1486, Church of Sant'Aurea; 1483–1486, Fortress; 1483–1486, Houses; Ostia, Italy. 1491–1492, Fortresses (renovations and additions), Jesi; Offida; and Osimo; Italy.

BIBLIOGRAPHY

DE FIORE, GASPARE 1963 *Baccio Pontelli: Architetto Fiorentino.* Rome: Edizioni dell'Ateneo.

DE LA CROIX, HORST 1972 *Military Considerations in City Planning: Fortifications.* New York: Braziller.

PONTI, GIO

Gio Ponti (1891–1979) was a professor of interior design in the department of architecture at the Polytechnic Institute of Milan, a member of the Higher Council of Fine Arts, and a long-time member of the board of managers for the Triennial of Milan. The mood of a "return to order" prevalent in Italy and the rest of Europe in the 1920s was expressed by Ponti in a highly sophisticated way for an upper middle class public. Through his works and through the magazine *Domus,* of which he was the editor from 1928, he promoted a renewal of Italian architecture and decorative arts, drawing upon the legacy of the Viennese Secession and the Wiener Werkstätte and transforming the "classical" language into a Rationalist vocabulary.

Representative of a moderate avant-garde which had acquired a position of prestige in the press, Ponti belonged to the youngest generation of Rationalists. Even in the period following World War II, he was able to make a valid contribution to the architectural panorama of Italy with works such as the Pirelli skyscraper (1955–1958).

SILVIA DANESI SQUARZINA
Translated from Italian by
Shara Wasserman

WORKS

1930–1931, Banca Unione (with E. Lancia), Milan. 1931, Villa Bouilhet, Paris. 1933, Lictor Tower (with C. Chiodi), Milan. 1934, School of Mathematics, University of Rome. 1934–1939, Department of Letters, University of Padova, Italy. 1935–1936, Italian Institute, Vienna. 1938–1939, Montecatini Office Building (with A. Fornaroli and E. Soncini); 1955–1958, Pirelli Skyscraper (with others); Milan. 1974, Shui-Hing Department Store, Hong Kong. 1978, Shui-Hing Department Store, Singapore.

BIBLIOGRAPHY

BALDESSARI, LUCIANO 1939 *L'architettura moderna in Italia.* Rovereto, Italy.

Cinquante anni di architettura italiana dal 1928 al 1978. 1979 Milan: Domus.

Espressione di Gio Ponte. 1954 With a preface by James Plaut. Milan: Guarnati.

The Expression of Gio Ponti. 1967 With a preface by Charles Eames. Minneapolis, Minn.: Walker Art Center.

LABÒ, MARIO 1936 *Architettura e arredamento del negozio.* Milan: Hoepli.

MINNUCCI, GAETANO 1936 *Scuole.* Milan: Hoepli.

MORETTI, BRUNO 1934 *Ville.* Milan: Hoepli.

MUZIO, GIOVANNI 1931 "Alcuni architetti d'oggi in Lombardia." *Dedalo* 1931.

PAGANO, GIUSEPPE 1936 *Tecnica dell'abitazione.* Milan: Triennale.

PAPINI, ROBERTO 1930 *Le Arti d'oggi.* Milan and Rome.

PATETTA, S. DAMIEN DI 1976 *Il Razionalismo e l'architettura in Italia durante il Fascismo.* Venice, Italy: Biennale della Venezia.

PIACENTINI, MARCELLO 1930 *Architettura d'oggi.*

Rome: Cremonese.
PICA, AGNOLDOMENICO 1941 *Architettura moderna in Italia.* Milan: Hoepli.
PONTI, GIO 1933 *La casa all'italiana.* Milan: Domus.
PONTI, GIO 1944 *Il Coro.* Milan: Uomo.
PONTI, GIO 1944 *Politica dell'Architettura.* Milan: Garzanti.
PONTI, GIO 1945 *L'Architettura e un cristallo.* Milan: Italiana.
PONTI, GIO 1945 *Verso la Casa Esatta.* Milan: Italiana.
PONTI, GIO 1956 *Paradiso Perduto.* Milan: Guarnati.
PONTI, GIO (1957)1960 *In Praise of Architecture.* New York: Dodge.
PONTI, GIO 1957–1960 *Milano Oggi.* Milan: Moderna.

Ponzio.
San Sebastiano fuori le mura (reconstruction; completed by Giovanni Vasanzio).
Rome.
1609–?

PONZIO, FLAMINIO

Born in Viggiu (Lombardy), Flaminio Ponzio (c.1559–1613) came to Rome in the mid-1580s and remained there for his entire career. His architectural formation is unknown, but in Rome he may have studied with his countryman Martino Longhi the Elder (see LONGHI FAMILY). In 1593, he was among the founding members of the Accademia di San Luca, and under Clement VIII (1592–1605) he served as architect of the Acqua Vergine. All of his important works, however, are dated after 1600. His own palazzo (1600), formerly in Via Alessandrina and now reconstructed in Piazza Campitelli, and his rebuilding of RAPHAEL's Sant' Eligio degli Orefici (1602) typify the basically conservative nature of his work just after the turn of the century. During the reign of Paul V Borghese, which began in 1605, Ponzio was the official papal architect. His first and most important work for the new pontiff was the Pauline Chapel in Santa Maria Maggiore (1605) which was built to match the adjacent Sistine Chapel of Sixtus V by DOMENICO FONTANA (1585). Although the two chapels are identical in plan and tectonic membering, Ponzio's is richer in surface ornamentation than its predecessor. His use of colored marbles, gilt stuccoes, and inlaid stones consciously rejects the harsh Counter-Reformatory aesthetic of Fontana's chapel. Ponzio also planned to reconstruct the entire rear elevation of the church, but only the façades of the Pauline Chapel and its sacristy were carried out.

Concurrent with his activity at Santa Maria Maggiore, Ponzio was also engaged in the construction of the east wing of the Quirinal Palace and minor additions to the Vatican Palace. From 1605 to 1612, he was in charge of the rebuilding of the Palazzo Borghese; the west wing and the two-story loggia connecting courtyard and garden are attributed to him. Other residential work for the Borghese during these years included commissions for the family's garden palace on the Quirinal (now Palazzo Rospigliosi-Pallavicini) and for two newly acquired villas in Frascati. More problematic is the attribution of the Villa Borghese on the Pincio, executed after 1613 by GIOVANNI VASANZIO, possibly on Ponzio's earlier design.

For Paul V, Ponzio is also believed to have designed the monumental fountain of the Acqua Paola on the Janiculum. Although a favorite of this pope, he was passed over for the important post of architect of St. Peter's, a position occupied by CARLO MADERNO since 1603. Ponzio entered the competition of 1606 for St. Peter's façade (won by Maderno), but his entry has been lost. His most successful ecclesiastical commission was the rebuilding of San Sebastiano fuori le mura, begun in 1609 and completed after his death by Vasanzio. The façade's lower story consists of an open arcade on paired columns similar to that of his garden loggia at the Palazzo Borghese.

Although Ponzio rejected the complexities of sixteenth-century Mannerism, he never succeeded entirely in rejecting its formalism. His position thus lay somewhere between the conservatism of Martino Longhi the Elder and the more dynamic, progressive style of Carlo Maderno.

JOHN VARRIANO

WORKS

1592–1605, Acqua Vergine; 1600, Palazzo Ponzio; 1602, Chapel of San Diego, San Giacomo degli Incurabili; 1602, Sant'Eligio degli Orefici (rebuilding); 1605, Pauline Chapel, Santa Maria Maggiore; 1605–1612, Palazzo Borghese; 1607, Chapels of Sant Andrea, Santa Barbara, and Santa Silvia, San Gregorio Magno; 1608, Fountain, Acqua Paola; 1608, Granaries, Santa Maria degli Angeli; 1608, Villa Borghese, Frascati; 1609–?, San Sebastiano fuori le mura (reconstruction; completed by Giovanni

Vasanzio); 1611, Palazzo Borghese al Quirinale (now Palazzo Rospigliosi-Pallavicini); n.d., House of Cavaliere d'Arpino, Palazzo Sciarra-Colonna; Rome.

BIBLIOGRAPHY

BAGLIONE, GIOVANNI (1642)1935 *Le vite de' pittori, scultori, et architetti.* Reprint. Rome: Calzone.

CREMA, LUIGI 1940 "Flaminio Ponzio architetto milanese a Roma." *Atti del IV Convegno Nazionale di Storia dell'Architettura* Oct.:281–308.

HEILMANN, CHRISTOPH 1970 "Acqua Paolo and the Urban Planning of Paul V Borghese." *Burlington Magazine* 112:656–663.

HIBBARD, HOWARD 1962 *The Architecture of the Palazzo Borghese.* American Academy in Rome.

HIBBARD, HOWARD 1971 *Carlo Maderno and Roman Architecture: 1580–1630.* University Park: Pennsylvania State University Press.

POOLE, GEORGE TEMPLE

George Temple Poole (1856–1934) was born in England and was trained as an architect and engineer. He arrived in Western Australia in 1886 and was appointed Colonial Architect in 1887 at a time of gold rushes and a great increase in public works. He resigned from that position in 1896 to practice privately; he joined C. F. Mouritzen in 1925. The Arts and Crafts movement influenced his public buildings and houses, although his style ranged from Renaissance Revival to early modern.

JOHN WHITE

WORKS

1886–1896, Insane Asylum, Fremantle; 1890, Treasury Building, Perth; 1893, Post and Telegraph Office, Geraldton; 1894, Central Railway Station, Perth; 1895, Courthouse, Cossack; 1895, Courthouse, York; 1895, Post Office, Cossack; 1895, Post and Telegraph Office, York; 1896, Courthouse, Albany; 1896, Courthouse, Roebourne; 1896, Customs House, Cossack; 1896, Government Observatory, Perth; 1896, Hospital, Albany; 1896, Lands Department, Perth; 1896, Lighthouse, Cape Leeuwin; 1896, Museum and Art Gallery, Perth; 1896, Post Office, Albany; 1896, Royal Mint, Perth; 1897, Hospital, Coolgardie; 1897, Hospital, York; 1897, Government Buildings, Cue; 1897, Public Offices, Coolgardie; 1897, Warden's Court, Coolgardie; 1929, Capitol Theater and Temple Court (with C. F. Mouritzen), Perth; Western Australia.

BIBLIOGRAPHY

MOLYNEUX, I. 1981 *Looking Around Perth.* Fremantle, Australia: Wescolour Press.

OLDHAM, RAY, and OLDHAM, JOHN 1981 *George Temple Poole: Architect of the Golden Years, 1885–1897.* Perth: University of Western Australia Press.

PITT, MORISON, M., and WHITE, JOHN (editors) 1979 *Western Towns and Buildings.* Perth: University of Western Australia Press.

POPE, JOHN RUSSELL

Born in New York, John Russell Pope (1874–1937) began studying architecture under WILLIAM R. WARE at Columbia University. He graduated in 1894, winning two Columbia prizes, one to the American Academy in Rome and one for travel. In Italy and Greece for two years, he made measured drawings of antique edifices. Late in 1896, he went to Paris, where he attended the Ecole des Beaux-Arts (1897–1899). Returning to New York in 1900, Pope commenced practice. Prolific, he did big houses for bankers and businessmen (Levi P. Morton's in Washington, D.C.; Ogden L. Mills's in Woodbury, Long Island; Marshall Field's in Huntington, Long Island; and so on), master plans for educational institutions (Yale, Dartmouth, and Johns Hopkins), and public buildings of national importance. His designs revived the Gothic, the Georgian, the eighteenth-century French, and the classical styles. The classical buildings are the most distinguished; they have the clear form and grand spirit evident in work by the American architect Pope admired most, Charles F. McKim (see MCKIM, MEAD, AND WHITE). Pope was the foremost inheritor of McKim's severe classicism; he was aptly called "the last of the Romans."

RICHARD CHAFEE

WORKS

1910, Temple of the Scottish Rite, Washington. c.1919, Union Station, Richmond, Va. 1925, Lincoln Memorial, Hodgenville, Ky. c.1925, Marcus L. Ward Home for Aged and Respectable Bachelors and Widowers, Maplewood, N.J. 1927, University Baptist Church, Baltimore, Md. 1927–1929, 1937, Baltimore Museum of Art, Md. 1928, Estate of Marshall Field III, Huntington, N.Y. 1928, First Presbyterian Church, New Rochelle, N.Y. 1929, Constitution Hall of the Daughters of the American Revolution; 1930, National City Christian Church; Washington. 1932, Calhoun College; 1932, Payne Whitney Gymnasium; Yale University, New Haven. 1933–1935, National Archives Building, Washington. 1936, Theodore Roosevelt Memorial, American Museum of Natural History, New York. 1937, American Battle Monument, Montfaucon, France. 1937, Duveen Sculpture Gallery, British Museum, London. 1937, Jefferson Memorial (not completed until 1943 by EGGERS AND HIGGINS); 1937, National Gallery of Art (not completed until 1941 by Eggers and Higgins); Washington. 1937, Sculpture Hall, Tate Gallery, London.

BIBLIOGRAPHY

CROLY, HERBERT 1911 "Recent Work of John Russell Pope." *Architectural Record* 29:441–511.

HUDNUT, JOSEPH 1941 "The Last of the Romans: Comment on the Building of the National Gallery of Art." *Magazine of Art* 34:169–173.

"John Russell Pope, Architect, 63, Dead." 1937 *New York Times* Aug. 28.

"John Russell Pope." 1937 *Journal of the Royal Institute of British Architects* 45:102.

STANTON, PHOEBE 1972 "A Note on John Russell Pope, Architect, 1874–1937." Part 2, pages 60–69 in The Baltimore Museum of Art, *Annual IV: Studies in Honor of Gertrude Rosenthal.* Baltimore: The museum.

SWALES, FRANCIS S. 1924 "Master Draftsman, VIII: John Russell Pope." *Pencil Points* 5:64–80, 90.

POPE, RICHARD SHACKLETON

Richard Shackleton Pope (1792?–1884) was clerk to ROBERT SMIRKE and CHARLES R. COCKERELL for whom he supervised the building (1821–1823) of the Philosophical Institution in Bristol, where he settled. He established a large practice, designing in the classical and the Gothic styles, from 1849 in partnership with J. Bindon and J. A. Clark, and latterly with his son Thomas. He was district surveyor of Bristol from 1831 to 1872.

R. WINDSOR LISCOMBE

WORKS

RICHARD SHACKLETON POPE

1827–1828, Court of Justice (with G. Dymond); 1830, Cattle Market (rebuilt in 1874), Temple Meads; 1830, Wool Hall, Saint Thomas Street; *1832, Bridewell; 1837–1838, Royal Western Hotel (now the Brunel House); 1839–1840, Saint Mary-on-the-Quay Church; 1843–1846, The Guildhall; *1844, Central Police Station; 1844–1847, Buckingham Baptist Church, Clifton; 1845, Plan of Victoria Street (with S. C. Fripp; built in 1870); 1848–1849, Meat Market; Bristol, England.

POPE, JOHN BINDON, AND JAMES ADAM CLARK

1852, Byrdon Place and Codrington Place, Clifton; 1855, Vegetable Market; 1856, Stuckey's Bank (now the Westminster Bank), Saint Nicholas Street; Bristol, England.

POPE AND BINDON

1860, Emmanuel Church, Old Market; *1862, Saint James's Church, Clifton; 1867, Assize Courts, Small Street; 1866, Avonwood House, Clifton Down; Bristol, England.

POPE AND THOMAS POPE

1873, Fishmarket, Bristol, England.

BIBLIOGRAPHY

GOMME, ANDOR; JENNER, MICHAEL; and LITTLE, BRYAN 1979 Pages 160, 238–241, 255, 272, 360–362, 440–441 in *Bristol: An Architectural History.* London: Lund Humphries.

POPOV, IVAN

Ivan Pavlov Popov (1912–1973) was a renowned architect and architectural educator with almost thirty years of teaching experience.

Born in Sliven, Bulgaria, he graduated summa cum laude from the Brno Polytechnic Institute, Czechoslovakia, in 1936, and started his professional career in the private office of GEORGI RADEV OVCHAROV. During his professional life (1937–1973), he won, as the head or as a member of design teams, thirty-five first or second prizes in architectural competitions and built the majority of these projects.

He joined Stancho Belkovski (see BELKOVSKI AND DANCHOV) at the Central Architectural Design Organization in Sofia, but his main affiliation was with the department of architecture at Sofia's Polytechnic Institute (1944–1973).

Popov believed in organic unity between form and function and in classical approaches to space, proportion, and scale.

MARIA POPOVA

WORKS

1937–1940, Sanatorium, Narechen, Bulgaria. 1938, High School, Asenovgrad, Bulgaria. 1939, High School, Botevgrad, Bulgaria. 1941, Hotel St. Elizabeth, Plovdiv, Bulgaria. 1949, Bank and Hotel, Zlatitsa, Bulgaria. 1951–1953, Communist Party Headquarters; 1951–1953, Ministerial Council, Sofia. 1957, Village Library, Sheinovo, Bulgaria. 1971–1974, Higher Institute of Civil Engineering and Architecture, Sofia. 1973–1974, Sanatorium (new wing), Narechen, Bulgaria.

BIBLIOGRAPHY

BERBENLIEV, P. 1975 "Edna Godina bez Arkhitekt Ivan Popov." *Arkhitektura* 1:27–28.

BŬLGARSKA AKADEMII͡A NA NAUKITE 1965 *Kratka istorii͡a na Bŭlgarskata arkhitektura.* Sofia: The academy.

POPOV, IAN 1955 *Proportsii v Bŭlgarskata Arkhitektura.* Sofia: Nauka i Izkustvo.

POPOV, IVAN P. (1962)1971 *Klasicheski Arkhitekturni Formi.* Sofia: Tekhnika.

POPOV, IVAN P. 1963 *Metodi za Opredeliane na Svetlopropuskaemostta na Prozorechnite Konstruktsii.* Sofia: Godishnik na VISI.

POPOV, IVAN P. (1965)1969 *Vŭvedeniev Arkhitekturnoto Proektirane.* Sofia: Tekhnika.

POPOV, IVAN P. 1969 *Postroiavane na Senki vurhu Klassicheski Arkhitekturni Formi v Ortogonalna Proektsii͡a.* Sofia: Tekhnika.

POPOV, IVAN P. 1970 *Suvremenna Arkhitektura: (1850–1914).* Sofia: Tekhnika.

POPP, ALEXANDER

Alexander Popp (1891–1947) was a pupil and collaborator of PETER BEHRENS and later succeeded him as professor (1938–1945) at the Vienna Academy of Fine Arts. Together with Behrens, he built the Cigarette Factory (1929–1935) in Linz, at that time the most extensive skeletal building in Austria, monumental and strictly functional in attitude. Popp also designed the first structures of the former Reichswerke Hermann Göring—now VOEST—in Linz, functional steel or reinforced concrete skeletal buildings with exterior walls of clinker brick.

SOKRATIS DIMITRIOU
Translated from German by
Beverley R. Placzek

WORKS

1929–1935, Austria Tabakwerke AG (with Peter Behrens); 1938–1945, Buildings of the Reichswerke Hermann Göring; Linz, Austria

BIBLIOGRAPHY

ACHLEITNER, FRIEDRICH 1980 *Oberösterreich/Salzburg/Tirol/Vorarlberg.* Volume 1 in *Österreichische Architektur im 20. Jahrhundert.* Vienna: Residenz.

PÖPPELMANN, MATTHÄUS DANIEL

As architect to the ambitious Augustus the Strong of Saxony, Matthäus Daniel Pöppelmann (1662–1736) designed one of the most extraordinary structures of the eighteenth century, the Zwinger in Dresden. Pöppelmann was the best of a new breed, the architect as state official, educated and active entirely within the recently established *Bauamt* (office of public works). He belonged to a first generation of designers, among them JOHANN BERNARD FISCHER VON ERLACH in Austria, the DIENTZENHOFER BROTHERS in Bohemia, CASPAR MOOSBRUGGER in Swabia, and ANDREAS SCHLÜTER in Prussia, who, between 1680 and 1720, created a new architecture that was splendidly developed in central Europe for the next three-quarters of a century.

Pöppelmann left his hometown of Herford, Westphalia, which had been reduced to poverty by the Thirty Year War, and found his way to Dresden, the major city of Electoral Saxony, where he is documented in 1680 as employed by the *Bauamt.* Appointed *Baukondukteur* eleven years later, his position required the preparation of drawings and cost estimates, the review of financial records for construction, the supervisor of less significant building operations, and travel throughout Saxony to inspect new sites and advise on building damage. He assumed the responsibility for Augustus's most important design commissions when promoted to *Landbaumeister* (state architect) in 1705, and in 1718, at the age of fifty-six, became *Oberlandbaumeister* (senior state architect): the official course of his career was more steady than spectacular.

Pöppelmann's training and position represent a departure from tradition. Until this time, an architect was educated within the engineers' corps (as was JOHANN BALTHASAR NEUMANN), as an artist (as were the ASAM BROTHERS), or by means of books and travel, (that is, an amateur in the best sense of the term, as was Anselm Franz, Freiherr von Ritter zu Grünsteyn). Now the increasing amount of building promoted by the Saxon court required an effectively organized office of operations. Pöppelmann was the first architect of stature whose career was determined by this office from start to finish. The *Bauamt* in Saxony was initially organized and managed by Johann Georg Starcke, who set the tone for Dresden's official architecture with his palace in the Grosser Garten. After Starcke's death in 1695, Count August Christoph von Wackerbarth ran the office, until he was succeeded by JEAN DE BODT in 1728. Of the other architects in the *Bauamt,* the most important were Marcus Conrad Dietze and Johann Friedrich Karcher, who was primarily in charge of garden design and festivals. Activity at the *Bauamt* was dominated by Friedrich Augustus II, known as Augustus the Strong, the elector of Saxony (1694–1733) and king of Poland (1697–1704, 1709–1733). An aficionado of architecture and to a degree trained as an architect, he commonly provided the initial design ideas for projects, supervised their development, and closely followed construction. Not even the enthusiasm of the Schönborn, greatest patrons of the eighteenth century, matched the intensity with which Augustus pursued his architectural interests.

On March 25, 1701, a substantial part of the Dresden palace burned out, and for the next two decades Augustus pushed his architects to provide him with an appropriate successor building. From this considerable activity, only the Zwinger was ever realized, an orangerie expanded in size and program to accommodate royal festivals and the marriage festivities of Augustus's son. The projects record a succession of grand designs in the service of unfounded ambition. Augustus sent Dietze to Italy from 1701 to 1703 so that he could steep himself in palace architecture. When he returned, Dietze proposed an entirely new structure consisting of wings and courts arranged in rectangular patterns and spread over a terrain far larger than any of the imperial fora in Rome. In 1704, not long after developing this project, he died in a fire, and from then on Pöppelmann was in charge of palace operations. Pöppelmann's designs, encompassing his most active years as state architect, are a creative tour de force; the Zwinger alone suggests how impressive they would have been if built.

The first of Pöppelmann's projects, conceived on an imposing scale, are skillfully composed, well-balanced units enlivened by generous amounts of statuary and ornament on surfaces, frames, and skylines. In plans and elevations, his earlier response to architectural developments in Berlin between 1695 and 1703 are replaced by an obvious sympathy for the seventeenth-century Roman palazzo, the Parisian *hôtel,* and Claude Perrault's east façade of the Louvre. In 1710, Augustus sent Pöppelmann on a study trip to Prague, Vienna, and Rome. After his return, the architect produced an extraordinary series of façade elevations for the palace. The orders, rather than being distributed evenly and with restraint along the length of the façade, are gathered into dramatic sculptural groups about large entryways; the wall is transformed to a slender grid supporting huge windows that are richly framed; elaborate towers and domes are introduced as decisive verticals. Behind these designs stand impressions of Lucas von Hildebrandt's Viennese palace façades and the church fronts by Martino Longhi the Younger (see Longhi Family), Carlo Rainaldi, and Pietro Berrettini da Cortona. Yet they remain distinctive individual creations, at once festive and architectonic.

Pöppelmann's final palace project (1716–1718) was undertaken after his return from study in Paris in 1715 and before 1718, when the Zwinger, but not the palace, was irrevocably committed to completion. A complex and sophisticated arrangement of variously shaped courts and building wings are composed on parallel, perpendicular, and diagonal axes. The buildings are ingeniously shaped to the irregular, built edge of the city, but extended from it and at enormous length into a site bordered by new fortifications. Palace and Zwinger are joined in a single complex, an idea that Pöppelmann had begun to work with before his departure to Paris. Derived in plan from the seventeenth-century *hôtel* and in elevation from several sources—Michelangelo, Giovanni Lorenzo Bernini, and the Italian and French Louvre projects—the richly decorated ensemble is an apotheosis of Pöppelmann's palace plans and the most splendid of Augustus's pretensions to royal grandiloquence. Like the earlier projects, its scale exceeded the financial resources to which Augustus had access, and the effort remained a paper showpiece.

By 1718, with the marriage of the elector's heir imminent, an appropriate building was required to serve the festivities; the Zwinger was the only reasonable choice. The northern arcaded exedra, its three pavilions, the western wing, and the *Kronentor* ("crown gate" or entryway) were all standing. Augustus had already decided to make the Zwinger an enclosed garden rather than only an orangerie. Accordingly, the structure was built on a symmetrical plan of two exedra, each with three pavilions; long wings connected these units, creating a large court; and rectangular structures for a theater/opera and a ballroom (both since demolished) were attached to the exterior of the southern exedra. The notion of a curved, arcaded exedra controlling a large open space extends back to structures such as the fora of Trajan and Augustus in Rome, and Pöppelmann compared his design to spaces like these. The form had been picked up in central Europe about 1700; specifically in Dresden, Karcher had constructed an amphitheater in 1699 that employed a curved arcade with pavilions at the ends and apex, precisely the forms Pöppelmann would use in the Zwinger, but with far greater elegance.

Pöppelmann. Zwinger. Dresden, Germany. 1705/1708–1722

Pöppelmann. Zwinger. Dresden, Germany. 1705/1708–1722

The lively plan of the Zwinger is taken up in the animated, richly sculpted elevations and in the juxtapositions of low arcades and tall pavilions and entryway. The sculptor Balthasar Permoser and his team of carvers were extensively involved in the undertaking, so that architecture, sculpture, and decorative elements heighten one another with astonishing vigor—a circumstance that Pöppelmann especially praised. Freestanding stairs swing out into the space, are drawn up and into pavilions, and connect various levels of the building. They would have underscored in stone the variety of moving waters that were to be part of the design, though little was realized and less survives: Pöppelmann devised a cascade tower, grottoes, pools, and fountains that were to be located throughout the complex and even inside some buildings. The Zwinger, more than a lively setting for festivals, became its own festival of architecture. As if acknowledging that the building was as much on display as it served the purposes of display, Pöppelmann incorporated viewing platforms into the design: a wide stylobate, terraces, and passageways inside the arcades and on their roofs. The spectator is invited to experience the Zwinger from many vantage points close to the building, in it, and upon it, a sophisticated and distinctive self-presentation of the structure. After 1719, Pöppelmann proposed opening the east flank of the Zwinger (which had been enclosed for the marriage celebration with a wooden tribune) toward the Elbe as a long court ending in hemicycle and tower. But nothing more came of this than of any of the other palace projects, and in the early 1720s, further designing of the Zwinger–palace complex was abandoned.

Soon after the royal marriage of 1719, Pöppelmann was at work on another structure for festivities. The Palace at Pillnitz, a few kilometers up river from Dresden, was begun during the winter of 1720–1721 as a smaller, seven-bay building. Put up in a few months, Augustus then wished it enlarged; this entailed a higher roof, a four-column portico, and five-bay pavilions to either side. Realized in a "Chinese" mode—pagoda-shaped roofs, oriental motifs and decoration—it remains one of the liveliest, largest, and most elaborate buildings in this fashion. Brightly colored, many of the architectural elements were illusionistically painted on the exterior, lending an air of lively impermanence to this solidly constructed building. A more fashionable and festive structure has rarely been achieved.

Pöppelmann's effectiveness as an architect can also be measured by his ability to adjust to a variety of building situations. At the hunting lodge of Moritzburg, he adapted his work to an existing structure and the remodeling by others. For the Jägerhof in Dresden-Neustadt he demonstrated that he could integrate the new design of a large building, its extensive courts, and an oval amphitheater with existing structures; and in a second project, that he could satisfy the same program with an idealized plan independent of the setting. The stud farm at Graditz and the Peterstor in Leipzig reveal his talent for locating new construction within very different settings—a landscape on the one hand, an urban environment on the other—but in such a way that the site in either case is both acknowledged and transformed.

The rebuilding and enlarging of the so-called Dutch Palace in Dresden marks a shift in Pöppelmann's position as architect to Augustus. During the first phase of alterations (1715–1719), Pöppelmann was in charge of the project, but already in 1722–1723, when another story was added to the building, Zacharias Longuelune, brought to Dresden in 1715 by Augustus, had become influential. Longuelune's work, based on Parisian training tempered by a stay in Berlin, was not dissimilar to that of Jean de Bodt, also French-trained. The tone of the palace design was established by Longuelune. It is a linear, flat composition of wall panels and windows, played off against the Louvre-like entryway. Pöppelmann's curved roofs over the corner wings and sparse touches of ornament are reduced to weak reflections of his vigorous creations at the Zwinger and Pillnitz. Yet for Augustus, the palace was oriental in character, an appropriate setting for his Japanese and Meissen porcelain—thus the change to its present name, Japanese Palace, even before completion. Although one of Augustus's larger and more prestigious undertakings, the palace as built suffers from changing design sensibilities that immobilize the exterior.

In central Europe for most of the eighteenth century, the church was the most important building type: most discussed, most respected, most built, richest in architectural interpretations. Pöppelmann's churches, however, are few and undistinguished. Augustus had converted to the Roman Catholic faith for political reasons, but Protestantism remained strong in Saxony. The Protestant church tended to be a plain structure that held large numbers of people; its architectural and theoretical underpinnings were developed by JOSEF FURTTENBACH and LEONHARD CHRISTOPH STURM in the seventeenth and early eighteenth centuries. The most elaborate Protestant church built during the eighteenth century stood in Dresden, GEORG BÄHR's Frauenkirche. From the outset, Pöppelmann showed little interest in obtaining this commission, and Bahr was soon in sole charge. The few churches Pöppelmann did build were small, rectangular shells. His most impressive design was for the Dreikönigskirche in Dresden-Neustadt (1731–1739), but even this project was taken over by Bahr after construction had been begun. Bahr opened the interior by pushing the piers close to the walls and placing a dome over the center of the building, which decisively changed Pöppelmann's original design.

Pöppelmann was responsible for much utilitarian construction throughout Saxony, undertakings such as fortifications, houses, gates, bridges, roads, dams, and embankments. His best known effort in this regard was the widening of the twelfth-century bridge across the Elbe. Promoted by Augustus to exceed the most glorious bridges in central Europe, Pöppelmann dramatically reduced costs and construction time by ingeniously widening the bridge. He cantilevered raised sidewalks from the edges of the original structure, and used iron railings to minimize the additional weight. Ordinances regulating bridge cleaning and traffic followed, making this a link vital to the economy and cityscape of Dresden: Bernardo Bellotto's shimmering views of the city display its aesthetic prominence.

From the later 1720s on, as Augustus began to favor Longuelune for larger design projects, Pöppelmann turned increasingly to the administration of the *Bauamt* and the completion of its many undertakings. In the early 1730s, a succession of deaths closed off part of his architectural life, Permoser in 1732, Augustus himself in 1733, and Wackerbarth in 1734. His own health gave out in 1735, and he had his will drawn up; on 17 January 1736 he died in Dresden.

CHRISTIAN F. OTTO

WORKS

1705/1708–1722, Zwinger (gardens, alterations, additions, and structures); 1715–1732, Dutch Palace (restoration and enlargement; with Zacharias Longuelune and Jean de Bodt; now the Japanese Palace); Dresden, Germany. 1720–1722, Palace, Pillnitz, near Dresden, Germany. 1721, Peterstor, Leipzig, Germany. 1722ff., Hunting Lodge (alterations and rebuilding), Moritzburg, Germany. 1727, Elbe Bridge (Augustus Bridge); 1731–1739, Church of the Epiphany (Dreikonigskirche, with George Bahr), Neustadt; Dresden, Germany.

BIBLIOGRAPHY

ASCHE, SIGFRIED (1966)1978 *Balthasar Permoser und die Barockskulptur des Dresdner Zwingers.* Berlin: Deutscher Verlag für Kunstwissenschaft.

GURLITT, CORNELIUS 1924 *August der Starke: Ein Fürstenleben aus der Zeit des deutschen Barock.* 2 vols. Dresden, Germany: Sibyllen.

HECKMANN, HERMANN 1954 *Matthäus Daniel Pöppelmann als Zeichner.* Dresden, Germany: VEB Verlag der Kunst.

Pöppelmann. Palace. Pillnitz, near Dresden, Germany. 1720–1722

HECKMANN, HERMANN 1972 *Matthäus Daniel Pöppelmann: Leben und Werk.* Munich and Berlin: Deutscher Kunstverlag.

HEMPEL, EBERHARD 1961 *Der Zwinger zu Dresden, Grundzüge und Schicksale seiner künstlerischen Gestaltung.* Berlin: Deutscher Verein für Kunstwissenschaft.

SPONSEL, JEAN-LOUIS 1924 *Der Zwinger, die Hoffeste und die Schlossbaupläne zu Dresden.* Dresden, Germany: Stengel.

PORDEN, WILLIAM

William Porden's (1755?–1822) reputation rested upon additions to The Pavilion, Brighton (1803–1812), and reconstruction of Eaton Hall, Cheshire (1804–1812) in an elaborate Regency Gothic, his major style. He studied with JAMES WYATT (was possibly his assistant 1784–1785), exhibiting at the Royal Academy from 1779, and became surveyor to the second Earl Grosvenor 1785–1821, designing Eccleston Church, Cheshire (1806?–1809) and refurbishing Grosvenor House, London (1807–1808). Primarily a country house architect, he remodeled Putney Park, Surrey (1794) in the neoclassical style.

R. WINDSOR LISCOMBE

WORKS

*1787–1789, Phillimore Place, Kensington; 1790, Ebury Chapel, Chelsea; London. 1794, Putney Park (remodeled), Surrey, England. 1795–1796, South Kelsey Church, Lincolnshire, England. 1803–1812, The Pavilion (additions); 1804, Mrs. Fitzherbert House (now the Young Men's Christian Association); Brighton, England. 1804–1812, Eaton Hall (reconstruction); 1806?–1809, Eccleston Church; Cheshire, England. 1807, Shottesbrooke Park, Berkshire, England. *1807–1808, Grosvenor House (refurbished), London.

BIBLIOGRAPHY

ACLOQUE, GUY, and CORNFORTH, JOHN 1971 "The Eternal Gothic of Eaton." *Country Life* 149:304–307, 360–364.

CONNOR, PATRICK 1978 "Unexecuted Designs for the Royal Pavilion at Brighton." *Apollo* 107:194–196.

CORNFORTH, JOHN 1973 "Old Grosvenor House." *Country Life* 154:1538–1541.

HOBHOUSE, HERMIONE 1971 Pages 53, 88–89 in *Thomas Cubitt: Master Builder.* London: Macmillan.

ROBERTS, HENRY D. 1939 *History of the Royal Pavilion, Brighton.* London: Country Life.

PORTA, GIACOMO DELLA

With the death of GIACOMO VIGNOLA in 1573, Giacomo della Porta (1532/1533?–1602) became the leading Roman architect of the late sixteenth century. Of Lombard origin, he was born in Porlezza, although Rome became the stage for the prodigious activity that earned him the title of "Architetto del Popolo Romano." Not only did he complete several projects started by MICHELANGELO, but as architect to the popes and the Roman nobility, he was associated with all the major building enterprises of the day.

The son and grandson of sculptors, he began his career making stucco decorations, and learned the technical and formal aspects of architecture through apprenticeship and association with Guidetto Guidetti, Vignola, and perhaps Michelangelo. His unusual sense for decorative details and his formidable technical competence derived from a training based more on practical knowledge than on speculative thinking. He was a practitioner who rose from the ranks.

Porta. Il Gesù. Rome. 1571–1584

Della Porta's first important commission, while still associated with Guidetti, was the Oratorio dell' Arciconfraternita del Santissimo Crocifisso di San Marcello (1562–1568). On the death of Guidetti, della Porta was appointed to supervise the works on the Capitoline Hill (1564). He modified Michelangelo's plans by adding a large window to the central bay of the Conservators' Palace (1565–1584) and a fourth opening to the oval design of the pavement. The façade and staircase of the Palazzo Senatorio (1593–1602) are also his work.

In 1573, he succeeded Vignola as architect in chief of St. Peter's, a position he held until his death. He built the western arm of the crossing and, under the pontificate of Sixtus V, he erected in collaboration with DOMENICO FONTANA the great dome (1586–1592) on which his fame primarily rests. Michelangelo's plan was changed, and the double-shelled structure, vertically articulated by buttresses, ribs, and lantern, was given a pointed profile. In addition the Chapel of Gregory XIII (1574–1578), begun by Michelangelo and Vignola, was completed, and the Chapel of Clement VIII (1594–1601) was built.

The Oratorio del Crocifisso had been a modest commission, but it was an important stepping stone in his professional career. The appointment to St. Peter's came following a recommendation to Pope Gregory XIII from Tommaso dei Cavalieri, the patrician friend of Michelangelo who, as a member of the confraternity, had played an important role in the construction of the oratory. The confraternity had Alessandro Farnese as its cardinal protector, and it was Farnese who, having turned down Vignola's plan for the façade of Il Gesù, the mother church of the Jesuit order, accepted the design submitted in 1571 by della Porta. He completed the façade and the great barrel vault in 1577, and directed building operations until the church was completed in 1584. In the oratory, the balanced composition of the façade may still have indicated an indebtedness to Vignola; in Il Gesù, della Porta turned clearly away from him and replaced the serenely harmonious equilibrium of Vignola's project with a new dynamic system. The central portal was strongly emphasized and became the climax of a system of forces: pilasters, bays, openings, sculptural decorations, and broken entablature are now all in function of the central bay that assumes the aspect of an emphasized vertical unit.

The tendency toward verticalism and an implicit understanding of Michelangelo's style are also revealed in the façade of San Luigi dei Francesi (1580–1584), and in the small church of Santa Maria ai Monti (1580), where strongly projected pilasters, rising between the side chapels, break up the continuous space of the aisless Gesù-type nave. In the nave of Sant'Andrea della Valle (1591), the pilasters became powerful clusters and created with their vigorous movement into the transverse arches of the vault a series of compartmentalized bays that stressed the verticality of the interior. For the first time in Rome, twin towers flanked the two-story façade of Sant'Atanasio ai Greci (c.1580–1583) and Trinità dei Monti (c.1583) probably originated in his design.

In the octagonal church of Santa Maria Scala Coeli (1582–1584), della Porta turned to the problem of a centrally planned building. Its dome (unlike St. Peter's which it antedates) is deeply set in the drum, and seems to arrest with its rigid, flattened shape all interior vertical flow; the exterior demonstrates the architect's interest in vigorous sculptural forms through bold juxtapositions of planes and corners, flat and convex surfaces. The problem of a domed, centralized church and its relationship to an adjacent longitudinal structure also engaged his attention in a number of unrealized projects: in the University of Rome, a centrally planned church should have completed the harmonious, rectangular courtyard of the Sapienza (1594), and in Florence he was asked by the Grand Duke Ferdinando I to build a large funerary chapel behind the choir of the Medicean church of San Lorenzo (1598).

Della Porta's palaces carry some of the most illustrious names in sixteenth-century Rome. Palazzo Farnese (c.1573), where he added the upper loggia to the garden façade, had set the style for palace design. From its long, smooth façade interrupted by evenly spaced windows and a central door, della Porta developed a distinctive new type. In Palazzo Crescenzi-Serlupi (1585), the horizontal alignment of the windows is underlined by a continuous band, the mezzanine, the heavy cornice; yet, since the windows are grouped at intervals which progressively accelerate toward the central axis of the door, another rhythm is created in a complex counterpoint of verticals and horizontals. For the Aldobrandini family, della Porta created one of the greatest villas in Frascati (1601), later completed by CARLO MADERNO who also modified his design for the gardens' "water-theatre."

Della Porta was also responsible for many of the fountains which carried water to Rome from the new papal aqueducts. They usually consist of superimposed basins of beautiful proportions enlivened by sculptural decorations and the effects of water that splashes from the highest into the lower bowls.

Porta. San Luigi dei Francesi. Rome. 1580–1584

Porta. Trinità dei Monti. Rome. c.1583

Della Porta's work was a transition between the classical style of cinquecento and baroque architecture. He reacted against the correctness of Vignola by synthetizing—rather than rejecting—the classical vocabulary, and transmitted Michelangelo's lesson by simplifying his complexities and eliminating his ambiguities. His search for new forms, which often resulted in an inventive and decorative treatment of surfaces, was not consistently or decisively sustained. Yet, his concentration on the decorative interaction of all parts, unified dynamic movement and vertical clarity represented in late sixteenth century architecture a progressive trend—and his legacy to the masters of the baroque.

JOSEPHINE VON HENNEBERG

WORKS

1562–1568, Oratorio dell'Arciconfraternita del Santissimo Crocifisso di San Marcello; c.1564, Santa Caterina dei Funari (façade); 1564–1573, Santa Maria Maggiore (Sforza Chapel); c.1565–1571, San Giovanni in Laterano (Massimo Chapel); 1565–1584, Conservators' Palace, Capitoline Hill; 1571–1584, Il Gesù (façade, barrel vault, and completion of construction); 1572–1578, Fountain, Piazza del Popolo (now in Piazza Nicosia); c.1573, Palazzo Farnese (upper loggia on the garden side); 1573–1579, Senator's Palace (interior), Capitoline Hill; 1574–1578, North and South Fountains, Piazza Navona; 1574–1578, St. Peter's (Chapel of Gregory XIII); 1575, Fountain, Piazza del Pantheon; 1578–1585, Cordonata (ramp) and Piazza, Capitoline Hill; c.1580, Palazzo Capizucchi Gasparri, Piazza Campitelli; 1580, Palazzo Serlupi-Lovatelli, Piazza Campitelli; 1580, Santa Maria ai Monti; c.1580–1583, Sant'Atanasio dei Greci; 1580–1584, San Luigi dei Francesi (façade); 1581–1584, Fountain, Piazza Colonna; 1581–1584, Fountain of the Turtles, Piazza Mattei; 1582–1584, Santa Maria Scala Coeli; 1582–1588, Fountain of the Egyptian Lions, bottom of the ramp to the Capitoline Hill; 1582–1591, Palazzo Ruggieri, Corso Vittorio Emanuele; 1582–1602, San Giovanni dei Fiorentini (nave); c.1583, Palazzo

Maffei-Marescotti, Via dei Cestari; c.1583, Trinità dei Monti (façade); 1584–1587, Palazzo Aldobrandini-Chigi (beginning), Piazza Colonna; 1585, Palazzo Crescenzi-Serlupi, Via del Seminario; 1586–1587, St. Peter's (dome; with Domenico Fontana); 1587–1592, Fountain, Piazza San Marco; 1588–1589, Fountain, Piazza Santa Maria dei Monti; 1589, Fountain, Piazza Campitelli; 1589, Fountain, Piazza Montanara; 1589–1590, Fountain, Piazza Ara Coeli; 1589–1593, Fountain, now in Piazza del Quirinale; 1590, "La Terrina" Fountain, Piazza Chiesa Nuova; 1591, Fountain, now in Via del Progresso; 1591, Sant'Andrea della Valle (nave); c.1593, Palazzo Paluzzi Albertoni, Piazza Campitelli; 1593–1602, Senator's Palace (façade), Capitoline Hill; 1594–1601, St. Peter's (Chapel of Clement VIII); *1594–1604, Palazzo Giustini-Piombino (completed by Carlo Lombardi); 1596–1597, Pucci Tomb, Santa Maria sopra Minerva; 1597–1602, San Giovanni in Laterano (transept); 1599, San Nicola in Carcere (façade); 1599, San Paolo alle Tre Fontane; 1600, Santa Maria sopra Minerva (Aldobrandini Chapel); Rome. 1601, Villa Aldobrandini, Frascati, Italy.

BIBLIOGRAPHY

ACKERMAN, JAMES S. 1971 *The Architecture of Michelangelo.* Harmondsworth, England, and Baltimore: Penguin.

ARSLAN, WART 1927–1928 "Forme Architettoniche Civili di Giacomo della Porta." *Bollettino D'Arte* Series 2 6:508–528.

BAGLIONE, GIOVANNI (1642)1935 *Le Vite de' Pittori, Scultori, ed Architetti.* Reprint. Rome: Calzoni.

BATTISTI, EUGENIO 1961 "Disegni Cinquecenteschi per San Giovanni dei Fiorentini." *Quaderni dell'Istituto di Storia della Architettura* 31–48:185–194.

GIOVANNONI, GUSTAVO 1935 "Chiese della seconda metà del Cinquecento in Roma." Pages 177–235 in *Saggi sulla Architettura del Rinascimento.* Milan: Fratelli Treves Editori.

HEYDENREICH, LUDWIG H., and LOTZ, WOLFGANG 1974 *Architecture in Italy, 1400–1600.* Harmondsworth, England, and Baltimore: Penguin.

HIBBARD, HOWARD 1961 "The Early History of Sant'Andrea della Valle." *Art Bulletin* 43:289–318.

LEFEVRE, RENATO 1971 "Della Porta e Maderno a Palazzo Chigi." *Palladio* 21:151–158.

ONOFRIO, CESARE D' 1957 *Le Fontane di Roma.* Rome: Staderini.

ONOFRIO, CESARE D' 1963 *La Villa Aldobrandini di Frascati.* Rome: Staderini.

PECCHIAI, PIO 1950 *Il Campidoglio nel Cinquecento, sulla Scorta dei Documenti.* Rome: Ruffolo.

PECCHIAI, PIO 1952 *Il Gesù di Roma Descritto ed Illustrato.* Rome: Società Grafica Romana.

PROJA, GIOVANNI BATTISTA 1970 *S. Nicola in Carcere.* Rome: Marietti.

RUFINI, E. 1957 *San Giovanni dei Fiorentini.* Rome: Marietti.

SCHWAGER, KLAUS 1961–1962 "Kardinal Pietro Aldobrandinis Villa di Belvedere in Frascati." *Römisches Jahrbuch für Kunstgeschichte* 9–10:289–382.

SCHWAGER, KLAUS 1975 "Giacomo della Porta's Herkunft und Anfänge in Rom: Tatsachen, Indizien, Mutmassungen." *Römisches Jahrbuch für Kunstgeschichte* 15:109–141.

THELEN, H. 1961 "Der Palazzo della Sapienza in Rom." *Miscellanea Bibliothecae Hertzianae* 1:258–307.

TIBERIA, VITALIANO 1971*a* "Alcune note su Giacomo della Porta." *Palladio* 21:181–183.

TIBERIA, VITALIANO 1971*b* "San Giuseppe dei Falegnami: notizie storiche." *Palladio* 21:184–188.

TIBERIA, VITALIANO 1974 *Giacomo della Porta: un architetto fra Manierismo e Barocco.* Rome: Bulzoni.

VENTURI, ADOLFO 1939 *Storia dell'Arte Italiana. XI: Architettura del Cinquecento, II.* Milan: Hoepli.

VON HENNEBERG, JOSEPHINE 1970 "An Early Work by Giacomo della Porta: The Oratorio del Santissimo Crocifisso di San Marcello in Rome." *Art Bulletin* 52:157–171.

VON HENNEBERG, JOSEPHINE 1977 "Documentation: Emilio dei Cavalieri, Giacomo della Porta, and G. B. Montano." *Journal of the Society of Architectural Historians* 36:252–255.

WASSERMAN, JACK 1964 "Giacomo della Porta's Church for the Sapienza in Rome." *Art Bulletin* 46:501–510.

WITTKOWER, RUDOLF 1964 *La Cupola di San Pietro di Michelangelo: Riesame Critico delle Testimonianze Contemporanee.* Florence: Sansoni Editore.

PORTMAN, JOHN

Born in South Carolina and educated in Atlanta, Georgia, John Portman (1924–) had a vision to design cities not just individual buildings. He certainly changed the face of Atlanta in his role of entrepreneur-architect and developer who conceived, designed, financed, and promoted this large-scale urban complex.

Although not usually praised for their architectural beauty, Portman's buildings are "crowd-pleasers" and show concern for the kinetics of people traffic. His first major endeavor was the Peachtree Center in downtown Atlanta (1961), a collection of buildings that includes the Merchandise Mart and the Hyatt Regency Hotel (1967). Portman uses what he calls "the elements of surprise," unexpected architectural gestures intended to create excitement, such as the revolving Polaris restaurant on the top of the Hyatt Regency or his playfully lighted, glass-enclosed, capsule-shaped elevator that scurries up and down the exterior wall of a building. Portman liberally uses "human environmental connections" such as trees, plants, birds, and water to aid the desired exchange between people and structure. His dramatic use of light and space is carefully conceived to help relieve the impending feelings of claustrophobia caused by modern urban congestion.

LYNDA GREENBERG

WORKS

1961, Peachtree Center; 1964, John Portman House; 1967, Hyatt Regency Hotel; Atlanta, Ga. 1971, Hyatt Regency O'Hare Hotel, Chicago, 1975, World Trade Mart, Brussels. 1977, Renaissance Center, Detroit, Mich.

BIBLIOGRAPHY

BARNETT, JONATHAN 1966 "John Portman: Atlanta's One-man Urban Renewal Program." *Architectural Record* 139, no. 1:133–140.

LEITNER, BERNHARD 1973 "John Portman: Architecture Is Not a Building." *Art in America* 61, no. 2:80–82.

PORTMAN, JOHN, and BARNETT, JONATHAN 1976 *The Architect as Developer.* New York: McGraw-Hill.

PORTMAN, JOHN, and BARNETT, JONATHAN 1977 "An Architecture for People and Not for Things." *Architectural Record* 161, no. 1:133-140.

PORTOIS, PETER

Peter, or Pierre, Portois (1812–1900) made unsubstantiated claims to be the first American architect with Ecole des Beaux-Arts training. After practicing in his native Belgium, he came to California with the Gold Rush. He built fine neoclassic commercial structures three decades before the style appeared elsewhere in the United States.

ANNE BLOOMFIELD

WORKS

*1851, Adelphi Theater; *1854, Wright's Bank Building; *1857, Hibernia Society and Bank Building; *1863, West End Hotel; *1875, Commercial Hotel; San Francisco.

BIBLIOGRAPHY

BUCHANAN, AGNES FOSTER 1906 "Some Early Business Buildings of San Francisco." *Architectural Record* 20:15–32.

"Death of One of the City's Pioneers." 1900 *San Francisco Examiner* August 21:4.

Great Register of the City and County of San Francisco. 1867 13080, July.

KIRKER, HAROLD (1960)1973 Pages 52, 82–83, 213, and plates 19, 26, 32 in *California's Architectural Frontier: Style and Tradition in the Nineteenth Century.* Santa Barbara, Calif., and Salt Lake City, Utah: Peregrine Smith.

VANDALL 1876 *San Francisco City Directory* 10.

PORUMBESCU, NICOLAE

Nicolae Porumbescu (1919–) graduated from the Institute of Architecture in Bucharest in 1947. His name is connected with many outstanding achievements in contemporary architecture. Following the approach of his predecessors in applying traits of traditional Rumanian architecture to modern designs, he has succeeded in giving each of his buildings an individual character. His most recent works give evidence of a new restlessness, showing elaborate baroque details.

CONSTANTIN MARIN MARINESCU

WORKS

1951, Hotel, Winter Sport Center, Brasov, Rumania. 1953, People's Fraternity Theater; 1960, State Circus; 1965, Urban Development Plan, Balta Alba; Bucharest. 1970, Urban Renewal Plan, Suceava, Rumania. 1981, Polytechnic Institute (with others), Iashi, Rumania.

BIBLIOGRAPHY

IONESCU, GRIGORE 1969 Pages 146–147 in *Arhitectura in Romania: Perioda anilor 1944–1969.* Bucharest: Editura Academiei Socialiste Romañia.

IONESCU, GRIGORE 1972 Pages 484–564 in *Histoire de l'Architecture en Roumanie.* Editura Academiei Republicii Sociliste Romañia.

"The Municipality of Iashi City." 1981 *Architectura* 2-3:9–81.

POSI, PAOLO

Among the followers of the late baroque in Rome was the architect and decorator Paolo Posi (1708–1776). Born in Siena, Italy, he began his career in earnest when he succeeded GABRIELE VALVASSORI as architect to the powerful Colonna family in Rome (1732).

His most important work was the façade of the national church of the Sienese in Rome, Santa Caterina on the Via Guilia (1760). Based on earlier churches, such as PIETRO BERRETTINI DA CORTONA's Santi Martina e Luca, Posi's small-scale work reduces the giant movement of masses characteristic of his baroque model to a kind of decorative whim. In place of the grand gesture, the two wings of the façade curl around to hug the central bay in a motion that is almost witty.

Posi was also responsible for the choir of the Church of Santa Maria dell'Anima (1750) in Rome. In this high hall church (the property of the German community in Rome), the sharp, brilliantly lighted space illuminates the choir with a high-spirited splash of color.

In some of Posi's works, such as his decorations for the Festa della Chinea, one sees the beginning of the dissolution of a baroque energy and the assertion of more rigid, academic values. Posi was also active as a restorer at the Pantheon, and he was appointed architect to St. Peter's, though he seems not to have done much work there.

His most noted work in Siena was the campanile for the Church of San Francesco (1765).

Nicholas Adams

WORKS

1750, Santa Maria dell'Anima (renovation and decoration of choir); 1757, Pantheon (renovation of attic zone); 1760, Santa Caterina dei Senesi (façade); Rome. 1765, Church of San Francesco (campanile), Siena, Italy.

BIBLIOGRAPHY

Portoghesi, Paolo 1970 *Roma Barocca: The History of an Architectonic Culture.* Cambridge, Mass.: M.I.T. Press.

POST, GEORGE BROWNE

On December 13, 1911, the American Institute of Architects bestowed the Gold Medal, its most prestigious award, on George Browne Post (1837–1913) for his distinguished services to the profession. This practice was introduced in 1907, and in the four years intervening the medal had been offered to only two other architects, namely, Sir Aston Webb of England and Charles Follen McKim (see McKim, Mead, and White), a leader along with Post of what has been called the "Eastern Establishment" in the United States. Post was seventy-four at the time, in the twilight of a long, active, and illustrious career. A photograph taken for the occasion pictures him as a man of impressive stature, of corpulent figure, a florid complexion, and a flowing handlebar mustache: a portrait of a prominent and successful businessman of the period.

Highlights of that career show that he contributed importantly, as a designer and engineer, to the origin and rise of the skyscraper from its inception around 1870 onward. Along with Richard Morris Hunt and William F. McKim, he was invited to participate in the planning for the Chicago Columbian Exposition of 1893 and was assigned the Manufacturers and Liberal Arts Building, the largest structure at the Fair.

It was at this point that he began to collect the long series of honors which were to come his way. From 1893–1897 he was president of the Architectural League of New York; president of the AIA from 1896–1899; and president of the local New York chapter in 1904. In 1901 he was decorated a Chevalier de la Legion d'Honneur, the first of many international awards. Between 1901–1909 he was director of the Municipal Arts Society; received an honorary degree of doctor of law from Columbia University in 1908; elected president of the Fine Arts Federation of New York in 1898; president and charter member of the National Arts Club from 1898–1905; appointed by the secretary of state a delegate to the World's Congress of Architects in London; made honorary corresponding member of the Royal Institute of British Architects in 1907; chosen by President Theodore Roosevelt to be on the National Advisory Board on Fuels and Structural Materials 1906–1909; elected an associate of the National Academy of Design in 1907 and an academician of the Academy in 1908; appointed in 1908 a member of the Permanent Committee of the International Congress of Architects; selected by Roosevelt a member of the Bureau of Fine Arts in 1909. These assignments and others indicate in what high respect George Post was held both in and outside of his profession.

Post's practice was widespread. Jobs were going on not only in New York but also in New Jersey, Connecticut, Pennsylvania, Ohio, Michigan, Wisconsin, Washington, Virginia, and Canada. Although he was primarily a commercial architect, he designed fashionable and expensive residences for the Vanderbilt and Huntington families on Fifth Avenue in New York, more than thirty houses for his neighbors in his hometown of Bernardsville, New Jersey, and many more on the East Coast. The firm had over twenty-five hotels to its credit, a state capitol and other municipal buildings, plans for college campuses, and designs for individual buildings. Add to these categories churches, hospitals, apartment complexes, restaurants, and theaters and one has an idea of the nature and scope of the firm's operation.

Despite the extraordinary honorary and professional demands on his time and energy, Post found relaxation and inspiration in travel abroad almost every year, an office statement reveals, returning laden down with sketchbooks filled with drawings of buildings and details that caught his attention. He was an accomplished water colorist and was personally responsible for many of the firm's renderings.

Post was born in New York City. His ancestry can be traced back to Lieutenant Richard Post who settled in Southhampton, Long Island, in 1640 and to Colonel Benjamin Church who came from Duxbury, Massachusetts, in 1639. Perhaps this explains in part the military training he received at Churchill's School, Ossining, New York, in his early years. In 1858, he graduated from New York University with a B.S. in civil engineering. Being mainly interested in architecture, he entered the office of Richard M. Hunt as a student draftsman. He remained there until 1860 when he formed a partnership with a fellow student, Charles D. Gambrill. The Civil War put a temporary end to this relationship and in 1861 Post was commissioned a captain in the 22nd Regiment of the New York State National Guard. He served for four months in 1862 and a similar period in 1863, became an aide to General Ambrose Burnside, saw action in the Battle of Fredericksburg, and subsequently rose to the rank of colonel.

By January 1864, he was once again working with Gambrill. This association continued until 1866. The New York New Building Docket 1007 contains an entry dated October 16, 1867 by Mead and Post, indicating that by the fall of that year Post had another partner, possibly the same person who later was associated with William McKim and STANFORD WHITE in the celebrated firm of McKim, Mead, and White. Alternate Plan # 21 of February 21, 1868 was submitted solely by Post, suggesting that by this time Post was on his own and was preparing to enter the competition for the Equitable Life Assurance Building which was to catapult him to fame.

The Equitable Life Assurance Building (1868–1870) in New York, a milestone in American architecture, was the first building planned with the passenger elevator in mind. This made possible increased height and rental revenue, thus giving rise to a large number of structures in the 1870s and early 1880s that were referred to as "elevator buildings." These averaged between 100 and 120 feet in height or twice the size of the ordinary commercial edifice. The winning design was submitted by ARTHUR GILMAN and Edward Kendall, but Post was asked to rethink the structural solution with an eye to reducing the cost. Since all of the submissions show an eight-story building, it can be assumed that the elevator was a competition requirement and therefore probably was the brainchild of Henry Hyde, chairman of the building committee. Nevertheless, Post enthusiastically supported the idea and, despite the warnings of conservative real estate agents, agreed to lease the "unrentable upper stories." Upon completion, the edifice was an immediate success and Post was offered substantially more than double the price he paid, but he chose not to accept.

His association with the Equitable was long-lasting and had a remarkable effect on Post's career. In 1872, he finished the Troy Savings Bank. Thereafter followed the Williamsburgh Savings Bank in Brooklyn (1875) and the Western Union Building in New York (1873–1875). This structure, along with the Tribune Building erected at the same time by R. Hunt, were the first two skyscrapers raised in the world. The former was 230 feet tall, the latter 260 feet, or about four times the height of the average business building of the era.

Of these two buildings, Montgomery Schuyler (1902) writes: "the pupil evidently surpassed his master. Because in the original Tribune Building, Mr. Hunt confronted with a novel problem, was fain to resort to a group of stories, instead of a single story as the new architectural unit, whereas Mr. Post in his first essay, hit upon the arrangement of a triple division into a base, shaft and capital, following Aristotle's requirement." In addition, it should be noted that in designing the shaft, Post employed a functional rather than an eclectic mode of vertical piers and horizontal beams and spandrels with window openings to form a rational grid pattern, a composition which the architect may have seen in the nearby Park Row Stores built by Griffith Thomas (see THOMAS AND THOMAS) in 1850. The Western Union was a milestone in many respects. Future tall buildings were to discard the expensive and unrentable mansards, the pavilions, and the double-storied orders which had little or nothing to do with the interior spaces, and adopted instead the flat roof with cornice and a gridlike, sparsely decorated façade.

From this time on Post's commissions multiplied despite the severe depression of 1873–1879. (His New York Hospital dates from 1875–1876, the Long Island Historical Society Building from 1878–1879, and the Smith Building in New York from 1879–1880.) Economic recovery made possible some of Post's major works, such as the Post Building (1880–1881), where he broke away from the block plan so common from the 1820s through the 1860s to the U-shaped formula which made possible greater amounts of well-lighted office space and thus enhanced revenue. This usage was further refined in the Mills Building in New York (1881–1883) which can be called the first modern office building. It was ten stories above ground, 156 feet high, covered an area of 23,000 square feet, had ten elevators, was wired with 5,588 of Edison's newly invented incandescent lights, had a steam-heating system to replace the ancient coal-burning fireplaces, three convenient entrances from the several streets for the employees of the eight hundred tenants, and a grand lobby brightly lit by a rotunda with skylight.

In the New York Produce Exchange (1881–1885) Post proved his engineering skill. He admirably solved the difficult problems involved in producing a very large unencumbered space of thirty-two hundred square feet for the exchange business together with a ring of three hundred offices for its members. His arcaded Renaissance style inspired commercial design for years to come and probably led to his invitation to the Chicago Exposition and the Manufacturers and Liberal Arts Building (1893), which also required considerable amounts of unobstructed space. When completed, the Ex-

George Browne Post. New York Stock Exchange. 1901–1904

position structure covered thirty-four acres. The central hall, entirely clear of columns, was 387-feet wide, 210-feet high, and 1278-feet long, a vastness unprecedented at the time. The exterior featured as a centerpiece a Roman triumphal arch with two smaller versions at each end. These were strung together by an arcade of fifty-eight smaller arches running the length of one side of the façade.

The best known examples of Post's arcaded manner were the old New York Times Building (1888–1890), the Union Trust Company Building (New York [1889–1890]), the Prudential Life Insurance Company Building (Newark [1890]), the Havemeyer Building (New York [1891–1892]), the Weld Building (New York [1895–1898]), and the Park Building (Pittsburgh [1896]). Of these the Times, the Union Trust, the Prudential, and especially the Erie County Savings Bank Building (Erie [1890–1893]) bear witness by their rough-textured masonry surfaces to the powerful influence still exerted by H. H. RICHARDSON's Romanesque Revival mode.

Toward the end of the century, Post turned to a more austere Roman Revival style based primarily on the Pantheon in Rome. The Bank of Pittsburgh (1894) had a pedimented façade supported by six Corinthian columns with a squarish block at the rear. His most famous structure was the New York Stock Exchange (1901–1904), which displays much the same features. The Cleveland Trust Company Building (1907–1908) adds a Roman dome which covers a noble space for the firm's transactions.

In 1905 Post's two sons, William S. and James O., entered the firm as equal partners under the name of George B. Post & Sons, easing the burden of management for their father who died suddenly on November 28, 1913 at the family home in Bernardsville, New Jersey.

WINSTON WEISMAN

WORKS

1868–1870, Equitable Life Assurance Company Building; New York. 1872, Troy Savings Bank, N.Y. *1873–1875, Western Union Building; 1874–1875, Chickering Hall; New York. 1875, Williamsburgh Savings Bank, Brooklyn, N.Y. 1875–1876, New York Hospital. 1878–1879, Long Island Historical Society Building, Brooklyn, N.Y. 1879–1880, Smith Building; 1880–1881, Post Building; 1881–1883, Mills Building; 1881–1885, Produce Exchange; 1882–1893, Cornelius Vanderbilt House; 1883–1885, Cotton Exchange; 1884, Mortimer Building, New York. 1884–1885, Hamilton Club, Brooklyn, N.Y. 1888–1890, New York Times Building (now part of Pace College); 1889–1890, Pulitzer Building; 1889–1890, Union Trust Company Building; New York. 1890, Prudential Life Insurance Company Building, Newark, N.J. 1890–1893, Erie County Savings Bank, Buffalo, N.Y. 1890–1894, C. P. Huntington House; 1891–1892, Havemeyer Building; New York. 1893, Manufacturers and Liberal Arts Building, Chicago Exposition. 1894, Bank of Pittsburgh. 1895–1898, Weld Building; New York. 1896, Park Building, Pittsburgh. 1896, 636–638 Broadway, New York. 1897–1899, Saint Paul Building; 1897–1908, The College of the City of New York; 1898–1899, Vincent Building; 1901–1904, New York Stock Exchange; New York. 1904–1907, Wisconsin State Capitol, Madison. 1907–1908, Cleveland Trust Company, Ohio. 1910–1911, 334 Fourth Avenue, New York. 1911–1912, Hotel Pontiac, Detroit. 1911–1912, Statler Hotel; 1912, Williamson Building; Cleveland, Ohio.

BIBLIOGRAPHY

"The College of the City of New York." 1907–1908 *Architects' and Builders' Magazine* 9:287–300.

"House of Cornelius Vanderbilt, Esq., New York, N.Y." 1881 *American Architect and Building News* 9:247.

MIKKELSEN, MICHAEL A. 1917 "The Wisconsin State Capitol, Madison, Wisc." *Architectural Record* 42:194–233.

"Recent Bank Building of the United States." 1909 *Architectural Record* 10:77–85.

SCHUYLER, MONTGOMERY 1902 "The New Stock Exchange." *Architectural Record* 12:413–420.

STURGIS, RUSSELL (1898)1977 *A Review of the Work of George B. Post.* Reprint. New York: Da Capo. Originally published in the *Architectural Record,* no. 4.

"The Union Trust Company's Building, Broadway, New York, N.Y." 1893 *American Architect and Building News* 42, Oct.:39.

WEISMAN, WINSTON 1953 "New York and the Problem of the First Skyscraper." *Journal of the Society of Architectural Historians* 12:13–21.

WEISMAN, WINSTON 1972*a* "The Chicago School Issue." *Prairie School Review* 9:6–30.

WEISMAN, WINSTON 1972*b* "The Commercial Architecture of George B. Post." *Journal of the Society of Architectural Historians* 12:13–21.
"Where Architects Work: Geo. B. Post's Workshop." 1900 *Architectural Record* 10:77–85.

POST, PIETER

Pieter Post (1608–1669), who was born in Haarlem, the Netherlands, belonged to a family of artists. His father was an artist in stained glass, and his brother Frans was the painter who accompanied Prince Johan Maurits van Nassau-Siegen on his voyage to Brazil.

Pieter Post is mainly known as an architect who worked in the style of the Dutch classicism. He was, however, an able painter and draftsman, as witness the many drawings and engravings he made mainly of his own work. Like LIEVEN DE KEY and JACOB VAN CAMPEN, he was a member of the Haarlem Guild of Saint Luke.

It is probable that Post's interest in architecture had been stimulated by Van Campen. As a pupil of Van Campen, Post was a good, industrious, but sometimes dry follower of the principles of the Dutch classicistic style. In his time, he was much appreciated; he received many commissions. His early independent works show clearly the Van Campen influence (Swanenburg House, Halfweg [1645]; ten Bosch House, The Hague [1647]) in the use of the classic orders and measurements not only in the façades, but also in the disposition of the rooms and the rich interior decorations (de Onbeschaamde House, Dordrecht [1650]; the State Assembly Hall, The Hague [1652]). His later works tend to be sober brick buildings, with almost no decorations (gunpowder magazine, Delft [1660–1662)]; Sonnenburg Castle [1661–1667]; front buildings, Heeze Castle [1662–1665]), a common feature of late seventeenth-century architecture in Holland.

Post started his career in 1633, working on the small palace of Johan Maurits van Nassau, the so-called Mauritshuis in The Hague. At the same time, Constantijn Huygens, the secretary of Stadholder Frederik Hendrik, was building his town palace in a similar style, next to the Mauritshuis. Huygens, knowing Post as an able and hard-working person, employed him as an engineer. Through Huygens, the attention of the stadholder was drawn to the young architect. In 1640, Post was engaged as supervisor of the works on the Noordeinde Palace (the Oude Hof) in The Hague. In 1645, he was appointed as architect and painter to the stadholder, and in 1646 he was promoted to architect-ordinaris. From this year until his death in 1669, Post supervised all the stadholderly works. His best-known work in this respect is the Huis ten Bosch in The Hague, originally built as a country house for Amalia van Solms, Frederik Hendrik's wife. The main feature is a large cruciform, domed hall, the *Oranjezaal,* with a light cupola, the so-called salle à l'Italienne, a motif introduced in the Netherlands in the Mauritshuis. After the death of Frederik Hendrik in 1647, the *Oranjezaal* was turned into a mausoleum and was richly decorated under the direction of Huygens and Van Campen. The small, centralized building was enlarged with side wings in the eighteenth century.

For Prince Johan Maurits van Nassau as governor of Brazil, Post probably designed the town-plan of Mauritsstad (about 1637), the Vrijburg Palace, and several houses, all in Brazil. For Johan Maurits as stadholder of Cleves and grand master of the Order of the Knights of Saint John, Post designed the palace of Sonnenburg, now in East Germany, a sober brick building, to be compared with the rear façade of the Huis ten Bosch. In Cleves, Post supervised the restoration and extension of the Schwanenburg Castle (1664) and made a design for the further development of the town (1664).

In addition to the activities for his royal commissioners, Post worked as an architect for administrative bodies such as the Polder Authorities, municipalities, the States of Holland, and as a private architect as well. The result of the diversity of commissioners was a diversity of works: town halls, churches, weigh stations, assembly halls, country houses, interior decoration, and town planning.

Post's main work for the Rhineland Polder Authorities is the decoration of the Hall and Courtroom in the Leiden Gemeenlandshuis with Ionic pilasters and painted timber barrel vaults and gilt-leather walls. By order of the States of Holland, Post improved the interior design of the

Pieter Post.
Noordeinde Palace (with others).
The Hague.
1640

Pieter Post.
Town Hall.
Maastricht, Netherlands.
1656–1664

Pieter Post.
Weigh Station.
Gouda, Netherlands.
1668

State Assembly Hall in The Hague (1652–1657), built a gun factory in the same town (1666–1668), and a gun powder magazine in Delft (1660–1662). The last two buildings were erected in a very sober way: plain brick walls with almost no decoration but a huge coat of arms of the States of Holland. The Haarlem municipality charged Post with the design of a town extension (1640) and of the Nieuwe Kerk (1645). For the Amsterdam municipality, Post designed a new town hall (1647), and in Middelburg, he gave his assistance during the construction of the Oostkerk. His most ambitious work, however, is the Maastricht town hall, designed in 1656 and executed in 1659–1664. The building, a square block situated in the center of the market square and built of stone, is crowned with a tower. The projected façades, with tiers of pilasters, show a harmonious, perhaps a little petty, elevation with large pediments. An arched porch with a double flight of stairs leads up to the most remarkable feature of the town hall: the interior with a huge central hall, marked by perfect arches and galleries, with rises into the roof. The Hall served as a *Vierschaar* (High Court of Justice) as well. The specific disposition of the rooms behind the galleries on the left- and right-hand side of the flight of stairs is due to the dual seigniory of the town of Maastricht. Of his weigh stations, the Leiden *Waaghuis* annex buttermarket of 1657–1659 is considered to be the most charming example. The ground level, treated in a rustic way, is superimposed by a Doric order, finished off by a pediment with sculptured reliefs by Rombout Verhulst. Compared to the Gouda Weigh Station of 1668, the Leiden one is more elegant and refined; an impression of plumpness, characteristic of this type of building, has been cleverly avoided.

Of his many private commissions, Huis De Onbeschaamde in Dordrecht (1650–1653) stands out. It is a distinguished, rather sober, and characteristic brick building with giant Corinthian pilasters over the middle bays, crowned with a pediment. Fruit and flower garlands decorate the façade, and the steep roof is crowned with ornate chimneys. The interiors are richly decorated.

Pieter Post.
De Onbeschaamde House,
123-125 Wijnstraat.
Dordrecht, Netherlands.
1650–1653

CATHERINA L. VAN GRONINGEN

WORKS

1633, Mauritshuis (with others), The Hague. *1639–1642, Vredenburch House, De Beemster, Netherlands. 1640, Noordeinde Palace (with others); *1640–1645, Aan de Boschkant House (interior decoration); The Hague. 1641–1643, Hofwijck (with others), Voorburg, Netherlands. 1645, Rhineland Polder Authority House, Swanenburg, Halfweg, Netherlands. 1645–1647, Ten Bosch House, The Hague. (A)c.1650, Admiralty Building, Hellevoetsluis, Netherlands. (A)c.1650, Beverschaap House; 1650–1653, De Onbeschaamde House, 123–125 Wijnstraat; Dordrecht, Netherlands. (A)1652–1654, Sluices, Halfweg, Netherlands. 1652–1657, Assembly Room of the States of Holland (interior decoration), The Hague. 1656–1664, Town Hall, Maastricht, Netherlands. 1657–1659, Weigh Station; 1657–1669, Hall and Courtroom, Rhineland Polder Authority House, Breestraat; 1658, Castle of Leiden (gateway); Leiden, Netherlands. 1660–1662, Gun Powder Magazine, Schie, near Delft, Netherlands. 1660, Nieuwkoop Almshouse; 1660, 't Vergulde Hooft House; The Hague. 1661, Church (elevation of the tower), Middenbeemster, Netherlands. 1661–1667, Sonnenburg Castle, near Kostrzyn, Germany. 1662–1665, Heeze Castle (design of façade and outbuildings), Netherlands. *1662–1665, Rijxdorp House, Wassenaar, Netherlands. 1664, Schwanenburg Castle (alterations), Cleves, Germany. 1665, Church (wooden spire), Buren, Netherlands. *1666–1668, Gun Factory, The Hague. 1668, Weigh Station, Gouda, Netherlands.

BIBLIOGRAPHY

BLOK, G. A. C. 1934 "Pieter Post: De bouwmeester van de Waag." *Oudheidkundige Kring "Die Goude"* 1934:104–110.

BLOK, G. A. C. 1937 *Pieter Post: 1608–1669.* Siegen, Germany: Vorländer.

BLOK, G. A. C. 1953 "Het Familiewapen Van Den

Bouwmeester Pieter Post?" *Gens Nostra* 8, no. 2:23–29.

HAAGEN, J. K. VAN DER 1967 "Het Generaliteits-Kruitmagazijn aan de Schie." Pages 187–228 in *Delftse Studiën.* Assen, Netherlands: Van Gorcum.

Les ouvrages d'Architecture ordonnez par Pierre Post. 1715 Leiden, Netherlands: Pieter van der Aa.

ROSENBERG, J.; SLIVE, S.: and KUILE, E. H. TER (1968)1977 *Dutch Art and Architecture: 1600–1800.* 3d ed. Baltimore: Penguin.

SLAGTER, J., and BURG, W. F. VAN DER 1940 "Pieter Post als architect van Rijnland." *Bulletin, Koninklijke Nederlandse Oudheidkundige Bond* 1940:57–61.

TERWEN, J. J. 1979 "The Buildings of Johan Maurits van Nassau." In E. van den Boogart (editor), *Johan Maurits van Nassau-Siegen, 1604–1679: A Humanist Prince in Europe and Brazil.* The Hague.

POSTHUMUS MEYJES, C. B.

After his training at the Technical University in Delft, Netherlands, Christiaan Bernard Posthumus Meyjes (1858–1922) joined the Dutch Iron Railway Company in Amsterdam. Around 1886, he settled there as an independent architect.

Characteristic of Posthumus Meyjes's work is the solid craftsmanship of his buildings. His designs were never very progressive. Until the beginning of the twentieth century, Posthumus Meyjes worked in the Dutch neo-Renaissance style, but later he came ever more under the influence of H. P. BERLAGE.

WIM DE WIT

WORKS

1882–1884, H.I.J.S.M. Office, Amsterdam. 1885, Station, Delft, Netherlands. *1889–1890, Poor-relief Board Orphanage, Amsterdam. 1894–1897, Snouck van Loosenpark, Enkhuizen, Netherlands. 1897–1914, Nieuwe Kerk (restoration); 1900–1902, Associatiecassa Office; 1902–1904, Leesmuseum; Amsterdam. 1907, Bank Mees and Sons, Rotterdam, Netherlands. 1908, Nieuwe Zijds Chapel; 1914–1920, Amstleven Office; Amsterdam.

BIBLIOGRAPHY

EVERS, HENRI (1911)1918 *De architectuur in hare hoofdtijdperken.* 2d ed. Amsterdam: Veen.

GUGEL, EUGEN 1902 *Geschiedenis van de bouwstijlen in de hoofdtijdperken der architectuur.* Rotterdam, Netherlands: Bolle.

ROY VAN ZUYDEWIJN, H. J. F. DE 1969 *Amsterdamse Bouwkunst 1815–1940.* Amsterdam: De Bussy.

POTAIN, NICOLAS MARIE

Nicholas Marie Potain (1713–1796) won the Grand Prix of the Académie d'Architecture in 1738. On returning to France after his stay in Rome, he became *architecte du roi* and *contrôleur des bâtiments de Fontainebleau.* He became a member of the Académie d'Architecture in 1756.

A protégé of ANGE JACQUES GABRIEL, Potain supervised the construction of the Place Louis XV (now Place de la Concorde) in Paris between 1754 and 1770.

In 1766, he presented to the municipality of Nantes, in western France, projects for the construction of a stock exchange, but they were judged too expensive. He proposed a new series of projects in 1778. In 1776, he presented a project for a military hospital in Lille, France.

After his trip to Italy, he became very interested in theaters. His studies reveal a fertile imagination in harmony with the theories of Charles Nicolas Cochin.

In 1767, he published his *Traité des ordres d'architecture.*

GÉRARD ROUSSET-CHARNY
Translated from French by
Richard Cleary

POTTER, EDWARD T.

Edward Tuckerman Potter (1831–1904) was early to adopt the English High Victorian Gothic and to accept EUGÈNE EMMANUEL VIOLLET-LE-DUC's advocacy of iron construction as appropriate to the Gothic style. Though widely separated in time, his Church of the Good Shepherd (1867–1869) and Caldwell Hart Colt Memorial Parish House (1894–1896) in Hartford, Connecticut, comprise a coordinated, inventively ornamented, polychromatic Gothic complex. In Yonkers, New York, his round-arched Saint John's Church (1871–1872) is a unique adaptation of his High Victorian Gothic to the style of the original Colonial church, part of which is incorporated into the structure. Potter's resplendently colorful Mark Twain House (1873–1874) in Hartford, done in partnership with the Beaux-Arts trained Alfred H. Thorp, reflects the revival in France of a rustic, northern European

Edward T. Potter. Mark Twain House (with Alfred H. Thorp). Hartford, Connecticut. 1873–1874, 1881

Edward T. Potter. Nott Memorial. Schenectady, New York. 1858–1859, 1872–1878

domestic type known as the "villa normande."

Born in Schenectady, New York, Edward Potter was the grandson of Eliphalet Nott, president of Union College, Schenectady, and the son of Alonzo Potter, the Episcopal bishop of Pennsylvania. Edward and his half-brother WILLIAM A. POTTER became specialists in church and collegiate architecture.

After graduating from Union College in 1853, Edward Potter apprenticed with RICHARD UPJOHN for about two years. In 1858, he designed the domed, centrally planned building first projected by JOSEPH-JACQUES RAMÉE in 1813 as the centerpiece of his Union campus. Work was halted at the foundation level in 1859 and not resumed until 1872; in 1871 Potter transformed his sixteen-sided, neoclassical design, which in 1859 had included a porch with arches having voussoirs of alternate colors of stone as in JACOB WREY MOULD's All Souls' Church in New York, to his High Victorian Gothic. The resultant Nott Memorial, which has an exposed interior iron skeleton, is among the best known American monuments of the style. From 1863 to about 1873, Potter was loosely associated with CHARLES W. CLINTON, and for most of his career his office was in New York.

Potter's first High Victorian Gothic building was the First Dutch Reformed Church in Schenectady (1861, 1862–1863) which was seminal to his later churches in its general form and details, conservative polychromy—dark gray sandstone walls trimmed in a lighter gray sandstone and brownstone—and transeptlike wing separated from the nave by a movable wood and glass screen. This plan anticipated the so-called Akron Plan of evangelical churches. The seminaturalistic carving of the foliated capitals followed the prescriptions of JOHN RUSKIN and the example of DEANE AND WOODWARD's Oxford Museum. Potter's carved ornament was often programmatic and pictorial, as, for instance, the historiated capitals of the hall of the George Hunter Brown House (1867) in Millbrook, New York, the gun parts on the Armorer's Porch of the Colt Church, and the nautical and marine imagery of the eccentric Colt Parish House, which as a whole is reminiscent of a sailing vessel.

In 1867, Potter began using cast-iron columns in his churches, following the lead of such English Low Church architects as E. BASSETT KEELING and deviating from contemporary American practice. In the early 1870s, Potter shed most of Upjohn's conservative Gothic Revivalist influence. Stimulated by the second volume of Viollet-Le-Duc's *Entretiens sur l'Architecture* (1872), and by ideas of polychromy and domestic style emanating from France, he produced some of his finest work.

In 1877, Potter retired from practice, settling in Newport, Rhode Island. The Colt Parish House is the only building of his design built afterward. His later years were spent writing poetry and music, devising inventions, and developing an ingenious and humane system of tenement and apartment housing designed for the standard New York lot. His model was awarded a medal in the anthropological section of the Chicago World's Fair of 1893, and his well-published system contributed to the climate of reform that instigated the 1901 New York Tenement House Law.

SARAH BRADFORD LANDAU

WORKS

1858–1859, 1872–1878, Nott Memorial; 1861, 1862–1863, First Dutch Reformed Church; Schenectady, N.Y. *1864, 1865–1867, 1873–1875, New England Congregational Church, Chicago. *1864–1865, Brown Brothers & Company Banking House, New York. 1865, 1866–1869, Packer Hall, Lehigh University, Bethlehem, Pa. *1865, 1867–1869, Beth Eden Baptist Church, Philadelphia. 1865, 1868–1872, All Saints' Memorial Church, Providence, R.I. *1867, George Hunter Brown House, Millbrook, N.Y. 1867–1869, Church of the Good Shepherd, Hartford, Conn. 1867–1873, Trinity Episcopal Cathedral, Davenport, Iowa. *c.1868–1870, Hospital of the Society for Relief of the Ruptured and Crippled; *1868–1871, Church of the Heavenly Rest; New York. *1870, 1873–1877, Saint John's Episcopal Church, Jacksonville, Fla. 1871–1872, Saint John's Church, Yonkers, N.Y. 1871–1873, Harvard Church, Brookline, Mass. 1873–1874, 1881, Mark Twain House (with Alfred H. Thorp); 1894–1896, Caldwell Hart Colt Memorial Parish House; Hartford Conn.

BIBLIOGRAPHY

CHAFEE, RICHARD 1966 "Edward Tuckerman Potter and Samuel L. Clemens: An Architect and His Client." Unpublished M.A. thesis, Yale University, New Haven.

HITCHCOCK, H. R. 1968 "Ruskin and American Architecture, or Regeneration Long Delayed." Pages 166–208 in John Summerson (editor), *Concerning Architecture: Essays on Architectural Writers and Writing Presented to Nikolaus Pevsner.* London: Penguin.

LANDAU, SARAH BRADFORD 1976 "The Colt Industrial Empire at Hartford." *Antiques* 109:568–579.

LANDAU, SARAH BRADFORD 1979 *Edward T. and William A. Potter: American Victorian Architects.* New York and London: Garland.

LANDAU, SARAH BRADFORD 1981 "Mark Twain's House in Connecticut." *Architectural Review* 169:162–166.

MENDEL, MESICK, and COHEN ARCHITECTS 1973 *The Nott Memorial: A Historic Structure Report.* Albany, N.Y.

POTTER, EDWARD TUCKERMAN 1864 *The Capitals of the Banker Screen in the First Reformed Church, Schenectady, New York.* Privately Printed.

POTTER, EDWARD TUCKERMAN 1868 *A Statement of the Considerations Influencing the Design of the First Dutch Reformed Church, Schenectady, New York.* New York: Baker & Godwin.

POTTER, EDWARD TUCKERMAN 1869 *World Pictures in Capitals.* Philadelphia: Lippincott.

POTTER, EDWARD TUCKERMAN c.1903 *Concentrated Residence Studies.* Privately Printed.

POTTER, WILLIAM A.

The buildings of William Appleton Potter (1842–1909), especially the Chancellor Green Library (1871–1873) at Princeton University, the South Congregational Church (1872, 1873–1875) in Springfield, Massachusetts, and the Evansville, Indiana, Customhouse (1875–1879), invested the American High Victorian Gothic with monumentality and classic dignity. Potter's work represents both the apogee and the decline of the style, the latter under both the influence of H. H. RICHARDSON, and the nascent revival of Renaissance forms in the 1870s. Potter's suburban houses, produced with ROBERT H. ROBERTSON, his partner from 1875 to 1881, were early to adopt features of the English-imported Queen Anne and early to participate in the Shingle style.

The son of Bishop Alonzo Potter and the half-brother of EDWARD T. POTTER, William was born in Schenectady, New York, but spent his youth in Philadelphia. After his graduation from Union College, Schenectady, in 1864, he worked briefly as a laboratory instructor in analytical chemistry at Columbia University before touring Europe in 1865. In 1867, having decided to become an architect, he joined Edward Potter's New York office. The commission for the Chancellor Green Library at Princeton established his reputation, and he and his firm designed seven buildings there, five of which were built in the 1870s. Geometrically determined proportions, softened by cusped arches banded in gray and brown sandstone, stained glass, and carved ornament reminiscent of Edward Potter's, govern the forms of the octagonal brown-stone-walled library and its symmetrically arranged wings.

The architect's finest work, the South Congregational Church in Springfield, Massachusetts, departs from Edward Potter's style in respect to its greater design unity, bolder handling of Gothic motifs, and more consistent proportions. Strikingly composed in sympathy with the corner site, the rounded west end, the tall tower, the transepts, and the chapel are united by yellowish Ohio stone band courses striping red Longmeadow stone walls. Large motifs counterpointed by small ones, for example, the enormous rose windows offset by single rows of tiny windows below, distinguish this and other Potter buildings of the 1870s. Beginning with the Berkshire Athenæum (1874–1876) in Pittsfield, Massachusetts, Potter emphasized regularity and balance in the design of public buildings, foreshadowing the "return to order" of the 1880s. Ornament became less an independent attraction and more an embellishment, in contrast to his half-brother's buildings. Potter's first obviously Richardsonian design was Potter and Robertson's round-arched project for the Brown University library of 1875.

In January 1875, Potter was appointed to succeed ALFRED B. MULLETT as supervising architect of the United States Treasury. About the same time, the Potter and Robertson firm, with Robertson as the junior partner, was formed in New York. Several of Potter's combined post office,

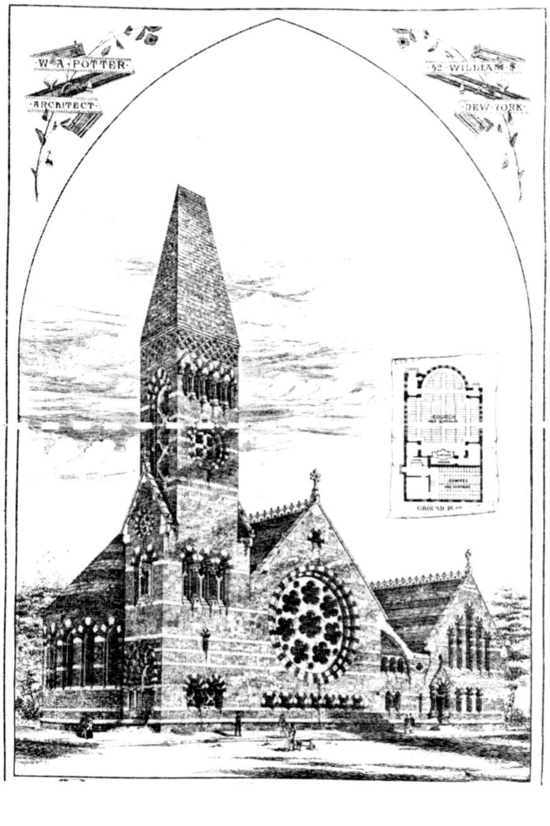

William A. Potter. South Congregational Church. Springfield, Massachusetts. 1872, 1873–1875

courthouse, and customhouse buildings followed the precedent set by the Berkshire Athenæum in regard to general form and style. Of these, the châteaulike Fall River Customhouse and Post Office (1875–1881) and the buff limestone, brownstone-trimmed Evansville Customhouse were his most successful Gothic designs. For the Atlanta Courthouse and Post Office (1875, 1876–1880), partly modeled after the sixteenth-century Villa Medici in Rome, Potter employed a round-arched variation of his High Victorian Gothic. The arcaded brick façades of the Grand Rapids Courthouse and Post Office (1875, 1876–1879) were also influenced by Richardson, specifically by the project for the Cheney Block. In July 1876, Potter resigned his government post and returned to full-time private practice.

Several of Potter and Robertson's houses designed after 1876 combined Old English half-timbering and shingled gables with partially open plans anchored by Colonial-style center hallways. The C. H. Baldwin House (1877–1878) in Newport, Rhode Island, which was largely inspired by Richardson's Watts Sherman House, includes an impressive three-story hall in the tradition of earlier Newport houses. The partly shingled Adam-Derby House (1878) in Oyster Bay, Long Island, and the almost completely shingled E. H. Van Ingen House (1879–1880) in Washington, Connecticut, approach the mature Shingle style.

After 1880, Potter's work was less innovative but continued to demonstrate a marked ability to adapt buildings to conditions of site and function. His master plan for Union College, Schenectady, of 1881, of which only Powers-Washburn Hall (1881–1883) was built, attempted to complete the neoclassical scheme of JOSEPH-JACQUES RAMÉE and also to resolve the conflict between Ramée's early nineteenth-century buildings and Edward Potter's High Victorian Gothic Nott Memorial. His Union Theological Seminary (1881, 1882–1884), undertaken with the assistance of his nephew JAMES BROWN LORD and Teachers College buildings (1892, 1893–1894, 1896–1897), both in New York City, are conservatively Gothic complexes designed to accommodate disparate institutional activities within the confines of New York sites.

Potter's Richardsonian Romanesque buildings, especially Princeton University's Alexander Hall (1891–1894) which is partly derived from the Palais du Trocadéro by J. A. G. DAVIOUD and J. D. Bourdais and which has a stage area decorated by Cosmatilike marble paneling and furnishings, are among the best known examples of the style. His First Reformed Dutch Church (1895, 1896–1897) in Somerville, New Jersey, and quadrangular Pyne Library (1896–1897) at Princeton belong to the early development of the Academic Gothic. Climaxed by a square, parapeted tower, the church evokes the fifteenth-century English parish church without being correctly neo-Perpendicular. The Pyne Library, one of the first of Princeton University's Collegiate Gothic buildings, compromises successfully with the freer Gothic style of the adjoining Chancellor Green Library.

SARAH BRADFORD LANDAU

WORKS

1871–1873, Chancellor Green Library; *1872–1874, John C. Green Science Bulding; Princeton University, N.J. 1872, 1873–1875, South Congregational Church, Springfield, Mass. 1874–1876, Berkshire Athenæum. Pittsfield, Mass. *1875–1876, University Hotel (with Robert H. Robertson); 1875–1877, Stuart Hall (with Robertson), Princeton Theological Seminary; 1875–1877, Witherspoon Hall (with Robertson); Princeton, N.J. *1875–1879, Courthouse and Post Office, Covington, Ky. 1875–1879, Customhouse and Post Office, Evansville, Ind. *1875–1881, Customhouse and Post Office, Fall River, Mass. *1875, 1876–1879, Courthouse and Post Office, Grand Rapids, Mich. *1875, 1876–1880, Courthouse and Post Office, Atlanta, Ga. 1875, 1876–1882, Post Office and Courthouse, Nashville, Tenn. *c.1877, Bryce Gray House (with Robertson), Long Branch, N.J. 1877–1878, C. H. Baldwin House (with Robertson), Newport, R.I. 1878, Adam-Derby House (with Robertson), Oyster Bay, N.Y. 1879–1880, E. H. Van Ingen House (with Robertson), Washington, Conn. *1881–1883, Powers-Washburn Hall, Union College, Schenectady, N.Y. *1881, 1882–1884, Union Theological Seminary (with James Brown Lord), New York. 1887–1889, Christ Church, Poughkeepsie, N.Y. 1887–1889, Holy Trinity Church Complex (now Saint Martin's Episcopal Church); *1888, c.1890–1892, Saint Agnes' Chapel Complex (parish house extant); New York. 1891–1894, Alexander Hall, Princeton University, N.J. 1892, 1893–1894, 1896–1897, Teachers College, New York. 1895, 1896–1897, First Reformed Dutch Church, Somerville, N.J. 1896–1897, Pyne Library (now East Pyne Building), Princeton University, N.J.

BIBLIOGRAPHY

HITCHCOCK, H. R. 1968 "Ruskin and American Architecture, or Regeneration Long Delayed." Pages 166–208 in John Summerson (editor), *Concerning Architecture: Essays on Architectural Writers and Writing Presented to Nikolaus Pevsner.* London: Penguin.

LANDAU, SARAH BRADFORD 1979 *Edward T. and William A. Potter: American Victorian Architects.* New York and London: Garland.

SCHUYLER, MONTGOMERY 1909 "The Work of William Appleton Potter." *Architectural Record* 26:176–196.

WODEHOUSE, LAWRENCE 1973 "William Appleton Potter, Principal *Pasticheur* of Henry Hobson Richardson." *Journal of the Society of Architectural Historians* 32:175–192.

POWELL and MOYA

Arnold Joseph Philip Powell (1921–) and John Hidalgo Moya (1926–) were together at the Architectural Association School in London from 1939, when FREDERICK GIBBERD was principal. They both worked as assistants in his office after leaving the school. It was probably Gibberd's individual approach to modern design that pointed the way to their own future practice. In 1946, they were awarded first prize in a competition for rebuilding thirty-three acres of Thameside land in Pimlico, London, as housing. This enabled them to set up in partnership. In 1951, they gave the Festival of Britain its progressive "vertical feature," the Skylon. Powell and Moya's designs are characterized by a practicality that provides different buildings with distinct identities and that brings out the distinctive qualities of materials. Even at Oxford and Cambridge they avoided a too obvious monumentality and produced buildings which are now very much at one with their historic surroundings. Attention to detail has meant that, in institutional buildings such as schools and hospitals, there is evidence of a care which has often been supposed to be inconsistent with large scale. In 1974, they were awarded the Gold Medal of the Royal Institute of British Architects, the first architectural practice—as opposed to individual—to have been so honored.

BRIAN HANSON

WORKS

1946–1962, Churchill Gardens Estate, Grosvenor Road; 1951, Skylon, Festival of Britain, South Bank; 1956, Mayfield School, West Hill, Putney; London. 1961. Festival Theatre, Chichester, Sussex, England. 1961–1972, Princess Margaret Hospital, Swindon, Wiltshire, England. 1966, Wexham Park Hospital, Slough; 1966–1975, Wycombe General Hospital, High Wycombe; Buckinghamshire, England. 1967, Cripps Building, Saint John's College, Cambridge. 1968, Blue Boar Quad, Christ Church, Oxford. 1970, British Pavilion (with Takaki and Dodd), Expo 70, Osaka, Japan. 1973, Plumstead Manor School, Woolwich, London. 1974, Wolfson College, Oxford. 1976, Museum of London.

BIBLIOGRAPHY

BOOTH, P., and TAYLOR, N. J. W. 1970 *Cambridge New Architecture: A Guide to the Post-war Buildings.* 3d ed. London: Hill.

BRUCKMANN, H., and LEWIS, D. N. 1960 *New Housing in Great Britain.* Stuttgart, Germany, and London: Tiranti.

GARDINER, S. 1974 "Powell and Moya's Dash for Freedom." *Journal of the Royal Institute of British Architects* 81:8–11.

MAXWELL, ROBERT 1972 *New British Architecture.* London: Thames & Hudson.

MILLS, EDWARD D. 1953 *The New Architecture in Great Britain (1946–1953).* London: Standard Catalogue.

NAIRN, IAN 1964 *Modern Buildings in London.* London Transport.

POYET, BERNARD

Bernard Poyet (1742–1824), who was born in Dijon, France, studied architecture with CHARLES DE WAILLY and traveled to Italy as a second-place winner of the Prix de Rome competition of 1768. There, he took special interest in the buildings of BALDASSARE PERUZZI and GIACOMO BAROZZI DA VIGNOLA. In France, Poyet became *maître des bâtiments de la ville de Paris,* and in this capacity he designed many projects for the city's development and embellishment, including a radial design for a new Hôtel Dieu (1785). He was appointed to the Conseil des Bâtiments Civils in 1815 and elected to the Institut de France in 1818.

RICHARD CLEARY

WORKS

*1777, Hôtel Callet; *1778, Maison des Enfants d'Orléans; *1780, Stables for the duc de Chartres; 1798, Rue des Colonnes (with NICOLAS JACQUES ANTOINE VESTIER); 1806–1807, Palais-Bourbon (Chambres des Députés; portico); Paris.

BIBLIOGRAPHY

ACADÉMIE DE FRANCE À ROME 1976 *Piranèse et les français: 1740–1790.* Rome: Elefante.

BRAHAM, ALLAN 1980 *The Architecture of the French Enlightenment.* London: Thames & Hudson.

GALLET, MICHAEL 1972 *Paris Domestic Architecture of the Eighteenth Century.* Translated by James C. Palmes. London: Barrie & Jenkins.

HAUTECOEUR, LOUIS 1952–1953 Volumes 4 and 5 in *Histoire de l'architecture classique en France.* Paris: Picard.

KAUFMANN, EMIL (1955)1968 *Architecture in the Age of Reason.* Reprint. New York: Dover.

ROSENAU, HELEN 1964 "Antoine Petit und sein Zentralplan für das Hôtel-Dieu in Paris: Ein Beitrag zur Architektur-Typologie." *Zeitschrift für Kunstgeschichte* 27:228–237.

POZZO, ANDREA

In his interpretation of the masters of the Roman high baroque, Andrea Pozzo (1642–1709) prepared the way for the style of the early eighteenth century in Rome. Born in Trento, Italy, Pozzo entered the Society of Jesus in Milan as a lay brother in 1665. Following a two-year novitiate in Genoa, he resettled in Milan where he resided, excepting trips to Genoa and Venice, until 1681. In that year,

Pozzo.
Il Gesù (Altar of Sant'Ignazio).
Rome.
1695–1699

on the advice of the painter Carlo Maratti, Father Oliva, General of the Jesuits, called Pozzo to Rome. His previous training and continuing career as a painter are the keys to understanding Pozzo's approach to architecture. For him, architecture proceeded from painted illusions of space, and he believed that a good architect is one who is first a good painter and a master of perspective. Equally important is the fact that Pozzo made no qualitative distinction between fictitious, provisional, and real architecture.

Pozzo's first commissions were for fictitious architecture. The sham drum and ciborium in San Francesco Saverio, Trento (1676–1679), and the fake dome and baldachin in the Gesù (1681–1684), Frascati, Italy, were probably the result of economic considerations. The sham dome of Sant'Ignazio, Rome (1684–1685), on the other hand, was necessitated by a legal suit which prevented the erection of a true cupola. The frescoed altar of 1685 in the left transept of the same church was replaced by a marble structure around 1750; however, the design of the original is preserved in Pozzo's treatise.

Pozzo's transition to constructed architecture is represented by the decoration of the choir of Sant'Ignazio, Rome (1685–1701), in which he abandoned his first idea of combining real and illusionistic architecture in favor of a more conventional scheme. Except for the altar rail, Pozzo was responsible for the design of the altar of Sant'Ignazio (1695–1699) in the Gesù in Rome. His basic conception derived from GIOVANNI LORENZO BERNINI's Cornaro Chapel in Santa Maria della Vittoria, Rome. Less directly, Bernini was also the source of inspiration for the altar of San Luigi Gonzaga (1697–1699) in Sant'Ignazio, Rome. Here, his model was the provisional altar erected before 1671 in Sant'Agnese in Piazza Navona by Mattia de Rossi (see DE ROSSI FAMILY), one of Bernini's pupils.

Pozzo designed several works whose construction he did not personally oversee. The high altar of the Cathedral of Foligno, Italy (1697–1703), is modeled on that of Saint Peter's in Rome. Around 1697, Pozzo prepared a project for the high altar of Santa Maria delle Grazie in Arco, Italy, which was not executed until 1705–1710. Here he employed a *serliana* in conjunction with motifs derived from FRANCESCO BORROMINI. In 1699 and 1700 respectively, Pozzo designed Jesuit-type plans for the Churches of Sant'Ignazio in Dubrovnik and the Cathedral of Ljubjana, Yugoslavia. The plan for San Francesco in Trento, Italy (1700–1711), on the other hand, was borrowed from CARLO RAINALDI's Santa Maria in Campitelli, Rome.

On his way to Vienna in 1702, Pozzo stopped in Montepulciano, Italy, where he designed the Oratorio di San Bernardo, transformed the fourteenth-century Church of Santa Maria dei Servi, and undertook the completion of the Gesù. Although these vary considerably in plan, Pozzo used the same type of articulation—clustered pilasters and encased columns—in each. Later on during his journey through Italy, he left designs for the high altars of the Collegiate Church at Lucignano d'Arezzo and of San Sebastiano in Verona.

Between 1703 and 1709, Pozzo transformed the interior of the Jesuit Universitätskirche in Vienna. In addition to painting a dome over the center of the nave, he inserted convex *coretti* into the chapel arcades and scenographically isolated the choir. In 1702, he sent plans to Belluno, Italy, for a Jesuit church there. Pozzo's hand is now hard to recognize because of subsequent alterations. For the funeral of Leopold I in 1705, Pozzo designed a catafalque for the Universitätskirche, Vienna. Unlike the common type, Pozzo's consisted of a single painted canvas, which rose to the vault, depicting the memorial in a domed crossing. His last architectural work in Vienna was the ciborium of the Franziskanerkirche (1706) in which he finally was able to realize in concrete form the illusionistic scheme of Mondovi.

Pozzo's influence was exceptionally widespread as a result of his two-volume treatise, published in 1693 and 1700, which by 1708 had been translated into all major European languages. In addition to the methods of perspective projection, the treatise contains engravings of his real and ephemeral architecture, as well as unexecuted projects. The three schemes for the apse of the Gesù in Rome (vol. 1, pp. 71–73) had considerable impact north of the Alps. Elements of his three projects for the east front of San Giovanni in Laterano in Rome of 1699 (vol. 2, pp. 83, 85, 87) reappear in almost all of the later proposals for this façade. His designs for ciboria which, according to Pozzo, could serve either as ephemeral or real architecture also were emulated. In particular, the *Fabbrica quadrata* (vol. 1, p. 64) constructed in modified form in the Franziskanerkirche, Vienna, set the standard for later architects in Austria and southern Germany. The engravings, furthermore, are an invaluable record of Pozzo's stylistic proclivities. For instance, the project for a round church and college (vol. 2, pp. 88–91; 109–111) is modeled after works not only by Bernini and CARLO FONTANA, but also by Borromini. Pozzo's ability to synthesize seemingly incompatible sources was of great importance for the next generation of Roman architects. The engravings of the *Quarant'ore* decorations for the Gesù, Rome, of 1685 (vol. 1, p. 71) and 1695 (vol. 2, p. 47) embody one of the major aims of seventeenth-century art. Pozzo established a continuum between the real and fictional space by adjusting the architecture of the painted flats to that of the nave and by allowing the apse to show through. He eliminated the barrier between the real space of the spectator and the imagined space of the sacred drama, between the earthly and the spiritual, transforming the spectator into an active participant.

CATHIE C. KELLY

WORKS

1676–1679, San Francesco Saverio (high altar and sham cupola), Mondovi, Italy. 1681–1684, Il Gesù (high altar), Frascati, Italy. 1684–1685, Sant'Ignazio (sham cupola); *1685, Il Gesù (*Quarant'ore*); *1685, Sant'Ignazio (left transept altar); 1685–1701, Sant'Ignazio (choir); *1695, Il Gesù (*Quarant'ore*); 1695–1699, Il Gesù (altar of Sant'Ignazio); 1697–1699, Sant'Ignazio (altar of San Luigi Gonzaga); Rome. 1697–1703, Cathedral (high altar), Foligno, Italy. 1699–1725, Sant'Ignazio, Dubrovnik, Yugoslavia. 1700–1705, Cathedral, Ljubljana, Yugoslavia. 1700–1711, San Francesco Saverio, Trento, Italy. 1702, Oratorio di San Bernardo; 1702, Santa Maria dei Servi; Montepulciano, Italy. 1702(?), San Sebastiano (high altar), Verona, Italy. 1702–1704, Collegiata di San Michele (high altar), Lucignano d'Arezzo, Italy. 1702–1714, Il Gesù, Montepulciano, Italy. 1703–1709, Universitätskirche (high altar and *coretti*), Vienna. 1704, Chiesa dei Gesuiti, Belluno, Italy. 1705–1710, Santa Maria delle Grazie (high altar), Arco, Trento, Italy. 1706, Franziskanerkirche (high altar), Vienna.

BIBLIOGRAPHY

BENEVENUTI, EDOARDO 1912 "La vita del Padre Pozzo scritta da Francesco Baldinucci." *Atti dell'imperiale regia academia di scienze, lettere, e arti degli Agiati in Rovereto* 18:207–237.

BJURSTRÖM, PER 1972 "Baroque Theater and the Jesuits." Translated by Patrick Hort. Pages 99–110 in Rudolf Wittkower and Irma B. Jaffe (editors), *Baroque Art: The Jesuit Contribution.* New York: Fordham University Press.

CARBONERI, NINO (editor) 1961 *Andrea Pozzo architetto (1642–1709).* Trento, Italy: Collance artisti trentini.

ENGGASS, ROBERT 1974 "The Altar-rail for St. Ignatius's Chapel in the Gesù in Roma." *Burlington Magazine* 116:178–189.

ENGGASS, ROBERT 1976 "Un problème du baroque romain tardif: Projets de sculptures par des artistes non sculpteurs." *Revue de l'art* 31:21–32.

GONCALVES, FLAVIO COSTA 1973 "Arquitectura E A. talha no noroeste de Portugal durante o seculo XVIII." Volume 2, pages 515–516 in *Actas del XXIII Congresso Internacional de Historia del Arte.* Spain: University of Granada.

GRISERI, ANDREINA 1967 *Le metamorfosi del Barocco.* Turin, Italy: Einaudi.

JACOB, SAVINE 1976 "Zu zwei römischen Architekturzeichnungen der Berliner Kunstbibliothek." *Römisches Jahrbuch für Kunstgeschichte* 16:289–304.

KERBER, BERNHARD 1971 *Andrea Pozzo.* Berlin and New York: De Gruyter.

KOWALCZYK, JERZY 1975*a* "Andrea Pozzo a późny barok w Polsce Cz. I. Traktat i oltarze." *Biuletyn Historii Sztuki* 37:162–178.

KOWALCZYK, JERZY 1975*b* "Andrea Pozzo a późny barok w Polsce Cz. II. Freski sklepienne." *Biuletyn Historii Sztuki* 37:335–350.

KOWALCZYK, JERZY 1977 "Andrea Pozzo e il tardo Barocco in Polonia." Pages 111–129 in Jan Slaski (editor), *Barocco fra Italia e Polonia.* Warsaw: Pánstwowe Wydawnictwo Naukowe.

LAVAGNINO, EMILIO; ANSALDI, GIULIO R.; and SALERNO, LUIGI (editors) 1959 *Altari barocchi in Roma.* Rome: Banco di Roma.

MARINI, REMIGIO 1959 *Andrea Pozzo Pittore (1642–1709).* Trento, Italy: Edizioni C.A.T.

MONTALTO, LINA 1957 "Il problema della cupola di Sant'Ignazio da P. Orazio Grassi e Fratel Pozzo ad oggi." *Bollettino del centro di studio per la storia dell'architettura* 11:33–62.

MONTALTO, LINA 1958 "Andrea Pozzo nella chiesa di Sant'Ignazio al Collegio Romano." *Studi romani* 6:668–679.

OENSLAGER, DONALD 1975 *Stage Design: Four Centuries of Scenic Invention with Drawings for the Theater from His Collection.* New York: Viking.

OGDEN, DUNBAR H. 1978 *The Italian Baroque Stage: Documents by Giulio Troili, Andrea Pozzo, Ferdinando Galli-Bibiena, Baldassare Orsini.* Translated with commentary by Dunbar E. Ogden. Berkeley: University of California Press.

PASCOLI, LIONE 1730–1736 *Vite de' pittori, scultori, ed architetti moderni.* 2 vols. Rome: De Rossi.

PECCHIAI, PIO 1952 *Il Gesù di Roma descritto ed*

illustrato. Rome: Società grafica romana.

PORTOGHESI, PAOLO 1970 *Roma Barocca: The History of an Architectonic Culture.* Translated by Barbara Luigia La Penta. Cambridge, Mass.: M.I.T. Press.

POZZO, ANDREA 1693–1700 *Perspectiva pictorum et architectorum.* 2 vols. Rome: Komareck Bohemi.

WEIL, MARK S. 1974 "The Devotion of the Forty Hours and Roman Baroque Illusions." *Journal of the Warburg and Courtauld Institutes* 37:218–248.

WILBERG-VIGNAU, PETER 1966 "Andrea Pozzo Innenraumgestaltung in S. Ignazio." Unpublished Ph.D. dissertation, University of Kiel, Germany.

PRAMPOLINI, ENRICO

Enrico Prampolini (1894–1956), a leader of second-generation Italian Futurism (or neo-Futurism), wrote widely on architecture, but completed only two major works. The Pavilion of Futurist Architecture in Turin (1928), with its active volumes and integrated lettering, exemplifies key principles of Futurism. Influenced by ANTONIO SANT'ELIA's machine-inspired, visionary, and individualistic architecture, Prampolini argued in 1926 in his "Manifesto of Futurist Architecture" (1974) for a style of "lyricism and dynamism" which "addresses not only technical problems . . . but also the dynamics of daily life," creating "a spiritual vision of the modern world." Prampolini attacked the pure functionalism of Rationalist architecture and the historicizing of Novecento. Yet, his Monument to the Fallen in Como (1930–1933), an ironically staid translation of a Sant'Elia design for a Power Station, was a collaboration with the Rationalist GIUSEPPE TERRAGNI. Prampolini also urged that Futurism should be the basis of Fascist architecture, and he submitted designs for Mussolini's 1942 Esposizione Universale Romana.

Prampolini's greatest contributions were in theater and set design, and he devised geometric, optical, and mechanical scenery intended to replace actors. Much of this "dynamic scenography" expresses the aesthetics of unrealized Futurist architecture. He developed the "polymaterial" work of art—abstract mixed-media reliefs that often functioned as murals. He edited *Noi* and *Stile Futurista* (with Fillia) and had many contacts with the international avant-garde.

GERALD D. SILK

WORKS

1928, Pavilion of Futurist Architecture, Turin, Italy. 1930–1935, Monument to the Fallen (with Giuseppe Terragni), Como, Italy.

BIBLIOGRAPHY

BUCARELLI, PALMA 1961 *Enrico Prampolini.* Rome: Galleria Nazionale d'arte moderna. Exhibition catalogue.

CLOUGH, ROSA TRILLO 1961 *Futurism: The Story of a Modern Art Movement.* New York: Philosophical Library.

CRISPOLTI, ENRICO 1969 *Il Mito della Macchina e Altri Temi del Futurismo.* Rome: Celebes.

DRUDI GAMBILLO, MARIA, and FIORI, TERESA 1958–1962 *Archivi del Futurismo.* Rome: De Luca.

"Futurismo Architettura." 1971 *Controspazio* 3, nos. 4–5: entire issue

KIRBY, MICHAEL 1971 *Futurist Performance.* New York: Dutton.

LISTA, GIOVANNI 1974 *Futurisme: Manifestes, Proclamations, Documents.* Lausanne, Switzerland: L'Age d'Homme.

PRANDTAUER, JACOB

Born in Stanz near Landeck, Austria, Jacob Prandtauer (1658–1726), one of the great architects of the Austrian baroque, was one of a group of artists that returned to Lower Austria from the Tyrol after years of Turkish raids.

At the age of seventeen, Prandtauer was taught masonry and architecture by Hans Georg Asam who had visited Italy and who recognized the progressive potential of the new baroque architecture. In 1680, Prandtauer was in contact with the Carlones (see CARLONE FAMILY), an Italian family of masons and sculptors who influenced his architecture with their use of frescoes and stuccoed vaults.

From 1683 to 1685, Prandtauer studied in Munich where he could fully appreciate and analyze the stuccoed ceilings of Andreas Faistenberger. The Theatiner Church in Munich, designed by Enrico Zuccalli (see ZUCCALLI FAMILY) was also of great influence on Prandtauer's future work as was the Kajetaner Church in Salzburg by Caspar Zuccalli.

Prandtauer worked as a sculptor for Albert Ernst, duke of Courland, on his Castle in Thalheim. While he was working there in 1689, the duke also gave him his first commission for the extension to a terrace garden and the design of a new pavilion. There followed commissions for numerous sculptures in 1690, as well as for a small chapel and a tower, allowing him to demonstrate his craftsmanship. The chapel, composed of five bays, had a straight choir, simple cross-vaults and a rather plain façade; the tower of the chapel was an octagon, typical of the seventeenth-century regional style, topped with an understated roof.

Throughout his career, Prandtauer's designs appeared as a synthesis of local traditional design and the revolutionary impulse of the baroque architectonic language. His design for the scriptorium of the Monastery of Sankt Pölten in 1969 (with its several floor levels, niches, and obelisques) showed an original sensitivity to north Italian influences. The cloister enunciated the first clear steps of Prandtauer's baroque architecture. In the late 1690s, Prandtauer received commissions for several additions to the Ochsenburg Castle near Sankt Pölten. The cloister arcades had character similar to that of Joching's monastery. In his design for a country residence in Schwaighof, Prandtauer combined a baroque style on the exterior with rather simple plasterings on the interior in the same manner as at the Joching monastery. To the contemporary method of plastering, which was to juxtapose the different planes, Prandtauer added in his Schwaighof design three-dimensional forms to create more unity.

Prandtauer's mastery of traditional craftsmanship made him skeptical of the baroque in his first commissions. Between 1694 and 1700, he remodeled and extended an old parish house and combined several commercial buildings into a summer residence in Haitzendorf. As part of the same complex, a church was also remodeled and a new parish house built. The façade of the commercial building remained simple, as opposed to the living quarters, which were more ornamented to give them a strong horizontal look and a general dynamic feeling. This was contrasted on the first floor with a vertical rhythm of portals and entrances. Prandtauer later added a garden pavilion (1708) with a small front stair and a mansard roof, whose careful proportions achieved an elegant silhouette. In 1703, Prandtauer was commissioned to extend a cellar in Wielandsthal which he built as a large domed building with vaulted windows. The exterior treatment was clearly baroque while on the inside, rusticated plaster was realized according to the local tradition.

In 1689, Prandtauer had remodeled and completed a four-wing courtyard for the Benedictine Monastery of Weikendorf. The columns integrated in the walls, the high arcades, and the minimal ornamentation achieved a feeling of plasticity, anticipating the later design for Melk Abbey. Through his designs for several bridges in the Wienerwald over the Danube, Prandtauer established the reputation that brought him the commission for Melk Abbey, which was to become his masterpiece.

The great Benedictine Abbey at Melk, Austria, dramatically located on a site towering above the Danube, occupied Prandtauer until the end of his life. He first rebuilt the church in a very sculptural baroque. The prior at Melk had asked Prandtauer to follow the baroque character of Carlo Antonio Carlone's design for Saint Florian's Abbey. In spite of this demand, Prandtauer emphasized the dramatic effect of light with a higher construction than the one achieved at Saint Florian and opened an imposing central vertical space. By integrating the columns within the curving of the walls, the design allowed more natural light and produced a three-dimensional effect that was expressed on the exterior as well. A particular way of vaulting the ceiling followed that at Saint Florian to allow a better setting for the paintings. The interior design of the church suffered from the numerous consultants who overdecorated the surfaces with statues and paintings even though such renowned craftsmen as M. Steinl and A. Bedduzzi participated in the work. It appears that no general consensus was reached on the extent of the ornamentation, on which the abbey's prior had been so insistant. As a result, Prandtauer's original idea for the interior decoration was largely distorted. For the exterior, Prandtauer developed a complex façade for the church, the deep layers of ornamentation exhibiting his original exploration of the baroque. The façade had a general vertical rhythm which was counteracted by a secondary horizontal organization created by the window sills, all of which was then topped by the curvilinear verticality of twin towers. His friend Carlo Antonio Carlone provided him with documents on FRANCESCO BORROMINI and GUARINO GUARINI from whom Prandtauer borrowed the formal motifs. For the general design, Prandtauer was influenced by JOHANN BERNHARD FISCHER VON ERLACH's churches in Salzburg. Similarly, KILIAN IGNAZ DIENTZENHOFER's design for the Church of Saint Nicholas in Prague and LUCAS VON HILDEBRANDT's design for the choir of Saint Lawrence in Gabel were contemporary influential examples. Prandtauer, in his design for Melk Abbey, realized a personal synthesis of the vernacular architectural tradition with the Austrian baroque. He never intended to create a style or make an architectural statement, but he was influential until the mid-eighteenth century. Melk remains, by its dramatic site, the impact of its façade, and the interior space, one of the great monuments of the baroque.

Following Melk Abbey, Prandtauer obtained mainly religious commissions. In 1706, he designed Sonntagberg Pilgrimage Church in a quieter environment as a reduced version of Melk Abbey. Calling for lighter ornamentation, the plan was based, as was Melk, on the presence of a cross-vaulted structure. The dominant tower was simpler than the one at Melk but its massive aspect created a monumental effect. The design for the Carmelite Abbey of Sankt Pölten in 1708 marked a return to his clear ornamentation as shown by the windows and a small number of sculptures. The general impression created at the Carmelite Abbey was of a simple spatial effect without all the distractions that were generated by the baroque designs in contemporary buildings. The crossing of the transept into the nave softened and refined the longitudinal rhythm which Prandtauer had achieved repeatedly in his previous designs.

In 1708, Prandtauer undertook the completion of Garsten Abbey after the death of Carlo Antonio Carlone, including both the guest range and the Christkindl Church. Prandtauer respected the drumlike shape of the church (as originally designed) although he preferred a long nave. In charge of the completion of Sankt Florian, Prandtauer worked on the opened staircase; he later designed the Marble Hall (1718–1722) and the Summer House (built posthumously).

Around 1709, Prandtauer started to work on the Monastery of Klosterneuberg which he organized around large cloisters. This hierarchical layout was typical of seventeenth-century buildings. Connected to a main axis, the larger halls were arranged in a crescendo fashion. Prandtauer's original idea was to use a revised version of palazzo architecture introduced by Fischer von Erlach in Upper Austria and inspired by the northern Italian Palladian (see ANDREA PALLADIO) style. Its clearest Austrian manifestations were in neoclassical monumental façades. The construction of the monastery started in 1713, with the collaboration of fine German craftsmen who had worked earlier for Fischer von Erlach.

In 1715, he undertook the completion of Herzogenburg Monastery, which had originally been planned by Fischer von Erlach. Respecting the over-all concept, Prandtauer realized the details in his own style, adapting the work to the taste of the official architecture of the emperor. In Herzogenburg, Prandtauer was placed in charge of large commercial buildings for which his skill was then fully developed; he mastered the positioning of small and large rooms in such a way that the scale appeared broken down. This hierarchy achieved a high artistic effect and expressed on the exterior the different functions of the interior spaces. Prandtauer used this same concept of scale manipulation in large commercial buildings for the Meierhof in Kremsmünster (1717–1722) and the Dechantei in Saint Florian (1712).

When designing Hohenbrunn Castle in 1724, Prandtauer adopted a strict baroque–classic mannerism in which he integrated motifs of triumphal vaults. Using stucco and skylights for the interiors, he shaped the buildings in a longitudinal rhythm associated with short and vertical cross-sections.

Back in Saint Pölten to work on the Romanesque abbey church, Prandtauer completely transformed the interior into the current baroque style. Personally committed to the completion of the nave, he participated even financially. The rich ornamentation and the wall niches were similar to those of the Melk Abbey (just completed in 1721).

In his last two projects, for the churches of Ravelsbach (1721–1726) and Wullersdorf (1725), Prandtauer designed in a classical manner. The interior walls were lightly curved and the general decoration echoed this effect by its rather plain character.

In the last twenty years of his career, Prandtauer was an adviser throughout the country for the rebuilding and the restoration of numerous religious buildings. Moving from one project to another, he made many different design decisions. Having mastered the current baroque style, he adapted to the various local traditions with overlaps of Roman Italian, northern Italian, and German influences. His flexibility in different situations, with an authentic search for Austrian simplicity, made him free of what could have been a stylistic dogma; he raised his architecture and ornamentations to an original craftsmanship.

MARC DILET

WORKS

1689, Benedictine Monastery (remodeling and completion), Weikendorf, Austria. 1690, Castle of Thalheim (chapel and pavilions), Austria. 1694–1700, Parish House and Cellar, Haitzendorf, Austria. 1696, Bridges, Zehendorf and Joching, Austria. 1696–1700, Sankt Pölten Abbey, Schwaighof, Austria. 1698, Castle (additions), Ochsenburg, Austria. 1702–1706, Church and Monastery (new construction and rebuilding), Melk, Austria. 1702–1707, Church (remodeling), Weikendorf, Austria. 1703, Cellar Extension, Wiesenthal, Austria. 1706–1718, Pilgrimage Church, Sonntagberg Church, Austria. 1708, Garden Pavilion, Haitzendorf, Austria. 1708–1712, Carmelite Church and Monastery, Saint Pölten, Schwaighof, Austria. 1708–1715, Garsten Monastery (completion), Saint Florian, Austria. 1713, Monastery, Klosterneuburg, Austria. 1714, Monastery, Herzogenburg, Austria. 1715–1726, Church (remodeling), Ponsee, Austria. 1716, Refectory, Melk, Austria. 1717–1722, Meierhof, Kremsmünster, Linz, Austria. 1718–1722, Marble Hall, Saint Florian, Austria. 1719–1726, Court of Kremsmünster, Linz, Austria. 1720, Dechantei, Saint Florian, Austria. 1721–1722, Church (remodeling of the nave), Saint Pölten, Schwaighof, Austria. 1721–1726, Church, Ravelsbach, Austria. 1724–1726, Hohenbrunn, Austria. 1725, Church, Wullersdorf, Austria. 1725–1728, Monastery, Herzogenburg, Austria.

BIBLIOGRAPHY

BACHMANN, LUISE GEORGE 1949 *Die andere Schöp-*

fung: Ein Baumeister Roman. Paderborn, Germany: Schoningh.
HEMPEL, EBERHARD 1965 *Baroque Art and Architecture in Central Europe.* Translated by Elizabeth Hempel and Marguerite Ray. Harmondsworth England: Penguin.
HOTZ, WALTER 1938 *Melk und die Wachbau.* Berlin: Rembrandt.
HANTSCH, HUGO 1926 *Jakob Prandtauer: Der Klosterarchitekt des osterreichischen Barock.* Vienna: Krystall.
KERBER, OTTMAR 1947 *Von Bramante zu Lucas von Hildebrandt.* Stuttgart, Germany: Kohlhammer.
MILLON, HENRY A. 1961 *Baroque and Rococo Architecture.* New York: Braziller.
RIESENHUBER, MARTIN 1924 *Die kirchliche Barockkunst in Österreisch.* Linz, Austria: Christlichen Kunstblätter.
SCHIER, WILHELM 1938 *Das Benediktinerstift Melk a.d. Donau.* Vienna: Filser.
SEDLMAYR, HANS 1930 *Österreichische Barockarchitektur: 1690–1740.* Vienna: Filser.
VOLKSHOCHSCHULE LANDECK 1960 *Bildner, Planer und Poeten im Oberen Inntal: Festschrift der Volkhochschule Landeck anlässlich des 300. Geburtstages Jakob Prandtauer's geleitet von Hermann Kuprian.* Innsbruck, Austria: Wagner.

PRATT, ROGER

Roger Pratt (1620–1685) was a country gentleman whose family seat was Ryston in Norfolk, England. He professed to the law, but the death of his father in 1640 enabled him to undertake a grand tour from 1643 to 1649, traveling in Flanders, Holland, France, and Italy, and making extensive observations of architecture. Around 1645, the year he matriculated in law at Padua University, he was living in Rome with John Evelyn, another expatriate from the nastiness of Cromwellian England. Pratt's study of continental architecture was probably as thorough as Evelyn's, but unlike Evelyn, Pratt was determined to put these studies to good and practical use. His diaries and papers are full of clever and sensible observations and he codified all this under various useful headings, such as "Notes on the Building of Country Houses" or "Rules for the Guidance of Architects." ANDREA PALLADIO, VINCENZO SCAMOZZI, or SEBASTIANO SERLIO are laid under tribute, but Pratt was more than just a textbook theorist, for to deep reading he added succinct interpretations of Italian and French architecture.

All this led to his becoming, as Howard Colvin aptly writes, "one of the pioneers of classical architecture in England," and this was expressed in a series of magisterial country houses that for consistency of style and treatment have no peer. The first was Coleshill House (c.1650), Berkshire, for

Pratt. Coleshill House. Berkshire, England. c.1650

his distant cousin Sir George Pratt, and it is interesting that here Pratt persuaded his cousin to demolish a partly built home that may well have been designed by JOHN WEBB, if not INIGO JONES. Whereas Webb's house had the traditional orders of architecture as applied to the façades, Pratt's is astylar, or unadorned by columns or pilasters; and in his succeeding houses, all astylar, Pratt can be described, to coin a word, as a master of astylism. Coleshill is a synthesis of long years of study, drawing upon Jones and both French and Italian architecture, in the latter case most notably Genoese palaces. Kingston Lacy, Dorset, followed in 1663, along with, in the same year, Horseheath, Cambridgeshire; then came Pratt's greatest achievement in Clarendon House, Piccadilly (1664), built for the first earl of Clarendon. All these houses adopt the double pile plan with the hall backing upon a saloon on the middle axis, plain façades with perfect proportioning of windows to wall, a hipped roof usually with dormer windows, and often a balustraded platform with a central cupola. As one who lived in Norfolk, Pratt may well have known of Jones's prophetic Prince's Lodging at Newmarket (1619) and benefited from it, and a study of Pratt's work cannot exclude the influence of that other gentleman architect, WILLIAM SAMWELL. Both men established the country house type dominant throughout the decades of the 1660s through the 1690s, and Clarendon House in particular was immensely influential because of its central and urban position. Derivatives are Belton House (1685), Lincolnshire, possibly by William Winde, and Denham Place (1688), Buckinghamshire, by WILLIAM STANTON, who had been the mason contractor at Belton.

Pratt was one of the architectural luminaries at the Restoration, one of the new junta so to write, and with HUGH MAY and Sir CHRISTOPHER WREN, he advised on the repair of Saint Paul's Cathedral. He was also one of the commissioners to supervise the rebuilding of London after the Great Fire of 1666, and it was probably for these services that he was knighted in 1668.

JOHN HARRIS

WORKS

*c.1650, Coleshill House, Berkshire, England. 1663, Horseheath Hall, Cambridgeshire, England. 1663, Kingston Lacy, Dorset, England. 1664, Clarendon House, Piccadilly, London, 1669, Ryston Hall, Norfolk, England.

BIBLIOGRAPHY

GUNTHER, R. T. (editor) 1928 *The Architecture of Sir Roger Pratt, Charles II's Commissioner for the Rebuilding of London After the Great Fire: Now Printed for the First Time From His Note-Books.* Oxford University Press.

SUMMERSON, JOHN (1963)1971 *Architecture in Britain, 1530–1830.* Rev. ed. New York: Penguin.

PRICE, BRUCE

Born in Cumberland, Maryland, Bruce Price (1845–1903) practiced briefly in Baltimore and Wilkes-Barre, Pennsylvania, before moving to New York in 1877. His early work was primarily domestic, culminating in the design and layout of Tuxedo Park, New York (1885–1890), a vacation community financed by Pierre Lorillard IV. The Shingle style houses Price built at Tuxedo, with their compact massing and axial plans, were extremely influential, especially for the work of the young FRANK LLOYD WRIGHT. The most notable of his later works, usually eclectic in inspiration, are the Romanesque Revival Windsor Station, Montreal (1888–1889), and a twenty-story office block in New York (1894–1896) for the American Surety Company.

TIMOTHY F. RUB

WORKS

1885–1890, Tuxedo Park (houses and community buildings), N.Y. 1888–1889, Windsor Station, Montreal. 1892–1893, Chateau Frontenac Hotel, Quebec City, Canada. 1894–1896, American Surety Building, New York.

BIBLIOGRAPHY

SCULLY, VINCENT 1971 *The Shingle Style and the Stick Style.* Rev. ed. New Haven: Yale University Press.

STURGIS, RUSSELL (1899)1977 *The Works of Bruce Price.* Reprint. New York: Da Capo. First published in the June 1899 issue of the *Architectural Record.*

PRICE, UVEDALE

Although Uvedale Price (1747–1829) was not the first critic in eighteenth-century Britain to write about the Picturesque and its relation to the fine arts, he was the style's arch-theoretician. His published work on the subject shows him to have been discerning, sensible, and evocative. Immensely influential upon landscape gardening and architectural theory and practice was Price's insistence on the character of the Picturesque as an aesthetic category distinct from the Sublime and the Beautiful. He emphasized its "variety and intricacy," its "sudden and broken" lines and surfaces, its projected tension between the natural and the contrived, between accident and order. An aristocratic product of Eton and Oxford, in touch with the best kindred minds of his time, such as RICHARD PAYNE KNIGHT, JOHN NASH, and HUMPHRY REPTON, Price lived an independent and semiretired life on his estate in Foxley, Herefordshire, but his influence has reached well into the twentieth century.

MARCIA ALLENTUCK

BIBLIOGRAPHY

ALLENTUCK, MARCIA 1974 "Sir Uvedale Price and the Picturesque Garden." Pages 59–76 in Nikolaus Pevsner (editor), *The Picturesque Garden and Its Influence Outside the British Isles.* Washington: Dumbarton Oaks.

HUSSEY, CHRISTOPHER 1967 *The Picturesque.* London: Cass.

PRICE, WILLIAM

Although William Price (1861–1916) had no academic architectural training, during the 1880s he studied evenings at the School of Applied Arts Division, School of Industrial Arts in Philadelphia. Throughout his career, Price worked in the Philadelphia area.

Before 1900, his practice consisted primarily of country estates, but after 1900 he expanded his commissions to include hotels, factories, and commercial buildings. Many of his projects used the new technology of steel and reinforced concrete. His style was an unusual merging of European and American sources and personal sensibilities.

PATRICIA C. PHILLIPS

WORKS

1898–1914, Traymore Hotel (additions), Atlantic City, N.J. 1901–1911, Rose Valley Planned Community, Pennsylvania. 1914–1919, Chicago Freight Terminal.

BIBLIOGRAPHY

SKY, ALISON, and STONE, MICHELE 1976 *Unbuilt America.* New York: McGraw-Hill.

THOMAS, GEORGE E. 1975 "William Price (1861–1916): Builder of Men and Buildings." Unpublished Ph.D. dissertation, University of Pennsylvania, Philadelphia.

PRICHARD, JOHN

John Prichard (1817–1886), born in Llangan, Wales, was the twelfth son of the vicar-choral of Llandaff. He was a pupil of T. L. Walker, who was a pupil and executor of A. C. Pugin. Prichard worked with Walker and A. W. N. PUGIN on the third volume of *Examples of Gothic Architecture* (1836).

Prichard set up practice in Llandaff and was diocesan architect from 1847 until his death. From 1852 to 1863, he was in partnership with JOHN POLLARD SEDDON.

Prichard, "a true disciple of Pugin," was also influenced by JOHN RUSKIN, and his work at Ettington Park (1858–1865) is one of the best examples of polychrome Ruskinian Gothic. BASIL CHAMPNEYS was his pupil.

ROGER DIXON

WORKS

1843–1882, Llandaff Cathedral (additions), Cardiff. 1849–1850, Saint Swithin, Ganarew, Herefordshire, England. 1849–1851, Saint Teilo, Merthyr Mawr, Glamorgshire, Wales. Begun 1854, Saint John the Baptist, Canton, Cardiff. 1858–1863, Saint Mary, Aberavon, near Port Talbot, Wales. 1858–1865, Ettington Park, Warwickshire, England. c.1859, School, Llandough, Glamorganshire, Wales. 1859–1860, Saint John, Maindee, Gwent, Wales. 1860–1863, Probate and Episcopal Registries, Llandaff, Cardiff. 1861–1864, Christ's College, Brecon, Wales. 1869–1871, Saint Margaret's, Roath, Cardiff. 1877, Saint Cadfarch, Penegoes, Wales. 1882, Saint Catherine, Baglan, Glamorganshire, Wales. 1885, Bute Mortuary Chapel, Saint Margaret's, Roath, Cardiff.

BIBLIOGRAPHY

CLARKE, BASIL (1938)1969 *Church Builders of the Nineteenth Century.* Reprint. Newton Abbot, England: David & Charles.

GIROUARD, MARK (1971)1979 *The Victorian Country House.* Rev. ed. New Haven: Yale University Press.

HASLAM, RICHARD 1979 *Powys.* Harmondsworth, England: Penguin.

HILLING, JOHN B. 1976 *The Historic Architecture of Wales.* Cardiff: University of Wales.

PHYSICK, JOHN, and DARBY, MICHAEL 1973 *Marble Halls.* London: H.M. Stationery Office.

PUGIN, A. W. N. ET AL. (1831)1895 *Examples of Gothic Architecture.* 3 vols. Reprint. Edinburgh: Grant.

TYACK, GEOFFREY 1979 "A Victorian Architectural Correspondence." *Architectural History* 22:78–87.

PRIMATICCIO, FRANCESCO

Primaticcio. Grotto, Jarden des Pins. Fontainebleau, France. 1543

Painter-sculptor-architect Francesco Primaticcio (1504/1505–1570) was one of the prime agents for the transfer of the architectural style of the High Renaissance and Mannerism from Italy to northern Europe. Born in Bologna and strongly influenced by the painter Parmigianino, he worked with GIULIO ROMANO in Mantua, Italy, before moving to France in 1532, where he was employed almost without break until his death in Paris. Though his fame rests largely on his painting and his remarkable stucco sculpture, he was also an able architect.

Primaticcio's key early experience was as an assistant to Giulio Romano between 1526 and 1531 at the Palazzo del Té, Mantua. There, he worked as a decorator—painting and sculpting—though not, so far as we know, as an architect. Nonetheless, his work with Giulio Romano was extremely important for it was on the basis of this that he was invited by Francis I in 1532 to come to France to work on the construction and decoration of his country residence at Fontainebleau.

In conjunction with Rosso Fiorentino, who was already there, and Niccolò dell'Abbate and Pelligrino Tebaldi, who arrived later, they formed a group of Italian artists known later as the school of Fontainebleau. Primaticcio's lissome stucco sculpture and highly colored gracile figures are the hall mark of the Fontainebleau/Italian style. Although Primaticcio and his team of Italian workmen were involved in the decoration of many rooms, very little has survived. In at least one case (Chambre du Roi, 1533–1536), a room design was supplied by Giulio Romano.

During his years in France, Primaticcio returned to Italy on a couple of occasions. In 1540, he went to Rome and returned with the architect GIACOMO BAROZZI DA VIGNOLA. Though largely active as a painter and stuccoist, he also built a number of architectural works of which the Grotto des Pins of 1543, modeled on the Grotto of Giulio Romano at Mantua, is the most distinguished. Primaticcio may also have seen MICHELANGELO's *Slaves,* two of which had been sent to France.

In his later years, Primaticcio turned more to architecture. The wing of Fontainebleau known as the Aile de la Belle Cheminée of 1568 and the fu-

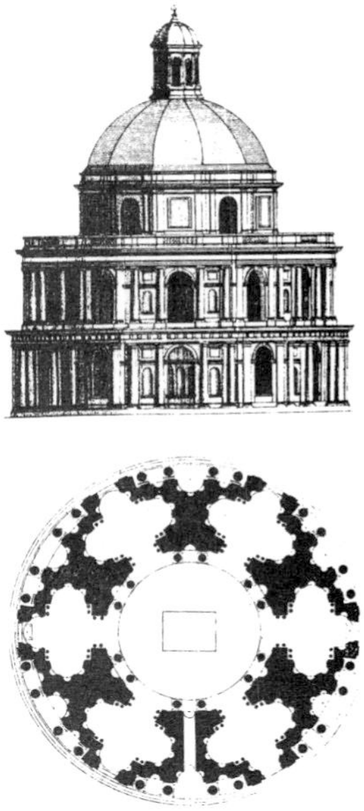

Primaticcio. Chapelle des Valois (funerary chapel completed by others). Saint Denis, Paris. 1563

nerary chapel of the Valois at Saint Denis, designed in 1563 but not built until after Primaticcio's death, are examples of this heightened architectural activity. The former reflects Primaticcio's reawakened classicism under the influence of Vignola while the latter, an elaborately sculpted chapel, recalls early sixteenth-century church/chapel designs such as DONATO BRAMANTE's Tempietto and Michelangelo's early plans for the Julius II Tomb, as well as Antonio da Sangallo's (see SANGALLO FAMILY) model of St. Peter's. This work, since destroyed, was largely brought to completion by JEAN BULLANT.

Primaticcio received numerous honors in his lifetime. His final trip to Italy was in 1563 when, as an old man, he returned to his native city of Bologna where he met GIORGIO VASARI, then in the process of rewriting his *Lives of the Artists*.

NICHOLAS ADAMS

WORKS

1533–1536, Palais de Fontainebleau (Chambre du Roi, Chambre de la Reine); 1543, Grotto, Jarden des Pins; Fontainebleau, France. 1555, Grotto, Château de Meudon, France. *1563, Chapelle des Valois (funerary chapel completed by others after Primaticcio's death), Saint Denis, Paris. 1568, Palais de Fontainebleau (Aile de la Belle Cheminée), France.

BIBLIOGRAPHY

BLUNT, ANTHONY (1957)1977 *Art and Architecture in France 1500–1700.* 2d ed. Harmondsworth, England: Penguin.
DIMIER, LOUIS 1900 *Le Primatice.* Paris: Leroux.
LERSCH, T. 1970 *Die Grabkapelle der Valois in St. Denis.* Munich.

PRIMOLI, JUAN BAUTISTA

Juan Bautista Primoli (1673–1747) was born in Milan. Soon after entering the Society of Jesus, he sailed for Buenos Aires in 1717, and completed his novitiate in Córdoba in 1719.

In Buenos Aires, he drew the plans for the Chapter Houses, continuing works in the Superior College and other Jesuit buildings in Córdoba between 1720 and 1729. A year later, he traveled to the Jesuit Missions of the Guaraníes, where he designed his most spectacular works. In San Miguel (1733) and in Santíssima Trinidad (1740), he applied a classical language to his three-naved churches, rich in stone relief and wall paintings.

His work has often been mistakenly ascribed to ANDRÉS BLANQUI, a fellow Jesuit, to whom he was closely connected in his work. Primoli stands out mostly as the experienced builder capable of technological renewal, such as was applied in the Jesuit Missions of the Guaraníes.

RAMOŃ GUTÍERREZ

WORKS

1720–1729, Superior College and Novitiate (works); (A)1727, Santa Catalina (cloister of the estancia); Córdoba, Argentina. 1731, Bridge on the Igarupá River, Misiones, Argentina. 1731, Church of the La Cruz Mission, Corrientes, Argentina. 1733, Church of San Miguel; 1740, Church of Trinidad; 1745, Church of Concepción de la Sierra; Misiones, Argentina.

BIBLIOGRAPHY

BUSANICHE, HERNÁN 1955 *La arquitectura en las Misiones Jesuíticas Guaraníes.* Santa Fe, Argentina: El Litoral.
BUSCHIAZZO, MARIO J. 1969 *Estancias Jesuíticas.* Buenos Aires: Filmediciones.
FURLONG, GUILLERMO 1946 *Arquitectos argentinos durante la dominación hispánica.* Buenos Aires: Editorial Huarpes.
FURLONG, GUILLERMO 1962 *Misiones y sus pueblos guaraníes.* Buenos Aires: Ediciones Theoría.
GUTÍERREZ, RAMÓN (1976)1978 *Evolución urbanística y arquitectónica del Paraguay.* 2d ed. Corrientes, Argentina: Departamento de Historia de la Arquitectura, Universidad Nacional del Nordeste.

PRISBREY, TRESSA

Without training or machinery, Tressa Prisbrey (1895–) hand-built thirteen small buildings in Santa Susana, California, out of bottles set in concrete to house her collection of treasures salvaged from the city dump. Pencils, shot glasses, hanging gourds, and discarded dolls fill her Pencil House, Shell House, Cleopatra's Bedroom, and other surrounding garden shrines and pavements studded with auto headlights, broken pottery, old license plates, and more.

JANET KAPLAN

WORK

1950s–1970s, Bottle Village, Santa Susana, Calif.

BIBLIOGRAPHY

McCOY, ESTHER 1974 "Grandma Prisbrey's Bottle Village." Pages 76–85 in Walker Art Center, *Naives and Visionaries.* New York: Dutton.
PRISBREY, TRESSA 1967 *Grandma's Bottle Village.* n.p.: Privately printed.

PRITCHARD, THOMAS

Thomas Farnolls Pritchard (1723–1777) will always be famous for the design of the cast-iron bridge at Shrewsbury (1767) and his role in the cast-iron bridge erected at Coalbrookdale (1767), the first in the world. He also commanded a huge architectural practice centered in Shropshire, where he was active from around 1745 to at least 1777. A Georgian architect handling classical and Gothic designs, his interiors were always elegant in the trim of decoration.

JOHN HARRIS

WORKS

1749, Saint Julian's Church, Shrewsbury; 1759, Tern Hall, Attingham; 1761, Swan Hill Court House, Shrewsbury; 1764, Hatton Grange; 1767, Cast-iron Bridge, Shrewsbury; 1767, Coalbrookdale Bridge; 1774, The Guildhall, Ludlow; 1777, Ironbridge, Coalbrookdale; Shropshire, England.

PRITCHETT, JAMES PIGOTT

Born in Pembrokeshire, England, James Pigott Pritchett (1789–1868) was educated as architect and sculptor in London. In 1813, he joined Charles Watson in York. His early work was strictly Greco-Roman, combined with technological advances in heating and ventilation. His designs from the 1820s for public buildings and churches were in the Gothic Revival style. He worked independently from 1831. His masterpiece of later years was Huddersfield Railway Station (1846–1847).

IVAN HALL

WORKS

1814, Wooley Park (lodge and gateway), West Yorkshire, England. 1816, Lendal Independent Chapel, York, England. 1818, Brafferton Vicarage, North Yorkshire, England. *1824, Ramsden Street Noncomformist Chapel, Huddersfield, West Yorkshire, England. 1827–1831, The Deanery, York, England. 1829, Saint Peter's School; 1829–1830, Saving's Bank, Saint Helen's Square; York, England. 1830, Nether Hoyland Church, South Yorkshire, England. 1832, Oakamoor Church, Staffordshire, England. 1835, Meltham Church, West Yorkshire, England. 1840, Vicarage, New Malton, North Yorkshire, England. 1846, Friend's Meetinghouse, Ackworth; 1846–1847, Railway Station, Huddersfield; 1847–1848, Flounder's Institute, Ackworth; 1861, Wesleyan Chapel, Sheepscar, Leeds; West Yorkshire, England.

BIBLIOGRAPHY

BIDEAULT, MARYSE, and LAUTIER, CLAUDINE 1977 "Saint-Nicaise de Reims: Chronologie et nouvelles remarques sur l'architecture." *Bulletin Monumental* 135:295–330.

BRANNER, ROBERT 1965 *St. Louis and the Court Style in Gothic Architecture.* London: Zwemmer.

GIVELET, CHARLES 1897 *L'église et l'abbaye de Saint-Nicaise de Reims: Notice historique et archéologique.* Reims, France: Michaud.

PROMIS, CARLO

Carlo Promis (1808–1872), Piedmontese architect and historian of architecture, after graduating in architecture from the university at Turin, Italy, in 1828, spent eight years in Rome in architectural and archeological studies. His first published work was devoted to epigraphical information on marble workers in Rome from the tenth to the fifteenth centuries (1836). This volume was followed by his publication of FRANCESCO DI GIORGIO MARTINI's treatise on civil and military architecture (1841), the first of a series of studies on military architecture and initial publication of treatises from the fifteenth through the seventeenth centuries. While publishing periodically, Promis continued his archeological investigations (he was appointed inspector of ancient monuments in 1837) and practiced and taught architecture. As professor of architecture at the University of Turin (1843–1869), he was responsible for the training of several generations of architects, including CARLO CEPPI and his contemporaries.

His architecture shows less interest in neo-Gothic than in early Christian (Basilica Christiana, project, 1845) and Renaissance styles, and he seems to have been attracted to buildings of the late fifteenth century in north Italy with profuse surface decorations (Casa Rizzetti, Turin, 1846). He prepared many projects for streets and piazzas in Turin, but probably his most influential plan was that for the area around the new railroad station at Porta Nuova. Once the appropriateness, adaptability, and civility of these buildings became known, they, or buildings similar, were extended east and west along Corso Vittorio Emanuele, and north and south on via Sacchi, via XX Settembre, via Lagrange, and via Nizza, providing a permanent, unifying skeletal network for the Porta Nuova sector.

HENRY A. MILLON

WORKS

1847, Casa Rizzetti; 1851, Piazza Carlo Felice (buildings on east and west forming the piazza); 1853, Housing, Piazza Solferino; Turin, Italy.

BIBLIOGRAPHY

CASTELLAZZI, GIOVANNI 1871–1875 *Fabbriche moderne inventate da Carlo Promis.* Turin, Italy: Bocca.

CAVALLARI-MURAT, AUGUSTO 1969 "Carlo Promis come urbanista: Auvio per una bibliografia riabilitativa." *Atti e Rassegna tecnica* no. 7.

CAVALLARI-MURAT, AUGUSTO 1976–1977 "Sperimentazione stilistica di Carlo Promis per Carlo Alberto: Una basilica cristiana (1845)." *Bollettino della Società Piemontese di Archeologia e Belle Arti* 30–31:62–73.

HITCHCOCK, H. R. (1958)1977 *Architecture: Nineteenth and Twentieth Centuries.* 4th ed., rev. Baltimore: Penguin.

LUMBROSO, GIAC. 1877 *Memorie e lettere di C. Promis.* Turin, Italy: Bocca.

MEEKS, CARROLL L. V. 1966 *Italian Architecture: 1750–1914.* New Haven: Yale University Press.

PROMIS, CARLO 1836 *Notizie epigrafiche degli artefici marmorari romani dal X al XV secolo.* Turin, Italy.

PROMIS, CARLO 1841*a* *Cinque dissertazioni dell'arte dell'ingegnere e dell'artigliere in Italia. . . .* Turin, Italy: Trattato di architettura.

PROMIS, CARLO 1841*b* *Trattato di architettura civile e militare di Francesco di Giorgio Martini.* 2 vols. Turin, Italy: Chirio e Mina. Includes *Vita di Francesco di Giorgio Martini architetto senese del secolo XV.*

PROMIS, CARLO 1844 *Della necessità dell'erudizione degli architetti.* Turin, Italy.

PROMIS, CARLO 1862 *Le antichità di Aosta. . . .* Turin, Italy: Stamperia Reale.

PROMIS, CARLO 1863 *Gl'ingegneri e gli scrittori militari Bolognesi del XV e XVI secolo.* Turin, Italy: Stamperia Reale.

PROMIS, CARLO 1873 *Gli architetti e l'architettura presso i romani.* Turin, Italy: Stamperia Reale.

PROMIS, CARLO 1875 *Vocaboli latini di architettura, posteriori a Vitruvio, oppure a lui sconosqiuti.* Turin, Italy: Stamperia Reale.

RICCI, MATTEO 1873 *Carlo Promis, cenni necrologici.* Turin, Italy: Favale.

PROST, HENRI

Leon-Henri Prost (1874–1959) pioneered in city and regional planning. A Beaux-Arts student of Marcel Lambert, professor of stereotomy, whose surveys of the Athenian Acropolis were praised for their *vue d'ensemble* (1874), Prost gained his exemplary knowledge of construction at the Ecole Spéciale d'Architecture as well as from Lambert.

Prost's lifelong concern to integrate economic activity into aesthetically satisfying, habitable environments was evidenced in his Imprimerie Nationale (1902), which won the Prix de Rome. At the Villa Medici in Rome, Prost's contemporaries' grand schemes for antique Rome (Paul Bigot), Selinonte (Jean Hulot), and Tusculum and the Cité Industrielle (TONY GARNIER) encouraged him to request permission to survey the whole complex of the Hagia Sophia in Constantinople.

Prost won the competition for an infrastructure plan for Antwerp (1910) just after helping to found the Société Française des Urbanistes. He used the canal around the old fortified town to link it with the engineering polygon of Berchem. In 1913, Prost met a most sympathetic patron, General Lyautey, administrator of Morocco. For Casablanca, Prost planned a port development using reclaimed land. He then moved on to drafting planning codes for Meknes, Fez, and Marrakech, where he designed new towns to accommodate Europeans and modern economic activity which were linked to the *medinas* by green spaces. In Rabat, the director-general's residence was the focal point of an administrative complex interlaced with green boulevards.

Prost was called to do a Master Plan for the district of Var, France, in 1922. It became the prototype regional plan in France for conserving natural beauty while providing adequate auto routes and economic development. He then worked almost ten years to see his Regional Plan for Paris decreed in 1934.

Prost went back to Istanbul in 1935, where an enlightened city government gave him two years to survey traffic, provisioning, bazaars, handicrafts, land parcelling, and archeological remains. Prost directed the resulting Master Plan, decreed in 1937, until 1951 when he returned to Paris. In 1957, invited to Istanbul as a member of the Planning Commission, he witnessed the creation of the new Ministry of Urbanism to implement his scheme.

ELIZABETH MCLANE

WORKS

1913–1917, Casablanca Master Plan, Morocco. 1913–1917, Fez Master Plan, Morocco. 1913–1917, Marrakech Master Plan, Morocco. 1922, Regional Planning Regulations, Var, France. 1928–1939, Paris Regional Plan. 1939–1958, Istanbul Master Plan.

BIBLIOGRAPHY

ACADÉMIE D'ARCHITECTURE 1960 *L'Oeuvre de Henri Prost: Architecture et Urbanisme.* Paris: The academy.

DELORME, J. C. 1977 "De Henri Prost à Michel Ecochard." *Architecture Mouvement Continuité* no. 42:6–12.

GABRIEL, ALBERT 1960 "Henri Prost et son Oeuvre à Stamboul." *Revue Archéologique* Apr.–June:211–217.

GRÉBER, JACQUES 1960 "Henri Prost: 1874–1959." *Vie Urbaine* no. 1:1–18.

"Hommage à Henri Prost." 1975 *Académie d'Architecture* no. 65:39–47.

LUCAN, JACQUES 1977 "Casablanca." *Architecture Mouvement Continuité* no. 42:5.

PROST, HENRI 1952 "Hommage à Forrestier." *Urbanisme* 21, nos. 304:74–75.

PROST, LOUIS 1937 "Hommage à Tony Garnier." *Construction Moderne* 53, supp.:3–9.

ROYER, JEAN 1965 "Henri Prost—L'Urbanisation." *Urbanisme* 34, no. 88:2–31.

ROYER, JEAN 1975 "Henri Prost: A Very Great Patron, 1874–1959." *Architectes* no. 57:18–21.

PROUVE, JEAN

The son of Victor Prouvé, one of the leading figures in the brilliant decorative arts movement in Nancy, France, around 1900, Jean Prouvé (1901–) was a major innovator in the field of prefabricated structures. Although he had some education in engineering, he was principally trained in the craft of iron-working. His first independent work in iron dates from 1918 but he established his own shop, in Nancy, only in 1923. There, he designed and made iron grilles and other architectural elements to the order of such leading architects as ROBERT MALLET-STEVENS.

Prouvé's reputation grew rapidly, and in 1931 he reorganized his workshop to allow for expanded and diversified production. The new firm made not only isolated elements but also entire prefabricated structures of metal parts. These metal parts were cleverly shaped so that they achieved a maximum of stability per unit volume of material, according to a technology devised and constantly refined by Prouvé and a growing number of associated engineers and fabricators. Prouvé's design innovations always accompanied improvements in the means of production of building parts made with an eye to achieving both an ever greater economy of labor and materials in manufacture and an increased functional efficiency in use. (The parallel of his work with R. BUCKMINSTER FULLER's research is pertinent.) Working as a designer of structural and infill elements in collaboration with successive architects, including TONY GARNIER and LE CORBUSIER, and production teams, Prouvé participated in a kind of collective production of architecture like that advanced in theory and practice by WALTER GROPIUS as necessary in the context of an industrialized society.

If, during the 1930s, Prouvé's workshop had made great advances in the techniques of prefabricating special and prototypical constructive elements, these techniques had been mainly, and certainly most elegantly, applied to the production of individual structures. But from 1939 on, under the conditions of wartime production in France, these techniques found a more appropriate application (in terms of Prouvé's own theoretical objectives) in the industrialized production of large numbers of identical structures, necessarily cheap and easy to transport, erect, and remove. Among such structures designed and built by Prouvé's firm were hospitals, schools, factories, emergency dwellings, and military barracks. Some of these were designed in conjunction with PIERRE JEANNERET.

Immediately after World War II, Prouvé and his associates became involved in the mass production of quickly assembled houses as part of the French reconstruction effort. In spite of many difficulties relative to the conditions of their manufacture, these units were remarkable for the finesse of their design. In the late 1940s, through alliances made with major steel and aluminum concerns, the Prouvé firm underwent dramatic expansion. The consistently high quality of their significantly increased output is notable in the light of certain severe conflicts of interest that emerged between Prouvé and the financial management of his enlarged company. These conflicts eventually induced him to abandon it in 1953. At this time Prouvé moved from Nancy to Paris, where he worked as an independent designer of architectural components until he founded a new firm in 1956. In the 1960s, his most notable achievements lay in the domain of lightweight sheathing elements pressed from sheet metal and applicable to a wide variety of building types.

ALFRED WILLIS

WORKS

*1936–1937, Roland Garros Aero-Club, Buc, France. *1937, Pavilion of the Union of Contemporary Artists, Paris World's Fair. 1938–1939, Maison du Peuple (market), Clichy, France. 1939, Prototypical Emergency Houses. 1947–1948, Experimental School, Vantoux, France. 1949, Fédération du Bâtiment Building, Paris. 1950, Houses, Meudon, France. 1950, Marne Printing Works, Tours, France. 1950–1951, Exhibition Hall, Lille, France. 1951, Firehouse, Bordeaux, France. 1951, School Complex, Villejuif, France. 1956, Pump Room, Evian, France. *1958, Luxembourg Pavilion, Brussels World's Fair. 1961, French Atomic Energy Commission Building, Pierrelatte, France. 1966, Ermont Youth Center, Val d'Oise, Paris. 1967, Exhibition Hall, Grenoble, France. 1967, Houses and School, Saint-Michel-sur-Orge, France. 1967–1968, School, Orléans, France. 1968–1970, Prototypical Total Service Stations. 1969–1970, Ecole Nationale d'Architecture, Nancy, France.

BIBLIOGRAPHY

Architecture 1954 2, nos. 11–12: entire issue.

BANHAM, REYNER 1962 "Jean Prouvé: The Thin Bent Detail." *Architectural Review* 131, Apr.:249–252.

HUBER, BENEDIKT, and STEINEGGER, JEAN CLAUDE (editors) 1971 *Jean Prouvé Prefabrication: Structures and Elements.* Translated by Alexander Lieven. New York: Praeger.

Jean Prouvé. 1964 Paris: Musée des Arts Décoratifs. Exhibition catalogue.

Jean Prouvé Constructeur. 1981 Rotterdam, Netherlands: Museum Boymans-van Beuningen. Exhibition catalogue.

PROUVÉ, JEAN 1929 *Le Métal.* Paris: Moreau.

RABENECK, ANDREW 1971 "Jean Prouvé." *Architectural Design* 41, July:431–432.

RAGON, MICHEL 1972 Volume 2 in *Histoire mondiale de l'architecture et de l'urbanisme modernes.* Tournai, Belgium: Casterman.

WINTER, JOHN 1980 "Prouvé, Jean." Pages 645–646 in Muriel Emanuel (editor), *Contemporary Architects.* New York: St. Martin's.

"The Work of Jean Prouvé." 1963 *Architectural Design* 33: 511–525.

PRUTSCHER, OTTO

The architect and artisan Otto Prutscher (1880–1949) was born in Vienna where he studied at the Kunstgewerbeschule under Franz Matsch and JOSEF HOFFMANN. He traveled to Paris and London on a Rothschild grant in 1895. In 1903 he became an assistant at the Graphische Lehr- und Versuchsanstalt in 1909, a professor at the Kunstgewerbeschule and in 1918 an inspector for the Fortbildungsschulwesen, Vienna, in 1918. Prutscher's architectural projects and interiors evince the static, ultra-refined, Art Deco classicizing characteristic of Hoffmann's work around 1910 and of much Viennese architecture of the period. Prutscher also designed furniture, textiles, silverware, jewelry, ceramics, leather goods, glassware, wallpaper, and lighting for numerous Viennese firms, including the Wiener Werkstätte.

SHELLEY SMITH KELLAM

WORKS

n.d., Bienenfeld Villa, Baden, Austria. n.d., Flemmich House, Jägerndorf, Austria. n.d., Heinrichshof Café, Vienna. n.d., Kapsch House, Mitterbach bei Mariazell, Austria. n.d., Municipal Housing on the Stöbergasse, Längenfeldgasse, Harkurtstrasse, and Güpferlinggasse; n.d., Österreichischer Werkbund Department Store, Kärntnerring; Vienna. n.d., Rothberger Villa, Baden, Austria. n.d., Wertheim House, Mariazell, Austria. n.d., Wiener Dianabad Warm Water Baths; n.d., Zykan (main entrance), Kohlmarkt; Vienna.

BIBLIOGRAPHY

EISLER, MAX 1916 "Otto Prutscher." *Die Kunst* 34, Feb.:166–172.

EISLER, MAX 1917 "Otto Prutschers Villa in Jägerndorf." *Die Kunst* 36, Mar.:182–190.

RUSSELL, FRANK (editor) 1980 *Art Nouveau Architecture.* New York: Rizzoli.

SAXL, FRITZ 1913 "Zwei Landhäuser von Otto Prutscher." *Der Architekt* 19:61–62, plates 136–139.

WEISER, ARMAND 1924 "Otto Prutscher." *Die Kunst* 50, Sept.:272–282.

PUGIN, AUGUSTUS CHARLES

Augustus Charles Pugin (1768–1832), a French émigré, lived most of his life in England. He is best known for his books of accurate illustrations of English and French medieval buildings published between 1821 and his death. From 1800 to 1820, he had specialized in architectural and topographical illustrations in aquatint, engraving, and watercolor. From 1817 on, he trained students in architectural drawing and dealt in foreign, particularly French, and English books on art and architecture.

Pugin came from France sometime before May 1792, when he registered as a student of painting at the Royal Academy. Shortly thereafter, he was employed by JOHN NASH who was his principal employer for seventeen years during which Pugin attempted to found an independent career through exhibition, sale, and publication of his watercolors. He exhibited first at the Royal Academy in 1799.

In 1802, Pugin married Catherine Welby, the daughter of a barrister. Augustus Welby Northmore Pugin (see A. W. N. PUGIN), their only child, was born in 1812. Mrs. Pugin was a person of considerable energy and intellectual power, and assisted her husband in the management of his work.

In what was clearly an effort to become an independent publisher, he joined J. C. Nattes in 1804 in the publication of two books, one of which was *A Tour of Oxford* which contained architectural views; neither was successful. Pugin then produced and marketed inexpensive prints of public occasions, among them the funeral of Lord Nelson and the trial of Lord Melville. Pugin was elected to associate membership in the Society of Painters in Water Colours in 1807, an indication of his standing in the field for he was one of two selected from a panel of seventeen candidates.

The decisive change in his fortunes came when in the same year Rudolph Ackermann embarked on large-scale publication of topographical books with colored aquatint plates. Pugin was one of his specialists in architectural illustration. Between 1808 and 1810, working with Thomas Rowlandson, Pugin produced the plates for the *Microcosm of London.* Many of the plates for *The Repository of Arts, Literature, Commerce, Manufactures, Fashions and Politics,* a periodical begun by Ackermann in 1809, were taken from Pugin watercolors. Ackermann republished some of the popular *Repository* illustrations as separate books. Pugin's *Gothic Furniture* appeared in this form, and many of the plates in JOHN BUONAROTTI PAPWORTH's *Select Views of London* were also his. Between 1810 and 1815, Pugin participated in the work on the remarkable illustrated books on Westminster Abbey, the universities of Oxford and Cambridge, and the public schools, all published by Ackermann.

After Waterloo, as public interest in places abroad was increased by travel, Ackermann published less English and more foreign topography, with the result that Pugin, though he continued to work on occasion with him, became more and more involved with personal projects as he exploited the reputation he had acquired. John Nash continued to employ him to prepare finished drawings. Pugin began to use draftsmen, some of whom were also his students, who traveled in parties under his supervision to sketch the subject he required. He established contact with potential clients, one of whom was the earl of Essex. He undertook to publish books on architecture and topography. *Specimens of Gothic Architecture* (1816), with plates by Pugin and F. Mackenzie and published by J. Taylor, though illustrative of Gothic, did not supply the patterns for architects whom Pugin perceived needed examples when they were asked to build in the style, which was rapidly gaining popularity. He followed this with a *Series of Views in Islington and Pontonville* (1819), a delightful work, published jointly with Ackermann. His first major book of the kind on which his reputation as a specialist in Gothic would rest was *Specimens of Gothic Architecture* (1821–1823) for which E. J. Willson wrote the text.

Between 1821 and his death, Pugin and his staff produced eight books of plates, five of which were on Gothic, with texts by J. Britton, W. H. Leeds, and others. He was, however, a remarkable artist of architectural subjects in general, a talent revealed in the Ackermann books and in his work on the illustrations of the Brighton Pavilion (1826) commissioned by Nash. He was also a creative publisher as his use of lithography in *Ornamental Timber Gables* (1831) shows.

In 1819, Pugin, his family, and a group of students visited France, and thereafter they traveled regularly there and in England to prepare drawings for books in process. A. W. N. Pugin accompanied his family and began to assist his father in the work of drawing, training that would lead him into the practice of architecture; on his father's death, he inherited the responsibility for the completion of *Examples of Gothic Architecture* which had begun to appear in installments in 1831.

Pugin did not design many buildings. Although he appears to have aspired to be known as an architect, in the lists of artists and architects published in the Annals of the Fine Arts (1816–1820), he is listed only as an artist. The author of an obituary in *Arnold's Magazine of the Fine Arts,* who clearly knew Pugin well and appreciated his talent, stated that he had designed buildings for the marquis of Downshire and the earl of Essex and that he had designed several private houses. In association with James Morgan, he designed the Diorama in Regent's Park. Isambert Kingsom Brunel was a friend and, in 1830, a collaborator with Pugin on plans and advice for the General Cemetery now known as Kensal Green.

Augustus Charles Pugin. Plate from Specimens of Gothic Architecture.

Pugin trained men who, in the decades that followed, became members of the architectural community, illustrators of architecture, publishers of books on the arts. Among them were Benjamin Ferrey, Sir James Pennethorne, Joseph Nash, Talbot Bury, F. T. Dollman, T. L. Walker, and his own son, A. W. N. Pugin, who was to bring added fame to the family name.

Pugin's life was not easy. He found it difficult to earn a living from the variety of tasks that came his way. The fact that he was French at a time when there was considerable prejudice directed at émigrés made his early years in England even more troubled. By all accounts, he was a fine painter in watercolors who turned to architectural illustration because of his association with Nash, Ackermann's requirements, and his own discovery that he did it well and that there was a demand for it as a specialty. Not until his fifty-second year did he begin the books on Gothic that were to make him famous for the precision of his draftsmanship, his knowledge of the Gothic, and the acumen he displayed in the selection of examples.

At the time of his death, it was said that Pugin had "performed for gothic architecture services similar to those which Stuart [see JAMES STUART] and his fellow-labourers effected for that of Greece" (Arnold's Magazine of the Fine Arts, 1883).

PHOEBE B. STANTON

BIBLIOGRAPHY

Arnold's Magazine of the Fine Arts 1833 1:320–327.

FERREY, BENJAMIN 1861 *Recollections of A. N. Welby Pugin and his Father, Augustus Pugin.* London: Stanford.

NORMAND, CHARLES P. J. 1829 *A New Parallel of the Orders of Architecture.* Translated and with two new plates by A. C. Pugin. London: Pugin.

PUGIN, AUGUSTUS CHARLES 1819 *A Series of Views in Islington and Pentonville from Original Drawings made in the Year 1818.* With a description of each subject by E. W. Brayley. London: Ackermann.

PUGIN, AUGUSTUS CHARLES (1821–1823)1870 *Specimens of Gothic Architecture selected from various Antient Edifices in England.* Letterpress by Edward James Willson. 2 vols. London: Bohn.

PUGIN, AUGUSTUS CHARLES (1825–1828)1838 *Illustrations of the Public Buildings of London with Historical and Descriptive Accounts of Each Edifice.* Edited and written by J. Britton. Text altered, rewritten and enlarged by W. H. Leeds. London: Taylor, Pugin, Britton.

PUGIN, AUGUSTUS CHARLES (1828)1833 *Pugin and Le Keux's Specimens of the Architectural Antiquities of Normandy. Historical and Descriptive Essays Accompanying a Series of Engraved Specimens of the Architectural Antiquities of Normandy. Edited by J. Britton, the Subjects Measured and Drawn by Augustus Pugin, Architect; and Engraved by John and Henry Le Keux.* London. Nattali.

PUGIN, AUGUSTUS CHARLES 1829–1833 *Paris and Its Environs, Displayed in a Series of Picturesque Views.* Engraved under the superintendence of Mr. C. Heath. London: Jennings & Chaphn.

PUGIN, AUGUSTUS CHARLES 1831 *Gothic Ornaments Selected From Various Buildings in England and France.* Drawn on stone by J. D. Harding. London: Preistley & Weale.

PUGIN, AUGUSTUS CHARLES (1831)1851 *A Series of Ornamental Timber Gables, From Existing Examples in England and France, Of the Sixteenth Century.* Drawn on stone by B. Ferrey, with descriptive letter-press by Edw. James Willson. London: Bohn.

PUGIN, AUGUSTUS CHARLES 1831–1836 *Examples of Gothic Architecture; Selected From Various Antient Edifices in England . . . Accompanied by Historical and Descriptive Accounts.* Text for vols. 1–2 by E. J. Willson, vol. 3 by T. L. Walker. 3 vols. London: The author.

TRAPPES LOMAX, M. 1932 *Pugin.* London: Sheed & Ward.

WEDGEWOOD, ALEXANDRA 1977 *Catalogue of the Drawings Collection of the Royal Institute of British Architects: The Pugin Family.* London: Gregg.

PUGIN, AUGUSTUS WELBY NORTHMORE

Augustus Welby Northmore Pugin (1812–1852), English Gothic Revival architect, designer of the decorative elements of architecture in the arts of furniture, stained glass, vestments, tiles, embroidery, metalwork, and book design, was also a notable architectural and religious polemicist. His drawings, for buildings and commissions in the decorative arts and as his personal record of places he visited and studied and of objects of medieval art he admired, constitute one of the largest bodies of such material surviving from the career of any English architect. They illustrate the brilliance of his draftsmanship, the extent and depth of his knowledge of medieval art in England and on the Continent, and the devotion with which he worked with its inspiration. Because his creativity was integrated in purpose and taste with the revival of Roman Catholicism in England, Pugin became a leading figure in the reawakening of feeling for the history and traditions of the Church in the minds of English Catholics and, for a time, a force in the Oxford movement. He wrote extensively on architecture and the decorative arts. He commented on and described his own buildings, in the hope that they would play a part in the reformation of taste he sought. He published on liturgical practice as it related to the design of the costume and vessels employed in the ceremony of the Church. He greatly added to the nature and definition of the principles which he felt must underlie all fine architecture and excellence in the decorative arts. His book, *The True Principles of Pointed or Christian Architecture,* first published in 1841, was as fundamental a statement by Pugin and, subsequently, as influential as were his buildings and the great quantity of his works in the decorative arts. *Contrasts; Or, A Parallel Between The Noble Edifices Of The Fourteenth And Fifteenth Centuries, And Similar Buildings Of The Present Day; Shewing The Present Decay Of Taste,* which appeared first in 1836, was so brilliant and caustic a comment on architecture that it warranted another and expanded edition in 1841. It remains the best known and admired tract on the struggle between the styles and the nature of the practice of architecture produced in the nineteenth century. It is also a comment on Pugin's religious beliefs.

Events in Pugin's life and his willingness to involve himself in controversy for causes he felt worthy added luster to his actions in his lifetime and imparted to his biography, after his premature death at the age of forty, something of the quality of legend. He was in many ways a typical Romantic, emotionally involved with his art, thwarted in the realization of his ideals, a public figure in the defense of his beliefs, a critic of his times. Pugin's career was astonishingly short, but his productivity was enormous in the few years he had to work. He began independent practice in 1836 and attained immediate recognition. He was most in demand between 1839 and 1844, when, encouraged by his support, he did his finest work. Though he continued to practice with success after 1845, his reign as arbiter of taste was then challenged by other architects who were prepared to serve the Roman Catholic and Gothic Revival causes. There can be no doubt that Pugin's imperious demands for purity of style and intolerance for patrons and architects who would compromise diminished his clientele. Never physically strong, Pugin was increasingly afflicted with illness as his practice shrank. Medical attention failed to repair his health, and in February 1852, he became acutely disordered. In June, he was judged insane and for a month was a patient at Bethlem Hospital. When he showed little improvement, he was removed, treated privately in London, and finally taken to his home in Ramsgate where he suffered a seizure and died on September 14. Overwork and the demands of his profession have been considered as causes of this illness; it now appears that Pugin was also physically ill and disposed to nervous disorders.

Pugin was a convert to Roman Catholicism, a bold public step taken in 1835, his twenty-third year, after the death of his parents and an aunt who together constituted the older generation of his family. The decision surely had much to do with his growing feeling for medieval art and knowledge of the history of the Church. Conversion also defined Pugin's own view of his role. In 1840 he wrote, "I have ever considered ecclesiastical architecture and faith connected . . . [D]oes not all power come from God and how can those who do not fear him derive a blessing on their efforts." He described himself as "the scholar and representative of the Glorious Catholic architects who lived in antient days and to whom the merit of all our present performances are in justice to be referred." Although this statement emphasizes Pugin's feeling that his task required suppression of originality, which could compromise the revival of past excellence, his actual performance in design and in the development of his power as a warrior for the Gothic cause in ecclesiastical and artistic matters inevitably displays much that is personal.

Pugin was the son of AUGUSTUS CHARLES PUGIN. The younger Pugin grew up in a bilingual household that was simultaneously school, drawing studio, architectural library, and bookshop. He traveled to Paris with his parents and parties of students in 1819, 1821—the year in which he said he did his first drawing—1824, 1827, and 1828 and subsequently traveled through England on expeditions to prepare for the books on which his father was engaged. According to Pugin's own account, he worked on designs for furniture for Morel and Seddon, who in 1827 was preparing the fittings for Windsor, and it has also been reported that he was employed as a stage carpenter. He began his own business in furniture design and manufacture and failed. He married in 1831 but his wife died in childbirth in 1832, leaving him with an infant daughter. His father died in December 1832, and his mother in May 1833. By the spring of 1834, when he was but twenty-two, Pugin was married for a second time and expecting the birth of his second child, EDWARD WELBY PUGIN, who after his father's death would be the litigious defender of the family name in the prolonged struggle with CHARLES BARRY and his family over A. W. N. Pugin's role in the design of the Houses of Parliament.

A. W. N. Pugin had not been trained as an architect in the way usual for men of his generation. He had grown up with it and he never was to endure the period of articled apprenticeship, the usual preface to practice. Between 1833 and 1836, he worked as a creator of books, producing three volumes of designs for the decorative arts and one of the details of medieval timber houses and the first edition of his famous book, *Contrasts*. He also founded the relationship with Charles Barry which was to lead from employment on the details of the King Edward VI Grammar School in early 1835 to participation in the preparation of Barry's competition design for the Houses of Parliament after September of that year and into 1836, when Barry's design was sent to the judges. When Barry received the award, Pugin returned to work with him on the detailed drawings required for the estimates. In 1837, Pugin moved to establish his own practice and make public his beliefs on the connection which should exist between religion and the arts.

The work for Barry on the creation of the Parliament House proposal which was to take first prize, the design and construction of Saint Marie's Grange, a house near Salisbury, England, for himself and his young family, and the publication of *Contrasts* in 1836 constitute the first episode in Pugin's professional life.

Barry, who was a distinguished and able architect, had come to Pugin, an artist with imaginative talent in the drawing of Gothic detail, to obtain his assistance in embellishing the building which he had designed. Barry knew Pugin was capable of this sort of work because he had undoubtedly seen the volumes of drawings Pugin had prepared. Between 1832 and 1835, Pugin had traveled widely in England and abroad to study medieval architecture, and in the training of his mind and hand he had set himself problems not unlike those usual in French academic architectural education and designed imaginary buildings. These volumes illustrated the scintillating power of his draftsmanship and his ability to bring his imagination, his knowledge of Gothic, and nineteenth-century tastes into accord. Together, in the Houses of Parliament, Barry as architect and Pugin as artist were to build one of Pugin's imaginary buildings. This was to be a lifework for Pugin who intermittently assisted Barry as the vast work progressed. Thus, Pugin was to be involved with a youthful project even as he progressed in his own designs beyond his early tastes. It should be noted that the original Parliament House decorations and details belong in date with the four books of ornamental designs Pugin produced and Ackermann published in 1835 and 1836. The latter show heavy Continental influence, but they share with the imaginary buildings and the Parliament House a decorative richness Pugin was to display but rarely in his own architectural practice.

Saint Marie's Grange, Pugin's first building, designed and built in 1835, though now altered by the addition of bay windows and a stair hall, represents his response when practical requirements were dominant. Pugin said that his house was "the only modern building that is compleat in every part in the antient style." The house is unusual for its time in the way in which it reproduces the vernacular building of the late Middle Ages. It illustrates in Pugin a preference for architecture that is not ornate and the direct way in which he could use building materials and exploit the site. Pugin had built a house which was Gothic rather than Gothick, idiosyncratic but not piquant, plain to the point of severity, and relying on the expression of its masses, roofs, towers, and materials for effect.

Contrasts was first published by Pugin from Saint Marie's Grange. When work on the competition drawings ended in 1836, and as the judges began their deliberations, Pugin and Barry separated temporarily. In the interval before the estimate drawings were begun Pugin turned to the preparation of a book he had long had in mind. The idea of illustrating the fallibilities of nineteenth-century architecture by comparison with the buildings of the fifteenth century, which Pugin seems in 1836 to have felt to be medieval, had been lurking in his mind since 1832. Drawings of that year show him toying with this idea. In 1836, his experience with competition, with the state of a profession in which he could function as an anonymous hired artist, his acerbic estimate of nineteenth-century society and of the architecture its leading designers produced, and, finally, his own newly won religious feeling united to produce one of the most attractive and successful books on architectural taste in the nineteenth century. The text declares that the nineteenth century cannot claim architectural excellence. On the contrary, if "architectural beauty is the fitness of the design to the purpose for which it is intended, and that the style of a building should correspond with its use that the spectator may at once perceive the purpose for which it was erected" then in the attainment of the medieval builders could be read the excellence of their age, and conversely, the loss of these artistic qualities after the Reformation revealed the failure of that society. The nineteenth century but continued the decline then begun. The ancient churches are tourist sights, they are not repaired; the builders of new churches seek low-cost structures and even rent cellar space beneath the hall to merchants. A medley of exotic styles prevails, none expressing more than vagaries of fancy occasioned by the taste of a designer or his capricious patron. The training of architects is impoverished. The system of the selection of architects is dishonest. Vulgarity and show have replaced excellence, because, an important point for Pugin, the "pretended Reformation" has altered society for the worse, and the arts mirror its degradation. Pairs of plates comparing medieval buildings, real and imagined by Pugin, with nineteenth-century structures; the frontispiece, a plate on the Trade of architecture; and the tailpiece, a balance in which the new is weighed against the old and "found wanting," are among Pugin's finest statements. He challenged the reigning taste and architects in England, appealed to patrons to renew their commitment to social and religious values, continued to declare that medieval art reflected a "better" society, and adduced principles of design by which excellence might be assessed.

Patrons who could afford the richness of Pugin's early decorative taste sought him out when *Contrasts,* his other books of illustration in the decorative arts, and his conversion to Roman Catholicism brought him fame. Two were wealthy Roman Catholic laymen, Charles Scarisbrick and John Talbot, earl of Shrewsbury, who had begun or were contemplating major additions to their houses. The third was the Church; in 1837, Pugin established relationships with the clergy at Oscott College where he lectured on medieval art and prepared designs for the interior of the chapel. Within a year, he had received commissions for ten churches in England and Ireland and began to work at Scarisbrick and Alton Towers.

Augustus Welby Northmore Pugin.
Hospital of Saint John.
Alton, Staffordshire, England.
1840 and later

The two princely domestic commissions elicited from Pugin further evidence of his capacity in florid yet well-scaled and historically informed decorations. The churches, a task in which he had no experience but many opinions, were challenging; money was limited and there were liturgical and historical requirements. Pugin had condemned what he called "the mushroom creeds" among the Protestants who built cheap churches; now he was to demonstrate his belief that "the ancient and orthodox style of architecture" could be built not cheaply but at the same cost as debased design. Of the churches Pugin built at this time in his career three survive, changed but still representative of his intent; they are the Church of Our Blessed Lady and Saint Thomas of Canterbury (1838) in Dudley, Worcestershire; Church of Saint Mary (1839), Derby, Derbyshire; and Saint Mary's, Uttoxeter, Staffordshire (1839). As Saint Mary's was being finished, Pugin wrote a description of it that indicates his aspirations and values. He described the style as early thirteenth century. (The windows were lancet arches without tracery; there is a round window in the entrance wall and a western gable terminates in a belfry.) There is no mention of the fact that the interior has no aisles, but Pugin does refer to the color of the stained wood of the roof. Tribute is paid to the earl of Shrewsbury who helped to pay for the stained glass. Then Pugin launches into what is clearly for him—and he hopes for his readers—the meaning of the building. Beginning with a discussion of the altar and its appointments he moves in his description reverently through the chancel, discussing the furniture and history of the liturgy. Those who oppose the restoration of ancient ecclesiastical architecture are "sunk in modern ignorance and prejudice. . . . [*M*]*ore effect can be produced, and greater space gained,* for a given sum in pointed architecture than in any other style whatever" (emphasis added). Pugin gave precedence to the altar. When this sacred responsibility had been met, elaboration of the architecture could occur, and Pugin clearly meant to build more richly, for the church at Derby is large and elegant. But the simplicity of his small, less expensive early churches reveals an aspect of Pugin's talent that, though overshadowed by his extravagant achievements, should not be underestimated. From it would come some of his finer buildings: modest, well-proportioned, expressive of their materials, and simply but carefully furnished.

Saint Mary's, Derby, belongs to the earliest of Pugin's phases; its tall, slender Gothic would gradually disappear from his work. The churches at Macclesfield, Dudley, and Hulme followed in 1839 and 1840. That at Macclesfield was a larger

Augustus Welby Northmore Pugin.
Alton Castle.
Staffordshire, England.
1840 and later

and more effective version of the Derby formula, but those at Dudley and Hulme initiate the series of practical, less expensive, and therefore less elaborate churches. Pugin did not include the church at Dudley in the illustration of his buildings which he prepared for *An Apology for the Revival of Christian Architecture* (1843) but Saint Wilfrid's, Hulme, is there, replete with a tall spire which it never acquired. The simplicity of Saint Wilfrid's is responsible for some of its effectiveness; the church is brick with stone dressings, the buttresses are well-proportioned, the windows are lancets easy to fill with stained glass. The interior is broad and open despite the division into nave and aisle, and so simply furnished that all attention is focused on the chancel. It is also the first of Pugin's churches to have an asymmetrical west front, for the tower stands at the end of the north aisle.

The finest of this early parish church type is the Church of Saint Michael the Archangel, Gorey, begun in 1839. As was to be the case with all Pugin's work in Ireland, it surpassed his English projects in materials, quality of building, size, and conception, a difference that can be accounted for by the cost and the supply of labor available in Ireland as well as by the fact that the Roman Catholic Irish were willing to invest in buildings of this kind. Saint Michael's is also remarkable in that in deference to the early medieval architecture of Ireland, Pugin chose Norman and kept the masses big and heavy and virtually devoid of ornament. The plan is cruciform and the dimensions are impressive; Saint Michael's is almost as large as Saint Chad's Cathedral (1839–1841), Birmingham, one of Pugin's more valiant efforts to build impressively. Although Pugin's English churches, and particularly his performances at Saint Giles, Cheadle, Staffordshire, and in his cathedrals are best known, no estimate of his capacities is accurate unless the Irish projects are considered. Chief among them must be the Gorey church, for it demonstrates how well he could work without decorative extravagance to attain architectural val-

Augustus Welby Northmore Pugin.
Saint Mary's.
Derby, England.
1837–1839

Augustus Welby Northmore Pugin.
Saint Michael the Archangel.
Gorey, Ireland.
1839

ues of mass, spatial relationships, the employment of light, the direct statement of building materials and, what was for him an essential, his commitment to historical style.

For Pugin and his developing career, Saint Chad's Cathedral, Birmingham, was a commission of the utmost importance. It celebrated the rising power of the faith in Birmingham where his contact with Roman Catholic clients had begun and where Pugin knew and admired the men who were associated with the Church and its activities. The cathedral was sufficiently endowed to permit him to hope that its richness would inspire Roman Catholics to build churches that were "Catholic and not like protestant conventicles with altars in them." He had begun to work on the reform of vestments and Saint Chad's was to have a full complement in the medieval pattern of which Pugin approved. Because of restricted funds, Pugin decided to expend on the interior rather than the exterior. "When the means are ample enough, every part of the church should be rendered as splendid as possible: but if one portion must be sacrificed surely no one would hesitate for an instant in deciding that its interior should claim especial attention, and that the material fabric should resemble the king's daughter described by the Psalmist as all glorious within." Pugin cited the cathedral of Munich as his model, for his cathedral, like it, would present "a great mass of perforated brick walls and high roofs," a statement one can credit because its architecture is certainly more German than English in its inspiration. The fourteenth-century stalls were from Cologne. The brass lectorium (now in the Metropolitan Museum, New York) and the cantors' chairs were brought from the Cathedral of Louvain, gifts of the earl of Shrewsbury. The glass of the windows over the altar was copied from "the fine old glass" that remained in Bristol and Tewkesbury. Pugin stated that "the defects may be considered as his own, while the beauties and merits must in justice be attributed to the glorious race of old Catholic artists, whose noble works he is so zealously striving to restore, and which are so exquisitely beautiful that the bare imitation of them is a work of extreme difficulty," a reiteration of his resolution to be a faithful follower of medieval precedents. For all this, the church and the remarkable Bishop's House nearby were creative works, fresh in conception and taste, in proportions and in forms, precisely because Pugin extracted a variety of features and qualities he admired from a diverse set of admired medieval sources and combined them in ways that were in the end personal.

Saint Chad's holds a special place in the chronology of Pugin's work, for it is the last of his buildings in which he employed the exaggerated tall spatial organization evident at Derby and characteristic of his first studies for important and large churches. Even as Saint Chad's was being built, Pugin was designing the next generation of his buildings, churches for Cheadle, Liverpool, and great churches for Southwark and Nottingham.

The years between 1839 and 1844 were singularly productive and satisfying for Pugin. He had acquired the patrons he most wished to attract. He possessed public attention, esteem, and the power to influence the taste of the Roman Catholic clergy and laity. He had few competitors as experienced in design and as attractive and well-known as he. He designed many buildings in these years and initiated the first of what were to be three partnerships with John Hardman of Birmingham to produce ecclesiastical metalwork from his designs for the general market and respond to orders for unique objects.

The churches of this second phase of his career, which typify his abilities and the changes he was making as he moved away from his earlier more florid and dramatic style, are Saint Oswald's (1840), Liverpool (now destroyed), and Saint Marie's (1839–1840) Warwick Bridge, Cumberland, both smaller churches, one for an urban setting and the other for a country parish. Saint Giles (1840–1846), Cheadle, Staffordshire a large parish church of extraordinary richness, is, though remarkable and a masterpiece of Victorian art, atypical of both Pugin's usual work and of the taste of the Church. The patronage of the earl of Shrewsbury made it possible for Pugin to realize many of his enthusiasms for decoration. The remarkable Cathedral Church of Saint Barnabas (1841–1844) in Nottingham and the Cathedral of Southwark (1840–1848) both, though different from one another, are also quite unlike Saint Chad's, Birmingham. Finally, a series of monastic and school buildings illustrate his grasp of residential and institutional Gothic design.

Because Pugin was so dramatic a personality and because he could and did on occasion produce designs overwhelming in their richness, it has been common to stress that aspect of his work. But to do so is to underemphasize the less ornamented, simpler, and, as architecture, most satisfying of his buildings. The proportions of the forms of exterior and interior, the direct treatment of its materials, the simplicity of the interior, and the dignity of its organization and appointments, were all part of Pugin's conscious plan for Nottingham. He said, "I have not one tracery window, no pinnacles or any ornament externally. It will be the greatest triumph of external simplicity and internal effect yet achieved. . . . I must have *outline* and *breaks* or the building will go for nothing." It can be said that large and elaborate churches inherently possess these possibilities. The effort Pugin made to achieve them is plain when a church such as Saint Barnabas, Nottingham, is compared with either Saint Chad's, Birmingham, or Saint Mary's, Derby; the latter two, though remarkable, are dainty rather than massive, elegant rather than stately. That Pugin actually sought direct architectural effect is proven in the small churches where sheer size could have no part in his achievement. Saint Marie's, Warwick Bridge, a church without aisles, modestly appointed with every liturgical requirement, is as firm and forthright as Saint Barnabas. Pugin had begun to employ local materials and to restore not only Gothic but also that variety of the style that fitted comfortably with the local, vernacular architecture. More often than is generally recognized, Pugin built this kind of church. Among them Saint Alphonsus (1840–1841), Barntown, Wexford, Ireland; Saint Mary's (1842–1844), Brewood, Staffordshire; and finally his own church, Saint Augustine's (1845–1852), Ramsgate, Kent, remain as demonstrations of his power as an architect.

These remarkable buildings share with the more elaborate schemes, such as Saint Giles a common feeling for the proportion of the whole. In passing from his early work to his mature style, Pugin changed the shape of his spaces and the form of his buildings. The tendency to make buildings that were tall in relation to their width is replaced by a preference for compact, wider, and proportionately lower interiors. It is in what may be his finest building, Saint Mary's Cathedral, Killarney, Ireland, begun in 1842 and completed only after the famine and after the death of Pugin, that the full realization of this architectural sense is expressed in large scale.

The years 1841 and 1842 were constructive ones for Pugin and his cause. The two articles published in the *Dublin Review* (May 1841 and February 1842) and subsequently republished as *On the Present State of Ecclesiastical Architecture in England* (1843) allowed Pugin to summarize his own achievement and to set forth his conclusions on correct liturgical practice and design and on the nature of Gothic precedents, and to publish etchings of his own work, in which his past performance and his ideas about design could be illustrated. In the first article, in describing the parish church, he emphasized the necessity, established by

Augustus Welby Northmore Pugin.
Saint Giles's.
Cheadle, Staffordshire, England.
1840–1846

Augustus Welby Northmore Pugin.
Saint Giles's (west door).
Cheadle, Staffordshire, England.
1840–1846

Augustus Welby Northmore Pugin.
Saint Giles's (tiles, floor, porch).
Cheadle, Staffordshire, England.
1840–1846

Augustus Welby Northmore Pugin. Saint Mary's. Brewood, Staffordshire, England. 1842–1844

Augustus Welby Northmore Pugin. Saint Mary's. Brewood, Staffordshire, England. 1842–1844

tradition, for a spire, which he says may be placed in various ways in reference to the body of the building. At Saint Giles, for example, he had placed the tower at the west end "rising directly from the ground." But this was not necessarily the pattern, for medieval builders made their plans *"essentially convenient and suitable to the required purpose, and decorated them afterwards."* Their beauty is "so striking because it is *natural*" and thus Pugin is prepared to repudiate symmetry in church design which had been, even in his own work, an inheritance from the classical tradition. Pugin's statement that *"until the present regular system of building both sides of a church exactly alike be broken up no real good can be expected"* announces that, in addition to his change of proportions of the interior and the building mass, Pugin has added asymmetry. His later designs would be freer and more "natural," therefore more Gothic.

The sources of these changes in Pugin's Gothic may be debated. It would appear that as he grew in knowledge of the style and in control of his own abilities his appreciation of Gothic changed until he perceived that late Gothic lacked the virtues imparted by integrity of expressed construction. In *True Principles,* also published in 1841, he noted that "among the many other symptoms of decline apparent in the later works in the pointed style" the "four centered arch" must join the building of pendant vaults in the Chapel of Henry VII in Westminister Abbey. He also acknowledged that he had himself been in error when, earlier in his work, he had succumbed to the beauties of Continental Gothic examples and stressed height at the expense of severity, an error in judgment he corrected in time and with the assistance of the counsel of the Roman Catholic antiquary Dr. Rock. Pugin focused his attention and admiration on English and Gothic and, within its variety, on that of the fourteenth century, an appreciation which undoubtedly contributed to the revised proportions, comparative severity, and asymmetry of his mature buildings. But despite his announced admiration for a particular period Pugin did not reproduce it, though he was certainly capable of doing so and said such was his intent.

In 1841, Pugin also rewrote the text of *Contrasts,* dispensing with the earlier version, and after subtracting one of his original pairs of plates, the house of JOHN SOANE and a late medieval house in Rouen, he added five new contrasts, among them the contrasted towns and care of the poor which alone are enough to make Pugin famous. Brilliant though the old and new plates were, the text was equally revealing of Pugin's temper. He had decided that the Reformation had not descended upon England but, rather, had been caused by her "internal decay." An alarming parallel could be drawn between past and present, for degeneracy will follow the decline of "Catholic principles." Pugin had also acquired new authorities upon whom to found his views: he had begun to read Durandus, whose exposition of Christian symbolism he adopted; two members of the circle of Lammenais, A. F. Rio, historian of Christian art,

Augustus Welby Northmore Pugin. Drawing of Saint Augustine's. Ramsgate, Kent, England. 1845–1852

and Charles Le Comte de Montalembert, expressing theories on the role of the Catholic Church in art and society and opposing the destruction of medieval monuments in France; in which the sermons of Savonarola Pugin found admonitions which resembled those he was preparing for the Roman Catholics of England. Through continued study of Paganism and "neglect of the sublime truths of the Catholic faith, you will become ashamed of the cross of Christ and imbibe the proud luxurious spirit and feelings of Paganism; til weak in faith and good works, you will fall into heresies, or infidelity itself." He acknowledged that his earlier assumption that Protestantism had been the cause of "Catholic degeneracy" was wrong. The pagan principle within Roman Catholicism has been equally, if not most, to blame. The text of the revised *Contrasts* is directed toward English Roman Catholics, the general public, who treated ancient buildings as curiosities, and to royalty and governments because they failed to support these national treasures. His comments on Westminister Abbey are particularly revealing of his position.

The True Principles of Pointed or Christian Architecture was published by John Weale in 1841 (second edition, Bohn, in 1843.) Pugin stated that general principles from which excellent design derived could be observed through study of any fine architecture, regardless of style. These laws were, he said, as immutable as those "that govern the arts of grammar and harmony," but that "they can be violated with greater impunity owing to their being less understood." This comment, and that which follows, come from the manuscript of a prospectus Pugin drafted for his book in order that Weale might advertise its publication. Pugin summarized his principles by saying "1. that all ornaments of true pointed edifices were merely introduced as decoration to the essential construction of these buildings; 2. that the construction of pointed architecture was varied to accord with *the properties of the various materials employed* shown by antient examples of stone, timber and metal construction; 3. that no features were introduced in the antient examples of stone, timber and metal construction; 4. that no features were introduced in the antient pointed edifices which were not essential either for convenience or propriety; 4. that pointed architecture is most consistent as it decorated the useful portions of buildings instead of concealing them; 5. that the defects of modern architecture are principally owing to the departure from antient consistent principles." By the time the prospectus was printed another principle had been added as 5: "the true principles of architectural proportion are only found in Pointed Edifices," and the original 5 had become 6.

Pugin set out to prove that in Gothic architecture all his principles of design could be seen at work and that this remarkable aesthetic unity was reason enough for a Gothic Revival. In a display of circular reasoning he justified Gothic through examination of its stylistic purity although he intended to recommend it for religious reasons and because of its association with English history and tradition. Difficulty arose when he, or Weale, perceived that had "the true principles" been observed in the revival of the classical style it, too, would attain excellence, which was not Pugin's intent. Pugin was using classical architectural aesthetic theory to appraise and condemn impoverished revivals of antiquity and at the same time demonstrate the inherent excellence of medieval architecture and craftsmanship. The unwelcome possibility that someone might observe that classical architecture designed according to true principles could be acceptable must have led to the addition of principle 5.

The sources for a book as important as *True Principles,* which forecast the aesthetic theory of functionalism, must be examined. Pugin appears to have read John Robison's *A System of Mechanical Philosophy* (1822), for in volume 1 appear some of the ideas which were to become Pugin's principles. Robison says, for example, "Our architects' . . . aim . . . is to make a beautiful object. The sources of the pleasures arising from what we call *taste* are so various, so complicated, and even so whimsical, that it is almost in vain to look for principle in the rules adopted by our professed architects." He uses the term "true principles of taste in architecture" and he observes that "Gothic architecture is perhaps entitled to the name of rational architecture; and its beauty is founded on the characteristic distinction of our species. It deserves cultivation; not the pitiful, servile, and unskilled copying of the monuments; this will produce incongruities and absurdities equal to any that have crept into the Greek architecture," sentiments and a vocabulary with which Pugin must have felt comfortable. Robison and Pugin repeat the Vitruvian (see VITRUVIUS) statement that Doric is the result of the petrifaction of a wooden architecture. Robison comments specifically on the structure of Saint Paul's and the way in which CHRISTOPHER WREN made "the whole of the upper order a mere screen" to which he gave "the appearance of habitation by the mock windows or niches" a point of which Pugin makes much in his book. There was a copy of A. F. FRÉZIER's *La Théorie et la Pratique de la Coupe des Pierres et de Bois* (1754) in the library of A. C. Pugin when it was sold at auction in 1833. Frézier could have been known to the younger Pugin who read French, and Robison, who in the 1770s wrote the lectures which became the book of 1805 and who cites other French writers could not have overlooked an authority so near his own generation. The belief that a relationship existed between England's national greatness and Gothic is not new. Pugin comments that "national feelings and national architecture are at so low an ebb, that it becomes an absolute duty in every Englishman to attempt their revival. . . . Our ancient architecture can alone furnish us with the means of doing this successfully." JOHN CARTER, in *The Builder's Magazine* (1774 and following) and in his later writing had repeatedly asserted that Gothic would "remind us of the heroic acts of those defenders of their country . . . of our long race of sovereigns . . . of our duty to our Creator, to ourselves and to mankind."

But to the ideas of the authorities who confirmed his thoughts Pugin added observations of his own. The plates of illustration in *True Principles* are witty and memorable, unique in English architectural literature. The essay on moldings he incorporates in his text, the comment on scale in architecture, the astute descriptions of the shortcomings of modern baronial and classical designs for houses, all his commentary on the decorative arts are together notable. *Contrasts* had assured Pugin a place among English architectural writers; *True Principles* enhanced his reputation.

Two years after the appearance of *True Principles,* Pugin published *An Apology for the Revival of Christian Architecture:* in it he cogently elaborates points he had made but not developed satisfactorily in the earlier book. Pugin was willing to name architects whose work he deplored, and CHARLES R. COCKERELL, WILLIAM TITE, and Soane were among those whom he accused of producing "another stale dish of illadapted classicisms." The mordancy of his wit and the accuracy of his criticisms amuse, but the book is rewarding because in it Pugin finally arrives at the center of the theory he had but in part put forward in *True Principles.* Gothic architecture is not merely beautiful and Christian and national: it could be built economically, and, without violence to its integrity, modern building methods and materials could be used in its revival; it represented, as he had said in *True Principles,* the full realization of his principles of design. In a tightly written paragraph he explained both to himself and his readers the question that had made *True Principles* puzzling, "The restorers of Christian architecture are more consistent followers of classic *principles* than all these boasted Greeks; they understand antiquity, and apply the ancient consistent rules to the new dispensation." Pugin was in essential agreement with FRANÇOIS BLONDEL who in 1675 had written, "All the pleasure we derive from artistic beauty depends on the observation of rule and measure: on proportion," and it may be Blondel to whom Pugin refers when he uses the *classic* with reference to his principles. In a discussion of building and "Modern Inventions and Mechanical Improvements," Pugin argues that nothing in Gothic Revivalism requires the revival of medieval techniques of building and that had energy from steam and metal construction been available Gothic builders would have used them. "We do not want to arrest the course of inventions, but to confine these inventions to their legitimate uses, and to prevent their substitution for nobler arts," but his discussion makes it clear that he perceives no principle that calls for a visual expression of these building techniques.

The plates in *An Apology* equal any in his earlier books. In the frontispiece, Pugin assembled his own churches in a bird's-eye view, set against a rising sun. Other plates show his proposals for Christian art and the whole concludes with a display of liturgical metal work from his own designs and manufactured in Birmingham. His satiric illustrations of the debased taste he deplored are again remarkable, apt, and downright funny; *Punch,* which recognized a master caricaturist when it saw one, paid Pugin's plate on the entrance of a commercial cemetery a compliment by publishing a drawing of its own proposal according to *True Principles* for the front of the British Museum.

An Apology was Pugin's last book on architecture. He was engaged in the preparation of the text and seventy-three plates reproduced in colored lithography for *The Glossary of Ecclesiastical Ornament* (Bohn, 1844), its professed aim being to educate the people of England in "minor matters" of Christian detail, patterns in "Christian design," and the symbolism of medieval religion so that correct forms could accompany "the mighty movement . . . in favour of the revival of the *architecture* of the middle ages" Pugin felt sure had arrived.

From its bibliography through its hundreds of definitions, each equipped with historical references and citations from authorities, the *Glossary* is a work of scholarship that ranks with the best of such books. Pugin had become a Christian antiquary. The frontispiece and the final plate, entitled *The End* and illustrating a fully Gothic and Christian funeral, show the densely ornamented world of Pugin's Gothic revival in rich lithographic color.

Floriated Ornament (Bohn, 1849) is, despite the brilliance of his earlier books, the most personal and attractive of all Pugin's publications. Having perceived that "the great difference between antient and modern artists is their adaptation of nature for decorative purposes," Pugin prepared a series of designs based on actual plants, for which he supplied botanical names. He pointed out that modern designers, regrettably, did not make an accommodation between the surface being decorated and the object being illustrated; his designs would show that decoration could be managed in "such a manner as not to destroy the consistency of the peculiar feature or object they were employed to decorate." *Floriated Ornament* illustrates the second of Pugin's principles, "that all ornament should consist of the enrichment of the essential construction of the building," and the theoretical statement contained in its introduction and its plates deserve to be recognized as part of his didactic writing.

After 1849, Pugin was confronted with new men in the Church who did not share his belief that the revival of Gothic art and architecture and the restoration of Roman Catholicism in England were one. John Henry Newman, Faber, and Bishop Wiseman were among those Pugin and his colleagues now had to oppose. In a book, *An Earnest Appeal for the Revival of Ancient Plain Song* (1850) and in an open letter to *The Tablet,* Pugin put his case succinctly and in a way that would not endear him to the clergymen who were attempting to provide churches for the growing Roman Catholic populace. Pugin said that though he submitted "in the most elaborate manner to the dogmas of faith as proposed by the Church," he would continue to campaign against "the temporal causes that have exercised so fatal an influence on religion" by which he meant "the important element of modern Paganism, which has corrupted and debased the externals of religion to a lamentable extent." In conclusion he declared, *"I shall never rest till I see the majestic architecture that was originally generated by the Catholic faith—again a living expression of the majesty of Catholic rites."* Newman was to say of Pugin, with some justice, that "the cannons of Gothic architecture are to him points of faith, and everyone is a heretic who would venture to question them."

Throughout his short but productive professional life, Pugin admired and was influenced by le Comte de Montalembert, whose active, outspoken, and intelligent participation in politics and Roman Catholic life in France kept alive and developed the idea of Roman Catholic liberalism. Montalembert was, like Pugin, half French, half English, son of an émigré. He had many friendships in England where he spent a good deal of time with members of Pugin's circle. In 1832,

Augustus Welby Northmore Pugin.
Etching of The Grange.
Ramsgate, Kent, England.
1843–1844

Montalembert had joined Victor Hugo and Chateaubriand to campaign against the destruction of medieval buildings and proposed the Committee for the Arts and Monuments established in 1837. Pugin quoted Montalembert in the second edition of *Contrasts.* In his conflicts with Bishop Wiseman and Newman, Pugin assumed a position not unlike Montalembert's in France: a loyal Roman Catholic but willing to work for a cause in which he believed but which was unpopular with the officers of the Church.

After 1844, Pugin's life and practice changed. The death of his second wife, removal of his household from London to Ramsgate, the foundation of business arrangements with John Hardman of Birmingham, and the establishment of a relationship with John G. Crace in the production of furniture all conspired to remove Pugin from the position of prominence he had earlier held. Other designers, perceiving the rise of taste for Gothic architecture, appeared to serve the Roman Catholic community; they were also more tractable and less demanding upon their clients. Pugin's mental and physical health began to decline. He was seriously ill in 1846 and, although he recovered and returned to design, the threat of illness remained. He had completed his major work for his greatest client, the earl of Shrewsbury. After 1844, Pugin returned to collaboration with Charles Barry on the Houses of Parliament, his time on the detailed drawings for the building and its ornament and the fitting out of the interior. Pugin remained the pre-eminent Roman Catholic artist-architect, but the character of his professional activities changed. In 1846, the leaders of the Ecclesiological Society, a movement to return the established church to medieval art, men with whom Pugin had had cordial relations, disowned him.

Despite these reverses and the heavy load of work occasioned by the Houses of Parliament and his various business enterprises, Pugin continued to develop. The ease with which he prepared the myriad of details for the internal and exterior enrichments of the Houses of Parliament, and the assurance displayed in the drawings for Crace and

Hardman indicate that he had attained a maturity not present even in his finest earlier work. The churches of Saint Peter (1845–1848), Marlow, Buckinghamshire; Saint Lawrence (1845–1847), Tubney, Berkshire; and the chapels at Saint Edmund's College (1846–1852), Ware, Hertfordshire, and Bicton Grange (1850), Devonshire, all late works, show that he had absorbed the lessons derived from his scholarship in medieval art and architecture and had begun to generate a strong personal style which would be noted by his contemporaries and architects who would follow him.

Pugin's talent as an artist, of which his surviving drawings are evidence, was astonishing even in time when drawings recording buildings and details were part of the activity of any practicing architect and many amateurs. His ability to conjure up the reality and excitement of a building scheme through drawings was a gift of his total knowledge of the style to which he was devoted, his visual imagination, and his religious conviction. His productivity as a designer and architect was prodigious; his buildings in England and Ireland and his work in the decorative arts established a standard of design his competitors were forced to meet.

The Houses of Parliament was a major nineteenth-century monument and Pugin's participation in it his major work. Richer in ornamentation and larger than any other Pugin building, it was for the late years of his life, when for Pugin the major preoccupation with the design began, in a style with which he was not artistically and intellectually in sympathy. Charles Barry was responsible for the conception of the whole, for the architecture and engineering problems, and for the management of the prolonged struggle with the physical problems of construction and with Parliament. Pugin prepared the designs for the tissue of ornament with which the building is covered and for the many details of hardware, stained glass, furniture, wallpapers, and tiles that distinguish the interior. Together, Barry and Pugin created a Gothic Revival secular building on a scale equal to that of any public building in the classical mode. Pugin could with justice say that its "long lines of fronts and excessive repetition are certainly not in accordance with the ancient spirit of civil architecture but its detail is most consoling" and go on to write that "this building is the morning star of the great revival of national architecture and art: it is a complete and practical refutation of those men who venture to assert that pointed architecture is not suitable for public edifices."

Pugin's buildings together compose an astonishing body of work, consistent in its loyalty to Gothic Revivalism and yet demonstrating a steady, inventive progression from the fragile delicacy of the church at Derby to the strength and original adaptation of Gothic forms that appears in the church at Marlow and the cathedral at Killarney. Had he lived Pugin would surely have continued to evolve his own version of an architecture based upon Gothic inspiration and "true principles." The originality of his brick buildings, of which the Bishop's House in Birmingham was an excellent example, demonstrates the direction he took when free from the obligation to ecclesiastical requirements.

In his books, Pugin commented extensively on the design of the decorative arts, a field in which he felt his "principles" also applied and in which his achievement was remarkable. His knowledge of medieval metalwork and stained glass was profound, and his insistence that precedents be followed in design of both and that they be manufactured carefully resulted in remarkable objects. At the same time, he was prepared to argue that repetition, even large-scale production of objects to be sold for less than the prices required for custom manufacture, would in no way violate his high standards. In collaboration with Crace, he planned to open a shop where furniture, textiles, and wallpapers of good design could be purchased at reasonable prices.

Despite his dazzling design achievement, Pugin is best known for his publications; he wrote for Roman Catholic journals, published books, and carried on epistolary controversies over matters of religion. He possessed a literary ability that makes the thousands of his surviving letters a lively record of his thought and responses to persons and ideas. Pugin brought together ideas on architecture that had been developed by generations of classical theorists and combined them with his own enthusiasm for Gothic and the age from which it came. In the process, he composed a statement on design that, with the exception of his addiction to Gothic, would survive long after him.

PHOEBE B. STANTON

WORKS

(A)1835, Church of Our Lady and Saint Margaret, Oxborough, Norfolk, England. 1835–1836, King Edward VI Grammar School (decorations; surviving portion later moved), Warwickshire, England. 1835–1836, Saint Marie's Grange (later altered, perhaps by Pugin); 1837, Clarendon Park (gatehouse); Alderbury, Wiltshire, England. 1837, Saint James's (much altered), Reading, England. 1837–1838, Oscott College (chapel and completion of buildings), Sutton Coldfield, Warwickshire, England. 1837–1839, Saint Mary's (church and presbytery), Derby, England. 1837–1845, Scarisbrick Hall (additions by E. W. Pugin), Ornskirk, Lancashire, England. 1837?–1846 and later, Alton Towers (additions), Staffordshire, England. 1838, Church of Our

Blessed Lady and Saint Thomas of Canterbury, Dudley, Worcestershire, England. 1838, Saint Anne's (later altered), Keighley, Yorkshire, England. 1838, Saint Augustine's, Solihull, Warwickshire, England. 1838, Saint Peter's College (chapel and interior fittings), Wexford, Ireland. 1838–1841, Saint Alban's, Macclesfield, Cheshire, England. *1839, Convent of Mercy, Bermondsey, London. 1839, Loreto Abbey (chapel altar and roof of crossing), Rathfarnum, Ireland. 1839, Saint Mary's, Uttoxeter, Staffordshire, England. 1839, Saint Michael the Archangel (church and convent), Gorey, Ireland. 1839–1840, Saint Marie's (now Church of Our Lady and Saint Wilfrid's), Warwick Bridge, Cumberland, England. 1839–1841, Metropolitan Cathedral of Saint Chad (including *Bishop's House), Warwickshire, England. 1839–1842, Saint John's (school, presbytery, and decoration of chancel), Banbury, Oxfordshire, England. 1839 and later, Mount Saint Bernard's Abbey (chapel later altered), Coalville, Leicestershire, England. 1840, Castle Rock (entrance and interior details), Leicestershire, England. 1840, Church of Our Lady, Warwick Bridge, Cumberland, England. Begun 1840, Saint Cuthbert's College (much altered), Durham, England. *1840, Saint Oswald's (chapel and school), Liverpool, England. 1840, Saint Wilfrid's (church and presbytery), Warwick Bridge, Cumberland, England. 1840, Saint Winifride's Chapel, Shepshed, Leicestershire, England. 1840–1843, Saint Winifride's (church, presbytery, and school), Neston, Cheshire, England. 1840–1844, Saint Alphonsus, Barntown, Wexford, Ireland. 1840–1846, Saint Giles's (church, Saint Joseph's Convent, presbytery, and school), Cheadle, Staffordshire, England. 1840–1848, Saint George's Cathedral (damaged; restored after 1945), Southwark, London. 1840–1852, Saint Cuthbert's College (completed later by others; Pugin's design altered), Durham, England. 1840 and later, Convent of the Sisters of Mercy (later additions by E. W. Pugin), Handsworth, Birmingham, England. 1840 and later, Garendon Hall (additions); 1840 and later, Grace Dieu Manor (decoration and additions); Leicestershire, England. 1840 and later, Hospital of Saint John and Alton Castle (including adjoining presbytery and house; now the Convent of the Sisters of Mercy and Saint John's School for Boys), Alton, Staffordshire, England. 1841, Ackworth Grange (*Jesus Chapel and amendations to the house), Pontefract, Yorkshire, England. (A)1841, Saint Mary's (additions and remodeling; with JAMES GILLESPIE GRAHAM), Edinburgh. 1841, Saint Swithin's (decoration of chancel ceiling), Leadenham, Lincolnshire, England. 1841, School, Spetchley, Worcestershire, England. 1841–1842, Saint Augustine of England (presbytery), Kenilworth, Warwickshire, England. 1841–1842, Saint Mary's, Stockton-on-Tees, Durham, England. 1841–1842, Saint Wilfrid's, Hume, Manchester, England. 1841–1844, Saint Barnabas's (presbytery), Nottingham, England. 1841–1844, Saint Mary's (with JOSEPH A. HANSOM), Newcastle-upon-Tyne, Northumberland, England. *1841–1847, Convent of Mercy; *1841–1847, Saint Marie's; Liverpool, England. 1841–1848, Oxenford Grange (farm buildings, bridge, and gatehouse); 1841–1848, Peper Harrow House (renovations and various works); Surrey, England. 1841–1851, Bilton Grange (renovations and additions), Rugby, Warwickshire, England. 1842, Saint Anne's (altar and reredos), Leeds, England. 1842–1843, Saint Peter's (presbytery), Woolwich, London. 1842–1844, Saint Mary's (church, presbytery, and school), Brewood, Staffordshire, England. 1842–1845, Saint John the Evangelist (interior much altered), Kirkham, Lancashire, England. 1842–1852, Saint Mary's (restoration and repairs), Beverley, Yorkshire, England. 1842 and later, Saint Mary's, Killarney, Ireland. 1843–1844, The Grange, Ramsgate, Kent, England. 1844, Girl's School, Chirk, Denbighshire, England. 1844, Ratcliffe College (main front and general plan; not completed until later by Hansom and E. W. Pugin), Ratcliffe-on-the-Wreake, Leicestershire, England. 1844, Saint Nicholas's (repairs and additions), Peper Harrow, Surrey, England. 1844–1850, Saint Mary's (repairs and additions), Wymswold, Leicestershire, England. *1844–1851, Cathedral of Our Lady and Saint Thomas (largely rebuilt), Northampton, England. 1844–1852, Houses of Parliament (interior decoration; with CHARLES BARRY), Westminster, England. 1844 and later, Oswaldcroft (now the Home for Incurables), Liverpool, England. 1844 and later, Saint Wilfrid's College, Cotton College, Staffordshire, England. 1845–1846, Glebe Farm; 1845–1846, Parish Church (restoration of the chancel); Rampisham, Dorset, England. 1845–1846, Parish Church, Tagoat, Ireland. 1845–1846, Saint Marie's Church (now a chapel), Rugby, Warwickshire, England. 1845–1846, Saint Mary's (later damaged), West Tofts, Norfolk, England. 1845–1846, Woodchester Park (not completed until later by others), near Stroud, Gloucestershire, England. 1845–1847, Saint Lawrence's (church, rectory, and school), Tubney, Berkshire, England. 1845–1848, Saint Peter's, Marlow, Buckinghamshire, England. 1845–1850, Convent of Mercy, Nottinghamshire, England. 1845–1850, Our Lady of the Annunciation (later altered), Bishop Eton, Liverpool, England. 1845–1852, Saint Augustine, Ramsgate, Kent, England. 1845–1852, Saint Patrick's College, Maynooth, Ireland. 1846–1847, Adare Manor (many interior details); 1846–1847, Village Church (additions); Adare, Ireland. 1846–1848, Convent (later additions and details by E. W. Pugin), Birr, Ireland. 1846–1852, Saint Edmund's College (chapel and house; now Saint Hugh's School), Ware, Hertfordshire, England. 1846 and later, Chirk Castle (renovations and additions), Denbighshire, England. 1847, Rectory, Lanteglos-by-Camelford, Cornwall, England. 1847, Saint Anne's Bede Houses, Lincoln, England. 1847–1848, Burton Closes (additions and interior decorations), Bakewell, Derbyshire, England. 1847–1849, Saint Oswald's (chancel), Winwick, Liverpool, England. 1847–1849, Saint Thomas's (church and presbytery), Fulham, London. 1848, Manor House (now Manor School), Wilburton, England. 1848, Saint Cuthbert's (chapel), Durham, England. 1849, Eastnor Castle (interior decoration), Ledbury, Herefordshire, England. 1849, Jesus College (chapel decoration), Cambridge. 1849–1850, Lismore Castle (with John G. Crace; furniture and decoration), Ireland. 1850, Aston Cemetery Chapel, Birmingham, England. 1850, Leighton

Hall (interior decorations), Welshpool, Montgomeryshire, England. 1850, Rolls Mortuary Chapel, Bicton Grange, Devonshire, England. 1850, Saint George's Cathedral (Petre Chantry interior), Southwark, London. 1851, Church of Our Lady Star of the Sea (decoration of the chancel and Chapel of Saint Joseph), Greenwich, London. n.d., Chapel of the Holy Trinity (including a convent, school, and presbytery), Radford, Oxfordshire, England. n.d., Saint Mary's (portions), Chelsea, London. n.d., Tomb of the Reverend George Augustus Montgomery, Saint John the Baptist, Bishopstone, Wiltshire, England.

BIBLIOGRAPHY

BOASE, THOMAS SHERRER ROSS 1959 *English Art.* Volume 10 in *The Oxford History of English Art.* London: Oxford University Press.

BOGAN, BERNARD 1948 *The Great Link: A History of Saint George's, Southwark, 1786–1848.* London: Burns & Oates.

BURY, SHIRLEY 1967*a* *Copy or Creation: Victorian Treasures from English Churches.* London: Worshipful Company of Goldsmiths.

BURY, SHIRLEY 1967*b* "In Search of Pugin's Church Plate." *Connoisseur* 165:29–35.

BURY, SHIRLEY 1969 "Pugin's Marriage Jewellry." *Victoria and Albert Museum Yearbook* 1:85–96.

BURY, TALBOT 1852 "Obituary." *The Builder* 25, no. 10:605–607.

CLARK, KENNETH (1928)1964 *The Gothic Revival.* Harmondsworth, England: Penguin.

EASTLAKE, CHARLES (1872)1975 *A History of the Gothic Revival.* Watkins Glen, N.Y.: American Life Foundation.

FERREY, BENJAMIN (1861)1978 *Recollections of A. N. Welby Pugin and His Father, Augustus Pugin.* London: Scolar.

GERMANN, GEORG 1972 *Gothic Revival in Europe and Britain: Sources, Influences and Ideas.* Translated from the German by Gerald Onn. London: Lund Humphries.

GWYNN, DENIS R. 1946 *Lord Shrewsbury, Pugin and the Catholic Revival.* London: Hollis & Carter.

HITCHCOCK, H. R. (1954)1972 *Early Victorian Architecture in Britain.* 2 vols. Reprint. New York: DaCapo.

HOUGHTON, WALTER E. (1957)1966 *The Victorian Frame of Mind.* New Haven: Yale University Press.

MILBURN, DAVID 1964 *A History of Ushaw College.* England: Ushaw Bookshop.

PEVSNER, NIKOLAUS 1951–1974 *The Buildings of England.* Harmondsworth, England: Penguin.

PEVSNER, NIKOLAUS 1943 "A Short Pugin Florelgium." *Architectural Review* 94:31–34.

PIPER, JOHN 1945 "St. Marie's Grange: The first home of A. W. N. Pugin." *Architectural Review* 98:90–93.

PORT, MICHAEL HARRY 1961 *Six Hundred New Churches.* London: SPCK.

PORT, MICHAEL HARRY (editor) 1976 *The Houses of Parliament.* New Haven: Yale University Press.

PUGIN, AUGUSTUS WELBY NORTHMORE 1835 *A Letter to A. W. Hakewill, In answer to his reflections on the style for rebuilding the Houses of Parliament.* London: Ackermann.

PUGIN, AUGUSTUS WELBY NORTHMORE (1835–1836)1972 *Gothic Furniture 1835. Designs for iron + brass work, 1836. Designs for gold and silversmiths 1836. Details of antient timber houses. 1837.* 4 vols. in 1. Reprint. Farnborough, England: Gregg International.

PUGIN, AUGUSTUS WELBY NORTHMORE (1836)1969 *Contrasts; Or, A Parallel Between The Noble Edifices Of the Middle Ages And Similar Buildings Of The Present Day; Shewing The Present Decay of Taste: Accompanied by appropriate text.* Reprint of 1841 ed. Originally published with the title *Contrasts; Or, A Parallel Between The Noble Edifices Of The Fourteenth and Fifteenth Centuries, And Similar Buildings Of The Present Day; Shewing The Present Decay of Taste: Accompanied by appropriate text.*

PUGIN, AUGUSTUS WELBY NORTHMORE 1837 *An apology for a work entitled "Contrasts"; being a defense of the assertations advanced in that publication, against the various attacks lately made upon it.* Birmingham, England: Stone.

PUGIN, AUGUSTUS WELBY NORTHMORE 1838*a* "West Front of Rouen Cathedral." *London and Dublin Orthodox Journal of Useful Knowledge for 1838* February 17:97–99.

PUGIN, AUGUSTUS WELBY NORTHMORE 1838*b* "Jube of St. Ouen." *London and Dublin Orthodox Journal of Useful Knowledge for 1838* March 3:129–131.

PUGIN, AUGUSTUS WELBY NORTHMORE 1838*c* "Doorway of Cloister, Abbey of St. Wandrille." *London and Dublin Journal of Useful Knowledge for 1838* March 13:161–164.

PUGIN, AUGUSTUS WELBY NORTHMORE 1838*d* "Fireplace in the Abbey of St. Amand, Rouen." *London and Dublin Orthodox Journal of Useful Knowledge for 1838* March 31:193–196.

PUGIN, AUGUSTUS WELBY NORTHMORE 1838*e* "Chasuble of Cloth of Gold, embroidered, formerly belonging to La Sainte Chapelle de Vie le Comte." *London and Dublin Journal of Useful Knowledge for 1838* April 14:225–230.

PUGIN, AUGUSTUS WELBY NORTHMORE 1838*f* "Monumental Brass of the Fifteenth Century." *London and Dublin Journal of Useful Knowledge for 1838* May 12:289–292.

PUGIN, AUGUSTUS WELBY NORTHMORE 1838*g* "West Front of St. Lawrence's Church, Nuremberg." *London and Dublin Journal of Useful Knowledge for 1838* May 26:321–323.

PUGIN, AUGUSTUS WELBY NORTHMORE 1839 *A Letter on the Proposed Protestant Memorial to Cramner, Ridley, & Latymer, addressed to the Subscribers to and Promoters of that Undertaking.* London: Booker and Dolman.

PUGIN, AUGUSTUS WELBY NORTHMORE (1841)1973 *The True Principles of Pointed or Christian Architecture: Set Forth in Two Lectures Delivered at St. Marie's Oscott.* Reprint. New York: St. Martin's.

PUGIN, AUGUSTUS WELBY NORTHMORE (1843*a*)1969 *The Present State of Ecclesiastical Archi-*

tecture in England. (*Republished from the Dublin Review*). Reprint. Oxford University Press.

PUGIN, AUGUSTUS WELBY NORTHMORE (1843*b*)1969 *An Apology for the Revival of Christian Architecture In England.* Oxford: St. Barnabas.

PUGIN, AUGUSTUS WELBY NORTHMORE (1844)1868 *Glossary of Ecclesiastical Ornament and Costume, Compiled from Antient Authorities and Examples illustrated by Extracts from the Works of Durandus, Georgius, Bona, Catalani, Gerbert, Martene, Molanus, Thiers, Mabillon, Ducange Etc. Faithfully translated by the Rev. Bernard Smith.* Rev. ed. London: Quaritch.

PUGIN, AUGUSTUS WELBY NORTHMORE 1846*a* "Lectures on Ecclesiastical Architecture Delivered to the Students of St. Mary's College, Oscott. Lecture the First." *Catholic Weekly Instructor* Feb. 1 and 7.

PUGIN, AUGUSTUS WELBY NORTHMORE 1846*b* "Lectures on Ecclesiastical Architecture Delivered to the Students of St. Mary's College, Oscott. Lecture the Second." *Catholic Weekly Instructor* Feb. 14 and 21.

PUGIN, AUGUSTUS WELBY NORTHMORE (1849)1894 *Floriated Ornament: A Series of Thirty-one Designs.* London: Bohn.

PUGIN, AUGUSTUS WELBY NORTHMORE 1850*a* *Some Remarks on the Articles Which Have Recently Appeared in the "Rambler" Relative to Ecclesiastical Architecture and Decoration.* London: Dolman.

PUGIN, AUGUSTUS WELBY NORTHMORE 1850*b* *An Address to the Inhabitants of Ramsgate.* London: Dolman.

PUGIN, AUGUSTUS WELBY NORTHMORE (1850*c*)1905 *An Earnest Appeal for the Revival of the Ancient Plain Song.* New York: Benziger.

PUGIN, AUGUSTUS WELBY NORTHMORE 1850*d* *Some Remarks on the Articles Which have Recently Appeared in the "Rambler" Relative to Ecclesiastical Architecture and Decoration.* London: Dolman.

PUGIN, AUGUSTUS WELBY NORTHMORE (1851*a*)1875 *Church and State; or Christian liberty. An earnest address on the establishment of the hierarchy . . . together with letters from Dr. Newman, Canon Liddon and the Right Hon. W. E. Gladstone.* London: Dolman. Originally published with the title *An Earnest Address on the Establishment of the Hierarchy.*

PUGIN, AUGUSTUS WELBY NORTHMORE 1851*b* *A Treatise on Chancel Screens and Rood Lofts, Their Antiquity, Use, and Symbolic Signification.* London: Dolman.

PUGIN, AUGUSTUS WELBY NORTHMORE 1851*c* *Letter to the Editor of the Tablet March 15, 1851.* London: The author.

PURCELL, EDMUND SHERIDAN 1900 *The Life and Letters of Ambrose Phillipps De Lisle.* 2 vols. London and New York: Macmillan.

ROPE, EDWARD GEORGE 1935 *Pugin.* Ditchling, England: Pepler & Sewell.

SIRR, HARRY E. G. 1917–1928 "Augustus Welby Pugin: A sketch." *Journal of the Royal Institute of British Architects* 25:213–226.

STANTON, PHOEBE B. 1951 "Pugin at Twenty-one." *Architectural Review* 110:187–190.

STANTON, PHOEBE B. 1952 "Some Comments on the Life and Works of Augustus Welby Northmore Pugin." *Journal of the Royal Institute of British Architects* Series 3 60, no. 2:47–64.

STANTON, PHOEBE B. 1954 "Pugin: Principles of Design versus Revivalism." *Journal of the Society of Architectural Historians* 13, no. 3:20–25.

STANTON, PHOEBE B. 1968*a* *The Gothic Revival and American Church Architecture, An Episode in Taste.* Baltimore: The John Hopkins University Press.

STANTON, PHOEBE B. 1968*b* "The Sources of Pugin's *Contrasts.*" Pages 120–139 in John Summerson (editor) *Concerning Architecture.* London: Allen Lane.

STANTON, PHOEBE B. (1971)1972 *Pugin.* New York: Viking.

SUMMERSON, JOHN 1948 "Pugin at Ramsgate." *Architectural Review* 103:163–166.

SUTTON, JOHN 1847 *A Short Account of Organs Built in England from the Reign of King Charles Second to the present time.* With five designs by A. Welby Pugin. London: Masters.

TRAPPES-LOMAX, MICHAEL 1932 *Pugin: A Medieval Victorian.* London: Sheed & Ward.

WATERHOUSE, PAUL 1897–1898 "Life and Work of Welby Pugin." *Architectural Review* 3:167–175, 211–221, 264–273; 4:23–27, 67–73, 115–118, 159–165.

WHITE, JAMES F. 1962 *The Cambridge Movement, the Ecclesiologists and the Gothic Revival.* Cambridge University Press.

WILLIAMS, RAYMOND (1958)1966 *Culture and Society, 1780–1950.* New York: Harper.

PUGIN, EDWARD WELBY

Edward Welby Pugin (1834–1875) was educated by his father, A. W. N. PUGIN, a noted British architect. He began independent practice at age eighteen, after the death of the elder Pugin. He dominated later partnerships with James Murray of London, George Coppinger Ashlin of Dublin, and J. Bethune of Ghent. Pugin's best works were creative, formally aggressive Gothic Revival buildings which adumbrated a later nineteenth-century tendency to move away from the constraints of historical accuracy. More than one hundred Roman Catholic churches and schools and several private mansions were listed in his obituary in *The Builder.* Pope Pius IX made him a Knight of Saint Sylvester in 1859 for his church of Notre Dame in Dadizele, Belgium.

ALICE H. R. HAUCK

WORKS

1850–1860, Saint Mary the Immaculate, Warwick, England. 1853, Our Lady of Help Cathedral, Shrewsbury, England. 1857–1859, Notre Dame, Dadizele, Belgium. 1858, Bishop Eton Monastery, Childwall; 1859, Our Lady of Reconciliation; Liverpool, England. 1860–1868, Scarsbrick Hall (additions), Lancashire, England. 1862, Saints Augustine and John, Dublin. 1863, Convent of Our Lady of Charity and Refuge, Burlestree, Herefordshire, England. 1864, Saint Francis, Gorton, Manchester, England. 1866, Sacred Heart, Dublin. 1866, Saint Gregory, Stratford-upon-Avon, England. 1868–1875, Cathedral (not completed until 1919), Queenstown (now Cobh), Ireland. 1874, Carlton Towers, Carlton-in-Belne, Yorkshire, England.

BIBLIOGRAPHY

DIXON, ROGER, and MUTHESIUS, STEFAN 1978 *Victorian Architecture.* London: Thomas & Hudson.

FERREY, BENJAMIN (1861)1978 *Recollections of A. W. N. Pugin.* With an introduction by Clive Wainwright. Reprint. London: Scholar.

GIROUARD, MARK (1971)1979 *The Victorian Country House.* 2d ed., rev. New Haven: Yale University Press.

WARE, DORA 1967 *A Short Dictionary of British Architects.* London: Allen & Unwin.

WEDGEWOOD, ALEXANDRA 1977 *The Pugin Family.* Farnborough, England: Gregg.

PUGLIANE, COSIMO

Cosimo Pugliane (?–1618) worked as an architect in Pisa during the early seventeenth century. He built the Palazzo Lanfreducci, later called Upezzinghi. From 1603–1605, he built the Logge di Banche in Pisa after a design of BERNARDO BUONTALENTI. It is a loggia of twelve pilasters originally intended as a market for wool and silk.

HOWARD SHUBERT

PUIG BOADA, ISIDRO

Isidro Puig Boada (1891–) was born in Barcelona, Spain. Director of works on the Sagrada Familia in Barcelona since 1950, he first met ANTONIO GAUDÍ Y CORNET in 1913. In 1929, he published *The Temple of the Sagrada Familia,* re-edited in 1952 and 1979. He is also the author of the *The Church of the Güell Colony* (1976) and *The Mind of Gaudi* (1981).

JUAN BASSEGODA NONELL
Translated from Spanish by
Judith E. Meighan

WORKS

1931, Casa in Vallvidrera, Barcelona, Spain. 1950, Cathedral of Solsona (restoration), Spain. 1954, Church of Balaguer; 1958, Church of Artesa de Segre; 1961, Church of Pujalt; Lerida, Spain.

BIBLIOGRAPHY

"Los noventa ãnos de Isidro Puig Boada." 1981 *La Vanguardia* 21, no. 4:25.

RÀFOLS, JOSÈ F. 1951 Volume 2 in *Diccionario biográfico de Artistas de Cataluña.* Barcelona, Spain: Millá.

PUIG I CADAFALCH, JOSEP

Josep Puig i Cadafalch (1867–1957) is the architect in Spain whose work reflects most clearly the adventure of the Secession and who, from the ascendancy of the language of *Modernismo,* proposed the use of the vocabulary of the changing phases of the central European avant-garde. If LLUÍS DOMENÈCH I MONTANER was the architect of the discovery of a national Catalan architecture in the midst of the general cultural Renaixensa in Catalonia and of the assertion of Catalan political autonomy, Puig i Cadafalch is the traveler, the archeologist, and the investigator who persisted in conquering medieval localisms. His was a new Catalonia which had its model in the civic ideal represented by England and Austria. The new Catalonia began with the first electoral triumph in 1901 of the nationalist party *Lliga Catalana,* which meant the election of Domenèch i Montaner as deputy and the beginning of the important political career of Puig i Cadafalch who eventually became the president of the *Mancomunitat,* the highest political organ of Catalonia between 1917 and 1924.

His architecture was initiated in the historicism of José Vilaseca and, fundamentally, of his teacher Domenèch i Montaner. The Amatller House (1898–1900) is from this period. In the façade, the different arts and traditional crafts are applied with precision, crowned by a pediment with a silhouette of evident German influence. The Terrades House (1904–1905) is Puig's most Wagnerian work. In many of his works Puig used brickwork, but it is in the Casarramona Factory (1911) that he profited most fully from the constructive possibilities of the cohesive wall system, a technique used in Catalonia since the fourteenth century.

Puig gave much attention to the interiors of his buildings. Dark corners, the screening out of light by means of window lattices, stained glass, glass galleries in the façade, and central patios or columned vestibules with skylights are featured in many of his houses. But it is not only the theme of light that characterized the domesticity and comfort of his interiors; the proper treatment of scale in each element that composed the rooms and the visual articulation of the spaces between them mitigate the excessive monumentality of many of his works. One of the best examples is his own house in Argentona (1897–1900), the result of the union of three houses of the village, in which the continuity of the spaces gives an unusually organic style.

In contrast and as parallel to the modernist "evocation of the North," Puig, adopting popular and historicist local themes, evolved toward compositions derived from vernacular Catalan architecture. Precedents of this are the Modernista Houses Garí (1898), and Macaya (1901) with their walls covered with stucco and graffiti and structured around a patio with exterior stairs to the main floor, in the manner of traditional fifteenth- and sixteenth-century construction.

In the group of family residences constructed in 1904, the reinterpretation of certain popular traditions of Catalan baroque reached a new stylistic approach under the direct influence of the Austrian Secessionists and, in particular, JOSEPH MARIA OLBRICH. These are constructions of small scale with large white walls and windows framed in stone, under which the ornamentation is reduced to graphics and to concentrations of verdant mosaics of vegetal themes, which, a few years later, Eugeni D'Ors codified in his *Glossari* and developed in *Noucentisme* the basis of a new classic figurative system of Mediterranean inspiration.

This moderated architecture marks the third stage of Puig i Cadafalch: the monumentalism of the Exposition of the Electrical Industries which took place in Barcelona in 1915 and which was later transformed into the International Exposition of 1929. Puig planned this exposition which was meant to be both the apotheosis of the spirit of Catalan capitalism, and a strategy to introduce the model of the new city. The initial plan and general disposition of the urbanization with a monumental avenue of waterfalls and the palaces was inspired by the Paris Exposition of 1900. Although only the twin palaces with baroque ornamentation were constructed according to Puig's plan, the project was conceived as a circle designed as a continuous mall of homogeneous structural elements. Also of this period is the Pich House (1921), the first attempt to assimilate the modern American architecture, inspired by the works of Louis H. Sullivan, to the buildings in Catalonia.

Parallel to the realization of his architectural works and to his political career, Puig i Cadafalch was an indefatigable investigator and historian. Among his 161 published works stands out the monumental history of Romanesque Catalan art that appeared between 1909 and 1918. This extensive theoretical production gained him international recognition and many honors and academic distinctions. Not only his personal work but also his political activity as president of the Institute of Catalan Studies had been to encourage archeological investigation and the institutionalization of Catalan Renaixensa effort.

ADOLF MARTÍNEZ I MATAMALA
Translated from Spanish by Judith E. Meighan

Puig i Cadafalch. Casa Amatller. Barcelona, Spain. 1898–1900

Puig i Cadafalch. Casa Trinxet. Barcelona, Spain. 1904

WORKS

*1893–1894, Joyería Macia, 18 Calle Fernando; 1895–1896, Casa Martí (Els Quatre Gats), 3 bis. Calle Montesión; 1897–1900, Casa Josep Puig i Cadafalch, Calle Dolors Monserdá, Plaza General Mola, Argentona; 1898, Casa Coll i Regás, 55 Calle Argentona, Mataró; 1898, Casa Garí (El Cros), Argentona; 1898–1900, Casa Amatller, 41 Paseo de Gracia; 1901, Casa Macaya, 8 Paseo General Mola; Barcelona, Spain. 1901–1902, Castillo Quadras, Maçanes, Gerona, Spain. 1902–1903, Hotel Términus, 282 Calle Aragón; 1903–1905, Casa Terrades (Casa de Los Punxes), 416–420, Avenida Diagonal; 1903–1907, Casa Serra, 126 Rambla de Catalunya; *1904, Casa Llorach, 263 Calle Muntaner; 1904, Casa Quadras, 373 Avenida Diagonal; *1904, Casa Trinxet, 268 Calle Córcega; 1905, Casa Sastre i Marqués, 44 Calle Eduardo Conde; 1911, Casa Company (altered), 203 Calle Casanova; 1911, Fábrica Casarramona, 36–44 Calle México; 1917, Casa Josep Puig i Cadafalch, 231 Calle Provenza; 1917–1923, Exposición International (various works); 1917–1923, Royal Palace (for Alfonso XIII and Victoria Eugenia), Parque de Montjuic; 1921, Casa Pich i Pon, 9 Plaza de Catalunya; 1923, Casa Guarro, 36 Via Layetana; 1924, Casa Casarrmona, 48 Paseo de Gracia; Barcelona, Spain.

BIBLIOGRAPHY

BOHIGAS, ORIOL 1948 "Josep Puig i Cadafalch, arquitecto octogenario: La obra no realizada." *Destino* 556:12–13.

BOHIGAS, ORIOL 1973 *Reseña y Catalogo de la Arquitectura Modernista.* Barcelona, Spain: Lumen.

BOHIGAS, ORIOL 1979 "Gracias y desgracias de los lenguajes clásicos en Barcelona." *Arquitecturas-bis* nos. 30–31.

CIRICI, ALEXANDRE 1966 "La Arquitectura de Puig i Cadafalch." *Cuadernos de Arquitectura* 63:49–52.

CIRICI, ALEXANDRE 1970 "Puig i Cadafalch: Somni, Civilització i riquesa." *L'Art Català Contemporani* 1970:62.

FLORENSA, ADOLFO 1967 "Puig i Cadafalch: Arquitecto, político i historiador de l'art y arquélogo." *Cuadernos de Arquitectura* 68:75–78.

JARDÍ, ENRIC 1975 *Puig i Cadafalch: Arquitecto, político i historiador de l'art.* Barcelona, Spain: Ariel.
L'oeuvre de Puig i Cadafalch, architecte, 1896–1904. 1904 Barcelona, Spain: Parera.
RAFOLS, J. F. 1956 "Puig i Cadafalch." *Cuadernos de Arquitectura* 28:1–7.

PURCELL, JAMES

Nothing at present is known of the life or education of James Purcell (?–1856). He came out to St. John's, Newfoundland, in 1842 as a mason to superintend the building of the Roman Catholic Cathedral. In the same year, he designed the small cruciform Christ Church for the Anglicans at Quidi Vidi. In 1843 he prepared a design for a proposed Anglican Cathedral at St. John's only to find his design rejected by a new and ecclesiologically-minded bishop. His major work was the Classic Revival Colonial Building (1850–1853) in St. John's. He was also responsible for the design of the Presentation Convent and School at St. John's.

SHANE O'DEA

WORKS

1842, Christ Church, Quidi Vidi, Newfoundland. 1844–1850, Colonial Building; 1850–1853, Presentation Convent and School; St. John's, Newfoundland.

PURCELL and ELMSLIE

Though brief in time, the post-1900 Prairie movement in American architecture was rich not only in the number and quality of buildings but also in the diversity of its points of view. Next to LOUIS H. SULLIVAN and FRANK LLOYD WRIGHT, the partnership of William Gray Purcell (1880–1965) and George Grant Elmslie (1871–1952) produced a number of what have come to be acknowledged as major monuments of the Prairie school. Though the careers of both Purcell and Elmslie were at times closely connected with Sullivan and Wright, their buildings turned out to express a highly personal version of the Prairie mode.

Purcell was born in Wilmette, near Chicago. His father, Charles A. Purcell, was active in the Chicago business world where he was a member of the Chicago Board of Trade. William Gray Purcell was raised by his grandparents in Oak Park, close to the Studio home of Frank Lloyd Wright. Purcell's grandfather, William Cunningham Gray, was a writer of national reputation and was the editor of the Midwestern magazine, *The Interior.* Purcell was educated in Oak Park and then went on to study architecture at Cornell University, from which he graduated in 1903. He first worked for a few months in the Chicago office of HENRY IVES COBB, then entered Louis Sullivan's office where he remained until the end of 1903. Early in the following year, he traveled to the West Coast working initially for JOHN G. HOWARD in Berkeley, and then with the Seattle firm of CHARLES H. BEBB and Leonard L. Mendel. In 1906, he traveled to Europe with a Cornell colleague, George Feick, Jr., and when they returned they established the firm of Purcell and Feick in Minneapolis. In 1909, George Grant Elmslie, who had been consulted on a number of occasions by the firm, became a partner. Between 1909 and 1913, the firm was that of Purcell, Feick, and Elmslie. In 1913, after Feick's departure, the firm became Purcell and Elmslie, and it continued under this name until the partnership was dissolved in 1922.

George Grant Elmslie was born on a small farm near Huntley, Scotland. His early education was at the Duke of Gordon Schools in Scotland. His family (including eight sisters and one brother) left Scotland in 1884 and went to Chicago where his father had obtained a managerial position with the Armour Company. Elmslie attended public schools in Chicago between 1884 and 1887. In 1888, he entered the office of J. LYMAN SILSBEE where he met Wright and also GEORGE MAHER. In the following year, he was engaged by the firm of ADLER AND SULLIVAN. When Wright left this firm in 1893, Elmslie assumed the position of chief draftsman. He continued his close association with Sullivan from 1895, when the Adler and Sullivan partnership was dissolved, until 1909 when he joined Purcell and Feick in Minneapolis.

Within the Sullivan office, much of the ornamentation of such buildings as the Guaranty Building, Buffalo, New York, (1894–1895), the Bayard Building, New York (1897–1898), the façade of the Gage Building, Chicago (1898–1899), and the Carson Pirie Scott Store, Chicago (1899–1904) was delineated by Elmslie. He was as well responsible for almost all of the ornament of Sullivan's National Farmer's Bank, Owatonna, Minnesota (1907–1908), and for the design of the Henry Babson Residence in Riverside, Illinois (1907), and the Harold Bradley House, Madison, Wisconsin (1909).

Before Elmslie's entry into the firm, Purcell and Feick had designed a cruciform-plan Prairie house and a small cottage for J. D. R. Steven in Eau Claire, Wisconsin (1909), a lakeshore house for Catherine Gray in Minneapolis (1907), and a suburban house in River Forest, Illinois (1909), for Purcell's father. Their two largest projects between 1907 and 1909 were variations on cruciform schemes: their unbuilt scheme for the First National Bank, Winona, Minnesota (1907), and the Stewart Memorial Church, Minneapolis (1909). All of the houses and other projects drew from the concurrent work of Sullivan, Wright, and the American Arts and Crafts movement.

Like Sullivan, Purcell and Elmslie designed a number of small banks throughout the upper Midwest. Their theme was that of a miniature brick jewel box, with the interior lighted by broad windows and skylights of colored opaque glass, and ornamented with colorful patterns of terra cotta, glass mosaics, stencil, and designs in sawed wood. The largest of their banks was The Merchants Bank of Winona, Minnesota (1911–1912); one of the smallest was the First State Bank, LeRoy, Minnesota (1914). Other commercial works by the firm included the Edison Shop, Chicago (1912–1913), where they explored in miniature the theme of the skyscraper, and two glass-walled factories which they built in New Haven and Chicago for the Alexander International Leather and Belting Corporation (1917–1918).

Purcell and Elmslie were intensely interested in obtaining institutional commissions, especially churches, but all of these projects remained unbuilt. The firm enthusiastically entered the competition for the new Capitol (Parliament) Building for Canberra, Australia (1914), but with Australia's entrance into World War I, the competition was cancelled. Another casualty of the war was their exotic design (part Prairie and part traditional Chinese) for the Y.M.C.A. Institutional Building and Church in Sieng Tan, China (1917). In their Woodbury County Courthouse, Sioux City, Iowa (1915–1917), designed with William L. Steele, the firm did realize the largest public building to be designed by any member of the Prairie school. For this building, Purcell and Elmslie took the theme of the classical box, articulated by engaged piers, and coupled it with the skyscraper image of American business.

The single-family free-standing house formed the major portion of Purcell and Elmslie's practice. They worked out numerous variations of the American Arts and Crafts square two-story stucco box. Some were larger and more elaborate, such as the Oscar Owre House, Minneapolis (1911–1912), others were compact and minimal as was the case in the C. T. Backus House (Minneapolis, 1915). The single-room bungalow, an often explored idea in the 1910s and 1920s, was impressively realized in Purcell's own cottage in Rose Valley, Pennsylvania (1918), where the combined dining and sleeping space had walls of sliding glass.

Two of their largest dwellings, the summer house for Harold Bradley, Woods Hole, Massachusetts (1911), and the lakeshore house for E. W. Decker, Holdridge, Lake Minnetonka, Minnesota (1912–1913), employed a cross-axial plan, the principal axis of which terminated in an extensive half-circle living bay. The culmination of their domestic designs was Purcell's own multilevel house in Minneapolis (1913), where the single great room was pressed into the ground to enjoy an intimate view of a pool and fountain, and was raised at the other end to look over the lake. In this house, as well as in many of their commercial, institutional, and domestic structures, they designed the built-in and free-standing furniture, carpets, draperies, stenciled patterns for the walls, intricately patterned leaded-glass windows, and ornament in terra cotta and sawed wood.

In 1922, the firm was dissolved and Elmslie established his practice in Chicago. Purcell moved to Portland, Oregon, where he continued in active

Purcell and Elmslie. First State Bank. LeRoy, Minnesota. 1914

Purcell and Elmslie. Woodbury County Courthouse (with Steele). Sioux City, Iowa. 1915–1917

practice through the 1920s. Elmslie's work of the decade continued to be Prairie-esque, but increasingly abstracted. This can be seen in his Capital Building and Loan Association Building, Topeka, Kansas (1922–1924), and his Western Springs Congregational Church, Western Springs, Illinois (1925–1926). Purcell's work became more picturesque and openly romantic. His own house in Portland, Oregon (1920), and the nearby Sidney Bell House (1927) display a picturesque layering of interior spaces. Purcell continued his involvement with low-cost and speculative housing. He designed and in many cases built speculative housing in both Portland and Minneapolis; he was an important figure in the American Institute of Architects Small Home Bureau, and he advocated the design of bungalow courts and garden apartments to solve the problem of low-cost housing.

After a serious illness at the end of the 1920s, Purcell moved to southern California where, while continuing to design some housing, he devoted most of his time to writing. Elmslie's practice essentially came to an end with the advent of the Depression, although he did collaborate on the design of several public schools; he produced a series of modern and Art Deco houses, none of which was built.

DAVID GEBHARD

WORKS

PURCELL AND FEICK

1907, Catherine Gray House, Minneapolis, Minn. 1909, J. D. R. Steven House and Cottage, Eau Claire, Wis. 1909, C. A. Purcell House, River Forest, Ill. 1909, Stewart Memorial Church, Minneapolis, Minn.

PURCELL, FEICK, AND ELMSLIE

1909, H. P. Gallaher House, Lake Minnetonka, Minn. 1910, Exchange State Bank, Grand Meadow, Minn. 1910, E. W. Powers House, Minneapolis, Minn. 1910–1911, First National Bank, Rhinelander, Wis. 1911, Lyman E. Wakefield House; 1911–1912, Oscar Owre House, Minneapolis, Minn. 1911, Harold C. Bradley Summer House, Woods Hole, Mass. 1911–1912, Merchants Bank, Winona, Minn. 1912–1913, E. W. Decker Summer House, Holdridge, Lake Minnetonka, Minn. 1912, Edison Shop, Chicago.

PURCELL AND ELMSLIE

1913, Edna S. (William Gray) Purcell House, Minneapolis, Minn. 1915, E. S. Hoyt House, Red Wing, Minn. 1913, Madison State Bank, Minn. 1913–1914, Community House and Parsonage, First Congregational Church, Eau Claire, Wis. 1914, First State Bank, LeRoy, Minn. 1914, Edison Shop, San Francisco. 1914, Margaret Little House, Berkeley, Calif. 1914–1915, Harold C. Bradley House, Madison, Wis. 1915, C. T. Backus House, Minneapolis, Minn. 1915–1916, Henry Babson Service Buildings, Riverside, Ill. 1915–1917, Woodbury County Courthouse (with William L. Steele), Sioux City, Iowa. 1916, Louis Heitman House, Helena, Montana. 1916, Farmers and Merchants State Bank, Hecter, Minn. 1916, Offices for Alexander International Leather and Belting Corporation, Philadelphia. 1917–1918, Factories, Alexander International Leather and Belting Corp., New Haven. 1917, Charles Wiethoff House, Minneapolis. 1918, William Gray Purcell Bengalow, Rose Valley, Pa. 1917–1920, First National Bank, Adams, Minn.

WILLIAM GRAY PURCELL

1920, William Gray Purcell House; 1923, Third Christian Science Church; 1927, Sidney Bell House; Portland, Oregon. 1927, Charles A. Purcell House, River Forest, Ill. 1927–1928, H. M. Peterson House, Minneapolis, Minn.

GEORGE GRANT ELMSLIE

1921–1924, Old Second National Bank, Aurora, Ill. 1922, American National Bank, Aurora, Ill. 1922–1924, Capital Building and Loan Association, Topeka, Kan. 1925–1926, Congregational Church, Western Springs, Ill. 1926, Healy Chapel, Aurora, Ill. 1929, Forbes Hall, Yankton College, Yankton, S.D. 1936, Oliver Morton School (with William S. Hutton), Hammond, Indiana.

BIBLIOGRAPHY

ANDREWS, WAYNE (1955)1978 *Architecture, Ambition, and Americans.* Rev. ed. New York: Free Press.

BROOKS, HAROLD ALLEN 1972 *The Prairie School: Frank Lloyd Wright and His Midwest Contemporaries.* University of Toronto Press.

CONDIT, CARL W. 1964 *The Chicago School of Architecture.* University of Chicago Press.

ELMSLIE, GEORGE GRANT 1946 "Sullivan Ornamentation." *Journal of the American Institute of Architects* 6:155–158.

ELMSLIE, GEORGE GRANT 1952 "The Chicago School: Its Inheritance and Bequest." *Journal of the American Institute of Architects* 18:32–40.

GEBHARD, DAVID 1953 *Purcell and Elmslie: Architects.* Minneapolis, Minn.: Walker Art Center. Exhibition catalogue.

GEBHARD, DAVID 1960*a* *A Guide to the Existing Buildings of Purcell and Elmslie.* N.M.: Roswell Museum and Art Center.

GEBHARD, DAVID 1960*b* "Louis Sullivan and George Grant Elmslie." *Journal of the Society of Architectural Historians* 19:62–68.

GEBHARD, DAVID 1965 *The Work of Elmslie and Purcell: Architects.* Park Forest, Ill.: Prairie School.

HAMLIN, TALBOT F. 1941 "George Grant Elmslie and the Chicago Scene." *Pencil Points* 22:575–586.

PURCELL, WILLIAM GRAY 1912 "Walter Burley Griffin, Progressive." *Western Architect* 18:93–95.

PURCELL, WILLIAM GRAY 1914 "Spencer and Powers, Architects." *Western Architect* 20:35–39.

PURCELL, WILLIAM GRAY 1961 "Architecture and the People." *Journal of the American Institute of Architects* 36:31–33.

PURCELL, WILLIAM GRAY, and ELMSLIE, GEORGE GRANT 1913 "Illustrating the work of Purcell,

Feick and Elmslie, Architects." *Western Architect* 19, no. 1:entire issue.

PURCELL, WILLIAM GRAY, and ELMSLIE, GEORGE GRANT 1915 "Illustrating in this issue the work of Purcell and Elmslie, architects." *Western Architect* 21, no. 1:1–20.

PURCELL, WILLIAM GRAY, and ELMSLIE, GEORGE GRANT 1915 "Illustrating the work of Purcell and Elmslie." *Western Architect* 22, no. 1:entire issue.

SPENCER, BRIAN A. (editor) 1979 *The Prairie School Tradition.* New York: Whitney Library of Design/Watson-Guptill.

PYTHEOS

Together with Satyros, Pytheos (?–330 B.C.) was architect of the Mausoleum at Halikarnassos, begun around 354 B.C. Distinguished by its huge size and elaborate sculptural programs, it was one of the ancient world's seven wonders and exerted considerable influence on later architects. Pytheos was the architect as well of the Temple of Athena at Priene, dedicated by Alexander the Great in 334 B.C. This building embodied a canon of proportions for the Ionic order. Pytheos wrote books on his works, now lost; the buildings themselves are known today only through fragmentary remains.

B. M. BOYLE

WORKS

*Begun c.354 B.C., Mausoleum (with Satyros), Halikarnassos, Greece. *c.340–334 B.C., Temple of Athena, Priene, Greece.

BIBLIOGRAPHY

English translations of the ancient texts can be found in the volumes of the Loeb Classical Library series, published by Harvard University Press and Heinemann.

ASHMOLE, BERNARD 1972 *Architect and Sculptor in Ancient Greece.* New York: New York University Press.

DINSMOOR, WILLIAM B. (1902)1975 *The Architecture of Ancient Greece.* Reprint of 1950 ed. New York: Norton. Originally published with the title *The Architecture of Ancient Greece and Rome.*

LAWRENCE, ARNOLD W. (1957)1975 *Greek Architecture.* Harmondsworth, England: Penguin.

PLINY, *Historia naturalis,* Book 36.31.

VITRUVIUS, *De architectura,* Books 1.1.12 and 7.Praef.12.

QUAGLIO FAMILY

For more than three centuries (seventeenth–twentieth), the prolific Quaglio family, originally from Laino in the Italian-Swiss Alps, were theater set designers and architects to the Courts of Vienna, Mannheim, and Munich. Lorenzo Quaglio (1730–1804) was rooted in the Bibiena tradition, while Angelo (1778–1815) introduced the neo-Gothic style and Simon (1795–1878) revived the closed room set and achieved fantastic light and color effects in his exotic "Magic Flute" sets (1818, 1839–1840). For King Maximilian II of Bavaria, Domenico Quaglio (c.1786–1837) reconstructed the neo-Gothic Castle of Hohenschwangau (1833–1837).

BARRY BERGDOLL

WORKS

GIOVANNI-MARIA QUAGLIO

n.d., Parish Church (façade), Novate, near Chiavenna, Italy.

LORENZO QUAGLIO

*1767, Opera House (extension; with Joseph Quaglio), Mannheim Schloss, Germany. *1775–1780, Comedy Theater (remodeled from Grain and Fruit Warehouses), Mannheim, Germany. *1780, New Comedy Theater (interior decoration), Frankfurt. (A)1780. Schloss Wain, near Laupheim, Württemberg, Germany. 1783–1790, Town Hall, Lauingen, Germany.

GIULIO QUAGLIO

1798, Court Theater (interiors), Dessau, Germany.

DOMENICO QUAGLIO

1833–1837, Schloss Hohenschwangau (rebuilding and interiors), Upper Bavaria, Germany.

BIBLIOGRAPHY

THE ARTS COUNCIL OF GREAT BRITAIN (editor) 1972 *The Age of Neo-Classicism.* London: The council. Exhibition catalogue.

DUNCKER, ALEXANDER 1846 *Kostüme und Decorationen der Oper Catharina Cornaro von Franz Lachner.* Berlin: The author.

SIMONSON, LEE 1933 *The Stage is Set.* New York: Harcourt.

QUAGLIO, JOHANN MARIA VON (1811)1823 *Praktische Anleitung zur Perspektive mit Anwendung auf die Baukunst.* 2d ed. Munich: Kunst-Anstalt an der Feyertags-Schule.

TROST, BRIGITTE 1973 *Domenico Quaglio, 1787–1837. Monographie und Werkverzeichnis.* Munich: Prestel.

QUARENGHI, GIACOMO

Giacomo Quarenghi (1744–1817) was born in Rota d'Imagna, in the province of Bergamo, Italy. It was in Bergamo that he completed his literary

Q

studies and started to dedicate himself to painting. In 1763, he was sent by his father to Rome, where he frequented the studio of Anton Raphael Mengs. He himself recounts in a letter that his friendship with Brenna (perhaps Vincenzo Brenna, an architect and painter, later active in Russia), his practice in the studios of architects ANTOINE DERIZET and Nicola Giansimoni, but above all else his reading of ANDREA PALLADIO's treatise persuaded him to dedicate himself to architecture.

His first important work, of pure classical inspiration, was the interior renovation of the Benedictine Church of Saint Scholastica (1771–1777) at Subiaco, in the province of Rome. English friends secured various commissions for him, such as the plan for the chapel of Lord Arundell (1776) in the Castle of Wardour, Wiltshire.

In his Roman period, interrupted by two study tours across Italy, he blended his work as an architect with an obvious activity in design: his views and fantasies reveal his admiration for Canaletto, Francesco Guardi, and GIOVANNI BATTISTA PIRANESI.

Due to Baron Grimm's interest, Quarenghi in 1779 received an invitation to go to Russia, to the court of Catherine II, whose preferred architect he would become. A tireless worker, he planned and built many constructions for the Russian court and for noble families, especially in St. Petersburg and the neighboring imperial holdings of Peterhof (today Petrodvorets) and Tsarskoye Selo (today Pushkin): in his works, his love for classicism, filtered through Palladio's example, is expressed; but at the same time, an attention to contemporary architects, such as CLAUDE NICOLAS LEDOUX and ROBERT ADAM and JAMES ADAM is also revealed.

After the death of Catherine II (1796), he continued to work at the courts of Paul I and Alexander I. Through his architectural works, Quarenghi contributed in a marked way to the delineation of the harmonious appearance of present-day Leningrad, especially because of the significant position of buildings such as the Academy of Sciences (1783–1789) and the Theater of the Hermitage (1783–1787), positioned along the Neva river. His capacity to insert buildings within the landscape, as happened in the case of the Imperial Manor at Tsarskoye Selo, with its elegant pavilion for music (1782–1788) and the great Alexander Palace (1790–1796), was also admirable.

Quarenghi returned to his homeland only for a brief period between 1810 and 1811. He died in St. Petersburg in 1817.

VANNI ZANELLA
Translated from Italian by
Florette Rechnitz Koffler

WORKS

1771–1777, Santa Scolastica (interior remodeling), Subiaco, Rome. 1776, Wardour Castle (altar for the chapel), Wiltshire, England. *1781–1789, English Palace, Petrodvorets; 1782–1788, Music Pavilion, Tsarskoye Selo (now Pushkin); near Leningrad. 1783–1787, Theater of the Hermitage; 1783–1789, Academy of Sciences; 1785–1790, State Bank; 1789–1796, Court Pharmacy; St. Petersburg (now Leningrad). 1790–1796, Alexander Palace, Tsarskoye Selo (now Pushkin), near Leningrad. 1790–1800, Yussupov Palace, St. Petersburg (now Leningrad). 1790–1805, Gallery of Shops, Moscow. 1798–1800, Church of the Knights of Malta; 1804–1807, Institute of Catherine; 1804–1807, Cavalry Guard's Riding Hall; 1806–1808, Smolny Institute; St. Petersburg.

BIBLIOGRAPHY

The Age of Neo-Classicism. 1972 London: Arts Council of Great Britain.

KORSUNOVA, MILIZA 1969 *Giacomo Quarenghi at the Galleria dell'Accademia in Venice. Master Drawings* 7, no. 3:308–310.

QUARINI, MARIO LUDOVICO

Mario Ludovico Quarini (1736–c.1800) was a follower and collaborator of BERNARDO ANTONIO VITTONE whom he may have met as early as 1757 in Chieri, Italy. They shared an extensive building practice from 1760 to 1770. Quarini engraved the illustrations for Vittone's treatise on the role of the architect, and supervised construction after Vittone's death. In 1773, he was elected citizen of Turin, and in 1785, he was nominated *architetto regio.*

Quarini's buildings in Chieri are representative of his three professional periods. San Filippo (1759), built before partnership with Vittone, is vertical and dynamic. It has a façade of two orders of unplastered brick. The slender columns layered three deep, the curved niches containing statues, and the framed trompe l'oeil windows result in a deeply sculpted composition. The side façade of the Palazzo Comunale (1771), for which Vittone had designed the main façade, is quieter being endowed with an imposing balustrade above the cornice line, but the entablature of the giant order is broken by the upper floor windows, and the capitals are unorthodox. The façade of San Bernardino (1792), built after Vittone's death, recalls the façade composition of San Giacomo in Balangero: the pediment front is supported by paired columns and flanked by towers. This static, plastered façade reinterprets the seventeenth-century elements in the new neoclassical idiom.

By contrast, his three buildings in Fossano,

constructed almost simultaneously, are more cohesive and constitute a conscious attempt to relate to the new neoclassical trends. However, the vault of San Giacomo (1789), in whose treatment of the niches above the piers there is an unmistakable quote from the dome of Santa Maria in Piazza in Turin, shows that Quarini could not entirely leave behind his master's flamboyant lessons.

MARTHA POLLAK

WORKS

1759, San Filippo (façade), Chieri, Italy. 1770–1771, Parish Church (presbytery and façade), San Benigno Canavese, Italy. 1771, Palazzo Comunale (side façade), Chieri, Italy. 1776, Abbey, San Benigno Canavese, Italy. 1777, Annunziata, Fossano, Italy. 1778–1779, Almshouse, San Benigno Canavese, Italy. 1779–1780, Palazzo Comunale; 1779–1781, Cathedral; Fossano, Italy. 1789, San Giacomo, Balangero, Italy. Completed 1792, San Bernardino (façade), Chieri, Italy.

BIBLIOGRAPHY

BAUDI DI VESME, A. 1968 Volume 3, page 881 in *Schede Vesme.* Turin, Italy.

CARBONERI, NINO 1959 "Note quariniane." *Bollettino Cuneo* 42:50–53.

CARBONERI, NINO 1963 "Architettura." *Mostra del Barocco piemontese* 1:81–83.

MOCCAGATTA, V. 1958 "L'architetto M. L. Quarini e le sue opere." *Atti e rasegna tecnica della Soc. degli ing. e degli archit. in Torino* 12:153–194.

MOCCAGATTA, V. 1976 "Le vicende construttive del Palazzo comunale di Riva di Chieri gia Radicati di Brozolo (1738–1797) e il primo progetto museale per le raccolte di antichita di Torino (c.1780–1795)." *Bolletino d'Arte* 61, July:263–295.

QUARONI, LUDOVICO

Ludovico Quaroni (1911–), architect, town planner, and teacher, has made some of the most significant contributions to the architectural discipline in post-World War II Italy.

After taking his degree in Rome in 1934, he began an illustrious career that has spanned all the developments in Italian architecture from the 1930s to the present. Quaroni began his teaching activity at the University of Rome in the 1930s as assistant to ENRICO DEL DEBBIO and MARCELLO PIACENTINI. Since then, he has also taught at the universities of Florence and Naples.

After spending five years in India as a prisoner of war, Quaroni returned to Rome in 1946 to help launch the architectural and urbanistic reconstruction of his country. The Tiburtino Quarter of 1950 in Rome is but the first of his many initiatives that helped revive Italy after the war. Quaroni's most important work in the following years has included low-cost housing and the master plans of numerous cities including Rome, Bari, Ravenna, Ivrea, and Reggio Calabria. He has also worked in North Africa and the Middle East. In 1956, he was awarded the prestigious Olivetti Prize in Urban Planning. His contributions to the Association for Organic Architecture and to the National Institute of Urban Planning are noteworthy. Recognized as one of the major protagonists in urban planning in Italy, Quaroni has contributed to the field through his prolific publishing and professional activity. In his work as a dedicated teacher, Quaroni has combined the fields of architecture, town planning, and sociology, and has influenced several generations of students.

ELLEN R. SHAPIRO

WORKS

1948–1958, Cathedral, Francavilla a Mare, Italy. 1950, Tiburtino Quarter (with others), Rome. 1952, Master Plan (with others), Ivrea, Italy. 1954, Master Plan (with others), Rome. 1956, Master Plan (with others), Ravenna, Italy. 1956, San Gottardo Church (with others), Genoa, Italy. 1964–1965, 167 Casilino Quarter (with others), Rome. 1964–1968, Cassa di Risparmio Bank (with others), Ravenna, Italy. 1965–1973, Master Plan (with others), Bari, Italy. 1968–1970, Master Plan (with others), Reggio Calabria, Italy. 1969, Casbah (renewal; with others), Tunis.

BIBLIOGRAPHY

BANDERA, ANTONIO ET AL. (editors) 1963 *Aspetti dell'arte contemporanea.* Rome: Edizioni dell'Ateneo.

CRESPI, RAFFAELLA 1957 "Profili di architetti: Quaroni." *Comunità* 11. no. 54:52–59.

DE FEO, GIOVANNA, and VALERIANI, ENRICO (editors) 1981 *Architetture italiane degli anni '70.* Rome: De Luca.

ESPAÑOL, JOAQUIÑ 1974 "Ludovico Quaroni." *Arquitecturas* no. 3:17–21.

MUSATTI, RICCARDO 1950 "Profilo di Ludovico Quaroni." *Comunità* 6:42–43.

QUISTELLI, ANTONIO 1973 "Progetti dello Studio Quaroni: Dieci anni di esperienze didattiche e professionali." *Controspazio* 5, no. 2:8–42.

TAFURI, MANFREDO 1964 *Ludovico Quaroni e lo sviluppo dell'architettura moderna in Italia.* Milan: Edizioni di Comunità.

ZEVI, BRUNO 1960 "Ludovico Quaroni: 1936–1944." *L'architettura cronache e storia* 52:692.

QUATREMERE DE QUINCY, ANTOINE CHRYSOSTHÔME

Born in Paris, Antoine Chrysosthôme Quatremère de Quincy (1755–1849) studied first law and then sculpture. In 1776, he traveled to Italy, visiting Naples in 1779 with Jacques Louis David, returning to Paris in 1780 to study architecture. In 1783 and 1784, he was again in Italy. In 1785, he won a prize for an essay on Egyptian architecture compared with that of Greece, thus initiating his career as scholar and ardent upholder of the classical ideal. In 1791, he transformed the Church of Sainte Geneviève into the Pantheon. From 1816 to 1839, he served as permanent secretary to the Academie des Beaux-Arts and sought to control all official building.

R. D. MIDDLETON

WORK

1828–1829, Saint Germain des Prés (pulpit; with ETIENNE HIPPOLYTE GODDE and Georges Jacquot), Paris.

BIBLIOGRAPHY

QUATREMÈRE DE QUINCY, ANTOINE CHRYSOSTHÔME 1788–1825 *Dictionnaire d'Architecture.* In *Encyclopédie Méthodique.* Paris: Panckoucke.

QUATREMÈRE DE QUINCY, ANTOINE CHRYSOSTHÔME 1803 *De l'Architecture Egyptienne considérée dans son origine, ses principes et son goût, et comparée sous les mêmes rapports à l'architecture grecque.* Paris: Barrois.

QUATREMÈRE DE QUINCY, ANTOINE CHRYSOSTHÔME 1814 *Le Jupiter Olympien ou l'Art de la Sculpture Antique considéré sous un nouveau point de vue. Ouvrage qui comprend un essai sur la sculpture polychrome, l'analyse explicative de la toreutique et l'histoire de la statuaire en or et en ivoire chez les Grecs et les Romains . . . .* Paris: Debure. In some copies the publication is postdated to 1815 to allow a dedication to Louis XVIII.

QUATREMÈRE DE QUINCY, ANTOINE CHRYSOSTHÔME 1823 *Essai sur la Nature; Le But et les Moyens de l'Imitation dans les Beaux-Arts.* Paris: Treuttel & Würtz.

QUATREMÈRE DE QUINCY, ANTOINE CHRYSOSTHÔME 1828 *De l'Invention et de l'innovation dan les Beaux-Arts.* Paris: Firmin-Didot.

QUATREMÈRE DE QUINCY, ANTOINE CHRYSOSTHÔME 1830 *Histoire de la vie et des oeuvres des plus célèbres architectes du XIe siècle jusqu'à la fin du XVIIIe.* 2 vols. Paris: Renouard.

QUATREMÈRE DE QUINCY, ANTOINE CHRYSOSTHÔME 1832 *Dictionnaire Historique d'Architecture.* 2 vols. Paris: Leclère.

QUATREMÈRE DE QUINCY, ANTOINE CHRYSOSTHÔME 1834 *Recueil de Notices Historiques lues dans les Séances Publiques de l'Académie royale des Beaux-Arts.* Paris: Leclère.

SCHNEIDER, RENÉ 1910*a* *L'Esthétique classique chez Quatremère de Quincy (1805–1823).* Paris: Hachette.

SCHNEIDER, RENÉ 1910*b* *Quatremère de Quincy et son Intervention dans les Arts (1788–1830).* Paris: Hachette.

QUESTEL, CHARLES AUGUSTE

Born in Paris, Charles Auguste Questel (1807–1888) entered the Ecole des Beaux-Arts in 1824, where he studied under Antoine Marie Peyre (see PEYRE FAMILY), ABEL BLOUET, and FÉLIX DUBAN. After a visit to Italy (1831–1832), he worked under Duban in 1834 before winning the competition for the Church of Saint Paul at Nîmes (1835), an early and competent essay in neo-Romanesque, although he was to become more adept at Quattrocento reinterpretations.

R. D. MIDDLETON

WORKS

1838–1849, Saint Paul, Place de la Madeleine, Nîmes, Gard, France. 1846–1878, Arena (restoration), Arles, Bouches du Rhône, France. 1847–1851, Fountain (with Jules Pradier), Place de Libération, Nîmes; 1848, Monument to Saint Louis, (with Pradier), Place Saint Louis, Aigues-Mortes; Gard, France. 1851–1879, Château de Versailles (restoration and alterations), Seine et Oise, France. 1854–1861, Saint Martin d'Ainay (restoration and furnishing of the main altar, and the pulpit), Place de l'Abbaye d'Ainay, Lyon, Rhône, France. 1859–1861, Hospital, rue de Saint Ouen, Gisors, Eure, France. 1862–1867, Hôtel de la Préfecture, (with Riondel père) Place de Verdun, Grenoble, Isère, France. 1863–1876, 1879–1888, Asile d'Aiénés de Sainte-Anne, rue Cabanis, Paris. 1864–1870, Musée Bibliothèque, (with J. F. Hector Riondel), Place de Verdun, Grenoble, Isère, France. 1868–1876, Galerie Dorée (restoration); 1868–1876, Hôtel de La Vrillière (Hôtel de Toulouse; additions), rue de la Vrillière; Paris.

BIBLIOGRAPHY

CHARVET, ETIENNE LÉON GABRIEL 1899 Pages 321–324 in *Lyon artistique. Architectes: Notices biographiques et bibliographiques.* Lyons, France: Bernoux & Cumin.

DELABORDE, HENRI 1890 *Institut de France. Académie des Beaux-Arts. Notice sur la vie et les ouvrages de M. Questel.* Paris: Firmin-Didot.

DELABORDE, HENRI, and BAILLY, ANTOINE NICHOLAS LOUIS 1888 *Institut de France. Academie des Beaux-Arts. Funérailles de M. Questal: Discours de M. le V$^{te.}$ H. Delaborde et de M. Bailly.* Paris: Firmin-Didot.

FOUCART, BRUNO 1976 "Questel et la Bibliothèque-Musée de Grenoble (1862–1872)." *Bulletin de la Société de l'Histoire de l'Art Français: Année 1975* 1976:281–301.

RAULIN, GUSTAVE LAURENT 1888 "Notice sur la vie et les oeuvres de Charles-Auguste Questel." *L'Architecture* 1888:52–56. Also published as *Charles-Auguste Questel, sa vie, ses oeuvres, 1807–1888.* Paris: Imprimeries Réunies.

SOUBIES, ALBERT 1911 Pages 250–295 in *Les Membres de l'Académie des Beaux-Arts: 3e série 1852–1876.* Paris: Flammarion.

RABIRIUS

Rabirius's (late first century A.D.) name appears only in the *Epigrams* of the Roman poet Martial; apparently the two men were friends. In one epigram (7.56), dating from 92 or 93, he is said to have "built by wondrous art the mansion of the Palatine," that is, the new palace of the emperors in Rome. In the other (10.71), written about 95 or 96, Martial in mourning the death of Rabirius's parents speaks of him as still alive. These spare references make it possible to add a name to the extremely short list of the Roman architects who created and brought to maturity, in and near the capital, the style that depended as much or more on the telling use of vaulted interior space as on the traditional, wooden-roofed classical architecture of the Orders. Rabirius's career could hardly have failed to overlap either that of SEVERUS or that of APOLLODORUS, and could easily have overlapped both. But nothing certain is known of him other than what Martial says and what can be learned from the wide-spread ruins still visible atop the Palatine Hill. He was perhaps descended from a distinguished Republican family prominent in the first century B.C.; that he was a professional of the first rank is clear from his selection by the emperor Domitian for the most important commission in his gift. His talent can be fairly gauged by the results.

Quite understandably, students of imperial architecture have tried to find evidence of his work beyond the Palatine, especially in the monuments of the Flavian dynasty (of which Domitian was the last), such as the Colosseum, the Baths of Titus, the rebuilding of the Forum of Caesar, Domitian's Villa at Albano, and so on. Although these efforts have yielded nothing positive, it is reasonable to believe that Domitian, and indeed his immediate predecessors, used Rabirius for major projects. There is a bit of evidence to suggest that he may have begun Trajan's Forum, early in the second century, but most authorities agree that that vast undertaking was entirely the work of Apollodorus.

What the despot Domitian required of Rabirius was not to remodel or enlarge the Palatine structures created for earlier emperors, but to create further to the south an entirely new complex which, by the time it was completed (c.96), covered some forty thousand square meters. Parts of Nero's palaces were covered over, and the rock of the Palatine was cut and shaped to take the several wings and levels of the new structure. On the north, at Forum level, a vast, vaulted guardhouse-vestibule was built; on the southwest, high above the stands and track of the Circus Maximus, a lofty imperial box. The palace was divided into three

R

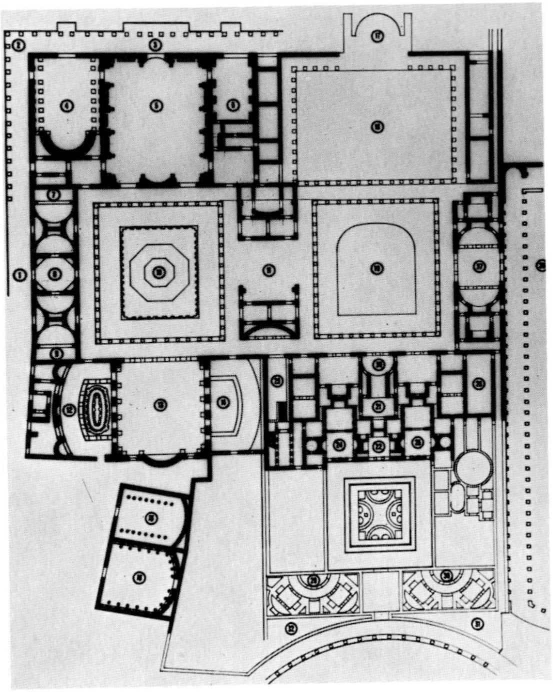

Rabirius.
Plan of Domitian's Palace.
Rome.
80s–90s

main parts, the Domus Flavia or public wing, furthest to the north, parallel to which lay the Domus Augustana or private quarters, with one part, toward the circus, composed of a sunken, lower level of apartments ranged round a deep-set open court. The third unit was in the shape of a small stadium but was gotten up as a garden with fountains and was used as a promenade and for entertainments.

Domitian, who, it was said, had the "building disease" (Plutarch, "Poplicola," 15.5), presumably demanded and certainly got an architectural expression of his ecumenical imperial claims. Because both the Flavia and the Augustana center round spacious peristyles, the palace has been called Hellenistic in style, but in fact it was the spacious, vaulted public rooms that gave the Domus Flavia its character; smaller ones, intricately interrelated, were the essence of the Domus Augustana. For example, in the emperor's basilica or audience hall of the Domus Flavia, a barrel-vaulted roof at least 27-meters high covered a longitudinal space at the end of which, centered in a wide apse and under a semidome, the imperial figure sat. The curves of the apse and its vault above could appear to an observer to be generated from that fixed central point, upon which not only the visitor's attention but the controlling lines of the architecture were focused. Similar principles were employed in other parts of the Flavia. Everywhere was the compass work, in both plan and elevation, that particularly distinguishes this style of architecture. Domed octagons, expanded by niches, are set into the fabric of the structure in several places, and there were elaborate fountains constructed on narrow oval plans.

The structure of the entire palace, except for the columns of the peristyles, façades, and certain of the halls, was of concrete, brick-faced below the springing lines of the vaults. Enormous concrete foundations have been excavated, of a size that would have satisfied even GIOVANNI BATTISTA PIRANESI. On the inner surfaces of the halls and apartments, large, thin sheets of colored and polished marbles were attached, and the pavements of the state halls were laid in patterns composed of colored marble rectangles, circles, and triangles. Presumably some of the vaults were encrusted with mosaics, but of them nothing remains. The visual effects of the interiors were largely dependent on this nonstructural, cosmetic sheathing of the working fabric, a method of design and construction that had become increasingly popular over the preceding decades. To some, for whom proper classical architecture is that of the Greeks and the earlier Romans, this style and its effects have been seen as meretricious and inartistic. Such opinions fail to take adequate notice of the significance of the great shift in architecture that took place in the first century A.D., a shift for which Rabirius was surely partly responsible. For it was then that the Orders and traditional trabeated construction were married, first hesitantly, and then with increasing success, to the new vaulted architecture of tinted interior spaces, one with very different objectives from that of the past.

In evaluating Rabirius's work it is important to notice that he planned and arranged his internal vaulted shapes with a surer hand than Severus did in the wing of Nero's Domus Aurea. He exploited the symbolic seamlessness of vaults of circular evolution in parts of halls where right angles would be

Rabirius.
Domitian's Palace.
Rome.
80s–90s

more suggestive of finite, fixed places. He forswore the traditional, usually inviolable alignment of the plan of one story above another, using the roof of the lower level of the Domus Augustana to carry different shapes and sizes of rooms than those below. He gave his patron as much that was novel as Severus had given his, and he strove to create an architectural language of majesty and dominion. His palace was in use at least until the sixth century, and its influence can be seen again and again in palaces, villas, and churches in Europe and beyond.

WILLIAM L. MACDONALD

WORK

80s–90s, Palace of the Caesars on the Palatine, Rome.

BIBLIOGRAPHY

English translations of the ancient texts can be found in the volumes of the Loeb Classical Library series, published by Harvard University Press and Heinemann.

FINSEN, HELGE 1962 *Domus Flavia sur le Palatin; Aula Regia-Basilica.* Hafniae, Denmark: Munksgaard.

MACDONALD, WILLIAM L. 1965 Volume 1, chapters 3 and 6 in *The Architecture of the Roman Empire.* New Haven: Yale University Press.

MARTIAL, *Epigrams,* 7.56, 8.36, and 10.71.

PLUTARCH, *Lives,* "Poplicola," 15.5.

STATIUS, *Silvae,* 4.2 (dining with Domitian in the Domus Flavia).

WARD-PERKINS, J. B. 1956 "Roman Concrete and Roman Palaces." *The Listener* 56:701–703.

RAFFAELLO SANZIO

See RAPHAEL.

RAGUE, JOHN FRANCIS

Born in Scotch Plains, New Jersey, builder-architect John Francis Rague (1799–1877) worked for MINARD LAFEVER in New York City and practiced in Springfield, Illinois, from 1831, in Milwaukee, Wisconsin, from around 1845, and in Dubuque, Iowa, from 1854, where he retired after 1857.

WESLEY I. SHANK

WORKS

1837–1854, Illinois Capitol, Springfield. 1840–1850s, Iowa Capitol, Iowa City. 1850–1851, North Hall; 1851–1855, South Hall; University of Wisconsin, Madison. 1857–1858, Dubuque County Jail; 1857–1858, City Hall; late 1850s, Edward T. Langworthy House; Dubuque, Iowa.

BIBLIOGRAPHY

HITCHCOCK, H. R., and SEALE, WILLIAM 1976 *Temples of Democracy: The State Capitols of the USA.* New York: Harcourt.

HOFFMAN, M. M. 1933–1935 "John Francis Rague—Pioneer Architect of Iowa." *Annals of Iowa* Series 3 19:444–448.

SHANK, WESLEY I. 1979 *The Iowa Catalog: Historic American Buildings Survey.* Iowa City: University of Iowa Press.

WOODMAN, BETSY H. 1969 "John Francis Rague: Mid-nineteenth Century Revivalist Architect (1799–1877)." Unpublished M.A. thesis, University of Iowa, Iowa City.

RAGUZZINI, FILIPPO

Filippo Raguzzini (c.1680–1771) is perhaps the best-known representative of the Roman rococo, a style which Rome never fully accepted, but which flourished episodically throughout the first half of the eighteenth century and most openly during the pontificate of Benedict XIII (1724–1730). Relatively little is known of Raguzzini's origins, and documentary evidence concerning the buildings attributed to him is remarkably sparse. He was born in Naples and executed his first designs in the provincial center of Benevento before his arrival in Rome in 1724. In this early period, Raguzzini was strongly influenced by the works of seventeenth-century Neapolitan architects such as COSIMO FONZAGA, which is especially evident in the Chapel of San Gennaro in the Chiesa dell' Annunziata, Benevento (c.1710). The sculptural qualities of the orders and the play of mass and void in this chapel are subordinated to a decidedly pictorial composition of surface patterns and the rich chromatic effects of marble intarsia. Moreover, deliberate disparities of scale within the chapel and the absence of classical decorum and clarity resulting from the subordination of ornament to architecture result in a design which is typical of southern Italy in this period.

In 1724, Raguzzini was called to Rome by Pope Benedict XIII, a native of Benevento, who was undoubtedly familiar with his work there. Benedict XIII was Raguzzini's great patron, and it was during Benedict's pontificate, a relatively short period of six years, that virtually all of Raguzzini's major buildings were constructed. Although the pope did indeed favor Raguzzini with architectural commissions, almost to the exclusion of the Roman architectural establishment, with few exceptions these commissions were small in scale and architecturally unassuming. Benedict XIII was not a builder-pope in the tradition of his eighteenth-century predecessor Clement XI, but was more concerned with the restoration of existing buildings. In fact, the bulk of Raguzzini's work in Rome consisted of modest restorations such as that of San Sisto Vecchio (1725–1727), where his intervention was limited to the consolidation of the existing structure and the resurfacing of the interior and exterior elevations with stucco.

A few commissions distinguish themselves from this pattern, offering greater scope for the display of Raguzzini's inventive powers, and it is to these that we must turn in order to chart the development of his personal style. One of these is the Chapel of San Domenico in Santa Maria sopra Minerva (1724–1725), most likely the first project undertaken by Raguzzini upon his arrival in Rome. A comparison of this Roman chapel with that of San Gennaro in Benevento reveals that although Raguzzini's southern love of rich surface pattern and polychromy persists, it is now subordinated to the system of orders which functions in a more sculptural way to mold a three-dimensional space. The increased clarity and monumentality of form that characterize Raguzzini's first Roman designs are even more apparent in the Ospedale di San Gallicano (1725–1726), where the role of ornament is reduced to a minimum and the emphasis is placed on the spare planar geometry of the exterior, relieved only by the curvilinear forms of the chapel projecting at center. It should be noted that this hospital was unusually advanced from the point of view of sanitary design, in particular with regard to ventilation, and that many features of the exterior (the continuous balcony, for example) were responses to functional as well as formal concerns.

Raguzzini is best known for the Piazza Sant'Ignazio (1727–1735), which constitutes the most mature expression of his genius. Working within the existing street pattern, Raguzzini constructed five apartment blocks which defined a square in front of the great Jesuit Church of Sant'Ignazio. These buildings are related to one another by means of three tangent ellipses which determine their curving ground plans and façade elevations. The light rococo forms of Raguzzini's structures are in conscious contrast to the monumentality of Alessandro Algardi's colossal baroque façade, to which they do not relate in scale, materials, or pretensions. Moreover, the traditional relationship between a major architectural monument and its urban setting has been reversed. Raguzzini's square does not exist primarily to set off the church, which cannot in any case be viewed comfortably from within its confines; rather, it is from the ample stairs of the church that the observer is invited to view the domestic structures which define the piazza. The audience has been invited on stage, as it were, to enjoy the ongoing spectacle of city life, which takes place in the stalls and boxes that Raguzzini, with consummate skill, has carved out of the surrounding urban fabric. It is precisely Raguzzini's inversion of the accepted relationships in baroque planning and scenography that gives the Piazza Sant'Ignazio its charm and compelling interest.

Raguzzini's mature designs show an increasing refinement and complexity. The convex façade of Santa Maria della Quercia (1727–1731), for example, expresses at once the interior space it molds while vigorously moving forward to activate the space without. At the same time, architectural ornament—even the use of the orders—is reduced to eloquent abstraction based more on the play of light and shade than on the forms themselves. In such mature designs Raguzzini is strongly influenced by FRANCESCO BORROMINI, whose reputation was enjoying a revival in Rome during this period. Significantly, both architects were criticized for what their contemporaries termed the Gothic tendencies of their personal styles. It is fascinating to speculate how much further Raguzzini might have pursued his reinterpretation of Borromini had his fortunes not been tied so closely to Benedict XIII. Following the pope's death in 1730, Raguzzini was denied important commissions and had to content himself with the rather limited opportunities which fell his way. To be sure, Raguzzini continued as a member of the Academy of Saint Luke, was elected to the prestigious Congregazione dei Virtuosi al Pantheon, and held public offices such as that of Architetto del Popolo Romano. He is also known to have participated in the competition for the Lateran façade, but by the 1730s the pronounced classicism of architects such as ALESSANDRO GALILEI and patrons like Neri Corsini was on the ascendancy. The combination of these radical shifts in taste and patronage effectively terminated Raguzzini's brief but brilliant Roman career.

JOHN PINTO

WORKS

c.1710, Chapel of San Gennaro, Chiesa dell' Annunziata; before 1724, Palazzetto De Simone; Benevento, Italy. 1724–1725, Chapel of San Domenico, Santa Maria sopra Minerva; 1725–1726, Ospedale di San Gallicano; 1725–1727, San Sisto Vecchio (restoration); 1726, Cappella del Crocifisso (restoration); c.1726, Cappella del Presepio, Santa Maria in Trastevere; 1726, Santa Maria del Rosario; Rome. 1726–1729, San Bartolomeo, Benevento, Italy. 1727, Casino Lercari, Albano, Italy. 1727–1728, Cappella Savelli, Santa Maria in Aracoeli, Rome. 1727–1731, Santa Maria della Quercia; 1727–1735, Piazza Sant'Ignazio; 1728, San Filippo Neri (façade); 1728–1730, Santi Quirico e Giulitta (façade); 1729–1734, Chiesa del Divino Amore; 1731, Spanish

Steps (restoration); 1741, Villa Gentili; Rome. 1767, Palazzo Terragnoli, Benevento, Italy.

BIBLIOGRAPHY

BONELLI, MASSIMO 1974 "Per una interpretazione di Filippo Raguzzini." *Capitolium* 49, nos. 10–11:29–33.

GOLZIO, VINCENZO 1934 "Nuovi documenti su Filippo Raguzzini." *Archivo d'Italia* 2:145–149.

LORET, MATTIA 1934 "L'architetto Raguzzini e il rococò in Rome." *Bollettino d'Arte* 27:313–321.

LOTTI, LUIGI 1962 "La Villa Gentili, oggi Dominici, e la sua attribuzione a Filippo Raguzzini." *Palatino* 6:11–15.

ROTILI, MARIO 1951 *Filippo Raguzzini e il rococò romano.* Rome: Palombi.

SCATASSA, ERCOLE 1913–1914 "Benedetto XIII e i suoi artisti beneventani." *Rassegna bibliografica dell'arte italiana* 26:111–119, 156–161; 27:138–141.

VENDITTI, ARNALDO 1972 "Un'opera del Raguzzini: Il Palazzo Terragnoli a Benevento." *Studi di Storia dell'Arte in onore di Valerio Mariani* 1972:215–226.

RAINALDI, GIROLAMO

Girolamo Rainaldi (1570–1655), father of Carlo Rainaldi, divided his time between Rome and various cities in northern Italy. He trained in Rome with DOMENICO FONTANA and emerged as an independent architect at about the time of the latter's departure for Naples in 1594. Girolamo's earliest works, the Aldobrandini Memorials in Santa Maria in Aracoeli (1595–1605), Rome, and the casa professa and sacristy of Il Gesù (1600–1620), Rome, establish a basic stylistic repertory of mannerist devices from which he seldom deviated throughout the course of his career. After the death of GIACOMO DELLA PORTA in 1602, Rainaldi succeeded to the post of architect of the *Popolo Romano,* but it was his older contemporary CARLO MADERNO who received the most important Roman commissions in the first quarter of the seventeenth century.

During the pontificate of Paul V, Rainaldi, an unsuccessful entrant in the competition for the façade of St. Peter's, was active chiefly in the construction of chapels and lesser monuments in Rome. The most significant of these is the Colonna Chapel in San Giovanni in Laterano (1606), a polychromed and richly ornamented ensemble whose altar is enframed on either side by his favorite motif of paired columns carrying tiny segmental pediments.

In the 1620s and 1630s, Rainaldi was principally occupied with commissions outside of Rome. In 1621, he began the Church of Santa Teresa at Caprarola which remains foremost among his independent endeavors. The most remarkable feature of this small church is its longitudinal plan with a broad cross-axis in the nave instead of the traditional transept and domed crossing before the high altar. This unexpected conflict of directional movement, mannerist though it was, soon became a recognizable feature of such incontestably baroque plans as Carlo Rainaldi's Santa Maria in Campitelli, Rome (1662). Less interesting are the interior and exterior elevations of Santa Teresa, which follow more conventional compositional models. In 1623, however, Rainaldi began work on the highly significant façade of Santa Lucia in Bologna. Although this work remains incomplete, his surviving drawing for the project indicates a compounded aedicular façade that looks backward to prior north Italian solutions and ahead to the fully developed baroque realizations of his son Carlo and others.

Rainaldi did not receive his most important appointment until 1644 when, at the age of seventy-four, he was made chief papal architect to Innocent X. In that capacity, he built the Palazzo Pamphilj in Piazza Navona (1645–1650), a vast building whose monotonously flat, somewhat incoherent façade relies upon the most conservative design principles. Girolamo ended his career in 1652–1653 as architect of the adjacent Church of Sant'Agnese in Agone, a commission completed after his death by Carlo with the intervention of FRANCESCO BORROMINI.

Girolamo Rainaldi's roots were in the sixteenth century, and throughout his career he remained steadfastly aloof from the bolder contemporary architectonic developments of the baroque. Ironically, perhaps, his overall importance lies in

Rainaldi. Palazzo Pamphilj. Rome. 1645–1650

his introduction of a few outdated but potentially significant north Italian devices to Roman architects coming to maturity in the mid-seventeenth century.

JOHN VARRIANO

WORKS

1595–1605, Aldobrandini Memorials, Santa Maria in Aracoeli; 1600–1620, Il Gesù (casa professa and sacristy); 1603–1604, Santa Maria della Scala (second chapel on the left aisle); 1603–1611, Aldobrandini Chapel, Santa Maria sopra Minerva; 1605–1621, Pauline Chapel (high altar), Santa Maria Maggiore; 1606, Colonna Chapel, San Giovanni in Laterano; Rome. 1621, Santa Teresa dei Scalzi, Caprarola, Italy. 1623, Santa Lucia (façade; incomplete), Bologna, Italy. 1634–1636, Chiesa dell'Annunziata (vaulting), Parma, Italy. 1645–1650, Palazzo Capitolino (completion; after Michelangelo and Giacomo della Porta); 1645–1650, Palazzo Pamphilj; 1647, San Girolamo della Carità; 1652–1653, Sant'Agnese in Agone (completed by others); Rome.

BIBLIOGRAPHY

BALDINUCCI, FILIPPO 1681–1728 *Notizie de' professori del disegno da Cimabue in qua.* Florence: Santi Franchi.

EIMER, GERHARD 1970–1971 *La fabbrica di S. Agnese in Navona.* 2 vols. Stockholm: Almqvist & Wiksell.

FAGIOLO DELL'ARCO, and CARANDINI, SILVIA 1977–1978 *L'effimero barocco.* 2 vols. Rome: Bulzoni.

FASOLO, FURIO 1961 *L'opera di Hieronimo e Carlo Rainaldi:* Rome: Edizioni Ricerche.

NOEHLES, KARL 1962 Review of Furio Fasolo, *L'opera di Hieronimo e Carlo Rainaldi. Zeitschrift für Kunstgeschichte* 25:166–177.

PASSERI, GIAMBATTISTA 1772 *Vite de' pittori, scultori ed architetti.* Edited by J. Hess. Rome: Barbiellini.

WITTKOWER, RUDOLPH 1937 "Carlo Rainaldi and the Roman Architecture of the Full Baroque." *Art Bulletin* 19:242–313.

RAINALDO

An inscription on the façade of the cathedral of Pisa, Italy, records Raynaldus (Rainaldo; 13th century) as its author (*prudens operator et ipse magister*). It is not clear, however, whether the façade dates from around 1120 or from 1240–1260. It is also not known if Rainaldo was an architect or at least an artist rather than an administrator.

CHRISTINE SMITH

WORK

(A)c.1250?, Pisa Cathedral (façade), Italy.

BIBLIOGRAPHY

SANPAOLESI, PIERO 1975 *Il Duomo di Pisa.* Pisa, Italy: Nistri-Lischi

SMITH, CHRISTINE 1980 "The Date and Authorship of the Pisa Duomo Façade." *Gesta* 19, no. 2:95–108.

RAINER, ROLAND

Born in Klagenfurt, Austria, Roland Rainer (1910–) has been a prime influence on younger Austrian architects in the decades following World War II. As an urban planner, teacher, writer, and architect, Rainer has espoused the fundamental notion that building is as much concerned with nature and open space as it is with solid structure. More important still is the sanctity of the individual, which, according to Rainer, must take precedence in any design formulation, particularly in the case of city planning and housing.

As the chief planning officer for the city of Vienna between 1958 and 1963, Rainer's Municipal Hall (1958) and his various housing developments were designed with these goals in mind. Earlier, his 1954 design (with Carl Auböck) of low, prefabricated detached housing had become typical of the rebuilding program which Austria undertook following World War II, for which Rainer and his followers were largely responsible. Although his work was focused on Vienna, Rainer conceived a number of other planning schemes such as for Linz, Ternitz, and Kuniglberg, a suburb of Vienna.

Throughout his career, Rainer has communicated his theoretical ideas by writing and teaching. Since 1956, he has been director of the architecture master class at the Akademie der Bildenden Künste in Vienna. Previously, he had been professor of housing and town and country planning at the Technische Hochschule in Hannover, Germany, from 1953 to 1954, and professor of building and design at the Technische Hochschule in Graz, Austria, in 1955. He received the Austrian National Prize for Architecture in 1962 and was made an Honorary Fellow of the American Institute of Architects in 1973.

Also in 1973, Rainer journeyed to China where, he believed, the priorities of urban life were more humane and less constricting than those of Western society. Horizontality, for example, rather than verticality is one of the keys to a healthy urban environment. Rainer put forth his impressions of Chinese society and its architecture in his book, *Die Welt als Garten: China* (1979).

PETER L. DONHAUSER

WORKS

1954, Prefabricated Housing (with Carl Auböck), Vienna. 1956, Terraced Housing, Ternitz, Austria. 1957, Artist's House, Kitzbühel, Austria. *1957, "Town of the Future," Interbau Exhibition, Berlin. 1958, Municipal Hall; 1958, Böhler Brothers Office Building, 12 Elisabethstrasse; Vienna. 1960, Steinbruch House, Burgenland, Austria. 1961, Municipal Hall, Swimming Pool, and Housing Development, Ternitz, Austria.

1963, Evangelical Church, Simmering; 1963, Housing Development, Mauerberggasse; Vienna. 1963, Lido, Ternitz, Austria. 1964, Municipal Hall (with Säume and Hafemann), Bremen, Germany. 1965, Municipal Hall, Ludwigshafen, Germany. *1966, Austrian Pavilion, Plovdiv, Bulgaria. *1967, Austrian Pavilion, Expo '67, Montreal. 1969, Puchenau Garden City (phase I), Linz, Austria. 1973, High School, Kagraner Anger; 1973, Television Center, Kuniglberg; Vienna. 1976, Roman Catholic Pastoral Center, Puchenau; 1978, Puchenau Garden City (phase II); Linz, Austria.

BIBLIOGRAPHY

KAMM, PETER (editor) (1965)1973 *Roland Rainer: Bauten, Schriften und Projekte.* Tübingen, Germany: Wasmuth.

RAINER, ROLAND 1947 *Die Behausungsfrage.* Vienna: Gallus.

RAINER, ROLAND 1948 *Ebenerdige Wohnhäuser.* Vaduz: Liechtenstein Verlag.

RAINER, ROLAND 1953 "Space and the Modern Highway." *Landscape* 2:2–7.

RAINER, ROLAND 1967 "Sports Hall, Vienna." *Architect and Building News* 232, no. 3:109–112.

RAINER, ROLAND 1972 *Livable Environments.* Zurich: Artemis.

RAINER, ROLAND 1978 *Kriterien der wohnlichen Stadt.* Graz, Austria: Druck.

RAINER, ROLAND 1979 *Die Welt als Garten: China.* Graz, Austria: Druck.

RAMEE, DANIEL

Architect and writer of many books and articles on religion, politics, and architectural history, Daniel Ramée (1806–1887) was born in Hamburg, Germany, and died in Paris. His father was JOSEPH JACQUES RAMÉE. He visited the United States with his family in 1812–1815 and later traveled extensively throughout Europe. Ramée's major architectural work was for the Commission des Monuments Historiques, restoring the cathedrals of Noyon, Senlis, Beauvais, and the abbeys of Saint Riquier and Saint Wulfran at Abbéville. He wrote an early history of architecture emphasizing racial differences in design, and his intimate knowledge of languages allowed him to make many translations of his own and other works. His *Dictionnaire* (1868*b*), in four languages, is still very useful.

PAUL F. NORTON

BIBLIOGRAPHY

CASTEL, LOUIS 1860 "Histoire générale de l'architecture par Daniel Ramée, Architecte." *Gazette des Beaux-Arts* 7:110–118.

RAMÉE, DANIEL 1843 *Manuel de l'histoire générale de l'architecture chez tous les peuple, et particulièrement de l'architecture en France au Moyen-âge.* 2 vols. Paris: Paulin.

RAMÉE, DANIEL 1859 *Monographie du château de Heidelberg.* Paris: Morel.

RAMÉE, DANIEL 1868*a* *L'architecture et la construction pratique mises à la portée des gens du monde.* Paris: Firmin-Didot.

RAMÉE, DANIEL 1868*b* *Dictionnaire général des termes d'architecture.* Paris: Reinwald.

VAPEREAU, GUSTAVE (1858)1884 *Dictionnaire universal des contemporains.* Rev. ed. Paris: Hachette.

RAMEE, JOSEPH JACQUES

While studying architecture in Paris, Joseph Jacques Ramée (1764–1842) was strongly influenced by J. N. L. DURAND, FRANÇOIS JOSEPH BÉLANGER, and CLAUDE NICOLAS LEDOUX. He fled France in 1793 owing to supposed Royalist leanings. In Hamburg, he started a furniture manufactory with Andreas Masson. Frequently in Copenhagen, he designed several imposing houses there. He and P. E. LeSueur decorated, in Pompeian manner, Erich Erichsen's mansion.

David Parish, a Hamburg merchant's son, persuaded Ramée to plan his properties in America. Ramée arrived in 1812, designed buildings at Ogdensburg, New York, for Parish, met President Nott of Union College in Schenectady, New York, and planned that campus. Proceeding to Baltimore, he designed Calverton Mansion for banker Dennis A. Smith. In competition for the Washington Monument (1814–1815) in Baltimore, he took second place. Finding little work in America, he sailed for Belgium in 1816 and thence to France (1823).

PAUL F. NORTON

WORKS

1799–1801, Erichsen Mansion (interior), Copenhagen. 1800–1802, Sophienholm, near Frederiksdal, Denmark. *1803, Bourse, Hamburg, Germany. 1806–1808, Øregaard, Hellerup, Denmark. 1813–1821, Early Buildings, Union College, Schenectady, N.Y. *1815–1816, Calverton Mansion, Baltimore.

BIBLIOGRAPHY

HISLOP, CODMAN, and LARRABEE, HAROLD A. 1938 "Joseph Jacques Ramée and the Building of North and South Colleges." *Union Alumni Monthly* 27:112–127.

MADSEN, HANS HELGE 1968 *Interiørdekorationer i Erichsens Palae, fra arkitekten J. J. Ramée's virke i København.* Copenhagen: Handelsbank.

NORTON, PAUL F. 1981 "The Architect of Calverton." *Maryland Historical Magazine* 76:113–123.

TUNNARD, CHRISTOPHER 1964 "Joseph Jacques Ramée and Union College." *Union Worthies* 19:5–15.

RAMÉE, JOSEPH JACQUES 1923 *Jardins irréguliers et maisons de campagne, de tous genres et de toutes dimensions,*

exécutés dans différentes contrées de l'Europe et de l'Amérique septentrionale. Paris.
RAMÉE, JOSEPH JACQUES n.d. *Parcs et jardins, composés et exécutés dans differens contrées de l'Europe et des états unis d'Amérique.* Paris: Rittner & Goupil.
RAMÉE, JOSEPH JACQUES n.d. *Recueil de cottages et maisons de campagne. . . .* Paris.

RANA, CARLO AMEDEO

Carlo Amedeo Rana (1714–1804), military engineer and architect, was born and died in Susa, Italy. Rana taught mathematics to artillery officers (1739–1780), wrote texts on military architecture, published a volume of twenty-three plates of stage designs (undated, perhaps 1760–1780), and was appointed royal architect in 1780. Although he had numerous commissions, he is best known for his Santi Michele e Solutore at Strambino, Italy, which is a skillful combination of neoclassical ornament on a rococo structure and plan.

HENRY A. MILLON

WORKS

1787–1790, Santo Bononio, Settimo Rottaro, Italy. 1764–1786, Santi Michele e Solutore (del Rosario), Strambino, Italy.

BIBLIOGRAPHY

BAUDI DI VESME, ALESSANDRO 1968 Volume 3, page 894 in *Schede Vesme.* Turin, Italy: Stamperia Artistica Nazionale.
BRAYDA, CARLO 1939 "Carlo Andrea Rana, Ingegnere Militare e Regio Architetto." *Rassegna Municipale Torino* 8.
BRAYDA, CARLO; COLI, LAURA; and SESIA, DARIO 1963 *Ingegneri e architetti del sei e settecento in piemonte.* Turin, Italy: Società degli ingegneri e degli architti.
VIGLIENO-COSSALINO, FERDINANDO 1969 *Carlo Andrea Rana, Architetto in Piemonte.* Ivrea, Italy: Fratelli.

RANSOME, ERNEST LESLIE

Ernest Leslie Ransome (1844–1917) was born in Ipswich, England, where his family had manufactured agricultural machinery since the late eighteenth century and several of Ernest's forebears had made notable innovations, both in this field and in others. Between 1844 and 1867, his father had developed a patented "concrete stone" and embarked upon its manufacture. After serving an apprenticeship in the main family works, Ernest crossed the Atlantic to exploit his father's patent in the United States. He settled in San Francisco as the building boom that followed the completion of the Union Pacific Railroad in 1869 was about to begin, and established a business there to manufacture concrete blocks. Building commissions followed and led to a series of more significant innovations in the use of bar reinforcement in concrete—seemingly largely independent of parallel developments in Europe and guided more by inventive flair than by systematic testing or theoretic understanding.

Ransome's first notable innovation, in 1884, was to use bars of twisted square section in place of round bars to obtain good bond with the surrounding concrete. For the concrete floor of a wine cellar constructed in 1888 he embedded pairs of these bars at intervals near the soffit and arched up the soffit between them, so that the bars acted as true tensile reinforcement. This was much more economical than the earlier use of cast-iron joists to carry the whole load. But both here and in other buildings at this time, construction was otherwise conventional with massive outer walls and cast-iron columns internally. He achieved the full concrete frame, permitting almost continouous external fenestration where desired, around 1900. At this time, he was also thinking further about unit construction, now in larger units of reinforced concrete. This called both for durable formwork that could be used repeatedly and for efficient and economical means of bonding units together. A series of patents between 1902 and 1909 covered the main requirements. However, by this time, many others were entering the field and Ransome's rather simple intuitive approach to the design of the reinforcement was becoming outmoded by the more rigorous approach developed in France and Germany.

ROWLAND MAINSTONE

WORKS

1888, Bourn and Wise Wine Cellar, Saint Helena, Calif. 1897–1898 Pacific Coast Borax Company Factory, Bayonne, N.J. 1902, Kelly and Jones Factory, Greensburg, Pa.

BIBLIOGRAPHY

RANSOME, ERNEST LESLIE, and SAUBREY, ALEXIS 1912 *Reinforced Concrete Buildings.* New York: McGraw-Hill.

RAPHAEL

Raphael (1483–1520) was, in Nikolaus Pevsner's words, the greatest exponent of High Renaissance classicism, not only in painting, but in architecture as well. He was born in Urbino as the son of the painter Giovanni Santi; his name was actually Raffaelle Sanzio. Not much is known of his earliest years except that his training was wholly that of a painter. He entered the workshop of Perugino in Peugia around 1500, went to Florence in 1504 and on to Rome, almost certainly in 1508. His remarkable if fragmentary achievements in architecture all belong to the later years of his tragically short life.

Raphael began practicing architecture actively as the career and the life of DONATO BRAMANTE was coming to an end; he succeeded Bramante in the role of principal papal architect and inherited his cultural legacy, in particular, one of Bramante's most important accomplishments, namely the tectonic sense of space adopted from Roman imperial architecture. However, Raphael began immediately to develop his own personal style. His long experience as painter led him to conceive of architecture as a visual art, and he experimented with refinements of optical correction seen through foreshortened vistas. A synthesis of Bramante's style and the most fertile of the current trends as expressed in the "triumphal" architecture of Giuliano da Sangallo (see SANGALLO FAMILY) allowed him to blend into his architecture rich figurative images, thus satisfying the antiquarian taste and the demands of his self-glorifying patrons. Already in one of his early works (Agostino Chigi's Stables, Rome [1512–1513]), Raphael appears to be a master of the classical orders, using the canon of proportions in a system of superimposed orders; his deep knowledge of the theory and practice of ancient architecture did not, however, bind him to it. On the contrary, adopting a direction which had been Bramante's, Raphael first used an abbreviated order (interior of Sant' Eligio, Rome [1515]) later replaced them with abstract elements used to represent the interior arrangement on the exterior walls (Villa Madama, Rome, [1518–1519]). His firsthand knowledge of ancient architecture and its way of unifying spaces, its modeling of walls, and its use of materials and decorative elements, allowed him to free himself gradually from the Quattrocento interpretation of that architecture. He first reduced the importance of vertical axes, one of the main compositional devices of fifteenth-century architecture, and later completely abandoned them (Branconio Palace). Similarly, he substituted for Bramante's disposition of the installations on longitudinal axes a balanced composition of spaces much closer to the static use of space of ancient architecture (final project for Villa Madama [1518–1519]).

Raphael came closer than anyone else before him to achieving an understanding of the spirit of classical architecture, deeply felt and relived in all its aspects, and this understanding allowed him to transform it freely into an architecture totally new in its compositional laws and functional system.

On August 1, 1514, at the age of thirty-one, after having achieved the highest success in his career as a painter, Raphael was officially appointed *magister operis* in charge of the most important architectural undertaking in progress in Rome at that time: the building of St. Peter's, which, in fact, he had been directing since April of that year. From the text of the breve confirming this appointment it appears that Bramante himself had suggested the name of the man who should continue his work and that this man was at the time considered excellent in painting and well versed in architecture—Raphael. In the six subsequent years, until his death in April 1520, Raphael directed for Pope Leo X some of the main works in Rome, from the Vatican Palace (from 1514–1515) to the Villa Madama (from 1518), and carried on an intense architectural activity for various other patrons, nearly all of whom were attached to the papal court.

Among the known works of Raphael only two had for certain been begun before the St. Peter's commission (starting from 1512–1513): the memorial chapel for Agostino Chigi in Santa Maria del Popolo and, for the same patron, the stables in the villa later called Farnesina.

With regard to the Chigi Chapel, the instructions for the completion of the works which Agostino Chigi, in August 1519, included in his will, mention Raphael, which confirms GIORGIO VASARI's attribution. The beginning (1512–1513) has been deduced from the date (1516) of the completion of the cupola mosaics. This, however, does not mean that the architectural details of the lower section were also completed, since it was common usage at the time to work on the finishing details from the highest stories down to the lowest stories. Certainly at the death of Agostino Chigi (1520), the mosaics of the drum had not yet been completed. For the sculptures and pyramids, the Chigi heirs drew up a contract in February 1521 with Lorenzetto, a disciple of Raphael. The work progressed very slowly and the chapel was opened to the public only in 1554. Subsequent additions and modifications in the seventeenth century did not substantially alter the final project, although some were fairly important, such as the transformation of the altar, the addition of two statues in the niches after removing the ones previously in place, and the simplification of the decoration on the pyramids.

Vasari's attribution of the stables was confirmed by an autograph drawing (Uffizi, E1474). A payment of May 1514 proves that on that date the work was already in progress; therefore, we date the beginning of the project in the previous year, or better 1512–1513, at which time Raphael received other commissions from Agostino Chigi. The stables were already in use in April 1518, though not quite completed; they were largely demolished in 1808 but were amply documented in several drawings of the sixteenth century.

The affinity of both the chapel and the stables with Bramantesque prototypes confirms the cultural derivation of Raphael the architect from Bramante, as was suggested by Vasari in the passages on their relationship. In the Chigi Chapel, the square format with rounded corners and the system of pendentives and pillars carved out of niches recall the solution for the crossing in St. Peter's. In the Chigi Stables, however, Raphael realized a variation on the theme of the Caprini Palace, substituting the half-columns—possibly inspired by the neighboring villa of BALDASSARE PERUZZI—he used double pilasters instead of Bramante's half-columns, and repeated them on two levels, the lower windowless level taking the place of the rusticated base. Although the vocabulary derives from a Bramantesque repertory, the two works are quite different from the architecture of Bramante. The Chigi Chapel shows a heightened preference for polychromy in the use of precious materials and for elegance in the design of the various details. Furthermore, since the whole is the work of a single artist, we observe a hitherto unprecedented integration of the diverse visual arts. The architecture unites a number of symbolical figures placed according to a precise architectural order; the themes of the Resurrection and of immortality unify the triumphal arch motive and the pyramids with the statues in the niches, with some of the reliefs in the festoons between the capitals, and with the mosaics in the cupola, with the projected altarpiece, and with the bronze relief intended for the base of a pyramid, executed in part with modifications after the death of Raphael.

Raphael.
Chigi Chapel.
Rome.
1512–1513 (not completed until later by others)

Raphael unlike Bramante, designed the superimposed orders of the Chigi stables according to a classical canon of proportions. Yet, he does not slavishly apply the orders to this building. To the façade facing the street, with superimposed orders, he juxtaposes sides without orders, as he would later do again, though less conspicuously, in the Branconio Palace. In fact, on the southern side of the stables, the disposition of the windows which implied the presence of a staircase was incompatible with the continuation of the organization of the street façade; also, an encircling wall on the whole prevented the two heterogeneous projects being seen at the same time, thus diminishing the shortcomings of their juxtaposition. This choice bears witness to a shift of interest from the abstract concept of the order to concrete conditions of vision that would ultimately lead Raphael effectively to refine the devices of optical correction of architecture. This inclination obviously springs from a rich pictorial experience, from which also derives the sensitivity toward the polychromy of materials and the ability to orchestrate, by using varied artistic techniques such a complex iconographic program as the Chigi Chapel. In this chapel, however, we see an individual relationship with ancient architecture, especially with the Pantheon, which Raphael wants to emulate in the elegance of detail and in the richness of materials. In the interior of the Pantheon one finds one of the best preserved examples of paneling in marbles of diverse colors, and from its vestibule Raphael adopted the fluted pilasters with bases, the elegant Corinthian capitals, and the flat panels that articulate the wall surface between the pairs of pilasters on the entrance side.

All this presupposes Raphael's careful and continued study of ancient monuments and contemporary buildings. This is confirmed in the first examples of architecture depicted in his paintings and in the few drawings of architecture by his hand before 1512, none of which can be safely related to a precise commission. It has been noted that Raphael often recalled and used forms that were familiar to him from a number of buildings of the last decades of the fifteenth century of his native city, Urbino; for example, drawing number 474–475 in the Wicar Museum (c.1500) shows an order of arches on columns above which is an order of pilasters similar to the solution of the main courtyard of the ducal palace in Urbino, except for the addition of a tympanum on the aedicula of the window. The capitals of the same courtyard can also be seen in paintings of architecture, as in the Annunciation on the predella of the Oddi altarpiece (1502–1503). Another building in Urbino, San Bernardino, attributed to FRANCESCO DI GIORGIO MARTINI, is the inspiration for a plan drawing (c.1506) of a chapel or small church with four circular columns at the corners of the central space in the Ashmolean Museum in Oxford (no. 517v); the sixteen-sided temple painted in the background of the *Marriage of the Virgin* (1504) appears instead as an original elaboration on a theme, that of a religious building with centralized plan, which in those years was the object of numerous experiments, both in practice and in treatises. In addition to the refined proportions, which would be a constant characteristic of his works and to other elements from Urbino, such as the windows in the drum, one can see in the capitals of the pilasters inside the portico, obtained through a projecting trabeation, a sign of Raphael's inclination toward designing the orders in an abbreviated manner. This preference appears in a number of architectural images in paintings at the time of his collaboration with Perugino and is more decisively confirmed in the last Roman works of Bramante, which show elements of synthesized order or in which components have been substituted by abstract forms. This inclination is evident throughout Raphael's activity, from the interior of Sant' Eligio degli Orefici (1514–1515) to the Villa Madama (from 1518).

Even though we do not have evidence in drawings and paintings, certain architectural trends emerging in Florence, where he resided from 1504 to 1508, had a lasting effect on Raphael's work. In particular, a tendency evinced in paintings executed during the years of Lorenzo the Magnificent and by archeological research and especially inspired by triumphal arches contributed to the formation of his taste. This tendency led him to design architectural projects of large size and significant figuration, a tendency already evinced during the years of Lorenzo the Magnificent in paintings showing architecture. Giuliano da Sangallo's style later influenced Raphael in a direct way when they collaborated in the building of St. Peter's (1514–1515) and even more in the competition for the façade of San Lorenzo in Florence (1515–1516) for which they both produced projects. But already during his stay in Florence, Raphael came to know various aspects of work by Giuliano da Sangallo: the reliefs in the courtyard of the Palace of Bartolomeo Scala, Santa Maria delle Carceri in Prato, the polychromy of the Gondi Chapel in progress at Santa Maria Novella, and the order of columns with horizontal trabeation in the vestibule of the Sacristy of Santo Spirito and in the atrium of Santa Maria Maddalena de' Pazzi.

Raphael. Marriage of the Virgin. 1504

At most a few years later, while he was still living in Florence, Raphael had his first direct contact with the architecture of ancient Rome. It is fairly probable that during an undocumented visit to Rome in 1506–1507 he designed the views of the vestibule and the interior of the Pantheon (Uffizi, A 164). Another trip to Rome probably took place even earlier, in 1502, according to a recent hypothesis that moves the traditional date of two successive renditions of a memorandum on the study of the monuments of ancient Rome—without date, names of author, or addressee but believed to have been written by Raphael to Leo X with the help of Baldassare Castiglione—from 1519 to 1513–1514. If this is the case, Raphael already possessed that critical knowledge of ancient architecture he started working as an architect, which would explain the maturity of his work on the Chigi Chapel. This hypothesis, however, is contradicted in the text of the same letter, where the author states: "I have been in Rome not quite twelve years," and this would seem to mean that he has been residing there for that length of time, namely, since 1508. Whatever the date of the memorandum, the writer clearly shows how useful it was to measure and draw the monuments accurately and to produce their objective representation in plan, perspective, and cross-section to whoever should wish to base a new architecture on the profound knowledge of the ancient manner.

At the same time, the author appears careful to compare the results of direct examination of the monuments with the literary sources; he understands the canons of the architectural orders expressed by VITRUVIUS and expresses the desire, clearly manifest in numerous works, to approach even more closely than Bramante the manner of the ancients, recapturing the richness of decoration and materials. In fact, Raphael, who employed a more and more precise antiquarian understanding in his activity as a painter, moved ever closer to antiquity in his architecture, a trend that reached its culmination in the Villa Madama. To this end, he availed himself of every possible means of research and of the best possible collaboration available in Rome.

In 1514, in order to meet the challenge of the St. Peter's commission, he made a careful study of Vitruvius's treatise as translated by the humanist M. Fabio Calvo, with whom he was in contact, and Raphael annotated a manuscript of the translation; furthermore, in order to interpret this and other ancient and contemporary treatises, first of all the one by LEON BATTISTA ALBERTI, he was able, in the building yard of St. Peter's, to obtain the opinion of two other connoisseurs of Vitruvius: Giuliano da Sangallo who since 1488, in his project for the palace for the king of Naples, had drawn inspiration from sections of the Vitruvian description of the *domus,* and FRA GIOCONDO, the octogenarian architect and humanist who published the first illustrated edition of *De architectura* which he prepared in more than two decades of study.

Also in 1514, Raphael visited the ruins in Rome accompanied by the antiquarian Andrea Fulvio, and in 1516 he went to visit the ancient architecture of Tivoli with Pietro Bembo, Baldassare Castiglione, and other literary personalities. Of all the drawings he made on these and other occasions and about which we have ample documentation, especially for the last two years of his life, only two sheets still exist with views and elevations of the Pantheon (Uffizi, A 164 r. & v. and Royal Institute of British Architects, vol. XIII, f. 1r. & v.). In addition to direct investigation of monuments and consultation of Latin literary sources, we surmise that Raphael used every kind of ancient images, from coins to miniatures, as viable means to satisfy his interest in the original aspect of classical architecture. These sources are indeed abundantly used in the pictorial activity of his workshop, Indeed, the *Antiquae urbis Romae cum regionibus Simulachrum,* is illustrated with figures derived from coins and miniatures from the Vatican Vergil, which was most certainly known to Raphael. Printed in 1527 by M. Fabio Calvo, it is the only remaining example, though remote, of the Raphaelesque program to restore graphically an integral image of ancient Rome. For example, the possible as yet uncertain knowledge of pyramids represented on ancient coins might justify the unusual, slender shape of the pyramids in the Chigi Chapel.

In the autumn of 1508, Raphael moved to Rome where, according to Vasari, he had been summoned to paint in the Stanze on a recommendation by Bramante. Working in the Stanze of the Papal Palace, he found himself surrounded by the most important Bramantesque building sites, from the new one in St. Peter's to the Belvedere Courtyard and the Loggie of San Damaso's courtyard.

Thus, Raphael immediately encountered the work of Bramante who had attempted to develop a new vocabulary stemming from an objective examination of Roman architecture, recapturing its synthetic mastery of structurally articulated spaces and experimenting with the possible combinations of the classical orders. The results he achieved in tackling a vast number of themes, in the research on various types of space, and in defining, in the Caprini Palace, a solution that was to be very successful in the sixteenth century, inducing many people, and among them Raphael himself, to credit Bramante with having come closer than anyone else to the grand manner of the ancients and so to have given birth to the new architecture.

At Bramante's death (1514), Raphael inherited the direction of the works, and because of this, he found it necessary to confront the style of his predecessor, to analyze it and master it in order either to adopt it or to reject it. But the influence on Raphael of Bramante's inventions are evident still earlier, in painted architectural images in the Stanze. The pedestal of one of the pilasters in St. Peter's appears in the *Disputa* (1509–1511), and the interior of St. Peter's under construction inspired the building in the background of the *School of Athens* (1509–1511). The attribution to Bramante of the drawing of this background is disputed. However, though the vocabulary is Bramantesque, the articulation of the relief of the walls and the fact that the building does not have all the characteristics of a working model (for example, the incredible intensity of the light in the space under the dome as well as other incongruities in the area of the crossing) justifies the belief that Raphael was the sole author.

Still close to Bramantesque prototypes are three works that Raphael began to construct at the end of 1514 and the beginning of 1515: the small Church of Sant' Eligio degli Orefici, the Palace of Jacopo da Brescia, and the completion of the Loggie of San Damaso. Whereas the first work still has a great deal in common with the phase represented by the Chigi Stables, in the da Brescia Palace and especially in the interior of the Loggie, the development from Raphael's early style to his mature style is evident.

The exchange of a piece of land for another in December 1514 on the occasion of the replanning of a street that joined Via Giulia to another street along the Tiber allowed the guild of the goldsmiths to incorporate the area on which stood an old church they owned and to rebuild it, fulfilling a resolution made in 1509. The construction of this church, Sant' Eligio, was in progress the following year and continued very slowly. In 1522, the goldsmiths assembled in the new church, but the dome was built only in 1535–1536 and its cornice completed in 1542. Some decades later, in 1575, began the work of consolidation until, the church being in ruin, FLAMINIO PONZIO, between 1602 and 1604, rebuilt the vaults and set the dome on a higher drum. In 1620, the façade was totally redone. Of the Cinquecento building, modified in the proportions of the dome and the drum and the distribution of the light, there remains little more than the plan. The original appearance can, however, be hypothetically reconstructed from two drawings dating from the middle of the sixteenth century, one of which bears, in the hand of Sallustio Peruzzi, the attribution to Raphael. This attribution, due to the reliability of the source (indirectly Sallustio's father, Baldassare Peruzzi), although late, is generally accepted; the graphic rendition, furthermore, is compatible with Raphael's style in 1514–1515, and therefore the project probably did not undergo significant modifications during the execution, which continued for such a long time after his death.

In Sant' Eligio, Raphael effected a synthesis between the simpler type of Santa Maria delle Carceri and the Bramantesque central-plan churches, especially Santi Celso and Giuliano. The Greek-cross plan with square central area and low drum with oculi recalls Santa Maria delle Carceri, while the tendency to unify the space as well as the diagonally cut pilasters that support the semicircular dome and the offset attachment of the apse are derived from Bramante. The individual forms also recall Bramante, from the windows in a style later called Serlian (see SEBASTIANO SERLIO) to the piers of the interior, and the capitols fused with the cornice, following that taste for synthesis already noted in Raphael. The cubic mass of the Greek cross is defined on the exterior façade by pairs of Doric pilasters on a high base, with canonic proportions, as in the Chigi Stables. These pilasters support a Doric trabeation with triglyphs, as in the Palace of Jacopo da Brescia, and, as in the latter, the articulation of the pilasters continues in the attic story, separated by abstract reliefs and indentations, after the style of Bramante.

The Palace of Jacopo da Brescia, physician to Leo X, was erected on a lot given to him in January 1515; in August of the following year, it was already largely built. It stood on a small trapezoidal area at the intersection of Borgo Sant'Angelo and Borgo Nuovo, the street leading to St. Peter's whose completion was carried out by Giuliano da Sangallo in 1514–1515. (The palace was later demolished and badly reconstructed on another site in the twentieth century, on the occasion of the construction of the Via della Conciliazione.) The attribution to Raphael is not documented, but the mastery of Bramante's vocabulary and especially the refinement of optical effects that the palace reveals are not attributable to any other architect working in Rome in those years and lead us to overcome the doubts raised by the somewhat clumsy proportions of the stories and by the stocky shape of the Doric pilasters and counter-pilasters. The façade of the palace corresponds to the style of the Caprini Palace in the division between the rusticated ground floor with shops and the upper stories with architectural orders. Besides the general scheme, Bramante is recalled by the Doric order with triglyphs in the *piano nobile* and the articulation of pilasters and counter-pilasters similar to that of those in the Ionic order of the Belvedere. But with the addition of a third story, barely higher than a mezzanine, to the *piano nobile,* Raphael reduced the dominance that this story had in the façade of the Caprini Palace, thereby joining to the two-story Bramantesque style his own variant of two-and-a-half stories, possibly already anticipated in the Chigi Stables and later repeated in Palazzo Bronconio and Palazzo Alberini. The treatment of the individual parts also leads us further from Palazzo Caprini: for the vertical emphasis that prevailed there he substituted the contrast between the vertical emphasis of the order and a base containing long horizontal rustication devoid of obvious vertical joints; in the series of pilasters on the *piano nobile* and in the indentations of the walls that frame the windows of the upper story, a taste is shown for a richer articulation of the wall relief; and in the *piano nobile* the strong projection of the window sills, their tympana, and the sills that support them heralds Raphael's development toward the use of more plastic forms.

Another important element in the development of Raphael's architecture is the fact that the long façade of the palace was arranged to be viewed from a privileged direction such as from St. Peter's Square. Starting from the left corner, the one closest to the square, the distance between the half-columns was progressively diminished, thereby giving to the distant viewer the illusion of a greater extension than the actual modest size allowed by the lot. This perspectival control of the view, amply investigated first in painting and later in theatrical scenery, allowed Raphael later to prevent deformations of perspective in the façade of the Pandolfini Palace in Florence (1516–1517) and to give a more regular appearance to the façade of the palace that had been planned as his own home on Via Giulia (1519–1520). On the short side of the da Brescia palace, the pilasters were rhythmically placed with two short lateral intervals and a greater one at the center, in the manner of a triumphal arch. It is notable, however, that the triumphal arch is merely alluded to, since no arcade appears and the two central pilasters together with the curvilinear frontispiece that tops them, would rather indicate an aedicula. The central bay was meant to show, in the frieze, the epigraphy of the owner and underneath reliefs of the papal coat of arms and a lion's head were to appear.

On the subject of Raphael's role in the continuation of the construction of the Loggie in the Vatican Palace, Vasari writes that he made a wooden model "with greater order and ornamentation than was done by Bramante." The Loggie, adjoining the Palace of Nicolas III, had been planned by Bramante no later than 1508 since during the following year the first loggia of Tuscan-Doric order was being built above the ground floor. At the death of Bramante, the construction had undoubtedly reached the height of the second loggia, which was in the Ionic order; indeed, above one of the doors on the landing of this floor was carved the name of Julius II.

Having prepared the new model, Raphael was probably able to resume work on the interior of the second loggia; in 1517, or perhaps in 1516, the frescoes and stuccos, which were finished at the end of 1519, were already begun. According to Vassari, at the time of Raphael's death, the construction of the third loggia, already in an advanced state at the end of 1519, had not been completed.

There has been extensive discussion concerning the attribution of the three orders of loggie and the identification of the changes applied by Raphael to Bramante's project since neither project is known. The stylistic homogeneity of the Loggie leads us to surmise that Raphael, having obtained the direction of the building, undoubtedly interrupted at the point of the Ionic order, carried on in the manner of Bramante. At any rate, the synthetic manner with which the orders are handled corresponds to that phase of Bramante's stylistic evolution that Raphael adopted ever since his first works and for which he always maintained a strong affinity; the trabeation on Composite columns, which in the third order takes the place of arcades on pilasters framed by architrave orders, cannot necessarily be interpreted as a variant introduced by Raphael to Bramante's project, since this was not an unfamiliar solution for a top story.

On the other hand, Raphael's own mark is easily recognizable in the interior architecture of the second loggia. In the ceiling, Raphael adopted sail-vaults, instead of the calottes used by Bramante in the lower story, which better lent themselves to painting and this also achieved the effect of giving each single bay greater weight and making the longitudinal axis more rhythmic. This effect is further reinforced by the treatment of the upper part of the wall between the pilasters which is deeply recessed while the lower part of the wall functions as a base to the windows with triangular tympana which are modeled in high relief. The result is a relief of the surface that is even stronger than in the *piano nobile* of the da Brescia Palace. In the drawing of the portal and in the convex base supporting the windows, inspired by ancient convex friezes, there appears a freedom in the use of classical elements that would be further developed in the Villa Madama. Raphael's work in the Loggie, according to Vassari, so highly pleased the pope that he commissioned him with all the work of painting and architecture being done in the papal palaces.

In 1516, Raphael directed the work on the rooms of Cardinal Bibbiena in the papal palace, of which there remain only two fragments: the *stufetta,* completed in June of that year, and a small loggia adjoining the third order of loggie which was built a little later and which opened to the Court of the Maresciallo.

Some letters by Pietro Bembo to Cardinal Bibbiena mention the dates during which these works were in progress and confirm the attribution of the *stufetta* to Raphael. The small loggia was discovered and restored in the twentieth century; and together with the paintings executed by his school, its architecture was ascribed to Raphael, an attribution never contradicted.

In both rooms, Raphael attempted to imitate ancient painting, both in technique and in subject, with *grotteschi* and other images which were executed by his students. The *stufetta* is a small square room, each side little more than two meters, with a cross-vault ceiling and two walls containing framed niches under which appear marble panels worked in relief; on the other two walls are a door and a window, arched and framed like the niches. All the elements are joined by a cornice that outlines the lower border of the lunettes and of the calottes of the niches and by a flat band that joins the lower cornices. The joining of the various elements, the delicately framed niches, and the impact of the lower wall are a prelude to similar details in the façade of the Branconio Palace. The small loggia, on the other hand, is an exercise on the theme of a rhythmic truss, with ached openings between pairs of Tuscan pilasters of peperino marble where normally one would find niches. On the opposite narrow wall, painting takes the place of architecture, and to the small arched openings of the first wall correspond false painted niches containing statues. The narrow niches at the opposite end of the façade of the Branconio Palace were undoubtedly also painted because, unlike the central larger ones, they are represented without shadows in the accurate reproduction (Uffizi, A 230).

Baccio Bandinelli tells us that, while in Florence at the end of 1515 and the beginning of 1516, Leo X summoned Raphael from Rome to enter a contest for the façade the Florentine church of San Lorenzo. Of Raphael's project nothing remains; instead, there remain for this project several designs by Giuliano da Sangallo who elaborated highly plastic façades using the triumphale arch motive, articulated by half-columns and containing niches with ample space for statues and reliefs. Sangallo's drawings, which Raphael was able to see on that occasion, were a determining factor in the design of the Branconio Palace, drafted toward the end of 1516, and in the development of a style richer in plastic elements.

In the Branconio Palace, Raphael achieved the full individuality of his style and introduced important new elements. He proposed a palace façade totally independent of any preceding one; he adapted the plan of a large palace with a courtyard surrounded by porticoes on all sides to the smaller palace, reducing the portico to one single side of an eccentric courtyard (contemporary with that of The Palazzo Baldassini by Antonio da Sangallo the Younger); he adopted for portico and loggia an ancient system of columns with architrave; and, as he had previously done in the two street façades of the Jacopo da Brescia Palace, he extended to the courtyard the device of combining façades of different styles.

Vasari, writing about this palace, says that Raphael provided drawings for several palaces in the Borgo, among which was that of Giovan Battista Branconio dell'Aquilla, a courtier of Leo X. In the latter months of 1516, Branconio obtained the land on which to build his palace, which was completed in July 1520 at the latest. If we calculate that the construction took approximately three years, Raphael probably prepared the project between the end of 1516 and 1517. The palace, which faced the section of Borgo Nuovo closest to St. Peter's, was demolished to make room for Bernini's colonnade, but it is known through numerous drawings of the sixteenth century. The oldest ones are to be found on a page of the notebook of Domenico da Varignana and allow us to examine some stages in the elaboration of the project. In elevation and cross-section, they show us a version different from the one eventually realized; next to it, and with some difficulty, was inserted at a later date another cross-section similar to the one actually constructed. In the rejected version, the extension of the ground plan, the division into ground floor and *piano nobile,* each with its own mezzanine, plus a second story of lesser height and the number of axes coincide with the final project. The two lower stories are inspired by an ancient building, the exedra of the Market of Trajan, then known as The Palace of Trajan, while the second-story windows topped by tympana without sills and the numerous balustrades recall an image of the same exedra drawn and completed with hypothetical additions by Giuliano da Sangallo. Some immaturity, especially in the ground plans, have made Raphael's authorship questionable; nonetheless, the importance of the return to the Market of Trajan and the presence of Raphaelesque motifs would suggest that he was in some way responsible for it. In fact, the series of aediculae on the *piano nobile* with tympana joined by a continuous trabeation is common to this version and to the final one, and the motif of the arcades framed by the classic order and alternately topped by tympana was also adapted to a Doric loggia with three arcades in an original project by Raphael for a villa for the Medicis, probably a preliminary study for the Villa Madama and thus dated 1517–1518 (Ashmolean Museum, 549). The variation reproduced by Domenico da Varignana could therefore be an initial endeavour elaborated, if not by Raphael himself, then by one of his students, following in part his instructions.

In the realized project, the relationship to Trajan's Market was so remote that it was not noted until close examination of the preceding version. On the ground floor, an order of half-columns with abbreviated Doric trabeation frames a series of arcades on pilasters that encompass also the windows of the mezzanine, whereas in the lower story of the Trajan exedra, there were no traces of columnar order, although it does appear in several pictorial Renaissance reconstructions. The uniform series of arcades alternately framed by aediculae with tympana on the *piano nobile* of the Trajan Market is replaced by rectangular windows placed into aediculae which alternate with niches on narrower stretches of wall. The tendency to make the rhythm more complex, avoiding the simple repetition of like elements, and the need to make every opening of the *piano nobile* correspond with one on the ground floor where the shops were placed, explain the transformations made to the motif of the Trajan exedra, where the aediculae frame and differentiate the arcades on an axis with the opening of the shops, while the intermediate ones correspond to a solid wall on the ground floor. In the preliminary project, the openings were made to correspond by enlarging the arcades and narrowing the solid areas between the doors of the shops; in the final one, Raphael accentuated the distinction between more important elements—the arcades framed by the aediculae—and the intermediate ones, shrinking the intervals between the two aediculae and replacing an intermediate arcade with an arched niche. A strong element—an aedicula with a window—is alternated with a weak one—a niche—in a pattern similar to that of the rhythmic truss which, as we have seen, Raphael confronted at the same time in Cardinal Bibbiena's Loggetta (1516–1517). The idea of introducing the niche as a weak element may have stemmed from the same Trajan exedra where, according to several Cinquecento drawings, the arcades were joined by niches, although in a manner different from the one employed in the Branconio Palace. The aediculae are realized with Ionic half-columns rather than with the Tuscan pilasters of the Market and are thus more sculptural, halfway between these and the Corinthian columns of the aediculae in the Pantheon, the other probable model often cited; the aediculae in the Pantheon were certainly the inspiration for the rectangular cornice of the windows and for the articulation of the lower portion of the aediculae.

Of equal importance is the abundance of stucco reliefs and statues, which gave to the palace a graceful appearance immediately appreciated by contemporaries. The rich decoration seen in the Chigi Chapel for the first time has an equivalent on the street façade of a palace, as well as in its courtyard. The idea could have been born from an idealized rendition of the Trajan complex; the writings of ancient historians praised its abundance of statues and trophies, as proven by statues, reliefs, and shields that were being unearthed in the excavations in the area of the exedra and of the Trajan Forum. Also, the preferences of the patron, a goldsmith and a collector of ancient coins, probably influenced the choice of the decoration. We have not as yet discovered the drawings of the ornamentation of the Branconio Palace, which would confirm whether the subjects of the panels, the relief medallions, and the statues in the niches were connected in a program as complex as that of the Chigi Chapel. From the drawings made of the façade and the courtyard, it can be seen that a leading motif could have been that of the eagle and of Jupiter's myths, the eagle being his symbol; therefore, the name of the native city of the patron (Aquila, meaning eagle) seems to have inspired the choice of one of the themes of the images which not only recreated an ancient ornamentation but also conferred prestige on the patron, relating him to antiquity. At any rate, even though we cannot know Raphael's thoughts as he drew inspiration from the so-called Palace of Trajan, it is unlikely that the choice was accidental. In fact, for Dante, whom Raphael knew well, Trajan was one of the most beneficent rulers of that empire whose emblem the eagle had become.

In the matter of placing sculptural ornamentation of ancient derivation on a façade, Raphael had an almost obligatory source of references in ancient triumphal arches, which were nearly as rich with suggestions as was the Domus Aurea for the decoration of interiors. In fact, nearly all the figurative elements in the façade of the Bronconio Palace have precedents in the *tondi* with symbolical figures and in the reliefs of the attic stories with reliefs of various city gates and triumphal arches. In addition to the statues placed on the axes of the half-columns, other, more architectural details of the palace presuppose a familiarity with triumphal arches; among these is the corner solution of the ground floor order with the half-column pulled forward allowing the plane of the wall to emerge. In order to design a triumphal façade, Raphael did not need to rely on antiquity alone; he could return to that tendency which Bramante approached in the ornamentation of the Santa Casa of Loreto and of which he was well aware through the recent project of Giuliano de Sangallo for San Lorenzo already mentioned. With the latter, the Branconio Palace shares a number of elements in addition to the sculptural strength of the half-columns and of the aediculae of the façade and of the courtyard, even though it differs distinctly from it in that it abandons the axial placement of the vertical elements of the order. An examination and re-evaluation of mural architectures of the imperial age was not governed by a system of orders superimposed on vertical axes, as, for instance, in the Market exedra and the interior of the Pantheon, persuaded Raphael to shed the Quattrocento predilection for that system. It is not, then, a pre-Mannerist desire to contradict the tectonic significance of the order but rather a closer approach to the variety of ancient wall architecture, rich in multiple experiences, not all transferable to a scheme of vertical axes. The ancient architectural motifs fused with figurative elements also inspird by ancient prototypes in themes and iconography are joined in a modern complex according to new compositional laws and to satisfy the representative needs of the patron.

The Palace for the bishop of Troia belongs to the same stylistic phase as the Branconio Palace, and Vasari tells us that it was designed by Raphael, his only architectural work realized outside of Rome.

The patron, Giannozzo Pandolfini, a friend of Leo X and of Raphael, held a lease on some gardens and buildings belonging to the church in an area of suburban Florence, the Via Sangallo, and there he had begun a construction later incorporated into the left wing of the palace designed by Raphael. Raphael was able to inspect the lot and the existing buildings when he went to Florence in the winter of 1515–1616, but he could complete the final project only after Pandolfini, in February 1516, achieved a compromise with the monastery that owned the land regarding the conditions for the continuation of the work. In July 1516, the pope approved the franchise of the assets already in Pandolfini's possession, and in June 1517 the same monastery conceded another piece of land and a church, which completed the area on which the palace was to be built. It was only then that the execution of Raphael's project was started. According to Vasari it was directed first by Giovan Francesco da Sangallo and, after his death (1530), by his brother Aristotile. Giovan Francesco probably also had a hand in the design of the project, since an alternative drawing for the portal of the palace (Uffizi, A 1822) is attributed to him. As a collaborator in the building of St. Peter's he had been working with Raphael since October 1514; furthermore, other drawings attributed to him and relating to other projects evolved by Raphael and his workshop, such as the Villa Madama (1518) and the Alberini Palace (1518), lead us to surmise that Giovan Francesco was an active member in the group of Raphael's collaborators.

The palace was never completed and of the initial project we cannot reconstruct anything but the street façade, and that only in part. Following a known prototype for suburban palaces, Raphael had designed an elongated and somewhat low building, with two stories and nine axes of windows. We can assume that the initial phase of the work was completed in 1520, according to the epigraph in the frieze of the cornice, and perhaps already in 1521 Giannozzo Pandolfini occupied the new building permanently. The entire façade on Via Sangallo, which exists today, must have been completed in the left side, but interrupted at the beginning of the *piano nobile* on the right side. In 1524, the palace still seemed to be far from completion and, after the death of the patron in 1525, the work was continued very probably by the same Giovan Francesco da Sangallo who, between 1527 and 1529, prepared for the heir a reduced project that shows the archaic façade with a loggia with an arcade on columns which laterally defines the two-storied structure. At the death of Giovan Francesco, the work continued under the direction of Aristotile da Sangallo, who perhaps may have cooperated with his brother even before then.

With the Pandolfini Palace, Raphael developed yet another type of palace, different from the palace of Jacopo da Brescia and the Branconio Palace. The width of the lot allowed him to express his preference for a façade developed mainly horizontally, adding just one story to the ground floor. The superiority of the *piano nobile* was obtained not so much through the proportions as through the recession of the upper part of the façade, and with the design of the lower story, characterized as a base level by the lateral corners and the portal

Raphael. Pandolfini Palace. Florence. 1516–1517 (not executed until later by Giovanni Francesco and Aristotile da Sangallo; never completed)

with a strong rustication and by the Tuscan pilasters of the aeduculae. The surface of the façade, outlined by rusticated corners and divided horizontally by a stringcourse, is articulated only by a double order of aediculae with bases, and all of which these elements, like the portal, project strongly from the surface of the wall. The orders appear only in the aediculae with Tuscan pilasters on the ground floor and Ionic half-columns in the *piano nobile.* The latter, as well as the tympana joined by a continuous trabeation and the balustraded balconies, recall the Bronconio Palace, begun very probably some months before the beginning of the Pandolfini Palace. Between the aediculae, in place of the arched niches of the Branconio Palace, we find shallow rectangular insets similar to the rectangular niche at the extreme right of the exedra of the Trajan Market; they reappear in 1519 in a drawing of a stage set attributed to Raphael (Uffizi, A 242). In the portal, the rusticated corners, and the stringcourse, the Pandolfini Palace recalls the style of Antonio da Sangallo; the palace is in fact the culminating point at which the styles of the two architects who were in close contact in the building of St. Peter's were closest. Of particular note are the similarities between the Pandolfini Palace and the Farnese Palace in Rome, especially the rustication of the corners and of the portal, where even the number of the radial masonry blocks is the same, and the balustraded window that underlines the central axis of the façade, though it was never completed in the Florentine palace. When the Pandolfini Palace was designed, the Farnese Palace by Antonio da Sangallo was most certainly in progress and thus may have yielded some suggestions. For some parts of the Farnese Palace initiated after 1517, such as the aediculae and the central window at the *piano nobile,* Raphael's project may have influenced the construction by Sangallo.

Finally, the optical refinements of the palace totally Raphaelesque, set for an angled view for a person approaching from the center of the town. As opposed to the da Brescia Palace, the axes of the furthest aediculae were placed at a progressively increasing distance in order to avoid the effect of the aediculae, due to their strong impact, looking as though superimposed one on top of the other.

The aediculae with half-columns, a motif that Raphael favored during the years of the Branconio and Pandolfini Palaces, appear also in the studies for the outer wall of the southern ambulatory of St. Peter's, where they are joined by an order of Doric half-columns with complete trabeation. They are drawn in plans and elevations made by Antonio da Sangallo as principal assistant to Raphael.

In April 1514, Raphael had become *magister operis* of Saint Peter's side by side with Fra Giocondo, who bore the same title, and with Giuliano da Sangallo as *operis administer et coadiutor.* With their cooperation Raphael was able to confront the problems that arose following the death of the patron, Pope Julius II, in the preceding year, and the death of Bramante. Bramante had begun the construction in April 1506 starting with the western choir, following an executive project that we do not know but that must from the very start have provided for a longitudinal plan since the realized form of the choir, never modified during the course of the work directed by him, was in accord only with a church of longitudinal plan. Furthermore, we can suppose that the nave was no longer than three bays, as can be seen in a drawing by Bramante (Uffizi, A 20), because it could not have had any affect on the Benediction Loggia of Pius II and other contiguous buildings which by 1505–1508 were either enlarged or begun.

The program had become much more grandiose after the election of Pope Leo X in 1513. The new pope, according to Raphael's own statement, wanted to allocate for St. Peter's a much larger annual sum than previously allocated by his predecessor and persuaded him to increase the length and the width of the nave and to add a monumental vestibule, as appears in several plans by Giuliano da Sangallo of 1513–1514. This new plan was also perhaps inspired by contemporary new projects by Bramante. Under the circumstances, Raphael, as soon as he took up his new duties, probably executed a model which he presented to the pope, obtaining his approval, as indicated in a letter to Castiglione. This model is not known either, and by and large Raphael's ideas on St. Peter's during the initial phase of his direction are not yet as well documented as are his subsequent projects. His only original drawing related to St. Peter's belongs indeed to this period, but it merely represents rapid sketches of the nave and of the vaults and chapels (Uffizi, A 1972 r and v). On the other hand, we do know the stage of the construction shortly after Raphael took over his responsibilities from a relief reproduced in folio 31 of the Coner Codex (1515). Besides the pilons of the crossing and of Bramante's western choir, the plan shows the pilasters next to the crossing at the beginning of each of the three arms. This and other reliefs permit us to rule out that in the summer of 1514, when he already prepared the new model, Raphael adhered to a ground plan like the one attributed to him by Serlio, in which the choir is flanked by a system of cross-shaped structures with smaller domes. The realization of that system was in fact prevented by the execution of the niche called "di Fra Giocondo" placed at the end of the southern nave next to the southwest pilon of the crossing for which the foundations were laid in July–August 1514.

In his final project for St. Peter's, Raphael returned to the idea of the minor domes and ambulatories that appear in the ground plan by Serlio and which are reproduced in ground plan, perspective, and cross-section in the notebook of Domenico da Varignana (1516–1517). The longitudinal plan with a nave of five bays, two lateral naves, and chapels reaches in length and width measurements similar to those in the ground plans of Giuliano da Sangallo of 1513–1514; the central nave and the lateral naves are divided by pillars with pairs of giant pilasters derived from the pilasters of the crossing, and the same system is adapted to the articulation of the chapels; finally, the hall is preceded by a large vestibule. Even though the motif of the minor domed crossings and the ambulatories that surround both the apses of the dransept and of the choir have their origin in Bramantesque projects such as the drawing Uffizi A 20, the articulation of the longitudinal space with the lateral chapels is fairly close to that of the ground plan in Uffizi A 7 by Giuliano da Sangallo.

Raphael faced a new problem in the main façade, that now was no longer behind the atrium of the old basilica as in Bramante's working project. He solved it with a highly original application of the gigantic order: in the central section of the vast façade, two pairs of colossal Corinthian pilasters placed on high bases supported a large tympanum resting on two pillars precisely aligned with those that in the interior outlined the central nave; the Corinthian order is intersected by a minor order of architraved Doric columns that bisects the central section of the façade in two superimposed porticoes and, articulated in columns and half-columns, proceed across the whole façade, onto the lower section of the bell towers that border it, and turn the corners where, on the exterior of the ambulatories, they are combined with the aedicula motif as developed in the drawings of Antonio da Sangallo the Younger. In designing the ambulatories, Raphael began the precise sculptural articulation that later characterized the projects of Antonio da Sangallo the Younger and, resulted in an unsuccessful wooden model in 1538–1539, which was rightly judged inadequate to the scale of the monument. In his choice, however, Raphael was motivated by the concern, frequent in his works, to reveal on the exterior the disposition of the interior, in this case that of the ambulatory. The same desire to make a correspondence between interior and exterior is also revealed in the main façade where, however, the intersection between a minor Doric order of trabeated columns and an order of giant Corinthian pilasters yields results of far greater monumentality, anticipating the façade of the Conservatori Palace by Michelangelo. Raphael's ideas on St. Peter's, however, are known to us only through drawings.

From the end of 1517, or probably from the summer of 1518 on, Raphael worked on the Villa Madama, the most complex project of his entire career after St. Peter's. The land allotted for the villa, a few miles from the Vatican at the foot of Monte Mario toward the valley of the Tiber, was leased in 1517 to Leo X by the Chapter of Saint Peter's. The pope closely followed the progress of the work in which his cousin, Cardinal Giulio de' Medici, who was indicated by his contemporaries as the sole patron, showed an equal interest. The pope wished to avoid being officially involved, probably because the villa was destined to remain in the private ownership of the Medici.

Preparations for the construction began in the fall of 1518. Following a method already used in the building of St. Peter's and here further refined, several clearly detailed drawings, precisely outlined and in scale, were prepared. The initial ground plan (Uffizi, A 273), a final one (Uffizi, A 314), several studies, and an intermediate project are described in a letter attributed to Raphael. Of all these drawings only one is, perhaps, his own, all the others being by the hand of some one of his assistants. Working with Raphael were other architects with whom he also collaborated on St. Peter's: Antonio da Sangallo the Younger and almost certainly Giovan Francesco da Sangallo, in addition to GIULIO ROMANO who had joined his workshop as a painter. Antonio da Sangallo the Younger, whose participation in the project is confirmed by drawings he made for the second project, provided rational solutions for individual problems, as in the case of a staircase facing the entrance toward Rome and in front of the vestibule, and translated Vitruvius's directions on theaters into a working project for an open-air theater included in the villa. It is probable that Raphael's increased awareness of antiquity, evident in the second project, was due to Sangallo's collaboration as well as to his tendency to conceive of space in a less uniform and more rhythmic way than did Bramante. Giovan Francesco da Sangallo was perhaps the draftsman of the initial ground plan, but we have no remaining drawings by Giulio Romano who, however, was undoubtedly responsible for some of the designing while Raphael lived. We cannot exclude the possibility that both men contributed to the elaboration of the initial project. Preparatory studies for this stage are not known, but numerous factors have allowed us to clarify, in favor of Raphael, some ambiguous and contradictory statements by Vasari, who attributes the main part to Giulio Romano. A recent factor in Raphael's favor was the discovery of a Cinquecento description of a villa which is considered an anonymous copy of a lost letter by Raphael concerning the Villa Madama and mentioned by Castiglione. In addition, we have a poem regarding the villa dedicated to Giulio de' Medici in 1519 in which the only artist mentioned is Raphael, and Sebastiano Serlio in his writings mentions Raphael with regard to the Villa Madama.

With the commission for their suburban villa, Leo X and Giulio de' Medici had assigned to Raphael the task of creating a monument that would exalt the greatness of its patrons and at the same time create in a rational manner an ambiance rich with suggestions and references to the refined way of life of the ancients: a complex of buildings, gardens, and other open spaces where the pope and his court could entertain important guests amidst all kinds of conveniences while enjoying theatrical presentations, hunts, and other diversions.

The importance attributed by Raphael to the beauty of the panorama and to the comforts that were to make the villa superior to all others, appears quite clearly from his description of the project. In order to realize these aspirations he used various elements popular in contemporary villas and palaces and an unprecedented amount of suggestions and ideas taken from ancient villas. In the initial project (Uffizi, A 273), the plan with three courtyards laid out along a longitudinal axis, recalls Bramante's Belvedere; in addition to features proper to aristocratic living quarters of the time, such as a chapel, a secret garden, and ample stables, there are others suggested by Vitruvius, Pliny, and other Latin authors on the subject of villas—a *dieta,* a *xisto,* a *hypodromo*— as well as a fish pond, a theater, a dome-covered salon and nymphaea, borrowed directly from ancient architecture, especially from the Villa Adriana. A section of Vitruvius (vol. 6, p. 5) which states that the layout of villas differs from that of urban habitations above all in that in a villa the section closer to the entrance was a peristyle rather than an atrium, allowed Raphael, by substituting a small entrance court for the peristyle, to adopt the sequence inspired by Vitruvius, of vestibule, atrium, passageway. This sequence, in its modern interpretation, had already been used more or less in its entirety, in urban palaces, especially by Antonio da Sangallo the Younger in the Farnese Palace in Rome. Also, in the palace designed by Giuliano da Sangallo for the king of Naples. More than once, in the initial project for the Villa Madama, antiquity is apparent, as seen through the interpretations of Giuliano da Sangallo and Bramante: the sequence vestibule–atrium–passageway recalls Giuliano and Antonio da Sangallo the Younger, the loggia facing the Tiber, the domed ceiling of the central aisle and the short sides ending in semicircular apses containing niches is very similar to Bramante's nymphaeum of Gennazzano.

The construction of the lower story was begun according to the ground plan Uffizi A 273, but shortly after the start there was a change in the plan, as described in a letter by Raphael. The most important new item is a circular court replacing the rectangular one at the center of the complex; other modifications that must have necessarily ensued are not described in the letter because at the time of the writing, Raphael could not yet have resolved all the contradictions born of this variation. Some of these problems are the object of partial studies by Antonio da Sangallo the Younger who, at the end of 1518 and in 1519 also drew the final plan (Uffizi, A 314). Here, the circular courtyard is securely placed, the central body of the building has become more compact, and the façade toward the Tiber, previously asymmetrical, is now totally symmetrical. The open-air theater is larger than in Uffizi A 273 and shows a more advanced understanding of Vitruvius's passages on the subject; furthermore, in the vicinity of the fish pond a *cenatio* was added. The circular courtyard owes its main inspiration to Pliny's Villa Laurentina, which he describes as equipped with a portico in the shape of a D, wrongly transcribed as O in a faulty rendition of his *Epistles.* A knowledge of the villas described by Pliny was already proven by the *dieta* in the initial project. *Cenatio,* circular court, Vitruvian theater, are all symptoms of the stronger tendency toward antiquity that characterized the second project. Rather than the patrons' suggestion, one notes here a new approach by the artist and a sharing of ideas between him and Antonio da Sangallo the Younger. However, as in the synthesis realized in the first project between the Bramantesque spaces of ancient inspiration, the sculptural treatment of the walls of the courtyards, antiquarian tendencies of Giuliano da Sangallo, and the motifs derived from literary sources or directly from ancient architecture, all of which can be ascribed to no other than Raphael, so also the change of compositional criteria revealed in the final project appears to be the coherent development of tendencies of the same architect. The comparison between the two plans is significant. In the initial one, the longitudinal axis, as the expression of a composition regulated by a central perspective, is prevalent from one end of the construction to the other, from the entrance all the way to the garden beyond the loggia. In the Uffizi A 314, the axis exhausts itself in the static space of the circular

Raphael.
Villa Madama.
Rome.
1518 (continued by Giulio Romano; never completed)

courtyard, and even before that, it is interrupted by the stair in front of the vestibule, while the altered dimensions of the vestibule and atrium diminish the possibility of a unified view of the sequence of spaces. Beyond the circular courtyard, in the loggia facing the garden, the arcade placed on the axis acquires a width equal to that of the others, while the loggia itself is expanded in the direction of the courtyard by the addition of two exedrae. Similarly, in the loggia facing the Tiber, the series of doors is moved from the longitudinal axis to a position tangential to the outer wall; the result is the strange eccentricity of the window at the extreme left of the garden façade.

In these modifications one discerns a tendency toward a more static conception of spaces, proper to the architecture of the imperial time, and a tendency to arrange them in a rhythmic sequence as previously seen in the interior of the second loggia of the Vatican Palace. The motifs of diverse origin seen in the first project are assimilated in accord with this new tendency.

The construction progressed following the drawing Uffizi A 314 with variations so negligible that that plan can be considered nearly identical with the working plan.

In June 1520, two months after the death of Raphael, the construction of the loggia toward the garden was finished as was that of two adjacent halls; their decoration was begun with the participation of Giulio Romano as painter. The following year, when the villa under constuction was represented in the background of that artist's *Battle of Ponte Milvio,* it had nearly reached the stage at which it would remain until its restoration in the twentieth century. Indeed, after the death of Leo X in December 1521, the construction no longer progressed with the initial speed, and Giulio de' Medici, even after being elected pope in 1523, concerned himself more with finishing the ornamentation in the completed wing and arranging the gardens than with the construction of the main building. Of this, only the northern hemicycle of the circular courtyard, the loggia facing the garden, and the intermediate parts adjoining these two bodies had been completed. From 1524 on, the work appears to have been directed by Antonio da Sangallo the Younger, who probably succeeded Raphael immediately after the latter's death.

In the realized fragment and in the prospect toward the valley, several of the characteristics observed in Raphael's style reappear. In the circular courtyard with half-columns and strongly projecting aediculae, we find the sculptural motifs of the Branconio Palace and of the crossing of St. Peter's, while the decoration of the interior of the loggia facing the garden is equal in richness to that of the interiors of the Chigi Chapel, of the Loggie, and of the Branconio Palace. In the garden façade, the use of abstract forms in place of the elements of the classical order reappears. Fasciae and piers projecting slightly from the walls flank gigantic Ionic pilasters, the classical order being used to indicate, on the facade, the interior disposition. Here also, the main motif—a projection in the form of an arcade with a lunette shaped as a thermal window—is born from the need to make the interior discernible; in this case a domed hall, to the left of the loggia facing the Tiber, had been planned but never executed. Rather than to Raphael, we can attribute to Giulio Romano the design of details such as the rusticated masonry cornices of the windows in the lower story, a chimney inspired very freely from the volute of an Ionic capital, and many more which anticipate Mannerist experimentation.

At the time he was working on the Villa Madama, Raphael also devoted himself to at least two other works of architecture. According to Vasari, he participated in the competition for San Giovanni dei Fiorentini (1518) with a project about which we know nothing and at the same time, oversaw a project, certainly elaborated in his workshop, that was used in the completion of the Alberini Palace.

This palace had probably been started soon after 1512 because that year the section of Via de Banchi on which it faces was straightened and furthermore, in 1515, the rooms of the *piano nobile* appear to have been completed. When in 1515 the building, still under construction, was leased with a promise of completion, one of the witnesses to the deed was the architect Pietro Rosselli, probable author of the first project. The commission was probably given to Raphael no earlier than 1518 since the style of the section credited to him scarcely fits with an earlier date; this dating is further confirmed by the date of a sheet of drawings in which Giovan Francesco da Sangallo outlines the project of the lower stringcourse of the palace (Uffizi, A 863 v).

The plan of the shops on Via de Banchi and of the part of the *piano nobile* executed before 1518, strongly affected the new project. The rusticated base in travertine marble of the lower story discouraged the use of strongly projecting members that would have had to extend beyond the existing wall; furthermore, the moderate height of the *piano nobile* and consequently of its windows was already predetermined by the construction already completed. Raphael was concerned to make the *piano nobile* more monumental in order to balance the façade. By adding a row of mezzanine windows to the *piano nobile* he achieved a succession of stories similar to that of the Branconio Palace. The lower story and the *piano nobile,* each with its own mezzanine are distinctly separate one from the other, while a second story of inferior height is separated from the *piano nobile* by a cornice. In the Alberini Palace, finally, he added a gallery above the cornice; it is barely visible from the ground and is therefore missing in nearly all the drawings of the sixteenth century.

The Alberini Palace marks Raphael's further progress toward overcoming the separation of the classical by orders, synthesizing them or substituting other elements for them. The *piano nobile* is articulated by flat pilasters or, rather, piers with well-defined capitals, obtained by a projection of elements under the cornice of simplified trabeation. The weight of these pilasters is further diminished by the comparison with the stronger relief of the cornices that frame the windows. In the upper floor, a similar articulation is obtained with elongated vertical panels, outlined by frames that correspond to the lower pilasters but do not rest on the underlying horizontal members, thus remaining suspended on the brick wall in the same manner as the frames that outline the windows. Many of these elements are of Bramantesque origin and some of them, such as the panels outlined by frames, come directly from the drum of the Tempietto in San Pietro in Montorio; others, such as the piers in the interior of Sant' Eligio, had been used before by Raphael. The "ear-shaped" windows of the second story have a precedent in the palace of Jacopo da Brescia and in the Branconio Palace, and the elegant design of some profiles, such as that of the portal which was introduced with the new project in the façade on Via de Banchi is also credited to Raphael. The palace, therefore, seems to have been designed according to a precise stylistic orientation rooted in Raphael's experience. However, the quality, inferior to that of his other works and not entirely justifiable by the dictates of the existing section, makes it difficult to attribute it entirely to him. Similarities appear in the Stati-Maccarani Palace in Rome, designed by Giulio Romano, whose subsequent works in Mantua are totally different from the Alberini Palace. Therefore, it is reasonable, and compatible with Vasari's statements that Giulio Romano executed the design on Raphael's order, to suppose that the commission was executed with the collaboration of Giulio Romano, then less than twenty years old, still at the beginning of his career as an architect and deeply tied to the style of his master.

In 1519, Raphael sent to Federico Gonzaga the project for a memorial monument, presumably for the marquis of Mantua, Francesco Gonzaga, which, in the absence of autograph drawings, was tentatively called a design for a pyramidal tomb and attributed to his workshop. If we exclude the attribution, thus far hypothetical, of a project for the villa of Baldassare Turini, later known as the Villa Lante, in Rome, the last certain and documented project of Raphael remains the one for his own palace on the Via Giulia. On March 24, 1520, the Chapter of Saint Peter's granted to Raphael the right to lease a parcel of land outlined by streets on all sides, located on the Via Giulia, in the vicinity of San Giovanni dei Fiorentini, under the condition that it would be built upon within five years. Raphael died a few days later, on April 6, and his project was never realized. The dealings that led to the acquisition of the land had probably begun some time earlier, and he had prepared a project, known through the plan of the ground floor and of the *piano nobile* (Uffizi, A 310, 311) that had been copied perhaps by Bernardino della Volpaia, a collaborator of Antonio da Sangallo the Younger, had copied when Antonio da Sangallo was commissioned to prepare a new project for the use of the area.

Many of the most important elements noted in his works, particularly those of the last years of his activity are merged in Raphael's palace. The composition is determined by optical perspectives; the program of the Villa Madama, which furnished the living quarters with every comfort, is adapted to the theme of a private urban palace; and in the courtyard the spaces inspired by antiquity, with exedrae and walls indented by niches, join this palace stylistically to the Villa Madama.

Raphael had planned to trim the irregularity of the trapezoidal lot to his advantage, obtaining two palaces within one building: a larger one for himself with an entrance on the Via Giulia, featuring a courtyard porticoed on three sides and closed on the fourth by a semicircular exedra, and a smaller courtyard similar to the former in plan, with an entrance on the opposite side. As far as we can tell from the plans, all four façades would have been articulated by an order of gigantic pilasters placed at unequal distances in order to conceal at first glance the different dimensions of the two contiguous façades, and using devices as effective as those employed in the palace of Jacopo da Brescia.

The acute angle of the lot, facing San Giovanni dei Fiorentini, was to have been reduced and resolved, repeating in a single bay the solution of the longer sides, perhaps with the addition of a tympanum which, as on the narrow side of the palace of Jacopo da Brescia, would recall the image of a triumphal arch. By here adopting the giant order, Raphael took a further stride toward the reduction to secular purposes of this system, a system initially employed in religious buildings and papal constructions. Raphael himself had proposed its use in his project for the façade of St. Peter's and, later, for the Villa Madama, and now, with this choice, he expressed the dignity which he desired to attribute to his own house—in which he was never to live. He died at the age of 37 after a brief fever. Together with Leonardo and Michaelangelo the most brilliant figure the High Renaissance brought forth. He was, as he wished, buried in the Pantheon from whose architecture he had received so much inspiration.

Pier Nicola Pagliari
Translated from Italian by
Shara Wasserman

WORKS

1512–1513, Chigi Chapel (not completed until later by others), Santa Maria del Popolo; *1512–1518, Chigi Stables (not completed); from 1514, St. Peter's (not completed until later by others); after 1514, Vatican Palace (various works); *1515, Jacopo da Brescia Palace; 1515, Sant' Eligio degli Orefici (not completed until later by others); from 1515, San Damaso's Courtyard (completion of the Loggie); 1516, Cardinal Bibbiena's Rooms; 1516–1517, Cardinal Bibbiena's Loggetta; *1516–1517, Branconio Palace; Rome. *1516–1517, Pandolfini Palace (not executed until later by Giovanni Francesco and Aristotile da Sangallo; never completed), Florence. 1518, Villa Madama (continued by Giulio Romano; never completed); Rome.

BIBLIOGRAPHY

Cavalcaselle, G. B., and Crowe, J. A. 1882–1885 *Raphael: His Life and Works.* London: Murray.

Chastel, André 1959 *Art et Humanisme à Florence.* Paris: Presses Universitaires.

Frommel, Christoph L. 1969 "La Villa Madama e le tipologia della villa romana nei Rinascimento." *Bollettino Palladio* 11:52.

Fulvio, Andrea 1527 *Antiquitates Urbis per Andream Fulvium Antiquarium. Ro. Nuperrime aeditae.* Rome.

Geymüller, Heinrich 1884 *Raffaello Sanzio studiato come architetto.* Milan: Hoepli.

Milizia, Francesco 1787 "Dell'Architettura civile." Volume 1, pages 129–130 in *Roma delle Belle Arte del disegno.* Bassano, Italy.

Passavant, J. D. 1839–1858 *Raffael von Urbino und sein Vater Giovanni Santi.* Leipzig.

Ray, Stefano 1974 *Raffaello architetto.* Rome: Laterza.

Ricci, Amico 1857–1859 *Storia dell'architettura in Italia dal sec. IV al XVII.* Modena, Italy: Regio-ducal camera.

Serlio, Sebastiano 1540 In *Il terzo libro di Sebastiano Serlio Bolognese.* Venice, Italy: Marcolino da Forli.

Tafuri, Manfredo 1966 *L'architettura del Manierismo enl Cinquecento europeo.* Rome: Officina Edizioni.

Weiss, Roberto 1969 *The Renaissance Discovery of Classical Antiquity.* London: Blackwell.

Wittkower, Rudolf 1962 *Architectural Principles in the Age of Humanism.* London.

Vasari, Giorgio (1568)1973 *Le opere di Giorgio Vasari, con nuove annotazione e commenti.* 9 vols. Edited by G. Milanese. Reprint. There are many English translations and selections from Vasari's *Lives,* the standard one by G. du C. de Vere was published in two volumes in London by the Medici Society in 1912–1915.

RAPP and RAPP

Cornelius Ward Rapp (1861–1927) and George Leslie Rapp (1878–1942) were sons of a carpenter-architect in Carbondale, Illinois. C. W. first assisted his father, then opened his own practice in Chicago around 1891. George graduated from the University of Illinois's school of architecture in 1899 and subsequently worked for Chicago architect Edward Krause. In 1906, the brothers formed a partnership, Rapp and Rapp, and soon became known for their designs of movie theaters. The Rapps began work for the Balaban and Katz chain in 1917, creating some of the country's early movie palaces (for example, the Tivoli and Chicago Theaters, both 1921), which served as paradigms for the type. The firm continued its association when the circuit merged with Paramount-Publix Theaters in 1925, expanding their practice nationwide.

Rapp and Rapp designed over 400 theaters, the majority of them during the 1920s. Most schemes were derived from about eight schematic types, modified and combined according to the requirements of each program. Eighteenth- and ninteenth-century French classical sources provided the primary inspiration for their lavish interiors. Together with THOMAS W. LAMB and John Eberson, Rapp and Rapp were the most important and influential American theater architects of the period.

During the 1930s, the firm diversified, designing a variety of commercial and industrial buildings. While retaining the original name, it was reorganized shortly before World War II, continuing operations until 1965.

RICHARD W. LONGSTRETH and STEVEN LEVIN

WORKS

1910, Majestic Theater, Dubuque, Iowa. 1915, Al Ringling Memorial Theater, Baraboo, Wisc. 1921, Chicago Theater, Chicago. 1921, Corn Palace, Mitchell, S.D. *1921, Tivoli Theater; 1925, Uptown Theater; 1926, Bismarck Hotel and Theater; 1926, Oriental Theater; Chicago. *1926, Paramount Theater, Times Square, New York. 1928, Paramount Theater (extensively altered); 1929, Loew's Kings Theater, Brooklyn, N.Y. 1931, Paramount Theater, Aurora, Ill.

BIBLIOGRAPHY

BARRY, JOHN F. ET AL. 1976 "Times Square Paramount." *Annual of the Theatre Historical Society* no. 3.

DUCI BELLA, JOSEPH 1971 "The Chicago Theatre: 1921–1971." *Marquee: Journal of the Theatre Historical Society* 3, no. 3:6–10.

HALL, BEN M. (1961)1975 *The Golden Age of the Movie Palace.* New York: Potter. Originally published with the title *The Best Remaining Seats.*

Marquee: Journal of the Theatre Historical Society 1977 9, no. 2:special issue.

MILLER, PETER R. ET AL. 1981 "Chicago Theatre." *Annual of the Theatre Historical Society* no. 8.

"Movie Theatre History in Wisconsin." 1980 *Marquee: Journal of the Theatre Historical Society* 12, no. 4:3–20.

NAYLOR, DAVID 1981 *American Picture Palaces.* New York: Van Nostrand.

RAPP, CORNELIUS W., AND RAPP, GEORGE L. 1927 *The Recent Work of C.W. and Geo. L. Rapp, Architects, Chicago, New York.* New York: Architectural Catalog Company.

SEXTON, RANDOLF W. (1927–1930)1977 *American Theatres of Today.* 2 vols. in 1. Reprint. New York: Vestal.

RAPSON, RALPH

Ralph Rapson (1914–) is distinguished as both architect and teacher. Born in Alma, Michigan, he graduated from the University of Michigan (1938). He studied with ELIEL SAARINEN at Cranbrook from 1938 to 1940 and remained to work in Saarinen's office. He served as head of the department of architecture (1943–1946) in the Institute for Design, Chicago, working under LÁSZLÓ MOHOLY-NAGY. From 1946 to 1954 he was assistant professor in the School of Architecture at the Massachusetts Institute of Technology, Cambridge, and during this period was one of the chief designers for the Department of State's Embassy Staff Apartments in Paris (1951–1953).

During the early 1940s, Rapson's work reflected strong interest in new building technologies. The clear ordering of his early plans gave way in the late 1950s to a more personally expressive series of complicated forms, as seen in the Pillsbury House (1963), Wayzata, Minnesota, or the Santa Cruz Performing Arts Center (1967–1971). Cedar Square West (1971–1974) in Minneapolis, Minnesota, demonstrates his sensitive yet strong management of urban-scaled complexes and indicates a significant design synthesis.

DAVID G. DE LONG

WORKS

1942, Willow Run Schools (with Eero Saarinen), Mich. 1951–1953, United States Embassy Staff Apartments (with John van der Meulen), Neuilly, Paris. 1955–1957, Saint Peter's Lutheran Church, Edina, Minn. 1960–

1963, Tyrone Guthrie Theater; 1963, State Capitol Credit Union Branch Office; Minneapolis, Minn. 1963, Phillip Pillsbury, Jr., House, Wayzata, Minn. 1966–1972, Rarig Center for the Performing Arts, University of Minnesota, West Bank Campus, Minneapolis. 1967–1971, Performing Arts Center, University of California, Santa Cruz. 1971–1974, Cedar Square West, Minneapolis, Minn. 1975, Recreation Facilities Building, Southern Illinois University, Carbondale.

BIBLIOGRAPHY

HEYER, PAUL 1966 Pages 55–59 in *Architects on Architecture.* New York: Walker.

RAPSON, RALPH 1977 "The Ten Commandments of Architectural Design." *Architecture Minnesota* 3, Nov.-Dec.: 15–18, 29–31.

RASCHDORFF, JULIUS

Trained at the Berlin Bauakademie, Julius Carl Raschdorff (1823–1914) served as city architect in Cologne from 1854 to 1872, designing many schools and public buildings. Through the restoration of Cologne's churches, City Hall (1860–1870), and Gürzenich Festival Hall (1855–1857), he studied German Renaissance architecture, which he combined with French Renaissance elements in his own work. From 1878, he was a professor at the Berlin Bauakademie. His career culminated in the grandiose design for the new Protestant Cathedral on the Lustgarten (1890) in Berlin.

BARRY BERGDOLL

WORKS

1855–1857, Gürzenich Festival and Concert Hall (restoration and extension), Cologne, Germany. 1856, City Hall (with Friedrich von Schmidt), Trier, Germany. 1860–1862, Saint Aposteln *Gymnasium;* 1860–1870, City Hall (restoration); *1861, Wallraf-Richartz Museum (designed by Friedrich August Stüler); Cologne, Germany. 1865–1866, Zivilkasino (executed by Emmerich of Trier), Saarbrücken, Germany. 1868–1877, Castle (restoration; with Hermann Ende), Cochem, Germany. 1869, School Administration Library; 1870–1872, Municipal Theater; Cologne, Germany. 1878–1880, Post Office, Brunswick, Germany. 1881–1884, Technische Hochschule (completed according to the plans of Richard Lucae and Friedrich Hitzig); c.1882, Tower of Saint Gertrud, Stockholm. 1882–1884, Chemical Laboratory, Technische Hochschule; 1884, Saint George English Church, Montbijoupark, Berlin. 1884–1889, Mausoleum of Kaiser Friedrich III, Friedenskirche, Potsdam, Germany. 1890–1905, Protestant Cathedral, Berlin.

BIBLIOGRAPHY

BÖRSCH-SUPAN, EVA 1977 *Berliner Baukunst nach Schinkel, 1840–1870.* Munich: Prestel.

HÄSSLIN, JOHANN JAKOB 1955 *Der Gürzenich zu Köln.* Munich: Prestel.

HOFFMANN, BERNHARD 1914 "Julius Raschdorff." *Zentralblatt der Bauverwaltung* 34:500–502.

RASCHDORFF, JULIUS 1862 "Das Kaufhaus Gürzenich in Köln." *Zeitschrift für Bauwesen* 12:3–20, plates 1–8.

RASCHDORFF, JULIUS 1878 *Abbildungen deutscher Schmiedewerke.* Berlin: Ernst & Korn.

RASCHDORFF, JULIUS 1879 *Entwürfe und Bauausführungen im Stile deutscher Renaissance.* Berlin: Wasmuth.

RASCHDORFF, JULIUS 1886–1922 *Palast-Architektur von Ober-Italien und Toscana von XIII. bis XVII. Jahrhundert.* Berlin: Wasmuth.

RASCHDORFF, JULIUS 1895 *Rheinische Holz- und Fachwerkbauten des XVI. und XVII. Jahrhunderts.* Berlin: Wasmuth.

RASCHDORFF, JULIUS 1896 *Der Dom zu Berlin.* Berlin: Reichsdruckerei.

RASCHDORFF, JULIUS 1899 *Kaiser Friedrich III. Mausoleum zu Potsdam.* Berlin: Wasmuth.

WEYRES, WILLY, and MANN, ALBRECHT 1968 *Handbuch zur Rheinischen Baukunst.* Cologne, Germany: Greven Verlag.

RASPALL, MANUEL J.

Manuel J. Raspall i Mayol (1877–1937), born in Barcelona, Spain, is one of the most original exponents of late Modernist style. His works are easily identifiable by the fancy of their ornamental rhetoric, their affectation, and Raspall's care over details, materials, and color.

Raspall obtained his degree in architecture in 1905. He carried out his professional career in Barcelona, mainly in the region of the Vallés (Comarca del Vallés), a rural environment. He thus became rather isolated from contemporary art and culture. He drew on his own inspiration for his works, although eclecticist and archeologist influences can be seen in them.

His work can be divided into three stages, the two first being *modernista,* differing in their decoration. The third stage, more academic, incorporated Catalan folk rhetoric into architectural language, possibly due to JOSEP PUIG I CADAFALCH's influence.

MIGUEL PÉREZ I SÀNCHEZ

WORKS

1905, Cloelia's Farm, Cardeu; 1906, Beach House, La Garriga; c.1906, Clapés House, Granollers; 1907, Ametlla del Vallés Coffee Shop; c.1908, Can Millet de Baix, L'Ametlla del Vallés; 1908, Nadal's Palace; 1909, Teixidor's Pharmacy; c.1910, Gambús House, El Figaró; c.1910, House in Church's Square, La Garriga; 1910, Miret House, Sant Antoni de Vilamajor; 1910, Valentí Pons House; 1911, Barbey House, La Garriga;

1911, Iris Villa, La Garriga; 1912–1916, La Garriga Hospital (improvements); 1914–1916, Reig House, La Garriga; 1925, Viader's Farm, Cardedeu; Barcelona, Spain.

BIBLIOGRAPHY

BOHIGAS, ORIOL 1961 "Raspall: Arquitecto." *Cuadernos de Arquitectura* 44:77–88.

BOHIGAS, ORIOL, and POMÉS, LEOPOLDO 1968 *Arquitectura Modernista.* Barcelona, Spain: Editorial Lumen.

CUSPINERA Y FONT, LLUIS 1978*a* *La Garriga: Guïa Arquitectónica.* Barcelona, Spain: Obral Cultural de "La Caixa."

CUSPINERA Y FONT, LLUIS 1978*b* "M. J. Raspall." Volume 12 in *Gran Enciclopédia Catalana.* Barcelona, Spain: The encyclopedia.

HERNANDEZ-CROS, J. EMILI; MORA, GABRIEL; and POUPLANA, XAVIER 1973 *Arquitectura de Barcelona.* Barcelona, Spain: COACB.

RASTRELLI, BARTOLOMMEO

Bartolommeo Francesco Rastrelli (c.1700–1771) was the most distinguished architect practicing in Russia in the middle of the eighteenth century. He accompanied his father Carlo, a sculptor, when the latter was called from Paris to Saint Petersburg in 1715. As a young man Rastrelli returned to Paris to study with ROBERT DE COTTE and, between 1725 and 1730, he may have visited Germany, Austria, and Italy. Upon Rastrelli's return to Russia in 1730, he built the Annenhof, a wooden palace complex in Moscow, for the Tsarina Anna Ivanovna, who appointed him court architect in 1736. It was during the reign of Elizabeth, however, that Rastrelli's position became pre-eminent; for more than twenty years he was awarded virtually every major imperial commission. Following Elizabeth's death Rastrelli fell out of favor, and the fanciful rococo style which is his hallmark was supplanted by the more severe neoclassical forms favored by Catherine II.

Rastrelli's great accomplishment was his formulation of a consistent late baroque style which reflected contemporary design in western Europe while incorporating traditional Russian architectural forms. Perhaps the finest examples of Rastrelli's imaginative fusion of rococo and Russian elements are the Cathedral of Saint Andrew in Kiev (1747–1748) and the Smolny Convent in Leningrad (1748–1755). Rastrelli's point of departure in designing both buildings clearly was the ecclesiastical architecture of seventeenth-century Moscow, churches which were characterized by Greek-cross plans generating a picturesque grouping of a dominant central cupola surrounded by four subsidiary domes. Other details, for example, the freestanding lanterns of Saint Andrew, may be traced to such European centers as Turin. Rastrelli's inspired composition of flaring silhouettes, coupled with his effective use of color and sculptural masses, characterize his highly original personal style, which transcends mere eclecticism.

Rastrelli's secular commissions far outnumbered his ecclesiastical buildings. The Stroganov Palace in Saint Petersburg (1750-1754) again shows an imaginative synthesis of native and foreign sources, and also displays Rastrelli's superb, if consciously unorthodox, manipulation of the classical orders. His best known secular buildings, the renovations of summer palaces at Peterhof (1747–1752) and Tsarskoe Selo (1749–1756), and the rebuilding of the Winter Palace in Saint Petersburg (1754–1762), are characterized by their enormous scale and horizontal expansion, necessitated in large part by preexisting structures. As a result, Rastrelli's concern for volumetric structures—so evident in his church designs and in smaller buildings like the garden pavilion of Mon Bijou at Tsarskoe Selo (1750)—was subordinated to the need to articulate long, seemingly endless façades. This he accomplished brilliantly, employing boldly projecting columns to break up the façade plane into vertical units and orchestrating these into grand rhythmic compositions. His success is most apparent in the Winter Palace, painted turquoise with white trim, which assumes the character of urban scenography when its theatrical façade, reflected in the waters of the Neva, is viewed from the Strelka.

JOHN PINTO

Rastrelli. Fourth Winter Palace. St. Petersburg (Leningrad). 1754–1762

WORKS

*c.1730, Annenhof Palace Complex, Moscow. *1732, Third Winter Palace, Saint Petersburg (Leningrad). 1736–1740, Biron Palace, Mitau, Russia. *1741–1744, Summer Palace; 1743–1757, Vorontsov Palace; *1744–1750, Anichkov Palace; Saint Petersburg (Leningrad). 1747–1748, The Cathedral of Saint Andrew, Kiev, Russia. 1747–1752, Summer Palace (renovation), Peterhof, Russia. 1748–1755, Smolny Convent, Saint Petersburg (Leningrad). 1749–1756, Grand Palace (renovation); *1750, Mon Bijou Pavilion; Tsarskoe Selo (Pushkin), Russia. 1750–1754, Stroganov Palace; 1754–1762, Fourth Winter Palace; Saint Petersburg (Leningrad). 1755–1762, Grotto, Tsarskoe Selo (Pushkin), Russia.

BIBLIOGRAPHY

ARKIN, DAVID E. 1954 *Rastrelli.* Moscow.

DENISOV, IU. M. 1963 *Zodchii Rastrelli.* St. Petersburg (Leningrad).

GRABAR', IGOR' IMMANUILOVICH 1910–1914 Volumes 3 and 4 in *Istoriia russkago iskusstva.* Moscow: Knebel.

HAMILTON, GEORGE H. 1954 *The Art and Architecture of Russia.* Baltimore: Penguin.

LO GATTO, ETTORE 1939 *Gli artisti italiana in Russia.* Rome: Libreria dello Stato.

KOZ'MIAN, GALINS KUZ'MINICHNA 1976 *F. B. Rastrelli.* St. Petersburg.

LUKOMSKI, GEORGIO 1924–1925 "Bartolomeo Rastrelli architetto italiano in Russia." *Architettura e Arti Decorative* 4:337–358.

RATTENBURY, F. M.

Born in Leeds, England, articled to Lockwood and Mawson, Francis Mawson Rattenbury (1867–1935) emigrated to British Columbia, Canada, in 1892. Winning the international competition for the Parliament Buildings (1893–1898), Victoria, blending English neo-Renaissance with Richardsonian Romanesque, he worked extensively for the provincial government, Canadian Pacific Railway, and the Bank of Montreal, predominantly in the château and Beaux-Arts styles, exemplified by the Empress Hotel, Victoria (1903–1908) and the Vancouver Courthouse (1906–1911); his houses were mainly Queen Anne. He returned to England in 1930, and was murdered in Bournemouth in 1935.

R. WINDSOR LISCOMBE

WORKS

1893–1898, Parliament Buildings, Victoria, British Columbia. 1895–1896, Courthouse, Nanaimo, British Columbia. 1896–1897, Bank of Montreal, Government Street, Victoria, British Columbia. 1899, Bank of Montreal, Nelson, British Columbia. *1899–1903, Patrick Burns Mansion, Calgary, Alberta. *1900–1903, Hotel Vancouver (major additions), British Columbia. 1901–1902, Cable Station, Bamfield, Vancouver Island. 1901–1903, Government House; 1903–1908, Empress Hotel; Victoria, British Columbia. 1906–1909, Courthouse, Nelson, British Columbia. 1906–1911, Courthouse, Vancouver, British Columbia. 1907, Merchants' Bank (now Bank of Montreal); 1911–1915, Parliamentary Library and Government Offices; 1923–1924, Second Canadian Pacific Railway Steamship Terminal; 1923–1925, Crystal Garden; Victoria, British Columbia.

BIBLIOGRAPHY

LISCOMBE, RHODRI WINDSOR, and BARRETT, ANTHONY A. 1979–1980 "Two Recently Discovered Drawings by F. M. Rattenbury." *RACAR* 6, no. 2:113–115.

LISCOMBE, RHODRI WINDSOR, and BARRETT, ANTHONY A. n.d. "F. M. Rattenbury." Forthcoming publication.

SEGGER, MARTIN 1976 "The Architecture of Samuel Maclure and Francis Mawson Rattenbury. In Search of Appropriate Form." *Canadian Collector* 11:51–55.

RAYMOND, ANTONIN

Born in Kladno, near Prague, Czechoslovakia, Antonin Raymond (1888–1976) graduated from the Technical College of Prague in 1910. In 1916, he emigrated to the United States where he learned about the works of ADOLF LOOS and FRANK LLOYD WRIGHT. He joined Wright's Taliesin in 1916. He went to Tokyo with Wright in 1919 to help him in the building of the Imperial Hotel. He was so interested in the simple and functional crafts and architecture of Japan that he decided to work there; he established his own office in 1920. He worked in Japan except for the war period.

His prize winning work, the Reader's Digest Office in Tokyo (1950–1952), was far beyond the Japanese level and shocked Japanese fellow architects. He was again awarded a prize in 1964 for the campus of the Nanzan University in Nagoya. His private residences, which show the influence of Japanese wooden structures, have been highly praised.

HIROSHI YAMAGUCHI

WORKS

1934, Saint Paul's, Karuizawa, Nagano Prefecture, Japan. 1951, Antonin Raymond House; 1950–1952, Reader's Digest Office; Tokyo. 1958–1961, Gunma Music Center, Takasaki, Japan. 1962–1964, Nanzan University Campus, Nagoya, Japan. 1965–1966, Shibata Catholic Church, Niigata Prefecture, Japan.

BIBLIOGRAPHY

RAYMOND, ANTONIN (1970)1973 *Antonin Raymond: An Autobiography.* Rutland, Vt.: Tuttle.

RAYMOND, JEAN ARNAUD

Jean Arnaud Raymond (1742–1811) was successively the student of JACQUES FRANÇOIS BLONDEL and JACQUES GERMAIN SOUFFLOT; he won the Grand Prix of the French Académie d'Architecture in 1766.

In 1768, he realized works for the archbishop of Narbonne. In 1766, he prepared a project for draining the Pontine Marshes. He created decorations for the Place du Peyrou and projects for the Palais des Etats of Languedoc in Montpellier. Between 1783 and 1786, he designed projects for prisons in Montpellier and Toulouse, the reconstruction of the Church of La Daurade in Toulouse, and the Church of Saint Rémy in Bordeaux. He also built the Chambre Souveraine du Clergé and the repository of the diocesan archives in Toulouse. In the same city, he decorated the archepiscopal palace for Monseigneur Loménie de Brienne. He also built the church of Ile-Jourdain and, in Aix-en-Provence, the chapel of the archbishop.

In Paris, he constructed in 1784 the Hôtel Saint Priest, 170 Faubourg Saint-Honoré, the Hôtel de Bonneval, Rue du Parc-Royal, and the *hôtel* and salesroom of Elizabeth Louise Vigée-Lebrun. At the Louvre, one finds his work today in the halls of Greco-Roman antiquities. There, he had realized the decoration for the summer apartments of the queen-mothers and the structural work of the bath suite.

His project for the Arc de Triomphe de l'Etoile was engraved by Louis Normand.

GÉRARD ROUSSET-CHARNY
Translated from French by Richard Cleary

BIBLIOGRAPHY

GALLET, MICHEL 1960 "La maison de Madame Vigée-Lebrun." *Gazette des Beaux-Arts* Series 6 56:275–284.

REDMAN, HENRY

Henry Redman (?–1528) was one of the leading English masons of his period. First recorded working at Westminster Abbey in 1495, he succeeded his father Thomas Redman as chief master mason there in 1516, and in 1519 was appointed master mason to the king jointly with William Vertue. He is most important, however, as the favorite mason of Cardinal Wolsey, the greatest builder of the time in England. Redman's work for Wolsey presumably included Hampton Court Palace, but this is not documented.

IAN CHILVERS

WORKS

(A)1515–1525, Hampton Court Palace (later extended by JOHN MOLTON), Middlesex, England. *1515–1529, York Place (later Whitehall Palace; later extended by Molton), London. 1516–1520, Lupton's Range (with William Vertue), Eton College, Berkshire, England. 1516–1523, Saint Margaret's (chancel and tower; later rebuilt and altered), Westminster; *1519, Greenwich Palace (two tiltyard towers); London. 1525–1528, Cardinal College (most of the east and west ranges and all of the south range; with John Lebons; now Christ Church), Oxford.

BIBLIOGRAPHY

HARVEY, JOHN H. 1943 "The Building Works and Architects of Cardinal Wolsey." *Journal of the British Archaeological Association* Series 3 8:50–59.

HARVEY, JOHN H. (1947)1948 *Gothic England: A Survey of National Culture 1300–1550.* Rev. ed. London: Batsford.

HARVEY, JOHN H. 1954 *English Mediaeval Architects.* London: Batsford.

REED and STEM

Formed by Charles A. Reed (1857–1911) and Allen H. Stem (1856–1931), the firm of Reed and Stem (1889–1911) designed more than one hundred stations for major railroad lines. The firm's original office was in St. Paul, Minnesota, where both men came to practice architecture, Reed after graduating from the Massachusetts Institute of Technology and Stem after studying at the Indianapolis Art School. In 1904, the firm opened an office in New York City and, with WARREN AND WETMORE, formed the New York Central and Hudson River Railroad Company Architects for the purpose of building Grand Central Station. Following Reed's death, Stem continued to practice architecture in Saint Paul.

DENNIS MCFADDEN

WORK

1903–1913, Grand Central Station (with Warren and Wetmore), New York.

BIBLIOGRAPHY

"C. A. Reed, Architect, Dead." 1911 *New York Times* Nov. 14, p. 13.

"Allen H. Stem." 1931 *Pencil Points* July:547.

MEEKS, CARROLL L. V. 1956 *The Railroad Station: An Architectural History.* New Haven: Yale University Press.

REGNAULT DE CORMONT

See ROBERT DE LUZARCHES.

REID, JAMES WILLIAM

Educated at the Massachusetts Institute of Technology and the Ecole des Beaux-Arts in Paris, James W. Reid (1851–1943) went to California in 1886 to design the imposing Hotel del Coronado, the first hotel with electricity throughout. In 1888, Reid and his brother Merritt opened a successful San Francisco practice, which included that city's first skyscraper, the Call Building (c.1897).

GWEN W. STEEGE

WORKS

1886–1888, Hotel del Coronado, San Diego, Calif. *c.1897, Call Building (later Claus Spreckels Building, then Central Tower); 1908, Cliff House, San Francisco.

BIBLIOGRAPHY

BANHAM, REYNER 1966 "Coronado: Or, Don't Smoke in Bed." *Architects' Journal* 143:317,319.

BUCKLEY, MARCIE 1970 *The Crown City's Brightest Gem.* San Diego, Calif.: Hotel del Coronado.

GREIBNER, ROBERT 1972 "Hotel del Coronado: A Jewel in the Crown City." *Historic Preservation* 24, no. 2:4–7.

REID, ROBERT

Robert Reid (1774–1856) was the principal government architect in Scotland during the first half of the nineteenth century. Reid was the son of a mason and a native of Edinburgh, but little else is known of his early life until he designed Edinburgh Law Courts (1804–1810). On the strength of this work and his subsequent major public and university commissions, Reid eventually became the master of works and architect to the king in Scotland in 1824.

Reid is best known for his Jacobean and neoclassical buildings in the Adam (see ROBERT ADAM) manner and for his layouts for the Edinburgh New Town. However, his finest work is a little-known picture gallery of considerable merit at Paxton House, Berwickshire (1812–1813).

JOHN MCASLAN

WORKS

1802–?, Edinburgh New Town (layout; with William Sibbald); 1802–1806, Bank of Scotland on the Mound (with Richard Crichton); Edinburgh. 1803–1807, Perth Academy (now County Library), Perth, Scotland. 1804–1810, New Law Courts, Edinburgh. 1811–1812, Customhouse, Leith, Scotland. 1811–1814, Saint George's Church (now Register House annex), Edinburgh. 1812–1813, Paxton House (east wing), Berwickshire, Scotland. 1824–1830, Downpatrick Gaol, County Down, Ireland. 1829–1831, United College (east wing), Saint Andrew's, Scotland.

BIBLIOGRAPHY

MORRISON, J. A. 1812 *A Guide to the City of Perth.* n.p.

REID, ROBERT 1809 *Observations on the Structure of Hospitals for the Treatment of Lunatics.* Edinburgh.

ROWAN, ALISTAIR 1967 "Paxton House, Berwickshire." *Country Life* 31:470–473.

YOUNGSON, A. J. 1966 *The Making of Classical Edinburgh.* Edinburgh University Press.

REIDY, AFFONSO EDUARDO

The career of Affonso Eduardo Reidy (1909–1964) manifested LE CORBUSIER's intense influence in Brazil after his 1936 trip when he spent three weeks lecturing and working with Reidy and other young architects on the design for the Brazilian Ministry of Education and Health Building. Born in Paris, Reidy grew up in Brazil and began his architectural education at the National School of Fine Arts while working for D. Alfred Agache. Agache had been invited to Brazil in 1927 and remained until 1930, laying out a traditional Beaux-Arts plan for the urban renovation of Rio de Janeiro. The combination of Agache's eclecticism and the antiquated curriculum at Rio's school of fine arts made Reidy an unlikely advocate of modern architecture, but after his first exposure to twentieth-century theories he fought against the academic colonialism that pervaded Brazilian architecture until the early 1930s.

In 1931 Reidy joined the teaching staff of the school of fine arts as GREGORI WARCHAVCHIK's assistant. He also received special commendation for his design for the Inn of Good Intentions (1931–1932), a hostel for the homeless. This two-story structure surrounded an interior courtyard

Reidy.
High School and Primary School in Pedregulho Housing Project.
Rio de Janeiro.
1947

and anticipated LE CORBUSIER's *brise-soleil* (sun breakers) with exterior venetian blinds which prevented the entrance of direct sunlight.

From 1936 until 1943, Reidy worked on the design and construction of the Ministry of Education and Health Building, the first government-sanctioned modern structure in Brazil, which suddenly brought international acclaim to Brazil's flowering modern architectural movement. In 1947, Reidy was appointed to the Department of Public Housing in Brazil and designed Pedregulho, a low-income housing project contained in an eight hundred-foot serpentine structure which naturally followed the hilly landscape of the twelve-acre site. Reminiscent of Le Corbusier's 1929 sketches for the reurbanization of Rio de Janeiro, Reidy put to use his town planning skills by incorporating community facilities into the complex and won first prize at the São Paulo Biennial in 1951 for his efforts. He used a similar design for the thirty-five-acre Gávea (1950–1952) residential neighborhood development. In both projects he turned obstacles into assets, thereby achieving a new regionalism in tropical architecture. He creatively adapted these structures to irregular sites, substituted ramps for costly elevators, and enclosed public areas around the apartments with perforated tiles and bricks in order to take advantage of cooling breezes.

Rio's Museum of Modern Art (1954–1960), Reidy's last project, inspired young Brazilians with its daring use of high technology and pure sense of architectonic aesthetics. Exploiting the sea view of the site which used reclaimed land on Rio's Guanabara Bay, Reidy designed a structural frame consisting of twenty-eight reinforced concrete ribs which supported and suspended the large glassed-in exhibition area—a glass and concrete version of Le Corbusier's 1937 tent design for the Paris Pavillon des Temps Nouveau. Reidy's architectural and urban planning endeavors exemplified the maturation of Le Corbusier's ideas in Brazil and the architectural prowess of an innovative architect.

ELIZABETH D. HARRIS

WORKS

1931–1932, Inn of Good Intentions; 1936–1943, Ministry of Education and Health Building (now the Palácio Da Cultura; with LÚCIO COSTA, OSCAR NIEMEYER, JORGE MOREIRA, Carlos Leão, and Ernani Vasconcellos); 1947, Pedregulho Housing Project; 1950–1951, Marechal Hermes Community Theatre; 1950–1952, Gávea Residential Neighborhood; 1954–1960, Museum of Modern Art; Rio de Janeiro. 1960, La Caisse De Prevoyance (experimental high school), Ascuncion, Paraguay.

BIBLIOGRAPHY

FRANCK, KLAUS 1960 *The Works of Affonso Eduardo Reidy.* Introduction by Sigfried Giedeon. New York: Praeger.

REILLY, CHARLES HERBERT

Charles Herbert Reilly (1874–1948) was less important as an architect than as an influential teacher and writer. He modeled the Liverpool School of Architecture on American Beaux-Arts lines and made it one of the most influential in Britain. Through the books of the school's work, he helped encourage the *néo-grèc* style fashionable just before World War I. Reilly much admired American classicism and sent his best pupils, such as Herbert J. Rowse to American offices. Reilly acted as consultant for the design by CARRÈRE AND HASTINGS for Devonshire House in Piccadilly, London (1924–1926); a decade later, again as consultant, Reilly brought Continental modernism to London with the Peter Jones Department Store, designed by his pupil WILLIAM CRABTREE (1936).

Born in London, Reilly had first been articled to his father, Charles Reilly, who worked in the City of London. He then worked in the office of JOHN BELCHER before becoming a junior partner in 1900 to Charles Stanley Peach, the pioneer power station architect. While associated with Peach, Reilly submitted a classical design in the competition for Liverpool Cathedral (1901–1902). From 1904 until 1933, Reilly was professor of Architecture at the University of Liverpool. He built comparatively little, but he was a prolific writer, publishing several books and many regular articles in the architectural journals. In 1937, he published his autobiography.

GAVIN STAMP

WORKS

CHARLES HERBERT REILLY AND C. S. PEACH

1900–1904, Electric Power Station, Ipswich, England. *1902–1904, Grove Road Power Station (never finished); 1903–1905, Duke Street Italian Garden Substation, Mayfair; 1903–1904, Colonial House, Tooley Street; London.

CHARLES HERBERT REILLY

1908–1910, Saint Barnabas', Shacklewell Row, London. 1911, Belmont, Chesterfield, England. 1911, 7–8 Buckingham Street, London. 1911, Wavertree Parish Church (additions), Liverpool, England. 1920, Accrington War Memorial, Lancashire, England. 1920, Durham County War Memorial, Durham, England. n.d., Gilmore Hall; n.d., Students' Union; University of Liverpool, England.

BIBLIOGRAPHY

The papers of Charles Reilly are in the archives of the University of Liverpool, England.

"Obituary." 1948 *Architectural Association Journal* 63, Feb.:174.

REILLY, CHARLES HERBERT 1921 *Some Liverpool Streets and Buildings in 1921.* England: Liverpool Daily Post and Mercury.

REILLY, CHARLES HERBERT 1924a *McKim, Mead and White.* London: Benn.

REILLY, CHARLES HERBERT 1924b *Some Manchester Streets and Their Buildings.* Liverpool (England) University Press.

REILLY, CHARLES HERBERT 1931 *Representative British Architects of Today.* London: Batsford. A selection of biographical articles published in *Building.*

REILLY, CHARLES HERBERT 1932 *The Theory and Practice of Architecture.* London: Gollancz.

REILLY, CHARLES HERBERT 1937 *Scaffolding in the Sky.* London: Routledge. Reilly's autobiography.

REILLY, CHARLES HERBERT n.d. *Selected Etchings by Piranesi.* Westminster, London: Technical Journal.

STAMP, GAVIN, and BOYD HARTE, G. 1979 *Temples of Power.*

REINHARD and HOFMEISTER

L. Andrew Reinhard (1891–1964) trained at the Mechanics Institute and studied at the Beaux-Arts Institute of Design. In the 1920s, he was a junior designer for Benjamin Wistar Morris and RAYMOND M. HOOD, among others, and worked for the developer John R. Todd. In 1928, he became an associate and then partner of Henry Hofmeister (1891–1962), who trained by apprenticeship with WARREN AND WETMORE where he worked for seventeen years on hotels in the Grand Central area of Manhattan and in Atlantic City, New Jersey. Reinhard and Hofmeister specialized in office building interior layouts. Through Todd, they became one of three associated firms working on Rockefeller Center (1928–1941). Subsequently, they designed the Chrysler Building East (1928).

CAROL HERSELLE KRINSKY

WORKS

1928, Chrsyler Building East; 1928–1941, Rockefeller Center (with Raymond M. Hood, Jacques Andre Fouilhoux, and Harvey Wiley Corbett, Wallace K. Harrison, and William H. MacMurray).

BIBLIOGRAPHY

"Henry Hofmeister." 1962 *Architectural Forum* 116:4.

KRINSKY, C. H. 1978 *Rockefeller Center.* New York: Oxford University Press.

"Obituary." 1964 *New York Times* Aug. 3, p. 25, col. 3.

TODD, JOHN REYNARD (1947)1948 *Living a Life.* New York.

RENACCO, NELLO

Nello Renacco (1915–), born in Turin, Italy, graduated from the Turin Politecnico. He was a partner of MARIO PASSANTI from 1939 until the latter's death in 1976. His interest in the theory and principles of new towns in England and Scandanavia led him to form interdisciplinary teams for planning studies. Renacco's teams worked on master plans for Torino-Falchera (1950–1954), Ivrea (1950–1953), Torino-Lucento (1954), Torino-La Vallette (1956), and Loano (1963–1964).

HENRY A. MILLON

WORKS

1944–1946, Regional Plan for Piedmont (with Giovanni Astengo and Rizzotti), Italy. 1950–1953, Master Plan (with Ludovico Quaroni), Ivrea, Italy. 1950–1954, Torino-Falchera Housing (with Astengo, Molli-Boffa, Mario Passanti, and Rizzotti), Italy. 1954, Torino-Lucento Housing (with Astengo, Rizzotti, and Grass); 1956, Torino-La-Vallette Master Plan; Turin, Italy. 1963–1964, Loano Master Plan, Italy.

RENARD, BRUNO

The founder of the Tournai school of neoclassicists, Bruno Renard (1781–1861) distinguished himself as an architect, restorer, archeologist, and professor. Born of a cultivated family, and supported by his uncle, the French architect D. Bourla, he studied in Paris (c. 1800–1807) under the leading designers of the Empire style, CHARLES PERCIER AND PIERRE FONTAINE, from whom he inherited his refined taste and analytic spirit. His most original achievement is the industrial complex of Le Grand-Hornu (1820–1835), which in many ways continues the tradition of CLAUDE NICOLAS LEDOUX.

MAURICE CULOT
Translated from French by
Shara Wasserman

WORKS

1820–1835, Grand Hornu (workshops and worker's city); 1822–1824, Concert Hall; 1822–1824, Public Square (plan); 1833–1835, Slaughterhouses; 1842–1835, Cathedral (restoration, including belfry); Tournai, Belgium.

BIBLIOGRAPHY

MARTINY, VICTOR GASTON 1979 *L'Architecture en Belgique des origines à 1900.* Brussels: Vokaer.

PUTTEMANS, PIERRE (1974)1976 *Modern Architecture in Belgium.* Translated by Mette Willert. Brussels: Vokaert.

TAYLOR, BRIAN BRACE 1976 "Le Grand-Hornu; 1820–1835." *L'Architecture d'Aujourd'hui* 183:103–112.

VAN HASSETT, A. 1864 "Bruno Renard: Membre de l'Academie." *Annuaire de l'Académie Royale de Belgique* 30:109–114.

RENIE, ANDRE MARIE

André Marie Renié (1789–1853) was born in Paris and studied with Antoine Vaudoyer (see VAUDOYER AND VAUDOYER) and Charles Percier (see PERCIER AND FONTAINE). One of many French architects who practiced abroad, Renié worked in Germany at the court of the duke of Saxe-Coburg-Gotha. At Coburg, he completed the Palace in an English Gothic style (1816–1840) and designed a playhouse.

LISA B. REITZES

WORK

1816–1840, Palace at Coburg (completion), Germany.

BIBLIOGRAPHY

HAUTECOEUR, LOUIS 1943–1957 *Histoire de l'Architecture classique en France.* 7 vols. Paris: Picard.

RENNIE, JOHN

John Rennie (1761–1821), born into a prosperous Scottish family, was educated at Edinburgh University and afterwards was London agent for BOULTON AND WATT, the celebrated steam engine builders. His abilities as an engineer earned him commissions to plan several important canals, and in designing the bridges and aqueducts for these he first showed that he was possessed of remarkable architectural talents. The Dundas and Avoncliffe Aqueducts (1797) on the Kennet and Avon Canal, harmonizing with the architecture of the nearby City of Bath, and Lune Aqueduct (1797), crossing the tidal estuary of the River Lune at Lancaster, are outstanding examples of this type of work and are still in use; but there were many more, and even the standard bridges are graceful structures.

Rennie. Dundas Aqueduct (Limpley Stoke). Bath, England. 1797

Further commissions included many fine road bridges. Spanning the River Thames in London were London Bridge, constructed by his son John (sold in 1963 and reerected at Lake Havasu City, Arizona), Waterloo Bridge (1817), and Southwark Bridge (1814), this last of cast iron. The list of his bridges is a lengthy one, but large or small they were all individually designed to suit the particular circumstances. Only two, Kelso (1800) and Waterloo, had similar architectural treatment. All the others showed a wide range of original design. In addition a great number which had no conscious architectural features were yet distinctive with the application of engineering principles.

In his numerous dock and harbor works, Rennie designed a number of buildings such as the Custom House (1821), Entrance Arch (1821), and lighthouse (1821) at Holyhead, and the main entrance (now demolished) to the East India Docks (1806) at London, but it is for his bridges large and small, of which hundreds still exist, that he is best remembered.

C. T. G. BOUCHER

WORKS

*1795, Bulk Aqueduct; 1795, Wyre Aqueduct; 1796, Conder Aqueduct; 1796, Yarrow Aqueduct; Lancashire, England. 1797, Avoncliff Aqueduct, near Bath, England. 1797, Dundas Aqueduct (Limpley Stoke), Bath, England. 1797, Lune Aqueduct, Lancaster, England. 1800, Kelso Bridge, Roxburgh County, Scotland. 1804, Whiteadder Bridge, Scotland. *1806, East India Docks (main entrance), London. 1806, Musselburgh Bridge, Scotland. *1807, Darlaston Bridge, Staffordshire, England. 1814, Newton Stewart Bridge, Wigton County, Scotland. *1814, Southwark Bridge, London. 1815, Stratford on Avon Railway Viaduct (adjoining the Bancroft Gardens), Stratford on Avon, England. *1817, Waterloo Bridge, London. 1818, Stoneleigh Bridge, Warwickshire, England. 1819, Bridge of Earn, Perth County, Scotland. 1820, Crammond Bridge, Scotland. 1821, Custom House; 1821, Entrance Arch; 1821, Lighthouse; Holyhead, Anglesey, North Wales. 1821, New Galloway Bridge, Kirkcudbrightshire, Scotland. *1825–1831, London Bridge (constructed by his son John and completed in 1831; transferred to United States and rebuilt, beginning 1963).

BIBLIOGRAPHY

BOUCHER, CYRIL T. G. 1963 *John Rennie, 1761–1821: The Life and Work of a Great Engineer.* Manchester (England) University Press.

REYBURN, WALLACE 1972 *Bridge Across the Atlantic: The Story of John Rennie.* London: Harrap.
SMILES, SAMUEL 1862 Volume 2, part 7 in *Lives of the Engineers.* London: John Murray.

RENWICK, JAMES

Few nineteenth-century architects achieved the recognition accorded James Renwick (1818–1895) during his lifetime. Active in New York City for more than half a century, he gained national attention with his first building, New York's prestigious Grace Church and later an international reputation as architect of Saint Patrick's Cathedral. Although primarily remembered as a church architect, the prodigious output of Renwick and his firm include museums, schools, theaters, hotels, commercial buildings, city and country residences, and many types of institutional facilities.

From the outset, Renwick experimented with both form and method; in the words of the distinguished contemporary critic Montgomery Schuyler, "he was never a purist." Trained as an engineer, he independently acquired a thorough knowledge of historic architecture and throughout his life maintained a keen interest in contemporary stylistic and structural developments. This was reflected in his innovative use of traditional forms and early employment of newly developed materials, mechanical devices, and structural systems. Thus, he became known early in his career as both a gifted designer and an architect with considerable technical expertise.

Notwithstanding his ability and dedication, Renwick's rapid success was partially due to advantages inherited at birth and augmented by his marriage in 1851 to Anna Lloyd Aspinwall, daughter of one of the richest men in America. Born in his grandmother's country house in Bloomingdale, just north of New York City, he was the second son of Margaret Brevoort, daughter of a wealthy landowner, and James Renwick, at that time a successful merchant and engineer. The descendant of seven generations of Brevoorts in America and four in the Renwick line, he was born into a small but influential social aristocracy. In addition, he would benefit from long-standing family traditions which prized and encouraged all forms of artistic and intellectual pursuits.

Renwick's early education consisted of English, mathematics, geography, and classical and modern languages. In 1831, at the customary age of twelve, he entered Columbia College where the curriculum also included physics, chemistry, mechanics, and astronomy. He was graduated in 1836, having lost a year because of an eye accident, and in 1839 was awarded an M.A. degree.

Unquestionably the greatest influence on the careers of Renwick and his two brothers, Henry Brevoort and Edward Sabine, both eminent engineers, was their father, the elder James Renwick. In 1820, following the bankruptcy of the family's mercantile business, the elder Renwick eagerly accepted the professorship in physics (then called natural philosophy) and chemistry at Columbia College. Soon known as one of the country's foremost engineers, he was also an expert astronomer and mineralogist, a leading art collector and patron, a prolific author on both scientific and historical subjects, as well as an accomplished artist, architectural historian, and amateur architect who found time to supervise the construction of buildings for friends. Devoted to his family (which also included a daughter, Laura), he not only trained his three sons as engineers but whenever necessary, unhesitatingly used his influence to further their careers.

Upon young James's graduation in 1836, his father helped in obtaining his appointment as an engineer on the Erie Railroad and, the following year, as a second assistant engineer for the Croton Aqueduct Commission. He remained in that capacity until the completion of the system in 1842, superintending the construction of the huge Distributing Reservoir which stood at Fifth Avenue and Forty-second Street. During that time, he was licensed as a city surveyor, for which he had been trained by his father. Of all the ways he was indebted to the elder man, none was more profound than the encouragement to pursue an architectural career and the guidance he received in his studies. Certainly, Professor Renwick's assurance of his son's capabilities was a determining factor in the decision by the vestry of Grace Church in July 1843 to select the twenty-four-year-old Renwick's design over those submitted by leading architects.

Renwick's only previous executed design had been the Bowling Green Fountain (1843), constructed while he was preparing the plans for Grace Church. An irregular grouping of large uncut black stones over which water followed a desultory course, this early attempt at the picturesque was so ridiculed it was replaced in only a few years.

In marked contrast, Grace Church (1843–1846) and RICHARD UPJOHN's somewhat earlier Trinity Church (1841–1846) had the distinction of being the first American buildings to evidence a genuine understanding of the medieval Gothic mode. Renwick's design was derived from both English and French sources and was described by the architect as "a small cathedral" in "the early Flamboyant," more commonly known as the Decorated style. Reportedly the first American example of an undulating tracery pattern, it would also appear to have been the earliest use of a cruciform plan. Despite the criticism of the plaster vaulting and the wooden spire (Renwick had strongly recommended stone), the lavishly decorated white marble church and rectory prominently situated at the bend of Broadway and Tenth Street was widely acclaimed.

Except for the French-inspired Romanesque Church of the Puritans (1846–1847) in New York for the Congregationalists, Renwick's other urban churches of the 1840s were for theologically conservative denominations and were variations of the Gothic mode of Grace Church. In New York City, multi-gabled Calvary Church (1846–1847) was to have been of white marble, later changed to brownstone, and was patterned on the twin-towered French cathedrals with triple entrance doors. Renwick economized in the South Dutch Church (1848–1849) by using a single corner tower and spire, brick for the side walls—stuccoed, sanded, and painted to simulate the buff freestone of the front—and exposed wood in the vault. Chicago's Second Presbyterian Church (1849?–1851) and Trinity Church (1850–1851) in Washington had similar five-bay entrance façades, but the corner towers and spires of the Chicago church differed and at Trinity were identical. The design of that façade, in fact, was originally the central elevation of Renwick's Gothic Revival entry in the 1846 competition for the new Smithsonian Institution (1847–1855) in Washington.

Renwick. Smithsonian Institution. Washington. 1847–1855

Renwick. Smithsonian Institution. Washington. 1847–1855

Contrary to the rules of that contest, Renwick submitted not one but two designs and a marbleized model of his prize winning scheme derived from English, French, and German Romanesque Revival sources (the entrance elevation of which was a modified version of the main façade of the Church of the Puritans). Despite the avowed preference of building committee chairman Robert Dale Owen for the round-arched style, Renwick's sole reason for submitting the symmetrical Gothic scheme was his conviction that it was the only suitable form for monumental public buildings. (This was shortly reaffirmed by his Free Academy, 1847–1849, in New York, modeled on the Dutch medieval town hall.)

The clearest indication of Renwick's faith in the Gothic as most appropriate for the Smithsonian was the title page he designed for Owen's *Hints on Public Architecture* (1849). For this essay advocating the Romanesque Revival style, Renwick ironically set the title within a traceried Gothic window enframed by a rusticated border containing vignettes of various architectural styles. Significantly, the focal point was not the view of the Smithsonian, relegated to the bottom of the page, but a Gothic doorway highlighted at the top.

Though Renwick considered the Romanesque (also referred to as Norman, Lombard, Byzantine, or simply Round style) inappropriate for grandiose public buildings, he began using this mode in 1848 for such diverse purposes as civic monuments, residences, commercial buildings, and city and country churches, frequently combining the Romanesque with other styles. The white marble triumphal arch for the proposed Clinton Monument (1848), for example, had considerable Romanesque detailing on an otherwise classical form, and Renwick's commercial designs were generally Italianate with an occasional touch of the medieval style.

A similarly eclectic mixture of Romanesque and Gothic was prevalent in his church architecture. Two designs which he termed "Lancet or early Gothic" and "modernized Romanesque or Round style" were published in *A Book of Plans for Churches and Parsonages* (1853). Both included similar stepped gables in the entrance façades, side towers, and buttresses, their primary difference being in the shape of the windows. Renwick's original of "modernized" Romanesque included window tracery, a deviation from historic precedent he predicated on the assumption that the Romanesque had "progressed . . . instead of changing into the Gothic."

Among his executed designs, Saint Stephen's (1853–1854), a brownstone church for Manhattan's wealthiest Roman Catholic parish, was substantially Romanesque. But for the Clinton Avenue Congregational Church (1854–1855) in fashionable Brooklyn Heights, Renwick set the "modernized" Romanesque openings into another adaptation of his Gothic Smithsonian proposal.

The most significant expression of Renwick's high regard for the Romanesque was in his parents' residence (1849–1851) on lower Fifth Avenue, a site that was originally part of Grandfather Brevoort's farm. Just as the Smithsonian was the first public building in that style, the Renwick house appears to have been the earliest and one of the rare residential uses of the Romanesque. Unusual, too, was the choice of brick, generally limited to utilitarian and speculatively built structures. Typical of Renwick's eclectic manner, the bold Romanesque details—the heavily corbeled and decorated cornice; the carved, presumably stone tracery, moldings and corbels of the windows; and the colonnettes flanking the deeply recessed front door—were combined with such nonmedieval elements as the side gable (a vertical counterpoint to the bay windows on the first floor) and the urbane arrangement of the front parlor windows opening onto an iron balcony. In the 1850s, Renwick would employ a common iron balcony as a unifying element in the English basement rowhouses (1855) he designed in the Italianate style on Ninth Street west of Fifth Avenue.

In the 1850s, Renwick was the architect of several of New York's elegant hotels. The Clarendon (1850–1851) on Union Square was a lively medley of colors and forms, a combination of yellow brick, terra-cotta window heads (one of the earliest uses of that material), and brownstone trim. The fundamentally Italianate design, according to contemporary accounts, included such Elizabethan details as tracery in the ground floor windows and paneled pilasters to the full height of the building. Shortly after in the Saint Denis Hotel (1851?–1852), designed for his mother, Renwick had the opportunity to be far more extravagant with Elizabethan embellishments. One contemporary critic considered it "bizarre and fantastical . . . (but) far from unpleasing," noting that the vast amount of terra-cotta ornament cost much less than if it were of stone. Conversely, there was nothing startling about the LaFarge House (1852 burned 1854; rebuilt 1854–1856), the largest of Renwick's early hotels. A typical white marble Italianate palazzo with cast-iron storefronts, it had little to distinguish itself from the myriad of others in that popular form.

Renwick. Corcoran Gallery. Washington. 1859–1871

Renwick's first tentative venture into the Second Empire style was the Cruger Mansion (1853–1854), a luxurious but, as Henry James termed it, "eccentric" house for a similarly unconventional client. Georgian in feeling with rough stone walls with quoins, a recessed two-story portico, and various Palladian (see ANDREA PALLADIO) motifs, it was crowned by a low mansard roof with dormers. Five years later, Renwick designed the first American building in which the complex decorative and spatial characteristics of that new style were properly combined, the Corcoran Gallery (1859, discontinued 1861; 1870–1871), renamed the Renwick Gallery, in Washington. In his description, Renwick acknowledged the new Louvre as his source but stressed that the details and proportions were "entirely different." Dissimilar, too, was the combination of brick with brownstone trim and the use of wrought-iron floor beams. Two interior courtyards and numerous skylights assured the essential natural illumination.

Renwick's conversion from the Gothic for major public buildings and his gradual mastery of what was commonly called "the modern French style," was also evident in two municipal hospitals on Blackwell's Island in New York. The castellated Smallpox Hospital (1853–1856?) was followed by the Second Empire Island Hospital (1858–1861), designed after his first trip to Europe. Plans for that building were completed within a month after the original hospital burned. Ostensibly modeled on the Tuileries, the only common elements between the French palace and this enormous but architecturally sparse "palace of the suffering poor" were the mansard roofs, here with only a single dome over the main entrance, and the sprawling, symmetrical plan. Notwithstanding the lack of time and money rather than of talent, this stolid stone structure surprisingly had more in common with the much earlier Cruger Mansion than the elegant Corcoran Gallery designed about a year later.

In the case of Vassar College (1861–1865), it was not a limited budget but the client who adversely influenced the design. Matthew Vassar, a retired Poughkeepsie brewer, returned from a grand tour of Europe determined to become a great public benefactor. One of the highlights of his trip had been the Tuileries which at his insistence was the model for the main building of the new college. Renwick's interpretation was admirable, a simplified brick version of that elegant Renaissance palace in which the overall form and massing rather than the ornamentation were emphasized. Noteworthy, too, were the extensive use of iron as a fire retardant material and the sophisticated heating, ventilation and plumbing systems. Unfortunately, there was an inherent flaw: the incompatibility of the monumental, urbane building with its rural, picturesque site, for which Vassar was solely responsible.

Conversely, the white marble Albemarle Hotel (1859–1862) was well-suited to its fashionable Madison Square location. Closely resembling a château, the building's graceful curved motif was repeated in the round arches of the windows, along the corner of the building, and in the conical pavilion of the mansard roof.

At this point, Renwick's practice had grown to the extent that by 1858 he made Richard Tylden Auchmuty a partner and two years later, Joseph Sands. One of the reasons for this expansion was the increase in commercial work. Generally classical in style, of masonry, and frequently with iron fronts on the first and occasionally the second floor, Renwick's commercial buildings were among the earliest to use iron as a fire resistant structural material. The Bank of the State of New York (1855–1856), for example, had full iron floor framing—girders, beams, and sheet iron troughs for the infill.

In the same decade, Renwick was selected as architect of Saint Patrick's Cathedral (1858–1879; spires 1885–1888); the archbishop's brother-in-law, William Rodrigue, was appointed as his associate. It was Renwick, however, who had sole responsibility for the entire design including the principal chapels, many of the side chapels, and virtually all of the interior furnishings. (Renwick's role as the designer was commemorated in the stained glass window portraying him delivering the plans to Archbishop Hughes.) He continued in this capacity until the end of his life, personally overseeing all additions including the archbishop's residence (1880–1882) and the rectory (1882–1883) in the rear of the cathedral facing Madison Avenue. Although Saint Patrick's was considered Renwick's finest achievement, it was, in reality, the greatest disappointment of his professional career.

The cathedral was to have been the magnificent consummation of the Decorated Gothic Revival church designs he had been developing since

Renwick.
Saint Patrick's Cathedral.
New York.
1858–1879

the 1840s. According to Renwick, the chief sources were the similarly twin-towered, triple-portalled Cathedrals of Rheims, Amiens, and Cologne and the naves of Yorkminster, Exeter, and Westminster, which he considered the most "advanced" examples of that era. The original plan for Saint Patrick's featured a monumental stone tower over the crossing, the first large masonry vault in the United States, and at the east end, an apse with a processional aisle and a chevet of chapels. But this extraordinary demonstration of Renwick's architectural and engineering skills was so diminished for financial reasons that in one respect, the completed building was a parody of his original concept.

By the time the cornerstone was laid in 1858, the crossing tower had been eliminated and the apse was first modified and then postponed. (It was eventually built after Renwick's death but not to his design). When the cost far exceeded the $1,000,000 estimate, it was decided to economize further by using plaster and wood lathe instead of masonry for the vault. Unfortunately, the buttresses necessary for the masonry vault had been completed before that change and because of their apparent uselessness have been criticized ever since. When the walls of the cathedral were only a few feet high, Renwick had abandoned the Decorated mode for his major church commissions in favor of the Italian Gothic or Romanesque. Though related to earlier work such as Saint Stephen's, these designs were far more robust, less self-conscious about stylistic details, and more concerned with the synthesis of form and fabric. In addition, combinations of richly colored, highly textured materials produced dazzling polychromatic effects.

These churches followed two formats. The earliest was that of the Church of the Covenant (1863–1865) in the Murray Hill section of New York—stone with alternating colors outlining the arched openings, the main entrance surmounted by an arcade of windows with a rose window above, and gables at all roof terminations and over the doors. For the Irvington Presbyterian Church (1868?–1869) in Westchester County, Renwick added a handsome campanile and belfry.

Saint Bartholomew's (1871–1872) in New York was the stylistic culmination of Renwick's use of this format, literally as well with a campanile almost twice the height of the nave. Situated on Madison Avenue and Forty-fourth Street, an elegant new residential area, Saint Bartholomew's eclipsed Trinity and Grace as the most fashionable Protestant Episcopal church. Commonly referred to as "the Vanderbilt Church" after one of its chief benefactors, the church, including the land, cost about $400,000. Described by one contemporary critic as "Lombardo-Gothic," by another as "Byzantine," and by Montgomery Schuyler as "Italian Romanesque," the critics unanimously lavished praise on the extraordinary richness of the interior and exterior polychromy. It was a design Renwick considered significant, the only one his firm exhibited at the 1876 Centennial Exhibition in Philadelphia.

The other style Renwick favored for these predominantly Italian inspired churches was the Gothic advocated by John Ruskin and promul-

Renwick.
Nave vaults of Saint Patrick's Cathedral.
New York.
1858–1879

Renwick.
Saint Patrick's Cathedral.
New York.
1858–1879

gated by such High Victorian English architects as WILLIAM BUTTERFIELD and GEORGE E. STREET. Saint Ann's Protestant Episcopal Church (1867–1869) in Brooklyn Heights was Renwick's first church of this type. Built at a cost of more than $250,000, the brownstone church and chapel had sharply contrasting bands of white stone with alternating colors in the flat trim of the windows and doors. Despite this emphasis on the horizontal and the liveliness of the design, the impression was one of great bulk and height, partly due to the two-story side aisles necessitated by the interior galleries and the absence of clearstories. The polychromy of the interior was dazzling and included Ruskinian iron columns with naturalistic capitals.

About ten years later, Renwick designed what Schuyler and, more recently, Paul Goldberger considered the most superb of the Renwick churches, All Saints' Roman Catholic Church (1882–1893) in Harlem. Construction was delayed because of financial difficulties and then proceeded slowly as funds were raised. The overall arrangement of the main façade was, with only minor exceptions, the same as that of Saint Ann's. Instead of stone, All Saints' was of an orange-yellow brick inlayed with buff and trimmed in terra cotta. The small scale of these materials and the multiplicity of sizes, shapes, and colors were echoed in such varied and innovative elements as the polygonal ends of the transepts and the graceful wheel windows of the clearstories. The result was both delicate and complex, the antithesis of Saint Ann's.

In Renwick's public architecture, the transition from the Second Empire to the High Victorian styles began in the late 1860s and was more gradual than in his ecclesiastical work. Booth's Theater (1867–1869) in New York City was designed about a year later than Saint Ann's, yet it was the most purely French of his public buildings in that style.

Unlike the majority of post-Civil War examples, Booth's was richly ornamented but not verbose. Renwick achieved this ideal by balancing the decorative elements with expanses of solid wall and by avoiding the undulation of the commonly used projecting bays. The effect was one of restrained elegance. Much of the over $1,000,000 cost was for specially designed heating and cooling systems, novel mechanical equipment for scenery changes, and particularly the extensive fire precautions. All of the walls (even the interior partitions) were masonry and, together with the roof, were reported to have been lined with sheet iron. These extraordinary structural measures and the interior arrangement which enabled the theater to be emptied in five minutes, received considerable publicity.

The Young Men's Christian Association Building (1868–1869) in New York gave some indication of Renwick's new interest in High Victorian forms. A vivid combination of brownstone with yellow stone detailing, the fundamentally Renaissance clubhouse included several unorthodox elements—the horizontal bands favored by the High Victorians, medieval designs in the window trim, and a slightly asymmetrical entrance façade.

The following year, Gothic windows and decorative patterns were featured in the North Western Dispensary (1869), one of New York's free clinics. In this utilitarian building, the polychromatic designs of stone against brick and the pointed windows outlined with alternating colors gave a substantial architectural lift to this otherwise simple rectangular structure. There was no need for such devices in the luxurious Daniel Willis James Residence (1869–1870) on Park Avenue designed the same year. Considered one of the finest of its type, the exterior of this free-standing mansion was a rich combination of costly materials—brownstone, limestone, and polished granite in several colors—and of meticulously carved medieval ornament.

Possibly the most dynamic of Renwick's High Victorian Gothic designs was a proposal that failed to get much beyond the design stage, his entry in the New York Masonic Hall competition in 1870. Borrowing heavily from GEORGE GILBERT SCOTT's similarly unsuccessful 1857 design for the London Foreign Office (which in turn owed much to the Oxford University Museum), the main difference in the Renwick version was the central tower set jauntily at an angle rather than squarely over the central entrance as in the prototype.

Two municipal hospitals designed in the late 1860s clearly illustrate this shift from the Renaissance to the High Victorian forms. In the construction of the Foundling Hospital (1867–1869) on Randall's Island, the transition is conspicuous. The central pavilion was completed first, a typical Second Empire composition. Though the wings were added only a year later in a harmonious scale and form, they were not rigidly symmetrical and included the popular High Victorian bands of narrow windows in assorted sizes and shapes. With the sprawling New York City Hospital for the Insane (1869–1871) on neighboring Ward's Island, the transformation had been completed. In brick, with a profusion of yellow stone ornament and medieval towers posted at the corners of the mansard roofs, the last of Renwick's massive hospitals displayed an unabashedly medieval air.

Concurrent with the stylistic change in Renwick's public architecture was a shift to elaborate

Italianate forms for commercial buildings. These were usually of masonry with iron fronts on the ground floor and occasionally on the second story as well, a structural system Renwick seemed to have preferred to that of the full iron front. One of the exceptions, however, was the Appleton Building (1870–1871) on lower Broadway, New York, an eclectic but constrained composition of Italianate flat arched windows, an attic story arcade of round headed openings, and a steep mansard roof with dormers.

A decade later in the enlarged front for the New York Stock Exchange (1880–1882), Renwick adapted one of the chief advantages of cast-iron architecture, an abundance of light provided by the great expanse of windows, to the then popular neoclassical monumentality associated with the Beaux-Arts. He accomplished this by encasing the large openings in a white marble framework encrusted with Renaissance ornament and crowning this frontispiece with an elegant pyramidal roof.

Another instance in which he chose to blend two traditions was for the restoration, reconstruction, and enlargement of the Roman Catholic Cathedral of Saint Augustine (1887–1888) in Florida. Renwick was vacationing in that resort when fire destroyed all but the exterior coquina walls of the late eighteenth-century Mission style church. As part of the rebuilding program, it was decided to increase the seating capacity and simultaneously "perfect the proportions" by adding transepts and a larger chancel. In a further effort to make this modest cathedral more prepossessing, a six-story freestanding bell tower was built at the side, cast in place of Portland cement mixed with coquina shell which was also used to stucco the extension. Renwick chose to model the new tower not on the Mission style of the church but on its unusual (but supposedly original) formal Georgian entrance.

During his long career, Renwick is reported to have designed many expensive city and country houses. Comparatively few, however, have been identified and for those, generally only fragmentary information has been found. (Renwick's private and professional papers were destroyed or scattered, making even the identification of the less publicized designs extremely difficult.) Judging by those that are known, his residential designs were highly individualized, varying according to each client's personal preferences and needs.

Two Gothic Revival country houses, though in the same style and of approximately the same date, expressed very divergent ways of life. *Martinstow* (1851) in West Haven, Connecticut was the home of Peter Ames, a wealthy descendant of early settlers. The exterior of this picturesque board and batten cottage was enlivened by triangular dormer windows, medieval trimmings cut out of wood, and small diamond-shaped window panes. By contrast, the pretentious 157-foot long stuccoed Longstreet Castle (1852–1854) ws designed for a Syracuse clothier, presumably modeled on the ancestral home of his English wife and reported to have cost several hundred thousand dollars. The medievalized interior of plaster vaults and cornices, heavily carved woodwork, marble mantelpieces, and stained glass closely resembled that of the rectory of Grace Church (1847). Among the many other buildings on the huge estate were a similarly castellated stable and another structure built solely for a ten-pin bowling alley.

"French Gothic" was the way Renwick described *Greyston* (1863–1864?), the stone cottage of his perennial client, William E. Dodge, overlooking the Hudson in Riverdale, New York. The cottage was asymmetrical with pointed arches in the long, rustic piazza and in the doors and windows, and the only French note was the mansard roof punctuated by decorative gables and the odd triangular dormer windows he had previously used in the Ames cottage. Of unquestionably French derivation, the Second Empire *Winyah Park* (1865) in New Rochelle, just north of New York City, was the residence of Richard Lathers, a client with a passionate interest in architecture whose earlier Italianate villa was by ALEXANDER JACKSON DAVIS. According to the surviving views, it had all the accoutrements of the French style including a towering pavilion above the mansard roof and a comparably elegant interior decor.

None of Renwick's residential commissions received greater personal attention than two houses for his close friends, Almy and Frederic Gallatin. They had selected East Hampton on Long Island's south shore as a summer residence, a resort without the rigid social protocol of Newport or Tuxedo Park. Renwick's design was similarly unpretentious. Modest in size and almost square, the frame cottage (1877?–1878) was the typical amalgam of various historic forms, some of which were associated with the Gallatins' heritage. Among these, the clearly expressed structural system and the pointed vertical boarding were representative of the chalet, possibly a reference to the husband's Swiss ancestry, while the mansard with its delicate crest rail and conical turret may have alluded to the wife's French Goelet forebears. Similarly, there was nothing startling about their spacious brownstone townhouse (1881–1883) on the southwest corner of Fifth Avenue and Fifty-third Street, a staid Italianate composition, particularly when compared to the neighboring marble replicas of French châteaux.

Joseph Sands died in 1880 but it was not until 1883 that Renwick promoted his wife's distant cousin, JAMES LAWRENCE ASPINWALL, and William H. Russell to partnerships in the firm. Although this enabled the sixty-five-year old Renwick to spend more time enjoying his favorite leisure activities—fishing, sailing, and accumulating additional paintings and decorative objects (particularly those of Chinese or Japanese origin) on his frequent travels—he continued to be actively involved in his practice until virtually the end of his life.

As late as 1890, Renwick embarked on the most grandiose scheme of his long career, the proposed National Gallery of History and Art in Washington. The idea was conceived by Franklin Webster Smith, an amateur architect and enthusiastic advocate of reinforced concrete construction, and Renwick's firm spent six months preparing the original designs. Basically an outdoor museum on sixty to seventy acres (an area near the Washington Monument was recommended), it would have as its focal point a replica of the Parthenon, one-and-a-half times the size of the original, crowning the summit and flanked by two smaller temples. Beneath, at gradually descending levels, stretched a *via sacra* lined with statues of the "great and good" and spanned by the memorial "Lincoln Arch." On either side, long narrow galleries enclosed vast courtyards. Each section depicted through its architecture and contents a major era in the history of civilization; the courtyards contained full-size, furnished replicas of such monuments as, for example, the Taj Mahal. All of the construction was to be of reinforced concrete. Although never built, this monumental Beaux-Arts classical arrangement was revolutionary, a forerunner of the first completed American example of that form, the 1893 World's Columbian Exposition in Chicago. Thus at seventy-two, Renwick continued to have the determination and the physical and mental energy to seek fresh challenges and to explore new solutions, qualities that characterized his entire career.

SELMA RATTNER

WORKS

*1843, Bowling Green Fountain; 1843–1846, Grace Church; 1846–1847, Calvary Church; *1846–1847, Church of the Puritans; 1847, Grace Church (rectory); *1847–1849, Free Academy; New York. 1847–1855, Smithsonian Institution, Washington. *1848–1849, South Dutch Church; *1849–1851, James Renwick, Sr., House; New York. *1849?–1851, Second Presbyterian Church, Chicago. *1850–1851, Clarendon Hotel, New York. *1850–1851, Trinity Church, Washington. 1851, *Martinstow* (Ames House), West Haven, Conn. 1851?–1852, Saint Denis Hotel; *1852, LaFarge House (burned 1854; rebuilt 1854–1856); New York. *1852–1854, Longstreet Castle, Syracuse, N.Y. *1853–1854, Cruger Mansion; 1853–1854, Saint Stephen's Church; 1853–1856?, Smallpox Hospital; New York. *1854–1855, Clinton Avenue Congregational Church, Brooklyn, N.Y. *1855, Rowhouses, 37–41 West 9 Street; *1855–1856, Bank of the State of New York; 1858–1861, Island Hospital; 1858–1879, Saint Patrick's Cathedral; *1859–1862, Albermarle Hotel; New York. 1859–1871, Corcoran Gallery (work stopped from 1861–1870), Washington. 1861–1865, Vassar College, Poughkeepsie, N.Y. 1863–1864?, *Greyston* (Dodge House), Riverdale, N.Y. *1863–1865, Church of the Covenant, New York. *1865, *Winyah Park* (Lathers House), New Rochelle, N.Y. *1867–1869, Booth's Theater; *1867–1869, Foundling Hospital; New York. *1867–1869, Saint Ann's Church, Brooklyn, N.Y. 1868?–1869, Irvington Presbyterian Church, N.Y. *1868–1869, Young Men's Christian Association Building; *1869, Northwestern Dispensary; *1869–1870, Daniel Willis James House; *1869–1871, New York City Hospital for the Insane; *1870–1871, Appleton Building; *1871–1872, Saint Bartholomew's Church; New York. 1871–1874, Second Presbyterian Church, Chicago. *1877?–1878, Gallatin House, East Hampton, N.Y. 1880–1882, Archbishop's House (Catholic); *1880–1882, Stock Exchange (enlargement); *1881–1882, Gallatin House; 1882–1883, Saint Patrick's Cathedral (rectory); 1882–1893, All Saints' Church; 1885–1888, Saint Patrick's Cathedral (spires); *1886–1887, Protestant Episcopal Diocesan House; New York. 1887–1888, Cathedral of Saint Augustine (enlargement), Fla. 1887–1888, Warehouse, 808 Broadway, New York.

BIBLIOGRAPHY

CANTOR, JAY E. 1971 "The Public Architecture of James Renwick, Jr." Unpublished M.A. Thesis, University of Delaware, Newark.

HAMLIN, TALBOT F. (1935)1943 "James Renwick." Volume 15, pages 507–508 in *Dictionary of American Biography.* Edited by Dumas Malone. Reprint. New York: Scribner.

HUMPHREY, EFFINGHAM 1942 "The Churches of James Renwick, Jr." Unpublished M.A. Thesis, New York University.

McKENNA, ROSALIE THORNE 1949 "A Study of the Architecture of the Main Building and the Landscape of Vassar College, 1860–1970." Unpublished M.A. Thesis, Vassar College, Poughkeepsie, N.Y.

McKENNA, ROSALIE THORNE 1951 "James Renwick, Jr. and the Second Empire Style in the United States." *Magazine of Art* 44:97–101.

PIERSON, WILLIAM H., JR. 1978 *American Buildings and their Architects: Technology and the Picturesque, the Corporate and the Early Gothic Styles.* Garden City, N.Y.: Doubleday.

RATTNER, SELMA 1969 "Renwick's Design for Grace Church: Religious Doctrine and the Gothic Revival." Unpublished M.A. Thesis, Columbia University, New York.

RATTNER, SELMA 1972 "Renwick's Church for

Blacks." *Historic Preservation* 24:32–35.
RATTNER, SELMA n.d. *James Renwick, Architect: Establishment and Innovation.* Manuscript in preparation.

REPTON, HUMPHRY

From 1788 until his death, Humphry Repton (1752–1818) came to be regarded as the foremost exponent of English landscape gardening, a position to which there had been no serious claimant since the death of CAPABILITY BROWN in 1783. Unlike his predecessor, Repton had no early training in the practical aspects of this art, having been intended for a mercantile career. The eldest of eleven children, he was born in Bury-St.-Edmunds where his father was a Collector of Excise. The family later moved to Norwich where he attended the Grammar School until he was twelve when it was decided that he should be sent to Holland to learn the language, Norwich having strong trade links with that country. Returning shortly before his sixteenth birthday, he joined a textile firm but found the work uncongenial and consoled himself by devoting his spare time to literature, music, and sketching in which he showed a particular talent. When he was eighteen, he became engaged to Mary Clarke but was not allowed to marry her until he came of age in 1773. A son was born in 1775, the first of sixteen children of whom only seven were to survive infancy.

The death of Repton's father in 1775 brought him a legacy sufficient to free him from business employment, and three years later he purchased a small property at Sustead near Aylsham. Here for some years he was able to enjoy the life of a country gentleman of modest means and made the acquaintance of two influential owners of nearby estates. One was Robert Marsham of Stratton Strawless from whom he learned much about husbandry and agriculture. The other was William Windham of Felbrigg, a friend of Dr. Johnson and Edmund Burke, and a distinguished statesman. Windham made his extensive library available to Repton and took him to Ireland as his secretary for some months when holding an official appointment under Lord Northington in 1783. Repton had by this time produced a number of local views which were used to illustrate a volume of Blomefield's *History of Norfolk,* but failing investments and a rapidly increasing family brought a financial crisis in 1784 and he was forced to sell his "little earthly paradise." Moving his family to a cottage near Romford in Essex, he spent the next four years producing a small volume of essays entitled *Variety,* a number of art criticisms, and a *catalogue raisonnée* for Boydell's Shakespeare Gallery.

So far, garden design had not seriously occupied Repton's attention, although he had visited a number of works by Brown and WILLIAM KENT and had expressed an admiration for them. The idea that he himself should adopt the laying out of parks and gardens as a profession came to him one night in the summer of 1788, and having familiarized himself with printed works on the subject by such authors as William Gilpin and Thomas Whately, he approached a number of friends to whom he thought his advice might be of use. An encouraging response began in September with a commission from Jeremiah Ives of Catton near Norwich. Early in 1789, he was at work on designs for Brandesbury and Sheffield Park (1791), and by the end of that year he had established the reputation which he was to hold for nearly three decades.

In general, Repton's schemes followed Brown's principles although he elaborated them with thicker plantations and a wider variety of trees as these became increasingly available from abroad. He also began to introduce an element of formality around the house by way of balustraded terraces and steps, as well as conservatories (more elaborate and decorative than the older hothouses), and "winter corridors" for exercise in bad weather. A number of his commissions were for the introduction of new features within grounds originally laid out by Brown, as at Holkham (1789), Corsham (1796–1800), and Longleat (1803), and in cases where he alone was concerned with the landscaping, the area involved was rarely as extensive as in his predecessor's undertakings. A measure of Repton's success was undoubtedly due to his skill as an artist. He would present his clients with proposals set out in small leather-bound volumes, the copper-plate text being illustrated by watercolors of "before" and "after" views. Of the so-called Red Books he claimed to have prepared more than four hundred, although less than half are documented and fewer have survived.

A drawback which Repton encountered at the outset was his lack of architectural training. Some of his commissions involved external improvement to an existing house or proposals for a new one, and although from 1800 his two sons, JOHN REPTON and GEORGE REPTON, had finished their training and were able to assist him, he was at first dependent on the help of such friends as WILLIAM WILKINS or JAMES WYATT and SAMUEL WYATT, whose names feature in the Red Books for Northrepps, Bracondale, Little Green, Tatton, and Garnons. In 1795, however, Repton became acquainted with JOHN NASH, a rising architect who saw in Repton's ever growing clientele chances for his own participation. It was agreed that Repton should recommend Nash where architectural ad-

Repton.
Wentworth Woodhouse (landscaping).
Yorkshire, England.
1790

vice was involved, and that the latter should pay him $2\frac{1}{2}$ percent on the cost of work carried out. The arrangement began with alterations to the house and grounds at Corsham, but although it continued for about five years and saw such successful creations as Southgate Grove, Sundridge Park, and Luscombe, Repton was soon to find that Nash was an unsatisfactory partner and that he was exploiting Repton's eldest son who had gone to work in Nash's office as a draftsman. In spite of the ensuing rift, there is no doubt as to the influence of Repton's landscaping theories on Nash's subsequent work, notably in the conception of Regent's Park, Blaise Hamlet, and the alterations in Saint James's Park.

During the same period, Repton was drawn into controversy with two authors with whom he had previously been on friendly terms. In 1794, the publication of RICHARD PAYNE KNIGHT's didactic poem *The Landscape* coincided with that of UVEDALE PRICE's *Essay on the Picturesque.* Both upheld the artistic superiority of wild and rugged scenery over the smooth serenity of landscapes by Brown and his followers, including those of Repton, whose Red Book for Tatton Park was singled out for ridicule in a footnote by Knight. As Repton was on the point of publishing the first of his own books on garden design, he was able to insert a note in defense of himself and his predecessor. The incident, however, generated considerable heat, and argument for and against the picturesque movement was to continue among the cognoscenti for several years.

Repton.
Drawing of Woburn Abbey from Fragments on the Theory and Practice of Landscape Gardening.
1818

The book which Repton published early in 1795 under the title of *Sketches and Hints on Landscape Gardening* was followed by *Observations on Landscape Gardening* in 1803 and a short essay entitled *An Inquiry into the Changes of Taste* in 1806. His designs for orientalizing the Brighton Pavilion, prepared for the Prince of Wales in 1806, but thwarted by the machinations of John Nash, were published two years later, and his last printed work, *Fragments on the Theory and Practice of Landscape Gardening,* was prepared with the help of his son John in 1818. The text of the garden books relied heavily on quotations from his various Red Books, and the illustrations were from his own drawings. The original volumes are now rare, but in 1840 John Claudius Loudon published an edition containing these books together with the essay on *Changes of Taste* and the Brighton Pavilion designs. This collected edition was prefaced by a *Biographical Notice* signed "A. B.," and doubtless written by a member of the Repton family basing the facts on a *Memoir* by Humphry himself, the manuscript of a small portion of which has recently passed through a London sale-room.

In January 1811, Repton was seriously injured in a carriage accident from which he only partially recovered. He and his wife continued to live in the Hare Street cottage, and in time he was able to resume a limited amount of work with the help of his son John. To this period belong the highly successful new house and landscaped surroundings of Sheringham Bower (1812–1819) and the alterations to the gardens at Ashridge (c.1814) where the introduction of a Monk's Garden, Rosarium, and American Garden are evidence of the desire in his later works to enliven the grounds near a house with specialized areas.

A good deal of time from 1814 on was given to the preparation of his last book, the *Fragments,* in which he recognized that landscape gardening on the grand scale was on the decline. Social change and the advent of the industrial revolution had already seen the breaking up of many estates and a new type of owner who, as he remarked sadly, "gives up beauty to gain, and prospect for the produce of his acres." Repton also found time to write a number of short poems and to make sketches dedicated to various friends. Of these, several are preserved in a portfolio now in the Avery Library, Columbia University, New York. He died suddenly from a seizure on 24 March, 1818, and was taken to Aylsham in Norfolk for burial in a family grave adjoining the south wall of Saint Michael's Church.

DOROTHY STROUD

WORKS

1788, Catton (landscaping), Norfolk, England. *1789, Brandesbury (landscaping), Middlesex, England. 1789, Holkham (landscaping), Norfolk, England. 1789–1803, Welbeck (landscaping), Nottinghamshire, England. 1790, Bulstrode (landscaping), Buckinghamshire, England. 1790, Wentworth Woodhouse (landscaping), Yorkshire, England. 1791, Sheffield Park (landscaping), Sussex, England. *1791, Thoresby (landscaping), Nottinghamshire, England. 1795, Burley-on-the-Hill (landscaping), Leicestershire, England. 1796–1800, Corsham (landscaping), Wiltshire, England. 1797, Southgate Grove (landscaping), London. 1798, Attingham (landscaping), Shropshire, England. 1799, Luscombe (landscaping), Devonshire, England. 1799, Panshanger (landscaping), Hertfordshire, England. 1800, West Wycombe Park (landscaping), Buckinghamshire, England. 1802, Brentry House (and landscaping), Avon, England. 1803, Longleat (landscaping), Wiltshire, England. 1803–1807, Stanage (landscaping and alterations to house), Norfolk, England. 1805–1813, Uppark (landscaping and alterations to house), Sussex, England. 1810, Endsleigh (landscaping), Devonshire, England. c.1810, Apsley Wood Lodge (small house and garden), Bedfordshire, England. 1812–1819, Sheringham Bower (house and landscaping), Norfolk, England. c.1814, Ashridge (landscaping), Hertfordshire, England. n.d., Catton (landscaping, for James Ives) near Norwich, England.

BIBLIOGRAPHY

LOUDON, J. C. (editor) 1840 *The Landscape Gardening and Landscape Architecture of the Late Humphry Repton, Esq.* London.

KETTON-CREMER, ROBERT WYNDHAM 1948 *A Norfolk Gallery.* London: Faber.

HUSSEY, C. 1967 *The Picturesque.* London: Cass; Hamden, Conn.: Archon.

KNIGHT, RICHARD PAYNE 1794 *The Landscape.* London: Bulmer.

MALINS, EDWARD 1966 *English Landscaping and Literature.* London: Oxford University Press.

PRICE, UVEDALE 1794 *Essay on the Picturesque.* London: Robson.

REPTON, HUMPHREY 1795 *Sketches and Hints on Landscape Gardening.* London: Bulmer.

REPTON, HUMPHRY 1803 *Observations on the Theory and Practice of Landscape Gardening.* London: Bensley.

REPTON, HUMPHRY 1818 *Fragments on the Theory and Practice of Landscape Gardening.* London: Bensley.

STROUD, DOROTHY 1962 *Humphry Repton.* London: Country Life.

REPTON and REPTON

The first and fourth sons of HUMPHRY REPTON, John Adey Repton (1775–1860) and George Stanley Repton (1786–1858) each contributed to the family practice, for example, in 1806 collaborating on a design for Brighton Pavilion. John was the more active, assisting his father from 1802 and especially after the father suffered a severe carriage accident in 1811. He trained with William Wilkins Senior who encouraged his antiquarian interests; together, they undertook a detailed study of Norwich Cathedral (1798–1800). From 1796 to 1802, he worked for JOHN NASH, with whom George was to train. Later, George Repton and Nash remodeled the Royal Opera House, Haymarket, London (1816–1818). Both exhibited at the Royal Academy, John between 1798 and 1804, and George from 1801. Stylistically, their respective tastes lay chiefly with the Elizabethan and Picturesque Tudor. In 1817, George married the daughter of Lord Chancellor Eldon, and around 1820, he established an independent country house practice, adopting a Palladian (see ANDREA PALLADIO) style. Besides his English architecture and landscaping, John improved estates in Holland and Germany. He became a supporter of the Cambridge Camden Society, as reflected in his last major commission, Holy Trinity, Springfield, Essex (1842–1843).

R. WINDSOR LISCOMBE

WORKS

JOHN ADEY REPTON

*1797–1798, Corsham Court (alterations; with John Nash), Wiltshire, England. 1802?, Brenty Hill (with Humphry Repton), Gloucestershire, England. *1809–1811, Harleston House (remodeling; with Humphry Repton), Northamptonshire, England. 1813–1819, Sheringham Hall (with Humphry Repton), Norfolk, England. 1813?–1831, Cobham Hall (remodeling; with Humphry Repton), Kent, England. 1817–1819, Bourn Hall (reconstruction; with Humphry Repton), Cambridgeshire, England. 1830–1835, Buckhurst Park (remodeling), Sussex, England. 1842–1843, Holy Trinity, Springfield, Essex, England.

GEORGE STANLEY REPTON

*1816–1818, Royal Opera House (remodeling; with John Nash), Haymarket; *1819–1820, Saint Philip's

Chapel, Regent's Street; London. 1820, Assembly Rooms, Aberystwyth, Dyfed, Wales. *1822, Sandgate Chapel, Kent, England. 1826–1827, Follaton House (renovation; now Council Offices), near Totnes, Devonshire, England. 1828–1829, Wolterton Hall (additions), Norfolk, England. 1830, Dumbleton Hall, near Evesham, Gloucestershire, England. 1832–1841, Winchester College (major additions), Hampshire, England. 1833, Kingston Chapel, near Corfe, Dorset, England. 1838–1840, Camerton Court, Somerset, England. 1842, Chipping Norton Town Hall, Oxfordshire, England.

BIBLIOGRAPHY

BRITTON, JOHN, and PUGIN, AUGUSTUS CHARLES 1825 Volume 1, pages 72–79, 102–106 in *Illustrations of the Public Buildings of London.* London: B. Taylor.

CONNER, PATRICK 1978 "Unexecuted Designs for the Royal Pavilion at Brighton." *Apollo* 106:192–199.

CRAIGER, J. E. L. 1969 "The Pump House on Cobham Hall Estate." *Archaeologia Cantiana* 84:161–174.

HARRIS, JOHN 1971 Pages 149, 171, 176, 178 in *A Catalogue of British Drawings for Architecture, Decoration, Sculpture and Landscape Gardening in American Collections 1550–1900.* Upper Saddle River, N.J.: Gregg.

HUSSEY, CHRISTOPHER 1958 Pages 168–174 in *English Country Houses: Late Georgian.* London: Country Life.

ISHAM, GYLES 1969 "Laxton Hall." *Northamptonshire Antiquarian Society* 66:18–21.

LEVER, JILL ET AL. 1976 Pages 114–121 in *Catalogue of the Drawings Collection of the Royal Institute of British Architects. O–R.* Farnborough, England: Gregg.

LISCOMBE, R. WINDSOR 1980 Pages 15, 16, 84, 87 in *William Wilkins 1778–1839.* Cambridge University Press.

NARES, GORDON 1957 "Wolterton Hall, Norfolk." *Country Life* 122:116–119, 166–169.

PIERCE, S. ROLAND 1965 *Norwich Cathedral at the End of the Eighteenth Century.* Farnborough, England: Gregg.

REPTON, HUMPHRY, and ADEY, JOHN 1816 *Fragments on the Theory and Practice of Landscape Gardening.* London: Taylor.

REPTON, HUMPHRY; STANLEY, GEORGE; and ADEY, JOHN 1808 *Designs for the Pavilion at Brighton.* London: Stadler.

STROUD, DOROTHY 1962 *Humphry Repton.* London: Country Life.

SUMMERSON, JOHN 1938 "A Repton Portfolio." *Journal of the Royal Institute of British Architects* Series 3 40:313–324.

SUMMERSON, JOHN 1980 Pages 35, 40, 41, 51, 54–55, 57, 88, 111, 140, 149 in *The Life and Work of John Nash: Architect.* Cambridge, Mass.: M.I.T. Press.

TEMPLE, NIGEL 1976 "In search of the Picturesque." *Architectural Review* 160:96–100.

WARD, J.D.U. 1948 "Landscape comes to Oxford." *Architectural Review.* 103:189–190.

REPULLES I VARGAS, ENRIQUE

Enrique Repulles i Vargas (1845–1922) was a turn-of-the-century Spanish eclectic architect. Born in Avila, he received his architectural degree in Madrid in 1869. His career was not notable until 1885 when he won a competition for the Madrid Stock Exchange (1885–1893). Henceforth, he dedicated himself to monumental architecture. His project for the Gothic Revival Basílica Teresiana in Alba de Tormes, Spain (unfinished), won a silver medal at the Exposition Universelle in Paris in 1900. Repulles i Vargas also restored a number of buildings in the neomedieval style. He was known as an architectural critic and entered the Academy of San Fernando in Madrid in 1896.

ELIZABETH A. T. SMITH

WORKS

1879, Church of Hortaleza, Spain. 1885–1893, Stock Exchange; 1894, Plaza de la Armería (completion); Madrid. 1898, Basílica Teresiana (unfinished), Alba de Tormes, Spain. 1898, Casa Consistorial, Valladolid, Spain. 1906, Santa Cristina; 1907–1909, Convent of La Divina Pastora, Madrid. 1908, City Hall, Valladolid, Spain. 1910, Oratorio del Olivar; n.d., Paseo de Rosales; n.d., San Ginés; n.d., San Jerónimo (restoration); Madrid. n.d., San Vicente (restoration); Avila, Spain. n.d., Old and New Salamanca Cathedrals (restoration), Spain. n.d., Toledo Cathedral (restoration), Spain.

BIBLIOGRAPHY

GAYA NUÑO, J. A. 1966 *Arte del siglo XIX.* Madrid: Editorial Plus-Ultra.

NAVASCUES PALACIO, PEDRO 1973 *Arquitectura y arquitectos madrileños del siglo XIX.* Madrid: Instituto de Estudios Madrileños.

NAVASCUES PALACIO, PEDRO 1971 "El problema del eclecticismo en la arquitectura española del siglo XIX." *Revista de las Ideas Estéticas* 114:23–37.

REPULLES I VARGAS, ENRIQUE 1900 *Proyecto de Basílica de Santa Teresa de Jesús en Alba de Tormes.* Salamanca, Spain: Calatrava.

REVELEY, HENRY WILLEY

Born in England, Henry Willey Reveley (1788–1875) was educated in Italy, where his family had moved. He graduated as an engineer from Pisa University. He returned to England in 1822, and after further study was appointed civil engineer at Cape Town in 1826. Several years later, he joined an expedition to Swan River Colony, Western Australia, as civil engineer, where he was responsible for many public buildings. In 1838, he returned to England, where he lectured and wrote without resuming his practice.

JOHN WHITE

WORKS

1827, Saint Andrew's Presbyterian Church, Cape Town. 1830, Colonial Jail (The "Round House"), Fremantle, Western Australia. *1835, Commissariat Store; 1837, Courthouse; *1839, Public Offices; Perth, Western Australia.

BIBLIOGRAPHY

LEWCOCK, RONALD 1963 *Early Nineteenth Century Architecture in South Africa.* Cape Town: Balkema.

WHITE, J. G. 1976 "Henry Reveley: Architect and Engineer." *Journal of the Royal Western Australian Historical Society* 8, no. 8:24–42.

Revell. Tornitaso Apartment Houses. Tapiola, Finland. 1960

REVELL, VILJO

The strong, independent architectural rationalism of Viljo Gabriel Revell (1910–1964) introduced many international ideas to his native Finland as he developed systematized yet expressive forms for residential, industrial, and commercial structures. Revell was born in Vaasa, a coastal town in western Finland. He was educated at the University of Technology in Helsinki (1928–1936), and he practiced in Helsinki for the rest of his life.

Revell was part of the first generation of Finnish architects to be inculcated with the ideals of functionalism, and the multipurpose Glass Palace, Helsinki (1935), built while Revell, Niilo Kokko, and Heims Riihimäki (partners, 1934–1936) were still students, embodied new spatial and constructive tendencies. In 1936 and 1937, Revell and AARNE ERVI assisted ALVAR AALTO in the design of the Finnish Pavilion for the Paris Exposition (1937). However, Revell's subsequent work reflected more the international tendencies toward simplicity and reduction of detail than did Aalto's highly individual later buildings.

Revell served as director of the Reconstruction Office (later the Finnish Standards Committee), founded by the Finnish Association of Architects in 1942. Research work there deepened his concern for the standardization of building systems and the problems of prefabricated construction. When he resigned in 1949 to devote himself to his architectural practice, many new opportunities for construction had arisen. Revell frequently entered competitions, and he won more than fifteen prizes after that for the Teollisuuskeskus Building in Helsinki, the first large postwar Finnish commercial structure, in 1948.

The search for new techniques and materials led Revell not only to the industrial modernism of the Teollisuuskeskus Building's strip windows and cylindrical columns, but also to the use of industrialized construction components. The Mäntyviita-Sufika residential buildings in Tapiola (1954) were among the earliest Finnish attempts at prefabricated wood-frame housing, while the rectilinear Hyvon-Kudeneule Factory (1954–1955) employed precast, prestressed beams and roof slabs and prefabricated insulated wall panels. Revell had developed an aesthetic of serial repetition in the sinuous *Blue Ribbon* housing project (1952), and even the Kärjensivu Rowhouses (1954–1955) suggest indefinite replication, with limited dwelling spaces compensated by varying views into the natural landscape.

Meticulous detailing and taut proportions characterize the Didrichsen Villa (1957–1958) and the Kaskenkaatajantie Apartments, Tapiola (1959). Nevertheless, the splayed angles and curvilinear rooftop elements of the Tornitaso Apartments (1960) which accent the skyline of Tapiola and the paraboloid roof of the Funeral Chapel, Tampere (1961), show Revell's response to contemporary international trends toward free forms. It is in the Toronto City Hall (1961–1965), based on a competition entry with Heikki Castrén, Bengt Lundsten, and Seppo Valjus (1958), that Revell's talent for representative monumentality is most evident. Despite the introduction during later design development of columnar supports and ambiguous details, the building's concave towers and circular Council Chamber convey a powerful imagery based on progressive technology.

Revell's office was a training ground for many

of Finland's gifted architects, and assistants were always involved in Revell's projects from the start, working independently while responding to his criticism. This collaborative working method ensured continuity after Revell's death, and the successor firm of Castrén, Jauhiainen, Nuuttila grew to be the largest architectural office in Finland. Their expertise in office-block design stemmed in part from Revell's own late commercial projects.

THOMAS G. BEDDALL

WORKS

1935, Glass Palace (with Niilo Kokko and Heimo Riihimäki); 1951–1952, Teollisuuskeskus Building (with Keijo Patäjä); Helsinki. 1954, Mäntyviita-Sufika Housing, Tapiola, Finland. 1954–1955, Hyvon-Kudeneule Knitwear Factory (with Osmo Lappo); Hanko, Finland. 1954–1955, Kärjensivu Rowhouses; 1957–1958, Didrichsen Villa; Helsinki. 1959, Kaskenkaatajantie Apartment Houses; 1960, Tornitaso Apartment Houses; Tapiola, Finland. 1960–1961, Garrison Annex (with Heikki Castrén), Guards' Barracks, Helsinki. 1960–1962, Commercial Center, Vaasa, Finland. 1961, Vatiala Funeral Chapel, Tampere, Finland. 1961–1965, City Hall (with John B. Parkin Associates), Toronto. 1962–1963, KOP Bank Building, Turku, Finland.

BIBLIOGRAPHY

ÅLANDER, KYÖSTI (editor) 1966 *Viljo Revell: Works and Projects.* New York: Praeger.

GUSTAVS, ERLAND 1974 "The Revell Legacy." *Canadian Architect* 19, no. 6:30–36.

HERTZEN, HEIKKI VON, and SPREIREGEN, PAUL D. (1971)1973 *Building a New Town: Finland's New Garden City, Tapiola.* 2d ed., rev. Cambridge, Mass.: M.I.T. Press.

"Neues Rathaus in Toronto." 1966 *Bauen und Wohnen* 20, no. 8:287–293.

"Projet pour l'Hôtel de Ville de Toronto, Canada." 1962 *L'Architecture d'aujourd'hui* 33, no. 100:54–59.

"Toronto City Hall and Civic Square, Ontario." 1965 *Canadian Architect* 10, no. 10:44–68.

"Toronto City Hall: Civic Design." 1965 *Journal of the Royal Architectural Institute of Canada* 42, no. 9:37–58.

"Zentrumsgebäude in Helsinki." 1968 *Werk* 55, no. 4:224–228.

REVETT, NICHOLAS

Nicholas Revett (1720–1804) was born in Brandeston, Suffolk. When studying painting in Rome in about 1742, he met JAMES STUART. Supported by the Society of Dilettanti, he and Stuart were in Athens from then until 1753, measuring and drawing buildings for *The Antiquities of Athens* (1762). From 1764 to 1766, Revett took part in an expedition financed by the Society of Dilettanti, published as *The Antiquities of Ionia* (1769–1797). His small architectural practice was closely dependent on classical models. Through his publications and his connections with the Society of Dilettanti rather than as an architect, he was an important influence in the development of the English neoclassical style.

LESLEY LEWIS

WORKS

c.1766, Standlynch (now Trafalgar House; portico and some interior decoration), Wiltshire, England. 1770–1771, West Wycombe Park (west portico), Buckinghamshire, England. 1778, Church of Ayot Saint Lawrence, Hertfordshire, England. 1778–1780, West Wycombe Park (Round Temple and *Temple of Flora), Buckinghamshire, England.

BIBLIOGRAPHY

CROOK, J. MORDAUNT 1972 *The Greek Revival: Neo-Classical Attitudes in British Architecture, 1760–1870.* London: Murray.

JACKSON-STOPS, GERVASE 1978 *West Wycombe Park.* London: National Trust.

LAWRENCE, LEWLEY 1938 "Stuart and Revett: Their Literary and Architectural Careers." *Journal of the Warburg Institute* 2, no. 2:128–146.

STUART, JAMES, and REVETT, NICHOLAS (1762)1968 *The Antiquities of Athens.* Reprint. New York: Arno.

WIEBENSON, DORA 1969 *Sources of Greek Revival Architecture.* London: Zwemmer.

RHIND, DAVID

David Rhind (1808–1883) trained with A. W. N. PUGIN, after which he spent a year in Rome. A fellow student who became a lifelong friend was CHARLES BARRY. Fond of Italianate styles, he set up practice in Edinburgh.

BRUCE WALKER

WORKS

1838, Scott Monument, George Square, Glasgow, Scotland. 1840, Haggs Church, Stirlingshire, Scotland. 1849–1853, Daniel Stewart's College, Edinburgh. 1854–1855, Commercial Bank, 8–16 Gordon Street, Glasgow, Scotland. 1872, Heriot Watt College, Chambers Street, Edinburgh.

BIBLIOGRAPHY

EDINBURGH ARCHITECTURAL ASSOCIATION 1907 *Exhibition Catalog.* Edinburgh Architectural Association.

"The Late Mr. David Rhind." 1883 *The Builder* 44:635.

WALKER, DAVID 1969 "Old Towns Revisited: Era of Banks and Churches." *Country Life* 146:502–504.

RHOIKOS OF SAMOS

Rhoikos of Samos (?–540 B.C.) was architect of the eighth altar of Hera at Samos (c.575 B.C.). A platform 120 feet square supported the altar itself, the whole being remarkable both for its size and for the splendor of its details. The altar was placed on the axis of the Heraion, itself shortly to be rebuilt by Rhoikos and THEODOROS. The new (fourth) Heraion (c.575–550 B.C.) was the first colossal Ionic dipteral temple, having no less than 132 columns altogether. It was the prototype for the colossal temples to follow, although destroyed by fire about fifty years after it was begun.

B. M. BOYLE

WORKS

*c.575 B.C., Eighth altar of Hera; *c.575–550 B.C., Fourth Temple of Hera; Samos, Greece.

BIBLIOGRAPHY

English translations of the ancient texts can be found in the volumes of the Loeb Classical Library series, published by Harvard University Press and Heinemann.

DINSMOOR, WILLIAM B. (1902)1975 *The Architecture of Ancient Greece.* Reprint of 1950 ed. New York: Norton. Originally published with the title *The Architecture of Ancient Greece and Rome.*

LAWRENCE, ARNOLD W. (1957)1975 *Greek Architecture.* Harmondsworth, England: Penguin.

PAUSANIAS, *Graeciae descriptio,* Book 10.38.3.

RICCHINO, FRANCESCO MARIA

Francesco Maria Ricchino (1583–1658) was one of the most imaginative and innovative architects of the early seventeenth century. Born in Milan, he studied first with LORENZO BINAGO, a Barnabite monk and one of the first Milanese architects to break from the strong local tradition of classicism. Binago's designs, particularly San Alessandro in Milan (begun 1602), incorporated a central plan with an extended longitudinal axis. Although in many features Binago was a late Mannerist, his juxtaposition of different-sized domed spaces at San Alessandro was a precedent for the style instigated by his talented student. Cardinal Federico Borromeo arranged for Ricchino to complete his education in Rome. In 1603, on his return from Rome, Ricchino proposed plans for the façade of the Cathedral of Milan.

Ricchino designed his first independent building, the Church of San Giuseppe in Milan, in 1607. The structure essentially combines two Greek-cross spaces into a congregational area and a sanctuary. San Giuseppe was an emancipation from the existing academic mode, a break with tradition relative in importance to CARLO MADERNO's Santa Susanna in Rome. Although construction was completed in 1616, the façade was not finished until 1630. Ricchino attempted to arrange a unity between the façade and the interior but he could not maintain the proper relationship and ostensibly created an external decoration. The front of the church is predominantly two aediculae placed one atop the other in geometrical proportion to the height of the body of the church and the octagonal structure of the upper tier. The façade does produce a type of unity, however, and it became exceedingly popular with later baroque architects.

The majority of Ricchino's best designs were done in the 1620s; during this decade, he completed his most unique and influential building, the Collegio Elvetico in Milan (1627). Ricchino was able to solve the disunity of the exterior and the interior by making the center of the façade concave. The concavity is offset with a convex balcony, while a stringcourse and a projecting cornice maintain a rectilinear integration.

When he was appointed to the post of architect to the Cathedral of Milan in 1631, Ricchino received the highest distinction afforded a Milanese architect. In 1651, he returned to the concave façade in the design of the exquisite Palazzo di Brera, originally a Jesuit College; the building is known for its intricate courtyard. Many of Ricchino's later churches have been destroyed but his remaining centrally planned buildings and the creation of the first concave façade of the baroque era serve as a legacy of his achievements. Ricchino left a void that was never filled by high baroque Lombard architects.

JEFFREY HUGHES

WORKS

1607, San Giovanni Battista; 1607–1630, San Giuseppe; 1625, Ospedale Maggiore (central cortile); 1627, Collegio Elvetico; 1631, Palazzo Annoni; 1645–1648, Palazzo Durini; begun 1651, Pallazo di Brera; Milan.

BIBLIOGRAPHY

CATANEO, E. 1957 *Il San Giuseppe del Richini.* Milan.

NORBERG-SCHULZ, CHRISTIAN 1971 *Baroque Architecture.* New York: Abrams.

WITTKOWER, RUDOLF (1958)1973 *Art and Architecture in Italy: 1600 to 1750.* 3d ed., rev. Baltimore: Penguin.

RICCI, LEONARDO

Leonardo Ricci (1918–) was born in Florence, Italy. He studied architecture at the University of

Florence under Giovanni Michelucci and received his degree in 1941. Since 1945, Ricci has taught at the University of Florence, where he became head of the faculty of architecture in 1971.

In partnership with LEONARDO SAVIOLI and G. Gori from 1944 to 1949, Ricci worked on several renewal projects for war-devastated Italy. Since 1949, he has had his own practice and has designed private homes, multiple dwellings, and residential villages. He did the layouts for the Italian Pavilion at *Expo '67* in Montreal.

Ricci's early work draws on the architectural idiom of FRANK LLOYD WRIGHT. His later work, in which interior structures are sculpturally expressed on the exterior and which has an organic quality, has been categorized as International Brutalism. Ricci's social awareness of people's contrasting needs for privacy and communication is often expressed in his buildings where bridgelike structures provide access to cavelike dwelling areas.

ANNA LEE SPIRO

WORKS

1946–1947, Bridge over Arno River (with G. Gori, E. Brizzi, and Leonardo Savioli), Figline, Valdarno, Italy. 1948–1951, Flower and Fruit Market (with E. Gori, G. Gori, Brizzi, and Savioli), Pescia, Italy. 1951–1953, Village (sixteen villas), Monterinaldi, Florence. 1957, Borghese-Mann House, Forte dei Marmi, Italy. 1959, Goti Spinning Factory, Campi Bisenzio; 1962–1974, Montepiano Residential Village; Florence. 1963, Experimental Village, Riesi, Sicily, Italy.

BIBLIOGRAPHY

"Abitazione a Firenze." 1969 *Architecture: Formes et Fonctions* 15:216–219.

"Architettura a Scala Urbana." 1969 *L'Architettura: Cronache e Storia* 17, no.1:24–33.

DEZZI BARDESCHI, MARCO 1973 *Italian Architecture 1965–70.* Florence. Exhibition catalogue.

"The Involved Man: Leonardo Ricci." 1960 *Progressive Architecture* 41:144–151.

"La Nascita di un Villaggio per una Nuova Comunità, in Sicilia." 1963 *Domus* 409:5–13.

RICCI, LEONARDO 1967 "Exploratory Research in Urban Form and the Future of Florence." *Arts and Architecture* 84, no.2:25, 32–34.

RICCI, TIBERIU

Tiberiu Ricci (1913–1979) graduated from the Institute of Architecture in Bucharest in 1938. He taught there from 1944 to 1978. His works stand out for their compositional clarity. He is the author, with others, of a book on architectural acoustics (1972).

CONSTANTIN MARIN MARINESCU

WORKS

1949–1960, Television Center; 1950, Housing Estate May 1, Calea Griviţei; 1956–1957, Concert and Radio System Station; Bucharest.

BIBLIOGRAPHY

IONESCU, GRIGORE 1965 Volume 2 in *Istoria Arhitecturii in Romania.* Bucharest: Editura Academiei Republicii Romaĥe.

IONESCU, GRIGORE 1969 *Arhitectura in Romania: Perioda anilor 1944–1969.* Bucharest: Editura Academiei Republicii Socialiste Romaĥia.

IONESCU, GRIGORE 1972 "Saptezeci si cinci de ani de la infiintarea invatamintului de arhitectura din Romania." *Arhitectura* 20:35–42.

MAMBRIANI, ALBERTO 1969 *L'Architettura Moderna nei Paesi Balcanici.* Bologna, Italy: Capelli.

PATRULIUS, RADU 1973–1974 "Contributii Romanesti in Arhitectura Anilor '30." *Arhitectura* 21, no.6:44–52; 22, no.1:53–59.

RICCI, TIBERIU ET AL. (1972)1974 *Acustica Arhitecturala.* Bucharest: Editura Tehnica.

SASARMAN, GHEORGHE 1972 "Inceputurile gindirii teoretice in arhitectura româneasča (1860–1916)." *Arhitectura* 20, no. 6:44–46.

RICHARDSON, ALBERT E.

Albert E. Richardson (1880–1964) was an important figure in English twentieth-century architecture as an architect, a teacher, and a writer. His influence encouraged the adoption of Beaux-Arts teaching methods and of a stripped neoclassical sytle, although his own tastes moved more and more toward the Georgian.

Born in London, Richardson was articled to Victor Page and was assistant to E. Hellicar and to LEONARD STOKES, but he spent his most significant apprenticeship as assistant to Frank T. Verity, whose work was very French in manner. In 1908, Richardson set up in partnership with his fellow assistant Charles Lovett Gill. In his several important articles in the *Architectural Review* in 1911–1916 and through his magnificent book, *Monumental Classic Architecture* (1914), Richardson promoted a reappraisal of nineteenth-century *neo-grèc,* particularly the work of CHARLES R. COCKERELL and HENRI LABROUSTE. His own buildings of the 1910s and 1920s reflect this source of influence; his early commercial work was Soanian (see JOHN SOANE) in character but it was reduced more and more to a subtle classical grid analogous to the work of AUGUSTE PERRET.

Richardson's domestice practice was usually Georgian in style and he had a profound knowledge of eighteenth century architecture. He was also much involved in the preservation and restoration of historic buildings, particularly in the town of Ampthill, Bedfordshire, which he made his home. Toward the end of his life, working in a hostile and unsympathetic architectural climate, Richardson played the role of the "Last of the Georgians," but his buildings of the 1950s are far from his least. From 1919 until 1946, Richardson was professor at the Bartlett School of Architecture at the University of London, where he was famous for his facility at rapid drawing. He was president of the Royal Academy in 1954–1956.

GAVIN STAMP

WORKS

1907–1911, Regent Street Polytechnic (with Frank Verity); 1910, 10 and 19 Berkeley Street; London. 1912, New Theatre, Manchester, England. 1912–1930, Cottages, Fordington, Dorset, England. 1912–1930, Cottages, Princetown, Dartmoor, Devon, England. 1912–1930, Duchy of Cornwall Estate, England. 1912–1930, Farmhouse, Stoke Climsland, England. 1914–1915, Moorgate Hall; 1922, 65–66 Leadenhall Street; 1923–1949, University College (later additions and alterations by William Wilkins, Gower Street; 1924–1925, Leith House, Gresham Street; 1926–1928, Stone House, Hounsditch and Bishopsgate; London. 1927, Dulverton Town Hall, England. 1930–1931, Saint Margaret's House, Wells Street, London. 1932, Eaton Socon Church (restoration), Bedfordshire, England. 1936–1937, Clifton House, Euston Road, London. 1937, Jockey Club, Newmarket, Suffolk, England. 1939–1941, Holy Cross Church, Greenford, Middlesex, England. 1943, Town Hall, Higham Ferrers, England. 1947–1968, Saint James's Church (restoration), London 1948–1952, Chancellor's Building; 1948–1952, Memorial Building; Christ's College, Cambridge. 1950, Woburn Abbey (alterations), Bedfordshire, England. 1950–1953, Trinity House (restoration and enlargement), Trinity Square; 1952, Saint Alfege's Church (restoration), Greenwich; London. 1954, Assembly Rooms (restoration), Bath, England. 1954–1959, Associated Electrical and Industries Building, Grosvenor Street, London. 1954–1961, Principal's Building; 1954–1961, Wolfson Building; Saint Hilda's College, Oxford. 1956–1959, Bracken House (*Financial Times* Building), Cannon Street, London.

BIBLIOGRAPHY

HOUFE, SIMON 1980 *Sir Albert Richardson.* London: White Crescent Press.

RICHARDSON, ALBERT E. 1914 *Monumental Classic Architecture in Great Britain and Ireland During the Eighteenth and Nineteenth Centuries.* London: Batsford.

RICHARDSON, ALBERT E. 1924 "The Modern Movement in Architecture." *Journal of the Royal Institute of British Architects* Series 3 31:267–274.

RICHARDSON, ALBERT E. 1931 *Georgian England.* London: Batsford.

RICHARDSON, ALBERT E. 1949 *An Introduction to Georgian Architecture.* London: Arts & Technics.

RICHARDSON, ALBERT E. 1951 *Southill: A Regency House.* London: Faber.

RICHARDSON, ALBERT E. 1955 *Robert Mylne, Architect and Engineer, 1733 to 1811.* London: Batsford.

RICHARDSON, ALBERT E., and CORFIATO, HECTOR (1938)1952 *The Art of Architecture.* 3d ed. London: English Universities Press.

RICHARDSON, ALBERT E., and CORFIATO, HECTOR 1948 *Design in Civil Architecture.* London: English Universities Press.

RICHARDSON, ALBERT E., and EBERLEIN, H. D. 1925*a* *The English Inn Past & Present.* London: Batsford.

RICHARDSON, ALBERT E., and EBERLEIN, H. D. 1925*b* *The Smaller English House of the Later Renaissance: 1660–1830.* London: Batsford.

RICHARDSON, ALBERT E., and GILL, C. LOVETT 1911 *London Houses from 1660 to 1820.* London: Batsford.

RICHARDSON, ALBERT E., and GILL, C. LOVETT 1924 *Regional Architecture of the West of England.* London: Benn.

TAYLOR, NICHOLAS 1966 "Sir Albert Richardson—A Classic Case of Edwardianism." *Architectural Review* 140:199–205.

RICHARDSON, CHARLES J.

Charles James Richardson (1809–1871) was born in London and became a pupil of Sir JOHN SOANE. He was notable as a protagonist of the "Jacobethan" Revival. From 1845 to 1852, he was master of the architectural class of the school of design at Somerset House.

Richardson formed a large collection of drawings, 549 of which are now at the Victoria and Albert Museum in London, including drawings by JOHN VANBRUGH, ROBERT ADAM, JOHN THORPE, and CHARLES H. TATHAM. He was surveyor of Lord Hartington's South Kensington Estate and supervised the building of the earl's house in Kensington Palace Gardens (1851–1853).

ROGER DIXON

WORKS

1849–1850, Vintners (enlarged and refronted), Maidstone, Kent, England. 1851–1853, 13 Kensington Palace Gardens (with Edward John Tarver; now the Soviet Embassy); 1856, Jackson Mansions, Queen's Gate, Kensington; London.

BIBLIOGRAPHY

BOLTON, A. R. (editor) 1924 *The Works of Sir John Soane.* London: Sir John Soane's Museum.

"Charles James Richardson." 1892 Volume 7, pages 41–42 in the *Dictionary of Architecture.* London: Richards.

HITCHCOCK, H. R. (1954)1972 *Early Victorian Architecture in Britain.* Reprint. 2 vols. New York: Da Capo.

NEWMAN, JOHN 1969 *West Kent and the Weald.* Harmondsworth, England: Penguin.
RICHARDSON, CHARLES JAMES 1837 *Observations on the Architecture of England During the Reigns of Queen Elizabeth and King James I.* London: Weale.
RICHARDSON, CHARLES JAMES 1841–1848 *Studies from Old English Mansions.* 4 vols. London: McClean.
RICHARDSON, CHARLES JAMES (1848)1852 *Studies of Ornamental Design.* Enlarged ed. London: Weale.
RICHARDSON, CHARLES JAMES 1870 *Picturesque Designs for Mansions, Villas, Lodges, etc.* London: Atchley.
SHEPPARD, F. H. W. (editor) 1973–1976 Volumes 37 and 38 in *Survey of London.* London: Athlone Press, University of London.

RICHARDSON, GEORGE

George Richardson (?–c.1813) embarked on a career of illustrating architectural publications. *New Vitruvius Britannicus* (1802–1808) is noted for documenting contemporary English architecture and for an innovative acquatint technique depicting texture and volume that departed from earlier traditions established by COLEN CAMPBELL, John Woolfe, and JAMES GANDON. Little is known of Richardson's architectural career except that he served as a draftsman and designer for the Adam brothers (see ADAM FAMILY) and was responsible for several decoration and plasterwork designs.

RICHARD LORCH

WORK

1774, Kedleston Hally, Derbyshire, England.

BIBLIOGRAPHY

FLEMING, JOAN 1962 *Robert Adam and His Circle.* Cambridge, Mass.: Harvard University Press.
HARRIS, JOHN (editor) 1971 *A Catalogue of British Drawings for Architecture, Decoration, Sculpture, and Landscape Gardening 1550–1900 in American Collections.* Upper Saddle River, N.J.: Gregg.
RICHARDSON, GEORGE (1774*a*)1968 *A Book of Ceilings, in the Style of Antique Grotesque.* Reprint of 1776 ed. Farnborough, England: Gregg.
RICHARDSON, GEORGE (1774*b*)1798 *Aedes Pembrochianae.* 13th ed. England: Salisbury Press.
RICHARDSON, GEORGE 1778–1779 *Iconology, or a Collection of Emblematical Figures, Moral and Instructive.* London: Scott.
RICHARDSON, GEORGE (1787)1969 *Treatise on the Five Orders of Architecture.* Reprint. Farnborough, England: Gregg.
RICHARDSON, GEORGE 1792 *New Designs in Architecture.* London: The author.
RICHARDSON, GEORGE 1793*a* *Capitals of Columns and Friezes Measured from the Antique.* London: Taylor.
RICHARDSON, GEORGE 1793*b* *New Designs of Vases and Tripods.* London: The author.
RICHARDSON, GEORGE (1794)1795 *Original Designs for Country Seats or Villas.* London: The author.
RICHARDSON, GEORGE (1802–1808)1970 *The New Vitruvius Britannicus.* Reprint. New York: Blom.

RICHARDSON, H. H.

Henry Hobson Richardson (1838–1886) was the most creative and influential American architect of his generation. He was the first in the nineteenth century to develop an uniquely personal style which then became a national style; he was also the first American-born architect to have an influence in Europe. More than any other architect of his time, he was intuitively responsive to those underlying forces that were shaping American life, and he had both the discipline and the imagination to direct those forces into the commanding reality of his buildings. Immense in conception, brilliantly planned, bold and direct in revealed structure, yet provocative in texture and detail, his works are marked by an urgent inner vitality that had no counterpart in the contemporary architecture of either Europe or America.

Richardson was born at the Priestly Plantation in Louisiana. His father, a native of Bermuda, was a cotton merchant in New Orleans; his mother was the granddaughter of the famous British dissenter, scientist, Joseph Priestly. Until he was sixteen, Richardson was educated in a private school in New Orleans. Then, after a year at the University of Louisiana, he went to Harvard College. Sometime during his senior year he decided on architecture as a career, and immediately following his graduation in 1859, his stepfather sent him to Europe to study. After spending the summer in the British Isles, he settled in Paris. Sometime in 1860, he was received into the atelier of Jules-Louis André, and in the fall of the same year, after an earlier unsuccessful attempt, he was admitted to the Ecole des Beaux-Arts. The only American architect to precede Richardson in this distinction was RICHARD MORRIS HUNT. Things went exceedingly well until the outbreak of the Civil War cut off his funds and brought to an end his active participation at the Ecole. Forced to support himself, he went to work for the architect THÉODORE LABROUSTE, the older brother of HENRI LABROUSTE, and later for JACQUES IGNACE HITTORFF. He returned to the United States in the fall of 1865 and settled in New York. Two years later, he formed a limited partnership with Charles Gambrill, in which the two men shared the various functions of an office yet worked independently of one another. In fact, the vast majority of Richardson's commissions came from the New

England area, and in 1874 he moved his family and office to Brookline, Massachusetts, where he practiced for the rest of his life. The partnership with Gambrill was terminated in 1878.

Richardson's disciplined training in France gave him four important attributes: a supreme dedication to architecture; a disciplined and highly professional method of design; a keen awareness of the critical function of planning and its corollary, the three-dimensional geometry of the building itself; and a passion for masonry construction. Stylistically, however, Richardson's mature work reflected neither the theoretical teachings of the Ecole nor the contemporary high style architecture of France. To be sure, a few of his very early designs were executed in the manner of the Second Empire. Typical were his Western Railway Offices (1867–1869) and the Agawam National Bank (1869–1870), both in Springfield, Massachusetts. Actually, however, except for a certain sureness of detail, little distinguishes these buildings from other Second Empire work being done in the United States. In two of his early houses, the Dorsheimer House (1868) in Buffalo, New York, and his own house, Arrochar (1868), on Staten Island, New York, the treatment of the mansard roofs was more American in character than French, and at Arrochar, which was a wooden house, the walls show a considerable influence from the uniquely American Stick style. At the same time, Richardson also experimented with the medieval modes then popular in the United States. His first commission, the Church of the Unity (1866–1869), also in Springfield, was conceived as an English parish church in the Victorian Gothic style as was his Grace Church (1867–1869) in Medford, Massachusetts. His Worcester (Massachusetts) High School (1869–1870), surely his least successful early design, combined a number of high Victorian ingredients.

Richardson made a conscious effort in his early works to understand and use the current architecture of America. Yet, in light of his subsequent development, it is equally clear that among the then popular styles only the Romanesque attracted him. His first major exposition of that style was the Brattle Square Church in Boston (1870–1872). There were, to be sure, scattered Romanesque details in the Worcester High School, especially in its soaring campanile tower, but the Brattle Square Church was the first of Richardson's buildings in which the Romanesque determined the character of the design.

Richardson's preference for the Romanesque was motivated in part by his firsthand knowledge of the Romanesque Revival churches which were under construction in Paris while he was there, such as Saint-Augustin or Saint-Ambroise. But his enthusiasm also had deep roots in his own native architecture. By the time he came on the scene, the United States had already experienced a lively and pervasive Romanesque Revival of its own, and it is altogether possible that this development may have aroused his initial enthusiasm for the style. Yet, it was not the prevailing American version, based on the Romanesque of Lombardy and the Rhineland, that ultimately attracted him but that of central France. He saw in the sturdy churches of Auvergne a strong and deeply organic mode of building in stone which had an extraordinary affinity with his own architectural instincts. Here was an architecture of essences, of unencumbered walls, of bold arches, and piers supporting and enclosing clearly articulated spaces, an architecture that gave him exactly what he needed. Through the sheer force of his imagination he molded this simple but powerful idiom into a style uniquely his own.

The first hints of Richardson's personal style appeared in the Brattle Square Church, the competition for which he won in 1870. Although his design is conspicuously Romanesque, it is generically rather than specifically so, and in its asymmetrical balance as well as its style, its roots are equally found in the varied asymmetrical arrangements then common in American church architecture. But Richardson's treatment of the medieval forms is quintessential: the quarry-faced masonry walls are dominant with muscular arched openings sharply cut and held in the plane of the wall. Ornament is virtually eliminated, except for the crown of the tower, and the simplicity, the largeness, and the structural vitality—hallmarks of Richardson's style—coalesced here for the first time.

A number of demanding commissions followed the Brattle Square Church: the State Hospital in Buffalo, New York (1872–1878), a large-scale project which tested the professional skills which he had acquired at the Ecole des Beaux-Arts; the Hampden County Court House in Springfield, Massachusetts (1871–1873); and the North Congregational Church, also in Springfield (1872–1873). In all these buildings, Richardson experimented further with the elements of the Romanesque, sometimes mixing them with other medieval forms, but always treating them with growing strength and simplicity. Equally important, they were all constructed of rock-faced masonry, a technique which Richardson was to use with great power and expressiveness.

Although Richardson's enthusiasm for stone masonry was first aroused in Paris, his mature realization of its expressive potential was prompted by his own native environment. In the New England

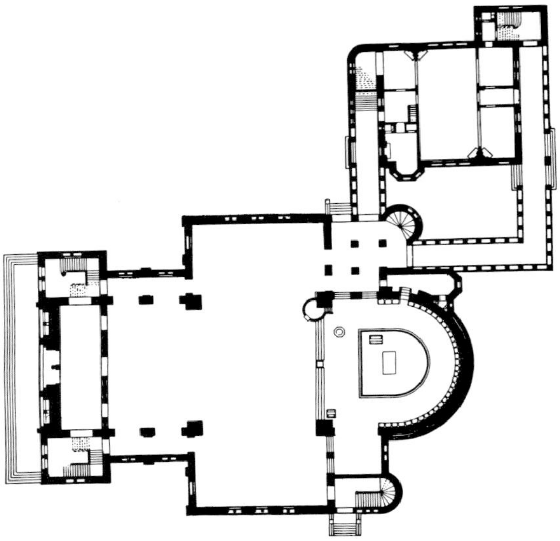

Richardson. Plan of Trinity Church. Boston. 1872–1877

landscape, granite outcroppings and glacial fieldstone fences were commonplace, and this ever present stimulus could not help but intensify his love of stone. More than that, in the Boston area there was already an established tradition for monumental stone construction which began in the austere dressed masonry walls of the neoclassical era and came to a climax in the quarry- and rock-faced polychrome walls of the medieval revivals during the third quarter of the nineteenth century. By the time Richardson arrived in New England, therefore, rough and colorful stone surfaces were everywhere and he was drawn to them like iron to a magnet.

If the Brattle Square Church marked a point of decision in Richardson's career, the enormous opportunity provided by Trinity Church, Boston, opened the floodgates of his creative powers and brought him to national prominence. He won the competition in June 1872, in a field of five other contestants, including Richard Morris Hunt. The original design underwent considerable alteration during the next two years, but by the spring of 1873 the plan of the church had been determined and work was begun on driving the 4,000 piles necessary to support the structure. Full construction did not begin until 1874 after Richardson had moved to Brookline. The church was consecrated in 1877, although the interior decoration was not finished until after 1879, and the chancel in particular was later altered. As intended by Richardson, his successors added a new porch to the west front in the 1890s. At the same time, the crowns of the two balancing west towers were made more elaborate so as to relate them better to the central tower. Except for some internal changes, it is in this condition that the church survives today.

In a manner never before seen in the United States, Richardson's design was based on the Romanesque of central France. The church itself is cruciform with a short nave, transepts, and an apse, all building in a pyramidal mass to a broad central tower, a composition Richardson identified with the churches of Auvergne. Specific Romanesque sources are also apparent; for example, the west façade as finished in Richardson's time was based on that of Saint-Giles-du-Garde in southern France and the great central tower was adopted from a turret of the old cathedral in Salamanca, Spain. In every instance, however, the original motifs were skillfully modified to adopt them to the general scheme, and Richardson was never again quite so overtly eclectic.

Richardson's highly individual use of rock-faced masonry on a monumental scale also matured at Trinity. The warm, slightly pinkish Milford granite is laid in random rectangular ashlar, varying substantially in size, with some of them large enough to suggest the gigantic dimensions so typical of the architect's mature work. Just enough red pigment was mixed with the mortar of the pointing to homogenize the wall and emphasize the variety of surface rather than geometry of the joints, and the whole is enlivened by the contrasting red of the darker Longmeadow stone trim and pattern work. This textural and chromatic liveliness is both enhanced and unified by the extraordinary quality of the masonry. Richardson was uncompromising in his demands for constructional excellence, and he was fortunate in having for his contractor for most of his buildings the firm of Norcross Brothers of Worcester, Massachusetts. The field partner in that firm, O. W. Norcross, was an engineer of unusual inventiveness and a master of stone construction. Because of this, he was immediately responsive to the largeness of Richardson's thinking and sympathetic to the architect's compelling preference for stone. This, together with the skill and talent of his specially trained craftsmen, made it possible for Richardson to achieve exacting standards and contributed much to the living quality of his buildings.

Designed and constructed to proclaim the weight and density of stone, the walls of Trinity also cohere, flat and curved alike, into a balanced system of ascending solids which is the exact outward press of the spaces within; and it is in the definition, flow, and connection of those spaces that the ultimate meaning of Trinity is to be found. To be sure, the origins are Romanesque and there are Romanesque details—round arches, colonnettes, piers, and carved capitals—but as an architectural concept the soaring open space of the sanctuary itself has no counterpart in any Romanesque church, French or otherwise. The vital core is the crossing, formed by four massive clustered

Richardson. Trinity Church. Boston. 1872–1877

piers. From these spring a complex system of arches on half arches which, in profile, have the exact configuration of a section taken from corner to corner through a dome on pendentives. The space envelope of Trinity, however, is mural, not domical. The great arches, together with their supporting piers, carry the walls of the stone tower, the flat ceiling of which is 103 feet above the floor. This creates, at the very center of the church, a magnificent uninterrupted vertical rectangle of space twice as high as it is wide.

For liturgical reasons the chancel is the largest auxiliary space, and it is raised above the main floor of the church by a series of steps. But here any concession to liturgy ends. The nave and both transepts are wider than they are long, and the aisles, which appear in the nave only, are reduced to simple passageways. In Richardson's design, therefore, those spatial components that play such independent roles in a medieval church, are radically compressed and made to flow into the dramatic space of the crossing to form a single coherent volume.

Richardson's unorthodox handling of Romanesque space was directly motivated by one of the principal functions of Trinity. The rector, Phillips Brooks, was a Low-Church Episcopalian; he was also a preacher of extraordinary eloquence, and

Richardson. Trinity Church. Boston. 1872–1877

Trinity was conceived from the beginning as a dramatic auditorium church in which his persuasive powers could be experienced to optimum advantage. As a building type the auditorium church went back in American architecture to the Congregational meetinghouses of colonial times. It also received special attention during the nineteenth century for non-Episcopal and Low-Church Episcopal congregations alike. In developing the form at Trinity, Richardson not only responded to the special nature of his client but he also embraced a longstanding convention from his New England architectural heritage.

If Richardson's responsiveness to his client's special needs is embodied in the interior space of Trinity, his extraordinary sensitivity to the means and materials of structure is no less manifest in his handling of the vast ceiling. In contrast to the flat ceiling in the tower, those sections that cover the wide sweeps of the nave, transepts, and the butt of the chancel have the appearance of large barrel vaults, carried on bracketlike half-vaults. Richardson was fully aware that in a true Romanesque church the vaults would have been made of stone, but to support masonry vaults as large as those at Trinity would have required buttressing of such magnitude and complexity as to be prohibitive. For this reason he turned to a traditional American technique and made his entire ceiling of wood and plaster. In doing this, however, he made no attempt whatsoever to imitate masonry construction. In fact, as the visible profile of the main truss sections suggests, the framing which is hidden behind the vaultlike surfaces is similar in principle to that of the great hammerbeam ceilings of late Gothic England. At the same time, on the curved face of the ceiling itself every rib of the fabric is shown in a shape and at a scale that clearly reveal that it is wood, and the plaster surfaces between the ribs are made to reaffirm their nonsupporting function through an overall system of polychrome decoration. The entire interior of Trinity is painted. Designed and executed by Richardson's friend, John La Farge, it is a glorious polychrome display of figural compositions and abstract patterns. Richardson called Trinity his "color church," and for sheer articulated splendor it was unmatched by any other church in America.

Even before the great church was finished, Richardson's achievement at Trinity was recognized, and it placed him at the very top of his profession, a position which he never relinquished during the remaining years of his life. Curiously, however, this same achievement did not put him in demand as a church architect. He subsequently designed seven other churches but only two were ever built, the Emmanuel Church in Pittsburgh (1883–1886) and the Baptist Church in Newton, Massachusetts (1884). The five unexecuted projects included the monumental Episcopal Cathedral for Albany, New York (1882–1883), one of Richardson's largest and most impressive designs.

The flowering of Richardson's individual style at Trinity was facilitated by the final establishment in Brookline of his architectural office, and the subsequent maturation of his working method. Richardson's personal involvement in the design process was at two levels. The first, which his earliest biographer, Mrs. Van Rensselaer, called the "initiative impulse," was fundamental and took the form of bold vibrant sketches which brought to life the essences of his concept. These were then turned over to his staff who put them to scale, and provided the drawings and specifications necessary to bring them to concrete reality. Richardson's second role was his continuous criticism and "oversight" in the development of the design and the construction of the building. His guidance was charismatic. His genius flowed into and through his assistants and assured his personal touch throughout the building down to the smallest detail.

Of the few commissions Richardson received while working on Trinity, the most provocative was his involvement in the completion of the New York State Capitol (1875) in Albany. It had been designed by THOMAS FULLER in 1867, but because of bad management and political interference it ran grossly over cost and was only half finished in 1875 when Richardson, LEOPOLD EIDLITZ, and FREDERICK LAW OLMSTED were asked to serve on an advisory committee to study the matter. In the end, Eidlitz and Richardson were commissioned to finish the building, with Olmsted functioning as treasurer.

For Richardson, the architectural outcome of the capitol enterprise was too diluted by compromise and by other hands to be clearly identified as his work, although the west staircase and the Senate Chamber (recently restored) were distinctly his, with the latter among his finest interiors. On the other hand, certain consequences of the experience would affect his growth as an architect. The first was the furthering of his relationship with Olmsted, his neighbor on Staten Island before the move to Brookline. They had already collaborated on other projects and during these years had become close friends. Olmsted's thinking was undoubtedly a critical stimulus in Richardson's growing awareness of the organic relationships between architecture and the natural environment. Their association in the Albany undertaking only served to deepen the bonds between them.

The quality of Richardson's contributions to the building also enhanced his professional reputation, especially in the area of civic architecture. During the nine years remaining to him, after the completion of Trinity, he was to receive three such commissions. The first was for the Ames Memorial

Richardson. Allegheny County Courthouse and Jail. Pittsburgh. 1883–1888

Town Hall in North Easton, Massachusetts (1879–1881), the second for the City Hall in Albany (1880–1882). The latter was considerably the larger, but the two designs were similar in their pyramidal outline, a concept of massing that appears frequently in the work of Richardson and that clearly was inspired by the churches of Auvergne.

By far the most important and most complex of Richardson's civic commissions was the third—that for the Allegheny County buildings in Pittsburgh. He won the competition in February 1884. Although finished after his death, it was a work in which the architect took special pride. The principal building, which occupies a city block, contains spaces for county administrative offices and records and for all the rooms and chambers associated with the county court system, including a law library. The jail was on an irregular adjacent block shaped in the form of a pentagon with its right angles and base side facing the courthouse. The two buildings were connected across the intervening street by an enclosed bridge carried on a massive segmental arch.

Both the large-scale formality and the complexity of the Allegheny County commission gave Richardson the best opportunity of his career to use to full advantage his training at the Ecole des Beaux-Arts. The main building, as prescribed in the program, is a rectangle surrounding an open court, with all parts balanced symmetrically around either the main or cross axes. On the long axis, the culmination of the façade is a 300-foot campanile. Throughout the building, the architect's command of the Beaux-Arts principles of design is eminently apparent. Through an ingenious division of the vertical space between three major floors and two mezzanines and through a fluid interlocking of horizontal and vertical access, the many functions of the building are logically separated or joined to provide ready access to public rooms, isolation of those that are private, and efficient security control. And all of this was achieved within the strictures of classical symmetry with the most important rooms symbolically placed in axial positions. In one of the truly brilliant architectural solutions of the nineteenth century, all the complexities of the internal spatial relationships are expressly articulated on the exterior of the building through both the fenestration and the massing.

On the interior, the centerpiece of the design is the main hall and grand staircase. Gigantic arches and arcades sweep and ascend with Piranesian (see GIOVANNI BATTISTA PIRANESI) grandeur to demonstrate the physical energy of arch construction

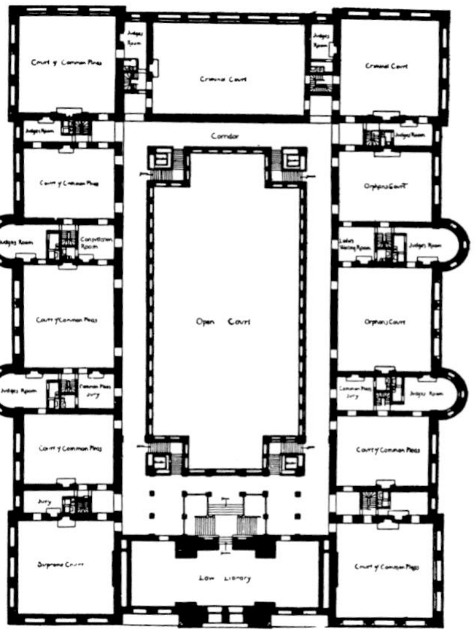

Richardson. Second floor plan of Allegheny County Courthouse. Pittsburgh. 1883–1888

Richardson. Main stairway of Allegheny County Courthouse. Pittsburgh. 1883–1888

with a visual drama unmatched in the architecture of nineteenth-century America. But equally expressive in the courthouse is Richardson's handling of metal. Although the metal-framed ceilings in the smaller compartments of the grand staircase are enclosed, in the upper ceiling of the stairwell itself the metal beams and segmental vaults of the fireproof construction are openly shown, as they were originally in other large public spaces of the building. In the supreme courtroom, for example, the large metal girders that support the metal joists and their segmental vaults were completely exposed and were even painted to relate them in color to the walls; and in a lively touch of decorative animation the heads of the rivets were gilded.

The formal restraint of the courthouse gives way in the jail to a weighty picturesque irregularity. A long two-story unit occupies the entire side of the block facing the courthouse. The fenestration is sparse and asymmetrically grouped in response to functional need. Behind, three long cell blocks radiate from an octagonal guard tower to form a T, the arms of which are unequal in length because of the irregular shape of the site. A formidable stone wall encloses the exercise yard.

The dramatic contrast between the visual character of the courthouse and that of the jail makes it obvious that Richardson conceived the two buildings as wholly different, each shaped and determined by its own special requirements, each symbolic of its own truths. Indeed, the only thing they have in common is the granite from which they are made, and even this is treated differently. Instead of the alternating courses of smaller stones that lighten and formalize the courthouse walls, those of the jail are laid in rock-faced regular ashlar, the individual stones of which are consistently gigantic in size and bold in projection. Like the arches of the grand stairway, the craggy precipitous walls of the jail intone the power of stone masonry, but here the theme is developed in harsher chords. The coda comes in the cyclopean arched door to the jail with its nine-foot voussoirs, a motif he had seen on a recent trip to Spain. More than any other detail in the entire complex, this colossal motif symbolizes the towering genius of Richardson at one of the supreme moments of his career.

Richardson. Allegheny County Jail. Pittsburgh. 1883–1888

Richardson's remarkable capacity to design for function, so superbly manifest in the Allegheny County buildings, reached special levels of power and simplicity in his most renowned building, the Marshall Field Wholesale Store in Chicago. Commissioned in 1885, it was not finished until 1887, a year after the architect's death; it was torn down in 1930 to make way for a parking lot.

Whereas the internal space requirements for the Allegheny County buildings were complex in the extreme, those for the Field Store were of the utmost simplicity: a cluster of regular cubical spaces for administrative offices and multiple floors of completely uninterrupted open space for the display and handling of dry goods, none of which posed serious weight problems. Richardson's solution was large, bold, and simple. A rectangular box, seven stories high, with a flat roof, it occupied an entire city block. The construction was load-bearing masonry, developed around a system of massive piers that rose from foundation to cornice. These piers formed the springs for a series of superposed arcades. The principal arcade, resting on the base of the building, had a single arch per bay. Above it was one with two arches per bay, and still further up was one with four.

This doubling of the rhythm in ascending arcades has been compared to a number of potential sources from the commercial architecture of his time, but especially to George Browne Post's Produce Exchange Building in New York (1884–1886), which was remarkably similar. At the same time, however, the idea was nurtured by the architect himself over a period of years in his own commercial work, beginning with the Cheney Building in Hartford, Connecticut (1875–1876), and the Hayden Building in Boston (1869). In both of these, he broke from the Second Empire style of his early commercial works in Springfield and turned instead to the Romanesque and to the ascending multiplication of the round-arched arcade. He used the same wall treatment in the Ames Bedford Street Store in Boston (1882–1883). All three were built before Post's Produce Exchange and were logical precursors of the Marshall Field Store.

Richardson's structural bay arrangement, with its dynamic multiplying rhythms, marked three sides of the building, but the other long side was completely different. Here, the center of the wall was held back to create a shallow court between two short wings, the ground floor of which contained a loading platform protected from the weather by a suspended glass roof. The two wings terminated in stone façades of two bays, identical to those on the rest of the building. Surviving drawings indicate, however, that the wall of the center section was of brick with extremely narrow piers supporting ten vertical strips of broad segmental arched windows. The result was a virtual wall of glass. Indeed, this open pier-and-arched-spandrel construction was identical to that employed in major industrial buildings of the period. The interior construction is particularly important as it relates to this "factory" wall. From the basement through the third floor, the framing was iron with the vertical posts sheathed in terra cotta. From the fourth floor to the roof, however, the internal structure was entirely wood, with wooden posts supporting enormous wooden beams, which in turn carried oak floors of at least four inches thick. This was a fire-resistant technique known as "slow-burning construction" which was in common use for industrial building, and its appearance in the Marshall Field Store ties Richardson to his practical as well as his aesthetic roots in American architecture.

The Marshall Field Store was extolled by Richardson's contemporaries, particularly LOUIS H. SULLIVAN, on whom it had considerable influence and for whom it became a *cause célèbre.* Many modern critics have also considered it as one of the greatest buildings of the nineteenth century, and for good reasons. Its wonder lies in the urgency of its simplicity, in the immense power with which a vital segment of American life was both satisfied and symbolized. In part, its austerity was engendered by the client, Marshall Field himself, a nononsense businessman who demanded the most for the least. But in an equally important sense, the building represented the ultimate destiny of Richardson's growth as an architect. Here, the fullness of his abundant style was reduced to absolute essentials: to integrated rhythmic sequences, to the relationships between solid and void, to proportion and scale, and to the seductive manipulation of surfaces. In the miraculous rightness of these things, Richardson transformed a direct, even commonplace solution to a pragmatic problem into an architectural work of electrifying eloquence.

Richardson.
Marshall Field Store.
Chicago.
1885–1887

Although Richardson used consistent functional concepts for specific building types, his intelligent responsiveness to the uniqueness of each individual commission assured the integrity of each solution. Thus, throughout his entire career, no two buildings were ever identical, and each was readable for precisely what it was. The railroad stations which he designed for various small towns in New England, for example, all had a low one-story block for a ticket office and waiting room, an open shed along the tracks, and a porte-cochère, with all elements contained under a single hovering roof structure. These charming little stations, such as the one in North Easton (1881–1884), were all built of rock-faced masonry. Yet, no two were alike, and when called upon to design a large station for New London, Connecticut (1885–1886), Richardson's solution was different altogether; it was emphatically symmetrical, two stories high, and made of brick.

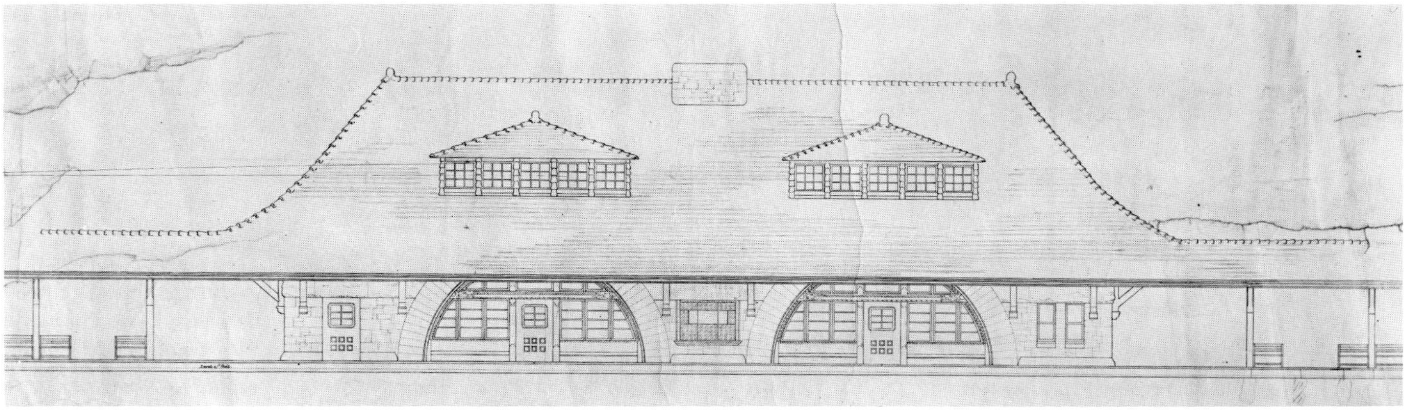

Richardson.
Old Colony Railroad Station.
North Easton, Massachusetts.
1881–1884

Along with his responsiveness to function, Richardson was also keenly aware of the relationship between each building and its environment, both natural and man-made, and in many instances this concern had a considerable effect on the ultimate design. In some, the nature of the site played an extremely subtle role. Among the most interesting were two very important buildings which he designed for his alma mater, Harvard. The earlier, Sever Hall (1878–1880), was intended to fill a pressing need for classroom space. Because this required identical spaces in a variety of sizes and shapes, the most logical solution was a symmetrical arrangement within a rectangular mass. As usual, Richardson's distribution of interior space is clearly articulated in discreet modulations of the walls, and in the varied and complex fenestration. But the use of the symmetrical rectangular box had another and equally important motivation: Sever Hall was built in Harvard Yard, where the university's venerable architecture—simple rectangular blocks, most of them brick, a few stone—formed clustered frames for academic life. Sever was the first of four buildings that ultimately formed another such cluster, and to harmonize with the prevailing texture of the older Yard, the building was brick. To be sure, it was pressed brick, darker in tone and harder and smoother in texture than the brick of the earlier buildings, and red pigment was added to the mortar to homogenize the wall. Moreover, a considerable amount of molded and cut brick was used to ornament and enliven surfaces, thus reflecting the Queen Anne taste then so popular in Boston. The only hint of the Romanesque is the archivolted round-arched opening that frames the west door. Otherwise, in its rectangular shape, its hipped roof, its classical pediments, and the basic scale of its structural material, Sever concedes with subtle grace to its architectural ambiance, without in any way sacrificing its intensely Richardsonian character.

Unlike Sever, which was conceived as an integral part of Harvard Yard, Austin Hall (1880–1884) was situated outside the Yard in a newly developing area that would later be known as the North Yard. Designed to house the thriving Harvard Law School, it was like Sever primarily a classroom building, although it also included the law library and a number of professor's offices. Like Sever, too, the basic plan is symmetrical, but it differs from the earlier building in that the main two-story rectangular block has lateral one-story wings (lecture halls) and a large two-story wing to the rear (first floor, large lecture hall; second floor, library and reading room). The treatment of the triple-arched entrance loggia is also more conspicuously Romanesque than anything at Sever, and to the right of this loggia a circular stair tower is asymmetrically placed. Except for the first floor fenestration, however, which differs in response to the off-center tower, the building is balanced absolutely around the central loggia arch, with all the major components of the interior clearly revealed by the massing and window groupings.

This elaborate massing was surely made possible by the less restrictive nature of the site, and it marked a dramatic break with the architectural conventions of the old Yard. So, too, did the shift from brick to rock-faced masonry. Here, the walls are random ashlar livened by animated polychrome patterns, including diaper work and marquetry. The resulting surface and chromatic richness, together with the more picturesque massing, accomplished two things for Richardson: it set Austin Hall apart in its unencumbered environment as a fresh and forceful statement in his own vigorous vocabulary, and it related the building to the polychrome splendor of Memorial Hall (1871–1874), WARE AND VAN BRUNT's grandiloquent Victorian Gothic pile which had just been completed, two hundred yards to the east. It, too, was outside the Yard, and together, the two buildings pointed to a provocative new direction in the architecture of Harvard, at the same time that they measure the gap between Richardson and his contemporaries.

In those buildings by Richardson such as Sever Hall, the Allegheny County Courthouse, and the Marshall Field Store, where the complex demands of collective man were best suited by formal geometry, we see the disciplined planner, the architect in touch with his time and place; the passionate side of Richardson's talent was reluctantly subdued by the constraints of symmetry and order. In those buildings given over to the life of the individual, however—particularly in his libraries and houses—the artist prevailed over the pragmatist, and here his creative fires burned brightly, even fiercely, to warm and illuminate both the work and the man.

In his first library—the Winn Memorial Library (1876–1879) in Woburn, Massachusetts—Richardson fully realized the highly individual solution to the problems of a library which he was to use for all five such commissions. It was an extended horizontal massing, asymmetrically balanced around an arched entrance opening and a clearly articulated stair tower. Internally, the main entrance gave directly onto a hall or control area, and immediately adjacent was the reading room. There was considerable variety among his five libraries as to exactly how these various functions were related. In all of them, however, the book repository itself was a horizontal block to the left of the entrance in which the fenestration of the façade was a continuous strip window directly beneath the eaves of a pitched roof. On the interior, the stacks were arranged in a series of two-story alcoves, constructed and ornamented entirely in wood; a second story in the main block provided additional space for a variety of functions.

The Winn Memorial Library was the most elaborate of Richardson's five designs, and in the Ames Memorial Library in North Easton, Massachusetts, commissioned just six months later, his treatment was enormously simplified. Although the Crane Memorial Library in Quincy, Massachusetts (1880–1882), is even simpler and represents Richardson's mature style in its most distilled form, the Ames Library has the freshness of early discovery and represents Richardson's solution with such vitality that it may be taken as typical of the group.

The principal block of the North Easton Library is square and gabled, front to back. The façade is symmetrically balanced around an enormous arched opening. Springing from the water table instead of from conventional piers or posts and sweeping up to and even into the stringcourse at the second floor, this gigantic motif appears here in Richardson's work for the first time. His source was the early Christian architecture of Syria, as illustrated in de Vogüé's *Syrie Centrale,* the second volume of which appeared in 1877, which Richardson seems to have acquired at that time. As a demonstration of the sheer power of stone masonry, it gave him exactly what he needed. He used it with daring and versatility, and it became a vital hallmark of his mature style.

To the left and slightly behind the main entrance façade and incorporated almost entirely into the principal block, was the stair tower, which rose through the full two-and-a-half stories of the building and was crowned by a triple-arched opening with a pyramidal top. Although this motif forms the peak of the compositional pyramid, the profile of the book stack wing is low and the actual thrust of the building is earthbound and horizontal. This, together with the rough surfaces of the magnificent rock-faced random ashlar, creates the impression of a live outcropping of granite as much as it does a building, and in harmony with this effect, the adjacent Town Hall, built two years later, was actually constructed on an outcropping. Although this may seem a fortuitous coupling of building and earth, it was in fact carefully planned with Olmsted, who made the Richardson buildings the climax of his landscape scheme for the immediate area. Seen in this dramatic context, the shadowed opening of the library seems as much like the mouth of a cave as it does the entrance to a building.

Although the Ames Library very quickly turned out to be too small to accommodate the rapid growth of the library's holdings (as did all of Richardson's libraries), this little gem is one of the most highly coherent and articulated of all of his small buildings; at the same time, it is one of the most attractively sensuous. In fact, nowhere is

Richardson.
Ames Memorial Public Library.
North Easton, Massachusetts.
1877–1879

Richardson's poetic responsiveness to the natural quality of materials more superbly apparent: the outside of the building is a world of stone experienced through the roughness and boldness of the rock-faced walls, the sparkling surfaces, and the earth-induced harmony of color; on the inside is a miraculous world of wood, of superb fine-grained butternut delicately scaled, shaped, and polished to a honey-colored patina of the most lustrous kind. It is precisely because Richardson encouraged the materials to do what they wanted to do and to be what they wanted to be that his buildings came to celebrate with Whitmanesque intensity the fruits of the natural world.

Of the wide variety of buildings designed by Richardson, none was more organically derived from nature than his houses. They are not built on the earth, they grow out of it; in shape, color, texture, even in material substance, they are its natural progeny. In part, this was the direct consequence of the special role of nature in the American romantic movement. Because of the dominating presence of the wilderness in their environment, nineteenth-century Americans saw nature not just as an object of philosophical reflection but also as a living reality, and the early generation of romantics responded to their physical world with guileless wonder. By Richardson's time, however, this attitude had broadened and hardened. As exploration and the railroad opened up more and more of the land, as the camera filled in the specific physical details, as the rapidly developing earth sciences (particularly biology and geology) revealed the organic structure of the earth, the landscape was no longer seen through a veil of light and atmosphere. Instead, it became an exciting structured organism, a substantial resource which would yield to the hand and the machine. Its attraction was not so much its visual excitement as its weight and density. Its largeness was exhilarating, its abundance seductive, and no creative figure of the period was more in accord with this materialistic view than Richardson. The immensity of his forms, the directness and boldness of his structural solutions, and the sensuous pleasure with which he probed and used the organic qualities of materials all celebrate with poetic intensity what Walt Whitman called the "far-swooping elbowed earth."

Nearly 40 percent of Richardson's work consisted of private houses, each unique because it was designed for a particular individual and a particular setting. At the same time, Richardson's houses share a dynamic and varied asymmetry both in plan and in massing. The most immediate roots of this are to be found in the asymmetrical schemes developed during the early picturesque movement in America. But equally influential, in a different way, was English domestic architecture of the 1860s and 1870s, especially that of R. NORMAN SHAW. Here were not only all the ingredients of the picturesque, but here too was the rich vocabulary of one of the most sparkling styles of the Victorian era, the Queen Anne. As the term implies, the style took something of its character from the last years of the age of CHRISTOPHER WREN, but in fact it was much more than that. In its efforts to be "old English" it was a sophisticated melange of styles, as much late medieval and early Renaissance as it was baroque.

Several features of this dynamic idiom were naturally attractive to Richardson, foremost of which was an open plan that centered around a living hall. As a room type, the living hall was reminiscent of the great halls of the English medieval house, and a prominent feature, therefore, was an ample fireplace. In contrast to its medieval prototype, however, the living hall also contained a spacious breaking staircase which led to the second floor. Together, these elements formed a warm and dynamic space at the very heart of the house, which was quite different from the medieval hall. First introduced into this country by Richardson in the Andrews House, Newport, Rhode Island (1872), the living hall became for him a vital core around which other living spaces such as the drawing room, the dining room, and the library were freely arranged in an open fluid plan.

Among Richardson's houses, the earliest example of the living hall that still survives is the Watts Sherman House in Newport, Rhode Island (1874–1875). The main entrance is through a shallow vestibule that opens immediately into the stairwell; to the right is the living hall itself. With the exception of the railing on the first landing, which forms a low partial screen between the two spaces, the stairwell is completely open to the living hall. On the wall diagonally across is a massive hooded fireplace. Broad doors on either side of the fireplace open into the library and drawing room respectively; the end of the drawing room is a wall of glass which presses out from the rear of the house in a five-sided bay. On the other side of the living hall, behind the stairwell, is the dining room, the entire end of which is a broad commanding fireplace. The living hall is the largest room in the house and extends from front to back through the entire building. Clearly intended as the focal space for life in the house, it was also warm and rich in its appointments. A triple window at the front end contained glowing stained glass by John La Farge (now in The Museum of Fine Arts, Boston); a similar but larger group window on the rear wall also had La Farge glass. The high paneling, the chimney breast, and the staircase were entirely of dark mahogany.

The exterior of the Sherman House was the first clear statement in this country of the Queen Anne style. Its design followed very quickly the publication (1871), in the English architectural periodical *Building News,* of important works by Shaw, and there is no doubt that the Sherman House was inspired by these illustrations. The complex irregular massing, the high gabled roofs and soaring clustered chimneys, the overhanging upper stories, the broad bands of small-paned hooded windows, the variations in wall treatment, all of these are characteristic of Shaw's domestic work. But this is the only one of Richardson's executed houses to be so directly influenced by Shaw. Just as the overt eclecticism at Trinity was never again repeated in Richardson's later work, so too the Watts Sherman House stands alone in its obvious derivation from Shaw. But even here there are important differences in the way Richardson handled the Shavian elements. First, there is the largeness and boldness of his massing. Shaw's lively projections are blunted by Richardson, and underlying the entire composition is the controlling Auvergnat clustered pyramid. Much more important is Richardson's treatment of the wall surfaces. In Shaw's work, they were a combination of hard-pressed brick on the first floor, and tile above; the first floor of the Sherman House is rock-faced stone; the upper floors, except for a modest amount of half timber, are wooden shingles. The textures of the walls are thus rougher and more organically related to nature than the English tiles. Moreover, the use of shingles draws on the American preference for wood which had its roots in colonial times. Richardson had already used shingles in the Andrews House, which was an all wooden structure, and his further use of the material here was to broaden the base of what would become a major movement in American domestic architecture.

Both the Andrews and the Watts Sherman House were designed for a semirural setting in an exclusive residential section of Newport, and their open asymmetry was appropriate for that setting. Richardson's next important domestic commission was for the rectory of Trinity Church in Boston (1879–1880), and when finished it became the first of an important group of urban houses conceived in terms quite different from those designed for the open countryside. Built of brick, with ornamental terra-cotta panels and stone trim, the house has something of the crispness of the English Queen Anne although few of its specific details; the treatment of the walls is simpler and bolder. In keeping with the constraints of its city site, the façade also hints at symmetry, with two gabled pavilions balanced formally around a central connecting unit. Window groupings, however, are poised asymmetrically around a great sweeping arch which is itself off center and forms the opening to the entrance porch. The result is a quiet tension which energizes but does not violate the contained shallow lot which the house totally occupies.

Richardson.
Watts Sherman House.
Newport, Rhode Island.
1874–1875

Richardson relied on this part-formal, part-dynamic arrangement for all of his urban residences, and although each solution was different from all the others, they were all masonry buildings. The Anderson (1881), Adams, and Hay Houses (both 1884–1886) in Washington were brick; the Sard House (1882–1883) in Albany and the MacVeagh House (1885–1886) in Chicago were stone. So is the Glessner House (1885–1886) in Chicago. Although finished after Richardson's death, this remarkable house is one of his most provocative works; it is also one about which a great deal is known. Built for the Chicago businessman John Jacob Glessner, it is located on the southwest corner of Prairie Avenue and Eighteenth Street, in what was then a fashionable new part of the city; George W. Pullman lived across the street, and down the block was the house of Marshall Field, designed by Richard Morris Hunt.

Richardson's design for the Glessner House was entirely conditioned by the long narrow shape of the corner lot. Placed directly on the street, the L-shaped building encloses the entire corner. The formidable walls are rock-faced granite, and the window openings on the street are few and small. The main façade is the short arm of the L on Prairie Avenue and is symmetrically balanced around the

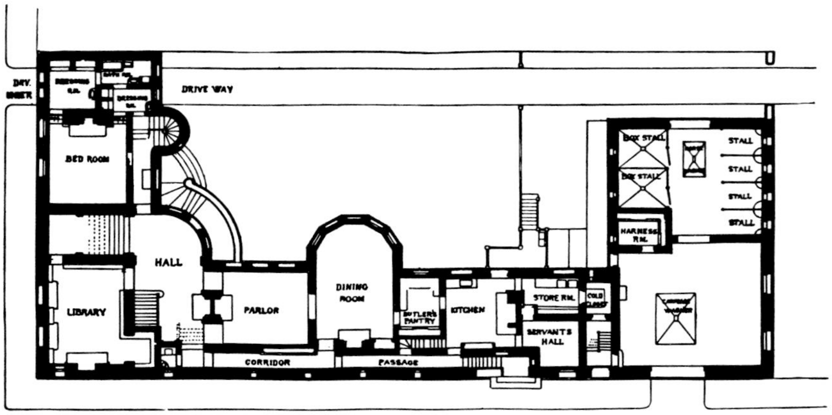

Richardson.
Plan of Glessner House.
Chicago.
1885–1887

heavy arched and linteled entrance door. The wall of this façade continues to the left beyond this symmetrical unit, however, to accommodate a carriage entrance to the inner court; thus, the total effect is asymmetrical, and the short chimneys are unequally spaced. The long side of the house on Eighteenth Street is completely asymmetrical with irregular clusters of windows dynamically poised around the sweeping arched opening of the rear entrance; at the end is a gabled carriage house. The exclusive effect of the powerful stone masonry, together with the small windows, is to shut out the city, physically as well as visually. In the courtyard, however, the building is both open and animated. The inner corner of the L is marked by a curved bay around which is balanced a larger polygonal bay and a smaller round stair tower, both with conical roofs. The windows on the court face either south or west and are both large and numerous; even on days when the sun is obscured by clouds, the interior spaces are flooded with light. The complex projections of the mass also articulate various segments of the interior space which, as in all Richardson's domestic plans, flow through and out of the living hall. The vital core of the design reveals itself in the circular corner bay.

One of the interesting aspects of Richardson's city dwellings is the vibrant restraint with which he handled the massing. If the lot was large enough to give him room, he did indulge in moderate projections, but where space was tight, as at the Glessner House, he relied entirely upon the simple solid wall. Although nature itself was by necessity excluded from the man-made cityscape, Richardson seems nevertheless to have seen the street as a kind of canyon with his walls as the cliffs and his openings as the natural fissures in the rock; and even though the masonry is lighter and more formal than in his buildings for less constrained sites, the living quality of surface, especially in the rock-faced masonry, is still very much a factor. The vital connection with nature is thus never completely broken.

It was in his rural and suburban dwellings, all designed for open and frequently expansive landscape settings, that Richardson was able to give free rein to all his romantic impulses; and of all the houses conceived for such contexts, the Ames Gate Lodge in North Easton, Massachusetts, is the most uninhibited, the most organic, and the most poetic. It rejected with brash ebullience the most revered conventions of American domestic architecture, and spoke instead an urgent new and natural language, at once expressive of the expectations of its patron and of the architectural brilliance of its creator. The most original house yet to be built in the United States, it remained so until the early twentieth century, when the Prairie houses of FRANK LLOYD WRIGHT, for which it was a clear antecedent, made their appearance in the Chicago suburbs.

The commission for the Ames Gate Lodge, received in March of 1880, was itself unusual. It not only called for an entrance gate to the Ames estate and a dwelling for a gatekeeper, but it was also to have guest rooms and a large Bachelor Hall on the second floor where the young men of the family could retreat with their college friends. A third element, which Richardson placed on the other side of the gate, was an ample room for the storage of plants in winter. Several things about Richardson's design are remarkable. First is the highly original massing. Although the main two-story block builds conspicuously toward the architect's favored pyramidal form, it does so in a broad and completely asymmetrical manner. There are bold varied projections on all sides of the basic rectangular block, and even the planes of the hipped roof are not set at corresponding angles; to accommodate the projection of a wellhouse, the west plane is considerably longer than that on the east. Moreover, the eave line is low, and when combined with that of the extended one-story plant house, it creates an earth-hugging horizontality that is unlike any house yet designed in the United States. At the same time, a widely projecting window hood on the west end of the house and the continuous horizontal bands of windows immediately under the eaves lighten the roof and make it seem to hover above the weighty irregular walls. It is primarily this, together with the earthbound horizontality, that pointed directly to Wright's Prairie houses (Heurtley House, 1902, Oak Park, Illinois).

If the horizontality of the Ames Gate Lodge presses it to the earth, its rough stone walls provide the organic connection. Made entirely of enormous boulders, they make it appear as much like a deposit of stones in a glacial moraine as a building erected by the human hand. Only the unifying

Richardson. Ames Gate Lodge. North Easton, Massachusetts. 1880–1881

logic of the sandstone arches, lintels, and trim and the neat surfaces of the red tile roof keep it in the realm of man-made things. For in spite of its primeval naturalism, the Ames Gate Lodge was indeed built by man, with consummate skill and sensitivity, and it contains within its overwhelming realism poetic passages of extraordinary poignance. One example is the great arch that spans the driveway. For sheer power it is one of the most moving structural elements Richardson ever conceived; it is also a magnificent evocation of latent energy. This is seen in the way the roof above, itself presumably resolute in its determination to preserve the eave line, yields to the pressure of the arch in a long gentle curve. It is as though roof and arch had grown together, over eons of time, and in the end the stronger had prevailed. Nowhere in American architecture of the nineteenth century are both the organic nature of materials and the logic of structure more eloquently joined than in this brilliant detail, and it is precisely such insights that set Richardson apart from his fellow architects and make him the most creative genius of his time.

It is impossible fully to understand the Ames Gate Lodge without exploring further the relationship between Richardson and Olmsted. Olmsted designed the grounds of the Ames estate, and the two men would later work together on the North Easton Town Hall project. It is hard to escape the notion, therefore, that because of the location of the Gate Lodge on a gentle knoll overlooking Olmsted's landscape, and because of the raw natural character of its walls, the building was designed with the setting clearly in mind. To be sure, Richardson had already used boulder construction for Grace Church, Medford, Massachusetts (1867–1869), although on a more modest scale, and its appearance in the Gate Lodge was thoroughly consistent with his enthusiasm for stone. But Olmsted was also a lover of stone. He used natural outcroppings whenever he could in his landscape designs, and it seems certain that the bold geological character of Richardson's masonry was intended by both to evoke the appearance of a natural rock formation. This conclusion gains considerable credence from the fact that one of the four signature stones found on the wellhouse balcony was Olmsted's. The others were those of Frederick L. Ames, the patron, Richardson, and LOUIS C. TIFFANY, who designed the overmantel and the bench screen that formed the inglenook in the Bachelor Hall.

Olmsted may also have brought to Richardson's attention the work of the mid-century picturesque movement in America, some of which was even then beginning to point toward Richardson. This was particularly true of the late work of ALEXANDER JACKSON DAVIS at Llewellyn Park in Orange, New Jersey. Llewellyn Park was a highly successful and widely acclaimed residential park with a brilliantly planned landscape setting, and it is unthinkable that Olmsted was not thoroughly familiar with it. Davis not only worked with Llewellyn Haskell in the planning of the park, but he was also responsible for a number of its houses, including a highly romantic gatehouse. There is little evidence to indicate a direct influence of Davis on Richardson, but the points of similarity between their works are sufficiently striking to suggest the strong probability that Richardson was well aware of Davis, especially through his later work at Llewellyn Park, and found in him a kindred spirit. Each man, in his time, was a leader in the picturesque movement in

Richardson. Stairhall of Paine House. Waltham, Massachusetts. 1884–1886

America, each was responsive to the natural qualities of materials, and each had a keen sense of the house in relation to its setting. A comparison, for example, between Richardson's Paine House (1884–1886) in Waltham, Massachusetts, and Davis's Castlewood (1857) in Llewellyn Park reveals with striking clarity the commonality of their vision and justifies the conclusion that important ideas in the work of Richardson had already flowered in American architecture. In developing them as he did with his own special touch of genius, he was reaping a harvest that had already been sown and nurtured by his predecessors. Seen in this light, the productive relationship between Richardson and Olmsted, which contributed so much to the naturalism of the architect's style, was very much like that between Davis and the landscape gardener ANDREW JACKSON DOWNING, who in a similar manner opened Davis's eyes to the relationship between the house and nature.

Richardson. Stoughton House. Cambridge, Massachusetts. 1882–1883

Richardson's innovative use of shingle as a wall cover in his domestic buildings, seen in the Paine House in combination with fieldstone, assumed its consummate form in a number of all-wooden houses (the Bryant House, 1880–1881, Cohasset, Massachusetts; the Channing House, 1882–1883, Brookline, Massachusetts) of which the Stoughton House (1882–1883) in Cambridge, Massachusetts, is one of the best preserved. In this splendid house, Richardson synthesized with extraordinary subtlety the principal ingredients of his mature domestic style: a bold compact but horizontal massing and its internal consequence, a fluid open plan developed around the living hall; the vitalization of the surface by the gently rough but warm and yielding texture of the shingle; and the suggestion through both shape and material substance of an organic relationship between the house and the earth upon which it stands. These ingredients became the basis of the most important and original development in American domestic architecture of the nineteenth century, the Shingle style. Although Richardson's untimely death precluded his continuing participation in this movement, his contemporaries and followers (particularly MCKIM, MEAD, AND WHITE, PEABODY AND STEARNS, WILLIAM R. EMERSON, and JOHN C. STEVENS) produced a spectacular galaxy of shingle houses throughout the Northeast, especially in romantically appropriate settings along the New England sea coast; and countless others, following their example, carried the style to every corner of the land. These houses were peculiarly American, and they provided the link between the wooden houses of the early picturesque movement and the later domestic work of Frank Lloyd Wright.

The Shingle style was one of Richardson's most fruitful contributions to American architecture. But in equal measure, his total architectural output was also influential, to the point, in fact, where by 1890 "Richardsonian" had become a national style. In the hands of countless imitators, from New York to Chicago to San Francisco, from Texas to Minnesota, from Florida to the Pacific Northwest, this idiom appeared in public buildings, commercial buildings, churches, libraries, railroad stations, mansions, and even a gas house, in the general diffusion of a personal style unparalleled in the earlier history of American architecture. Richardson-inspired buildings also appeared in England, New Zealand, Australia, Canada, the Netherlands, Scandinavia, and especially Germany where the shingle house had a considerable influence. Richardson's work was also discussed in foreign architectural literature.

Throughout his mature years, Richardson suffered from an incurable kidney disorder which finally took his life, and because of its debilitating effects some of his very last work was actually done from his sick bed. Yet, no architecture of the period is so vital and alive, so bursting with energy, so filled with delight. It represents the total outpouring of an immense heart in response to a full and abundant life. In the words of his friend and patron Phillips Brooks, the rector of Trinity Church, "his life passed into his buildings by ways too subtle even for himself to understand . . . the man and his work are absolutely one. The man is in the work, and the work is in the man."

WILLIAM H. PIERSON, JR.

WORKS

*1866–1869, Church of the Unity, Springfield, Mass. 1867–1869, Grace Church, Medford, Mass. *1867–1869, Western Railroad Offices, Springfield, Mass. 1868, Arrochar, Staten Island, N.Y. *1868, Dorsheimer House, Buffalo, N.Y. 1869, Hayden Building, Boston. *1869–1870, Agawam National Bank, Springfield, Mass. *1869–1870, High School, Worcester, Mass. 1870–1872, Brattle Square Church, Boston. 1871–1873, Hampden County Courthouse, Springfield, Mass. *1872, Andrews House, Newport, R.I. 1872–1873, North Congregational Church, Springfield, Mass. 1872–1877, Trinity Church, Boston. 1872–1878, State Asylum for the Insane, Buffalo, N.Y. 1874–1875, Watts Sherman House, Newport, R.I. 1875–1876, Cheney Building, Hartford, Conn. 1875 and later, New York State Capitol, Albany. 1876–1879, Winn Memorial Public Library, Woburn, Mass. 1877–1879, Ames Memorial Public Library, North Easton, Mass. 1878–1880, Sever Hall, Harvard University, Cambridge, Mass. 1879, Ames Monument, Sherman, Wyo. 1879–1880, Rectory, Trinity Church, Boston. 1879–1881, Ames Memorial Town Hall; 1880–1881, Ames Gate Lodge; North Easton, Mass. 1880–1881, Bryant House, Cohasset, Mass. 1880–1882, City Hall, Albany, N.Y. 1880–1882, Crane Memorial Public Library, Quincy, Mass. 1880–1884, Austin Hall, Harvard University, Cambridge, Mass. 1880–1884, Boylston Street Bridge; 1880–1884, Charlesgate West Bridge; Boston. 1881, Anderson House, Washington. 1881, Boston and Albany Railroad Station, Auburndale, Mass. 1881–1882, Browne House, Marion, Mass. *1881–1883, Higginson House, Boston. 1881–1884, Boston and Albany Railroad Station, Palmer, Mass. 1881–1884, Old Colony Railroad Station, North Easton, Mass. *1882–1883, Ames Store, Kingston and Bedford Streets, Boston. 1882–1883, Channing House, Brookline, Mass. 1882–1883, Sard House, Albany, N.Y. 1882–1883, Stoughton House, Cambridge, Mass. 1882–1885, Ames Store, Washington Street, Boston. 1883, Boston and Albany Railroad Station, Framingham, Mass. 1883, Connecticut River Railroad Station, Holyoke, Mass. 1883–1884, Boston and Albany Railroad Station, Chestnut Hill, Mass. 1883–1885, Converse Memorial Public Library, Malden, Mass. 1883–1886, Billings Library, University of Vermont, Burlington. 1883–1886, Emmanuel Church; 1883–1888, Allegheny County Courthouse and Jail; Pittsburgh. 1884, Ames Cottage, North Easton, Mass. 1884, Baptist Church, Newton, Mass. 1884, Boston and Albany Railroad Station, Brighton, Mass. 1884, Boston and Albany Railroad Station, Eliot, Mass. 1884, Boston and Albany Railroad Station, Waban, Mass. 1884, Boston and Albany Railroad Station, Woodland, Mass. *1884–1886, Adams House; 1884–1886, Hay House; Washington. 1884–1886, Paine House, Waltham, Mass. 1885, Boston and Albany Railroad Station, Wellesley Hills, Mass. 1885–1887, Glessner House; 1885–1887, MacVeagh House; *1885–1887, Marshall Field Store; Chicago. 1885–1887, Union Station, New London, Conn. *1885–1888, Chamber of Commerce Building, Cincinnati, Ohio. 1886–1887, Ames Store, Harrison Avenue, Boston.

BIBLIOGRAPHY

Around the Station: The Town and the Train. Focus of a New England Town's Growth. 1978 Framingham, Mass.: Danforth Museum. Exhibition catalogue.

BROOKS, PHILLIPS 1886 "Henry Hobson Richardson." *Harvard Monthly* 3:1–7.

BROWN, GLENN 1931 *1860–1930: Memories.* Washington: Roberts.

BROWN, ROBERT F. 1977 "The Aesthetic Transformation of an Industrial Community." *Winterthur Portfolio* 12:35–64.

BUNTING, BAINBRIDGE 1967 *Houses of Boston's Back Bay: An Architectural History, 1840–1917.* Cambridge, Mass.: Belknap.

CHAFEE, RICHARD 1977 "Richardson's Record at the Ecole des Beaux Arts." *Journal of the Society of Architectural Historians* 36:175–188.

CHESTER, ARTHUR H. 1888 *Trinity Church in the City of Boston: An Historical and Descriptive Account.* Cambridge, Mass.: Wilson.

CINCINNATI ASTRONOMICAL SOCIETY 1914 *Richardson, the Architect.* Cincinnati, Ohio: The society.

COMES, JOHN THEODORE 1906 "The Allegheny County Court House." *International Studio* 28:appendixes 3–7.

COOK, CLARENCE 1878 "Recent Church Decoration." *Scribner's Monthly* 15:569–577.

COOLIDGE, CHARLES A. 1927 "Henry H. Richardson." In Mark Antony DeWolfe Howe (editor), *Later Years of the Saturday Club: 1870–1920.* Boston: Houghton Mifflin.

CORTISSOZ, ROYAL 1913 "H. H. Richardson." In *Art and Common Sense.* New York: Scribner's.

"The County Buildings at Pittsburgh." 1885 *Harper's Weekly* 29, Feb. 28:141–142.

CUTTER, WILLIAM R. 1890 "A Model Village Library." *New England Magazine* New Series 1:617–625.

EATON, LEONARD K. 1966 "Richardson and Sullivan in Scandinavia." *Progressive Architecture* 47:168–171.

EATON, LEONARD K. 1972 *American Architecture Comes of Age: European Reaction to H. H. Richardson and Louis Sullivan.* Cambridge, Mass.: M.I.T. Press.

FERRIDAY, PETER 1973 "A Painter with a Passion for Success." *Country Life* 153:222, 224.

FLEMING, MALCOLM K. 1975 "The Saving of Henry Hobson Richardson's Union Station, New London, Connecticut." *American Art Review* 2:29–40.

FORBES, J. D. 1958 "Shepley, Bulfinch, Richardson and Abbott, Architects: An Introduction." *Journal of the Society of Architectural Historians* 17:19–31.

FRIEDLAENDER, MARC 1970 "Henry Hobson Richardson, Henry Adams and John Hay." *Journal of the Society of Architectural Historians* 29:231–246.

GASS, JOHN B. 1896 "American Architecture and Architects, with Special Reference to the Works of the Late Richard Morris Hunt and Henry Hobson Richardson." *Journal of the Royal Institute of British Architects* 3, Feb. 6:229–232.

GMELIN, LEOPOLD 1899 "American Architecture from a German Point of View." *The Forum* 27:690–704.

HALE, EDWARD 1894 "H. H. Richardson and His Work." *New England Magazine* New Series 11:513–532.

HALE, JONATHAN 1973 "Sic Transit." *Architectural Forum* 140, Nov.:74–81.

Henry Hobson Richardson: The Allegheny County Courthouse and Jail, Part I. An Exhibition of Selected Drawings from the Competition. 1977 Pittsburgh.

HILL, LEROY, DRAPER, JR. 1962 *The Crane Library.* Quincy, Mass.: Trustees of the Thomas Crane Public Library.

HITCHCOCK, H. R. (1936)1966 *The Architecture of Henry Hobson Richardson and His Times.* Cambridge, Mass.: M.I.T. Press.

HITCHCOCK, H. R. 1950 "Richardson's American Express Building: A Note." *Journal of the Society of Architectural Historians* 9:25–30.

HITCHCOCK, H. R. 1966 *Richardson as a Victorian Architect.* Baltimore: Barton-Gillet.

HITCHCOCK, H. R. 1975 "An Inventory of the Architectural Library of H. H. Richardson." *Nineteenth Century* 1, Jan.:27, 31; Apr.:18–19.

HITCHCOCK, H. R. 1980 "Richardson's New York Senate Chamber Restored." *Nineteenth Century* 6, Spring:44–47.

HOMOLKA, LARRY J. 1966 "Richardson's North Easton." *Architectural Forum* 124, May:72–77.

HUFF, WILLIAM S. 1958 "Richardson's Jail." *Western Pennsylvania Historical Magazine* 41, Spring:41–59.

HUXTABLE, ADA LOUISE 1971 "Keeping the There There." *New York Times,* May 16, sec. 2, p. 21.

KLUKAS, ARNOLD W. 1975 "Henry Hobson Richardson's Design for the Emmanuel Episcopal Church, Pittsburgh." *American Art Review* 2, July–Aug.:64–76.

KOCH, ROBERT 1975 "Glass as Ornament: From Richardson to Wright." *Princeton University, Record of the Art Museum* 34:28–35.

KOWSKY, F. R. 1980 "William Dorsheimer House: A Reflection of French Suburban Architecture in the Early Work of H. H. Richardson." *Art Bulletin* 62, Mar.:134–147.

LANGTON, W. A. 1900 "The Method of H. H. Richardson." *Architect and Contract Reporter* 63, Mar. 9:156–158.

LEWIS, DUDLEY ARNOLD 1962 "Evaluations of American Architecture by European Critics: 1875–1900." 2 vols. Unpublished Ph.D. dissertation, University of Michigan, Ann Arbor.

MCKEE, HARLEY J. 1957 "Building for the State of New York: 1790–1890." *Empire State Architect* 17, May–June:33, 50; July–Aug.:17, 27; Sept.–Oct.:55, 81.

Monographs of American Architecture 1886–1888 Vols. 1, 3, and 5. Boston: Ticknor. Volume 1: *Austin Hall, Harvard Law School, Cambridge, Mass.* Volume 3: *Ames Memorial Buildings.* Volume 5: *Trinity Church, Boston, Mass.*

"Mr. Richardson's Work at North Easton, Massachusetts." 1886 *American Architect and Building News* 19, May 8:223–224.

MUMFORD, LEWIS 1924*a* "American Architecture: The Realization of Industrialism." *The Freeman.* 8, Feb. 27:584–586.

MUMFORD, LEWIS (1924*b*)1955 *Sticks and Stones: A Study of American Architecture and Civilization.* 2d ed., rev. New York: Dover.

MUMFORD, LEWIS (1931)1955 *The Brown Decades: A Study of the Arts of America, 1865–1895.* 2d ed., rev. New York: Dover.

MUMFORD, LEWIS (1952)1972 "The Regionalism of Richardson." In *Roots of Contemporary American Architecture.* New York: Dover.

NEWMAN, M. W. 1972 "Granite Hut." *Architectural Forum* 137, Nov.:34–41.

NORTON, BETTINA (editor) 1978 *Trinity Church: The Story of an Episcopal Parish in the City of Boston.* Boston: Wardens and Vestry of Trinity Church.

O'GORMAN, JAMES F. 1964 "On Richardson and Sullivan and Wright." *Connection* Feb.:7–11.

O'GORMAN, JAMES F. 1969 "Henry Hobson Richardson and Frank Lloyd Wright." *Art Quarterly* 32, Autumn:292–315.

O'GORMAN, JAMES F. 1973 "O.W. Norcross, Richardson's 'Master Builder': A Preliminary Report." *Journal of the Society of Architectural Historians* 32:104–113.

O'GORMAN, JAMES F. 1974 *H. H. Richardson and His Office: A Centennial of His Move to Boston, 1874. Selected Drawings.* Cambridge, Mass.: Department of Printing and Graphic Arts, Harvard College Library.

O'GORMAN, JAMES F. 1976 "A Tragic Circle." *Nineteenth Century* 2, Autumn:46–49.

O'GORMAN, JAMES F. 1978 "The Marshall Field Wholesale Store." *Journal of the Society of Architectural Historians* 37:175–194.

O'GORMAN, JAMES F. 1979 "On Vacation with H. H. Richardson: Ten Letters from Europe, 1882." *Archives of the American Art Journal* 19:2–14.

OLMSTED, FREDERICK LAW 1886 "H. H. Richardson." *American Architect* July.

PARIS, W. FRANKLYN 1955 "H. H. Richardson:

1838–1886." *New York University Hall of American Artists* 10:49–59.

PHILLIPS, J. H. 1914 "The Evolution of the Suburban Station." *Architectural Record* 36, Aug.:122–127.

PICKENS, BUFORD L. 1940 "H. H. Richardson and Basic Form Concepts in Modern Architecture." *Art Quarterly* 3, Summer:273–291.

PRICE, CHARLES 1965 "Henry Hobson Richardson: Some Unpublished Drawings." *Perspecta* 9–10:199–210.

RANDALL, RICHARD H., JR. 1962 *The Furniture of H. H. Richardson.* Boston: Museum of Fine Arts. Exhibition catalogue.

REININK, A. W. 1970 "American Influences on Late Nineteenth Century Architecture in the Netherlands." *Journal of the Society of Architectural Historians* 29:163–174.

"A Reminiscence of Richardson." 1892 *Inland Architect and News Record* 20, Sept.:15.

"The Report on the New York State Capitol." 1876 *American Architect and Building News* Mar. 11:82–83.

RETTING, ROBERT B. (editor) 1972 *Architecture of H. H. Richardson and His Contemporaries in Boston and Vicinity, 1972 Annual Tour, Society of Architectural Historians, Tour Notes.* Philadelphia: The society.

RICHARDSON, H. H. 1895 *The Billings Library; The Gift to the University of Vermont of Frederick Billings, H. H. Richardson Architect.* Boston: Heliotype.

"Richardson's Office Practice." 1887 *American Architect and Building News* 22, Oct. 1:154.

ROSEBERRY, CECIL R. 1964 *Capitol Story.* Albany: State of New York.

RUDD, J. WILLIAM 1968 "The Cincinnati Chamber of Commerce Building." *Journal of the Society of Architectural Historians* 27, May:115–123.

SCHEYER, ERNST 1953 "Henry Adams and Henry Hobson Richardson." *Journal of the Society of Architectural Historians* 12, Mar.:7–12.

SCHUYLER, MONTGOMERY 1891*a* "The Romanesque Revival in New York." *Architectural Record* 1, July–Sept.:7–38.

SCHUYLER, MONTGOMERY 1891*b* "The Romanesque Revival in America." *Architectural Record* 1, Oct.–Dec.:151–198.

SCHUYLER, MONTGOMERY (1961)1964 *American Architecture, and Other Writings.* Edited by William H. Jordy and Ralph Coe. New York: Atheneum.

SCULLY, VINCENT J., JR. (1955)1971 *The Shingle Style and the Stick Style: Architectural Theory and Design from Richardson to the Origins of Wright.* New Haven: Yale University Press.

SHEPHERD, WALTER 1939 "Von Herkomer's Folly." *Country Life* 86, Oct.–Dec.:636.

"Some Incidents in the Life of H. H. Richardson." 1886 *American Architect and Building News* 20, Oct. 23:198–199.

STEBBINS, THEODORE 1968 "Richardson and Trinity Church: The Evolution of a Building." *Journal of the Society of Architectural Historians* 27:281–298.

"Trinity Church" 1877 *American Architect and Building News* 2, Aug. 11:254, 258–259.

"Trinity Church Decoration." 1876 *American Architect and Building News* 1:345.

TSELOS, DIMITRI 1970 "Richardson's Influence on European Architecture." *Journal of the Society of Architectural Historians* 29:156–162.

VAN BRUNT, HENRY 1879*a* "The Decoration of Trinity Church, Boston." *American Architect and Building News* 5, no. 178:164–165.

VAN BRUNT, HENRY (1879*b*)1969 "The New Dispensation in Monumental Art." In William A. Coles (editor), *Architecture and Society: Selected Essays of Henry Van Brunt.* Cambridge, Mass.: Belknap.

VAN BRUNT, HENRY (1886)1969 "Henry Hobson Richardson, Architect." In William A. Coles (editor), *Architecture and Society: Selected Essays of Henry Van Brunt.* Cambridge, Mass.: Belknap.

VAN RENSSELAER, MARIANA GRISWOLD 1884 "Recent Architecture in America." *Century* 28:48ff, 333–334, 512–515.

VAN RENSSELAER, MARIANA GRISWOLD 1885 "Recent Architecture in America." *Century* 29:323ff.

VAN RENSSELAER, MARIANA GRISWOLD 1886 "Recent Architecture in America." *Century* 31:677–687; 32:3ff, 17, 20, 206, 421ff.

VAN RENSSELAER, MARIANA GRISWOLD (1888)1969 *Henry Hobson Richardson and His Works.* With an introduction by William Morgan. New York: Dover.

VAN TRUMP, JAMES D. 1957 "The Romanesque Revival in Pittsburgh." *Journal of the Society of Architectural Historians* 16:22–28.

VAN TRUMP, JAMES D. 1958 "The Church Beyond Fashion. . . ." *The Charette* 38, Apr.:26–29.

VAN TRUMP, JAMES D. 1974 "Revived Romanesque in Pittsburgh." *Carnegie Magazine* 48, Mar.:108–113.

VAN ZANTEN, DAVID T. 1964 "H. H. Richardson's Glessner House." *Journal of the Society of Architectural Historians* 23:106–111.

WEBSTER, J. CARSON 1950 "Richardson's American Express Building." *Journal of the Society of Architectural Historians* 9:20–24.

WEINBERG, HELENE BARBARA 1974 "John La Farge and the Decoration of Trinity Church." *Journal of the Society of Architectural Historians* 33:323–353.

WIGHT, PETER B. 1886 "H. H. Richardson." *Inland Architect and Builder* 7, May:59–61.

WILLARD, A. R. 1980 "Recent Church Architecture in Boston." *New England Magazine* New Series 1:641–662.

ZAITZEVSKY, CYNTHIA 1973*a* "A New Richardson Building." *Journal of the Society of Architectural Historians* 32:164–166.

ZAITZEVSKY, CYNTHIA 1973*b* "The Olmsted Firm and the Structures of the Boston Park System." *Journal of the Society of Architectural Historians* 32:167–174.

RICKER, N. C.

Nathan Clifford Ricker (1843–1924) was a pioneer figure in architectural education, the first architectural graduate of collegiate rank in the United States, and a seminal figure in the profession.

Ricker.
Altgeld Hall, University of Illinois (library with James M. White).
Urbana.
1896–1897

Born in Maine, well-prepared in mathematics, languages, and science, and a skilled craftsman, he combined practical architectural experience (following the Chicago fire) with theoretical studies at the University of Illinois to graduate in March 1873. After supplementary study at the Bau-Akademie in Berlin and on his return to Urbana, he led the department of architecture for the next thirty-seven years. In 1878, he was elected dean of engineering, a position he held for twenty-seven years along with the headship of architecture.

Early recognition of the need of architectural students to be acquainted with significant literature led Ricker to translate more than forty volumes ranging from EUGÈNE EMMANUEL VIOLLET-LE-DUC's ten-volume *Dictionnaire Raisonné* to OTTO WAGNER's *Moderne Architektur.*

Ricker's own structural studies resulted in the publication of three books and three technical bulletins. In 1903, he was successful in establishing the University of Illinois Engineering Experiment Station, the first in any American university.

Along with teaching, research, and administration, Ricker was largely responsible for the university's building program during its early years. This included Harker Hall (Chemistry Laboratory) (1877–1878), Drill Hall (Gymnasium Annex) (1889–1890), Natural History Building (1892–1893), and Altgeld Hall (the library), in association with James M. White (1896–1897).

Always active in the profession, Ricker worked closely with DANKMAR ADLER of Chicago in drafting and obtaining passage of the Illinois Architectural Act of 1897—the first legislation in the country to provide for the registration of architects. Ricker also served eighteen years as chairman of the Examining Board, retiring in 1917 when he believed the procedure was well-established.

ALAN K. LAING

WORKS

1877–1878, Harker Hall (Chemistry Laboratory); 1889–1890, Drill Hall (Gymnasium Annex); 1892–1893, Natural History Building; 1896–1897, Altgeld Hall (library with James M. White); University of Illinois, Urbana.

BIBLIOGRAPHY

Many drawings by N. C. Ricker are in the collection of The University of Illinois Archives.

BANNISTER, TURPIN C. 1953 "Pioneering in Architectural Education." *Journal of the American Institute of Architects* 20:3–8, 76–81.

BANNISTER, TURPIN C. (editor) 1954 Volume 1 of *The Architect at Mid Century.* New York: Reinhold. Report of the Commission for the Survey of Education and Registration of the American Institute of Architects.

KIMBALL, SIDNEY F. 1913 "The Department of Architecture: Development, Condition, Ideals." *Alumni Quarterly* (University of Illinois) 7:87–96.

LAING, ALAN K. 1973 *Nathan Clifford Ricker, 1843–1924: Pioneer in American Architectural Education.* Urbana: University of Illinois Press.

O'DONNELL, THOMAS E. 1926 "The Writings and Translations of Dr. N. Clifford Ricker." Urbana, Ill: Unpublished manuscript.

RICKER, N. C. 1922 "The Story of a Life." Urbana, Ill: Unpublished manuscript.

SOLBERG, WINTON U. 1968 *The University of Illinois 1867–1894: An Intellectual and Cultural History.* Urbana: University of Illinois Press.

RICKMAN, THOMAS

Thomas Rickman (1776–1841) was an English church architect during the Commissioners' era in the early nineteenth century.

In Liverpool in 1808, Rickman turned his keen observational powers to local Gothic churches. Within a few years, he developed into a leading scholarly authority on medieval antiquities. His *Attempt to Discriminate the Styles of English Architecture from the Conquest to the Reformation,* which appeared in seven editions between 1817 and 1881, was the most successful of several such treatises of the day.

As a practicing architect, Rickman put this self-taught expertise to good use. In collaboration with John Cragg, a Liverpool iron-master, Rickman designed three Liverpool churches between 1813 and 1816, and soon became adept not only at reproducing medieval details in iron, but also at reusing the components themselves. The formation of the Church Building Commission in 1818 provided Rickman with a bonanza of opportunities, notwithstanding severe criticism of his initial project by JOHN NASH, ROBERT SMIRKE, and

JOHN SOANE, and despite the fact that he never obtained the superintendence of a London church. His ample practice, which included a variety of public and private edifices as well as churches, was directed first from Liverpool and then from Birmingham.

The enormity of Rickman's *oeuvre* attests to his physical energy, eclectic tastes, elegant draftsmanship, popularity with patrons, mastery of details both compositional and administrative, and to the competence of his partners—notably Henry Hutchinson and R. C. Hussey. With the advents of Anglican ecclesiology and the crusading Roman Catholic reforms of A. W. N. PUGIN in the mid-1830s, Rickman's late Georgian Gothic quickly became obsolete, but today his work deserves fuller recognition.

GERALD L. CARR

WORKS

1813–1814, Saint George, Everton; 1814–1815, Saint Michael, Toxteth; 1815–1816, Saint Philip, Hardman Street; Liverpool. 1819–1822, Saint George, Birmingham, England. 1822–1823, Christ Church, Brunswick Square, Gloucester, England. 1822–1825, Saint George, Chorley; 1822–1825, Saint Peter, Preston; Lancashire, England. 1822–1826, Saint Peter, Hampton Lucy, Warwickshire, England. 1823–1825, Saint Paul's, Preston, Lancashire, England. 1825–?, Lough Fea House, County Monaghan, Ireland. *1825–1827, Saint Peter, Dale End, Birmingham, England. 1825–1829, Ombersley Church, Worcestershire, England. *1826–1829, Saint Thomas, Birmingham, England. 1827–1829, Saint John, Oulton, Yorkshire, England. 1827–1831, Saint John's College, The New Court, Cambridge. 1829–1831, Holy Trinity, Bristol, England. 1829–1832, Drapers' Hall, Coventry, England. 1831–1832, Saint Mary the Virgin (west tower), Saffron Walden, Essex, England. 1832–1835, Matfen Hall, Northumberland, England. 1835–1837, All Saints, Stretton-on-Dunmore, Warwickshire, England. 1838–1839, Christ Church, Clevedon, Somerset, England.

BIBLIOGRAPHY

CARR, GERALD L. 1976 "The Commissioners' Churches of London, 1818–1837." Unpublished Ph.D. dissertation, University of Michigan, Ann Arbor.

PORT, MICHAEL H. 1961 *Six Hundred New Churches.* London: S.P.C.K.

RICKMAN, THOMAS (1819)1881 *An Attempt to Discriminate the Styles of English Architecture from the Conquest to the Reformation.* 7th ed. Oxford: Parker.

RIDDLE, THEODATE POPE

One of the earliest women to practice architecture in America, Theodate Pope Riddle (1868–1946) brought to her work a conscious sense of the past, a sensitivity to the use of natural materials, and a particular concern with the process of construction. After graduating from Miss Porter's School in Farmington, Connecticut, in 1886, she restored several nearby homes, was privately tutored at Princeton University, which did not admit women, and worked closely with STANFORD WHITE on the design of her parents' estate, Hill-Stead. By 1910, she was a registered architect with offices in New York and Connecticut. In 1918, Riddle became a member of the American Institute of Architects; eight years later, she was elected an A.I.A. Fellow, one of the first women so honored.

Among her projects are workers' housing, educational institutions, residential estates, and the reconstruction of and addition to the Theodore Roosevelt Birthplace. Riddle's most ambitious work, for which she planned both the academic program and the physical environment, was Avon Old Farms School (1920–1929) in Avon, Connecticut. Inspired by English Cotswold architecture, she translated that picturesque idiom of masonry, half-timbering, and steep slate roofs into a highly original, robust complex.

JUDITH C. PAINE

WORKS

1898–1901, Hill-Stead (Alfred Pope House, with Stanford White), Farmington, Conn. 1906–1909, Westover School; c.1912, Joseph P. Chamberlain Estate; Middlebury, Conn. 1915, Worker's Housing (three double cottages), Farmington, Conn. 1916, Hop Brook School (later altered), Naugatuck, Conn. 1917, Dormer House (Mrs. Charles O. Gates Estate), Locust Valley, N.Y. 1923, Theodore Roosevelt Birthplace (reconstruction, interior restoration, and design of adjacent building), New York. 1920–1929, Avon Old Farms School, Conn.

BIBLIOGRAPHY

ANDREWS, WAYNE (1955)1978 *Architecture, Ambition and Americans.* Rev. ed. New York: Free Press.

"Avon Old Farms: A School for Boys." 1925 *American Architect* 128, no. 2484:391–394.

BOYD, JOHN TAYLOR, JR. 1919 "Some Principles of Small House Design." *Architectural Record* 46:408.

BRANDEGEE, ARTHUR L. 1906 *Farmington, Connecticut: The Village of Beautiful Homes.* Farmington, Conn.: Brandegee & Smith.

BURCHARD, JOHN, and BUSH-BROWN, ALBERT 1966 *The Architecture of America.* Boston: Little, Brown.

"Dormer House." 1919 *Country Life in America* 35, no. 4:56–57.

FERREE, BARR 1910 "'Hill-Stead': The Estate of Alfred Atmore Pope, Esq., Farmington, Connecticut." *American Homes and Gardens* 7, no. 2:45–51.

GREEN, CONSTANCE 1948 *History of Naugatuck, Connecticut.* Naugatuck: The author.

Hitchcock, H. R. (1958)1971 *Architecture: Nineteenth and Twentieth Centuries.* Baltimore: Penguin.

Isham, Norman M., and Brown, Albert F. (1900)1965 *Early Connecticut Houses.* Reprint. New York: Dover.

Jones, Richard F., Jr. 1962 *A Jones Family History.* Bloomfield, Conn.: Privately printed.

McKin, Mead, and White (1914–1918)1981 *A Monograph of the Work of McKim, Mead & White.* Reprint. New York: Architectural Book Publishing Company.

Mumford, Lewis (1931)1955 *The Brown Decades.* 2d ed. Reprint. New York: Dover.

Paine, Judith 1979 *Theodate Pope Riddle: Her Life and Work.* Washington: National Park Service.

"Portfolio." 1929 *The Architect* 12, no. 6:639–651.

Torre, Susan (editor) 1977 *Women in American Architecture: A Historic and Contemporary Perspective.* New York: Watson-Guptill.

RIDOLFI, MARIO

Mario Ridolfi (1904–) was one of the most complicated members of the MIAR. (Movimento Italiano Architettura Razionale), his work being quite independent of the canons of Rationalist orthodoxy. Especially during his early years, Ridolfi's works echoed the two components of his own cultural formation: the academic tradition of the Roman school and an orientation toward German Expressionism. After World War II, Ridolfi played an active part in the debate over reconstruction, stressing the necessity to standardize materials, principles, and building elements in view of the industrialization of the construction industry. At the same time, Ridolfi underscored the need to protect the urban context and the values of the ambiance, not only for historical and artistic purposes, but also for the psychological goal of humanizing architecture through the recovery of regional traditions. Of the many subjects of Ridolfi's study, his work on the house has been a fundamental contribution to Italian culture.

Ridolfi entered the Scuola Superiore di Architettura in Rome in 1924, and there he began a collaboration with Adalberto Libera that lasted through their early careers. Ridolfi's early work was characterized by the alternation between "rarefied classicism" and compositional techniques linked to the Roman baroque (and here the influence of Enrico Del Debbio and Pietro Aschieri could be seen) with works that were clearly Rationalist. Among works in the first group are the competition for the school in Piazza d'Arme in Rome (1926); the library in a garden (1927); and the elliptical residence competition (1927). The Rationalist works include the projects for the restaurant tower and hotel presented at the 1928 Exhibition of MIAR and the thesis project for a seaside Colony at Castelfusano (1929). The Expressionist matrix emerged after his direct contact with German culture and was evident in works such as the Post Office in Piazza Bologna (1933) or the competition for the Palazzo del Littorio (1934), both in Rome.

Ridolfi's trip to Germany and Switzerland in 1933 and his contact with "small-scale rationalism" brought about a change in his work: the analysis of simple elements such as fixtures or furnishings brought him to that "architecture of elements" which allowed him to overcome the antithesis between Rationalism and the Roman school. After the trip, he began to emphasize the theme of the house, a subject which had already interested him and in which he had already executed work of some significance. He also began to make definite his adherence to the language of Rationalist architecture, as shown in the residences in Via de Villa Massimo (1934) and Via San Valentino (1936), Rome, both done in collaboration with the German engineer W. Frankl. Ridolfi's design for the model home at E'42 (1940) testified further to his didactic and experimental interest in the theme of the house.

The immediate postwar period signaled Ridolfi's definitive shift away from the Rationalist experience. His adherence to the new organic tendencies could also be seen in his work as co-director of the new magazine *Metron* (1945). With his editorial work on the *Manuale dell'Architetto* (published in 1946 by the Centro Nazionale delle Ricerche, but the result of research conducted since 1940), Ridolfi furnished an essential contribution to the formation of a new generation that during the postwar reconstruction was involved particularly with subsidized housing. The INA Casa project Tiburtino (1949–1954), Rome, represented for Ridolfi and the other designers an occasion for experimenting with a new design method inspired in part by American sociology and in part by the populism of the Roman baroque. Numerous interesting works derived from the brief success of Ridolfi's new-realist poetics, including the INA Casa quarter in Cerignola (1950) and the houses in Viale Etiopia (1951–1954), Rome, all of which aroused interest throughout Europe, but the brief period ended with the failure of the Tiburtino experience. After the 1950s, Ridolfi continued his studies with consistency, always in collaboration with Frankl. Among other things, he produced the very effective Olivetti Nursery School in Ivrea (1955–1963) and a series of interventions in the city of Terni, the dominant being research on vernacular architecture. After the bitter failure of the Agip Tower Hotel project (1968), which represented a synthesis of all of Ridolfi's work, he retired to Marmore and has since dedicated his time to studying single-family housing typologies.

The interest in the artisan building experience testifies to his love of the crafts which he also transmitted to subsequent generations. Ridolfi also has the distinction of having brought German Expressionism to the attention of Italian architects during his youth and, through the recovery of a vernacular language of architecture, of having furnished Italian postwar and post-Rationalist culture with an impetus for a renewal of the architectural language.

CESARE DE' SETA
Translated from Italian by Diane Ghirardo

WORKS

*1927, Library in a Public Garden, Rome. *1933, Post Office, Piazza Bologna; 1934 House, via di Villa Massimo: Rome. *1936, A. Bordoni Technical Institute (with Wolfgang Frankl), Pavia, Italy. *1936, Palazzina Colombo (with Frankl), via San Valentino; *1940, Rech and Festa Company House, Housing Exhibition, E'42; 1942, Low-cost House for the Castiglione firm, Rome. 1948–1949, INA Casa Apartments, Terni, Italy. *1949–1954, INA Casa Quarter (with Ludovico Quaroni and others), via Tiburtina, Rome. *1950, INA Casa Housing Quarter (with Frankl), Cerignola, Italy. *1951–1954, INA-Assicurazioni Apartments (with Frankl), viale Etiopia, Rome. *1955–1963, Olivetti Nursery School (with Frankl), Canton Vesco, Ivrea, Italy. 1960–1961, Middle School (with Frankl), Terni, Italy. *1968, Project for an Agip Motel (with Frankl), Settebagni, Italy.

BIBLIOGRAPHY

"Architettura di Mario Ridolfi." 1974 *Controspazio* 6, no. 1: entire issue; no. 3: entire issue.

CANELLA, GUIDO, and ROSSI, ALDO 1956 "Architetti italiani: Mario Ridolfi." *Communità* 10: June–July:50–55.

CELINI, FRANCESCO; D'AMATO, CLAUDIO; and VALERIANI, ENRICO (editors) 1979 *Le architetture di Ridolfi e Frankl.* Rome: De Luca.

RIED, BENEDIKT

Benedikt Ried (1454–1534), whose name is spelled in a variety of ways, was born in Upper Austria and died in Bohemia.

He was active mainly in Bohemia. Written sources mention him for the first time in 1489. He was the leading personality of late Gothic architecture in central Europe. His name is connected with the fundamental reconstruction of the Castle of Prague under King Vladislav Jagiello. Ried might have been sent to Prague as a fortification architect by the king's brother-in-law, George the Rich of Landshut. In a period of about twenty years, Ried accomplished several works. First of all, he rebuilt the ancient palace of Emperor Charles IV, having constructed there the new monumental Throne Hall, today called the Vladislav Hall. The hall, of unusual dimensions (62 x 16 x 13 m.), was vaulted by a late Gothic net vault with curved ribs, but its space concept was imbued with the new Renaissance feeling. Of Ried's pupils the best known is Jakob Heilmann who was active in Saxony.

JOŘINA HOŘEJŠÍ

BIBLIOGRAPHY

FEHR, GÖTZ 1961 *Benedikt Ried: Ein deutscher Baumeister zwischen Gotik und Renaissance in Böhmen.* Munich: Callwey.

HOŘEJŠÍ, JIŘINA, and VACKOVÁ, JARMILA 1968 "An der Wende des Zeitalters: Hofkunst um 1500 in Böhmen." *Alte und moderne Kunst* 13.

RIEMERSCHMID, RICHARD

The contribution of Richard Riemerschmid (1868–1957) to the development of modern design in Germany, especially in his native Munich, was seminal. Although he studied painting, he became an architect, executing a number of buildings, interiors, and two garden city projects. Most of his life, however, was devoted to teaching and to designing objects of applied art including furniture, lighting, glassware, ceramics, and textiles. His buildings—mostly country houses, such as his own house in Pasing, Germany, of 1896—as well as his furniture and interior designs, blended the German vernacular with the influence of the English Arts and Crafts movement into a personal version of the northern *Jugendstil.* Riemerschmid was a founding member of many of the prominent associations of progressive designers including the Vereinigte Werkstätten für Kunst in Handwerk (1896)—which he founded with PETER BEHRENS, BRUNO PAUL, Bernhard Pankok, and other designers active in Munich—and the Deutscher Werkbund (1907), of which he was president from 1921 to 1924.

CHRISTOPHER WILK

WORKS

1896, Richard Riemerschmid House, Pasing, Germany. 1899, Music Room, Dresden Exhibition, Germany. *1900, Room for a Lover of Art, World's Fair, Paris. 1901, Schauspielhaus (interior); 1925, Banqueting and Exhibition Halls, Deutsches Museum; Munich.

BIBLIOGRAPHY

BAUER, A. 1911–1912 "Richard Riemerschmid." *Die Kunst* 26:345–368.

BREUER, ROBERT 1910–1911 "Die Gartenstadt Hellerau." *Deutsche Kunst und Dekoration* 27:447–465.

MUTHESIUS, HERMANN 1904 "Die Kunst Richard Riemerschmids." *Dekorative Kunst* 12:249–283.

RÉE, PAUL JOHANNES 1905–1906 "Richard Riemerschmid." *Dekorative Kunst* 14:265–304.

RIEZLER, WALTER 1908 "Neue Arbeiten von Richard Riemerschmid." *Deutsche Kunst und Dekoration* 22:164–214.

RIETVELD, GERRIT

From the 1920s through the early 1960s Gerrit Thomas Rietveld (1888–1964), a Dutch designer, contributed to the formation of a modern design canon. Born in Utrecht, he began his career as a craftsman, expanded the scope of his work to include architecture, and became an internationally acclaimed figure in the art world. Aside from occasional trips, he lived his entire life in Utrecht.

Rietveld's formal education ended at the age of eleven, when he apprenticed in his father's cabinetmaking shop. From 1906 to 1911 he worked as a designer for a local jewelry firm; in 1911 he established his own cabinetmaking studio; and in 1919 he became an independent architect. Throughout these early years he developed skills in architectural drawing and techniques in night classes conducted by the Utrecht architects P. Houtzagers and P. J. Klaarhamer.

In 1919, through contacts with ROBERT VAN'T HOFF and the painter Bart van der Leck, Rietveld began an association with De Stijl, a group of loosely affiliated Dutch and European artists, initiated in 1917 and spearheaded by THEO VAN DOESBURG through his editorship of the periodical *De Stijl*.

Rietveld. Schröder House. Utrecht. 1924

Rietveld's first public recognition came with design of his famous Red-Blue Chair (1918). Rietveld established discrete, rectilinear planes for horizontal and vertical support, and suspended them within modular, three-dimensional Cartesian coordinates of wooden linear members. The separate pieces, overlapping at intersections, reach beyond points of contact, thus extending the volume of the chair into the ambient space. Distinction of parts is further emphasized by the red and blue of back and seat, seen against the yellow-tipped black of the supporting frame. The pristine space composition, which embodied the major tenets of De Stijl, was a design seed for Rietveld's subsequent work, and eventually was incorporated into the wider sphere of twentieth-century design. A photograph of the chair was published in *De Stijl* (1919) and is exhibited today in major modern art museums throughout the world as an icon of early modernism.

Throughout his career Rietveld designed a number of shops, the most historically important of which was the G. Z. C. Jewelry Store in Amsterdam (1920–1922). Rietveld's open and light design—a radical departure from the then current norm—consisted of independent areas, each outlined by red, blue, or yellow frames. The luminous glass cases were arranged, as with the Red-Blue Chair, along a three-dimensional coordinate system, and channeled space continuously from the street through the shop. Floor, ceiling, and walls were coordinated into a total environmental design; space was punctuated by clusters of bare bulbs interspersed throughout. Not only was the short-lived store the first major large scale work in Rietveld's career, it also marked the first architecturally scaled concrete example of De Stijl purist thought. Its artistic success, however, was offset by its economic failure, and the shop was destroyed shortly after completion.

The well-known Schröder House in Utrecht (1924), programmed and designed in collaboration with its owner, shows Rietveld's mastery of a fresh design syntax. Similar to its furniture progenitor, open volumes are asymmetrically defined in the small building by independent planes, perpendicularly linked like slotted and overlapping playing cards which extend beyond their intersections. The Berlin chair (1923), composed almost entirely of vertical and horizontal planes asymmetrically assembled—the Red-Blue chair is symmetrical—was a proximate small-scale model for the house.

Like traditional Japanese domestic interiors, the upper level, which follows Schröder's vision, can be subdivided into a variety of spaces by sliding panels. Sleeping, living, working, and dining areas are thus accommodated within a relatively small space. The lower level, originally consisting of foyer, kitchen, studio, work, and sleeping units, is composed of interpenetrating cubicles, joined visually by glass bands beneath the ceiling.

Although considered quintessential avant-garde design, Rietveld's masterfully organized small spaces fall within a well-established Dutch tradition—one of the smallest countries in the world with one of the highest population densities—of skillfully planning maximum use of minimal spaces. Rietveld extended this minimalist practice qualitatively. His economical use of space admirably satisfies utilitarian needs; but his open, flexible, and impeccably proportioned interiors promote a sense of well-being, as they seem to expand far beyond their physical boundaries. Rietveld created usable spaces, but avoided the functionalist dogma that was developing in European architectural circles during the late twenties. "Functional architecture," he argued, "must not just slavishly satisfy existing needs; it must also reveal living conditions. It must not simply establish space; it must intensively experience space" (Brown, 1958, pp. 160–161)

The Schröder House is, in fact, a small building but the Rietveld design makes it appear much larger than it is. Originally facing open farmland, its loosely-defined volumes swell into the space surrounding it. Free from historical association and bearing no likeness to natural forms, the house clashes with its archaic surroundings. The Schröder House quickly became a landmark of modern architecture—one of the first domestic examples of twentieth-century informality.

During the late 1920s and 1930s Rietveld designed a number of shops, executed several multiple-dwelling designs, and experimented constantly with formal and technical projects for furniture and housing. Especially noteworthy was the Garage and Chauffeur's Quarters (1927–1928) in Utrecht. Prefabricated concrete planks of one by three meters were integrated within a framework of steel "I" members. The planks were sealed with black enamel sprinkled with white, creating a luminous gray vertical-horizontal planar system within the black lines of the steel.

During the same period Rietveld began designing chairs to be stamped out of one piece of material, anticipating current industrial designs in compound-curved, fiberglass forms. In his chairs of bent plywood, seat and back were integrated into continuous simple curves, the seating sup-

Rietveld.
Stoop House.
Velp, Netherlands.
1951

ported by bent metal tubes. In 1929 he began his life-long work on a so-called "core" system of housing, consisting of prefabricated kernels incorporating vertical circulation, plumbing, heating, and electricity. Living spaces were to be arranged around the industrially-constructed center.

Rietveld was a Dutch delegate to the Congrès Internationaux d'Architecture Moderne conferences at La Sarraz, Switzerland (1928), and Frankfurt (1930); and he designed and built low-cost housing for the Werkbund Siedlung in Vienna (1930–1932). In Utrecht, he executed one group (1930–1934) of row houses across from the Schröder House, and another on Robert Schumannstraat (1932); he also built many single houses during the decade, some of which radically departed from the rectilinear purity characteristic of Rietveld's work. The best of the group is the Verrijn-Stuart Summer House at Breukelerveen (1941).

Built over water and accessible only by rowboat, at a distance the summer house looks like a ragged pile of debris. Restricted by local regulations specifying that houses in the isolated area must have pitched roofs and must conform to the rustic character of existing buildings, Rietveld constructed the most rustic house imaginable on a wooden frame, and covered it with shaggy clapboards. Its tilted roof is thatched and the interior ground level floor is finished with round sections of tree trunks embedded in adhesive. Virtually all surfaces and lines are curved, some concave, some convex. Living, dining, and kitchen areas are on the lower level; a sleeping loft overlooks the dining space via a balcony. The compressed living zone flows into the soaring dining area, which overlooks a dramatic stretch of trees and water. Nothing could be more formally alien from Rietveld's characteristic work; yet the playful informality of the dynamically interlocked spaces is pure Rietveld.

During the Great Depression he designed a

line of "Crate Furniture" (1934) manufactured from pre-cut boxwood, one of the earliest examples of inexpensive, knockdown furniture designed to be assembled by the owner. Rietveld's wooden Zig-Zag chair (1934), one of his better known works, is still in production and has been copied extensively in recent years.

During World War II, modern architecture, De Stijl, and Rietveld were of little public interest. But Rietveld reentered the architectural world during the 1950s with a large number of commissions for private houses and a government commission for the Netherlands Pavilion at the Biennale, Venice (1954). He also designed the Juliana Hall and the entrance to the Trade Fair (1956) and housing in Hoograven (1954–1957), both in Utrecht; the De Ploeg Textile Factory at Bergeyk (1956); the Instituut voor Kunstnijverheidsonderwijs in Amsterdam (1956–1968); Akademie voor Beeldende Kunst, Arnhem (1957–1963); and the De Zonnehof (1959–1960), an exhibition hall in Amersfoort.

Of all the relatively large-scale productions of his last years, the temporary Sculpture Pavilion at Sonsbeek Park (1954) is the most artistically successful. Located originally in a wooded area near Arnhem, the pavilion is a classic example of Rietveld's ability to create much with little. He used wood, glass, and concrete-block to establish loosely affiliated surfaces which seem to move centrifigually, as in a pinwheel, from its spatial center. Blocks are stacked on their sides with visible openings allowing for a variety of textured surfaces, against which works can be exhibited. Some blocks are filled, others left open. Inside and outside are literally one, as the ingeniously composed planes of varying heights and lengths slide parallelly and perpendicularly in a thoroughly spatial composition in the tradition of his early works.

In 1961 J. Van Dillen and J. Van Tricht became Rietveld's partners. Thus, many of Rietveld's last works, such as the Rijksmuseum Vincent van Gogh in Amsterdam (1963–1972), were built by his associates after his death. From the 1940s on, Rietveld taught part-time in Rotterdam, The Hague, Arnhem, and Amsterdam.

As the size and number of commissions increased during his last few years, so did national recognition, resulting in awards and honors, among them the Sikkens Prize, the Order of Oranje-Nassau, and the Crown Order of Belgium. His colleagues made him an honorary member of the Bond van Nederlandse Architecten and he received an honorary doctorate from the Technische Hogeschool at Delft a few months before he died in June, 1964.

Rietveld saw himself primarily as a man of action, not a man of thought. With little confidence in formal education, words, and the value of "history," he assumed in 1932 that "art is action" (Brown, 1965).

Paradoxically, this unusually active autodidact, who had so little faith in words, published approximately sixty articles. Collectively, they outline an intellectual position which clearly demonstrates that his preoccupation with the creation of simple lucid forms and spaces was not motivated by an art for art's sake aesthetic, but was based on a deeply held ethical conviction that a building should promote the well being of its inhabitants.

Having little regard for the preciosity of "Art" as it is often defined and practiced, Rietveld aimed to establish life-enhancing surroundings that would increase awareness of the visual, and more specifically spatial, reality of one's environment. Aiming for an expansion of consciousness, he was motivated, he said, by selfishness. Dismissing the notion that art is a "Cultural" activity, Rietveld wrote in 1931 that "art will destroy itself; only a great artist can create pure artless work, . . . [which] . . . is not a luxurious excess or, even worse, a kind of spiritual sublimity which stands outside, above, or beside society. Art is an important economic factor which creates awareness and sharpens discrimination. Art is not self-sufficient; the words 'L'art pour l'art' are as degrading as the words 'applied art'" (*ibid.*).

As a contingent activity, architecture was for Rietveld a transitory environmental arrangement calculated to serve the human needs of the moment. He aimed for practicality in his work but avoided a narrow functionalism, since his flexible spaces were calculated to adjust to changing needs over long periods of time.

He avoided monumentality as he believed this approach, through its historical, aesthetic, and cultural associations, distracts from the quality of the life of the inhabitants the building is intended to serve. On the other hand, a functional approach, which is necessarily based on a fixed notion of activities, tends to freeze an inherently changing situation.

Thus buildings, for Rietveld, were not vehicles for values nor were they intended to be rational responses to precise functional requirements. Instead, architecture was viewed by him as a complex artifact that allows us to enter reality. "Architecture is not a matter of beauty or ugliness, but of clarity. . . . Good architecture is a fragment of reality which forces a partial expansion of ourself. . . . It is the background of our life, neither more beautiful nor ugly; but if it is good: clear" (*ibid.*).

THEODORE M. BROWN

WORKS

*1920–1922, G. Z. C. Jewelry Store, Amsterdam. 1924, Schröder House; *1927–1928, Garage and Chauffeur's Quarters, 10 Waldeck Pyrmontkade; Utrecht. *1928, Zaudy Shop, Wesel, Germany. 1930–1932, Row Houses, Wiener Werkbund Siedlung, Vienna. 1930–1934, Row Houses, Erasmuslaan; 1932, Row Houses, Robert Schumannstraat; Utrecht. 1941, Verrijn-Stuart Summer House, Breukelerveen, Netherlands. 1951, Stoop House, Velp, Netherlands. *1954, Netherlands Pavilion, Biennale, Venice, Italy. *1954, Sculpture Pavilion, Sonsbeek Park, Arnheim, Netherlands. 1954–1957, Housing, Hoograven; 1956, Juliana Hall and Entrance, Trade Fair; Utrecht. 1956, De Ploeg Textile Factory, Bergeyk, Netherlands. 1956–1964, Instituut voor Kunstnijverheidsonderwijs (now Gerrit Rietveldacademie; not completed until 1968), Amsterdam. 1957–1963, Academie voor Beeldende Kunst, Arnhem, Netherlands. 1958–1959, Van Doel House, Ilpendam, Netherlands. 1959–1960, De Zonnehof, Amersfoort, Netherlands. 1961–1964, Van Sloobe House, Heerlen, Netherlands. 1963–1964, Rijksmuseum Vincent van Gogh (completed by J. Van Dillen and J. Van Tricht in 1972), Amsterdam.

BIBLIOGRAPHY

BANHAM, REYNER (1960)1967 *Theory and Design in the First Machine Age.* 2d ed. New York: Praeger.

BERTHEUX, WIL 1972 *G. Rietveld Architect.* Amsterdam: Stedelijk Museum. Exhibition catalogue.

BROWN, THEODORE M. 1958 *The Work of G. Rietveld, Architect.* Utrecht: Bruna & Zoon.

BROWN, THEODORE M. 1965 "Rietveld's Egocentric Vision." *Journal of the Society of Architectural Historians.* 24:292–296. Quotations in the text are from this article.

BROWN, THEODORE M. 1968 "Mondrian and Rietveld, The Divining Rod and the Compass." *Nederlands Kunsthistorisch Jaarboek* 19:205–214.

BUFFINGA, A. 1971 *G. Th. Rietveld.* Amsterdam: Meulenhoff.

FANELLI, GIOVANNI 1968 *Architettura Moderna in Olanda 1900–1940.* Florence, Italy: Marchi & Bertolli.

JAFFE, HANS LUDWIG C. 1956 *De Stijl/1917–1931.* Amsterdam: Meulenhoff.

MULDER, BERTUS 1975 *Rietveld Schröder Huis 1925–1975.* Utrecht: Bruna & Zoon.

OVERLY, PAUL 1969 *De Stijl.* London: Studio Vista.

PETERSEN, AD (editor) 1968 *De Stijl.* 2 volumes. Amsterdam: Athenaeum. Facsimile reprint of the periodical, complete from 1917–1932.

Rietveld, 1924. Schröder Huis. 1963 Amsterdam: Steendrukkerij De Jong.

WILSON, COLIN ST. JOHN 1964 "Gerrit Rietveld: 1888–1964." *Architectural Review* 136:399–402.

RIGOTTI, ANNIBALE

Annibale Rigotti (1870–1968) was born in Turin, Italy. From 1893 to 1896, Rigotti worked in Constantinople with RAIMONDO D'ARONCO, and in 1907 he was in Bangkok. He entered many competitions and taught in Parma, Florence, Turin, and Venezia. He soon replaced the neoclassic forms of his master, Cresentino Caselli, with neo-Gothic and neopicturesque styles and became a knowledgeable and authoritative exponent of the evolving early modern architecture. Among his many works are the cemetery in Treviso (1893), the Palazzo Municipale in Cagliari (1898), an influential skeletal Tudor Gothic structure; the Esposizione Internazionale delle Arti Figurativi, Turin (1901; with d'Aronco); the Circolo degli artisti in Turin (1915); and many buildings in Thailand.

HENRY A. MILLON

WORKS

1893, Cemetery, Treviso, Italy. 1896, Municipal Theater, Sitov, Bulgaria. 1897, Public School, Sommariva, Italy. 1898, Palazzo Municipale, Cagliari, Italy. 1901, Turin Esposizione Internazionale delle Arti Figurativi (with Raimondo D'Aronco); 1913, Cassa di Risparmio; 1915, Turin Circolo degli artisti; 1930, Vegetable and Fruit Market (with Giorgio Rigotti); Turin, Italy.

BIBLIOGRAPHY

BORASI, VINCENZO 1960–1961 "Sulla paternità artistica del Palazzo Communale di Cagliari." *Bollettino della Società Piemontese di Archeologia e Belle Arti* 14–15:169–180.

MARCONI, PAOLO, and ZEDDI, NANNI 1964–1965 "Annibale Rigotti e il Palazzo Comunale di Cagliari." *L'architettura* 10, no. 113:772–776.

LEVA PISTOI, MILA 1969 *Torino: Mezzo secolo di architettura.* Turin, Italy.

RIPLEY, THOMAS

Thomas Ripley (c.1683–1758) rose from laborer to comptroller of the Office of Works in succession to JOHN VANBRUGH in 1726. Ripley was not an extreme Palladian, but more an executant of designs by others. Blatherwyck Hall, Northamptonshire (1720), and Wolterton Hall, Norfolk (1727), demonstrate his competence in handsome but plain architecture. He was patronized by Sir Robert Walpole to whom he owed the surveyorship of Greenwich Hospital (1729) and who may have secured him the job of designing the Admiralty, Whitehall (1723). Ripley also worked extensively for other Walpoles.

JOHN HARRIS

WORKS

1718, Customs House, Liverpool, England. 1720, Blatherwyck Hall, Northamptonshire, England. 1723, Admiralty, Whitehall, London. 1727, Wolterton Hall, Norfolk, England.

RISTORO, FRA, and SISTO, FRA

According to his obituary, written in the sixteenth century, Fra Ristoro (1225?–1283?) entered the convent of Santa Maria Novella as a lay brother around 1250. Together with Fra Sisto (1225?–1289), he was charged with overseeing works for the Florentine Commune (for example, the rebuilding of Ponte alla Carraia 1260s–1270s) and with the design for the present Church of Santa Maria Novella (1279). Many other works have been attributed to the two lay brothers, the most important one being the design of Santa Maria sopra Minerva, Rome (1280s), but these are difficult to substantiate.

CHRISTINE SMITH

WORKS

(A)1260s–1270s, Bargello; (A)1260s–1270s, Ponte alle Carraia (reconstruction); (A)1260s–1270s, Ponte alle Grazie (reconstruction); Florence. (A)1260s–1270s, San Domenico, Pistoia, Italy. (A)1260s–1270s, San Remigio; (A)1260s–1270s, Santa Maria Novella; (A)1280s, Santa Maria sopra Minerva; (A)1280s, Vatican Palace (vaults); Rome.

BIBLIOGRAPHY

MEERSSEMAN, GERARD G. 1972 "Origini del tipo di Chiesa Umbro-Toscano degli Ordini Mendicanti." Pages 63–77 in *Il Gotico a Pistoia nei suoi rapporti con l'arte Gotica Italiana.* Pistoia: Centro Italiano di studi di storie e d'arte. Rome: Tipografia Centenari.

ORLANDI, STEFANO (editor) 1955 *Necrologio de S. Maria Novella: 1235–1504.* Florence: Olschki.

Rizzo.
Doge's Palace (courtyard, east side).
Venice.
After 1483

RIZZO, ANTONIO

Antonio Rizzo (1430–1498?) emerged as an architect in Venice in the latter half of the fifteenth century. Born in Verona (or Como?), he was trained as a sculptor and continued working in sculpture while accepting building commissions. As early as the sixteenth century, some confusion surrounded his name and he has been variously identified in the literature as Antonio Bregno or Antonio Dentone. Few works can be attributed to him with any degree of certainty.

Rizzo must have come to Venice in the early 1460s. The earliest records of him in the city are as a sculptor for the tomb of Orsato Giustiniani, today known only from an eighteenth-century drawing. His first major commission was for the tomb monument of Doge Nicolò Tron in the Church of Santa Maria Gloriosa dei Frari in Venice (c.1476–1479). Containing twenty-two free-standing figures and six reliefs, it was the largest such monument erected in Venice at that time. It is the only monument which is generally agreed to be by Rizzo. His only signed work was that of the statue of Eve (c.1480) in the niche of the façade of the Arco Foscari, the principal entrance into the Palazzo Ducale in Venice. The statue of Adam in the opposite niche is also presumed to be by him.

Rizzo's most important architectural commission was the reconstruction of the east portion of the Palazzo Ducale which was destroyed in a fire of 1483. He held the position of *protomaestro,* or chief architect, until 1498. The articulation of the east wing, with its prolific application of ornament in relief produces an effect which is decidedly more pictorial than architectural. The design of the lower part of the back façade of the palazzo along the Rio della Canonica has also been attributed to Rizzo. It is notable for its rusticated socle, an unusual feature in Venice.

Construction of the monumental outdoor staircase on the east side of the courtyard of the palazzo began in 1485. Ever since the placement of JACOPO SANSOVINO's enormous sixteenth-century statues of Mars and Neptune at the top of the staircase, it has been known as the Scala dei Giganti. As a free-standing staircase on a large scale, the Scala dei Giganti has been considered the first monumental example of its kind.

Lack of funds halted the building of the staircase several times. Forced to flee Venice in 1498 for having embezzled palace funds, Rizzo was not heard from again.

CARLA PUPPIN

WORKS

*c.1464, Tomb of Orsato Giustiniani (originally in

Sant' Andrea della Certosa); Venice, Italy. c.1476–1479, Tomb Monument of Doge Nicolò Tron, Santa Maria Gloriosa dei Frari; c.1480, Statues of Adam and Eve, Arco Foscari (façade), Palazzo Ducale; After 1483, Palazzo Ducale (remodeling of east wing); 1485–c.1495, Scala dei Giganti Palazzo.

BIBLIOGRAPHY

McAndrew, John 1980 *Venetian Architecture of the Early Renaissance.* Cambridge, Mass.: M.I.T. Press.

Munman, Robert 1968 "Venetian Renaissance Tomb Monuments." Unpublished Ph.D. dissertation, Harvard University, Cambridge, Mass.

Munman, Robert 1973 "Antonio Rizzo's Sarcophagus for Nicolò Tron: A Closer Look." *Art Bulletin* 55:77–85.

Muraro, Michaelangelo 1961 "La Scala senza Giganti." In M. Meiss (editor), *De Artibus Opuscala XL: Essays in Honor of Erwin Panofsky.* 2 vols. New York University Press.

Paoletti, Pietro 1893 *L'Architettura e la scultura del Rinascimento a Venezia.* Venice: Organia-Naya.

Pohlandt, Von Wiebke 1971 "Antonio Rizzo." *Jahrbuch der Berliner Museen* 13:162–207.

Venturi, Adolfo 1924 Part 2 in *Architettura del quattrocento.* Volume 8 in *Storia dell'Arte Italiana.* Milan: University of Hoepli.

ROA, YVES

Working within the general vocabulary of the International style, Yves Roa (1927–), who was born in Tunisia, combines in his architecture industrial materials and techniques with a sensitivity toward nature. In his suburban homes outside of Paris, he added traditional materials such as stone and wood which he exploits for their natural beauty and warmth.

Mehrangiz Nikou Sexton

WORKS

1961, E.D.F. Administrative Unit, Melun, France. 1961, E.D.F. Laboratory, Saint Denis, France. 1963, Weekend House, near Paris. 1966, House, Demmarie-les-Lys, France. 1979, Intercontinental Okoume Palace Hotel (with Clement Cacoub), Libreville. 1979, Residence for Visiting Heads of States (with Cacoub), Abidjan.

BIBLIOGRAPHY

"E.D.F. Laboratoire d'Essais Spéciaux à Saint Denis." *L'Architecture d'aujourd'hui* 32, no. 95:30–32.

"E.D.F. Unité Administrative à Melun," 1961 *L'Architecture d'aujourd'hui* 32, no. 95:92–93.

"Habitation de fonction à Dammarie-les-Lys." 1966 *L'Architecture Française* 27, nos. 289–290:62–64.

"Intercontinental Okoume Palace at Libreville." 1979 *Mur Vivant* 52:92–93.

"Weekend House near Paris." 1963 *Arts and Architecture* 80:14–15.

ROBBIA, LUCA DELLA

Although he may take third place in importance among sculptors of the early Italian Renaissance behind Donatello and Lorenzo Ghiberti, Luca della Robbia (1399/1400–1482) was nonetheless a significant figure. He is also of some special interest for the history of architecture. He not only realized architectural ideas of Filippo Brunelleschi in the decorative passages of some of his sculpture, but also contributed sculptural ornament to many important buildings of the early Renaissance.

Born in Florence, the son of a worker in the Florentine wool trade, Luca may have been trained as a goldsmith, like Brunelleschi. It is probable that he worked in the shop of Ghiberti (either between 1423 and 1424 or 1427 and 1429) before he moved to the shop of Nanni di Banco at the Cathedral in Florence. There, he learned the blend of Nanni's monumental classicism and Ghiberti's Gothic sweetness that was to serve him throughout his sculptural career.

Robbia. Detail from Museo dell'Opera del Duomo (cantoria). Florence. 1431

Luca della Robbia's first major independent commission was the Cantoria or Singing Gallery of 1431 for the Cathedral in Florence (now Museo dell'Opera del Duomo, Florence). In reality an organ loft, this work shows strong evidence of Brunelleschi's influence and possible participation. The paired Corinthian pilasters that divide the figural fields recall Brunelleschi's late works, such as the Tribunes for the Cathedral. Indeed, it is likely that a work in the crossing of the Cathedral, under Brunelleschi's great cupola would have been directed, at least in part, by the great architect himself.

Luca also provided enameled terra-cotta figures for the walls of Brunelleschi's Pazzi Chapel (1442–1452). This technique of enameled terracotta became Luca's characteristic form, and it has been suggested by John Pope-Hennessey (1980,

Robbia. Museo dell'Opera del Duomo (cantoria). Florence. 1431

Robbia.
Detail from Pazzi Chapel (apostles and saints), San Croce.
Florence.
1442–1452

Robbia.
Pazzi Chapel (apostles and saints), San Croce.
Florence.
1442–1452

p. 37) that Brunelleschi may even have invented this colorful technique. Certainly Luca's works for the Pazzi Chapel must be seen as an organized response to Donatello's roundels for Brunelleschi's Old Sacristy (San Lorenzo, Florence). Instead of the polychromed perspective system used by Donatello and opposed by Brunelleschi, Luca used a bichromatic color system of blue and white in the Pazzi Chapel. The heiratic poses of the Pazzi Chapel figures and their careful disposition within the space reinforce the architectural harmony of Brunelleschi's work.

In later years, Luca devoted himself almost completely to terra-cotta statuary and became known as one of the best Florentine decorative sculptors. He continued to collaborate with architects, as in the highly colored ceiling of the Chapel of the Crucifixion of 1449 (San Miniato al Monte, Florence) in which he aided MICHELOZZO DI BARTOLOMMEO and in the decoration for the Chapel of the Cardinal of Portugal in the same church (1461–1462) where he aided Antonio Rossellino. The latter work is one of the great collaborative masterpieces of the early Renaissance. In addition to della Robbia and Rossellino, Piero and Antonio Pollaiuolo and Alesso Bladovinetti worked there.

Luca was responsible for setting up a workshop of some size and economic importance. Using simple means of reproduction, Luca was able to mass-produce copies of his works so that they are found not only throughout Italy but also throughout the world.

NICHOLAS ADAMS

WORKS

1431, Museo dell'Opera del Duomo (cantoria); 1442–1452, Pazzi Chapel (apostles and saints), San Croce; 1449, Chapel of the Crucifixion (ceiling decoration), San Miniato al Monte; 1461–1462, Chapel of the Cardinal of Portugal (ceiling decoration), San Miniato al Monte; Florence.

BIBLIOGRAPHY

POPE-HENNESSY, JOHN 1980 *Luca della Robbia.* Ithaca, N.Y.: Cornell University Press.

ROBERT, HUBERT

Painter and garden designer, Hubert Robert (1733–1808) collected and illustrated rural scenes in the 1740s. He was in Rome from 1754 to 1765 as a pensionnaire of the French Academy, and in 1763 guided CLAUDE-HENRI WATELET through this city. He later visited and sketched at Watelet's Moulin-Joli. His earliest independent garden design may be for the MARQUIS DE GIRARDIN at Ermenonville (1770s), where he is probably responsible for at least the design of the Brasserie and Jean-Jacques Rousseau's tomb. In 1778 he became "dessinateur des jardins du Roi" at Versailles. He was a key figure in the transition from the gardening vocabulary and techniques developed at Ermenonville to those of later gardens where the sentimental and moral associations and the imitation of painting were replaced by a direct working with nature to create theatrical effects. His ability to achieve these was unsurpassed. Méréville, where he replaced FRANÇOIS-JOSEPH BÉLANGER in 1786, is his *chef d'oeuvre,* and the finest mature example of the French picturesque garden.

DORA WIEBENSON

WORKS

1770s, Ermenonville Garden, France. From 1780, Betz Garden (with Duc d'Harcourt), France. From 1786, Méréville Garden, France.

BIBLIOGRAPHY

CAYEUX, JEAN DE 1968 "Hubert Robert dessinateur de jardins et sa collaboration au Parc de Méréville." *Bulletin de la Société de l'histoire de l'art français* 1968:127–133.

CHOPPIN DE JANVRY, OLIVIER 1969 "Méréville." *L'Oeil* 180, Dec.:30–41, 83, 96.

NOLHAC, PIERRE DE 1910 Pages 56–60 in *Hubert Robert: 1733–1808.* Paris: Goupil.

ROBERT DE COUCY

See JEAN D'ORBAIS.

ROBERT DE LUZARCHES

Robert de Luzarches (or Lusarches), Thomas de Cormont, and Regnault de Cormont were successive architects of the Cathedral of Notre-Dame at Amiens, France, from around 1220 to around 1290. This is known from an inscription installed in the center of the labyrinth in the nave pavement by Regnault in 1288.

En lan de grace mil II^{c}
Et XX fu leuvre de cheens
Premierement encommenchie
Adonc yert de cheste evesquie
Evart ecesques benis
Et roy de France Loys
Qui fu filz Phelippe le Sage.
Chil qui maistre yert de loeuvre
Maistre Robert estoit nommes
Et de Lusarches surnommes
Maistre Thomas fu apres luy
De Cormont, et apres
Ses filz maistre Regnault, qui mettre
Fist a chest point chy ceste lettre
Que lincarnation valoit
XIII^{c} ans en faloit.

The information obtained is principally the sequence of the three architects: that Robert de Luzarches was the first master who began the church in 1220; that he was followed by Thomas de Cormont for an unspecified period; and that Thomas was followed by his son, Regnault de Cormont, who installed the inscription twelve years before the year of the Incarnation 1300, that is, in 1288.

This inscription being the only documentation concerning Robert, Thomas, and Regnault at Amiens, there is considerable disagreement about the tenures and contributions of each to the cathedral.

Robert de Luzarches is correctly considered the designer of the cathedral since it was he who first established its scale (but possibly not its size in the sense of length) and its aesthetic effect. Robert's actual work may have been limited to the outer walls of the nave and the nave aisles with their vaults.

Cathedral of Notre-Dame (nave labyrinth inscription). Amiens, France. 1288

Robert was followed as master by Thomas de Cormont beginning around 1235. The traditional view is that the nave was completed by Robert and that Thomas was responsible for the lower parts of the east side of the transept, the choir aisles and ambulatory, and the radiating chapels of the choir. Robert Branner proposed that Thomas was called to Paris in the early 1240s (September 1241?) to build the Sainte-Chapelle for Louis IX. French scholars emphatically deny this possibility, and Alain Erlande-Brandenburg (1977) has more recently proposed that Thomas designed and erected the west façade and the upper parts of the nave of Amiens, dated from 1236 on, rejecting the traditional attribution of this work to Robert.

Whatever happened to Thomas, his son Regnault replaced him and was master for nearly fifty years, from around 1240 to at least 1288. Regnault was responsible for the choir above the triforium and for the transept terminals (and possibly for the crossing vault). Regnault's work is fairly uniform despite the long period required for it and the fact that work was interrupted by a fire in 1258 and slowed down in the period 1248–1254 when the bishop accompanied the king, Louis IX, on a crusade to Egypt. The donation of a window for the hemicycle clearstory by Bernard d'Abbeville in 1269 indicates the main vaulting must have been complete or nearly so by that date. Comparison with manuscript miniatures shows that the choir buttresses, Regnault's work, were serving as models no later than 1300.

The specific tenures at Amiens of its three architects are less significant than their cumulative effect. From EUGÈNE EMMANUEL VIOLLET-LE-DUC (1854–1868) through Paul Frankl (1947), Amiens has been considered the most "rational" of the French Gothic cathedrals, the epitome of possibilities within the style. Robert de Luzarches can be assigned no buildings previous to Amiens, but he was thoroughly familiar with Parisian work and may have been trained in or around that city. Robert took several dramatic steps which made Amiens different from any building which had come before and which set Gothic architecture on a new course. Amiens in all likelihood was the first Gothic building executed entirely from designs drawn before construction was begun, and Robert rejected a geometric basis of design in favor of an arithmetical system. In addition, he perfected if he did not actually invent a novel system of systemization and prefabrication of parts.

These approaches to design permitted what was Robert de Luzarches's principal accomplishment, the aesthetic effect of Amiens. Robert categorically renounced the massive structure of Chartres and Reims in favor of the skeletal thinness of Soissons, a building he surely knew, in order to create a building characterized by a brittle tenseness of surface and precision of details. This aesthetic, despite changes in details by Thomas and by Regnault, enforced an aesthetic unity throughout this vast (133.50 meters interior length; 42.30 meters interior height) building.

The employment of bar tracery designs, beginning with Robert but continued and developed by Thomas and, especially, by Regnault, made Amiens a characteristically Court style building with influence as far away as Cologne. The collective achievements of Robert de Luzarches, Thomas de Cormont, and Regnault de Cormont were revolutionary. It is with reason that JOHN RUSKIN characterized Amiens as "Gothic [architecture] clear of Romanesque tradition, pure, authoritative, unsurpassable, and beyond criticism."

CARL F. BARNES, JR.

BIBLIOGRAPHY

The labyrinth inscription of Amiens giving the names of its successive architects was destroyed in 1828, but was recorded in the early fourteenth century in the Registre des Distributions du Chapître, *volume 2, folio 247, Archives de la Somme, Amiens, France. Fragments were preserved in the Musée de Picardie in Amiens.*

BARNES, CARL F., JR. 1978 "Cross-media Design Motifs in XIIIth-Century France: Architectural Motifs in the Psalter and Hours of Yolande de Soissons and in the Cathedral of Notre-Dame at Amiens." *Gesta* 17, no. 2:37–40.

BRANNER, ROBERT 1962 "Paris and the Origins of Rayonnant Gothic Architecture Down to 1240." *Art Bulletin* 44:39–51.

BRANNER, ROBERT 1965 Pages 61–67, 138–140 in *St. Louis and the Court Style in Gothic Architecture.* London: Zwemmer.

DURAND, GEORGES 1901–1903 *Monographie de l'église Notre-Dame cathédrale d'Amiens.* Paris: Picard; Amiens, France: Yvert & Teller.

DURAND, GEORGES 1936 "Bibliographie de la cathédrale d'Amiens." *Congrès Archéologique de France* 99:9–27.

ERLANDE-BRANDENBURG, ALAIN 1977 "La façade de la cathédrale d'Amiens." *Bulletin Monumental* 135:253–293.

FRANKL, PAUL 1947 "A French Gothic Cathedral: Amiens." *Art in America* 35:295–299.

KIMPEL, DIETER 1977 "Le développement de la taille en série dans l'architecture médiévale et son rôle dans l'histoire économique." *Bulletin Monumental* 135:195–222.

PRAK, NIELS LUNING 1966 "Measurements of Amiens Cathedral." *Journal of the Society of Architectural Historians* 25:209–212.

VIOLLET-LE-DUC, EUGÈNE EMMANUEL (1854-1868) 1967 *Dictionnaire raisonné de l'architecture française du XIe au XVIe siècle.* 10 vols. Reprint. Paris: Nobele.

ROBERTO BROTHERS

The Roberto Brothers—Marcelo (1908–1964), Milton (1914–1953), and Mauricio (1921–)—have been responsible for five decades of innovative tropical architecture in Brazil. A distinctive Roberto style has never emerged; instead, each structure bearing their names has uniquely responded to specific needs. The oldest brother, Marcelo, graduated in 1930 from the National School of Fine Arts (which all three brothers attended) and began his firm in 1931 after traveling to Europe. Milton joined the firm in 1934, and in 1935 the brothers won their first and Brazil's first architectural competition for the Brazilian Press Association Building (1935–1936). Aware of LE CORBUSIER's *brise-soleil* (sun breaker) designs for the 1933 Algiers project, they faced two sides of the rectilinear block with vertically fixed sun breakers. As the first large office building in Brazil to use reinforced concrete and sun breakers and to depart from the eclectic structures which pervaded at the time, the building established a precedent for the development of modern architecture in Brazil.

In 1937, the Robertos won their second competition, Santos Dumont Airport, which led to a successful experimentation with sun breakers in the shape of an exterior eggcrate which allowed an unobstructed view but deflected sunlight from directly entering the airport terminal.

Mauricio, began to work with his brothers in 1941, three years before finishing his architectural degree. The first structure to bear all three names was the Instituto de Resseguras Headquarters (1942), which anticipated later worldwide developments by breaking away from the box shape with four distinct, asymmetrical façades. Their Tijuca resort development (1943) was noted as one of the ten best modern works of architecture in the world.

Movement and variety distinguished Roberto designs long before these qualities became internationally popular. Mauricio stated that the striking diversity of each Roberto project was a combination of their objective approach, which he attributed to the influence of FRANK LLOYD WRIGHT, and the continual influx of new ideas as each brother joined the firm. They attacked architectural problems directly by seeking the simplest solutions with available materials. Foremost in their projects has been control of Brazil's intense sunlight. Experimenting with different designs for sun breakers, they created a most original design for the Seguradores Office Building (1949); Mauricio updated it for his Academy of Letters Building (1972–1977) in Rio. Movable shutters hung on frames two feet from the building allowed individual control of the sun's intensity from the interior.

Milton died in 1953, four years after becoming president of the Brazilian Institute of Architects. Marcelo and Mauricio continued to maintain the same level of excellence in architecture and each expanded their involvement in the field of urbanism. Marcelo had been head of the department of architecture and urbanism at Brazil's Federal University in Rio de Janeiro since 1938 and concentrated on urbanism until his death. Fortunately, Mauricio has sustained the firm, and recently his son, Marcio, joined him, adding to the regenerating tradition of the Roberto name in Brazilian architecture.

ELIZABETH D. HARRIS

WORKS

1935–1936, Brazilian Press Association Building; 1937, Santos Dumont Airport; 1942, Instituto de Resseguros do Brasil Headquarters; Rio de Janeiro. 1943, Resort Development, Barra da Tijuca, Brazil. 1945, Apartment Building on Nossa Senhora da Copacabana; 1949, SOTREQ-Caterpilar Offices and Showroom; 1949, Seguradores Office Building; 1962, Parque Eduardo Guinle Club; Rio de Janeiro. 1970, Bank of Brazil Headquarters, São Luis, Brazil. 1972–1977, Brazilian Academy of Letters Building, Rio de Janeiro.

Roberto Brothers. Seguradores Office Building. Rio de Janeiro. 1949

BIBLIOGRAPHY

FERRAZ, GERALDO 1956 "Individualidades na História da Atual Arquitetura no Brasil—IV. M.M.M. Roberto." *Habitat* 6, June:49–66.

GOODWIN, PHILIP L. 1943 *Brazil Builds: Architecture New and Old, 1652–1942.* New York: Museum of Modern Art.

ROBERTS, HENRY

Henry Roberts (1803–1876) is remembered chiefly as a pioneer of working class housing. The son of a merchant of the City of London, he was articled to CHARLES FOWLER. He entered the Royal Academy School in 1825 and worked for ROBERT SMIRKE before making an extensive tour of Italy and other parts of the continent. He set up practice in 1830. He became honorary architect of the Society for Improving the Condition of the Labouring Classes and designed a number of model dwellings including those built for Prince Albert as part of the Great Exhibition of 1851. His numerous publications on working class housing included *The Dwellings of the Labouring Classes,* first published in 1850, which was translated into French. He retired to Italy and died in Florence in 1876. GEORGE GILBERT SCOTT worked for him.

ROGER DIXON

WORKS

1832–1835, Hall of the Fishmongers' Company, London. *1837, Escott House, Ottery Saint Mary, Devon, England. 1840–1841, Saint Mary, Elvetham, Hampshire, England. *1844–1846, First London Bridge Station (rebuilt 1851); 1849–1850, Model Family Houses, Streatham Street, Bloomsbury; 1851, Model Houses in Hyde Park (now in Kensington Park); London.

BIBLIOGRAPHY

GRAVES, ALGERNON (1905)1970 *The Royal Academy of Arts.* Reprint. East Ardsley, England: S. R. Publishers.

"Henry Roberts." 1887 Volume 7, pages 51–52 in Wyatt Papworth (editor), *The Dictionary of Architecture.* London: Architectural Publication Society.

METCALF, PRISCILLA 1977 *The Halls of the Fishmongers' Company.* Chichester, England: Phillimore.

ROBERTS, HENRY (1850)1867 *The Dwellings of the Labouring Classes.* Expanded ed. London: Society for Improving the Condition of the Labouring Classes.

TARN, JOHN N. 1971 *Working-class Housing in 19th-century Britain.* London: Lund Humphries.

ROBERTSON, HOWARD MORLEY

Howard Morley Robertson (1888–1963) was born in Utah and educated in England. He obtained his diploma in architecture from the Ecole des Beaux-Arts in Paris in 1913 and worked for a time in architectural offices in Boston and New York. He entered into partnership with J. Murray Easton in London in 1919. Robertson was principal, then director of education, at the Architectural Association School from 1920 to 1935, years in which a number of soon-to-be-eminent students passed through the school. He shared with F. R. Yerbury, the association secretary, a passionate interest in continental architecture, which Yerbury would photograph and Robertson would write about. Continental influences are ever present in his work of the 1920s and 1930s. Though Robertson could at times be avant-garde, his architecture tended to be in a simplified Renaissance style. He was knighted for his work.

BRIAN HANSON

WORKS

Before 1925, Bathing Pool and Pavilion, Golf Hotel, and Residences, Prestatyn, Wales. 1925, British Pavilion, International Exposition, Paris. 1925, Royal Horticultural Society Hall (with J. Murray Easton); 1929, Savoy Court and Hotel (with Easton); 1929–1932, Liberty's Department Store (with Easton), Great Marlborough Street; 1930, Offices, 52 Cornhill; London. 1930, Oxford University Press Warehouse, Neasden, London. 1932, Royal Bank of Canada, 6 Lothbury; 1932–1933, Nurses' Home and Children's Hospital, 37–46 Guilford Street; London. 1935, British Pavilion, International Exposition, Brussels. 1936, British Pavilion, World's Fair, Johannesburg. 1936, British Pavilion, World's Fair, New York. 1937, Flats, Avenue Close; 1937, Flats, Saint Edmund's Terrace; 1938, Metropolitan Water Board Laboratories, London. 1939, City of London Electricity Supply Company Showrooms. 1946–1947, Sanatorium, Uppingham School, Rutland, England. 1949, SS Rangitane (interiors). 1949, SS Rangitoto (interiors). 1950, Flats, Church Street; 1950, Flats, Saint John's Wood Road; London. 1951, Hatfield Technical College, Hertfordshire, England. 1951, SS Ruahine (interiors). 1952–1963, Plan, University of Reading, Berkshire, England. 1956, Bank of England Printing Works, Loughton, Essex, England. 1956, Faculty of Letters, University of Reading, Berkshire, England. 1958, Bank of England Returned Note Building, Loughton, Essex, England. 1961, Shell Centre Building, London. 1961–1967, Lloyd's Bank Regional Head Offices, Birmingham, England.

BIBLIOGRAPHY

BANHAM, REYNER 1953 "Howard Robertson." *Architectural Review* 114:160–168.

"Men of the Year—Howard Robertson." 1953 *Architects' Journal* 117:68.

ROBERTSON, HOWARD 1922 "Modern Dutch Architecture." *Architectural Review* 52:46–50.

ROBERTSON, HOWARD 1924*a* "Modern Sweden." *Architectural Review* 56:24–31.

ROBERTSON, HOWARD (1924*b*)1955 *The Principles of Architectural Composition.* London: Architectural Press.

ROBERTSON, HOWARD 1924–1925 "The Architecture of Finland." *Architectural Review* 56:215–219; 57:34–39.

ROBERTSON, HOWARD 1926 *Architecture Explained.* London and New York: Benn.

ROBERTSON, HOWARD 1927 "Architecture 1927—at the RIBA Galleries." *Architectural Review* 61:217–219.

ROBERTSON, HOWARD 1928 "Architecture 1928." *Architectural Review* 63:220–222.

ROBERTSON, HOWARD (1932)1952 *Modern Architectural Design.* Rev. ed. London: Architectural Press.

ROBERTSON, HOWARD 1938 "Architecture in Ankara." *Architect and Building News* 154:39–41.

ROBERTSON, HOWARD 1939 "The New York World's Fair." *Journal of the Architectural Association* 55:33–34.

ROBERTSON, HOWARD 1940 "Architecture 1919–1939." *The Builder* 158:151–153.

ROBERTSON, HOWARD 1942 "The Contributory Industries: What Are They, and How Can They Help Re-employment." In *The Post-War Home: A Series of Lectures on Its Interior and Equipment.* London: Studio.

ROBERTSON, HOWARD 1944 *Architecture Arising.* London: Faber.

ROBERTSON, HOWARD 1947*a* "Design of Interiors." *Journal of the Architectural Association* 62:93–96.

ROBERTSON, HOWARD 1947*b* "Quality in Architecture." *Architects' Journal* 106:409–410.

ROBERTSON, HOWARD 1947*c* *Reconstruction and the*

Home. London and New York: Studio.
ROBERTSON, HOWARD 1948 "The American Scene." *Architect and Building News* 193:268–271.
ROBERTSON, HOWARD 1949 "The Seven Vamps of Architecture." *The Builder* 176:360–363.
ROBERTSON, HOWARD 1952 "Inaugural Address." *Journal of the Royal Institute of British Architects* 60:3–8.
ROBERTSON, HOWARD 1954 "The Architects' Dilemma." *Journal of the American Institute of Architects* 21:55–58.
ROBERTSON, HOWARD, and YERBURY, F. R. 1928 *Examples of Modern French Architecture.* London: Benn.
ROBERTSON, HOWARD, and YERBURY, F. R. 1928–1930 "A Pictorial Review of Modern Architecture in Europe." *Architecture* 58:295–302; 62:357–360.

ROBERTSON, R. H.

A successful and prolific New York architect, the Philadelphia-born Robert Henderson Robertson (1849–1919) designed buildings of all types for prominent clients and organizations. Educated in Scotland and at Rutgers College, where he graduated in 1869, Robertson was in the Philadelphia office of Henry Sims from 1869 to around 1872. Then, in New York, he worked briefly for GEORGE B. POST and in 1873 and 1874 for EDWARD T. POTTER. From 1875 to 1881, he was WILLIAM A. POTTER's partner. Afterward, he was occasionally associated with others.

Robertson's Phillips Presbyterian Church (1873–1874) in New York City owed much to the Potters' High Victorian Gothic churches. At an early date, his Timpson Cottage (1875) in Seabright, New Jersey, included Old English motifs; and as early as 1881, he was practicing the Richardsonian (see H. H. RICHARDSON) Romanesque, an outstanding example of which was his Mott Haven Railroad Station (1885–1886) in New York. Robertson's skyscrapers contribute to the variety of lower Manhattan's skyline; and his Renaissance-inspired Saint Paul's Methodist Episcopal Church (1895–1897) in New York, is, according to Herbert R. Broderick, "now a rare example of a transitional mode between the picturesque freedom of the 1870s and 80s . . . and the more rigidly codified *Beaux-Arts* classicism" that followed.

SARAH BRADFORD LANDAU

WORKS

For additional works built between the years 1875 and 1880 see William A. Potter.

*1873–1874, Phillips Presbyterian Church, New York. *1875, Theodore Timpson Cottage, Seabright, N.J. *1881, Church of the Holy Spirit (later All Souls' Protestant Episcopal Church), New York. 1881–1882, Burden Ironworks Office Building, Troy, N.Y. *1881–1882, John Sloane House; 1883–1885, Saint James's Church (reconstructed 1924 by RALPH ADAMS CRAM); *1885–1886, Mott Haven Railroad Station; 1885–1887, Young Women's Christian Association Building; New York. c.1886, Library at Drew University, Madison, N.J. 1886–1887, First Methodist Episcopal Church (now the Community Baptist Church), Yonkers, N.Y. 1887–1889, John W. Auchincloss House (Hammersmith Farm), Newport, R.I. 1887–1902, William Seward Webb House and Farm Buildings, Shelburne, Vt. 1888–1889, United Charities Building; 1889–1890, Lincoln Building; *1889–1890 Rutgers Riverside Church; 1890–1892, McIntyre Building; 1891–1892, Mohawk Building; 1891–1892, Saint Luke's Episcopal Church; New York. 1893, Hodge Hall, Princeton Theological Seminary, N.J. 1893–1894, Corn Exchange Bank; 1894–1895, American Tract Society Building; 1895–1897, Saint Paul's Methodist Episcopal Church and Parish House (now the United Church of Saint Paul and Saint Andrew); 1896–1898, New York Bank for Savings; 1896–1899, Park Row Building; 1899–1902, Lying-In Hospital of New York; New York.

BIBLIOGRAPHY

BRODERICK, HERBERT R. 1980 "United Methodist Church of St. Paul and St. Andrew." Unpublished report, Avery Architectural Library, Columbia University, New York.
FRANCIS, DENNIS STEADMAN 1980 *Architects in Practice, New York City, 1840–1900.* New York: Committee for Preservation of Architectural Records.
LANDAU, SARAH BRADFORD 1979 *Edward T. and William A. Potter: American Victorian Architects.* New York and London: Garland.
MENDEL, MESICK, COHEN, ARCHITECTS 1976 *The Burden Iron Company Office Building.* Albany: Mendel, Mesick, Cohen, Architects.
SCHUYLER, MONTGOMERY 1896 "The Works of R. H. Robertson." *Architectural Record* 6, Oct.–Dec.:184–219.

ROBILANT, FILIPPO NICOLIS DI

Filippo Nicolis di Robilant (1723–1783) was a count, architect and planner, and officer. A member of the *Consiglio degli Edili* from 1773, he received many minor commissions. His work shows an appreciation of aspects of GUARINO GUARINI (Turin, San Giovanni Decollato, 1751), FILIPPO JUVARRA (Casale Monferrato, Palazzo Gozzani di San Giorgio, from 1778), and BERNARDO ANTONIO VITTONE (Turin, Santa Pelagia, 1769–1772). One of a number of able nobles practicing architecture, Nicolis di Robilant displays in his early work at Sant'Albano Stura, Santa Croce an interest in Guarini's structural vaulting forms that culminated in San Giovanni Decollato, in which the spatial sequence and interlaced ribs of the domed sanctuary recall both Guarini and Vittone. In 1769, he designed Santa Pelagia for the Augustinian nuns who had earlier received designs for the church from Juvarra and Vittone. In the centrally planned Santa Pelagia, di Robilant follows Vittone's austere color and stucco decoration while realizing his finest work by emphasizing vertical structural continuity, flowing expansive space, and dramatic lighting from the upper levels of the hemicycles and dome.

The interiors of di Robilant's Palazzo Gozzani di San Giorgio display in the vaults a similar affection for dramatic structure (salon and main stair vault), but the wall articulation on interior and exterior is sober and traditional and derives from GIOVANNI LORENZO BERNINI and Juvarra. The construction was supervised by PIETRO BONVICINI.

HENRY A. MILLON

WORKS

1750, Sant'Albano Stura, Santa Croce; 1751, San Giovanni Decollato (Misercordia); 1769–1772, Santa Pelagia; Turin, Italy. 1778–?, Palazzo Gozzani di San Giorgio Casale Monferrato, Italy.

BIBLIOGRAPHY

BRAYDA, CARLO; COLI, LAURA; and SESIA, DARIO 1963 *Ingegneri e architetti del sei e settecento in Piemonte.* Turin, Italy: Societa Ingegnerie Architetti.

CARBONERI, NINO 1958 "La cappella del suffragio nel duomo di Mondovì." *Bolletino della Società per gli Storici Archeologici ed artistici nella provincia de Cuneo* 41:515.

CARBONERI, NINO 1963*a* Volume 1, pages 73–75 in *Architettura, Mostra del Barocco Piemontese.* Turin, Italy.

CARBONERI, NINO 1963*b* "La chiesa di San Sebatiano a Carru ad altre opere di Filippo Nicolis di Robilant." *Bolletino della Società per gli Studi Storici Archeologici ed Artistici della provincia di Cuneo* 50:3–11.

CARBONERI, NINO 1963*c* "Per un profilo dell'architetto Filippo Nicolis di Robilant." *Palladio* 13:183–196.

CHEVALLEY, GIOVANNI 1947 "Le terme di Aix in Savoia dell'architetto Filippo Nicolis di Robilant." *Bolletino della Società Piemontese di Archeologia e di Bella Arte* New series 1:128–133.

TAMBURINI, LUCIANO 1968 *Le chiese di Torino.* Turin, Italy: Le bouqiniste.

ROBINSON, P. F.

Peter Frederick Robinson (1776–1858) was a pupil of HENRY HOLLAND and of WILLIAM PORDEN. He moved permanently to Boulogne, France, about 1840. His Egyptian Hall in London (1811–1812) was the most prominent example of the early Egyptian Revival in England. His style, highly picturesque and often imitated, was characterized by irregular plans and elevations, elaborate bargeboards, and Tudor ornamentation. Robinson was an early advocate of the preservation and restoration of vernacular architecture. His pupils included H. F. LOCKWOOD.

JOHN ARCHER

WORKS

1807, Hans Town Assembly Rooms, London. 1808, Seaman's Cottage, Sandgate, England. 1808, Villa for W. Phillimore, Kensington. *1811–1812, Egyptian Hall; London. *1813, Town Hall and Market Place, Lampeter (LLanbedr), Wales. *1822–1823, Mickleham Church (alterations), England. *1825, Christ Church, Leamington, England. 1825–1827, The Querns, near Circencester, England. *1826–1835, Castle Jail (prison, governor's house, gatehouse, alterations), York, England. 1827, The Holmwood, near Dorking, England. *c.1828, Swiss Cottage, London. 1830, Stora Sundby (remodeling), Sodermanland, Sweden. 1831, Singleton House (major alterations), Swansea, Wales. c.1835, Villa (in The Park), Nottingham, England. c.1838, Seaside Villa, near Oystermouth, England.

BIBLIOGRAPHY

DOBAI, JOHANNES 1977 Volume 3 in *Die Kunstliteratur des Klassizimus und der Romantik in England.* Bern: Benteli.

HITCHCOCK, H. R. (1954)1972 *Early Victorian Architecture in Britain.* 2 vols. Reprint. New York: Da Capo.

LYALL, SUTHERLAND 1974 "Minor Domestic Architecture in England and Pattern Books 1790–1840." Unpublished Ph.D. dissertation, University of London.

MCMORDORIE, MICHAEL 1975 "Picturesque Pattern Books and Pre-Victorian Designers." *Architectural History* 18:43–49.

"P. F. Robinson." 1848–1892 In The Architectural Publication Society, *The Dictionary of Architecture.* 8 vols. London: Richards.

ROBINSON, P. F. (1823)1850 *Rural Architecture.* 5th ed. London: Bohn.

ROBINSON, P. F. 1824 *An Attempt to Ascertain the Age of the Church of Mickleham, in Surrey.* London: Carpenter.

ROBINSON, P. F. (1827*a*)1853 *Designs for Ornamental Villas.* 4th ed. London: Bohn.

ROBINSON, P. F. (1827*b*)1847 *Vitruvius Britannicus.* 2d ed. London: Bohn.

ROBINSON, P. F. (1830*a*)1837 *Designs for Farm Buildings.* 3d ed. London: Bohn.

ROBINSON, P. F. (1830*b*)1837 *Village Architecture.* 4th ed. London: Bohn.

ROBINSON, P. F. (1833)1837 *Designs for Gate Cottages, Lodges, and Park Entrances.* 3d ed. London: Bohn. Originally published with the title *Designs for Lodges and Park Entrances.*

ROBINSON, P. F. 1837 *Domestic Architecture in the*

Tudor Style. London: Williams.
ROBINSON, P. F. (1838)1853 *A New Series of Designs for Ornamental Cottages and Villas.* London: Bohn.

ROBINSON, THOMAS

Thomas Robinson (c.1702–1777), a Yorkshireman said to have resembled a pair of scissors, was an enthusiastic amateur follower of LORD BURLINGTON. He rebuilt the family house of Rokeby (1725–1730) in an individual Palladian (see ANDREA PALLADIO) manner later developed at Claydon (c.1760). He completed Castle Howard (1753–1759) with a Palladian wing matching ill with JOHN VANBRUGH's work. When governor of Barbados (1742–1747), Robinson designed official buildings there.

ANDOR GOMME

WORKS

1725–1730, Rokeby Hall, Yorkshire, England. 1745?, Armoury and Arsenal, Pilgram, Barbados. 1753–1759, Castle Howard (west wing), Yorkshire, England. 1760, Bishop Auckland Castle (gateway), Durham, England. 1760–1780?, Claydon House, Buckinghamshire, England. 1763–1765, Saint Mary's Church, Glynde, Sussex, England.

BIBLIOGRAPHY

HUSSEY, CHRISTOPHER (1955)1965 *English Country Houses: Early Georgian, 1715–1760.* Rev. ed. London: Country Life.
LEES-MILNE, JAMES 1970 *English Country Houses: Baroque, 1685–1716.* London: Country Life.
TIPPING, H. AVRAY 1921–1928 *English Homes, Period V: Early Georgian, 1714–1760.* London: Country Life; New York: Scribner.
WHISTLER, LAWRENCE 1954 *The Imagination of Vanbrugh and his Fellow Architects.* London: Batsford.

ROBINSON, WILLIAM

William Robinson (c.1643–1712) was born in England. He became surveyor-general of Ireland in 1671 and resigned in 1700. His principal works were buildings in Dublin Castle, the Royal Hospital Kilmainham (1679–1687), Saint Mary's Church (1701), Marsh's Library (1703–1704), all in Dublin, and parts of Charles Fort Kinsale (1678). He left Ireland in 1709 and died in London in 1712.

MAURICE CRAIG

WORKS

1678–?, Charles Fort Kinsale (parts); 1679–1687, Royal Hospital Kilmainham; 1701, Saint Mary's Hospital; 1703–1704, Marsh's Library; *n.d., Dublin Castle (some buildings); Dublin.

BIBLIOGRAPHY

LOEBER, ROLF 1974 "Sir William Robinson." *Irish Georgian Society Bulletin* 17, nos. 1–2:3–9.
LOEBER, ROLF 1979 "Engineers in Ireland 1600–1730." *Irish Sword* 1979:289–298.
LOEBER, ROLF 1981 *A Biographical Dictionary of Architects in Ireland 1600–1720.* London: Murray.

ROBSON, EDWARD ROBERT

Edward Robert Robson (1836–1917) is primarily known as the first specialist in school architecture in Britain. The son of a prosperous builder in Durham, he was articled to JOHN DOBSON of Newcastle from 1853 to 1856, and from 1857 to 1860 was in GEORGE GILBERT SCOTT's office in London. He was in practice in Durham and Liverpool before being appointed first architect to the new London School Board in 1871. Robson was responsible for the over-all supervision as well as the design of many new elementary schools being built in London from 1872 to 1889, continuing in an advisory capacity until 1904. The London School Board style, as it became known, of which he and JOHN JAMES STEVENSON, Robson's partner from 1871 to 1876, were largely responsible, was an aspect of the vernacular classical revival of late nineteenth-century England. He published an influential book, *School Architecture,* in 1874.

BETTY ELZEA

WORKS

1878, Berger Road School, Hackney; 1881, Royal Institute of Painters in Watercolours, Piccadilly; 1886, People's Palace (since altered), Stepney; 1888, New Gallery (rebuilt 1920), Regent Street; London.

BIBLIOGRAPHY

GREGORY-JONES, DAVID 1958 "Towers of Learning." *Architectural Review* 123:393–398.
GIROUARD, MARK 1977 *Sweetness and Light: The Queen Anne Movement, 1860–1900.* Oxford: Clarendon Press.
ROBSON, EDWARD ROBERT (1874)1972 *School Architecture.* With an introduction by Malcolm Seaborne. Leicester (England) University Press. New York: Humanities Press.
ROBSON, PHILIP A. 1916–1917 "Edward Robert Robson, F.S.A.: A Memoir by His Son." *Journal of the Royal Institute of British Architects* Series 3 24:92–96.

ROCA, FRANCISCO

Francisco Roca y Simó (1874–1940), born in Barcelona, Spain, graduated from the School of Architecture of Madrid (1903). His early architectural works are in Palma de Majorca, Spain. Imbued with the theories of historicism and modernism, Roca fell under the influence of ANTONÍ GAUDÍ, LLUÍS DOMÈNECH I MONTANER, and JOSEP PUIG I CADAFALCH, forerunners of the *Renaixensa Catalán.*

In 1913, Roca traveled to Argentina, settling in Rosario. His most significant works included the Spanish Club (1913–1916), the Cabanellas Palace (1916–1918), the Spanish Mutual Assistance Association (1916–1917), and *La Europea* (1916), a confectioner's shop and tea parlor. He returned to Spain in 1919, but his Spanish buildings lack the expressive strength of his works in Latin America.

Roca's work in Argentina, along with that of his contemporary JULIÁN GARCÍA NUNEZ, is the best produced by Catalonian Modernists outside Spain because of both its plastic and symbolic vigor and the high quality of the building techniques.

GRACIELA M. VIÑUALES

WORKS

1909–1910, Menorquina Pension; 1910, College of Notaries; Palma de Mallorca, Spain. 1913–1916, Spanish Club; 1916, *La Europea;* 1916–1917, Spanish Mutual Assistance Association; 1916–1918, Cabanellas Palace; 1918, Remonda Montserrat Building; Rosario, Argentina.

BIBLIOGRAPHY

BAUSERO, LUIS 1968 *Historia del Palacio Legislativo de Montevideo.* Montevideo.

GUTIERREZ, RAMÓN 1971 "Presencia y continuidad de España en la Arquitectura rioplatense." *Hogar y arquitectura* 97.

ORTIZ, FEDERICO ET AL. 1968 *La arquitectura de liberalismo en la Argentina.* Buenos Aires: Editorial Sudamericana.

SEBASTIAN LOPEZ, SANTIAGO, and ALONSO FERNANDEZ, ANTONIO 1973 *Arquitectura Mallorquina moderna y contemporánea.* Palma, Spain: Estudio General Luliano.

SEGUI AZNAR, MIGUEL 1972 "Arquitectura modernista en Mallorca." *Bulletín de la Cámara de Comercio de Palma* 674.

ROCCO, EMMANUELE

An engineer graduated at the Scuola d'Applicazione of Naples, Italy, in 1875, Emmanuele Rocco (1852–?) was a prominent figure in the urban renewal of Naples at the end of the nineteenth century. He designed railroads and bridges and, in the eclectic "Umbertino-floreale" style, the Santa Brigida quarter and many apartment buildings, including a remarkable one at the Parco Margherita in Naples. He executed the Galleria Umberto I (1887–1890), the steel-and-glass-covered civic heart of the new Naples, in collaboration with Paolo Boubée, Antonio Curri, and Ernesto di Mauro.

MANFREDI G. NICOLETTI

BIBLIOGRAPHY

DE FUSCO, RENATO 1959 *Il floreale a Napoli.* Naples: Edizioni scientifiche italiane.

VENDITTI, ARNOLDO 1961 *Architettura neoclassica a Napoli.* Naples: Edizione scientifiche italiane.

ROCHE, MARTIN

See HOLABIRD and ROCHE.

ROCHE and DINKELOO

The firm of Kevin Roche (1922–), John Dinkeloo (1918–1981), and Associates has designed some of the nation's most provocative civic and corporate architecture in the last twenty years. Roche and Dinkeloo, both earlier associates in the office of EERO SAARINEN, formally became partners in 1966 after completing the work Saarinen left following his death in 1961.

Born in Dublin, Kevin Roche came to the United States in 1948 after receiving his bachelor of architecture degree from the National University of Ireland three years earlier. He spent a semester at the Illinois Institute of Technology with LUDWIG MIES VAN DER ROHE and later met Eero Saarinen. Roche became Saarinen's principal design associate in 1954 after having joined the firm in 1950. In 1950 also, John Dinkeloo met Saarinen and himself became a partner in 1956. Dinkeloo had graduated from the University of Michigan and, by the age of twenty-eight, had become chief of production and coordinator of structural and mechanical work in the Chicago office of SKIDMORE, OWINGS, AND MERRILL.

Along with senior partner and administrator Joseph Lacy, Roche and Dinkeloo did not lose a single client following Saarinen's death but instead successfully completed his major projects, among which were the TWA Terminal at John F. Kennedy International Airport (1956–1962) in New York and the John Deere and Company Headquarters (1961–1964) in Moline, Illinois. In addition, they received major commissions of their own, the first of which was the elegant multileveled Oakland Museum (1961–1968) in Oakland, California.

Once established as successful architects in their own right, Roche and Dinkeloo formed a model partnership. Dinkeloo was the technologist, an expert in construction and industrial methods; Roche was the designer. Stark, angular contrasts between concrete, masonry, steel, and glass defined their buildings which were almost purely sculptural in form: the Ford Foundation Headquarters (1963–1968) in New York, the Creative Arts Center of Wesleyan University (1965–1973) in Middletown, Connecticut, the hotel and office building of the United Nations Development Corporation (1969–1975) in New York, and the master plan for the Metropolitan Museum of Art (1967–1974, 1976) also in New York.

PETER L. DONHAUSER

WORKS

1961–1968, Oakland Museum, Calif. *1962–1964, International Business Machines Pavilion, World's Fair, New York. 1962–1967, Richard C. Lee High School, New Haven. 1962–1969, Administration, Student Union, and Physical Education Buildings, Rochester Institute of Technology, N.Y. 1963–1968, Ford Foundation Headquarters, New York. 1963–1965, Cummins Engine Company Components Plant, Darlington, Durham, England. 1964–1974, Fine Arts Center, University of Massachusetts, Amherst. 1965–1969, Knights of Columbus Headquarters, New Haven. 1965–1969, United States Post Office, Columbus, Ind. 1965–1971, Power Center for the Performing Arts, University of Michigan, Ann Arbor. 1965–1972, New Haven Veterans Memorial Coliseum. 1965–1973, Creative Arts Center, Wesleyan University, Middletown, Conn. 1966–1972, Aetna Life and Casualty and Computer Building, Hartford, Conn. 1966–1972, Irwin Union Bank and Trust Company, Columbus, Ind. 1967–1971, College Life Insurance Company of America Headquarters, Indianapolis, Ind. 1967–1974, 1976, Metropolitan Museum of Art Master Plan; 1969–1975, United Nations Development Corporation Hotel and Office Building; New York. 1970–1973, Cummins Engine Company Sub-Assembly Plant, Columbus, Ind. 1970–1974, Richardson-Merrell, Incorporated Headquarters, Wilton, Conn. 1970–1974, Worcester County National Bank, Mass. 1972–1981, Indiana and Michigan Power Company, Fort Wayne, Ind. 1973–1976, Kentucky Power Company Headquarters, Ashland. 1974–1979, Denver Center for the Performing Arts, Colo. 1975–1979, John Deere and Company Headquarters, Moline, Ill. 1976–1981, International Business Machines Corporation Thomas J. Watson Research Center (addition), Yorktown Heights, N.Y. 1976–1982, J. M. Moudy Building, Texas Christian University, Fort Worth. 1976–1982, Union Carbide Corporation World Headquarters, Danbury, Conn. 1977–1982, Bell Telephone Laboratories (expansion), Holmdel, N.J. 1977–1982, General Foods Corporation Headquarters, Rye, N.Y. 1978–1982, John Deere Insurance Company Headquarters, Moline, Ill.

BIBLIOGRAPHY

COOK, JOHN W., and KLOTZ, HEINRICH 1973 *Conversations with Architects.* New York: Praeger.

"Fresh Forms and New Directions from a Special Kind of Problem Solving." 1968 *Architectural Record* 143, May:145–168.

FUTAGAWA, YUKIO 1975 *1962–1975.* Volume 1 in *Roche, Kevin and John Dinkeloo and Associates.* Tokyo: A.D.A.

HEYER, PAUL (1966)1978 *Architects on Architecture: New Directions in America.* Enl. ed. New York: Walker.

"Kevin Go Bragh." 1965 *Progressive Architecture* 46, May:190–195.

"Kevin Roche and John Dinkeloo: 1964–1974." 1974 *Architectural Forum* 140, Mar.:16–85. Includes articles by Robert Coombs, Ludwig Glaeser, Paul Goldberger, Carleton Knight II, William Marlin, Vincent Scully, and Suzanne Stephens.

MCQUADE, WALTER 1963 "The New Saarinen Office." *Architectural Forum* 118, Apr.:113–119.

STERN, ROBERT A. M. (1969)1977 *New Directions in American Architecture.* Rev. ed. New York: Braziller.

RODIA, SIMON

Without plans, machinery, scaffolding, or engineering training, Simon (Sam) Rodia (1879–1965) built a complex of open-work towers made of steel rods covered with a sparkling mosaic of broken pottery, seashells, and bottle glass, materials he salvaged from empty lots, beaches, and railroad beds in and around Los Angeles. The spires, joined by horizontal spokes connecting to circular hoops, rise as high as 100 feet. His wooden house, destroyed by fire in 1957, was set within the complex. Declared hazardous by the city of Los Angeles, the towers were threatened with demolition until an engineer's stress test proved them structurally sound. They have since been designated a cultural monument.

JANET KAPLAN

WORK

1921–1954, Watts Towers, Los Angeles, Calif.

BIBLIOGRAPHY

COMMITTEE FOR SIMON RODIA'S TOWERS IN WATTS 1961 *The Watts Towers.* Los Angeles: The committee.

LANGSNER, JULES 1951 "Sam of Watts." *Art and Architecture* 68, July: 23–25.

TRILLIN, CALVIN 1965 "I Know I Want to Do Something." *New Yorker* 41, May 29: 72–120.

TRILLIN, CALVIN 1974 "Simon Rodia: Watts Towers." Pages 20–31 in Walker Art Center, *Naives and Visionaries.* New York: Dutton.

RODRIGUEZ AYUSO, EMILIO

Emilio Rodriguez Ayuso (1845–1891) was born in Madrid where he attended the School of Architecture, graduating in 1869. In 1874, he built, in collaboration with Lorenzo Alvarez Capra, the new bull ring of Madrid, a building with a mixed structure of cast iron on the interior and tile on the exterior. The work implied, stylistically, the birth of the Mudejar Revival in Spain at a time when the eclectic and historicizing styles dominated the architectural scene. In subsequent works Rodriguez overcame this literal dependence on a historical style to arrive at solutions of greater expressive freedom. The building for the Aguirre Schools (1884) and the annex to the Homeopathic Hospital (1876), both in Madrid, are good indications of this markedly free and creative language. The neo-Mudejar would find wide acceptance among the architects of the period, especially among those in Madrid, giving rise to an architecture characterized by tiled façades composed in an orderly way, in which the allusions to the Mudejar became, in certain instances, irrelevant and evolved toward a new language of great formal attraction.

Carlos Flores Lopez
Translated from Spanish by Tomlyn Barns

WORKS

*1874, Bull Ring (with Lorenzo Alvarez Capra); *1875–1876, Palace for the Marquess of Anglada; c.1876, Homeopathic Hospital (new wing); 1882, Library, Palace of the Senate; 1884, Aguirre Schools; Madrid.

BIBLIOGRAPHY

Castellanos, Santiago, and Repullés, Enrique María 1892 *Album de homenaje a Emilio Rodriguez Ayuso.* Madrid.

Flores Lopez, Carlos 1966 "Rodriguez Ayuso y su influencia sobre la arquitectura madrileña." *Hogar y Arquitectura* 67:50–63.

González Amezueta, Adolfo 1969 "Arquitectura neomudéjar en Madrid." *Arquitectura* 125:3–74.

RODRÍGUEZ TIZÓN, VENTURA

Ventura Rodríguez Tizón (1717–1785) was the greatest architect of the eighteenth century in Spain. His work was primarily neoclassical in style, but over the years it reflected shifts from the full-blown Italian baroque influence in Spain to that of a simplified, reductive form of building characteristic of the Enlightenment age.

The life and work of Ventura Rodríguez can be divided into three periods: the formative, the eclectic, and the enlightened. In the first phase, from 1731 to 1736, he began his career as a draftsman at the royal palace of Aranjuez, working under Etienne Marchand. From 1735 through the 1750s, he worked under Giovanni B. Sacchetti at the Royal Palace in Madrid. The impact of this formative period lies in his assimilation of the Italian baroque tradition as propagated in Spain by Sacchetti and Filippo Juvarra. His two major commissions of this period, the Church of San Marco in Madrid (1749–1753) and the Chapel of El Pilar at the Church of El Pilar in Saragossa (1750), reflect the clearly Italianate tendencies typical of court architecture. The eclectic period of Ventura Rodríguez extends from 1760–1766, following his dismissal from the royal works in 1759. In search of new commissions, he adapted his style toward a more rigorous and austere approach as early as the reductive block church form of the Convent of the Agustinos Filipinos of 1759 in Valladolid. He arrived at a complete reversal of his earlier ornate baroque style in the Country House of the Infante Don Luis of 1763 at Boabdilla del Monte, Spain.

Ventura Rodríguez early assimilated the growing influence of French neoclassical design propagated by the Spanish Academy, in which he was active from 1752 to 1785. In these years, he executed secular commissions in accord with the spirit of the Spanish Enlightenment; the College of Surgery in Barcelona (1761–1764) is representative of a new type of functional edifice. Becoming more closely allied with the rationalist policies of the government, he was named municipal architect of Madrid in 1764. The enlightened phase of Ventura Rodríguez began in 1766 with his appointment as inspector of buildings for the Council of Castile, in charge of reviewing all plans for secular construction. Between 1766 and 1785, he executed a group of remarkable small works, both secular and religious. The parish churches of Vélez de Benandalla (1776) and Talará (1783) in the province of Granada are representative in their stark, simplistic forms and functional purpose as spiritual and focal centers for their respective towns. Rodríguez's arrival at this extremely classicizing building style resulted both from his involvement with the governmental campaign of enlightenment and from the visual and structural translation of an idea directly into form.

Ventura Rodríguez was the terminal figure of baroque architecture in Spain; his career ended with the complete adaptation of the classical style. In addition to the significance and wide-ranging influence of his architecture, he was a major force in shaping the neoclassical theory and practice of

Rodríguez. San Marco. Madrid. 1749–1753

Rodríguez. Pamplona Cathedral. Spain. 1783

the Spanish Academy. He was appointed its director of architecture in 1752.

ELIZABETH A. T. SMITH

WORKS

1749–1753, San Marco, Madrid. 1750, Church of the Monastery of Santo Domingo de Silos, Burgos, Spain. 1750, Chapel of the Virgin, Nuestra Señora del Pilar, Saragossa, Spain. 1752, San Julían (main altar and chapel), Cuenca Cathedral; 1753, Trasparente, Cuenca Cathedral; Spain. *1754, San Norberto (façade), Madrid. 1755, Chapel of San Pedro de Alcantara, Arenas de San Pedro, Spain. 1755, La Encarnación (remodeling of nave), Madrid. 1759, Convent of the Agustinos Filipinos; 1760–1763, Royal Palace (restorations); Valladolid, Spain. 1761–1764, College of Surgery, Barcelona, Spain. 1761–1764, Jaén Cathedral (sagrario), Spain. *1762, Municipal Slaughter and Curing House for Pork Products, Madrid. 1763, Infante Don Luis House, Boabdilla del Monte, Spain. 1767, San Sebastián (façade), Azpeita, Spain. 1770, Almería Cathedral (traschoir), Spain. 1771, Collegiate Church, Santa Fe, Spain. 1772, Chapel of the College of the Poor Damsels of Santa Vitoria (completion and restorations), Córdoba, Spain. 1772, Zamora Cathedral (main altar), Spain. 1773, Palace of Liria, Spain. 1775, La Encarnación (completion), Loja, Spain. 1776, Parish Church, Vélez de Benandalla, Spain. 1777, Fountain of Apollo (with M. Álvarez), Madrid. 1777, Nuestra Señora de la Asunción (main altar and presbytery), Rentería, Spain. 1777, Parish Church, Alvia del Taha, Spain. 1777–1784, Parish Larrabezúa, Spain. 1779, Basilica of Covadonga, Spain. 1779, Santa María la Mayor, Algarinejo, Spain. 1780, Parish Church, Cajar, Spain. 1780, Santos Sebastián e Ildefonso, Olula del Río, Spain. 1783, Pamplona Cathedral (façade), Spain. 1783, Parish Church, Talará, Spain.

BIBLIOGRAPHY

CALZADA, ANDRÉS 1933 *Historia de la arquitectura española.* Barcelona, Spain: Labor.

CHUECA GOITIA, FERNANDO 1942 "Ventura Rodríguez y la escuela barroca romana." *Archivo Español de Arte* 15:185–210.

ÍNÍGUEZ ALMECH, FRANCISCO 1935 "Don Ventura Rodríguez." *Arquitectura* 17:75–112.

ÍNÍGUEZ ALMECH, FRANCISCO 1949 "La formación de don Ventura Rodríguez." *Archivo Español de Arte* 22:137–148.

KUBLER, GEORGE, and SORIA, MARTIN (1959) *Art and Architecture in Spain and Portugal and Their American Dominions 1500–1800.* Baltimore: Penguin.

LORENTE JUNQUERA, MANUEL 1946 "La evolución arquitectónica en España en los siglos XVIII y XIX." *Arte Español* 30:74–79.

REESE, THOMAS F. 1976 *The Architecture of Ventura Rodriguez Tizón in the Development of the Eighteenth Century Style in Spain.* 2 vols. New York: Garland.

SCHUBERT, OTTO 1924 *Historia del barroco en España.* Translated from German by Manuel Hernández Alcalde. Madrid: Editorial Saturnino Calleja.

ROEBLING, JOHN AUGUSTUS, and ROEBLING, WASHINGTON AUGUSTUS

John (1806–1869) and Washington (1837–1926) Roebling, father and son, were the foremost American engineers of suspension bridge construction in the nineteenth century. John, born in Mühlhausen, Thuringia, on June 12, 1806, graduated with a degree in civil engineering from the Royal Polytechnic Institute of Berlin in 1826. Georg Friedrich Hegel, Roebling's professor of philosophy, aroused in the young student a lifelong enthusiasm for metaphysics. Although his thesis, on the suspension bridge at Bamberg, Bavaria, marked the beginning of an interest that resulted in some of the greatest structural achievements of the age, it was nearly twenty years before

Roebling and Roebling. Brooklyn Bridge. New York. 1869–1883

he established himself as a builder.

Because of limited opportunities and the bureaucratic inertia in the eastern German states, John Roebling and his brother Karl immigrated to Pennsylvania in 1831, where they became farmers. By 1837, the poor quality of the soil and his lack of talent for the agricultural life led John Roebling to accept the position of Pennsylvania state engineer. His duties were chiefly to survey and supervise the construction of canals, locks, and dams. In 1841 he invented the first twisted wire-rope cable, and in 1849 he established a factory at Trenton, New Jersey, for its manufacture. The invention foreshadowed the technique of supporting the deck of suspension bridges by means of wire cables in place of the much weaker wrought iron chains of earlier forms. Roebling had already been given an opportunity to demonstrate the value of his invention in his design of the cable-suspended aqueduct to carry the Pennsylvania State Canal (1844–1845) over the Allegheny River. The success of this unprecedented work brought commissions for a series of four similar aqueducts (1846–1850) built to convey the Delaware and Hudson Canal over various streams, including the Delaware River, in northeastern Pennsylvania.

These remarkable spans, capable of supporting extremely heavy loads, gave Roebling a national reputation as a bridge engineer, and by 1850 he was called upon to design larger and more daring structures. During the 1850s, after all the Delaware and Hudson aqueducts had been opened, he completed three major works and placed under construction the largest span of his lifetime. The reconstruction of the storm-damaged bridge over the Ohio River at Wheeling, West Virginia, a structure designed by Charles Ellet, was accomplished in 1854. Roebling's successful design, which was distinguished chiefly by stays radiating outward and downward from the tops of the towers to the panel points of the deck, demonstrated that he was one of the world's leading authorities on the aerodynamic stability of long suspended spans. He also built the Niagara River Bridge (1851–1855), the first and the last suspension bridge for standard railway loads, and the highway span over the Allegheny River at Pittsburgh (1857–1860). Four years earlier the great work built to unite Cincinnati, Ohio, and Covington, Kentucky, was inaugurated, but storms, ice, financial difficulties, depression, and Civil War delayed completion for ten years. The 1,057-foot length of deck between the towers made it the longest clear span in the world at the time. The supporting structure was considerably strengthened in 1898 to carry railway traffic.

The greatest challenge still lay ahead, though he never saw any part of the physical fabric. The New York Bridge Company was prepared to initiate construction of the long-proposed bridge over the East River between New York and Brooklyn, and in 1867 the directors appointed John Roebling chief engineer of the project. During a final survey in June 1869, an injury to his foot necessitated the amputation of the toes. He died of the resulting tetanus infection on the 22d of the following month. The construction of the celebrated Brooklyn Bridge, however, was triumphantly completed in the spring of 1883. John Roebling was a prolific writer as well as a bridge builder and theorist: his chief published work was *Long and Short Span Railway Bridges* (1869); among his unpublished writings was an extremely long manuscript on metaphysical speculation.

Washington Augustus Roebling was born in Saxonburg, Pennsylvania, on May 26, 1837. After graduation from Rensselaer Polytechnic Institute, he served an engineering apprenticeship in the wire mill that his father had founded at Trenton. He joined the older man in the design of suspension bridges and the supervision of their construction shortly before the completion of the Allegheny River Bridge at Pittsburgh in 1860. He enlisted in the Union Army at the beginning of the Civil War and rose from the rank of private to that of lieutenant colonel. His duties as an officer were concerned to a great extent with engineering work, which included the construction of temporary suspension bridges over the Rappahannock and Shenandoah rivers. At the conclusion of the war he rejoined his father and served with him during the last two years of construction on the Cincinnati Bridge (1865–1867). After his return from travel and study in Europe during the years 1867–1868 he was appointed assistant chief engineer of the New York Bridge Company and chief engineer in 1869, following the death of his father. His health was permanently impaired by caisson disease, contracted in 1872 during a descent into one of the underwater chambers, and as a consequence of his crippled state, he had to direct the operations on Brooklyn Bridge from a house near the Brooklyn tower.

Washington Roebling was never able to work for sustained periods of time throughout the remainder of his long life. He assumed the presidency of John A. Roebling's Sons Company in 1876, but he was forced to resign the office in 1884. He lived in Troy, New York, whence he returned sporadically to Trenton. He resumed the presidency of the company briefly in 1920, during the manufacture of the cable for the Bear Mountain Bridge over the Hudson River (1922–1924). He died in Troy on July 21, 1926, a martyr, like his father, to the building of the East River span. Although the great suspension bridges that now unite the cities around New York Harbor and San Francisco Bay far exceed the Brooklyn Bridge in size, the 1595-foot main span of the latter, easily the longest in the world at the time, belongs to the heroic age of long-span bridge construction. It eventually took on the character of a national symbol, while its building became a part of the national legend of striving and overcoming. It is one of the few strictly engineering works to achieve such a status.

CARL W. CONDIT

WORKS

*1844–1845, Pennsylvania Canal Aqueduct, Allegheny River. *1846, Highway, Monongahela River, Pittsburgh. 1846–1850, Delaware and Hudson Canal Aqueducts: *Lackawaxen, *Neversink, and *Roundout Rivers. *1851–1855, Rail and Highway, Niagara River Bridge, Niagara Falls, N.Y. and Ontario, Canada. *1857–1860, Highway, Allegheny River, Pittsburgh. 1856–1867, Highway and Street Railway, Ohio River, Cincinnati. 1869–1883, Brooklyn Bridge, New York.

BIBLIOGRAPHY

CONDIT, CARL W. 1960 *American Building Art: The Nineteenth Century.* New York: Oxford University Press.

CONDIT, CARL W. 1968 *American Building: Materials and Techniques From the First Colonial Settlements to the Present.* University of Chicago Press.

ROEBLING, JOHN AUGUSTUS 1869 *Long and Short Span Railway Bridges.* New York: Van Nostrand.

"Roebling, John Augustus." 1935 Volume 16, pages 86–89 in *Dictionary of American Biography.* New York: Scribner.

"Roebling, Washington Augustus." 1935 Volume 16, pages 89–90 in *Dictionary of American Biography.* New York: Scribner.

SCHUYLER, HAMILTON 1931 *The Roeblings: A Century of Engineers, Bridge-builders, and Industrialists; the Story of Three Generations of an Illustrious Family, 1831–1931.* Princeton University Press.

STEINMAN, DAVID B. 1945 *The Builders of the Bridge: The Story of John Roebling and His Son.* New York: Harcourt.

STERN, JOSEPH S., JR. 1966 *The Great Suspension Bridge at Cincinnati, Ohio.* Cincinnati: Committee for the Celebration of the Centennial of the Great Suspension Bridge.

TRACHTENBERG, ALAN 1965 *Brooklyn Bridge: Fact and Symbol.* New York: Oxford University Press.

VOGEL, ROBERT M. 1971 *Roebling's Delaware and Hudson Canal Aqueducts.* Washington: Smithsonian Institution Press.

ROGERS, ISAIAH

Isaiah Rogers (1800–1869) was a leading American architect from before 1830 until the late 1860s. He is remembered primarily as a hotel architect, but his major works, almost none of which have survived urban economic pressures, were of many types. He was born in Marshfield, Massachusetts, a sixth-generation descendant of John Rogers, who settled there in 1647. In 1817, Isaiah left his family's farm and apprenticed himself to Jesse Shaw, a Boston housewright. By 1821, he was in Mobile, Alabama, where in 1822 he won a competition for a theater, built in 1824. In 1822, he joined the Boston architect SOLOMON WILLARD. By 1826, Rogers was practicing independently, Willard

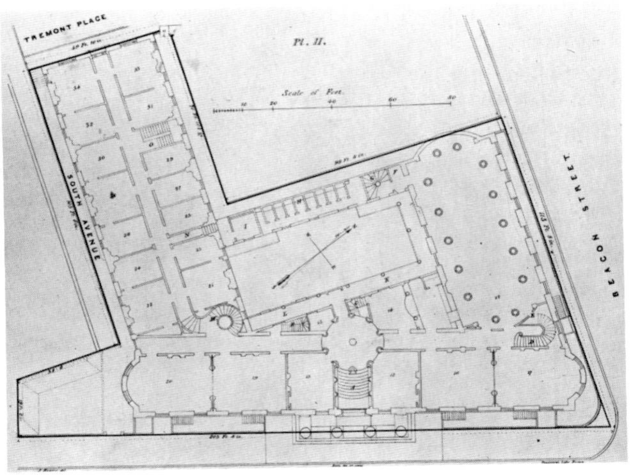

Rogers.
Plan of Tremont House.
Boston.
1828–1829

Rogers.
Tremont House.
Boston.
1828–1829

having left to manage his Quincy, Massachusetts, granite business. Willard supplied granite for Rogers, and in 1842 they jointly leased a Quincy quarry. Until 1844, most of Rogers's principal works were Greek Revival with monolithic granite columns.

Rogers's first nationally important work was the Tremont House of 1828–1829 in Boston, which set a new standard for hotel design and is generally regarded as initiating American leadership in this field. It was unsurpassed for the dignity of its exterior and the convenience of its plan, the latter ingeniously masking the irregularity of the site. William H. Eliot's book, *A Description of Tremont House* (1830), spread Rogers's fame among his contemporaries. The brick Bangor House, a Maine version of the Tremont House erected in 1833–1834 by Charles G. Bryant and Lyman Seavey from Rogers's plans, and the handsome Suffolk Bank in Boston, its granite front composed of a tetrastyle-in-antis Ionic colonnade above a high basement, followed. In 1833, Richard Bond joined Rogers in a partnership that ended in 1834, when Rogers left for New York to design the famous Astor House, an even larger and more mechanically advanced hotel than Tremont House.

Rogers.
Merchants' Exchange.
New York.
1836–1842

Rogers's work in New York included the distyle-in-antis Bank of America (1835) on Wall Street; the Ionic octastyle Middle Collegiate Dutch Reformed Church (1837–1839), its pediment surmounted by a tholos belfry and spire; and the magnificent Merchants' Exchange (1836–1842), his masterpiece. Behind its Schinkelesque (see KARL FRIEDRICH SCHINKEL) granite Ionic colonnade there was a great marble rotunda vaulted by a brick Pantheon dome eighty feet in diameter, destroyed when four stories were added by MCKIM, MEAD, AND WHITE after 1907. The Exchange was one of only four American buildings illustrated in the 1849 Brockhaus *Bilder-atlas.* Rogers designed the elegant Exchange Hotel (1839–1841) in Richmond, Virginia, with an engaged tetrastyle-in-antis colonnade flanked by elliptical bays; the distyle-in-antis Exchange Bank (1840–1841) in Richmond; and the Egyptian Revival Granary Burying Ground Gate and fence (1839–1840) in Boston (sculpted by Solomon Willard) before his return to Boston in 1841. On December 6, 1836, Rogers became a founder of the American Institution of Architects, precursor of the American Institute of Architects.

For the Boston Merchants' Exchange Rogers used even larger masses of monolithic granite than in its New York counterpart. The majestic front had four engaged piers between sixty-ton antae supporting a low pediment. The Corinthian order was *sui generis.* Rogers's second Boston period was characterized by stylistic and typological variety. His Egyptian Jew's Cemetery Gate (1841–1842) in Newport, Rhode Island; the Gothic granite mansion for Enoch Reddington Mudge (1843–1844) in Swampscott, Massachusetts; the Gothic Howard Athenaeum (1846) in Boston, an innovative theater with a sloping parquet instead of a flat pit; the Greek Revival Quincy Town House (1844–1845; misattributed to Solomon Willard); and Harvard Observatory (1844–1845) in Cambridge all date from before 1847, when he returned to New York to build the Astor Place Opera House (1847). Thenceforth, most of his work was in a restrained Italianate manner.

In 1848, Rogers settled in Cincinnati, Ohio, where his Burnet House, an Italianate five-part composition with a dome-and-belvedere-crowned central pavilion, was completed in 1850. The *Illustrated London News* called it the world's best hotel. The Gothic, iron-fronted Tyler Davidson Store (1849–1850), villas for George Hatch and Winthrop B. Smith (both 1850–1851), and Saint John's Episcopal Church (1849–1852), which had a Romanesque stone concentric-arched front flanked by diagonally set towers, in Cincinnati; the Battle House (1851–1852) in Mobile, Alabama; and the Greek Revival Capital Hotel (1852–1853) in Frankfort, Kentucky, which had a five-part front; all antedated November 1853, when Rogers, who had a branch office in Louisville, made Henry Whitestone his partner. The remodeling of the Galt House in Louisville and rebuilding of the Louisville Hotel (1850–1856), the arcaded Italianate W. B. Reynolds Store (1855–1856) in Louisville, and the Commercial Bank of Kentucky (1855–1856) in Paducah, remarkable for its early extensive use of terra cotta, were typical of the firm's work.

In February 1855, Solomon Willard Rogers, who had assisted his father since 1846, became a partner. Whitestone left in 1857, and Rogers withdrew from Louisville. Thereafter, the firm was styled Isaiah Rogers and Son, although ALFRED B. MULLETT, who joined as draftsman in 1857, became a partner in 1859 or 1860, departing by 1861. Those years were occupied by the Oliver House (1858–1859) in Toledo, Ohio, which has an elliptical center (planned for a dome) joining wings that recede in a shallow V (interior gutted in 1920); the arcaded Italianate Maxwell House (1859–1869) in Nashville, Tennessee, which lasted until 1961, and the vast Longview State Hospital (before 1856–1860) in Cincinnati, Ohio, which had offset wings flanking a domed entrance pavilion containing a lofty rotunda. Rogers revised and completed Henry Walter and JAMES KNOX WILSON's Hamilton County Courthouse (1855–1861) in Cincinnati and the Ohio Capitol (1858–1861) in Columbus before July 23, 1862, when he was appointed chief of the Bureau of Construction in the Treasury Department and moved to Washington, where he built the west wing of the United States Treasury (1862–1865).

On June 30, 1863, Rogers became supervising architect of the Treasury Department. He resigned on September 30, 1865, and returned to Cincinnati, where he built Pike's Opera House in 1866. He was an inventor, holding patents for bridges issued in 1841, 1856, and 1863, and a "burglar-proof" safe (1863). Joseph Jenkin's Masonic Temple and the anonymous Brazer's Building in Boston, Charles F. Reichardt's Charleston (South Carolina) Hotel, Henry Whitestone's (second) Galt House in Louisville, George Purvis's (second) Saint Charles Hotel in New Orleans, and Mullett's United States Courthouse in Portland, Maine, and his San Francisco Mint have all been misattributed to Isaiah Rogers.

DENYS PETER MYERS

WORKS

*1822–1824, Mobile Theater, Ala. 1826, Commercial Wharf (later altered), Boston. *1826, Masonic Hall, Augusta, Ga. *1827, Tremont Theater; *1828–1829, Tremont House; Boston. 1829–1830, Lowell Town House (later altered), Mass. 1833, First Parish Church (alterations), Cambridge, Mass. 1833–1834, Bangor House (later altered), Maine. 1833–1834, Robert Bennet Forbes House (alterations), Milton, Mass. *1833–1836, Suffolk Bank, Boston. *1834–1836, Astor House; *1835, Bank of America; New York. 1836–1838, Stephen Salisbury House, Worcester, Mass. 1836–1842, Merchants' Exchange (later altered); *1837–1839, Middle Collegiate Dutch Reformed Church; *1838–1839, Merchants' Bank; *1839, Benjamin L. Swan House; *1839, David Thompson House; New York. 1839–1840, Granary Burying Ground Gate and Fence, Boston. *1839–1841; Exchange Hotel; *1840–1841, Exchange Bank; Richmond, Va. *1840–1842, Merchants' Exchange, Boston. 1841–1842, Jew's Cemetery (gate and fence); 1842, Touro Synagogue (gate and fence); Newport, R.I. *1843–1844, Enoch Reddington Mudge Mansion, Swampscott, Mass. *1844–1845, Boston Female Orphan Asylum. 1844–1845, Harvard Astronomical Observatory (later altered), Cambridge, Mass. 1844–1845 Quincy Town House, Mass. 1845, Horace L. Kent House (later altered), Richmond Va. *1846, Howard Athenaeum, Boston. *1847, Astor Place Opera House, New York. *1848–1850, Burnet House; 1849–1850, Commercial Bank; *1849–1850, Tyler Davidson Store; *1849–1852, Saint John's Episcopal Church; 1850–1851, George Hatch Villa; *1850–1851, Winthrop B. Smith Villa; Cincinnati, Ohio. *1850–1852, Phillips House (hotel), Dayton, Ohio. *1850–1856, Louisville Hotel, Ky. *1851–1852, Battle House, Mobile, Ala. *1852–1853, Capital Hotel, Frankfort, Ky. *1854, Metropolitan Hall, Chicago. *1854, Newcomb Building; 1855, Fifth Ward School; Louisville, Ky. *1855–1856, Commercial Bank of Kentucky, Paducah. 1855–1856, W. B. Reynolds Store, Louisville, Ky. *1855–1861, Hamilton County Courthouse (completion), Cincinnati, Ohio. *1856, Louisville Medical Institute, Ky. 1858–1859, Oliver House (later altered), Toledo, Ohio. Before *1856–1860, Longview State Hospital; 1861, Hamilton County Jail; Cincinnati, Ohio. 1858–1861, Ohio State Capitol (completion), Columbus. *1859–1869, Maxwell House, Nashville, Tenn. 1862–1865, Treasury United States Building (west wing), Washington. *1866, Pike's Opera House, Cincinnati, Ohio.

BIBLIOGRAPHY

Isaiah Rogers's manuscript diaries (1838–1856, 1861, and 1867) are in the Avery Architectural Library, Columbia University, New York.

Biographical Encyclopaedia of Ohio of the Nineteenth Century. 1876 Cincinnati: Galaxy.

DRUMMOND, JOSIAH H. 1898 *John Rogers of Marshfield and Some of His Descendants.* Portland, Me.: Smith & Sale.

ELIOT, WILLIAM HAVARD 1830 *A Description of Tremont House.* Boston: Gray & Bowen.

HAMLIN, TALBOT (1944)1964 *Greek Revival Architecture in America.* Reprint. New York: Dover.

HITCHCOCK, H. B. (1963)1977 *Architecture: Nineteenth and Twentieth Centuries.* Baltimore: Penguin.

KILHAM, WALTER H. JR. 1946 *Boston After Bulfinch.* Cambridge, Mass.: Harvard University Press.

MYERS, DENYS PETER 1951 "Isaiah Rogers in Cincinnati." *Bulletin of the Historical and Philosophical Society of Ohio* 9:121–132.

MYERS, DENYS PETER 1966 "The Recently Discovered Diaries of Isaiah Rogers." *Columbia Library Columns* 16:25–31.

WHIELDON, WILLIAM W. 1865 *Memoir of Solomon Willard.* Boston: Monument Association.

ROGERS, JAMES GAMBLE

James Gamble Rogers (1867–1947), a product of formal training at the Ecole des Beaux-Arts in Paris, became one of the most adept and creative of a group of American architects designing in the eclectic style. He was little influenced by the new directions in architecture emerging in the early twentieth century, and between 1915 and 1935, he produced a large body of institutional buildings notable for their elegant detail and sensitive spatial organization.

Rogers's most distinguished work was done at Yale University, where the Memorial Quadrangle and Harkness Tower (1916–1919) remain among the most refined and powerful examples of collegiate Gothic architecture anywhere. The tower became the focus of the campus and the centerpiece of the residential college plan, instituted in 1928 as the result of a gift from Edward S. Harkness and modeled on the undergraduate college organization at Oxford and Cambridge. Rogers designed the majority of the colleges at Yale and in addition was responsible for the major buildings donated to Yale by the Sterling family, starting with the massive neo-Gothic Sterling Memorial Library (1924–1930), for which BERTRAM GROSVENOR GOODHUE had originally been given the commission. When Goodhue died in 1924, the commission went to Rogers who then went on to design the Sterling Law Buildings (1926–1930) and the Hall of Graduate Studies (1927–1930), both neo-Gothic buildings donated by the Sterling Family.

JAMES G. ROGERS III

WORKS

1916–1919, Memorial Quadrangle and Harkness Tower, Yale University, New Haven. 1923–1928, Columbia Presbyterian Hospital, New York. 1924–1930, Sterling Memorial Library; 1926–1930, Sterling Law Buildings; 1927–1930, Hall of Graduate Studies; 1928–1933, Yale College Residential Colleges; Yale University, New Haven. 1932–1934, Butler Library, Columbia University, New York.

ROHAULT DE FLEURY FAMILY

The Rohault de Fleury family was active in Paris from 1800, when Hubert (1777–1846) was one of the few students at JULIEN DAVID LEROY's Ecole spéciale de l'architecture, to the late 1860s when his son Charles (1801–1875) withdrew from practice to write on religious subjects. Trained at the Ecole des Beaux-Arts, Charles's son Georges (1835–1905) wrote on medieval architecture. As a whole, the work of the Rohault de Fleury family illuminates the practice of an architectural office in Paris during the first sixty years of the nineteenth century, the social and political context of the time, and the role of architects in planning pre-Haussmannian Paris.

Hubert, a superb draftsman, was awarded the Prix de Rome in 1802. On his return from Rome in 1806, he was appointed as one of the inspectors for the construction of the Arc de Triomphe at the Place de l'Etoile, but the expected series of brilliant public commissions did not follow. Considerably younger than the architects who worked for Bonaparte's regime, Hubert waited until 1819 for his first public commission. Then, as chief architect of the prefecture of the police, he was charged with a number of barracks and buildings for the prefecture, which would remain his chief client. In 1819, Hubert was also appointed co-architect with ETIENNE HYPPOLITE GODDE to restore the Thermes de Julien for ANTOINE QUATREMÈRE DE QUINCY's commission.

Hubert's major period of activity was during the 1820s when he was principally involved in vast projects in the new suburbs, related to the health, feeding, and security of Paris's rapidly expanding population. Although mostly unbuilt, these schemes are remarkable as evidence of urban planning and for their elegantly conceived and rendered neoclassical buildings: slaughterhouse complexes on the plaine de Grenelle (1824), the park of Clichy, where the Lavoir was built (1827), and the forêt de Bondy (1827); and a vast horse infirmary in the new Poissonnière suburb (1824–1825). Hubert's many unbuilt hospital projects include additions to JACQUES GONDOUIN's Ecole de Chirurgie (1820–1824). He finally designed and built some pavilions for the Institution Sainte-Perrine (1830).

It was Hubert's fate, probably due to timing and a conservative personality, that the public buildings he did erect were inherently low-budget; the fish and butter market buildings of 1821 and additions to police barracks. Ironically, his only complete and acclaimed work, the barracks in the rue Mouffetard (1821–1824), is best known for his son's addition of 1827. The barracks tell much of Hubert and of Charles: Hubert's part is stucco and stone, severe yet serenely neoclassical; Charles's, a flamboyant, rusticated investigation of the Florentine Renaissance.

Charles was a man of his time, a student of the Ecole Polytechnique (1820–1822) and the Ecole des Beaux-Arts, but more innovative than most. His eclectic experiments continued. He followed his father's neoclassical vocabulary in a series of small houses and villas in the suburbs of Paris (1835–1842), but his Galerie de minérologie et de géologie (1833–1834) had Roman influences; his Hippodrome (1844–1845) was Moorish; and he chose early Renaissance for the Pavillon de Rohan (1853) and the Hôtel Sauvage (1861–1862); Louis XIII for the Hôtel de Préfecture, Poitiers (1859–1866). More significantly, he was also a pioneer of iron architecture. His very early straightforward iron-and-glass greenhouses (1833) at the Muséum d'Histoire Naturelle were immediately visited by JOSEPH PAXTON. In the 1830s, he also experimented with hydraulic cements and iron floor systems. Charles succeeded JACQUES MOLINOS as architect of the Muséum d'Histoire Naturelle and was responsible for its development from 1833 to 1862.

In the 1850s, Charles's office was crowded with work for elegant villas and *hôtels de ville,* and huge apartment and commercial blocks at the Place de l'Etoile (1857–1858) and the Place de l'Opéra (1855) with JACQUES IGNACE HITTORFF and others.

The height of Charles's career was his appointment as architect for the new opera in 1859; the bitter depth followed in 1860, when the Empress Eugénie caused a competition to be called, which resulted in the Opéra of CHARLES GARNIER. Charles Rohault de Fleury developed his ideas for the new opera and its site over many years, beginning at least in 1838 when he drew a façade which either paralleled or was influenced by GOTTFRIED SEMPER's Dresden Opera (1838–1841). Charles produced no major work after the opera debacle and turned to his religious writings. The Place de l'Opéra, however, belongs to him: its plan, that of the surrounding streets, and, in good part, its buildings.

PHYLLIS LAMBERT

WORKS

HUBERT ROHAULT DE FLEURY

*1819–1820, Caserne de Gendarmerie Hôtel Soyecourt; 1819–1822, Préfecture de la police (addition), rue Lamoignon; 1819–1823, Palais des Thermes de Julien (restoration with Etienne Hippolyte Goode); 1821–1824, Caserne de la rue Mouffetard; *1822, Caserne de Sapeurs (pompiers), rue de la Paix; *1824, Rohault de Fleury House, rue d'Auguesseau; (A)1825–1830, Caserne de Gendarmerie, rue Saint-Martin; *1827, Lavoir à Clichy; *1828–1830, Institution de Sainte-Pérrine; Paris.

CHARLES ROHAULT DE FLEURY

1827, Caserne de la rue Mouffetard (addition); 1833, Muséum d'histoire naturelle (Serres chaudes); 1833–1834, Muséum d'histoire naturelle (Galerie de Minéralogie); 1833–1834, Muséum d'histoire naturelle (Bâtiment de singes); *1844–1845, Hippodrome; 1853–1855, Pavillon de Rohan, rue Saint-Honoré; (A)1854–1861, Hôtel du Prince Soltykoff, rue Saint-Arnaud; (A)1855, Chambre des Notaires; 1855, Hôtel du Louvre (with H. J. Hittorff, A. Armand, and J. A. F. Pellechet); (A)1856, Hôtels Fontenilliat, Champs Elysées; 1857–1858, Hôtels Place de l'Etoile (with Hittorf); Paris. 1859–1866, Hôtel de Préfecture, Poitiers, France. (A)1861–1862, Hôtel Sauvage, Champs Elysées; Paris.

BIBLIOGRAPHY

The Rohault de Fleury Archive is in the Canadian Centre for Architecture, Montreal.

COUZY, HÉLÈNE 1973 "Travaux aux Halles dans la première moitié du XIXe siècle. . . ." *Bulletin, Société de l'histoire de l'art français* 1973:247–254.

FRANCE, MINISTÈRE DE L'EDUCATION NATIONALE, DIRECTION DES ARCHIVES DE FRANCE 1958 Volume 1 in *Catalogue général des cartes, plans et dessins d'architecture.* Paris: Imprimerie nationale.

GOURLIER, BIET; TARDIEU, GRILLON; and TARDIEU, FEU 1825–1850 *Choix d'édifices publics projetés et construits en France depuis le commencement du XIXe siècle.* 3 vols. Paris: Colos.

HIX, JOHN 1974 *The Glass House.* Cambridge, Mass.: M.I.T. Press.

KRAFFT, J. CH., and THIOLLET 1849 *Choix des plus jolies maisons de Paris et des environs.* Paris: Bance.

NORMAND, LOUIS MARIE n.d. *Paris Moderne, ou, Choix de maisons construites dans les nouveaux quartiers de la capitale et dans ses environs.* Paris: Normand.

ROHAULT DE FLEURY, CHARLES 1870 *Mémoire sur les instruments de la passion.* Paris: Lesort.

ROHAULT DE FLEURY, CHARLES 1874 *L'Evangile: Etudes iconographiques et archéologiques.* Tours, France.
ROHAULT DE FLEURY, CHARLES 1876 *Musée d'histoire naturelle. . . .* Paris.
ROHAULT DE FLEURY, CHARLES 1878 *La Sainte Vierge: Etudes archéologiques et iconographiques.* Paris: Poussielgue.
ROHAULT DE FLEURY, CHARLES, and ROHAULT DE FLEURY, GEORGES 1883–1889 *La Messe: Etudes archéologiques sur ses monuments.* Paris: Morel.
ROHAULT DE FLEURY, GEORGES 1866 *Les monuments de Pise au moyen âge. . . .* Paris: Morel.
ROHAULT DE FLEURY, GEORGES 1870–1873 *La Toscane au moyen âge: Architecture civile et militaire.* Paris: Lacroix.
ROHAULT DE FLEURY, GEORGES 1874 *La Toscane au moyen age: Lettres sur l'architecture civile et militaire en 1400. . . .* Paris: Morel.
ROHAULT DE FLEURY, GEORGES 1877 *Le Lateran au moyen âge.* Paris: Morel.
ROHAULT DE FLEURY, GEORGES 1884 *Oeuvre de C. Rohault de Fleury architecte.* Paris: Librairie centrale d'architecture.
ROHAULT DE FLEURY, GEORGES 1903 *Gallia Dominicana: Les couvents de St.-Dominique au moyen âge.* Paris. Lethielleux.

ROHE, LUDWIG MIES VAN DER

See MIES VAN DER ROHE, LUDWIG.

ROMEIN, THOMAS

Thomas Romein (1811–1881), born in Leeuwarden, Netherlands, finished his training at the Academy in Rotterdam, where he came into contact with the latest international trends in architecture. Back in Leeuwarden in 1834, he became a surveyor with the Provincial Public Works. From 1843 until his death, he was city architect of Leeuwarden.

As a private architect, he designed several classicist churches, country houses, and public buildings, the most important of which is the Palace of Justice, Leeuwarden, and the Grietenijhuis (town hall) of Menaldum, Netherlands.

MARIET J. H. WILLINGE

WORKS

1835, Mennonite Church, Akkrum, Utingeradeel; 1836, Reformed Church, Arum, Wonseradeel; 1840, Clubhouse Amicitia, Leeuwarden; 1841, Countryhouse, Saint Anna Parochie, Het Bildt; 1843, Haersmastate, Drachten, Smallingerland; 1843, Reformed Church, Terband, Heerenveen; 1843, Riniastate, Oudemirdum, Gaasterland; 1843, Town Hall, Menaldum; 1843–1844, Reformed Church, Saint Jacobiparochie, Het Bildt; 1844–1845, Main Guard (rebuilding), Leeuwarden; 1845, Harmonie, Harlingen; 1845–1847, Council Hall (interior), Leeuwarden; 1846–1852, Palace of Justice, Leeuwarden; 1852, Mennonite Church, Dokkum; 1878–1880, Exchange and Weighbuilding, Leeuwarden; Friesland, Netherlands.

BIBLIOGRAPHY

BOSCHMA, C. 1964 *Thomas Romein: Een classicistisch bouwmeester in het Friesland van de negentiende eeuw.* Assen, Netherlands: Opus Musivum.
MUSEUM BOYMANS-VAN BEUNINGEN 1941 *Nederland bouwt in baksteen: 1800–1940.* Rotterdam, Netherlands: The museum.

RONDELET, JEAN BAPTISTE

Born in Lyons, France, the son of a master mason, Jean Baptiste Rondelet (1743–1829) moved to Paris in 1763 to study under JACQUES FRANÇOIS BLONDEL. From 1770, he worked under JACQUES GERMAIN SOUFFLOT on the Church of Sainte Geneviève and became his trusted technical adviser. After a stay in Italy (1783–1784), he again took up work on Sainte Geneviève, although it was only between 1791 and 1812, under the guidance of A. C. QUATREMÈRE DE QUINCY, that he completed the structure.

R. D. MIDDLETON

BIBLIOGRAPHY

CHARVET, ETIENNE LÉON GABRIEL 1899 Pages 340–344 in *Lyon artistique. Architectes: Notices biographiques et bibliographiques.* Lyons, France: Bernoux & Cumin.
CHEVALIER, PIERRE, and RABREAU, DANIEL 1977 *Le Panthéon.* Paris: Caisse Nationale des Monuments Historiques et des Sites.
MATHIEU, MAE 1940 *Pierre Patte: Sa vie et son oeuvre.* Paris: Presses Universitaires de France.
MATHUSEK-BAUDOUIN, MARIE NOËLLE 1980 "Biographie de Jean Rondelet." Pages 155–157 in *Soufflot et son temps: 1780–1980.* Paris: Caisse Nationale des Monuments Historiques et des Sites.
MONVAL, JEAN MONDAIN 1918 *Soufflot: Sa Vie—son oeuvre—son esthétique (1713–1780).* Paris: Lemerre.
RONDELET, ANTOINE J. B. 1852 *Notice Historique sur l'église de Sainte-Geneviève.* Paris: Remquet.
RONDELET, JEAN BAPTISTE 1788–1820 Articles in volumes 1 and 2 in Antoine Chrysosthôme Quatremère de Quincy (editor), *Encyclopédie Méthodique.* Paris: Panckoucke. Rondelet wrote 129 entries relating to construction.
RONDELET, JEAN BAPTISTE (1789)1790 *Mémoire sur l'Architecture considérée généralement, avec des observations sur l'administration relative à cet art, et le projet d'une école pratique qui serait chargée de tous les ouvrages publics.* Paris: Gueffier.
RONDELET, JEAN BAPTISTE 1799 *Prospectus d'un traité*

théorique et pratique sur l'art de bâtir . . . sollicitant une place à l'Institut. Paris: Herault.

RONDELET, JEAN BAPTISTE 1802–1817 *Traité théorique et pratique de l'art de bâtir.* 7 vols. Paris: The author.

RONDELET, JEAN BAPTISTE 1820 *Commentaire de S. J. Frontin sur les aqueducs de Rome: Traduit du Latin avec le texte en regard . . . suivi de la description des principaux aqueducs construits jusqu' à nos jours.* Paris: The author.

ROOSENBURG, DIRK

Dirk Roosenburg (1887–1962) was born in The Hague, Netherlands, and settled there as an independent architect in 1916 after having studied at the Technical University in Delft and after having worked at H. P. BERLAGE's office. He soon made a name for himself because of his technical capabilities. He obtained commissions from big companies such as KLM, Philips, Oranje Nassau coal mines, and the Ministry of Public Works. One of his most famous works is the office of the Rijksverzekeringsbank (State Insurance Bank) in Amsterdam (1937–1939).

WIM DE WIT

WORKS

1920–1929, Philips Factory, Offices, and Laboratory, Eindhoven, Netherlands. 1928, Villa Windekind, The Hague. 1931, Oranje Nassau Mines Office, Heerlen, Netherlands. 1932, Zuyderzee Works Sluices, Den Oever, Netherlands. 1937–1939, Rijksverzekeringsbank Office, Amsterdam. 1940–1947, KLM Office (with P. Verhave and J. Luyt), The Hague.

BIBLIOGRAPHY

"In Memoriam ir. D. Roosenburg." 1962 *Bouwkundig Weekblad* 80:56–65.

Nederland Bouwt in Baksteen. 1941 Rotterdam, Netherlands: Museum Boymans-van Beuningen.

ROY VAN ZUYDEWIJN, H. J. F. DE 1970 *Haagse huizen en gebouwen.* Amsterdam: De Bussy.

ROOT, JOHN WELLBORN

John Wellborn Root (1850–1891) achieved the distinction, in his short career, of developing a design sensibility responsive to both the technical demands of the tall office building and the historical mandate for an eclecticism appropriate to the times. Twelve years younger than H. H. RICHARDSON and six years older than LOUIS H. SULLIVAN, Root was one of the few American architects of this period to work successfully in the Richardsonian manner and the only one whose accomplishments in design and criticism could rival those of Sullivan.

Root was born in Lumpkin, Georgia, and raised in Atlanta, where he studied drawing at home. When that city was occupied by Union troops in 1864, Root was sent to Liverpool, England, to continue his studies at the Clare Mount School in Wallasey. In 1866, he returned to the United States, and in 1869 he graduated in civil engineering from New York University. For about a year, he worked in the office of JAMES RENWICK, then for two years in the office of JOHN B. SNOOK, where he served as superintendent of construction. Early in 1872, PETER B. WIGHT, recently moved from New York to Chicago to take part in the rebuilding of the city after the 1871 fire, called for Root to join him as foreman in the office of Carter, Drake, and Wight. Later that year, DANIEL H. BURNHAM entered Wight's office as a draftsman, and by the middle of 1873, Burnham and Root had started their own partnership.

During the eighteen years of their practice together, Burnham and Root designed and built (or were preparing to build) as many as 216 private houses, thirty-nine office buildings, twenty-six apartment buildings and hotels, twenty-three railroad stations, twelve stores and warehouses, twelve schools and hospitals, eight churches, and twenty other structures (Hines, 1974, p. 403; cf. pp. 372–378). Burnham was responsible for developing and managing the office organization which made it possible to carry out this volume of work. Root was the partner in charge of design. Burnham was most often the one who secured the commissions, and he also contributed to working out the floor plans of buildings. From these initial ideas, Root elaborated most of the aspects of the design of a building, occasionally attending even to the drawing of details. During the evolution of a project, Burnham offered criticism of Root's designs, and draftsmen contributed ideas of their own. The resulting visual form of the building can be credited to Root's controlling sensibility in responding to suggestions made by his clients, his partner, and his assistants.

Although the firm had a steady supply of residential commissions through two decades, the most memorable works of Burnham and Root are a series of tall office buildings designed for downtown Chicago during the 1880s. Structural innovations introduced by this firm made possible the construction of taller and taller buildings, and their Montauk Block (ten stories), Monadnock Block (sixteen stories), and Masonic Temple (twenty-two stories) set new height records in Chicago in their time. In the Montauk Block (1881–1882), one of the footings was constructed

Root.
The Rookery.
Chicago.
1885–1887

of a grillage of steel rails encased in cement, a space-saving substructure as strong as a more massive pyramidal footing of stone. All the footings of the Rialto Building (1883–1886) were constructed using this new technique, as were those in The Rookery (1885–1888), the Monadnock Block (1889–1891), and other buildings of the late 1880s.

Although the Montauk Block had masonry bearing walls, it was the first Chicago building to have an interior frame entirely of iron members, sheathed in lightweight, fireproof tile. The Rand-McNally Building at the end of the decade (1888–1890) was the first building with an all-steel frame and with a complete exterior cladding of lightweight terra cotta.

The aesthetic possibilities of the large interior light court were first fully realized in The Rookery, with its bright, two-story atrium beneath an iron and glass vault. Above this space is an open light court. The principal street elevations of The Rookery were still of load-bearing masonry construction, but the elevations facing the light court were designed to provide a maximum amount of window area. A skeletal frame carried the uninterrupted brick spandrels, and the closely spaced windows, the terra-cotta bands above them, and the continuous sills emphasized the horizontal sense of these interior elevations.

The Monadnock Block, widely considered to be Root's masterpiece, was designed with exterior masonry bearing walls, because Peter Brooks, the client (also of the Montauk Block and The Rookery), was skeptical about the durability of an all-steel frame. Suggestions for an "avoidance of ornamentation" came from Brooks in his initial correspondence of 1884. The next year, Root produced a relatively austere design relying on stylized Egyptian motifs and subtly tapered profiles. The project was shelved in 1886 and not resumed until 1889. Further suggestions for stripping away ornament may have come from Burnham and the drafting staff, but it was Root who worked diligently during the fall of 1889 to shape a design in which the major profiles of the brown brick exterior could be made to subsume both the urge for ornament and the urge for simplicity.

Root's last major work would be the first phase of the design and construction of the Reliance Building (1889–1891). This phase included only the remodeling of the store fronts of an existing building for the new tenant, Carson, Pirie, Scott, and Company, using large sheets of plate glass and granite piers with low-relief ornament, and also the preparation of foundations to carry the fifteen-story steel-frame structure to be built several years later. Root's overall design has not survived, and the rest of the building was elaborated in 1894 by Burnham's new designer, CHARLES B. ATWOOD. At the time of his death early in 1891, Root was assisting Burnham with the site planning and architectural conceptualization for the World's Columbian Exposition.

The best known buildings of John Wellborn Root have been variously celebrated for his inclusion of pioneering structural components, his treatment of surface, and his embodiment of interior or exterior volume. His less successful buildings are a result of the large amount of design work for which he took responsibility in the busy firm and of an ambivalence in balancing the demands of masonry construction, ornamental elaboration, and structural innovation.

Root was active in the musical and theatrical life of Chicago, and in 1882, he married Dora Louise Monroe, sister of the poet Harriet Monroe who would publish the first full-length biography of him in 1896. He was one of the organizers of the Western Association of Architects in 1884, its first secretary, then president. When this organization merged with the American Institute of Architects in 1889, Root was elected to serve as national secretary, a position he held until his death. He was a popular speaker at meetings of the Western Association of Architects and the Chicago Architectural Sketch Club during the late 1880s, and many of the papers he prepared for these occasions were published in the *Inland Architect.* Root learned much from the writings of EDWARD GARBETT, GOTTFRIED SEMPER, and EUGÈNE EMMANUEL VIOLLET-LE-DUC. His own writings show his interest in the analytic solution of programmatic requirements, the metaphoric expression of ethical values in buildings, and the historical determinism of style: "Styles are found truly at the appointed time, but solely by those who, with intelligence and soberness, are working out their ends by the best means at hand, and with scarce a thought of the coming new or national style" (Root, [1885–1890] 1967, p. 133).

J. A. CHEWNING

WORKS

*1874, Sherman House; *1881–1882, Montauk Building; *1882–1883, Chicago, Burlington, and Quincy General Office Building; *1883–1886, Rialto Building; *1884–1885, Insurance Exchange Building; *1885–1887, Phenix Building; 1885–1887, The Rookery (interior light court redesigned by FRANK LLOYD WRIGHT in 1905); *1886–1887, Art Institute (later the Chicago Club); 1886–1887, Saint Gabriel's; *1886–1887, Pickwick Flats; Chicago. *1886–1888, Board of Trade Building, Kansas City, Mo. 1887–1888, Lake View Presbyterian Church; *1888–1890, Rand-McNally Building; *1889–1890, Edward H. Valentine House; *1889–1891, Chicago (Great Northern) Hotel; 1889–1890, Monadnock Building (not completed until 1892); 1889–1891, Reliance Building (completed according to revised designs by Charles B. Atwood in 1894–1895); *1890–1891, Masonic Temple (not completed until 1892); Chicago. 1890–1891, Mills Building (not completed until 1892), San Francisco. 1890–1891, Union Depot, Keokuk, Iowa. *1890–1891, Woman's Building (not completed until 1892), Chicago.

BIBLIOGRAPHY

CONDIT, CARL W. 1964 *The Chicago School of Architecture: A History of Commercial and Public Building in the Chicago Area, 1875–1925.* University of Chicago Press.

EATON, LEONARD K. 1972 "John Wellborn Root and the Julian M. Case House." *Prairie School Review* 9:18–22.

HINES, THOMAS S. 1974 *Burnham of Chicago: Architect and Planner.* New York: Oxford University Press.

HITCHCOCK, H. R. (1929)1972 *Modern Architecture: Romanticism and Reintegration.* Reprint. New York: Arno.

HOFFMANN, DONALD 1967 "John Root's Monadnock Building." *Journal of the Society of Architectural Historians* 26:269–277.

MONROE, HARRIET (1896)1966 *John Wellborn Root: A Study of His Life and Work.* Reprint. Park Forest, Ill.: Prairie School Press.

OVERBY, OSMUND R. 1963*a* "Monadnock Block." Unpublished report, Historic American Buildings Survey, Library of Congress, Washington.

OVERBY, OSMUND R. 1963*b* "Rookery Building." Unpublished report, Historic American Buildings Survey, Library of Congress, Washington.

ROBERTSON, THOMAS BURNS 1942 "John Wellborn Root, Architect (1850–1891)." Unpublished M.A. thesis, New York University.

ROOT, JOHN WELLBORN (1885–1890)1967 *The Meanings of Architecture: Buildings and Writings by John Wellborn Root.* Edited by Donald Hoffmann. New York: Horizon.

SCHUYLER, MONTGOMERY (1891)1961 *American Architecture and Other Writings.* Edited by William H. Jordy and Ralph Coe. Cambridge, Mass.: Harvard University Press.

STARRETT, THEODORE 1912 "John Wellborn Root." *Architects' and Builders' Magazine* 13:429–431.

TALLMADGE, THOMAS E. 1941 *Architecture in Old Chicago.* University of Chicago Press.

ROPER, DAVID RIDALL

David Ridall Roper (1774?–1855) was a competent Regency Greek Revivalist, although ARTHUR BOWYER CLAYTON assisted in the design of his most important works, Saint Mark's Church, Kennington (1822–1824), and the Shot Tower, Lambeth (1826), London. Roper was also a surveyor who, with Samuel Robinson, valued property for the Regent Street development in London. Elected president of the Surveyors' Club in 1813, he had a number of pupils, including his sons, Joshua and David.

R. WINDSOR LISCOMBE

WORKS

*1805?, Albion Fire Office, Southwark; 1811–1813, Brockwell Hall, near Dulwich; 1812, Surrey Chapel Almshouses, Southward; 1819, Grove Chapel, Camberwell; 1822–1824, Saint Mark's Church, Kennington; 1825–1826, Haberdashers' (Aske's) Almshouses (now Shoreditch Technical Institute), Hoxton; *1826, Shot Tower, Lambeth; London.

BIBLIOGRAPHY

"Survey of London." 1956 Volume 26, pages 31–33 in F. H. W. Sheppard, *The Parish of St. Mary Lambeth: Part II. Southern Area.* London: Athlone.

RORICZER FAMILY

Among the dynasties of masons such as the PARLER, Ensinger (see ULRICH VON ENSINGEN), and Böblinger (see HANS AND MATTHÄUS BÖBLINGER) families which dominated large-scale projects in southern Germany, the Roriczer clan would be the least important were it not for the theoretical booklets published by Mathes Roriczer.

Wenzel Roriczer (Veclav Rorycz?) probably came from the Parler lodge in Prague to Regensburg, and was hired as the architect of Saint Peter's Cathedral in 1411. The imperial capital of the Upper Palatinate had suffered a series of setbacks, and the cathedral construction was to last through the city's submission to the duke of Bavaria in

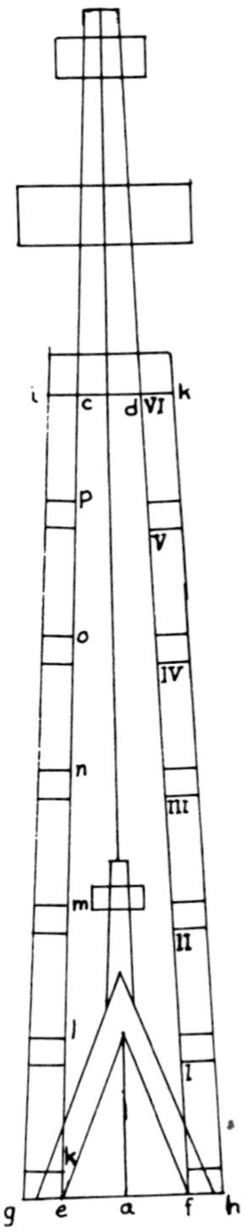

Mathes Roriczer. Drawing from The Booklet of Correct Finials. *1486*

Mathes Roriczer. Drawing from Geometria Deutsch.

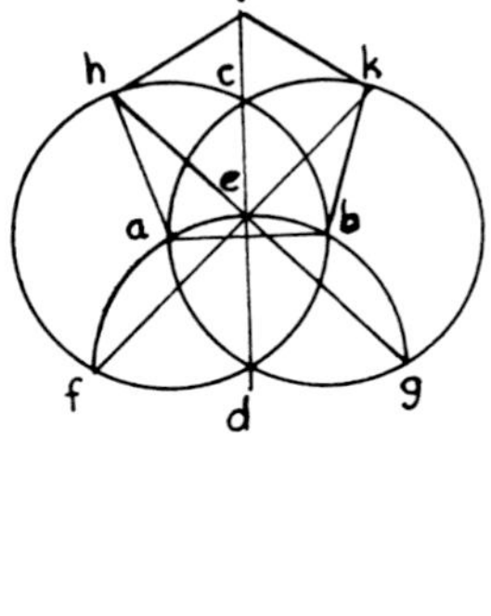

1486 and its swing back to the imperial fold in 1492. Wenzel further developed the west façade and the lower stories of the twin towers. He died in 1419, leaving a young son, Konrad. His widow married Andreas Engel who took over work on the cathedral in 1436 and also supervised the construction of Saint George in Noerdlingen as well as the Frauenkirche in Ingolstadt, Saint Lorenz in Nuremberg, and the cathedral complex in Eichstätt. In 1440, Engel transferred some of his duties in Eichstätt to his stepson Konrad Roriczer, who also participated in and eventually took control over the construction of the choir of Saint Lorenz in Nuremberg from 1454 to 1466. In 1456, Konrad inherited the cathedral lodge at Regensburg and radically redesigned the façade from a two-tower project to an elaborate one-tower scheme, which was rejected. Instead, he had to settle for the highly original entrance hall on a triangular plan for which the elevation drawing of around 1475 still exists. In 1462, he served as a consultant in Vienna, and in 1474 he performed the same service for the Frauenkirche in Munich. He is last mentioned in October 1477.

Konrad's oldest son Mathes (Matthew) was born in the 1430s. In 1461, he was sent to Noerdlingen to transmit and explain his father's design for the tower of Saint George, and he may have worked there briefly. The following year, he began to work in the lodge of Saint Lorenz in Nuremberg as parlier, and in 1463, he passed his master's exam. He immediately acquired Nuremberg citizenship and took on an apprentice. As a master mason, he participated in the erection of the exterior choir walls and their finials, the construction of the huge roof, and the initial stages of vault construction before being fired for unstated reasons in 1466. From 1468 to 1472, he worked with Hans Boeblinger on the sophisticated tower of the Frauenkirche in Esslingen and constructed the tabernacle which was eventually used for the Böblinger tombs. There followed a stay in Eichstätt, where he constructed the chapter sacristy. In 1473, he was one of the consultants assessing the vaults of the Frauenkirche in Munich. On March 24, 1476, he acquired Regensburg citizenship and replaced his father as master of the works at the cathedral from January 6, 1478, through October 1492. He completed the top of the entrance hall, the upper west façade with a monumental crucifix, the pulpit (1482), the third story of the north tower, the elegant Eichel turret (1487–1488), and an exquisite tabernacle (1493); he probably also designed the Altar of the Three Kings. A drawing by Hans Holbein the Elder of around 1490 shows him as a rather frail, contemplative skeptic at the time when he was supervising three printing projects concerning geometry and the design of finials and gables. He probably died in 1495.

In March of the same year, his brother Wolfgang became a citizen of Regensburg and took over the cathedral lodge. He completed the façade, further stories of the towers, a baldachin, and an exquisite baptismal font. Involved in factional politics, he chose the wrong side and was beheaded on May 30, 1540, thus abruptly ending the architectural dominance of the Roriczer family which had persisted for more than a century.

On June 28, 1486, Mathes Roriczer published his first and best known tract *Das Büchlein von der fialen Gerechtigkeit* (The Booklet of Correct Finials). The dedicatory inscription states Roriczer's purpose: the construction of finials in plan and elevation through the use of geometric principles developed by "men of knowledge" such as the Parlers. The following sixteen pages explain the design process which requires a sequence of numerous predictable steps. The plan of the finial is derived from a base square into which a second and third square are inscribed at 45° angles. These squares are then aligned with the sides of the original square, resulting in a cubic base and the body of the finial with its recessed long rectangles. The height of the finial is an arbitrary septuple multiplication of the base. Mathes Roriczer also dealt with the construction of the pyramidal pinnacle above the body of the finial, using a 1 : 7, that is, a very steep, proportion. The position and size of the crockets and of the three cross-flowers at the top are also determined by geometric and arithmetic steps. These procedures, which require arbitrary modular multiplications, are relatively primitive when compared to the purely geometric determination that governs the shape and size of each segment of large pinnacles in earlier theoretical drawings.

A second, more fundamental treatise published by Mathes Roriczer has become known as *Geometria Deutsch.* The eight-page text and illustrations starkly describe the geometric procedures necessary to halve a right angle; to construct a pentagon, a hexagon, an octagon; to determine the length of the circumference of a circle; to find the center of a circle from a segment; and to construct a square equal in surface to that of an equilateral triangle. This tract, which allows for the solution of complex geometric problems using the compass and a straight-edge, is related to a manuscript copy of the anonymous *De inquisicione figurarum* which was available in Munich, the *Geometria trium fratrum,* and possibly to Erhard Ratdolt's Euclid edition which appeared in Venice in 1482.

The final product of Roriczer's press is a four-page tract on gables which he probably authored in reaction to the goldsmith Hans Schmuttermayer's essay on finials and gables published c.1488–1489. Roriczer's tract of around 1490 developed a slightly steeper and more complex arch and included the necessary plan, an elevation of the whole, and the three cross-flowers. Schmuttermayer's booklet corroborates the pervasiveness of Gothic architectural geometry around 1500. Mathes Roriczer gave us a mnemonic, somewhat arbitrary insight into the extraction of the elevation from the groundplan through the use of the quadrature and additional geometric steps which began to be practiced in the 1220s and which were to influence subsequent architectural treatises of the Renaissance such as Dürer's *Unterweysung der Messung.*

FRANÇOIS BUCHER

BIBLIOGRAPHY

BUCHER, FRANÇOIS 1976 "Micro-architecture as the 'Idea' of Gothic Theory and Style." *Gesta* 15, nos. 1–2:71–89.

GELDNER, FERDINAND 1965 *Matthäus Roritzer: Das Büchlein von der Fialen Gerechtigkeit.* Wiesbaden, Germany: Pressler.

RECHT, ROLAND 1980 "Le Traité de géométrie de Mathieu Roriczer." *Dossiers Histoire et Archéologie* (now called *Les Dossiers de l'archéologie*) 47:24–25.

SHELBY, LONNIE R. 1977 *Gothic Design Techniques: The Fifteenth-century Design Booklets of Mathes Roriczer and Hans Schmuttermayer.* Carbondale: Southern Illinois University Press.

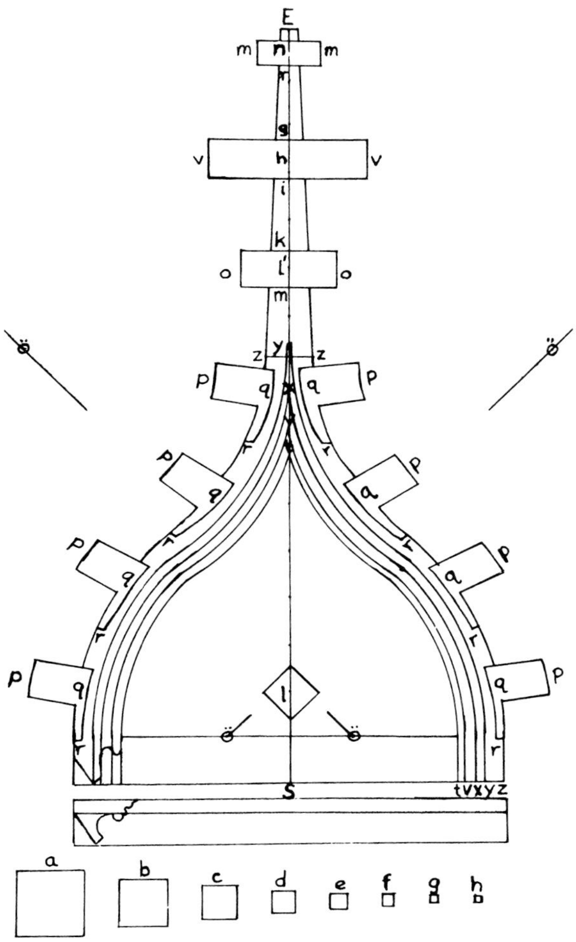

Drawing from Hans Schmuttermayer's Booklet on Gables. *1488–1489*

ROSEN, ANTON S.

Anton S. Rosen (1859–1928) graduated from the Technical School in Copenhagen in 1877 and from the Royal Academy in 1882. He was a student of Vilhelm Dahlerup and worked in his office until 1896. Rosen had a happily mixed style of his own, influenced by everything new in technology and design from ALFRED MESSEL to LOUIS H. SULLIVAN. His vital and imaginative talent and his care for color and texture made him the foremost Art Nouveau architect in Denmark.

LISBET BALSLEV JØRGENSEN

WORKS

1906–1907, Office Building, 34 Vesterbrogade (Savoy); 1907, Office Building, 16 Frederiksberggade (Metropol); Copenhagen. 1909, Denmark Exhibition, Århus. 1907–1910, Palads Hotel, Copenhagen. 1912–1917, Gerthas Minde (garden city), Odense, Denmark. 1914–1915, Tuborg Administration Building, Copenhagen. 1915, Denmark's House, San Francisco.

BIBLIOGRAPHY

JØRGENSEN, AXEL 1952 "Rosen, Anton Sophus." Volume 3, pages 73–75 in *Weilbachs Kunstnerleksikon.* Copenhagen.

MØLLER, VIGGO STEN 1980 *Arkitekten Anton Rosens arbejder.* Copenhagen: Rhodos.

ROSENBERG, EUGENE

Having studied engineering, Eugene Rosenberg (1907–) transferred in 1928 to the Prague Academy of Fine Arts to study architecture. In 1929, he worked intermittently for LE CORBUSIER. He arrived in England in 1939 with a reputation for modernism gained through his work in Prague, and entered the circle of English modernists—EDWIN MAXWELL FRY, FREDERICK GIBBERD, and FRANCIS YORKE. He formed a partnership with Yorke and with Cyril Mardall in 1944 (see Yorke, Mardall, and Rosenberg) which continued to design buildings imbued with the rationalist spirit of the early years of modernism for more than thirty years.

BRIAN HANSON

WORKS

1929, Housing Holešovice, Czechoslovakia. 1931–1933, Red Cross Tuberculosis and Maternity Clinics, Topolčany, Czechoslovakia. 1936, Humanita (workers' cooperative housing), Prague. 1937, Grammar School, Bratislava, Czechoslovakia. 1950, Barclay Secondary School (with F. R. S. Yorke and Cyril Mardall), Stevenage, Hertfordshire, England. 1956, Sheppard School (with Yorke and Mardall), Tulse Hill; 1961, Yorke, Rosenberg, and Mardall Offices (with Yorke and Mardall), Greystoke Place; London. 1963–1972, Keddies Department Store (with Yorke and Mardall), Southend, Essex, England. 1965–1971, Warwick University (buildings, with Yorke and Mardall), Coventry, England. 1966–1974, Saint Thomas' Hospital (with Yorke and Mardall), Lambeth; 1968, Heathrow Airport (Cargo Area Canteen and Airside Operations Building, with Yorke and Mardall); London. 1968–1972, Zambia University (buildings, with Yorke and Mardall), Lusaka. 1969, Stansted Airport (terminal building, with Yorke and Mardall), Essex, England. 1970–1972, Leeds Royal Infirmary and Ancillary Building (extensions, with Yorke and Mardall), Yorkshire, England. 1972, WD and HO Wills Offices and Factory (with Yorke, Mardall, and Skidmore, Owings and Merrill), Bristol, England. 1973–1975, Ashmolean Gallery, Oxford, England.

BIBLIOGRAPHY

"Arcades, Offices, and Flats, Prague." 1940*a* *Architect's Journal* 92:29–33.

"Block of Flats." 1940*b* *Architect's Journal* 91:407–412.

Kadlečíková, M. 1964 "Conversations with an Overseas Architect." *Domov* 1964:3.

Rosenberg, E. 1943 "Rebuilding and the Human Environment." *Nove Ceslosloven*sko Nov.

Yorke, Rosenberg, Mardall 1972 *The Architecture of Yorke, Rosenberg, Mardall, 1944–1972.* Introduction by Reyner Banham. London: Lund Humphries; New York: Crane Russak.

ROSENBERG, LOUIS CONRAD

Born in Portland, Oregon, Louis Conrad Rosenberg (1890–) showed a precocious talent in drawing. He won a scholarship to the Massachusetts Institute of Technology and a traveling fellowship, the latter deferred because of World War I. He taught at the University of Oregon and served in the army. While in Rome in 1921, he took up etching. Success in this medium led to a major career in printmaking.

Marion Dean Ross

BIBLIOGRAPHY

McMillan, Gail 1978 "Catalog of the Louis Conrad Rosenberg Collection." Unpublished manuscript, University of Oregon Library, Eugene.

Rosenberg, Louis Conrad 1922 *The Davanzati Palace, Florence, Italy.* New York: Architectural Book Publishing Company.

Rosenberg, Louis Conrad 1929 *L. C. Rosenberg, A.R.E.* With an introduction by Malcolm C. Salaman. London: The Studio; New York: Rudge.

Rosenberg, Louis Conrad 1930 *Louis C. Rosenberg.* With an appreciation by Kenneth Reid. New York: Crafton Collection; London: Colnaghi.

ROŠKOT, KAMIL

Kamil Roškot (1886–1945) developed his style from Jan Kotěra's rationalistic conception of modern architecture, which was characterized by clear tectonics and joint brickwork. Greatly impressed by his many trips to Italy and Tunisia, where he familiarized himself with the classical architecture of the Mediterranean area, Roškot, who was born in Vlašim, Bohemia, developed in the late 1920s a lapidary, puristic form of the new style. He also became a bold, monumental town planner. However, his uncompromising positions prevented the practical realization of his ideas, in spite of his many successes in competitions. His personal qualitites and exemplary work earned him the respect of his contemporaries.

The Theater at Ústí nad Orlicí (1934–1935), the Tomb of Czech Kings in the crypt of Saint Vitus Cathedral in Prague (1934–1935), the Czechoslovak state pavilions in Milan (1927), Chicago (1933), and New York (1939), as well as a number of unrealized designs are evidence of Roškot's great talent which stretched beyond the clichés of the International style doctrine.

Vladimír Šlapeta

WORKS

1923, Apartment House, Letná, Prague. *1927, Czechoslovak State Pavilion, Milan. 1933, Czechoslovak State Pavilion, Chicago. 1934–1935, Tomb of Czech Kings, Saint Vitus Cathedral, Prague. 1934–1935, Theater, Ústí nad Orlicí, Czechoslovakia. *1938–1939, Czechoslovak State Pavilion, New York.

BIBLIOGRAPHY

Černý, František, and Šlapeta, Vladimír 1978 *Kamil Roškot, 1886–1945, architektonické dílo.* Olomouc, Czechoslovakia: Galene výtvarného umění. Exhibition catalogue, with a list of works.

Černý, František, and Štěpánck, Josef 1946 *Kamil Roškot-Výstava životního díla.* Prague: Museum of Arts and Crafts. Exhibition catalogue.

Komonen, Markku, and Šlapeta, Vladimír 1979 *Kamil Roškot 1886–1945, Arkkitehti.* Helsinki: Museum of Finnish Architecture. Exhibition catalogue.

Schweighofer, Anton; Šlapeta, Vladimír; and Podrecca, Boris 1981 *Kamil Roškot 1886–1945:*

Das architektonische Werk. Vienna: Künstlerhaus. Exhibition catalogue.

ŠLAPETA, VLADIMÍR 1978 "Kamil Roškot—L'opera architettonica." *Lotus International* 20:63–95. Text in English and Italian.

ROSS, GEORGE ALLEN

George Allen Ross (1878–1946), a Montreal architect educated at the Massachusetts Institute of Technology and the Ecole des Beaux-Arts in Paris, trained under CARRÈRE AND HASTINGS of New York City. With his partners David MacFarlane and later Robert H. Macdonald, he designed the Château Laurier Hotel, Ottawa (1912), and the Dominion Square Building, Montreal (1928–1929).

ROBERT HILL

BIBLIOGRAPHY

SMITH, J. ROXBURGH 1946 "Obituary." *Journal of the Royal Architectural Institute of Canada* 23, Apr.:103.

ROSSELLINO, BERNARDO

Born in the village of Settignano near Florence, Italy, Bernardo di Matteo Gambarelli called Rossellino (1409–1464) probably received his training as a stonemason in the family workshop (see GAMBARELLI FAMILY). Rossellino, who also worked as a sculptor, began his architectural career with his design for the upper portions of the façade of the Misericordia Palace in Arezzo, Italy (1433–1435). Returning to Florence, he worked at the Aranci Cloister of the Badia (1436–1438) and designed the Cloister of Santa Maria alle Campora (1436), one of the first such structures built in the Renaissance style. During the 1440s, his designs for the Portal of the Sala del Consistoro in the Palazzo Pubblico of Siena, Italy (1446) and for the architectural frame of his Tomb of Leonardo Bruni in Santa Croce, Florence, Italy (1446–1448), showed his allegiance to the classical revival. Rossellino's sympathy for *il modo antico* extended beyond surface details to an understanding for the harmonious relationships and grandeur found in antique art. These qualities are evidenced in the finest architectural accomplishment of his early years: the Spinelli Cloister at Santa Croce in Florence (1448–1452). During the same years, he remodeled eight houses into the core of the Rucellai Palace, replacing one of them with a handsome courtyard.

The second phase of Rossellino's architectural career began with a stay in Rome (August 1451–1455) and his employment on the building staff of Pope Nicholas V. GIORGIO VASARI probably is in error in attributing numerous projects in and around Rome to Rossellino; documents show he was responsible only for supplying hoists for the Torre Nova (1452) at the Vatican and for the renovation of the Roman church of Santo Stefano Rotondo (1453). His years in Rome did provide him with a firsthand knowledge of antiquity and a familiarity with the theories of LEON BATTISTA ALBERTI with whom he may have collaborated on the never-executed plans for the Vatican Palace, the Borgo district, and a new St. Peter's. Upon his return to Florence, he remodeled some structures into a palace for Tommaso Spinelli (1459?–1464?), remarkable for its architectural sculptures, use of sgraffito decorations, and for the perspectival illusionism of the entrance passage.

Rossellino's greatest artistic achievement came with a commission from Pope Pius II Piccolomini to rebuild the town of Pienza, Italy. Here, Rossellino designed (1459–1464) the Piccolomini Palace, the cathedral, Communal Palace, and town square; he also supervised the remodeling of the Bishop's Palace, Canons' Residence, palaces for several cardinals, and houses for members of the curia staff and citizenry. For the Piccolomini Palace, he used three tiers of pilasters to articulate three sides of the building and superimposed loggias on the fourth, or garden, façade. The cathedral combines a Germanic hall-church interior with a classicizing front. The real significance of Pienza, however, lies not in the individual units but in its total urban concept, the basic ideas for which may have originated in the earlier designs for Pope Nicholas V's

Rossellino. Palazzo Piccolomini. Pienza, Italy. 1459–1464

Rossellino. Cathedral. Pienza, Italy. 1459–1464

Vatican projects. In Florence, Rossellino adapted his scheme for the Piccolomini Palace for the façade of the Rucellai Palace (1462), usually attributed to Alberti. In 1461, he was made superintendent of the construction of the Florence Cathedral, an appointment which recognized his position as the leader of the most important architectural workshop in the city.

CHARLES RANDALL MACK

WORKS

1433–1435, Fraternità di Santa Maria della Misericordia (façade), Arezzo, Italy. 1436, Cloister, Santa Maria alle Campora; 1436–1438, Aranci Cloister (with others), The Badia; Florence. 1446, Sala del Consistoro (portal), Palazzo Pubblico, Siena, Italy. 1446–1448, Tomb of Leonardo Bruni (architectural frame), Santa Croce; 1448–1452, Palazzo Rucellai (core and courtyard); 1448–1452, Spinelli Cloister, Santa Croce; Florence. 1453, Santo Stefano Rotondo (renovation), Rome. 1459?–1464?, Palazzo Spinelli, Florence. 1459–1464, Rebuilding of Pienza (Cathedral, Palazzo Piccolomini, Palazzo Comunale, Palazzo Vescovile, Palazzo Canonica, Palazzo Ammannati, and other palaces and houses), Italy. 1461, Chapel of the Cardinal of Portugal (workshop), San Miniato ai Monte; 1462, Palazzo Rucellai (façade); Florence. 1463, San Pietro (bell tower), Perugia, Italy. 1463, St. Peter's (benediction loggia), Rome.

BIBLIOGRAPHY

CARLI, ENZO 1966 *Pienza, la città di Pio II.* Rome: Editalia.

FABRICZY, CORNELIUS VON 1900 "Ein Jugendwerk Bernardo Rossellinos und spätere unbeachtete Schöpfungen seines Meissels." *Jahrbuch der Königlich-Preussischen Kunstsammlungen* 21:33–54, 99–113.

HARTT, FREDERICK; CORTI, GINO; and KENNEDY, CLARENCE 1964 *The Chapel of the Cardinal of Portugal, 1434–1459, at San Miniato in Florence.* Philadelphia: University of Pennsylvania Press.

HEYDENREICH, LUDWIG 1937 "Pius II als Bauherr von Pienza." *Zeitschrift für Kunstgeschichte* 6:105–146.

MACK, CHARLES RANDALL 1972 "Studies in the Architectural Career of Bernardo di Matteo Gamberelli Called Rossellino." Unpublished Ph.D. dissertation, University of North Carolina at Chapel Hill.

MACK, CHARLES RANDALL 1974 "The Rucellai Palace: Some New Proposals." *Art Bulletin* 56:517–529.

PLANISCIG, LEO 1942 *Bernardo und Antonio Rossellino.* Vienna: Schroll.

PREYER, BRENDA 1975 "Giovanni Rucellai and the Rucellai Palace." Unpublished Ph.D. dissertation, Harvard University, Cambridge, Mass.

SAALMAN, HOWARD 1966 "Tommaso Spinelli, Michelozzo, Manetti and Rossellino." *Journal of the Society of Architectural Historians* 25:151–164.

SALMI, MARIO 1977 "Bernardo Rossellino ad Arezzo." Pages 254–261 in Maria Duprè Dal Poggetto and Paolo Dal Poggetto (editors), *Scritti di storia dell'arte in onore di Ugo Procacci.* Milan: Electa Editrice.

SANPAOLESI, PIERO 1942 "Costruzioni del prima Quattrocento nella Badia Fiorentina." *Rivista d'arte* Series 2 24:143–179.

SANPAOLESI, PIERO 1963 "Precisazioni sul Palazzo Rucellai." *Palladio* New Series 13:61–66.

SCHULZ, ANNE MARKHAM 1977 *The Sculpture of Bernardo Rossellino and his Workshop.* N.J.: Princeton University Press.

TYSZKIEWICZ, MARYLA 1928 *Bernardo Rossellino.* Florence: Stamperia Polacca.

ROSSETTI, BIAGIO

Biagio Rossetti (1447?–1516) was the pre-eminent architect of Renaissance Ferrara (Italy). Born there around 1447, he died in his native city in 1516. Rossetti is first documented in 1467 as an assistant and collaborator of Pietro Benvenuti, court architect of Borso d'Este. At the death of Benvenuti in 1483, Rossetti became ducal architect and munitions engineer for Ercole d'Este. The position gave him superintendence of virtually all architectural and military projects in the city and territories of Ferrara until the accession of Alfonso I d'Este in 1505. In 1490, he built his own residence, Casa Rossetti, a modest two-story brick house that reflects vernacular design principles but is distinguished by a deft personal handling of fenestration and terra-cotta decoration.

Rossetti was responsible for one of the most important urban planning projects of the entire fifteenth century: the Erculean Addition to Ferrara, designed for Ercole I in 1492. The scheme was intended to advance Ferrara as a populous, prestigious and powerful north Italian capital. More than doubling the area of the old city, the Erculean

Addition consisted of a polygonal circuit of low, terraced walls with round towers and four gates traversed by two main streets, Via Prione from east to west, and Via degli Angeli from north to south. The twin foci of the plan were the intersection of the two streets and a large, eccentrically placed market square, Piazza Nuova. At the intersection, Rossetti began three palaces that declared the scope and scale of a new aristocratic neighborhood. For Sigismondo d'Este he built the imposing Palazzo dei Diamanti (1493–1516), named for its faceted marble revetment; accompanying it are the Palazzo Turchi-Di Bagno (1493) and Palazzo Prosperi-Sacrati (1493), brick buildings with ornamental marble pilasters marking corners of the intersection. For the Piazza Nuova, which measures about one hundred by two hundred meters, Rossetti designed the Palazzo Rondinelli (1494–?) and the Palazzo Strozzi-Bevilacqua (1494–?), both of which feature spacious ground floor arcades facing the square.

Rossetti erected four major ecclesiastical structures in Ferrara. San Francesco, located within the old city, was begun in 1494 on a plan which recalls that of FILIPPO BRUNELLESCHI's San Lorenzo in Florence. The nave is covered by flattened domes on pendentives between transverse arches, the aisle bays are domed, and the recessed chapels have barrel vaults. Santa Maria in Vado, also in old Ferrara, was initiated one year later. Here, the nave was given a wooden ceiling while the aisle bays, without recessed chapels, have groin vaults; the arcade columns are raised on high pedestals. In the Erculean Addition, Rossetti began the Church of San Benedetto in 1496. Severely damaged in World War II but subsequently rebuilt, San Benedetto is an aisled Latin-cross church with semicircular chapels, transepts, and choir. Its barrel-vaulted nave has two domes, and the arcading rests on alternating square and rectangular piers. San Cristoforo alla Certosa, begun in the Erculean Addition in 1498, is an aisleless monastic church with sail vaults over paired bays in the nave, transepts, and choir, and with a raised hemispherical dome at the crossing. In all of these works, Rossetti creatively adapted Tuscan and Lombard ideas to his own cool, classicizing idiom, successfully investing Ferrara with the style and measure of a progressive modern city.

RICHARD J. TUTTLE

WORKS

1475?–1499, San Niccolò (apse); 1485–?, San Giorgio (campanile); 1490, Casa Rossetti; 1493, Palazzo Prosperi-Sacrati; 1493, Palazzo, Turchi-Di Bagno; 1493–1516, Palazzo dei Diamanti (not completed until 1567 by others); 1494, Palazzo Mosti; 1494–?, Palazzo Rondinelli; 1494–?, San Francesco; 1494–?, Palazzo Strozzi-Bevilaqua; 1495–?, Santa Maria in Vado; 1496–?, San Benedetto; 1498–?, Cathedral (apse); 1498–?, San Cristoforo alla Certosa; 1500?–?, Palazzo di Giulio d'Este; 1500?–?, Palazzo di Ludovico il Moro; 1500?–?, Palazzo Roverella; Ferrara, Italy.

Rossetti. Palazzo dei Diamanti. Ferrara, Italy. 1493–1516 (not completed until 1567 by others)

BIBLIOGRAPHY

ROSENBERG, CHARLES M. 1978 "The Erculean Addition to Ferrara: Contemporary Reactions and Pragmatic Considerations." *The Early Renaissance, Acta* 5:49–67.

ZEVI, BRUNO 1960 *Biagio Rossetti, architetto ferrarese, il primo urbanista moderno europeo.* Turin, Italy: Einaudi. Reissued without transcriptions of archival documents in 1971 (revised 1973) as *Saper vedere l'urbanistica. Ferara di Biagio Rossetti, la prima citta moderna europea,* published in Turin, Italy, by Einaudi.

ROSSI, DOMENICO

The son of Francesco Rossi and Catterina Sardi (whose brothers, Padre Francesco and GIUSEPPE SARDI, brought him up), Domenico Rossi (1657–1737) was sent from his native Lugano to Venice at the age of eight to be schooled by his uncle Francesco, a priest at San Giulian; but the latter stated in 1674 that the rambunctious Domenico had instead been apprenticed as a stonecutter to BALDASSARE LONGHENA. Rossi's fundamental biographer, TOMMASO TEMANZA, confirms this and also that he went on to work with Alessandro Tremignon as well; Domenico seems to have assisted his architect uncle Giuseppe Sardi on Palazzo Flangini and the San Lazzaro facade, which strongly influenced his earliest buildings.

Until Rossi turned fifty, he was a public engineer for the Venetian sanitary board and treasury, and worked also in the Republic's overseas dominions of Istria and Greece. He was an expert on fireworks and he may have traveled in the Levant with the future Doge Francesco Morosini (whose

Rossi. San Stae. Venice, Italy. 1710–1712

ballistics experts blew up the Parthenon in Athens in 1687). His pyrotechnic celebrations for the Venetian Pope Alexander VIII Ottoboni's election in 1689 may have earned him the first of several trips to Rome; during a later visit to the papal capital with his son-in-law Giovanni Antonio Scalfarotto in 1710, he evidently met and was strongly influenced by Cardinal Pietro Ottoboni's brilliant theater architect, FILIPPO JUVARRA.

Rossi's architectural career began in earnest when he won a prestigious competition for the Grand Canal façade of San Stae in 1709; his Roman sojourn of the next year was probably offered as an incentive for future patronage by the Counts Manin of Udine, who employed him for the next quarter-century on their native cathedral (1713–1718), on rebuilding the Jesuit church in Venice (1714–1729), and especially on an enormous villa (completed 1738) and two family chapels in the Friuli (Passariano, 1710s–1730s, and Udine, 1732–1736). Rossi's other principal patrons were the Corner (for example, Palazzo della Regina, 1723–c.1730), who apparently introduced him as early as 1700 to their Venetian neighbor Count Girolamo Savorgnan, for whose family Domenico executed both a Venetian palace interior and a great country house before 1708. Since the latter was at Osoppo in the Friuli and since the Savorgnan are known to have arranged Rossi's introduction to the Dolfin family (Venetian palace, before 1709; Archiepiscopal Palace, Udine, 1708–1725), the Dolfin may well have arranged Domenico's introduction to the Counts Manin and his crucial Roman visit (his last trip there was undertaken to present a design in the Lateran façade competition of 1732).

His masters Longhena and Sardi inculcated in Rossi a deep sensitivity to dramatic chiaroscuro as the foil to a powerful structure. His façade of San Stae, boldly presenting a novel interpenetration of Palladian orders, sparkles above the Grand Canal with a combination of formal inventiveness and coloristic splendor that makes Rossi the foremost Venetian architect of the first third of the eighteenth century—a pre-eminence in which he was brilliantly succeeded, for an equal term, by GIORGIO MASSARI.

DOUGLAS LEWIS

WORKS

Early 1680s?, Palazzo Flangini (with Giuseppe Sardi), Grand Canal; (A)1687?–1690s, Palazzo Rizzi, Santa Maria Maggiore; Venice, Italy. c.1700, Cathedral (high altar; originally in the Venetian Church of the Incurabili), Vittorio Veneto, Italy. 1704–1707, San Stae (high altar and nave altars); *1706–1710, Cappella Zane (completion of work begun by Antonio Gaspari), San Stin; 1706–1710, Palazzo Zane (remodeling of garden pavilion); 1706–1723, San Girolamo (high altar by Domenico Piccoli), Venice, Italy. (A)1707, San Michele, San Daniele del Friuli, Italy. (A)before 1708, Palazzo Savorgnan (interiors), Cannaregio, Venice, Italy. *Before 1708, Palazzo Savorgan, Osoppo, Italy. 1708–1709, Palazzo Dolfin, San Pantalon, Venice, Italy. 1708–1725, Palazzo Dolfin (the Archiepiscopal Palace), Udine, Italy. 1710–1712, San Stae (façade); 1710s?, Palazzo Maffetti, San Polo; Venice, Italy. (A)1710s–1730s, Villa Manin (expansion not completed until 1738 by Giovanni Ziborghi), Passariano, Italy. 1712, Palazzo Riva, Santa Giustina; 1713, Palazzo Cavagnis, San Giovanni Laterano; Venice, Italy. 1713–1718, Cathedral (remodeling of choir and transepts; with Padre Giuseppe Pozzo), Udine, Italy. 1714–1729, Santa Maria Assunta dei Gesuiti (church and façade; with Pozzo and Giambattista Fattoretto); 1718–1719, Santa Maria Formosa (altar of Santa Barbara; with Giuseppe Torretti); Venice, Italy. (A)1720s?, Villa Sandi at Maras, Belluno, Italy. 1723–c.1730, Palazzo Corner della Regina (with Giovanni Antonio Scalfarotto), Grand Canal, Venice, Italy. 1732–1736, Cappella Manin (with Torretti), Udine, Italy.

BIBLIOGRAPHY

BASSI, ELENA 1962 "Domenico Rossi." Pages 207–232 in *Architettura del Sei e Settecento a Venezia.* Naples: Edizioni Scientifiche Italiane.

HOWARD, DEBORAH 1981 Pages 195–198 in *The Architectural History of Venice.* New York: Holmes & Meier; London: Batsford.

LEWIS, DOUGLAS 1979 *The Late Baroque Churches of Venice.* New York: Garland.

OLIVATO, LOREDANA 1973 "Palazzo Cornaro della Regina." *Antichità Viva* 12, no. 3:27–49.

RIZZI, ALDO 1971 *La Villa Manin di Passarinao.* Udine, Italy: Del Bianco.

TEMANZA, TOMMASO 1963 Pages 38–41 in Nicola Ivanoff (editor), *Zibaldon de' Memorie Storiche.* Venice, Italy, and Rome: Istituto per la Collaborazione Culturale. The work is an unpublished manuscript of 1738ff.

ROSSI, KARL I.

Karl Ivanovitch Rossi (1775–1849) was born and worked in Russia where he studied architecture before spending two years in Rome. He worked in St. Petersburg, then the capital, where his projects and buildings made him one of the leading figures of Russian architectural classicism. He designed the major part of the center of St. Petersburg which owes him its monumental character. Rossi was the descendant of several generations of Russian architects, originally hailing from Italy.

ANATOLE KOPP

WORKS

1819–1825fi Mikhailovski Palace; 1819–1829, General Headquarters and Palace Square; St. Petersburg, Russia.

BIBLIOGRAPHY

EGOROV, I. A. 1969 *The Architectural Planning of Saint Petersburg.* Translated by Eric Dluhosch. Athens: Ohio University Press.

Vseobchtchaia istoria arkhitektury. 1963 Moscow.

ROTH, ALFRED

Born in Wangen, Switzerland, Alfred Roth (1903–) studied painting and chamber music before he became one of KARL MOSER'S students at the Eidgenössische Technische Hochschule in Zurich. His subsequent close cooperation with LE CORBUSIER as designer in charge of the two houses at the Weissenhofsiedlung in Stuttgart (1927) established his contact with various leading figures of the Modern movement. In his book *Begegnung mit Pionieren* (1973), he later wrote about his encounters with Le Corbusier and many others, among whom Piet Mondrian and HENRY VAN DE VELDE probably made the most lasting impression.

Roth's career as an independent architect began in 1928, when he opened a small office in Göteborg, Sweden. After his return to Switzerland (1930), he worked on the interiors of the Neubühl Housing Development in Zurich and joined the Swiss Congrès Internationaux d'Architecture Moderne (CIAM) group. It is interesting to note that his only major housing project realized in Switzerland was a commission that came from within the CIAM circle: the famous Doldertal Apartments in Zurich (1935–1936), built with his partner Emil Roth and in collaboration with MARCEL BREUER for the art historian SIEGFRIED GIEDION, CIAM's general secretary. The fortunate combination allowed for the imaginative and subtle spatial organization and detailing for which the Doldertal Apartments are well known. Yet they inevitably placed the project outside the thematic sphere of social housing, CIAM's main preoccupation around 1930.

Besides the Doldertal Apartments, Roth built little during the 1930s, but he was a prolific writer. From 1934 on, he edited *Weiterbauen,* the periodical of the Swiss CIAM group; at the same time, he contributed newspaper articles to the artistic avant-garde's struggle for public recognition. Finally, he published *The New Architecture* (1939), an overview of the architecture of the 1930s. He was editor of *Werk* from 1942 to 1956 and managed to create an international audience both for the magazine itself and for the architecture (mostly Swiss and modern) documented in its high-quality glossy pages. The most important by-product of his editorial activity was his book *The New School* (1950). Apart from constituting an indispensable compendium on the topic, this book documents Roth's strong belief in education as a means of human and cultural emancipation. He sees architecture primarily as a means rather than as an end in this emancipatory process of humanity. In fact, according to him not the least important among architecture's purposes is to contribute "to the consolidation of the consciousness of our times" (1939, p. 8).

In his capacity as an architect no less than in that as a polemicist, Roth seems indefatigable in his crusade in favor of design quality at the service of people's lives. He has built in the United States, Sweden, and Yugoslavia, and since the 1960s has been involved in important projects in the Middle East, where schools again occupy center stage. Among his Middle Eastern projects, the Sabbag Commercial Center in Beirut (1968–1970) is probably the most important architectural achievement. Regrettably, no project of comparable caliber by Roth was realized in his own century; there, his *oeuvre* consists primarily of houses (such as his own house in Zurich, 1960, which he shares with a group of students), schools, and a number of carefully designed extensions to GOTTFRIED SEMPER'S and Gustav Gull's main building of the ETH in Zurich (1962–1972).

STANISLAUS VON MOOS

WORKS

1929–1930, Apartments, Göteborg, Sweden. 1935–

1936, Doldertal Apartments (with Emil Roth and Marcel Breuer); 1939, Pavilion of Commerce (with Emil Roth), Swiss National Exhibition; Zurich. 1948–1949, Swiss Tourist Office, London. 1950–1952, Primary School, Berkeley. 1960, Roth House; 1961–1962, Primary School; 1962–1972, Main Building, Machine Laboratory, Natural Science Institute (extension), ETH; Zurich. 1966–1969, Secondary School, Skopje, Yugoslavia. 1966–1980, Schools, Kuwait. 1968–1970, Sabbag Commercial Center, Beirut. 1978–1980, Abu Nuseir New Town (with others), near Amman, Jordan.

BIBLIOGRAPHY

GROSS, ROLAND 1963 "Zum siebzigsten geburtstag von Alfred Roth." *Werk* 6:705–708.

GUBLER, JACQUES 1975 *Nationalisme et internationalisme dans l'architecture moderne de la Suisse.* Lausanne, Switzerland: L'Age d'Homme.

ROTH, ALFRED (1927)1977 *Zwei Wohnhäuser von Le Corbusier und Pierre Jeanneret.* Stuttgart, Germany: Krämer.

ROTH, ALFRED (1950)1966 *The New Schoolhouse.* Rev. ed. New York: Praeger.

ROTH, ALFRED 1973 *Begegnung mit Pionieren.* Basel: Birkhäuser.

ROTH, ALFRED (editor) 1946 *USA baut: Moderne Amerikanische Architektur.* Winterthur, Switzerland: Buchdruckerei Winterthur.

ROTH, ALFRED (editor) 1976 *The New Architecture.* Zurich: Verlag für Architektur.

ROTH, EMERY

Prominent and skillful in the design of apartment houses, Emery Roth (1871–1948) was also one of the few Art Nouveau experimenters in New York. His early multiple dwellings, like 509 West 121st Street (1910–1911) and 601 West End Avenue (1915–1916), show strong influences of Art Nouveau and other nontraditional styles, but by the 1920s Roth was working within a straightforward classical formula. It was in this period that he was most successful, and the twin-towered San Remo (1928–1929) contains some of the best apartment layouts of the time. By the 1940s his sons had taken over the firm, and their designs became bland and commercial, although they enjoyed great success with office developers.

CHRISTOPHER GRAY

WORKS

1901–1903, Belleclaire Hotel; 1910–1911, 509 West 121 Street; 1915–1916, 601 West End Avenue; 1928–1929, Beresford Apartments, Central Park West; 1928–1929, San Remo Apartments, Central Park West; 1938–1940, Normandie Apartments; 1949–1948, Look Building (not completed until 1950); New York.

ROUSSEAU, PIERRE

Pierre Rousseau (1751–1810) obtained the second prize of the French Académie d'Architecture and was a *pensionnaire du roi* in Rome in 1773. He built the Théatins tenements, 25 Quai Voltaire, Paris, between 1778 and 1780. He was the architect of tenements on the Rue Royale and the Rue de Bellechasse, of the Hôtel Dreuneuc, Rue de Provence, and the *hôtel* at 26 Rue de La Rochefoucauld. In 1783, he realized a gracious and measured residence, the Hôtel de Salm (today the Palais de la Légion d'Honneur). He also built the muniment room and the Chinese pavilion of the Hôtel de Montmorency, Boulevard Montmartre, Paris.

As architect of the town of Clermont-Ferrand and the *département* of Puy-de-Dôme, he designed the markets at Issoire and the prisons of Riom.

GÉRARD ROUSSET-CHARNY
Translated from French by
Richard Cleary

ROUSSET, PIERRE NOËL

Pierre Noël Rousset (?–1795) won the second prize of the French Académie d'Architecture in 1731 and in 1732. He was admitted to the Académie and also was elected to the academies of Florence and Bologna.

Around 1750, he decorated the Danger House and the Hôtel de Meulan, Rue des Capucines (formerly the Hôtel Legendre d'Armini built by ROBERT DE COTTE). He also worked on the Hôtel de Bourbon, 46–50 Rue Neuve-des-Petits-Champs and on the house of Monsieur Boucher, Rue Vivienne.

In 1753, he built the Larcher château on Ile-Saint-Denis, a house in Viry-Châtillon, and the kitchens of the Château de Livry. In 1768, Rousset completed the Hôtel Brochant des Tournelles, Rue Perrault.

Along with MATHURIN CHERPITEL, Rousset lost the contract for the Hôtel d'Uzès in Paris to CLAUDE NICOLAS LEDOUX; nevertheless, he received the commission for building the town hall of Uzès in Gard.

GÉRARD ROUSSET-CHARNY
Translated from French by
Richard Cleary

BIBLIOGRAPHY

GANAY, ERNEST DE 1933 "Fabriques aux jardins du XVIIIe siècle: Edifices de la Chine et de l'Orient, temples, belvédères, pavillons." *Revue de l'Art Ancien et Moderne* 64:49–74.

GANAY, ERNEST DE 1955 "Fabriques aux jardins du XVIIIe siècle." *Gazette des Beaux-Arts* Series 6 45:287–298.

ROZEHNAL, BEDŘICH

Bedřich Rozehnal (1902–) lived and worked in Brno, Czechoslovakia. He taught at the Technical University of Brno (1945–1960) and at the Jan Evangelista Purkyně University in Brno (1964–1971). His style issued from the principles of LE CORBUSIER's architecture which he applied to a field that was of primary interest for him, namely, the construction of hospitals. University Pediatric Hospital in Brno (1947–1953), his architectural masterpiece, is one of the most remarkable buildings in Czechoslovakia to be built in the first years after World War II.

VLADIMÍR ŠLAPETA

WORKS

1931, Pazdera Department Store, Brno-Tuřany, Czechoslovakia. 1937, Hospital, Nové Městona Moravě, Czechoslovakia. 1939–1947, Hospital, Dačice, Czechoslovakia. 1939–1947, Hospital, Kykov, Czechoslovakia. 1947–1953, University Pediatric Hospital, Brno, Czechoslovakia.

BIBLIOGRAPHY

DORGELO, A. 1960 *Modern European Architecture.* Amsterdam, London, New York, and Princeton, N.J.: Elsevier.

KUDĚLKA, ZDENĚK 1967 *Bedřich Rozehnal architekonická tvorba: 1927–1967.* Brno, Czechoslovakia. Exhibition catalogue.

ROZEHNAL, BEDŘICH 1949 *Cesta k řešení nemocničí otázky města Brna.* Brno, Czechoslovakia: The author.

ŠLAPETA, VLADIMÍR 1980 "Poznámky k dielu Bedřicha Rozehnala." *Projekt* 3, no. 235:44–49, 54.

RUBIÓ I BELLVER, JOAN

Joan Rubió i Bellver (1871–1952), a Catalan architect, was born in Reus and died in Barcelona, Spain. He graduated from the School of Architecture in Barcelona in 1892 and immediately entered the studio of ANTONIO GAUDÍ Y CORNET with whom he collaborated continuously until 1905. He specialized in the development of technical solutions for the projected structural complexes of Gaudí, in particular, Park Güell and the Church of the Güell Colony. His relation with Gaudí was of great influence in the diffusion of the ideas of the master and in the systematic codification of the current thought that was known as *gaudinismo.* Rubió's determination to leave eclecticism behind resulted in a reflection on the technical conditions of architecture, and he attempted to overcome the situation of his time through the architecture of Gaudí. Rubió wrote several monographs on the theoretical problems of architecture. The technology of the primitive constructions in stone, the methods of calculation in Gothic structures, and the problem of architectonic synthesis in the Christian church are some of the themes developed in his work.

Rubió began to construct his first buildings around 1900. The Macario Golferichs House (1901), the laundries of Sanatorio del Tibidabo (1903), the Isabel Pommer House (1906), the Fornells House (1903), the Roviralta House (El Frare Blanc) (1913), and the Manuel Dolcet House (1907) in Barcelona are the most notable of this period. In all these, traditional artisan work was combined with new ways of using brick, resulting in a brilliant chromaticism and a great expressive richness. He collaborated also with FRANCISCO BERENGUER I MESTRES on various buildings in the Güell Colony. Attributed to him are the so-called House of the Director and the Co-operative Building.

In later public buildings and in churches and chapels, Rubió developed the principles that he considered the basis for *gaudinismo* through the use of parabolic arches, a central plan, and the clear expression of structure and the construction materials. The Chapel of San Miguel de la Roqueta in Ripoll (1912) and the baldachin for the Monastery of Ripoll (1912) are the primary models for those that followed: the Laboratories Serra de Reus (1912) and the churches of Raymat (1918) and Foment de Pietat (1916) in Barcelona. The works of his last period show a tendency toward the grandiose and a certain dramatism, for example, the Raventos stores of Raymat (1924), the Cuadrada House of Reus (1926), the buildings for the Industrial University of Barcelona (1927), and the Old Age Home of Igualada (1931).

Rubió i Bellver was part of the Catalan autonomist movement, being an elected member of the Barcelona Municipal Government in 1905. Later, he collaborated with Prat de la Riba in the Union of Catalonia as director of architectural services.

IGNASI DE SOLÀ-MORALES
Translated from Spanish by
Judith E. Meighan

WORKS

1901, Macario Golferichs House; 1903, Fornells House; 1903, Sanatorio del Tibidabo (laundry building); 1906, Isabel Pommar House; 1907, Manuel Dolcet House;

Barcelona, Spain. 1912, Chapel of San Miguel de la Roqueta, Ripoll, Spain. 1912, Laboratories Serra de Reus, Spain. 1912, Monastery of Ripoll (baldachin), Spain. 1913, Roviralta House, *El Frare Blanc;* 1916, Church of the Foment de Pietat; Barcelona, Spain. 1918, Church; 1924, Raventos Stores; Raymat, Spain. 1926, Cuadrada House, Reus, Spain. 1927, Industrial University of Barcelona, Spain. 1931, Old Age Home, Igualada, Spain.

BIBLIOGRAPHY

BOHIGAS, ORIOL 1973 *Reseña y catálogo de la arquitectura modernista.* Barcelona, Spain: Lumen.

CIRICI PELLICER, ALEJANDRO 1951 *El arte modernista catalán.* Barcelona, Spain: Ayma.

RÀFOLS, JOSÉ 1949 *Modernismo y modernistas.* Barcelona, Spain: Destino.

SOLÀ-MORALES, IGNASI DE 1975 *Joan Rubió i Bellver y la fortuna del gaudinismo.* Barcelona, Spain: Gaya Ciencia.

RUDOLPH, PAUL MARVIN

Paul Marvin Rudolph (1918–) was born in Elkton, Kentucky. After an itinerant upbringing as the son of a Methodist minister, Rudolph pursued an undergraduate education, first at Athens College, Alabama (1934–1936), then Alabama Polytechnic Institute (1936–1940), studying architecture. Following a year of professional practice in Birmingham, Alabama, he entered the Harvard Graduate School of Design in 1941 under WALTER GROPIUS. His time at Harvard, interrupted by three years of naval duty (1943–1946), was spent in the company of fellow students EDWARD L. BARNES, ULRICH FRANZEN, ROBERT GEDDES, JOHN M. JOHANSEN, PHILIP JOHNSON, and I. M. PEI. After graduation in 1947, Rudolph entered into a partnership with Ralph Twitchell in Sarasota, Florida, that lasted until 1952. Since then, he has practiced alone in Sarasota, Boston, New Haven, and New York. From 1958 to 1965, Rudolph acted as chairman of the department of architecture at Yale University.

Rudolph. Art and Architecture Building, Yale University. New Haven. 1958–1962

Rudolph's architecture is generally characterized by irregular silhouette, monolithic and textural surfaces, and dramatic interior spaces. Those forms derive from two sources. His early work, particularly the Finney (1947), Healy (1948), and Walker (1952) Guest Houses in Florida and the Applebee Residence (1956), Auburn, Alabama, alludes to the "Harvard box," Gropius's paradigm of three-dimensional, cellular architectural space. Rudolph's academic training at Alabama Polytechnic provides the second source: an emphasis on drawing which led to an even more fundamental understanding of the two-dimensional surfaces orchestrating architectural space. Both interests are well displayed in the mature Micheels House, Westport, Connecticut (1972), whose varied external articulation suggests a complex juxtaposition of compartmental spaces, yet whose internal surfaces coordinate fairly uniform spatial trays, frontally disposed. Rudolph's Milam House, Jacksonville, Florida (1960–1962) and the Art and Architecture Building at Yale University (1958–1962) investigated this kind of combative formal play at earlier dates.

A second project for Yale University, his Married Students Dormitory (1960–1961), marks Rudolph's entry into specifically urban problems. The scheme repeats a basic housing module, creating a townscape in miniature, hence expanding Rudolph's early understanding of cellular architecture. The Dormitory spawned a succession of important large-scale projects, mostly unexecuted, including a resort community for Stafford Harbor, Virginia (1966), Graphic Arts Center, New York (1967), Lower Manhattan Expressway Project (1967–1972), Buffalo Waterfront Development (1969–1972), and housing proposals for Hong Fok Investment Holdings in the Far East (1979–). Simultaneously, Rudolph demonstrated a second, spatial attitude toward urban form, deploying buildings as so many space-shaping surfaces. Inaugurated with his undervalued Jewett Arts Center at Wellesley College (1955–1958), this spatial emphasis reappears in a number of Rudolph's campus plans, particularly Tuskegee Institute, Alabama (1958) and Southeastern Massachusetts University, North Dartmouth (1963), and in the provocative Boston Government Service Center (1962–1971), which the architect coordinated. This last project, still incomplete, pioneers new terrain for present-day urban design. Unlike standard functionalist planning practice, which continues to polarize program and historic urban form, Rudolph seeks to fuse these oppositions here. The Government Center interprets a difficult program in the spatial terms of the historical city, coordinating its various programs in a continuous, low-rise structure bent to shape a fan-shaped piazza, the whole greater than the sum of its parts. A commentary on the weaknesses of doctrinaire modernism, this complex further underscores the ability of Paul Rudolph and others of his generation to evaluate their teachers and then to formalize a substantive critique.

RICHARD BECHERER

WORKS

1947, Finney Guest House; 1948, Healey Guest House (Cocoon House); 1951, Wheelan Cottage; Siesta Key, Fla. 1952, Walker Guest House, Sanibel Island, Fla. 1955–1958, Jewett Arts Center, Wellesley, Mass. 1956, Applebee House, Auburn, Ala. 1957, Blue Cross/Blue Shield Building, Boston. 1957–1958, Riverview High School, Sarasota, Fla. 1957–1959, Greeley Memorial Laboratory, New Haven. 1958–1959, Sarasota High School, Fla. 1958–1962, Art and Architecture Building, Yale University; 1959–1963, Temple Street Parking Garage; 1960–1961, Married Students Dormitory, Yale University, New Haven. 1960–1962, Milam House, Jacksonville, Fla. 1960–1964, Endo Laboratories, Garden City, N.Y. 1960–1969, Tuskegee Institute Interdenominational Chapel, Ala. 1961–1962, Wallace House, Athens, Ala. 1962–1966, Crawford Manor, New Haven. 1962–1971, Government Service Center (with others), Boston. 1963, Orange County Courthouse, Goshen, N.Y. 1963, Southeastern Massachusetts University, North Dartmouth. 1963–1966, Creative Arts Center, Hamilton, N.Y. 1967, Tracey Towers Apartments, New York. 1968, Stadium, Damman, Saudi Arabia. 1968–1970, Oriental Masonic Gardens Housing, New Haven. 1968–1971, First Church, Boston. 1968–1972, Green House, Cherry Ridge, Pa. 1969–1971, Natural Science Building, SUNY, Purchase, N.Y. 1970–1977, Burroughs Wellcome and Company, Incorporated, Corporate Headquarters, Research Triangle Park, N.C. 1972, Micheels House, Westport, Conn. 1974, Pitts Theological Library, Altanta, Ga. 1975–1981, Chapel, Chandler School of Theology, Atlanta, Ga. 1979–, Housing for Hong Fok Investment Holdings, Hong Kong. 1979, Housing for Hong Fok Investment Holdings, Singapore.

BIBLIOGRAPHY

COOK, JOHN W., and KLOTZ, HEINRICH 1973 Pages 90–121 in *Conversations with Architects.* Foreword by Vincent Scully. New York: Praeger.

FRANZEN, ULRICH, and RUDOLPH, PAUL 1975 *The Evolving City: Urban Design Proposals by Ulrich Franzen and Paul Rudolph.* Text by Peter Wolf. New York: Whitney Library of Design.

MILLON, HENRY A. 1960 "Rudolph at the Cross Roads." *Architectural Design* 30, no. 12:497–504.

MOHOLY-NAGY, SIBYL 1970 *Introduction to the Architecture of Paul Rudolph.* With captions by Gerhard Schwab and comments by Paul Rudolph. New York: Praeger.

"New Directions: Paul Rudolph, Philip Johnson, and Buckminster Fuller." 1952 *Perspecta* 1:18–37.

"100 by Paul Rudolph/1946–74." 1977 *Architecture & Urbanism* 80, July: special issue.

POMMER, RICHARD 1972 "The Art and Architecture Building at Yale, Once Again." *Burlington Magazine* 114, no. 837:853–861.

RUDOLPH, PAUL 1956 "The Six Determinants of Architectural Form." *Architectural Review* 120, no. 4:183–190.

RUDOLPH, PAUL 1957 "Regionalism in Architecture." *Perspecta* 4:12–19.

RUDOLPH, PAUL 1972 *Paul Rudolph: Drawings.* Edited by Yukio Futagawa. Tokyo: A.D.A.

RUDOLPH, PAUL (1974)1979 *Paul Rudolph: Dessins d'Architecture.* 3d ed. Fribourg, Switzerland: Office du Livre.

SPADE, ROBERT 1971 *Paul Rudolph.* New York: Simon & Schuster.

STERN, ROBERT A. M. (1969)1977 Pages 30–41 in *New Directions in American Architecture.* Rev. ed. New York: Braziller.

VERONESI, GIULIA 1961 "Paul Rudolph." *Zodiac* 8:148–161.

RUSCONI, GIOVANNI ANTONIO

Although active as a painter and an architect, Giovanni Antonio Rusconi (1520?–1587) is noted chiefly for his extensive illustrations to an edition of VITRUVIUS's *Ten Books on Architecture* published in Venice after his death in 1590. In this work, an Italian translation of the original, Rusconi used Palladian (see ANDREA PALLADIO) architectural forms but bent them in a stricter, less manneristic form. His illustrations were particularly influential in the early eighteenth century among the progenitors of Italian neoclassicism such as Giovanni Poleni, the teacher of TOMMASO TEMANZA.

Rusconi's architectural career was spent mainly in the Venetian area. He was an assistant to Andrea Palladio and helped him on many projects. He is noted for a splendid floating theater built for the Compagnia degli Accessi in Venice (1564).

Born either in Canton Ticino or Como, he died in Venice.

NICHOLAS ADAMS

BIBLIOGRAPHY

RUSCONI, GIOVANNI ANTONIO 1590 *Della Architettura di Gio. Antonio Rusconi con centosessanta figure disegnate dal Medesimo secondo i precetti di Vitruvio e con chiarezza a brevità dischiarate.* Venice, Italy.

RUSCONI SASSI, LUDOVICO

Ludovico Rusconi Sassi (1678–1736) received his training at the Accademia di San Luca in Rome. His competition drawings (1696 and 1702) indicate that he had looked at all of the major seventeenth-century Roman architects except GIOVANNI LORENZO BERNINI. Following the completion of his studies in 1702, Rusconi Sassi entered the service of Cardinal Pietro Ottoboni; by 1705, he was the principal architect of this important patron, a position which he held until his death.

His earliest works, the Aedicula (1715–1716) on the Via del Pellegrino behind the Cancelleria and the Odescalchi Chapel (1719–1722) in Santissimi Apostoli in Rome, were strongly influenced by FRANCESCO BORROMINI. Nonetheless, the Cappela Paolucci (1723–1724) in San Marcello al Corso, Rome, confirms Lione Pascoli's inclusion of Rusconi Sassi in the circle of CARLO FONTANA. In his *Accademico di Merito* drawing (1722–1724), he combined these different trends. The *Quarant'ore* apparatus (1725) in San Lorenzo in Damas, Rome, was apparently dependent on Fontana.

Between 1727 and 1733, Rusconi Sassi terminated the Church of San Salvatore in Lauro, Rome. To the nave constructed by OTTAVIANO MASCHERINO and to the crossing elevated to the level of the entablature by Francesco Fontana he added the choir and Cortonesque (see PIETRO BERRETTINI DA CORTONA) dome. The original aedicula of the Madonna di Loreto, which was replaced in 1791, was Berninian in inspiration. For the Church of San Giuseppe alla Lungara (1730–1734), also in Rome, Rusconi Sassi took up the theme of San Carlo alle Quattro Fontane: an elongated octagon covered by an oval dome. In contrast to Borromini's church, Rusconi Sassi made these geometrical forms more clearly recognizable. The Borrominian elements are even more marked in the model produced in conjunction with the competition (1732) for the façade of San Giovanni in Laterano, Rome. However, Rusconi Sassi also had Carlo Fontana's project (1699) for the same church in mind.

Rusconi Sassi Odescalchi Chapel, Santissimi Apostoli. Rome. 1719–1722

Lastly, Rusconi Sassi executed two chapels for Cardinal Ottoboni. Although transformed in the early nineteenth century, the Chapel of the Holy Sacrament (1732/1733–1736) in San Lorenzo in Damaso is still mostly the work of Rusconi Sassi. A slightly concave rear wall animates an otherwise simple conception. In Porto, near Fiumicino, he added the Chapel of the Holy Sacrament (1735) to the Church of Santa Lucia as a pendant to Carlo Fontana's Chapel of Sant'Erasmo. Using Fontana's basic scheme as a point of departure, Rusconi Sassi endowed the space with a sense of movement and plasticity.

The union of the classicizing style of Fontana and the more unorthodox one of Borromini in Rusconi Sassi's work is characteristic of many architects working in Rome at the time. His very limited interest in Bernini, however, sets him apart from Fontana's other pupils, in particular FILIPPO JUVARRA and NICOLA MICHETTI. Furthermore, the Borrominesque aedicula and the Odescalchi Chapel were executed at least a decade earlier than the structures normally cited in connection with the so-called Borrominian revival. Thus, Rusconi Sassi was one of the pioneers in this movement.

CATHIE C. KELLY

WORKS

1715–1716, Aedicula, via del Pellegrino; 1719–1722, Odescalchi Chapel, Santissimi Apostoli; 1723–1724, Paolucci Chapel, San Marcello al Corso; *1725, San Lorenzo in Damaso (*Quarant'Ore*); 1727–1733, San Salvatore in Lauro (completion); 1730–1734, San Giuseppe alla Lungara; 1732, San Giovanni in Laterno (model for façade); 1732/1733–1736, Chapel of the Holy Sacrament, San Lorenzo in Damasco; Rome. 1735, Chapel of the Holy Sacrament, Santa Lucia, Porto Fiumicino, Italy.

BIBLIOGRAPHY

ASTOLFI, CARLO 1933 "Storia del convento e chiesa

di S. Salvatore in Lauro oggi S. Maria di Loreto dei Marchegiani." *Rassegna marchigiana* 11:173–188, 210–231, 252–272.

ASTOLFI, CARLO 1942 "Benemerenze dei Piceni nell'edilizia romana." *Studia Picena* 17:161–167.

DONATI, UGO 1942 *Artisti ticinesi à Roma.* Bellizona, Italy: Istituto editoriale ticinese.

FANANO, E. 1959 *S. Salvatore in Lauro del Pio sodalizio dei Piceni.* Volume 52 in *Chiese di Roma illustrate.* Rome: Marietti.

FASOLO, FURIO 1949 *Le chiese di Roma nel '700.* Rome: Danesi.

FASOLO, FURIO 1954 "Architettura di Zagarolo: Postilla cugli architetti." *Istituto di storia dell'architettura: Quaderni* no. 6:7–11.

GIGLI, LAURA 1977 *San Marcello al Corso.* Volume 131 in *Chiese di Roma illustrate.* Rome: Istituto di studi romani.

GRIONI, JOHN S. 1975 *Le edicole sacre di Roma.* Rome: Editalia.

HAGER, HELLMUT 1971 "Il modello di Ludovico Rusconi Sassi del concorso per la facciata di San Giovanni in Laterano (1732) ed i prospetti a convessità centrale durante la prima metà del Settecento a Roma." *Commentari* 23:36–67.

KELLY, CATHIE COOK 1980 "Ludovico Rusconi Sassi and Early Eighteenth-century Architecture in Rome." Unpublished Ph.D. dissertation, Pennsylvania State University, University Park.

MARCONI, PAOLO; CIPRIANI, ANGELA; and VALERIANI, ENRICO 1974 *I disegni di architettura dell'Archivo storico dell'Accademia di San Luca.* 2 vols. Rome: De Luca.

PASCOLI, LIONE (1730–1736)1965 *Vite de'pittori, scultori, ed architetti moderni.* 2 vols. Reprint. Amsterdam: Israel.

SANTILLI, FRANCESCO 1925 *La basilica dei SS. Apostoli.* Volume 15 in *Chiese di Roma illustrate.* Rome: Casa editrice Roma.

SCHIAVO, ARMANDO 1956 *La Fontana di Trevi e le altre opere di Nicola Salvi.* Rome: Istituto poligrafico dello stato.

SCHIAVO, ARMANDO 1964 *Il palazzo della Cancelleria.* Rome: Staderini.

SCHIAVO, ARMANDO 1972 "Veduta di Giuseppe Valeriani del S. Lorenzo in Damaso." *Studi romani* 20:228–234.

VIZZARI, DOMENICO 1966 *La chiesa di San Giuseppe alla Lungara: Note illustrative.* 2 vols. in 1. Naples: Ardor.

WEIL, MARK S. 1974 'The Devotion of the Forty Hours and Roman Baroque Illusions." *Journal of the Warburg and Courtauld Institutes* 37:218–248.

ZOCCA, EMMA 1959 *La basilica dei SS. Apostoli Roma.* Rome: Canella.

RUSKIN, JOHN

John Ruskin (1819–1900) was the most important British architectural critic of the nineteenth century. Tolstoy and Proust regarded him as one of the greatest of all writers. His influence is to be seen in the Gothic Revival of the High Victorian period and of the Arts and Crafts movement that followed it.

Ruskin, the only son of a rich sherry merchant of Scottish origins, showed early promise as a writer and a poet. He was educated largely at home but had early exposure to architecture and mountain landscape, traveling with his parents to the Lake District, to France, Germany, Switzerland, and Italy.

In 1837, he went up to Christ Church Oxford as a gentleman commoner. His mother, anxious for her son's health, took rooms in Oxford to be near him and required him to report to her daily. While still an undergraduate, Ruskin contributed a number of articles on "The Poetry of Architecture" under the *nom de plume* of Kata Phusin to J. C. Loudon's *Architectural Magazine.* Loudon regarded Ruskin as "the greatest natural genius that ever it has been my fortune to become acquainted with" (Collingwood, 1893, p. 58).

Ruskin had become interested in J. M. W. Turner as early as 1836. His father sympathized with this interest and bought a number of Turner's paintings, as did Ruskin himself. In May 1843, when Ruskin was twenty-four, the first volume of *Modern Painters* was published in which he described Turner as "this consummate artist," being "above other men in knowledge of truth" (Ruskin, 1843, pp. 445, 446).

In 1845, Ruskin made an extended visit to Italy, his first without his parents. He met up with J. D. Harding, the artist from whom he had received drawing lessons. Together, they sketched Venice; Ruskin bought a number of early daguerreotypes of the city. It was Ruskin's first long working visit to the city, and the result of this and other architectural studies was *The Seven Lamps of Architecture,* published in 1849. This influential book, written in a rhetorical and highly individualistic style, starts by advocating the moral quality in architecture in two chapters called the Lamp of Sacrifice and the Lamp of Truth: "All the fair devices that ever were fancied, are not work worth a lie. Leave your walls as bare as a planed board, or build them of baked mud and chopped straw, if need be; but do not rough-cast them with falsehood" (Allen, 1883, p. 55).

The Lamp of Power is a discourse on the aesthetic of the sublime. It is followed by the Lamp of Beauty which proclaims nature as the source of architectural beauty. In the Lamp of Life, Ruskin took to craftsmanship: "I believe the right question to ask, respecting all ornament, is simply this: Was it done with enjoyment—was the carver

Ruskin.
Drawing from The Seven Lamps of Architecture.
1849

happy while he was about it?" (Allen, 1883, p. 173). The Lamp of Memory is a plea for the long-term view—"When we build, let us think we build for ever" (Allen, 1883, p. 186)—and contains an attack on restoration: "Restoration, so called, is the worst manner of Destruction" (Allen, 1883, p. 194). Finally, the Lamp of Obedience claims that there is no need for a new style of architecture and advocates the use of "1. The Pisan Romanesque; 2. The early Gothic of the Western Italian Republics, advanced as far and as fast as our art would enable us to the Gothic of Giotto; 3. The Venetian Gothic in its purest development; 4. The English earliest decorated" (Allen, 1883, p. 208). Ruskin's illustrations to the Seven Lamps, many of which are derived from Venetian sources, reinforced the message of the text.

Ruskin had planned a book on Venice during his visit in 1845. The first of his three-volume work, *The Stones of Venice,* appeared in 1851, and analyzes Venetian architecture detail by detail: the wall, the shaft, the capital, the roof cornice. The second volume, published in 1853, discusses the Byzantine and Gothic architecture of the city and contains the celebrated chapter on "The Nature of Gothic." Here, he sees in classical perfection the slavery of its workmen and compared it with the freedom of the Gothic craftsman, praising its very imperfection. "And it is, perhaps, the principal admirableness of the Gothic schools of architecture that they thus receive the results of the labour of inferior minds; and out of fragments of imperfection, and betraying that imperfection in every touch, indulgently raise up a stately and unaccusable whole" (Allen, 1903, pp. 157–158). For Ruskin, the craftsman must be the designer: "We are always in these days endeavouring to separate the two; we want one man to be always thinking, and another to be always working, and we call one a gentleman, and the other an operative; whereas the workman ought often to be thinking, and the thinker often to be working, and both should be a gentleman, in the best sense."

He was to some extent to see his principle realized in the Oxford Museum, designed by DEANE AND WOODWARD, a scheme with which he was closely connected through his friend Dr. Acland. In April 1856, he gave an address at the Workmen's Reading Rooms to the men employed in building the Museum and spoke of the true happiness that lies in good work well done.

In 1868, Ruskin was appointed first Slade Professor at Oxford, and he gave a series of popular lectures expounding his views on art and architecture. These and other lectures he gave were frequently published and kept his views before the public, so that by the middle of his career he was the most influential critic in Britain.

In his later life, social, economic, and political questions took an increasing amount of his time. His social criticism was as forceful as his artistic, and he thundered against the commercialism of his day. In 1871, he founded Saint George's Guild, an agricultural and industrial cooperative. The experiment was a failure.

In 1848, he had married Effie Gray but their marriage, which was never consummated, was anulled in 1854. Effie later married John Millais, the Pre-Raphaelite painter, with whom the Ruskins had taken a holiday in Scotland in 1853.

In 1871, Ruskin bought Brantwood, a house by the shore of Lake Coniston. Continuous overwork undermined his constitution, and in 1878 he had the first of the attacks of mental illness which were to be increasingly frequent in his later years.

Ruskin's architectural influence can be seen during his lifetime on buildings throughout Britain and abroad—from Bombay to Boston. His ideal of craftsmanship inspired WILLIAM MORRIS and the Arts and Crafts movement, and his views on preservation were a potent force in the foundation of the Society for the Protection of Ancient Buildings. Ruskin's influence continued into the twentieth century; he was read by architects such as HENRY VAN DE VELDE, FRANK LLOYD

WRIGHT, and WALTER GROPIUS, and helped form their view of architecture.

ROGER DIXON

BIBLIOGRAPHY

BELL, QUENTIN 1978 *Ruskin.* New York: Braziller.

COLLINGWOOD, W. G. (1893)1922 *The Life of John Ruskin.* 11th ed., rev. London: Methuen.

COOK, EDWARD T. 1911 *The Life of John Ruskin.* 2 vols. London: Allen.

COOK, EDWARD T., and WEDDERBURN, ALEXANDER (editors) 1903–1912 *The Works of John Ruskin.* 39 vols. London: Allen.

CONNER, PATRICK 1979 *Savage Ruskin.* London: Macmillan.

EVANS, JOAN 1954 *John Ruskin.* New York: Oxford University Press.

GARRIGAN, KRISTINE O. 1973 *Ruskin on Architecture.* Madison: University of Wisconsin Press.

HANSON, BRIAN 1981 "Carrying Off the Grand Canal." *Architectural Review* 169, Feb.:104–109.

HEWISON, ROBERT 1976 *John Ruskin: The Argument of the Eye.* London: Thames & Hudson.

HITCHCOCK, H. R. 1968 "Ruskin and American Architecture or Regeneration Long Delayed." In John Summerson (editor), *Concerning Architecture.* London: Allen Lane.

PEVSNER, NIKOLAUS 1969 *Ruskin and Viollet-Le-Duc.* London: Thames & Hudson.

PEVSNER, NIKOLAUS 1972 *Some Architectural Writers of the Nineteenth Century.* Oxford: Clarendon.

RUSKIN, JOHN 1843–1860 *Modern Painters.* 5 vols. London: Smith, Elder.

RUSKIN, JOHN (1849)1883 *The Seven Lamps of Architecture.* Kent, England: George Allen.

RUSKIN, JOHN (1851–1853)1903 *The Stones of Venice.* 3 vols. Kent, England: George Allen.

UNRAU, JOHN 1978 *Looking at Architecture with Ruskin.* London: Thames & Hudson.

WALTON, PAUL H. 1972 *The Drawings of John Ruskin.* Oxford: Clarendon.

RUSSELL, ROBERT

Robert Russell (1808–1900) was effectively the first architect to practice in Melbourne. He was born in London in 1808, articled to WILLIAM BURN of Edinburgh, worked for JOHN NASH from 1829 on the extensions to Buckingham Palace, and emigrated to Sydney in 1833 to become acting assistant to the town surveyor, Francis Clarke, a colleague from Nash's office. He was government clerk of works at Melbourne in 1838 and entered private practice upon his dismissal in 1839. His work is of a conservative Georgian character and from about 1850 he practiced mainly as a surveyor.

MILES LEWIS

WORKS

1839, Yarra Cottage; 1839–1842, Church of Saint James (later Pro-Cathedral); 1840–1841, Bank of Australasia; Melbourne.

BIBLIOGRAPHY

The correspondence and drawings of Robert Russell are in the collection of the Archives Authority of New South Wales, Sydney, Australia. His sketches are in the State Library of Victoria, Melbourne.

FOOTE, ROBERT J. 1981 "Robert Russell (1808–1900)." Unpublished B. Arch. thesis, University of New South Wales, Sydney.

FREELAND, JOHN MAXWELL 1963 *Melbourne Churches 1836–1851.* Carlton, Australia: Melbourne University Press.

PRESTON, HARLEY 1967 "Russell, Robert." Volume 2, pp. 409–411 in *Australian Dictionary of Biography.* Carlton, Australia: Melbourne University Press.

RUSSELL, ROBERT TOR

Robert Tor Russell (1888–1972) was responsible for much of the fabric of New Delhi, where he maintained a classical treatment for a variety of different buildings. He went out to India in 1914–1915 as an assistant to JOHN BEGG. After war service, Russell was appointed chief architect to the government of India (1919). In New Delhi, he and his staff designed official housing, shopping centers, police stations, post offices, and other official buildings. Russell retired from India in 1939.

GAVIN STAMP

WORKS

1920s, Connaught Place; 1930, House for Commander in Chief (now Nehru Museum); n.d., East and West Hostels; New Delhi.

RUUSUVUORI, AARNO

Aarno Ruusuvuori (1925–) has been one of the leading architects and most influential representatives of Constructivist architecture in Finland since the 1950s. His work is characterized by strong conceptual principles, sophisticated use of technology, elegant detailing, and simple and bold massing, often in exposed concrete and glass. These qualities are successfully employed in his churches and industrial buildings, but also in the renovation projects, where Ruusuvuori juxtaposes new elements in historical context. As a professor at Helsinki University of Technology (1963–1966) and as a director of the Museum of Finnish Architecture (1975–1978), Ruusuvuori has been influential in developing the theoretical basis for rationalist architecture. In 1978, he was appointed Finnish state professor of arts for a five-year period.

PIRKKO-LIISA LOUHENJOKI

WORKS

1961, Church and Parish Center, Hyvinkää, Finland. 1964, Huutoniemi Church and Parish Center, Vaasa, Finland. 1964–1966, Weilin & Göös Printing Works, Tapiola, Espoo, Finland. 1966, Prefabricated System House, Bökars, Finland. 1967, Marimekko Printing Works; 1967, Roihuvuori Elementary School; Helsinki. 1968, Police Headquarters, Mikkeli, Finland. 1970, Helsinki City Hall (renovation). 1972, Rauhanummi Chapel and Cemetery, Hyvinkää, Finland. 1972, Stunkel House, Grenolier, Switzerland. 1973, Paragon Office Building, Helsinki. 1976, Real Estate Development Center, Addis Ababa. 1979, Parate Printing Works, Helsinki. 1980, Apartment Hotel Al Rashid, Riyadh, Saudi Arabia.

BIBLIOGRAPHY

"Aarno Ruusuvuori." 1967 *Kokusai Kentiku* 34, no. 4:13–60.

DONAT, JOHN (editor) 1965 Volume 2 in *World Architecture.* London: Studio Vista.

Finnish Architecture. 1975 The Hague: Museum of Finnish Architecture and the Netherlands Congress Center. Exhibition catalogue.

"Paragon Office Building, Helsinki, Finland." 1974 *Architecture and Urbanism* 4, no. 45:24–28.

RICHARDS, J. M. 1978 *800 Years of Finnish Architecture.* Newton Abbot, England: David & Charles.

SALOKORPI, ASKO 1970 *Modern Architecture in Finland.* London: Weidenfeld & Nicolson.

SALOKORPI, ASKO 1980 "Ruusuvuori, Aarno." Page 694 in Muriel Emanuel (editor), *Contemporary Architects.* New York: St. Martin's.

SMITH, G. E. KIDDER 1964 *The New Churches of Europe.* New York: Holt.

TEMPEL, EGON 1968 *New Finnish Architecture.* Translated by James C. Palmes. London: Architectural Press.

S

SAARINEN, ELIEL, and SAARINEN, EERO

Gottlieb Eliel Saarinen (1873–1950) was born in Rautasalmi, Finland. He studied both painting and architecture in Helsinki from 1893 to 1897. In 1896, he formed an architectural office with HERMAN GESELLIUS and ARMAS ELIEL LINDGREN which lasted until 1905, after which Saarinen practiced two more years with Gesellius alone.

In 1904, Saarinen married his second wife, Louise (Loja) Gesellius who was a noted artist in her own right and a frequent collaborator with her husband. The Saarinen family, in fact, has a rather unique position in the history of modern design. Eva-Lisa (Pipsan), their daughter, was a frequent collaborator and interior designer. However, it was their son, Eero Saarinen (1910–1961), born in Kirkkonummi, Finland, who succeeded his father and became one of the greatest architects of his generation. Between them, their work spans two continents and some eight decades.

The first commission given to the young firm of Gesellius, Lindgren, and Saarinen was the Tallberg Apartments in Helsinki (1897); the building had decidedly medieval overtones and a series of towers with conical roofs. National Romanticism is the term generally used to describe Finnish architecture at the turn of the century, an eclectic mixture of Scandinavian medieval architecture, continental Art Nouveau, and the Romantic Revival of H. H. RICHARDSON. The Pohjola Fire Insurance Company Building in Helsinki (1899–c.1902) was their first building in the National Romantic style.

The commission that established the international reputation of Gesellius, Lindgren, and Saarinen, however, was the Finnish Pavilion for the 1900 Exposition in Paris (1899–1900). Both the plan and the general massing are derived from Richardson's libraries of the late 1870s and the 1880s. The most prominent features were the low pointed entrance arch and the tapered tower with elaborate pinnacle. The interiors featured murals and furniture by Ayel Gallén-Kallela.

Their newly won success brought the Saarinen office numerous commissions for apartment buildings and public structures during the 1900s. The Olofsborg Apartment House in Helsinki (1901) was perhaps their best commercial design during this period. It is typical of other commissions with its horizontal masonry base with arches; stuccoed upper walls punctuated with fenestration, bays, and towers; and steep roof broken by chimneys, gables, and turrets. The National Museum in Helsinki (1902–1904) was certainly one of the largest commissions to be given to the office, but the de-

Eliel Saarinen. Huitträsk (with Gesellius and Lindgren). Kirkkonummi, Finland. 1902

Eliel Saarinen. Suur-Merijoki (with Gesellius and Lindgren). Near Viipuri, Finland. 1902–1903

sign is less original with its eclectic overtones. Its importance lies in the use of a bold entrance tower; one of the newel posts inside showed perhaps the earliest use by Saarinen of a stepped massing on a vertical tower form.

Gesellius, Lindgren, and Saarinen's greatest Finnish domestic commission was for their own home/studio, *Huitträsk,* near Kirkkonummi, begun in 1902 and modified considerably over succeeding decades. The complex of three houses was built outside Helsinki on a steep hillside overlooking a lake, thus following the Arts and Crafts ideal of artists living and working in the country. The plan consists of two large picturesque masses endorsing a central courtyard, with terraced gardens at either end. The lower stories were built of large boulders partially stuccoed, while the upper walls were rustic bays; the whole was capped with massive, steep roofs. Saarinen's own house was notable for its great hall and numerous fireplace inglenooks; it contained some of his finest early furniture designs. *Huitträsk* is perhaps the greatest sample of National Romanticism to survive in Finland.

Though smaller than *Huitträsk, Suur-Merijoki* (1902–1903), near Viipuri (now in Russia), was a magnificent country villa. The exterior massing with its corner turret and sunken porte-cochère recall American houses such as Richardson's Ames Gate Lodge, North Easton, Massachusetts (1880–1881), and PEABODY AND STEARNS's *Kragsyde,* Manchester-by-the-Sea, Massachusetts (c.1882). The importance of the house, though, lies in the interiors, perhaps the most comprehensive and beautiful Saarinen domestic interior design of the early 1900s.

Eliel Saarinen's most famous public building in Finland is, of course, the Railroad Station in Helsinki. The office won the competition in 1904, and the building went through at least six revisions before completion in 1914. The initial design was somewhat ecclesiastical and was certainly less avant-garde than Sigurd Frosterus's *Jugendstil* entry. The prize allowed Saarinen to travel in Germany, Austria, and Britain for comparative studies; this trip was no doubt responsible for the Viennese influence seen in the final design. The prominent tower, in particular, seems to be derived from JOSEF HOFFMANN's Palais Stoclet in Brussels (1905–1911). The station, however, was a very advanced design for its time, especially in its exposed concrete vaulting inside.

The office executed another railroad station in Viipuri (1904–1913), which has traditionally been thought to be largely the work of Gesellius. Though smaller, the station is more advanced in plan with its multiple levels for movement of passengers and anticipates the Dulles Airport (1958–1962) by Eero Saarinen.

The Helsinki Railroad Station required a decade for completion. The first major design to show the new German/Austrian influence after Saarinen's travels was the competition entry for the Haus eines Kunst Freundes, Essen-Ruhr, Germany (1904). The earlier picturesque massing was replaced by a cubic mass: small blocks for the lower walls and white stucco with geometric banding for the upper walls. The roof was far less permanent, and the front deviation featured a semicircular gable. In plan, the main rooms formed a cross-axis with an open spatial flow. This project thus shows a decided influence from the Wagnerschule and the Wiener Werkstätte, though the interiors were still somewhat in the National Romantic style.

Any traces of Saarinen's earlier style were absent in the design for Dr. Paul Remev's country estate, Molchow-Haus, Mark Brandenburg, Germany (1905–1909). The house was almost square in plan; the exterior walls were completely stuccoed with the exception of a low masonry basement course. The main façade had a massive triangular gable; the recessed entrance with semihexagonal bays and a stylized Palladian window above was strangely reminiscent of FRANK

Eliel Saarinen. Railroad Station. Helsinki. 1904–1914

LLOYD WRIGHT's Oak Park Residence of 1889, though this is clearly quite early for Wright's work to have been known in Europe. For the interior, Saarinen was given complete freedom, and he produced a stunning series of proto-modern rooms that rival those of Suur-Merijoki in their sumptuousness.

The Saarinen office was quite productive during the last half of the decade, but the commissions now tended to be for public buildings as the firm became more established. Among the best designs were the competition entry for the Palace of Peace, The Hague (1905), and the town halls for Lappeenranta (1906) and Joensun (1909–1913). Other projects such as that for a rather classicizing art exhibition hall for Helsinki (1908) clearly showed a debt to JOSEPH MARIA OLBRICH's exhibition galley in Darmstadt, Germany (c.1907).

In the previous four years, Saarinen's work had shown a growing preference for symmetrical plans and masses. Major buildings retained the familiar tower, but it was now used less as an asymmetrical vertical accent. In 1908, Saarinen published a remarkable visionary design for a public building. The drawing showed a symmetrical form, but the tower had now been moved to the center and was greatly expanded to form a pyramidal mass. This was perhaps the earliest usage by Saarinen of a practice that he was to employ with increasing regularity well into the 1930s. In the same year, in fact, Saarinen used a smaller variation of this pyramidal design for his project for the Finnish House of Parliament, Helsinki.

This movement toward more symmetrical masses led Saarinen, like many of his European contemporaries, toward a neoclassical revival by 1910. Such projects as that for an industrial exposition in Helsinki (1910) still show the influence of Olbrich and his Austrian contemporaries; but the formal courts, colonnades, and pergolas are frankly neoclassical. Other projects such as those for a palace in Sofia (c.1912) featured neobaroque façades and gardens. During the 1910s, Saarinen also designed a series of neoclassical projects for Helsinki: a town hall and government building (1913) for the neoclassical section of Helsinki, which would have formed handsome counterparts to JOHANN CARL LUDWIG ENGEL's buildings; an imposing neobaroque concert hall (1914) opposite the train station; and a monumental crematorium for Helsinki (1916), which featured a rotunda with quadrant colonnades enclosing a semicircular court. With the outbreak of World War I and the subsequent revolution in Russia and its duchy Finland, few of these neoclassical designs were executed, the most notable exception being the rather formal Villa Keirkner (c.1915–1918) in Helsinki.

During the same decade, Saarinen devoted a considerable amount of his energies to urban design projects. One of his most impressive plans was for Canberra (1912), for which he won second prize. The early schemes, in particular, with their formal waterways, axes, and grandiose neoclassical buildings approach the monumentality of ETIENNE LOUIS BOULLÉE.

Canberra, however, was but one of several major city plans undertaken by Saarinen in the 1910s: Munkkiniemi in Finland (1910–1915), Revel in Estonia (1911–1913), and a master plan for greater Helsinki (1916–c.1918). All of these projects showed the influence of CAMILLO SITTE. A smaller project for the thoroughfare Centralgaten in Helsinki (1916) was a prototype for ALVAR AALTO's Rautatalo Office Building executed at the same site about 1953.

An examination of Saarinen's work during this turbulent decade reveals a schism, not unlike that found in contemporaries such as PETER BEHRENS: his public buildings were largely designed in a neoclassical style, while his commercial buildings allowed more original solutions. The latter were mostly projects for Helsinki stores of about six stories, the Hubers Office Building (1910), a commercial building (1911), and the Stockmann Department Store (1916). The design generally featured an arcade on the ground level, a symmetrical façade articulated with a rhythm of vertical piers rising to a prominent roof, and an entrance marked by a pavilion which broke the roofline and ended in an elaborate gable. Saarinen's only realized commercial building during this period was for the Kästyöläispankki in Helsinki (1920), a rather retardataire design which recalls Richardson's Marshall Field Wholesale Store, Chicago (1885–1887).

By the end of the decade, Saarinen was searching for a new direction in his work, as is readily apparent in the numerous sketches for a Finnish national museum, the Kalevalatolo, Munkkiniemi (1919–1921). Designed for a peninsula, the project had a series of courts formed by low buildings from which rose a massive, bluntly tapered tower.

It was, however, in another tower design—the Chicago Tribune Tower (1922)—that Saarinen found a new direction in his work and a new country. The designer won second place to JOHN MEAD HOWELLS and RAYMOND M. HOOD's Gothic Revival entry. However, it won the day in the architectural press and established Saarinen at the age of forty-nine at the forefront of his contemporaries. The Tribune Tower was, in fact, a continued refinement of the stepped-tower form that had begun in the early 1900s and had had its first major embodiment in the Helsinki Railroad Station. In this instance, the skyscraper's steel frame had modified the form; but the primary aesthetic concern for Saarinen was always to be a search for form, the title, in fact, of his 1948 book. New technology and expressed functionalism were clearly of less importance.

Eliel Saarinen. Kingswood School for Girls. Bloomfield Hills, Michigan. 1929–1930

Saarinen's Tribune entry, moreover, was indicative of the larger question of his place in twentieth-century architecture. The design avoided the academicism of the many classical and Gothic Revival entries but never attained the avant-gardism of several of the German and Dutch entries. With his strong ties to the nineteenth century, Saarinen never forsook the past but rather modified it to modern demands. He thus claimed a unique position in American architecture in the second quarter of the twentieth century: Saarinen did not approach the genius of Wright, whose work transcended all rules, nor did he embrace a dogma such as the International style of WALTER GROPIUS or MARCEL BREUER. It was this moderate course that made his work so accessible and so influential for the average American architect.

Eliel Saarinen sailed for the United States in February 1923; his family joined him in April. His first project in America was a massive redevelopment of the Chicago lakefront (1923). This daring project called for sunken expressways with pedestrian parks and plazas above, multilevel subterranean garages and railroads, and a skyscraper hotel reminiscent of the Tribune Tower.

The following year, Saarinen accepted a teaching position at the University of Michigan at Ann Arbor. For nearby Detroit, he envisioned a similar waterfront master plan (1924) at reduced scale. The prominent element in this design, however, was a rather classicizing memorial hall, once again illustrating Saarinen's moderation.

In the same year, Saarinen met George Booth, a Detroit publisher, and began the greatest commission of his American career. Saarinen was given the task of designing a complex of children's schools and an advanced-level art academy in Bloomfield Hills, Michigan. His initial concept was for a complex on the scale of Versailles with gardens and lakes. Over the course of the next two decades, he built the Cranbrook School for Boys (1924–1930), faculty housing (1928ff.), studios for resident artists (1926ff.), the Kingswood School for Girls (1929–1930), the Institute of Science (1931–1933), and a museum and library (1940–1943). In addition, Saarinen served as president of Cranbrook Academy (1932–1942) and helped to develop one of the most influential art schools in America. During his lifetime, the faculty included Carl Milles, Maija Grotell, Loja Saarinen, CHARLES O. EAMES, Marianne Strengell, Eero Saarinen, and Harry Bertoia. The younger faculty and students, in particular, were to have a profound effect on post-World War II Western design.

The Boys' School is a rather picturesque grouping of brick buildings around multilevel courtyards. The brick-and-stone detailing is among the finest of any American buildings of the period. In many respects, the complex is quite traditional and recalls RAGNAR ÖSTBERG's Stockholm Town Hall (1909–1923). It was also the first instance involving the collaboration of his two children, Eva-Lisa and Eero.

If the Boys' School retained European overtones, Kingswood School clearly showed the influence of Saarinen's Midwest rival, Frank Lloyd Wright, in its pronounced horizontality and hipped roofs. Most important, Kingswood illustrates the Arts and Crafts ideal of the collaboration of fine and applied arts. Everything was designed or selected by Saarinen down to the smallest detail. The furniture was designed by Eero Saarinen, then in his late teens; the textiles were woven by Loja Saarinen and the Cranbrook Looms; and Eva-Lisa Saarinen Swanson assisted with wall and ceiling treatments.

With the work at Cranbrook, Saarinen undertook few outside commissions during the 1920s. One of the best projects was for a Christian Science Church for Minneapolis, Minnesota (1925). The exterior featured the now familiar stepped centralized mass; the tripartite plan, however, recalls Wright's Unity Temple (1906). Saarinen's other major independent project of this time was an entry for the League of Nations competition (1927) in Geneva, which had similar massing and detailing though expanded into a massive tower.

As noted earlier, all members of the Saarinen family were actively involved in commissions. By 1930, however, Eero Saarinen was a mature young man and began formal studies in sculpture in Paris; he later studied architecture at Yale. More important, he practiced in Finland from 1934 to 1936, which gave him not only distance from his father but also allowed him to see the work of avant-garde European designers such as ERICH MENDELSOHN and Alvar Aalto. One of his earliest Finnish projects was a rather modern design for the Helsinki Post Office (1934) for which he won third prize. From about 1934 onward, he collaborated with Jarl Eklund and his father on the Swedish Theater in Helsinki. The executed neoclassical design by Eklund was decidedly inferior to the younger Saarinen's numerous sketches in the manner of Mendelsohn. In particular, Saarinen's remarkable designs for the so-called Forum (1935) in Helsinki recall the German architect with their sleek, carved glass walls.

During the 1930s, Eliel Saarinen also maintained strong ties to Finland. He continued to receive commissions and enter competitions there but did not actually execute any designs.

On his return to Bloomfield Hills, Eero Saarinen joined his father's office: the firm was first known as Saarinen and Saarinen (1937–1939) and subsequently as Saarinen, Swanson and Saarinen with the addition of a brother-in-law, J. Robert F. Swanson. The only interruption was Eero Saarinen's wartime service in Washington (1942–1945).

The acclaim accorded the Cranbrook buildings brought a series of commissions for campus master plans for some two decades. They included the Stevens Institute of Technology, Hoboken, New Jersey (1931–1934); Goucher College, Baltimore, Maryland (1930); Antioch College, Yellow Springs, Ohio (1944); Drake University, Des Moines, Iowa (1946–c.1955); and Brandeis University, Waltham, Massachusetts (1948–c.1951).

Likewise, the elder Saarinen's faculty in handling large complexes of buildings led to several important urban design commissions. They included projects for the Flint Civic Center, Flint, Michigan (1937–1944); New Castle, Indiana (1944), and the Detroit Cure Center (1938–c.1951).

Eliel Saarinen's ability to design monumental buildings on an urban scale is perhaps best illustrated in his Art Deco Alexander Hamilton Memorial for Chicago (1933–c.1939). This project was one of Saarinen's best designs of the 1930s and if built would have been in marked contrast to the neoclassical monuments to the founding fathers in Washington, D.C.

The return of the younger Saarinen in the late 1930s caused a noticeable change in the style of the office, and his influence was decisive in their four most important buildings just before World War II. Eero Saarinen was obviously very much aware of the International style and the Constructivists, and his influence is apparent in a movement away from the centralized, stepped massing of his father toward a more articulated massing that expressed the function and plan of the building. The detailing and choice of materials, however, still very much reflected the stamp of the elder Saarinen.

One of the earliest commissions to reflect this change was the Kleinhans Music Hall in Buffalo, New York (1938-1940). The two horseshoe-shaped auditoriums with joint lobby are expressed in powerful sculptural forms. The building was noteworthy also for the reflecting pool, a motif that became a Saarinen trademark.

The Crow Island School in Winnetka, Illinois (1939–1940), designed jointly with the firm of Perkins, Wheeler, and Will, had a remarkably innovative plan with its use of one-story classroom

Eliel and Eero Saarinen. Tabernacle Church of Christ. Columbus, Indiana. 1939–1942

wings off a central spine. It was one of the most advanced school designs in the second quarter of the century.

The Tabernacle Church of Christ in Columbus, Indiana (1939–1942), is considered the Saarinens' finest ecclesiastical commission. It is, however, almost completely derived from a series of Finnish church designs, starting with ERIK BRYGGMAN's church at Sortavala (1929), the Tehtaapuisto church in Helsinki (1930), and his chapel at Turku (1938–c.1941). The Saarinen design, nonetheless, remains one of the most beautiful churches in America. The building is a carefully articulated composition of cubic blocks grouped around a sunken courtyard, large reflecting pool, and campanile.

Certainly the most widely acclaimed design of the Saarinen office during this period was their first-prize entry for the Smithsonian Art Gallery in Washington, D.C. (1939). The project featured the familiar elements of articulated geometric massing, an enclosed courtyard, a reflecting pool, and sculpture used as an architectural element. It would have been one of the few modern buildings on the capitol mall with true monumentality.

Two commissions from the 1940s which seem to be largely the work of Eliel Saarinen are the Cranbrook Academy of Art Museum and Library (1940–1943) and a projected chapel for Stephens College, Columbia, Missouri (1947). The former is somewhat classicizing in its central propylaeum, but the design is, in fact, derived from the modern Musée des Arts Modernes and the Palais du Chaillot which Saarinen no doubt saw at the 1937 Paris Fair. The Stephens Chapel recalls an earlier Josef Hoffmann design. In this case, the centralized chapel has become a circular form in a reflecting pool, a motif to be used by the younger Saarinen in his chapel designs for Drake University and the Massachusetts Institute of Technology, Cambridge (1953–1956).

During this time, Eero Saarinen undertook a number of independent projects which make an instructive comparison to the work of the office: an art center for Wheaton College, Norton, Massachusetts (1938); a national theater for William and Mary College, Williamsburg, Virginia (1939); and a community center for the U.S. Gypsum Company (1941–1942). The most important of these independent designs were for the periodical *California Arts and Architecture:* a design for prefabricated housing (1943) with Oliver Lundquist and two designs for steel-framed Case Study Houses (1945–c.1951) with Charles Eames. The latter two were executed with modifications as the Eames and John Entenza residences in Pacific Palisades, California.

Eero Saarinen also collaborated with Eames on a remarkable series of furniture designs for the Organic Design in Home Furnishings competition (1940–1941) at the Museum of Modern Art, New York. From the 1940s onward, Saarinen did numerous designs for Knoll, establishing himself as one of the most important furniture designers of the century. The most notable examples were the womb chair (1946–1948) and the Nos. 71 and 72 chair series (c.1956).

Eero Saarinen's interest in industrial design was indicative of a generational gap between father and son. With the exception of some silver designs in the 1930s, virtually all of Eliel Saarinen's designs were custom-made. His ties to the nineteenth-century Arts and Crafts movement were simply too strong to allow him to embrace new technology and industrial materials. Eero Saarinen shared many of his father's romantic ideals, but he clearly saw the value of the machine aesthetic.

This difference between father and son is seen clearly in their most important commission of the 1940s: the General Motors Technical Center in Warren, Michigan (1945–1955). The initial design under the elder Saarinen's control was for a complex of streamlined buildings grouped around a large, irregularly curved pool. Due to his father's failing health and death on July 1, 1950, the subsequent revisions and final design were largely the work of Eero Saarinen. As executed, the General Motors Center is clearly indebted to LUDWIG MIES VAN DER ROHE's Illinois Institute of Technology campus plan, Chicago (1939–1941).

Charles Eames (1971) has noted that in designing the General Motors complex, Eero Saarinen made an important change in his design approach. This "systems approach" involved a detailed analysis of a problem with innumerable sketches. The goal was to find a unique form and structure to express a concept architecturally. This accounts in large part for the variety in Saarinen's subsequent work, for his was "a legacy of concept and procedure, rather than of form" (Eames, 1971, p. 26).

General Motors remains one of the finest post-World War II corporate complexes. Its international recognition made Eero Saarinen & Associates (formed 1950) one of the most important corporate architectural firms in America and brought a steady series of clients through the 1950s. Perhaps the most important of these commissions were for corporate offices in park settings: the Thomas J. Watson Research Center for International Business Machines, Yorktown, New York (1957–1961); the Bell Laboratories, Holmdel, New Jersey (1957–1962); and the Deere & Company Headquarters, Moline, Illinois (1957–1963).

Academic commissions also continued to come in to the Saarinen office. The most important examples were a new campus for Concordia College, Fort Wayne, Indiana (1953–1958); a dormitory complex (1955–1958) and law school (1956–1960) for the University of Chicago; a dormitory for the University of Pennsylvania, Philadelphia (1957–1960); and the Samuel F. B. Morse and Ezra Stiles Colleges at Yale University, New Haven, Connecticut (1958–1962).

It was, however, a series of powerful sculptural designs in the 1950s for which Eero Saarinen is perhaps best remembered. One of the earliest indicators was the parabolic arch design for the Jefferson National Expansion Memorial competition in St. Louis, Missouri. Saarinen won the competition in 1948, but it was not completed with modifications until 1964. It was the domed Kresge Auditorium and circular chapel for the Massachusetts Institute of Technology (1953–1956) that seemed to be the harbinger of this change in his work. The design for the Ingolls Hockey Rink at Yale (1956–1959) carried this search for concave-con-

Eero Saarinen.
Kresge Auditorium, Massachusetts Institute of Technology.
Cambridge.
1953–1956

Eero Saarinen.
Terminal, Trans World Airways, Kennedy Airport.
New York.
1962

Eero Saarinen.
Dulles Airport.
Chantilly, Virginia.
1958–1962

Eero Saarinen.
Columbia Broadcasting System Headquarters.
New York.
1960–1964

vex sculptural forms even further. Saarinen's undisputed masterpieces remain the soaring terminal for Trans World Airways at Kennedy International Airport (1956–1962) and the serene pavilion for the Dulles International Airport, Chantilly, Virginia (1958–1962). Both personify the sensation of flying as no other twentieth-century buildings.

Shortly before his death, Saarinen began the sketches for a skyscraper for the Columbia Broadcasting System (1960–1964) in New York. His design for a soaring tower of black granite triangular piers—a startling contrast to the curtain-wall skyscrapers of the period—was his last major commission to be realized. Almost forty years before, the competition for the Chicago Tribune Tower had brought both father and son to the United States. Eliel Saarinen was never to build a skyscraper, that uniquely American form; and his son did not live to see his only tall building finished. They left a legacy, however, as two of the finest designers of the Modern movement.

R. Craig Miller

WORKS

ELIEL SAARINEN

1897, Tallberg Apartment Building, Helsinki. *1899–1900, Finnish Pavilion (with Herman Gesellius and Armas Lindgren), International Exposition, Paris. 1899–c.1902, Pohjola Building (with Gesellius and Lindgren); 1901, Olofsborg Apartment Building (with Gesellius and Lindgren); Helsinki. 1902, Huitträsk (with Gesellius and Lindgren), Kirkkonummi, Finland. 1902–1903, Suur-Merijoki (with Gesellius and Lindgren), near Viipuri, Finland. 1902–1904, National Museum (with Gesellius and Lindgren), Helsinki. 1904–c.1913, Railroad Station (with Gesellius), Viipuri, Finland. 1904–1914, Railroad Station, Helsinki. 1905–1909, Paul Remer Residence (with Gesellius), *Molchow-Haus,* Mark Brandenburg, Germany. 1909–1913, Town Hall, Joensun, Finland. c.1915/1916–1918, Villa Keirkner; 1916, Centralgatan City Plan (partially executed); 1920, Kästyöläisankki Building; Helsinki. 1924–1930, Cranbrook School for Boys; 1928–1929, Saarinen House; Bloomfield Hills, Mich. *1929, Dining Room, Exhibit at Metropolitan Museum of Art; 1929–1930, Hudnut Building (with Ely Jacques Kahn); New York. 1929–1930, Kingswood School for Girls; 1931–1933, Cranbrook Institute of Science; Bloomfield Hills, Mich. *1934–1935, Room for a Lady, Exhibit at Metropolitan Museum of Art, New York. 1938–1940, Kleinhans Music Hall (with F. J. and W. A. Kidd), Buffalo, N.Y. 1940–1943, Cranbrook Museum and Library, Bloomfield Hills, Mich.

EERO SAARINEN

1945–1949, Charles Eames Residence (with Charles Eames); 1945–1950, John Entenza Residence (with Eames); Palisades, Calif. 1945–1956, General Motors Technical Center (with Smith, Hinchman, and Grylls), Warren, Mich. 1946–1957, Metropolitan Milwaukee War Memorial, Wisc. 1948–1964, Jefferson National Expansion Memorial, St. Louis, Mo. 1953–1956, Kresge Auditorium and Chapel (with Anderson and Beckwith), Massachusetts Institute of Technology, Cambridge. 1953–1957, Irwin Miller Residence (with Alexander Girard and Dan Kiley), Columbus, Ind. 1953–1958, Concordia College, Fort Wayne, Ind. 1955–1958, Dormitory Complex, University of Chicago. 1955–1959, United States Chancellery Building, Oslo. 1955–1960, United States Chancellery Building (with Yorke, Rosenberg, and Mardall), London. 1956–1959, Ingalls Hockey Rink, Yale University, New Haven. 1956–1960, University of Chicago Law School. 1956–1962, Terminal, Trans World Airways, Kennedy Airport, New York. 1957–1960, University of Pennsylvania Dormitory, Philadelphia. 1957–1961, Thomas J. Watson Research Center, International Business Machines, Yorktown, N.Y. 1957–1962, Bell Laboratories, Holmdel, N.J. 1957–1963, Deere and Company Headquarters, Moline, Ill. 1958–1962, Dulles Airport (with Ammann and Whitney), Chantilly, Va. 1958–1962, Samuel F. B. Morse and Ezra Stiles Colleges, Yale University, New Haven. 1960–1964, Columbia Broadcasting System Headquarters, New York.

ELIEL AND EERO SAARINEN

1938, Berkshire Music Center Master Plan and Symphony Pavilion (pavilion executed in modified design by Joseph Franz), Tanglewood, Mass. 1939–1940, Crow Island School (with Perkins, Wheeler, and Will), Winnetka, Ill. 1939–1942, Tabernacle Church of Christ, Columbus, Ind. 1942, Berkshire Music Center Summer Opera House and Chamber Music Hall, Tanglewood, Mass. 1944–1948, Edmundson Memorial Museum (with Brooks-Borg); 1946–c.1955, Drake University Campus Plan (with Brooks-Borg; partially executed); Des Moines, Iowa. 1947–1949, Christ Church Lutheran (with Mills, Gilbertson, and Hays), Minneapolis, Minn. 1947–1957, Stephens College Chapel, Columbia, Mo. 1948–c.1951, Brandeis University Campus Plan (partially executed), Waltham, Mass.

BIBLIOGRAPHY

Fayans, Stefan 1909 "Baukunst und Volk." *Moderne Bauformen* 8, no. 8:337–353.

Gaidos, Elizabeth (editor) 1972 *The Creative Spirit of Cranbrook.* Bloomfield Hills, Mich.: Cranbrook Academy.

"General Motors Technical Center." 1945 *Architectural Record* 98:98–103.

"General Motors Technical Center." 1951 *Architectural Forum* 95:111–123.

"General Motors Technical Center." 1954 *Architectural Forum* 101:100–119.

"Gesellius, Lindgren, und Saarinen." 1907 *Moderne Bauformen* 6, no. 4:137–162.

"GM's Industrial Versailles." 1956 *Architectural Forum* 104:122–129.

Grut, Torben A. 1912 "Den Internationella Stadsplane afdelningen För Ordnande Af Ny Hufvudstad I Australien." *Arkitektur* 12:141–157.

HAUSEN, MARIKA 1967 "Gesellius-Lindgren-Saarinen vid Sekelskiftet." *Arkkitehti/Arkitekten* 9:6–12.
HAUSEN, MARIKA 1977 "The Helsinki Railway Station in Eliel Saarinen's first versions 1904." *Taidehistoriallisia Tutkimuksia* 3:57–114.
HUDNUT, JOSEPH 1939 "Smithsonian Competition Results." *Magazine of Art* 32:456–459, 488–489.
HUDNUT, JOSEPH (commentator) 1941*a* "Crow Island School, Winnetka, Ill." *Architectural Forum* 75:79–92.
HUDNUT, JOSEPH 1941*b* "Kleinhans Music Hall, Buffalo, N.Y." *Architectural Forum* 75:35–42.
KAUFMANN, EDGAR, JR. 1962 "Inside Eero Saarinen's TWA Building." *Interiors* 121:86–93.
"The Kingswood School for Girls, Cranbrook, Michigan." 1932 *Architectural Forum* 56:37–60.
LARRABEE, ERIC, and VIGNELLI, MASSIMO 1981 *Knoll Design.* New York: Abrams.
MCCUE, GEORGE 1978 "The Arch: An Appreciation." *Journal of the American Institute of Architects* 67:57–63.
MCQUADE, WALTER 1962 "Eero Saarinen, A Complete Architect." *Architectural Forum* 116:102–119.
MACOMBER, HENRY P. 1933 "The Michigan Home of Eliel Saarinen." *House Beautiful* 74:133–136.
NOYES, ELIOT F. 1941 *Organic Design in Home Furnishings.* New York: Museum of Modern Art.
ÖHQUIST, JOHANNES 1920 "Ein Finnischer Städtebauer." *Der Städtebau* 17, nos. 3–4: 21–27.
"One Family of Forms." 1962 *Progressive Architecture* 43:158–165.
OSBORN-BERLIN, MAX 1908 "Ein modernes Märkisches Waldschlösschen (Molchow-Haus bei Alt-Ruppin)." *Moderne Bauformen* 7, no. 6:217–239.
"Portfolio of Current Architecture." 1928 *Architectural Record* 64:475–505.
"Recent Work of Eero Saarinen." 1959 *Zodiac* 4:30–67.
REID, K. 1936 "Eliel Saarinen, Master of Design." *Pencil Points* 17:463–494.
SAARINEN, ALINE B. (editor) 1962 *Eero Saarinen on His Work.* New Haven: Yale University Press.
SAARINEN, EERO 1952 "Our Epoch of Architecture." *Journal of the American Institute of Architects* 18:243–247.
SAARINEN, ELIEL 1915 *Munkkiniemi-Haaga Ja Suur-Helsinki.* Helsinki: Osakeyhtiö M. G. Stenius.
SAARINEN, ELIEL 1944 *The City.* New York: Reinhold.
SAARINEN, ELIEL 1948 *Search for Form.* New York: Reinhold.
"Saarinen Challenges the Rectangle." 1953 *Architectural Forum* 98:126–133.
The Saarinen Door. 1963 With an introduction by Eva Ingersol Gatling. Bloomfield Hills, Mich.: Cranbrook Academy.
SÍREN, J. S. (editor) 1955 *Eliel Saarinen, Muistonäyttely.* Helsinki: J. Simeliusen Perillisten Kirjapaino Oy.
SPADE, RUPERT 1968 Introduction in *Eero Saarinen.* New York: Simon & Schuster.
SULLIVAN, LOUIS 1923 "The Chicago Tribune Competition." *Architectural Record* 53:151–157.
TEMKO, ALLAN 1962 *Eero Saarinen.* New York: Braziller.
TILGHMAN, DONNELL 1928 "Eliel Saarinen." *Architectural Record* 63:393–402.
WANSCHER, VILHELM 1923 "The Chicago Tribune Building." *Architekten* 25:22–28.
"Der Wettbewerb um einen Bebauungsplan für die Bundeshauptstadt von Australien." 1913 *Der Städtebau* 10, no. 7:73–77; no. 8:86–88.

SABINE, WALLACE CLEMENT

Born in Ohio, Wallace Clement Sabine (1868–1919) studied optics and electricity at Ohio State University and Harvard University, but his subsequent experiments in the propagation and reverberation of sound established him as the founder of the modern science of architectural acoustics. He is best known as the consultant for Boston's acclaimed Symphony Hall (1898–1900). Sabine wrote on "whispering galleries" and on the possible influence of cathedral acoustics on the development of polyphonic music in Europe. He obtained patents for ceramic acoustical tiling and Akoustolith. The "Open Window Unit," which he defined as the measure of sound absorption, was renamed the "sabin" after his death.

NICOLAS B. COLLINS

WORKS

1895, New Fogg Art Museum (now Hunt Hall; correction of lecture room acoustics with RICHARD MORRIS HUNT), Cambridge, Mass. 1898–1900, New Boston Music Hall (now Symphony Hall; with MCKIM, MEAD, AND WHITE).

BIBLIOGRAPHY

CORNELIUS, CHARLES OVER 1919 "Wallace Clement Sabine." *Architectural Record* 46, Sept.:286–287.
ORCOTT, WILLIAM DANA 1933 *Wallace Clement Sabine: A Study in Achievement.* Norwood, Mass.: Plympton.
SABINE, PAUL E. 1919 "The Life Work of the Late Wallace Clement Sabine: An Appreciation." *American Architect* 116, part 1:1–3.
SABINE, WALLACE CLEMENT (1922)1964 *Collected Papers on Acoustics.* New York: Dover. This volume contains most of Sabine's writings on acoustics that were originally published between 1900–1915 in such journals as the *American Architect, Brickbuilder, Engineering Record,* and *Proceedings of the American Academy of Arts and Sciences.*

SABSOVITCH, L. M.

L. M. Sabsovitch (20th century) was born and worked in Russia. He belonged to the team of economists engaged in the preparation of the First Five Year Plan (1928–1932). His main known contributions are in the field of town planning and housing. During the debate over the physical planning which went on in the Soviet Union between 1929 and 1931, Sabsovitch was the leader of the "Urbanist" orientation, as opposed to the "Deurbanists" whose leader was M. OKHITOVITCH. The Urbanist proposition consisted in a decentralized scheme of planning relying on the construction of new industrial towns, progressively replacing the ancient ones, located close to the sources of raw materials and not exceeding 30,000 to 50,000 inhabitants. These towns were to be built in accordance with the projected "Reconstruction of the Way of Life," a major goal of the Soviets in the 1920s. This "New Life" was to rely on the collectivization of most of the functions until then performed within the family cell: meal preparation, laundry, child rearing, and so on. A rigorous zoning was to be enforced. Sabsovitch tried to prove through economical and financial calculations that all the towns and villages of the Soviet Union could be reconstructed, along his principles, within the scope of two five-year plans. The resolution of the Central Committee of the Bolshevik Party on May 29, 1930, condemning the discussions of the 1929–1931 period and denouncing them as utopical put an end to Sabsovitch's known activity.

ANATOLE KOPP

BIBLIOGRAPHY

KOPP, ANATOLE (1967)1970 *Town and Revolution.* Translated by Thomas Burton. New York: Braziller.

SABSOVITCH, L. M. 1929 *Goroda buduchtchejo.* Moscow.

SACCHETTI, GIOVANNI BATTISTA

Giovanni Battista Sacchetti (1700–1764), a pupil and follower of FILIPPO JUVARRA from 1718, was born in Turin, Italy, and died in Madrid. Sacchetti compiled the canonical list of Juvarra's works from 1714 to 1734. He assisted Juvarra with preparation of models and drawings. He executed the ephemeral memorials at the death of the princess of Carignano (1722), two queens (1728 and 1735), and King Vittorio Amedeo of Savoy (1732). He supervised the construction of San Filippo in Turin for Juvarra from 1734. After the death of Juvarra in early 1736, Sacchetti was called to continue his work on the Royal Palace in Madrid. There, he developed Juvarra's design and built a new model more in accord with the wishes of the king, while retaining much that Juvarra had proposed. The palace, begun in 1738 and completed in 1764, extremely well-sited along a sloping hillside, is one of the major eighteenth-century palaces of Europe. Although large, it conveys a sense of majesty and dignity appropriate to its purpose. At the same time, the building is harmoniously integrated with the other buildings of the complex and with the street level, the courtyards, the lower garden level, and the much lower slopes to the west—a significant and insufficiently appreciated achievement. Sacchetti also completed the palace of San Idelfonso at Segovia, Spain, and designed a church for the Monastery of the Visitation in Madrid that was not executed. His submergence in the work of Juvarra and our lack of detailed documentation makes a characterization of his own architecture difficult.

HENRY A. MILLON

WORKS

1722, Ephemeral Memorial (at the death of the Princess of Carignano); 1728, Ephemeral Memorial (at the death of the Queen of Savoy); 1732, Ephemeral Memorial (at the death of King Vittorio Amedeo of Savoy); 1734, San Filippo (supervised construction for Filippo Juvarra); Turin, Italy. 1736–?, Palacio Granja (executant architect), San Idelfonso, Segovia, Spain. 1736–1764, Palacio Real (modified and executed Juvarra's design), Madrid.

BIBLIOGRAPHY

BATTISTI, EUGENIO 1958 "Juvarra a San Ildefonso." *Commentari* 9, no. 4:273–297.

BAUDI DI VESME, ALESSANDRO 1968 Volume 3, pages 955–956 in *Schede Vesme.* Turin, Italy: Stamperia Artistica Nazionale.

BRAYDA, CARLO; COLI, LAURA; and SESIA, DARIO 1963 Page 63 in *Ingegneri e architetti del settecento in Piemonte.* Turin, Italy: Società degli ingegneri e degli architti.

PLAZE, F. J. DE LA 1975 *El Palacio Real de Madrid.* Madrid: Editorial Patrimonio Nacional.

VIALE FERRERO, MERCEDES (1966)1970 Pages 102–103 in *Filippo Juvarra: Scenografo e architetto teatrale.* New York: Blom.

SACCONI, GIUSEPPE

Giuseppe Sacconi (1854–1905) is best known as the designer of the enormous and florid monument to Vittorio Emanuele II (1884–1905) which all but dwarfs the Capitoline Hill in Rome. In fact, the "Vittoriano" was an unfortunate hybrid: its white Brescian marble, altogether out of keeping with Roman architecture, was not Sacconi's choice, and the monument itself was greatly changed after his death by GAETANO KOCH, M. Manfredi, and PIO PIACENTINI. The setting of the monument was also altered, through renovation and road construction in the surrounding areas, under Mussolini.

More characteristic of Sacconi's real architectural inclinations were the delicate and refined façade of the Palazzo delle Assicurazioni Generale on the Piazza Venezia (1902–1907, completed by G. Cirilli) and his work in historic preservation and renovation. Sacconi was superintendent of monuments for Ascoli Piceno and Umbria from 1891 to 1905, and was extremely active in restoration projects in these areas and in Rome. In this work, he occasionally collaborated with LUCA CARIMINI and GUGLIELMO CALDERINI.

BARBARA MILLER LANE

WORKS

1878–1883, Church of San Francesco (reconstruction), Force, Ascoli Piceno, Italy. 1884–1905, Victor Emmanuel II Monument (not completed until 1911 by M. Manfredi, Gaetano Koch, and Pio Piacentini), Rome. 1890s, Cathedral (restoration), Ascoli Piceno, Italy. 1890, Sanctuary of Santa Casa (restoration and new buildings; with Luca Carimini), Loreto, Italy. 1890–1905, Quadriportico, San Paolo fuori Mura (not completed until 1910 with Guglielmo Calderini), Rome. 1900–1905, Chapel in Memory of Umberto I (not completed until 1910 by G. Cirilli), Monza, Italy. 1902–1905, Palazzo delle Assicurazioni Generale (façade; not completed until 1907 by G. Cirilli), Piazza Venezia, Rome.

BIBLIOGRAPHY

ACCASTO, GIANNI; FRATICELLI, VANNA; and NICOLINI, RENATO 1971 *L'architettura di Roma capitale: 1890–1970.* Rome: Golem.

ACCIARESI, PRIMO 1911 *Giuseppe Sacconi e l'opera sua massima.* Rome: Tipografia dell'Unione editrice.

CEDERNA, ANTONIO 1980 *Mussolini Urbanista: Lo sventramento di Roma negli anni del consenso.* Bari, Italy, and Rome: Laterza & Figli.

MARANESI, D. FRANCESCO 1929 *Un grande architetto marchigiano: Giuseppe Sacconi.* Fermo, Italy: Premiato Stabilmento Cooperativo Tipografico.

MEEKS, CARROLL L. V. 1966 *Italian Architecture: 1750–1914.* New Haven: Yale University Press.

MOROSINI, LUIGI 1929 *Giuseppe Sacconi: La Vita e L'opera.* Rome: Biblioteca d'Arte.

PORTOGHESI, PAOLO 1968 *L'ecletismo a Roma: 1870–1922.* Rome: De Luca.

SACCONI, GIUSEPPE 1883 *Relazione del progretto per il monumento nazionale a Vittorio Emanuele II.* Rome.

SAPORI, FRANCESCO 1946 *Il Vittoriano.* Rome: La Libreria dello stato.

SACRISTE, EDUARDO

Eduardo Sacriste (1905–), one of the leaders of the Modern movement in Argentina, was born and educated in Buenos Aires, although most of his activity as an architect was in the northern city of Tucumán, where he settled in 1946. There, he worked at the new School of Architecture with ENRICO TEDESCHI and others. He also worked as professor of design in England, India, the United States, and at many Argentine universities.

In his buildings and his writings, his concern with the private house as a building type is obvious. In these, he crystallized his most interesting achievements.

ALBERTO NICOLINI

WORKS

1936, Juan B. Terán House; 1947, Di Lella House; 1948, Garden State School; 1948–1958, Children's Hospital; 1949, Gómez Omil House; 1960, Schujman House; 1961, Crisóstomo Alvarez, 661 Apartment Building; 1968, Comercio del Norte Insurance Company; Tucumán, Argentina. 1968, Clericó Country House, El Galpón, Salta, Argentina. 1976, Lichinsky House, Tucumán, Argentina.

BIBLIOGRAPHY

SACRISTE, EDUARDO (1959)1962 *Building Footprints.* Buenos Aires: Editorial Universitaria.

SACRISTE, EDUARDO 1960 *Usonia.* Buenos Aires: Ediciones Infinito.

SACRISTE, EDUARDO 1968 *Qúe es la Casa?* Buenos Aires: Editorial Columba.

SACRISTE, EDUARDO 1973 *Charla a Principiantes.* 2d ed. Buenos Aires: E.U.D.E.B.A.

Sacconi. Victor Emmanuel II Monument. Rome. 1884–1905 (not completed until 1911 by Manfredi, Koch, and Piacentini)

SAELTZER, ALEXANDER

Alexander Saeltzer, a German architect with a significant practice in mid-nineteenth century New York City, designed the Gothic Revival synagogue for the Congregation Anshe Slonim (1849). He also designed two important Italian Renaissance palazzo-style buildings, the Astor Library (1849–1853), and the private banking house of Duncan, Sherman & Company (1855–1856).

LOIS SEVERINI

WORKS

1849, Congregation Anshe Slonim Synagogue; 1849–1853, Astor Library; 1855–1856, Duncan, Sherman & Company Building; New York.

BIBLIOGRAPHY

KRAMER, ELLEN W. 1968 "Contemporary Descriptions of New York City and Its Public Architecture ca. 1850." *Journal of the Society of Architectural Historians* 27, no. 4:264–280.

WOLFE, GERARD R. 1975 *New York: A Guide to the Metropolis.* New York University Press.

SAENZ DE OIZA, FRANCISCO JAVIER

Born in Cáseda, Navarra, Spain, Francisco Javier Saenz de Oiza (1918–) completed his studies in Madrid where he received his architectural degree in 1946.

After a study trip to the United States, Oiza soon became well known in Spain, winning some of the most important competitions of those years. But it was in the construction of the Aránzazu Basilica (in collaboration with the architect Laorga) that Oiza's desire to break with the architecture then in style manifested itself in an energetic simplification of traditional models, accompanied by a new use of materials. Convinced that the renewal of architecture should accompany social changes brought about by technological developments, Oiza became a member of a group of architects who defended the Modern movement. With them, he participated in the construction of a series of suburbs of Madrid, the *Poblados Dirigidos.* Oiza was later involved in housing programs undertaken by cooperatives in various suburbs on the outskirts of Madrid, among which one must single out the Puerta of Angel, Batán, and Erillas.

Temperamentally restless and critical and sensitive to the international changes in style, Oiza, at the end of the 1950s, began to develop a more open architecture in which it will not be difficult to discern his admiration, at that time, for FRANK LLOYD WRIGHT, ALVAR AALTO, and LOUIS I. KAHN. This new attitude culminated in what is considered one of his most successful works, Torres Blancas, Madrid (1959–1968), commissioned by Juan Huarte, a businessman and lover of the arts. The skyscraper theme in the Banco de Bilbao produced a sheer volume that mixes structural purity and precision of details.

JOSÉ RAFAEL MONEO
Translated from Spanish by Tomlyn Barns

WORKS

1950, Basilica of Arázazu (with Laorga), Spain. 1956, Poblado Dirigado of Entrevias (with Alvear and Sierra); 1956, Poblado Dirigado of Fuencarral (first phase); Madrid. 1958, Single-family Housing, Durana, Alava, Spain. 1959–1968, Torres Blancas, Madrid. 1960, Single-family Housing, Talavera, Toledo, Spain. 1972–1981, Bank of Bilbao, Madrid.

BIBLIOGRAPHY

L'Architettura 1969 No. 151:special issue.

DOMENECH GIRBAU, LUIS 1968 *Arquitectura española contemporánea.* Barcelona, Spain: Blume.

FLORES LOPEZ, CARLOS 1961 *Arquitectura española contemporánea.* Madrid: Aguilar.

FULLAONDO, JUAN DANIEL 1970 *La Escuela de Madrid.* Buenos Aires: Summa.

FULLAONDO, JUAN DANIEL 1968 *Agonía, Utopía, Renacimiento.* Madrid: Nueva Forma.

Zodiac 1965 No. 15:special issue.

SAINTENOY, PAUL

Paul Pierre Jean Saintenoy (1862–1952), grandson of J. P. CLUYSENAAR, studied architecture at the academies of Brussels and Antwerp. His finest works are those in the Art Nouveau style which he practiced briefly around 1900. His later designs in a rather heavy-handed modernistic manner generally lack the crispness of his masterpiece, the Old England Store in Brussels (1899–1900). Saintenoy wrote extensively on subjects in art and architectural history.

ALFRED WILLIS

WORKS

1893–1899, Hôtel de Clèves et Ravenstein (restoration); 1895, Delacre Pharmacy; 1895, House, 81 Avenue Louise; 1899–1900, Old England Store (with others); 1900, House, 34 rue de Taciturne; Brussels. *1904, Belgian Pavilion, Exposition of St. Louis, Mo. 1907, Provincial Government House, Hasselt, Belgium. 1932, North Railway Station (with Jacques Saintenoy and Jean Hendrickx-Van den Bossche), Brussels.

BIBLIOGRAPHY

BORSI, FRANCO (1974)1977 *Bruxelles 1900.* New York: Rizzoli.

Le Livre Bleu. 1950 Brussels: Ferd. Larcier.

"Paul Saintenoy." 1953 *Académie Royale de Belgique: Bulletin de la Classe des Beaux-Arts* 38:55.

PUTTEMANS, PIERRE 1976 *Modern Architecture in Belgium.* Volume 5 in *History of Architecture in Belgium.* Brussels: Vokaer.

RUSSELL, FRANK (editor) 1979 *Art Nouveau Architecture.* New York: Rizzoli.

SAINTENOY, PAUL 1910 *Notes de Voyage d'un architecte en Amérique.* Louvain, Belgium: Wouters-Ickx.

SAINTENOY, PAUL n.d. "L'architecture." Pages 631–634 in *Livre d'or de l'indépendance belge.* Brussels and Antwerp, Belgium: Leclercq.

SAKAKURA, JUNZŌ

Born in Gifu Prefecture, Japan, Junzō Sakakura (1904–1968) graduated from Tokyo University with a degree in literature. He went to France in 1929 and worked at LE CORBUSIER's atelier in Paris from 1931 to 1936. In 1936, he designed the Japanese Pavilion for the Paris International Exhibition of Decorative Arts held the following year, for which he was awarded the Grand Prix.

Establishing his own office in Tokyo in 1940, he tried to introduce to Japan the architecture of rationalism on which Le Corbusier had insisted. After World War II, with many architects working for him, he achieved a remarkably large number of works. In 1960, he was awarded a prize of the Architectural Institute of Japan for his design of the Hashima Municipal Office (1959). After Sakakura's death, Fumitaka Nishizawa took over as head of Sakakura Associates.

TAKASHI HASEGAWA

WORKS

*1937, Japanese Pavilion, International Exhibition, Paris. 1951, Museum of Modern Art, Kamakura, Kanagawa Prefecture, Japan. 1959, Hashima Municipal Office, Gifu Prefecture, Japan. 1961, Institute of Shionogi Seiyaku Company Limited, Osaka, Japan. 1966, Museum of Modern Art (annex), Kamakura, Kanagawa Prefecture, Japan. 1969, Kanagawa Prefecture Office, Yokohama, Japan.

BIBLIOGRAPHY

SAKAKURA, JUNZŌ 1975 *Ōkinakoe.* Tokyo.

SALMON and GILLESPIE

James Salmon (1874–1924), the third generation of an established Glasgow architectural family, was one of the most original Scottish designers and thinkers of his time. He was apprenticed to William Leiper and joined his father's practice in 1890. He began his own successful partnership with John Gaff Gillespie (1870–1926) in 1897 in the firm of Salmon, Son, and Gillespie. Much is known of Salmon, but details of Gillespie's life are obscure.

Salmon believed implicitly that it was essential to develop a contemporary Scottish architectural style that retained visual links with the past yet used modern materials and building techniques. With his partner, he most effectively demonstrated these principles in the design of two Glasgow office buildings: the elegantly detailed Hatrack Building (1899) and the steel-framed and concrete-clad Lion Chambers (1905–1906).

Although Salmon is generally regarded as the more important of the two architects, Gillespie's unbuilt winning entry for the British Architects' 1909 competition to design an office building in concrete shows that he too was a most inventive designer.

Salmon and Gillespie, who were excelled only by JOHN J. BURNET and CHARLES RENNIE MACKINTOSH in the originality of their Glasgow buildings of the period, dissolved their partnership in 1913. Neither architect was to produce any further works of note independently when building work resumed in Scotland after World War I.

JOHN MCASLAN

WORKS

JAMES SALMON, JR.

1897, Mercantile Chambers; 1899, The Hatrack Building; 1902, Lloyd Morris Memorial Church; 1905–1906, Lion Chambers; 1906, Catholic Apostolic Church (north aisle and narthex); 1914, Church Hall, Dalmarnock; 1924, Redlands Hospital for Women (additions); Glasgow, Scotland.

JOHN GAFF GILLESPIE

1893, Scottish Temperance League Building, Glasgow, Scotland. 1897, 1901, Martine Hotel, Troon, Scotland. 1899, British Linen Bank No.1; 1899, House, 12 University Gardens; 1899–1900, British Linen Bank No. 2; 1905, British Linen Bank No. 3 (upper floor extension); Glasgow, Scotland. 1907–1908, Municipal Buildings, Stirling, Scotland. 1911, Pollock Golf Clubhouse; Glasgow, Scotland. 1913, Steel Company of Scotland Offices, Blochairn, Scotland.

SALMON AND GILLESPIE

1899, Anderson Savings Bank; 1899, Church Hall, Denistoun; Glasgow, Scotland.

BIBLIOGRAPHY

GOMME, ANDOR, and WALKER, DAVID 1968 *Architecture of Glasgow.* London: Lund Humphries.
"Obituary to James Salmon." 1924 *Journal of the Royal Institute of British Architects* 31:513.
SALMON, JAMES 1908 "The Decoration of Steel and Reinforced Concrete." *Builder's Journal* 27:269–273.
SERVICE, ALASTAIR (1975)1977 *Edwardian Architecture.* London: Oxford University Press.
WALKER, DAVID 1966 "Salmon, Son, Grandson and Gillespie." *Scottish Art Review* 10, no. 3:17–21, 28–29.
WALKER, DAVID 1975 "The Partnership of James Salmon and John Gaff Gillespie." In Alastair Service (editor), *Edwardian Architecture and Its Origins.* London: Architectural Press.

SALMONA, ROGELIO

Rogelio Salmona (1929–) has combined traditional materials with asymmetrical designs to stimulate a regional revival in modern Colombian architecture. Born in Paris, he studied in Colombia, returning to Paris in 1948 to join LE CORBUSIER's atelier. Eleven years later, he settled in Bogotá after working on the Paris UNESCO Building for three years.

The diversity of Salmona's architectural repertoire ranges from wedge-shaped brick apartments at Timiza (1964–1965) to the snaillike high-rise of the El Parque residences (1965–1970), also of brick. In 1977, he won Colombia's *Premio Nacional de Arquitectura,* and as a professor of architecture he has encouraged Colombians to find inspiration within their own architectural heritage.

ELIZABETH D. HARRIS

WORKS

1959–1961, El Polo Apartment House (with Guillermo Bermudez); 1964–1965, Timiza Communal Housing Project; 1965–1970, Residencias El Parque; 1967–1973, Headquarters for the Colombia Society of Architects; 1975–1980, Museum of Modern Art; Bogotá.

BIBLIOGRAPHY

BAYÓN, DAMIÁN, and GASPARINI, PAOLO 1977 *Panorámica de la Arquitectura Latino-Americana.* Barcelona: Editorial Blume.

BERTY, ANNE 1981 *Architectures Colombiennes.* Paris: Moniteur.

BULLRICH, FRANCISCO 1969 *New Directions in Latin American Architecture.* New York: Braziller.

SALMONA, ROGELIO 1972 "Architettura di Rogelio Salmona: Considerazioni sull'architettura moderna in Colombia." *Controspazio* 4, Aug.:38–51.

Salvi. Trevi Fountain. Rome. 1732–1751

SALVI, NICOLA

Nicola Salvi (1697–1751) was born in Rome, where he studied with Antonio Valeri and Antonio Canevari. As a pupil Salvi drew after the works of MICHELANGELO, PIETRO DA CORTONA and GIOVANNI LORENZO BERNINI, and virtually memorized the architectural treatise of VITRUVIUS. In 1713 Salvi's precocious literary and artistic talents were recognized by his election to the Accademia degli Arcadi. Other professional honors followed, including membership in the Accademia di San Luca (1733) and the Congregazione dei Virtuosi al Pantheon (1745). In 1727, following Canevari's departure for Portugal, Salvi took charge of his master's Roman studio, and it is from this time that his first identifiable designs date. The most interesting of these was a large temporary structure set up in the Piazza di Spagna in 1728 which functioned as an architectural backdrop to an elaborate fireworks display. This theatrical *macchina* prefigured Salvi's scenographic design for the Trevi Fountain.

In 1732 Salvi participated in both the great architectural competitions organized by Pope Clement XII. While Salvi's projects for the Lateran façade were unsuccessful, one of the designs he submitted for the Trevi Fountain won him the commission to build what is generally acknowledged to be the most spectacular fountain in the world. The construction of the Trevi Fountain was an extremely protracted affair, but by 1735 the architecture was structurally complete and by Salvi's death in 1751 the ornamental rock formations and full scale models of most of the sculpture were in place. Salvi's design for the Trevi, while showing specific influences from the work of earlier baroque masters, is an inspired and highly original composition. Salvi effected a fusion of architecture, sculpture, and water into a monomorphic unity by theatrical means. The spontaneous visual expression of water is enriched by Salvi's complex iconographical program symbolizing the sovereign role played by this element in nature. The architectural component of the Trevi is essentially a classical reduction of high baroque design, while aspects of the sculpture and ornament (especially Neptune's shell) are closer to the rococo style popular in contemporary France.

After 1744 Salvi's poor health severely limited his activity. In fact, he never executed another design approaching the scale and importance of the Trevi, but several of his smaller buildings attest to the range and quality of his work. Among the most important of these are his interior remodeling of Santa Maria dei Gradi in Viterbo (1737), the chapel of Saint John in Saint Roch, Lisbon

(1742; executed in Rome under Salvi's supervision and then shipped to Portugal), and the expansion of Bernini's Palazzo Chigi-Odescalchi in Rome (1745). Like his great contemporary and friend, LUIGI VANVITELLI, Salvi's historical significance rests largely in his ability to express the scenographic potential of architecture and in his more tempered, classicizing interpretation of traditional baroque forms. Perhaps, as FRANCESCO MILIZIA wrote, the Trevi Fountain is the finest eighteenth-century building in Rome; in any case, it certainly is Salvi's masterpiece.

JOHN PINTO

WORKS

*c.1727, San Paolo fuori le mura (baptistry); *1728, Piazza di Spagna (fireworks apparatus); 1732–1751, Trevi Fountain; 1735, Palazzo Monte di Pieta (expansion); Rome. 1737, Santa Maria dei Gradi (renovation), Viterbo, Italy. 1742, Chapel of Saint John, Saint Roch, Lisbon. *1743–1746, Villa Bolognetti (chapel and gate); 1745, Palazzo Chigi-Odescalchi (expansion); Rome.

BIBLIOGRAPHY

COOKE, LESTER H. 1956 "The Documents Relating to the Fountain of Trevi." *Art Bulletin* 38:149–173.

MATTHIAE, GUGLIELMO 1954 "Nicola Salvi minore." *Palladio* 4:161–170.

MILIZIA, FRANCESCO 1826–1828 Volume 5, pages 376–380 in *Opere Complete di Francesco Milizia risquerdante le belle arti.* Bologna, Italy: Stamperia Cardinali e Frulli.

MOSCHINI, VITTORIO 1929 "La prima opera di Nicola Salvi." *Roma* 7:345–347.

ONOFRIO, CESARE D' 1957 *Le Fontane di Roma con documenti et disegni inediti.* Rome: Staderini.

SCHAVO, ARMANDO 1956 *La Fontana di Trevi e le altre opere di Nicola Salvi.* Rome: Istituto Poligrafico dello Stato.

SALVIN, ANTHONY

Born in Worthing of an ancient Durham family, Anthony Salvin (1799–1881) worked briefly for John Paterson of Edinburgh before coming to London about 1822. There, he mixed in artistic circles and may have worked for JOHN NASH. In 1826 and 1828, he received commissions for two lavish Tudor mansions, Mamhead and Moreby Hall. His reputation thus established, he went on to design a long series of opulent country houses and also carried out additions and alterations to many important older houses.

Though adept in many styles, Salvin was especially associated with the Tudor and Elizabethan modes. Harlaxton Manor (1831–1838), one of the most extravagant houses of the time, was an ebullient yet scholarly restoration of a great Elizabethan palace, while Scotney Castle (1835–1843) was a sensitive adaptation of the simpler Elizabethan manor house. Later, at Thoresby Hall (1864–1875) and other large mansions, he continued the style of Harlaxton, though without its panache.

Salvin was also recognized as an authority on medieval castles, a specialty which was reflected at

Salvin. Harlaxton Manor. Lincolnshire, England. 1831–1838

Peckforton Castle (1844–1850), an unstinting effort to build a modern aristocrat's mansion in the image of a thirteenth-century fortress, and at Alnwick Castle (1854–1865). Here, the duke of Northumberland commissioned him to rebuild one of Britain's largest medieval castles, furnishing it in the Italian Renaissance style. Salvin also restored a number of important government castles, including the Tower of London (1854–1869) and Windsor Castle (1858–1867).

Though principally known for his country houses, Salvin also designed a number of churches. In 1839–1840, he took part in the group effort to redesign and adorn the new church at Kilndown, which became, under the direction of Viscount Beresford and A. J. B. Beresford Hope, a showcase for liturgical furnishings in the Ecclesiological mode. At Cambridge, he worked directly for the Ecclesiological Society, directing the restoration of the Church of the Holy Sepulchre (1841–1843), a controversial project also intended as a model of Ecclesiological principles.

Though few of Salvin's works appeared in the architectural journals, he always had a large clientele, mainly aristocratic, and he maintained a high reputation in the profession. He was a Fellow of the Society of Antiquaries (1824) and of the Royal Institute of British Architects (1836), of which he also served as vice-president; in 1863, he received its Gold Medal. He collaborated for many years with his brother-in-law, the landscape gardener William Andrews Nesfield, and numbered among his pupils and assistants JOHN L. PEARSON and R. NORMAN SHAW, as well as his nephew WILLIAM E. NESFIELD.

E. N. KAUFMAN

WORKS

1826–1838, Mamhead, Devonshire, England. 1828–1832, Moreby Hall; 1830–1836, Methley Hall (restoration); Yorkshire, England. 1831–1836, Farham, Sussex, England. 1831–1838, Harlaxton Manor, Lincolnshire, England. 1835–1843, Scotney Castle, Kent, England. 1838–1842, Rufford Abbey, Lancashire, England. 1840–1841, Christ Church (additions and alterations), Kilndown, Kent, England. 1841–1843, Church of the Holy Sepulchre (restoration), Cambridge. 1844–1850, Peckforton Castle, Cheshire, England. 1846–1851, Hafod, Dyfed, Wales. 1853–1869, Tower of London (restoration and additions). 1854–1863, Keele Hall, Staffordshire, England. 1854–1865, Alnwick Castle (rebuilding), Northumberland, England. 1858–1867, Windsor Castle (restoration and additions), Berkshire, England. 1864–1875, Thoresby Hall, Nottinghamshire, England. 1869, Albury House, Surrey, England.

BIBLIOGRAPHY

EASTLAKE, CHARLES L. (1872)1970 *A History of the Gothic Revival.* Edited with an introduction by J. Mordaunt Crook. Reprint. New York: Humanities Press.

GIROUARD, MARK (1971)1979 *The Victorian Country House.* Rev. ed. New Haven: Yale University Press.

HUSSEY, CHRISTOPHER 1958 *English Country Houses: Late Georgian, 1800–1840.* London: Country Life.

"The Late Mr. Anthony Salvin, Architect." 1881 *The Builder* 41:809–810, 818, 893.

WHITE, JAMES F. 1962 *The Cambridge Movement: The Ecclesiologists and the Gothic Revival.* Cambridge University Press.

SALVISBERG, OTTO R.

Some of the buildings of Otto Rudolf Salvisberg (1882–1940), such as the Siedlung Schillerpromenade in Reinickendorf, Berlin (1929–1931), have entered the standard literature on modern architecture, yet on the whole this architect has not received the attention he deserves. This may be due to the fact that he lacked any aura of a pioneer, that he wrote comparatively little—while building a lot—and that the last decade of his life was almost entirely dedicated to work in Switzerland, a country that never granted particular fame to any of its architects. Born near Berne, he started studying at the Technikum in nearby Biel but never graduated. After a few years of traveling, mostly in southern Germany, he worked for Hans Curjel and KARL MOSER in Karlsruhe, Germany (1906) and later for the firm of Thiersch und Hocheder in Munich. In 1908, he joined the firm of Paul Zimmerreimer in Berlin, where he soon became designer in charge of some of the firm's most important projects, such as the Lindenhaus, a large concrete office building in Berlin-Kreuzberg (1912–1913).

Although foreshadowing aspects of later *Grossstadtarchitektur,* Salvisberg's numerous early projects and buildings boast of historic references, and this is equally true for his CAMILLO SITTE-inspired social housing complexes built in various parts of Europe and vacillating, according to local context, from Bavarian folk rococo to picturesque neomedieval. During the 1920s, he went through a rather decorative Expressionist phase, but finally he reduced his palette to a *sachlich* elementarism, thereby managing to purge the traditions of residential building from explicit historicist elements without abolishing the sense of bourgeois opulence traditionally associated with the genre.

Salvisberg became one of Berlin's most sought after architects for villas and private residences. Even the most restrained among these, such as the large, brick-faced residence of the art collector Flechtheim in Berlin-Grünewald (1928–1929), has a comfortable and reassuring aura; it exudes a modernity that opened the eyes of many potential clients for the language of the new architecture while at the same time obstructing their view of the more radical manifesto-architecture of WALTER GROPIUS, LUDWIG MIES VAN DER ROHE, and Häsler.

As a designer of social housing complexes, Salvisberg stood on the side of the radical avant-garde. His best known contribution to this theme is the already mentioned Gross-Siedlung Schillerpromenade in Berlin-Reinickendorf (1929–1931).

Parallel to his work in and around Berlin, Salvisberg unfolded a rather extensive activity in Switzerland, where he had opened a second office in 1923, in partnership with Otto Brechbühl. In 1924, the team won the competition for a new building in the Bernese hospital complex of the Lory Spital (built 1926–1929). When in 1930 the Technische Hochschule (ETH) in Zurich offered him Karl Moser's chair, Salvisberg accepted. Switzerland soon turned out to be a far more fertile territory than Germany for the kind of architectural culture he represented. Furthermore, it happened to offer his buildings a chance of physical survival—Salvisberg's only true "Berlinesque" office building still extant is the curved main building of the SUVA, Switzerland's public insurance agency, in Berne (1930–1931). His generously laid-out and beautifully detailed University- and Hospital buildings in Berne and Zurich are still admirable in their laconic and competent rationality. The most beautiful among his university buildings are the Machine Laboratory and the Central Heating Plant of the ETH in Zurich (1930–1933) next to the school's main building by GOTTFRIED SEMPER and Gustav Gull. Partly reusing older buildings, this vast complex has a street façade of simple gravity, interior galleries from where to gaze at the machinery displayed in the large covered hall, and a high cubic chimney which constituted for a long time the only "modern" element in Zurich's skyline.

STANISLAUS VON MOOS

Salvisberg.
Machine Laboratory and Heating Plant, ETH.
Zurich.
1930–1933

WORKS

1912, Villa Neutze, Dahlem; *1912, Prächtel Office Building (with Paul Zimmerreicher); *1912–1913, Lindenhaus Office Building (with Zimmerreicher); Berlin. 1919, Pohland House, Falkenstein, Vogtland, Germany. 1923–1924, Tang House, Dahlem; *1924–1925, Freimiethäuser, Lichterfelde; 1924–1926, Rowhouses, Lichterfelde; 1925, Salvisberg House, Südende; Berlin. 1926–1929, Lory Spital (with Otto Brechbühl), Berne. 1928–1929, Flechtheim House, Grünewald; 1929–1931, Gross-Siedlung Schillerpromenade, Reinickendorf; *1929–1930, Deutsche Krankenversicherung Office Building, Schöneberg; Berlin. 1929–1930, Elfenau Mothers Home (with Brechbühl); 1930–1931, SUVA Office Building (with Brechbühl); 1930–1931, University Buildings (with Brechbühl); Berne. 1930–1931, Salvisberg House; 1930–1933, Machine Laboratory and Heating Plant, ETH; Zurich. 1934, Barrell House; 1936–1940, La Roche Administration Building and Factories; Basel. 1937–1939, Children's Hospital; 1939–1940, Dreikönigsegg Apartment Building; Zurich.

BIBLIOGRAPHY

LICHTENSTEIN, CLAUDE 1977 "Salvisberg und das 'neue Bauen.'" *Werk/Archithese* 10:7–14.

MOOS, STANISLAUS VON 1977 "Architektur auf den zweiten Blick." *Werk/Archithese* 10:3–6.

PLATZ, GUSTAV A. 1927 *Die Baukunst der neuesten Zeit.* Berlin: Propyläen.

POSENER, JULIUS 1977 "Salvisberg in Berlin." *Werk/Archithese* 10:23–25.

SALVISBERG, OTTO R. 1929 "Architektenschule." *Werk* 16:209.

SALVISBERG, OTTO R. 1933 "Technik und Formausdruck im Bauen." *Tecknische Rundschau* 51:1–5.

SALVISBERG, OTTO R. 1934 "Grundlagen der Gestalltung im Krankenhausbau." *Nosokomeion* 1934:229ff.

WERTHEIM, PAUL 1914 "Architekturen von Otto Salvisberg, Verlin." *Moderne Bauformen* 13:113–137.

WERTHEIM, PAUL (editor) 1927 *Neuere Arbeiten von O. R. Salvisberg.* Berlin: Hübsch.

SAMBIN, HUGUES

Typical of many Renaissance artists and craftsmen, Hugues Sambin (1520–c.1600) had a broad and accomplished range of talents. Active in the

French city of Dijon, Sambin was an architect, sculptor, engineer, and carpenter whose only documented work is the pair of sculpted doors at the Palais de Justice in Dijon (1583). However, on the basis of these decorations, a number of other edifices in this city with similar ornamentation have been attributed to Sambin.

Born near the small town of Gray in France, Sambin was a student of Boudrillet de Troyes who exposed him to various design methods and approaches including the specific ornamental works of Du Cerceau (see DU CERCEAU FAMILY) and HANS VREDEMAN DE VRIES; the sculptural program on the doors at the Palais de Justice, for example, certainly incorporates motifs prevalent in their work (caryatids, candelabras, fruit, palmettes, lion's heads). Other houses in Dijon which carry many of the same ornamental schemes on their façades include the Maison Milsand, Rue des Forges (1561), whose scorpion-and-arrow designs are characteristic of Sambin; the Maison Chasseret, 8 Rue Stephen-Liègeard (1560); the Hôtel Fyot de Mineure, 23 Rue Amiral-Roussin; and the Hôtel Le Compasseur, 66 Rue Vannerie, whose unusual decoration of winged masks is also from Sambin.

According to contemporary records, Sambin was also official city architect of Dijon by 1584; in the same year, he supervised the construction of a number of windmills just outside the city. In addition, in his capacity as engineer, he appears to have been involved in artillery and water diversion projects for the army. In 1572, Sambin published a treatise entitled *Oeuvre de la diversité des termes.* He died at the turn of the century, although the exact date of his death is unrecorded.

PETER L. DONHAUSER

BIBLIOGRAPHY

FYOT, EUGÈNE 1925 "Influence Didactique de Hugues Sambin sur le Décor d'Architecture." *Bulletin Archéologique* 1925:207–236.

HAUTECOEUR, LOUIS 1948 Volume 1 in *Histoire de l'Architecture Classique en France.* Paris: Picard.

SAMONÀ, GIUSEPPE

Giuseppe Samonà (1898–) has produced a vast array of architectural works throughout Italy as well as major contributions to the field of urban planning. He has also proven himself an able critic and historian in books and articles on such diverse subjects as ANTONIO SANT'ELIA, FRANK LLOYD WRIGHT, low-cost housing, and the Cathedral of Cefalù.

Samonà took his degree in civil engineering in 1922 at the University of Palermo. His earliest works display a simplified monumentalism, a quality which he found in industrial architecture and stressed in his interpretation of the Modern movement. It was only after 1930, when he became familiar with the works of LE CORBUSIER, that Samonà began to use International style elements in his own projects. His approach to that style was, however, a cautious and very personal one, and some critics have suggested an influence of the Wagnerschule and ERIC MENDELSOHN on his work.

During the 1930s, the architect won several competitions sponsored by the Fascist government. Samonà's Post Office in the Appio quarter of Rome (1933–1936) was one of the winning entries in the Regime competition that gave four new major post offices to the Italian capital.

One of the founders of the University Institute for Architecture in Venice in 1924, Samonà was director of the school from 1945–1971. In addition to publishing important studies in the field of urban planning, Samonà has created new quarters in various Italian cities, including housing in Mestre (1951–1956) and Palermo (1956–1958).

In his most recent work, such as the Theater in Sciacca (1970–1974), the architect has revealed an interest in the poetics of pure form.

ELLEN R. SHAPIRO

WORKS

1933–1936, Post Office, Appio Quarter, Rome. 1950–1954, Villa Scimemi, Mondello, Palermo, Italy. 1950–1956, National Institute for Assistance for Work Accidents Headquarters (with others), Venice, Italy. 1951–1956, National Insurance Institute Housing (with others), San Giuliano, Mestre, Italy. 1953, Traumatology Hospital, Bari, Italy. 1956–1958, Borgo Ulivia Quarter (with others), Palermo, Italy. 1956–1958, National Institute of Social Welfare Headquarters, Messina, Italy. 1959, Public Housing Committee Quarter (with others), San Giuliano, Mestre, Italy. 1961–1963, Electric Light Company Headquarters, Palermo, Italy. 1970–1974, Banca d'Italia (with others), Padova, Italy. 1970–1974, Theater, Sciacca, Italy.

BIBLIOGRAPHY

AYMONINO, CARLO (editor) 1975 *Giuseppe Samonà: 1923–1975, Cinquant'anni di architettura.* Rome: Officiana.

CUZZER, ALDO 1959 "I grandi concorsi." *La Casa* 6:246–271.

DE FEO, GIOVANNA, and VALERIANI, ENRICO (editors) 1981 *Architetture italiane degli anni '70.* Rome: De Luca.

LOVERO, PASQUALE (editor) 1975 *Giuseppe Samonà: L'unità architettura-urbanistica, Scritti e progetti 1929–1973.* Milan: Angeli.

SAMWELL, WILLIAM

William Samwell (1628–1676) was a gentleman architect of considerable accomplishment. His designs were distinguished by the sophistication of their planning and their exploitation of spatial possibilities in a manner that prefigured the larger seats of the eighteenth century. This resulted in houses in which a successful balance was achieved between the grand public and the convenient private rooms. His achievement has until recently been undervalued, but the demolished Eaton Hall (1675–1682), the remodeled and ruinous Grange Park (c.1670), and his remodeling of Ham House (1672–1674) provide evidence of a contribution to Restoration architecture as significant as that of the better-known gentleman architects HUGH MAY and ROGER PRATT.

JOHN BOLD

WORKS

1668–1671, King's House (partly demolished), Newmarket, Suffolk, England. c.1670, Grange Park, Hampshire, England. 1672–1674, Ham House, Surrey, England. *1673–1674, The Royal Mews, Charing Cross, London. 1674–1686, Felbrigg Hall, Norfolk, England. *1675–1682, Eaton Hall, Cheshire, England.

BIBLIOGRAPHY

DUNBAR, JOHN G. 1975 "The Building Activities of the Duke and Duchess of Lauderdale, 1670–1682." *Archaeological Journal* 132:202–230.

MERCER, E. 1970 "William Samwell and the Grange." In Howard M. Colvin and John Harris (editors), *The Country Seat.* London: Allen Lane.

SANDERSON, JOHN

John Sanderson (?–1774) was a competent Palladian (see ANDREA PALLADIO) follower of the school of LORD BURLINGTON. He designed country houses on his own but was also content to work as professional assistant to gentleman amateurs, including SANDERSON MILLER and Thomas Prowse. His talented interior designs show a leaning toward rococo.

ANDOR GOMME

WORKS

*1730?, Kelham Hall, Nottinghamshire, England. *1731, Stratton Park, Hampshire, England 1745–1747, Saint John's Church, Hampstead, London. 1747–1748, Kirtlington Park (interiors), Oxfordshire, England. 1750, Pusey House, Berkshire, England. 1754, Hagley Hall (interiors), Worcestershire, England. 1755–1770?, Kimberley Hall, Norfolk, England.

BIBLIOGRAPHY

HUSSEY, CHRISTOPHER (1955)1965 *English Country Houses: Early Georgian, 1715–1760.* Rev. ed. London: Country Life.

WOOLFE, JOHN, and GANDON, JAMES 1970 Volume 4 in *Vitruvius Britannicus.* New York: Blom.

SANDYS, FRANCIS

Francis Sandys (?–1815) was an Irishman patronized by the earl of Bristol, for whom he built the huge fantastic oval of Ickworth House (begun 1796) to an outline design by Mario Asprucci. Curves figure prominently in all Sandys's houses, which are notable for ambitious volumetric effects. His career ended early with the failure of his new jail at Durham (1809).

ANDOR GOMME

WORKS

1795, Finborough Hall, Great Finborough; 1796–1830, Ickworth House; 1800?, Worlingham Hall; 1804, Assembly Rooms, Bury St. Edmonds; Suffolk, England. *1809–1813, County Jail, Worcester, England. 1813–1815, Dorchester Bridge, Oxfordshire, England.

BIBLIOGRAPHY

HUSSEY, CHRISTOPHER 1956 *English Country Houses: Mid-Georgian, 1760–1800.* London: Country Life.

RANKIN, PETER 1972 *Irish Building Ventures of the Earl Bishop of Derry: 1730–1803.* Belfast, Northern Ireland: Ulster Architectural Heritage Society.

SANFELICE, FERDINANDO

Ferdinando Sanfelice (1675–1750) was a member of a Neapolitan group of architects classified under the term *barocchetto.* One of the most prolific Neapolitan architects of the early eighteenth century, Sanfelice studied with the painter Francesco Solimena who was the instrumental force behind the group. The biographer De Dominci attributed numerous palaces to Sanfelice, and he has consequently been associated with domestic architecture. His style was dependent on a native formalism, ranging from severe mural surfaces to a profusion of ornament. His Palazzo Sera Cassano (1725–1726), a sloping structure with a rhythmic façade, denotes his freedom in handling the mannered tradition. Sanfelice was most accomplished in the design of monumental staircases, where he sought to interject a visual complexity into the vaulted vestibule.

JEFFREY HUGHES

WORKS

1701, Santa Maria delle Periclitani, Pontecorvo, Italy. 1725–1726, Palazzo Serra Cassano; 1728, Palazzo Sanfelice; c.1735, Chiesa delle Nunzitelle; Milan.

BIBLIOGRAPHY

WITTKOWER, RUDOLF (1958)1973 *Art and Architecture in Italy: 1600 to 1750.* 3d ed., rev. Baltimore: Penguin.

SANGALLO FAMILY

For over a century, members of the celebrated Sangallo family of artists stood at the forefront of the Renaissance architectural profession. Beginning around 1480, the name "da Sangallo," derived from the district near the Porta San Gallo in Florence, was assumed by three generations of the Giamberti and Cordiani families, among whom Giuliano, Antonio the Elder, and Antonio the Younger were the major figures. The founder of the dynasty was Francesco Giamberti (1404–1480), a woodworker and decorator who attended the court of the de' Medici.

Giuliano da Sangallo. Giuliano da Sangallo, Francesco's son, was born in Florence about 1443 and died there in 1516. He was probably first trained by his father in wood sculpture, an art he practiced throughout his life. At an early age, however, he was apprenticed to Francesco di Giovanni, called Il Francone, a military engineer with whom he went to Rome around 1465 and later collaborated on fortifications. In Rome, both men were employed by the Vatican but their accomplishments are unknown. At this time Giuliano initiated a study of ancient architectural monuments which he recorded in several sketchbooks now preserved in the Vatican Library and in the Biblioteca Comunale of Siena. In the early 1470s, Giuliano returned to Florence, where he developed a style reflecting his Roman experience. In the small courtyard of the Palazzo of Bartolomeo Scala, now part of the Palazzo Ghirardesca, he employed a neo-antique pier-and-pilaster system of arcading along with monumental pictorial reliefs. This was followed by the Villa Medici at Poggio a Caiano near Florence, designed for Lorenzo the Magnificent around 1480, the first large-scale realization of a humanist villa in the manner of the ancients. Dominating the crest of a gentle hill, the building rises from an arcaded terrace-platform derived from the Roman cryptoporticus, and its entrance features an Ionic porch with a broad pediment. The villa's square layout, distinguished by rigorous symmetry and the rational disposition of interior volumes, centers upon a large barrel-vaulted hall that evokes the grandeur of Roman thermae.

Backed by Lorenzo the Magnificent, in 1484 Giuliano obtained the commission for Santa Maria delle Carceri in Prato. The church has a Greek-cross plan, barrel vaults in the arms and a dome on pendentives at the crossing. For the articulation of the interior Giuliano turned back nearly fifty years to models such as the Pazzi Chapel of FILIPPO BRUNELLESCHI. In a similar display of traditionalism, he adopted a Brunelleschian mode in his Ionic atrium of Santa Maria Maddalena dei Pazzi (1492), and in the octagonal Sacristy of Santo Spirito (1489–1495) executed in collaboration with IL CRONOCA. For the rectangular vestibule to the Sacristy, however, Giuliano produced a powerfully original system of free-standing Corinthian columns bearing a richly carved barrel vault.

Giuliano da Sangallo. Villa Medici. Poggio a Caiano, Italy. 1480–1497?

Giuliano da Sangallo. Santa Maria delle Carceri. Prato, Italy. 1484–1491

With the death of Lorenzo the Magnificent in 1492 and the expulsion of the di' Medici from Florence two years later, Giuliano was deprived of his principal source of patronage. New support came from Cardinal Giuliano della Rovere, who may have employed the architect in Rome and who commissioned him to build the Palazzo Rovere in Savona (1494). Giuliano was active concurrently in Florence, where he built the Palazzo Gondi (1490–1501) and made a wood model for the Palazzo Strozzi (1498). Both palaces represent progressive elaborations of the Palazzo Medici of MICHELOZZO DI BARTOLOMMEO.

Giuliano was one of the foremost military architects of the Renaissance. In 1488, he began Poggio Imperiale near Poggibonsi, whose city wall and citadel exhibit the earliest coherent realization of large angle bastions. The bastion system was subsequently developed in partnership with his brother Antonio the Elder at the fortresses of Arezzo (1502–1503), Borgo San Sepolcro (1502–1505) and Pisa (1509–1512). Their coastal fortress at Nettuno (1501–1503) south of Rome represents a milestone in the history of military architecture.

In 1503, Giuliano della Rovere assumed the papal throne as Julius II, and the architect went to Rome expecting important commissions from his former patron. His hopes were frustrated, however, when the pope placed his most ambitious projects in the hands of DONATO BRAMANTE. Discontented with only minor commissions, Giuliano returned to Florence until the election of Pope Leo X in 1513. He was appointed building administrator of St. Peter's with the architects RAPHAEL and FRA GIOCONDO in 1515, but his contribution to the basilica was negligible. In the year before his death, Giuliano submitted designs for the façade of San Lorenzo in Florence which exercised a decisive influence on the projects of his friend MICHELANGELO.

Some of Giuliano's most progressive architectural ideas are found in three unexecuted palace projects known from drawings: the royal residence for Ferdinand I of Naples (1488), the vast suburban palace for Lorenzo the Magnificent in Florence (1490?), and the papal palace for Leo X on the Piazza Navona, Rome (1513). The designs attest to an unrivaled grasp of Imperial Roman planning principles, scaling, and structure. Of the Florentine architects of the period, Giuliano is the true successor to Brunelleschi and LEON BATTISTA ALBERTI, and he came closest to the incipient style of the High Renaissance.

Antonio da Sangallo the Elder. Antonio da Sangallo the Elder, Giuliano's brother, was also a leading sculptor, military engineer, and architect. Born in Florence about 1453, he died in 1534. His

Antonio da Sangallo the Elder.
Madonna di San Biagio.
Montepulciano, Italy.
1518–1534

earliest documented work was the refortification of the Castel Sant'Angelo, Rome (1493), which was followed by the papal fortress of Civitacastellana (1494–1497). Then, for nearly twenty years, he worked in subordinate collaboration with Giuliano on military architecture. In 1495, he assumed direction of Giuliano's fortifications at Poggio Imperiale and is recorded there as late as 1513. Similarly, he superintended construction of the fortresses at Arezzo, Borgo San Sepolcro, Pisa, and Nettuno. Between 1505 and 1515, he designed and built the Fortezza Vecchia at Leghorn. In Florence, along with minor jobs in the Palazzo Vecchio and the Cathedral, Antonio the Elder executed with Baccio d'Agnolo the Loggia de' Servi (1517–1529) opposite the Ospedale degli Innocenti of Brunelleschi, thus giving all but definitive form to the Piazza della Santissima Annunziata.

Antonio the Elder's last years were spent at the southern Tuscan town of Montepulciano. There, he began and largely completed his masterpiece, the Madonna di San Biagio (1518–1534), a pilgrimage church located just outside the city walls. Following a Greek-cross plan reminiscent of Giuliano's Santa Maria delle Carceri at Prato, the church is oriented by virtue of an apselike sacristy to the south and two campanili flanking the north façade. The arms of the church are barrel-vaulted and the central dome is supported by a high drum on pendentives. Executed entirely in travertine, the Madonna di San Biagio is articulated both inside and out by a single order of massive Doric pilasters and half-columns which invests it with a sense of strength and solidity virtually unequaled in contemporary ecclesiastical architecture. Several patrician palaces at Montepulciano have been traditionally attributed to Antonio the Elder, but without secure documentation. These include the Palazzo Nobili-Tarughi, the Palazzo Contucci-Del Monte, and the Palazzo Cervini. To him is also given the Palazzo del Monte, now the Palazzo Comunale, in the town of Monte San Savino.

Antonio da Sangallo the Younger. Antonio da Sangallo the Younger was one of the great masters of the Renaissance, attaining the highest degree of professional, social, and economic success in Rome, where he dominated the architectural scene during the second quarter of the sixteenth century. Born in Florence in 1484, the son of Antonio Cordiani and Smeralda Giamberti, a sister of Giuliano and Antonio the Elder, he died in Terni on September 28, 1546. Probably trained by his uncles, he was taken by Giuliano to Rome around 1503. Soon after, he entered the workshop of Bramante, who employed him first as a carpenter and then as a draftsman and supervisor at projects such as St. Peter's (from 1511), the Cortile del Belvedere at the Vatican (from 1510), and the harbor and fortress at Civitavecchia (around 1513). After Bramante's death in 1514, he continued at St. Peter's under Raphael, whom he assisted at the Villa Madama (1517–1518). Thus, by his mid-thirties, Antonio the Younger had acquired practical experience on a variety of building projects under the leading masters of the High Renaissance. He was exceptional in his time for practicing no other art but architecture.

Antonio the Younger developed an independent practice around 1515. At this time, he became the personal architect of Cardinal Alessandro Farnese, for whom he began the Palazzo Farnese in Rome, greatly enlarging the original project when his patron became Pope Paul III in 1534. An immense symmetrical block surrounded by streets and fronted by a spacious piazza, the palace engaged the architect until his death, after which it was significantly advanced and altered by Michelangelo and finished by GIACOMO DELLA PORTA. The building exhibits features typical of Antonio the Younger's palace style: a façade conceived as a neutral plane framed by rusticated angle quoins, divided horizontally by incisive stringcourses, and organized in bays by plain rectangular and aedicular windows with a rusticated portal. The interior courtyard, by contrast, is richly articulated by a full complement of superimposed classical orders directly inspired by antique models such as the Theater of Marcellus. Outside Rome, Antonio the Younger produced other Farnese projects, including the pentagonal fortress of Caprarola (1521?–1527?), later transformed into a villa by GIACOMO BAROZZI DA VIGNOLA, and the palatial strongholds of Capodimonte (begun by 1518) and Gradoli (1536?), as well as the fortified town of Castro (1537), later destroyed.

Antonio da Sangallo the Younger. St. Peter's (wood model). Rome. 1538–1543

At the death of Raphael in 1520, Antonio the Younger was named architect-in-chief of St. Peter's with BALDASSARE PERUZZI, a position he occupied alone from 1536. His conception of the church was embodied in the large wood model (1538–1543), now kept in St. Peter's, that was executed by his pupil Antonio Labacco. The project involved a return to Bramante's initial notion of a Greek-cross church with a central dome, but it added a high, towered façade as a semi-independent structure which introduced a longitudinal emphasis. Highly ambitious in scale, the scheme called for a complex multistoried exterior elevation that was criticized by contemporaries. When Michelangelo took over as architect in 1546, the entire project was abandoned.

As first architect to popes Clement VII and Paul III, Antonio the Younger received numerous official commissions. While he was continuously employed within the Vatican palace, where he built the Sala Regia and the Pauline Chapel (1540–1546) and added much to the Cortile del Belvedere, he also designed the Zecca, the papal mint of Rome (1525–1527), built much of the Apostolic Palace at Loreto (1526–1534), and conceived the Pozzo di San Patrizio at Orvieto (1527–1535), a deep well with horse ramps forming a double helix. Under Paul III, he became a leading expert and practitioner of military architecture with projects such as the pentagonal For-

Antonio da Sangallo the Younger. Palazzo Farnese (later altered by Michelangelo and Della Porta). Rome. 1515?–1546

tezza da Basso at Florence (1534–1536), the Papal Fortress at Ancona (1537), and the Rocca Paolina at Perugia (1540–1541). In Rome, his outstanding achievement in this field is represented by two prestigious projects, only partly realized, for a series of bastions along the Aventine Hill and around the Porta Ardeatina (1537–1542), and for the bastioned walls of the Vatican Borgo, including the impressive but unfinished Porta di Santo Spirito (1543–1546).

Such large and far-flung enterprises did not deter the acceptance of numerous private secular and religious commissions. The architect's professional success and status were declared publically by his own handsome three-story palace in the Via Giulia (1534?–1543), and by the beginnings of a second, larger Sangallo residence (Palazzo Sacchetti, 1543) in the same street in Rome.

The immense productivity of Antonio the Younger was facilitated by an efficient workshop made up of collaborating family members. The group was somewhat disdainfully dubbed the *setta sangallesca* (Sangallo sect) by GIORGIO VASARI, but it may be considered the veritable prototype of the modern architectural firm. Its activity is documented by several thousand drawings of antique monuments, contemporary buildings, and ongoing Sangallo projects now kept in the Cabinetto dei Disegni of the Uffizi Gallery, Florence. Many drawings were done by Antonio the Younger's brother, Giovanni Battista called Il Gobbo ("the hunchback," 1496–1552), who produced an illustrated translation of VITRUVIUS's *De architectura,* now in the Biblioteca Corsiniana, Rome. Further assistance was provided by Giovanni Francesco (1482–1530) and Bastiano, called Aristotele (1484–1551), sons of Maddalena Giamberti, a sister of Giuliano and Antonio the Elder. Giovanni Francesco assisted Raphael at St. Peter's, the Villa Madama, and the Palazzo Pandolfini in Florence, and he worked on fortifications at Cortona, Leghorn, Pistoia, and Pisa. Bastiano, who was a painter and celebrated scenographer, assisted at St. Peter's before superintending the fortifications of Antonio the Younger at Florence, Castro, and Perugia. Francesco, called Il Margotta (1494–1576), was the son of Giuliano. A successful sculptor, he collaborated with Antonio the Elder at Montepulciano, and carried out fortification work for the Florentine Republic at Pistoia, Prato, and Florence. In 1543, he succeeded Baccio d'Agnolo as chief architect of the Cathedral of Florence.

RICHARD J. TUTTLE

WORKS

GIULIANO DA SANGALLO

1472?–1480?, Palazzo of Bartolomeo Scala (now Ghirardesca), Florence. 1480–1497?, Villa Medici, Poggio a Caiano, Italy. 1484–1491, Santa Maria delle Carceri, Prato, Italy. 1489–1495, Santo Spirito (vestibule and sacristy; with Il Cronaca); 1490–1501, Palazzo Gondi; 1492, Santa Maria Maddalena dei Pazzi (atrium); Florence. 1494, Palazzo Rovere, Savona, Italy. 1499–1500, Basilica of the Santa Casa (cupola), Loreto, Italy. 1509–1512, Fortress, Pisa, Italy.

ANTONIO DA SANGALLO THE ELDER

1493, Castel Sant'Angelo (fortification and restoration), Rome. 1494–1497, Fortress, Civitacastellana, Italy. 1502–1507, Santissima Annunziata, Arezzo, Italy. 1506–1534, Fortezza Vecchia, Leghorn, Italy. 1517–1529, Loggia de'Servi (with Baccio d'Agnolo); Florence. 1518–1534, Madonna di San Biagio, Montepulciano, Italy.

ANTONIO DA SANGALLO THE YOUNGER

1515?–1519?, Castello Farnese, Capodimonte, Italy. 1515?–1519, Palazzo Baldassini; 1515?–1546, Palazzo Farnese; Rome. 1517, Chapel of the Sacrament, Cathedral, Foligno, Italy. 1517–1518, Serra Chapel, San Giacomo degli Spagnuoli, Rome. 1518?–1527, Palazzo Ferratini, Amelia, Italy. 1520?–1530?, Santa Maria di Loreto, Rome. 1521?–1527?, Castello Farnese, Caprarola, Italy. 1522–1527, Palazzo Regis (Le Roy or Farnesina) ai Baullari; 1525–1527, Zecca (Palazzo del Banco di Santo Spirito), Rome. 1526–1534, Apostolic Palace, Loreto, Italy. 1527–1535, Pozzo di San Patrizio, Orvieto, Italy. 1530, Cesi Chapel, Santa Maria della Pace, Rome. 1534–1536, Fortezza da Basso, Florence. 1534–1543, Casa Sangello in Via Giulia, Rome. 1536?, Palazzo Farnese, Gradoli, Italy. 1537, Papal Fortress, Ancona, Italy. 1537–1542, Bastione Ardeatina; 1538, Santo Spirito in Sassia (façade); 1538–1543, St. Peter's (wood model); 1540–1546, Pauline Chapel and Sala Regia, Vatican Palace; 1543–1546, Palazzo Sacchetti (Sangallo); 1543–1546, Fortifications of Vatican Borgo and Porta Santo Spirito; Rome.

GIULIANO DA SANGALLO AND ANTONIO DA SANGALLO THE ELDER

1495–1513, Fortifications of Poggio Imperial, near Poggibonsi, Italy. 1501–1503, Fortress, Nettuno, Italy. 1502–1503, Fortress, Arezzo, Italy. 1502–1505, Fortress, Borgo San Sepolcro, Italy.

BIBLIOGRAPHY

ACKERMAN, JAMES S. 1954 "Architectural Practice in the Italian Renaissance." *Journal of the Society of Architectural Historians* 13:3–11.

CLAUSSE, GUSTAVE 1900–1902 *Les San Gallo.* 3 vols. Paris: Leroux.

FABRICZY, CORNELIUS VON 1902*a* "Giuliano da Sangallo: Chronologischer Prospekt." *Jahrbuch der Preussischen Kunstsammlungen* 23:1–42.

FABRICZY, CORNELIUS VON 1902*b* *Die Handzeichnungen Giulano's da San Gallo.* Stuttgart, Germany: Gerschel.

FALB, RUDOLF (editor) 1902 *Il taccuino senese di Giuliano da San Gallo.* Siena, Italy: The author.

FOSTER, PHILIP ELLIS 1978 *A Study of Lorenzo de' Medici's Villa at Poggio a Caiano.* New York and London: Garland.

FROMMEL, CHRISTOPHER L. 1964 "Antonio da Sangallos Cappella Paolina." *Zeitschrift für Kunstgeschichte* 27:1–42.

FROMMEL, CHRISTOPHER L. 1973 *Der römische Palastbau der Hochrenaissance.* 3 vols. Tübingen, Germany: Wasmuth.

GIOVANNONI, GUSTAVO 1959 *Antonio da Sangallo: Il Giovane.* Rome: Tipografia Regionale.

HUELSEN, CHRISTIAN VON (editor) 1910 *Il libro di Giuliano da Sangallo: Codice Vaticano Barberiniano latino 4424.* 2 vols. Leipzig: Harrassowitz.

LISNER, MARGRIT 1969 "Zum bildhauerischen Werk der Sangallo." *Pantheon* 27, March:99–119; May:190–208.

MARCHINI, GIUSEPPE 1943 *Giuliano da Sangallo.* Florence: Sansoni.

MIARELLI MARIANI, GAETANO 1976 "La critica del Vasari e la setta sangallesca." Pages 567–585 in *Il Vasari storiografe e artista: Atti del Congresso internazionale, 1974.* Florence: Istituto Nazionale di Studi sul Rinascimento.

SEVERINI, GIANCARLO 1970 *Architetture militari di Giuliano da Sangallo.* Pisa, Italy: Lischi.

VASARI, GIORGIO (1568)1973 *Le opere di Giorgio Vasari, con nuove annotazioni e commenti.* 9 vols. Edited by G. Milanesi. Reprint. Florence: Sansoni. Originally published in 1550 with the title *Le vite de più eccelenti architetti.* There are many English translations and selections from Vasari's *Lives;* the standard one by G. du C. de Vere was published in ten volumes in London by the Medici Society in 1912–1915.

SANMICHELI, MICHELE

The most versatile of the great High Renaissance architects of northern Italy, Michele Sanmicheli (1484/1485–1559) is as distinguished for his masterpieces of military architecture as for his achievements in ecclesiastical and secular design, of which he executed an almost unparalleled variety both in public and private commissions. Together with JACOPO SANSOVINO, he was principally responsible for introducing into Venetian dominions the developed central Italian mode of High Renaissance architecture, as both had practiced it in Rome. But Sanmicheli had the distinction unique in this pivotal epoch (a distinction shared among Renaissance architects of this rank only by ANDREA PALLADIO, a generation later) of being a native subject of the Venetian Republic. He was born in Verona into a substantial family of masons, deriving from Porlezza in Lombardy. His father, Giovanni, had moved to Verona by 1482, and worked on the civic Loggia until 1493. He died shortly afterward, although GIORGIO VASARI (who as a close friend is the principal contemporary source for information about Sanmicheli) said that Michele received his early training from his father and his uncle Bartolomeo. The latter had come with his brother to Verona, bringing his two young sons, Paolo and Matteo. Paolo worked as a lifelong collaborator with his distinguished cousin; since Michele remained unmarried, Paolo's son Giangirolamo became Michele's most brilliant disciple, specializing in works of fortification.

Sanmicheli as a youthful apprentice must have had almost as keen an interest in Verona's great relics of Roman antiquity as in recent models of early Renaissance architecture in the Veneto, particularly since the relationship between these styles strongly preoccupied his influential Veronese compatriots, FRA GIOCONDO and GIOVANNI MARIA FALCONETTO. But Vasari tells us that he went at the age of sixteen to Rome, the essential proving-ground of both ancient and modern classicism; and there, in 1500 or 1501, he must have come immediately and profoundly under the influence of DONATO BRAMANTE. It has even been suggested that Sanmicheli constitutes Bramante's most authentic successor, and this is true to the extent that Bramante afforded him the continuing vision of a grave and sober monumentality, inventively adapted to the creation of a new "imperial" architecture. Indeed, Michele as a north Italian already sensitive to antiquity seems to have felt a congenial rapport with the remaining Urbinate and Lombard components of Bramante's style, to an extent not shared even by a fellow student of these same years, his close friend and contemporary, Antonio da Sangallo the Younger (see SANGALLO FAMILY), who came to Rome in 1503. Antonio, trained in the context of a similar but more distinguished family of Florentine architects, seems to have gravitated naturally to the "purer" classicism of RAPHAEL's architectural idiom, which informs his own dry and correct style. Only a year or eighteen months Sanmicheli's senior, he called Michele by the nickname "el Verona," and the two remained closely associated through the full quarter-century of Michele's central Italian career.

It was probably Antonio's and Michele's mutual patron Cardinal Giulio de' Medici, later Pope Clement VII, who obtained Sanmicheli's first independent professional appointment as superintendent of works at Orvieto Cathedral, in November of 1509—a post he held, with brief interruptions, for fifteen years. In supervising the vast façade, on whose upper parts his work was concentrated, Michele gained practical experience in two complementary aspects of Renaissance architecture, engineering and design, although Sangallo was frequently consulted in the latter activity and Sanmicheli's preponderant contribution at Orvieto seems to have been technical. Even in two more private commissions, a funeral chapel for an Orvietan family and the main body of Montefiascone Cathedral (1519?; apparently requested of him by Cardinal Alessandro Farnese, later Pope Paul III), Sanmicheli produced essentially two variants on his friend Sangallo's plan (1507) of Santa Maria di Loreto in Rome: the internal spaces of both the Cappella Petrucci (1516–1523) and the upper church in Montefiascone are niched octagons, examples of a centralized design to which Sanmicheli was to return in his late villa chapel at Fumane (1558?), and, with variants, in his projects for the Lazzaretto chapel and the Madonna di Campagna in Verona.

The successive, mature phase of Michele's career was launched when Clement VII, threatened by the foreign military pressures that were to culminate in the Sack of Rome in 1527, dispatched Sangallo and Sanmicheli together on a tour of inspection and repair of city walls in the northern tier of the Papal States, on the borders of Lombardy and Emilia. They surveyed the fortifications at Ravenna, Rimini, Cesena, Forlì, Faenza, and Imola; more important, they supervised new works at Parma and especially at Piacenza, where Sanmicheli was personally responsible for strengthening the civic defenses during the early months of 1526. The experience exercised a decisive influence on his professional development. He may possibly have assisted Bramante on the fortification of Civitàvecchia (1508); but we know nothing of the intervening experience, before 1526, that must have recommended him as a papal consultant on military engineering. In this context, however, it is perhaps especially indicative that his colleague Antonio had continued work on the same fortress at Civitàvecchia, in 1515–1519. Antonio had been trained in the orbit of Giuliano da Sangallo and Antonio da Sangallo the elder, both of whom are now recognized to have figured critically in the development of the modern fortification system that combined triangular bastions with thick curtain walls as adaptations to the increasing use of heavy artillery. Vasari claimed that Michele invented this system, but in fact he seems to have learned its rudiments from the accumulated experience of the Sangallo family: Sanmicheli's pre-eminence lay in designing and constructing its earliest massive application, in the colossal chain of walls, bastions, and gates with which he was commissioned by the Venetian Republic to fortify his native town of Verona.

How and exactly when Michele became a consultant on the fortifications of Verona is not clearly understood; we know that he had returned home by the winter of 1526–1527, and that a date of 1527 was inscribed on the first example of the new system to be adopted at Verona, the triangular bastion of the Maddalene. This seminal work (the earliest such bastion surviving in Europe) is mentioned in documents as the work of a competitor whom Sanmicheli almost immediately replaced, an engineer named Michele da Leoni. It is smaller than Sanmicheli's immediately successive examples, and it stands on the left (east) bank of the Adige, while his documented versions all defend the right bank, along a new perimeter connecting two major bends in the river. Even so, it seems most highly unlikely that Sanmicheli's presence in Verona should not be reflected (at least by consultation, as a contemporary annalist in fact implied) in the design of this epoch-making bastion, prefiguring as it does a form of which he was immediately and decisively to become the acknowledged master.

Michele's thirty-year sequence of official appointments to the government of Venice, its mainland territories, and its overseas empire now seems most likely to have developed as a consequence of an initial and highly prestigious private commission, documented by the one surviving drawing which can reasonably be identified as his—a beautiful plan of 1528 in the Correr Museum in Venice for a palace project on the Grand Canal. It was made for the exceedingly influential Procurator of Saint Mark, Vettor Grimani, the major patron of Sansovino; Grimani's closest associate in the Procuracy (the principal agency for public commissions in the city center of Venice) was his fellow officer Antonio Cappello, who was serving in 1528 as Venetian commander at the river port of Legnago, in the southern Veneto. Here, Sanmicheli obtained his first documented Venetian appointment, with a commission to fortify the twin centers of Legnago and Porto on opposite banks of the Adige. The two halves of his star-shaped plan created a single fortress whose brilliant design attracted the enthusiastic admiration of the Venetian commander-in-chief, Francesco Maria della Rovere, duke of Urbino; under this high patronage, Michele's official career was assured, and his superintendence of the fortifications of Verona was established in the following year. Shortly afterward, he and the duke made an inspection tour of Venetian citadels, from Chiusa in the Friuli through Padua, Vicenza, Peschiera, and Brescia, to Orginuovi and Bergamo on the Lombard frontier; for all of them the architect eventually designed new fortifications, as he did as well for the duke's own fortress of Senigallia in the Urbinate. Sanmicheli's expertise in military architecture soon attracted wide attention and foreign requests so persuasive that the Republic was obliged early in 1531, for example, to lend him for three months to their ally Francesco II Sforza, duke of Milan. Michele prepared an impessive series of designs, to the immense gratification of that prince, for his fortress cities of Alessandria, Pavia, and Lodi.

But the Venetian Republic had by now fully grasped the extraordinary strategic importance of Michele's skills, and—under the direct supervision of the Council of Ten—he was dispatched early in the 1530s on a lifelong series of appointments to create and maintain a network of modern fortresses in the Venetian empire overseas. The towns in the Levant whose fortifications he personally inspected, with the dates of his designs as they are known, include Capodistria (Koper) on the Istrian peninsula (in 1550); the three cities of Zara (Zadar, 1534 and 1537), Sebenico (Šibenik, before 1556), and Cattaro (Kotor, c.1547) on the Dalmatian coast; Corfu in 1537–1538 and 1542–1543; presumably Nauplion (?); Famagosta in Cyprus (before 1559); and, most important, the four great citadels of Crete: Candia (Heraklion, 1539–1591), Chania (1538), Rettimo (1539), and Sitia. Since fortification architecture necessarily changed with technological developments in warfare, none of Michele's fortresses (except his works at Verona) remains intact. Chania and especially Candia, whose bulk stupefied contemporary observers, were his masterpieces in the Levant; for Zara (1534–1543) and Sebenico (1556) he designed splendid gates, but these were actually built with modifications by Giangirolamo Sanmicheli; the one at Zadar survives and is a fine example of the latter's style.

Michele's extensive criss-crossing of the Adriatic, Ionian, and Aegean seas brought him—as perhaps the unique Renaissance architect of the West—into constant association with the ancient centers of Hellenic architecture: we may plausibly expect him to have had a first-hand acquaintance of the ruins of Athens, as he certainly did of the Morea and the Archipelago. He not only knew baseless Doric to have been the primary order in Greek art, but used it (with rusticated drums) on the city façade of his Porta Palio (1548–1550) in Verona; Vasari specifically noted its appearance there and recognized the whole work as "the crowning miracle" of Michele's career. Indeed, it displays both aspects of his genius in that it presents a novel and compelling architectural image and dominates the center of his stupendous triple triad of the Verona walls (where three great gates are each flanked by two bastions, making a nine-part sequence of outer defenses). Sanmicheli's most impressive achievement, however, is that he resisted narrow specialization in the military architecture of which he became the foremost European authority; many of his private buildings also at-

Sanmicheli.
Porta del Palio.
Verona, Italy.
1548–1559

Sanmicheli.
Palazzo Bevilacqua.
Verona, Italy.
Before 1532?

tained an exceptional distinction, and some reached the exalted level of the Porta Palio and the Porta Nuova, which Vasari aptly characterized as "highly advanced, extremely original, and very beautiful."

Sanmicheli's early palace designs are precocious manifestations of High Renaissance design in the north, coming as they do immediately on the heels of the Sack of Rome. His project of 1528 for Vettor Grimani's palace on the Grand Canal is a masterly adaptation of Roman grandeur to a Venetian site, in addition to being one of the most distinguished drawings of its date and type. Although not built, its elements were directly incorporated into the planning of Palazzo Canossa, Michele's first securely dated palace in Verona. The latter's patron was the bishop of Bayeux, who also ordered Sanmicheli's delicate choir screen in Verona Cathedral and who recommended the architect to his son-in-law, who commissioned Michele's splendidly detailed Palazzo Bevilacqua. Both the Venetian palace project and the roughly contemporaneous Palazzo Lavezola-Pompei (1527–1535?) in Verona show strong evidences of influence from SEBASTIANO SERLIO, who also reached Venice from Rome by the spring of 1528. It was doubtless through Serlio that Michele had access to the drawings of BALDASSARE PERUZZI (whom he may also have known in Rome); partly on the basis of them, he developed his imaginative plan for the Villa Soranzo, which he arranged to have frescoed by his young friends Paolo Veronese and Giambattista Zelotti. Among his other painter friends, Sanmicheli was also particularly close to Torbido, Vasari, and Titian; he knew MICHELANGELO well, and in Venice he frequented the sophisticated humanist circle of Cardinal Pietro Bembo, whose commemorative monument he designed in the Santo at Padua. Working on the fortifications of Padua in 1539–1540, he met Alvise Cornaro and Giangiorgio Trissino and became one of the principal influences on the artistic development of their mutual protégé, Palladio. The broad cultural awareness that Michele derived from such associates is reflected in the extraordinarily open-minded inventiveness with which he approached his commissions: apropos of another monument in Padua (that of his patron Alessandro Contarini), Sanmicheli remarked that its unusual pyramidal configuration signaled a new approach to tomb design by freeing the genre from conceptual dependence on the formal patterns of chapels and altars (as reported by Vasari).

Sanmicheli's finest ecclesiastical work is his early Cappella Pellegrini (1527–1557) in Verona, and his greatest domestic achievement is his last, the magnificent palace that he began in 1557 for Girolamo Grimani on the Grand Canal in Venice. The domed cylinder of the Pellegrini Chapel

Sanmicheli.
Pellegrini Chapel, Church of San Bernardino.
Verona, Italy.
1527?–1557

Sanmicheli.
Palazzo Grimani at San Luca.
Venice, Italy.
1557–1559 (not completed until 1561–1568 by Grigi and 1570–1575 by Rusconi)

(1527–1557) is delicately detailed, serene and abstracted on its perfectly centralized plan; the more elaborate internal membering of its lower zone creates the illusion of an expanded diameter above the cornice and of a great floating hemisphere of quietly articulated space. The Palazzo Grimani, which may justly be called the quintessential Renaissance palace, is sober and imposing in its image of republican gravity, but conceived on a truly imperial scale. Its powerful order and arcades, brilliantly disposed in a far grander configuration than had been achieved even in Rome itself, accentuate a dominant skeletal structure within which the traditional Venetian wall planes are almost dissolved away. Its forms constitute a triumphant revival of the ancient empire, but its mode of distilled monumentality evokes Hellenic experience as well. This inspired union of Eastern severity and Western grandeur, at a level of sublime quality and on a vast scale, give both it and its inventor a unique place in European architecture.

DOUGLAS LEWIS

WORKS

1513–1532, Cathedral (partial completion of central gable); 1514–1559, Cathedral (spires, not completed until 1590); 1516–1523, Crypt Chapel and *Chancel Tomb of Girolamo Petrucci, Church of San Domenico; Orvieto, Italy. 1519?, Cathedral (main body), Montefiascone, Italy. 1527?–1535?, Palazzo Lavezola (Pompei); 1527?–1557, Pellegrini Chapel, Church of San Bernardino; Verona, Italy. 1528–1535, Legnago Fortifications, Italy. 1528–1535, Porta San Martino, Legnago, Italy. 1529/1531–1537, Palazzo Canossa; 1530–1531, Barbarigo Bastion; before 1532?, Palazzo Bevilacqua; Verona, Italy. (A)1532?–1537, Palazzo Grimani at San Severo, Venice, Italy. 1533, Palazzo del Podesta (portal); 1533–1551, Porta Nuova; 1534–1541, Cathedral (choir screen); 1535, Faler Bastion; Verona, Italy. 1535, 1543–1544, Fort of San Andrea, opposite Lido, Venice, Italy. 1538, San Bernardino Bastion, Verona, Italy. After 1538?, Palazzo Bragadin (portal) at Santa Formosa, Venice. (A)1538–1542, Villa Brenzone, Punta San Vigilio del Garda, Italy. 1539–1556, Corner Bastion, Padua, Italy. *1539?–1542, Villa Corner, Piombino Dese, Italy. 1540, San Zeno Bastion, Verona, Italy. *1540–1551, Villa Soranzo (La Soranza), Treville di Castelfranco, Italy. 1541?, Villa Saraceno (Palazzo delle Trombe), Finale di Agugliaro, Italy. 1542, Palazzo Lando-Corner (Corner-Spinelli; remodeled main halls and ceiling with Giorgio Vasari), Venice, Italy. 1544–1558, Tomb of Alessandro Contarini; after 1547, Monument to Cardinal Pietro Bembo, Basilica of Sant'Antonio; Padua, Italy. 1547–1550, Porta San Zeno; 1547–1550, Spagna Bastion; 1547–1559, Church of Santa Maria in Organo (lower order of façade not completed until 1592); Verona, Italy. (A)1548–1556, Palazzo Gussoni at Santa Fosca, Venice, Italy. 1548–1559, Porta del Palio; 1551, San Francesco Bastion; Verona, Italy. (A)Before 1555, Palazzo Roncale, Rovigo, Italy. (A)1555, Bucintoro Boathouse (façade), Venice, Italy. (A)1555?, Palazzo Guastaverza, Verona, Italy. 1555–1564, Palazzo Corner at San Polo; 1557–1559, Palazzo Grimani at San Luca (completed 1561–1568 by Gian Giacomo dei Grigi, and 1570–1575 by Giannantonio Rusconi), Venice, Italy. 1558?, Chapel of Villa Della Torre, Fumane, Italy. Before 1559, Dome (completed 1604) and Campanile, Church of San Giorgio in Braida; 1559, Church of the Madonna di Campagna (constructed 1559–1561), Verona, Italy.

BIBLIOGRAPHY

GAZZOLA, PIERO (editor) 1960 *Michele Sanmicheli; Catalogo.* Venice, Italy: Neri Pozza.

LANGENSKIÖLD, ERIK 1938 *Michele Sanmicheli, the Architect of Verona: His Life and Works.* Uppsala, Sweden: Almqvist & Wiksells.

LEWIS, DOUGLAS 1972 "Un disegno autografo del Sanmicheli." *Bollettino dei Musei Civici Veneziani* 27, nos. 3–4:7–36.

Michele Sanmichele: studi raccolti dall'Accademia di Agricoltura, Scienze e Lettere di Verona. 1960 Verona, Italy: Valdonega.

PUPPI, LIONELLO 1971 *Michele Sanmicheli: Architetto di Verona.* Padua, Italy: Marsilio.

VASARI, GIORGIO 1960 *Michele Sanmichele: Architettore veronese.* Verona, Italy: Valdonega.

VASARI, GIORGIO (1568)1973 *Le opere di Giorgio Vasari, con nuove annotazioni e commenti.* 9 vols. Edited by G. Milanesi. Reprint. Florence: Sasoni. Originally published in 1550 with the title *Le vite de più eccelenti architetti.* There are English translations and selections from Vasari's *Lives;* the standard one by G. du C. de Vere was published in ten volumes in London by the Medici Society in 1912–1915.

SANSOVINO, JACOPO

Jacopo Sansovino (1486–1570), the eldest son of Antonio (1460–1531) and Francesca Tatti, was baptized in the Florentine parish of San Pier Maggiore on 3 July 1486; he died in Venice, where he spent the great majority of his working life. He very early came to be called by the toponymic applied also to his teacher, Andrea Contucci, as a reference to the latter's native town of Monte San Savino in Tuscany. Like Contucci, whose shop in Florence he is thought to have entered in 1502, Jacopo became a proficient master in both sculpture and architecture; but unlike his master, Jacopo's brilliance and creative powers as an architect were fully equal to his celebrated talents as a sculptor. In this sense, his career as well as his sculptural and architectural oeuvres are paralleled most closely by the similar achievements—at an even more extraordinary level—of MICHELANGELO, whose compatriot and rival he was. But a more fundamental difference than the subjective index of quality distinguishes Michelangelo and Sansovino, as the dominant mid-sixteenth-century architects respectively of Central and Northern Italy. The artistic ferment of Florence and Rome encouraged Michelangelo's inventive genius to the constant creation of wholly new architectural forms: the force of his reputation then established this idiosyncratic vocabulary as one of the principal sources of a revolutionary Mannerist style, which became the dominant Central Italian mode for the remainder of the sixteenth century. In a parallel of influence but in sharp contrast of effect, Sansovino was inspired by the social and artistic conservatism of his adopted Venice to perpetuate a confident image of High Renaissance classicism far beyond the heyday of Mannerist experimentation, so successfully that his personal style may be said to have shaped the development of Venetian architecture from the middle of the sixteenth through the end of the eighteenth centuries.

During his Florentine apprenticeship of 1502–1505, Sansovino was influenced by his master Andrea principally in sculpture; the latter's close associate Giuliano da Sangallo (see SANGALLO FAMILY) seems to have been his mentor in architecture. Andrea's and Giuliano's collaboration on the vestibule and sacristy of Santo Spirito (1488–1496), for example, would have provided Jacopo with a paradigm of brilliant spatial articulation, enlivened by a concentrated richness of classical ornament.

Following the election of Pope Julius II, both Andrea and Giuliano went to Rome, respectively in 1505 and 1506: Jacopo accompanied them, was lodged in Giuliano's house in the Borgo, and was introduced by him not only to Pope Julius, but also to DONATO BRAMANTE. Jacopo would have been intimately associated with this senior exponent of High Renaissance design through his assistance on Andrea Sansovino's tombs for two papal nephews in the choir that Bramante had just built for the Church of Santa Maria del Popolo. Andrea also became the supervising executant of Bramante's designs for the Santa Casa at Loreto, in the papal church which had been domed, and for which also façade projects had been submitted, by Giuliano da Sangallo.. Andrea's Popolo tombs and Giuliano's Loretan façade designs (Uffizi Gallery, Florence), as well as Bramante's Santa Casa, Palazzo Caprini, and other works all became formative influences on Jacopo's architectural style. Although during this first Roman sojourn of 1506–1511 he was obliged to devote himself rather to sculpture than to architecture, Jacopo did acquire (through his first recorded work, a bronze reduction of the newly discovered Laocoön) the loyal enthusiasm of his first crucially important Venetian patrons, Cardinal Domenico Grimani and his father Antonio Grimani. These wealthy Venetian noblemen were involved in excavating a splendid series of antique sculptures from the hillside property on which they were building a new villa, opposite the present Palazzo Barberini. Although there is no direct evidence or early tradition for Jacopo's involvement in the project, GIORGIO VASARI tells us that he was mainly occupied on his first residence in Rome with the restoration of antiquities; and his future relations with the Grimani family strongly suggest that he may also have had a hand in the design or execution of the Vigna Grimana on the Quirinal.

Jacopo returned to Florence around 1511 and remained there until the summer or fall of 1518. His architectural work in Florence is associated with the triumphal entry into the city of the Medici Pope, Leo X, on 30 November 1515. For this event, Sansovino created an elaborate temporary façade for the Florentine cathedral in wood and plaster, of which we have several contemporary descriptions. On the lower order there were three great arches framing the doors, placed between four pairs of colossal columns on high supporting blocks; the taller central portion of the façade was screened with an upper register of two more column pairs supporting a pediment. The twelve columns were coupled to enclose deep niches containing heroic sculptures; above these were bronze-colored figural reliefs, of which a *Story of Susanna* alone survives, in the Victoria and Albert Museum in London. Jacopo's festival screen (whose forms recur in many of his mature works) was thus intimately related to Giuliano da Sangallo's façade drawings mentioned above. These very projects, moreover, though apparently designed for Loreto before 1513, were reworked by Giuliano on the same sheets as entries in Pope Leo's 1515–1516 competition for the façade of the church of San Lorenzo in Florence. Sansovino and Michelangelo, as well as several other architects, were also involved in this competition. Because of the pope's enthusiasm for Jacopo's temporary cathedral façade, Jacopo at first seemed destined to receive the architectural commission for San Lorenzo, and Michelangelo the sculptural; but the latter's unwillingness to collaborate meant that Sansovino was eventually excluded, even after he had taken Baccio d'Agnolo's wooden model of his design to the papal court in 1516. In a letter of 30 June 1517, Jacopo bitterly protested Michelangelo's giving him no share even in the sculptures, in such vituperative terms that he must effectively have annulled any future professional relationships with Buonarroti. Within a year, Sansovino had moved once more to Rome.

The three years from 1518 to 1521 that Jacopo spent in the papal capital must have been among his most successful, although little now remains to document his architectural designs. His new residence in Rome is attested, however, by his presence on 23 October 1518 at an arbitration of the site for his first surviving building, the Palazzo Gaddi in the Via del Banco di Santo Spirito, at the southern end of the Ponte Sant'Angelo. Only the epitaph has been preserved from a tomb he was simultaneously commissioned to build for the Cardinal of Aragon (d.1519); the structure itself, perhaps, may never have been erected. His two earliest churches were approved for execution to his designs but were immediately assigned for construction (possibly in partnership or collaboration) to his colleague Antonio da Sangallo the Younger. For both the longitudinal plan of San Marcello (1519–?) and the centralized design of San Giovanni dei Fiorentini (1518–1521), in fact, we depend upon drawings by Antonio for our shadowy knowledge of Jacopo's projects; Vasari tells us only that Sansovino's design for San Giovanni (successfully submitted in competition with Sangallo, RAPHAEL, and BALDASSARE PERUZZI) had a large central dome with four smaller ones in the corners, and compares it to plates published by SEBASTIANO SERLIO.

Jacopo's son Francesco Sansovino was born in Rome in 1521, possibly early in the year; the architect's last recorded involvement with the foundations of San Giovanni dei Fiorentini is dated 7 January 1521. After this point Antonio da Sangallo took over that project, and Sansovino left Rome for the north (saving face, as Vasari tells us, by claiming the need to recuperate from a fall) even before a serious setback to papal patronage was occasioned by the death of Leo X at the end of the same year. It has been assumed that Jacopo returned to Florence; but in view of his recent rebuffs both there and in Rome it is far more likely that the election on 6 July 1521 of Antonio Grimani as doge of Venice was the magnet that drew Sansovino for the first time toward the city that would provide the bulk of his life's work. Francesco Sansovino repeatedly stated, both in print and in official depositions, that his father lived forty-seven years in Venice; but this span was not continuous, since Jacopo was in Rome again at least from 1525 to 1527. Calculating backward from his death date, therefore, we may regard it as virtually certain that Jacopo moved to Venice for the first time in 1521. This chronology has the advantage of clarifying several mysterious aspects of Jacopo's career. We may now understand why his next Roman tomb, for the newly rising Church of San Marcello, should commemorate a Venetian family of prelates: it was commissioned by Jacopo Orso of Chioggia in honor of his brother, the bishop of Agen (d.1511), and their uncle the Cardinal Sant'Angelo (d.1503). Vasari's undeveloped connection of Sansovino with the villa built in the Veneto in the 1520s by Federico Priuli is legitimized by that nobleman's very close kinship with the Grimani family: he was also an intimate friend of Federico Gonzaga of Mantua, with whom Sansovino is otherwise inexplicably connected by the time of the Sack of Rome in 1527. Finally, it was in 1521 that a sister of Marc'Antonio Giustinian, another prominent Venetian friend of Jacopo's, was married to the doge's grandson, Vettor Grimani, who became Sansovino's most powerful patron in Venice. After two years in which we must assume that he came to know Jacopo very well, Vettor was elected to the high office of Procurator of Saint Mark on 26 January 1523; his grandfather died on 7 May, and Doge Andrea Gritti was elected on the 20th; in the few weeks before the death on August 27th of Sansovino's early patron Cardinal Domenico Grimani, Jacopo had been recommended to the new doge (presumably by letter from Rome, through the cardinal's nephew Vettor) and given a ducal mandate to advise on the restoration of the domes of Saint Mark's. This great task in fact occupied

Sansovino.
Library of Saint Mark.
Venice, Italy.
1536–1560 (not completed until 1591 by Scamozzi)

Sansovino's first years in Venice, but it was suspended by one more intrusion of Roman events in his peripatetic life. On 18 November 1523, the Florentine Cardinal Giulio de' Medici was elected pope as Clement VII, and within a little over a year Jacopo had traveled south once more, under the promise of renewed activity on San Giovanni dei Fiorentini. That frustrating commission was decisively terminated by the Sack of Rome, and Jacopo fled for the last time to the north; stopping in Venice, he was persuaded by Doge Gritti to undertake further restorations on the ducal basilica, and he remained in Venice (save for one brief visit to Florence in 1540) for the rest of his life.

The triumphant history of Sansovino's career in Venice has been very thoroughly studied and is easily accessible in modern publications. His Venetian architectural works include four great public buildings, six churches, two charitable institutions, three large palaces, one surviving villa, and innumerable smaller projects, the most important of which are included in the list below. Barely more than eighteen months after his arrival, he was appointed (on 7 April 1529) as *Proto* or superintendent of the Procuracy of Saint Mark, the institution responsible for architectural activity in the center of the city; in this capacity he entered on a lifetime of professional collaboration with Vettor Grimani, the latter's associates Antonio Capello and Zuanne da Lezze, and other enlightened patrons who became thoroughly committed to his aesthetic principles and architectural policies. Chief among these was Sansovino's consistent effort to monumentalize and ennoble the Piazza San Marco: his Mint, Library, Loggetta, and church of San Geminiano were newly created as its four principal ornaments, and they were connected by continuous extensions of the Procuracies to form those stupendous combinations of open spaces and festive buildings that have achieved universal admiration since their completion in the seventeenth century. Together with his great Scala d'Oro (Golden Stair 1557–1558) in the Ducal Palace, these buildings not only brilliantly define the public forum of the Venetian state, but also uniquely encapsulate "the myth of Venice"—a vision of her government as the world's oldest and "Most Serene" Republic, heir to "a quarter and a half of a quarter of the ancient Empire," as her chronicles attested—in a profoundly persuasive and successful way. Indeed, Sansovino's most extraordinary achievement is that he managed to appropriate the Roman High Renaissance ideal of a *reborn* antique splendor as the expressive image of a *living* Mediterranean empire. His exalted architectural and sculptural iconographies might actually be recognized as having rallied Venetian confidence in this imperial destiny and (even as her overseas dominions fell away to the Turks) may thus have supported the concept of Venice's creative role in the Christian West—until all her institutions, including her long-standing architectural traditions, were overthrown by Napoleon.

It has sometimes been maintained that the architecture of Venice's last independent centuries was essentially neo-Palladian (see ANDREA PALLADIO); however, Sansovino's successor left neither palaces nor public buildings in the city, and even

Sansovino. Villa of Alvise Garzoni. Pontecasale, Italy. 1530s

Sansovino. Palazzo Corner (della Ca'Grande), San Maurizio. Venice, Italy. 1545?–1566

his famous churches (because they were so much more complex) were emulated not much more frequently than Sansovino's brilliantly simple cube and plain façade at San Martino (1540?–1570) or his harmonious oval at the Incurabili. What few public buildings were left to be built after Jacopo's regularization of the city center—the continuations by Vincenzo Scamozzi of the Library and Procuratie Nuove—became virtual reproductions of Sansovino's paradigms. In palace building, above all, the successive geniuses of Baldassare Longhena, Giuseppe Sardi, Domenico Rossi, and Giorgio Massari found no higher challenge than to rearticulate more plastic and more lively interpretations of Jacopo's soberly classical Palazzo Dolfin and Villa Garzoni, or especially the dominating majesty of his Ca'Corner—the biggest palace in the city and one of the most perfect adaptations of a Bramantesque idiom to the grandiose requirements of the later Renaissance and baroque.

Sansovino had many pupils intimately identified with his sculptural style, but no direct disciple in architecture: indeed, his greatest follower, Alessandro Vittoria, insensitively introduced a series of late Mannerist complexities to the façade for San Giuliano, (1566–1570) and also elsewhere was more interested in his own versions of originality than in perpetuating Sansovino's richly elaborated classical vocabulary.

Sansovino's Library of Saint Mark was hailed by no less a contemporary than Palladio as the finest work of architecture to be built since the time of the ancients, and it did in fact accomplish a radical reorientation of Venetian style. Its bold massing and deep three-dimensional articulation achieve an unusual structural power, dramatically enlivened by the intense chiaroscuro of its sculptural ornament. Like the Logetta beside it, the Marciana Library is perhaps more profoundly understood as an elaborate, civic-scaled sculpture than as a work of architecture. It was this dynamic interplay of form and structure that constituted Sansovino's principal legacy to succeeding generations, most brilliantly reinvoked in the following century by Baldassare Longhena.

Douglas Lewis

Sansovino. Piazza San Marco (loggetta). Venice, Italy. 1537–1540

WORKS

*(A), 1506–1511, Villa Grimani? (with others), Rome. *1515, Cathedral of Santa Maria del Fiore (wooden festival façade; with Andrea del Sarto); *1515, Wooden Triumphal Arch (for entry of Pope Leo X), Porta Sal Gallo, Florence. *1518–1521, San Giovanni dei Fiorentini (with Antonio Da Sangallo the Younger); 1518?–1530s, Palace of Giovanni Gaddi (Strozzi-Niccolini); *1519–1533, Santa Maria sopra Minerva (Monument of Cardinal Alvise of Aragon); 1519–?, San Marcello al Corso (rebuilding; with Sangallo); 1521?–1527, San Marcello al Corso (Monument of Giovanni Michiel, Cardinal of Sant'Angelo, and Antonio Orso, Bishop of Agen); Rome. *(A)1521/1525?–1531, Villa of Frederico Priuli (with others), Treville di Castelfranco, Italy. 1530s, Villa of Alvise Garzoni, Pontecasale, Italy. 1530–1532, Chapel of the Assumption and the Monument of Bishop Gelasio Nichesola, Verona Cathedral, Italy. 1531, Five Doric Shops, Ponte della Pescaria; 1531, 1535–1570, Scuola Grande della Misericordia (not completed until 1589); 1533–1570, San Francesca della Vigna; *mid-1530s–1542?, Santo Spirito in Isola (façade and choir); 1535–1547, State Mint (Zecca); Venice, Italy. 1536–1540, Santo Croce di Gerusalemme (Monument to Francisco Quiñones, Cardinal of Santa Croce), Rome. 1536–1560, Library of Saint Mark (not completed until 1591 by Vincenzo Scamozzi); 1536–1550, Palace of Giovanni Dolfin; 1536–?, Santa Maria Mater Domini (Altar of the Virgin and other work); 1537–1540, Piazza San Marco (loggetta); 1540?–1570, San Martino (not completed until 1633–1653); 1544–1562?, Palazzo Moro; 1545–1547, Ca' di Dio; 1545?–1566, Palazzo Corner (della Ca'Grande), San Maurizio; (A)1549?–1566, San Fantin (choir); 1553–1557/1562, 1566–1570, San Giuliano (with Alessandro Vittoria; not completed until 1593); *1554–1557, Fabbriche Nuove at Rialto; 1555, 1557–1558, Scala d'Oro (with Michele Sanmichele), Ducal Palace; 1555?–1561, San Salvatore (Monument of Doge Francesco Venier and other work); 1557–1558, San Geminiano (*façade, roof, and dome); 1557–1558, San Sebastiano (Monument of Archbishop Livio Podocataro); (A)1557–1570, Santa Maria dei Crociferi (now dei Gesuiti; Monument of the Da Lezze Family); (A)1558–1566, State Mint (third story); *1565–1568, Church of the Incurabili; 1568, San Basso (*sacristy and high altar); Venice, Italy.

BIBLIOGRAPHY

GIOVANNONI, GUSTAVO (1917)1935 "Un'opera sconosciuta di Jacopo Sansovino in Roma." Pages 121–142 in *Saggi sulla architettura del Rinascimento.* 2d rev. ed. Milan: Treves.

HOWARD, DEBORAH 1975 *Jacopo Sansovino: Architecture and Patronage in Renaissance Venice.* New Haven: Yale University Press.

HOWARD, DEBORAH 1981 *The Architectural History of Venice.* New York: Holmes & Meier; London: Batsford.

LEWIS, DOUGLAS 1972 "Un disegno . . . e la notizia del committente del Sansovino per S. Francesco della Vigna: Nuovi appunti per il mecenatismo artistico del Procuratore Vettor Grimani." *Bollettino dei Musei Civici Veneziani* 17, nos. 3–4: 7–36.

LEWIS, DOUGLAS 1979 "Sansovino and Venetian Architecture." *Burlington Magazine* 121, no. 910:38–41.

LORENZETTI, GIULIO 1929 *Itinerario sansoviniano a Venezia.* Venice, Italy: Comitato per le onoranze sansoviniane.

LOTZ, WOLFGANG (1963)1977 "The Roman Legacy in Sansovino's Venetian Buildings." Pages 140–151, 164–171 in *Studies in Italian Renaissance Architecture.* Cambridge, Mass.: M.I.T. Press.

MARIACHER, GIOVANNI 1962 *Il Sansovino.* Milan: Mondadori.

TAFURI, MANFREDO (1969)1972 *Jacopo Sansovino e l'architettura del '500 a Venezia.* Padua, Italy: Marsilio.

VASARI, GIORGIO (1568)1973 *Le opere di Giorgio Vasari, con nuove annotazioni e commenti.* 9 vols. Edited by G. Milanesi. Reprint. Florence: Sansoni. Originally published in 1550 with the title *Le vite de' più eccelenti . . . architettori.* There are many English translations and selections from Vasari's *Lives;* the standard complete translation by G. du C. de Vere was published in ten volumes by the Medici Society in 1912–1915.

SANT'ELIA, ANTONIO

For an architect with no built works safely attributed to him, Antonio Sant'Elia (1888–1916) has been an extraordinarily important figure in twentieth-century architecture. Sant'Elia's reputation hinges entirely on a brief manifesto published in his name in 1914 and on a series of drawings for a Futurist architecture and a Futurist city. Despite the modest proportions of his oeuvre, Sant'Elia's designs and ideas electrified many young Italian architects and helped usher in a new spirit in the architecture of postwar Italy; in addition, Sant' Elia's words and designs have since been viewed elsewhere as emblematic of the changes which occurred in architecture after World War I.

Born in Como, Sant'Elia studied architecture in Milan and subsequently in Bologna, where he completed his degree in 1912. He worked for municipal offices in Milan for a time, and although he finally set up his own practice in Milan, he primarily worked for other offices. During the brief period between 1914 and his departure with the Italian military in 1915, Sant'Elia was associated with a group of Italian artists who called themselves Futurists, including Carlo Carrà, Umberto Boccioni, GIACOMO BALLA, Gino Severini, and especially Filippo Tomaso Marinetti. As early as 1909, Marinetti had inaugurated the polemical activities of his Futurist group; the Futurists defined themselves as a group which exalted industrialism and technology as the hallmark of the world of the future. Into an Italian cultural environment where the dominant styles were classicism and Art Nouveau, but which was also beginning the explosive process of industrialization, the Futurists proclaimed a new vision of an art which exploited the aesthetic possibilities of air machines, electric power, and automobiles, and in which new materials of the new industrial age would replace the traditional materials of artists. Marinetti explicitly claimed that nothing matched the turbulent beauty of a power station, and Boccioni proposed to incorporate the decidedly untraditional materials of glass and metals into a new sculptural aesthetic; in both cases, the Futurist rebellion was implicitly aimed at the snobbism and static character of the dominant elite culture.

The exact point at which Sant'Elia came into contact with the Futurists is not known, but in 1911 and 1912 his designs were still heavily influenced by the Italian Secessionist movement. By 1912, however, Sant'Elia, MARIO CHIATTONE, and Ugo Nebbia had formed the *Nuove Tendenze* (New Tendencies) group, and in 1914 they held their first exhibit. The exhibition catalog carried a preface, the *Messaggio,* signed by Sant'Elia. Barely two months later, Sant'Elia's *Manifesto of Futurist Architecture* appeared, the text of which was much like that of the *Messaggio,* with the exception of some additions at the beginning and at the end and the frequent insertion of the words Futurist or Futurism. Exactly who was responsible for the additions is unknown, but there is reason to believe that the additions represent Marinetti's views. Italian scholars have expended considerable energy trying to dissociate Sant'Elia from Marinetti, largely because of the latter's subsequent enthusiastic involvement with Mussolini and Fascism. No reliable evidence exists to document the degree of influence which Marinetti exerted on Sant'Elia, but the important point is that Sant'Elia's ideas as expressed in the *Messaggio* were fully consistent with those of Marinetti's Futurism. Both Sant'Elia and Marinetti rejected the anachronistic aesthetics of the past and both embraced a cultural vision based upon a new social and technological order. The sections which were added to the *Messaggio* included more rhetorical flourishes but did not substantively alter Sant'Elia's ideas.

The document itself is a remarkable piece of work, especially since it was written before World War I and by a virtually unknown and untried architect. In the opening lines of the *Messaggio,* Sant'Elia declared that the new architecture did not consist of a decorative style but rather of an acceptance of the special conditions of modern life and, with this, the willingness to employ all available scientific and technological resources to create a new house responsive to the demands of modern life. No longer could tradition guide the building process, for new materials such as reinforced concrete ruled out the old canons of architecture and totally altered the methods of construction. Sant'Elia further observed that forcing light and slender reinforced concrete support systems to imitate old and massive supporting members was simply grotesque—an observation which Rationalist architects were to take up with particular vigor during the 1920s and 1930s. Buildings could no longer be monumental, heavy, and static—no more cathedrals and assembly halls, but rather railroad stations, superhighways, and colossal ports. Sant'Elia envisioned a new city in which dynamism was the informing motif: externally visible elevators, glass, concrete and iron giving visual shape to an architecture of dynamic simplicity. From the problem of the individual decorative element, Sant'Elia urged a broader view which encompassed larger masses, even to the level of the city. Following a ringing denunciation of ornament, Sant'Elia concluded the *Messaggio* with a summary of three terse denunciations of what he despised and four proclamations of what the principles underlying the new architecture should be.

Whether or not Sant'Elia knew the Futurists before he composed his *Messaggio,* the affinity of his ideas to those of the Futurists is unmistakable: both perceived a world characterized by a high degree of mobility and by an increasingly sophisticated technology. Marinetti's additions to the *Messaggio* also inveighed against the attempt to mask the modern building skeleton with carnival decorations, and ridiculed the sterility of empty formal exercises. As a corollary to the anti-monumentalism of Sant'Elia's *Messaggio,* Marinetti added the specific claim that the new architecture would be transient: each generation would have to build its own city, and people would outlast their houses.

The *Nuove Tendenze* exhibit consisted of drawings by Sant'Elia and Chiattone, and these drawings, along with many more which Sant'Elia executed between 1912 and 1915, presented images of the new city and new architecture of which the architects dreamed. From the rough sketches of "Architectural Dynamism" to the more fully rendered and detailed images of modern urban sites, Sant'Elia evinced a unified perception of the shape of the architecture of the future. Powerful as these images are, perhaps even more important was Sant'Elia's acknowledgment of the centrality of communications and movement in his vision of Milan in the year 2000. The concept which underlay his city was a transportation network often three to seven levels deep from which the tall shafts of apartments and offices emerge. He even placed an airplane runway on one level of a rebuilt central train station for Milan.

Despite the adamant insistence in the *Messaggio* and the *Manifesto* that in the new age architects should be antimonumental, clearly the architecture of Sant'Elia's vision is monumental, even if it is not dedicated to church and aristocracy but to industry and the machine. Perhaps the most ironic testimony of this is the monument to Sant'Elia in his hometown of Como. Built under the guidance of ENRICO PRAMPOLINI and GIUSEPPE TERRAGNI, the design of the structure is based upon Sant'Elia's rough sketches of "Architectural Dynamism" and is a monument to both the dead of World War I and the architect himself. But the monumental scale and exuberant presence of the structures Sant'Elia conceived is here reduced to modest, even puny, dimensions, almost a caricature of the mammoth buildings Sant'Elia planned them to be. That precious few of these architectural visions were rendered in plan or elevation, thus underlining their monumentality, and that they are uncompromisingly symmetrical betrays the fact that the rupture with traditional canons was not as complete as Sant'Elia asserted it to be in the *Messaggio.*

Nonetheless, the novelty and audacity of Sant'Elia's ideas are undeniable; he may have been influenced by the Parisian Gustave Kahn in his proposals for a multilevel, multifunctional transportation grid binding together the various parts of his city, but Sant'Elia gave expression to a far more comprehensive and in many ways eerily prophetic program. It is impossible to speculate on what direction his work might have taken after World War I; his death on the battlefield in 1916, two months after the death of Boccioni, not only cut off a promising architectural career but also arrested the further development of a Futurist architectural program. Marinetti doggedly promoted Sant'Elia's *Manifesto* and drawings following the war, keeping alive both his memory and the powerful images themselves. Sant'Elia's skyscraper city certainly remained the most potent image, but the ideas in the *Messaggio* and *Manifesto* were picked up first outside of Italy—probably influencing LE CORBUSIER among others—and eventually in Italy as well, particularly the insistence on the structural and hence aesthetic possibilities of new materials. In the late 1920s and 1930s, the young generation of Italian architects often viewed itself as having assumed the mantle of Sant'Elia. A volume of essays published in 1935, *Dopo Sant'Elia* (Milan: Editoriale Domus), recognized the fundamental changes in the conception of architecture which had occurred in the twentieth century and accepted Sant'Elia's work as marking off the new era from the old. Although the formal components of Italian architecture during the Fascist period drew more upon sources outside of Italy, Sant'Elia remained an inspiration and the spiritual ancestor of many of Italy's most important architects in the twentieth century.

DIANE GHIRARDO

BIBLIOGRAPHY

BANHAM, REYNER (1960)1970 Pages 99–137 in *Theory and Design in the First Machine Age.* New York: Praeger.

CALVESI, MAURIZIO 1958 "Il futurista Sant'Elia: Un'analisi del 'Manifesto.'" Volume 1, pages 110–129 in *Le due avanguardie: Studi sul futurismo.* Bari, Italy: Laterza.

FRAMPTON, KENNETH 1980 *Modern Architecture: A Critical History.* New York and Toronto: Oxford University Press.

SANT'ELIA, ANTONIO (1914)1970 "Messaggio" and "Manifesto of Futurist Architecture." In Ulrich Conrads (editor), *Programs and Manifestoes on 20th-Century Architecture.* Translated by Michael Bullock. Cambridge, Mass.: M.I.T. Press.

TISDALL, CAROLINE, and BOZZOLLA, ANGELO 1977 *Futurism.* London: Thames & Hudson.

VENTURY, LIONELLO; PICA, AGNOLDOMENICO; PAGANO, GIUSEPPE ET AL. 1935 *Dopo Sant'Elia.* Milan: Domus.

SANTI DI TITO

Primarily a painter but also an architect, Santi di Tito (1536–1603) was born in Sansepolcro, Italy, and did most of his work in and around Florence, Italy. Santi worked in a neo-fifteenth-century style with touches of Mannerism. His major architectural accomplishment, the Palazzo Zanchini in Florence (1583–?), combined elements derived from DONATO BRAMANTE, the BAGLIONI FAMILY, and BARTOLOMMEO AMMANNATI.

CHARLES RANDALL MACK

WORKS

1568–1569, San Tommaso d'Aquino (oratory); (A)c.1571, San Pier Gattolini (façade); 1583–?, Palazzo Zanchini; (A)1586–?, Santa Maria in Campo; Florence. 1599–1603, Convento di San Michele a Doccia (not completed until 1605), Fiesole, Italy. c.1600, Casa di Santi di Tito; c.1600, Palazzo Nonfinito (grand staircase); Florence. c.1600, Pieve cupola, Monte Vetturini, Italy. c.1600, Villa dei Collazzi, Florence. c.1600, Villa Le Corti, San Casciano Val de Pesa, Italy. c.1600, Villa Strozzi ("il Boschetto" a Monteoliveto), Florence.

BIBLIOGRAPHY

ARNOLDS, GÜNTER 1934 *Santi di Tito, pittore di*

Sansepoloro. Arezzo, Italy: Petrarca.
BORSI, FRANCO 1974 Pages 364–370 in *Firenze del Cinquecento.* Rome: Editalia.
BUCCI, MARIO 1971–1973 *Palazzi di Firenze.* 4 vols. Florence: Vallecchi.
CHIARELLI, RENZO 1939 "Contributi a Santi di Tito architetto." *Rivista d'arte* 21:126–155.

SANTINI AICHEL, JAN BLAŽEJ

Jan Blažej (Johann Blasius) Santini Aichel (Aichl) (1677–1723) was one of the most important architects of the eighteenth century in Bohemia and indeed one of the most interesting creative figures of his time in Europe. Born in Prague, the grandson of the *Baumeister* Antonín Aichel, Aichel's family may have originated in the Ticino area near Lake Lugano, whence came so many other artists and architects, such as FRANCESCO BORROMINI, and particularly a host of architects and *Baumeister* who were active in Bohemia, including Pietro Ferrabosco, Giovanni Baptista Alliprandi, and Carlo Lurago, with whom Antonín Aichl was befriended. Santini Aichel was the eldest child of the stonemason Santin Aichel, who worked in Prague and was associated with Jean Baptiste Mathey.

Although it is possible that Santini Aichel received some instruction either from his father or from Mathey, he was in fact trained as a painter, perhaps with the Imperial Painter Christian Schröder. He ended his formal training around 1696, and it is likely that he thereafter spent two or three *Wanderjahre* traveling abroad. Santini Aichel's itinerary can only be surmised from the influences that are presumably found in his later work: from them it can be hypothesized that he visited Austria, where he could have seen the work of JOHANN BERNHARD FISCHER VON ERLACH, and Italy, where he could have seen the architecture of Borromini.

Around 1700, Santini Aichel returned to Bohemia, where he is documented as having been employed by the Cistercian cloister at Zbraslav (Königsaal) near Prague. In the early years of his career until 1704, he is known to have worked with his brother Jakub František (Jakob Franz). Later, either because of his own original lack of training or because of increasing demands for his services, Santini Aichel collaborated with a number of *Baumeister,* masons, and architects, and, most important, with the architect František (Franz) Maximilian Kaňka, who completed several buildings designed by Santini after his death. Although Santini Aichel personally directed the construction of several churches himself, including those at Kladruby (1716) and Rajhrad (1721–1723), he is more often documented as a draftsman and designer of projects. He is also known to have given advice on projects he did not himself design. Santini Aichel may thus be regarded as representing the beginnings of a move toward separation and specialization in the stages of the design process in Bohemian architecture.

Santini's work at Zbraslav began a long association with the older ecclesiastical orders in Bohemia, who continued to provide him with a major source of patronage. The Cistercians, Benedictines, and Premonstratensians all gave him important commissions, and a Cistercian even referred to him later as "unser Santini" (our Santini).

Santini Aichel's first major commission for the Cistercians, his design of the Church of the Assumption of the Virgin at Sedlec (1702–1705), also gives early evidence of his imagination as a designer. At Sedlec, the abbot Jindřich Snopek, after having first employed Pavel Ignaz Bayer, engaged Santini to reconstruct the church which had been the order's first in Bohemia, but which had remained a ruin since its destruction by the Hussites in 1421 and again during the Thirty Years' War. At Sedlec, Santini Aichel consequently used an essentially Gothic vocabulary that recalls the past age of glory of the Roman Catholic Church in Bohemia, but in a way that no medieval architect would have done. The ribs on the vaults of the nave and choir serve no functional purpose, but like the tracery of the windows form an almost playful interlace that is reminiscent of architecture of the Jagellonian period in Bohemia, as exemplified in the oeuvre of Benedikt Ried (REJT). The balloon vaults in the side aisles of the church are also not to be found in earlier Gothic architecture of the Middle Ages, and in general the forms employed by Santini on the exterior as well as the interior of the church are treated in a plastic if not indeed in a painterly manner that may even be compared with decorative elements of eighteenth-century architecture elsewhere.

The Cistercian Church in Sedlec thus represents the first in a series of creative responses by Santini to monastic commissions to build in a Gothic manner, of which the next prominent example is the Church of the Birth of the Virgin in Želiv (1712–1720). There Santini Aichel supplied the Premonstratensian abbot Jeronym Hlína with a design in which not only the decorative use of ribs, as at Sedlec, but also the whole conception of space and mass in the building transforms the Gothic idiom into a new architectural dialect. The play of concave and convex forms in the tribune in the interior, while recalling Ried's architecture, also bears comparison with aspects of seventeenth-century architecture in Italy. Hence Santini Aichel's architecture is often called "Baroque Gothic" or "Gothicizing Baroque."

Santini Aichel drew from aesthetic, religious, and intellectual currents that were found not only in a long local Gothic tradition in which Gothic forms were regarded as particularly appropriate to church architecture but also in a conscious movement of historical and religious revival that sought to imbue the past with new meaning, and among other things revived or created cults of Bohemian saints. Thus both for formal and cultural reasons, even where Santini Aichel's Gothicizing buildings superficially resemble similar manifestations elsewhere in Europe, as in the architecture of NICHOLAS HAWKSMOOR or of the later Gothic Revival, his work must be considered an independent creation. This is seen most clearly in the church Santini built at Kladruby (1712–1726). Santini's intentions there are aptly described by his patron, the abbot Maurus Finzguth, who in 1720 spoke of the cupola placed over the crossing as *"amplissima more Gotico nondum visa"* (most ample, in a Gothic style not hitherto seen). Santini's efforts may thus be interpreted as intended to generate a new architectural manner or style (*mos*) out of the use of medieval elements. The elevation of the nave at Kladruby accordingly combines ogive with rounded arches, and its vault is given over to an interplay of functionless intertwining ribs.

Throughout his career, Santini also designed pilgrimage churches where the conception of ground plans and spaces is no less inventive than the treatment of forms in his cloister churches. The Saint Anne Chapel (1705–1707) in Panenské Břežany is built in the form of an equilateral triangle; the Chapel of the Name of the Virgin in Mladotice (1708–1710) is hexagonal in shape; the chapel at Marianské Týnice (1711–1732) forms a Greek cross; and the chapel of Saint John Nepomuk in Běstvina (c.1720) is star-shaped. Similar unusual ground plans, recalling the work of Borromini and GUARINO GUARINI, can be found in some of Santini's designs for cloister churches, such as that of Saint Bernard, built for the Cistercians at Plasy (1711–1732), and the Benedictine Church of Saints Peter and Paul at Rajhrad (1721–1732). The unusual ground plans of Santini's churches often serve a symbolic function, as they do in Borromini's work: the six-sided star plan at Běstvina, for instance, alludes to the stars that were supposed to have appeared over the spot of his martyrdom and at his birthplace.

In Santini Aichel's designs the symbolic or ideological use of ground plans and of forms was taken further even than Borromini had done and

Santini Aichel.
Cloister Church.
Kladruby, Czechoslovakia.
1712–1726

Santini Aichel.
Church of Saint John Nepomuk.
Zelená Hora near Žd'ař nad Sazavou, Czechoslovakia.
1719–1720

Santini Aichel. Karlová Koruna (later Schloss Karlskrone). Chlumec nad Cidlinou, Czechoslovakia. 1721–1723

may be seen to culminate in the remarkable pilgrimage church of Saint John Nepomuk on the Zelená Hora (Green Mountain) near Žd'ař nad Sazavou (1719–1720). There, the abbot Vaclav Vejmluva, who had already created a religious and cultural center at Žd'ař associated with the restitution of the Pre-Hussite church and who had earlier patronized Santini, had the architect design a chapel to honor Nepomuk, whose cult and birthplace were associated with Žd'ař, and to house a recently rediscovered relic of Nepomuk's tongue. The complicated ground plan consists of a ten-sided polygon in which is inscribed a five-pointed star; the whole is set within the ambit of a sequence of ten chapels forming an external decagon. In the masterful design of interlocking spaces in the chapel, the ribs and pilasters composed of Gothic elements recall Nepomuk's era. The popular Bohemian saint is also evoked by the star-shaped forms in ground plan and stucco decoration, and by the tongue shapes that form the points of the stars, and some of the doors, windows, and stucco patterns.

From the earliest days of his career, Santini Aichel also worked for the high nobility in Bohemia. In 1722, it was even said that Santini was at work for forty noble families. His important designs for domestic residences begin with the Bishop's Palace in Hradec Kralove (1704–1716) and continue with designs for such distinguished structures as the palaces built for Count Moržin (later known as the Palais Černin [1713–1714]) and Count Kolovrat (later Thun-Hohenstein [1716–1725]) in the Malá Strana (Small Side) in Prague. The façades of the latter two buildings were decorated with works by the two outstanding Bohemian sculptors of the century, Matthias Bernhard Braun and Ferdinand Maximilian Brokoff. In their sculptural decoration and elevation, Santini's Prague palaces may be related to the architecture of Fischer von Erlach.

Whereas elements in Santini's plans for the Schloss Karlová Koruna (later Schloss Karlskrone) in Chlumec nad Cidlinou may also be traced back to Fischerian ideas, the actual completion of this late work (1721–1723) has no direct counterpart in Fischer's *oeuvre.* At Chlumec, Santini Aichel developed a plan consisting of a cylindrical central core with radiating quadratic blocks. The interior disposition of mass and space varies at each story, resulting in highly original and surprising combinations. Chlumec may be regarded as the culmination of a tradition of spatial and formal inventiveness in Bohemian palace architecture that indeed dates back to Ferdinand of the Tyrol's Schloss Stern (later Villa Hvězda) (1555–1556) on the White Mountain near Prague.

The wonderful flow of Santini Aichel's inventions was cut short by his death in 1723. Among his architectural followers are F. M. Kaňka, who had worked with him and completed a number of his buildings; Johann Ferdinand Schor may also be considered to have been influenced by Santini Aichel, at least in his decorations for Saint Veit's in Prague, for which Santini Aichel had submitted designs for the celebration of St. John Nepomuk's beatification in 1721. The Gothic Revival of the later eighteenth and nineteenth centuries also had a forerunner in Santini Aichel. Yet it is not only the precedent in his architecture that merits attention. Santini Aichel's unique combinations of forms, mass, and space, as demonstrated at their best on the Zelená Hora near Žd'ař, deserve consideration from practicing architects of post-modernist inclination as well as from historians of architecture.

THOMAS DACOSTA KAUFMANN

WORKS

c.1700–1727, Cistercian Cloister Zbraslav of the Virgin; near Prague. 1702–1705, Church of the Assumption and of John the Baptist, Sedlec, Czechoslovakia. 1704, Church of Saint James Major, Kopidlno, Czechoslovakia. 1704–1716, Bishop's Palace, Hradec Kralove, Czechoslovakia. 1705–1707, Chapel of Saint Anne, Panenské Břežany, Czechoslovakia. 1706/1710–1722, Cloister Church, Žd'ař nad Sazavou, Czechoslovakia. 1708, Church of Saint Libora, Jesence, Czechoslovakia. 1708, Church of Saint Prokop, Chotoun, Czechoslovakia. 1708–1710, Chapel of the Name of the Virgin, Mladotice, Czechoslovakia. 1710–1714, Church of the Holy Trinity (façade), Rychnovmad Kněžnou, Czechoslovakia. 1711–1732, Cistercian Cloister and Church of Saint Bernard, Plasy, Czechoslovakia. 1711–1732, Chapel, Mariánské Týnice, Czechoslovakia. 1712–1720, Church of the Virgin, Želiv, Czechoslovakia. 1712–1726, Cloister Church, Kladruby, Czechoslovakia. 1713–1714, Palace of Count Moržin (later the Palais Černin), Prague. 1714–1717, Church of Saint Clement, Hradec Kralove, Czechoslovakia. 1716–1725, Kolovrat (later Thun-Hohenstein) Palace, Prague. 1719–1720, Church of Saint John Nepomuk, Zelená Hora near Žd'ař nad Sazavou, Czechoslovakia. c.1720, Church of Saint John Nepomuk, Běstvina, Czechoslovakia. 1720/1722–1734, Cistercian Prelature, Žd'ař, Czechoslovakia. 1721–1723, Karlova Koruna (later Schloss Karlskrone), Chlumec nad Cirlinou, Czechoslovakia. 1721–1732, Church of Saints Peter and Paul, Rajhrad, Czechoslovakia.

BIBLIOGRAPHY

FRANZ, HEINRICH GERHARD 1950 "Gotik und Barock im Werk des Johann Santini Aichel." *Wiener Jahrbuch für Kunstgeschichte* 14:65–130.

FRANZ, HEINRICH GERHARD 1962 *Bauten und Baumeister der Barockzeit in Böhmen.* Leipzig: E. A. Seemann.

KALISTA, ZDENĚK 1970 *Česká barokní gotika a její Žd'árské ohnisko.* Brno, Czech.: Blok.

KOTRBA, VIKTOR 1974 "Johann Santini—sein Werdegang und seine Architektur." *Umění* 22:185–196.

KOTRBA, VIKTOR 1976 *Česká barokní gotika: Dílo Jana Santiniho-Aichla.* Prague: Academia.

PEVSNER, NIKOLAUS 1957 "Bohemian Hawksmoor." *Architectural Review* 121:113–114.

RICHTER, VACLAV 1966 "Santinis Pläne für die Kirche auf der Zelená Hora." *Sborník Prací Filosofické Fakulty Brněnské University, Řada Uměnovědna* 12:25–28.

SVACHA, ROSTISLAV 1979 "K vývoji díla Jana Santiniho." *Umění* 27:382–400.

TIETZE, HANS 1909 "Wiener Gotik im XVIII. Jahrhundert." *Kunstgeschichtliches Jahrbuch der K.K. Zentralkommission* 3:162–186.

SANTOS DE CARVALHO, EUGÉNIO DOS

Eugénio dos Santos de Carvalho (1711–1760) was the designer principally responsible for the reconstruction of fifty central acres of Lisbon after the great earthquake of 1755. To contemporaries, this harmonious rebuilding of Lisbon's core to serve commerce stood for rationalism in economics, in city planning, and in architecture. It was ordained by the king's chief minister, Sebastião José de Carvalho e Melo, known by his later title as the marquess of Pombal. The task was supervised by an aging but most competent engineer, Manuel de Maia. Santos rose to become Manuel de Maia's principal aide amid urgent activity, competitive ambitions, and pressures from powerful traders and ecclesiastics. His rectangular street plan was chosen over alternative schemes; in it he may have been influenced by a time-tested British naval base on Minorca. At the edge of the ample harbor formed by the Tagus river, Santos laid out a vast square, the Praço do Commércio, known as the Terreiro do Praço. At its edge, uniform buildings housed port authorities, government services, and facilities for commercial associations. Behind the square lay regular blocks with business premises at ground level and three stories of dwellings above. The nearly uniform structures were bound by regulations for safety and economy. Specially designed wood framing was faced with stucco, stone trimmed. Maia ensured adequate water and sanitation as well as proper street widths, while Santos designed well-proportioned, logically detailed façades. Double-hipped tile roofs, a north European device providing extra space, were contributed by Santos's assistant, Carlos Mardel, Hungarian by birth, who had made his mark in Portugal thanks to a light, balanced sense of design; he had created a charming country house for the chief minister. After Santos's death, Mardel's designs in part of the rebuilt area were less severe than earlier structures though still governed by Maia's unyielding rules of economy. Lisbon's civic architecture had been traditionally sober, and it seems fitting that Santos's elegantly restrained work has become known as a forerunner of rationalist trends in twentieth-century urban design.

EDGAR KAUFMANN, JR.

BIBLIOGRAPHY

FRANCA, JOSE-AUGUSTO 1965 *Une ville des lumières: La Lisbonne de Pombal.* Paris: S.E.V.P.E.N.

KUBLER, GEORGE, and SORIA, MARTIN 1959 *Art and Architecture in Spain and Portugal and Their American Dominions: 1500 to 1800.* Baltimore: Penguin.

SMITH, ROBERT C. 1968 *The Art of Portugal: 1500 to 1800.* New York: Meredith.

Santos de Carvalho. Ruas da Prata and São Julião (with Carlos Mardel). Lisbon. c.1755–1770

SARDI, GIUSEPPE

Born in Morcote on Lake Lugano in Italian Switzerland, Giuseppe Sardi (c.1621–1699) was prominent in Venice before he was thirty. His two earliest commissions came from a merchant, Jacopo Galli: the 1649–1655 façade of the Scuola di San Teodoro, recalling JACOPO SANSOVINO's San Geminiano and especially the Scuola di San Girolamo by Antonio and Tommaso Contini (see CONTINI FAMILY), and a similar but larger façade of 1649–1663 for San Salvatore. The beautiful canal front of 1673 for San Lazzaro, based on the central section of ANDREA PALLADIO's façade for San Francesco della Vigna, was also commissioned by Calli. Sardi's great Mocenigo Monument (1654–1655) at San Lazzaro is actually an inner screen-façade separating the church from a deep vestibule. It was followed by his twin masterpieces, the richly sculptured front for Santa Maria del Giglio (1678–1680) and a splendid aedicular façade finished in the same year for BALDASSARE LONGHENA's Church of the Scalzi (which differs from the Giglio façade in its motif of nested pediments). Among Sardi's three palaces, the most significant is Palazzo Flangini, on which a lavish sculptural decoration is rigorously controlled. In his last decade, Sardi went gently mad; his robust and elaborated style deeply influenced his nephew, DOMENICO ROSSI.

DOUGLAS LEWIS

WORKS

1649–1655, Scuola Grande di San Teodoro (façade); 1649–1663, San Salvatore (façade); *(A)San Tomà (façade, reconstr. 1742–1755 by Francesco Bognolo); c.1653–1657, Madonna dell'Orto (monument of Girolamo Cavazza); 1654–1655, San Lazzaro dei Mendicanti (monument of Alvise Mocenigo); Venice, Italy. 1657–1669, San Francesco (altar of the Passion of Christ), Padua, Italy. 1659/1660–1664, Santa Maria Gloriosa dei Frari (altar of Sant'Antonio); before 1663, Palazzo Surian on the Cannaregio (prob. expanded c.1685); before 1663, Palazzo Savorgnan on the Cannaregio (completed 1680s–1690s by Domenico Rossi?); 1664–1666, Ospedaletto di Santi Giovanni e Paolo (refectory, dormitories, and spiral stair); 1664?–1682?, Palazzo Flangini on the Grand Canal (with Domenico Rossi); 1668–1671, San Pantalon (high altar and tabernacle); Venice, Italy. 1673–1677, Villa Zane, Altino, Italy. 1673–1680s?, San Lazzaro dei Mendicanti (nave altars and façade, with Domenico Rossi?); 1678–1680, Santa Maria del Giglio (façade and two altars, completed 1683?); late 1670s–1680, Santa Maria di Nazareth deli Scalzi (façade); (A)1682–1688, Santa Croce degli Armeni; 1688, Santa Maria del Carmine (reconstruction of campanile); Venice, Italy.

BIBLIOGRAPHY

BASSI, ELENA 1962 "Giuseppe Sardi." Pages 184–206 in *Architettura del Sei e Settecento a Venezia.* Naples: Edizioni Scientifiche Italiane.

BASSI, ELENA 1976 *Palazzi di Venezia: Admiranda Urbis Venetae.* Venice, Italy: La Stamperia di Venezia.

HOWARD, DEBORAH 1981 Pages 188–192 in *The Architectural History of Venice.* New York: Holmes & Meier; London: Batsford.

LEWIS, DOUGLAS 1979 *The Late Baroque Churches of Venice.* New York: Garland.

SARTORIS, ALBERTO

Alberto Sartoris (1901–) was born in Turin, Italy. For political reasons, his father, a woodcarver, emigrated to Geneva, Switzerland, with his family soon after Alberto's birth. Sartoris was educated in Switzerland, graduating from the Ecole des Beaux Arts of Geneva in 1919. He returned to Italy, worked briefly for RAIMONDO D'ARONCO, and from 1922 until 1926 worked for ANNIBALE RIGOTTI in Turin.

Beginning in the 1920s, Sartoris participated in various international avant-garde art movements. He met members of the Italian Futurist movement at the 1921 Futurist exhibition in Geneva. That same year, he began to correspond regularly with THEO VAN DOESBURG. He was one of the founders of the Congrès Internationaux d'Architecture Moderne (CIAM). His circle of acquaintances continued to grow and included LE CORBUSIER and Anatoli Lunacharsky. In 1930, he participated in the *Cercle et Carré* exhibition in Paris and, between 1931 and 1936, in the activities of the Abstraction—Creation group.

In Italy, he was a member of the Movimento Italiano per l'Architettura Razionale. His 1928 pavilion at the Turin exhibition is one of the first examples of Rationalist architecture in Italy. In 1929, he became editor of the periodical *La città futurista.*

Although Sartoris has often been identified as a Futurist, the severe character of his graphic style, his preference for axometric projections, and the rigid rectilinear character of his designs derive more from Dutch *De Stijl* and Italian rationalist ideas than from the formal language of Futurism. Sartoris did share the Futurists' tireless enthusiasm for propagandizing on behalf of modern art and architecture. He published numerous articles in Italian and Swiss journals, and organized numerous exhibitions. In 1932, he published *Gli elementi dell'architettura funzionale,* a profusely illustrated compendium of contemporary world architecture. In 1935 and 1936, he traveled extensively in South America, lecturing on modern architecture.

Since World War II, Sartoris has lived in Lausanne, Switzerland. A member of the faculties of the Ecole Polytechnique Fédérale de Lausanne and the Académie Cantonale des Beaux-Arts de Sion, Sartoris has continued to write and lecture extensively on modern art and architecture. He is a member of numerous important international associations. He has played a key role in the development of modern architecture in both Switzerland and Italy, serving as an important link between developments in those countries and the international scene.

DENNIS DOORDAN

WORKS

*1928, Exhibition Pavilion, Turin, Italy. 1932, Church of Notre Dame, Lourtier, Switzerland. 1934–1935, Morand-Pasteur House, Saillon, Switzerland. 1938–1939, Villa-Studio for Italo and Vincenzo De Grandi, Corseaux, Switzerland. 1960, Apartment Building, Lutry, Switzerland.

BIBLIOGRAPHY

ABRIANI, ALBERTO 1972 *Alberto Sartoris, mezzo secolo di attività.* Turin, Italy: Gallerie d'arte Martano.

GUBLER, JACQUES 1978 *Alberto Sartoris: Architekt.* Zurich: ETH.

SARTORIS, ALBERTO (1932)1941 *Gli elementi dell'architettura funzionale.* 3d ed., rev. Milan: Hoepli.

SARTORIS, ALBERTO 1948–1954 *Encyclopédie de l'architecture nouvelle.* 3 vols. Milan: Hoepli.

SASAKI, HIDEO

Born and educated in California, Hideo Sasaki (1919–) came to study at Harvard University in 1946 and later served as chairman of the landscape architecture department (1958–1968). Influential as a teacher, Sasaki developed his landscape design office simultaneously, encompassing architecture and planning in Sasaki Walker Associates (1952–), Sasaki, Dawson, Demay Associates (1966–1978) and Sasaki Associates (1978–). His characteristically urban spaces at the Place Bonaventure Hotel, Montreal (1966–1967) and Greenacre Park, New York (1972), integrate strong geometric forms with rich plant textures and sculptural fountains or pavilions. Sasaki's corporate and campus plans and resort community designs draw on a similar vocabulary to establish coherent networks of landscaped spaces.

THOMAS G. BEDDALL

WORKS

1952, Jaycee Headquarters, Tulsa, Okla. 1957, Upjohn Company General Office Building, Kalamazoo, Mich. 1958–1968, Sea Pines Plantation Master Plan, Hilton Head Island, S.C. 1959–1961, Foothill College, Los Altos Hills, Calif. 1960–1964, Constitution Plaza, Hartford, Conn. 1961, Bell Telephone Laboratories, Holmdel, N.J. 1961, Master Plan, University of Colorado, Boulder. 1964, Master Plan, University of Massachusetts, Amherst. 1966–1970, Copley Square Development, Boston. 1969, Place Bonaventure Hotel Roof Garden, Montreal. 1972, Greenacre Park, New York.

BIBLIOGRAPHY

"Back Bay's Sedate Square." 1970 *Architectural Forum* 133, no. 3:60–63.

"Castle in the Sky—Hotel Bonaventure." 1967 *Interiors* 127, no. 3:102–117.

DIXON, JOHN MORRIS 1966 "Colorado U: Respect for a Robust Environment." *Architectural Forum* 125, no. 3:54–63.

"Roof Garden of the Place Bonaventure." 1971 *Architecture and Urbanism* 11, Nov.:90–96.

ROWAN, JAN C. 1960 "Design of Exterior Spaces." *Progressive Architecture* 41, no. 7:108–126.

SASAKI, HIDEO 1950 "Thoughts on Education in Landscape Architecture." *Landscape Architecture* 40, no. 4:158–160.

SCHMERTZ, MILDRED F. 1964 "Insuring the Growth of Hartford." *Architectural Record* 135, no. 3:178–187.

SCHMERTZ, MILDRED F. 1966 "Distinguished Architecture for a State University." *Architectural Record* 139, no. 5:165–183.

SATŌ, TAKEO

Born in Nagoya, Japan, and educated at Waseda University, Takeo Satō (1899–1972) was appointed assistant professor immediately after graduation from the university in 1924; he became professor in 1938. He is known as the pioneer in the field of architectural acoustics in Japan, in which he took his doctorate in 1935. He had also shown his outstanding ability as an architectural designer and was one of the leaders of the Japanese Modern movement. Leaving the university, he established his own architect's office in 1951. The strictly geometric, primary shapes, in his works were part of his designs throughout his life.

TAKASHI HASEGAWA

WORKS

1927, Ohkuma Memorial Hall, Waseda University, Tokyo. 1944, Iwakuni Chōkokan Museum, Yamaguchi Prefecture, Japan. 1958, Asahikawa City Office; 1971, Hokkaidō Kaitaku Memorial Museum, Sapporo; Hokkaido, Japan.

BIBLIOGRAPHY

Gendainihon Kenchikuka Zenshū. 1975 Volume 7. Tokyo.

Takeo Satō: Architect. 1963 Tokyo.

SAULNIER, JULES

Jules Saulnier (1828–1900), a French architect, is best remembered for his design of the Menier Chocolate Works. The building was set on four iron girders across piers embedded in the river Marne, from which came the power for the plant. The building was erected around an iron frame that carried all the weight, allowing the walls to be, as Saulnier put it, "entirely plain from top to bottom, with no projections." The walls were then filled with decorative polychrome bricks and overlaid with diagonal traces, like those of wood construction, that held the structure rigid. All this was much praised, but the building had little influence on later architecture.

DAVID CAST

WORK

1871–1872, Chocolat Menier Factory, Noiseul-sur-Marne, France.

BIBLIOGRAPHY

GIEDION, SIGFRIED (1941)1967 *Space, Time and Architecture: The Growth of a New Tradition.* 5th ed. Cambridge, Mass.: Harvard University Press.

GUEDES, PEDRO (editor) 1979 *The Macmillan Encyclopedia of Architecture and Technological Change.* London: Macmillan.

VIOLLET-LE-DUC, EUGÈNE EMMANUEL (1863–1872) 1965 *Entretiens sur l'architecture.* Reprint. Ridgewood, N.J.: Gregg.

SAUVAGE, HENRI

Frédéric Henri Sauvage (1873–1932) was the son of a tradesman who moved to Paris from Rouen to start a wallpaper and decorative fabric business. Henri joined the atelier of JEAN LOUIS PASCAL at the Ecole des Beaux-Arts, where he formed warm friendships with architects Henri Provensal and Charles Duval and painters Francis Jourdain (son of Frantz) and Jacques Majorelle (brother of Louis). FRANTZ JOURDAIN drew his son's friends into a group prepared to develop new trends in plastic and decorative arts, architecture included. They met in the studio of sculptor Alexandre Charpentier.

Sauvage left Pascal's atelier in 1895 to begin his own career of artistic production in all the decorative arts and architecture. Supported by his friendship with the Majorelles and his marriage to Marie-Louise Charpentier in 1896, he designed shop interiors for the decorators Jansen, Rue Royale (1898), Paris, and the Café de Paris (1898). After producing Art Nouveau furniture designs for the House of Majorelle, manufacturers of Nancy, he was commissioned to do the Villa Majorelle, Nancy (1898–1901).

Sauvage directed his own wallpaper business from 1896 to 1904 and continued to design wallpapers, fabrics, furniture, ceramics (for Bigot), book bindings, and jewelry throughout his career. His first clearly attributed architectural work is the glazed shopping gallery Argentine, Avenue Victor Hugo, Paris (c.1900). In 1901, he began the project for a low-cost housing block, Rue Fernand Flocon, Paris, a building type that would occupy him for the rest of his architectural career.

Until World War I, Sauvage's low-cost and bourgeois apartment buildings, done with his partner Charles Sarazin, incorporated either the medievalizing or the Art Nouveau tendencies of their group. Finally, the 1912 Immeuble à Gradins, 26 Rue Vavin, Paris, stated the formal direction which Sauvage's postwar architecture would take.

The stepped-back succession of floor levels was an attempt to play upon Parisian cornice-line and ridge-line regulations in order to increase light and air. Enormously massive masonry (20 m. thick at ground level in the approved project) indicate a lacuna in the solution of structural problems, recognized by the City's architectural service as it denied the first application for a building permit. Sauvage is, however, credited with effective progress in interior design in his low-cost housing: prefabricated wall panels without moldings requiring maintenance and tiled kitchens and baths.

After the war, Sauvage widened his repertory and built two cinemas, Gambetta (1920) and Les Sèvres (1922). He also designed several pavilions for the 1925 Exposition des Arts Décoratifs et Industriels in Paris. In 1926, he built a garage for 1,000 vehicles and the new Samaritaine department store (with his old mentor, Frantz Jourdain), both in Paris. His last work was the Restaurant Vert Galant (1932) designed in the great tradition of the *belle époque* which he helped to launch.

ELIZABETH MCLANE

WORKS

1898, Café de Paris; 1898, Shop Jansen (interior), Rue Royale; Paris. 1898–1901, Villa Majorelle, Nancy, France. c.1900, Galerie Argentine, Avenue Victor Hugo; 1901, Apartment House, 1 Rue Fernand Flocon; 1904, Low-cost Housing, 7 Rue Tretaigne (with Charles Sarazin); 1912, Immeuble à Gradins, 26 Rue Vavin (with Charles Sarazin); 1920, Cinema Gambetta; 1922, Cinema Les Sèvres; *1925, Pavilions, Exposition des Arts Décoratifs et Industriels; 1926, Garage Rue Campagne-Première; 1926, La Samaritaine (with Frantz Jourdain), Rue du Pont Neuf; 1932, Restaurant Vert Galant, Quai des Orfèvres; Paris.

BIBLIOGRAPHY

BORSI, FRANCO, and GODOLI, EZIO 1976 *Paris, 1900.* Brussels: Vokaer.

CULOT, MAURICE, and GRENIER, LISE 1978*a* "Henri Sauvage, 1873–1932, L'Âme Fantastique." *Architectural Association Quarterly* 10, no. 2:16–27.

CULOT, MAURICE, and GRENIER, LISE 1978*b* "Henri Sauvage's Quixotic Mind." *Architecture and Urbanism* 11:113–128.

JOURDAIN, FRANTZ 1902 "La Villa Marjorelle à Nancy." *L'Art Décoratif* 47:202–208.

RIOTER, LEON 1909 "L'Art à L'École." *L'Art Décoratif* 1:92–99.

SAUVAGE, HENRI, and SARAZIN, CHARLES 1904 *Éléments d'Architecture Moderne.* Paris: Schmid.

VITRY, PAUL 1925 "L'Exposition des Arts Décoratifs Modernes, L'Architecture." *Gazette des Beaux-Arts* 12:1–18.

SAVAGE, JAMES

Born in London and there trained under DANIEL ASHER ALEXANDER, James Savage (1779–1852) became a student at the Royal Academy in 1798. He worked mostly on public buildings, and his interest in methods of construction made him a successful designer of bridges and churches. He built the first stone vault of the Gothic Revival at Saint Luke's, Chelsea (1820–1824), where he is buried.

JILL ALLIBONE

WORKS

1808–1816, Richmond Bridge, Dublin. 1815–1820, Tempsford Bridge, Bedfordshire, England. 1820–1824, Saint Luke's, Chelsea; 1827–1829, Saint James, Bermondsey; London. 1827–1829, All Saints, Upper Norwood, Surrey, England. *1828–1830, Holy Trinity, Sloane Street, Chelsea; 1828–1830, Holy Trinity, Tottenham Green; London. 1829–1831, Saint Mary the Virgin, Ilford, Essex, England. 1829–1831, Saint Mary, Speenhamland, Berkshire, England. *1832–1833, Saint Michael, Burleigh Street, Strand, London. 1835, Saint Thomas the Martyr, Brentwood, Essex, England. *1836, Union Workhouse, Dartford, Kent, England. 1836–1838, Saint Paul, Addlestone, Surrey, England. 1843–1847, Union Workhouse, Tenterden, Kent, England.

BIBLIOGRAPHY

EASTLAKE, CHARLES LOCK 1872 Pages 141–142 in *A History of the Gothic Revival.* London: Longmans.

"The Late Mr. James Savage, Architect." 1852 *The Builder* 10:377.

REDGRAVE, SAMUEL 1878 Pages 378–379 in *A Dictionary of Artists of the English School.* London.

SAVAGE, H., and SAVAGE, C. W. 1852 *Memoir of James Savage.* Farnborough, England: Gregg. Communication to the Royal Institute of British Architects.

SAVIOLI, LEONARDO

Leonardo Savioli (1917–), born in Florence, Italy, is an architect and painter. Since graduating from the Florence School of Architecture in 1941 he has taught urban, architectural and interior design, and landscape architecture at that school. His architecture is characterized by a sculpturesque use of reinforced concrete.

DENNIS DOORDAN

WORKS

1962–1964, Villa Sandrone, Arezzo, Italy. 1962–1968, Residential Quarter (with M. Dezzi Bardeschi, U. Giorgini, F. Gori, and D. Santi), Sorganne, Italy. 1963–1965, Villa Taddei (with Santi), San Domenico di Fiesole, Italy. 1964, Villa Bayon (with Santi), San Gaggio, Italy. 1964–1967, Via Piagentina Apartment Building (with Santi); 1965, Arno River Bridge; Florence. 1965, Mattolini House (with Santi), Castello, Italy.

BIBLIOGRAPHY

EMANUEL, MURIEL (editor) 1980 *Contemporary Architects.* New York: St. Martin's.

GOBBI, GRAZIA 1976 *Itinerario di Firenze moderna: Architettura 1860–1975.* Florence: Centro Di.

KOENIG, GIOVANNI KLAUS 1968 *Architettura in Toscana: 1931–1968.* Turin, Italy: ERI.

SAVIOLI, LEONARDO 1953 "Dal 1900 al 1950." *Urbanistica* 23, no. 12:29–42.

SCAMOZZI, OTTAVIO BERTOTTI

See BERTOTTI-SCAMOZZI, OTTAVIO.

SCAMOZZI, VINCENZO

Vincenzo Scamozzi (1548–1616), apparently the only child of Gian Domenico Scamozzi (c.1526–1582) and Catterina Moschini, was born in Vicenza on 2 September 1548 (rather than in 1552 as is usually said), and died at his house in the parish of San Severo in Venice on 7 August 1616. He was the most important Venetian architect and theoretician between the death of ANDREA PALLADIO (1580) and the first activity of BALDASSARE LONGHENA (1616), which coincided with the year of his death; his dry academic style marks a conservative or even reactionary interlude between the innovative activities of these more original masters. Although he is principally remembered as the author of one of the last and most ambitious Renaissance treatises on building (*L'Idea della architet-*

tura universale, published in Venice in 1615), Scamozzi is unusual among sixteenth-century theorists in having produced as well a large body of architectural works. To some degree, his substantial oeuvre is a function of his unique availability in the northeast Italian vacuum that followed the deaths of MICHELE SANMICHELI (1559), JACOPO SANSOVINO (1570), and Palladio; but Scamozzi's calculated revisions of these predecessors' models gave him a severe though self-conscious classical style, which exactly coincided with the prevailing aesthetic of his patrons. With these clients and colleagues, however, as with the world at large, Scamozzi's relations were mixed. He never married (in order, as he said, that he might devote himself to his work); and although he retained the loyalty of certain older sponsors—such as Marc'Antonio Barbaro and Giacomo Contarini, who had also befriended Palladio—their deaths in the mid-1590s precipitated a more difficult situation for his work, involving a noticeable decline in commissions. In 1595, indeed, Scamozzi was dismissed from his principal ecclesiastical job, the Church of the Tolentini, as a result of public litigation in which he was accused of technical incompetence and personal irascibility. Even the cosmopolitan INIGO JONES became so exasperated with his braggadocio as to call him "purblind," and his character as we glimpse it from the pages of the *Idea* is argumentative, egotistical, and tendentious. His building style is very largely based on that of Palladio (so closely, in fact, that in his early Palazzo Thiene-Bonin we are still not sure whether he may have adapted a Palladian design), but he was so jealous of the older master's reputation that he mentions Palladio's name only rarely and tangentially in his treatise. Notwithstanding these drawbacks, above all the historical mischance of functioning as a personally unattractive intermediary between the warmly humane geniuses of Palladio and Longhena, Scamozzi still commands respect: he created at least a dozen architectural masterpieces—among a wide range of villas, palaces, public buildings, and churches—and his theoretical writings are a kind of *summa* of Renaissance thought.

Scamozzi was almost unique in the historical roster of Venetian architects, but highly characteristic of his generation, in being a classically educated "gentleman artist" of independent means. His upbringing and training are thus closely paralleled by the humanist preoccupations within which Sansovino's and Palladio's sons in Venice, or FEDERICO ZUCCARI in Florence and Rome, developed personal status as members of intellectual elites rather than becoming mere practitioners of artisans' skills. Gian Domenico Scamozzi is one of the principal keys to this cultural transformation of his son, but his own personality is poorly understood. He is documented in Vicenza as a successful surveyor and building contractor, dealing especially in lumber; he is often called a "carpenter," and his architectural talents seem to have been correspondingly limited, though perhaps somewhat wider than this description implies. He particularly admired SEBASTIANO SERLIO (probably without the benefit of personal acquaintance, since he would have been only fifteen when Serlio left the Veneto in 1541), from whose writings he made a topical index, published in the first compendium edition of Serlio's books in 1584. This posthumous contribution, however, was edited by Gian Domenico's theorizing son, so thoroughly as to cause Vincenzo's fundamental eighteenth-century biographer TOMMASO TEMANZA (as well as modern scholars) to suspect that the paternal contribution may have been small indeed. That suspicion involves also a prefatory *Discorso* (published in the revised Serlio edition of 1600 and now assigned definitely to Vincenzo), as well as the larger question of Gian Domenico's possible activity as a designer rather than a builder. The elder Scamozzi's Vicentine humanist colleague Lodovico Roncone wrote an introduction to the "Scamozzian" editions of Serlio, in which he enumerated almost all of young Vincenzo's projects through 1584: to this list he prefixed the names of three other buildings, as works of Gian Domenico's. From the earliest of these, inscribed 1560, there remains only a modest portal; and there are reasons for doubting a clear ascription to the senior Scamozzi in the case of the other two. The Palazzo Testoni in Vicenza, probably of 1571, is formally so close to documented works of Vincenzo's (Palazzo Trissino al Duomo, Palazzo Ravaschieri) as to nurture the doubt that Gian Domenico may only have executed a parallel design by his son: a situation which can now be demonstrated as a virtual certainty for the third of Roncone's attributions. This is "Scamozzi & Son's" jointly executed Villa Ferramosca at Barbano, where Gian Domenico evidently created an archaizing loggia on the western side, while a surviving drawing by Vincenzo demonstrates his authorship—at the precocious age of twenty—of the main east block and wings. A highly sophisticated pair of large palaces with related façade compositions, the Villa Verlati of 1574–1576 and the attributed Palazzo Caldogno inscribed 1575, attest to Vincenzo's independent mastery of design (even if he occasionally relied on his father for assistance in execution) by the time of his twenty-fifth year. Together with his imposing realization of Palazzo Thiene-Bonin, they prepared at least in part for his first truly important and perhaps most brilliant accomplishment, the building which assured his lasting reputation before he had reached the age of thirty.

This was the plague retreat of the *Rocca* for Vettor Pisani, the most perfect post-Palladian villa and in many ways a formal and iconographic improvement even over its celebrated models. Set atop a high hill, the low cube of its almost uninflected exterior is dominated on three sides by an open "serliana" (a "Palladian" or "Venetian" window), and on the front by an open loggia recessed behind a simple column screen, supporting a pediment. All four of these airy spaces open as satellites onto a domed circular hall, lighted by an open oculus: the rooms in the corners are thus literally enveloped by cooling breezes, and the whole fabric is permeated with light and air in perhaps a more successful way than any comparable structure. Scamozzi's brilliance of invention is balanced by a truly classical sense of restraint, as the sober stone ornament is set in crystalline geometries on plain white plastered walls. This handling emphasizes a three-dimensional plasticity that shapes a sculptural entity within the architectural frame, and makes of this densely compacted yet open pavilion a magical metaphor of natural space. Scamozzi in his long life may never again have reached such a level of sublime abstraction, so boldly conceived; but his Villa Molin at Mandria of twenty years later (1597) shows similarly concentrated masses around a soaring central hall, while his matched pair of twin pavilions for the Villa Cornaro al Paradiso (1607–1616), an innovation established only after the preparation of his treatise plate, reflects GIACOMO BAROZZI DA VIGNOLA at Bagnaia and looks forward to the dualities of the emerging baroque.

This initial decade of Scamozzi's career culminated in a two-year study trip to Rome, where Vincenzo returned again in 1585–1586, and apparently twice more in the 1590s. Temanza (evidently benefiting from a lost document) reported that Scamozzi arrived in Rome on 31 October, 1579, and in March 1580 published two impressive engravings of Diocletian's and the "Antonine" Baths, before moving to Naples in May of 1581. Upon returning to the Veneto later that year, he settled in Venice, where one of his first works was to publish forty commentaries and three introductory chapters for a series of Roman topographic prints by Giambattista Pittoni, as *Discorsi sopra le Antichità* (editions in 1582, 1583; a youthful treatise on perspective scenography in six books—written about 1574—is now lost, but was called *Dei Teatri e delle Scene*).

Apparently within weeks of his arrival in Venice at the end of 1581, Vincenzo had begun to develop designs for two of his most significant works, whose commissions were awarded him respectively in March and April of 1582: the Church of San Gaetano for the Theatines in Padua, and the great fabric of the Procuratie Nuove on the Piazza San Marco in Venice. The Theatine church is a large cubic hall with angled corners, articulated with colossal Composite pilasters supporting the ribs of a high domical vault: this single volumetric cavity is artfully introduced by a richly carved façade, on which answering Composite pilasters boldly express a strong structural rhythm. The great Venetian palace for the "New Procuracies" became Scamozzi's largest work, for it was constructed over the course of eighty years as the final element to enclose the Piazza San Marco, whose entire southern side it fills. Rather than the misattributed plan for the fortress city of Palmanova, it is on the Procuratie Nuove that Vincenzo's claim to interest as an urbanist must be based. The two lower stories of its immense façade exactly continue those of Sansovino's adjoining Library of Saint Mark (whose opposite end, alongside the

Scamozzi. Procuratie Nuove. Venice, Italy. 1581–1598/1599 (later altered; completed in 1663 by Longhena)

Mint, Scamozzi was simultaneously finishing); above these, he added to the Procuracies a third floor closely derived from Palladio's 1578 project for the Ducal Palace. The resulting screen forms a continuous front for the individual houses of the Procurators of Saint Mark, each occupying five bays. Scamozzi himself completed two of these units, with the courtyard behind: to it, and to his first ten façade bays west of the Library, he gave a much more copious ornament than his successors could afford.

The commissions for these prominent works assured Scamozzi's metropolitan reputation by 1582, the same year in which Marc'Antonio Barbaro secured for him the design of a great ducal tomb, in the now gutted Church of the Carità (although widely thought to have perished without a depiction, the Da Ponte monument is recorded on a Scamozzi drawing in Venice's Museo Correr, as well as in an engraving by Dionisio Valesi, two images which have not heretofore been associated). Vincenzo's immediate supervisor for a remodeling of the Marciana Library anteroom as a museum of antiquities (1587 and following) was Procurator Francesco Priuli, and the association affords a new date for Scamozzi's elaborate structure at that nobleman's villa in Treville. The Villa Priuli (1597) façade, in turn, is the closest parallel to the extended front, identically ordered, on his celebrated theater for a new Gonzago dukedom at Sabbioneta (1588). This innovative structure, the second surviving theater building of the Renaissance, reflects Vincenzo's immediately preceding work on remodeling the stage of the first, Palladio's Teatro Olimpico in Vicenza. Instead of Palladio's broad semicircular *cavea* set within a wide squarish building, however, Scamozzi pioneered at Sabbioneta a long narrow shoebox-shaped hall, within whose deep perspective the stage achieves an ideal scenographic illusionism, with regard to the tightly clustered seats surmounted by the ducal loge at the back.

The Theatine order, briefly pleased with Scamozzi's San Gaetano in Padua, commissioned him in 1590 to design their major church in Venice, and the architect's original drawings demonstrate the sad results of his dismissal in 1595 from San Nicolò. Its ambitious domed triconch with deep nave was radically simplified by the supervising brethren, and Vincenzo's façade was not executed at all. His designs for this project probably did have a major effect, though, in helping him to obtain commissions abroad, for he traveled widely (Rome, 1598?; from Hungary to France, 16 August 1599–14 May 1600) in the wake of his Venetian debacle. In 1604, he was engaged to design a cathedral for the bishop of Salzburg, Wolf Dietrich von Raitenau: although its foundations were begun, the bishop's successor had them replaced by the footings of a competitor's design, whose execution does at least palely reflect Scamozzi's project. The latter constitutes one of the most interesting plans for a great Italian Renaissance church, combining as it does close reminiscences of RAPHAEL's and BALDASSARE PERUZZI's designs for Saint Peter's in Rome, with many up-to-date north Italian motifs as well. Two final commissions for ecclesiastical projects in Venice produced Vincenzo's hospital church of San Lazzaro (1601–1636), and his façade of San Giorgio Maggiore (1607–1611). San Lazzaro is almost unknown, yet it is highly important as the prototype for a substantial number of Venetian parish and monastic churches in the seventeenth and eighteenth centuries. Its chapel-flanked rectangular space with a coved ceiling and square chancel, chastely ornamented with simple pilasters and plain entablatures, gave it a reproducibility that assured its enduring popularity. In much the same way, Vincenzo's revision of the façade for San Giorgio,

Scamozzi.
Teatro Olimpico (extensions of stage and perhaps the rustic gate).
Vicenza, Italy.
1584–1585

Scamozzi.
San Lazzaro dei Mendicanti.
Venice, Italy.
1601–1636

twenty-five years after Palladio's death, simplified and regularized its members (by applying their intended projections once more to the flat plane) in such a persuasive way that its descendants have become extraordinarily widespread.

At the end of his life, Scamozzi did achieve that most coveted Venetian opportunity, a commission for a palace on the Grand Canal. His Palazzo Contarini at San Trovaso (1609–1616) is one of his most diagnostic works, for it sums up his curiously arid approach to classical composition. The façade is severely flat, with broad expanses of absolutely plain marble sheathing. The shallow pilaster strips of thinly articulated orders mark off the bays and support delicate entablatures, whose function is barely more than that of stringcourses between the floors. Enormously elongated windows give a self-consciously archaic flavor to the whole, and indeed the fenestration patterns and floor positions repeat exactly those of a Gothic palace which the same patrons owned next door. The closest parallels to this design are works by early Venetian Renaissance masters of more than a century earlier, that is before Sanmicheli and Sansovino introduced into Venice their masterpieces of developed High Renaissance style. Most predictably of all, the Palazzo Contarini almost exactly reproduces the planar, cerebral effect of Sebastiano Serlio's published palace projects and thus brings Scamozzi's career back full circle to that bookish master on whose analysis Vincenzo's father founded his training.

Despite the opinions of himself and of succeeding centuries, Scamozzi's place in the history of architecture is far more appropriately established by his buildings than by his treatise. *L'Idea della architettura universale* was published at the author's expense, within the year of his death, with only six of its intended twelve, but later ten, books actually issued (Part One, Books I, II, III; Part Two, Books VI, VII, VIII; Pallucchini gives a thorough list of subsequent editions). George L. Hersey (1976) has managed to extract what few novel ideas are imbedded in its vast mass of turgid prose; its few plates are technically fine but made long before publication. The influence of the work as a whole may be said to have been nil: Book VI on the orders, however, became for centuries (and in every language) a standard handbook for architects and craftsmen. Scamozzi's much more interesting text is a manuscript daybook, now published by Barbieri, in which he recorded significant sights on his journey from Paris to Venice in 1600. Its attractive small sketches of French cathedrals especially show him to have been one of the few Renaissance architects with a real sensitivity to Gothic art.

Scamozzi. Palazzo Contarini. Venice, Italy. 1609–1616

Scamozzi had only one pupil, who briefly encountered him in his last years through sheer propinquity, having been born and raised in the same neighborhood of San Severo in Venice. The fact that this youngster was Baldassare Longhena, who was destined to revolutionize Venetian architecture through his independent rediscovery of the masters before his teacher, means that Scamozzi's career is truly a closed chapter in the history of art.

DOUGLAS LEWIS

WORKS

1568–c.1575, Villa of Girolamo Ferramosca (with Gian Domenico Scamozzi), Barbano, Italy. (A)1572/1577–1586/1593, Palazzo Thiene-Bonin, Vicenza, Italy. 1574–1576, 1590–1615, Villa of Leonardo Verlati, Villaverla, Italy. 1575–1578, Rocca Pisani (Vettor Pisani Villa), Lonigo, Italy. 1576–1579, Trissino-Trento (Pierfranceso Trissino Palace; with Gian Domenico Scamozzi), Vicenza, Italy. 1580s, Villa of Francesco Priuli (north wing), Treville di Castelfranco, Italy. 1580–1592?, Villa Almerico-Capra (La Rotonda; completion of Andrea Palladio's design, with construction of its stable), Vicenza, Italy. 1581–1586, San Gaetano da Thiene, Padua, Italy. 1581–1598/1599, Procuratie Nuove (continued with a different interior design by Francesco Smeraldi and completed in 1663 by Baldassare Longhena), Piazza San Marco, Venice, Italy. (A)1582?, Palazzo Cividale, Vicenza, Italy. 1582–1591, Library of Saint Mark (completion of Jacopo Sansovino's design), Venice, Italy. 1584–1585, Teatro Olimpico (extensions of stage and perhaps the rustic gate), Vicenza, Italy. 1587–1596, Library of Saint Mark (antisala), Venice,

Italy. 1588, Villa Cornaro (reconstruction), Poisolo di Castelfranco, Italy. 1588–1590, Theater (for Duke Vespasiano Gonzaga), Sabbioneta, Italy. 1590, Villa of Girolamo Contarini (revised in construction), Loreggia, Italy. 1590–1595, San Nicolò da Tolentino, Venice, Italy. 1591–1594, San Gaetano da Thiene (monastery), Padua, Italy. (A)1591–1595, Villa of Girolamo Cornaro (completion), Piombino, Italy. 1591–1597, Villa Duodo and Chapel of San Giorgio, Monselice, Italy. 1592–1616, Palace of Galeazzo Trissino al Corso, Vicenza, Italy. *1594–1600, Villa of Valerio Bardellini, Monfumo, Italy. 1596, Villa of Girolamo Ferretti, River Brenta, Sambruson del Dolo, Italy. 1596–1597, Villa of Girolamo Cornaro (stable), Piombino, Italy. 1597, Villa of Nicoló Molin, Mandria, Italy. *1597, Villa Priuli, Carrara Padovano Italy. 1597–1598, Villa Godi, Sarmego, Italy. 1601, Palazzo del Bò (university façade), Padua, Italy. 1601–1606, San Giacomo di Rialto (altar of Scuola degli Orefici; with Girolamo Campagna); 1601–1636, San Lazzaro dei Mendicanti Church and Hospital; Venice, Italy. 1604–1607, 1611–1612, Cathedral of Saints Rupert and Virgil (completed in 1614–1628 by Santino Solari), Salzburg, Austria. 1605, Santi Giovanni e Paolo (sacristy door; with Alessandro Vittorio), Venice, Italy. 1605–1616, Villa Duodo (six chapels for via Romana), Monselice, Italy. 1607–1611, San Giorgio Maggiore (façade); *1607–1616, Villa Cornaro al Paradiso (twin pavilions); Venice, Italy. *1609, Domenico Trevisan Villa, San Donà di Piave, Italy. 1609–1616, Palazzo Contarini; 1614, Palazzo Loredan (east wing; demolished in 1659 and rebuilt in 1660); Venice, Italy.

BIBLIOGRAPHY

BARBIERI, FRANCO 1952 *Vincenzo Scamozzi.* Vicenza, Italy: La Cassa di Risparmio.

DE LA CROIX, HORST 1966 "Palmanova: A Study in Sixteenth-century Urbanism." *Saggi e Memorie di Storia dell' Arte* 5:23–41.

DONIN, RICHARD KURT 1948 *Vincenzo Scamozzi und der Einfluss Venedigs auf die Salzburger Architektur.* Innsbruck, Austria: Rohrer.

GALLO, RODOLFO 1958–1959 "Vincenzo Scamozzi e la chiesa di San Nicolò da Tolentino." *Atti dell'-Istituto Veneto di Scienze, Lettere e Arti* 117:103–122.

HERSEY, GEORGE, L. 1976 *Pythagorean Palaces.* Ithaca, N.Y.: Cornell University Press.

LEWIS, DOUGLAS 1977 "Girolamo II Corner's Completion of Piombino, with an Unrecognized Building of 1596 by Vincenzo Scamozzi." *Architectura* 7:40–45.

PUPPI, LIONELLO, and PUPPI, LOREDANA OLIVATO 1974 "Scamozziana—progetti e alcune altre novità grafiche con qualche quesito." *Antichità Viva* 13, no. 4:54–80.

SCAMOZZI, VINCENZO (1600)1959 *Taccuino di viaggio da Parigi a Venezia.* Edited by Franco Barbieri. Venice, Italy, and Rome: Istituto per la Collaborazione Culturale.

SCAMOZZI, VINCENZO (1615)1964 *L'Idea della architettura universale.* Reprint. Ridgewood, N.J.: Gregg.

TEMANZA, TOMMASO (1778)1966 *Vite dei più celebri architetti e scultori veneziama.* Edited by Liliana Grassi. Reprint. Milan: Edizioni Labor.

TIMOFIEWITSCH, VLADIMIR 1965 "Das Testament Vincenzo Scamozzis vom 2. September 1602." *Bollettino del Centro Internazionale di Studi di Architettura* 7:316–328.

SCAPITTA, GIOVANNI BATTISTA

Giovanni Battista Scapitta (1653–1715) was born in Valenza in the Monferrato, Italy, and practiced in Casale Monferrato, where he was associated with and was succeeded by his nephew Vincenzo Scapitta. The diary of De Conti (written in the late eighteenth century) attributes the Palazzo Treville (1730) and Santa Caterina (1725) to Scapitta; however, it has since been shown that both were begun earlier. The Treville palace has an unusually developed scenographic perspective plan, including atrium, courtyard, and passages radiating through the building to the gardens behind, perhaps derived from Ferdinando and Francesco Bibiana and Lombard sources, combined with a delicate and refined relief stucco decoration of the vaults. Santa Caterina, a longitudinal oval in plan, also appears precocious in the second decade but is, in any case, notable.

HENRY A. MILLON

WORKS

(A)1714, Santa Caterina, Casale Monferrato, Italy. (A)1712–c.1790s, Palazzo Gozzani di Treville, Italy.

BIBLIOGRAPHY

CARBONERI, NINO 1963 Volume 1, pages 64–65 in *Architecture, Mostra del Barocco Piemontese.* Turin, Italy.

CARBONERI, NINO 1965 "La Parrocchiale di Pobietto e la Chiesa di San Pietro a Casale Monferrato." *Bollettino della Società Piemontese di Archeologia e Belle Arti.* New Series 19:43–48.

CORNAGLIA, E. 1968 *Giovanni Battista Scapitta architetto e Vincenzo Scapitta agrimensore.* Casale Monferrato, Italy.

TORNIELLI, VITTORIO 1957 *Architetture di otto secoli del Monferrato.* Casale Monferrato: Arte Grafiche.

VIALE FERRERO, MERCEDES 1966 Pages 60–65, plate 17, in *Ritratto di Casale.* Turin, Italy.

SCARPA, CARLO

Carlo Scarpa (1902–1978) was born in Venice, Italy. After receiving a certificate of the Academy of Fine Arts in architecture in 1926, he became assistant to Guido Cirilli at the University Institute of Architecture of Venice. He taught there and remained a practicing architect until his death in 1978.

Scarpa was very quick to get rid of a perfectly mastered academic education and joined the Modern movement. During the Fascist regime, he became a passionate supporter of Rational architecture. In his first works, between the two world wars, he aligned himself with LE CORBUSIER, LUDWIG MIES VAN DER ROHE, WALTER GROPIUS, ADOLF LOOS, and with their programmatic statements and trends.

After the war, his projects for the exhibitions of Paul Klee (Venice Biennale 1949), Giovanni Bellini (at the Ducal Palace in Venice, 1949), and Mondrian (Rome, 1956) already show a master's technique in the arrangement of museum materials, for which he became widely known. The Museo dell'Accademia (1947–1956) and Museo Correr (1953–1960) in Venice, the Palazzo Abatellis (Palermo, 1953–1954), the Gipsoteca Canova (Possagno, 1956–1957), and the Museo di Castelvecchio (Verona, 1964) are some of his works in this period. His entire body of works gives evidence of his faithfulness to the Modern movement. This is seen even in his last, unfinished projects: Cemetery Brion (San Vito d'Altivole, 1970), Ottolenghi House (Bardolino, 1975), Banca Popolare di Verona (1973), and housing blocks (Vicenza, 1975) where concrete, steel, and glass harmonize with forgotten traditions. A legend since the very beginning of his career, he has been defined as the "poet architect" of a typically Venetian tradition; in his last project, for the Picasso Museum (Paris, 1975), Scarpa denied once again that narrow definition and used Le Corbusier's famous ramp of Villa Savoye as a link between the temporary underground museum and the garden. But Scarpa's purity of style and uncompromising ethical stand are very far removed from Le Corbusier's. Scarpa remained to the last one of the best contemporary teachers and professionals.

PHILIPPE DUBOY

WORKS

1927–1947, Glassware for Venini Company, Murano, Italy. 1936–1937, 1956, University (Ca Foscari); 1941, Tomb of Rizzo Family, Cemetary of San Michele; 1947–1956, Museo dell'Accademia; 1949, Exhibition Paul Klee, Biennale of Art; 1950, Pavilion of the Book, Biennale of Art; Venice, Italy. 1953, Exhibition Antonello di Messina, Town Hall, Messina, Italy. 1953–1954, Palazzo Abatellis, Palermo, Italy. 1953–1960, Museo Correr, Venice, Italy. 1954–1956, Galleria degli Uffizi (first rooms with IGNAZIO GARDELLO and GIOVANNI MICHELUCCI), Florence. 1954–1956, Venezuela Pavilion, Biennale of Art; 1955, Manlio Capitolo (public court); Venice, Italy. 1955–1961, Veretti House, Udine, Italy. 1956–1957, Gipsoteca Canova, Possagno, Italy. 1957–1958, Show Room Olivetti; 1960, Exhibition ERICH MENDELSOHN, Biennale of Art; Venice, Italy. 1960, Memorial of FRANK LLOYD WRIGHT (exhibition), Triennale of Art, Milan. 1961, Exhibition (the sense of color and the mastery of water), Italia 61, Turin, Italy. 1961, Gavina Shop, Bologna, Italy. 1961–1963, Querini-Stampalia Foundation (ground floor and garden), Venice, Italy. 1964, Museo di Castelvecchio, Verona, Italy. 1964–1968, Zentner House, Zurich. 1967, Exhibition (the poem), Italian Pavilion, Montreal. 1968, Exhibition of Carlo Scarpa, LOUIS I. KAHN, PAUL RUDOLPH AND FRANCO ALBINI (pursuit of new structures), Biennale of Art, Venice, Italy. 1969, Exhibition of Mendelsohn's drawings, University of California, Berkeley. 1970–1978, Cemetery Brion (completed after his death), San Vito d'Altivole, Italy. 1973–1978, Banca Popolare di Verona (completed after his death), Italy. 1975, Monument to the Memory of the 1972 Terrorist Outrage, Brescia, Italy. 1975–1978, Ottolenghi House (completed after his death), Bardolino, Italy. 1975–1978, Housing blocks (completed after his death), Vincenza, Italy.

BIBLIOGRAPHY

A.M.C. 1973 50:entire issue.

BRUSATIN, MANLIO 1972 "Carlo Scarpa architetto." *Controspazio* 4, nos. 3–4.

KAHN, LOUIS, and CANTACUZINO, SHERBAN 1974 *Carla Scarpa: Exhibition at Heinz Gallery.* London: Royal Institute of British Architects.

PORTOGHESI, PAOLO 1979 "Carlo Scarpa, Cemetery Brion-Vega, S. Vito, Treviso, Italy." *Global Architecture* no. 50:entire issue.

Progressive Architecture 1981 62, no. 5:entire issue.

Rassegna 1981 7:entire issue.

SANTINI, PIER CARLO 1979 "Carlo Scarpa, Olivetti Show-room, S. Marco, Venezia, Italy 1957–58. Querini-Stampalia, Venezia, Italy 1961–63. Castelvecchio Museum, Verona, Italy, 1958–1964." *Global Architecture* no. 51.

YOKOYAMA, TADASHI, and TOYOTA, HIROYUKI 1977 "Carlo Scarpa." *Space Design* no. 153:7–162.

SCHACHT, EMIL

Born in Denmark, Emil Schacht (1854–1926) studied in Hannover, Germany, and Copenhagen. He emigrated to the United States in 1874, returned to Denmark where he married, and came back to America, first to Omaha, Nebraska, and in 1884 to Portland, Oregon. He had a large residential and commercial practice, first alone, later with his son, Martin Schacht.

MARION DEAN ROSS

WORKS

*1905, Oriental Building, Lewis and Clark Exposition; 1906–1907, Lenox Hotel; c.1910, John A. Veness House; 1912, Police Headquarters; Portland, Oregon.

BIBLIOGRAPHY

Further information on Emil Schacht can be found in the Special Collections of the University of Oregon Library, Eugene.

VAUGHAN, THOMAS, and FERRIDAY, VIRGINIA GUEST (editors) 1974 *Space, Style and Structure.* 2 vols. Portland: Oregon Historical Society.

SCHAROUN, HANS

Although usually grouped with the German Expressionist architects of the post-World War I era, Hans Scharoun (1893–1972) is distinguished for his ability to integrate principles of orthodox modernism, Expressionism, and the tenets of *das neue Bauen* (new building), a design philosophy articulated by HUGO HÄRING. Notwithstanding the changed nature of his commissions after World War II and the concomitant change in the image quality of his designs, Scharoun's work provides continuity between German architecture of the 1920s and that of the postwar era. His most significant achievements and the ones that most accurately reflect the social and architectural philosophies that he refined throughout his career, are the large cultural buildings built after World War II including theaters, concert halls, libraries, and schools.

Born in Bremen, Germany, Scharoun spent his youth in the port city of Bremerhaven. Appropriately, marine imagery later appears in his architecture as in the German Maritime Museum (1970), Bremerhaven. Having studied architecture at the Technische Hochschule in Berlin-Charlottenburg from 1912, Scharoun entered the military in 1915 in the Division of Reconstruction, East Prussia, where he remained until 1918. Following his military service, Scharoun established an architectural practice in Insterburg, remaining there until 1925. Competition projects and a few houses comprised his work. Scharoun took part in the Arbeitsrat für Kunst organized in 1919. In his projects, Scharoun experimented with traditional design principles as well as allowing his architectural fantasies to inform his work. Thus, his project for rebuilding the Cathedral Square at Prenzlau (1919) was rigid and classical in plan, while the designs for the Gelsenkirchen Cultural Center (1920) and the Matheus Müller Works extension (1920) were characterized by the attempt to integrate (despite their functional irrelevance) the crystalline shapes and planning principles suggested by colleagues in *Die Gläserne Kette* (the Glass Chain).

In 1926, Scharoun joined *Der Ring,* to which LUDWIG MIES VAN DER ROHE, HANS POELZIG, BRUNO TAUT and MAX TAUT, ERIC MENDELSOHN, LUDWIG HILBERSEIMER, and Hugo Häring belonged. To Häring, Scharoun owed his rejection of aesthetics as the determinant of architectural form and his commitment to an organic ideal according to which form becomes an expression of function. As such, Scharoun insisted that the plan can be developed only by a complete understanding of the program. Because each function determines its own form, and a building may combine seemingly inconsistent forms, an arbitrarily imposed shape is precluded.

From 1915 to 1932, Scharoun taught at the Staatliche Akademie für Kunst und Kunstgewerbe in Breslau. His architecture, which had evolved from a static and classical early phase, began to reflect the principles of the International style. A detached house in reinforced concrete for the Weissenhof Siedlung, Stuttgart (1927), is Scharoun's first important built work and illustrates his interest in creating form that expresses its function irrespective of aesthetic considerations. Before the Nazis imposed restrictions on building, Scharoun designed a mobile house (his building for the German Garden and Industry Exhibition at Liegnitz, 1927, is the best example) and projected a number of housing developments. The apartment blocks that he designed for Siemensstadt, Berlin (he was responsible for overall planning of the housing estate), are notable for their unconventional orientation to one another, and the individual flats include central living/dining areas, which serve also as circulation space. During the Nazi years, Scharoun lived in Siemensstadt, building a few private houses, generating plans for housing developments, and painting utopian conceptions in watercolors.

The Schminke House (1933) indicates the direction in which Scharoun's architecture was moving when the Nazis "outlawed" modern architecture. Two axes, which are suggested by the site, largely determine the plan, which is free and open, divided only by movable partitions. Balconies, which are supported on free-standing columns, extend from the living and bedroom areas, and curves replace external angles. The house serves as a screen between garden and road while suggesting continuity of interior and exterior.

Although the private houses of 1933–1943 have rather traditional exteriors, in accordance with German restrictions, Scharoun continued to experiment with free planning. As Berlin City Planning officer, Scharoun produced a radical reconstruction plan for the city, which he exhibited in 1946. Consistent with the scarcity of building projects in Germany after the war, he produced only a few architectural projects in the later 1940s. Nonetheless, he was active in planning and teaching, participating in the re-establishment of the architectural faculty of the Berlin Technische Hochschule, where he was the senior professor in the town planning department until 1958, and heading the Institute for Building Studies at the German Academy of Sciences (1947–1951).

The architecture produced between 1950 and 1972 (the year of his death), represents the culmination of Scharoun's development, in that it sums up ideas about architecture as a determining factor in social interaction. The Darmstadt School (1951) which remained only a project, was a model for the Geschwisterschule (1956–1962) in Lunen and the Volkschule at Marl (1961–1968). While the individual classroom served as the basis for the design, Scharoun intended to stress the communal nature of the educational experience. Scharoun's interest in representing the various social and physical functions of education with different forms resulted in a fragmented plan. His ability to reconcile seemingly contradictory aims is evident in the Kassel Theater scheme (1952, with Herman Mattern), also never executed, which served as a prototype for the Mannheim Theater (1953) and the Wolfsburg Theater (1965–1972). The social and cultural significance of the theater is emphasized by making it a prominent landmark in the townscape, but an organic relation with the landscape is also created. Thus, Kassel Theater's undulating form reflects the hilly profile of the city.

The Berlin Philharmonic Hall (1959–1963) is Scharoun's best-known work and perhaps best illustrates his design methodology. Overall siting and orientation serve to regularize the exterior shape of the building; the form was generated by a desire to accommodate the internal functions—the hallmark of Scharoun's planning. His great State Library in Berlin, built on the same principles, was not completed until after his death.

SUSAN STRAUSS

Scharoun.
Berlin Philharmonic Hall, Tiergarten.
1959–1963

WORKS

1917, Community Hall, Kattenau, East Prussia. 1920, Two Houses, Pregelstrasse; 1922, Single-family Houses; 1923–1924, Apartment Blocks, Parkring; Insterburg, East Prussia. 1924–1925, Public Buildings, Bad Mergentheim Spa, Württemberg, Germany. 1927, Mobile Wooden House, German Garden and Industry Exhibition, Liegnitz, Germany. 1927, Single-family House, Weissenhofsiedlung, Stuttgart, Germany. 1928–1929, Apartment Block, Kaiserdamm, Charlottenburg, Berlin. 1929, Single People's Apartment Block, Deutscher Werkbund Exhibition, Breslau, Germany. 1933, Schminke House, Lobau, Saxony, Germany. 1937–1938, Noack House, Potsdam, Germany. 1940, Housing, Kaiserstrasse, Bremerhaven, Germany. 1949, Institute of Building Conversion, German Academy of Sciences, Berlin. 1954–1959, Romeo and Juliet Flats, Zuffenhausen, Stuttgart, Germany. 1956–1962, Geschwister Secondary School, Lunen, Westphalia, Germany. 1959–1963, Berlin Philharmonic Hall, Tiergarten. 1961–1968, School, Marl, Westphalia, Germany. 1963–1971, German Embassy, Brasilia. 1965–1972, City Theater (not completed until 1973), Wolfsburg, Germany. 1966, Architecture Building, Technical University of Berlin. 1966, Chapel of Saint John, Glockengarten, Bochum, Germany. 1967–1972, State Library (not completed until 1978), Berlin. 1970, Church and Parish Center, Rabenberg, Wolfsburg, Germany. 1970, German Maritime Museum, Bremerhaven, Germany.

BIBLIOGRAPHY

CONRADS, ULRICH, and SPERLICH, HANS 1960 *Phantastische Architektur.* Stuttgart, Germany: Hatje.

"Hans Scharoun." 1967 *Aujourd'hui* 10, nos. 57–58:2–61.

JONES, PETER BLUNDELL 1973 "Scharoun, Häring and Organic Functionalism." *Architectural Association Quarterly* 5, no. 1:48–57.

JONES, PETER BLUNDELL 1975 "Late Works of Scharoun." *Architectural Review* 157, Mar.:140–154.

JONES, PETER BLUNDELL 1976 "Ship Shape Scharoun: German Maritime Museum, Bremerhaven." *Architectural Review* 159, Mar.:154–162.

JONES, PETER BLUNDELL 1978*a* *Hans Scharoun.* London: Gordon Fraser Gallery.

JONES, PETER BLUNDELL 1978*b* "Hans Scharoun: An Introduction." *Architectural Design* 48, no.7:492–495.

JONES, PETER BLUNDELL 1978*c* "Organic versus Classic." *Architectural Association Quarterly* 10, no.1:10–20.

JONES, PETER BLUNDELL 1979 "Scharoun's Staatsbibliothek: State Library, Berlin." *Architectural Review* 165, June:330–341.

LANIER, R. S. 1964 "Acoustics in-the-round at the Berlin Philharmonic." *Architectural Forum* 120, May:98–105.

MESSINA, VITTORIO LETI; TAUT, MAX; and LAUTERBACH, HEINRICH 1969 *Hans Scharoun.* Rome: Officina Edizione.

PEHNT, WOLFGANG 1973 *Expressionist Architecture.* London: Thames & Hudson.

PFANKUCH, PETER 1974 *Hans Scharoun: Bauten, Entwürfe, Texte.* Berlin: Akademie der Künste.

"Philharmonie de Berlin." 1964 *L'Architecture d'Aujourd'hui* 34, no. 115:54–61.

SEGAL, WALTER 1973 "Scharoun." *Architectural Review* 153, Feb.:98–102.

STABER, MARGIT 1962 "Hans Scharoun: Ein Beitrag zum organischen Bauen." *Zodiac* 10:52–93.

SCHEERBART, PAUL

Paul Scheerbart (1863–1915), born in Danzig, East Prussia, was a German Expressionist writer whose whimsical, mystical short stories and novels often dealt with futuristic glass architecture. Although he died in Berlin in 1915, through his close friendship with BRUNO TAUT his ideas had a lasting influence on Expressionist designs after World War I. Scheerbart's best known book is *Glass Architecture* (1914). This work was dedicated to Taut, who in turn dedicated his Glass House at the Cologne Werkbund Exhibition, also of 1914, to Scheerbart. In *Glass Architecture,* as well as in his other writings, Scheerbart saw glass structures, and particularly buildings using stained glass, as an expression of a heightened sensory awareness. In his most utopian works he called for the rejection of an old "brick culture" and for a world in which glass architecture stands for a new anarchistic society. Glass imagery was to be used in Scheerbart's sense—as a metaphor of social change—by Expressionist artists and architects belonging to the Arbeitsrat für Kunst and the Gläserne Kette. Scheerbart's concepts of a crystalline transformation of both architecture and society also affected WALTER GROPIUS's opening manifesto of the Bauhaus in April 1919, as well as several unusual glass skyscraper projects by LUDWIG MIES VAN DER ROHE. In a bastardized form, the glass skyscraper became a central feature of the American phase of the International style.

ROSEMARIE HAAG BLETTER

BIBLIOGRAPHY

BANHAM, REYNER 1959 "The Glass Paradise." *Architectural Review* 125:87–89.

BLETTER, ROSEMARIE HAAG 1975 "Paul Scheerbart's Architectural Fantasies." *Journal of the Society of Architectural Historians* 34:83–97.

SHARP, DENNIS (editor) 1972 *Glass Architecture by Paul Scheerbart and Alpine Architecture by Bruno Taut.* Translated by James Palmes and Shirley Palmer. New York and Washington: Praeger. Originally published in German as two separate works in 1914 and 1919 respectively.

SCHELLING, H. G. J.

In the period between 1920 and 1960, H. G. J. Schelling (1888–1978), together with S. van Ravesteyn, determined the architecture of the Dutch Railway Company. In the service of this company since 1916, Schelling held the responsibility for the construction of railway stations in the northern part of Holland. Especially after World War II, he was noted for his bare, reinforced concrete structures.

MARK À CAMPO

WORKS

1939, Amstelstation, Amsterdam. 1950, Railway Station, Enschede, Netherlands. 1951, Railway Station, Hengelo, Netherlands. 1952, Railway Station, Zutphen, Netherlands. 1953, Railway Station, Leiden, Netherlands. 1954, Railway Station, Arnhem, Netherlands.

BIBLIOGRAPHY

DOPPER, H., and PORTIER, G. 1976 *De geschiedenis van de Nederlandse Stations.*

SCHINDLER, R. M.

R(udolph) M(ichael) Schindler (1887–1953) worked in isolation in Los Angeles. He was out of step with the International style and shunned eclectic styles. His work rarely appeared in architectural journals, and because of his unconventional dress and jovial manner he was not considered a "serious" architect by his colleagues.

Nearly all of his commissions were houses, rarely large, and always built at a low cost. Complex spatial relationships interested him more than fine workmanship and materials. He is now a cult figure and his work is zealously protected.

He was born in Vienna, where his father was an artisan in metal who had practiced his craft in New York before opening an import business in Vienna.

Schindler enrolled in the Royal Technical Institute in 1906, and in 1910 he was accepted by the Wagner School of the Academy of Art. He attended both schools simultaneously for one year, receiving a degree from the Institute in 1911 and from the Academy in 1913. He was employed as a draftsman in the firm of Mayr and Mayer from 1911 to 1914. The firm credited him with the design and supervision of the Clubhouse for Actors (1911) in the historic core of Vienna.

Schindler's interest in America was quickened by OTTO WAGNER, ADOLF LOOS, and FRANK LLOYD WRIGHT, whose Wasmuth Portfolio he studied in 1910. He answered an advertisement in a Vienna newspaper for a draftsman with the Chicago firm of Ottenheimer, Stern, and Reichert, and left for Chicago in February 1914 to fulfill a three-year contract with the firm. Among the large buildings he designed for them between 1915 and early 1918 were the Elks Club and Buena Shore Club in Chicago.

By the time his contract had run out, his movements were hampered by the entry of the United States into the war; he appealed to Frank Lloyd Wright, who took him into his office in early 1918. The plans in which he participated were the Imperial Hotel, buildings for Aline Barnsdall on Olive Hill, Los Angeles, and several smaller projects. In 1919, he married Sophie Pauline Gibling, teacher of music at a progressive school and at the Hull House.

In December 1919, Wright sent Schindler to Los Angeles to oversee construction of Barnsdall's Hollyhock House. Only three of the many buildings planned for Olive Hill were executed, and at the end of 1921, with the Wright office closing, Schindler determined to start his own practice.

His most notable works of the 1920s were of concrete, each using a different structural system. His Kings Road House (1921–1922), Los Angeles, both his office and home, was a cooperative house for two young couples. The plan may have been the first to elevate women to equality; it was a response to the spirit of the suffragist movement and to Schindler's belief that the architect could foster talent in women by providing them a space of their own. The L-shaped plan, consisting of two equal-sized studios, entry hall, bath, and roof sleeping porch, was flipped and repeated; turning the two L plans in opposite directions created courts for outdoor living rooms. The L plans were linked by a single shared kitchen in which the wives, according to Schindler, performed the duties on alternate weeks to "gain periods of respite from the incessant household rhythm." Projecting from the kitchen was a guest studio.

The building material was tapered concrete panels poured on the slab floor, which was on the same level as the garden; the panels were tilted upright and joined by slits of glass. Large openings were concentrated in walls on the garden side of each studio, with clearstories for additional light. Among the Wrightian practices in Schindler's early houses were the lightweight movable partitions, from the Japanese by way of Wright, and geometric patterns of wood, in relief, or applied to the sash of glazed openings.

The Pueblo Ribera Court (1923), La Jolla, California, comprised twelve four-room cottages with roof terrace and walled patio. They were designed in pairs so that the plan could be flipped; thus, the masonry wall of one became a garden wall for the patio of the second. A "slip-form" structural system in concrete allowed forms to be lifted and reused, the joint being treated as integral decoration.

Schindler.
Schindler House.
Los Angeles.
1921–1922

The most famous work of the concrete period was the Lovell Beach House (1926), Newport Beach, California. The house was lifted above the ground on five freestanding concrete frames, poured in place, and the prefabricated enclosed

Schindler.
Lovell Beach House.
Newport Beach, California.
1926

space was hung by steel rods from the frames. The interweaving of enclosed space and frame created a spatial ambiguity. On the street elevation the frame was dominant but on the ocean side the interior space pressed forward through the two-story glass wall, and balconies and overhangs advanced beyond the frame or cut away from it.

In the Packard House (1924), Pasadena, California, thin concrete was sprayed against molds to form walls. The configuration of the house grew out of a tract restriction for steep roofs; to minimize the roof and at the same time produce space forms in the high living room Schindler mitered the gables and flattened the roof ridge. He turned tract restrictions to his advantage on other occasions. In the Bennati Cabin (1934), Lake Arrowhead, California, the steep roof was carried to the base to form an A shape. A variation of the Packard scheme occurred in the Tischler House (1949), Los Angeles, in which the gable end was broken up by a projecting dormer. In a tract requiring tile roofs, part of the exterior walls were covered with tile. Some of his most expressionist buildings grew out of tract restrictions, but there were minor houses of the 1920s in which expression came from the large-scale decorative details.

An early example of a house for a steep hillside was the three-story Wolfe House (1928), Catalina Island, California. Rather than integrate the house into the slope he let it hover above it, with three points of contact with the grade. In his later hillside houses in the Silver Lake area of Los Angeles he avoided carving out the slope by using pylons, central shafts, or other devices.

Schindler's work fell into three periods, which coincided roughly with the decades of the 1920s, 1930s, and 1940s. He abandoned concrete during the Depression years of the 1930s because of the cost, working entirely with wood framing and stucco skin. The materials responded easily to the cubic forms which were characteristic of the period. The cubism paralleled the *Stijl* movement in the Netherlands. Schindler's cubes, however, were so broken up that inner and outer space flowed together. There was surface movement; the stucco fascias widened or thinned, the line was interrupted by a downturn or an upturn expanded into a parapet wall.

Schindler. Buck House. Los Angeles. 1934

The variations in the style often arose from site difficulties. The Oliver House (1933), Los Angeles, presented the problem of pushing the house up a narrow steep slope to the view at the back. He set the house at an angle to the street, recessed the lower level, and cantilevered the dominant cubic form of the entrance level beyond it. The main rooms were arranged in an L around a view terrace at the top.

For his houses of the 1920s, Schindler designed furniture of redwood boards; in the 1930s he developed unit furniture of ash plywood, the units being combined for various uses. In the Oliver House the built-in sofa in the living room terminated in units forming shelves, cabinets, and tables.

The Buck House (1934), the finest of the cubistic work, resembles somewhat the forms the unit furniture could take. The forms are constantly in movement; they grow, break up, and reform. The entrance hall is in a low recessed cube between two higher cubes, which accounts for the glimpse of the sky above the front door.

Schindler's framing lent itself to such surprises. Instead of the standard balloon frame he devised one with the plate line at door height; this allowed him to break through the girdle of studs, without disturbing the plate line, for changes of ceiling height, for clearstories, and for the introduction of glazed openings at will.

Late in the 1930s, Schindler added a countermotion to the cubes by revolving the plan. The best use was in the Falk Apartments (1939), Los Angeles, where privacy for the roof terraces was accomplished by revolving the plan a quarter turn. He revolved the plan twice for some of the rooms to produce a variety of space forms. The scheme probably originated in 1937 in a group of shops just off a main boulevard; to make display windows visible from the boulevard he lifted them and gave a different orientation to each.

The plan revolution figured importantly in his work of the 1940s. Other changes arose out of the war and postwar economy. Plywood replaced plaster for interior walls; ceilings were of thick, grooved planking, which served as a base for the roofing material. The weight of the planking accounted for the change from flat to pitched roofs, and the weight determined the shortness of the span. Roofs dominated the form. In the Van Dekker House (1940), Canoga Park, California, there were no less than five shed roofs.

With the emphasis on roof came many in-sloping walls. This became the theme of the Kallis House (1945), North Hollywood, California. The site was depressed below street level, and the sloping glass admitted more light at the front and to an artist's studio detached from the house. He took advantage of the curve of the street to place the artist's studio at an angle to the main house; the two were connected by a raised terrace with a fireplace of stone, a material he had not used in the 1920s and 1930s.

Another solution for a site on a curve occurred in the planning of the Lechner House (1948), Studio City, California. An open-angled plan embraced a large terrace from which there was an uninterrupted view of a canyon.

Schindler's only church, Bethlehem Baptist Church (1944), replaced one destroyed by fire in the Watts area of Los Angeles. He faced a closed wall onto a heavily traveled street, giving it symbolic importance by the overlapping bands of stucco resembling masonry. The deeply recessed entrance was from a side street, the landscaped spaces along the approach planned as meeting places for the congregation. On the tower above the entrance was a four-sided cross which was visible inside the church through glazing in the roof.

His last houses were like unfinished ideas which might have developed into a new style. The Tischler House (1949), Los Angeles, California, in which color was released into the air through the blue of fiberglass roofing panels, went back to the Viennese Secession for the black and silver colors of the living room. The Janson House (1940), Los Angeles, was a constructivist tour de force on a site offering only enough land for a garage. The house grew out of the canyon floor; the living spaces were pods hung from, or resting on top of, a slender masonry shaft. On the street level were two equal-sized studio rooms with fiberglass walls and clearstories; clear glass provided a spectacular view of the canyon. The two studios were separated by a mechanical core in which were the bath and kitchen. The final work, the Skolnik House (1951–1953), Los Angeles, had a merry-go-round plan, above which floated a tentlike roof, the spaces below being divided by screen walls.

ESTHER MCCOY

WORKS

1921–1922, Schindler House, Los Angeles. 1923, Pueblo Ribera Court, La Jolla, Calif. 1924, Packard House, Pasadena, Calif. 1926, Lovell Beach House, Newport Beach, Calif. 1928, Wolfe House, Catalina Island, Calif. 1933, Oliver House, Los Angeles. 1934, Bennati Cabin, Lake Arrowhead, Calif. 1934, Buck House; 1935, Walker House; 1936, McAlmon House; Los Angeles. 1937, Rodakiewicz House, Beverly Hills, Calif. 1939, Falk Apartments, Los Angeles. 1940, Van Dekker House, Canoga Park, Calif. 1944, Bethlehem Baptist Church, Los Angeles. 1946, Kallis House; 1948, Lechner House; Studio City, Calif. 1949, Tischler House; 1949, Janson House; 1950–1953, Skolnik House; Los Angeles.

BIBLIOGRAPHY

ANDREWS, WAYNE (1947)1978 *Architecture, Ambition, and Americans: A Social History of American Architecture.* Rev. ed. New York: Free Press.

BENHAM, REYNER 1971 *Los Angeles.* New York: Harper.

GEBHARD, DAVID 1971 *Schindler.* New York: Viking.

HOLLEIN, HANS 1961 "Rudolf M. Schindler," *Der Aufbau* (Vienna) 16, no. 3:102–110.

HOLLEIN, HANS 1966 "Rudolf M. Schindler." *Bau* (Vienna) 21, no. 4:67–82.

JORDY, WILLIAM H. 1972 *Progressive and Academic Ideals at the Turn of the Twentieth Century.* Volume 3 in *American Buildings and Their Architects.* New York: Doubleday.

MCCOY, ESTHER 1960 *Five California Architects.* New York: Reinhold.

Vienna to Los Angeles: Two Journeys. 1979 Santa Monica, Calif.: Arts & Architecture Press. Introduction to letters between R. M. Schindler and Richard Neutra, and letters of Louis Sullivan to R. M. Schindler.

SCHINKEL, KARL FRIEDRICH

Pre-eminent German architect of the nineteenth century, Karl Friedrich Schinkel (1781–1841) served for a quarter of a century as state architect in Prussia, defining an epoch in Prussian architecture and establishing a design standard upheld by successive generations of Berlin architects. Trained in both the rationalist pragmatism of the German *Baumeister* tradition and the neoclassical tradition of Johann Joachim Winckelmann, Schinkel formulated a lucid and monumental architecture at once dependent on structural analysis and expressive of the highest ideals of restoration Prussia. Although he upheld Greece as an ideal model throughout his long career, he was no revivalist. Like his contemporary Georg Friedrich Hegel, often considered the Prussian state philosopher, Schinkel analyzed the structure of the past to isolate the strains from which the present could be constructed. All of his buildings are animated by a tension between his theory of the autonomous monument and his ability to cast buildings as focal points in a complex matrix of controlled views and suggestive architectural relationships. Both the formal integrity of Schinkel's designs and his concept of the professional architect as an agent of social ideas, "the ennobler of all human relationships" as he expressed it, have made Schinkel's career one of the most admired and studied in the history of modern architecture.

The son of the local inspector of churches and schools, Schinkel was born in Neuruppin, a town in the Mark Brandenburg province distinguished by its fine, royally sponsored housing. After the loss of nearly two-thirds of the town in a disastrous blaze in 1787 which also destroyed the family house and precipitated Schinkel's father's death, Neuruppin was rapidly rebuilt on a new rationalized plan. Thus, Schinkel's early years were spent amidst a town under reconstruction, an impressive model of architecture as public service with profound echoes in his mature career. His gifts as a draftsman were already manifested during his school years, first in Neuruppin and then at the distinguished Gymnasium zum Grauen Kloster in Berlin, where the widowed mother moved her six children in 1794. At the 1797 Academy Exhibition, Schinkel was so profoundly moved by the young FRIEDRICH GILLY'S design for a monument to the genius of Frederick the Great that he vowed to become an architect. Schinkel was not alone in his enthralled recognition of Gilly's own genius in the project; it affected an entire generation of architects through its powerful investment of antique forms with romantic ideals. Impatiently awaiting Gilly's return from a trip to Paris, Schinkel began his architectural training in 1798 under Gilly's father David, even boarding for a time in the Gilly household. Based on the model of JACQUES FRANÇOIS BLONDEL's academy, Gilly's architectural school taught construction as the basis of architecture and imbued pupils with a respect for materials and structure as determinants of form. A pioneer in the organization of formal architectural education as a path to state careers, David Gilly was an organizer of the Berlin Bauakademie in 1799. Schinkel, a member of the first class, was taught there in the tradition of Berlin neoclassicism by CARL GOTTHARD LANGHANS; by the staunch Hellenist, art historian, and theorist Alois Hirt; and by Gilly's friend HEINRICH GENTZ. It was nevertheless Friedrich Gilly's inspiring talent and close friendship which instilled Schinkel with the conviction that architecture could be the materialization of higher ideals. At his premature death in 1800, Gilly left Schinkel his designs which had circulated like precious secrets among the young architects studying in Berlin, including LEO VON KLENZE and Haller von Hallerstein, and which Schinkel preserved and mined for inspiration throughout his career. They were, indeed, more important to his formation of an individual vision of architecture than the group of Gilly commissions he was left to complete. In these remodelings and designs of small country houses and outbuildings, Schinkel established fruitful contacts with the aristocracy of the Mark Brandenburg. Gilly's severe, stereometric style and his devotion to the ideal of Greek architecture provided a model of monumental simplicity and geometrical clarity fundamental to Schinkel's own architecture. Although these early houses are strongly dependent on Gilly, in the Steinmeyer House in Berlin (1802–1805) there is already a hint of those qualities that would differentiate Schinkel's mature architecture from that of his masters Gilly and Gentz. Schinkel was increasingly interested in the surface as a skin and the possibility of making it represent the structural system of the building. His description of Gilly as "the creator of what I am" (Wolzogen, 1862, vol. 1, p. 173) was, however, no sentimental exaggeration. Friedrich Gilly had defined the themes of Schinkel's career in his appreciation of both the antique and the native brick Gothic tradition as architectures in which a harmonious aesthetic had given form to a cultural ideal. No doubt, Schinkel's decision to complete his formation by a trip to Italy and France was conceived in large part as a fulfillment of Gilly's own most cherished longing to study the monuments of antiquity at first hand.

Schinkel traveled to Italy with a fellow architectural student, J. G. Steinmeyer, son of his first Berlin patron. Following the traditional route from Berlin via Prague, Vienna, Trieste, Venice, and then through Lombardy and Tuscany, he arrived in Rome where he was soon introduced into the stimulating milieu of German artists there, which included the neoclassical painters Joseph Anton Koch and Gottlieb Schick who would exercise a great influence over Schinkel's developing style as a painter. In Rome, Schinkel complained that he was more often considered a promising landscape painter than an architect. Indeed, throughout his career, painting would be a subsidiary, if at times dominant, and always complementary activity to architectural design.

In the winter of 1803–1804, Schinkel traveled to Naples and toured Sicily where he fell under the spell of the richness and colorfulness of the Greek and medieval monuments. Whereas most architects of this period, both German and French, enjoyed royal or aristocratic support for their trips, Schinkel paid his own way and thus his *Bildungsreise* was characterized by an independence of mind from the outset. From Prague and Vienna on, medieval buildings captivated his attention. "For the most part, antiquity offers nothing new, for one is acquainted with it from childhood," he later explained to David Gilly in a letter from Paris

(Wolzogen, 1862, vol. 1, p. 166). From the medieval brick churches of Bologna and Ferrara to that unique admixture of Gothic and classic that is Milan Cathedral and the Islamic-tinged Norman Romanesque of Sicily, Schinkel studied the monuments of what he labeled then "Saracenic architecture" with an eye to his own designs and possible publication. He admired their truthful material expression, picturesque relation to natural settings, and even synthetic approach to the architectural past. In his travel drawings Schinkel did not, however, merely record the nonantique buildings, but he also subjected them to conjectural restoration and analytical regularization, seeking by clarifying their essential forms and compositions to impart that spirit of harmony and repose he cherished in antiquity. In Schinkel's hands, the traditional neoclassical journey of emulation, or gathering of models for future designs, was transformed into one of analysis and discovery. Schinkel was the first architect of the nineteenth century to distill from the architecture of the past a method rather than a model for contemporary architecture.

Carrying only one book, a volume of the writings of the contemporary philosopher Johann Gottlieb Fichte, Schinkel was also at the beginning of an engagement with the definition of his artistic role and with an interest in idealist philosophy that would shape his whole career. His travel diaries and letters reflect the influence of Fichte's analysis of the development of individual consciousness in the natural realm of physical objects. As though seeking to recreate Fichte's search for self-definition, Schinkel repeatedly sought out Italian promontories that would afford him panoramic vistas encompassing whole cities and their settings. This technique of deliberate spatial detachment was to be, as Kurt Forster (1982) has illustrated, a key to Schinkel's concept of space in his Berlin career as a panorama painter and architect; it also paralleled his approach to the architectural past. Just as towns and their monuments when seen from ahigh were comprehended in their larger geographical context, so from his standpoint in the nineteenth century—a century absorbed with a heightened concern for defining its own character—Schinkel saw the antique and the medieval heritage as two perfected moments in a continuous sequence. Once larger historical processes were understood, a new architecture could be postulated at once continuous with the past and expressive of its own time.

Fichte's insistence on the necessity for translating individual awareness into public action and his concept of moral vocation (*The Vocation of Man,* 1800) fired Schinkel with a sense of architecture as a public responsibility. Yet, there could hardly have been a less promising time to begin an architectural career in Prussia; the defeat at Jena in 1806 and the subsequent Napoleonic occupation marked the cessation of nearly all building activity. Working as a painter, Schinkel exploited his travel sketches in a series of idealized landscape paintings and lithographs. In order to support himself and, after his marriage in 1809, his young family, Schinkel painted some forty-five dioramas and panoramas for the popular Christmas-time presentations of the entrepreneur Wilhelm Gropius. In the illusionistic space of the panorama, the experience of Italy was first translated into a public medium, recreating for a wider audience that sensation of a privileged vantage point commanding both time and space. In the panorama—a phenomenon imported from England—the combination of illusionistic scene painting, artificial lighting, and frequently music created an immediate and realistic confrontation with distant places and events. From the Panorama of Palermo (1808) to imaginary historical reconstructions such as the Seven Wonders of the Ancient World (1812) and finally contemporary events such as the Defeat at Leipzig (1813), scenes were brought into harrowing juxtaposition with the individual viewer.

As early as 1806, Schinkel had been suggested for the post of court theater painter, but it was only in 1815 that he was able to execute the first of his designs. The renowned mystical sets for Mozart's *Magic Flute* (1815) had the same unity of effect and monumental impact as his earlier dioramas. Schinkel painted over one hundred sets for some forty plays, mostly between 1815 and 1820, an activity which acquainted him further with the structure of romantic comedy and drama first imparted by his friendship with the playwright Ludwig Tieck.

The dioramas not only won Schinkel public acclaim but also captured the imagination of Queen Luise, who commissioned Schinkel in 1809 to decorate several interiors in the Royal Palaces at Berlin and Charlottenburg. With the encouragement of Wilhelm von Humboldt, then minister of education, she had him appointed in March 1810 as *Oberbauassessor* in the Department of Public Works. Charged with reviewing "the aesthetic component" in all state-financed building, Schinkel had gained a foothold on the mountain of Prussian bureaucracy he would later dominate. By 1815, he was promoted to *Geheimer Oberbaurat* and given particular responsibility for Berlin. He began to conceive an architecture expressive of Prussia's imperial and social aspirations, yet shaped by the liberal reform tradition which had been established by influential Prussian bureaucrats during the Napoleonic occupation. The romantic patriotism of his projects during those years (1808–1809) and during the Wars of Liberation (1813–1815) reflect in image and program the ideals of architecture as a molding social agent which were more subtly incorporated in his mature designs. From the first, Schinkel's buildings were structured by the polarities of his position within the liberally minded bureaucracy and his close relationship with the royal family.

The romantic program for Queen Luise's bedroom at the Charlottenburg Palace (1810) continued the pictorial illusionism of the panoramas. By the simple means of white muslin stretched over rose-colored walls, light was reflected and filtered through the material to create a glowing effect of sunrise. This obscuring of the boundaries between the realms of architecture and nature, a demonstration of Schinkel's belief that "architecture is the continuation of nature in her constructive activity" (Peschken, 1979, p. 35), is also reflected in his paintings of Gothic cathedrals which appear to grow from their rocky settings (*Dom über einer Stadt,* Neue Pinakothek, Munich, 1813). Deeply affected by an exhibition of Caspar David Friedrich's paintings in Berlin in 1810, Schinkel adopted a more romantic landscape style in which nature, now more frequently the rugged northern landscape and always a record of human presence, is the carrier of religious and philosophical meaning. Schinkel's friendship with the Romantic writers Achem and Bettira von Arnim and Clemens Brentano, who met regularly in Schinkel's house in the Gross-Friedrichstrasse during these years, deepened his interest in the Middle Ages as a period in which German cultural unity and a higher Christian purpose had given rise to a harmonious cultural expression. The humiliation of the Napoleonic defeat gave this association a new nationalist immediacy. Fichte's *Reden an die Deutsche Nation* (Addresses to the German Nation), delivered during the bleak winter of 1807–1808, were lectures aimed to rouse Prussian cultural self-awareness and patriotism. They filled Schinkel with a renewed belief in the artist's duty to the nation. Beginning with his plans to rebuild the burned Petrikirche in Berlin (1809–1810, second project 1814–1815) and culminating in his grandiose scheme for a commemorative cathedral of the Wars of Liberation (1815), Schinkel charged the Gothic with symbolizing the national cause and thereby linked Prussia with a higher Christian purpose.

Queen Luise's death in 1810 was the focus of outpourings of patriotic fervor. Schinkel designed a cast-iron memorial (1811) which, financed by public subscription, was to be raised on the spot in Gransee where her coffin had rested overnight en route to Charlottenburg. Her death had assumed such symbolic import that the design of her mausoleum occasioned the earliest dispute over the appropriate historical style for a national monument. King Friedrich Wilhelm III commissioned a classical temple front to commemorate his loss and even provided a sketch for the interior. But Schinkel, in challenging the associational appropriateness of a temple, seized the opportunity to issue a manifesto celebrating the national Gothic. Clearly conscious of Gilly's epoch-making design to honor an earlier national hero, Frederick the Great, Schinkel presented a stunning view of a high Gothic shrine radiating light from its heavily wooded setting. In the text accompanying his watercolors at the 1810 Academy Exhibition, he declared classical architecture cold and meaningless in a building intended to represent the Christian celebration of death as the passage to a higher realm. Gothic alone, he maintained, was capable of filling the visitor with the feelings of "the infinite and eternal." Only there was "the spirit fully victorious over mass and material" (Wolzogen, 1863, vol. 3, p. 157). Evoking eighteenth-century notions of Gothic's natural origin, Schinkel compared the interior to a palm grove raised over the queen's sarcophagus, in turn held aloft by pristine white angels. But unlike eighteenth-century designs in the Gothic style, Schinkel's was no mere

Schinkel. Mausoleum for Queen Luise (with Gentz). Park Charlottenburg, Berlin. 1810–1840

Schinkel. Sarcophagus for Queen Luise (with Gentz). Park Charlottenburg, Berlin. 1810–1840

whimsical garden ornament but a declaration of Gothic architecture as the embodiment of the national spirit. Paradoxically, the mausoleum as built by Heinrich Gentz has a Doric temple front designed by Schinkel (1810–1811) to the king's specifications.

Gilly's monument is again evoked in Schinkel's selection of a reorganized Leipziger Platz as the site for a national cathedral to commemorate the Wars of Liberation. An original amalgam of a high Gothic nave and a domed crossing interpreted in anachronistic Gothic forms, this pilgrimage cathedral was to be raised on a plinth as a free-standing monument but set as the focal point of the streets radiating from the hexagonal Leipziger Platz. Symbolic of German unity in style, the cathedral would also serve as an agent of national renewal in its actual construction. Schinkel proposed creating a *Bauhütte,* an emulation of the teams of craftsmen who had erected the original Gothic cathedrals. Intended as a means of revitalizing Prussian crafts and industry, this was the first romantic suggestion of a concern that would preoccupy Schinkel in his official career and that would become a dominant theme of the Gothic Revival. At Cologne Cathedral, where restoration began under Schinkel's direction after his report of 1816, the Gothic style was raised to the rank of a national compaign in a politically fragmented land. But Schinkel's cathedral was specifically Prussian, indeed militaristic, in theme and depicted in its sculptural program the history of the state's highest honor: the Order of the Iron Cross. Itself designed by Schinkel in 1813, the Iron Cross was the iconic emblem of sacrifice for the war, since the turning-in of gold jewelry for the production of iron weapons—encapsulated in the slogan "*Gold gab'Ich für Eisen*" (I gave gold for iron)—had charged Berlin's iron industry with patriotic significance. Utopian from the start, the cathedral project was formally abandoned in 1816 as too grandiose. Its patriotic associations are preserved, however, in the giant Gothic pinnacle cast in iron after Schinkel's designs and erected on Templower Berg (now Kreuzberg) in 1818. Like so many later Schinkel designs, it was intended not only as an object to be seen on the horizon but also as an observation point for viewing the area and grasping one's place in a larger system both spatial and, by stylistic association, historical.

In the great series of public monuments—the Neue Wache, Schauspielhaus (Theater), and Altes Museum—that inaugurated Schinkel's public career, he returned to a stern classical imagery as the language most expressive of Restoration Prussia's confident aspirations and of the lofty humanist ideals of the reforming ministers von Stein and von Humboldt. In giving architectural form to Berlin's new cultural and political institutions, Schinkel as state architect sought to embody the king's declaration upon the foundation of the new Berlin University that intellectual and cultural power must replace what Prussia had lost in military might. The university, of which Fichte was the first rector, was organized by Schinkel's friend and patron Wilhelm von Humboldt, who during his brief ministry (1809–1810) undertook reform of Prussian education as the first step in an envisioned comprehensive plan for fostering public culture. A cosmopolitan whose household was a continual nodal point of intellectual discourse, Humboldt had hosted Friedrich Gilly in Paris in 1797 and Schinkel in Rome in 1804 and was now to be a major inspiration of Schinkel's early Berlin career. With Republican Greece as his ideal, Humboldt viewed education and public cultivation as the keys to a renewed cultural flourishing. The new bourgeois citizen was to be educated for sustained cultural participation under the protective eye of the absolute monarch. Fichte's philosophy of moral vocation and Humboldt's idealist program are reflected in Schinkel's formulation of the architect's role as "the ennobler of all human relationships," a goal that structured not only his individual designs but also their juxtapositions in the evolving panorama of Schinkel's Berlin monuments.

Although Schinkel presented a comprehensive plan for Berlin in 1817, the first of many destined to remain on paper, he was never to be given a free hand in planning. Friedrich Wilhelm III was a parsimonious and cautious patron. His son, the crown prince, was an enthusiastic pupil and friend of Schinkel but he increasingly put forth his own suggestions as necessary images for Schinkel's designs. Schinkel's recasting of the eighteenth-century *Residenzstadt* as the capital of the German state destined for hegemony among myriad smaller states was achieved only gradually and thanks to the longevity and consistency of his goal. Proceeding building by building, he created an incremental landscape of individual monuments and set vistas all tied to one another by a rich matrix of geometrical ordering and contrived views. Through fragmented spatial sequences and suggestive juxtapositions, Schinkel sought to lead the Prussian citizen to a new awareness of his situation among the national institutions and their relation to the monarch.

Schinkel's close friendship with the philosopher and aesthetician Wilhelm Solger, an old school friend with whom he enthusiastically read antique drama and studied ancient history, reinforced his renewed celebration of Gilly's Greek ideal as the model for a Prussian state architecture.

Schinkel. Schauspielhaus (theater and concert hall). Berlin. 1819–1821

Schinkel. Schauspielhaus (theater and concert hall). Berlin. 1819–1821

The radical shift from his grand Gothic schemes to a heroic classical state style is reflected most clearly in the evolution of the design for the Neue Wache, a small royal guardhouse in Unter den Linden next to the Armory. Schinkel abandoned his initial model of a medieval round-arched hall in the manner of the Florentine Loggia dei Lance in favor of that elemental and assertive Greek Doric design which has ever since symbolized Prussia's military origins. Loosely modeled, as Schinkel (1819–1840) claimed, on a Roman castrum, it combines a baseless Doric portico with a closed cubic mass contained by canted corner pylons, the whole reminiscent of Gilly's austere, reductive aesthetic. Despite its small size, Schinkel's assured handling of scale and proportion and the grand simplicity of the building's composition give it a monumental presence among its larger baroque and Palladian (see ANDREA PALLADIO) neighbors. Recessed from the street, the Neue Wache is tied into the geometric order of its immediate context by the skillful arrangement of trees and statuary, here executed by Schinkel's frequent collaborator, the sculptor Daniel Christian Rauch.

Behind the portico, the plan of the Neue Wache is asymmetrical, the first indication of Schinkel's ability to enclose increasingly complex and varied functions in a symmetrically ordered and geometrically lucid exterior determined by the building's immediate physical context and its symbolic role. In the *Zivilkasino* at Potsdam (1818), for instance, the organization of the façade responds to the established order of Potsdam's urban form without giving any indication of the skillful asymmetrical disposition of the varied functions, including a dance hall, within.

Schinkel was required to reuse the foundations and six Ionic columns from Langhans's earlier state theater (1800–1802), which had burned in 1817, in his design for the Schauspielhaus (1818–1821). Massed with characteristic simplicity, the Schauspielhaus adeptly accommodates a relatively small auditorium and stage house in the gabled central section with a concert hall and rehearsal/storage areas respectively in the symmetrical flanking lower sections. Although the silhouette is similar to the contemporary National Theater in Munich by KARL VON FISCHER (finished 1818), the Bavarian theater contains a more traditional baroque auditorium and has neither the clarity of intersecting volumes nor the strength of surface articulation of Schinkel's theater. Schinkel's essential departure from the composition by geometric solids of early German neoclassicism is first manifested in the reticulated system of stripped pilaster supports and horizontal entablatures which unifies the building's masses. Forming continuous bands of fenestration, this structural grid dissolves the wall surface into a screen that represents the structural purity of trabeation, the constructional system Schinkel deemed appropriate for public architecture. It is neither continuous with the actual structural system nor expressive of the subdivisions of the interior. Characteristically, the autonomy of the monument is expressed in the strong framing of the corners.

Thrust into the Gendarmenmarkt, the theater's Ionic portico visually engages the porticoes of the flanking French and German churches into a coherent urban ensemble. Representative of the notion of the theater as a temple of the arts, the portico and grand exterior stair are intended to elevate the visitor to the level of cultural participation, a theme repeated in Schinkel's other monuments. At the opening performance in May 1821, the privileged playgoer witnessed a stage backdrop painted by Gropius depicting the Schauspielhaus itself as seen from the Museum Insel. The building was thus represented as a symbol of the ennobling capacity of the art of theater. At the same time, the viewer's self-conscious reflection of his own situation was provoked. This contrived detachment is incorporated more subtly in the very structure of Schinkel's later designs which repeatedly feature viewing points from which the visitor is made aware of his position in a larger landscape.

The practice of architecture as a means of public cultivation central to all Schinkel's designs is given its most complete expression in his early masterpiece, the Altes Museum (1824–1830). The idea of a public museum was itself novel. Schinkel's building not only was to provide a model for later treatments of this typically nineteenth-century building type, but it was also calculated to initiate an emerging bourgeois audience to the viewing of the former aristocratic collections. In 1798, Friedrich Wilhelm II and Alois Hirt had first proposed arranging the royal collections for public exhibition, and in 1800, Schinkel had prepared an ideal view of a museum, but it was not until 1815, when Schinkel and Hirt arranged the royal treasures recovered from Paris in the former Academy Building, that serious discussion of a new building was voiced. The museum then took on new significance in the context of Humboldt's notion of the role of cultural institutions in the national education. Humboldt himself had opened his collection of antique sculpture to the public in the elegant villa Schloss Tegel which Schinkel remodeled for him in 1821–1824.

In the Altes Museum, Schinkel created one of his most harmonious works, at once a monument "complete in and of itself" and a lynchpin for the physical and economical reorganization of the Lustgarten and the canals behind. The rationalization of shipping and warehousing facilities, later completed by Schinkel's Packhofgebäude (customs, canal administration, and warehouses) of 1829–1832, was an essential feature in the king's agreement to the ambitious undertaking. The apparent influence of JEAN NICOLAS LOUIS DURAND'S textbook in the geometric clarity of the museum's plan of galleries flanking a central rotunda all contained within a rectangular outline was no indication of Schinkel's sympathy with the French theorist's utilitarian views. Indeed, the simplicity of the forms belies the subtle organization of a didactic spatial sequence calculated to elevate the public to a higher cultural and self-awareness. It was precisely these issues that arose in the Museum Building Committee where Alois Hirt took violent objection to the façade of eighteen colossal Ionic columns framed by closing antae and to the central rotunda, terming them useless extravagances. Schinkel protested that he sought to accommodate "the higher purpose" of a museum

Schinkel. Schloss Tegel. Berlin. 1821–1824

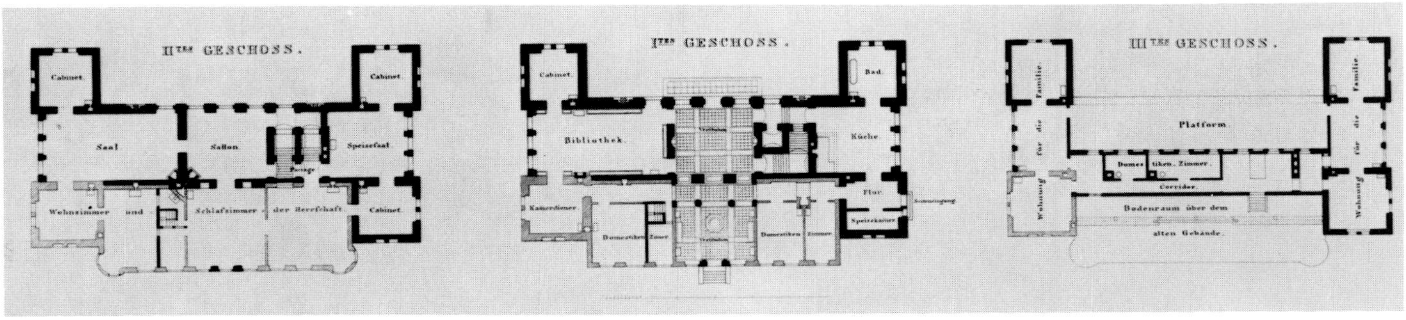

Schinkel. Schloss Tegel. Berlin. 1821–1824

rather than simply its "trivial function" of housing pictures.

The framed colonnade itself was displayed along with the Royal Palace and the Cathedral (remodeled by Schinkel in 1816–1820) in the replanted Lustgarten, a leafy "wall," according to Schinkel (1819–1840), "against which to exhibit monuments." A grand public image that mediates between the closed geometric solid of the museum and the public space, the colonnade recalls the antique *stoa poikile* in form, function, and association. Like that ancient promenade, Schinkel's stoa was decorated with murals, here arranged on two levels to express the two levels of galleries behind and representing the fine arts' place in the developmental history of mankind. Penetrating the stoa, the museum visitor was conducted on an initiatory journey culminating in the rotunda, a pantheon of the arts calculated to make him "more receptive to the enjoyment and understanding of what the building contained" (*ibid.*)

Set in a recess in the stoa's center, the stepped pyramidal mass of the staircase is at once a highly sophisticated spatial composition and an essay in the primitive origins of vaulted form. Arriving on the upper landing of this staircase which ambiguously mediates between indoors and outdoors, the viewer is suddenly afforded a view back through the colonnades to the royal palace and Berlin beyond. Thus, before entering the gallery, the visitor is not only conducted on a symbolic journey through architectural history from pure trabeated stoa to domed rotunda, but he also sees himself in a new relation to his everyday civic setting meant to equip him to comprehend the objects on display inside, all arranged in a didactic historical sequence.

Schinkel.
Altes Museum, Lustgarten.
Berlin.
1824–1830

Schinkel.
Altes Museum (staircase).
Lustgarten, Berlin.
1824–1830

The alternative Gothic and Classical projects which Schinkel prepared for the Friedrich Werder Church indicate how committed he was in the early 1820s to a rationalized classicism as the appropriate state style. In contrast to the mausoleum project, it was now Schinkel who proposed a classical design (1823) and the crown—this time the crown prince, who increasingly sought to influence his father's artistic policy—who argued for the Gothic style. Schinkel's Gothic church as ultimately constructed was not a new design but a translation into Gothic form and brick construction of the classical project. Schinkel did not simply change the ornamentation but also designed an equivalent in Gothic structural terms substituting an aisleless chapel with wall buttresses for the original sequence of four saucer-domed bays reminiscent of a Roman basilica. The late Gothic prototypes—an English college chapel for the exterior and the upper chapel at Marienburg for the interior—are evident; but all is severely treated, relying on proportion and dominant lines rather than on decoration for effect. Although Schinkel favored the classical design, he published both in his *Sammlung Architektonischer Entwürfe* as evidence that style was a question of image, while architecture was a matter of logical construction elevated by aesthetic feeling.

An interpretation of architectural history in structural terms is fundamental to the theories suggested in the notes and sketches that Schinkel prepared for a projected textbook, the *Architektonisches Lehrbuch,* which Goerd Peschken dates to the mid-1820s. Just as in his public architecture Schinkel sought to guide the citizenry to a higher cultural awareness, so in his textbook the architecture student would be carefully guided to an understanding of the creative processes of architecture. The student neither is given the perfected orders to copy in the manner of traditional architectural books nor is he offered a series of complete compositions as in Durand's influential text. Rather, architecture is analyzed tectonically as the formal expression of structural ideas that have been refined during the course of history, an approach grounded in the neoclassical theories of Winckelmann and Hirt. The classical orders are depicted as one moment, albeit a perfected one, in a continuous sequence. "In architecture," Schinkel explained, "everything must be truthful, any masking or hiding of construction is a mistake." Schinkel's evolutionary search for primordial form reflects the natural history studies of Goethe and Alexander von Humboldt. Once the natural history of the materials and structures of architecture and its evolution from trabeation to arcuation and finally to vaulting was understood, history could serve as the basis for continued architectural development. In the tradition of Schiller and Herder, then, Schinkel saw history as a continuing process. As Fichte had first directed him in Italy, Schinkel approached history throughout his career as a rich source of lessons, but he insisted repeatedly that "every work of art must possess an entirely new element, even if crafted within the character of a known style of beauty; without this new element it can possess interest for neither the creator nor the viewer" (letter to Crown Prince Maximilian of Bavaria, 1840). Schinkel's method was analytical and increasingly dialectical in his opposition of antique and Christian principles of architecture as the poles to be synthesized in modern architecture. Schinkel's textbook was never published. In 1820, he was appointed professor of architecture at the Fine Arts Academy of Berlin, but he rarely taught. Nonetheless, through example and official duties, his pedagogical influence was tremendous.

Schinkel worked extensively in close cooperation with the royal family in remodeling both their Berlin palaces and in creating country retreats expressive of their individual tastes. His Berlin interiors represent a new style of elegant representational space dependent more on refined proportion and color than on major architectural forms. In Prince August's Palace (1816–1817), for example, traditional baroque room sequences are blurred by the introduction of columnar screens, niches, and even mirrors. After Schinkel's second Italian tour with Dr. Gustav Waagen in 1824, he created a series of festive, Pompeiian-style interiors which continue the darker, deeper intensity of his late decorative palate. It was, however, the analytical study of Italian vernacular buildings that occasioned the most important development in Schinkel's architecture in the 1820s. In the series of "southern" retreats which Schinkel created in the Potsdam countryside from 1825, he not only realized a new asymmetrical mode of composition which harmoniously related building to landscape, but also created an architecture in which historical image was secondary to a form that arose from the conditions of design. The pristine outlines, asymmetrical massing, and harmony between human construction and nature in anonymous Italian

Schinkel. New Pavilion (now Schinkel Pavilion). Charlottenburg, Berlin. 1824–1825

structures were a major inspiration for Schinkel's creation of an architecture in which history was truly understood as process rather than prototype.

King Friedrich Wilhelm III had specified that the royal *casina* at Chiatamone near Naples, which had enchanted him during a visit in 1822, serve as a model for a pavilion to be built at Charlottenburg, in commemoration of his morganatic second marriage. Before he left for Italy in 1824, Schinkel drew plans for the pristine cubic structure which recalls the *casina* in its recessed loggias and continuous iron balcony around the upper story. The building is, however, no reproduction of an Italian original, but the result of a rigorous design exercise in the dynamics of its own geometric order, inflected to accommodate the existing order of the palace park. The only departure from the strict rectilinear organization of the plan is the semicircular Pompeiian bench in the *Gartensaal*. A favored motif of Schinkel's in garden design as a termination of the building's principal axes in their extension into nature, it is here reversed. The bench is not aligned with the house's axes but with that of the garden path outside and thus represents, within this autonomous cube, the intersection of the natural and the architectural order.

Although Schinkel's rural designs abandon the formal unity of his urban projects, these asymmetrical compositions nevertheless result from similar processes of geometric design. In his notes for the *Lehrbuch* he explained: "Every object with a specific function demands a correspondingly specific order. This order is either symmetry which everyone understands or relative order, which is understood only by those who know its principle" (Peschken, 1979, p. 19). The unexecuted design for a riverside *Lusthaus* near Potsdam is a simple example of relative order: its plan and elevations are the results of the interplay between a presupposed original symmetry and the displacements required to accommodate the program. The building thus contains in its formal order the record of its own design. Commissioned by the crown prince as a gathering place for his brothers, the princes who in the next decade would in turn charge Schinkel with designing their own country seats in close proximity to one another, the *Lusthaus* presages the themes of Schinkel's Potsdam work. Not only is each design "complete in and of itself," a stated goal of all Schinkel's architecture, but all are interrelated by reciprocal vistas. Treating them as elements in an evolving landscape, Schinkel created a rural equivalent to his Berlin designs. After his death, the work at Potsdam was continued under Friedrich Wilhelm IV by LUDWIG PERSIUS and later by FRIEDRICH AUGUST STÜLER.

Persius had supervised Schinkel's Potsdam work from 1825, beginning with Prince Karl's commission for the remodeling of an eighteenth-century house at Klein Glienicke into an Italianate villa. This occasioned the first of many collaborations between Schinkel and the landscape designer Peter Joseph Lenné, a specialist in the English picturesque manner. At Glienicke, Schinkel replaced a mansard with a flat roof, added a Doric portico, and gave the whole composition, centered around a tall companilelike tower, a sharp rectilinear profile and crisp stuccoed definition. Of the numerous garden structures designed by Schinkel, Persius, and later Ferdinand von Arnim, Grosse Neugierde (1835–1837), a circular tea pavilion modeled on the third century B.C. monument of Lysicrates at Athens, is the most revealing of Schinkel's approach to history. Set at the elevated corner of the estate, it commands extensive views along the Potsdam Road and the Havel River to the nearby castellated Tudor Gothic Schloss Babelsberg of Prince Wilhelm (1832–1835), as well as the skyline of Potsdam beyond, itself dominated by the dome of Schinkel's Nikolaikirche (1830–1837, dome added 1845ff). With its circular platform, the Grosse Neugierde once again introduces the experience of panoramic vision which had dominated Schinkel's earlier work; here, he permits the privileged visitor to comprehend an entire landscape carefully formed by Schinkel over the preceding decade from one viewing point.

In the Charlottenhof, a southern extension of the royal park at Sanssouci designed by Lenné for the crown prince, Schinkel realized his most complete work in the "villa mode." The temple-fronted Schloss Charlottenhof and the nearby "vernacular" Court Gardener's House are formally contrasted but suggestively juxtaposed and linked by vistas. A Christmas gift from the king on Friedrich Wilhelm's marriage to Princess Elisabeth of Bavaria in 1826, the Charlottenhof was an adroit remodeling of a modest eighteenth-century house into a formal Roman villa. In the tradition of the French *maison de plaisance,* the living rooms all on one level have direct visual and physical connection with nature and are small-scale evocations of a bourgeois lifestyle in contract with the pompous splendor of the nearby Frederician baroque palaces of Potsdam. Working from an initial sketch by the crown prince, Schinkel developed a composition exploiting differentiated ground levels and a tautly held balance between perfect symmetry and asymmetry in both house and garden. Extending its own geometric axial order to control not only the artificially elevated terrace set like a stage before the backdrop of the Doric portico with its delicate Pompeiian paintings, but also the surrounding garden, the house was to have been the centerpiece of an even grander composition including the reconstruction of an antique villa and natural hippodrome.

The Court Gardener's House (1829–1833), in contrast with the deliberate and formal artificiality of Schloss Charlottenhof, is a picturesque garden *fabrique* meant to evoke notions of life in harmony with nature. Based on the crown prince's and Schinkel's mutual enthusiasm for the anonymous vernacular of the Tuscan countryside, the extensive trellises and the formal play between open and closed forms and shifting planes which draw the natural world into the geometric order of the building merge it with the surrounding landscape. A study in asymmetrical composition anchored by the central tower around which it spirals, the building seems almost to have grown from its site and to have been added to over the ages. Despite its juxtaposition of antique fragments, wooden trellises and simple architecture, the house is no mere Italian revery; it is a theoretical conceit on the relation of form and structure to natural processes.

In 1826, Schinkel was sent to England to study new museums and their installations for his Altes Museum. Whereas the Italian vernacular provided the key to Schinkel's rural designs, it was the brick industrial vernacular of England that spurred him in his quest for a modern architecture appropriate for the emerging industrial Prussia. Schinkel traveled with his friend Peter C. W. Beuth, a member of the reform-minded Prussian bureaucracy who most influenced the early development of Prussia's industry and its arts and crafts education. In the early 1820s, Beuth and Schinkel had collaborated on an official pattern book entitled *Vorbilder für Fabrikanten und Handwerker* (1821–1830) providing Schinkel-designed models for everything from household objects to architectural ornament. The *Vorbilder* was conceived in the same paternalistic pedagogical spirit as Schinkel's public architecture

Schinkel.
Court Gardener's House.
Charlottenhof, Sanssouci,
Potsdam, Germany.
1829–1833

and his own publication of his architectural designs, the *Sammlung Architektonischer Entwürfe*. The books were intended to elevate didactically the public taste for well-designed objects while simultaneously assuring quality in Prussia's emerging industrial production. Although fascinated with the pure brick walls and cast-iron roof structures of modern English factories, Schinkel viewed England's industrialization with critical reserve. These buildings lacked the aesthetic elevation of architecture, and the social implications of the endless rows of terrace housing built to house the workers which Schinkel found so dreary were all too clear. England provoked Schinkel's technical experimentation, but it did not provide a model for an architecture expressive of the values that reigned in the Prussian bureaucracy and that had helped shape his own architectural philosophy.

The following year, Schinkel drew an uncommissioned design for a U-shaped bazaar building (1827) to be built on Unter den Linden which served as a manifesto for a new brick "functionalist" style; this would emerge as a major theme of his architecture in the late 1820s, culminating in his last important building, the Bauakademie (School of Architecture, 1831–1835). In these buildings, the design of the façade as a structural screen, first developed in the theaters of Berlin and Hamburg (1827), is unified organically with the building's actual structure. The generous open elevational grid of brick supports and expansive fenestration in the Bazaar building is the continuation of the axes of the supports within. The forms are not borrowed from a historical image but are a direct expression of the brick construction. The development of a modern brick architectural language was to become a major concern of architects throughout the German states in the 1830s, especially in the circles of HEINRICH HÜBSCH in Karlsruhe, FRIEDRICH VON GÄRTNER in Munich, and ALEXIS DE CHATEAUNEUF in Hamburg. Schinkel's appreciation of a brick aesthetic was first kindled by Friedrich Gilly's 1799 views of the medieval castle at Marienburg in East Prussia, which Schinkel himself had visited in 1819. Tempered by his close study of Italian brick architecture and inspired anew by the experience of England, he considered the material the best medium for realizing a synthesis of antiquity and the middle ages.

Although Schinkel continued to design in his classical state style and to use, as was traditional in Prussia, plaster detailing over brick structure, in such representational buildings as the Hauptwache in Dresden (1831–1833) and the Potsdam Nikolaikirche, he was intent on demonstrating that brick could be used for a range of building types from warehouses to country houses and even for the highest type, the church. Both Schinkel and the crown prince puzzled in the late 1820s over the appropriate form of a Protestant church which would at once distinguish it from Catholic models and illustrate its continuity with Christian tradition, a concern paralleled in the court patronage of Ludwig I of Bavaria (see G. F. ZIEBLAND). Together they developed grandiose plans to replace the Cathedral on the Lustgarten with an immense early Christian basilica which would have overshadowed the Altes Museum and the careful balance Schinkel had created among the monuments. Although the early Christian style was felt to be the true meeting point of antiquity and the Christian Middle Ages and thus a crucial juncture in both the architectural and religious development of the West, the crown prince insisted on a much more literal translation of this model into contemporary form than Schinkel's own experiments in brick architecture suggested. The five alternative designs for a church in the Oranienburg suburb achieved a more original synthesis. They not only defined model floor plans for Protestant worship, but they were also exemplars of an architecture based entirely on brick construction. The most striking of these, a longitudinal plan, combines North Italian Romanesque, the audience hall at Trier, and Schinkel's own brick Werder Church into a design defined by a round-arched fenestration module which dissolves the wall fully into a grid of supports and infill glass. Subject to the king's vacillations, the four modest churches eventually built were extremely reduced translations of Schinkel's intentions.

Schinkel designed a house with an exposed brick façade for the manufacturer Tobias Feilner, whose factory provided the brick and terra cotta for the Werder Church and, later, the Bauakademie. It was quite evidently an advertisement for Feilner's business and a patent demonstration that brick was as suitable for a bourgeois house as for a utilitarian structure. In the Bauakademie, Schinkel's most personal and, reputedly, favorite design, brick construction determines the form of a structure given the role of representing architecture itself among the panoply of Berlin public monuments. The headquarters of both the School of Architecture and the *Oberbaudeputation,* the building was commissioned not by the Crown but rather by the respective heads of the institutions whose ideals had formed the program: Beuth and Schinkel himself (director of the *Oberbaudeputation* from 1830). A realized prototype, the building was intended as a model for industrializing Prussia, an object lesson for the students and official architects whose work within was done under Schinkel's name and guidance. Here, the learning of architecture was formally linked with state practice, an institutionalization of Schinkel's own lifetime goal.

Schinkel. Bauakademie. Berlin. 1831–1836

In this proto-skeleton structure, the wall articulation distinguished clearly between the supporting piers and the "infill" fenestration panels. In the composition of these façades, traditional hierarchical structure is denied, both in proportion and in centering of the entrance. The forms are the exterior expression of the open grid of segmentally arched brick supports within. The brick itself, providing fireproof quarters for the library and model collections, provided the principal ornamentation in its vibrant red and violet polychromy and the bas-relief terra-cotta window and door enframements. Depicting "Moments from the developmental history of architecture," these represented the Greek and Gothic as completed styles. The suggestive open end of the historical pattern is their synthesis in the Bauakademie itself, home and source of modern Prussian architecture. As Schinkel's rural buildings had borne the form of their own design history, so the Bauakademie was the product of its own structural history. The segmental arched module of the cubic design was the tectonic synthesis of classical trabeation and Gothic arcuation. Like those past periods of structural perfection, the Bauakademie referred to no history but its own, the history of its material and structural emergence. Later Berlin architects saw the building as a model of utilitarian design; it served as the source for a characteristic Berlin municipal style of brick.

The 1830s witnessed a marked decline in Schinkel's executed work as his official duties multiplied and his health progressively failed. Reviewing and revising countless designs for Prussia's far-flung provinces, Schinkel spread an image of state architecture throughout the kingdom. Between 1831 and 1834, as *Oberbaudirektor,* he made official visits throughout Prussia and advised especially on the preservation of historic monuments. His influence was strong throughout Germany and even in Scandinavia. In 1838, Schinkel was promoted to the highest position within the bureaucracy, that of *Oberlandesbaudirektor*.

Although Schinkel developed the lessons of the Bauakademie in the unexecuted designs for a Royal Library (1835) entirely of brick, his late years were dominated by utopian designs for grandiose reconstructions of antique villas, which served the restoration monarchy's romantic notions. Prepared, for the most part, at the instigation of the crown prince, these projects have a retrospective character. While continuing the formal order developed in his Potsdam work, Schinkel treated the complex programs of these royal projects as architectural museums rich in commentary on his own long career defining the ideals of the state. Schinkel prepared picturesque reconstructions of Pliny's Laurentian and Tuscan villas (1833–1835) for the crown prince, who led Schinkel to believe that his *Architektonisches Lehrbuch* might finally be published if he included an Ideal Residence for a Prince as the culmination of the lessons. The design of the vast complex projected offices of the administrative bureaucracy as well as institutions of learning and culture for the public, all subsumed under the authoritative protection of the monarch. A full expression of the crown prince's romantic paternalism, the independent values of the reform bureaucracy were here subordinated to the final royal authority. On arcuated brick foundations, the various functions of the precinct rise above as discrete structures, each with its own historical image. Both a Greek Temple and Schinkel's earlier Gothic Cathedral designs tower above as the ideals synthesized in the enlightened Christian monarchy.

Contemporary with this ideal design, Schinkel prepared stunning watercolor plans to convert the Athenian Acropolis into a residence for the Bavarian Prince Otto (1835) named protector king of Greece by a European Congress of 1833. A monument to the triumph of the restored monarchy over popular uprising, Schinkel's design continued the theme of the antique villa discreetly subordinated to the forms of the larger landscape and the antique monuments which rise above the residence like great relics in an outdoor museum. But even in the sacred precinct of his Grecian ideal, Schinkel was no revivalist; the dazzling audience hall features a trussed roof based on English medieval and modern ceiling construction. The whole complex was to be painted brilliantly in bright color patterns, a reflection of the contemporary theories of polychromy with which JACQUES IGNACE HITTORFF and GOTTFRIED SEMPER had challenged the received ideal notion of the antique.

Working, as for the Acropolis design, from a picture of a site he had never seen, Schinkel prepared designs for Schloss Orianda, the final synthesis of his picturesque planning and his incorporation of panoramic views and landscape. The palace would crown a plateau over the Black Sea in the Crimea near Yalta (1838, unexecuted). The views of this palace for the crown prince's sister, the Csarina Alexandra of Russia, unite Schinkel's activity and vision as a landscape painter and as an architect. The carefully organized precinct, with its romantic juxtaposition of natural growth and the history of structure, was a swan song, not only of Schinkel's career but of a system of royal patronage that would not survive the first generation of Schinkel's pupils. The central Greek temple which rises above the complex as an ideal image commemorates that temple which had determined Schinkel's whole career: Gilly's romantic monument to Frederick the Great. It was a theme with enduring potency in nineteenth-century German architecture from Klenze's Walhalla to Stüller's and JOHANN HEINRICH STRACK's National Gallery set in the Berlin museum complex which, under the crown prince's guidance, took so much in its organization and imagery from Schinkel's late retrospective designs.

A total mental and physical collapse confined Schinkel to bed for the last year of his life. A plan for the reorganization of northern Berlin between Moabit and the Tiergarten was drawn up just days before, but like Orianda and so many earlier schemes for Berlin it was to remain on paper. Yet, the richness of Schinkel's work in both executed buildings and published designs provided the models for Berlin architecture for the next two generations. While Persius completed Schinkel's Potsdam work and Stüler his unfinished Berlin projects, the next generation of Bauakademie pupils continued to work in the name of Schinkel. If they more often translated his work into an image that could give form to the desires of Berlin's rapidly growing industrial bourgeoisie, especially in countless suburban villas which systematized Schinkel's Potsdam manner, they nonetheless maintained his aesthetic until the formation of the German Empire (1871) completely altered Prussian patronage and aspirations. As late as 1860, the popular author Theodor Fontane noted: "We are still living in a world of Schinkel's forms; very few of us know this, but it is true nonetheless" (Fontane, 1959, vol. 1).

Yet even after 1870, Schinkel's reputation survived the disdain of early modern architects for the nineteenth century. His influence has yet to be eclipsed. ADOLF LOOS declared Schinkel the last great architect and LUDWIG MIES VAN DER ROHE's debt is no less clear in his early domestic work than in his statement that all that could be learned about architecture could be learned from Schinkel's Altes Museum. Schinkel's birthday has been the occasion of a speech often dedicated to examining his contemporaneity since 1845, a pursuit recently rekindled by the celebration of his 200th birthday and a renewed interest worldwide in Schinkel's work and his approach to history on the part of contemporary architects.

BARRY BERGDOLL

WORKS

1800–1801, Estate Outbuildings, Neu Hardenburg, Germany. 1800–1801, Pomona Temple, Potsdam, Germany. 1801, Houses, Quilitz, Germany. *1801–1803, Schloss Buckow (remodeling), Kreis Lebus, Germany. *1802–1805, Steinmeyer House, Friedrichstrasse, Berlin. 1803, Bleichause; 1803, School; Quilitz, Germany. 1806, Tilebein House, Züllcow, near Stettin, Poland. *1810, Palace of Friedrich Wilhelm III (interior renovations); 1810, Schloss Charlottenburg (bedroom of Queen Luise); 1810–1840, Mausoleum for Queen Luise (with Heinrich Gentz), Park Charlottenburg; Berlin. 1811, Monument to Queen Luise, Gransee, Germany. 1812–1840, Schloss Ehrenburg, Coburg, Germany. *1816–1817, Prince August's Palace (interiors), Wilhelmstrasse; 1817–1818, Neue Wache (royal guardhouse), Unter den Linden; *1816–1820, Cathedral (remodeling), Lustgarten; Berlin. 1817, Monument to the Fallen, Grossbeeren, Germany. *1817, Prince Friedrich's Palace (interiors), Wilhelmstrasse; *1817–1818, Barracks, Lindenstrasse; Berlin. 1817–1818, Saalbau, Bad Freienwald Oder, Germany. 1818–1821, Kreuzberg Monument (later altered), Berlin. *1818–1824, Zivilkasino, Potsdam, Germany. *1819, Neue Wilhelmstrasse; 1819–1821, Schauspielhaus (theater and concert hall); Berlin. 1820, Catholic Church, Marienwerder, Germany. 1820–1823, Schloss Neuhardenburg, Quilitz, Germany. 1821–1824, Nikolaikirche, Magdeburg-Neustadt, Germany. 1821–1824, Schloss Tegel (remodeled), Berlin. 1821–1826, Luisenkirche (tower only), Charlottenburg; 1822–1824, Schlossbrücke (now Friedrich Engels Bridge); Berlin. 1822, Schloss Seifersdorf (remodeling), near Dresden, Germany. 1822–1824, Antonin Hunting Lodge, near Ostrowo, Poland. *1822–1825, Gatehouses, Lange Brucke, Potsdam, Germany. 1822–1825, Schauspielhaus (theater; plans later reworked by Cremer), Aachen, Germany. *1823, Arts and Crafts School (remodeling); *1823, Behrend Landhaus, Charlottenburg; *1823–1824, Gatehouses, Potsdam Gate; Berlin. 1823 and later, Schloss Stolzenfels (reconstruction), Stolzenfels, Rhine, Germany. *1824–1825, Ingenieur und Artillerieschule (Kriegsakademie; façade only); *1824–1825, New Pavilion (now Schinkel Pavilion; later rebuilt); 1824–1826, Kavalierhaus (Danziger Haus), Pfaueninsel; *1824–1826, Royal Schloss (crown prince's apartments); 1824–1826, Singakademie (altered in execution by Heinrich Ottmer); Berlin. 1824–1827, Schloss Neundorf, Germany. 1824–1829, Schloss Glienecke (including park structures); 1824–1830, Altes Museum, Lustgarten; 1824–1833, Scharnhorst Memorial, Invaliden Cemetery; *1825, Pavilion, Schloss Bellevue; Berlin. 1825–1827, Elisen Fountain, Aachen, Germany. 1825–1827, Lighthouse, Arcona, Rügen, Germany. *1825–1827, Theater (Schinkel's design altered in construction by C. L. Wimmel), Hamburg, Germany. 1825–1829, Gesellschafthaus, Friedrich Wilhelms Garden, near Magdeburg, Germany. 1825–1830, Friedrich Werder Church, Berlin. 1826, Schloss Charlottenhof (remodeling); 1826–1828, Unteroffiziersschule, Jägeralle, Potsdam, Germany. *1827, Konigliches Palais (Royal Chapel), Unter den Linden; *1827–1828, Prince Karl's Palace (interiors), Wilhelmplatz; *1827–1829, Gewerbeinstitut (additions); *1828–1829, Feilner House (fragments survive in the Märkisches Museum, East Berlin, and the Berlin Museum); *1829–1832, Packofgebäude; Berlin. 1829–1833, Court Gardener's House, Charlottenhof, Sanssouci, Potsdam, Germany. *1829–1833, Palais Redern, Berlin. 1829–1833, Peterhof Palace (chapel), near St. Petersburg, Russia. 1830, Pavillion, Roman Baths, Charlottenhof, Potsdam, Germany. *1830–1833, Prince Albrecht's Palace, Berlin. 1830–1834, Elisabeth Church, Invalidenstrasse, Berlin. 1830–1837, Nikolaikirche (dome added 1843–1849 by others; later restored), Potsdam, Germany. 1831–1833, Hauptwache, Dresden, Germany. 1831–1836, Leipzig University (main building). *1831–1836, Bauakademie, Berlin. 1832–1834, Nazarethkirche (later altered and rebuilt), Wedding; 1832–1834, Saint Johannes (later altered), Alt Moabit; 1832–1834, Saint Pault, Gesundbrunnen; *1832–1835, Observatory, Berlin. 1832–1835, Schloss Babelsberg (later extended), Potsdam, Germany. 1834, Chauseehaus, Schiffmühle, near Frienwalde, Germany. 1835–1837, Grosse Neugierde, Glienicke Park, Berlin. 1838–1840, Schloss Kamenz, Silesia, Germany. c.1840, Church, Krzeszowica, Poland. 1840–1845, Town Hall (not completed until later by others), Zittau, Germany.

BIBLIOGRAPHY

Architektur der DDR. 1981 30, no. 2:entire issue.

BAYER, JOSEPH 1919 "Goethe, Schinkel und die Gotik." Pages 64–85 in Robert Stia (editor), *Baustudien und baubilder: Schriften zur Kunst, aus dem Nachlass.* Jena, Yugoslavia.

BERLIN VERWALTUNG DER STAATLICHEN SCHLÖSSER UND GÄRTEN 1981 *Karl Friedrich Schinkel: Architektur, Malerei, Kunstgewerbe.* Berlin: Orangerie, Schloss Charlottenburg.

BLOCH, PETER 1973 "Das Kreuzberg-Denkmal und die patriotische Kunst." *Jahrbuch der Stiftung Preussischer Kulturbesitz* 11:142–159.

BOETTICHER, CARL 1857 *Carl Friedrich Schinkel und sein Baukünstlerisches Vermächtnis.* Berlin: Ernst & Korn.

BÖRSCH-SUPAN, HELMUT 1969 "Schinkels Landschaft mit Motiven aus dem Salzburgischen." *Zeitschrift für Kunstgeschichte* 32, nos. 3–4:317–323.

BÖRSCH-SUPAN, HELMUT (1970)1976 *Der Schinkel Pavillon im Schlosspark zu Charlottenburg.* Berlin: Verwaltung der Staatlichen Schlösser und Garten.

BÖRSCH-SUPAN, HELMUT 1976 *Das Mausoleum im Charlottenburger Schlossgarten.* Berlin: Verwaltung der Stattlichen Schlösser und Garten.

CARTER, RAND 1979 "Karl Friedrich Schinkel's Project for a Royal Palace on the Acropolis." *Journal of the Society of Architectural Historians* 38, no. 1:34–46.

DEUTSCHE BAUAKADEMIE (editor) 1951 *Über Karl Friedrich Schinkel.* Berlin: Henschel.

EINEM, HERBERT VON 1963 "Karl Friedrich Schinkel." *Jahrbuch der Stiftung Preussischer Kulturbesitz* 1:73–89.

ETTINGER, LEOPOLD 1945 "A German Architect's Visit to England in 1826." *Architectural Review* 97:131–134.

Farbe und Raum 1981 35, no. 3:entire issue.

FONTANE, THEODOR 1959–1975 Pages 97–117 in *Wanderungen durch die Mark Brandenburg, I: Die Graftschaft Ruppin.* Volume 9 in *Sämtliche Werke.* Munich: Nymphenburger.

FORSSMAN, ERIK 1981 *Karl Friedrich Schinkel: Bauwerke und Baugedanken.* Munich: Schnell & Steiner.

FORSTER, KURT 1982 *Karl Friedrich Schinkel.* London: Academy.

GEYER, ALBERT 1926 *Die historischen Wohnräume im Berliner Schloss.* Berlin: Deutscher Kunstverlag.

GIESE, LEOPOLD 1921 *Die Friedrichs-Werdersche Kirche zu Berlin.* Berlin: Zirkel.

GRISEBACH, AUGUST (1924)1981 *Carl Friedrich Schinkel, Architekt, Städtebauer, Maler.* Reprint. Munich: Piper.

GRISEBACH, AUGUST 1956 "Karl Friedrich Schinkel." *Die Grossen Deutschen* 2:548–558.

GROPIUS, MARTIN 1877 *Karl Friedrich Schinkel: Dekorationen Innerer Räume.* Berlin: Ernst & Korn.

GRUPPE, OTTO F. 1843 *Carl Friedrich Schinkel und die neue Berliner Dom.* Berlin: Lüderitz.

JACOBSTHAL, E. 1890 *Rückblicke auf die baukünstlerischen Prinzipien Schinkels und Böttichers.* Berlin: Deuter & Nicolas.

JOHNSON, PHILIP (1962)1979 "Schinkel and Mies." In Robert A. M. Stern (editor), *Writings/Philip Johnson.* Reprint. New York: Oxford University Press. Originally published as an article in *Program.*

KAUFFMANN, HANS 1963 "Zweckbau und Monument: Zu Friedrich Schinkels Museum am Berliner Lustgarten." *Eine Freundesgabe der Wissenschaft für Ernst Hellmut Vits* 1963:135–166.

KLOPFER, PAUL 1911 *Von Palladio bis Schinkel: Ein Charakteristik der Baukunst des Klassizismus.* Esslingen, Germany: Netf.

KNOPP, NORBERT 1977 "Schinkel's Idee einer Stilsynthese." Pages 245–254 in Werner Hager and Norbert Knopp (editors), *Beiträge zum Problem des Stilpluralismus.* Munich: Prestel.

KOCH, GEORG FRIEDRICH 1966 "Karl Friedrich Schinkel und die Architektur des Mittelalters." *Zeitschrift für Kunstgeschichte* 29, no. 3:177–222.

KRÄTSCHELL, JOHANNES 1892 *Karl Friedrich Schinkel in seinem Verhältnis zur gotischen Baukunst.* Berlin: Ernst.

KUGLER, FRANZ (1842)1954 "Karl Friedrich Schinkel: Eine Charakteristik seiner künstlerischen Wirksamkeit." Volume 3, pages 305–362 in *Kleine Schriften und Studien zur Kunstgeschichte.* Stuttgart, Germany: Ebner & Seubert.

KUNST, HANS-JOACHIM 1974 "Bemerkungen zu Schinkels Entwürfen für die Friedrich Werdersche Kirche in Berlin." *Marburger Jahrbuch* 19:241–258.

LEMMER, KLAUS J. (editor) 1973 *Karl Friedrich Schinkel: Berlin: Bauten und Entwürfe.* Berlin: Rembrandt.

LIPSTADT, HÉLÈNE, and BERGDOLL, BARRY 1981 "Karl Friedrich Schinkel: Architecture as Alchemy." *Progressive Architecture* 62, no. 10:72–77.

LOHDE, LUDWIG (1835–1837)1861 *Schinkels Möbelentwürfe, welche bei Einrichtung prinzlicher Wohnungen in den letzten zehn Jahren ausgeführt wurden.* 3d ed. Berlin: Duncker & Numblet.

LORCK, CARL VON (editor) (1937)1956 *Reisen in Deutschland.* Dresden, Germany: Jess. Originally published with the title *Deutschland in Schinkels Briefen und Zeichnungen.*

LORCK, CARL VON 1939 *Karl Friedrich Schinkel.* Berlin: Rembrandt.

MACKOWSKY, HANS 1922 *Karl Friedrich Schinkel, Briefe, Tagebücher, Gedanken.* Berlin: Propyläen.

MANTEUFFEL, CLAUS ZOGE VON 1976 "Schinkel und Semper—Idee und Ratioale Grundlage der Stilbildung." Pages 291–301 in E. Borsch-Supan (editor). *Gottfried Semper und die Mitte des 19. Jahrhunderts.* Basel: Birkhäuser.

NEUMANN, MAX 1942 *Menschen um Schinkel.* Berlin: Gruyter.

PESCHKEN, GOERD 1961 *Schinkels Bauakademie in Berlin: Ein Aufruf zu ihrer Rettung.* Berlin: Deutscher Kunstverlag.

PESCHKEN, GOERD 1966 "Schinkels nachgelassene Fragmente eines architektonischen Lehrbuchs." *Bonner Jahrbücher* 66:293–315.

PESCHKEN, GOERD 1968 "Technologische Ästhetik in Schinkels Architektur." *Zeitschrift des deutschen Vereins für Kunstwissenschaft* 1968:45–81.

PESCHKEN, GOERD 1979 *Das Architektonische Lehrbuch.* Berlin: Deutscher Kunstverlag. Part of Rave and Kuhn (1939–).

PEVSNER, NIKOLAUS (1952)1968 "Karl Friedrich Schinkel." Volume 1, pages 174–195 in *Studies in Art, Architecture, and Design.* London: Thames & Hudson.

PLAGEMANN, VOLKER 1967 *Das Deutsche Kunstmuseum, 1790–1870.* Munich: Prestel.

POSENER, JULIUS 1972 "Schinkel's English Diary." Pages 10–15 in *From Schinkel to the Bauhaus.* New York: Wittenborn.

POSENER, JULIUS (editor) 1981 *Festreden Schinkel zu Ehren: 1846–1980.* Berlin: Fröhlich & Kaufmann.

PUNDT, HERMANN G. 1972 *Schinkel's Berlin: A Study in Environmental Planning.* Cambridge, Mass.: Harvard University Press.

RAVE, PAUL ORTWIN 1942 *Genius der Baukunst.* Berlin: Mann.

RAVE, PAUL ORTWIN 1950 *Wilhelm von Humboldt und das Schloss zu Tegel.* Leipzig: Koehler & Amelang.

RAVE, PAUL, and KUHN, MARGARETE (editors) 1939– *Schinkels Lebenswerk.* 14 vols. Berlin: Deutscher Kunstverlag. Additional volumes in preparation.

RICHARDSON, ALBERT E. 1912 "Karl Friedrich

Schinkel: A Study." *Architectural Review* 31:61–79.

RIEMANN, GOTTFRIED 1971 "Frühe englische Ingenieurbauten in der Sicht Karl Friedrich Schinkels . . ." *Forschungen und Berichte* 13:75–86.

RIEMANN, GOTTFRIED 1973 "Englische Einflüsse im architektonischen Spätwerk Karl Friedrich Schinkels." *Forschungen und Berichte* 15:79–104.

SCHINKEL, KARL FRIEDRICH 1819–1824 *Dekorationen auf den beiden königlichen Theatern in Berlin.* Berlin: Wittich.

SCHINKEL, KARL FRIEDRICH (1819–1840)1981 *Sammlung Architektonischer Entwürfe.* Reprint. Berlin: Arani; Chicago: Exedra.

SCHINKEL, KARL FRIEDRICH 1848–1850 *Werke der höheren Baukunst.* Potsdam, Germany: Riegel.

SENAT VON BERLIN (editor) 1981 *Karl Friedrich Schinkels Werk und Wirkungen.* Berlin: Martin Cropius Bau. Exhibition catalogue.

SIEVERS, JOHANNES 1960 "Das Vorbild des 'Neuen Pavillons' von Karl Schinkel im Schlosspark Charlottenburg." *Zeitschrift für Kunstgeschichte* 23:227–241.

SPRINGER, PETER 1981 *Schinkels Schlossbrücke in Berlin: Zweckbau und Monument.* Berlin: Propyläen.

STAATLICHE MUSEEN ZU BERLIN 1980 *Karl Friedrich Schinkel: 1781–1841.* Berlin: The museum. Exhibition catalogue.

WAAGEN, GUSTAV (1844)1980 *Karl Friedrich Schinkel als Mensch und als Künstler.* Reprint. Düsseldorf, Germany: Werner.

WOLZOGEN, ALFRED VON (1862–1864)1981 *Aus Schinkels Nachlass.* 4 vols. Reprint. Berlin: Mäander.

WOLZOGEN, ALFRED VON 1864 *Schinkel als Architekt, Maler und Kunstphilosoph.* Berlin: Ernst & Korn.

ZADOW, MARIO 1980 *Karl Friedrich Schinkel.* Berlin: Rembrandt.

SCHLÜTER, ANDREAS

Andreas Schlüter (1659?–1714) was born in Danzig (now Gdánsk, Poland) and was trained there as a sculptor under David Sapovius. Nothing is known of his professional travel, perhaps to Italy, France, and Holland, which would have completed his artistic training. Probably from 1681, and certainly from 1689, he was active as a sculptor at the court of the Polish King Johann Sobieski in Warsaw. It is assumed that he had a part in the figurative ornament of Agostino Locci's extensions of 1679–1696 to Schloss Wilanow near Warsaw. Schlüter's collaboration with the Polish court architect Tyman van Gameren, an adherent of the North Italian academic tradition, was decisive for his later architectural activity. He created the ornamental sculpture for van Gameren's Krasinsky Palace in Warsaw (1689–1693), where he first acquainted himself with architectural problems. In 1694, he went to Berlin and became court sculptor to the Elector Frederick III of Brandenburg, whose court was striving both politically and artistically to gain the Prussian Royal Crown (1701). The Academy of Arts, founded in this context, gave Schlüter, who was named instructor of sculpture, the opportunity to travel to Rome, where he not only acquired plaster casts of antique statuary for the Academy but also was able to see Roman sculpture, decoration, and architecture with his own eyes. After returning to Berlin, he created the impressive sculptural cycle on the Arsenal, consisting of keystones with trophy helmets and warrior's heads. He also received the commission for his principal sculptural work, the equestrian statue of the Great Elector, intended for the urbanistically important site on the Long Bridge (Lange Brücke) between the Old City and the Palace.

A foreign architect was initially sought to continue the conversion of the Elector's Palace into a Royal Palace which had been begun earlier by JOHANN ARNOLD NERING. However, after both Domenico Martinelli and Nicodemus Tessin (see TESSIN FAMILY) had turned down the commission, Schlüter presented a model for the renovation which he had prepared independently in the interim. Given the commission in 1698, Schlüter was officially named *Schlossbaudirektor* in 1699. At the same time, he directed briefly the construction of the Arsenal (1698–1699), a building also begun by Nering, to which Schlüter wished to add a high attic decorated with relief sculpture. After the partial collapse of the vaults, however, the completion was taken over by JEAN DE BODT. Schlüter then devoted himself entirely to the Royal Palace, concentrating all of Berlin's artistic resources on this building which he executed with great organizational skill, tremendous speed, and a great expenditure of materials. His duties were not confined to the complete artistic planning but extended as well to the organization and supervision of the construction and the interior furnishing in all its details. The new palace façade facing the city was complete in time for Frederick I's accession to the throne in 1701. The extension of the garden wing and the new building of the staircase pavilion were structurally complete and part of the newly decorated interiors was also ready for use. The final decoration of the central stair hall, the alteration of Nering's arcaded galleries in the courtyard, as well as the continuing decoration of the state rooms and other apartments continued until 1706.

In 1701, Schlüter was named a member of the Berlin Academy of Sciences in recognition of "his [knowledge] of the science of building and its related mathematical and mechanical arts." From 1702–1704, he was director of the Academy of Arts. His position, which commanded the entire artistic life of the Berlin court at this time, was comparable to that of GIOVANNI LORENZO BERNINI in Rome. On the other bank of the Spree River, he built from 1702–1704 the palace of the count of Wartenberg, with a stately façade facing the Schlossplatz. The post office was later installed there. The small stables (1703–1706) and the foundry (1705–1707) were erected according to his designs. He gave these utilitarian structures austere façades and a clearly articulated massing. Schlüter was not involved architecturally at any of the other royal residences, including that at Charlottenburg. Only in Bad Freienwalde was a *Lusthaus* built in 1704–1707 after Schlüter's designs.

Also after his own designs, Schlüter had begun in 1702 to reface and heighten the Water Tower near the Mint, which belonged to the Berlin Schloss. With a high basement, two stories of commanding free-standing columns and a curved termination, it was to be the royal emblem of the capital with its clock, glockenspiel, and fountains. This building marked a transition in Schlüter's life. In 1704, as it reached two-thirds of the planned height of about 92 m, the tower tilted and threatened to collapse. Schlüter sought to save it with supports and iron armatures, but in 1706 he was forced to forestall the menacing collapse by partial demolition. An investigating commission determined that the irreparable damage was due to bad ground and insufficient foundations. They rejected Schlüter's reduced plan and decided for total demolition. In 1707, Schlüter was dismissed from the *Schlossbaudirektion* and replaced by JOHANN FRIEDRICH EOSANDER. Although Schlüter retained his post as court sculptor, he received only few commissions. In 1710, he resigned from the Academy of Sciences. Only in 1711–1712 was he again engaged as an architect, this time by Ernst Bogislav von Kameke for whom he built a country house in Berlin's Dorotheenstadt, which was of the Lusthaus type.

In 1713, after Frederick I's death, when artists were abandoning Berlin, Schlüter took up an invitation to St. Petersburg, where he was named architectural director to the court of Peter the Great. Here he pursued an industrious planning and design program for the court and the new, ambitious capital, an activity which B. Hallström (1961) has sought to reconstruct. He has shown that Schlüter probably originally prepared designs for the grotto near the Summer Palace, the Peterhof, and Monplaisir Palace, numerous palaces of the nobility, and the *Kunstkammer,* all of which were to be executed by others. The czar also engaged Schlüter intensively with mechanical problems. Schlüter's health was, however, weakening; he died exactly one year after his arrival in St. Petersburg, before he could even begin the realization of his ambitiously conceived plans. Nonetheless, his designs seem to have been the basis for the work of his collaborators and followers, Johann Friedrich Braunstein and Georg Johann Mattarnovi.

Schlüter, an architectural autodidact, had come to architecture through his sculptural works in Warsaw and Berlin. He ranks, thus, with MICHELANGELO, Bernini, and JOHANN BERNHARD

Schlüter.
Schloss (renovation and interior decoration; later expanded and completed by Eosander).
Berlin.
1698–1706

FISCHER VON ERLACH as one of the most significant sculptor-architects of European importance in postmedieval art history.

A quick perception, a fine sensibility for superlative achievements in past architecture, and a passionate artistic temperament enabled Schlüter to achieve a convincing synthesis of motifs and stylistic elements drawn from widely divergent and different stylistic epochs. A bold and original personal style was the result, one which achieved a baroque liveliness by contrasting tension of flat and sculpted elements. Schlüter's sculptural formulation of architecture was thus the source of that vigorous vitality which he instilled in his architecture. His chief work, the parts of the Berlin Schloss he completed, displayed this most clearly; the palace was, however, bombed in World War II and subsequently, for political reasons, dynamited. Schlüter had planned a cubic, four-winged complex around a central courtyard, an arrangement traditional in Roman and French palace design. Facing the city, the building presented a massive slab with a flat terrace roof fronted by a balustrade topped by statues. The progressively layered wall articulation, with robustly projecting window pediments, continued until the corner towers, which acted like broad shoulders highlighting the massiveness of the building. The entrance projection with its colossal superimposed freestanding columns gave the center of the façade a dominant triumphal motif. It featured wide rectangular openings in the interstices of each floor. The Michelangelesque articulation of the central window jambs with inset diminutive columns was repeated in the central bay of the corner towers. It also governed the wall articulation of the rooms and the stairhalls inside this wing of the palace. The entrance projection on the garden front was flat. Instead of colossal columns it was articulated by grouped pilasters which framed the large window openings, which thus read here to full effect. The contrast between recessed planes and projections was most pronounced in the courtyard: the stairhalls stood out distinctly between the tautly stretched, linking galleries. Here, always, two of the four stories were combined by members of a Corinthian order. Projecting columns carried statues on the lower part, and flat, fluted pilasters were set above. At the central stair, the ingenious combination of the columnar motif from the Roman Forum of Nerva together with the articulation system of Michelangelo's Palazzo dei Conservatori produced an effect of great tension. The contrast of direction between the articulating skeleton of large and small orders on the one hand and the wide fenestration on the other determined the dramatic, taut form of the building. Schlüter placed freestanding columns and arches only at important places. Otherwise he avoided columns in favor of a structured, generous system of flat, rectangular articulating elements, enriched with a few prominent sculptural accents.

In the country house for Count Kameke, which is typologically closely related to LUCAS VON HILDEBRANDT's Starhemberg Garden Palace in Vienna, a curvilinear modeling of the masses was predominent: the concavely recessed portal bay of the two-storied central block is highlighted by convexly swelling flanking bays. The coupled pilaster strip articulation of the façade culminates in an undulating cornice with statues above, which seem to take up the moving rhythms of the façade. The silhouette of the building is closed by single-storied side wings, which are very slightly recessed and have subtly emphasized corner projections.

In interiors, especially in the ceremonial spaces and the *Elisabethsaal* of the palace, Schlüter also realized outstanding works. Here he varied PIETRO BERRETTINI DA CORTONA's ceiling type masterfully, developed it further, and luxuriously enriched it with sculptural decoration. The lucid and refined wall articulation of these rooms was accented at principal junctures by high-relief stucco figures, which simultaneously heightened the contrast between architecture and sculpture and represented the function of the respective rooms.

Despite the misfortunes of his architectural career, Schlüter and his architecture had a tremendous effect. In Berlin, Martin Heinrich Böhme and PAUL DECKER were his pupils. More important was the marked influence of his architecture on architects from Fischer von Erlach, MATTHÄUS DANIEL PÖPPELMANN, and GEORG WENCESLAUS VON KNOBELSDORFF to KARL FRIEDRICH SCHINKEL, whose own skeletal, architectonic system owed much to involvement with and even restoration of Schlüter's Berlin buildings. After 1888, the historicizing "Wilhelmine baroque" consciously sought to design "in the spirit of Schlüter." Today, none of his architectural works survive.

FRITZ-EUGEN KELLER
Translated from German by
Barry Bergdoll

WORKS

1688?–1693?, Cathedral (high altar), Oliva, Poland. 1698–1699, Arsenal (begun by Johann Arnold Nering; not completed until later by Jean de Bodt); *1698–1706, Schloss (renovation and interior decoration; later expanded and completed by Johann Friedrich Eosander); *1701?–1704, Wartenberg Palace (Old Post Office); *1702–1706, Münzturm (Mint Tower); 1703–1706, Small Stables; Berlin. 1704–1707, Lustschloss,

Bad Freienwalde, Brandenburg, Germany. *1705–1707, Foundry; *1711–1712, Landhaus Kamecke; Berlin. 1713–1714, Art Gallery (not completed until later by others), St. Petersburg, Russia. 1713–1714, Monplaisir Palace (not completed until later by others); 1713–1714, Peterhof Palace (not completed until later by others); near St. Petersburg, Russia.

BIBLIOGRAPHY

GURLITT, CORNELIUS 1891 *Andreas Schlüter.* Berlin: Wasmuth.

HAGER, WERNER 1942 Pages 155–164 in *Die Bauten des deutschen barocks, 1690–1770.* Jena, Germany: Diederichs.

HALLSTRÖM, BJÖRN HENRIK 1961 "Der Baumeister Andreas Schlüter und seine Nachfolge in St. Petersburg." *Konsthistorisk Tidskrift* 30:95–126.

HEMPEL, EBERHARD 1965 *Baroque Art and Architecture in Central Europe.* Harmondsworth, England: Penguin.

HUBALA, ERICH 1965 "Das Berliner Schloss und Andreas Schlüter." Pages 311–344 in *Gedenkschrift Ernst Gall.* Munich: Deutscher Kunstverlag.

IWICKI, ZYGMUNT 1980 *Der Hochaltar der Kathedrale in Oliva: Ein Werk von Andreas Schlüter.* Freiburg, Germany: Hochschulverlag.

KELLER, FRITZ-EUGEN 1979 "Triumphbogen in der Berliner Architektur des 17. und 18. Jahrhunderts." Volume 1, pages 99, 103–105 in *Berlin und die Antike.* Berlin: Deutsches Archäologisches Institut.

KÜHN, MARGARETE 1977 "Andreas Schlüter als Bildhauer." Pages 105–181 in *Barockplastik in Norddeutschland.* Mainz, Germany: Zabern.

LADENDORFF, HEINZ 1935 *Der Bildhauer und Baumeister Andreas Schlüter.* Berlin: Deutscher Verein für Kunstwissenschaft.

PESCHKEN, GOERD 1967 "Neue Literatur über Andreas Schlüter." *Zeitschrift für Kunstgeschichte* 30:229–246.

PESCHKEN, GOERD, and KLÜNNER, WERNER 1982 *Das Berliner Schloss.* Berlin: Propyläen.